For John,

   With affection and great admiration — on an auspicious day for our Society and for Georgetown.

Alvaro

16.ii.2001

The Letters of
Dr Charles Burney

Dr Charles Burney. From the portrait by Sir Joshua Reynolds, 1781. 'I have lately sate for my Picture to Sr Jos. Reynolds . . . wch every body says is very like'— except Dr Johnson: 'we want to see *Burney* & he never comes to us in that dress.'

The Letters of
Dr Charles Burney

VOLUME I
1751–1784

Edited by

ALVARO RIBEIRO, SJ

CLARENDON PRESS · OXFORD
1991

Oxford University Press, Walton Street, Oxford OX2 6DP

Oxford New York Toronto
Delhi Bombay Calcutta Madras Karachi
Petaling Jaya Singapore Hong Kong Tokyo
Nairobi Dar es Salaam Cape Town
Melbourne Auckland

and associated companies in
Berlin Ibadan

Oxford is a trade mark of Oxford University Press

Published in the United States
by Oxford University Press, New York

British Library Cataloguing in Publication Data
Burney, Charles 1726–1814
The letters of Dr. Charles Burney.
Vol 1, 1751–1784
I. Title   II. Ribeiro, Alvaro
780.92
ISBN 0-19-812687-5

Library of Congress Cataloging in Publication Data
Burney, Charles, 1726–1814.
[Correspondence]
The letters of Dr. Charles Burney/edited by Alvaro Ribeiro.
p.   cm.
Contents: v. 1. 1751–1784.
1. Burney, Charles, 1726–1814—Correspondence.   2. Musicologists—
England—Correspondence.   I. Ribeiro, Alvaro, 1947–
II. Title.
ML423.B9A4   1990
780'.92—dc20   89-71098
ISBN 0-19-812687-5

Typeset by Best-set Typesetter Ltd
Printed in Great Britain by
The Alden Press, Oxford

To Marie Alves Ribeiro
music teacher

PREFACE

The hitherto unpublished letters of Dr Charles Burney (1726–1814) commence publication in this, the first of a projected four-volume edition. Burney, the great eighteenth-century English historian of music, was a lively and talented correspondent in an age marked by superlative letter-writers. His letters, and their replies, have been located in over seventy public and private manuscript collections on both sides of the Atlantic and as far afield as New Zealand. All of Burney's letters known to be preserved are to be published in this edition, arranged in chronological order and presented in their entirety, freed from the excisions and obliterations perpetrated on them by his daughter, the novelist Fanny Burney (1752–1840), who, as Madame d'Arblay, planned but never brought to fruition an edition of her father's correspondence. Of the 191 letters included in this first volume, 154 have never reached print, and the majority of the rest have only appeared in unreliable and frequently abridged texts.

The year 1784, when Burney was fifty-eight, has been selected as a natural terminal date for this volume. In that year Burney was elected to The Club, which included in its membership the leaders of the intellectual and professional circles of the day. Fashionable London also staged in 1784 the spectacular musical Commemoration of Handel, and King George III approved Burney as the official historian of the festival. These events signal Burney's attainment of fame and public recognition of eminence as a 'man of letters' in the most distinguished musical, literary, and social circles of the age. 1784 also marks the end of an era in Burney's life: in July that year the focus of the literary coterie at Streatham, Mrs Thrale, married the singer Gabriel Piozzi; and Samuel Johnson, Burney's revered friend, died in December. These, then, are the letters of Burney's active years which saw his remarkable rise from relatively humble origins to a position at the head of his chosen profession, music, and to possession of an international reputation as a scholar and author of the Continental *Tours*, the first two volumes of the famous *History of Music*, and the *Commemoration of Handel*.

ACKNOWLEDGEMENTS

It is a great privilege to acknowledge first the assistance and friendship of Burney's descendants. Mr John Comyn has not only placed at my disposal his choice collection of Burney papers and memorabilia, but has also welcomed me into the family itself as godfather to his son, Hugo Charles Burney Comyn. I am deeply honoured. Mr Michael Burney-Cumming has also generously granted me permission to publish that portion of the family papers in his possession. Other Burneys have consistently shown a keen interest in my work on their ancestor. To all I am most grateful.

All Burney scholars owe a debt of gratitude to Professor Joyce Hemlow for her pioneering work on the vast archive that is the Burney Papers. To her and to the team of scholars in the Burney Room at McGill University, Montreal, I am grateful for two years spent in their midst: 1975 to 1976, a sojourn made possible by a special grant from discretionary funds by Principal Robert E. Bell, and 1987 to 1988, made possible by an appointment to the Burney Project by Professor David Williams, Chairman of the Department of English. To my colleagues in the Project, Professor Lars E. Troide, who continues to edit the early journals and letters of Fanny Burney, and Professor Slava Klima, who will edit the ensuing volumes of Burney's letters, I am grateful for more kindnesses and advice than I am capable of expressing. The Project assistants have borne the brunt of many a long and tedious editorial operation: Mr Garry Bowers; Dr Stewart Cooke; Ms Linda Rozmovits; Dr Andrea Smith; and Ms Elsie Wagner. Whatever pleasure they may take in this volume will be small recompense for their labours.

I wish to express my gratitude to my former colleagues in the Osborn Collection at Yale for their manifold kindnesses and suggestions. It was a pleasure and a privilege to work with them. It was while I worked in the early 1970s for three years at Yale as the late Dr James Marshall Osborn's research assistant, much in the manner of an eighteenth-century apprentice to a master scholar, that 'Jim' encouraged me to take on the editing of Burney's letters. It is a source of considerable sorrow that I shall not now be able to present this volume to him, but I am confident that his memory lives on in the affection and gratitude of the many scholars who have benefited from his munificence and his insistence on the central importance to literary and historical studies of documentary evidence. Dr Stephen R. Parks, now Curator of the Osborn Collection, has generously facilitated my work every step of the way from initial xeroxing to final checking.

To Dr Lola L. Szladits and her staff at the Berg Collection in The New York Public Library I am indebted for much help in guiding me through the masses of Burney Papers in the Berg, and for permission to publish.

Of that portion of the now scattered Burney family archive used in this volume, I thank particularly the curators of the public collections and the owners of the private for permission to publish. Many have gone to great trouble to facilitate my work in its early stages by allowing me to hunt down, examine, and photocopy the manuscripts in their custody or possession: Ashmolean Museum, Oxford; Bancroft Library, University of California, Berkeley; Mr Roger W. Barrett, Chicago, Illinois; Beinecke Rare Book and Manuscript Library, Yale University; Bodleian Library, Oxford; Boston Public Library; British Library, London; Mary Couts Burnett Library, Texas Christian University, Fort Worth; Mr Michael Burney-Cumming, Polebrook, Oundle, near Peterborough; Cambridge University Library; National Library of Australia, Canberra ACT; Civico Museo Bibliografico Musicale, Bologna; Mr Gerald Coke, Jenkyn Place, Bentley, Hampshire; Mr John R. G. Comyn; Dixson Library, State Library of New South Wales, Sydney; Fitzwilliam Museum, Cambridge; Folger Shakespeare Library, Washington, DC; Mr James Gilvarry; Gesellschaft der Musikfreunde, Vienna; Staats-und Universitätsbibliothek, Hamburg; Hornby Library, City of Liverpool Public Libraries; Houghton Library, Harvard University; Donald and Mary Hyde Collection, Four Oaks Farm, Somerville, New Jersey; Dr Johnson's House, Gough Square, London; the late Ralph A. Leigh; National Portrait Gallery, London; Bibliothèque Publique de la Ville de Neuchâtel, Switzerland; McGill University Library; Mr W. G. S. Macmillan, Knapton Old Hall, North Walsam, Norfolk; Mr Victor Montagu, Mapperton, Beaminster, Dorset; Norfolk Record Office; Mr Thomas North, Rougham Hall, Norfolk; Bibliothèque Nationale, Paris; Pierpont Morgan Library, New York; Mr H. L. Platnauer, Birmingham; the late Frederick A. Pottle; The Royal Society of London; John Rylands University Library of Manchester; Mr John H. A. Sparrow, All Souls College, Oxford; Forster Collection, Victoria and Albert Museum, London.

The elucidation of Burney's text has taken me to many libraries and record offices on both sides of the Atlantic. I should like to express my thanks especially to the officials of the Bodleian Library, Oxford; British Library; McGill University Library; and Yale University Library, where I have done much of the work.

Because Burney's interests were so wide-ranging, it would have been preferable to have a polymath as the editor of his letters. Failing that ideal, I have drawn on the collective learning and assistance of the Revd W. M. Atkins; Fr Joop van Banning, SJ; Fr Michael Barnes, SJ; Professor Kalman Burnim; Professor Michael Cartwright; Professor Curt Cecil; Dr Mary Chan; the late Professor Thomas Copeland; Mrs Margaret Cranmer; Fr Richard Cronin, SJ; Professor Thomas Curley; Fr Brian Daley, SJ; Mr Tom Davis; Professor Vincent Duckles; Fr Francis Edwards, SJ; Dr David Fairer; Ms Christine Ferdinand; Dr David Fleeman; the late Dame Helen Gardner; Professor Joel Gold; Professor Kerry Grant; Dr Jean Gribenski; Professor Harlan Hamilton; Mr and Mrs Michael Kassler; Mr John Kenworthy-Browne; Professor William Kupersmith; the late W. S. Lewis; Mr Michel Noiray; Dr Pierluigi Petrobelli; Professor Cecil Price; Professor and Mrs John Riely; Professor Betty Rizzo; Dr Stephen Roe; Professor Peter Sabor; the late Dr Robert Shackleton; Dr Frederick Sternfeld; the late Dame Lucy Sutherland; Ms Elizabeth E. Tate; Professor Marshall Waingrow; Mr John

Acknowledgements

Wing; Mr William Woods; Mr Paul Yeats-Edwards; and Mr Yung Kai-Kin.

I acknowledge with deep respect the help rendered by several generations of members of my own college, Balliol College, Oxford. Their cheerful tolerance and combined erudition in many branches of learning have saved me from many blunders. For answers to what must have seemed an endless stream of queries, I am particularly grateful to the Hon. Dominic Asquith; Dr Penelope Bulloch; Dr Carol Clark; the Revd Dr Charles Everitt; Dr Kenneth Garlick; Mr Jasper Griffin; Mr Edward Jenkyns; Mr Rhion Jones; Mr Nicholas Kenyon; Dr Lawrence Keppie; Mr Hugh Lawson-Tancred; Mr Simon Lee; Dr Colin Lucas; the late J. C. Maxwell; Dr Paul Overton; Mr Vincent Quinn; Mr Stephen Shuttleworth; Mr Thomas Smith; Mr Henry Snow; Dr Cynthia Stallman; Dr Morgan Sweeney. I thank particularly Dr Roger Lonsdale of Balliol, whose watchful eye has perused this edition from beginning to end, whose wise and thoughtful counsel has directed my steps, and whose profound knowledge of Burney and the eighteenth century has furnished me with a shining example to follow.

The dedication of this volume to Marie Ribeiro, my mother, feebly acknowledges my greatest debt. A piano teacher by profession, she laboured for forty-nine consecutive years before her retirement to initiate one 'little Master' after another 'little Miss' in the rudiments of music. Thus possessed of an insider's intimate knowledge and understanding, she resonated in sympathy throughout with Dr Burney himself and the editor of his letters.

CONTENTS

LIST OF ILLUSTRATIONS

ABBREVIATIONS AND CUE TITLES

PERSONS

CB   Charles Burney (1726–1814)

CFBt   Charlotte Francis Barrett (1786–1870)

FB   Frances Burney (1752–1840)
FBA   after 1793 Madame d'Arblay

SEB   Susanna Elizabeth Burney (1755–1800)
SBP   after 1782 Mrs Phillips

MANUSCRIPT COLLECTIONS

Berg	The Henry W. and Albert A. Berg Collection, The New York Public Library.
BL	The British Library.
Bologna	Civico Museo Bibliografico Musicale, Bologna.
BRBL	The Beinecke Rare Book and Manuscript Library, Yale University, New Haven, Connecticut.
Burney-Cumming	Collection of Michael Burney-Cumming, 5 King's Arms Lane, Polebrook, Oundle, near Peterborough.
Coke	Collection of Gerald Coke, Jenkyn Place, Bentley, Hampshire.
Comyn	Family collection of John R. G. Comyn.
Folger	The Folger Shakespeare Library, Washington, DC.
Hamburg	Staats- und Universitätsbibliothek, Hamburg.
Hyde	Collection of Donald and Mary Hyde, Four Oaks Farm, Somerville, New Jersey.
Montagu	Collection of Victor Montagu, Mapperton House, Beaminster, Dorset.
Osborn	The James Marshall and Marie-Louise Osborn Collection, Yale University Library, New Haven, Connecticut.
Platnauer	Collection of H. L. Platnauer, Edgbaston, Birmingham.
PML	The Pierpont Morgan Library, New York.
PRO	Public Record Office, London.
R. A. Leigh	Collection of Ralph A. Leigh, Trinity College, Cambridge.
Rylands	The John Rylands University Library of Manchester.

| Sparrow | Collection of John H. A. Sparrow, All Souls College, Oxford. |

FREQUENTLY CITED WORKS

In all works London, for books in English, and Paris, for books in French, are assumed to be the place of publication unless otherwise indicated.

ADB	*Allgemeine Deutsche Biographie*, 55 vols., Leipzig, 1875–1910.
BD	*A Biographical Dictionary of Actors, Actresses, Musicians, Dancers, Managers & Other Stage Personnel in London, 1660–1800*, ed. Philip H. Highfill, Jr., Kalman A. Burnim, and Edward A. Langhans, Carbondale and Edwardsville, Ill., 1973– .
Boaden	*The Private Correspondence of David Garrick*, ed. J. Boaden, 2 vols., 1831–2.
Bradfer-Lawrence	H. L. Bradfer-Lawrence, 'The Merchants of Lynn', in *A Supplement to Blomefield's Norfolk*, ed. C. Ingleby, 1929, pp. 143–204.
Brofsky	Howard Brofsky, 'Doctor Burney and Padre Martini: Writing a General History of Music', *The Musical Quarterly*, lxv (1979), 313–45.
BUCEM	*The British Union-Catalogue of Early Music*, ed. Elizabeth B. Schnapper, 2 vols., 1957.
Burford Papers	William Holden Hutton, *Burford Papers, being Letters of Samuel Crisp to His Sister at Burford; and Other Studies of a Century (1745–1845)*, 1905.
Burke *Corresp.*	*The Correspondence of Edmund Burke*, ed. Thomas W. Copeland, *et al.*, 10 vols., Cambridge and Chicago, 1958–70.
Cat. Corr.	*A Catalogue of the Burney Family Correspondence 1749–1878*, comp. Joyce Hemlow, with Jeanne M. Burgess and Althea Douglas, New York, 1971.
'Cat. Fac. Mus.'	'Catalogue of the Books Tracts & Treatises ... on the particular Faculty of Music ... of the late Charles Burney ...' (BL Add. MS 18191).
Cat. Misc. Lib.	Leigh and Sotheby, *A Catalogue of the Miscellaneous Library of ... Charles Burney*, 9 June 1814. The Yale priced copy: X348/S71/1814/6/9.
Cat. Mus. Lib.	White, *A Catalogue of the ... Collection of Music ... of ... Charles Burney*, 8 August 1814. The Music Division of the Library of Congress priced copy.
CB Mem.	*Memoirs of Dr. Charles Burney 1726–1769*, ed. Slava Klima, Garry Bowers, and Kerry S. Grant, Lincoln, Neb., 1988. References are to fragment number.

CCR	*The Court and City Register.*
Clifford	James L. Clifford, *Hester Lynch Piozzi (Mrs. Thrale)*, 2nd edn. corrected, Oxford, 1968.
Country Clergyman	*Recreations and Studies of a Country Clergyman of the Eighteenth Century*, ed. Richard Twining, 1882.
DAB	*Dictionary of American Biography.*
Dawe	Donovan Dawe, *Organists of the City of London 1666–1850*, Padstow, 1983.
DBF	*Dictionnaire de biographie française*, 1929– .
DBI	*Dizionario biografico degli italiani*, Rome, 1960– .
De Castro	J. P. de Castro, *The Gordon Riots*, 1926.
DHBS	*Dictionnaire historique & biographique de la Suisse*, 7 vols. and *Supplément*, Neuchâtel, 1921–34.
Diderot *Corresp.*	Denis Diderot, *Correspondance*, ed. Georges Roth, 16 vols., 1955–70.
DL	*Diary and Letters of Madame d'Arblay (1778–1840)*, ed. Austin Dobson, 6 vols., 1904–5.
DNB	*Dictionary of National Biography.*
DSB	*Dictionary of Scientific Biography*, ed. C. C. Gillispie, 16 vols., New York, 1970–80.
DWB	*The Dictionary of Welsh Biography down to 1940*, 1959.
ED	*The Early Diary of Frances Burney 1768–1778*, ed. Annie Raine Ellis, rev. edn., 2 vols., 1907.
EJL	*The Early Journals and Letters of Fanny Burney*, ed. Lars E. Troide, *et al.*, vol. i–, Oxford, 1988– .
Fétis	*Biographie universelle des musiciens*, ed. François-Joseph Fétis, 2nd edn., 8 vols., 1860–5. *Supplément et complément*, 2 vols., 1878–80.
Foster	*Alumni Oxonienses*, ed. Joseph Foster, 1st ser., *1500–1714*, 4 vols., Oxford, 1891–2; 2nd ser., *1715–1886*, 4 vols., Oxford, 1887–8.
Frag. Mem.	Holograph fragments of Burney's 'Memoirs' which survive in Berg, BL, and Osborn.
Garrick *Letters*	*The Letters of David Garrick*, ed. David M. Little and George M. Kahrl, 3 vols., Cambridge, Mass., 1963.
German Tour	Charles Burney, *The Present State Music in Germany, the Netherlands, and United Provinces*, 2 vols., 1773; 2nd corrected edn., 1775.
GM	*The Gentleman's Magazine*, 1731–1880.
Grant	Kerry S. Grant, *Dr. Burney as Critic and Historian of Music*, Ann Arbor, Mich., 1983.
Gray *Corresp.*	*Correspondence of Thomas Gray*, ed. Paget Toynbee and Leonard Whibley, with corrections and additions by H. W. Starr, 3 vols., Oxford, 1971.
Handel Commem.	Charles Burney, *An Account of the Musical Performances in Westminster-Abbey, and the Pantheon, May*

	26th, 27th, 29th; and June the 3d, and 5th, 1784. In Commemoration of Handel, 1785.
Hawkins	Sir John Hawkins, *A General History of the Science and Practice of Music*, 5 vols., 1776.
HFB	Joyce Hemlow, *The History of Fanny Burney*, Oxford, 1958.
Hillen	H. J. Hillen, *History of the Borough of King's Lynn*, 2 vols., Norwich, 1907.
Hill–Powell	*Boswell's Life of Johnson*, ed. G. B. Hill, rev. L. F. Powell, 6 vols., Oxford, 1934–64.
Hist. Mus.	Charles Burney, *A General History of Music, from the Earliest Ages to the Present Period*, 4 vols., 1776–89. References to the first volume are to the rev. 2nd edn. (1789). Where the 1st edn. (1776) is specifically mentioned, it is cited as *Hist. Mus.* i (1776).
HMC	Historical Manuscripts Commission.
Hoboken	A. van Hoboken, *Joseph Haydn, Thematisch-bibliographisches Werkverzeichnis*, 3 vols., Mainz, 1957–78.
Horn	D. B. Horn, *British Diplomatic Representatives 1689–1789*, 1932.
Hyde, *Thrales*	Mary Hyde, *The Thrales of Streatham Park*, Cambridge, Mass., 1977.
Italian Tour	Charles Burney, *The Present State of Music in France and Italy*, 1771; 2nd corrected edn., 1773.
JL	*The Journals and Letters of Fanny Burney (Madame d'Arblay)*, ed. Joyce Hemlow, *et al.*, 12 vols., Oxford, 1972–84.
Johnson *Letters*	*The Letters of Samuel Johnson*, ed. R. W. Chapman, 3 vols., Oxford, 1952.
Kassler	Jamie Croy Kassler, *The Science of Music in Britain, 1714–1830: A Catalogue of Writings, Lectures and Inventions*, 2 vols., New York, 1979.
Leigh	R. A. Leigh, 'Les Amitiés françaises du Dr Burney', *Revue de littérature comparée*, xxv (1951), 161–94.
The London Stage	*The London Stage 1660–1800*, 5 pts. in 11 vols., Carbondale, Ill., 1960–8. References are to part, volume, page.
Lonsdale	Roger Lonsdale, *Dr. Charles Burney: A Literary Biography*, Oxford, 1965.
Manwaring	G. E. Manwaring, *My Friend the Admiral: The Life, Letters, and Journals of Rear-Admiral James Burney, F.R.S.*, 1931.
Maxted	Ian Maxted, *The London Book Trades 1775–1800: A Preliminary Checklist of Members*, Folkestone, 1977.

Mem.	Madame d'Arblay, *Memoirs of Doctor Burney, Arranged from His Own Manuscripts, from Family Papers, and from Personal Recollections*, 3 vols., 1832.
Mercer	Charles Burney, *A General History of Music*, ed. Frank Mercer, 2 vols., 1935.
MGG	*Die Musik in Geschichte und Gegenwart*, ed. Friedrich Blume, 14 vols., Kassel, 1949–68. *Supplement*, 2 vols., Kassel, 1973–9.
Michaud	*Biographie universelle ancienne et moderne*, ed. Louis-Gabriel Michaud, nouv. éd., 45 vols., 1843–[65].
Namier and Brooke	Sir Lewis Namier and John Brooke, *The House of Commons, 1754–1790*, 3 vols., 1964.
NDB	*Neue Deutsche Biographie*, Berlin, 1952– .
New Grove	*The New Grove Dictionary of Music and Musicians*, ed. Stanley Sadie, 20 vols., 1980.
OED	*Oxford English Dictionary*.
Plomer	H. R. Plomer, *et al.*, *A Dictionary of the Printers and Booksellers . . . in England . . . 1726 to 1775*, Oxford, 1932.
Rees	*The Cyclopaedia; or, Universal Dictionary of Arts, Sciences, and Literature*, ed. Abraham Rees, 45 vols., 1802–20. Burney contributed the musical articles in this work.
RES	*The Review of English Studies*.
RISM	Publications of the Répertoire International des Sources Musicales.
Rousseau *Corresp.*	*Correspondance complète de Jean Jacques Rousseau*, ed. R. A. Leigh, vol. i– , 1965– .
Scholes	Percy A. Scholes, *The Great Dr. Burney*, 2 vols., 1948.
Scholes, *Hawkins*	Percy A. Scholes, *The Life and Activities of Sir John Hawkins*, 1953.
Sedgwick	Romney Sedgwick, *The House of Commons, 1715–1754*, 2 vols., 1970.
Thraliana	*Thraliana: The Diary of Mrs. Hester Lynch Thrale (Later Mrs. Piozzi) 1776–1809*, ed. Katharine C. Balderston, 2nd edn., 2 vols., Oxford, 1951.
Tours	*Dr. Burney's Musical Tours in Europe*, ed. Percy A. Scholes, 2 vols., 1959.
UTET	*La Musica: Dizionario*, ed. Guido M. Gatti, Unione Tipografico-Editrice Torinese, 2 vols., Turin, 1968–71.
Venn	*Alumni Cantabrigienses*. Part I: to 1751, ed. John and J. A. Venn, 4 vols., Cambridge, 1922–7; part II: 1752–1900, ed. J. A. Venn, 6 vols., Cambridge, 1940–54.

Walpole *Corresp.*	*The Yale Edition of Horace Walpole's Correspondence*, ed. W. S. Lewis, *et al.*, 48 vols., New Haven, Conn., 1937–83.
'Worcester Memoranda'	'Memoranda of the Burney Family 1603–1845'. The MS is untraced, but a typescript is preserved of this family chronicle in the Scholes Papers in Osborn.

References to Shakespeare are to *The Complete Works*, ed. Peter Alexander, 1951.

CHRONOLOGY OF MAJOR EVENTS IN CHARLES BURNEY'S LIFE TO 1784

1726	7 Apr. (o.s.)	Born at Shrewsbury
1738–44		Schooling at Shrewsbury and Chester
1744	Aug.–Sept.	Moves to London as Thomas Arne's apprentice
1746	summer	Meets Fulke Greville and Wilbury circle
1747	summer	Meets Samuel Crisp
1748	29 Sept.	Greville purchases Burney's indentures from Arne
1749	24 May	Esther, his first daughter, born
	12 June	Marries Esther Sleepe
	29 Oct.	Elected organist of St Dionis Backchurch
	3 Dec.	Elected to Society of Musicians
1750	13 June	James, his first son, born
1751	Sept.	Illness obliges him to leave London for King's Lynn, Norfolk, where he accepts post of organist at St Margaret's Church; meets William Bewley
1752	13 June	Fanny born
1755	4 Jan.	Susan born
	16 Feb.	Correspondence with Samuel Johnson begins
1757	4 Dec.	Charles born
1760		Returns to London, lives in Poland Street; becomes fashionable music master
1761	4 Nov.	Charlotte born
1762	29 Sept.	Esther, his wife, dies
1764	June–July	Takes his daughters to Paris
	Nov.	Elected to Society of Arts
1765	June–July	Fetches his daughters from Paris
1766	21 Nov.	*The Cunning Man*, his translation of Rousseau's *Le Devin du village* performed at Drury Lane

1767		Appointed Extra Musician in the King's Band
	2 Oct.	Marries Elizabeth Allen
1768	20 Nov.	Richard Thomas born
1769	22 June	D.Mus., Oxon.
	25 Oct.	Publishes *An Essay towards a History of the Principal Comets*
1770	7 June	Departs on musical tour of France and Italy
	24 Dec.	Returns to new residence in Queen Square, Bloomsbury
1771	4 May	Publishes *Italian Tour*
1772	3 July	Departs on musical tour of the Low Countries, Germany, and Austria
	29 Aug.	Sarah Harriet born
	early Nov.	Returns to London
1773	23 Apr.	Publishes *German Tour*
	28 Apr.	Correspondence with Thomas Twining begins
	16 Dec.	Elected FRS
1774	20 May	Promoted Musician in Ordinary in the King's Band
	3 Aug.	Fails to establish a music school at the Foundling Hospital
	8 Oct.	Moves to St Martin's Street
1776	31 Jan.	Publishes first volume of *History of Music*
	23 Nov.	Sir John Hawkins publishes rival *History*
	12 Dec.	Gives first harpsichord lesson to Queeney Thrale; joins Streatham circle
1777		Correspondence with Mrs Thrale begins
1778	29 Jan.	Fanny publishes *Evelina*
1779	18 Feb.	Reads 'Account of an Infant Musician' (Crotch) to Royal Society; subsequently publishes *Account*
1780	June	Witnesses the Gordon Riots
1781	Jan.	Portrait painted by Sir Joshua Reynolds
1782	29 May	Publishes second volume of *History of Music*
	12 July	Fanny publishes *Cecilia*

1783	24 Apr.	Samuel Crisp dies
	5 Sept.	William Bewley dies
1783	18 Dec.	Burke obtains for him post as organist at Royal Hospital, Chelsea
1784	17 Feb.	Elected to The Club
	May–June	Handel Commemoration; King approves of him as historian of the event
	July	Mrs Thrale marries Gabriel Piozzi: end of Streatham circle
	13 Dec.	Samuel Johnson dies
1785	24 Jan.	Publishes *Commemoration of Handel*

INTRODUCTION

'The history of a hero, is to be found in his *public* transactions; and that of a man of letters, in his *private* correspondence.' Burney's observation in the Preface to his *Memoirs of the Life and Writings of the Abate Metastasio* (1796) might with equal truth be made of Burney himself. Like so many members of the illustrious circle of friends that surrounded Samuel Johnson in London in the latter half of the eighteenth century, Charles Burney, the first major historian of music in English, was not favoured with any particular advantage of birth or of wealth. Apprenticed at the age of eighteen to Thomas Arne, he pursued until the age of forty-three a moderately successful musical career as a teacher, church organist, and composer for the theatre. Burney, it should be noted, did not father a famous 'School' of performance; nor are his compositions of great renown. His rise from relatively humble origins to fame and social position in his own day, and his interest to us now, was achieved through his pen: in his publications and in his letters.

Roger Lonsdale, in *Dr. Charles Burney: A Literary Biography* (Oxford, 1965), has convincingly demonstrated how Burney, at the mid-point of his life, set out to turn his socially disadvantageous musical background to his benefit by the expedient of writing about his art. Burney, as Lonsdale accurately observes, transcended his original profession as a 'mere musician' to acceptance as a 'man of letters'. Lonsdale stresses Burney's unprecedented success in capturing for himself a 'polite literary audience for his books', which won for him 'an equally unprecedented welcome into the most distinguished intellectual and social circles of his time.' In addition to his published writings, his letters, here edited for the first time, show that Burney also employed the tool of the familiar letter in his striving for fame and recognition. The biographical interest of his letters, therefore, lies in the insight they furnish into the manner in which Burney exerted himself to inform, entertain, amuse, and win the affection and esteem of his correspondents. He made it his business to get to know and to retain the friendship of everybody of any 'consequence' in his day. His letters are filled with his irresistible charm, his natural talents for friendship, and his close observation of the musical, literary, artistic, theatrical, scientific, political, and social scenes of his time. Burney rarely writes a dull letter, for, as he himself put it, 'all letters to friends sh^d be a supplement to their last *Conversation*.'

The extent to which Burney consciously used the letter to his advantage has hitherto not been open to inspection by scholars of the late eighteenth century. Of the 191 letters arranged in chronological order in this volume, some 154 have remained totally unpublished, preserved now in public and private collections of manuscripts on both sides of the Atlantic and as far afield as New Zealand and Australia. The earliest letter to have come down to us belongs to 1751, when at the age of twenty-five Burney was obliged by ill-health to retreat to a country-organist's post in Norfolk. There he found an 'Execrably bad' organ, and a population totally ignorant of 'the most known & Common Musicall Merits'. It is illuminating, from the biographical point of view, to place this letter beside those written in 1784, the last year to be included in this volume. In 1784, we find Burney, thirty-three years later, aged fifty-eight, designated as it were 'by Royal Appointment', official historian of the Handel Commemoration, one of the most spectacular and celebrated musical events in England during the eighteenth century. Here too we find Burney consulted by the music-loving Earl of Sandwich for his opinion on appropriate venues for subsequent festivals in London for Handel's music.

Several other events in Burney's life have prompted the selection of 1784 as a natural termination-date of this volume. In February 1784, Burney won election to The Club, which signified in his own estimation his arrival at the pinnacle of contemporary literary society. In July that year Mrs Thrale married the 'mere musician', Gabriel Piozzi, thus bringing to an end the golden years of the Streatham coterie, which Burney had enjoyed since 1776. In December 1784 Samuel Johnson died. The Age of Johnson passes, and we find Burney magisterially assessing the qualifications of the potential Johnson biographers—a far cry from the 'insignificant' country organist who in 1755 plucked up sufficient 'impertinence' to write his first letter to Johnson.

Burney's literary and social achievements must nevertheless be seen against the background of his constant necessity to earn a livelihood. As London's most fashionable music master, he hurried during the season from one 'little Master' to another 'little Miss', waging, as he put it, 'A, B, C-Battles' with them. With a large family to support, and despite his social eminence, he reveals wryly to his son Charles in 1781, 'I still remain a drudge amid the smiles of Wealth & Power'. His literary work on the *History of Music*, which brought him the recognition he so eagerly sought, was prosecuted only during the summer holidays, in between bouts of illness, late at night and early into the morning. At the conclusion of the *History* in 1789 he would observe that it was a work 'for wch I had so heavily taxed every amusement, & Social enjoyment, & in order to gain time had drawn so deeply from my sinking fund, Sleep'. It is hardly surprising, then, that these letters of Burney's active years give the overall impression of having been written at a high pitch of tension and in great haste— 'I have no Time to be happy'.

In addition to the biographical interest of Burney's early correspondence, his letters are valuable for the information they contain. As a professional musician who wrote about 'Flutes & Fiddles', both as historian and critic of music and musicians, Burney's published writings are extensively quoted by musical scholars. His firsthand comments on music on the Continent in the *Tours*, his account of the Handel Commemoration in 1784, his observation of contemporary music-making in the fourth volume of the *History*, and the articles he penned late in life for Abraham Rees's *Cyclopaedia* are justly mined by writers on music today. The letters, however, reveal the private 'Profession de Foi musicale' behind, and sometimes significantly at variance with, the public published utterances.

In these letters, belonging to the years in which Burney collected his materials for and wrote his *History*, he reveals his critical principles. Regarding music as an 'innocent luxury', he admits contemporary and fashionable 'taste' as a valid legislator of the arts. He holds, furthermore, to the idea of progress in the history of music. It is not surprising, then, to find in him a modernist, whose musical taste is founded on the pronouncements of Rousseau and the encyclopédistes. Siding with Rousseau, he exalts the simple and melodious style of Italian, particularly Neapolitan, opera as exemplified in composers such as Pergolesi and Hasse. In contrast, he views French opera as stagnating under the pervasive influence of the outdated Lully and Rameau. With regard to instrumental music, he approves of German composers such as those of the Mannheim School who had advanced from the 'laboured contrivances' of 'Gothic' contrapuntal writing. He praises C. P. E. Bach, for example, for escaping 'the trammels of Fugues & crowded parts in which his Father so excelled.' Letters to Twining in 1783 and later are full of the praises of Haydn.

Burney's musical preferences were that of a practitioner of the art keeping abreast of the times. He was, as Percy Scholes remarked, 'a student of the living art'. To the fashionable man of taste, therefore, Sir John Hawkins's conviction that music had achieved 'its greatest perfection in *Europe* from about the middle of the sixteenth to the beginning of the seventeenth Century' was perverse obscurantism.

The five volumes of Hawkins's *History* appeared in November 1776, some ten months after the first volume of Burney's. Roger Lonsdale (pp. 189–225) has described fully how Burney's professional jealousy of and personal animosity towards Hawkins prompted him to arrange a devastating reception for the rival *History*. The story is a chronicle of the most inglorious chapter in Burney's biography.

Since the publication of the two *Histories* there has been controversy over their relative merits. It is therefore perhaps timely to remind the reader that the two *Histories* and their respective authors are so dissimilar that a study of Hawkins *vis-à-vis* Burney is necessarily a study of contrasts. The difference lies partly in the audiences for which they intended their volumes: Burney wished the history of his art to be read by a polite literary audience. Hawkins, as Thomas Twining observes perceptively, 'writes to antiquarians & *old-English* grubbers ... there is not among any set of people such a comfortable scratch-back confederacy as among these old-ruin diggers.' Burney, in contrast, wishes 'to have my Book so divested of Pedantry & Jargon that every Miss, who plays *o' top o' the Spinet* should make it her manual.' At the centre lies their fundamental difference in conception of what constitutes a history of music. To Hawkins a history was a dispassionate record of facts. In the antiquary's spirit, Hawkins carefully and accurately compiled an enormous and impersonal record. Questions of taste do not enter into his book, and the reader is free to form his own verdict. As such, Hawkins is invaluable today for his storehouse of information about music. To Burney, on the other hand, the writing of a history was inseparable from interpretation and evaluation. Burney's aim, as he so often reiterates in his letters, was to entertain as well as educate his reader. His *History* is consequently a highly personal review of music and musicians, and as a valuable record of the enlightened taste of his time contributes to our understanding of the eighteenth century. His private letters are therefore important for the light they throw on his musical assumptions and creed.

In no other correspondence preserved to this day does Burney so completely confess his opinions as in that with Thomas Twining. The correspondence with Twining opens in 1773 and Burney soon observes, 'I seem *inside-out* with you, & inclined to tell you every secret of my *Life*.' Taken as a whole, Burney's letters to Twining, and Twining's replies, provide a fascinating blow-by-blow account of the writing of the *History of Music*. Twining, a classical scholar, proved indispensable to the composition of the first two volumes of the *History*, always modestly maintaining, however, 'that there is a monstrous stride between seeing what *should* be done, & doing it'.

As the intimacy between the two correspondents grows, and as the *History* approaches more modern times, thereby rendering Twining's direct intervention less essential, Burney's letters to his friend include matters of more general interest than ancient music. It is to Twining that Burney gives the private history of the development of his own musical taste in the remarkable letter of 14 December 1781. Twining by this time had come to expect that Burney would 'as usual, tell me all you think, without a muzzle.' Burney pens to Twining his eyewitness account of the Gordon Riots of 1780 and his critical comments on the opera in London; he shares with Twining his enthusiasm for Pacchierotti's singing, his excitement over Captain Cook's voyages of discovery and the first successful attempts at flying. He also draws on Twining's sympathy in his grief over the deaths of Samuel Crisp and William Bewley in 1783. It is to Twining that Burney writes his most remarkable letter, that of 31 July 1784: a headlong, frantic epistle that fairly bursts with Burney's mingled rage and anxiety over publishing his *Commemoration of Handel*.

It is fortunate that Twining's replies to Burney in large part have also been preserved. The correspondence, it can be seen, was one between social and intellectual equals in which common interests and concerns are treated with that mixture of learning, wit, and close observation that characterizes the greatest correspondences of an age of letter-writers. Samuel Parr described Twining as 'possessing a talent for epistolary writing certainly not surpassed by any of his contemporaries. ... Whether he wielded an argument or tossed about an opinion, all was natural, original and most delightful.' Parr might with justice have said the same of Burney's letters to Twining.

Burney's four letters to Samuel Johnson are of a different order. Of great interest to Johnsonians, they show the deferential side of Burney's character and his relations with the man he regarded as the most illustrious of his age. These letters date from Burney's earlier years, before he became in 1769 'Doctor Burney'. Fortunately preserved in drafts, they show Burney carefully crafting his letters, rejecting inelegant phrases, finding the right tone of voice between brazen familiarity and fawning obsequiousness. Not having heard from Johnson for a long time, Burney initially writes in his letter of 14 October 1765 that his 'Esteem & veneration' for the great man 'were a little weakened perhaps by' Johnson's long silence. This phrase is then carefully re-drafted to read 'wch had slumbered a little perhaps during your long Silence'—implying thereby no abridgement of esteem but rather an interlude of refreshing repose. These letters to Johnson, and similar compositions to the powerful, wealthy, or eminent, were not written with the heart *'au bout de la langue'* and may be regarded as literary productions in their own right.

In delightful contrast to the lofty strains of the letters to Johnson stands Burney's sequence of letters to Mrs Thrale. He exercises in these letters the considerable epistolary art of seeming artlessness. His affection for Mrs Thrale and the pride he took in her virtual adoption of his daughter Fanny after the sensational appearance of *Evelina* in 1778 are apparent. With delicacy of touch Burney seasons these letters with his jokes, his puns, his wry comments on the Johnsonian and social circles, and his unique brand of self-deprecatory humour. The lightness of treatment appears to have extended even to the casual dating of his letters: Burney seems to have caught from Mrs Thrale the insouciance of heading his letters to her 'Monday Morn^g' or 'Thursday Night'. The editing of these letters poses formidable dating problems, matched only by their annotation where W. S. Lewis's injunction to all editors of letters must be firmly borne in mind: 'Don't sit on the soufflé'.

The central glory of the vast archive of Burney family papers that has been preserved shines in the series of correspondences which passed between members of the family. Burney fathered a large and talented brood in whom he instilled the importance of writing informatively and entertainingly to one another. It is a normal characteristic to find in letters that pass between brothers and sisters, or between parents and children, the shorthand of a family code—not so the Burneys. As Mrs Thrale herself noted: 'The Family of the Burneys are a very surprizing Set of People; their Esteem & fondness for the D^r seems to inspire them all with a Desire not to disgrace him; & so every individual of it must write and read & be literary' (*Thraliana*, i. 399). And so from the briefest 'alive', to their exchanges of 'a few pleasing words', to their long journal-letters, the Burneys took pains and pleasure in writing to one another. Joyce Hemlow has observed that the family correspondence constitutes a 'saga more dramatic, more varied, interesting, and moving than fiction ... a history of changing manners and customs ... to rival that provided in the Paston Letters.'

Part of this family saga is to be found in Burney's letters to his children. 'So now you've a Letter to swear by', Burney concludes his verse-epistle to the ten-year-old Fanny, and his letters proceed in similar vein, full of affection and intimacy, rejoicing in family triumphs, consoling in family calamities. The turning-point in Burney's life is marked by a brief note to 'My dear Girls' on his successful annexation of D.Mus. to his name in June 1769, and this volume published by the press of his own university concludes, it is hoped appropriately, with Doctor Burney writing to his favourite daughter, Susan Phillips, on the subject of Doctor Johnson.

All his life Burney rather fancied himself as a bit of a poet. He was given to composing occasional verses for his family and friends to mark birthdays and weddings and anniversaries. For the most part he presented these verse compositions by hand to their recipients. But in cases where it can be demonstrated from external evidence that he must have sent his poems through the post, the verses are treated in this edition as letters and find their place in the run of the correspondence. It is not always easy to decide which set of verses he actually posted and which he presented by hand. In exercising editorial discretion to establish the canon of Burney's verse correspondence, I have preferred to err perhaps on the side of severity and exclusion on the grounds that his poetical effusions will neither greatly enhance Burney's literary reputation nor significantly enrich the available corpus of eighteenth-century verse.

Three major runs of Burney letters do not find their rightful place in this edition: his letters to Esther Sleepe, his first wife, must be assumed to have been destroyed after her untimely death in 1762; his correspondence with Elizabeth Allen, his second wife, was consigned by Burney himself to the flames in November 1796 after her decease; and his letters to William Bewley.

Preserved in the Osborn Collection at Yale are over fifty brilliant letters from Bewley to Burney, which, to judge from their content and style, was a correspondence to rival the Burney–Twining exchange. We have fragmentary copies of only two of Burney's letters to Bewley. Bewley clearly responded in kind to Burney, whose son, Charles, in an appreciative obituary of Bewley wrote: 'His style might be considered as a model for epistolary compositions: at once easy and elegant: learned without pedantry, pleasant without affectation.' Bewley, the retiring surgeon of Great Massingham, Norfolk, fully aware of the fatal cancer within him, emerged from his obscure retreat to pay a farewell visit to his friends, and died in Burney's house in September 1783. He had probably destroyed the letters from his correspondents before leaving Massingham on his final journey. Yet the hope remains that in some hitherto unexamined hoard of old family papers these letters will one day come to light.

It would be perverse to conclude an introduction to the early letters of Charles Burney without mentioning, albeit fleetingly, the entertainment they afford. In an age of superlative letter-writers, Burney need not be assigned a humble position. His gift for the apt and eminently quotable phrase, his deep humanity in distress, the range and scope of his interests and observations attract our attention and engage our affection. Burney himself, as we have seen, considered that all letters to friends should supplement their 'last *Conversation*'. It was a principle that did not pass unnoticed by his contemporaries. His brother-in-law, Arthur Young, the traveller and agricultural reformer, wrote in his *Autobiography*, posthumously published in 1898:

In a letter from Dr. Burney . . . he rallied me with much wit on my culture of the earth instead of the Muses. This friend of mine had a happy talent of rendering his letters lively and agreeable, indeed they were a picture of the man, for I never met with any person who had more decided talents for conversation, eminently seasoned with wit and humour, and these talents were so at command that he could exert them at will.

Burney's letter to Young is, alas, not preserved.

TEXTUAL INTRODUCTION

A *Provenance*

When Burney died at the age of eighty-eight in April 1814, his papers passed by his wish to his daughter, Fanny Burney d'Arblay, who had already, while her father was still alive, assisted him in sifting through his correspondence. In the years that followed, Madame d'Arblay continued to work intermittently on her father's manuscripts, finally publishing in 1832 her *Memoirs of Doctor Burney, Arranged from His Own Manuscripts, from Family Papers, and from Personal Recollections*. The *Memoirs* appeared in three volumes to which it was Madame d'Arblay's intention to add a fourth containing Burney's correspondence. To this end she carefully read through the letters at her disposal, classified them with her characteristic dots and crosses, docketed them with her comments, assiduously altered her father's salutation 'Dear Fan' to her preferred 'Dear Fanny', traced over pale or faded ink, and surreptitiously, in a hand approximating Burney's own, with an interpolated word or two, made 'Papa' in his letters sound more religiously orthodox than he was. She also cut away with her scissors or obliterated with her heavily inked pen passages which she considered unfit to meet 'the public eye'.

Madame d'Arblay never fulfilled her ambition to print her father's correspondence, for, as she lamented in a letter to her step-brother, Stephen Allen, in May 1833, 'I am extremely perplext relative to publishing the Correspondence. I have very many Letters *to* my dear Father, but very few of his own, as he kept copies of scarcely any. Even Mr. Bewley's, which are of first rate merit, are often unintelligible without their answers—of which I have only here & there a scrap or fragment' (*JL* xii. 791).

The 'killing mass' of family papers, which by successive deaths in the family had fallen into Madame d'Arblay's hands, was divided at her own death in 1840 into two. By the terms of her will (PRO, Prerogative Court of Canterbury, Arden 88), her father's papers, with the important exception of her own letters to Burney, passed to her nephew, Burney's grandson, Charles Parr Burney (1785–1864). Madame d'Arblay's own papers, together with her letters to Burney, she bequeathed to her niece, Charlotte Francis Barrett (1786–1870). Mrs Barrett proceeded to edit with scissors and paste-pot her aunt's letters and journals to produce her seven-volume *Diary and Letters of Madame d'Arblay* (1842–6). We are not here directly concerned with the fortunes of the Barrett papers, and how they came to rest divided between the Berg Collection in The New York Public Library, and the Barrett Collection in the British Library. Their history has been fully described by Joyce Hemlow in the Introductions to her *Catalogue of the Burney Family Correspondence 1749–1878* (New York, 1971), and *The Journals and Letters of Fanny Burney (Madame d'Arblay)*, i (Oxford, 1972), as well as by Lars E. Troide in the Introduction to *The Early Journals and Letters of Fanny Burney*, i (Oxford, 1988).

Burney's papers, together with those of his son, Charles (1757–1817), the classical scholar, descended in the male line through Charles Parr Burney to the fifth Charles Burney (1840–1912), Master in the Chancery Division. The papers had been augmented by members of this branch of the family, who were industrious autograph collectors. The fifth Charles Burney fathered six daughters, one of whom, Fanny, later Mrs Atherton Cumming (1869–1954), inherited that portion of the family papers, portraits, and mementoes, which now forms the family collection of her grandson, Mr John Comyn. This collection will one day pass to his son, Hugo Charles Burney Comyn, born in 1980.

The inheritance of another daughter of the fifth Charles Burney has passed into the collection of Mr Michael Burney-Cumming. The bulk, however, of the fifth Charles Burney's family archive appears to have fallen to another of his daughters, Miss Mabel Burney (1870–1953). It was shortly after her death in 1953 that these papers found their way to the public auction rooms, where, in a series of notable sales, the late James Marshall Osborn of Yale bought them for his splendid collection of eighteenth-century manuscripts, now housed in the Beinecke Rare Book and Manuscript Library, Yale University. Subsequent sales at Sotheby's have added to the riches of the Osborn Collection, which now holds about sixty per cent of the Burney Papers that have descended in the male line of the family.

Stray collections of Burney's letters also descended in the families of their recipients. These documents have come to rest in public and private repositories scattered around the world. No effort has been spared by two generations of Burney scholars to locate them, but all are resigned to the sober truth that it is a foolhardy editor who claims his edition to be 'definitive'.

B *The Text and Conventions*

Each letter is headed with the name of the recipient, place of writing, and date. Names of recipients, places, and dates supplied by the editor have been enclosed within square brackets [ ].

The document is then briefly described in the head-note: ALS (auto-graph letter signed); AL (autograph letter, not signed); LS (letter signed, not autograph); L (letter, neither autograph nor signed). This is followed by an indication of whether the preserved document is a fragment of a letter, an extract, a draft, a copy, or in verse. Neither Burney nor Madame d'Arblay distinguished consistently between a draft and a copy. It is sometimes evident that Burney preserved his draft as a record of the letter actually sent, calling it a 'Copy'. Where possible, the hand of an amanuensis has been identified.

The location of the document is then given within parentheses. Major locations are given in abbreviated form, and are identified in the Abbreviations and Cue Titles list. Press-marks and folio or page numbers are included where they assist in locating the document. Mention is made, where appropriate, of the state of preservation of the letter, whether mounted, fragile, torn, or with leaves cut away.

Then are noted in sequence the address; franks; postmarks; endorse-ments and dockets, with line-breaks indicated by the solidus |. Madame d'Arblay's editorial symbols with which she classified Burney's letters into various categories of interest for inclusion in her projected edition of the correspondence are retained and have been interpreted:

> ※ ※ A release of top choice in interest.
>
> ※ ⚜ A release of secondary interest; also signifying 'Examined & Amalgamated with others'.
>
> ※ ⚜ ※ A release of tertiary interest.
>
> ✕ ✕ ✗
>
> ✕ ✖ *l* A release of doubtful interest.
>
> ○ Examined, to be destroyed.

Other MS drafts or copies of the same letter are listed, followed by the publication history, if any. Publication of brief extracts is not noted. An 'Editor's Note' explains any peculiarity in the source used.

The text follows, reproducing as closely as possible what Burney wrote. Square brackets [ ] enclose editorial insertions to complete the sense where Burney inadvertently omits a word or mark of punc-tuation. Conjectural readings, where the MS is incomplete, damaged, or torn, are enclosed within angle brackets ⟨ ⟩. Deletions and obliter-ations of Burney's text by subsequent hands, notably by Madame d'Arblay's, where it has been possible to retrieve the text, are indicated by half-brackets ⌐ ¬, following the procedure of the Hemlow and Troide editions of Fanny Burney. Where the editor has been unable to resurrect the words or phrases buried beneath Madame d'Arblay's swirling *e*'s, *o*'s and *m*'s, the admission of defeat has been noted thus: [xxx *3 words*] or [xxx *2 lines*].

Burney's spelling and abbreviations (including the ampersand) are retained, with the exception of the MS dot under superscripted abbreviations, e.g. w^{ch}, L^{d}, wth. Burney's capitalization is frequently perplexing. In the interests of readability, proper names have been capitalized by the editor, who has also capitalized the beginning of a sentence if preceded by a full stop. It was not the usual practice in the eighteenth century, nor was it Burney's, to capitalize after marks of interrogation and exclamation. Lower case has been retained in these cases.

Burney's punctuation has been followed. His use of the dash—often indicates the haste with which he wrote. He occasionally leaves a gap of about five to eight spaces in the line. These spaces have been interpreted as indicating a new paragraph. No attempt has been made to regularize or to render grammatical Burney's letters or phrases in foreign languages, since to do so would falsify the impression of his proficiency in these languages.

Only significant textual variants and, in the case of drafts, original phraseology are noted in the footnotes, e.g. MS Book] *interlined above deleted* volume. The rejected readings are given exactly as written, with concluding punctuation only if present in the MS. Where Burney interlines an alternative word or phrase but does not delete his original, the original reading has been followed, with the alternative dropped to the notes. Where these textual notes involve a phrase, a double-cue system is used, e.g. ⁸⁻⁸ and editorial comments appear in italic type. In addition to showing Burney at work on his letters, these notes are also intended as a record of Madame d'Arblay's editorial efforts on her father's letters. It may be assumed throughout that where Madame d'Arblay found Burney's 'Fan' she altered it to 'Fanny', a name she preferred for herself throughout her life.

Two letters in his volume pose an intriguing dilemma in textual criticism. Burney to Joseph Warton, 12 August 1771 and Burney to James Lind, 19 September 1774 have come down to us in printed texts. Also preserved are Burney's MS drafts of these letters, but not the letters actually sent through the post. On the assumption that the documents actually sent stand behind the printed text, the published sources have in both cases been taken as the copy-text. Significant variants from Burney's draft, where it can be demonstrated that the printers misread Burney's hand, inserted editorial matter, or deliberately omitted a passage, are incorporated in the text presented in this edition, with the alteration noted in the Annotation.

c *The Annotation*

The Annotation follows the general principle that the better known an event or person is, the less needs to be said by way of identification. Cross-references in the annotation, it should be observed, direct the reader to the notes cited as well as to the place in the text of the letter from which the note is dropped.

In dating, 1 January has been taken as the opening of the year. Until 1752, for official purposes, but by no means consistently, Englishmen tended to use the old reckoning from 25 March, Lady Day, so that Joseph Snookes, for example, who may have been born on 5 February 1724/5 is here given a 1725 date of birth.

Quotation from MS letters to Burney and other MS sources extracted in the annotation follows the conventions of transcription of the text as stated above. In citing published references, London, for works in English, and Paris, for works in French, are assumed to be the place of publication unless otherwise indicated. For reasons of brevity the number of volumes comprising a multi-volume work is not given unless specifically called for: reference is made only to the volume cited.

In an attempt to keep the identification of persons to manageable proportions, stress has been placed on their activities at the time Burney writes or refers to them. Thus a peer of the realm, a clergyman, or a musician who may have held a succession of posts, appointments, or preferments is normally identified by the creations and the post he or she held at the time of Burney's allusion. Oxford degrees have been normalized to modern usage: the degree first, followed by the faculty.

While every effort has been taken to explain obscurities adequately and to hold a decent silence with regard to the obvious, it is not always apparent, in the case of a writer whose interests were as catholic as Burney's, what the obvious is. In the increasing specialization of our day, what may be self-evident to a music historian may not be so to a literary scholar or a social historian and vice versa. Burney's editor must inevitably subscribe to Samuel Johnson's dictum in the Preface to his edition of Shakespeare:

It is impossible for an expositor not to write too little for some, and too much for others. He can only judge what is necessary by his own experience; and how long soever he may deliberate, will at last explain many lines which the learned will think impossible to be mistaken, and omit many for which the ignorant will want his help. These are censures merely relative, and must be quietly endured.

To Mrs Burney[1]   King's Lynn,
                              [*c.*30 September 1751][2]

AL fragment (Osborn). Second leaf missing.
    Docketed by FBA: ✳ Beautiful Testimony | of the consummate Virtues, as well | as endearing attractions of my honoured | Mother—1ˢᵗ Wife of Dr. B. | F. d'A.   *Publ.:* *Mem.* i. 88–90, extracts with alterations.

                              Lynn Rˢ Monday Morn

Now My Amiable Friend, let me unbosom myself to thee, as if I was to Enjoy the incomparable Felicity of thy Presence.—And first, let me exclaim at the unreasonableness of Man's Desires, at his unbounded Ambition & Averice, & at the inconstancy of his Temper, wᶜʰ impels him the Moment he is in Possession of the Thing that once employ'd all His Thoughts & wishes, to wish to relinquish it, & to fix his Mind's Eye on some Bauble that becomes his Point of View & that if attain'd he wou'd wish as much to Change for a Toy of perhaps Less Consequence to His interest & Quiet. O thou Constant Tenant of My Heart! (to apply the Above to My self) thou art the only Good *I* have been *Constant* to, the Only Blessing I have been thankful to Providence for, & the only one I feel I shall ever Continue to have a True Sense of. Ought I not to Blush at this Character Suiting Me! indeed I ought, & Do. Not that I think it One peculiar to Myself, I believe 'twou'd fit More than half Mankind. But it shames me to think How little I knew my self, when I fancy'd I shou'd be Happy in this Place, O God! I find it impossible I shou'd ever be so. Wou'd you believe it! that I have more than an Hundred Times Wish'd I had Never Heard its Name. Nothing but the Hopes of acquiring an independent Fortune in a Short Space of Time will keep me Here, tho' I am too deeply enter'd to retreat without great loss. But Happiness Can't be too dearly Purchas'd. I greatly dislike this Place, in short, & wou'd gladly Change it for London at any Rate. The People, tho' not Wanting in any

---

[1] Esther Burney, née Sleepe (1725–62), CB's first wife, whom he had married on 25 June 1749. See *CB Mem.* 49 n. 3, and Dawe, pp. 12–13, 85. At the time of the present letter she had borne CB three children: Esther (b. 24 May 1749); James (b. 13 June 1750); and Charles (3 June 1751–2). CB, now 25 years old, journeyed alone to King's Lynn, leaving his wife and infant children behind in London.

[2] CB could not have left London for Norfolk much before mid-Sept. 1751 (Fanny Burney was born on 13 June 1752). He probably arrived in King's Lynn in time for Michaelmas 1751. The tenor of the letter suggests that it may have been written on the morning after his first Sunday service as organist at St Margaret's Church.

I

Civillitys to Me are far from What I like.[3] I know not What use may do. For S^r Jn° T., Whom I had the Greatest Hopes from, upon a Nearer View does not answer My Expectations.[4] The Organ is Execrably bad, out of an hundred & fifty that I suppose there are in London, I dare say there is no One so bad.[5] & Add to that a Total Ignorance of the most known & Common Musicall Merits that runs thro' the Whole Body of People I have yet Convers'd with, Even S^r J: who is the Oracle of Apollo in this Country is extreamly Shallow, I say the bad Organ & the Ignorance of My Auditors must totally extinguish the few Sparks of Genius for Composition I may have, & entirely Discourage Practice.[6] For Wherin wou'd any Pains I May take to Execute a Meritorious tho' Difficult Piece of Music, be repaid if like Orpheus I am to Perform to Stocks & Trees. In short, I wish I Cou'd Make a good retreat, that is Without Offending the Gentlemen Who have been at pains as they thought to Serve Me, & before 'tis too late to be reinstated in My London "Business.[7] I wish to know (& I shall enquire to Morrow) how the 100£ that the Organ Salary is Made is to be paid;[8] if Quarterly, 'twou'd be Time enough for St Dionis if I

---

[3] See Mme d'Arblay's interlined comment, n. 13.

[4] Sir John Turner (1712–80), 3rd Baronet, MP for King's Lynn (1739–74), described by Henry Fox as 'shallow and conceited' (Namier and Brooke, iii. 570), had twice (1737, 1748) served as Mayor of Lynn, and was to do so again in 1768. With the death of John Barlow (buried 25 Apr. 1751), the incumbent organist at St Margaret's, the post had fallen vacant and Turner offered it to CB on behalf of the Mayor and Corporation. See Scholes, i. 65–7; Lonsdale, pp. 37, 39–40; *CB Mem.* 65 n. 1.

[5] This organ, with which CB wrestled for his first two and a half years at St Margaret's, 'erected in 1676 ... was then an old one removed from a College in Cambridge ... [and] so much decayed in it's several parts as to be rendered useless' (Lynn Corporation Minutes, 12 Oct. 1752. The Town Hall, King's Lynn: Hall Book, KL/C7/13, fo. 251ᵛ). In CB's time the instrument contained nine stops in the great and three in the choir organ; it stood over the choir screen at the east end of the nave (for its specification, see *Ipswich Journal*, 8 Dec. 1753; also W. Taylor, *The Antiquities of King's Lynn* (Lynn, 1844), p. 35 and plate facing p. 31). The case and ornamentation were elaborate: 'The old organ at Lynn had on it a figure of King David playing on the harp cut in solid wood, larger than the life: likewise several moving figures which beat time, &c. ... Some modern organ-builders (perhaps, in complaisance to an absurd canon) set up the Royal Arms; and we see the British Lion, with gogle eyes and shaggy mane, grinning enough to fright all the congregation'. See *GM* xlii (1772), 565; also *CB Mem.* 70 n. 1.
Thirty-eight years later, CB recalled that 'the wooden pipes were so worm-eaten as to fall to pieces when taken out to be cleaned' (*Hist. Mus.* iii. 438 n.; Mercer, ii. 345 n.).

[6] CB's musical compositions until 1751 are listed in Scholes, ii. 340–2. See also *CB Mem.* 52–3 nn., 55 n. 4, 59–60.

[7] CB's consumptive illness and removal to Lynn had interrupted a blossoming career in London. See Lonsdale, pp. 36–7; *CB Mem.* 59, 63–4.

[8] 'As an encouragement to settle there' CB's salary as the organist at King's Lynn 'was made by subscription £100 a year ... encreased to that sum from £20 a year' (BL Add. MS 48345, fo. 22ᵛ; *CB Mem.* 65). The churchwardens' accounts show that the 'usual Salary' was in fact £30, and that the salaries of parish employees were due them each year at Lady Day, on 25 Mar. (Norfolk Record Office: PD 39/76 (S)).

return'd at X^mas or a little after.[9] & if any of My Schollars, as Miss Robinson,[10] Frasi,[11] Miss Douglas[12] had . . ."[13]

To Mrs Burney[1]
King's Lynn,
19 December 1751

Source: Mem. i. 91–4. Some lines of CB's verse letter were omitted by FBA, who inserted in their place a series of asterisks.

Lynn Regis.

Come, my darling!—quit the town;
Come!—and me with rapture crown.

*   *   *   *

If 'tis meet to fee or bribe
A leech of th' Æsculapius tribe,
We Hepburn[2] have, who's wise as Socrates,
And deep in physic as Hippocrates.
Or, if 'tis meet to take the air,

[9] In Oct. 1749, CB had won election to the post of organist at St Dionis Backchurch, Fenchurch Street, in the City of London, which carried an annual salary of £30 (*CB Mem.* 54).
This passage, obliterated by Mme d'Arblay, confirms that CB at this time considered his move to Lynn merely as a temporary though profitable sick-leave from his duties at St Dionis's. Lonsdale (p. 39 n. 2) correctly finds significance in CB's tardy resignation at Easter 1752 from his London post. See also Dawe, p. 85; and *Daily Advertiser*, 24 Jan. 1752.

[10] Possibly the daughter (*fl.* 1733–45) of John Robinson (*c.*1682–1762), the organist of Westminster Abbey. A contralto, she sang the part of Daniel at the first performance of Handel's oratorio *Belshazzar* (27 Mar. 1745). CB described her as 'a coarse singer, with an unpleasant toned voice; but that did not prevent her from becoming a great player on the harpsichord' ('Robinson, Miss' in Rees; see also 'Palschau' in Rees).

[11] Giulia Frasi (*fl.* 1742–72), Italian soprano who had become CB's pupil in 1749. See *CB Mem.* 56–7.

[12] Not identified. It is not certain that the name buried under the obliteration is 'Douglas'.

[13] MS Business . . . had] *obliterated by FBA, who then interlined* stet Business. NB. Dr. Burney afterwards became reconciled to Lynn, & as partial to its Inhabitants as they were, universally, to him.

[1] According to Mme d'Arblay, Mrs Burney, in response to CB's letter of [*c.*30 Sept. 1751], had 'pleaded for his accommodating himself to his new situation' (*Mem.* i. 90). For Mrs Burney's lively interest in reading, see n. 5 below; and *CB Mem.* 69.

[2] George Hepburn (1669–1759), MD, a Scot, physician to Sir Robert Walpole, had settled in King's Lynn early in the century 'as a physician; in which character he soon acquired high reputation, so as to be placed at the head of the profession in this part of the kingdom for near if not quite half a century' (W. Richards, *The History of Lynn* (Lynn, 1812), ii. 1028). See also Walpole *Corresp.* xl. 226; *EJL* i. 17 n. 45; *CB Mem. post* 65 n. 3.

3

You borne shall be on horse or mare;[3]
And, 'gainst all chances to provide,
I'll be your faithful 'squire and guide.
    If unadulterate wine be good
To glad the heart, and mend the blood,
We that in plenty boast at Lynn,[4]
Would make with pleasure Bacchus grin.
    Should nerves auricular demand
A head profound, and cunning hand,
The charms of music to display,
Pray,—cannot *I* compose and play?
And strains to your each humour suit
On organ, violin, or flute?
    If these delights you deem too transient,
We modern authors have, or antient,
Which, while I've lungs from phthisicks freed,
To thee with rapture, sweet, I'll read.
    If Homer's bold, inventive fire,
Or Virgil's art, you most admire;
If Pliny's eloquence and ease,
Or Ovid's flowery fancy please;
In fair array they marshall'd stand,
Most humbly waiting your command.
    To humanize and mend the heart,
Our serious hours we'll set apart.

          *   *   *   *

    We'll learn to separate right from wrong,
Through Pope's mellifluous moral song.
    If wit and humour be our drift,
We'll laugh at knaves and fools with Swift.
    To know the world, its follies see,
Ourselves from ridicule to free,
To whom for lessons shall we run,
But to the pleasing Addison?
    Great Bacon's learning; Congreve's wit,
By turns thy humour well may hit.
    How sweet, original, and strong,
How high the flights of Dryden's song!
He, though so often careless found,

---

[3] For CB's faithful mare Peggy, see *Mem.* i. 107–8, 133; and *CB Mem.* 68.
[4] King's Lynn was an important seaport, and importation of wine was one source of the wealth of its merchants. See Bradfer-Lawrence, pp. 151–203.

4

Lifts us so high above the ground
That we disdain terrestrial things,
And scale Olympus while he sings.
    Among the bards who mount the skies
Whoe'er to such a height could rise
As Milton? he, to whom 'twas given
To plunge to Hell, and mount to Heaven.
How few like thee—my soul's delight!
Can follow him in every flight?[5]
    La Mancha's knight, on gloomy day,
Shall teach our muscles how to play,
And at the black fanatic class,
We'll sometimes laugh with Hudibras.
    When human passions all subside,
Where shall we find so sure a guide
Through metaphysics' mazy ground
As Locke—scrutator most profound?
    One bard there still remains in store,
And who has him need little more:
A bard above my feeble lay;
Above what wiser scribes can say.
He would the secret thoughts reveal
Of all the human mind can feel:
None e'er like him in every feature
So fair a likeness drew of Nature.
No passion swells the mortal breast
But what his pencil has exprest:
Nor need I tell my heart's sole queen
That Shakespeare is the bard I mean.
    May heaven, all bounteous in its care,
These blessings, and our offspring spare!
And while our lives are thus employ'd,
No earthly bliss left unenjoy'd,
May we—without a sigh or tear—
Together finish our career!
Together gain another station
Without the pangs of separation!
    And when our souls have travelled far
Beyond this little dirty star,

[5] Mrs Burney's taste in literature appears in her correspondence with Mrs Greville, who wrote to her on 30 Jan. 1759: 'I go on with Old Spencer from time to time, but I don't believe that I shall finish it *Eftsoons*; *Nathless* many things please me much ... Old Spencer talks very plain English now & then' (Berg). See also CB to Mrs Greville, [?July 1756], n. 1.

5

Beyond the reach of strife, or noise,
To taste celestial, stable joys—
O may we still together keep—
Or may our death be endless sleep!

Lynn Regis, 19th Dec. 1751.

To Fulke Greville[1]   [King's Lynn, 1752?][2]

Source: Mem. i. 110–12. Some lines of CB's verse letter were omitted by FBA, who inserted in their place a series of asterisks.

TO FULK GREVILLE, ESQ., AT PARIS.

Hence, 'loathed business,' which so long
Has plunged me in the toiling throng.
Forgive, dear Sir! and gentle Madam![3]
A drudging younger son of Adam,
Who's forc'd from morn to night to labor
Or at the pipe, or at the tabor:
Nor has he hope 'twill e'er be o'er
Till landed on some kinder shore;
Some more propitious star, whose rays
Benign, may cheer his future days.[4]

Ah, think for rest how he must pant
Whose life's the summer of an ant!
With grief o'erwhelm'd, the wretched Abel[5]
Is dumb as architect of Babel.[6]

---

[1] Fulke Greville (1717–1806), MP for Monmouth (1747–54), CB's early patron, later author of *Maxims, Characters, and Reflections, Critical, Satyrical, and Moral* (1756). Mme d'Arblay describes CB's meeting him in the summer of 1746 at the shop of Jacob Kirkman (1710–92) the harpsichord maker (*Mem.* i. 24–35). Greville took CB to Wilbury, his seat in Wiltshire, introduced him to high society and at Michaelmas 1748 purchased his three remaining years of apprenticeship to Thomas Arne (1710–78) for £300. See *CB Mem.* 41–7 and Lonsdale, pp. 14–23.

[2] The date of this verse epistle is uncertain. In 1749 CB was supposed to accompany the Grevilles to Italy, but instead chose to marry Esther Sleepe and stay in England (Lonsdale, pp. 21–2; *CB Mem.* 50). The Grevilles stayed abroad until late 1753 or early 1754. It was from Paris that they sent CB a printed copy of Rousseau's *Le Devin du village*, published in 1753 (*CB Mem.* 109; Lonsdale, pp. 44, 70–1).

[3] Frances Greville, Fulke Greville's wife. See CB to Mrs Greville, [?July 1756], n. 1.

[4] CB's activities, besides his duties as organist at St Margaret's, consisted chiefly of giving lessons to pupils in and around King's Lynn. See *Mem.* i. 107–9; *CB Mem. post* 65 n. 6; Scholes, i. 67–76; Lonsdale, pp. 38–45.

[5] Abel Drugger, in Ben Jonson's *The Alchemist*, was one of Garrick's great roles. CB acquired this nickname 'from imitating Garrick . . . during the theatricals at Wilbury' (*Mem.* i. 111 n.).

[6] See Genesis 10:8–10; 11:1–9.

—Three months of sullen silence—seem
With black ingratitude to teem;[7]
As if my heart were made of stone
Which kindness could not work upon;
Or benefits e'er sit enshrin'd
Within the precincts of my mind.
 But think not so, dear Sir! my crime
Proceeds alone from want of time.
No more a giddy youth, and idle,
Without a curb, without a bridle,
Who frisk'd about like colt unbroke,
And life regarded as a joke.—
No!—different duties now are mine;
Nor do I at my cares repine:
With naught to think of but myself
I little heeded worldly pelf;
But now, alert I act and move
For others whom I better love.
 Should you refuse me absolution,
Condemning my new institution,
'Twould chill at once my heart and zeal
For this my little commonweal.—
O give my peace not such a stab!
Nor slay—as Cain did—name-sake Nab.[8]

   * * * *

 This prologue first premis'd, in hopes
Such figures, metaphors, and tropes
For pardon will not plead in vain,
We'll now proceed in lighter strain.

   * * * *

To Lord Orford[1]   King's Lynn, 18 September 1752

Source: The letter belonged to H. L. Bradfer-Lawrence, who permitted Percy A. Scholes to make a transcript in 1930, but refused permission to publish, as it was to

[7] Greville's letter from the continent is not preserved.
[8] See Genesis 4:1–16.

[1] George Walpole (1730–91), 3rd Earl of Orford (1751), grandson of Sir Robert Walpole (1676–1745), and nephew of Horace Walpole (1717–97). From his father Robert (1701–51),

have been included in a volume about Lynn celebrities which Mr Bradfer-Lawrence intended to write. The text follows Scholes's transcript, now in the Osborn Collection.

Addressed: To the Right Honorable The Earl of Orford, | at his House in London.[2]

My Lord,

Having advertized a concert at Swaffham in the Race Week for Wednesday the 27th inst. at 11 o'clock in the morning;[3] I thought it my duty to acquaint your Lordship with it, in humble hopes of your Lordship's patronage & presence,[4] particularly as the last time I had the honor of seeing your Lordship, you was pleas'd to command me whenever I made a concert to give you information of it.

I have hopes from your Lordship's love of music, & from the favourable & flattering reception you was pleased to condescend to honor [me] with; that the freedom of this application will be pardon'd.

I am my Lord, with the highest respect,
your Lordship's Most devoted
&
most obliged servant,
Charles Burney

Lynn Regis 18th Septr. | 1752.

To Fulke Greville [King's Lynn], July 1753[1]

AL verse copy (Osborn: shelves c 97, pp. 101–7).

Epistle. *To Fulk Grevile Esqʳ*
Once more, for Love of Ryme & Grevile,
I court the Nine in Speeches civil;

2nd Earl of Orford, George Walpole had inherited Houghton Hall, Norfolk, where CB enjoyed his 'constant patronage & regard' (*CB Mem.* 84).

[2] Lord Orford's London house was in Green Street, Grosvenor Square.

[3] Horse-races were run at Swaffham, 15 miles south-east of King's Lynn, on 3 days, 26–8 Sept. 1752. The *Norwich Mercury*, 22–9 Aug. 1752, carried a preliminary announcement of CB's concert and a full advertisement in the number for 16–23 Sept. The venue for the concert was the Crown Inn: 'The first VIOLIN, with a Solo, by Mr. FISHER from *Cambridge*, who will likewise perform a Solo on the VIOLONCELLO. First HAUTBOIS, with a Solo, by Mr. SHARP from *Stamford*: And the HARPSICHORD, with a Concerto and Lesson, by Mr. BURNEY.' Tickets, available at the Crown Inn and at CB's house in Lynn, were priced at 3s. For an account of CB's concert activities in and around King's Lynn, see Scholes, i. 85–7 and *CB Mem. post* 65 n. 1 and 71.

[4] CB's 'humble hopes' in Lord Orford's attendance were probably fulfilled: Orford raced his chestnut mare, Mischance, against 'Mr. Shaftoe's brown Gelding Tinker' for 4 miles over the Swaffham course. Stake-money was set at 100 guineas (*Norwich Mercury*, 29 Aug.–16 Sept. 1752).

[1] The date of this verse epistle is confirmed by CB's mention of Avison's recently published *Essay on Musical Expression* (nn. 16–17 below).

& much the Ears of them & *Sun*[2] drum
For pun, for Quibble, & Conundrum.
No more Old Handel's ample Page,
Or sweet Scarlatti's happy Rage,[3]
(wch well can draw or dry up Tears)
My Hands employ, or fill my Ears:
Neglecting Things within my Ken,
The Bow I quit to Wield the Pen.
Nor solemn Semibreve I swell,
Nor on the tardy Minim dwell,
The sable-Headed Crotchet Curse,
& fly them all for Jingling Verse.
   But wafted by a darting Ray,
Methinks I hear Apollo[4] say—
"Pray Younker mind your fidling Trade,
Nor e'er in Ryme Expect our Aid:
Altho' the healing Art be Mine,
To Which I Verse & Music Join,
Yet vainly think not Friend that you
Can have our Help in any Two
There's more to be attain'd in one
Than e'er our brightest earthly Son
Has yet been able to surmount
Tho Homer 'mongst those Sons you count
   Of all the Scrapers at our Shrine
Whose Music mortals call divine
There's none, how far soe'er he launches
E'er shone alike in all its Branches
One charms with TASTE perhaps a Nation
Yet wants the Rules of SOLMIZATION[5]
& Odds 'tis, if *profound* his Vein
He's Gifted with a Costive Brain.
   CORELLI[6] mov'd with even Gale

---

[2] Apollo, patron of the Muses.
[3] Domenico Scarlatti (1685–1757), harpsichordist and composer, founder of modern keyboard execution. See below n. 10.
[4] MS Apollo] *interlined over deleted* my Daddy.
The rest of the epistle, until the last 4 lines, is Apollo's address to CB, who 6 years earlier had founded with the Scottish composer and music publisher James Oswald (1711–69) the Society of the Temple of Apollo (*CB Mem.* 53; Lonsdale, pp. 30–1).
[5] 'Naming the notes in the scale according to the hexachord of Guido' (Rees).
[6] Arcangelo Corelli (1653–1713), CB wrote later, had inaugurated 'a memorable æra for the *violin, tenor,* and *violoncello* ... rendered them respectable, and fixed their use and reputation, in

9

While I, & Nature Swell'd his Sail
With modesty his Course he steer'd
Nor Rocks or Quicksands ever feer'd
For well alike to him were known
Both Musick's *Compass* & his own
Thus free from cankring Critick's Blame
He safe arriv'd at endless Fame.
　　He, dying, from his Lawrel Wreath,
His great Disciple[7] did bequeath
A Sprig, wch planted on his Brow
Did all his Master's Bays outgrow.
The sprightly Violin he taught
T'express each Passion Word & Thought
Nor from his Pen shall Envy see
Ought that's unworthy him or me
As Sister Pallas, not in vain
Witholds the Bard from Lyric Strain
　　For him each tuneful Briton's Heart
The Warmest Wishes still impart
For plain he points each trackless Road
I' th' Way to Fame he ever trod
& with Desert like this shall be
The Idol of Posterity[8]
　　PURCEL,[9] the Orpheus of your Climes
Ador'd by's own & after Times
Whose Mind so richly was endow'd
Whose Melodies so sweetly flow'd
Uniting with Poetic Fire
Such Sounds as I alone inspire
Had been (by me & Fancy Nurs'd)
In age the most enlighten'd, First.

all probability, as long as the present system of Music shall continue to delight the ears of mankind' (*Hist. Mus.* iii. 550; Mercer, ii. 437).

[7] MS Disciple] *CB notes in margin* Geminiani.

The Italian violinist, theorist, and composer Francesco Xaverio Geminiani (1687–1762), came to England in 1714 and in 1751 published his influential treatise, *The Art of Playing on the Violin.*

[8] Later in life CB's admiration for Geminiani diminished: 'As a musician, he was certainly a great master of harmony, and very useful to our country in his day; but though he had more variety of modulation, and more skill in diversifying his parts than Corelli, his melody was even inferior, and there is frequently an irregularity in his measures and phraseology' (*Hist. Mus.* iv. 645; Mercer, ii. 994).

[9] CB considered Henry Purcell (1659–95) 'an English musician of more extensive genius than perhaps our country can boast at any other period of time', and his vocal music 'as superior to Handel's as an original poem to a translation' ('Purcell' in Rees).

SCARLATTI,[10] blest with brightest Ray
That e'er illumin'd human Clay
Happy Enthusiast! whose Strains
(Offspring of Genius not of Pains)
Can raise the Soul to heav'nly Bliss
Or drive her down Grief's fell Abyss
By him such Sounds are oft combin'd
As other Mortal n'er c^d find
Such as in th'Idalian Grove[11]
Or playing at the Throne of Jove
Surrounded by the heav'nly Host
I alone 'mongst *Gods* can boast.
   Great HANDEL,[12] whose Extensive Soul
Essay'd to comprehend the Whole
Who ne'er to this or that confin'd
His Genius try'd in ev'ry kind,
Which was, (his works prove in Rehearsal)
Of all Mankind's most universal
   But if there's ought his Fame can blast
'Tis want of Elegance & Taste
& that, the Rabble's Ear to touch
He study'd & he writ too much
Yet sure these wants are well supply'd
By Beauties Time can never hide
As he of all the Wights before us

---

[10] CB later wrote in one of his musical notebooks the following hitherto unpublished estimate of Domenico Scarlatti: 'This is the only favourite Composer, for keyed Instrum^{ts} perhaps, whose works may be truely called *inimitable*. The style of Handel, Alberti, Eman. Bach & all other great & original Geniuses have been copied, & made the Standards of Perfection for a Time wherever they have been known: & even peculiarities & refinements of C.P.E. Bach have been imitated with excess throughout Germany; but neither Italy, Spain or England, where Scarlatti's Pieces have been universally admired, has produced a similar Genius or any one Production, that bears the least resemblance to his either in wildness, boldness of Invention & modulation, or in that spirited & Characteristic manner of shewing all the powers of the Harp^d even without Pedals or the Assistance of any other modern improvements, wch can vary the colouring of each Piece by the Musical *Chiar'oscuro*, of *Forte* & *Piano*. Scarlatti has the art of introducing light & shade into his Pieces by sudden transitions wch render them in particular places pathetic even during the most rapid movements. He knew the defects of the Harp^d too well to write slow movem^{ts} (adagios) for it: indeed his Genius seems too impetuous for such productions—however, he has supplied the want of them by Strokes of distress & passion without arriving at long sounds by dwelling on them beyond the vibrating Power of his Instrument, whose Tones are too transient either to sustain or Express them' (Osborn: shelves c 97, pp. 32–3). See also *CB Mem.* 43 n. 8; and *Tours*, ii. 220.

[11] A grove consecrated to Venus, near Idalion in Cyprus.

[12] CB's great and genuine admiration for Handel in his *Hist. Mus.*, *Handel Commem.*, and his article 'Handel' in Rees was tempered by his opposition to the 'cult of Handel' in England at the expense of modern music (see Grant, pp. 243–5, 287–90).

Supremely best can Swell the *Chorus*
& when his Fugues the *Organ* fill
Both Men & Gods revere his Skill.
　To PEPUSCH, Musick's Catechism
We gave to drive & keep out Scism
A BENTLEY in his Art was he
Whose Eye cou'd faults not Beauties see.[13]
　To ARNE[14] With Genius great endow'd
We *Ballads* gave to please the Croud.
　BOYCE[15] has the Art, with holy Rapture
To lull asleep the Dean & Chapter—
But wou'dst thou know them ev'ry One
Go read with Care Friend AVISON[16]
His flowry Eloquence displays
Their Gifts from Orpheus down to Hayes[17]
In Words wch well the Subject suit
As breath'd thro' sweet Euterpe's Flute

[13] Johann Christoph Pepusch (1667–1752), composer of German origin, came to England *c.*1704. CB had met him in 1746 (*CB Mem.* 35, 43 n. 5) as an old man, when Pepusch concerned himself with 'every thing concerning ancient harmonics, that was dark, unintelligible, and foreign to common and useful practice'. To the young admirer of modern Italian composers he appeared 'as a pedant totally devoid of genius', though later CB acknowledged Pepusch's devotion to ancient music ('Pepusch' in Rees).

Richard Bentley (1662–1742), classical scholar and critic, had been satirized by Pope and Swift as a pedant ('slashing Bentley') because of his passion for emending classical texts.

[14] Thomas Augustine Arne (1710–78), under whom CB had served as apprentice (1744–8) until Greville released him from his 'tutelage' (*CB Mem.* 21–31, 47). Of Arne's popular music, CB wrote: 'in his songs for the theatres and public gardens, he was ever triumphant over all competitors. At Vauxhall, particularly, ... his ballads ... were performed during many years with great applause, and were afterwards circulated all over the kingdom' ('Arne' in Rees).

[15] William Boyce (1711–79), Mus.D. (1749), organist, composer, and musical antiquary; editor of the three-volume collection of English *Cathedral Music* (1760, 1768, 1773). CB's name appears among the subscribers to the first volume, and his flippant suggestion here that Boyce's compositions induce slumber was not his considered opinion. CB later wrote: 'Dr. Boyce, with all due reverence for the abilities of Handel, was one of the few of our church composers who neither pillaged nor servilely imitated him. There is an original and sterling merit in his productions, founded as much on the study of our own old masters, as on the best models of other countries, that gives to all his works a peculiar stamp and character of his own, for strength, clearness, and facility, without any mixture of styles, or extraneous and heterogeneous ornaments' (*Hist. Mus.* iii. 620–1; Mercer, ii. 493–4).

[16] Charles Avison (1709–70), composer, musical theorist, and director of the Musical Society in Newcastle-upon-Tyne, was a pupil of Geminiani. In 1752 he published his controversial *An Essay on Musical Expression* (see also n. 17). CB later wrote of Avison: 'he was the first, and almost the only writer, who attempted' musical criticism in England, 'But his judgment was warped by many prejudices' (*Hist. Mus.* iii, p. vi; Mercer, ii. 7).

[17] William Hayes (1708–77), D.Mus. (1749), Heather Professor of Music at Oxford (1742–77), whom young CB had met in Shrewsbury (*CB Mem.* 16 n. 3). In Jan. 1753 Hayes had published anonymously critical *Remarks on Mr. Avison's Essay on Musical Expression*, to which Avison published *A Reply* on 22 Feb. 1753, followed by a second edition of his *Essay* later in the year. See 'Avison' in *New Grove*; Kassler, i. 30–4, 488–90.

And now our Mandate quick attend
Henceforth thy Thoughts on Music bend
Nor more in Jingling Nonsense piddle
But quickly reassume thy Fiddle
& if thou'dst not be disinherited
By Us wch richly thou hast merited
Go & thy Gamut well explore
In search of Sounds untuned before
(If ought thro' Music's wide Domain
Uncultur'd & unknown remain)
Go, nor Thy fleeting Hours mispend
In quest of Ryme will tire thy Friend.
   If not to these Commands Obedient
To punish we've a quick expedient
Thy Finger shall forget to move
(Thy Eye no more its Index prove)[18]
Nor shall Obedient to thy Will
The Honey of each page distil."
—Thus ended the celestial Hector[19]
His sharp—& worse than Curtain-Lecture;
& with his Racket, coil & fuss
I tumbled off my Pegasus.

                    July. 1753

To Mrs Burney   King's Lynn, 1753

Source: Mem. i. 131–3. Some lines of CB's verse letter were omitted by FBA, who inserted in their place a series of asterisks.

To Mrs. Burney.[1]

To thee, henceforth, my matchless mate,
My leisure hours I'll dedicate;
To thee my inmost thoughts transmit,
Whene'er the busy scene I quit.
   For thee, companion dear! I feel
An unextinguishable zeal;

---

[18] The eye will no longer direct the hand. CB later often complained of severe cramps in his hands, which interfered with his musical performance as well as his writing.

[19] Apollo, the speaker of this hectoring passage.

[1] According to Mme d'Arblay, CB sent this verse letter to his wife 'during a short separation, while still at Lynn' (*Mem.* i. 130).

13

A love implanted in the mind,
From all the grosser dregs refined.
Ah! tell me, must not love like mine
Be planted by a hand divine,
Which, when creation's work was done,
Our heart-strings tuned in unison?
   If business, or domestic care
The vigour of my mind impair;
If forc'd by toil from thee to rove,
'Till wearied limbs forget to move,
At night, reclin'd upon thy breast,
Thy converse lulls my soul to rest.
   If sickness her distemper'd brood
Let loose,—to burn, or freeze my blood,
Thy tender vigilance and care,
My feeble frame can soon repair.
   When in some doubtful maze I stray,
'Tis thou point'st out the unerring way;
If judgment float on wavering wings,
In notions vague of men and things;
If different views my mind divide,
Thy nod instructs me to decide.
My pliant soul 'tis thou can'st bend,
My help! companion! wife! and friend!
   When, in the irksome day of trouble
The mental eye sees evil double,
Sweet partner of my hopes and fears!
'Tis thou alone can'st dry my tears.
'Tis thou alone can'st bring relief,
Partner of every joy and grief!
E'en when encompass'd with distress,
Thy smile can every ill redress.
   On thee, my lovely, faithful friend,
My worldly blessings all depend:
But if a cloud thy visage low'r, ⎫
Not all the wealth in Plutus' power, ⎬
Could buy my heart one peaceful hour. ⎭
Then, lodg'd within that aching heart,
Is sorrow's sympathetic dart.

      *   *   *   *

   But when upon that brow, the seat
Of sense refin'd, and beauty sweet,

The graces and the loves are seen,
And Venus sits by Wisdom's queen;
Pale sadness takes her heavy flight,
And, envious, shuns the blissful sight.
   So when the sun has long endur'd
His radiant face to be obscur'd
By baleful mists and vapours dense,
All nature mourns with grief intense:
But the refulgent God of Day
Soon shews himself in bright array;
And as his glorious visage clears,
The globe itself in smiles appears.

Lynn, 1753.

To The Churchwardens and Parishioners of St Margaret's, King's Lynn[1]

King's Lynn,
1 February 1755

LS copy ('Churchwardens' accounts with vestry minutes and church rates 1752–1772' of St Margaret's Church, King's Lynn. Norfolk Record Office: PD 39/76(S)).
  Publ.: Musical Times, xlv (1904), 439; H. J. Hillen, *History of the Borough of King's Lynn* (Norwich, 1907), ii. 494; Scholes, i. 81.

High Street 1st Feb$\overline{ry}$ 1755

Gentlemen,
  The Subscription being Expired which first induced me to reside in this Town,[2] & my Success in other respects falling short of my Expectations; the Organ Salary is too inconsiderable to retain me in your Service.[3]

---

[1] In 1755, the churchwardens of St Margaret's were James Robertson and Thomas Hawkins. The copy of CB's letter in the churchwardens' accounts book is introduced with the preamble: 'Parish of Saint Margaret in King's Lynn in Norfolk. At a Meeting of the Parishioners this 3^d Day of February in the year of our Lord 1755, pursuant to publick Notice given in the Church on Sunday last for that Purpose—This Day a Letter from Mr Chas Burney Organist Dated the 1st Day of this instant February directed to the Churchwardens, & Parishion^{rs} of this Parish was read, and follows in these Words—'.

[2] For details about CB's High Street house, located in the Chequer Ward, see Hillen, ii. 492; Scholes, i. 74, 86 n. 2, and plate 8 facing p. 72. The churchwardens' accounts reveal that from 1753 to 1757, CB paid an annual rent of £10. 13s. 4d. From 1758 to 1760 he paid £7.

[3] See CB to Mrs Burney, [c.30 Sept. 1751], n. 8. In King's Lynn, CB's income was supplemented by subscription concerts. He organized two such musical evenings at the Town Hall, on 8 Feb. and 28 Aug. 1753 (*Norwich Mercury*, 27 Jan.–3 Feb.; 28 July–4 Aug.).

15

I am therefore oblig'd to inform you that I shall resign my Place of Organist at Michaelmas next, or sooner, if you can meet with a Person to your Satisfaction to Succeed me[4]—

And here permit me to Acquaint you, that the Fine Instrument[5] in your Possession requires great Time & Pains to keep it in Order, from the Multiplicity of its Stops; the chief whereof I can faithfully Assure you will soon become useless if neglected in this particular.[6] And give me Leave further to add, that the Tuning an Organ is no where understood to be a part of the Person's Business who performs upon it, & the less so, as very few Organists are Qualified for the Undertaking—

I thank you for the Honour conferr'd upon me by my Election, & am

Gentlemen,
y^r most Obedient,
and most Hble Servant
Ch: Burney

To Samuel Johnson

King's Lynn,
16 February 1755

ALS copy (William Luther Lewis Collection, Mary Couts Burnett Library, Texas Christian University, Fort Worth, Texas).

Endorsed by CB: Copy of 1st Letter | to Mr Saml Johnson | Feby 16. 1755. | N° 1. *Docketed by* FBA: ✳ I To D^r. Johnson | Feby 1755   *Publ.: The Harmonicon*, xi (1833), 53; *Mem.* i. 119–20.

The churchwardens' accounts at Easter 1754 record: 'Charles Burney Organist unpaid', and at Easter 1755: 'Mr Burney for 2 Y^r [£]60' (Norfolk Record Office: PD 39/76(S)). Anxiety over the prospect of a second year's unpaid service may in part have provoked CB to send in this letter of resignation before Lady Day and Easter 1755. CB must also have complained to his friend Samuel Crisp (*c.*1707–83) of low fees from Lynn music pupils. Crisp's reply is illuminating: 'Your underrate prices in the town, and galloping about the country for higher, especially in the winter—are they worthy of your talents?' (Crisp to CB, [1754?], untraced, quoted in part in *Mem.* i. 128–9; Lonsdale, p. 45 n. 2).

[4] In response to this letter, the Parish of St Margaret's resolved at the Vestry meeting held 'according to antient Custom' on Easter Monday (31 Mar.) 1755 to advertise a vacancy for the post.

[5] The new organ, built at CB's instigation by Johann Snetzler (1710–85), had been 'opened' by CB on 17 Mar. 1754. For a detailed account of the construction and specification of this instrument, see Scholes, i. 77–80; ii. 319–20.

[6] Much later CB recalled with satisfaction his part in the construction of this organ: 'Snetzler put a reed stop in the Lynn Org. under my eye, wch he called a *Fr. Horn.*—it was a louder and coarser kind of Hautboy' (CB to Callcott, 14 Jan. 1803). See also *Hist. Mus.* iii. 438 n.; Mercer, ii. 345 n.; and *CB Mem.* 70.

Lynn Regis, Norfolk.

Sir

Though I have never had the happiness of a personal knowledge of you, I cannot think myself wholly a stranger to a man with whose sentiments I have so long been acquainted:[1] for it seems to me as if the writer who was sincere had effected the plan of that Philosopher who wished that men had windows at their breasts, through which the affections of their hearts might be viewed.[2]

It is with great self-denial that I refrain from giving way to panegyric in speaking of the pleasure & instruction I have rec^d from your admirable writings; but knowing that transcendent merit shrinks more at praise, than either vice or dulness at censure, I shall compress my encomiums into a short compass, & only tell you, that I revere your principles & integrity in not prostituting your genius, learning, & knowledge of the human heart, in ornamenting vice or folly wth those beautiful flowers of Language, due only to wisdom & virtue. I must add that your periodical Productions seem to me models of true genius, useful learning, & elegant diction, employed in the service of the purest precepts of religion, & the most inviting morality.

I shall wave any further gratification of my wish to tell you, Sir, how much I have been delighted by your productions; & proceed to the *business* of this letter; wch is no other than to beg the favour of you to inform me, by the way that will give you the least trouble, *when*, & in *what manner*, your admirably-planned, & long-wished-for Dictionary, will be published?[3] If it should be by *Subscription*, or you sh^d have any books at your own disposal, I shall beg of you to favour me with 6 Copies for myself & friends, for which I will send you a [4]draught ⌐for the money, as soon as I shall know the requisite sum.⌐[4]

[1] 'Mr. Burney was one of the first and most fervent admirers of . . . the Rambler and the Idler. He took them both in; he read them to all his friends; and was the first to bring them to a bookish little coterie that assembled weekly at Mrs. Stephen Allen's' (*Mem.* i. 117–18). Christopher Smart (1722–71), the poet, had first called CB's attention to *The Rambler* (see Hill–Powell, i. 208 n. 3; Lonsdale, pp. 45–6). For a comprehensive account of CB's friendship with Dr Johnson, see R. Lonsdale, 'Johnson and Dr. Burney', in *Johnson, Boswell and Their Circle*, ed. M. M. Lascelles, *et al.* (Oxford, 1965), pp. 21–40.

[2] See Lucian, *Hermotimus*, 20. According to the tale, Momus, the faultfinder, judged a contest between Athena, Poseidon, and Hephaestus. Momus objected to Hephaestus's invention, Man, for he had no window in his breast through which his thoughts and sentiments could be seen. CB may have obtained his reference from Pope's published letters. See *The Correspondence of Alexander Pope*, ed. G. Sherburn (Oxford, 1956), i. 353; ii. 23; also 'A Window in the Breast', *The Oxford Book of Greek Verse*, ed. G. Murray (Oxford, 1931), p. 203.

[3] The *Dictionary* was to come out on 15 Apr. 1755 in two folio volumes, priced 90s. (W. P. Courtney and D. Nichol Smith, *A Bibliography of Samuel Johnson* (Oxford, 1925), pp. 54–5).

[4]–4 MS draught for . . . sum.] *FBA placed a period after* draught *and deleted the rest of the sentence.*

'I have no Dictionaries to dispose of for myself,' wrote Johnson in his answer of 8 Apr., 'but shall be glad to have you direct your friends to Mr. Dodsley, because it was by his recommendation that I was employed in the work' (Johnson *Letters*, i. 69).

17

I ought to beg pardon of the public, as well as yourself, Sir, for detaining you thus long from your useful labours; but it is the fate of men of eminence to be persecuted by insignificant friends, as well as enemies; & the simple cur who barks through fondness & affection is no less troublesome, than if stimulated by anger & aversion.

I hope however that your Philosophy will incline you to forgive the intemperance of my zeal & impatience in making these enquiries,[5] as well my ambition to subscribe myself with very great regard, Sir,

Your sincere admirer,
and most humble servant.
Cha[s] Burney.

Feb[y] 16. 1755.

To Samuel Johnson

King's Lynn,
14 April 1755

ALS draft (Hyde).
Endorsed by CB: To M[r] Johnson. 14th Apr. 1755. N° 2. This neither had nor required an immediate answer   *Docketed by* FBA: 2.(1) 14. April—1775 2 ✳   *Also* L copy incomplete (Osborn) in the hand of FBA.[1]   *Publ.*: *Mem.* i. 122–4; Mercer, ii. 1027–8; Scholes, i. 89–90.

Sir.

That you w[d] think my Letter[2] worthy of notice, was what I began to Despair of. & indeed I had framed & admitted several Reasons for your Silence, more than sufficient to exculpate you.

But so highly has your Politeness rated my Intentions, that I find it impossible for me to resist accepting the Invitation with which you have honoured[3] me of writing to you again,[4] though Conscious, that I have nothing to offer w[ch] can by any means merit y[r] attention.

---

[5] Johnson answered (8 Apr.): 'Your civilities were offered with too much elegance not to engage attention; and I have too much pleasure in pleasing men like you, not to feel very sensibly the distinction which you have bestowed upon me' (Johnson *Letters*, i. 68).

[1] This single leaf in Mme d'Arblay's hand is a fragment of the MS of the *Memoirs of Doctor Burney*. The text runs from the postscript of this letter to Johnson, 'Have you, Sir, ever met with a little French Book . . .', continues with connecting narrative, and concludes with the beginning of CB's next letter to Johnson, 26 Mar. 1757, as far as '. . . a great part of its furniture: but as praise is' (*Mem.* i. 123–5).

[2] Of 16 Feb. 1755.

[3] MS honoured] *interlined over deleted* favoured

[4] Johnson wrote (8 Apr.): 'When you have leisure to think again upon me, let me be favoured with another letter; and another yet, when you have looked into my Dictionary' (Johnson *Letters*, i. 69). See also *Mem.* i. 121–2; Hill–Powell, i. 286.

It is with the utmost Impatience that I await the possession of y[r] Great Work, In w[ch] every Litterary Difficulty will be solved, & curiosity Gratified, at least as far as English literature[5] is concerned. Nor am I fearful of letting Expectation rise to the [6]utmost summit in w[ch] she can accompany reason,[6] since I am Certain that no Disappointment will Ensue.

From what you are pleased to say concerning M[r] Dodsly,[7] I shall ever think myself much his Debtor, but yet I cannot help suspecting that you intended him a Compliment when you talked of *Recommendation*:[8] for is it possible that the World sh[d] be so blind, or Booksellers so stupid as to need other recommendation than your own? indeed I shall Honour both so far as to substitute *solicitation* in the place of the above humiliating term.[9] Such of my Friends as have not already ordered y[r] Dictionary, I have requested to apply to M[r] Dodsly.

Perhaps you will smile, when I inform you, that since first the rumour of your Dictionary's Coming Abroad this Winter was spread,[10] I have been supposed to be marvellously deep in Politics, for a man who has ever submitted without scrutiny or murmur to the Decrees of those under whose Guidance Provedence has placed him. Not a sun has set since the above [11]Time, without previously lighting[11] me to the Coffee House, nor has risen without renewing my Curiosity. But Time, the Great revealer of secrets has, at length, put an End to my solicitude. For, (if there be Truth in Bookselling Man) I can [12]now by unerring Calculation[12] foretell the Day & Hour when it will arrive at Lynn.[13]

Having Determined at the Close of the Ensuing summer to fix my future abode in London,[14] I cannot help rejoicing that I shall be an Inhabitant, & exulting that I shall be a fellow Citizen wth M[r] Johnson.

[5] MS literature] *interlined over deleted* Learning

[6-6] MS utmost ... reason,] *originally* summit that Reason can accompany her to

[7] Robert Dodsley (1703–64), poet, dramatist, and bookseller, who distributed Johnson's *Dictionary*.

[8] For Dodsley's 'recommendation', see above, CB to Johnson, 16 Feb. 1755, n. 4–4; also Hill–Powell, i. 182–3; iii. 405.

[9] MS humiliating term.] *interlined over deleted* Humbling Word.

[10] The imminent publication of Johnson's *Dictionary* caused much comment in the press, for which see J. H. Sledd and G. J. Kolb, *Dr. Johnson's Dictionary* (Chicago, 1955), pp. 110, 144–7; and Helen L. McGuffie, *Samuel Johnson in the British Press, 1749–1784, Chronological Checklist* (New York, 1976), p. 15.

[11-11] MS Time, ... lighting] *originally* Time, that has not lighted

[12-12] MS now ... Calculation] *originally* now Calculate

[13] The *Norwich Mercury* of 5 Apr. 1755 carried an advertisement of the *Dictionary* under the heading 'This Day was published', anticipating the actual publication date by ten days.

[14] When Mme d'Arblay published this letter in 1832, she omitted CB's express intention of returning to London after the summer of 1755 and altered the opening of the paragraph to read: 'If, which is probable, I should fix my future abode in London...' (*Mem.* i. 123).

& were it possible ever to be honoured with a small share of his Esteem I sh^d regard it as the Most gratefull Circumstance of my Life. & shall I add, that I have a female Companion whose Intellects are sufficiently Masculine to enter Into the true Spirit of y^r Writings, & Consequent⟨ly⟩ to have an Enthusiastic Zeal for them & their author? How Happy w^d y^r presence make us over our Tea, so often Meliorated by y^r producti⟨ons.⟩[15]

If, [16]in the mean tim[e],[16] y^r Avocations w^d permit you to bestow a Line or two upon me, without greatly incommoding yourself, You w^d communicate the Highest Delight to

Sir
y^r Most Obed^t
& Most Humble Servant
Cha. Burney.

Have you, Sir, ever happened upon a little french Book Entitled *Synonymes Francois*, par M. l'Abbe Girard?[17] I am inclined to imagine, if you have not seen it, that it w^d afford you, as a philologer some pleasure; it being Written with great spirit, &, as I think, Accuracy. But I sh^d rejoice either to have my Opinion Confirmed or Corrected by Yours. If you sh^d find any Difficulty in procuring this Book, Mine is wholly at y^r service.[18]

Lynn. R^s | Apr. 14th | 1755.

To Fulke Greville

King's Lynn,
6 December 1755

ALS (BL Egerton MS 3437, fo. 303).
Publ: Betty Rizzo, '"The High Road to Eminence": A New Letter from Charles Burney in Norfolk', *Notes and Queries*, n.s. xxxiii (1986), 61–3.

[15] For the Burneys' intellectual interests, see *CB Mem.* 68 n. 1 and 69; and above, CB to Mrs Burney, 19 Dec. 1751.

[16-16] MS in ... tim[e]] *interlined over deleted* at any Time

[17] The abbé Gabriel Girard (1677–1748), French grammarian, had published in 1718 *La Justesse de la langue françoise, ou les différentes significations des mots qui passent pour synonymes.* Subsequent editions, of which there were many, bore the title *Synonymes françois, leurs différentes significations, et le choix qu'il en faut faire pour parler avec justesse.*

[18] CB owned the 1737 Amsterdam duodecimo edition (*Cat. Misc. Lib.*, lot 712). It was while reading 'the abbé Gerard's synonimes' in company with Dr Johnson and Mrs Thrale in 1782 that Fanny Burney stumbled on Mrs Thrale's secret passion for Gabriel Piozzi (*JL* v. 427–8 and n. 6; vii. 535–8).

Though I addressed a Letter[1] to you at Wilbury some Time since, I have not the least Title to reproach you for taking y[r] own Time in answering it.

I have now a Matter of great importance to myself to lay before you; & in w[ch] I have the Most Pressing occasion for you[r] assistance. You must know that D[r] Green is dead,[2] & the place for w[ch] I have so long languished is thereby become vacant. You some Time since were so kind to say you sh[d] not scruple applying to L[d] Holderness[3] in my behalf, if Travers[4] had died; sh[d] you now think there w[d] be any impropriety in *Writing* to him for me, as I suppose you to be at Wilbury & unable to *see* him? if not, I sh[d] think a Line from you might be of Service to me.[5] As I suppose it natural for D[r] Boyce to be advanced to D[r] Green's place he being next him in rank,[6] either Boyce's place or Travers's w[d] amply Content me, as they will doubtless be removed.[7] When you have said what you think proper for me to my Lord—(if you sh[d] think it proper to write for me) I humbly think you might venture to assure his Lordsh[p] that I have not been entirely Idle since

[1] Not preserved.

[2] Maurice Greene (1696–1755), Mus.D. (1730), composer and organist, had died on 1 Dec. He had held the posts of organist of St Paul's Cathedral (1718), organist and composer of the Chapel Royal (1727), and Master of the King's Musick (1735). He had therefore been situated 'at the head of our cathedral Music, and the King's band' (*Hist. Mus.* iv. 667; Mercer, ii. 1010).

[3] Robert D'Arcy (1718–78), 4th Earl of Holderness (1722), Secretary of State for the Southern Department and Privy Councillor (1751), patron of music and poetry. CB had met Holderness at Bath in 1747, was subsequently 'honoured' by his 'notice' in London, and had 'most humbly dedicated' to him his first musical publication, *Six Sonatas for two Violins, with a Bass for the Violoncello or Harpsichord* (1748). See *CB Mem.* 45, 51–2; Scholes, ii. 340.

[4] John Travers (*c.*1703–58), organist and composer, formerly an apprentice of Maurice Greene, had held a royal appointment as one of the two organists of the Chapel Royal since May 1737.

[5] Greville complied with CB's request and sent this letter to Holderness with a covering note of his own, dated 'Friday Morn.' [12 Dec. 1755]: 'will L[d] Holderness accept of M[r] Grevile's best Comp[s] & allow Him to do what He is in general most disinclined to—He means—Sollicit?— M[r] G. had y[e] Enclosed by y[e] Post from the Little man his Lordshp. has done y[e] Honour to listen to, & He has indeed so much merit many ways that M[r] G. cou'd never decline any hint or desire to help Him forwards as much as might lay in M[r] Grevile's small Power' (BL Egerton MS 3437, fo. 302).

[6] William Boyce, already composer to the Chapel Royal (1736), had anticipated Greene's death by writing on 26 Nov. to the Duke of Devonshire 'to beg your Grace's Interest, that I may succeed him, as Master of His Majesty's Band of Musicians . . . I set the last birthday Ode for him [Greene], am now setting that for the New-Years-day, and have conducted all the perform- ances during his illness' ('Boyce' in *New Grove*). Boyce was duly nominated to the Mastership.

[7] Neither Boyce nor Travers relinquished their royal appointments as Chapel Royal com- poser and organist respectively. The vacancy created by Greene's death was filled on 13 Jan. 1756 by James Nares (1715–83), organist of York Minster (1735–56). When Travers died in June 1758, Boyce succeeded him as Chapel Royal organist as well. Of Boyce's pluralism CB later wrote: 'On the decease of Dr. Greene . . . he was appointed master of the king's band, and, in 1758, on the death of Travers, organist of the chapel royal; of which he had succeeded Weldon, in 1736, as composer; so that he enjoyed three honourable appointments at once, which used to be supplied by three several professors' ('Boyce' in Rees).

my residence in Norfolk, but have applied myself with unwearied application in my Business to Qualify myself for such a post as that for wch I am an humble petitioner. If it were allowed one to speak in one's own behalf, or if it w^d have Weight I c^d venture to affirm that neither Travers nor Boyce ever c^d beat me in playing, (& now they have past their meridian)[8] & as to Composition[9]—but I won't be indecent[10]—If I were so happy as to succeed in this application, I sh^d go to London with Great Speed & Courage—as I sh^d then be put in the high road to Eminence—[11]

⌐I often peep in the papers in hopes of seeing y^r Book advertised— when will this happen, & by w^t Title must I seek it?¬[12]—la mia moglie non sta bene—but begs her respects to Mrs G. & yourself. I hope to hear that you are all perfectly well, & that you still retain your usual good wishes & partiality for

Dearest Sir, y^r Most affectionately faithful Servt
Ch. B.

Lyn. 6 Decr 1755.

To Mrs Greville[1]   [King's Lynn, ?July 1756]

Source: Mem. i. 113–14.

[8] CB was now 29 years old, Travers about 52. Boyce, aged 44, was increasingly disabled by deafness.

[9] For CB's estimate of Boyce, see CB to Greville, July 1753, n. 15. Travers had 'attached himself to Dr. Pepusch, and confined his studies solely to the correct, dry, and fanciless style of that master. His compositions, however pure the harmony, can only be ranked with pieces of mechanism, which labour alone may produce, without the assistance of genius. His passion for fugues, resembled that of an inveterate punster, ... so Travers seems never to have seen or heard any series of sounds, without trying to form them into a fugue, and meditating when and where the answer might be brought in' ('Travers' in Rees).

[10] *Fribble:* 'Flesh and Blood can't bear it—I could—but I won't grow indecent' (Garrick, *Miss in Her Teens*, II. i). For CB and Fribble, see CB to Mrs Greville, [?July 1756], n. 1.

[11] For CB's subsequent attempts to obtain a royal appointment, see Scholes, ii. 321–7; Lonsdale, pp. 74–5, 169, 294–5, 314–15, 319–23.

[12] Greville obliterated this sentence which refers to his *Maxims, Characters, and Reflections*, published anonymously on 18 Mar. 1756 (*Daily Advertiser*).

[1] Frances Greville, née Macartney (*c.*1730–89), 3rd daughter of James Macartney (1692–1770), had married Fulke Greville in 1748; CB assisted at the secret ceremony, and later stood proxy for the Duke of Beaufort as godfather to her first daughter (*CB Mem.* 46–7; Lonsdale, pp. 20–1). She wrote verses, and her 'A Prayer for Indifference' (1759) was much admired in her day (*The New Oxford Book of Eighteenth Century Verse*, ed. R. Lonsdale (Oxford, 1984), pp. 483–5).

The Grevilles, says Mme d'Arblay, often acted at home 'sundry proverbs, interludes, and farces, in which young Burney was always a principal personage. In one, amongst others, he played his part with a humour so entertaining, that its nick-name was fastened upon him ...

WILLIAM FRIBBLE, ESQ.[2]

TO HER WHO WAS ONCE MISS BIDDY BELLAIR.[3]

Greeting.

No boisterous hackney coachman clown,[4]
No frisky fair nymph of the town
E'er wore so insolent a brow
As Captain Flash,[5] since Hymen's vow
To him in silken bonds has tied
So sweet, so fair, so kind a bride.
   Well! curse me, now, if I can bear it!—
Though to his face I'd not declare it—
To think that you should take a dance
With such a roister into France;[6]
And leave poor Will in torturing anguish
To sigh and pine, to grieve and languish.
   'Twas—let me tell you, Ma'am—quite cruel!
Though Jack and I shall fight a duel[7]
If ever he to England come
And does not skulk behind a drum.
   But—apropos to coming over,
I hope you soon will land at Dover
That I may fly, more swift than hawk,
With you to have some *serus* talk.[8]
The while, how great will be my bliss
Should you but deign to let me kiss—

that of a finical, conceited coxcomb, a paltry and illiterate poltroon; namely, Will Fribble, Esq. in Garrick's farce of Miss in her Teens [originally performed 17 Jan. 1747 at Covent Garden]. Mr. Greville himself was Captain Flash, and the beautiful Mrs. Greville was Miss Biddy Bellair; by which three names, from the great diversion their adoption had afforded, they corresponded with one another during several years' (*Mem.* i. 60).

[2] Fribble, whose delight it was to 'invent Fashions for the Ladies, make Models of 'em and cut out Patterns in Paper', was also given to composing extravagantly amorous verses to Biddy Bellair, introducing them thus: '*William Fribble*, Esq; to Miss *Biddy Bellair* — — greeting' (*Miss in Her Teens*, ii. i). This was Garrick's own part.

[3] 'A young Lady of Wit, Beauty, and Fifteen thousand Pounds Fortune ... but newely come out of the Country and just turn'd of sixteen' (i. i, ii).

[4] *Fribble* (to *Biddy*): 'You must know, Miss, there is not an Animal in the Creation I have so great an Aversion to, as those Hackney-coach Fellows' (ii. i).

[5] A blustering braggart, rival of Fribble.

[6] CB wrote these verses to Mrs Greville 'upon her going abroad' (*Mem.* i. 112). The Grevilles departed for a second continental sojourn in July 1756, a circumstance which suggests the date of this verse epistle.

[7] Although they posture at it, Flash and Fribble, cowards both, never actually cross swords for Biddy's hand.

[8] *Fribble:* 'Then pray let me have a little *serous* talk with you' (ii. i).

O may these ardent vows prevail!—
Your little finger's vermeil nail!
   Who am,
Till direful death to dust shall crumble,
My dearest *cretur!*[9] yours,

most humble,
WILL FRIBBLE.

To Samuel Johnson

King's Lynn,
26 March 1757

ALS copy (Berg).
  Endorsed by CB: To | Mr S. Johnson | 26th Mar. 1757. | N° 3.   *Docketed by* FBA:
3 | (2) | ✳ (NB N° 4. | omitted)   *Also* L copy incomplete (Osborn) in FBA's hand.[1]
Publ.: Mem. i. 124–6, there dated 27 Mar.; Scholes, i. 90–1.

Lynn in Norfolk
26 March 1757.

Sir.

Without exercising the greatest self-denial I sh^d not have been able thus long to withold from you my grateful Acknowledgements for the Delight & Instruction you have afforded me by means of your admirable Dictionary: a Work I believe, not yet equaled in any Language. For, not to Mention the Accuracy Precision & Elegance of the Definitions, The Illustrations of words are so judiciously & happily selected as to render it a Repository &, I had almost said, Universal Register of whatever is sublime or beautiful in english Literature.— Sunt verba & Voces, prætereaque, [3]Nihil,[2] so apt a motto for Dictionaries in general[3] cannot with the least degree of Propriety be applied in the Present Case, since in looking for *Words* we find *Things.* The Road indeed to the former is so flowry as not to be travelled with Speed, at least by me, who find it impossible to arrive at the Intelligence I want without bating by the way & revelling in Collateral Entertainm^t. Were I to Express all that I think upon this Subject,

---

[9] Garrick's effeminate Fribble addresses Biddy as 'my dear *Creeter*' (II. i), and (in her words) advises her 'what Ribbons become my complexion, where to stick my Patches, . . . which is the best Wash for the Face, and the best Paste for the Hands' (I. ii).

[1] See CB to Johnson, 14 Apr. 1755, n. 1.

[2] 'Beyond words and sayings there is nothing' (Horace, *Epistles*, 1. i. 34). The quotation figures as epigraph on the title-page of Rousseau's *Lettre sur la musique françoise* (1753).

[3-3] MS Nihil, . . . general] *altered from* Nihil. an adage wch so well describes the Contents of almost every other Dictionary

your Dictionary w^d be stripped of a great part of its Furniture. But as praise is never gratefully received by the justly deserving till a Deduction be first made for the Ignorance or partiality of him who bestows it; I shall support my opinion by a Passage from a Work of Reputation among our Neighbours, which if it have not yet Reached you I shall rejoice at being the first to Communicate, in hopes of augmenting the Satisfaction arising from honest Fame, & a Conviction of having conferred Benefits on Mankind; well knowing with how parsimonious & niggard a Hand men administer Comfort of this kind to Modest Merit.

'Le savant & ingenieux M. Samuel Johnson, qui dans l'incomparable Feuille Periodique, intitulée le *Rambler*, apprenoit à ses Compatriotes à Penser avec Justesse sur les Matieres les plus interessantes, vient de leur fournir des secours pour bien parler & pour ecrire correctement; Talens que personne peut'etre ne possede dans un degré plus Eminent que lui.—il n'y a qu'une Voix sur le succes des Efforts de l'Auteur pour Epurer, fixer & Enrichir une Langue dont son *Rambler* montre si admirablement l'abondance & la Force, l'Elegance & l'Harmonie.'

Bibliotheque des Savans. Tom. 3. p. 482.[4]

Tho' I had constantly in Remembrance the Encouragement with wch you flattered me in your Reply to my first Letter, yet knowing that Civility & politeness seem often to Countenance Actions which they would not perform, I could hardly think myself intitled to the permission you gave me, of writing to you again,[5] had I not lately been apprised of your Intention to Oblige the Admirers of Shakespear wth a New Edition of his Works by Subscription.[6] But, shall I venture to tell you, notwithstanding my veneration for you & Shakespear, that I c^d not partake of the Joy wch the selfish Publick seemed to feel on this Occasion[7]—no, far from it; I c^d not but be afflicted at reflecting that so exalted, so refined a Genius as the author of the Rambler sh^d submit to a Task so unworthy of him as that of a mere Editor. For who w^d not grieve to see a Paladio or a Jones[8] undergo the dull Drugery of carrying Rubbish from an old Building when he sh^d be tracing the Model of a New?—But I detain you too long from the main Subject of this Letter wch is to beg a place in y^r List of Subscribers for

---

[4] This laudatory notice actually appeared in the *Bibliothèque des sciences et des beaux-arts*, iii, pt. 2 (Apr.–June 1755), 482, not in the 'Bibliothèque des savans'. Much confusion has been caused by CB's misleading citation. See, for example, Hill–Powell, i. 323; J. H. Sledd and G. J. Kolb, *Dr. Johnson's Dictionary* (Chicago, 1955), p. 145.

[5] See CB to Johnson, 14 Apr. 1755, n. 4.

[6] Johnson's *Proposals for Printing, by Subscription, the Dramatick Works of William Shakespeare*, dated 1 June 1756, was published on 8 June.

[7] CB had clearly been 'apprised' of Johnson's scheme through the newspapers.

[8] Andrea Palladio (1508–80) and Inigo Jones (1573–1652), eminent architects.

The R^t Honble the Earl of Orford.
Miss Mason^9
Archdale Wilson Esq^{r10}
Richard Fuller Esq^{r11}
The Revd Mr Briggs Carey.^{12} & Sr y^r Most Hum^{le} & extreamly
                                        Devoted Servt
                                        Chas Burney.

P.S. I sh^d be glad if you w^d favour me with y^r Proposals not having yet seen them.^{13}

To Philip Case^1 [King's Lynn], 23 July 1759

Source: HMC, *Townshend*, 11th Report, Appendix, Part IV (1887), pp. 395–6, which says that the present letter was at Raynham, 'dated at Lynn and endorsed, "Mr Burney to Mr Case about Musick."'

^{9} Not identified.

^{10} Archdale Wilson (d. 1762?) may well have been the 'Long Wilson of Walsingham' about whom Bewley wrote to CB on 4 Aug. 1762 (Osborn): 'Have you heard that *Long Wilson* of Walsingham has shot himself, for no visible cause but the *taedium Vitae*; & that in his Will, wrote a day or two before the act, he formally begs pardon of God for the Sins he had committed & for that which he was about to commit. Now Wilson was a most strict & conscientious Unbeliever; but for fear of the worst clapp'd this into his Will by way of a *saving Clause*, or *Nonobstante*.—It could do no harm, you know: Nevertheless, to you & me, & all sober Christians it has very much the appearance of squeaking.'

^{11} Richard Fuller (*c.*1710–70) of Great Yarmouth, politician, had entered Caius College, Cambridge, in Feb. 1726, and in the same month also gained admission at the Inner Temple. On three occasions, in 1741, 1754, and 1756, he stood unsuccessfully as a parliamentary candidate for Yarmouth, against the interests controlled by the Townshends and Walpoles. See Namier and Brooke, i. 340.

^{12} The Revd Briggs Cary, or Carey (1733–93), son of John Cary (1692–1776), writing-master, Mayor of Lynn in 1740, 1754, and 1765. In 1755 Briggs Cary graduated BA from Peterhouse, Cambridge, was ordained Deacon on 15 July, and soon after accepted from Charles Bagge (1715–91), Vicar of Lynn, an appointment as Curate at £40 per annum. Ordained to the priesthood in 1757, he was in 1760 collated Rector of Stanhoe on the recommendation of Lord Orford. In addition to a considerable fortune inherited in 1752 from his maternal grandfather, Cary also enjoyed several ecclesiastical preferments (for which see T. A. Walker, *Admissions to Peterhouse* (Cambridge, 1912), p. 300; Bradfer-Lawrence, pp. 173–5). His slight but entertaining MS diary is preserved in the Norfolk Record Office (Bradfer-Lawrence Collection, II b).

^{13} Although Johnson wrote a reply to the present letter, he omitted to send it. Later in the year, as the original Christmas 1757 deadline for the publication of the edition of Shakespeare approached, CB wrote again in Dec. 1757. This fourth letter to Johnson has been destroyed, as Mme d'Arblay's dockets show on this letter and on that of 14 Oct. 1765 (see *post*). Johnson replied immediately to CB's fourth letter on 24 Dec. 1757: 'If you can direct me how to send proposals I should wish that they were in such hands' (Johnson *Letters*, i. 104). Later, on 8 Mar. 1758, Johnson wrote: 'I have sent you a bundle of proposals' (ibid., p. 106).

^{1} Philip Case (1712–92), lawyer, Comptroller of the Customs at Lynn, Wisbech, and Wells (1754), Deputy Clerk, then Clerk (1760) of the Peace for Norfolk, was a protégé of the powerful Townshends of Raynham. Admitted a freeman of Lynn by purchase in 1733, he became Mayor

Publ.: O. E. Deutsch, 'Burney, Handel and the Barrel Organ', *Musical Times*, xc (1949), 227.

Sir,

I fear I shall not be able to propose any useful hints as to the Furniture of the Barrel Organ you mentioned to me, unless I was informed what Stops it contained, what is its Compass, together with the Size & Number of its Barrels. However I will suppose it capable of performing the following Pieces, wch in the serious Way w^d if well adapted to the Instrument afford great pleasure to the admirers of such Compositions.

1. Corelli's 8th Concerto (or the favourite movem^t in it).[2]
2. He was despised & rejected—in Handel's Messiah.[3]
3. Powerful Guardian—set by D^o.[4]
4. Return O God of Hosts—in Samson.[5]
5. Tis Liberty alone—in Judas Maccabeus.[6]
6. Handel's Second Organ Concerto, or Part of it.[7]
7. Geminiani's 1st Concerto op. 2da, or D^o.[8]
8. King of Prussia's March.[9]
9. March of the 3^d Regiment of Guards.[10]
10. Hasse's 1st Concerto.[11]
11. Rende mi il Figlio mio, del Sig^r Cocchi, nel Ciro riconosciuto.[12]

in 1745, 1764, 1777, and 1786. Case amassed a great fortune and for half a century 'virtually controlled the public and social life of King's Lynn'. For a substantial account of his life and career, see Bradfer-Lawrence, pp. 192–201.

[2] Corelli's set of twelve *Concerti grossi* (Op. 6) was published in Amsterdam in 1714. The eighth concerto, in G minor, is associated with midnight Mass at Christmas—'Fatto per la notte di Natale'. CB probably refers specifically to the third movement, 'the beautiful adagio', of this concerto. See *Hist. Mus.* iii. 557 n.; Mercer, ii. 442 n.

[3] The air, Burney wrote later, 'has ever impressed me with the highest idea of excellence in pathetic expression, of any English song with which I am acquainted' (*Handel Commem.*, p. 79).

[4] In Handel's *Joseph and His Brethren*, first performed 2 Mar. 1744.

[5] Handel's *Samson* was first performed on 18 Feb. 1743.

[6] *Judas Maccabaeus* was first performed on 1 Apr. 1747.

[7] In B flat (Op. 4, no. 2).

[8] CB refers particularly to the *Allegro* finale of Geminiani's *Concerto grosso*, Op. 2, no. 1 (1732), which was well known as 'Geminiani's Minuet'. See R. Fiske, *English Theatre Music in the Eighteenth Century* (1973), p. 107.

[9] Published in 1758 to the words 'What Honours are to Fred'rick due', by Gualtero Nicolini (*fl.* 1758).

[10] Also called 'Captain Reed's or the Third Regiment of Guards March'. See 'Marches' in *BUCEM*.

[11] For Johann Adolf Hasse, see CB to Ebeling, Nov. 1771, nn. 7, 8. CB probably recommends his Concerto in F, Op. 4, no. 1 (1741), which was frequently republished under such titles as 'Hasse's celebrated concerto' and 'A favourite concerto' (*BUCEM*).

[12] Gioacchino Cocchi (*c.*1720–after 1788), Italian opera composer. His setting of Metastasio's *Ciro riconosciuto* was first performed in London in 1759. CB praises the aria as being 'happily set ... full of spirit and passion, and perfectly suited to the situation of the character by which it was performed. This is one of the first capital opera airs without a second part and *Da Capo*' (*Hist. Mus.* iv. 471; Mercer, ii. 857).

12. The Simphony & last Movem^t of Handel's Coronation Anthem.[13]

If these Compositions or any Part of them should be approved & practicable, it will be necessary to have them judiciously suited & adjusted to the Genius of the Organ & filled up with such Simphonies & accompanym^{ts} as will best compensate for the Want of a Voice in the Songs or a Number of Instruments in the other Pieces.—I am, Sir,—Your Most Obed^t & Most Humble Servant,

Chas. Burney.

To William Bewley[1]

Bristol,
[September 1762?][2]

AL fragment (Berg).
Docketed by FBA: ✻ 1761.

Hot-Wells, Bristol[3]

⌐Think not, my dearest Bewley, that you can ever be forgotten by any one who has had the Pleasure of your Acquaintance so long as the Miscreant Who now Writes to you. No, he will remember you as long as Sense, Wit, Taste, Humour, Integrity, Simplicity, or Friendship, can communicate to him the least degree of Pleasure.⌐ Nothing but an uninterupted Bustle, & unrelaxed application to Business[4] has kept me thus long from Massingham—I mean my Letter—for as to the Better Part of⌐my self (wth all due respect to my wife) I mean my own

[13] The 'Simphony' (i.e. the overture) and the 'last Movem^t' of the 'Anthem Composed for the Coronation of King GEORGE the Second, 1727' probably refer to the Introduction to 'Zadok the Priest', and 'My heart is inditing' (*Handel Commem.*, pp. 69, 107). See A. C. Bell, *Handel Chronological Thematic Catalogue* (Darley, 1972).

[1] William Bewley (1726–83), was born in North Shields near Newcastle in Northumberland. In 1749 he married Barbara Green (d. 1797) of Swaffham and settled in the village of Great Massingham, Norfolk, as surgeon and apothecary. Bewley, known as 'the philosopher of Massingham', had met CB in Norfolk (Lonsdale, pp. 41–2), and was 'a man for whom Mr. Burney felt the most enlightened friendship that the sympathetic magnetism of similar tastes, humours, and feelings, could inspire' (*Mem.* i. 105).

[2] The preserved fragment of CB's letter appears to be his reply to a letter from Bewley dated 4 Aug. 1762 (Osborn).

[3] If the conjectural dating of this fragment is accurate, it is the only piece of evidence to show that CB journeyed to Bristol Hotwells in the summer of 1762. In 1761, Mrs Burney, in declining health, had sought a cure at Bath and Bristol Hotwells, where CB joined her during the summer (*CB Mem. post* 87). It would appear that in 1762 Esther went to Bristol again to seek a cure, followed by her husband. See also *Mem.* i. 137; *HFB*, pp. 10–11; Lonsdale, p. 56.

[4] For CB's whirl of activities after his return to London from Norfolk in 1760, and his residence in Poland Street, see *CB Mem.* 85–92; *Mem.* i. 133–6; Scholes, i. 100–6; Lonsdale, pp. 53–6.

half ofⁿ my Self, my Mind, it has constantly had a Quotidian trip there ever since I left Norfolk— ...⁵

To Dorothy Young¹   [Poland Street,
                               October 1762]²

Source: Mem. i. 140–5.
Also publ.: Scholes, ii. 288–90.

I had not thought it possible that any thing could urge me to write in the present deplorable disposition of my mind;³ but my dear Miss Young's letter⁴ haunts me! Neither did I think it possible for any thing to add to my affliction, borne down and broken-hearted as I am. But the current of your woes and sympathetic sorrows meeting mine, has overpowered all bounds which religion, philosophy, reason, or even despair, may have been likely to set to my grief. Oh Miss Young! you knew her worth—you were one of the few people capable of seeing and feeling it. Good God! that she should be snatched from me at a time when I thought her health re-establishing, and fixing for a long old age! when our plans began to succeed, and we flattered ourselves with enjoying each other's society ere long, in a peaceable and quiet retirement from the bustling frivolousness of a capital, to which our

⁵ The remaining part of this letter must have contained a '*tickling* Catalogue' of compliments to his friend, for Bewley, referring to CB's 'treat of Septʳ last', wrote on 18–21 Mar. 1763: 'How can you, my dear Burney, if you mean me w[ell,] compliment me at so intemperate a rate,—*ad insaniam usque?* . . . Had you not a looking glass before you when you drew it up?' (Osborn).

¹ Dorothy Young (*c*.1721–1805) of King's Lynn, granddaughter of the eminent physician Dr George Hepburn, was a close friend of the Burneys, and had assisted at the birth of Esther's children at Lynn. Esther found in her and Mrs Stephen Allen a bookish 'congeniality of taste [which] brought on a close intimacy & friendship between them, wᶜʰ ⟨lasted till the⟩ termination of their several lives' (*CB Mem.* 69 n. 6). Although 'Dolly' was ugly and deformed, her 'feelings were so sensitive, that tears started into her eyes at every thing she either saw or heard of mortal sufferings, or of mortal unkindness' (*Mem.* i. 98). Later she published a volume entitled *Translations from the French by D. Y.* (Lynn, 1770) to which CB subscribed for six copies. See also Scholes, i. 75; and *EJL* i. 20 n. 54.

² This letter was written shortly after Mrs Burney's death on 29 Sept. 1762. Mme d'Arblay, who printed the text, says that it was 'found amongst [CB's] posthumous papers, so ill-written and so blotted by his tears, that he must have felt himself obliged to re-write it for the post' (*Mem.* i. 139).

³ CB's profound grief at the death of his wife is evident in some of the surviving fragments of his 'Memoirs' (*CB Mem.* 92–3). He drafted some elegiac verses on the cover of a letter from Bewley, [Winter 1762–3], (BL Egerton MS 3700A, fo. 20). See also *Mem.* i. 146–51.

⁴ Not preserved.

niggard stars had compelled us to fly for the prospect of establishing our children.[5]

Amongst the numberless losses I sustain, there are none that un-man me so much as the total deprivation of domestic comfort and converse—that converse from which I tore myself with such difficulty in a morning, and to which I flew back with such celerity at night! She was the source of all I could ever project or perform that was praise-worthy—all that I could do that was laudable had an eye to her approbation. There was a rectitude in her mind and judgment, that rendered her approbation so animating, so rational, so satisfactory! I have lost the spur, the stimulus to all exertions, all warrantable pursuits,—except those of another world. From an ambitious, active, enterprizing Being, I am become a torpid drone, a listless, desponding wretch!—I know you will bear with my weakness, nay, in part, par-ticipate in it; but this is a kind of dotage unfit for common eyes, or even for common friends, to be entrusted with.

You kindly, and truly, my dear Miss Young, styled her one of the greatest ornaments of society; but, apart from the ornamental, in which she shone in a superior degree, think, oh think, of her high merit as a daughter,[6] mother, wife, sister,[7] friend! I always, from the first moment I saw her to the last, had an ardent passion for her person, to which time had added true friendship and rational regard. Perhaps it is honouring myself too much to say, few people were more suited to each other; but, at least, I always endeavoured to render myself more worthy of her than nature, perhaps, had formed me. But she could mould me to what she pleased! A distant hint—a remote wish from her was enough to inspire me with courage for any under-taking. But all is lost and gone in losing her—the whole world is a desert to me! nor does its whole circumference afford the least hope of succour—not a single ray of that fortitude She so fully possessed!

You, and all who knew her, respected and admired her under-standing while she was living. Judge, then, with what awe and vener-ation I must be struck to hear her counsel when dying!—to see her meet that tremendous spectre, death, with that calmness, resignation, and true religious fortitude, that no stoic philosopher, nor scarcely christian, could surpass; for it was all in privacy and simplicity. Socrates and Seneca called their friends around them to give them that courage

[5] See *CB Mem.* 84.

[6] She was the daughter of Richard Sleepe (d. 1758), musician and London City wait, who married (1705) Frances Wood (d. by 1775), the much loved maternal grandmother of CB's children. See Dawe, pp. 12, 85; *CB Mem.* 49; *EJL* i. 18 n. 49, 60 n. 30.

[7] Of the many children of Richard and Frances Sleepe, the family correspondence shows that the Burneys were particularly close to James Sleepe (1716–94), and Mary Sleepe (1715–78?) who married (1743) John Sansom (d. *c.*1769). See *EJL* i. 171 n. 81, 172 n. 82.

that perhaps solitude might have robbed them of, and to spread abroad their fame to posterity; but she, dear pattern of humility! had no such vain view; no parade, no grimace! When she was aware that all was over—when she had herself pronounced the dread sentence, that she felt she should not outlive the coming night, she composedly gave herself up to religion, and begged that she might not be interrupted in her prayers and meditations.

Afterwards she called me to her, and then tranquilly talked about our family and affairs, in a manner quite oracular.

Sometime later she desired to see Hetty,[8] who, till that day, had spent the miserable week almost constantly at her bed-side, or at the foot of the bed. Fanny, Susan, and Charley, had been sent, some days before, to the kind care of Mrs. Sheeles in Queen Square,[9] to be out of the way; and little Charlotte was taken to the house of her nurse.

To poor Hetty she then discoursed in so kind, so feeling, so tender a manner, that I am sure her words will never be forgotten. And, this over, she talked of her own death—her funeral—her place of burial,[10]—with as much composure as if talking of a journey to Lynn! Think of this, my dear Miss Young, and see the impossibility of supporting such a loss—such an adieu, with calmness! I hovered over her till she sighed, not groaned, her last—placidly sighed it—just after midnight.

Her disorder was an inflammation of the stomach, with which she was seized on the 19th of September, after being on that day, and for some days previously, remarkably in health and spirits. She suffered the most excruciating torments for eight days, with a patience, a resignation, nearly quite silent. Her malady baffled all medical skill from the beginning. I called in Dr. Hunter.[11]

On the 28th, the last day![12] she suffered, I suppose, less, perhaps nothing! as mortification must have taken place, which must have

[8] Esther, the eldest child, was 13 years old when her mother died. The Burneys were much given to affectionate family nicknames. CB's six children by his first marriage who survived their mother were: Esther ('Hetty', 1749–1832); James ('Jemm', 1750–1821); Frances ('Fan' or 'Fanny', 1752–1840); Susanna Elizabeth ('Sue', 'Susey' or 'Sukey', 1755–1800); Charles ('Charley', 1757–1817); and Charlotte Ann ('Ottenburg', 1761–1838).

[9] Anne Elizabeth Sheeles, née Irwin (*fl.* 1735–75), married (1735) John Sheeles, or Shields (*fl.* 1735–65). She ran the 'great boarding-school in Queen Square Bloomsbury' at which CB held the post of music master from the time of his return from Norfolk in 1760 until about 1775 (*CB Mem.* 84; *EJL* i. 147 n. 17). For Fanny's account of her stay at Mrs Sheeles's, see *HFB*, p. 11; *JL* iv. 254.

[10] Mrs Burney's place of burial has not been discovered.

[11] William Hunter (1718–83), MD (1750), FRS (1767). By this time he had become the leading obstetrician in London, consulted by Queen Charlotte.

[12] 29 Sept. appears to be the correct death-date. It is supported by an entry in a fragment of CB's Index to his 'Memoirs': 'bereaved on Mich' day!' (*CB Mem.* 92). In the text of *CB Mem.* 92, CB states incorrectly that 'she expired on the 27th', followed by *HFB*, p. 11 and Lonsdale, p. 56.

31

afforded that sort of ease, that those who have escaped such previous agony shudder to think of! On that ever memorable, that dreadful day, she talked more than she had done throughout her whole illness. She forgot nothing, nor threw one word away! always hoping we should meet and know each other hereafter!—She told poor Hetty how sweet it would be if she could see her constantly from whence she was going, and begged she would invariably suppose that that would be the case. What a lesson to leave to a daughter!—She exhorted her to remember how much her example might influence the poor younger ones; and bid her write little letters, and fancies, to her in the other world, to say how they all went on; adding, that she felt as if she should surely know something of them.

Afterwards, feeling probably her end fast approaching, she serenely said, with one hand on the head of Hetty, and the other grasped in mine: 'Now this is dying pleasantly! in the arms of one's friends!' I burst into an unrestrained agony of grief, when, with a superiority of wisdom, resignation, and true religion,—though awaiting, consciously, from instant to instant awaiting the shaft of death,—she mildly uttered, in a faint, faint voice, but penetratingly tender, 'Oh Charles!—'

I checked myself instantaneously, over-awed and stilled as by a voice from one above. I felt she meant to beg me not to agitate her last moments!—I entreated her forgiveness, and told her it was but human nature. 'And so it is!' said she, gently; and presently added, 'Nay, it is worse for the living than the dying,—though a moment sets us even!—life is but a paltry business—yet

> Who, to dumb forgetfulness a prey
> This pleasing—anxious being e'er resign'd?
> Left the warm precincts of the cheerful day,
> Nor cast one longing, lingering look behind?'[13]

She had still muscular strength left to softly press both our hands as she pronounced these affecting lines.

Other fine passages, also, both from holy writ, and from what is most religious in our best poets, she from time to time recited, with fervent prayers; in which most devoutly we joined.

These, my dear Miss Young, are the outlines of her sublime and edifying exit ———— ———— What a situation was mine! but for my poor helpless children, how gladly, how most gladly should I have wished to accompany her hence on the very instant, to that other world to which she so divinely passed!—for what in this remains for me?

[13] Thomas Gray, 'Elegy Written in a Country Churchyard', ll. 85–8.

To Mrs Allen[1]   [Poland Street],
                                          1 December 1762

ALS (Berg), overwritten by FBA.
  Docketed by CB: To M^rs St. Allen, before her widow ⌐ hood,[2] on the death of my dear
1st wife, who died in Sept^r ⌐ 1762, Written Decr same year.   *And by* FBA: ✶ *Dec^r*
1762. ⌐ *Hist.* ⌐ NB. I have covered afresh ⌐ the pale Ink, which was ⌐ nearly effaced by
time. ⌐ F d'A. [For the rest of her comment, see n. 5 below.]

My dear Madam—

Letters of Condolence are full as difficult to answer as to write—at
least I find them so; or your's, full of Heart-felt Commiseration &
tenderness, had been reply'd to long since.[3] Indeed I have dreaded the
sight of all my most Intimate & dear Friends, since the Calamity that
has befallen us; particularly those who were best acquainted with the
worth of what we have lost—wonder not then, dear Madam, that I
have shun'd a Conversation with *you*, who were[4] so sensible of the
uncommon Mind & amiable Qualities of my ever-to-be-lamented.—
There is no *one* appellation sufficiently comprehensive to include *what*
she was to me!—but 'tis cruel to obtrude my melancholy & gloomy
thoughts upon you.—Afflictions run circular, & wheel about—if
we look round us, few or none escape at some Time or other the unexpected Deprivation of what is most dear & Essential to the Heart's
ease & mind's serenity!—one sh^d not, therefore, anticipate evils which
always arrive too soon—I will therefore tear myself from that subject
which will forever be uppermost in my thoughts, to thank you for the
Care you have taken of the Body, as well as the Consolation you have
afforded to the Mind.[5]—The very fat & fine Turkey you were so good

[1] Elizabeth Allen, née Allen (1728–96), of King's Lynn. On 22 May 1749 she had married
her cousin, Stephen Allen (1724–63), a wealthy Lynn corn merchant. She was noted for her
beauty, intelligence, and quick temper, and later (2 Oct. 1767) became CB's second wife. See
Mem. i. 97 and *CB Mem.* 69 n. 7.
[2] Stephen Allen died on 11 Apr. 1763. He was buried on 17 Apr. ('St. Margaret's Church,
King's Lynn, Register of Burials, 1678–1784', Norfolk Record Office: PD 39/35 (S)).
[3] Mrs Allen's letter to CB is not preserved. After her death on 20 Oct. 1796 CB destroyed
most of their correspondence (see Introduction, p. xxviii).
[4] MS were] *FBA overwrote* are
[5] On the blank fourth page of this letter Mme d'Arblay later wrote: 'This beautifully touching
Letter was written after the death of my incomparable Mother, to Mrs. Stephen Allen of Lynn,
afterwards my Mother in Law [i.e. stepmother],—but before her Widowhood, & while, far from
regarding her as successor to my unrivalled Mother, the desolate Widower had not yet conceived it possible he could ever have wished, or even have endured a second conjugal Partner.
But the Void—the Chasm—in his House as well as in his Mind, called aloud for what relief
could be bestowed by Female society—& the Beauty, as well as talents & cultivated parts of
Mrs. Stephen Allen, brought forward, through her impressive sympathy in his loss, the idea, &
then the trial, of a connection that might offer—what in This World could be offered, of

to[6] send Hetty arrived safe & inoffensive to Night—for wch you have mine together with Hetty's best acknowledgments. Your exceeding Friendly & benevolent Temptations thrown in my way for a Journey into Norfolk the Ensuing Holy days,[7] were rec^d with all due Gratitude— but I am so overhead & Ears in Bustle now for the rest of the Winter, that I stand no prudent Chance of making an escape before Whits- untide. Indeed Home is so little Home—& contains such innumer- able Mementos of my once Happy State, that it was fortunate for me to be dragg'd from it by Business, however reluctantly I quitted it— indeed, I had nothing for it but to plunge deeply & precipitately into Bustle![8] Thank God, people don't know how little I am able to think of Business when I am at it—otherwise I sh^d stand but a small Chance of getting any to do—but I am now insensibly got upon the very Topick I intended to avoid—another attempt at an Excursion, & I'll conclude.—How happy are you to have the Dear Sensible Dolly[9] with you!—to have the melancholy satisfaction of drying her tears too! a Satisfaction cruelly denied to us, who wish'd so much to do it, however unequal to the Task. Well! 'tis a dirty, shabby world—that's the truth on't—I rail, & fear I shall continue my abuse till I have done with it.—But that's no reason why I should not wish, as I fer- vently do, that you may ever have Cause to bless the Hour you Came into it & enjoy the Singular Felicity of Escaping Pain & Misfortune to your last Breath—!

I am, dear Madam,
with affectionate wishes for the
Health & Happiness of my good
Friend Mr Allen[10]—
Y^r most obliged
& Zealous[11] Servant
Chas Burney

1st Dec^r | 1762.

Reparation. And, but for the unhappy effects of a Temper the most unhappy, the experiment might have succeeded as completely as it did partially—for whatever there might be to lament of flaw or defect, he was warmly attached to her, & owed to her his chief though not unbroken after-Happiness.'

Joyce Hemlow first brought to light the full vehemence of the antipathy that developed between the second Mrs Burney and the children of the first (*HFB*, pp. 35–40 *et passim*).

[6] MS to] *FBA altered to* as to

[7] MS Holy days,] *FBA obliterated and interlined* spring

[8] 'At length obliged to plunge into business, & attend at a school,' CB found that 'having my mind occupied by my affairs was a useful dissipation of my sorrow; as it forced me to a temporary inattention to myself and the irreparable loss I had sustained' (*CB Mem.* 93).

[9] Dorothy Young.

[10] Stephen Allen had not been a 'good Friend' to CB on his arrival in King's Lynn in 1751. An item in CB's Index to his 'Memoirs' records: 'Mr Stephen Allen from a foe becomes a friend' (*CB Mem. post* 68).

[11] MS Zealous] *FBA overwrote* Devoted

34

To Mrs Allen [Poland Street,
late 1762?][1]

L incomplete copy, in the hand of FBA (Berg: FBA, 'Characters extracted from various writings of my dearest Father'). FBA introduced the extract with the heading: 'Character of my revered though nearly unknown Mother, taken from a Letter written by my Father to Mrs. Stephen Allen, afterwards his second wife.'
Publ: Mem. i. 145–6, with considerable alterations.

Even Prosperity is insipid without participation with those we love;—[2]& with respect to comfort & satisfaction—how wretchedness is accumulated Heaven knows! For[2] I have lost a soul congenial with my own—a Person[3] who in outward appertenances & internal conceptions condescended to assimilate [4]my own manners & ideas .... But all my feelings are not for myself;[4] my poor Girls have sustained a [5]loss more[5] extensive than they—poor Innocents! are at present sensible of. Unprovided as I should have left them with respect to Fortune, [6]they would have been better off with such a Mother! *always with them* than with me, who, though I am able to bustle for their subsistence, am *never* with them long enough to attend to their conduct, & the formation of their Minds. Their Mother,—feeble of body, & unable to endure the fatigue of acquiring subsistence for such a family by Labour, had such inexhaustible resources in her exalted & divine Mind & intellects, that if it had been *my* fate to relinquish Her & Life first, I should have been under no great apprehension for the welfare of my Children.[6] It would have grieved me [7]to leave her[7] oppressed by such a load of care, but I should[8] have had no doubt of her supporting [9]it, as

[1] When Mme d'Arblay printed her heavily edited version of the present letter in *Mem.* i. 145–6, she stated that it was written 'at a later period' than CB to Dorothy Young, [Oct. 1762]. It also appears to be later than CB to Mrs Allen, 1 Dec. 1762, in which CB opens his correspondence with her after the death of his wife.

[2-2] & with ... For] *Mem. text reads* for me, therefore, heaven knows, all is at an end—all is accumulated wretchedness!

[3] Person] *Mem. text reads* companion

[4-4] my own ... for myself;] *Mem. text reads* her ideas and manners with mine. Yet believe not that all my feelings are for myself;

[5-5] loss more] *Mem. text reads* loss far more

[6-6] they would ... Children.] *Mem. text reads* had it been my fate to resign her and life first, I should have been under no great apprehension for the welfare of my children, in leaving them to a mother who had such inexhaustible resources in her mind and intellects.

[7-7] to leave her] *Mem. text reads* indeed, to have quitted her

[8] should] *Mem. text reads* could

[9-9] it, as long ... Mind.] *Mem. text reads* it with fortitude and abilities, as long as life and health had been allowed her. Fortitude and abilities she possessed, indeed, to a degree that, without hyperbole, no human being can conceive but myself, who have seen her under such severe trials as alone can manifest, unquestionably, true parts and greatness of mind.

35

long as life & health were allowed her with Fortitude & Abilities. Indeed, without hyperbole, she was possessed of both to a degree which no one can conceive but myself, who had seen her in such situations, & under such severe trials, as alone can shew true parts & greatness of Mind.[9] I am thoroughly convinced she was [10]equal to[10] any situation, [11]exalted or humble, which this life can furnish. She was as well able to govern a Kingdom as a Family: And—with all that nice discernment, & quickness of perception, she—if occasion seemed to require it, could submit to such drudgery & toil as were fit only for the meanest domestic, with that resignation & Alacrity as are usually found only in those who have never known a better state. And with such a strength of Reason, & capacity for Literature as would have cut a figure at the head of any Academy in Europe, she never relinquished a moment the female & amiable softness of her own sex, with which Men are so charmed & captivated.[11]

To Fanny Burney [West Woodhay, mid-June 1763][1]

ALS verses (Berg).
Addressed: For | Fanny.   *Docketed by* FB: 1763 | Woodhay—Berkshire | Nº 1 | 63 *And by* FBA: ⌗ From Wood Hay in Berkshire, | From my dear Father, | When I was 10 years old. | Nº 1. | I | II.   *Publ.: ED* i, p. xlvi.

> My Fanny shall find
> That I have in Mind
> Her humble Request & Petition,

[10-10] equal to] *Mem. text reads* fitted for
[11-11] exalted ... captivated.] *Mem. text reads* either exalted or humble, which this life can furnish. And with all her nice discernment, quickness of perception, and delicacy, she could submit, if occasion seemed to require it, to such drudgery and toil as are suited to the meanest domestic; and that, with a liveliness and alacrity that, in general, are to be found in those only who have never known a better state. Yet with a strength of reason the most solid, and a capacity for literature the most intelligent, she never for a moment relinquished the female and amiable softness of her sex with which, above every other attribute, men are most charmed and captivated.

[1] This verse epistle is dated from a section of CB's fragmentary 'Memoirs' preserved in the Berg Collection. Recalling the events of 1763, CB wrote that he went on 'holidays' with 'Mrs Cibber & Mr & Mrs Sloper, June 9th to Westwood Hay near Newbury, and past 8 or 10 days there very pleasantly.' CB's eldest daughter, Hetty, was also of the party (*CB Mem.* 94). The verse epistle may well have been a birthday offering to Fanny, who turned 11 on 13 June 1763.

West Woodhay, Berkshire, was the seat of William Sloper (1709–89), MP (1747–56), who had married (1728) Catherine Hunter (*c.*1707–97). In 1737 Sloper had become the protector and subsequently lover of the celebrated actress and singer Susannah Maria Cibber, née Arne (1714–66). CB's friendship with Mrs Cibber dated from his 1744–8 apprenticeship under Arne, who was Mrs Cibber's brother (*CB Mem.* 31). See also Lonsdale, pp. 11, 57, 489; Mary Nash, *The Provoked Wife: The Life and Times of Susannah Cibber* (1977), pp. 22, 105–18, 249, 271–3, 312–13; Sedgwick, ii. 426.

Which said, if I'd write her
A Line, 'twould delight her
And Quite happy make her Condition.

I'm not such a Churl
To deny my dear Girl
So small & so trifling a Favour;
For I always shall try
With her Wish to Comply,
Though of Nonsense it happen to savour.

Tho' little I say,
I beg & I pray
That careful you'll put these Lines rare by:
For well they'll succeed
If my Love they should plead—
So now you've a Letter to swear by.

C.B.

To Mrs Allen [Poland Street, *c.*20 April 1764]

AL (Osborn). Partly overwritten by FBA; torn.
Endorsed by CB: To Mrs Allen | 1765 *Docketed by* FBA: ※ 1765 | To Mrs Ste: Allen | *Hist.*— | on the Marriage of Lady Susan Strangways with | Mr. Obrien, the most elegant & lively of Actors. | and an admirable character of Mason the Poet.

L^y^ Susan Strangways Marriage with Mr Obrien of Drury Lane Theatre has made a great Hubbub & Noise here[1]—nothing else has been talked of since except M. D'Eon's Quarrel with M. de Guerchy & his Publication of all the Letters of M. de Nivernois, M. de Choiseul, M. de Saint Foix &c relative to the Peace, wch every body is reading with great avidity—'tis a great 4to Vol. & I have not had time to Read much of it yet—but there seems in what I have run over to be a great deal of wit & cleverness in the Lett^rs^ of Messrs de Nivernois & D'Eon[2]—

[1] On 7 Apr. 1764, the day after she came of age, Lady Susannah Sarah Louisa Fox-Strangways (1743–1827), eldest daughter of the Earl of Ilchester, eloped with William O'Brien (d. 1815), actor, who had assisted in amateur theatricals at Holland House, in which the young members of the Fox and Lennox families participated (*DNB*). Lady Susan and Mr O'Brien were married at St Paul's Church, Covent Garden.

The Fox and Lennox families, by virtue of close family and friendly connections, were also dragged into the scandal of Lady Susan's improvident marriage.

[2] Charles-Geneviève-Louis-Auguste-André-Timothée d'Éon de Beaumont (1728–1810), the

But to return to L^y Susan. You must know that I had the Honour to teach her 3 Sisters L^y Lucy[3]—L^y Henrietta[4] & L^y Frances Strang-ways,[5] & therefore cannot help being very sorry for L^d & L^y Ilchester & the whole Family[6]—indeed the Duke of Richmond's,[7] Ld Kildare's,[8]

notorious French transvestite, swordsman, diplomatist, and secret agent (*DBF*; *DNB*; *BD*), published on 23 Mar. 1764 in London his *Lettres, mémoires & négociations particulières ... avec M. M. les ducs de Praslin, de Nivernois, de Sainte-Foy, & Regnier de Guerchy*. CB's copies of the octavo and quarto editions of this work are listed in *Cat. Misc. Lib.*, lots 494, 635.

D'Éon had arrived in England in Sept. 1762 as Secretary to the embassy of Louis-Jules-Barbon Mancini-Mazarini (1716–98), duc de Nivernais, who was to negotiate the terms of peace to end the Seven Years' War. After the signing of the Treaty of Paris (10 Feb. 1763), Nivernais returned to France (Apr. 1763), leaving D'Éon in temporary charge of the embassy. By July 1763, D'Éon had been raised to the dignity of Minister Plenipotentiary and, on secret instructions from King Louis XV, resolved to remain in England. He therefore refused to accept his orders of recall or to hand over secret diplomatic papers to the new French Ambassador, Claude-Louise-François de Régnier (1715–67), comte de Guerchy, who arrived in Oct. 1763. A bitter quarrel ensued between D'Éon and Guerchy over these and financial matters. Guerchy was an ally of the French Foreign Minister, César-Gabriel de Choiseul (1712–85), comte de Choiseul-Chevigny, created duc de Praslin (1762), and Claude-Pierre-Maximilien Radix de Sainte-Foy (b. c.1736), diplomatist, at this time 'chef des bureaux des affaires étrangères' (D'Éon, *Lettres*, 4to edn., p. xxxiii). The paper war between D'Éon and Guerchy led to D'Éon's scandalous publication in the *Lettres* of compromising and highly embarrassing correspondence with his superiors in the French diplomatic service. See Walpole *Corresp.* xxii. 190–1, 216–18; xxxviii. 238, 356–7, 370; O. Homberg and F. Jousselin, trans. A. Rieu, *D'Éon de Beaumont, His Life and Times* (1911), pp. 61–123; T. F. Gaillardet, trans. Antonia White, *The Memoirs of Chevalier D'Éon* (1970), pp. 112–91.

³ Lady Lucy Fox-Strangways (1748–87), second surviving daughter of the Earl of Ilchester, married (1771) the Hon. Stephen Digby (1742–1800), for whom see *HFB*, pp. 205–12, 493 n. H; and *JL* i. 137 n.

⁴ Lady Christian Henrietta Caroline Fox-Strangways (1750–1815), third surviving daughter of the Earl of Ilchester, married (1770) John Dyke Acland (1746–78). Lady Harriet (as she was generally called) performed heroic deeds during the War of American Independence. See *DNB*; Namier and Brooke, ii. 4–5; and Walpole *Corresp.* xxxii. 402.

⁵ Lady Frances Muriel Fox-Strangways (1755–1814), fourth surviving daughter of the Earl of Ilchester, married (1777) Valentine Richard Quin (1752–1824), created Baronet (1781), Baron Adare (1800), Viscount Mount-Earl (1816), Viscount Adare and Earl of Dunraven (1822). See *JL* iv. 254.

⁶ Stephen Fox (1704–76), who added the name 'Strangways' to 'Fox' in 1758, MP for Shaftesbury (1726–41), joint Secretary to the Treasury (1739–41), joint Comptroller of the Army Accounts (1747–76), created Lord Ilchester and Baron of Woodford-Strangways (1741), Lord Ilchester and Stavordale, Baron of Redlynch (1747), Earl of Ilchester (1756). He married (1736) Elizabeth Strangways-Horner (1723–92), heiress to the Melbury estate in Dorsetshire. The sons of this marriage were: Henry Thomas (1747–1802), 2nd Earl; Stephen Strangways Digby (1751–1836); and Charles Redlynch (1761–1836).

According to Walpole, Lord Ilchester was 'the most indulgent of fathers', who 'doted' on his eldest daughter, Lady Susan (Walpole *Corresp.* xxii. 219).

⁷ Charles Lennox (1735–1806), 3rd Duke of Richmond, great-grandson of King Charles II.

⁸ James FitzGerald (1722–73), 20th Earl of Kildare, created Marquess of Kildare (1761), Duke of Leinster (1766), had married (1747) Lady Emilia Mary Lennox (1731–1814), sister to the Duke of Richmond and confidante to her other sisters, Lady Caroline Holland (n. 9), and Lady Sarah Bunbury (n. 10). For the letters that passed between these sisters concerning Lady Susan's elopement, see B. FitzGerald, ed., *Correspondence of Emily, Duchess of Leinster* (Dublin, 1949–57).

Ld Holland's[9] & Sr Will. Bunburys[10] all are involved in the Disgrace. Except the Honour & the L^y 'tis a very bad Match for Obrien—for notwithstanding all that the News papers have asserted relative to the Lady's Fortune[11]—I can venture to assure you from undoubted authority y^t she has not six pence independent of her Father, & he as yet seems inexorable[12]—the whole Family is hurried out of Town[13]—& L^y Susan weeps & wails to every body she sees—quite as foolish—as the Match itself, surely—She confesses her Passion to have been of 3 year's Standing—that she has not closed her Eyes these 3 or 4 Months for thinking of the Step she was about to Make—& is *one & Twenty*—now for Heaven's sake what has happened since her Marriage wch it was not Natural for her to expect? *contempt* of the world & *anger* of Friends, surely were natural Consequences wch such *premeditation* must have presented to her mind one w^d think very strongly in her self-*Conflicts* before her *Fall*—for a *fallen angel* she now undoubtedly is in the Eyes of most Good People.

I must just tell you that I have lately been so happy as to renew an old Acquaintance wth the Charming Poet Mr Mason.[14] He has been at

[9] Henry Fox (1705–74), created Baron Holland of Foxley (1763), younger brother of Lord Ilchester, had eloped in 1744 with Lady Georgiana Caroline Lennox (1723–74), created Baroness Holland (1762). In 1726 he leased Holland House and bought it outright in 1768.

Probably recalling his own experience in an elopement, Lord Holland exerted himself to smooth the path of the erring couple. See Lord Ilchester, *Henry Fox, First Lord Holland* (1920), ii. 278–9; and Edith R. Curtis, *Lady Sarah Lennox, an Irrepressible Stuart, 1745–1826* (New York, 1946), pp. 147–53.

[10] The Revd Sir William Bunbury (*c*.1711–64), 5th Baronet, Vicar of Mildenhall, Suffolk (1736–64), Rector of Reed, Hertfordshire (1748–58). His considerable estates were to descend to his first son, Thomas Charles Bunbury (1740–1821)), who had married (1762) Lady Sarah Lennox (1745–1826). Lady Sarah's boon companion was Lady Susan Fox-Strangways. They acted together in the Holland House amateur theatricals (Walpole *Corresp.* ix. 335), and shared each other's confidences. Three days after the elopement, Lady Sarah wrote Lady Susan a long, affectionate, and supportive letter and in the months following was unrelenting in her efforts to assist her friend. See Lady Ilchester and Lord Stavordale, eds., *The Life and Letters of Lady Sarah Lennox, 1745–1826* (1901), i. 137 ff.

[11] The *London Evening Post*, 7–10 Apr. 1764, reported: 'It is whispered that a certain favourite Actor has played his part so well as to marry a Lady with a very considerable fortune . . .'. *Lloyd's Evening Post*, 6–9 Apr. 1764, also reported that 'Mr. O'Brien, of the Theatre Royal in Drury-lane' had married 'a young Lady of great family, with a very considerable fortune'.

[12] Lord Ilchester long remained inexorable. It was Lady Ilchester and her brother-in-law, Lord Holland, who took pity on the couple. Holland settled on Lady Susan an annuity of £400 for 3 years, tried to find some overseas diplomatic post for O'Brien, engineered the couple's emigration to New York, and at last won over his brother's acceptance. For these family stirs and the later career of the O'Briens, who remained happily married ever after, see *DNB* under 'O'Brien, William'; Lord Ilchester, *Henry Fox*, ii. 278–9; and Lady Ilchester and Lord Stavordale, *Life . . . Sarah Lennox, passim*.

[13] 'Yesterday [i.e. 11 Apr. 1764] the Right Hon. the Earl of Ilchester and Family set out from their House in Burlington-Street, for their Seat in Somersetshire' (*St. James's Chronicle*, 10–12 Apr. 1764; see also *Lloyd's Evening Post*, 11–13 Apr. 1764).

[14] The Revd William Mason (1725–97), poet and divine, had probably met CB at the house

my House to Tea & to hear Hetty &c—he is I must tell you nearly as good a Musician & Painter as Poet—plays very well the Harp^d & knows the thing thoroughly—but what pleases me most of all is his *Manner of Man*—he is innocently chearful (remember he's a Divine) in all respects natural & unassuming—no grotesk or Caricature Marks of Geniüs about him, but comfortably communicative & conver⟨si⟩ble without overawing or reminding you of his Superiority—for a superior Man he doubtless is to every one in his way except his Friend Mr Grey[15]—in short I like the Man as much as his writings, wch is saying a great deal for him, & more than I can say for any great Genius I have ever been acquainted wth in the Literary World. As a Divine I like him vastly—for tho' I may not pay so much respect to all the 39 Articles wch many good X^tians do, yet I love & revere Decency Propriety, Virtue & Benevolence wherever I meet with them. They unman me—or rather make a Man of Me—by expanding the Heart & letting in kindness & Philanthropy—[16]

What an unmerciful long Letter have I scratched—well, I fear it m⟨u⟩st be the last—the Nasty Parliament will have it so[17]—I wish all the Members—but *Philanthropy*—Well, I must gulp my Indignation down & conclude, Dearest Mad^m,

Yours Most Devoutly—

Pray put me in a way how to convey the Italian Prayer Book to you—without Coach or Boat[18]—

of Robert D'Arcy (1718–78), 4th Earl of Holderness, about the year 1748 when CB was still an apprentice to Arne. See Lonsdale, pp. 16, 69–70, 374. The first collected edition of Mason's *Poems*, dedicated to Lord Holderness, had recently appeared, published on 4 Jan. 1764 by Robert Horsfield (*London Chronicle*, 3–5 Jan. 1764).

[15] Thomas Gray (1716–71), the poet, had befriended Mason at Cambridge in 1747 when Mason, largely through Gray's advocacy, was nominated to a Fellowship in Pembroke College. See *DNB*; and Gray *Corresp.* i. 298 n. 33.

[16] MS Philanthropy—] *FBA added* with true Christianity.

[17] Widespread 'frauds and abuses' of the privilege of franking mail led to the passage in Parliament of a bill 'for preventing frauds and abuses in relation to the sending and receiving of letters and packets free from the duty of postage.' The bill received the Royal Assent on 19 Apr. 1764 (4 Geo. III, c.24), and the stringent new regulations came into force on 1 May. See *London Chronicle*, 17–19 Apr. 1764; *The Annual Register . . . for the Year 1764*, pp. 131–4; H. Robinson, *The British Post Office: A History* (Princeton, 1948), pp. 116–19; and Walpole *Corresp.* xxxviii. 368 and n. 10.

[18] Following the passage of the new Act, the General Post Office issued a notice dated 20 Apr. 1764 which appeared in the newspapers. Among other details relating to the new regulations governing the use of franks, it announced: 'And whereas great Numbers of Letters are privately collected and delivered contrary to Law, . . . all Carriers, Coachmen, Watermen, Wherrymen, . . . hereafter detected in the illegal collecting, conveying, or delivering of Letters and Packets, will be prosecuted with the utmost Severity' (*London Gazette*, no. 10410, 17–21 Apr. 1764).

To Fanny Burney   Paris, 13 June 1764[1]

ALS (Berg).

Addressed: To | Miss Fanny Burney | at Mr Burney's in | Poland Street, Soho, | Londres | Angleterre   *Pmk:* I⟨V⟩18   *Endorsed by* CB: N° 3.   *Docketed by* FBA: ⧧ 2 | most | Touching | account | of the | Sufferings | of my | adored | Sister | Susan | in her | Journey | to | Paris, |⌐tog¬| with | our | tender | Father | & | dear | sister | Esther. | June 13th 1764. | 1764

I write to my dear Fanny again, to tell her, to tell her Grandmama's, to tell her aunts, to tell her uncles to tell her Cozens,[2] to tell all Friends that we are now at Paris.[3]—'tis now Wednesday Night the 13th June— I am just come from the Comick Opera, wch is here Called the Comedie Italienne, where I have been extreamly well Entertained,[4] but am so tired with standing the whole Time, wch every Body in the *Pit* does, that I can hardly put a foot to the Ground, or a Hand to the Pen.

We did not get here till Monday Night, owing to poor Sukey's Cough[5] wch has been frightfully bad, & made me very unhappy. If it

---

[1] This was Fanny's twelfth birthday.

[2] Among the Burney relatives here alluded to are CB's mother, Ann, née Cooper (*c.*1690– 1775) and CB's unmarried sisters, Ann or Nancy 'Aunt Nanny' (1722–94) and Rebecca 'Aunt Becky' (1724–1809), who lived together in a house in York St., Covent Garden. CB's brother, Richard (1723–92), who had married (*c.*1745) Elizabeth Humphries (*c.*1720–71), lived in Worcester. Richard's family, Fanny's cousins, comprised in 1764: Charles Rousseau (1747–1819), Ann (1749–1819), Richard Gustavus (1751–90), James Adolphus (1753–98), Elizabeth Warren (1755–1832), Rebecca (1758–1835), and Edward Francesco (1760–1848). See genealogical table in *JL* i, facing p. lxix, and pp. lxxiv–lxxv; 'Worcester Memoranda'.

For Fanny's relatives on the maternal (Sleepe) side, see CB to Dorothy Young, [Oct. 1762], nn. 6, 7; *EJL* i. 18 n. 49, 171–2 nn. 81–2.

[3] CB had set out for Paris with 15-year-old Esther and 9-year-old Susan 'at the breaking up of Mrs Sheeles's school June 6th' for 'I wished to give my children as good an education as I c^d afford' as 'I found that learning French, for females . . . was absolutely necessary' (*CB Mem.* 103). For CB's reasons for taking Susan instead of Fanny to Paris, see *Mem.* i. 154–5; *HFB*, p. 15.

[4] Since its merger in early 1762 with the Opéra Comique, the Théâtre Italien, popularly called the Comédie Italienne, had nourished the vogue of the musical play, a genre known as *opéra-comique*.

The programme for 13 June 1764 offered three pieces: *Le Roi et le fermier*, a three-act comedy by Michel-Jean Sedaine (1719–97) based on Robert Dodsley's *The King and the Miller of Mansfield* (1737). Sedaine's play included *ariettes* set to music by Pierre-Alexandre Monsigny (1729–1817). The second item was *Le Médecin de l'amour*, a one-act *opéra comique* by Louis Anseaume (1721–84), with music by Jean-Louis Laruette (1731–92), composer, actor and tenor singer, who belonged to the troupe of the Théâtre Italien (C. D. Brenner, *A Bibliographical List of Plays in the French Language, 1700–1789* (Berkeley, 1947), items 11041, 2921). Of the afterpiece, *Fêtes marines*, little is known other than that it was performed 24 times at the Théâtre Italien between 24 May and 30 Aug. 1764. See C. D. Brenner, *The Théâtre Italien: Its Repertory, 1716–1793, with a Historical Introduction* (Berkeley and Los Angeles, 1961), pp. 277–9.

[5] Susan had 'a fearful tendency to a consumptive habit . . . that seemed to require the balsamic qualities of a warmer and clearer atmosphere' (*Mem.* i. 154–5).

had not been for that, our Journey w^d have been too happy I suppose
for this World. For we met with no kind of accident all the way, & had
very fine weather the whole Time except a few showers on Saturday &
Sunday wch only laid the Dust, a thing as much wanted in France as
in England. The weather is now very hot, & expected to continue so
for some Time; tho' they say it was for 3 weeks before we came as
cold at Paris & all over France as it c^d be any where in the Months
of May & June. Indeed we had Fires all the way till we came here.
But to return to the Poor dear Sukey—tho' she was brisk [&] well
in appearance when we set out from Calais at about 1 o'clock at Noon
on Thursday[6] I found by the Time we reached Boulogne wch is but
3 posts & a half or 21 Miles, she was too much tired to go on further
that Night, tho' it was only 5 o'Clock when we got into Boulogne.
She was very hot & Feverish & has been so at Times, besides her
Cough, ever since she came out.—We did not get into the Chaise next
Day, Friday,[7] till near 12 o'Clock and lay at Abbeville, 54 miles from
Bo[u]logne. There I indulged the poor Suke again by letting her Lye
in Bed till near 11, & we stopped again about 4 at Amiens 30 Miles
farther to dine, but she poor soul has had very little appetite ever since
she came out. We lay on Saturday Night[8] at Breteu[i]l, 21 Miles from
Amiens—determining next day to get up soon & to reach Paris on
[Sunday] at Night, wch might have been done by being in the Chaise
at 6 o'Clock in the Morning: but the sweet little Susey was so ill in the
Morning that I began to think we sh^d be able to get no farther on our
Journey—however about 11 we set off & reached Clermont, 21 Miles
nearer Paris where we dined & went only 15 Miles farther to Chantilly
that Night.[9] At this very delightful place we staid till near 4 o'Clock
on Monday[10]—Poor Sukey took a little Walk in those enchanting
Gardens, but had a most violent fit of coughing afterwards, & was
so tired she was forced to lie down till we set out for Paris where we
got on Monday Night between 8 & 9 o'Clock. [We] have a very Good
appartment at the Hotel d'Hollande[11] the very Room where Mr Lobb[12]

[6] 7 June.
[7] 8 June.
[8] 9 June.
[9] 10 June.
[10] 11 June.
[11] L'Hôtel des Ambassadeurs de Hollande, at 47 rue Vieille-du-Temple. See Comte d'Aucourt, *Les Anciens hôtels de Paris* (1890), p. 42; and 'Jacques Hillairet' (pseud. of A. A. Coussillan), *Dictionnaire historique des rues de Paris* (3rd edn., 1963), ii. 636–7.
[12] William Lobb (*c*.1736–65), BA (1755), MA (1758), Fellow of Peterhouse, Cambridge (1758), Taxor (1762). In July 1763 he had obtained licence to travel for 4 years (Venn), being 'Put on the Physic line' in Nov. (T. A. Walker, *Admissions to Peterhouse* (Cambridge, 1912), p. 301). CB could have met Lobb at Lynn through Briggs Cary, whose MS 'Diary' records on the inside cover, '1754 ... The Sophs that Year at Peter House were Cary ... Lobb' (Norfolk Record

lodged last year, & a bed in a Closet where I lie. Sukey I think is rather better since we got here, tho' during the Time of my writing this she has had a dreadfull Fit of Coughing & bleeding at the Nose. There is just underneath us a Lady Clifford[13] in this House, who very kindly sent upon hearing we were English to desire to see us. She is an elderly, sensible, plain Lady without Pride or Ceremony, & very kind to your Sisters desiring them to go in & out of her Appartme⟨nts⟩ as if they were their own—There lives with ⟨he⟩r Ladyship a very pretty little French you⟨ng⟩ Lady whose name is Rosalie[14] a little younger than Susey & an excellent play-fellow for her till she & Hetty get settled. I have not yet seen the French Lady who is to assist me in placing them—but shall to Morrow or next Day, when I have some Cloaths to appear among French People in. I have found out my Friend M[r] Strange,[15] with some difficulty—& have been with S[r] James Macdonald[16] not minding Dress with my Countrymen. I have been excessively wretched about the dear little Sufferer, Sukey, or Else this place & People w[d] have afforded me infinite amusement, but none greater than I have now in writing to my dear Children & Friends

Office: Bradfer-Lawrence Collection, II b); or later through Mason, as Lobb was also a friend of Thomas Gray (Gray *Corresp*. ii. 898; iii. 1297). According to CB, Lobb was one of 'four very extraordinary dilettanti musicians' at Cambridge: 'the most correct and certain *Sight's* man on the harpsichord or organ with whose performance we have been acquainted' ('Bates, Joah' in Rees). Lobb's abilities on the keyboard admitted him to the musical evenings in the Burney home. Thomas Twining, another of the four Cambridge 'dilettanti musicians', was to recall: 'I always recollected with much pleasure a very agreeable evening that I once passed at your house, with poor Lobb' (Twining to CB, 28 May 1773).

[13] Lady Elizabeth Clifford, née Blount (d. 1778), widow of Hugh Clifford (1700–32), 3rd Baron Clifford of Chudleigh, whom she had married in 1725. She was the eldest daughter of Alexander Pope's friend and correspondent, Edward Blount, of Blagdon, Devon. CB recounts that she was 'a Lady who, on acc[t] of her religion, had lived many years in a private manner, in the capital of France.—She was rather in years; but chearful, full of anecdote, and able to give me the life and character of every person of consequence at the court of Versailles, as well as in the city' (*CB Mem.* 104).

[14] Not identified.

[15] Robert Strange (1721–92), engraver, with Jacobite sympathies, had left England in 1760 after declining to engrave Allan Ramsay's portraits of the Prince of Wales and Lord Bute. He was to be knighted in 1787. His wife, Isabella, née Lumisden (1719–1806), was a witness at CB's second marriage on 2 Oct. 1767 (*CB Mem.* 113 n. 6). For the relations between the Burneys and the Stranges, see *JL* i. 142 n. 13.

[16] Sir James Macdonald (1742–66), 8th Baronet of Sleat, whom Boswell dubbed 'the *Marcellus* of Scotland' (Hill–Powell, iv. 82 n. 1). After a brilliant career at Eton and Christ Church, Oxford (matric. 9 May 1759), he went on the Grand Tour, but died at Rome on 26 July 1766, aged 24. 'Such extraordinary honours were paid to his memory, As had never graced that of any other British subject, Since the death of Sir Philip Sydney' (Hill–Powell, v. 152). For Sir James's account of Paris at this time, see his letters to William Weller Pepys in Alice C. C. Gaussen, *A Later Pepys* (1904), i. 274–6.

CB probably carried a letter of introduction to Sir James from his uncle, Alexander Montgomerie (1723–69), 10th Earl of Eglinton, who had also obtained for CB an introduction to David Hume (Lonsdale, p. 62).

in England, being my dear Fanny's most affectionate Father—C. Burney.

Beg of one of your Aunts to answer this immediately, & to direct to me according to my last Instructions.

Paris, Rue du Colombier.[17]

To Fanny Burney   Paris, 18[–20] June 1764

AL (Berg). Torn.
Addressed: To | Miss Fanny Burney | at Mr Burney's in Poland Street | Soho | London | Angleterre   *Pmk:* IV 26   *Endorsed by* CB: N° 4   *Docketed by* FBA: # 3 | Paris | sweet Susan's | amendment— | Esther's dress | Lady Clifford, | 1764

Paris. Monday 18th June 1764

I am sure it will please my dear Fanny &c &c very much, to hear that Sukey is a *great deal better*, tho' I were to write nothing Else. & indeed I have but little Time to spare—She continued very ill here till Saturday,[1] wth the most frightful fits of Cough^g & bleeding at the Nose I ever saw, wch has made me hitherto pass my Time very ill. It has soured all my Enjoyments here, or prevented them: as I could but seldom leave her, & when I did, her Situation & Sufferings were always uppermost in my Thoughts. She now, however, wakes in the morn^g & goes to sleep at Night without a Coughing Fit—& when she has one 'tis by no means so bad. She has better spirits & more appetite, both of wch were quite tost till within these two Days. No progress is as yet made about placing your Sisters here. It turns out a far more difficult thing to find a proper house for them than I imagined.

Wednesday Night[2]

I cannot send this away without telling you that Sukey is still better than when the above was written, & likewise that I have now Hopes of placing Hetty & her much to my Satisfaction. Indeed it will cost a good deal more money than I expected, but I am now too far advanced

---

[17] The present rue Jacob, near Saint-Germain-des-Prés, where Laurence Sterne lived in the spring of 1764 at No. 46 (Hillairet, *Rues de Paris*, i. 666). William Bewley, on learning of CB's plans to go to Paris, had written: 'Enquire after Tristram, the Prince of Biographers, the first of Writers, & whether there are any hopes of his going on with the *Book of Books*' (Bewley to CB, 1 June 1764, Osborn). Sterne, however, had left Paris at the end of May (A. H. Cash, *Laurence Sterne: The Later Years* (1986), p. 188).

[1] 16 June.
[2] 20 June.

to retreat.[3] It will be some Days yet ere this affair is adjusted. To Morrow is a great Festival[4] here, when all the Streets & Churches will be hung with Tapestry—& the finest Pictures in the King's Collections will be exposed. There will be likewise Processions of the Clergy in all parts of the City. Hetty & Susy have been out but very little yet, not having had proper Cloaths: & indeed if they had been ever so much dressed Sukey was unable to stir at Home or Abroad. I was on Sunday at the English Ambassador's Chapel (Lord Hertford)[5] & saw there a great many English People. Among whom was Mr Coleman, author of the Deuce is in him &c,[6] Mr Vaillant[7] the Bookseller—Mr Wilks[8]

[3] 'Lady Clifford gave me my choice of two methods of having my children well placed & educated. One was at a Convent at Blois, where the best French was spoken, and where the board, clothing, and Masters w^d cost no more than £20 a year for each! as they all wore a cheap black Uniform: no finery or distinctions ⌐was¬ allowed to excite envy or vanity in the rest; and the masters were poor priests, whose worldly passions were subdued, & ⌐they¬ c^d subsist upon a very small income. But the pensioners, ⌐or boarders must be all Catholics, and¬ submit to the discipline & religious ceremonies of the House.

The other proposition was ⌐the¬ placing my children in the hands, and under the care of some prudent & worthy female, who w^d suffer them, if protestants, to attend the English Ambassador's chapel, and allow ⌐ed¬ [them] to have such masters as I sh^d direct ⌐paying in proportion to their attendance & abilities.¬ This I preferred, though instead of £20 a year for each, it w^d cost me a hundred. For as it was my wish that my children sh^d be brought up in the religion of their Fathers, that is, the established religion of our country, I thought it best, ⌐whatever might be the expence,¬ to avoid putting them in the way to be prejudiced in favour of any religion ⌐but our own¬, as it might distract their minds, &, if opposed, render them miserable for the rest of their lives' (*CB Mem.* 104).

CB finally placed his daughters with Mme Anne Saintmard (*fl.* 1757–70), who became 'truly attached to them, & they to her' (Greville to CB, [14] Nov. 1764, Osborn; see also *Tours*, i. 13).

[4] The Feast of Corpus Christi; see also *Tours*, i. 15–17.

[5] Francis Seymour Conway (1718–94), 2nd Baron Conway (1732), created Viscount Beauchamp and Earl of Hertford (1750), Earl of Yarmouth and Marquess of Hertford (1793), Horace Walpole's cousin and correspondent. He served as British Ambassador to France from Oct. 1763 to June 1765.

[6] George Colman the elder (1732–94), dramatist. His two-act farce, *The Deuce is in Him*, was first performed as an afterpiece at Drury Lane on 4 Nov. 1763 to great applause (*The London Stage*, IV. ii. 1017). Colman had journeyed to Paris in May 1764 to recuperate from a brief illness (R. B. Peake, *Memoirs of the Colman Family* (1841), i. 105–8).

In 1763 CB had provided the musical setting to fourteen of the songs in the Garrick–Colman adaptation of *A Midsummer Night's Dream*. For an account of this unsuccessful production, see *CB Mem.* 100; Lonsdale, pp. 57–60; E. R. Page, *George Colman the Elder* (New York, 1935), pp. 87–8, 108.

[7] Paul Vaillant (*c.*1715–1802), conducted the family bookselling business at 87 the Strand, specializing in French and classical books. Sheriff of London in 1760 and Master of the Company of Stationers in 1770, Vaillant was known as the 'Father' of the Company. See W. B. Vaillant, *The Vaillant Family* (2nd edn., Weybridge, 1928), pp. 9–10.

[8] John Wilkes (1725–97), MP for Aylesbury (1757–64), had caused a furore with the publication of the *North Briton*, No. 45 (23 Apr. 1763). In Dec. 1763, Wilkes took refuge in Paris from the political and legal storm surrounding him at home, claiming ill health. Neither the House of Commons nor the Courts countenanced his claim. He was expelled the House on 20 Jan. 1764, and convicted of libel before Lord Mansfield on 21 Feb. His non-appearance to receive judgment led to his being declared an outlaw. David Hume in Paris wrote to his London publisher Andrew Millar on 23 May 1764: 'I never see Mr. Wilkes here but at Chapel, where he is a most

&c—Ld Beauchamp[9] son to the Ambassador has been very civil ⌐to me⌐ & has shewed me the House wch his Father Lord Hertford lives in & for wch his Lordship gives £800 a year. It is called l'Hotel de Brancas, the name of a French Duke[10] now living, & is the finest & best fu[r]nished & fitted up I ever saw.[11] Mr Hume, Secretary to the Embassy[12] is likewise very civil & Friendly to me, as is Lady Clifford who lives in the same House & is own Sister to the Dutchess of Norfolk.[13] Indeed she is uncommonly kind to your Sisters, who w^d not know what to do about dress but for her Ladyship; for Madame du Voisin[14] whom I depended on in these Matters is ready to Lie in, & consequently confined at Home. In short L^y Clifford has been so kind as to not only give her advice but Even personal assistance, by going

regular, & devout, and edifying, and pious Attendant. I take him to be entirely regenerate', to which Millar replied on 5 June: 'I take Mr Wilkes to be the same man he was, acting a part'. See *The Letters of David Hume*, ed. J. Y. T. Greig (Oxford, 1932), i. 444 and n. 5; and *CB Mem.* 104.

[9] Francis Seymour Conway, afterwards Ingram-Seymour-Conway (1743–1822), styled Viscount Beauchamp (1750–93), eldest son and heir of Lord Hertford.

[10] Louis-Léon-Félicité de Brancas (1733–1824), comte de Lauraguais, later duc de Brancas ('Brancas' in *DBF*).

[11] L'hôtel de Brancas, formerly known as l'hôtel de Lassay, and also as l'hôtel de Lauraguais, rue de l'Université in the faubourg S. Germain. The British Embassy moved there in Mar. 1764, to the delight of Lord Hertford, who wrote to Horace Walpole on 22 Mar.: 'Has my brother told you that I have hired the best house at Paris? It is charming. It is upon the river; it has a very large garden; it has the finest apartment, and is town and country, exactly what it should be for an ambassador who is to make a show and to live in it both summer and winter' (Walpole *Corresp.* xxxviii. 351).

[12] David Hume (1711–76) had accepted Lord Hertford's invitation in the summer of 1763 to join his Embassy, with a 'near Prospect of being appointed Secretary to the Embassy'. The royal appointment and annual salary of £1000, however, fell to Thomas Charles Bunbury. Despite Hertford's protests, Bunbury continued to enjoy the salary and the official title, while Hume did the work: 'I am not Secretary at all but do the Business of Secretary to the Ambassy, without any Character. Bunbury has the Commission and Appointments' (Hume to Edmonstoune, [Apr. 1764], in *New Letters of David Hume*, ed. R. Klibansky and E. C. Mossner (Oxford, 1954), p. 83). Hume received the official appointment only in July 1765 (E. C. Mossner, *The Life of David Hume* (Oxford, 1970), pp. 434–5, 492–3).

Hume's intimate friend, Michael Ramsay, had written a letter of introduction for CB on 5 June 1764: 'It is on my Friend Mr Burneys account that I have now the pleasure of writing to you. He has beein long a favourite of Lord Eglintoune's and I fancy He carrys a letter from his Lo[rdshi]p to you. He is a Musician by profession & perhaps One of the most Ingenious & deserving in that way that you have known. I ask his pardon for saying in that way: I might wth great Justice have mentioned his merit & ingenuity in many other respects, and one very properly entitled to the civilitys that may be in your way to show Him' (Royal Society of Edinburgh: Hume MSS, vol. vi, no. 105).

CB also presented for Hume's 'free & Undisguisd opinion' an anonymous volume 'which reflected upon some political and some poetical questions'. The author, in a letter to Hume from Spa, dated 6 Sept. 1764 (Hume MSS, v. 44), subsequently identified himself as Fulke Greville.

[13] Mary Blount (*c.*1702–73), second daughter of Pope's friend Edward Blount, had married in 1727 Edward Howard (1686–1777), who in 1732 succeeded his brother as 9th Duke of Norfolk.

[14] Not identified.

out herself & taking your Sisters with her to furnish them with what they are most i⟨n need⟩ of.

God bless you, my dear Fanny. Kiss ⟨Charles⟩ & Charlotte heartily for me, & remember me ⟨kind⟩ly to every body. Oh if you were to see w⟨hat a⟩ Beau they have made of me here!—but ⟨tho' I⟩ sh^d in my present dress, figure at a Birth Da⟨y i⟩n England,[15] yet here, I am not near so fine as ⟨a⟩ Tradesman, who have all fine figured or la⟨ced⟩ Silk Coats & Laced Ruffles—while mine are only Plain. Adieu, adieu, I shall present Hetty with this bit of paper to write down her dream upon, for she is now fast asleep at my Elbow.

[*Esther Burney completes the letter with a brief note on Paris fashions. See ED i, pp. xlix–l.*]

To Samuel Johnson

Poland Street,
14 October 1765

ALS draft (Hyde).
Endorsed by CB: To | Dr Johnson 1765 | N° 5:   *Docketed by* FBA: 5 ✳ | 14th Octr 1765 | NB N° 4 | omitted[1] *also* ✳ *at beginning of postscript.*

Sir

^2ʳThe Transaction I am going to mention to you happened so long since[3] that I am fearful I shall not be able to ^4recall it to^4 your Memory. About the year 1759 I had the Honour to wait on you, in Gough Square[5] with a ^6subscription of 5 Guineas for 5 Copies of your Shakespear^6 on the behalf of Mr Greville. Now as it did not occur to you to furnish[7] me wth Receits wch a certain Delicacy prevented me from mentioning— ^8the same delicacy made^8 me think it necessary to give Mr G. 5 of the

---

[15] The royal birthday celebration, when exceptionally splendid clothes were worn. See, for example, Pope's *Rape of the Lock*, i. 23. In 1770 CB again commented on the necessity of sartorial elegance in Paris: 'Dress, at Paris, is at its height of sumptuosity and importance' (*Tours*, i. 11).

[1] CB's letter 'N° 4' to Johnson, written in December 1757, was destroyed. See CB to Johnson, 26 Mar. 1757, n. 13.

[2-2] MS The Transaction ... wth 5.] *FBA deleted the first paragraph and added a note before the second* After some business.

[3] MS since] *interlined over deleted* ago

[4-4] MS recall it to] *interlined over deleted* explain *and alternative* revive in

[5] Johnson lived at 17 Gough Square, Fleet Street, from 1749 to 1759. The building is now preserved as national property and called 'Dr. Johnson's House'. CB's account of probably his first visit to Gough Square in 1758 is published in Hill–Powell, i. 328–30. See also J. L. Clifford, *Dictionary Johnson* (1980), pp. 15–25, 199–201.

[6-6] MS subscription ... Shakespear] *altered from* subscription to your Shakespear of 5 G^s

[7] MS furnish] *interlined over deleted* give

[8-8] MS the ... made] *altered from* & as the same Fine Delicacy wch made

47

Receits I had formerly been favoured wth by You for Persons whose Names I had begged you to insert in Your List of Subscribers & for whom the 1st Payment[9] had been [10]remitted to[10] you from Lynn. This being the Case I am unable to furnish my Friends by whom I am called upon with Rec[ts] to produce to M[r] Tonson.[11] If therefore Sir, you can [12]possibly recollect the Circumstance above mentioned sufficiently to be satisfied of its reallity (the only Condition upon w[ch] this application is wish'd to operate)[12] & have Rec[ts] remaining[13] in your Hands, I shall be extreamly obliged to you if you will favour me wth 5.[14][12]

I cannot let this opportunity escape me of thanking you in the most sincere & hearty manner for the uncommon Pleasure you have communicated to me by your most admirable Preface. It has awakened in me all that Esteem & venerati⟨on⟩ w[ch] your other[15] writings had inspired [16]but w[ch] had slumbered a little perhaps ⟨du⟩ring[16] your long Silence. My Zeal for Shakespear was never equal to that I had for you as a writer so long since as the year 1747 when I read your Plan of that Dictionary[17] for the Execution of w[ch] the world has not been nor can ever be sufficiently grateful. When I eagerly seized the opportunity of Subscribing to you as Shakespear's Editor it was less at the Instigation of my fondness for him (tho' by no means insensible to his surprising Powers) than of the ardent desire I had to sacrifice to your Genius. [18]Criticism had already done[18] so much for that Anomalous Author who is so seldom a proper object for its Labours[19]—now [20]soaring above now sinking below its Legislation[20]—that I expected but little addition to the Pleasure he had afforded me, even from you. I think

[9] Of one guinea. The 'Conditions' prefixed to Johnson's *Proposals* had stipulated that 'the price to subscribers shall be two guineas; one to be paid at subscribing, the other on the delivery of the book in sheets' (*The Yale Edition of the Works of Samuel Johnson*, vol. vii, ed. A. Sherbo (New Haven, 1968), p. 58). For Johnson's Norfolk subscribers, see CB to Johnson, 26 Mar. 1757.

[10-10] MS remitted to] *interlined over deleted* advanced

[11] Jacob Tonson (1714–67), the third publisher of that name, conducted the family business in the Strand. He was the principal publisher of Johnson's *Shakespeare*, which had just appeared on 10 Oct. 1765.

[12-12] MS possibly ... operate)] *altered from* by means of these Circumstance above mentioned sufficiently clear to be satisfied of the Truth *alternative* merit *deleted*.

[13] MS remaining] left *deleted*.

[14] MS wth 5.] *altered from* wth 5 to enable me to s[end] *and alternative* but can *all deleted*.

[15] MS other] *interlined over deleted* long

[16-16] MS but ... ⟨du⟩ring] *altered from* me w[ch] were a little weakened perhaps by

[17] *The Plan of a Dictionary of the English Language: Addressed to the Right Honourable Philip Dormer, Earl of Chesterfield; One of His Majesty's Principal Secretaries of State* had been published in quarto in early Aug. 1747. For a full bibliographical analysis and discussion of the *Plan*, see J. H. Sledd and G. J. Kolb, *Dr. Johnson's Dictionary* (Chicago, 1955), ch. 2.

[18-18] MS Criticism ... done] *altered from* so much had already been

[19] MS Labours] *interlined over deleted* powers

[20-20] MS soaring ... Legislation] *altered from* soaring beyond its Legislation now sinking into mere inanity

it but seldom happens that his Meaning *when worth knowing* is not [21]manifested or to be gathered from[21] the Context. How your Labours will convince me of the Contrary I have not had[22] Leisure to prove, having only, as yet, read your Preface, wch again I must say has afforded me more Pleasure, I had almost said Rapture, than any Production[23] of equal length I have ever read—the Richness & Elegance of the Language! the Elevation Originality & Ingenuity of thoughts! together with that mildness of Dissent so charming in Controversy & in all enquiries after Truth! [24]have enchanted me.[24] May your great Abilities be crowned with due Gratitude by the Public. If you can bear undisturbed the Squibs & Crackers of Mob-Criticks you have certainly Nothing to fear from the Artillery of whole Armies [25]of regulars—as they must infallibly become your Allies.[25]

I am, Sir, your much Obliged,
& most humble Servt
Ch. B.

Poland Street, Soho. | 14th Octr 1765.

I [26]very much wish a good Translation of your Preface may speedily be given to our Neighbours the French[26] who all greatly underate the merits of our Dramatick Poet, perhaps because they think we as much over-rate them.[27] [28]It w^d shew them[28] what our best writers think of him, & [29]convince them[29] that whatever veneration we may have for his wonderful Genius we are not so blinded by Prejudice & national Pride as to let his great & real Defects escape Censure. They call him a Goth & a Barbarian because his Faults are glaring & his Beauties for the most part not to be understood but by those who

[21-21] MS manifested ... from] *altered from* to be guessed at by
[22] MS not had] *altered from* not yet had
[23] MS Production] *interlined over deleted* writing
[24-24] MS have ... me.] *interlined over deleted* together
[25-25] MS of regulars ... Allies.] *altered from* of the most able & verteran Troops—as they must infallibly be on your Side
[26-26] MS very ... French] *altered from* sincerely wish I were able to give a good Translation of this Preface to the French
[27] MS them.] *interlined over deleted* his Merit.
CB alludes to the great eighteenth-century Anglo-French literary controversy over Shakespeare, at the centre of which stood Voltaire, who had declared in 1755 that Shakespeare was *'un barbare aimable, un fou séduisant'* (Boaden, ii. 408), and in 1761 had attacked Shakespeare in his controversial *Appel à toutes les nations de l'Europe*. Johnson in his 'Preface' dismissed Shakespeare's detractors, particularly Voltaire's attacks, as 'the petty cavils of petty minds' (*Works*, vii. 66). For accounts of the controversy, see T. R. Lounsbury, *Shakespeare and Voltaire* (1902), pp. 281–8; P. Van Tieghem, *La découverte de Shakespeare sur le continent*, in *Le Préromantisme* (1924–47), iii. 249–87; A. Gunny, *Voltaire and English Literature*, in *Studies on Voltaire and the Eighteenth Century*, clxxvii (Oxford, 1979), pp. 26–48.
[28-28] MS It ... them] *altered from* By it they w^d see
[29-29] MS convince them] *altered from* w^d be convinced

possess greater knowledge in our Language than Foreigners can perhaps ever arrive at. I well know that we have[30] Enthusia[s]ts among us who will be much surprised at the 〈C〉oncessions you have made & who will think after all the great Eloquence you have bestowed in his Favour, that you have betrayed the Ca〈u〉se of Shakespear & your Country, not considering that [31]his works form[31] 'A Wild, where Weeds & Flow'rs promiscuous shoot'[32] & that it is the Business of a Critical Botanist to class & desc〈rib〉e & not to praise or Censure indiscriminately.[33]

To Fulke Greville   [Poland Street, autumn 1768?][1]

L copy, in FB's hand (Berg).
Endorsed by CB: Copy of Letter ⎮ to ⎮ F. G. chiefly ⎮ ab^t Johnson & ⎮ Criticism
Docketed by FBA: ✻ *To Fulk Greville Esqr*, ⎮ on Johnson's ⎮ Shakespear— ⎮ —68.

Dear Sir,

I snatch a Moment from my eternal hurries to thank you for your Note[2] & Book: the latter I return, as I find myself in possession of the Reviews in which Johnson is Cut up,[3]—& indeed it is done by an able hand. I dipped last Night into the Critique, & saw plainly penetration & Reasoning Powers. But the thing which I love most in all discussions of matters not essential to human happiness, & the prosperity of the

---

[30] MS have] *altered from* have some
[31-31] MS his ... form] *altered from* the works of 〈Sh〉akespear compose *alternative* are
[32] Pope, *An Essay on Man*, i. 7. See also Johnson's 'Preface' to *Shakespeare*: 'the composition of Shakespeare is a forest, in which oaks extend their branches, and pines tower in the air, interspersed sometimes with weeds and brambles, and sometimes giving shelter to myrtles and to roses' (*Works*, vii. 84).
[33] MS indiscriminately] *interlined over deleted* in *alternative* by the Lump
Johnson replied to CB on 16 Oct.: 'I defend my criticism in the same manner with you. We must confess the faults of our favourite, to gain credit to our praise of his excellencies. He that claims either for himself or for another the honours of perfection, will surely injure the reputation which he designs to assist' (Johnson *Letters*, i. 178).

---

[1] The date of this letter may be inferred, but only tentatively, from the following pointers. Mme d'Arblay's postdating '–68' holds little weight, though CB's own endorsement, 'Copy of Letter ...' is written in a hand that would suggest this period. Greville had been abroad since early 1766 as British Minister to the Imperial Diet and Envoy Extraordinary to Bavaria, residing principally in Munich, from whence he departed on leave shortly after 28 May 1768 (Horn, pp. 42, 46). Greville and CB's discussion of Johnson's *Shakespeare* probably occurred soon after Greville's return from Germany.
[2] Not preserved.
[3] Possibly the anonymous and unfavourable notices by William Kenrick (1725?–79) in the *Monthly Review*, xxxiii (1765), 285–301, 374–89.

state,—I mean *Candour*, is wanting.—At least there seems to me a manifest *determination* to lower Johnson,—he can do nothing right in the Eyes of his Critic,—whether he praise, or censure Shakespear, he is to be *always* wrong. Johnson's hard words, which people cease to Cavil at now as they used to do in 1765,[4] are no longer hard words,— the general run of writers have adopted most of them; & *style*, as we agreed the other Day, is both purified & enriched throughout the Kingdom. Surely in the Periods, which Johnson's antagonist exhibits only to point out absurdities in them, there is a vigour of Mind, as well as Expression, which very few Writers, in any Language, ever possess.—Let his errors & false reasoning be pointed out,—let his too constant use of flowery & learned Language be censured, but allow him what he *has*,—originality & depth of Thought let the Vehicle of Conveyance be what it will. I never look on Johnson as a perfect Writer,—or Man,—but he has *Giant* Talents, & virtues which are known only to few of those who see nothing but Inflation of style,—& awkward bulkiness in his Figure. I have not Time to read his Preface to Shakespear now,—when I did, I was very much pleased with it,[5]—but perhaps I was as much disposed to give him credit for too great a share of Merit in his remarks, as his Critic too little. In short, the Reader's Mind Colours things wonderfully with respect to living Authors & their Works: you allow Johnson, & always did, great penetration, & are perhaps less biassed either by Friendship, or habit of Admiration, than myself: his Critic, that has struck you & Mrs. G. as a superior Writer, strikes me likewise as such: but if it c^d be known, I would lay a Wager that he's a sworn Foe to Johnson, as well as a furious Lover of Shakespeare. At the Time Johnson's Edition & Notes came out, I admired his Courage for daring to censure the real vices & defects of this wonderful Author, & yet, as I thought, defend him where defensible. There certainly has long been a Shakespeare *Mania* in this Country.—Garrick has abetted it for his own sake.[6]—But I hope, ere long, to talk over these matters as calmly & fairly as all subjects of mere amusem^t should be. I have niether seen nor read any of his plays for many years;—but there are strokes of *mental anatomy* in him that I never can forget, & that seem to me like Gleams from some Superior Being. I shall most gladly avail myself of the happiness you allow me &c &c

[4] For example, a correspondent to the *St. James's Chronicle*, 15–17 Oct. and 9–12 Nov. 1765, dubbed Johnson 'this Schoolmaster, and Treasurer of hard Words'.

[5] See CB to Johnson, 14 Oct. 1765.

[6] David Garrick (1717–79), with whom CB had been associated both professionally and socially from his earliest years in London. See Lonsdale, *passim*. For Garrick's productions of Shakespeare, see K. A. Burnim, *David Garrick, Director* (Pittsburgh, 1961). In 1769 Garrick was to organize the famous Shakespeare Jubilee at Stratford. See G. W. Stone, Jr. and G. M. Kahrl, *David Garrick: A Critical Biography* (Carbondale and Edwardsville, 1979), pp. 577–85.

To Esther and Fanny Burney   Oxford, 22 June 1769

L copy (Berg: Fanny Burney, MS of 'Juvenile Journal' for 1769, fo. 33).
Publ.: ED i. 56, in part; *EJL* i. 75.

Oxford, Thursday June 22[d]
past 2 o'clock

My dear Girls,

I know it will please you much to hear that the Performance of my Anthem[1] is just very well over, not one mistake of consequence—Barsanti[2] did extreamly well, & all was much applauded—I shall to-morrow have both my Degrees; (for I must first take that of Batchelor of musick)[3] with great unanimity & reputation—D[r] Hayes[4] is very

---

[1] The events which led CB to seek a doctorate in music at Oxford are related in Lonsdale, pp. 77–9. CB's Anthem, 'I will love Thee, O Lord, my Strength', is preserved in the Bodleian Library, MS Mus. Sch. Ex. c. 15. When it was first performed, it was 'received with universal Applause, and allowed by the Judges of Musical Merit to be the most ingenious and elegant Performance that was ever exhibited here on the like Occasion' (*Jackson's Oxford Journal*, 24 June 1769). 'My Academic exercise was performed at three (subsequent) annual choral meetings at Oxford; in the first & second of wch the principal soprano part was performed by Miss Barsanti, & the next by Miss Linley ere her Marriage with Mr Sheridan was published' (*CB Mem.* 115).

[2] Jane, or 'Jenny', Barsanti (*c.*1755–95), one of CB's pupils, made her professional début as a singer on this occasion. *Jackson's Oxford Journal* (24 June 1769) reported: 'Miss Barsanti's Voice and Manner of Singing were greatly admired . . . and this young Lady, who is a Scholar of Dr. Burney, and not above fourteen Years of Age, will, if we mistake not, in Time amply repay the Public any Indulgence, with which they are disposed to encourage the becoming Diffidence of modest Merit.' For her other singing engagements while in Oxford, see *EJL* i. 73–5. In his article on Jenny Barsanti's father, Francesco Barsanti (1690–1775) in Rees, CB explains that she 'had been bound apprentice to a master [presumably CB] who had undertaken to prepare her for a public singer, and with whom she had vanquished all the difficulties of the art in point of execution.' See also *BD*.

[3] By the Statutes of the University of Oxford, a candidate for the degree of B.Mus. was obliged to have spent 7 years in the study or practice of music and to be vouched for by testimony 'under the hands of credible witnesses'. His examination consisted of the production of a 'Canticum' in five parts to be performed in the School of Music. To proceed to the D.Mus., he had to pursue his professional studies for a further 5 years, and to present a 'Canticum' in six or eight parts. The candidate could matriculate as a member of the University just before his examination ('Degrees' in Rees; information kindly supplied by Dame Lucy Sutherland).

It was possible, however, for a doctoral candidate, on special application to Convocation through the Chancellor, to 'accumulate' the baccalaureate and doctorate. CB's application, in the form of a letter to Convocation from George Henry Lee (1718–72), 3rd Earl of Lichfield (1743), Chancellor of Oxford (1762–72), was proposed in Convocation on 21 June 1769. It stated that 'Charles Burney one of the King's Musicians extraordinary . . . is desirous of pro-ceeding to the Degree of Doctor in Music, but has been prevented from taking the Degree of Batchelor in that Faculty by a constant attendance on the Duties of his Profession for upwards of twenty Years at a considerable distance from the University. He therefore humbly prays that by the Favour of Convocation he may be permitted to accumulate the two Degrees paying Fees for both but doing Exercise for that of Doctor only in order to his being a Candidate for the Degree of Doctor in Music' (Oxford University Archives: 'Register of Convocation, 1766–1776', N.E.P. / *Subtus* / Register Bi, p. 102).

civil; & lends me his Robe with a very good Grace—Adieu—I know not when I shall get Home.— ⌜M^r & Mrs Pleydel[5] are here, & your three Cousins[6]—Park[7] & Pasquali[8] and all—⌝[9]

To William Mason

[Poland Street],
27 May 1770

L copy extracts, in FB's hand (Osborn). FB indicates passages omitted in her transcription by a series of crosses. These are here represented by asterisks.
Docketed by FBA: *To the Reverend Mr. Mason.*   *Publ.*: Scholes, i. 148–50.

27th May, 1770.

*   *   *   *

Several Friends, who through partiality, perhaps overated my abilities, have been desirous that I should write a History of Music:

Although the testimonial on CB's behalf by 'credible witnesses' does not appear to have survived, CB recalled that one of his referees was Dr William Boyce, 'who signed my certificate for a degree at Oxford, & with whom I always lived upon terms of friendship' (CB to Callcott, 14 Nov. 1803).

CB matriculated from University College on 20 June, and after the performance of his exercise on 22 June, supplicated for the degrees of B.Mus. and D.Mus. on 23 June 1769 (Foster; Scholes, i. 142–6; Lonsdale, p. 79).

[4] William Hayes, Heather Professor of Music, conducted the performance of CB's doctoral exercise.

[5] Charles Stafford Pleydell, or Playdell (d. 1779), had gone to India in 1744 as an employee of the East India Company, and married in 1759 Elizabeth, daughter of John Zephaniah Holwell (1711–98), Governor of Bengal. In 1768 the Pleydells returned to England and soon became close friends of the Burney family (see *EJL* i. 67 n. 50). In 1769 'the bewitching and accomplished Mrs Pleydel' became one 'amongst my new scholars' (*CB Mem.* 117). Fanny records that 'Mrs. & Mr. Pleydel payed Papa the Compliment of going to Oxford purposely to hear his Anthem' (*EJL* i. 75).

[6] Sons of CB's brother Richard, who lived at Worcester: Charles Rousseau, Richard Gustavus and James Adolphus (CB to Fanny Burney, 13 June 1764, n. 2).

[7] John Parke (1745–1829) had been engaged in 1768 as principal oboist at the Opera. He took his wife with him to Oxford, as CB recorded 40 years later in a letter to her, recalling 'the many times we met in a friendly way from the time of my taking my degree at Oxford, during your *Chickenhood*, compared with my mature age of 42' (CB to Mrs Parke, [c.1808]). CB compared Parke's playing favourably with that of the famous oboist Johann Christian Fischer (1733–1800): 'no tone approaches so near to that of Fischer, in richness and power, as that of . . . Park' ('Fischer' in Rees).

[8] Francesco Pasquali (*fl.* 1760–86), double-bass player and concert room proprietor, was a neighbour of the Burneys in Poland Street. In 1772 he built a concert room in Tottenham Street which became in 1786 the venue for the Concerts of Ancient Music. Pasquali is listed among the principal double-bass players in the orchestra for the Handel Commemoration in 1784 (*Handel Commem.*, p. 19). See *EJL* i. 75 n. 69.

[9] Fanny Burney records of this letter that CB 'was in so much haste, he has not even sign'd it' (*EJL* i. 75).

& it is an undertaking upon which I have already spent much Meditation, & for which I have been some time collecting materials. The
prospect widens as I advance. 'Tis a Chaos to which God knows
whether I shall have Life, leisure, or abilities to give order. I find
it connected with Religion, Philosophy, History, Poetry, Painting,
Sculpture, public Exhibitions & private life. It is, like Gold, to be
found, though in but small portions, even in lead-ore, & in the Coal
Mine; which are equivalent to heavy Authors, & the rust & rubbish of
antiquity. It is somewhat extraordinary that nothing of this kind has
been attempted in our language, which abounds with histories of
almost every other art, as well as of its Professors. Yet I see no reason
why the life of an eminent musician should not afford as much entertainment to the Public as that of a Painter. The Former [1]is more
frequently thrown into the highest society, his life is more chequered,
⌐& he obtains more easy access to the Great than the Latter.[1] Farinelli,[2]
for instance, who, after having been carressed by¬ almost every Prince
in Europe, became the favourite of one of the first Monarchs in the
World for Wealth & Power, at whose Court, at Madrid, he continued
till ⌐after¬ the Death of his Patron; after which he retired to enjoy the
otium cum dignitate[3] at Bologna, where he now lives, & is at this very
time building ⌐himself,¬ in the language of his Country, un Palazzo,
for the accommodation of himself & friends. Now amongst all the
Painters whose lives have been written by Vasari,[4] there is no ⌐one
except¬ Leonardo da Vinci, who furnishes such great & interesting
events.

Something must of course be said about the ancient music, of which
but little, it must be owned, is known: however, a musician, cæteris
paribus is as likely to conjecture what was possible & practicable, as
any other literary speculator. Few new Materials can at this time be
hoped for; but new conjectures may be hazarded; & I wish that you,
& your friend Mr. Gray, would honour my work so far as to enrich it
with a few of your notions upon some of the dark & most disputable
points in the ancient Music. That the Ancients had Harmony, or

---

[1-1] MS is more ... Latter.] *FBA altered by obliteration and interlineation to read* is as frequently
thrown into the highest society, & his life is more chequered because less habitually confined.

[2] Carlo Broschi (1705–82), known as 'Farinelli', the most celebrated castrato of his day, lived
at the Court of Philip V and Ferdinand VI of Spain from 1737–59. Wealth and honours were
showered upon him. CB was to visit Farinelli later in the year at Bologna. See *Tours*, i. 147–8,
151–7, 161; *Hist. Mus.* iv. 378–81, 412–17; Mercer, ii. 788–91, 813–17; Rees; C. Ricci, *Burney,
Casanova, e Farinelli in Bologna* (Milan, 1890).

[3] 'A peaceful life with honour' (Cicero, *Pro Sestio*, xlv. 98).

[4] Giorgio Vasari (1511–74), painter and architect, best known for his *Le Vite de' più eccellenti
architetti, pittori, et scultori italiani*, first published at Florence in 1550. CB owned two editions of
this work: Bologna, 1648; and Rome, 1759 (*Cat. Misc. Lib.*, lots 2007–8).

Music in parts, beyond unisons & Octaves, I am in very great doubt. The *Tibiæ impares*, with which the comedies of Terence were accompanied, must have been octaves to each other, as a pipe, or string half the length of another, produces that Concord.[5] The simplicity of the ancient Instruments to be found on antique basso relievos is such as I think encourages no high opinion of their effects singly, without the additional powers of voice & Song. The enharmonic Genus,[6] so to[t]ally lost to us, seems only practicable among the Ancients in their declamation, for which I have long been of opinion that they had a notation; else, by what rules of musical relation could the *Tibicen*, who, according to Plutarch, stood behind Gracchus, bring his voice down to its natural & sober pitch, when raised too high by passion?[7] In Alypius, there are different Notes for vocal & Instrumental purposes;[8] & I believe Aristotle mentions the notes of Declamation.[9] The sounds of Speech, according to the Abbé de Condillac, are inappreciable; &,

[5] 'The Roman comedy, in the time of Terence was accompanied *tibiis paribus et imparibus*, with *equal* and *unequal flutes*, occasionally. This is upon record in all the most ancient manuscripts of that author. What these *double flutes* were, or how played upon by one person, has much perplexed the learned, as well as practical musicians. For my own part, I had long been of opinion, that the *equal* flutes were *unisons*, and the *unequal* octaves to each other, blown by one mouth piece, before my journey into Italy; and the numerous representations I saw of them there in ancient sculpture, did not furnish me with any more probable conjecture' (*Hist. Mus.* i. 157–8; Mercer, i. 141–2). The Greek *aulos* and the Roman *tibia* were double-reed instruments, closer to the modern oboe than the flute. See 'Aulos' in *New Grove*; Kathleen Schlesinger, *The Greek Aulos* (1939); P. Bate, *The Oboe* (3rd edn., 1975), p. 12.

[6] The system of ancient musical tonality, which divided the interval of the perfect fourth into intervals of four semitones and two quarter tones. See 'Greece' in *Harvard Dictionary of Music*, ed. Willi Apel (2nd edn., 1970), p. 352; Isobel Henderson, 'Ancient Greek Music', in *New Oxford History of Music*, vol. i: *Ancient and Oriental Music*, ed. E. Wellesz (1957), pp. 336–403; Isobel Henderson and D. Wulstan, 'Introduction: Ancient Greece', in *A History of Western Music*, vol. i: *Music from the Middle Ages to the Renaissance*, ed. F. W. Sternfeld (1973), pp. 27–58. The Enharmonic Genus of the Greeks was one of the most troublesome topics for CB in writing the *History of Music*, and one for which Twining's assistance was invaluable. See CB to Twining, 13 July 1774; 28 June 1775.

[7] 'Orators, though not constantly accompanied by an instrument, had their voices sometimes regulated by one ... and this instrument served as a kind of *pitch-pipe*. Both Cicero and Plutarch, relate the well known story of the voice of the furious tribune, Caius Gracchus, being brought down to its natural pitch, after he had lost it in a transport of passion, by means of a servant placed behind him with one of these instruments' (*Hist. Mus.* i. 164; Mercer, i. 146). See Plutarch, *Life of Tiberius Gracchus*, II. 4–5.

[8] Alypius (*fl. c.*360 BC), Greek writer on music, whose *Introductio musica* (*Eisagōgē mousikē*) is the chief source of information on ancient Greek notation. CB relied heavily on him in affirming that in Greek notation 'two rows of ... characters were usually placed over the words of a lyric poem; the upper row serving for the voice, and the lower for instruments'. Alypius's treatise was included in Marcus Meibom's *Antiquae musicae auctores septem, Graece et Latine*, which issued in two volumes 'from the elegant press of Elzevir, Amst[erdam] 1652' (*Hist. Mus.* i. 9, 441; Mercer, i. 29, 349). CB owned a copy ('Cat. Fac. Mus.', item 100).

[9] 'Problems Connected with Harmony' (*Problems*, XIX), though pseudo-Aristotelean, is one of the earliest documents about ancient Greek music. See W. S. Hett's translation of the *Problems*, Loeb Classical Library (1936), i. 378–415; F. A. Gevaert and J. C. Vollgraff, *Les problèmes musicaux d'Aristote* (Gand, 1899–1903), pp. 46–9, 218–22.

consequently, too minute for Notation:[10] this may be true with respect to all modern Languages, except the Italian; but I am certain it would be very possible to reduce to Notes their manner of reading Poetry; which, together with their Recitatives, is perhaps a *reste* of the ancient music. No one of the ancient Genera is come down to us entire, except the Diatonic; which is ascending & descending by steps: whereas the Enharmonic seems to teach how to slide up & down the Banisters. As to their Instruments, neither the violin, nor any other Instrument played with a Bow, seems to be amongst them. The Syringia, Tibiæ, Utriculariæ, & the Polyaulos,[11] seem to have given rise to the future attempts at an Organ: & the Hydraulicon described by Vitruvius,[12] & which Claudian seems to mean in the following passage

> Et qui magna Levi detrudens murmura Tacta
> Innumera[s] voces [segetis] moderatus ainæ
> Intonet erranti digito penitusque trabali
> Vecte Laborantes in Carmina concitet undas,[13]

appears to resemble the present Organ in most respects but the manner of blowing it.

I agree with Rousseau in thinking the Canto Fermo a remnant of the Ancient Music of the Pagans;[14] as our present chanting & Responses in the Cathedral Service is of the plain Chant in the Romish Church; for Tallys,[15] who first adjusted the Gregorian Chant to English words at the time of the Reformation, I believe added little or nothing to what he found in the Latin Litany Responses, &c.

I have seen the first Book of our Church plain Chant by Tallis,

[10] CB refers to the *Essai sur l'origine des connoissances humaines*, part II, section i, ch. 6 (Amsterdam, 1746), ii. 92, 94, by Étienne Bonnot de Condillac (1714–80), abbé de Mureau, French philosophe and disciple of Locke.

[11] 'Polyaulos' is probably a mistranscription by Fanny Burney of 'plagiaulos' (πλαγίαυλος), or cross-flute. The other wind instruments were: the *syrinx*, 'composed of a number of reeds of different lengths tied together'; the *tibia*, 'originally a Flute, made of the shank, or shin bone of an animal' (*Hist. Mus.* i. 487; Mercer, i. 399); and the *tibia utricularis*, or Roman bagpipe.

[12] In *De Architectura*, x. viii. See *Hist. Mus.* i. 491; Mercer, i. 403; also Willi Apel, 'Early History of the Organ', *Speculum*, xxiii (1948), 191–216.

[13] 'Him too whose light touch can elicit loud music from those pipes of bronze that sound a thousand diverse notes beneath his wandering fingers and who by means of a lever stirs to song the labouring water' (*Panegyric on the Consulship of Fl. Manlius Theodorus*, ll. 316–19, *Claudian*, trans. M. Platnauer, Loeb Classical Library (1922), i. 361). CB quotes these lines again in *Hist. Mus.* i. 490; Mercer, i. 403; and in Rees under 'Hydraulicon'.

[14] Rousseau in his *Dictionnaire de musique* (1768), p. 379, defines 'Plain-chant' as 'le nom qu'on donne dans l'Église Romaine au Chant Ecclésiastique. Ce Chant, tel qu'il subsiste encore aujourd'hui, est un reste bien défiguré, mais bien précieux, de l'ancienne Musique Grecque, laquelle, après avoir passé par les mains des barbares, n'a pû perdre encore toutes ses premières beautés'.

[15] Thomas Tallis (c.1505–85), English organist and composer. On his Continental tours, CB confirmed his belief that Tallis adapted Gregorian Chant to English usage: 'It appears plainly

printed in the time of Henry the Eighth, & I have compared it with the Ambrosian & *Gregorian* Canto Fermo, & find a perfect resemblance.

Thus far for ancient Greek & Roman Music, & for ancient music since the time of Boetius, or rather Guido Aretine.[16] I have got together & consulted an incredible number of Books & Tracts on the subject with more disappointment & disgust than satisfaction, for they are, in general, such faithful copies of each other, that by reading two or three, you have the substance of as many hundred. It is far more easy to compile a dull Book of bits & scraps from these writers, than to get any one to read it after it is done. I have therefore determined to fly to Italy this Summer, & to allay my thirst of knowledge at the pure source,[17] which I am unable to do by such spare Draughts as are to be attained from the polluted Works through which it is conducted to us here. No one that I know of has gone into Italy meerly upon such an errand, though the Italians at present surpass the rest of Europe in no one art so much as in their Music. I shall consult the public Libraries at Milan, Florence, Venice, Rome, Naples, &c, for the first rise & progress of Music since Guido's time; & I shall endeavour, by hearing & conversing with the most eminent Professors, to inform myself of its present state.

*   *   *   *

In the Vatican, I expect to find the original Notes of the Melodies sung by the Troubadours,[18] who were the first Bards in modern song — — as *You* know better than I can tell you.

*   *   *   *

᠁I ought to make many apologies for the length of this Letter; but I hope your love for Music will render them somewhat less necessary. Indeed, I should add Poetry, as the history of one almost indispensably

to me that our old chants and responses were not new compositions by Tallis, at the time of the reformation, but only adjusted to English words' (*Tours*, i. 5).

[16] Anicius Manlius Torquatus Severinus Boetius, or Boethius (*c*.480–*c*.524), Roman philosopher and statesman, whose treatise in five books, *De Institutione Musica*, was instrumental in transmitting knowledge of ancient Greek musical art to the Middle Ages. For CB's censorious verdict on the value of Boethius's treatise, see *Hist. Mus.* ii. 31 n.; Mercer, i. 430 n. *x*; and CB to J. W. Callcott, 29 Jan. 1802 (Osborn).

Guido d'Arezzo, or Aretinus (*c*.991–after 1033), Benedictine monk, whose revolutionary musical practice and celebrated *Micrologus* (compiled after 1026) disseminated the system of solmization (*ut, re, mi, fa, sol, la*) which replaced the cumbrous Greek nomenclature of notes, applied the system of the 'Guidonian Hand' to directing a chorus, and established the use of the music staff of 4 lines. See *MGG*; *New Grove*.

[17] CB favoured this metaphor. See *Tours*, i, p. xxvii; and *Giambattista Martini, Piano generale per una storia della musica di Charles Burney con un catalogo della sua biblioteca musicale*, ed. V. Duckles (Bologna, 1972), p. viii.

[18] See *Tours*, i. 218.

includes that of the other. I find in Crescembeni much to my purpose; & also in P. Menestriers History of the Poets.⸗[19]

*   *   *   *

To Montagu North[1]

Poland Street,
27 May 1770

ALS (North Papers, Rougham, Norfolk).
  Addressed: To | The Revd Dr North | at Sternfield, near | Saxmundham | Suffolk
Pmk.: 28 MA   *Docketed by* North: Dr Burney | May 27, 1770. | Dr Burney May 27,
1770.

Dear Sir.

It gave me great concern that you sh^d be in Town, tho' for so short a Time, without my having the Honour & happiness of seeing you. But I was unfortunate in the attempts we both made. & I fear it will not be in my Power to indemnify myself for the Loss I have sustained, by waiting upon you in Suffolk for some Time, as I am now on the Wing for Italy, having determined to set out on my Journey thither on Tuesday 7 Night, the 5th of June.

Had the Books I have hitherto consulted, wch have been very numerous, supplied me with the Information I wanted relative to my intended History of Music, I sh^d not undertake a Journey that will cost me much Time, money & Fatigue. But these Authors are, in general, such faithful Copies of each other that by reading 2 or 3 of them you have the Substance of as many hundred. In hopes therefore

---

[19] Giovanni Mario Crescimbeni (1663–1728), Italian priest, poet, and critic, was a founder-member of the Academy of the Arcadians, which sought to promote and cultivate correct poetic taste. Among other works, he wrote a critical evaluation of all the Italian poets entitled *L'Istoria della volgar poesia* (Rome, 1698), and edited *Notizie istoriche degli Arcadi morti* (Rome, 1720–1).

  Claude-François Menestrier (1631–1705), Jesuit, was a prolific miscellaneous writer, scholar, and antiquary. See Michaud; *DBF*; C. Sommervogel, SJ, *Bibliothèque de la Compagnie de Jésus* (rev. edn., Louvain, 1960), vol. v, cols. 905–45.

  CB's reference to 'Menestriers History of the Poets' is misleading: he probably meant by his citation either Crescimbeni's *Istoria* or his *Notizie*. No list of Menestrier's voluminous publications contains a reference to a 'History of the Poets', though in several instances in his *History of Music*, CB cites as his authority Menestrier's *Des représentations en musique, anciennes et modernes* (1681).

[1] The Revd Montagu North (1712–79), DD (1767), Rector of Sternfield, Suffolk (1767), Prebendary of Windsor (1775–9), second son of the lawyer, music historian and theorist, the Hon. Roger North (*c.*1651–1734), of Rougham, Norfolk (*DNB*; *New Grove*). For CB's long friendship with the North family, see CB to Malone, 30 June 1799 (PML). See *GM* xlix (1779), 424; Venn.

of giving to my Book some marks of originality or at least of Novelty, I shall e'en go and allay my Thirst of Knowledge at the Source, & not content myself with the spare Draughts & Sips I am able to obtain from the poluted works thro' wch it is conducted to us here. If you can think of any thing I can do for you on that part of the Continent over wch I shall pass between Calais & Naples you will afford me much Pleasure, by communicating to me your Wishes before my Departure.

I am Dear Sir, with great Regard,
Your obliged & Most Humble Servt
Chas Burney.

Poland Street, May 27th | 1770.

To Fanny Burney   Dover, 6 June 1770

ALS (BL Egerton MS 3690, fo. 1).
Addressed: For | Fan   *Docketed by* FBA: ✳ IV. | Benignant Leave-taking | on setting out for France & Italy. | June 1770 | N° 10. | 1770.

My dear Fan—

I cannot set Sail[1] ere I have given you a Word & a Wish of kindness & affection. Continue to Love me & to believe that I Love you—& that my Family is never nearer my Heart than when I am obliged to be far from them. It has ever been *necessity* not *Choice* that has separated us. Had I an Ark like that of Noah, I w^d have taken you all in it—but—I have not Time to say ⟨m⟩ore than adieu.—I hope to live to make you ⟨all⟩ porcupines by the Wonders I shall have seen ⟨whe⟩n I come to relate them.—Farewell my Dr Fan—y^r Mama[2] will furnish y^r *Rent* as it becomes due—

C.B.

Dover—6. June | 1770.

[1] CB arrived at Dover on 'Tuesday, June 5th' and sailed to Calais on 7 June 'without any other accident than the very common one of being intolerably ill during the whole passage' (*Tours*, i. 1).
[2] CB's second wife, Elizabeth Allen, née Allen (1728–96), whom he had married on 2 Oct. 1767 (*CB Mem.* 113–14). Mrs Burney appears to have accompanied CB to Dover (*Tours*, i. 1), and no doubt delivered this note by hand to Fanny.

To David Garrick

Naples,
17[-18] October 1770

ALS (Victoria and Albert Museum, Forster Collection: 48. F. 43, fos. 97–8).
Addressed: To | David Garrick Esqr | In Southampton Street, Covent Garden |
London | Inghilterra   *Pmk:* NO 17 NAPOLI   *Publ.:* Boaden, i. 403–5;
Scholes, ii. 290–3.

Naples. Octr 17. 1770[1]

'Thus far into the Bowels of the Land have we marched on without
Impediment,'[2] except such as every Traveller must Encounter, who has
to deal with Italian Innkeepers—Camerieri—Vittorini—Postiglioni
&c &c.—but for the Honour of Italy, as well as for my own Honour,—
I must say that my reception & treatment among the Men of Learning
& Genius throughout my Journey have been to the last degree flattering. After the Acc^ts I had read & heard of this Country I expected
to meet with a People shy of strangers & difficult of Access. But, *au
Contraire*, in every great Town where I have stopt I have not only met
with politeness & Civility, but even with Kindness & Friendship. I
am almost ashamed to tell you how many Men of Eminence both in
the literary & Musical World have interested themselves in my Enterprise; but as you, who rank so high among the former Class in our
own Country, have kindly manifested your good wishes in an Effectual
Manner by your hearty recommendations to your Fr^ds at Paris,[3] I
shall venture to tell you, without fear of incurring the Character of a
Puffer, what reason I have to be satisfied wth the success of my Journey.
    When I left England I had two objects in view: the one was to get
from the Libraries & the *viva voce* Conversation of the Learned what

[1] Before he set out for France and Italy, CB had evidently outlined in conversation a proposed itinerary to his friend Samuel Crisp on Saturday 26 May 1770. On the following Monday,
28 May, Crisp wrote about 'one thing, that has lain upon my Mind, ever since I left you ... that
your route may be all plann'd & settled before hand' (Osborn). It appears from Crisp's letter
that CB's original plan had been to leave London in early June, and 'to be in London again some
time in October'. Crisp strongly objected to this hurried itinerary: 'something must be indulg'd
to natural Curiosity, especially in such an Animal as Yourself, who want to grasp at every thing.'
More particularly, Crisp warned CB about *'Mal aria'*, rampant in Italy 'precisely during part of
July, all August & September & part of October, ... & the Road between Rome & Naples,
precisely the most fatal spot, while the Mal Aria reigns ... ⌐I don't well see, how You can get to
& from Naples without great hazard ... You had better sacrifice two more winter months
advantage in London than risque Your life—stay at Rome till the danger is past; then go to
Naples, & content Yourself to return to England about Xmas⌐'. See also *Tours*, i. 238–9. CB
clearly heeded Crisp's advice by timing his arrival in Naples in mid-Oct.
    [2] *Richard III*, v. ii. 3–4.
    [3] For Garrick's letters to his Parisian friends on behalf of CB, see *Tours*, i. 25; Garrick *Letters*,
ii. 693–4; Lonsdale, pp. 85–6.

information I c^d relative to the Music of the ancients—& the other was to Judge wth my own Ears of the *present State* of Modern Music in the places thro' wch I sh^d pass from the Performance & Conversation of the first Musicians in Italy. I shall here only mention the Most remarkable of both sorts. As my general History must be a work of Time, I intend publishing, as soon as I get Home, in a Pamphlet or small volume, an Account of the *Present State* of Music in France & Italy, in wch I shall describe according to my Judgment & Feelings the merits of the several Compositions & performers I have heard in travelling thro' those Countries. At Turin I often saw & conversed wth the famous Padre Beccaria[4]—& the 2 Bezozzi's[5] not only performed to me for near Two Hours but were Friendly all the Time I was there—I found some things I wanted too in the King's Library—at Milan Padre Boscovich,[6] Padre Frisier,[7] Sig^r Oltrocchi Ambrosian Librarian,[8] D. Triulzi,[9] the Abbate Bonelli[10]—Padre Sacchi,[11] il Conte Po[12] &c—& on the side of practical Music the famous San Martini,[13]

[4] Giovanni Battista Beccaria (1716–81), Piarist priest and physicist, professor of experimental physics at the University of Turin (1748), FRS (1755), was a pioneer in the study of electricity. CB himself was 'pretty deeply bit ... by this new science' (Bewley to CB, 18 June 1770, Osborn). See *DBI*; *DSB*; *Tours*, i. 59–60. CB was in Turin from 11 to 14 July.

[5] The brothers Alessandro (1702–93) and Paolo Girolamo (1704–78) Besozzi, oboist and bassoonist respectively to the King of Sardinia. CB visited the brothers on 13 July 1770 (*Tours*, i. 57–8), and was highly impressed by their playing.

[6] Rudjer Josip Bošković (1711–87), celebrated Croatian Jesuit mathematician, astronomer, physicist, and diplomat: FRS (1761). Characterized by Željko Marković in *DSB* as 'perhaps the last polymath to figure in an important way in the history of science', Bošković had moved his work in 1770 to the department of optics and astronomy at the Scuole Palatine in Milan. See *Tours*, i. 68–9.

[7] Paolo Frisi (1728–84), Milanese mathematician, physicist, and astronomer, was a member of the Barnabite order. He had in 1764 been made professor of mathematics in the palatine schools at Milan and was an expert in hydraulics. See *Tours*, i. 83; *DSB*.

[8] Baldassarre Oltrocchi (1715–99), theologian, of the Congregation of Oblates, had been prefect of the Ambrosian Library since 1748. See C. von Wurzbach, *Biographisches Lexikon des Kaiserthums Oesterreich* (Vienna, 1856–91), xxi. 58; C. Frati, *Dizionario bio-bibliografico dei bibliotecari e bibliofili italiani* (Florence, 1933), pp. 419–20; *Tours*, i. 67–8, 79, 81–2.

[9] 'Don Triulzi', otherwise unidentified, whom CB met in the Ambrosian Library. He was 'a noble and learned clergyman ... very much in years' who had studied neumes and had 'formed some ingenious conjectures about them' (*Tours*, i. 79).

[10] Benedetto Bonelli (1704–83), Franciscan theologian and editor of the works of St Bonaventure (*DBI*), used his influence 'like *magic*' to gain for CB access to the manuscript treasures of the Ambrosian Library (*Tours*, i. 82).

[11] Giovenale Sacchi (1726–89), Barnabite priest and prolific author on musical theory and biography. See *Tours*, i. 82; 'Sacchi' in Rees.

[12] The Conte Giuseppe Po (*fl.* 1770–8), Milanese patrician, became a founder member of the Società Patriottica, established in 1776 for the promotion of agriculture, fine arts, and manufacture (*Storia di Milano*, ed. G. Treccani degli Alfieri (Milan, 1953–66), xii. 622 n. 4, 627; *Tours*, i. 79–80, 82–5).

[13] Giovanni Battista Sammartini, or San Martini (*c.*1701–75), organist, composer of over 2,000 ecclesiastical and secular works, and one of the early experimenters with symphonic form (*Tours*, i. 64 ff.; 'Martini' in Rees; CB to Twining, 14 Dec. 1781, n. 23).

Lampugnani,[14] il Padre Maestro Florione, of the Duomo[15] &c—At Brescia I stopt but two Days & only one at Verona & Vicenza—but at Padua I was 6 or 8 Days.[16] & there I found y[r] Fr[d] D[r] Marsili[17] Cav. Valcinieri[18]—Padre Colombo[19]—padre Vallotti[20]—Maestro di Capella al *Santo*, one of the greatest Composers for the Church now alive—& on the side of practice Sig[r] Guglietti,[21] poor Tartini's scholar & successor at S[t] Anthony's Church, from whom I got the *last drop of his Pen*, or, in other words, the last solo he Composed. At Venice I had high Entertainm[t] of all Sorts. For Learning & Theory I conversed w[th]

[14] Giovanni Battista Lampugnani (1706–88), Italian opera composer, succeeded Galuppi in 1743 as composer to the King's Opera House in London, where he stayed until about 1746. He spent his last years in his native Milan as a singing master and conductor or *maestro al cembalo* at the Teatro Regio Ducal. 'He was a pleasant old man, with the spirits and good nature of a young one' (Rees). See also *Tours*, i. 76.

[15] Giovanni Andrea Fioroni (*c.*1704–78), composer of sacred music and *maestro di cappella* at Milan cathedral since 1747. CB found his compositions examples of the survival of 'the ancient grave stile' (*Tours*, i. 65). See also 'Fioroni' in Rees.
   CB was in Milan from 16 to 25 July.

[16] 29 July–3 Aug.

[17] Giovanni Marsili (1727–95), MD, professor of botany and prefect of the botanical garden in the University of Padua, FRS (1758). He had published *Fungi carrariensis historia* (Padua, 1766). See P. A. Saccardo, *La Botanica in Italia* (Venice, 1895–1901), i. 104; ii. 68, 125; E. A. Cigogna, *Delle inscrizioni veneziane* (Venice, 1824–53), iii. 10–11; *Tours*, i. 97 ff.

[18] 'Cavaliere Valcinieri', otherwise unidentified, was the curator of the museum in Padua, which contained 'a great number of natural curiosities' (*Tours*, i. 103, 106–7).

[19] Giovanni Alberto Colombo, or Colombi (*fl.* 1745–72), Benedictine monk, professor of physics and philosophy at the University of Padua. He was a friend of Tartini, who had bequeathed to him his MSS concerning musical theory. See G. Tiraboschi, *Biblioteca modenese* (Modena, 1781–6), ii. 61; G. A. Moschini, *Della letteratura veneziana del secolo XVIII* (Venice, 1806–8), iii. 204; Cigogna, *Inscrizioni*, iv. 620; also *Tours*, i. 98–107.

[20] Francesco Antonio Vallotti (1697–1780), a Franciscan, had a reputation as the best organist of his time in Italy. He composed for the church and planned a four-volume theoretical work on music, *Della scienza teorica, e pratica della moderna musica*, of which he completed only the first volume (Padua, 1779). From 1730 until his death, Vallotti held the important post of *maestro di cappella* at the basilica church of St Anthony at Padua, called locally *il Santo*. For CB's appreciative short accounts of Vallotti, see *Tours*, i. 105 and 'Vallotti' in Rees.

[21] Giulio Meneghini (*fl.* 1756–81), known as 'Giulietto' or 'Tromba', succeeded his master, Giuseppe Tartini (1692–1770), as first violinist in the orchestra of the Basilica del Santo at Padua. CB shared with his friend William Bewley an enthusiasm for the compositions of 'the Divine Tartini' (Bewley to CB, 24 Apr. 1771, Osborn), which amounted almost to veneration. Deeply disappointed that the great violinist, teacher, theorist, and composer had died only 5 months before his arrival in Padua, CB visited all the people and places associated with Tartini 'with the zeal of a pilgrim at Mecca', and 'begged a copy' from Meneghini of Tartini's last two violin solos, 'regarding these last drops of his pen as sacred relics of so great and original a genius' (see *Tours*, i. 98–102, 107). On his return to Britain, CB brought out in the summer of 1771 *A Letter from the late Signor Tartini to Signora Maddalena Lombardini (now Signora Sirmen) Published as an Important Lesson to Performers on the Violin, Translated by Dr. Burney*, with the Italian and English texts on facing pages. See *Hist. Mus.* iii. 562–7; Mercer, ii. 446–50; and CB's article in Rees where he states categorically that Tartini was 'the greatest performer on the violin and composer for that instrument of the last century.' See P. Petrobelli, *Giuseppe Tartini, le fonti biografiche* (Venice, 1968).

Dr Reghellini,[22] the Abate Martini,[23] the Librarian of S. Marc's,[24] il Conte Tassis[25]—& for Modern Music with the famous Galuppi,[26] Latilla[27] & Sacchini[28]—at Bologna I almost lived in the Houses of the Celebrated Theorist & Historian Padre Martini,[29] whose Library

[22] Giovanni Reghellini (1710–72), physician and surgeon, had written a medical treatise, *Osservazioni sopra alcuni casi rari medici e chirurgici* (Venice, 1764). He dedicated one of the *Osservazioni* to his friend Giovanni Marsili. See Cigogna, *Inscrizioni*, iii. 11; *Tours*, i. 119.

[23] The abate Giovanni Martini (*fl.* 1770) was 'a learned Venetian dilettante, and an excellent judge of every species of music, ancient and modern'. He had travelled in Greece, and had 'studied all the Greek scales and knows ... as much as any one else, about the systems of Pythagoras, Ptolemy, and the writers collected by Meibomius, as well as of Rameau and Tartini' (*Tours*, i. 119–20). Martini founded an academy in Venice exclusively for the performance of the music of Marcello, a fellow Venetian, whom he greatly admired ('Martini, Abate' in Rees). Not to be confused with Sammartini or Padre Martini (nn. 13, 29).

[24] The librarian of the Marciana in 1770 was Antonio Maria Zanetti (*c.*1705–78), who had taken up the appointment in 1736 (Frati, *Dizionario*, pp. 577–8).

[25] Count Anton Thurn und Taxis (*c.*1735–1816), who had recently become general superintendent of posts in the Venetian state and Austrian possessions, was also an accomplished musician and composer. A scholar and friend of Tartini, he had inherited from the composer a quantity of MS scores with other papers. He published a defence of Tartini, possibly with the composer's collaboration, entitled *Riposta di un anonimo al celebre signor Rousseau circa al suo sentimento in proposito d'alcune proposizioni del Sig. Giuseppe Tartini* (Venice, 1769). See *Tours*, i. 100, 120, 126; UTET.

[26] Baldassare Galuppi (1706–85), composer, native of Burano, frequently called 'Il Buranello'. In 1762 he had been promoted from second to first *maestro di cappella* at St Mark's, and in 1768 appointed director of the Ospedale degli Incurabili, one of the four musical academies for which Venice was famous. CB enjoyed a 'long, profitable, and entertaining' visit with Galuppi while in Venice (*Tours*, i. 133–4), and thought that Galuppi had more influence than any other contemporary Italian composer on English dramatic music, owing to the steady popularity of his operas on the London stage (*Hist. Mus.* iv. 449, 539–40; Mercer, ii. 841–2, 910).

[27] Gaetano Latilla (1711–88), prolific composer for the stage, best known for his comic operas, had succeeded Galuppi in 1762 as second *maestro* at St Mark's. When CB met him in Venice, however, he had '"fallen from his high estate," and shrunk into a humble deputy organist' ('Latilla' in Rees; *Tours*, i. 116, 121–2). By 1774 Latilla had returned to Naples, where he had been educated.

[28] Antonio Maria Gasparo Gioacchino Sacchini (1730–86), composer, had been appointed (1768) director of the Ospedaletto, one of the Venetian musical academies. CB, at this time not yet on terms of familiarity with Sacchini, ranked him as a composer second only to Galuppi in Venice. Sacchini arrived in London in Apr. 1772 and stayed for over a decade, during which time CB got to know him well: 'He remained too long in England for his fame and fortune. The first was injured by cabals, ... and the second by inactivity and want of economy' (Rees). Sacchini finally moved to Paris where he died. See CB to Archer, 21–8 Feb. 1779.

CB stayed in Venice from 3 to 19 Aug.

[29] Giovanni Battista (Giambattista) Martini (1706–84), Franciscan, the leading authority of his day on music history and theory, composer, and teacher. In 1725 he had become *maestro di cappella* at the Church of San Francesco. The first volume of his projected five-volume *Storia della musica* had been published at Bologna in 1757. Of the later volumes, Martini published only the second (1770) and the third (1781). He died while working on the fourth. To his great relief, CB found in Padre Martini a source of assistance and encouragement rather than of rivalry in his plan to write his own history of music. See *Tours*, i. 145 ff.; Lonsdale, pp. 89–90.

While CB was in Bologna (21–31 Aug.), Padre Martini made a transcript of the Italian translation of CB's 'Plan for a General History of Music', which he took with him on his travels. This interesting document, preserved in Bologna in the Civico Museo Bibliografico Musicale

of Books relative to Music amounts to 16 or 17,000 Vol^s—he was very communicative & we compared *Notes* & have already opened a Cor[r]espondence—I had great Civilities from Farinelli[30] with whom I spent two whole Days. I visited here the famous Dottoressa Laura Bassa[31] upon the Merits of a recommendation from her Fr^d Padre Beccaria.—At Florence il Proposto Fossi[32]—Dr Guadagni[33]— Sig^r Bandini the grand Duke's Librarian[34]—il Canonico Domenico Cavalea[35]—& Dr Perelli,[36] were all open & Friendly—I was almost every Night at an *Academia* in the House of the famous improvisatrice Corilla[37]—The first rate Practical Musicians I found here, were

(MS 1.F.62), has been reproduced in facsimile in *Giambattista Martini, Piano generale per una storia della musica di Charles Burney con un catalogo della sua biblioteca musicale*, ed. V. Duckles (Bologna, 1972). See Brofsky.

[30] For CB's meetings with Farinelli, see *Tours*, i. 147–8, 151–7.

[31] Laura Maria Caterina Verati, née Bassi (1711–78), noted scientist, had taken her doctorate at the age of 20 in May 1732. In the same year she received a chair of natural philosophy in the University of Bologna. This extraordinary achievement for a woman in the eighteenth century was celebrated in two volumes of commendatory verses written by contemporary Italian poets. In addition to her scientific studies, she wrote poetry and held membership in the Academy of the Arcadians. In 1738 she married Giuseppe Verati, a physician.
When CB visited her, Laura Bassi showed him some of her experiments in electricity (*Tours*, i. 159–60).

[32] Ferdinando Fossi (*fl.* 1758–89), who held the ecclesiastical dignity of 'il Proposto di Or San Michele', was librarian at the Magliabechian Library (Frati, *Dizionario*, p. 236; Walpole *Corresp.* xxi. 170; *Tours*, i. 181–92).

[33] Giovanni Francesco Guadagni (1704–94) had distinguished himself as a student of experimental philosophy and mathematics at the University of Bologna. His subsequent peripatetic career as a *savant* and belletrist took him to Padua, Rome, Naples, Florence, and Turin. When CB visited him on 12 Sept. 1770, Guadagni made him 'a present of a very fine old Music-book by Orlando di Lasso' (*Tours*, i. 187). See A. Schivardi, *Biografia dei medici illustri bresciani* (Brescia, 1839–52), i. 199.

[34] Angelo Maria Bandini (1726–1803), scholar, philologist, and antiquary. In 1756 he took Holy Orders, attained the dignity of Protonotary Apostolic, and was appointed by the Emperor Francis I (1708–65), in his capacity as Grand Duke of Tuscany, principal librarian at the Laurentian Library. Among his many scholarly and literary achievements, he played a major part in the publication of the important annual review, *Novelle letterarie*, and published a catalogue of the Greek, Latin, and Italian MSS in the Laurentian Library (8 vols., Florence, 1764–78). Notices of Bandini abound: for the most useful, see *DBI*; Frati, *Dizionario*, pp. 45–7; for a checklist of Bandini's publications, see M. Parenti, *Aggiunte al dizionario ... di Carlo Frati* (Florence, 1952–60), i. 64–71.

[35] The 'Canonico Domenico Cavalea', otherwise unidentified, was 'a great Hebraist' who 'promised to send me his remarks upon Hebrew accents, which he thinks were the ancient characters for sound' (*Tours*, i. 189–90). CB includes Cavalea's observation in *Hist. Mus.* i. 255–6; Mercer, i. 213.

[36] Tommaso Perelli (1704–83), professor of astronomy at the University of Pisa since 1739. CB found him 'well read in ancient Music and ancient authors ... and has promised to *think* for me' (*Tours*, i. 190). See *Biografia degli italiani illustri*, ed. E. de Tipaldo (Venice, 1834–45), iv. 149–52; F. Inghirami, *Storia della Toscana* [*vols. XII–XIV*]: *Biografia* (Fiesole, 1843–4), iii. 62–4.

[37] Maria Maddalena Romola Fernandez, née Morelli (1728–1800), famed for her ability to compose extemporaneous verse on any subject, accompanying herself on the violin, took the name Corilla Olimpica when she was admitted to the Academy of the Arcadians. Later, 31 Aug. 1776, she was ceremonially crowned laureate in Rome. See A. Ademollo, *Corilla Olimpica* (Florence, 1887); *Tours*, i. 188 and n. 1.

Mansoli[38]—Nardini,[39] Campioni[40]—Dotel Figlio[41] &c—by the Time I got to Rom⟨e⟩ my Italian Acquaintance & Letters were much accumulated—I staid there near a month[42]—Several Friends & first rate artists there are on the hunt for me—& are making original Drawings of musical Instruments from Bassi rilievi & antient sculpture of the first Class. As to the Music of the Pope's Chapel, I shall be enabled to speak of it from the best authority my own Eyes & Ears can afford—Sig^r Santarelli the pope's Maestro di Capella[43] has loaded me with Civility & Friendly offices—is now getting made out for me Copies of the best Compositions that are in constant use in the Pope's Chapel—I have found out the Music of the *1st Opera* & *1st Oratorio* that ever were set to Music[44]—the D. of Dorset[45] had a very good Concert

[38] Giovanni Manzuoli (*c*.1720–82), castrato known as 'Succianoccioli', whose voice, according to CB, was second only to Farinelli's in power (*Hist. Mus.* iv. 484–5; Mercer, ii. 867–8). CB had heard him in London 6 years earlier (*CB Mem.* 106); when he heard the aging singer perform in his native Florence, he was still delighted by Manzuoli, though the power of his voice had faded (*Tours*, i. 183).

[39] Pietro Nardini (1722–93), violinist and composer, the most outstanding of Tartini's pupils. After Tartini's death in Feb. 1770, he had accepted the position of principal violinist at the court of the Grand Duke of Tuscany in Florence, where he set up his own school of violin playing (*Tours*, i. 184–91).

[40] Carlo Antonio Campioni (1720–88), composer and pupil of Tartini, was *maestro di cappella* to the Grand Duke of Tuscany, a post he had held since 1763 (*Tours*, i. 187, 190).

[41] Nicolas Dothel, or Dottel (*fl.* 1750–70), flautist and composer, known as 'Dottel Figlio'. Little is known about him. CB informs us that he played in the band of the Grand Duke (*Tours*, i. 184; Scholes, i. 122 and n. 3). A large number of his compositions for the flute are listed in *Einzeldrucke vor 1800*, ed. K. Schlager, RISM, ser. A, pt. I, vol. ii (1972), pp. 436–7.
  CB stayed in Florence from 1 to 16 Sept.

[42] From 20 Sept. to 14 Oct.

[43] Giuseppe Santarelli (1710–90), castrato and composer, had joined the choir of the Pontifical Chapel in 1749 and that of the Church of Santa Maria Maggiore in 1761. In the same year, he proposed reforms to rectify the abuses current in the papal choir. His proposals raised a storm of protest, which probably explains the non-publication of his learned work on church music, *Della musica del Santuario e della disciplina de'suoi cantori*, the first volume of which had been printed in Rome (1764), but not published. The second volume, 'in great forwardness' when CB met Santarelli in 1770, remains in MS and is preserved in the Civico Museo Bibliografico Musicale, Bologna (*Tours*, i. 229 and n. 2; 'Santarelli' in Rees; UTET).

[44] CB refers to *Euridice*, first performed in the Palazzo Pitti in Florence on 6 Oct. 1600 on the occasion of the wedding of Henry IV of France to Maria de' Medici. Ottavio Rinuccini (1562– 1621) wrote the libretto, which was set to music mainly by Jacopo Peri (1561–1633) with a few arias by Giulio Caccini (*c*.1545–1618) inserted. CB found the score of *Euridice* (published in 1600) in the Palazzo Rinuccini in Florence (*Tours*, i. 185; *Hist. Mus.* iv. 25–6; Mercer, ii. 515–16). The Rinuccini–Peri *Dafne* (first performed in 1598), which is now generally accorded pride of place as the first opera, is clearly not the work CB had examined. Peri's music is mostly lost, though Rinuccini's libretto reached print in 1600. See A. Loewenberg, *Annals of Opera, 1597–1940* (2nd edn., Geneva, 1955), vol. i, cols. 1–3; F. W. Sternfeld, The First Printed Opera Libretto', *Music and Letters*, lix (1978), 121–38.
  Santarelli had found for CB the score of the *Rappresentatione di Anima et di Corpo* by Emilio de' Cavalieri (*c*.1550–1602), which CB considered to be the first oratorio preserved. It was performed and published in Rome in 1600 (*Tours*, i. 224–5; *Hist. Mus.* iv. 86–90; Mercer, ii. 564–9). Recent musical scholarship disagrees with CB's opinion that Cavalieri's *Rappresentatione* can properly be called an oratorio. See e.g. P. H. Láng, *Music in Western Civilization* (New York, 1941), p. 346;

every Night, & took a great deal of Pains to get Curious & Clever performers together often on my Acc^t—I was presented to Cardinal Alessandro Albani,[46] the principal Librarian at the Vatican who gave me permission to go into it & to have whatever w^d be of use to my Work Copied. I spent Most of my Mornings in this Library & the abate Elie[47] one of the Custode, was very obliging & serviceable to me in my researches after *Canto Fermo, Contra Punto* Provençale Songs &c. & I have been pretty fortunate—the Card^l Albani is likewise *Prefetto* of the Pope's Chapel, & gave me leave to ransack the Archives there— but tho' this is sport & special fun to me—I forget that by the Time this arrives both your Hands and your Head will be too full to admit Flutes & Fiddles.[48] However, this I am sure of, that you have a heart wch glows with Friendship & will excuse my breaking in upon you at an unseasonable Time, when it is to Pay an old Debt from hence of several Years standing—I remember you sent me an Excellent Letter from Naples wch was never answered.[49]—& this is more an acknowledgement of the Debt than a payment of it—but d—n your Speeches, you'll say, & so I have done—first begging my best Respects to Mrs Garrick[50]—I shall stay here till after the 4th of Novr S. Charles's Day, wch you know is that on wch the serious opera begins—when the great Theatre is doubly illuminated[51]—I w^d not take L100 not to be here then: indeed it will cost me more—but Jomelli is here—& is the

D. J. Grout, *A History of Western Music* (rev. edn., 1973), pp. 322–4; H. E. Smither, *A History of the Oratorio* (Chapel Hill, 1977), i. 79–89; 'Oratorio' in *New Grove*.

[45] John Frederick Sackville (1745–99), 3rd Duke of Dorset, had set off on a tour of the Continent early in 1770 with his mistress, Anne ('Nancy') Parsons (*c*.1735–*c*.1814). See C. J. Phillips, *History of the Sackville Family* (1930), ii. 198–9.

[46] Alessandro Albani (1692–1779), nephew of Pope Clement XI, cardinal (1721), Librarian of the Vatican (1761–79), collector.

[47] Giovanni Elia Baldi (*c*.1728–99), called 'Elia', of the Vatican Library. Although a layman with a large family, Elia Baldi by virtue of his employment in the Vatican would have worn clerical dress and may have been called by the loosely applied honorific title 'abate'. From a lowly 'scopatore' in 1744, he rose to coadjutor to various 'scriptores' (1764, 1772), and became himself a 'scriptor graecus' in 1780. He worked mainly in the collection of coins and medals, helped compile catalogues of antiquities and Greek manuscripts, made collations for the Septuagint Bible, and addressed a memoir to Pius VI on the organization of the Vatican Library. See J. B. Odier, *La Bibliothèque Vaticane de Sixte IV à Pie XI, recherches sur l'histoire des collections de manuscrits* in *Studi e Testi*, cclxxii (Vatican, 1973), 182–3, 190 n. 3; also *Tours*, i. 205–6, 216, 291.

[48] The 1770–1 season had opened at Drury Lane on 22 Sept. with a performance of *Cymbeline* (*The London Stage*, iv. iii. 1498).

[49] Full of his impressions of the music and musicians he had heard in Italy, Garrick's letter to CB from Naples, 5 Feb. 1764 (Comyn), is published for the first time in its entirety in *CB Mem.* 102.

[50] Eva Maria Garrick, née Veigel (1724–1822), called Violette, had married Garrick in June 1749. She had been a ballet dancer. See Garrick *Letters*, i, pp. xxxv–xxxvii; and for CB's admiration of her, *CB Mem.* 108.

[51] The royal opera house in Naples, built in 1737 by Charles III (1716–88), King of the Two Sicilies (1734–59), King of Spain (1759–88), was named Teatro San Carlo in honour of the

Composer[52]—De amicis[53] & Aprile[54] are principals—the Gabriele[55] is still in Banishment at Palermo—I was with Piccini all the Morning —there's a pretty Comic opera of his now in run—as to Music—but the Libretto is terrible stuff[56]—I have been here but 3 Days—Mr Hamilton is at his Villeggiatura[57]—I dine with our little Consul[58] to Morrow & with Mr Hamilton in the Country on Sunday. Vesuvius begins to throw up Fire finely—& an Eruption is hourly Expected. Adieu my Dear Sir believe me yours most affectionately—

Ch. Burney

To Padre Martini   Naples, 20 October 1770

ALS (Bologna: I. 1. 26).
Addressed: Al Molto Reverendo | Il celebrarissimo P. Maestro | Martini | al S. Francesco in | Bologna   *Publ.:* Brofsky, pp. 322–3, in English translation.

monarch's patron, St Charles Borromeo (M. F. Robinson, *Naples and Neapolitan Opera* (Oxford, 1972), pp. 7–10). For CB's description of the San Carlo, see *Tours*, i. 271, 277–9.

[52] Nicolò Jommelli (1714–74), the celebrated composer of the Neapolitan school, had first set Metastasio's *Demofoonte* to music in 1743. He revised his score of the opera for the Naples revival which opened the San Carlo season on 4 Nov. 1770 (Loewenberg, *Annals*, i, col. 200). For CB's account of the performance, see *Tours*, i. 270, 277–9.

[53] Anna Lucia Buonsollazzi, née De Amicis (*c.*1733–1816), soprano, who had appeared in London in the 1762–3 season, did not in fact sing in the revival of Jommelli's *Demofoonte*. CB records (*Tours*, i. 270, 278–9) that the principal soprano was named 'Bianchi', who may have been Marianna Bianchi (*fl.* 1765–73), the wife of the composer Antonio Tozzi (*c.*1736–after 1812). See 'Tozzi, Antonio' in *New Grove*.

[54] Giuseppe Aprile (1732–1813), called 'Sciroletto' or 'Scirolino', castrato, composer, and voice teacher, sang the leading role in *Demofoonte*.

[55] Caterina Gabrielli (1730–96), coloratura soprano, also called 'La Coghetta'. Famous for her interpretations of rôles in operas by Gluck and Tommaso Traetta, she was also notorious for her caprice and scandalous love affairs. See *BD*; *New Grove*. Garrick had heard her sing in Naples in 1764, and had written about her performance to CB (5 Feb. 1764, Comyn). See above, n. 49.

[56] CB arrived in Naples on 16 Oct., and in the evening attended a performance of the comic opera *Gelosia per gelosia*, composed by Niccolò Vito Piccinni (1728–1800) to a libretto by Giovanni Battista Lorenzi (1721–1807). See *Tours*, i. 241–2; A. Cametti, 'Saggio cronologico delle opere teatrali (1754–1794) di Niccolò Piccinni', *Rivista musicale italiana*, viii (1901), 90.
CB spent the morning of 18 Oct. with Piccinni (*Tours*, i. 245–8), an event which helps to date the present letter accurately. See also CB to Archer, 21–8 Feb. 1779, n. 6.

[57] William Hamilton (1730–1803), diplomat, archaeologist, and vulcanologist, British Envoy Extraordinary and Minister Plenipotentiary at the court of Naples (1764–1800), FRS (1766), Knight of the Bath (1772). His 'villeggiatura', or house in the country, was called the Villa Angelica (Hamilton to CB, 23 Oct. [1770], Osborn). See B. Fothergill, *Sir William Hamilton, Envoy Extraordinary* (1969).

[58] Isaac Jamineau (*c.*1710–89), educated at Westminster School, Trinity College, Cambridge, and the Middle Temple; British Consul at Naples (1753–79), whom Garrick had also met at Naples (Garrick *Letters*, i. 400). See Venn; *GM* xxiii (1753), 345; lix (1789), 1056; Fothergill, *Hamilton*, pp. 127–30.

Molto reverendo e Veneratm̃o Padre.

Altro non m'avrebbe impedito fin adesso riconoscere e ringraziarle con ogni Gratitudine per i tanti suoi favori conferite mentre fossi Stato in Bologna che per Tema che non fosse privata la Communità del Tempo che lei impiega tanto per la sua profitto. Tengo tante Care le di lei Cortesie e sono talmente impresse nel mio Cuore che non posso mai dimenticarle, e stimerò sempre come la più fortunata e più lusinghevole avvenimento non solo del mio Viaggio in Italia ma della mia Vita l'onore della di lei Conoscenza.

Rincontrai à Firenze molti uomini dotti e di Prezzo che s'impacciavano molti nella mia ricchiesta che tanto più mi sorpresese quantocche la di lei grande opera rende inutile nell'Italia ogni tentativa alla Storia della Musica.

La di lei Lettera della quale fui favorito consegnai nelle mane del Sig^r Perkins[1] che mi ricevè colla somma politezza e mi fece mille amicizie quando Stetti à Firenze. Ho stabilito in questa Città una Corispondenza Col Sig^r Giuseppe Molini[2] chi avrà cura particolare delle due Edizioni del secondo volume della sua opera stupenda[3] e ne consignerà il Prezzo à chiunque sarà da lei nominato quando riceve i libri. La Speranza di trovargli à Firenze verso il mezzo di Novembre mi ha determinato di rippassare per questa Citta tornando in Inghilterra.[4]

Fra i molti uomini dotti ed illuminati à Roma che mi sono stati d'un gran giovamento nei miei ricercamenti, nessuno ne fù tanto che il Cavaliere Santarelli, la di lei Gentilezza intendimento e Benevolenza non possono figurarsi, per i quali sono interamente tenuto à lei come furono le conseguenze della di lei Lettera colla quale ero onorato à questo Musico compito.

[1] William Perkins (*fl.* 1760–71), 'an English Gentleman, who has resided a considerable time in this city [Florence] and in Bologna' was a skilled 'cellist, who attempted to make his instrument imitate the 'violin, flute, french-horn, trumpet, hautbois, and bassoon' (*Tours*, i. 182). He presented CB with a copy of his *Facile Difficile, or Mysterys of the Violoncello, Exposed in XI Sonatas or Duets* [1760?], which was sold for 2*s.* 6*d.* in the dispersal of CB's musical library (*Cat. Mus. Lib.*, lot 908). See also *Hist. Mus.* iv. 51 n.; Mercer, ii. 536 n.

[2] Giuseppe di Romualdo Molini (*fl.* 1770), merchant and bookseller in Florence, of a family with book-trade connections in Paris and London (*Tours*, i. 176), had undertaken to forward to his brother Peter in London the books CB had collected in Bologna and Florence (*Tours*, i. 192). See L. Molini, *Operette bibliografiche del Cav. Giuseppe Molini* (Florence, 1858), p. viii; CB to Crisp, 19–24 Dec. 1770, n. 13.

[3] The volumes of Padre Martini's *Storia della musica* were printed from the same setting of the text in two formats: a regular quarto, and a *de luxe* folio in which the text is surrounded by lavish decorative borders. The second volume of the *Storia* was published in 1770, but CB could not procure a copy before returning to England.

[4] When he revisited Florence on 24 Nov. on his return journey, CB was highly aggravated to discover that Molini had performed none of his promises: 'he had forgot even *what* he had promised to do for me before my return' (*Tours*, i. 304).

Giunsi à Napoli la 16 Corrente, e la mia prima inchiesta era per il Sig^re Jomelli, ma non l'ho ancora trovato, essendolo andate nella Campagna a villeggiatura qualche miglie lontano, e non tornerà sino alla mezzo della Settimana seguente, ma siccome non potei differire più l'assicurarla del mio rispetto e gratitudine riserve la relazione dell'Accoglimento del Sig^r Jomelli per un'altra Lettera dopo la ricevuta del secondo Volume della di lei opera.

Rimarrò à Napoli sin'ai 5 o 6 Novembre per Sentire un'opera della quale la Musica è composta dal Sig^re Jomelli per il Teatro reale, e poi, dopo un dimoro d'una Settimana à Roma bisogna tornar subito in Inghilterra—per la via di Firenze—Pisa—Genoa—Antibo, Lione, e Parigi—

Se non sarei così fortunato di trovare à Firenze il 2do Volume della sua Storia io stimerò la mia racolta de' Libri molta Imperfetta; se fosse pero possibile de trovare una Commodità di mandarvelo afinch'io potessi portarlo me Stesso in Inghilterra mi farebbe Molto Piacere e tanto più se fossero accompagnate d'una sua pretiosissima Lettera.[5]

Impresso con veri Sentimenti della di Lei erudizione, Pietà e Bontà di Cuo[re] a la più grande Venerazione del suo Carattere, resto Molto reverendo Padre

Napoli 20 8bre 1770
Umilissimo ed Obbligatissimo Servitore
Charles Burney.

To Samuel Crisp[1]

Calais and Queen Square,
19–24 December 1770

ALS (Osborn).
Addressed: To ⎮ Samuel Crisp Esqr ⎮ at Chesington, near Epsom ⎮ in Surry   *Pmk:*
24 DE   *Endorsed by* Crisp: N° 6. ⎮ Decr 19. 1770   *Docketed by* FBA: ☩ ✳ on ⎮

[5] Martini later sent CB a copy of this volume 'Per mezzo del Sig: Perkins' with a covering letter dated 16 Jan. 1771 (Osborn). At the end of May 1771 CB was still awaiting the arrival of the book (CB to Crisp, [31] May [1771]).

[1] Samuel Crisp (*c.*1707–83), who had befriended young CB in 1747 at Wilbury, was 'a man of infinite taste in all the fine Arts, an excellent Scholar, & who having resided many years in Italy, & being possessed of a fine tenor voice, sung in as good taste as any professed opera singer' (*CB Mem.* 43). Afflicted by the failure of his tragedy *Virginia* (1754), financial difficulties, and gout, Crisp had retired to Chessington in Surrey and lived as a recluse in the virtually inaccessible house of his friend Christopher Hamilton (1698–1758/9).

Although Crisp and CB had corresponded in the 1750s, the two friends did not meet for at least 16 years before they re-established contact in 1764 (*CB Mem.* 105). From then on visits to Crisp at Chessington Hall became a regular feature of life for CB and members of his family. See *HFB*, pp. 16–18; Lonsdale, pp. 18–19, 99; *JL* i. 144 n. 4; *EJL* i, p. xix.

the | Materials | acquired | in Venice, | Florence, | Rome, | Naples | &c | for the | History of | Musick. | Nº 2

Calais 19. Decr 1770

My dear Friend.

But few things have lain heavier on my Conscience than the seeming neglect of *you* in not writing once to Chesington during my whole Expedition on the Continent. But as you are more reasonable than other People, & are a better Judge of the difficulties I had to encounter, as well as of the various Enquiries & employments I had to fill up my Time, I trust you will not be the last of my Literary Creditors in forgiving the Debt, or at least in accepting this Composition for payment.—I rather Hope to find you in London if I sh^d ever get there:— but ⌜at present there is but little likelihood of it, for⌝ such infernal Winds have continued for many Days past, that one w^d think wth Trinculo that 'Hell was broke loose & all the Devils were here.'[2]—I have undergone incredible Fatigues in my Journey from Rome to Paris—[3]wch place I ⌜left on Sunday morning[4] & ⌝ travelled [3] Post Night & Day in order to get to England as fast as possible, but tho' I arrived here early Yesterday Morning ⌜I am not a bit the forwarder—⌝ I might[5] have slept Comfortably on the road instead of sitting[6] in a Cold Chaise in[7] that kind of Comfortless stupifaction wch beings feel who are neither a sleep nor a wake, Dead or[8] alive. I was hurried on board Capt Osburn's ship[9] ⌜here⌝ yesterday, the Instant I arrived, without being able to dry my things, all wet, &, I fear, spoilt by Eternal Rains, or to refresh myself.—But a storm wch had but just subsided came on again & we were all obliged to go back into the Town.[10]—

I long very much to tell you my adventures, viva voce, as well as to

[2] Or, more precisely, with Ferdinand, as reported by Ariel: 'Hell is empty, | And all the devils are here' (*The Tempest*, I. ii. 214–15).

[3-3] MS w^{ch} ... travelled] *FBA altered by interlineation and obliteration to* from wch place I travelled

[4] 16 Dec.

[5] MS might] *FBA added* as well

[6] MS sitting] *FBA added* all night

[7] MS Chaise in] *FBA altered to* Chaise, in

[8] MS or] *FBA altered to* nor

[9] 'Osburn', captain of the Channel packet-boat, has not been identified.

[10] While CB waited in Calais (*Tours*, i. 318), he sat for his portrait to Joseph Nollekens (1737–1823), the English sculptor who was then returning to England after 8 years of study in Italy. This portrait in black chalk was sold by Evans on 4 Dec. 1823 at the sale of Nollekens's prints and drawings (lot 260) as 'a Portrait of Dr. Burney, drawn at Calais in the year 1770', and came up for sale again at Sotheby's, 27 Jan. 1966 (lot 65), ascribed without supporting evidence to Charles Grignion the younger (1754–1804). It was bought by the late J. M. Osborn, who first reproduced it in a Christmas greeting card in 1968. H. E. Poole subsequently used the drawing as frontispiece to his edition for the Folio Society of CB's travel journal, *Music, Men, and Manners in France and Italy 1770* (1969). The correct attribution has re-emerged only recently. Mr J. Kenworthy-Browne, who is writing a biography of Nollekens, confirms that the inscription, with its characteristic misspelling 'Calis', is in Nollekens's hand. See Illustration 1.

Dr Burney at Calis in the year 1770

1. Dr Charles Burney. From a drawing by Joseph Nollekens, 1770. The drawing was executed at Calais while Burney waited for favourable winds to take him home to England at the end of his first Continental musical tour.

communicate to you my discoveries & to shew you my Journal, in order to avail myself of your Counsel as to the best manner of making them turn to some account in an honourable as well as profitable way. If the rest of the Musical World has half the Curiosity that I had, they will be glad of the Informations I can give them without the Trouble, Expense & even dangers I have experienced in order to qualify myself for their Service. I c^d give such a list of Names of the Men of Letters & Eminent Composers with whom I have Conversed—of the Vocal & Instrumental performers I have heard, of the Libraries I have [11]Consulted & of the acquisitions I have made in Books & MSS.[11] as I sh^d think w^d be very imposing did I not fear the imputation of *puffing*, a Vice of wch authors are so frequently Guilty, that Truth & fa[l]shood are equally suspected.

I hope I shall get all my Materials together in a few Months, but at present they are very much dispersed. The 1st Embarkation of Books &c I made was at Venice under the Care of our resident Mr Richie[12]— at Florence my Collection grew unwealdy again & I sent off another Chest, by way of Leghorn, addressed to Molini[13]—at Rome & Naples my acquisitions in Books, prints & Drawings were very great—of these a large Chest was made up & consigned to the Care of the worthy Mr Byers,[14] one of the best antiquaries & honestest Men at Rome—I have, however, with me the Choicest of my MSS & drawings of ancient Instruments, wch I am determined shall sink or swim with me.

I never got your Friendly Letter ⌐in behalf of the young Folks⌐ till the Day before I left Rome—⌐a large packet of Letters from England written in June & July last had by an unaccountable neglect in my Bankers lain at Paris & Lyon several Months.[15]—I was however glad to find that my Sentiments had been so conformable[16] to yours ere I ever knew what they were.⌐ I hope all that has been done in my

[11-11] MS Consulted ... made ... & MSS.] *FBA altered to* Consulted, ... made, ... & in MSS.

[12] Robert Richie (d. 1790), merchant, served as British chargé d'affaires (1769–71, 1775, 1786–90) at Venice, where he had settled. In 1776 he was appointed Consul at Venice. See *Tours*, i. 115–16, 140; *GM* lx (1790), 1148; Horn, p. 86.

[13] Peter Molini (*fl.* 1770–95), Italian merchant, language master, and bookseller, who conducted his business in London at 18 Haymarket, St James's, from 1773 (Maxted, p. 155). He was the brother of Giuseppe di Romualdo Molini, the bookseller whom CB had met in Florence (CB to Martini, 20 Oct. 1770, nn. 2, 4; *Tours*, i. 176, 192).

[14] James Byers, or Byres (1734–1817), Scottish architect and archaeologist, resided at Rome for nearly 40 years from 1750 to 1790 (*Tours*, i. 201). See also *DNB*; and B. Ford, 'James Byres, Principal Antiquarian for the English Visitors to Rome', *Apollo*, xcix (1974), 446–61.

[15] The address panel of Bewley to CB, 18 June 1770 (Osborn), shows the route these letters took. Bewley's direction 'A Monsieur | Monsieur Burney | chez Messrs Rougemont Freres | Paris' is deleted and redirected: 'Henry Scheres | a | Lyon'. CB subsequently endorsed the letter 'Sent to Italy'.

[16] MS conformable] *alternative* similar

Absence will turn out happily ⸢to the parties concerned.⸣ I am very sensible of the kind manner in wch you interested yourself in these Transactions.[17]—But you so well know the Nature of that Beast called Ma⟨n⟩ that if he has received 99 Favours from his Friend & he sh^d Chance to refuse him the hundredth, all the rest are cancelled—pray th⟨ink⟩ of this & don't let all your past Labours be lost, but sa⟨ve⟩ them from Oblivion by the addition of one more to the Number—come to Town & hear my Tale—& take the place I always assigned you of [18]Guide, Philosopher & Friend—[18] I have 1000 things to tell you—but none so true as that I love & honour you more than any one of my acquaintance & am wth a hundred &c &c—yours most affectionately.

Chas Burney

Queen Square, Monday Night[19]—just arrived after being detained at Calais by abominable Winds & weather till Sunday Morning.—Am heartily glad to find myself in old England again & very impatient to see you—do Come—

To Pierre Guy[1]

Queen Square,
[28 February 1771][2]

LS draft, in SEB's hand, with autograph revisions by CB (R. A. Leigh).

[17] Crisp's 'Friendly Letter' is not preserved, though its contents may be inferred from CB's oblique allusion here, which Mme d'Arblay nevertheless saw fit to obliterate very firmly. Crisp's letter no doubt contained a detailed account of the part he played in the removal, during CB's absence, of the Burney household from Poland Street to their new residence at 42 Queen Square, Bloomsbury. In addition to the convenience of inhabiting a larger house, Crisp deemed it expedient to remove the young Burneys from the influence of their Poland Street neighbour, Mrs Veronica Pringle, née Rennie (d. by 1791), a widow, and the attentions of her circle of 'droll and entertaining' young men, among whom in particular was Alexander Seton (1743–1801). Hetty had fallen in love with Seton before she married her cousin the accomplished harpsichordist Charles Rousseau Burney on 20 Sept. 1770; and Fanny, aged 18, was not averse to the young charmer: 'Papa has bought a house in Queen Square. It is settled by Mr Crisp—to my very great grief, that we are quite to drop Mrs. Pringle—that we may see no more of Mr. Seton' (*EJL* i. 139–40). See also *HFB*, pp. 31–5; *EJL* i. 39 n. 14, 41 n. 19, 139 n. 2.

[18–18] MS Guide ... Friend—] *FBA altered to* "Guide ... Friend—"! CB quotes Pope, *An Essay on Man*, iv. 390.

[19] Christmas Eve, 1770.

[1] Pierre Guy (1715–95), Parisian bookseller and publisher, 'one of the few people Rousseau suffers to approach him', had arranged CB's meeting with Rousseau in Dec. 1770 (*Tours*, i. 311–15). Guy had been a partner of Rousseau's publisher, Nicolas-Bonaventure Duchesne (1712–65), who, from about 1760, had increasingly entrusted Guy with the management of the business. After Duchesne's death in July 1765, Guy married Duchesne's widow and ran the affairs of the publishing house, bringing out Rousseau's *Dictionnaire de musique* (1767) under the imprint 'Chez la Veuve Duchesne'. See Rousseau *Corresp.* vii. 383.

[2] The letter can be accurately dated from Guy's reply: 'J'ay bien reçu La Lettre que vous avez pris la peine de m'écrire le 28e fevrier' (Guy to CB, 8 Apr. 1771, Osborn).

Endorsed by CB: Copy of a Letter to | *M. Gui*—March 1st | 1771. | C.B—   *Docketed*
by FBA: March. 1771   *Publ.*: Leigh, pp. 172–3; Rousseau *Corresp.* xxxviii. 190–4.

Queen Square, Bloomsbury. London.

Monsieur

Comme il m'est impossible d'oublier Jamais l'honneur que vous m'avez bien procuré de connoitre personnellement M. Rousseau—Je vous supplie de Croire que ce n'a pas eté par Negligence qu'il n'a pas reçu plu-tot les Livres que j'ai promis de lui envoyer.[3] Je suis trop sensible du prix de la permission que M. Rousseau a bien voulu m'accorder pour n'en pas faire le plus grand cas. Mais j'ai attendu jusqu'ici vainement L'occasion qui a present se presente de passer ces Livres en France—etant d'un trop gros volume pour la poste. Je serois charmé de profiter de cette occasion pour ecrire a M. Rousseau lui meme, de lui demander ses conseils sur l'Ouvrage dont j'eus l'honneur de lui montrer le plan,[4] & de lui temoigner toute l'estime & la veneration que j'ai pour sa personne et pour ses grands Talens. Mais etant si peu connu de lui, ce seroit abuser de sa Bonté de lui incomoder d'une Lettre de ma part.

[5]Depuis mon retour en Angleterre J'ai employé quelque Tems à ecrire[5] une espece de Journal de mon Voyage—dans lequel je dois donner l'*Etat Actuel de la Musique en France & en Italie* et en quelque sorte rendre compte au Public des Materiaux que [6]j'y ai trouvez dans mes recherches.[6] Ce Journal precédera [7]l'ouvrage que j'ai long Tems medité sur l'Histoire generale de la musique. M. Rousseau sera, pour ainsi dire, le Heros de cette Histoire[7] [8]car il faut convenir qu'il a fait plus de bien a la Musique que tous les Ecrivains ensemble sur ce qui regarde le Bon Gout & le rafinement de cet Art. & de plus je dirai hardiment au Public que parmi tant de miliers de Livres qui ont eté

---

[3] CB's account of his visit to Rousseau concludes: 'Ere I went away, I got him to consent to let me send him the music of Jomelli's *Passione*, with the London edition of his *Divin du Village*, my Cunning Man, and we parted exceeding good friends' (*Tours*, i. 315). Jomelli's *La Passione di nostro Signore Giesu Cristo. Oratorio ... poesia del Signor Metastasio*, had recently (1770) been published in London by Robert Bremner (*c.*1713–89), who had also published the second edition of *The Cunning Man* (1766), CB's adaptation of Rousseau's operetta, *Le Devin du village* (1752).

[4] 'I had the courage to offer him a copy of my plan in French, which had the appearance of great length ... He said he never read, and seemed coy, and afraid of it—However, he took it in his hand, and begun reading to himself, and ere he had got half way down the 1st page, he read aloud, and seemed caught by it' (*Tours*, i. 314).

[5–5] MS Depuis ... ecrire] *altered from* J'ai ete depuis mon retour en Angleterre tres occupe par ecrivan

[6–6] MS j'y ai ... recherches.] *altered from* j'ai trouvez dans mon Voyage.

[7–7] MS l'ouvrage ... Histoire] *altered from* mon Histoire Generale — dans le quel M. Rousseau sera mon Heros.

[8–8] MS car il ... degout.] *originally* & je dirai hardiment ... lire sans degout. & qu'il a fait

ecrit sur cette Matiere sa Lettre sur la Musique Francoise & son Dictionaire de Musiqu[e] sont presque les seuls qu'on puisse lire sans degout.[8]

[9]Il y a quelque Tems que j'ai eté reduit à l'Etat de garder le Lit[9] par une Maladie severe & obstiné qui m'empeche actuellement de rien faire que de dicter cette Lettre a une de mes Filles.—J'espere que votre Correspondant vous a mandé qu'il a reçu les Livres dont vous m'avez Chargé—& que vous me ferez la Justice de me croire avec Estime

Votre tres Humble
et très Obeissant Serviteur.
C.B.

Je vous prie de presenter mes tres Humble Respects a M. Rousseau.—

To Denis Diderot[1] [Queen Square, *c.*28 February 1771][2]

LS draft, in FB's hand (Osborn).
Docketed by FBA: à M. Diderot.

Dear Sir—

As I am convinced you Read English better than I can write french,[3] I shall make no apology for addressing you in that Language. After

plus de bien ... Art. *CB then reversed the sequence of the clauses by numbering them and altered the connecting phrases accordingly.*

In 1752 a battle erupted in Paris between the advocates of French and Italian music. Together with the *encyclopédistes*, Rousseau joined in the pamphlet war called the 'guerre (or querelle) des bouffons' with his crushing condemnation of French music, the *Lettre sur la musique françoise* (Nov. 1753). See A. R. Oliver, *The Encyclopedists as Critics of Music* (New York, 1947), ch. 7; *Tours*, i. 322–6. CB in his works frequently mentions Rousseau's *Lettre* with approval: see for example, *Tours*, i. 30; *Hist. Mus.* iv. 3–5, 615–16; Mercer, ii. 498–500, 970–1.

Based on the musical articles he wrote in 1749 for inclusion in the *Encyclopédie*, Rousseau's *Dictionnaire de musique* was published at Geneva in Nov. 1767, and Paris in 1768. For CB's opinion of this work, see *Hist. Mus.* iv. 628; Mercer, ii. 980. At one time CB himself considered an English translation of the *Dictionnaire*. See *Mem.* i. 164–5; Lonsdale, pp. 76, 407.

[9–9] MS Il y a ... Lit] *altered from* J'ai eté depuis quelque Tems oblige de garder mon Lit

[1] Denis Diderot (1713–84), whom CB had met on 14 Dec. 1770. They greeted one another 'as cordially as if we had been acquaintances of long standing', for CB had been one of the earliest subscribers to the *Encyclopédie* (*Tours*, i. 312; *CB Mem.* 69 n. 5). CB eventually possessed the complete *Encyclopédie* (1751–72) in folio: text in 17 vols., plates in 11 vols.; as well as the *Supplément* in 5 vols., 1776–7 (*Cat. Misc. Lib.*, lot 907, which in 1814 fetched 17 guineas). See also J. Lough, *The Encyclopédie in Eighteenth-Century England, and Other Studies* (Newcastle-upon-Tyne, 1970), pp. 1–24.

[2] The date of this draft may be adduced from its similarities in circumstance and phraseology to CB's letter to Guy, [28 Feb. 1771]. Both letters speak of a 'severe & obstinate' illness which forced CB to dictate them to an amanuensis.

[3] Diderot '*reads* English as well as his own language, without speaking a word' (*Tours*, i. 316).

finishing my musical enquiries upon the Continent & having enjoyed the conversation of men the most eminent for learning & genius, [4]I wished previous[4] to the publication of my gen. Hist. to give some acc^t [5]to my Country men[5] of ye success of my Voyage in a small work under the title of the present state of Music in France & Italy. The execution of this Design [6]and a severe & obstinate Indispo[sition] have hitherto prevented me from availing myself of the permission you so kindly & readily favoured me with of writing[6] to you, in order to thank you for y^r hospitality & Counsel, & the Papers you confided to my care, for wh^{ch} I not only think myself accountable to you, but to the Public[7]—& for the honour you did me in presenting me to Ma^{lle} Diderot,[8] with whose truly amiable character & excellent perform-ance on the Harp^d I was equally delighted.[9]

It grieves me to treat with seeming severity the Music of a Country which I respect so much as France but my strictures are chiefly con-fined to the Music of its serious operas & concert spirituel wh^{ch} have long been given up by the 1st persons for taste & genius there. [10]& according to my[10] feelings, from wh^{ch} I constantly & honestly speak, the expression of that Music seems vicious & unnatural—the melody dry & uninteresting—& the measure unmarked. This has been long discovered & acknowledged by Individuals, but a general reformation is not soon brought about. My *Brochure* w^d have been in the Press ere now, had not the indisposition above mentioned confined me to my Bed, from whence I am obliged to dictate this Letter. [11]It is my design to have[11] it translated into french—for tho' the former part [12]does not flatter[12] y^r Country men, the latter may amuse them, & thro' some

[4-4] MS I ... previous] *altered from* I wished to give some acc^t to my Countrymen of the success of my voyage in a small work previous

[5-5] MS to ... men] *altered from* of ye present s

[6-6] MS and ... writing] *altered from* has employed all the Moments I could spare from other avocations & have long deprived me of the happiness of writing

[7] Diderot showed keen interest in CB's 'Plan', and discussed it with him in detail: 'When we came to the articles Antient Music, Accents, Poetry, etc, he took out of his Cabinet a great heap of MSS. in his own hand writing sufficient for a folio upon the same subject which he gave me to make just what use I pleased of ... I shall look upon myself as accountable for these papers, not only to M. Diderot, but to the public' (*Tours*, i. 316). Despite intensive search, these papers have not been found. See Lonsdale, pp. 95–6.

[8] Diderot's 17-year-old daughter, Marie-Angélique (1753–1824), in whose musical education her father took a great deal of interest, was, in CB's flattering view, 'one of the finest harpsichord-players in Paris' (*Tours*, i. 317). In Sept. 1772 she was to marry Abel-François-Nicolas Caroillon, marquis de Vandeul, and, to Diderot's great disappointment, failed to progress further in music. See Leigh, pp. 175–6.

[9] MS delighted.] delighted. *then deleted* I sh^d much sooner have availed myself of ye permission you so readily & so kindly favoured me with of writing to you.

[10-10] MS & ... my] *altered from* the want of melody

[11-11] MS It ... have] *altered from* I have thoughts of having

[12-12] MS does not flatter] *altered from* is not flattering

new lights upon a subject which has not been treated[13] Ex professo by any author whom I have yet met with. I sh^d be very happy to submit the Translation to y^r Correction—for tho' I know you are so good a Patriot as to be tender of y^r Countrys honour in things of importance— yet y^r judgment & y^r taste will I trust, befriend my opinions in the present case—it is not such music as I Had the pleasure to hear Mlle Diderot perform, that I condemn—& upon that, as well as upon y^r admirable writings, I form my judgment of y^r taste in Music.[14] I must intreat you, Sir, to present my most humble respects to Mlle Diderot, together with 6 concertos by Wagenseil,[15] 6 Ditto by Jean Bach[16] & 2 Trios which [17]neither merit[17] her acceptance nor the Company they keep.[18] But instead of these I did intend myself the honour of sending her some thing [19]in MS, less unworthy her Hand & her judgment, but have been too ill to get[19] them transcribed—however, they shall be forth coming in a future parcel. I must likewise intreat you to [do] me the honour to present my respects to M. le Baron D'Holbach[20]—to M. l'abbe Morellet,[21] & to each of the members of that charming society into wh^{ch} I had the honour of being admitted, the Day I had 1st the happiness of being presented to you.

[13] MS treated] *interlined over deleted* Handled

[14] 'Though I had the pleasure of hearing her for several hours, not a single French composition was played by her the whole time, all was Italian and German; hence it will not be difficult to form a judgment of M. Diderot's taste in music' (*Tours*, i. 317). For a study of Diderot's musical ideas and writings, see J.-M. Bardez, *Diderot et la musique: valeur de la contribution d'un mélomane* (1975).

[15] Georg Christoph Wagenseil (1715–77), Austrian composer, music master to the Empress Maria Theresa (1717–80) and the imperial princesses. About 1765, two London publishers, John Walsh (1709–66) and Peter Welcker (d. 1775), separately issued sets of six Wagenseil keyboard concertos (see *BUCEM* and *New Grove*). It is likely that CB sent one of these sets to Angélique Diderot.

[16] Johann Christian Bach (1735–82), the 'London Bach', youngest surviving son of Johann Sebastian Bach (1685–1750). In 1762 J. C. Bach had settled in London as a composer and later as an impresario. In the following year he was appointed music master to Queen Charlotte. CB probably sent Bach's *Sei concerti per il cembalo* ..., opus 7, published in London *c*.1770 by Welcker. See *BUCEM*.

[17–17] MS neither merit] *altered from* are little worthy of

[18] CB refers to his own compositions, *Two Sonatas for the Harpsichord or Forte Piano with Accompanyments for a Violin and Violoncello*, published *c*.1770 in London by Robert Bremner (*c*.1713–89). See Scholes, ii. 347.

[19–19] MS in MS, . . . get] *altered from* less insignificant, had not my indisposition prevented my having

[20] Paul-Henri Thiry (1723–89), baron d'Holbach, materialist philosopher of German origin, man of letters, *encyclopédiste*, at whose hospitable home CB had first met Diderot (*Tours*, i. 312). Under the pseudonym 'Mirabaud', d'Holbach had published in 1770 his most controversial work, *Le Système de la nature*.

[21] The abbé André Morellet (1727–1819), economist and writer, elected in 1785 to the Académie Française. He contributed six articles to the *Encyclopédie*. See J. Lough, *The Contributors to the Encyclopédie* (1973), pp. 18, 93–4; *Tours*, i. 28 n. 5, 312, 316. Morellet is best known for his *Mémoires de l'abbé Morellet, de l'Académie Française, sur le dix-huitième siècle et sur la Révolution* (1821).

[22]I have the same petition to make to you in behalf of M. l'abbé Arnaud & M. Suard[23] to whose politeness & hospitality while at Paris, I have very singular obligations.[22] I have to intreat you to do me the honour to admit me into the number of those who most sincerely admire [24]your Writings & esteem[24] y^r Character

I[25]

Charles Burney

To Baron d'Holbach   Queen Square, 23 May 1771

ALS copy (Berg).
Endorsed by CB: Copy of a Letter | to M. le Baron | D'Holbach at | Paris May 25 | 1771   *Publ.:* Leigh, pp. 190–1.

London 23^d of May 1771

Sir.

The Happyness I enjoyed under your hospitable Roof when I was last at Paris, is still fresh in my memory.[1] Indeed I shall ever regard the Honour of your Acquaintance as one of the most pleasing Consequences of the Journey I undertook in search of Curious persons

---

[22-22] MS I have ... obligations.] *originally* the reasons above mentioned have prevented my writing to M^r l'abbe Arnaud & to M. Suard; to whose politeness & hospitality while at Paris, I have very singular obligations. Let me add one petition more to those above mentioned—namely that of begging you *the second sentence then partially deleted and altered to* I have the same petition to make to you in behalf of these Gentlemen & lastly *all deleted except the cue words* I have the same *which refer to the final wording written in full below the signature.*

[23] Jean-Baptiste-Antoine Suard (1733–1817), journalist, translator, and miscellaneous writer, to whom CB had been introduced by a letter from David Garrick. See Garrick *Letters*, ii. 693–4; *Tours*, i. 25, 29.

Associated with Suard in the editorship and management of the *Journal étranger* (1760–62), the *Gazette littéraire de l'Europe* (1764–66), and the *Gazette de France* (1762–71), the abbé François Arnaud (1721–84), littérateur, member of the Académie des Inscriptions et Belles-Lettres (1762), and the Académie Française (1771), had delighted CB at a dinner party given by Suard: 'we conversed so long and unreservedly on the subject of ancient and modern Music, that I was quite ashamed of it' (*Tours*, i. 29). For Arnaud's publications on music, see *DBF*. For the friendly and professional relations of Suard and Arnaud, see D.-J. Garat, *Mémoires historiques sur le XVIIIe siècle et sur M. Suard* (2nd edn., 1821); A. C. Hunter, *J.-B.-A. Suard, un introducteur de la littérature anglaise en France* (1925), ch. 3.

[24-24] MS your ... esteem] *altered from* you as a Writer

[25] The MS draft does not show the complimentary close.

---

[1] For CB's account of his visit to d'Holbach, see *Tours*, i. 312–13, 316. A wealthy man who maintained an excellent table and a fine wine cellar, d'Holbach entertained at his *salon* the most celebrated liberal thinkers and writers of his day. See A. C. Kors, *D'Holbach's Coterie: an Enlightenment in Paris* (Princeton, 1976).

& things. I should much sooner have made my acknowledgements for the favours I received during that Journey had not the Moments I had allotted to that grateful Task been wasted in sickness. After my recovery, all the time I could spare from other avocations was spent in attending the press during the Impression of a little Work[2] which I have the honour to send you as an excuse for my silence, tho' I fear it will want one for itself.

I hope my Friends at Paris who think much in the same way as myself as to French singing in the Old Serious Opera Stile, will pardon some Severities & Sarcasms which have escaped me in speaking of it. I respect the French Nation for a thousand good & great Quality's in its Inhabitants—& I love with a Cordial Affection many Individuals for their personal Merit & Amiable Characters; but I am at War with Vice wherever I meet with it: & as far as my feelings will enable me to judge the generality of Vocal *french Expression* is *Vicious*. & all the old & old fashioned Music, composed after Lulli's Model is, according to those same feelings, without Air, without Accent, & without Measure.[3] I speak not thus Contemptiously of French Music in order to exalt our own, for we have none that we can properly call our own, for that of Handel, a Saxon, is not ours, any more than that of Lulli, a florentine, belongs to the french. At present *your* Countrymen, Sir, seem the first people on the Globe for *Instrumental Music* both as to Composition & performance; as the Italians are now & have long been, superiour to all other people in a Musical Language & in *Vocal* Music.[4] I should be very happy if you would honour me with your opinion as to the General tenor of my reasoning upon the subject of Music & point out those Errours which it is impossible to escape in hasty Travelling as well as in hasty Writing. If you would Condescend to indulge me in this wish, my future more grave & more voluminous Work may be the better for it. I make the same request likewise to M. Diderot,[5]

[2] *The Present State of Music in France and Italy: or, The Journal of a Tour through those Countries, undertaken to collect Materials for a General History of Music. By Charles Burney, Mus. D.*, published by T. Becket and Co., had appeared on 4 May 1771 (*Public Advertiser*). CB himself refers to the book by the short title *Italian Tour*.

[3] Jean-Baptiste Lully, or Lulli (1632–87), Florentine composer who in 1646 settled at the French court. Patronized by Louis XIV, Lully created a distinctive French style of operatic art, different from the Italian. In CB's estimation, Lully's influence on his French successors impeded the improvement of vocal composition in France. 'Music remained stationary for near a century, in spite of the several attempts that were made in order to stimulate activity and enterprize ... The French ... seem to have enjoyed their lyric *sommeils* in great comfort and tranquillity till 1752' (*Hist. Mus.* iv. 608–9; Mercer, ii. 965). See also *Tours*, i. 18.

[4] Although settled in France, d'Holbach was a German. After his German tour in 1772, CB wrote: 'though Italy has carried *vocal* music to a perfection unknown in any other country, much of the present excellence of *instrumental* is certainly owing to the natives of Germany' (*Tours*, ii, pp. xii, 243–4).

[5] See CB to Diderot, 27 May 1771.

who knows & feels good Music & has thought of it in a more profound & philosophic as well as Sentimental Way, than most of his Countrymen.[6]

There seems to be a most unaccountable Obstinacy in the attachment of the french to their National Music. In every other Art or Science they are allowed by the rest of Europe to have great Merit; but they seem indifferent about their Fame in every thing but Music; & perhaps upon the same principle as a weak place in a fortification is watched & defended with all the forces that can be mustered upon the approach of an Enemy, they are more tenacious of their Musical honour, & keep double guard upon it at all Times & in all places.

Our friend Garrick is very well at present & often talks of his Parisian Friends[7] to whom he did me the honour to introduce me by his recommendatory Letters last Year. I am going to Morrow Night to see him Act, perhaps for the last Time, as he now talks seriously of quitting the Stage.[8] I beg leave to present my most humble respects to Madame la Baronne,[9] & to be numbered among those who are most ambitious of the honour of being remembered by you—being Sir, with the greatest truth

Your most Obliged
& Obedient Servant
Charles Burney.

Queen's Square | Bloomsbury.

---

[6] Seven months later, d'Holbach replied in a letter dated 15 Dec. 1771 (Osborn): 'Vous n'avèz pas dû craindre que votre façon de penser sur la musique françoise déplût aux personnes que vous avèz fréquentées à Paris. Les gens du goût sont partout de la même religion. L'attachement des françois à leur musique nationale est l'effet de l'habitude et du préjugé, qui jamais ne raisonnent et ne veulent céder. Il en est de la musique comme des ragoûts—auxquels on est accoutumé dès l'enfance et que l'on préfère à ceux des autres pays. Les françois tiennent à Lulli par la même raison que les allemands tiennent aux choux aigres, et les Espagnols au Saffran. Pour moi J'ai lu votre livre avec un très grand plaisir. Mr Diderot, beaucoup meilleur Juge que moi, m'en a paru très content; il me charge de vous le dire et de vous faire un million de compliments.'

[7] For Garrick's friends in Paris, and his relations with them, see F. A. Hedgcock, *A Cosmopolitan Actor: David Garrick and His French Friends* (1912).

[8] On Friday 24 May 1771 Garrick played Benedick in *Much Ado about Nothing* at Drury Lane. The performance was a benefit for the Theatrical Fund: 'No admittance into Pit or Boxes but with tickets. Ladies urged to come early to get to their places with greater Conveniency' (*The London Stage*, iv. iii. 1552). These circumstances suggest a date for a hitherto undated note to CB from Garrick (Garrick *Letters*, iii. 1271, there dated 'Monday [1771–1774]'), in which Garrick arranged three front-row seats for CB and said he had given orders for CB to be admitted 'the uncrowded way' via the stage door. Garrick's note may tentatively be dated Monday [20 May 1771]. He did not in fact retire from the stage until the 1775–6 season.

[9] Charlotte-Suzanne d'Holbach, née d'Aine (1733–1814), d'Holbach's second wife (Rousseau *Corresp.* xxv. 330; Kors, *D'Holbach*, pp. 158–9).

To Jean-Baptiste-Antoine Suard   Queen Square,
24 May 1771

ALS copy (Berg).
  Endorsed by CB: Copy of a Letter | to M. Suard at | Paris. May 25th | 1771   *Docketed*
by FBA: × M. Suard.   *Publ.* (in part): Leigh, pp. 191–2.

May 24th—1771

Sir.

   After so much politeness, so many friendly offices, so much hospitality as I was honoured with from you last summer, it was impossible for me to remain thus long silent without remorse. For if you think either yourself or your kindness to me were forgotten you neither think justly of your own worth nor of my Sensibility. The hastyness of my Journey on the Continent & the hardships & sudden changes of climate I experienc'd so impaired my health that I have scarce known what perfect Health is since my Arrival in England. & the little time I could steal from a sick bed & other indispensible avocations has been spent in preparing for the public a short account of the present State of Music in France & Italy according to the sensations excited in me by the performances I heard in the course of my Journey in quest of historical Materials relative to the Music of past Times. I have the honour to send you a Copy of this little work, which, as a Good French-Man I am ashamed you should see; at the same Time that as a Citizen of the World, a Friend to Mankind & an Illustrious & Liberal defender of Truth, I hope I shall be pardoned some severe strictures which have escaped me relative to your old Music & old Expression. I know that the first persons in the literary World among you not only tolerate Italian Music but love & adopt it; otherwise I should not have believed my Ears, or have dared to give way to my own feelings. As it is, those seem the best patriots among you who wish to get rid of what disgraces you so much in the Opinion of your Neighbours. & I cannot think the Italian Expression in singing, with which the rest of Europe is so pleased, is incompatible with your Language.[1] Indeed I have made the Experiment & have prevailed on

---

[1] Rousseau in his devastating attack on French music (*Lettre sur la musique françoise* (2nd edn., 1753), pp. 91–2) argued that the French language itself, with its proliferation of consonants and poverty in open vowel sounds, did not lend itself to musical setting: 'Je crois avoir fait voir qu'il n'y a ni mesure ni mélodie dans la Musique Françoise, parce que la langue n'en est pas susceptible ... les François n'ont point de Musique & n'en peuvent avoir; ou que si jamais ils en ont une, ce sera tant pis pour eux.' CB, however, points to French inertia in creative composition: 'the long and pertinacious attachment to the style of Lulli and his imitators in vocal

some Italians of Merit, as vocal performers, to sing several of M. Gretry's Airs[2] which are composed of a melody wholly Italian tho' to french words & have been rather more pleased than I usually am with Italian songs from Comic Opera's as the french contain more Meaning & Sentiment—& I did not think the language suffered by being pronounced in a Manner less Nasal, or the Music by being more accented & performed by a true *voce di petto*.[3]

I know not whether you will subscribe to my reasoning on the subject or whether you & M. l'Abbé Arnaud give up french expression as much as french Compositions of the Old Cast; but it will grieve me to think differently from two such excellent Judges of every part of Science, of Taste & of human nature. Few persons dissent will mortify me more, as it will make me doubt of my principles & even of my feelings to which I have perhaps too much trusted. Whatever are your thoughts & those of M. l'Abbé Arnaud I should be very glad to know them, as, if they differ much from mine I shall take myself severely to task & correct my Errours as far as Conviction will let me without mercy.

I was very sorry to see the Month of April expire without the Happyness of se[e]ing you in England; as you gave me hopes, Sir, of your arrival here[4] when I had last the honour of conversing with you, before it was at an End. Garrick is very well, & we never meet without talking of our paris Friends with great Affection. I hope Madame Suard[5] is in perfect health, & beg leave to present my most humble Respects to her. To M. L'Abbé Arnaud I hope I am not quite forgotten. I long very much for another musical conversation with him; which would only make me wish for a thousand more. I should be extreamly obliged to him for the exact scale of that chinese Instrument you were so kind to shew me,[6] as the few notes it contains in an

compositions . . . have doubtless more impeded its progress, than want of genius in this active and lively people, or defects in their language, to which Rousseau and others have ascribed the imperfections of their Music' (*Hist. Mus.* iv. 607, 616 n.; Mercer, ii. 964, 971 n.).

[2] André-Ernest-Modeste Grétry (1741–1813), French composer of Walloon descent, 'at present, the most fashionable composer of comic operas', whom CB had met in Paris on 22 June 1770 and with whom he had a long conversation on song writing (*Tours*, i. 31–3).

[3] 'Chest-voice', a technical term in singing to denote the register: as opposed to 'voce di testa' (head voice; falsetto), or 'voce di gola' (throat voice). 'The falset voice is literally *voce da testa*, and formed in the throat; never like the notes formed in the chest, called *voce di petto*' ('voice' in Rees).

[4] Suard, who had visited London for the first time about 1768, did not return for a second visit until Apr. 1773 (A. C. Hunter, *J.-B.-A. Suard, un introducteur de la littérature anglaise en France* (1925), pp. 127, 129).

[5] Amélie Suard, née Panckoucke (1750–1830), sister of the Parisian bookseller and publisher Charles-Joseph Panckoucke, had married Suard in Jan. 1766. See R. Doumic, 'Lettres d'un philosophe et d'une femme sensible: Condorcet et Madame Suard d'après une correspondance inédite', *Revue des deux mondes*, v (1911), 302–25, 835–60; vii (1912), 57–81; Garrick *Letters*, ii. 523–4; Rousseau *Corresp.* xxviii. 289.

[6] 'After dinner M. Suard shewed me a Chinese Instrument belonging to the Abbé Arnauld. It is in form like our Sticado—thin dry bars of light wood, very sonorous which rest on a hollow

Octave have given rise to some thoughts & experiments upon other wild national Musics than the Chinese, which when better ascertained & digested I shall have great pleasure in Communicating to M. l'Abbé.[7]

If any English Books are announced in such Journals as you have any concern in;[8] & you think mine worthy of being mentioned among them you will oblige me very much by procuring it such an Advantage. It is now time to conclude & to assure you that I am, with the most sincere regard

Sir,
your most obliged
& obedient servant
Charles Burney.

Queen Square, Bloomsbury | London.

To Denis Diderot[1]

[Queen Square],
27 May 1771

L incomplete copy, in the hand of FB (Berg).
Docketed by FB: Extract—May 27. 1771 | A Monsieur Monsieur Diderot. | Copy. | By order. | FB. Sec. & House Clerk.   *And by* FBA: ✕ To *M. Diderot*—   *Publ.:* Leigh, pp. 177–8; Diderot *Corresp.* xi. 40–2, in French translation; D. Diderot, *Œuvres complètes*, intro. R. Lewinter (1969–73), ix. 1031–2, in French translation.

... The National Music of your Country, it will require Ages to extirpate. The attachment to it of the generality of hearers in Public places seems to me to be much stronger than it ought to be, after the attempts that have been made by so many able Writers to correct the Public Taste. But you labour under the same disadvantage of *bad singing* in your Country, as we do in ours. Your Orchestras are good,

vessel in the form of the hulk of a little ship—There are but 17 notes on it—It has no semi-tones that I could find, and but five sounds from a note to its octave . . . The Abbé thinks this scale to be that of Pythagoras' (*Tours*, i. 317).

[7] See CB to Lind, 19 Sept. 1774, n. 8; to Raper, [?Sept.–Oct. 1777], n. 12.

[8] As editor of the *Journal étranger* and the *Gazette littéraire*, Suard had attempted to promote French interest in English literature. His career in literary journalism, however, had ended with the last issue of the *Gazette littéraire* in Feb. 1766. Although he continued with Arnaud to edit the *Gazette de France* until their dismissal in Sept. 1771, this official publication carried little matter of literary interest (Hunter, *Suard*, pp. 50–1, 85–7, 127–8; Walpole *Corresp.* v. 92–3; vii. 340).

[1] In reply to CB's first letter to him, [*c*.28 Feb. 1771], Diderot had sent CB a letter dated 15 May 1771 (Osborn) introducing the composer and chess-player, François-André Danican, called Philidor (1726–95), who brought the letter to CB. See *EJL* i. 154–5; Diderot *Corresp.* xi. 37–9.

& so are ours; & as far as Instruments are concerned, perhaps France, Germany & England have the superiority over Italy itself, from whence indeed it must be confessed that they have borrowed all their Taste, their knowledge of effects, & of Light & Shade. But for Vocal Music, which insinuates itself into the soul with so much more facility than Instrumental, French, German, English & all the People on the Globe must bow down to the Italians! It wants no great depth of philosophy to account for this, after feeling & admitting the Fact. The Language of Italy; the Musical schools; the great Number of good Vocal Performers constantly employed in the Churches & the Dramas, Serious & Comic, being almost always set to Music, will at least help to solve the Problem.

If I had had Health & Leisure to attend to a Translation of my Book into French, I would have retrenched many things in it which must be both useless & displeasing to the Natives of France. I speak of many things as an English Man who writes meerly for Englishmen to Read. But it appeared necessary to enliven my Narrative with many trivial circumstances unnecessary to a learned or speculative Reader; for their Number is too small to support an Author.[2] However in this small & feeble Publication, you will discover my Musical principles as to Expression, Effects, accompaniments, Lyric Poetry, &c. Where you find them erroneous, I entreat you to correct them, or at least to enable me to do it in my future greater & more serious Work, by pointing them out, when I have next the honour to hear from You. I am very impatient to see the Treatise of Harmony you mention.[3] It is saying every thing for it in my opinion, that You think it worth digesting & being made Public. But I think Genius & Taste are more frequently wanting than Science & the Mechanism of the Art, at least in France & England. But to shorten the Road to Science & to facilitate the means of turning it to the best account,—is to deserve well both of one's Country & of Posterity.[4] I have the honour to be,

---

[2] Fanny wrote of CB's *Italian Tour*: 'He prints this Book for himself' (*EJL* i. 146), that is, at his own risk, without benefit of subscribers or 'Bookselling, or other Craft' (CB to Arthur Young, 11 Oct. 1773).

[3] Diderot had written in his letter of 15 May: 'Le traité d'harmonie que je fais Imprimer touche a sa fin. Je ne manquerai pas de vous le faire passer.' This *traité* was the *Leçons de clavecin, et principes d'harmonie* (1771), by Anton Bemetzrieder (1739–1825?), Alsatian writer on music and Angélique Diderot's music master (*New Grove*). Diderot wrote the Preface to the *Leçons*, but the body of the text reveals he played a far greater part in its composition than is suggested by his assertion that he had merely been 'le correcteur' of Bemetzrieder's 'mauvais français tudesque'. See Leigh, p. 180 n. 3; Diderot, *Œuvres complètes*, ix. 113–544; J. Gribenski, 'A propos des *Leçons de clavecin* (1771): Diderot et Bemetzrieder', *Revue de musicologie*, lxvi (1980), 125–78; Kassler, i. 68.

[4] Diderot, summarizing the *Leçons de clavecin*, had written in his letter of 15 May, 'J'espere que vous y trouverez des vues nouvelles, une theorie plus generale que celle de la basse fondamen[t]ale qui a bien de la peine a rendre raison de plusieurs accords, ... outre ce merite, L'ouvrage en

with an affectionate attachment to your Person, & the highest regard for your Virtues & Science, dear Sir, y^r obedient & most obliged ser^t

Chas Burney.

faites moi la Grace, je vous supplie, de presenter mes tres humble respects a Mad^{lle} Diderot, & de me croire tres interessé en tout ce qui vous regarde.

To Pierre Guy *enclosing*   [Queen Square,
To Jean-Jacques Rousseau   late May 1771]^1

AL drafts (Osborn).
Endorsed by CB: Copie d'une Lett^{re} | a | M. Rousseau   *Docketed by* FBA: à M. Rousseau,   *Editor's Note:* CB drafted these letters on two conjugate folio leaves. The letter to Guy occupies the top half of p. 1, 'Monsieur. Je suis bien ... Passerai à Paris.' and runs from the bottom half of p. 3 to p. 4. The salutation occurs again at the resumption of the letter on p. 3, 'Monsieur. Je vous assure ...'. Between these two paragraphs of the letter to Guy, CB drafted incompletely the letter to Rousseau which runs from the bottom half of p. 1 to the top of p. 3.   *Publ.:* Rousseau *Corresp.* xxxviii. 223–5, 230–1 (as three separate letters).

[*to Guy*]

Monsieur.

Je suis bien sensible de l'Honneur que vous m'avez bien procuree d'une Lettre de la part de M. Rousseau dont je fais le plus grand Cas, et pour laquelle je vous supplie Monsieur d'accepter mes tres humble[s] remercimens.^{2} Mais j'ai encore une Grace à vous demander, c'est de presenter à Monsieur Rousseau Le Livre et La Lettre a son addresse que vous recevrez avec ce billet. S'il y a dans la Literature quelque chose de nouveau qui vient de paroitre ou sur la Musique *ex professo*, ou par rapport à L'histoire de cette Science vous me ferez un grand plaisir de la faire passer à mon Addresse en Angleterre par la premiere

---

aura Incontestablement un autre; c'est d'avoir donné a une Science qui jusqu'a present n'avoit eté que d'habitude, et d'experience, une forme ou l'on passe du plus connu, au moins connu, et par laquelle on arrive au dernier terme de l'art, qui est de faire de la musique très variée, et sans faute, quand on manque de genie; et d'en faire de belle, quand on a du genie.'

^{1} This letter to Guy, enclosing a copy of the *Italian Tour* and a letter to Rousseau, clearly belongs chronologically with the preceding letters to d'Holbach, Suard, and Diderot.

^{2} Under cover of his own letter to CB of 8 Apr. 1771 (Osborn), Guy had forwarded a letter from Rousseau: 'Voicy une Lettre de ce Grand homme, que je viens de recevoir dans le moment.' Rousseau's letter (see n. 10) can therefore be dated [8 Apr.] 1771. See Rousseau *Corresp.* xxxviii. 212–15.

occasion, et j'en paierez le Montant ou à Votre Correspondant ici ou par le moyen de quelqu'un de mes connoissance[3] qui Passerai à Paris.

[*CB here interrupts with his draft to Rousseau and resumes to Guy*]

Monsieur.

Je vous assure que je serois charmé d'etre bon à quelque chose par rapport de Monsr R. pour que je sent et je sentirai Jamais la plus grande Estime et consideration. [4]C'est en vain que j'ai fait toute la perquisition possible; de trouver le nom du[4] Ministre à qui la Lettre dont il s'agit fut addressée.[5] Mais il y a arrive tant de Changement de Tems en Tems dans notre Ministere que sans le date de la Lettre ou le noms de la personne, c'est impossible de tirer au Claire cette affaire. Or si dans la Conversation avec M. R. vous pourriez[6] vous en informer au juste, & me [7]faire me la Communique apres dans une lettre[7] je ne tarderois pas un moment de faire tout mon Possible pour procurer une Reponse a sa Lettre mais, comme je suis [8]sure que le Ministre[8] actuel n'est pas lui a qui La Lettre de M. R. fut addressée, si vous pouviez lui disposer d'ecrire de nouveaux a, My Lord North,[9] le Ministre actuel, je me chargerai tres volontier de lui rendre cette Lettre & d'en procurer sil est possible une reponse. Soyez assurer Monsieur qu'il n'y a rien au Monde qui me ferrois plus de plaisir que de rendre quelque Service à ce grand Homme. Mais il faut Menager sa delicatesse, et vous pouvez conter sur Moi que je tacherai avec soins d'agir en telle sorte que je ne la blesserai pas.

Je suis Monsr avec estime

Votre &c

[3] MS connoissance] *alternative* amis

[4-4] MS C'est en vain que j'ai ... trouver le nom du] *altered from* mais j'ai ... trouver qui fut le

[5] Guy, in a long postscript to his letter of 8 Apr., had requested CB's assistance in the delicate matter of Rousseau's Royal Pension. In May 1766, through the good offices of David Hume, George III had granted Rousseau a pension of £100, which he had declined. This issue of the pension had been one of the chief causes of the stormy public quarrel between Rousseau and Hume in 1766–7. Aware that Rousseau lived in frugal circumstances, Guy implored CB to try to discover why Rousseau had received no reply to a letter he had allegedly written to an unnamed British Minister supposedly on the subject of the pension. See Guy to CB, 8 Apr. 1771 (Osborn; Rousseau *Corresp.* xxxviii. 213); Lonsdale, pp. 101–3; L. G. Crocker, *Jean-Jacques Rousseau: The Prophetic Voice (1758–1778)* (New York, 1973), ch. 8; E. C. Mossner, *The Life of David Hume* (Oxford, 1970), ch. 35; R. A. Leigh, 'Rousseau's English Pension', in *Studies in Eighteenth-Century French Literature presented to Robert Niklaus*, ed. J. H. Fox, *et al.* (Exeter, 1975), pp. 109–22.

[6] MS pourriez] *altered by overwriting from original* pouviez *and deleted interlined alternative* puissiez

[7-7] MS faire ... lettre] *interlined over deleted* serois apres le plaisir de me l'ecrire

[8-8] MS sure ... Ministre] *altered from* certain que ce Ministre n'est

[9] Frederick North (1732–92), styled Lord North, 2nd Earl of Guilford (1790). As Chancellor of the Exchequer (1767–82), and First Lord of the Treasury (1770–82), he had been the head of the Administration since 1770.

[*to Rousseau*]

Monsr

Je suis tres flatté de vostre Souvenir[10] ainsi que par la Permission que vous avez bien voulu me donner de v^s fournir les Livres imprimés de Musique [11]dont j'ai eu le plaisir[11] de V^s faire tenir par les Soins de M. Gui. J'ai l'Honneur de penser precisement comme vous Monsr par rapport de la Passione d'Jomelli. Si cette belle Composition[12] a quelque defaut c'est qu'elle est trop travaillee—et c'est là le defaut ordinaire de ce grand Maitre depuis son sejour en Allemagne ou la Simplicité dans les ouvrage⟨s⟩ de l'Art ne plait pas. On y meprens quelquefois du bruit pour la Musique et la Travaille pour le Genie. Mais selon moi il n'y a rien de plus belle dans la Musique que [13]le *Simplex Mu*[*n*]*ditiis*[13] qui regne dans les ouvrage[s] de Pergolesi,[14] de Hasse et quelque fois dans ceux de Buranello et de Sacchini.—Depuis mon arrivé en angleterre j'ai eté occupé d'un petit ouvrage dont j'ai l'Honneur de v^s faire passer une Copie, sur l'Etat actuel de la Musique en France et en Italie. J'en ai parlé avec beaucoup de franchise et vous verrez Monsr une narration tres fidelle de tout ce que j'ai Senti par rapport de la Musique actuel de ces pais là dans Mon Voyage l'anné passé. Les Francois n'en Seront pas flattes. Mais M. il y a long Tems que vous m'avez appris de regarder les Fugues et les Morce[a]ux [de] Musique Savante comme des *Chef-d'oe*[*u*]*vres insupportable*,[15] et sans etre guidé par votre bon gout et vos lumiere j'ai toujours senti que

[10] A MS copy of Rousseau's letter to CB, [8 Apr.] 1771, is preserved in the Bibliothèque Publique de la Ville de Neuchâtel (MS R 291, fos. 140^v–141). While the original autograph is not preserved, the letter has reached print several times: *Mem.* i. 257–8; *Matériaux pour la correspondance de J. J. Rousseau*, ed. A. François (1923), p. 71; *Correspondance générale de J.-J. Rousseau*, ed. Th. Dufour (1924–34), xx. 111; and Rousseau *Corresp.* xxxviii. 214–15. To have received this complimentary communication from Rousseau himself was a great honour which CB cherished to the end of his life. See CB to Mme d'Arblay, 12 Oct. [1806] (Osborn); *Mem.* iii. 371–3; Scholes, ii. 309–10; Lonsdale, pp. 101, 436–7.

[11–11] MS dont ... plaisir] *interlined above alternative* que j'avois *and deleted* l'Honneur

[12] MS Composition] *alternative* ouvrage

[13–13] MS le ... *Mu*[*n*]*ditiis*] *alternative* cette elegante Simplicite

CB's interlined alternative reading elucidates this quotation from Horace, *Odes*, i. v. 5.

[14] Commenting on Jommelli's *Passione* which CB had sent as a gift (see CB to Guy, [28 Feb. 1771], n. 3), Rousseau wrote in his reply, 'cet ouvrage admirable me paroit plein d'harmonie et d'expression, il merite en cela d'être mis a coté du Stabat Mater de Pergolese, je le trouve seulement au dessous, en ce qu'il a moins de simplicité' (Rousseau to CB, [8 Apr.] 1771, Neuchâtel; see n. 10). Jommelli had been influenced by German music during his appointment as *kapellmeister* to the Duke of Württemberg at Stuttgart from 1753 to 1769.

The *Stabat Mater* of Giovanni Battista Pergolesi (1710–36) is one of his last compositions (*New Grove*). His comic intermezzo, *La Serva Padrona* (1733), at its revival in Paris in 1752, touched off the 'guerre des bouffons' in which Rousseau had participated (see CB to Guy, [28 Feb. 1771], n. 8–8).

[15] CB alludes to the article 'Fugue' in Rousseau's *Dictionnaire de musique*: 'on peut dire qu'une belle *Fugue* est l'ingrat chef-d'œuvre d'un bon Harmoniste.'

l'Expression des Francois en chantant est fausse et detestable. Mais ce n'est pas la seul prejugé dont vos ecrits m'ont gueris radicalement. —Je serai Charmé dans le petit Journal de mes sensations par Rapport de la Musique en France et en Italie si vous voudrez bien Marquer mes defauts et les Erreurs naturels d'un Voyageur dans un païs etranger qui ne dois pas se fier de ses propres sens.

On dit ici M. que vous avez fait Chanter votre belle Piece de Pygmalion dans un Chant Grec avec l'accompagnm^t des Flutes en Imitation au Moin de la Maniere de Chanter ou de reciter des Anciens dans les Piece[s] de Theatre.[16] S'il cela est Vrai je serroi tres Curieux de savoir vos Idees la dessus. C'est une Matiere tres delicate et dont on a parler beaucoup dans tous les Traitez ainsi que dans les Histoires de la Musique sans dire la Moindre chose qui m'a convaincu que les auteur de ces Livres ...

To Samuel Crisp   [Queen Square, 31]
                                        May [1771]

AL (Osborn), fragile and torn.
Addressed: To|Samuel Crispe Esqr|at Chesington, near|Epsom in|Surry   *Pmk:*
1 IV   *Endorsed by* Crisp: N° 8.|May 31.|1771   *Docketed by* FBA: ⌗ Rough|
First idea|of the|Plan|of the|History|of|Musick.|N° 3.|30 1771.

Friday, last of May
⌐I hardly knew what I wished of you in imposing upon you the Office of Critick for the Review[1]—what a quantity of writing have I

---

[16] Rousseau's dramatic scene *Pygmalion* was first performed at Lyons in May 1770, with music largely composed by Horace Coignet (1735–1821). Convinced that opera was not possible in the French language, Rousseau attempted this radical experiment in melodrama, a genre of dramatic presentation which became very popular in the late eighteenth century: spoken text alternating with instrumental music. The text of *Pygmalion* first reached print in Jan. 1771 in the *Mercure de France*, ii. 200–9, prefaced by an explanatory letter (p. 199) from Coignet: 'ce n'est point un opéra: [Rousseau] l'a intitulé, Scène Lyrique. Les paroles ne se chantent point, & la Musique ne sert qu'à remplir les intervalles des repos nécessaires à la déclamation. M. Rousseau vouloit donner, par ce spectacle, une idée de la Mélopé des Grecs, de leur ancienne déclamation théâtrale; il desiroit que la Musique fût expressive, qu'elle peignît la situation, &, pour ainsi dire, le genre d'affection que ressentoit l'Acteur'. In 1775 CB's friend William Mason translated *Pygmalion* into English. See 'Coignet' and 'Rousseau' in *New Grove*; Walpole *Corresp.* xxviii. 183–4.

[1] This passage, and others in this letter obliterated by Mme d'Arblay, reveals that CB had made arrangements for his friend Samuel Crisp to review the *Italian Tour* in the influential *Critical Review*, and that Crisp had sent for CB's perusal a manuscript copy of the critique prior to publication. Crisp's two-part article appeared in the *Critical Review* for June (xxxi. 421–32) and July (xxxii. 1–15) 1771. See Lonsdale, pp. 108–10.

involved you in!—⌐ you w^d have had my acknowledgm^ts sooner but I have had upon my Hands no less than 8 or 9 Letters for Paris, w^ch, together with some of my Books, in presents, I send by Strange,[2] who was to depart this Morning.—Did I tell you I had rec^d a Letter from Rousseau?[3]—Baretti brought me one likewise from Padre Martini last week[4] & ⌐Philidor⌐ (the famous Chess player & Composer of French ⌐Comic⌐ Operas) one from Diderot.[5]—So that I am ⌐now⌐ fairly in Correspondence wth the 3 principal Heros of my Journal, & the best Theorists & writers on the subject of Music in Europe.—

Never complain of want of νους or of spunk—for y^r Crit⌐ique⌐ is full of Fire. ⌐you have been before hand with me in the only doubts I had concerning the Expediency of such long Extracts[6]—I feared, like you, that they may either be too long for the Review, or too much satisfy the reader to make him inclined to purchase the Work—I believe I shall leave that Matter to Hamilton[7]—another thing I believe it will be prudent to soften—the attack upon *my* attack of Fr. Music is perhaps a little too strongly urged, in accusing me of *Injustice* & *prejudice*, two terrible Qualities in an Historian!—which it may even be dangerous to hint at—again—my *Enthusiasm* in favour of *Italian Music*, at wch the Critique wonders hits a little too hard[8]—& will certainly raise the allarm among the English Musicians—⌐ I have ⌐already⌐ had a

---

[2] Robert Strange, the engraver. See CB to FB, 13 June 1764, n. 15.

[3] i.e. Rousseau to CB, [8 Apr.] 1771. See CB to Guy and Rousseau, [late May 1771], nn. 2, 10, 14.

[4] Giuseppe Marc'Antonio Baretti (1719–89), man of letters, had settled in London in 1751. He had assisted CB on his musical travels by providing him with letters of introduction to relatives and friends in Italy. See L. Collison-Morley, *Giuseppe Baretti and His Friends* (1909), p. 227; *Tours*, i. 59, 79, 97, 119, 145; Giuseppe Baretti, *Epistolario*, ed. L. Piccioni (Bari, 1936), ii. 14, 16, 20, 31–2, 44, 62.

Baretti had returned late in Apr. 1771 from a 9-month visit to Italy. The brief letter of greeting he brought from Padre Martini to CB is dated from Bologna, 7 Apr. 1771 (Osborn), and is published in English translation by Brofsky, p. 325 (facsimile p. 326).

[5] i.e. Diderot to CB, 15 May 1771 (Osborn). See CB to Diderot, 27 May 1771, n. 1. CB's delight in these communications from the eminent is reflected in Fanny's Journal for 3 June: 'My Father has been honoured with Letters from the great Rousseau, M. Diderot, & Padre Martini, three as eminent as the Age has produced' (*EJL* i. 155–6).

[6] Extracts from the *Italian Tour* occupy some twenty-three of the twenty-seven printed pages of Crisp's review. CB's accounts of the Venetian and Neapolitan Conservatorios comprise a third of the extracts, perhaps because CB at this time advocated the establishment of a musical conservatory in England. See CB to Giardini, 21 June 1772; to Twining, 13 July 1774.

[7] Archibald Hamilton (*c.*1720–93), printer, publisher, and editor of the *Critical Review*, which he had founded in 1756. See Plomer, p. 114; *GM* lxiii (1793), 285.

[8] Crisp's 'attack' reads in part: 'in a man of Dr. Burney's general knowledge of the art, and who is to give us a fair and impartial account of the music of all nations, we cannot but wonder, his enthusiasm in favour of a different stile, should have hurried him into bitterness and invective against the French ... let the Italian have the preference, which it seems fairly entitled to; but must the French therefore, in contradiction to the general feelings of a whole nation, be anathematised without remorse?' (*Critical Review*, xxxii. 14–15).

Curious Letter from Dr Arne,[9] wch I must shew you, on the Subject. He is hurt at not being mentioned tho' the three foreigners, Giardini, Bach & Abel are.[10]—But I heard their music performed throughout Italy, whereas that of the poor D^r has never yet been able to Clamber the Alps.—& from the Title of my Book a Russian or Hottentot Musician has equal right to Complain of being neglected as Dr Arne an English Musician—in my Hist^y when I come to the Music & Musicians of this Country he doubtless ought to be Named with Eloge as the best Composer for the English Stage of his Time.—As Purcel was before him.[11]—I have many Folks still on my Hands—& know not when I shall be able to get to Ches[sington]—or to work seriously at my History.—Except Dr Arne's Letter, wch is likewise full of Flomery as to my *Manner of Writing* &c—I hear Nothing but praise —& all agree in finding my Nonsense *Entertaining*.—This will probably sell the Book & get Subscribers.—ꟼthe ⟨Cambridge?⟩ Critique is gone to Hamilton, by the penny Post.—in all likelihood he will ⟨prune?⟩ it [xxx *one word*] & I will tell him I had rathe[r] be whipped at the Cart's A——[12] than ⟨so?⟩ be praised & afterwards produce the anonimous Critick—ꟼ[13]

[9] Arne's letter of protest to CB is not preserved.

[10] 'I find all over Italy that Giardini's solos, and Bach's and Abel's overtures, are in great repute, and very justly so, as I heard nothing equal to them of the kind, on the continent' (*Tours*, i. 280). Later, CB wrote: 'the arrival of Giardini, Bach, and Abel ... brought about a total revolution in our musical taste' (*Hist. Mus.* iv. 673; Mercer, ii. 1015). As Arne was also actively engaged in contemporary London music-making, he was understandably incensed that he was not mentioned along with them.

For CB's acquaintance with Felice de'Giardini (1716–96), the celebrated violinist and composer who first appeared in London in 1750, see *CB Mem.* 58. Giardini had been leader, conductor, and impresario of the Italian Opera in London, and from 1770 to 1776 conducted the Three Choirs festival.

J. C. Bach was closely associated with Karl Friedrich Abel (1723–87), viola da gamba player, composer, and impresario. Abel had settled in England in 1759 and was appointed chamber musician to Queen Charlotte in 1765, from which year Bach and Abel had jointly run a famous series of fashionable winter concerts.

[11] Although Arne 'had formed a new style of his own, there did not appear that fertility of ideas, original grandeur of thought, or those resources upon all occasions which are discoverable in the works of his predecessor, Purcell, both for the church and stage; yet, in secular Music, he must be allowed to have surpassed him in ease, grace, and variety' (*Hist. Mus.* iv. 674–5; Mercer, ii. 1016; repeated in Rees under 'Arne').

[12] Where wrongdoers were flogged through the streets (see *OED* under 'Cart's-tail').

[13] Although several attempts to decipher completely this heavily obliterated passage have proved fruitless, a sufficient number of words have emerged to indicate a hitherto unsuspected connection between CB and the *Critical Review*. In the issues of the *Critical Review* for June and July 1771, in which Crisp's notice of CB's *Italian Tour* appears, is also printed an anonymous review of a new (1771) publication entitled *Principles and Power of Harmony* (xxxi. 458–63; xxxii. 15–24). CB himself mentions this volume in a last-minute footnote inserted in his *Italian Tour* (*Tours*, i. 101n.). Extensive extracts from the review of the *Principles* appear in CB's article in Rees's *Cyclopaedia* on Benjamin Stillingfleet (1702–71), subsequently revealed to be the author of the *Principles*. As it was CB's practice in his articles for Rees to quote passages from his own published writings, it seems certain that CB himself wrote the review. This conclusion is

I have got my Books, prints & music from Rome, tho' those from Venice are not yet arrived.—I shall first get over the Drudgery of Jewish Music—Padre Martini—Don Calmet[14]—the Bible—& some hebrew priests with whom I will Converse by Means of my Fr^d Franks,[15] will suffice for that part of my Enterprize.—The Classicks, Padre Martini's 2^d Vol. which I expect Dayly with the old Treatises in my possession & my drawings of ancient Instruments & remarks upon them, will suffice I hope for Greek & Roman Music till the Time of Guido—Then our Monkish Writers must be read—old Missals, & offices of the Church with different examples of Notation & remarks will bring me to the 14th Century, the Time when John de Muris invented the pres[e]nt Musical Characters[16]—After this a Field will be opened to range in of old Compositions & Treatises which will bring me to the Time of Leo the Tenth[17] when Contra Punto & Church Music were so much improved by Prenestine[18]—After this Materials will not be wanting—in the year 1600—operas & oratorios began, from the History & Series of which I hope to something more amusing to the reader as it will be less Laborious to the writer than the preceding Periods.[19]

confirmed by William Bewley, who reviewed the *Principles* in the *Monthly Review* (xlv. 369–77, 477–84). On 23 Oct. 1771 Bewley wrote to CB: 'I have been very idle as a R———r lately, & never sat down till the other day to the *Power & Principles &c*, which I really must get ready for next month—By the bye—a certain Cr. R———r has made me very shy of that article' (Osborn).

CB's connection with the *Critical Review* would explain how he contrived to get its editor to accept Crisp's review of his own *Italian Tour*.

[14] Antoine Calmet (1672–1757), called 'Dom Augustin', French Benedictine monk, Abbot of Senones in 1729 (*DBF*). In 'The History of Hebrew Music' (*Hist. Mus.* i. 224–57; Mercer, i. 191–214), CB draws heavily upon Calmet's *Dissertations qui peuvent servir de prolégomènes de l'Écriture Sainte* (1720), which was based on the prefaces to the various books of the Bible and the learned 'dissertations' on biblical topics that had appeared in Calmet's *Commentaire littéral sur tous les livres de l'Ancien et du Nouveau Testament* (1707–16).

[15] Naphtali Franks (1715–96), of Mortlake, Surrey, FRS (1764), was one of the leading lay members of the Great Synagogue in London. Franks was an accomplished amateur violinist, 'pas[s]ionately fond of Music', and had befriended the 21-year-old CB at Bath in the autumn of 1747. In 1750, Franks had invited CB to a private concert in his house to hear Giardini, who had recently arrived in England, and likewise in 1764 to hear the 8-year-old Wolfgang Amadeus Mozart (*CB Mem.* 45, 58, 107). Franks later subscribed to CB's *Hist. Mus.* See C. Roth, *The Great Synagogue, London, 1690–1940* (1950), pp. 62–4, 299; and *GM* lxvi (1796), 968.

[16] Jehan des Murs or Johannes de Muris (*c*.1300–*c*.1350), French musical theorist, mathematician, and astronomer. CB later wrote: 'The invention of *characters for time* has ... been given by almost all the writers on music of the last and present century, to John de Muris, who flourished about the year 1330, ... yet ... I am in possession of ... a stubborn proof of that discovery not being the property of John de Muris ... [who] though not the inventor of the *Cantus Mensurabilis*, seems by his numerous writings greatly to have improved it' (*Hist. Mus.* ii. 174–5, 207; Mercer, i. 529, 551).

[17] Giovanni de'Medici (1475–1521), Pope Leo X (1513), patron of the arts and learning.

[18] Giovanni Pierluigi (*c*.1525–94), named Palestrina after his birthplace, which was called in Roman times Praeneste.

[19] CB had originally planned to start his *History* with the eleventh century and the work of

Think over all this by the Time I see you & tell me if you know of any other method for me to Pursue.—

Jemm is arrived in the Downs, & Expects to get on shore in a few Days.[20] ⌐in the Course of your reading pray don't forget to set down Chapter & verse ⟨of⟩ whatever may be of use or amusement ⟨to⟩ my projected Work. I have still 50 Let⟨ters⟩ on my Hands—so for the present addio—

I have found out 2 or 3 Cursed typographi⟨cal⟩ blunders in things that I had marked & Correc⟨ted⟩ in the proofs—but which were overlooked by the Corrector, & be d——— to him—such as vole*ti* for vole*te*—V*a*cana—for V*a*ticana.—M*a*ssa for M*e*ssa &c—&c &c[21]— why the devil does not the public mak⟨e⟩ haste in buying up this cursed first Edit. in order to get a 2ᵈ more Correct?—Vale—⌐

To Joseph Warton[1]   Queen Square,
                                           12 August 1771

Source: John Wooll, *Biographical Memoirs of the Late Revᵈ Joseph Warton, D.D.* (1806), pp. 382–5;   *also* ALS draft, incomplete (Osborn). The text is taken from the printed source. Significant variant readings from the draft are footnoted. See Textual Introduction.

Queen's-square, Bloomsbury,
Aug. 12, 1771.

Sir,

Having received, from my friend Mr. Garrick, your kind communication of the contents of an old and scarce book on music, I hope I

Guido (CB to Twining, 28 Apr. 1773), but on reading further in 'a great Number of fogram musical Authors' had second thoughts, so that by the time he departed on his Italian tour, the *History* was to be all inclusive (CB to Mason, 27 May 1770; and the present letter). For CB's execution of his plan, see Grant, chs. 3, 9.

[20] CB's eldest son, James, had begun his naval career in Oct. 1760 at the age of 10, and in 1766 had received his warrant as Midshipman. In Feb. 1770, there being little scope for adventure or advancement in the peace-time Royal Navy, James had signed on as an ordinary seaman in the East Indiaman, *Greenwich*. The vessel sailed for Bombay, and on its return voyage reached Deal in the Downs on 28 May 1771, setting sail for London on the following day. James received his discharge on 27 June 1771. See Manwaring, ch. 1; *CB Mem.* 88–9; *EJL* i. 152; *Public Advertiser*, 30 and 31 May 1771.

[21] These mistakes in the first edition of the *Italian Tour* (pp. 261, 262, and v) were corrected in the second edition (1773) on pp. 271, 271, and vii. They are noted, with many more, in a MS list compiled and endorsed by CB 'Erràta to Ital. Tour' (Osborn).

[1] Joseph Warton (1722–1800), DD (1768), poet and literary critic, Headmaster (1766–93) of Winchester (*DNB*).

shall be pardoned for breaking in upon you somewhat abruptly with my acknowledgements.[2] Indeed I am the more encouraged to risk this letter, as your voluntary offer of assistance, to a person wholly unknown to you, but by a feeble and hasty publication, which I never flattered myself could be worthy your perusal, must proceed from benevolence of disposition, from a cordial affection for the arts in general, and from a spirit of universal philanthropy.

Franchinus Gaffurius,[3] or as the Italians call him il Gafforio,[4] was a very eminent and voluminous writer of the 15th and 16th centuries; and though I picked up last year in Italy several of his treatises, all which are scarce, yet I do not find the work you mention among them. Nor is the same edition of it as that in Winchester Coll. among the almost innumerable books in Padre Martini's library.[5] This good father has however three different editions of the Practicæ Musicæ— one printed at Milan, 1496; one at Brescia, 1497; and one at Venice, 1512. The work is frequently mentioned and quoted by subsequent writers on the subject of music, and seems to be the clearest, and the best of his productions; as it will perhaps give an idea of the principles upon which the composers of his time produced such admirable models of good harmony. He was but a very few years anterior to the famous Prenestina,[6] the best writer for the church since the invention of the modern scale and counterpoint.

I have long been drudging through 'all such reading as was never read'[7] with more patience than profit, I fear; for the jargon, pedantry, and inanity of musical writers, cannot be matched in any other art. I have lately had occasion to consult a work by Gafforio, which I found at Venice—De Harmonia Musicorum Instrumentorum [opus],[8] Mediol. 1518. In this he attempts to give an account of the modes and

[2] Warton had written to David Garrick: 'Understanding that you are a friend of Dr Burney, who is writing the history of Music, & who has already given us a most entertaining Musical Tour, I send you the enclosed to be communicated to Him. It is the Title & Contents of an old Treatise of Music which I have accidentally found in our College Library' (30 July 1771, Osborn). Garrick promptly forwarded Warton's letter and enclosure to CB under cover of a letter dated 9 Aug. [1771] (Garrick *Letters*, ii. 753–4; MS now in the Houghton Library, Harvard).

[3] Franchino Gafori (1451–1522), priest, musical theorist, and composer, *maestro di capella* of the Duomo in Milan from 1484 until his death (*New Grove*). His name is usually Latinized as 'Franchinus Gaffurius'. Warton drew CB's attention to the third edition of Gafori's *Practica musicae utriusque cantus* (Brescia, 1502), a copy of which is listed in the 1634 Catalogue of the Winchester College Library. The volume is now missing from Winchester.

[4] MS draft spells 'Gafforio' consistently.

[5] MS draft adds 'of wch I have a Catalogue'. CB's copy of Padre Martini's catalogue is not known to be extant.

[6] MS draft spells 'Prenestina': i.e. Palestrina. See CB to Crisp, [31] May [1771], n. 18.

[7] Alexander Pope, *Dunciad*, iv. 250. Warton had published the first volume of his influential *An Essay on the Writings and Genius of Pope* in 1756. CB owned the second edition (1762) of this volume (*Cat. Misc. Lib.*, lot 1950).

[8] MS draft includes 'opus', correctly. This folio volume is listed in 'Cat. Fac. Mus.', item 54.

genera of the ancient Greeks with as much confidence and solemnity as the rest of his brethren, without knowing any more of the matter than about what kind of music is used by the inhabitants of terra incognita. We have the words without the things—well-sounding terms of art, de belle parole, without ideas. Rousseau says of Rameau's famous *Generation Harmonique*, that it is a book, qu'il a fait fortune, sans etre lu[9]—this singular luck has happened to more books on music than one. I fancy it would be difficult to find among the admirers of Zarlino,[10] the prince of musicians, as he is often called, a single person who has been gifted with perseverance sufficient to read his Harmonic Institutions quite through.

But to return to Gafforio. In the work I just mentioned, he has been implicitly copied by other writers, ten deep: and among the rest, by Bontempi,[11] who in several particulars is the best writer on music that I have yet met with. [12]If therefore during the course of my Work I could with propriety be indulged with the loan of the book for a few days (of which, as it is a College book, I very much doubt) it should not only be taken great care of, but should be speedily returned with innumerable thanks.[12] The rest of Gafforio's writings that have come to my knowledge are, Theoricum Opus Armoniæ discipline, Neapolis, 1480—Auct. et emendat. Mediol. 1492: &[13] Angelicum ac divinum opus Musice maternâ Linguâ[14] Script. Mediolani, 1508. After saying thus far, I venture, Sir, to add, that if, in the course of your extensive reading, and still more deep and refined reflection, any thing should occur relative to my subject, and you would interest yourself so far in my plan as to communicate to me, I should not only be highly flattered by it, but the Work would be greatly benefited by a few hints from so excellent a judge of every species of literature; indeed the undertaking

[9] Jean-Philippe Rameau (1683–1764), French composer and theorist. His *Génération harmonique, ou traité de musique théorique et pratique* (1737), is listed in 'Cat. Fac. Mus.', item 117. Rousseau, in the *Dictionnaire de musique* (under 'Musique'), says of Rameau's theoretical writings, 'M. Rameau, dont les écrits ont ceci de singulier, qu'ils ont fait une grande fortune sans avoir été lus de personne.'

[10] Gioseffo (or 'Gioseffe') Zarlino (1517–90), Italian Franciscan composer and theorist, *maestro di capella* of St Mark's, Venice, from 1565 until his death. His *Le Istitutioni harmoniche* was first published at Venice in 1558 (*New Grove*). CB's copy is listed in 'Cat. Fac. Mus.', item 156.

[11] Giovanni Andrea Angelini (*c*.1624–1705), who adopted his patron's name, Bontempi, Italian composer, castrato, and theorist (*New Grove*). CB refers to one of Bontempi's three treatises on music, *Historia musica* (Perugia, 1695), a copy of which CB found in Italy. This copy is item 19 in 'Cat. Fac. Mus.' (see CB to Ebeling, 30 Mar. 1772, n. 16; to [Fountaine?], 3–[4] Nov. 1773, n. 3).

[12–12] MS draft gives alternative reading: 'deep as I now am in all such reading as was never read old Franchini Gafforio will be kindly rec[d] if wth propriety I may ask leave of Absence for him from Coll. during a few Days—'

[13] MS draft reads '&'.

[14] MS draft gives 'Linguâ', correctly. CB's copy is listed in 'Cat. Fac. Mus.', item 53.

which I have dared to attempt is so intimately connected with an art which you have so long and so happily exercised, that it is impossible to give a history of Music which will not necessarily include a history of Poetry. So small is my claim upon your leisure, that it grieves me to obtrude such a long letter upon you, but the opportunity our friend Mr. Garrick afforded me of answering your letter to him, and of jointly thanking you for it,[15] was too tempting to be resisted by one who has long been ambitious of assuring you that he has the honour to be, with the highest respect and regard, Sir,

Your obedient and most humble servant,
Chas. Burney.

To Montagu North[1]

[Queen Square, summer 1771][2]

ALS (North Papers, Rougham, Norfolk).

Dear Sir,

It was so much my Intention to write to you immediately after my return to England, that I procured Franks from your neighbour Sir John Rous[3] for that purpose; but Illness & incessant hurry have hitherto deprived me of that satisfaction though you were so kind to make the first advances towards the renewal of our correspondence. It has been a double mortification to me to let your very kind & obliging Letter remain so long without my acknowledgm[ts] for its contents w[ch] are every way so flattering.[4] Few consequences of my feeble endeavours to throw new lights on some parts of our favourite art have pleased me more than your approbation. You have thought so much & so deeply

---

[15] Garrick had written (9 Aug.): 'I must beg of You to thank y[e] D[r] & make our best Acknowledgments in both our Names' (see n. 2).

[1] Montagu North, who had inherited his father's papers and MSS, had written to CB on 31 May 1771 (Osborn), after reading the *Italian Tour*. CB 'long lived in friendship' with North, 'who had a very curious collection of Music, & was himself a good Musician' (CB to Malone, 30 June 1799, PML).

[2] This undated letter was written between the receipt of North's letter (n. 1) and CB's late summer visit to Norfolk.

[3] Sir John Rous (*c.*1728–71), of Henham Hall, Suffolk, 5th Baronet (1735), MP for Suffolk (1768–71). See Namier and Brooke, iii. 380.

[4] North in his letter of 31 May had written: 'I saw your late Book advertized in the Papers, & have bought & read it with the greatest Avidity. I have the Pleasure of finding that I agree with you in most Things.' North had also offered CB access to his collection of books and MSS. CB was to make extensive use of Roger North's MS 'Memoires of Musick . . . 1728' in his chapter on the history of seventeenth-century English music in *Hist. Mus.* iii. 323–516; Mercer, ii. 260–410.

& discriminately upon the subject yourself, that I have the advantage at least of being understood by you in many things wch will escape others. You must clearly have seen my discontent through all the soft & civil Terms I was able to give it, both with respect to composing & performing of Vocal Music.[5] The Voice already corrupted & vitiated in its Intonations by the Temperament of modern Instruments is overcharged with Harmony & suffocated by Instrumental performers who seem ambitious of being heard even when they have nothing to say. A dry & unmeaning Tenor[6] or 2^d violin part plaid louder then the principal is like a small shapeless stone stracted from it's place in a beautiful building—it is an excrescence one cannot help wishing either to lop off or to beat back into its place.—You must perceive though I have not said it, totidem verbis, that The Italians are far behind us in the construction of their Instruments & in their performance upon them;[7] but that in singing, the first & most essential part of music, they are before all the world. Our Church music is not so bad in itself as ill performed. But till we have music schools under the Direction of men of Taste & Genius, like the Conservatorios of Italy, & better salaries are given to the performers, our singing must be so barbarous as to ruin the best Compositions of our own or of any Country on the Globe.

You will soon see in print the whole music of the Popes Chapel, as performed there during passion week.[8] For it is not my Intention to keep in useless obscurity any of the Musical Curiosities I have collected in my Journey; & Tho' I hardly suppose the purchasers of such Compositions will be sufficient to pay the expense of publication, yet I shall run the risk of being a little out of pocket in hopes of gratifying the wishes of the curious in such matters. The Sonata you mention by Gregorio Allegri, I believe is printed, tho very Ill, in Kircher's Musurgia[9]—I scored it many years ago as a curiosity—the Harmony

---

[5] See, for example, 'The superior refinement of the Italian music cannot be fairly attributed to the great number of *artificial* voices with which Italy, to its dishonour, abounds; for vocal music seems at present in its highest state of perfection in the conservatorios of Venice, where only the *natural* voices of females can be heard; so that the greatest crime of which the Italians seem guilty is the having dared to apply to their softer language a species of music more delicate and refined, than is to be found in the rest of Europe' (*Tours*, i. 320).

[6] i.e. a viola.

[7] 'I have neither met with a *great* player on the harpsichord, nor an *original* composer for it throughout Italy. . . . It is at present so much neglected both by the maker and player, that it is difficult to say whether the instruments themselves, or the performers are the worst. To persons accustomed to English harpsichords, all the keyed instruments on the continent appear to great disadvantage . . . the keys are so noisy, and the tone so feeble, that more wood is heard than wire' (*Tours*, i. 236).

[8] For CB's edition of the Sistine Chapel Passion Week music, see CB to Ebeling, 30 Mar. 1772, n. 5.

[9] North had written (31 May): 'You mention your having gotten the famous Miserere of the

is good & the points are well managed—but there is little melody & life to shew the Genius of the violin in it—the knowledge of the bow wch modern performers possess in so superior a degree to those of the last Century, has made that a different & a very superior instrument to what it then was.[10]—I was very sincere in the request I made to my Countrymen of communicating to me their curiosities & counsel.[11] For as it is neither my Intention to write a panegyric nor a satyr upon the music of any country, but fully to relate what I find & feel, I hope for the honour of England, wch has had good music in its church at least as early as any country in the Xtian world except Italy, that I shall be enabled to do Justice to the Talents & Taste of its Inhabitants. I have been kept in London this summer by Business much later than usual. However I hope to get out of it ere long, in order to retire to some quiet place to desect my Thoughts & materials. If I sh^d be able to get into Norfolk for any Time I shall most certainly dedicate a few Days to you & Sternfield wch w^d afford me a very sensible pleasure, being with a most sincere regard,

> Dear Sir,
> your obedient
> & most obliged servant.
> Cha: Burney.

In the great hurry with which I was forced to publish my little Book which you see is a Temporary performance that from its very title required despach, I had not Time to see a 2^d proof of any of the sheets, many of my corrections in the first have escaped the printer, besides others that had before escaped me. I have therefore printed an Errata,[12]

Pope's Chapel [*Tours*, i. 230]: I have heard of that, but did not know it was composed by Gregorio Allegri. I have a Sonata of his in four Parts; which no doubt you have seen.' CB in response refers to the four-part 'Symphonia' for strings by Allegri included in the *Musurgia universalis* (Rome, 1650), i. 487–94, by Athanasius Kircher (1602–80), German Jesuit theologian, historian, and music theorist (*NDB*; *New Grove*), 'a man of immense, but indigested learning' (Rees). CB's copy of the *Musurgia* is listed in 'Cat. Fac. Mus.', item 75. For Gregorio Allegri (1582–1652), see CB to Ebeling, 30 Mar. 1772, n. 4.

[10] CB discusses Allegri's composition as an early example of a string quartet in *Hist. Mus.* iii. 547; Mercer, ii. 435: the '*Quartetto* ... does not manifest any great progress which the *violin tribe* had made towards perfection, about the middle of the last century.'

[11] CB had written at the end of his *Italian Tour*: 'I have mentioned some of the materials which I acquired, and to these may be added a great number, which I collected during many years in England, ... and as I am certain that no place abounds more with men of sound learning, or with collectors of curious compositions and valuable materials necessary to my intended work, than my own country; I humbly hope that I shall also be honoured with their counsel and communications' (*Tours*, i. 320–1).

North had written (31 May): 'as you mention in your Book, that, with all you have got by your Travells, you nevertheless do not intend overlooking your Friends; I hope I shall not be the one overlooked; but that I may hope for the Pleasure of your good Company some time this Summer at Sternfield.'

[12] Although an errata list to the first edition of the *Italian Tour* is preserved in MS in the

wch is so considerable as almost to make me ashamed to produce it. However I shall inclose one for your B^k in Case you sh^{ld} ever think it worth looking into a second Time. Most of the mistakes are in the forein words & names wch it is very hard to make printers exact in, who are utterly ignorant of their meaning. I hope you will honour me with another letter when you have Leisure to bestow a few words upon me.

To Denis Diderot

[Queen Square],
10 October 1771

L copy, incomplete (R. A. Leigh). Bottom half of the second leaf cut away. *Docketed by* FBA: Oct. 1771   *And by* ?: Extract of | a Letter to | M. Diderot. | written Oct: | 10. 1771.   *Publ.:* Leigh, pp. 183–5; Diderot *Corresp.* xi. 205–8, in French translation; D. Diderot, *Œuvres complètes*, intro. R. Lewinter (1969–73), ix. 1120–2, in French translation.

Extrait d'une Lettre à M: Diderot.[1]

... Le traité du *Melo Drame*[2] is well written, full of ingenious &

Osborn Collection, no printed version has been located. See also, CB to Crisp, [31] May [1771], n. 21.

---

[1] This is an extract from a much longer letter CB wrote to Diderot, the original of which is not preserved. What CB said in the missing paragraphs of his letter may be partially reconstructed from the extant incoming letters of Diderot.

CB's letter of 10 Oct. 1771 was written in reply to two letters he received from Diderot:

In a letter dated 18 Aug. 1771 (R. A. Leigh), Diderot thanked CB for the gift of the *Italian Tour* and expressed great satisfaction with the book. This letter Diderot transmitted to CB through Friedrich Melchior Grimm (1723–1807), the Bavarian diplomat and critic, who journeyed to London at this time. Grimm was also entrusted to deliver to CB a copy of Bemetzrieder's *Leçons de clavecin* (Diderot *Corresp.* xi. 95–9).

Diderot wrote again to CB on 26 Sept. 1771 (Osborn): 'Voici un service que j'attends de votre amitié et pour lequel je mets tout le monde en l'air. J'en ai écrit à Mr Grimm. J'en ai écrit à monsieur Jean Bach que j'ai connu pendant son séjour à Paris; et je prends la liberté d'en écrire à M^r le Docteur Burney. Il s'agit de me procurer un bon, mais un très bon piano-forte. Votre santé, vos occupations, monsieur, vous laisseront-elles le loisir de me rendre ce service? ... Comme il ne faut pas qu'au lieu d'un instrument, j'en aie trois, et que j'ai donné la même commission à mon ami, et à Monsieur Jean Bach, oserois je vous prier de vous concerter avec eux?' (Diderot *Corresp.* xi. 196–7).

CB probably received both letters in early Oct. on his return to London after spending late Aug. and Sept. in Norfolk (*Frag. Mem.*, Osborn; *EJL* i. 164, 172–4). He evidently set about complying with Diderot's request and, we surmise, wrote about the fruits of his investigations in the now not extant portion of his letter of 10 Oct. Diderot's undated reply to this letter is published in Leigh, pp. 185–8 and in Diderot *Corresp.* xi. 213–17, there conjecturally dated [28? October], on the strength of an 'OC 29' postmark. An examination of the MS (R. A. Leigh) shows this postmark (as well as another, '2 o'CLOCK T') to be of English origin, stamped when Diderot's letter actually arrived in London. Diderot's reply is therefore more convincingly dated [*c.*20 Oct. 1771], and reveals that CB promised to find 'le meilleur piano-forte qu'il y ait à Londres' suitable for Angélique Diderot to play: 'un petit piano-forte de Zumpe, avec les touches surajoutées', priced at 18 guineas.

[2] *Traité du mélo-drame, ou réflexions sur la musique dramatique* (1772) by Jean-Laurent Garcin

elegant thoughts, & the work of a person who has thought profoundly on the Subject—his views are enlarged, & his feelings delicate. But I am inclined to think him too severe on that bewitching species of melody called *Air*,[3] or as he calls it Ariette, it certainly impedes the business of the Drama, but then, if the Air is well written, & well sung by a fine voice, a true Lover of Music can easily forgive the delay it occasions, & is ready to *encore* even that frigid thing, as the Author calls it, an *Air* with a *da Capo*.[4]—But while all the french Airs are composed *en Rondeaux*,[5] it seems as if you had little title to condemn the *Da Capo* in the Italian. By what I have read of this work it seems as if the Author was desirous of destroying all Airs in the modern french Operas & bringing them to a level with those of Lully & Rameau, where the *Measure* is so frequently changed, that it is difficult to distinguish Air from Recitative.[6] Indeed the poets who wrote for these respectable Composers knew but little of true Lyric poetry—& crouded the Airs with so *many words* & *ideas*, & in *measures*[7] so incommensurate, with respect to *Melody*, that no symmetry or connection could be preserved in the Musical phrases.[8] Hence, in order not to offend against

(1733–81), Swiss minister, teacher, and botanist (*DHBS*). Copies of the *Traité* were evidently already circulating in 1771 (Rousseau *Corresp.* v. 251 n.). CB's copy is listed in 'Cat. Fac. Mus.', item 171. For a discussion of CB's views on the relationship of lyric poetry to music in dramatic presentations, see Grant, ch. 8.

[3] CB wrote in his article, 'Air, in *Music*' in Rees: 'Though Air sometimes implies the words of a song, as well as the melody in general; nice discrimination requires, that we should confine its import to melody, a tune, alone, and *song* to the words. A fine or pleasing air has nothing to do with the poetry, which may be fine, though ill set. And the air may be beautiful, even to nonsensical words.'

[4] 'Ital[ian] musical term, implying, after an air or movement seems finished, a return to the first part or strain, which is to be repeated from the beginning, to the corona, ∩, or final mark' ('Da Capo' in Rees).

In his *Traité*, Garcin condemns the 'invention assez moderne' of *da capo* on the grounds that 'le retour des memes idées musicales, n'offrant plus rien de nouveau, laisse morfondre l'attention de l'Auditeur' (pp. 142 n., 143). He devotes part of Chapter IV of his treatise to a discussion 'De l'Ariette dramatique & de ses parties', and begins Chapter V with an 'Examen de plusieurs Ariettes Italiennes, selon les régles du Mélo-Drame' ('Table des Principales Matieres', p. 379; see especially pp. 103–68 *passim*).

[5] 'An air of two or more strains, always returning to, and finishing with the first. ... Rousseau has very justly censured the writing and setting vocal rondeaus, in which the thought is begun in one strain, and continued or ended in another; or begins with a simile, of which the application is made in the second strain. The term *rondeau*, derived from *rondel*, is of great antiquity in France' ('Rondeau' in Rees).

[6] Diderot commented in his reply of [*c.*20 Oct.] on Lully's librettist, the poet and dramatist Philippe Quinault (1635–88): 'Les poëmes de Quinault sont délicieux à lire, et la musique de Lulli est plate; mais cette plate musique ayant été composée pour ces poëmes, et ces poëmes composés pour cette plate musique, quiconque a tenté jusqu'à présent de musiquer *Armide* autrement que Lulli a fait de la musique plus plate encore que celle de Lulli' (Diderot *Corresp.* xi. 215).

[7] 'The measure is that which regulates the time we are to dwell on each note. ... All measures and species of time in modern music are reduced to two proportions; the *binary, dual*, or *even measure*, in which the rise and fall of the hand are equal; and the *ternary, triple*, or *odd* measure, in which the fall is double to the rise' (Rees).

[8] CB here reiterates the opinions he had expressed in a conversation with Grétry: 'he agreed

propriety, in expressing the words & the Heterogeneous Ideas they contained, the Composer was obliged at every Instant to change the measure & style of his Melodies.—The Author, however seems to know & to feel the grace of Italian Melody; &, I believe, as far as he will allow the use of it in modern Operas, he would wish it to be Italian.[9] Upon the whole I should think that so great a friend to the Drama would be happier at a meer *play*, as declaimed & represented at the *Theatre François*; & that one whose Ears are extremely affected by the Charms of sound, would receive more pleasure at a private Concert than at an Opera or a play. For I very much suspect that poetry will always suffer by the florid stile of Modern Melody; & that our ears have been too long accustomed to it, to allow us to return back to the ancient Simplicity of Elementary Sounds, of only one note to one Syllable.[10] So that at an Opera the Lover of poetry, or the Lover of melody, or sometimes both, must be offended.

I am charmed with the beginning of the Leçons de Clavecin,[11] I have had time to read little more of it—the Dialogue & doctrine seem equally excellent & Mad^lle Diderot's prelude[12] est très savant en modulati⟨on.⟩ I have formed a design of proving the practicability of M: Bemetzrieder's Method upon one of my own daughters who plays pretty well on the Harpsichord;[13] but who has not learned as

with me entirely in my assertion, that there were in France, and elsewhere, men, at present, who wrote very pretty verses, full of wit, invention, and passion; admirable to read, but very ill calculated for songs . . . A song for music should consist only of *one subject* or *passion*, expressed in as *few* and as *soft words as possible*. Since the refinement of melody, and the exclusion of recitative, a song, which usually recapitulates, illustrates, or closes a scene, is not the place for epigrammatic points, or for a number of heterogeneous thoughts and clashing metaphors; if the writer has the least pity for the composer, or love for music, or wishes to afford the least opportunity for symmetry in the air, in his song, I say again, the thought should be *one*, and the expression as easy and laconic as possible' (*Tours*, i. 31–2).

[9] For example, Garcin asserts: 'Faites en effet abstraction de toute loi du Mélo-Drame, vous serez obligé de convenir qu'aucune Musique moderne ne peut le disputer à l'Italienne' (pp. 181–2); and 'il n'est point de Musique de Concert qui soit comparable à la Musique Italienne' (p. 183).

[10] Diderot replied: 'Je gage que ce Mr de Garcin est un érudit qui voudroit nous ramener à l'accompagnement des flûtes anciennes. Il ne faut, selon lui, produire des sons que pour renforcer les idées du poëte. Mais il ne voit pas que si le poëte n'a pas pressenti la puissance de l'art musical, n'en a pas préparé l'effet, le musicien n'a qu'à couper les cordes de son instrument. Je voudrois bien sçavoir si Mr de Garcin permet à l'acteur de chanter ou non?' (Diderot *Corresp.* xi. 215).

[11] CB's copy of the *Leçons* is listed in 'Cat. Fac. Mus.', item 12.

[12] For 'Le prélude de l'élève', see the *Leçons de clavecin*, pp. 303–6; Diderot, *Œuvres complètes*, ix. 479–82.

[13] Susan Burney, now aged 16, who 'had the best taste in all the Arts, particularly in Music, sung with a feeble but touching & impressive voice and in a style more truly Italian perhaps than any of Sacchini's Scholars' (*Frag. Mem.*, Osborn). Fanny records in her Journal under 4 Nov. 1771: 'Sukey & myself are extremely engaged at present, in studying a Book lately Published, under M. Diderot's direction, & which he sent to Papa, upon music. It promises to teach us Harmony & the Theory of music. M. Diderot's Daughter was taught by the method made use of in it. However, I have no expectation of going very deep in the science myself' (*EJL* i. 176–7).

yet, either accompaniment or Modulation. She knows the French Language pretty well, having been *en pension* two years at Paris, is very fond of Music, has a good Ear, & talents which I have not had leisure to cultivate; & is never so happy as when she can get a french Book, in which she can find the name of Diderot. This will be a fair Trial, & if she fails it will only prove the Superiority of Mad^lle Diderots Genius, which enabled her in so short a Time to acquire a knowledge in Modulation to which so few of her sex have *ever* arrived[14]—I make no doubt but that the principles which could satisfie M. Bemetzrieder's Philosopher,[15] are well founded. I shall however read the Book with the utmost attention, & honestly point out such places as may seem to me either dark or exceptionable. & this I shall do as to a friend, for you honour him with that appellation, & to a person who has so politely & kindly favoured me thus early with the sight of his ingenious Lessons, in your elegant Dress.[16] The first Dialogue is written with such wit & spirit, that it would make an admirable scene in a Comedy. I want much to know Who is the Author of the *Traité du Melo Drame*, as it is extremely well written, though I cannot subscribe to all the opinions it contains.[17]

Octr 10th 1771

To Christoph Daniel Ebeling[1]   [Queen Square], November 1771

L copy extract, in the hand of FB (Hamburg).
Endorsed by CB: To Mr Ebeling Vice-Director of | The Academy of Commerce at |

[14] 'Soyez sûr du succès de Mad^lle votre fille;' wrote Diderot in reply, 'à la seule condition qu'elle ira pas à pas, et qu'elle ne passera pas d'une leçon à une autre, que les précédentes ne lui soient très familières. Persuadez lui surtout de ne pas dédaigner des choses si élémentaires, qu'il lui sera difficile d'en sentir les conséquences' (Diderot *Corresp.* xi. 214).

[15] In the *Leçons de clavecin*, cast in dialogue form, Diderot appears as 'Le philosophe'.

[16] Concerning Bemetzrieder's *Leçons*, Diderot had written in his letter of 18 Aug.: 'Je vous prie de le lire avec attention. Je crois que ce traité est le seul qui jusqu'à présent conduise au but par principes et avec méthode; il me semble avoir réduit l'art à des règles aussi sûres et aussi invariables que les autres sciences. ... Je crois que cet ouvrage, digne d'être traduit dans tous les langues, ne sera pas oublié dans votre grand ouvrage. C'est moi qui l'ai écrit; c'est à ma fille qu'il est dédié. Si la lecture vous faisoit naître quelques objections, je puis vous répondre que l'auteur se feroit un plaisir d'y satisfaire' (Diderot *Corresp.* xi. 97–8).

[17] Diderot explained in his reply of [*c.*20 Oct.]: 'L'auteur du mélo-drame est un nommé Mr de Garcin, de Neufchâtel. C'est une dissertation de M^r le chevalier de Châtelux sur la nature de la poësie lyrique qui a donné lieu à l'ouvrage de Mr de Garcin' (Diderot *Corresp.* xi. 214).

CB endorsed Diderot's letter of [*c.*20 Oct.]: 'Lett^re de M. Diderot | Diderot. N° 4. | Answered Novr 17. | 1771'. CB's answer is not preserved.

[1] Christoph Daniel Ebeling (1741–1817), German man of letters, Master and Supervisor of the Commercial Academy of Hamburg (*NDB*; *MGG*; Scholes, i. 198–9; *Tours*, ii. 211–12).

1771

Hamburg.   *Docketed by* FBA: ✕ Extract from a Letter to Mynhère *Ebeling*, Nov^r
1771   *Publ.:* Scholes, i. 201–3.

... I know so much already of the candour of your Mind, & the soundness of your judgement, that I will venture to give you my *profession de Foi*, relative to the merits of your Countrymen. I have ever regarded them as *profound*, not only in Music, but in other arts & sciences; & so great is their industry, that they seem more frequently to go to the *bottom* of the things ab^t wch they enquire, than any other people of Europe. Indeed the search of truth is slow & laborious to such as are determined to find her; & this has perhaps provoked some impatient & superficial writers in other Countries to accuse them of dulness & prolixity. As to music I should not hesitate to give it as my opinion, that they are the *first* people in Europe at present both for the Composition & performance of *Instrumental music*. There are several of your Countrymen, but not mentioned in your Essay,[2] or letter, whose musical productions & performances have given me great delight. Such as Abel, Schobert, Echard, Eichner, Fischer, Wagenseil, Schwindl, Hayden,[3] &c. Abel has been many years in England, has composed excellent symphonies & Quartets for violins, &c, with two Books of very pleasing sonatas for the Harpsichord, accompanied by a violin & violincello.[4] & he is, moreover, the most perfect player of the Viol da gamba I have ever heard. Indeed his taste is the most exquisite & refined, & his judgment & learning the most perfect that I have ever met united in one performer; & I can conceive no one able to surpass him on any Instrument, except his fellow student, Mr C. P. E.

Impressed by CB's *Italian Tour*, Ebeling published a German translation of it in Hamburg, 1772, and had opened a correspondence with CB with a letter dated 20 Aug. 1771 (Scholes, i. 199–201; original MS now in the Staats- und Universitätsbibliothek, Hamburg). For Ebeling's letters to CB, see G. M. Stewart, 'Christoph Daniel Ebeling, Hamburger Pädagoge und Literaturkritiker, und seine Briefe an Charles Burney', *Zeitschrift des Vereins für Hamburgische Geschichte*, lxi (1975), 33–58.

[2] In his letter of 20 Aug. 1771, Ebeling had written, 'it went into my mind to communicate with You a litle Essay of an Advice to form a selected musical library which I published in one of our Magazines just when I got Your Book.' Ebeling's 'Versuch einer auserlesenen musikalischen Bibliotheck' had appeared in *Hamburger Unterhaltungen*, x (1770), 303–22, 504–34, a periodical edited by Ebeling. It is his most important contribution to music, and 'places him in the company of Burney, Hawkins and Gerbert as one of the first music historians' (*New Grove*).

[3] Karl Friedrich Abel (1723–87); Johann Schobert (*c.*1735–67); Johann Gottfried Eckard (1735–1809); Ernst Eichner (1740–77); Johann Christian Fischer (1733–1800); Georg Christoph Wagenseil (1715–77); Friedrich Schwindl (1737–86); Franz Joseph Haydn (1732–1809). See *New Grove*.

[4] In addition to the general reference to Abel's symphonies and chamber music, CB alludes specifically to Abel's *Six Sonatas for the Harpsicord with Accompanyments for a Violin or German Flute, and Violoncello* ... *Opera II* [1760]; and *Six sonates pour le clavecin, avec l'accompagnement d'un violon ou flute traversiere et d'un violoncelle* ... *Oeuvre V* [1764]. See W. Knape, *Bibliographisch-thematisches Verzeichnis der Kompositionen von Karl Friedrich Abel* (Cuxhaven, 1971), nos. 111–16, 117–22.

Bach,[5] who stands so high in my opinion, that I should not scruple to pronounce him the greatest writer for the Harpsichord now alive, or that has ever existed as far as I am able to judge, by a comparison of his works with those of others, & by my own Feelings when I hear them performed. I am very happy in finding that my opinions of almost all the Composers you have named, with whose works I am acquainted, are so like yours, that if you had not seen many of them in my Book before I had the honour of your Letter, it might seem in me an affected complaisance towards your decisions: but you will perceive from my writing, that we think alike of Jomelli, Galuppi, Piccini, Sacchini, L'Atilla,[6] &c.

But I will now go still further in my musical Creed; I confess to you, that of all the Composers of songs that have ever existed in any Country, Hasse stands the highest in my opinion.[7] He is possessed of grace, invention, propriety beyond all others. The Poet & the singer are equally respected by him, & he never sacrifices either to the pedantry of crowding his Score, or the vanity of Instrumental Performers. He has not perhaps the nervous grandeur, I had almost called it martial grandeur of Handel, which so well suited his age & the English nation; but he has more Melody, more simplicity, more taste, & more happiness in the expression of words.[8] I will go further, & confess that the History of the good Padre Martini so replete with learned authorities is what his Countrymen frequently call it, a seccatura; that Blainville

[5] Carl Philipp Emanuel Bach (1714–88), known as the 'Berlin' or 'Hamburg' Bach, second and most famous surviving son of J. S. Bach, under whom he studied, composer and keyboard player, had settled in Hamburg in 1768 (*New Grove*). The Bachs and Abels were family friends; C. P. E. Bach and Abel, despite their almost 10 years' discrepancy in age, might be called 'fellow students' in the sense that both at some time had been pupils of J. S. Bach. CB, who knew Abel personally, states categorically that Abel had been 'a disciple of Sebastian Bach' (*Hist. Mus.* iv. 678; Mercer, ii. 1018). For CB's account of his meeting with C. P. E. Bach the following year in Hamburg (arranged by Ebeling), see *Tours*, ii. 211–20.

[6] See CB to Garrick, 17–[18] Oct. 1770, nn. 26–8, 52, 56.

[7] Johann Adolf Hasse (1699–1783), one of the most widely admired composers, particularly of *opera seria*, in his day. See *New Grove* for an account of his career. CB was to meet Hasse on his German tour, and recorded the encounter in *Tours*, ii. 118–20. See also *Hist. Mus.* iv. 548–9; Mercer, ii. 918; Rees.

[8] In an unpublished and undated MS notebook which he entitled 'Materials Towards the History of German Music & Musicians', CB compared Hasse and Handel: 'Handel's operas did not exceed 40.—But his Oratorios amount to upwards of 20 & indeed Hasse has likewise Composed a great N° of oratorios, Masses, Cantatas, Duets, Misereres, Salvs Reginas, Stabat Maters &c wch are very much esteemed in Italy & Germany, so that he may be said to be as voluminous a Composer as Handel. W^ch was the best of the two I shall not pretend to determine. Both had great merit in a different way. Such as admire manliness of style, richness of Harmony & ingenuity of Contrivance will vote in favour of Handel: while others who admire an Elegant simplicity, refined Taste, clearness, & a judicious & happy Expression of Words, will give their Suffrage to Hasse. But nothing can be more illiberal & unjust than to exalt the one at the Expence of the other, especially when it is done, as is frequently the Case, sans connoissance de Cause, as the best Works of Hasse are but in few Hands in England, so that where 9 out of 10

is execrable, even among Frenchmen;[9] Marpurg's critische Einlietung in die Gaschichte &c of Music,[10] affords me very few materials for my Work, which I have not repeatedly found in others. He is too short even as far as he has gone. It seems to me rather an INDEX of a complete general History, than the work itself. & his severe decisions concerning the modern Italians, I can by no means subscribe to; namely that they are *elende componisten*: & particularly that Galuppi ist ein *schlechter* componist.[11] M. Marpurg must have decided without sufficient information concerning the works of modern Composers, or must be governed by prejudice. Tartini was alive when he wrote, who with Durante,[12] Vallotti, Galuppi, Jomelli, [L]Atilla, Perez,[13] Piccini, &c, are enough to mark any Age. & I believe there have seldom been more great Geniusses alive at any one period. But then they are accused of writing in too light a style—but Grace, Fancy, Feeling & clearness, are to me superiour to all other merits. There are Times for shewing learning & contrivance; but I think the best of all contrivances in Music, is to please people of discernment & taste, without trouble. A long & laboured Fugue, *recte et retro* in 40 parts,[14] may be a good Entertainment for the *Eyes* of a Critic, but can never delight the *Ears* of a Man of Taste. I was no less surprised than pleased to find Mr C. P. E. Bach get out of the trammels of Fugues & crowded parts in which his Father so excelled. Domenico Scarlatti did the same at a

think it blasphemy to name him in Competition wth Handel: yet on the Continent little more than the Name of Handel, carried thither by the English has been heard. How is it then possible either for the generality of English or Foreigners to form a Comparative Judgm^t Concerning the Merit of these great Composers?' (Osborn shelves c 100, p. [41]).

[9] Charles-Henri de Blainville (*fl.* 1710–77), French cellist, composer, and music theorist, whose *Histoire générale, critique et philologique de la musique* (1767) CB considered 'a work for which the author's materials seem to have been so scanty, that he was reduced to fill two-thirds of his thin quarto volume, with an indigested treatise on composition' (*Hist. Mus.* iv. 626; Mercer, ii. 979). CB's copy is listed in 'Cat. Fac. Mus.', item 16.

[10] Friedrich Wilhelm Marpurg (1718–95), prolific German writer on music, whose *Kritische Einleitung in die Geschichte und Lehrsätze der alten und neuen Musik* (Berlin, 1759) CB owned. His copy ('Cat. Fac. Mus.', item 92) is preserved in the British Library (556. c. 11).

[11] In the unpaginated Index at the end of the *Kritische Einleitung*, Marpurg gives the entry 'Galuppi, ein schlechter Componist'; to his entry '*Italiäner* sind heutiges Tages elende Componisten', CB added in his own copy (n. 10) in pencil the marginal comment: 'not true'.

[12] Francesco Durante (1684–1755), Neapolitan composer of church music and influential music teacher, whose pupils included Paisiello, Sacchini, Pergolesi, and Piccinni. See *Hist. Mus.* iii. 536; Mercer, ii. 426; Rees; *New Grove*.

[13] David Perez (1711–78), Spanish composer of operas and church music, born and educated in Naples. In 1752 he journeyed to Lisbon, and settled at the Portuguese Court as *maestro di cappella*. See *Hist. Mus.* iv. 570–2; Mercer, ii. 934–6; *New Grove*.

[14] CB alludes to Thomas Tallis's forty-part motet *Spem in alium*, which he later called 'this stupendous, though perhaps Gothic, specimen of human labour and intellect' (*Hist. Mus.* iii. 74–5; Mercer, ii. 67–8). CB possessed a MS copy described as 'Song of 40 Parts, original ancient score, MS', which was sold for 5*s*. (*Cat. Mus. Lib.*, lot 405). See P. Doe, *Tallis* (1968), pp. 41, 47–8.

Time when a Fugue followed every passage like its Shadow. They both struck out a style of their own. Scarlatti's full of Enthusiasm fire & passion, Bach's every thing, by turns, that music can express.[15]

The offer you so kindly make of procuring me Books, I accept with the utmost gratitude. It will enable me to do justice to your Countrymen, which, as you very truly observe, has not yet been done i[n] any attempt at a History of Music. I shall not rest till I am able to Read many of the Books you mention;[16] & if you will push your zeal for the interest of Music in general, & of my labours in particular so far as to send me over the following Books, if you can possibly procure them for me, you will serve & oblige me extremely, & I will instantly reimburse you whatever sum they may cost, upon knowing what it is, to Mr Böhmen,[17] or to any other friend or Correspondent you chuse in this Kingdom.

Joh. Mathewson's Ehrenptforte.[18]
Scheiben's Kritischer musickus.[19]
Marpurg's historisch krit: Beyträge[20]
Walther's Musikalisches Lexicon.[21]

[15] Giuseppe Domenico Scarlatti (1685–1757) studied under his father, Pietro Alessandro Gaspare Scarlatti (1660–1725). In his *German Tour*, CB again pointed out the similarities between Domenico Scarlatti and C. P. E. Bach: 'Both were sons of great and popular composers, regarded as standards of perfection by all their contemporaries, except their own children, who dared to explore new ways to fame' (*Tours*, ii. 220). See also R. Kirkpatrick, *Domenico Scarlatti* (Princeton, 1953), pp. 8–11.

[16] At this very time Fanny Burney recorded in her Journal: 'My Father is at present most diligently studying German. He has an unquenchable thirst of knowledge—& would in time, I believe, be the first Linguist in England' (*EJL* i. 174). Time never vouchsafed CB mastery of the German language: 'I am now so surrounded & bewildered with *Charman* books of all kinds, that I shall fret myself to Sauer-Kraut if you do not come & disentangle me soon' (CB to C. I. Latrobe, [1788]).

[17] Perhaps Johann Gottlob Böhme, or Böhmen (1717–80), German man of letters and Professor (1757) of History at Leipzig (*ADB*), whom Fanny Burney lists as a visitor to the Burney household in 1772 (*EJL* i. 181).

[18] Johann Mattheson (1681–1764), whose collection of biographies of contemporary musicians was published under the title *Grundlage einer Ehren-Pforte* (Hamburg, 1740). See 'Cat. Fac. Mus.', item 99.

[19] Johann Adolph Scheibe (1708–76), composer and theorist. *Der critische Musikus*, in which he attacked Italian operatic conventions, appeared first as a fortnightly, then as a weekly periodical at Hamburg between 1737 and 1740. CB acquired the second edition, collected under the title *Critischer Musikus* (Leipzig, 1745). See 'Cat. Fac. Mus.', item 131.

[20] Marpurg's *Historisch-kritische Beyträge zur Aufnahme der Musik* (Berlin, 1754–78), of which all parts had been published by 1762, save the sixth (1778). CB's set of these volumes was sold for 4s. 6d. (*Cat. Misc. Lib.*, lot 1064).

[21] Johann Gottfried Walther (1684–1748), German musician and lexicographer. His *Musikalisches Lexicon; oder, musicalische Bibliothec* (Leipzig, 1732), pioneered the mixture of biographical and technical articles in a single musical reference work. CB's copy is listed in 'Cat. Fac. Mus.', item 152.

Marpurg's Handbuch dey dem Generasbasse[22]

C. P. E. Bach's art das clav. zu spielen[23]

Marpurg von der Fuge Feanzösische[24]

Nichelman von der melodie[25]

Quantz Anweisung die Flöte Trav. zu spiel[26]

Ernst Gottl: Baron's Historisch Theo. & prat: untersuchung des Inst. des Laute[27]

Mathewson's Life of Handel, as translated & augmented.[28]

Some of the most ancient National Mel[o]dies or German Airs, such as were made before all Europe was overrun with Italian Music, would be very curious & useful in my work, if such can be procured.

I am extremely curious to see some of C. P. E. Bach's *vocal* Music. If you can get me the church music by him mentioned in your Essay,[29] & any new Harp^d Pieces of that Author, I shall receive [them] with great pleasure. Whatever Books & Music relative to my History that you think usefull & can procure for me, I beg of you to send with those above mentioned. I am certain you are an excellent Judge of what will do most honour to your Country men, & my work. It is my intention to give examples of style in different peri[o]ds & Countries.[30] I need

[22] *Handbuch bey dem Generalbasse und der Composition* ..., which had been published in three parts (Berlin, 1755–8). 'Cat. Fac. Mus.', item 93, shows that CB acquired the second edition of the work, which carried a revised first part (Berlin, 1762). It was sold for 12s. (*Cat. Mus. Lib.*, lot 923).

[23] *Versuch über die wahre Art das Clavier zu spielen* ..., in two parts (Berlin, 1753, 1762). CB's copy was sold for 15s. (*Cat. Mus. Lib.*, lot 877).

[24] *Abhandlung von der Fuge* ..., in two parts (Berlin, 1753, 1754), abridged and translated into French by the author as *Traité de la fugue et du contrepoint* (Berlin, 1756). CB acquired a copy of this translation ('Cat. Fac. Mus.', item 90).

[25] Christoph Nichelmann (1717–62), harpsichordist and composer, wrote a treatise on the nature of melody, *Die Melodie nach ihrem Wesen sowohl, als nach ihren Eigenschaften* (Danzig, 1755).

[26] Johann Joachim Quantz (1697–1773), flautist, wrote the *Versuch einer Anweisung, die Flöte traversiere zu spielen* ... (Berlin, 1752). CB's copy is listed in *Cat. Mus. Lib.*, lot 909.

[27] Ernst Gottlieb Baron (1696–1760), lutenist and writer on music, published the *Historisch-theoretisch und practische Untersuchung des Instruments der Lauten* (Nuremberg, 1727).

[28] Mattheson, who was an acquaintance of Handel, translated into German John Mainwaring's *Memoirs of the Life of the late George Frederic Handel* (1760), the first book-length biography of a composer. Ebeling had written to CB in his letter of 20 Aug.: 'the Life of Handel is very imperfectly written in english, but translated into German, corrected and augmented by Mr. Matheson an ancient friend of Mr. Handel's.' Mattheson's *Georg Friderich Händels Lebensbeschreibung* ... was published in Hamburg in 1761.

[29] Ebeling had listed in his 'Versuch', pp. 319–20, four sacred musical works by C. P. E. Bach: the *Magnificat* in D (Wq. 215); an otherwise unidentified 'Ostermusik, 1766'; the oratorio *Die Israeliten in der Wüste* (Wq. 238); and a 'Passion, 1770', which may be identified as the passion-cantata *Die letzten Leiden des Erlösers* (Wq. 233). See A. Wotquenne, *Thematisches Verzeichnis der Werke von Carl Philipp Emanuel Bach (1714–1788)* (Leipzig, 1905).

[30] CB's intended section in his *History of Music* on National Music did not materialize. See Lonsdale, pp. 143, 160.

say no more to one so well informed. I am already in possession of Marpurg's crit. Hist. of ancient Music,[31] & a friend has lent me Mathewson's Grosse general bass-schute—printed at Ham. 1731.[32] & Wolffgan Gaspar Printsens von Waldthurn Phrynis mitilenæus. Dresd. 1696.[33]

To John Alcock[1]   [Queen Square], 26 November 1771

L copy extract (Osborn).
Docketed by FBA: For Memoirs of Dr. Burney⎟To Dr Alcock.   *And by* ?: Lett^r to Dr Alcock⎟Farinelli   *And by* ??: Extract⎟of a Letter⎟To Dr Alcock⎟Novr 26⎟1771

... There is a circumstance relative to the Birth & name of Farinelli, which I did not chuse to mention during his Life,[2] which is, that he was the Son of a *Musical Baker*, at Naples, called Broschi & it was alluding to his father's trade that he was nick-named Farinelli,[3] or the little Baker, *Farina* being Italian for wheat Flour, is frequently extended to such as use it, or rather, perhaps, to such Bakers as are meal merchants, as is the case of some of ours. Jaycock[4] was a celebrated

[31] See above, nn. 10, 11.
[32] Mattheson's *Grosse General-Bass-Schule* ... (Hamburg, 1731), is listed in 'Cat. Fac. Mus.', item 98.
[33] Wolfgang Caspar Printz (1641–1717), composer and theorist, born at Waldthurn in the Upper Palatinate, whose important work *Phrynis Mitilenaeus, oder Satyrischer Componist* (Dresden and Leipzig, 1696), is 'one of the most extensive summaries of music theory written in Germany in the 17th century' (*New Grove*).

[1] John Alcock (1715–1806), B.Mus. (1755), D.Mus. (1766), English organist and composer. A school-fellow of Boyce, apprenticed to John Stanley, he had been organist of Lichfield Cathedral (1750–before 1765). He was currently organist of the parish churches of Sutton Coldfield, Warwickshire (1761–86), and Tamworth, Staffordshire (1766–90). For his works and antiquarian interests, see *New Grove*.
[2] Alcock had probably written to CB after reading in the *Italian Tour* CB's account of Farinelli's life and career (pp. 205–17; *Tours*, i. 153–7). Perhaps Alcock supplied CB with additional information about Farinelli, which he suggested should be included in the second edition of the *Tour*.
[3] After Carlo Broschi's death in 1782, CB included this explanation for the nickname 'Farinelli' in the last volume of the *History of Music*, published in 1789 (iv. 379 n.; Mercer, ii. 789 n.). Farinelli's father, Salvatore Broschi (1681–1717), was Royal Viceroy at Maratea and Cisternino (1706–9) and a music master and composer, not a baker. The castrato's professional nickname appears to have been derived from that of the Neapolitan family Farina, the boy's patrons (*New Grove*). See also A. Heriot, *The Castrati in Opera* (1956), pp. 95–110.
[4] Samuel Jeacocke (d. *c.*1748), carried on the business of a baker in Clerkenwell. A keen amateur musician, 'when a fiddle or a violoncello did not please him,' he would, 'to mend the tone of it, bake it for a week in a bed of saw-dust' (Hawkins, v. 351). See also 'Jeacock' in Rees.

musical Baker with us, in my Time. He was Brother to the famous President of the Robin-hood Club,[5] who was possessed of great natural parts, by the meer force of which, without Education, he was able to investigate abstruse subjects of human Reason, & to foil in Disputation, Persons greatly his superiors in point of Learning, as well as Birth & situation. I knew the Baker well.[6] He had amassed together a great collection of curious Books on Music, some of which I purchased at the sale of his Effects after his decease, 18 or 20 years ago. Tho' he played on no instrument well, but the Tenor,[7] he had attempted several others, & had a very singular faculty upon the Harpsichord, of playing the changes of any number of Bells, as far as 10,[8] for Hours together, in as quick succession as they are usually rung. He had in his younger Days, been a great Ringer & had literally the several Peals of 6. 8. or 10 Bells so much at his *finger's Ends*, that he played with facility from memory & reflection, what, if reduced to Musical Notation, would scarce be practicable to the greatest Performer in Europe. & yet his fingers were stiff, & unable to execute a Birth Day Minuet. I have formerly wrote down a series of changes upon 10 Bells, but so wild was the melody they produced, & so difficult to execute, that I never could equal the honest Baker in playing them. ...

To Christoph Daniel Ebeling

[Queen Square], 30 March 1772

L copy extract (Hamburg).
Endorsed by CB: Extract of a Letter to Mr Ebeling.|Extract of a|Lett^r to M. Ebeling|at Hambro—Mar. | 30th 1772.

London March 30. 1772.[1]

... The Italian composers for the church are innumerable; those of the 16th & 17th Centuries whose works still live, are chiefly o[f] the

---

[5] Caleb Jeacocke (1706–86), also a baker (*DNB*). From 1743 to 1761 he presided over the deliberations and potations of the debating society founded in 1613, which in 1747 moved the venue of its celebrated Monday meetings from the Essex Head in Essex Street to the Robin Hood in Butcher Row, Temple Bar (*The History of the Robinhood Society* (1764), pp. 119–32).

[6] Samuel, the musician. The ensuing sketch of Jeacocke's 'singular faculty' of playing bell-ringing changes on the harpsichord is substantially repeated in CB's article on Jeacocke in Rees.

[7] i.e. viola. Jeacocke 'played on several instruments, but mostly the tenor-violin' (Hawkins, v. 351).

[8] 'Which changes amounted to 3,628,800' ('Jeacock' in Rees). For CB's youthful interest in change-ringing, see *CB Mem.* 6.

[1] The present extract appears to be a reply to a missing letter from Ebeling, written earlier in 1772.

Roman School: as Palestrina, Luca Marenza,[2] Benevoli,[3] Allegri,[4] &c. Of the first & last of these 4, I have given a somewhat particular account in my preface to the compositions which are annually sung in the Pope's Chapel during Passion Week, of which I had the honour to send you a copy,[5] with the translation of a letter from Tartini,[6] as soon as printed, consigned to the care of our friend, Mr Böhmen. You will see in perusing the first mentioned publication, the dry, but chaste, correct, & simple Style of Church Music during the lives of those composers. Marenza was a very voluminous & agreable writer of Madrigals in 4, 5, 6, 7, & 8 parts—his short & detached subjects are pretty & ingenious for the time in which he flourished, which was the latter end of the 16 Century. I got a compleat collection of his Works at Rome by the assistance of Santarelli, the Pope's Maestro di Capella— they consist of 9 Volumes of different Works in separate parts & some in score, any one or more of which I will either lend, or get transcribed for you, if you have the least desire to be in possession of them.[7] He died in 1599. As to the works of Palestrina, they are almost in all hands. I have a great number of them. Among which two Vol^s of madrigals in 5 parts please me the most, & seem to me the best compositions of the kind that ever were produced by Man.[8] Benevoli was remarkable for writing in a great number of parts. I have 3 Masses by him—one for 12 equal Soprano's—one for 4 Choirs con-

[2] Luca Marenzio (1553–99), singer and composer, is chiefly noted as one of the most prolific Italian madrigalists. See *Hist. Mus.* iii. 201–8; Mercer, ii. 165–70; D. Arnold, *Marenzio* (1965).

[3] Orazio Benevoli (1605–72), *maestro di cappella* at the Vatican from 1646 until his death, much of whose church music is written for several choirs in a large number of parts. See *New Grove*.

[4] Gregorio Allegri (1582–1652), singer in the papal choir under Urban VIII, Pope (1623–44). Appointed to the papal choir (after 1630), Allegri wrote most of his sacred works for the Vatican, including the famous *Miserere* (*New Grove*; *Tours*, i. 232–4; *Hist. Mus.* iii. 525; Mercer, ii. 417).

[5] *La Musica che si canta annualmente nelle funzioni della settimana santa, nella cappella pontificia. Composta dal Palestrina, Allegri, e Bai. Raccolta e pubblicata da Carlo Burney. Mus. D.* CB's edition of the Holy Week music performed in the Sistine Chapel was published in London by Robert Bremner. The engraved title-page gives 1771 as the year of publication; the work was first advertised as 'This Day is published' in the *Public Advertiser*, 29 Jan. 1772.

Ebeling wrote in reply on 4 June 1772 (Hamburg): 'I received your kind present, which is a treasure for me, & I return you my sincere thanks for it. I had got the Miserere of Allegri but in a very bad copy, and as for the others I knew nothing of them. I wish to hear these pieces performed once, so I am enraptured with their simplicity full of expression. They are indubitable proofs that all stiles of music old and modern are very effectfull in the hand of geniuses.'

[6] *A Letter from the late Signor Tartini to Signora Maddalena Lombardini (now Signora Sirmen) Published as an Important Lesson to Performers on the Violin, Translated by Dr. Burney.* CB brought out this pamphlet, with the Italian and English texts on facing pages, in the summer of 1771.

[7] Of the large collection of Marenzio's madrigals listed in the sale of CB's music library (*Cat. Mus. Lib.*, lots 366, 369–73, 382), lot 372 appears to describe the set he acquired in Rome: 'madrigals for 5, 6, 7, and 8 voices, in 8 books, MS.' The lot fetched £2. 6s.

[8] CB refers to another musical MS in his library, listed in *Cat. Mus. Lib.*, lot 395 as: 'Palestrina— Madrigale, Motetti e Salmi a 5 Voc. *in score* MS.'.

sisting of 16 voices—& one in 24 real parts or Sei cori.[9]—This was composed in the beginning of the last Century upon the cessation of the plague wch then had raged at Rome. It was performed in St Peter's Church by near 200 Voices, the 6th Choir was placed in the cupola of that stupendous Building, & tradition says the effects produced by such a number of parts reinforced by so many voices was beyond description & imagination.[10] The rest of Italy has had a Series of Able Composers for the church, but to characterize their different Styles would be no easy Matter, as every Age has its *mode* of composition, which 2 or 3 original geniusses at most render prevalent. The rest come all under the denomination of Imitatores, servum, pecus.[11] Indeed during the 15th Century the Music of all Europe was so much of the same cast that no difference could be found but in the words to which it was applied, in that of Spain, France, Italy, Germany or England. No melody was admitted but what w^d afford an *Answer* or an imitation in the several parts—no rhythm was attended to in the words, & it is but very lately I think that music can be said to have any thing like it. At present it has in good compositions, its accents, its phrases, & its periods; all capable of being as strongly marked by the performer as those of Rhetoric or Poetry by an Orator, or declaimer. The Musical library of St Marks Church at Venice is so rich in Masses & other choral Music, that Lord Bute,[12] a Scots Nobleman, the year I was in Italy had a collection made from them to the amount of near 200 Volumes. The compositions of Lotti,[13] & Marcello[14] are most esteemed among these, & are still as frequently performed at Venice as those of Palestrina & Benevoli throughout Italy. About the middle of the last Century or somewhat later Mazzocchi was at the head of

---

[9] Listed in *Cat. Mus. Lib.* as lots 228–9. For CB's comments on Benevoli's 'curious productions' and wonderful 'powers of managing an unwieldy score', see *Hist. Mus.* iii. 525; Mercer, ii. 417–18.

[10] See *Hist. Mus.* ii. 11 n.; Mercer, i. 416 n., where the same story is related.

[11] 'Imitators, you servile herd'. Horace, *Epistles*, I. xix. 19.

[12] John Stuart (1713–92), 3rd Earl of Bute (1723), statesman and royal favourite (*DNB*). In bad health, Bute had left England for France and Italy in Nov. 1769, arrived in the vicinity of Venice in Dec. and returned to London in May 1771 (*Tours*, i. 96; Walpole *Corresp.* xxiii. 152, 161, 297, 302, 312).

[13] Antonio Lotti (*c.*1667–1740), singer and organist, elected *primo maestro di cappella* of St Mark's, Venice, in 1736. While in Venice CB had been moved 'even to tears' by one of Lotti's masses (*Tours*, i. 115).

[14] Benedetto Marcello (1686–1739), violinist and composer, was a student of Lotti. Marcello is celebrated for his musical setting of the first fifty psalms, *Estro Poetico-armonico* (Venice, 1724–6), which CB considered somewhat '*over-praised*: as the subjects of many of his fugues and airs are not only common and old-fashioned at present, but were far from new at the time these psalms were composed' (*Hist. Mus.* iv. 543; Mercer, ii. 912–13).

the Roman College;[15] & according to Bontempi it was under his direction that the regular System of study mention'd in the preface referred to above, was instituted, & most successfully pursued.[16] I have seen some excellent Motets & masses by Mazzocchi.—Clari of Pisa[17] & Perti of Bologna[18] are admirable in their way.—Clari's duets & Trio's are much in the Style of Steffano's[19]—& Perti wrote in many parts as correctly as Palestrina with more melody. I have an *Adoramus* for 4 voices by him which is very much esteemed all over Italy, & a Mass printed in 15 parts.[20] Among those of the present Century, Old Scarlatti,[21] Leo,[22] Feo,[23] Abos,[24] Durante, Pergolesi, Hasse & Jomelli stand ⟨out⟩ most as Composers for the church. I might add Fioroni of Milan, & Vallotti of Padua.[25] The Masses of Old Scarlatti are but little known. However Jomelli assured [me] that Italy never produced a greater man in that kind of writing.[26] When Hasse was Maestro of

[15] Virgilio Mazzocchi (1597–1646), composer, was *maestro* of the Cappella Giulia of St Peter's, Rome, from 1629 until his death. Palestrina was a predecessor, and Benevoli the successor of Mazzocchi in this appointment. See J. M. Llorens, *Le opere musicali della cappella giulia*, in *Studi e Testi*, cclxv (Vatican, 1971), pp. v–xxi; *New Grove*.

[16] Bontempi (see CB to Warton, 12 Aug. 1771, n. 11) studied under Mazzocchi in Rome. In the introductory preface (pp. iii–iv) to his edition of the papal Holy Week music, CB translated from Bontempi's *Historia musica* (Perugia, 1695), p. 170, the account of the rigorous daily schedule of study and practice introduced by Mazzocchi for musical students training for the Vatican choirs.

[17] Giovanni Carlo Maria Clari (1677–1754), composer, *maestro di cappella* at Pisa from 1736 to his death. His vocal chamber music, set to religious texts, enjoyed a vogue in England during the eighteenth century (see n. 19).

[18] Giacomo Antonio Perti (1661–1756), 'a solid grave composer of church Music', was *maestro di cappella* at San Petronio, Bologna (1696–1756), and one of Padre Martini's musical mentors (*New Grove*; *Hist. Mus.* iv. 51; Mercer, ii. 536).

[19] Agostino Steffani (1654–1728), composer of operas and church music, diplomat, and titular Bishop of Spiga (1706). His duets for two voices and continuo represent an important stage in the development of Italian vocal music (*New Grove*). 'There are perhaps no compositions more correct, or fugues in which the subjects are more pleasing, or answers and imitations more artful, than are to be found in the duets of Steffani ... [Clari's] style of duetti and terzetti certainly resembles that of Steffani, but we find no similarity of passage, and sometimes he is superior to the Abate in grandeur of subject, and elegance of phrase in his melodies' (*Hist. Mus.* iii. 535–6; Mercer, ii. 425–6).

[20] Perti's *Messa e salmi concertati a quattro voci, con strumenti e ripieni ... opera seconda* (Bologna, 1735), is listed in *Cat. Mus. Lib.*, lot 397. The *Adoramus* has not been traced.

[21] Alessandro Scarlatti (1660–1725), best known for his operas and cantatas, father of Domenico.

[22] Leonardo Ortensio Salvatore di Leo (1694–1744), leading Neapolitan composer 'equally celebrated as an instructor' (*Hist. Mus.* iv. 544–5; Mercer, ii. 914–15).

[23] Francesco Feo (1691–1761), composer and teacher, whom CB called 'one of the greatest Neapolitan masters of his time' (*Hist. Mus.* iv. 550; Mercer, ii. 919).

[24] Girolamo Abos (1715–60), Maltese composer, 'a good master of the Neapolitan school' (*Hist. Mus.* iv. 466; Mercer, ii. 854–5).

[25] For Fioroni and Vallotti, see CB to Garrick, 17–[18] Oct. 1770, nn. 15, 20.

[26] Jommelli 'spoke very much in praise of Alessandro Scarlatti, as to his church music, such as motets, masses, and oratorios' (*Tours*, i. 259).

the Conservatorio of la Pietà at Venice, he composed a Miserere which is annually sung there in Passion Week,[27] with as much veneration as that of Allegri is at Rome. *I* am in possession of this piece,[28] which is saying that *you* may be so, whenever you please. I have a list of Pergolesi's works somewhere, but cannot find it now. However, I believe he never composed more than two serious Operas, & a Burletta & a half, with 2 or 3 Intermezzi.[29] He was a very slow writer, as I have been assured by those who knew him Personally: his Instrument was the Violin. He absolutely killed himself by mental & bodily labour. He Died very young of a Consumption—not poisoned, as has been said, but emaciated by a Cough & too intense application. I procured at Naples all his Church Music not Printed. His Stabat Mater has long been so in England, & his salve Regina in France.[30] The MSS. I procured are as follow—Messa a due Cori con stromenti—Miserere—Messa a'5 voi.—Laudate e Confitebor a'Canto solo—Salve Regina & a Dixit.[31] I did not get a complete Score of his Olympiade, as the best songs have been long Printed in England. . . .[32]

. . . [33]It is very hard that Men of taste & feeling are to be judged by those that have none—I would have every Artist & Man of Genius, tried by his Peers. But even in our free Government, they are denied this priviledge, granted in our Courts of Judicature to all other Ranks & degrees of Men! . . .

[27] Hasse was associated with the Ospedale degli Incurabili (not the Pietà) in Venice. Numerous biographers have stated that Hasse was *maestro di cappella* of the Incurabili from 1727 to 1731 and wrote his celebrated *Miserere* for that institution in 1728. For a sceptical appraisal of both claims, see S. H. Hansell, 'Sacred Music at the *Incurabili* in Venice at the Time of J. A. Hasse—I', *Journal of the American Musicological Society*, xxiii (1970), 282–301, and his article 'Johann Adolf Hasse' in *New Grove*.

[28] *Cat. Mus. Lib.*, lot 252 lists a *Miserere* in MS by Hasse, which is possibly the work to which CB alludes.

[29] For a full listing of Pergolesi's secular vocal music for the stage, see M. E. Paymer, *Giovanni Battista Pergolesi, 1710–1736, a Thematic Catalogue of the Opera Omnia* (New York, 1977), pp. 37–56; for those CB owned, see *Cat. Mus. Lib.*, lots 566–8.

[30] Pergolesi died in 1736 at the age of 26. His *Stabat Mater* was first published in London by John Walsh the younger (1709–66) in *Le Delizie dell Opere* . . ., vol. v (1748), pp. 2–26, separately in 1749, and subsequently in many editions. The *Salve Regina* to which CB refers was published in Paris by Antoine Huberty (*c*.1722–91) in 1760. See W. C. Smith and C. Humphries, *A Bibliography of the Musical Works Published by the Firm of John Walsh during the Years 1721–1766* (1968), nos. 560, 1195; and Cari Johansson, *French Music Publishers' Catalogues of the Second Half of the Eighteenth Century* (Stockholm, 1955), p. 42.

[31] Listed in *Cat. Mus. Lib.*, lots 277, 276, 279, 280–1, 278. The *Dixit* is not listed.

[32] CB refers to *The Favourite Songs in the Opera call'd L'Olimpiade*, published by Walsh, *c*.1753; republished in *Le Delizie dell Opere* . . ., vol. vi (1753), pp. 1–21; vol. ix (*c*.1760), pp. 118–38 (Smith and Humphries, *Walsh*, nos. 1138, 561, 564).

[33] This paragraph is separated from the main body of the letter by a line and the endorsement 'Same Letter'.

To Baron d'Holbach

Queen Square,
2 June 1772

LS copy (Osborn: 'Letterbook, Musical Correspondence').
Addressed: A Monsieur Le Baron D'Holbach. | Rue Royale—butte de S. Rock—A Paris. *Docketed by* FBA: ✳

London, Queen's Square
Bloomsbury.

Sir.

It is very painful to me to think how insensible I must appear to the singular marks of your Goodness with which I have been honoured. Ingratitude for Benefits received contributes to harden the most benevolent hearts, & by degrees dries up the source of human kindness, & Philanthropy. But let me remove a little of this apparent Guilt from myself by assuring you that the German Books you were so kind to remember, & to procure & send me by the care of Col. Barre, did not arrive for several months after your most welcome Letter anounced them[1]—there had been a Stop at the Custom house, or elsewhere of the Colonels Baggage which occasion'd this delay. I find a great number of useful materials for my Historical Work in the writings of Marpurg, with which you have been so kind as to furnish me. As to his Genius & taste, I think them both inferior to his Learning—he is a favourer of the old fashion'd french Music, & consequently has but little toleration for other kinds. He treats with contempt due only to Ignorance & Dulness, some of the best modern Composers of Italy. He has written an excellent Book upon the Fugue[2]—at a time when, unluckily for him & his treatise, Fugues are regarded as remains of Gothic Barbarism—& exploded by all men of true taste. However, supposing his Musical tenets to be erroneous, there still remain historical facts in his Publications, relative to the lives of eminent Musicians—Musical Establishments—celebrated Organs & Organists of Germany, which are very much to my purpose. I have received lately from Hamburg, beside⟨s⟩ a great quantity of excellent Music by the best Composers of the North, several works upon the Theory of Music

---

[1] D'Holbach had written to CB on 15 Dec. 1771 (Osborn), informing him that he was sending 'les livres de Musique allemande que vous desiriez' in the care of Isaac Barré (1726–1802), soldier and politician, MP for Chipping Wycombe (1761–74), for Calne (1774–90), lieutenant-colonel (1761). See *DNB*; Namier and Brooke, ii. 50–4.

[2] *Abhandling von der Fuge*. See CB to Ebeling, Nov. 1771, n. 24.

& its History³—such as Bachs versuch über di wahre art das clavier zu spielen. 3 bander 4ᵗᵒ—Quantzens versuch einer anweisung die flöte Trav: zu spielen.—Hillers Nachrichten und anmerkungen die Musik betreffend—3 bander 4ᵗᵒ4—Mathesons Ehren-p.forte 4ᵗᵒ— Scheibens kritischer musikus.—Walthers Musicalisches Lexicon.— kritische Briefe über die Tonkunst, mit kleinen Clavier Stücken und singoden. 3 bander. 4ᵗᵒ5—Matheson's Lebenlauff von G. F. Händel— &c—These Books, together with those for which I am so much indebted to you, & the great number of German compositions I am now possessed of, are so far from repressing my Curiosity after the Musical Productions of the Germans that they excite a fresh desire to see & to hear more—And I am now on the Point of visiting the Principal Cities of the Netherlands, Germany & Holland in search of Musical Curiosity, & materials for my great Work.⁶ Rambling thus all over Europe after a single art will perhaps be thought by some a greater madness than that of which the Chevalier Quixote was guilty of in strolling only thro' the kingdoms of Spain after a single imaginary Mistress—But nothing is so subject to change as Fashion even among Men of Letters & Philosophers. We are told that Homer, Heroditus, Pythagoras, Plato, Pausanias &c travell'd to the remotest parts of the whole world in search of knowledge concerning men & things—mais nous avons changé tout cela—an Historian and Philosopher now find it more commode to travel thro' Books, & over Maps by the fire side, than to waste their Health, Time, & money in the search of Information elsewhere. To compile is much easier than to compose.—In the Journey I am now going to take I do not always expect to meet with a down Bed or a french Cook—perhaps I shall frequently, instead of these meet only with clean Straw & Pompernichel—but the Expectation of such Inconveniencies by no means abates my rage for Visiting every City I can get at between Brussels & Vienna—between Vienna & Hamburg—coming home thro' Holland. In the course of my Tour Dresden, Berlin, Manheim, Munich, &c will not be neglected. A Man

---

³ Only those works not listed in CB to Ebeling, Nov. 1771, are identified below.

⁴ Johann Adam Hiller, or Hüller (1728–1804), conductor, composer, and teacher, whose *Wöchentliche Nachrichten und Ammerkungen, die Musik betreffend* (Leipzig, 1766–70), was the earliest German musical periodical to include contemporary reviews and news. CB's set is listed in 'Cat. Fac. Mus.', item 65.

⁵ Marpurg's *Kritische Briefe über die Tonkunst, mit kleinen Klavier-Stücken und Singoden* (Berlin, 1760–4).

⁶ Early in May 1772, CB had startled his family after a Sunday concert at home. Sir William Hamilton, who had attended the *soirée*, planned to return to Naples in June: 'He said he should pass through Germany—"shall you—cried my Father—"why I believe *I* shall go to Germany this summer.—" ... I verily believe, though this was said *en passant*, that my Father will reflect upon it—for he has an insatiable rage of adding to the materials for his History' (*EJL* i. 219–20; also p. 224).

of Letters at Hamburg has done my Little Book the honour to translate it into German,[7] he has likewise apprised the Musical People in many places of my Intention to visit them—this—& Letters from Lord Sandwich[8] & other Friends of my Enterprize, to our Ministers & Consuls in the Several Northern Courts will I hope facilitate my Enquiries.

If you can point out to me any person or thing that will be serviceable to my undertaking & will honour me with a Line addressed to me Poste restante, at Brussels, Antworp or Vienna, I shall ever regard it as a Benefaction to my History, & a considerable Addition to the favours you have already so kindly conferred on him who has the honour to be

with the most profound respect
& Sincere Attachment
Chas Burney.

I have had the pleasure of frequently seeing M. Morellet,[9] & of dining with him twice at Garricks, where M. le Baron et Madame la Baronne, sa famille—aussi bien que tous les Hommes illustres de sa Societé, are never forgotten in our *toastes* a l'angloises—Messrs Diderot & Grimm[10]

---

[7] Ebeling's translation of CB's *Italian Tour* appeared under the title *Carl Burney's der Musik Doctors Tagebuch einer Musikalischen Reise durch Frankreich und Italien welche er unternommen hat um zu einer allgemeinen Geschichte der Musik Materialien zu sammlen. Aus dem Englischen übersetzt von C. D. Ebeling, Aufsehern der Handlungsakademie zu Hamburg* (Hamburg, 1772). It was published by Johann Joachim Christoph Bode (1730–93).

[8] John Montagu (1718–92), 4th Earl of Sandwich (1729), First Lord of the Admiralty (1771–82), with whom CB had become familiar after meeting him at Houghton, Norfolk, in summer 1771. See *DNB*; Lonsdale, pp. 111–12. In the Introduction to his *German Tour*, CB wrote: 'I am principally indebted to the patronage of the Earl of Sandwich, who, to assist me in calling the attention of the public to the history of his favourite art ... was pleased to honour me with recommendatory letters, in his own hand, to every English nobleman and gentleman who resided in a public character in the several cities through which I passed; the influence of which was so powerful as to gain me easy access to those who were not only the most able, but whom I was so fortunate as to find the most willing to forward my undertaking' (*Tours*, ii, p. xii).

[9] The abbé André Morellet visited England between Apr. and Oct. 1772, as the guest of William Petty (1737–1805), 2nd Earl of Shelburne (1761), created Marquess of Lansdowne (1784). Before touring the countryside, Morellet spent 6 weeks in May and June in London, where 'Garrick ... me donna pendant mon séjour toutes sortes de marques d'amitié' (*Mémoires inédits de l'abbé Morellet*, ed. P. E. Lémontey (2nd edn., 1822), i. 201–16). Morellet had spent the evening of Sunday 10 May in the Burney home (*EJL* i. 221–2).
In his letter of 15 Dec. 1771 to CB (Osborn), d'Holbach had written, 'vous trouverèz ci-joint une petite brochure de M L'abbé Morellet sur l'expréssion musicale, qu'il me charge de vous faire tenir; elle a eu un grand Succès ici.' Morellet's *De l'Expression en musique*, written in Italy in 1759, was inserted in the *Mercure de France* (Nov. 1771), pp. 113–43. CB considered this work 'full of ingenious ideas, and written with elegance' (*Hist. Mus.* iv. 626; Mercer, ii. 979).

[10] Friedrich Melchior Grimm (1723–1807), Baron (1775), man of letters, and one of Diderot's closest friends, had visited Britain in 1771, accompanying Prince Ludwig of Hesse-Darmstadt (1753–1830). Grimm had invited CB and Garrick to dine with the Prince on 15 Nov. 1771 at 'Thatch's House St. James Street' (Grimm to CB, 14 Nov. [1771], Folger MS Y.c. 1115 (1); see also CB to Diderot, 10 Oct. 1771, n. 1).

are frequently specified on these occasions. May I hope for the honour of being remembered of them sometimes?—

June 2^d 1772.

To Felice de'Giardini[1]

Queen Square,
21 June 1772

LS copy (Osborn: 'Letterbook, Musical Correspondence').
Addressed: Mr Giardini   *Docketed by* FBA: ✕

Dear Sir,

I am again going to ramble over different parts ⟨o⟩f Europe in search of further materials towards the History ⟨o⟩f Ancient & Modern Music. I should have been very happy ⟨i⟩n half an Hours Conversation with you before my Departure, ⟨w⟩hich will be in a few Days; but if it should happen to be inconvenient to you to name a Time when you can allow me that pleasure, I must beg the favour of you to send me, by the Bearer, my sketch of a plan for an English Conservatorio,[2] in order to make a few additions to it. If you should honour it so far as to wish to have it again in your possession, I shall most gladly replace it in the Hands of so perfect a Judge of the Subject, & one whose influence & countenance of it, would more contribute to its Success, than the Patronage of any one Person in the Kingdom. However, if no oppor-

[1] At a private concert in the home of Naphtali Franks in May 1750, CB had first met the great Italian violinist Felice de'Giardini (1716–96), whose recent arrival in England marked 'a memorable aera in the instrumental Music of this kingdom.' CB and the assembled company were thrown into the 'utmost astonishment' by the virtuoso's performance (*CB Mem.* 58). Giardini possessed, however, a mercurial temperament which CB blamed for some of his most acute professional disappointments: 'I was Three times engaged with him in business; but was so much the dupe of his Temper & inadmissible Demands, that against reason & Conviction, I consented to deliver in Proposals of his framing to those with whom we were in treaty wch were so offensive & impracticable as to overset the whole business' ('Biographical Dictionary', MS Osborn shelves c 97, pp. 39–41, 57). For CB's published accounts of Giardini, see *Hist. Mus.* iv. 460, 521–3, 669–72; Mercer, ii. 849–50, 895–6, 1012–14; for an account of CB's subsequent quarrels with him, 'Giardini' in Rees; R. Lonsdale, 'Dr. Burney's "Dictionary of Music"', *Musicology*, v (Sydney, 1979), 167–8; Lonsdale, pp. 78, 152, 227–8.

[2] As CB later related to Thomas Twining (see CB to Twining, 13 July 1774), the scheme to set up a musical conservatory in London on the model of the Italian conservatorios had 'haunted' him. He had drawn up 'the sketch of a plan' and had interested Giardini in it. Various sponsors were considered: the Royal Family, the Fund for Decayed Musicians, and public subscription. In 1774 CB and Giardini finally decided to approach the Governors of the Foundling Hospital. The earlier drafts of CB's plans are not preserved, but two MS drafts from the 1774 attempt are in the Osborn Collection (shelves c 32, 39). These drafts have been collated and edited by Jamie C. Kassler, 'Burney's *Sketch of a Plan for a Public Music-School*', *Musical Quarterly*, lviii (1972), 210–34. See CB to Crisp, [31] May [1771], n. 6.

tunity offers for your procuring it the protection of the Great among your acquaintance, after it is more digested, enlarged & corrected, I really think I shall venture to lay it before the Public at Large, by which it must, perhaps, be ultimately supported. At any rate, I see no disgrace that can accrue to me, for pointing out the practi[ca]bility & usefulness of such an Establishment,[3] as I think it sufficiently obvious & demonstrated, that 'to a Commercial People it would be profitable, or at least œconomical; & to a People who encourage & cultivate the arts it would be honourable.'[4] These being my present sentiments, at my return to England, which will not be till the beginning of Winter, I shall Print, either in a small Pamphlet, or in some other Form, a Prospectus for a Music School.[5] At all Events, I shall constantly hope for your counsel, concurrence & Friendship, in This, & in all my other ⟨mu⟩sical projects, not more from self interest, than the tru⟨e⟩ regard with which I am, dear Sir, your obliged &

most obed^t Ser^t
Charles Bur⟨ney⟩

Queen's Square | June 21st 1772.

To Count Firmian[1]

Queen Square,
22 June 1772

LS copy (Osborn: 'Letterbook, Musical Correspondence').
Addressed: A Son Excellence, M. le Comte Firmian— | A Milan.   *Docketed by* FBA: ×

[3] CB eventually wrote in 1774: 'There is at this Period, a benevolent principle infused into the Hearts of Persons of liberal Minds & affluent Fortunes, ... and it seems as if nothing more were wanting to engage attention, & facilitate encouragement with respect to any new Establishment, than to prove that it is practicable & Useful' (MS Osborn shelves c 39, p. 1; Kassler, 'Burney's *Sketch*', p. 228).
[4] The MS drafts of CB's 1774 'Plan' show his difficulties in phrasing this central appeal to public patriotism and economy. The final text reads: 'Now an Establishment for the cultivation of Musical Talents among our own Natives, would not only save the National Honour, but the National wealth; & thus be of use to us as a Commercial People on the side of Public Œconomy' (Kassler, 'Burney's *Sketch*', p. 229).
[5] CB's 'Plan' or 'Prospectus' never reached print in his lifetime. See Lonsdale, p. 150. Musical education is one of CB's recurring themes in his *German Tour*. At Munich, for example, he showed great interest in 'a *music school* at the Jesuits college' for '*poor scholars*', and at Dresden in 'the Singschüler or singing boys of the *music school*, commonly called *poor scholars*' (*Tours*, ii. 52–4, 150–2).

[1] Carl Joseph Gotthard (1718–82), Graf von Firmian, Austrian statesman, diplomat, and bibliophile, was Governor of Hapsburg-ruled Lombardy from 1759 until his death. CB characterized him as 'a sort of King of Milan' when they met there in July 1770 (*Tours*, i. 79–80, 83–5). See C. Frati, *Dizionario bio-bibliografico dei bibliotecari e bibliofili italiani* (Florence, 1933), pp. 226–7; Walpole *Corresp.* xxi. 271, 282, 339–40.

My Lord,

An address from one who has the honour of being so little know⟨n⟩ to your Excellence will I fear incur the censure of too great boldness—Indeed I have some reason to fear that the time & occasion of my being honoured by your Excellency's notice have long been forgotten—It was in the Month of July 1770 that I executed a small commission, with which I was charged by Mr Strange, of presenting to your excellence some of his Prints,[2] which office I eagerly undertook in hopes of attaining by it access to so illustrious a Personage, & one by whom English Travellers are in a particular Manner treated with Politeness & Hospitality. And this Circumstance of the Prints, slight as it was, procured me the honour of Dining with your Excellence, & a reception so flattering that I shall ever remember it among the most agreable Incidents of my Life. Unluckily my Stay at Milan was too short to afford me an opportunity of improving such favourable dispositions towards me by paying my Duty to your Excellence a second time; And my acquaintance, of a few hours, was not sufficient for me to take the Liberty of informing your Excellence that I had an Object for then visiting Italy, besides that of mere pleasure or common Curiosity—At my return to England I published an account of the motives & success of My Journey in an 8.vo ⟨vol⟩ume, under the title of, 'The present State of Music in France ⟨and⟩ Italy, or the Journal of a Tour through those Countries, under⟨ta⟩ken to collect materials for a General History of Music.'

I had for many years been meditating a History of Music, ⟨and⟩ collecting Materials for that purpose in my own country, but ⟨th⟩e Information I was able to gather there from the dead Letter of ⟨w⟩ritten evidence was so unsatisfactory that I determined to extend my Enquiries to the continent, & I was so content with the result of my Journey, & have been so much flattered by the favourable reception given to my account of it by the Public, that I am now on the Point of visiting the Principal cities of Holland, Germany & the Netherlands with a similar design.

Your Excellence is allowed, universally, to be so perfect a judge, & so unlimited a Protector of the Arts & of Artists, that I flatter myself, & indeed have been flattered by several persons of consideration among my countrymen not unknown to your Excellence, that such an Enterprize, when made known to you, would be honoured by your Countenance & extensive Influence, in facilitating my researches.

Lord Sandwich has been pleased to honour me with Letters to all our Ministers & Consuls resident in the several Cities through which

---

[2] See *Tours*, i. 83.

it is my design to pass.—But as Lord Stormont, our Ambassador at Vienna is upon the Point of quitting that Court, I fear his Lordship will be gone before my arrival there—.[3] In that case I may find it difficult to obtain admission into the Libraries, or access to the Learned that I may wish to consult—The Admirable Metestasio,[4] & the natural & elegant Composer Hasse,[5] I am told both reside at Vienna—Poetry & Musick owe so much to their Superiour abilities, that I have a great ambition to be personnall⟨y⟩ known to them; for in speaking of the Opera they will be deservedly the Hero's of my General History.

By this time your Excellence has penetrated the views with which I have ventured to address you, which I have done in English for 2 reasons: the one is your Excellency's known progress in our Language, & partiality to our Literature: the other, that I am somewhat more able to make my defence for the confidence with which I approach your Excellence in my own vernacular Tongue, than in any other Language.

The two first Cities I shall visit in my way to Vienna are Brussels & Antwerp—where according to Lod: Guicciardini[6] & the Abbé du Bos[7] modern Harmony, or Music in Parts, had its birth & first

[3] David Murray (1727–96), 7th Viscount Stormont (1748), 2nd Earl of Mansfield (1793), statesman and diplomat, had been British Ambassador Extraordinary and Plenipotentiary at the Imperial Hapsburg Court in Vienna since 1763. Although his transfer to the Court of Versailles was announced officially only on 10 Oct. 1772 (*London Gazette*, 6–10 Oct. 1772), his change of Embassy was already common knowledge in June (Walpole *Corresp.* v. 258). Stormont in fact left Vienna to take up his new post as Ambassador to France in Dec. 1772 (Horn, pp. 24–5, 38), and was therefore able to render CB considerable assistance when he arrived in Vienna in Aug. (*Tours*, ii. 76).

[4] Pietro Antonio Domenico Bonaventura Trapassi (1698–1782), called 'Metastasio', Italian poet and dramatist. Metastasio was the most famous librettist of the century: his libretti were set to music by all the major operatic composers. He had settled in Vienna in 1730 as the Imperial Court poet, remaining there till his death. Lord Stormont was to arrange CB's first meeting with Metastasio (*Tours*, ii. 101 ff.). CB greatly admired the poet: in 1779 Mrs Thrale recorded that Dr Johnson 'said he would change with nobody but Hugo Grotius. Burney rather wished to be Metastasio' (*Thraliana*, i. 377). In 1796 CB was to publish his *Memoirs of the Life and Writings of the Abate Metastasio* in three volumes.

[5] Hasse had moved to Vienna in 1761 and there collaborated with Metastasio in professional rivalry with Christoph Willibald Gluck (1714–87). See *Tours*, ii. 95 ff.

[6] Lodovico Guicciardini (1521–89), Florentine patrician, settled in Antwerp (1541), man of letters. His *Descrittione ... di tutti i Paesi Bassi, altrimenti detti Germania Inferiore*, first published at Antwerp in 1567, went through many editions and translations (R. H. Touwaide, *Messire Lodovico Guicciardini: Gentilhomme florentin* (Nieuwkoop, 1975)). CB's copy of the 1588 Antwerp edition of the *Descrittione* is listed in *Cat. Misc. Lib.*, lot 1133.

[7] The abbé Jean-Baptiste Du Bos (1670–1742), French diplomat and critic, whose *Réflexions critiques sur la poésie et sur la peinture* (1719) won him membership in the Académie Française (1720). In a section of his treatise entitled 'Quelques réflexions sur la Musique des Italiens. Que les Italiens n'ont cultivé cet art qu'après les François & les Flamands', Du Bos cites Guicciardini as the authority for his assertion that 'la musique reprit naissance dans les Pays bas, ou pour mieux dire, elle y fleurissoit déjà depuis long-temps avec un succès auquel toute l'Europe rendoit homage' (*Réflexions*, i. 665–70). CB owned two copies of this work, dated 1732 and 1733 (*Cat. Misc. Lib.*, lots 253, 252). See *Tours*, ii. 7, 10, 13–14; *Hist. Mus.* ii. 448–9; Mercer, i. 711.

cultivation. If in any of the Libraries, Churches or Convents proofs could be obtained of this very doubtful & curious point, they would be of no small Importance to my work.

My Timidity in addressing your Excellence upon the Subject of my Journey has made me postpone the sending this Letter so long that I fear it will be impossible for me to receive an Answer to it while in England, if it should be so fortunate as to be honoured with one: but if your Excellence should condescend to devise any means of assisting me in my Enquiries,—or should have the Goodness to point out to me either persons or things, that would be serviceable to my enterprize; a Letter addressed to, Le Docteur Burney, Anglois, poste restante, at Antworp, Brussels, or Vienna would ever be acknowledged as one of the most honourable Benefactions to my Work which I could aspire to.

I have the Honour to Assure your Excellence that I am, with the most profound respect

Your Excellencies most obliged
And most devoted Servant.
Chas Burney.

Queens Square | Bloomsbury | London. | June 22d 1772.

To Sir James Gray[1]

Queen Square,
25 June 1772

LS copy (Osborn: 'Letterbook, Musical Correspondence').
Addressed: To Sir James Gray, K.B.—   *Docketed by* FBA: ✕

Sir,

When I had the honour of seeing you last, you advised me to write to Count Firmian; it was a formal & a formidable kind of thing, which for some Time I was unable to set about. However, in these matters, as in many others, ce n'est que le premier pas qui coute. The Business is now done, but so late, I fear no good can be derived from it. Lord Sandwich has been so kind as to write Letters for me, to most of our Northern Ministers & Consuls. I believe Mr Harris is not so great a Musician as his Father;[2] nor remarkably touched with the charms of

---

[1] Sir James Gray (*c.*1708–73), 2nd Baronet (1722), KB (1761), diplomatist and antiquary, had held diplomatic posts in Venice (1744–53), Naples (1753–65), and Madrid (1767–9). See *DNB Supplement*; Horn, pp. 76, 85, 136. Having enjoyed the *Italian Tour*, Sir James had asked William Mason to introduce him to CB (Mason to CB, 9 May 1771, Osborn; *EJL* i. 152).

[2] James Harris (1709–80), MP for Christchurch (1761–80), a scholar universally nicknamed

Music. I cannot therefore expect that his zeal for my Enquiries will flow spontaneously. His Father is not in London, or I would have begged a Toccatina from him to his degenerate Son.[3] I only mean degenerate with Respect to Music, most certainly, for Mr H. the Minister is extreamly well spoken of in all other particulars: & as the Constable in one of Shakespeare's plays, says, 'these are gifts which God gives—'[4] —I am no more displeased with a Man for not loving or understanding Music, than with his not having black Eyes or being 6 Feet high.—In the present case, it would perhaps, have been more convenient for me, if the Father had been at Berlin, instead of the Son. As it is, the latter, like a craving Horse, will but want a little more spurring.—May I beg of you, sir, to stimulate him in my favour by a Line or two?[5]

As I expect to find Metastasio & Hasse at Vienna, I should be very glad of a Personal acquaintance with them; for in writing about the Italian opera, they will be the Heros of my General History⟨.⟩ I do hope, therefore, that my application to Count Firmian will be productive of something favourable in that particular.[6] & in other places, I hope I shall be able to scramble my way through difficulties, as well

'Hermes' after his treatise *Hermes: or, a Philosophical Inquiry concerning Language and Universal Grammar* (1751). A keen lover of music and the arts, he had also published *Three Treatises* (1744), concerning art; music, painting, poetry; and happiness (*DNB*; Namier and Brooke, ii. 588–9). Harris was an old friend of CB: in autumn 1747, Fulke Greville had taken young Burney along on a visit to Harris (*CB Mem.* 44; Lonsdale, p. 18).

'Hermes' Harris's son, James Harris (1746–1820), 'the foremost diplomat of his age' (Namier and Brooke, ii. 590), MP for Christchurch (1770–4; 1780–8), KB (1779), created Baron (1788), Earl of Malmesbury (1800), had begun his distinguished diplomatic career in 1768 as Secretary of Sir James Gray's Embassy at Madrid. He had arrived in Berlin in Feb. 1772 as Envoy Extraordinary to the Prussian Court (*DNB*; Horn, pp. 136, 108–9). CB's information that the younger Harris did not share his father's passion for music was correct. Harris wrote to his mother from Berlin, 10 Mar. 1772, asking her to send 'all the new and old country dances that have been or are now danced at London, ... It is probably the only music I shall trouble you for' (*A Series of Letters of the First Earl of Malmesbury, His Family and Friends, from 1745 to 1820*, ed. the Earl of Malmesbury (1870), i. 254).

[3] CB nevertheless did manage to get a 'Toccatina' from 'Hermes' Harris, who wrote to CB on 30 June 1772 from his home in the Close at Salisbury: 'Understanding from Mrs Castle, that you wished for a Letter of mine to my son, ... I have taken the liberty to send you the inclosed for y^r perusal, which, when you deliver it to him, you will be pleased to seal' (Osborn).

[4] Dogberry in *Much Ado about Nothing*, III. v. 38–40. CB quotes Dogberry again in the 'Preface' to his *Hist. Mus.* i, p. xii; Mercer, i. 18.

[5] Sir James replied: 'as you go by the way of Dover, you will pass by the end of my Garden, so that I may hope to see you without interrupting your journey, & have an opportunity of giving into your own hands a Letter for my friend Harris ... [who] in Spite of his Ears as a Minister of peace, must be a friend to Harmony' (Gray to CB, 28 June 1772, Osborn).

[6] Sir James also promised to give CB a letter of introduction to Hasse, who, 'besides superior talents in his Profession, is possess'd of many very amiable qualities, & I am persuaded will do you all service in a work, that will interest his own reputation as well as promote the honor of a Science in which he excells. C[ount] Firmian will probably have recommended you to him, & possibly to Metastasio. You have very properly named them together, as their joint productions have carried vocal performance to the highest degree of perfection' (ibid.).

as I did in Italy. The Germans have already done my little Book the Honour to translate it, &, contrary to my expectations, have been very civil to it in their Journals.[7] They are, in general, so jealous of the Italian Musicians, that I rather expected severity from them. However, this will inform them of my views in visiting their Country, & perhaps, put them a little on their Mettle in point of civility, as in performance.

It is my Design to set out next Week for Dover, & from thence to Ostend, whence I can soon get to Brussels & Antwerp. As to the rest of my route[, it] is unsettled, but I hope to see Vienna, Prague, Dresden, Leipsic, Berlin, Hamburg &c. & the Cities on the Rhine, & Holland in my way back. I have the Honour to be, with great Respect, Sir, your obliged & most Humble Servant

Ch. Burney.

Queen's Square, Bloomsbury— | June 25th 1772.

To Charles Davy[1]

Sittingbourne,
3 July 1772

AL draft fragment (Berg: 'Apology to Mr. Davy').
Endorsed by CB: July 3d Apology to Mr Davy | after answering Mr Smear concerning the motion | of the fundamental Base by seconds.   *Docketed by* FBA: ✻ ✳
Hist. | 1772

I wish I cd as easily satisfy myself in answering your polite & flattering Proposal of inscribing Mr Smear's work[2] to one so unworthy of such an honour as myself. I own I have my Fears for myself & doubts for you, Gentlemen, as to the expediency of such an honourable Testimony of

---

[7] See CB to d'Holbach, 2 June 1772, n. 7. Favourable notices of the *Italian Tour* had appeared in *Jenaische Zeitungen von Gelehrten Sachen* (1772), p. 312; *Neue Bibliothek der schönen Wissenschaften und der freyen Künste*, xiii (1772), 174.

[1] The Revd Charles Davy (1723–97), BA (1743), MA (1748), miscellaneous writer, Usher of the Perse School, Cambridge (1747), Rector of Topcroft, Norfolk (1764–97), of Benacre, Suffolk (1766–76), later of Onehouse (1776–97). See J. Venn, *Biographical History of Gonville and Caius College* (Cambridge, 1897–1958), ii. 46; *The Suffolk Garland: or, a Collection of Poems . . . Relative to that County* (Ipswich, 1818), pp. 17–18; *DNB*.

[2] The Revd Christopher Smear (*c*.1742–1802), BA (1763), MA (1767), Fellow of Caius College, Cambridge (1766–8), Curate of Westhall and Brampton, Norfolk (1765), later Rector of Chillesford, Suffolk (1781–1802), of Frostenden (1791–1802). In 1768 Smear and Charles Davy had issued *Proposals for printing by subscription An Essay upon the Principles and Powers of Vocal and Instrumental Music*. The 'Essay' did not reach print, though according to Thompson Cooper ('Davy, Charles' in *DNB*) 'the manuscript is still in existence.' See J. Venn, *Gonville and Caius*, ii. 76.

your regard: nor can I, in my vainest moments, think myself worthy of it, or that it will be righ[t] for you to confer such an honour upon one who pretends not, as yet, to have given sufficient proofs of depth in the *Theory* of Music, in any writings he has hitherto published, to entitle him to such Distinction. I want Weight for myself too much to be able to give it to others. But I entreat you, Gentⁿ, to regard my declining this Honour more as a Mark of fearful Diffidence than of Ingratitude, as no one can be more truely sensible of your partiality to my feeble endeavour to merit your approbation & that of the Public, than, Gentⁿ, y^r much obliged & Most obed^t Servt

Sittingborne, Kent. 1772[3]

To Thomas Twining[1]

Queen Square,
28 April 1773

ALS (BL Add. MS 39929, fos. 54–6^v).
Also: L copy extract (Osborn: 'Twining Letterbook No. 2', pp. 1–3).   *Endorsed by* Daniel Twining: 1. Renewal of acquaintance ǀ 2. Sends his Plan. ǀ 3. Sr J. Hawkins ǀ Insert after Orig^l p. 4 ǀ Mem 1833 copd partly, marked with pencil, to Dr C.P.B. ǀ (28 Apr. 1773); ǀ (28 April 1773)   *Publ.:* Scholes, *Hawkins*, pp. 238–9 (in part).

Dear Sir.

Few Consequences of the Enterprise in wch I have embarked have pleased me so much as the voluntary notice with which you have honoured me, and the interest which you kindly take in it's prosecution.[2]

---

[3] CB evidently wrote this letter en route to Dover at the beginning of his second musical tour.

[1] The Revd Thomas Twining (1735–1804), BA (1760), MA (1763), classical scholar and musician, Fellow of Sidney Sussex College, Cambridge (1760), Vicar of Fordham, Essex (1764–1804), and of White Notley (1768–1804), Rector of St Mary's, Colchester (1788–1804). A decade or more earlier, Twining had spent an evening with the Burneys, introduced by his Cambridge friend William Lobb (see CB to FB, 13 June 1764, n. 12), but had not kept up the acquaintance. Twining at that time had been one of 'four very extraordinary dilettanti musicians' at Cambridge. He was, according to CB, 'an admirable performer and leader on the violin, and an excellent judge of every species of music' (Rees, under 'Bates, Joah'). See Lonsdale, pp. 134–7; *DNB*.

In Feb. 1773, on one of his rare visits to London, Twining had called at CB's house in Queen Square 'in hopes of having the pleasure of half an hour's conversation . . . upon musical matters', but had missed meeting CB. Back at home in his vicarage at Fordham, 'buried in the country, reduced, for all his musical enjoyment, to a short-compassed harpsichord, & his own no voice, & absolutely cut off from all conversation upon the subject', Twining finally summoned up sufficient 'impertinence' to open a correspondence with CB with a letter dated 7 Apr. 1773 (copy, BL Add. MS 39933, fos. 69–71).

[2] In his letter of 7 Apr., Twining wrote, 'it would be a gratification of my curiosity that would give me great pleasure, if you would be so kind to inform me, *when* (if you are within sight of the time yourself,) your history of music is likely to appear.'

My People had neglected to tell me of your having called in Queen's Square last Feb^y, otherwise I should eagerly have seized so favourable an occasion of renewing an acquaintance of wch I have so often lamented the short duration.

Your Letter found me beset with all the '*Devils*' of this middle world.—The Scribling Demon at the Head of a Legion of inferior rank had scarce allowed me to eat or sleep for some weeks before; but at this Time I was labouring hard to Cast them out—I have at length got rid of them, & of two brats that I have sent into the wide World to shift for themselves.[3] ⌐But notwithstanding the pangs of Child Birth it will appear by a Label[4] prefixed to the back of one of them, that I, like other Breeders, forgetting or slighting former sufferings, determine to fall to again, & am preparing for another Pregnancy—& having now found the secret of producing Twins, a double Fœtus may perhaps ensue more enormous than the last.⌐

Without further Rodomontade, I shall send you a rough Sketch of my Plan,[5] such as I carried with me into Germany, & wch I had once a design to print, ⌐but the Hatton-Garden Knight[6] prevented me, by the slowness of his Motions.[7] I heartily wished him to come out first, but

---

[3] CB's *German Tour* appeared on 23 Apr. 1773 (*Morning Chronicle*), in two octavo volumes, priced at 10s. sewed, under the full title *The Present State of Music in Germany, the Netherlands, and United Provinces. Or, The Journal of a Tour through those Countries, undertaken to collect Materials for a General History of Music*. His publishers were 'T. Becket and Co. Strand; J. Robson, New Bond-Street; and G. Robinson, Paternoster Row'.

[4] Facing the title-page of the second volume of his *German Tour*, CB published a one-page 'Proposals for Printing by Subscription, a General History of Music, From the Earliest Ages to the Present Period', dated 'London, April 20th, 1773'. These 'Proposals' were also issued on a separate leaf in a quarto format, the only known copy of which is preserved in the Bodleian Library (shelf-mark: Vet. A5 a. 15(45)).

The first of the three 'Conditions' stated 'That the work shall be elegantly printed in Two Volumes Quarto ...'. The 'Proposals' also stipulated that the price for the two volumes for subscribers would be two guineas; that the first volume would appear in 1774; and that the whole enterprise would be abandoned unless 500 copies were subscribed for by Christmas 1773.

[5] Twining had asked CB for 'a general idea of your plan, tho' it were but the skeleton of a skeleton'. CB had printed an 'Advertisement' at the end of the first edition of his *Italian Tour* (1771): 'A General Plan of the author's intended *History of Music*, with Proposals for Printing it by Subscription, will be submitted to the public as soon as the work is sufficiently advanced to enable him to fix a time with any degree of certainty for its appearance.' For CB's 'Plan', the only known copy of which is preserved in Bologna, see CB to Garrick, 17–[18] Oct. 1770, n. 29.

[6] Sir John Hawkins (1719–89), attorney, magistrate, and CB's rival historian of music, occupied a house in Hatton Garden from 1761 to 1777. Hawkins had recently sought and been granted (on 23 Oct. 1772) the dignity of knighthood (*DNB*; B. H. Davis, *A Proof of Eminence: the Life of Sir John Hawkins* (Bloomington, 1973), pp. 83, 167, 240–6). See Introduction, pp. xxiv–v.

[7] The first volume of Hawkins's *A General History of the Science and Practice of Music* had been printed by the summer of 1771, and the second volume probably in the summer of 1772, though they were published only in 1776 (Davis, *Hawkins*, pp. 121–2). Twining, in his letter of 7 Apr., informed CB that Thomas Payne (1719–99), Hawkins's publisher, had shown him the first volume 'beginning, as usual, from Mercury &c &c with a crammed account of every thing that has been said, disputed, & conjectured, over & over again, about the music of the ancients.'

finding how Voluminous he would be, & that there was little likelihood of his being out soon, I did not Chuse to let him know my Ideas & resources for the work I had undertaken. I have therefore only offered to the Public proposals in a Common form, without endeavouring to raise Expectation by magnificent Promises.⌐ After the two Journeys I have taken I hope I shall have credit for persevering Diligence; & after mentioning the opportunities I have had for accumulating materials, I hope a display of them will be unnecessary.

⌐With respect to Brother H: I must own to you that when I first heard of his having Embarked in the same Business, my Courage was somewhat abated; I doubted of my competence for entering the Lists with such a Champion, till I fortunately met with his Edition of Walton's Angler,[8] & the Notes to this revived my ardor for Action, & I have ever since regarded him in the Light of a Rival by no means formidable. The Passage you mention I have for some Time had in soak for him,[9] in Case we sh^d ever be obliged to *Compare notes. Whereof* I hope there will be no occasion. I thank you heartily for what you tell me relative to his progress[10]—Modern Music & Musicians are likely to have little Quarter from such a writer, who besides his little knowledge in practice, delights so much in old musty Conundrums that he will not give a hearing to anything better. He confessed to me that he had not been at an opera these 20 years—that he *never* was at the annual Concert for the Benefit of decayed musicians[11]—That he neither liked Tartini's Compositions nor his Book.[12] (I'm sure he understands neither)—he made up to me two or three Times by way of acquaintance, & I naturally gave way to it & was as open & Frank as if he had been my Brother, till I heard several Stories ab^t him well

[8] *The Complete Angler*, edited by Hawkins, had first appeared in London in 1760. CB's copy is listed in *Cat. Misc. Lib.*, lot 1942.

[9] In a long footnote in his edition (p. 238 n.), Hawkins had declared that 'Music was in its greatest perfection in *Europe* from about the middle of the sixteenth to the beginning of the seventeenth Century; when, with a variety of treble-instruments, a vicious taste was introduced, and harmony received its mortal wound.' This musical creed CB considered tantamount to heresy (see Lonsdale, p. 190; Davis, *Hawkins*, p. 117).

[10] The MS copy of Twining's letter of 7 Apr., made by his half-brother, Richard Twining (1749–1824), omits the passage about Hawkins's progress, marking the omission with a series of crosses (BL Add. MS 39933, fo. 70ᵛ).

[11] Established in 1738 as a charitable fund for the support of indigent musicians and their families, the Royal Society of Musicians of Great Britain received its Charter from George III in 1790, 'till which period the institution went under the title of "The Fund for the Support of decayed Musicians and their Families"' ('Society' in Rees). CB gives an account of the Society in *Handel Commem.*, pp. 129–36. See also Pippa Drummond, 'The Royal Society of Musicians in the Eighteenth Century', *Music and Letters*, lix (1978), 268–89.

[12] Either Tartini's *Trattato di musica secondo la vera scienza dell'armonia* (Padua, 1754), or its English translation with commentary by Stillingfleet, *Principles and Power of Harmony* (1771), for which see CB to Crisp, [31] May [1771], n. 13.

authenticated which made me Shy—when I came from Italy & Called upon him, he conversed with me Pen in Hand, in the *Deposition* way.— This I did not much like—however I sent him my Book as soon as printed, & before Publication—I did the same by my Edition of the Miserere of Allegri & the rest of the Music performed in the Pope's Chapel during Passion Week—& wished heartily to forget that we were in each other's way. However I have been advised by several who know him better than myself not to be too intimate with him nor too Communicative. My feelings are ever repugnant to reserve Mystery & Suspicion, however they must in the present Case, I believe, take place.

If Sr John had ever had any Taste, the reading such a pack of old rubbish as he seems most to delight in w^d have spoilt it⁷—I set off with a determination to begin at the 11th Century when Guido is said to have invented the Scale wch is still in Use; but by reading a great Number of fogram musical Authors, they have so far Contaminated my Ideas as to incline me to dip into all the dark & unfathomable Stuff concerning Greek Modes & Hebrew Psalmody, ab^t which we know nearly as much, as of the Musical System used by the Inhabitants of the Planet Saturn.—Something *must* perhaps be said; but my Say will be more to Laugh at what others have written, perhaps, than to offer anything of my own Concerning them.—The History of *Counterpoint* is certainly all that concerns a History of music—& this wth a little Biography concerning Composers & performers will be chiefly attended to in the Course of my Work. I could wish to have my Book so divested of Pedantry & Jargon that every Miss, who plays *o' top o' the Spinet* should make it her manual.—But then what is to become of all the nobly Sounding Greek Terms of Hypate Hypaton, proslambanomenos, &c? God knows—for words without Ideas are my utter aversion.

I shall, you perceive, stand in need of anecdotes[13] to Compensate for this total neglect of Erudition, therefore, pray send me all you Can about the Shoe Buckles, Shoes, Slippers or even the Corns they have occasioned on the Feet of great men.

I thank you for telling me of Giraldus Cambrensis,[14] I have met

---

[13] Twining had written in his letter of 7 Apr.: 'Some years ago I had some conversation about music with Geminiani, from whom I picked up a few little anecdotes, & particulars of no great consequence, relating chiefly to Corelli; . . . If you think they may be of the least use to you, they are much at your service. In this age of anecdotes & personalities the *importance* of them will not be rigorously insisted on. I am persuaded, if you could have brought from Italy a drawing of one of Corelli's shoe buckles, it would have taken more readers of your history, than the most curious you have procured of ancient instruments'.

[14] What Twining told CB about the combative Welsh cleric and scholar, Gerald de Barri, called Giraldus Cambrensis (*c.*1146–*c.*1223), was omitted in the transcription of his letter of

with Quotations from him frequently in the Irish Historians, for I have drudged thro' all such reading as was never read[15] before I commenced Traveller—I hope you will favour me wth your Thoughts as frequently as you can during my Labours—they will be gratefully received—you see with how little Ceremony I have treated you—pray serve me in kind, & let me have the pleasure of hearing from you in a true Chit-Chat way, which you are happily Qualified for, & in which you can communicate such great pleasure to others with so little trouble to yourself. Another request, & I have done;—let me entreat you not to Come to London without affording me the Satisfaction of seeing you in Queen Square—as we sh^d do more Business in the Exchange of Sentiments during half an hour's Conversation, vivâ voce than by 100 Letters.

When you have read my Sketch of a Plan, I must beg of you to return it to me, as I have no other Copy of it.—Remember its Contents are what I promise *myself*, not the Public. Tell me your opinion of it,[16] I entreat you, & believe me to be with great regard, dear Sir,

your obliged & obed^t Servt
Cha. Burney.

Queen's Square ¦ 28th Apr. ¦ 1773.

To Christoph Daniel Ebeling [Queen Square], 15 July 1773

LS copy (Osborn: 'Letterbook, Musical Correspondence').
Addressed: To Mr. Ebeling, at Hamburg. *Docketed by* FBA: ✕·

July 15–1773.

Dear Sir,

I never was more mortified at the receit of a Letter in my Life, than by yours of the 20th of June;[1] beginning with an open Declaration of

---

7 Apr. (fo. 71ᵛ). Twining probably called CB's attention to the famous passage in Giraldus's *Descriptio Cambriae* (1194), which records part-singing among the Welsh as early as the twelfth century. CB discusses this important document in the history of early polyphony in *Hist. Mus.* ii. 107–10; Mercer, i. 482–4. See also 'Giraldus Cambrensis' in *New Grove*.

[15] Pope, *Dunciad*, iv. 250. CB also used this quotation in the Preface to his *History of Music* (i, p. x; Mercer, i. 17).

[16] Twining returned CB's Plan on 8 May, with a covering letter: 'you obliged me much, & made me very happy by your plan, & still more by your communication & agreeable letter, calculated, I fear, to open every sluice of impertinence' (BL Add. MS 39933, fo. 72ᵛ).

[1] Now preserved in the Staats- und Universitätsbibliothek, Hamburg. Postmarks show that Ebeling's letter arrived in London on 3 July. It was then redirected to CB at The Queen's

War.[2] The Passage which has chiefly given offence,[3] was inserted with so little rancour, or design of giving Pain to a Single Friend or Man of Merit, that I had utterly forgot it was in my Book, nor do I know now where to find it. As to the author who furnished it, however he may have transgressed the Bounds of Moderation, or perhaps of Justice; never entertain a Thought of my giving him up.[4] We English have an utter abhorrence & detestation of the Character of an *Informer*, & you yourself in your cooler moments would detest such *lacheté*—I'll give up the *Passage* with all my Heart, in a 2ᵈ Edition,[5] & you have my full leave to omit it in your Translation, nay, my *Wish* that you would send it to the D——l. But, if not, shew it no mercy in your Notes—brand it—& shew all the Patriotic indignation against it that you please, but spare the author, or rather, the retailer of it, for I was no more than the Transcriber of the Passage from a Letter which I received during the Time my Work was in the Press: throw it upon inadvertance, not malevolence, or prejudice, I beseech you.[6] I have shewn throughout

College, Oxford, where he had gone to attend the installation of Lord North as Chancellor of Oxford University at Encaenia, 7–9 July 1773 (see CB to Twining, 30 Aug. 1773, n. 9).

Ebeling, who had received a copy of the *German Tour*, expressed vehement protest at CB's strictures on the Germans and Germany. The text of Ebeling's letter is published in G. M. Stewart, 'Christoph Daniel Ebeling, Hamburger Pädagoge und Literaturkritiker, und seine Briefe an Charles Burney', *Zeitschrift des Vereins für Hamburgische Geschichte*, lxi (1975), 50–4.

[2] Ebeling opened his attack with an apocalyptic adaptation of Virgil's *Aeneid*, vi. 86–7: 'Bella horrida bella et Tamesin multo spumantem sanguine cerno!' ('I see wars, terrible wars, and the Thames foaming with much blood').

[3] In the first edition of the *German Tour*, ii. 24: '. . . it is not *nature*, but *cultivation*, which makes music so generally understood by the Germans; and it has been said by an accurate observer of human nature, who has long resided among them, that "if innate genius exists, Germany certainly is not the seat of it; though it must be allowed, to be that of perseverance and application".' The author of this offending quotation was the diplomatist, Louis Devisme (1720–76), British Minister Plenipotentiary to the Bavarian Court in Munich (1769–74), who had expressed these sentiments in a letter to CB dated 30 Nov. 1772 (Osborn). See *DNB*; Horn, p. 46.

CB, it should be noted, was not entirely blameless, for a scrutiny of Devisme's letter in which the quotation occurs reveals that he wrote in reply to a letter (now lost) from CB. From Devisme's remarks, it can be inferred that it was CB who first raised the issue of German genius. Devisme, in concurring with CB, however, provided him with a convenient quotable verdict for the *German Tour*. Devisme wrote in his letter of 30 Nov. 1772: 'I have again much obligation to you for all the particulars you send of Art & Artists, & for what I esteem more, your own observations. . . . Your manner of accounting for the progress of the Bohemians in musick is very natural. If innate Genius exists, Germany is certainly not the seat of it, but it is that of perseverance and application.' See C. B. Oldman, 'Charles Burney and Louis De Visme', *The Music Review*, xxvii (1966), 93–7; Scholes, i. 248–9; Lonsdale, pp. 124–7.

[4] In his letter of 20 June, Ebeling demanded, 'Who is that terrae filius that dares to judge a whole nation! By which degree of knowledge and genius, and observation and experience was he intitled to utter such an offending sentence? Does he understand the German language? What is his name? In the name of all Germanns, I desire you must deliver him to our revenge.'

[5] CB omitted the quotation from Devisme and toned down the entire passage in the second edition of his *German Tour* (1775), ii. 24–5 (*Tours*, ii. 138 and n. 1). See also CB's final retraction, *Hist. Mus.* iv. 606; Mercer, ii. 963.

[6] In their translation, published in Hamburg in 1773, Ebeling and Bode retained the passage,

my Book, the utmost Zeal & admiration of the Talents of Individuals in Germany, as well as affection for their Persons. If I have mentioned the Nakedness of the Land, & the wretchedness of the people, in some parts of my Tour, it was more to expose the Tyranny of the Government, & despotism of Princes, than to insult the people, whom I pitied with all my soul—a brave, honest & industrious race, by Nature, who are denied the common rights of humanity, to such a Degree, as to be rendered sour & unfeeling to others. You & I will not enter into so endless a Dispute, as the discussion of the claim of Superiority in the Germans or English, would occasion.[7] I pretend not to understand the Literary merit of your poets, Historians, &c. I will only say, that from the few persons of other Countries who understand German, perhaps more than any other defect, your Poets are much less known throughout Europe, by Translations, than our's. You read & Speak English fluently, but do not flatter yourself that you understand our Poets, or feel the beauties of our Versification, of our poetic phrases and expressions, as forcibly as the Natives of England do; you & all Foreigners, are in this particular like Deaf Men, who only hear the course & noisy parts of a Concert; you have the general Tenor & outline of a Poem, but not the Graces or Colouring; I judge myself in the same severe manner with respect to French & Italian, which I have read & studied near 30 years. But when I find the French & Italians in raptures with Poems & parts of Poems that give me no pleasure, & of which I cannot comprehend the Beauties, I immediately suppose myself ignorant of the finer parts of the Language, & that the ideas I annex to Words & Combinations of words, are wholly different from those of the Natives. You blaspheme against our Milton & Shakespeare without *Connoissance de Cause*. I never ventured to say that M[r] Klopstock was not equal to Milton, but gave him Credit for that exalted station, from your own report of him.[8] The other objections you make to my *Chien de Livre* I

---

but criticized it in an editorial note. See *Carl Burney's der Musik Doctors Tagebuch seiner Musikalischen Reisen. Dritter Band. Durch Böhmen, Sachsen, Brandenburg, Hamburg und Holland*, p. 12.

[7] Ebeling had written in his letter (20 June): 'I confess we are badly governed in some parts, but let even the polish and the poor human fellow creatures in Eastindia tell the world who are the bestmen the Germans who conquer'd Polonia, or the english who conquerred Bengala?'

[8] The passage now under discussion is CB's interview on 10 Oct. 1772 with the poet Friedrich Gottlieb Klopstock (1724–1803), 'who is called, the Milton of Germany'. CB in the *German Tour* then proceeded to quote from a letter he had received from Dr Jakob Mumssen (1737–1819), the Hamburg physician who had introduced CB to the poet: Klopstock's 'merit in the German language, will be best known to future ages; his odes require a reader of good natural sense, well acquainted with the history of his own country, its language, antiquity, and the harmony of verse; the more they are studied, the more they will please; they are by many reckoned unintelligible, merely because they are analogous to no other species of writing' (*Tours*, ii. 212–13; Mumssen to CB, 16 Oct. 1772, Osborn). Ebeling (20 June) had disputed this evaluation in a confused sentence in which he praised Klopstock ('such Genius the english never had') at the expense of Shakespeare ('he is no epical and lyric poet') and Milton.

feel no great uneasiness about—but remember this—that I would throw away my Pen, break my Ink-Bottle, & burn every bit of Paper in my House,[9] sooner than let others guide me in *all* my opinions about Men, Things & Countries. I never will ask any Nation, City or Individual what I shall say of them, as I am certain that their vanity & self love would lead me further from truth, than my own ignorance or prejudice. I am not so little acquainted with Human Nature, as to expect *all* I say will be approved by *all Men*. You set my *Welsh Blood* up a little,[10] but I shake my Ears, & am not only in perfect charity with you, but honour your patriotic spirit; nay further, it has always been my opinion, that the Man who feels not a love & attachment to his native Country, & who defends not its Honours, cannot be possessed of a good Heart. I love England—am proud of Breathing the same Air as Locke, Newton, Milton, Dryden—Shakespeare &c I bless myself in the liberty of our Government, & the Happiness it puts in our power, when I compare it to any other Country I have yet seen; but all this affection does not blind me so far as to make me defend indefensible Things. In the fine arts we have done but little, in Music, except for the Church, less than our nieghbours. I understand not your distinction about different parts of Germany;[11] I look upon the Empire through which I Travelled, as Germany in general, & all Europe speaks of it as such: in that Light, you ought to have done more in Literature than our *little* Island, not bigger much, than one of your Circles. When I say, I understand not your Distinctions, do not fancy that I mean Geographically; I learnt all your Divisions of Circles, Electorates, &c, at School; but I speak as the rest of Europe Speak— *ne vous* deplaise.

Pray give my affectionate Compliments to dear Mr Bach:[12] & to Mr Klopstock, however angry he is with me,[13] for I love & revere Men of Genius of all Countries, without reserve or distinction: I cannot think, however, Quantz a Genius, or that the K. of Prussia, who is so attached

[9] CB here indulges in a mischievously oblique allusion to Shakespeare: 'I'll break my staff, ⎮ Bury it certain fathoms in the earth, ⎮ And deeper than did ever plummet sound ⎮ I'll drown my book' (*Tempest*, v. i. 54–7).

[10] Ebeling had stigmatized CB (20 June): 'You un⟨gra⟩tefull offspring of ancient Germany! But I remember to t⟨ake⟩ heart you are a Welsh, and by this fact I believe it to be true.'

[11] Ebeling wrote (20 June): 'there is a general mistake that you believe Our nation is to be considered as one people. No Sir history and Geography will acquaint You that we are composed of different clans or even little nations quite different from one another in dialects, customs, nothwistanding many of them have been altered by administration, mixture with foreigners, transmigrations etc. but [you] always say the Germans in genere. You should say the Bavarians, Upper Saxons, lower Saxons etc.'.

[12] i.e. C. P. E. Bach, for whom see CB to Ebeling, Nov. 1771, n. 5.

[13] Ebeling reported that Klopstock 'would not reed your Book when he found the above mentioned sentence' on German genius (see n. 3).

to his Music, can love such a superiour Being in Music as Bach.[14] Many thanks to M[r] Bode for his Present,[15] & remembrance of me. When comes he to England? I have not Time to look for the Prices of the trifling Stuff I sent you. I go out of Town into Norfolk to Write at my History in quiet the rest of the Summer. There is no peace for me here. A M. Framery of Paris, who intends to Translate my History into French, has Criticised my account of French Music, & sent me a long, feeble & dull defence of it—even of the *Singing*. A cursed *seccatura* that I *must* answer.[16] Nothing but Panygeric will be believed: but my own feelings cannot be sacrificed to *Politesse*. I have niether Time or room here to take notice of some of your objections, though I think them not all unanswerable. I most cordially Shake you by the Thumb, & beg you to make my Book as palatable to your Countrymen & friends as you can. Yours in all affection

C.B.

To James Hutton[1]

[Queen Square],
17 July 1773

LS copy (Osborn: 'Letterbook, Musical Correspondence').
Addressed: To M[r] Hutton of Lindsey House, Chelsea.   *Docketed by* FBA: ✳

[14] In his *German Tour*, CB repeatedly grumbled at what he considered Frederick the Great's old-fashioned musical taste, which stemmed from his devotion to the German flute, 'an instrument which, from its confined powers, has had less good music composed for it, than any other in common use', and the King's consequent dependence on the compositions of his mentor, Quantz, whose 'taste is that of forty years ago'. Given this musical climate, therefore, C. P. E. Bach's 'style did not insinuate itself into the favour it deserved at the court of Berlin' (*Tours*, ii. 182, 217).

[15] Ebeling had written (20 June): 'I shall ... sent You five of Keisers opera's as a present of Mr. Bode'. These five operas were sent to CB together with Ebeling's next letter to him, 27 July 1773 (Hamburg). Reinhard Keiser (1674–1739), 'composed chiefly for Hamburg, and in general, to the German language' (*Tours*, ii. 119; *New Grove*).

[16] Nicolas-Étienne Framery (1745–1810), French man of letters and musician, edited the *Journal de musique historique, théorique et pratique* from 1770 to 1771 (*New Grove*). Neither Framery's letter nor CB's answer is preserved, though Fanny heard CB read to Garrick 'An Answer which he is preparing to some Complaints made by French Writers concerning his Censure of their music' (*EJL* i. 272–3). Framery's intended translation of CB's *History* did not materialize (Lonsdale, p. 128).

[1] James Hutton (1715–95), who may be regarded as the founder of the Moravian Church in England, had first visited Germany in 1739 (*DNB*). Hutton wrote to CB on 2 July 1773 (Osborn), objecting to CB's comments on the expense of travelling in Germany, the poverty of the people, and scarcity of food in the countryside. See *ED* i. 303–12; Lonsdale, pp. 124–5; D. Benham, *Memoirs of James Hutton; Comprising the Annals of His Life, and Connection with the United Brethren* (1856).

1773

Sir,

A few Words may raise doubts & suspicions which would require Volumes to remove. I know not what interest you may have in the honour of Germany; but it cannot be stronger than mine for my own honour, when my veracity is attacked. You have only read an Extract from my Book.[2] Had the Book itself fallen in your Hands, you would have seen various reasons given for excessive scarceness & dearness in all kinds of Things in many parts of Germany, all the Time I was there. I make not the least doubt but what you advance with respect to your cheaper way of Travelling there than myself, is most true; but then I must suppose two Things which can alone account for it; one may be your speaking the Language readily, or having more experience in the German Methods of avoiding Expence & impositions than myself: the other, your Journeys having happened in Times of greater plenty, perhaps before the last War,[3] which ruined many parts of that Country, particularly Saxony & Bohemia so much that they will not soon recover it.

You say not, sir, *when* you were last in Germany. & I cannot suppose it to have been since the great scarcity of Corn, by which so much sickness, Death, & wretchedness have been occasioned. I was assured, by our Minister at Dresden,[4] that 100.000 Lives have been lost by it since the last War in the Elector of Saxony's[5] Dominions only. & Bohemia was but just emerging from Disease & misery when I travelled through it. So that in places where *white* Bread used to abound, scarse *black* bread, or any Bread at all was to be found.[6] As to appearances in descending the Danube, I'll trust my own Eyes with respect to fertility, Cattle, &c,[7] though I always doubted them in Towns, with respect to Customs, & manners.

As to the price of Horses, & the number *forced* upon me, if it were necessary, I would make oath to the Truth of what I have advanced.

[2] In his letter of protest to CB, Hutton revealed that he had read only the first part of Bewley's anonymous review of the *German Tour* in the June issue of the *Monthly Review*. Bewley's favourable notice appeared in the *Monthly Review* in two parts, in June (xlviii. 457–69) and Sept. (xlix. 212–24).

[3] The Seven Years' War, which lasted from 1756 to 1763.

[4] John Osborn (1743–1814), educated at Westminster and Christ Church, Oxford, BA (1764), DCL (1777), FRS (1777), British Envoy Extraordinary to Saxony from 1771 to 1775 (G. F. R. Barker and A. H. Stenning, *The Record of Old Westminsters* (1928), ii. 706; Horn, p. 65).

[5] Frederick Augustus III (1750–1827), called 'The Just', Elector of Saxony. In 1806 he assumed the dignity of King Frederick Augustus I of Saxony.

[6] Hutton had written (2 July): 'Mr H. never found want of white Bread, & excellent too, in every even Market Town He went through'.

[7] Hutton had reported (2 July): 'the Parts near the Iser & the Danube He always heard were very fruitful, Corn particularly in abundance & Pasture also. & even in the Forests are abundance of domestic Cattle frequently, as Mr H. has seen with his own Eyes in other parts'.

When I arrived in Saxony, I found by a new *Reglement* which had just then taken place, that I was charged a Rixdoller, each Horse, instead of a Florin, the usual price for a *Station*. I was obliged to have 3 Horses—a Horse was charged for the *Schwager*, half a Horse for the Wagon, besides various Taxes, as *schossegeld*, Barriergeld, Drinkgeld, &c.[8] If you put all these together, it will appear that a *Station*, such as from Pirna to Dresden, which I believe is but two German Miles, Cost me ab[t] 4 Rixdollers. You understand, Sir, I suppose, that I Travelled extra-post, for this money, & not by the *post ordinaire*, which is abundantly Cheaper; but even this not so much as I expected, when I came to pay for my servant & Baggage besides other Fees & Taxes.

I must own that I did not so much think how my Narrative would please the Inhabitants of Germany as to relate Things simply, & as they were. I have the highest respect & veneration for the Electress Dowager of Saxony,[9] & for her Brother, the Elector of Bavaria.[10] I should be grieved to offend them, perhaps more than any great personages from whom I was honoured with notice; & if any parts of my Journal were softened, it was occasioned by the high respect & gratitude with which I am impressed for that Prince & Princess, but in general my remarks are given undisguised & plain, just as they were set down on the Spot in my Journal Book.

I am sorry to be obliged to trouble you with so long a defence of myself, which perhaps will arrive late, for I am but just come from Oxford, where I was when your note arrived in Queen Sq[r] & after all, it will not perhaps, be satisfactory, however, so hurried as I am with other Concerns, I should be grieved to be put upon my Defence in matters of small concern to the Work in which I am Engaged, which will require more Time & Labour than I shall be able to bestow upon it, however diligent & ambitious I may be of avoiding disgrace, though Honour & profit may be denied me. I am going into Norfolk tomorrow for the remainder of the Summer, at my return, I should be glad to

---

[8] See *Tours*, ii. 136. Hutton disbelieved CB's account, duly reported by Bewley in his review, of the hardships of travel in Germany. To CB's assertion that 'it cost me frequently at the rate of eighteen pence for each English mile', Hutton had responded in his letter of 2 July: 'it seems to M[r] H. here is a great mistake, as M[r] H. has travelled some thousand miles, at different times, in Germany & never paid any thing like that'.

[9] Maria Antonia Walpurgis (1724–80), widow of Frederick Christian (1722–63), Elector of Saxony, was a patron of the arts and an accomplished musician. She published her compositions under the initials E. T. P. A., standing for Ermelinda Talea Pastorella Arcada, her name as a member of the Academy of Arcadians (*Tours*, ii. 46–51; 'Maria' in *New Grove*).

[10] Maximilian III Joseph (1727–77), Elector of Bavaria from 1745 to 1777. An amateur musician himself, he had MS copies of his own 'Stabat Mater and Litany' made and sent to CB through Louis Devisme (*Cat. Mus. Lib.*, lot 403; *Tours*, ii. 49–51; Devisme to CB, 20 Sept. and 30 Nov. 1772, Osborn).

remove your doubts in Conversation, if you w^d do me the Honour to call in Queen Square, wth or without my friend Dr. Ha[w]kesworth.[11]

I am Sir,

your obedient

& most hu^{ble} Ser^t

Chas Burney.

July 17th 1773.

To Mrs Crewe[1] [Great Massingham], 8 August 1773

AL draft (Berg).
Docketed by FBA: ✻ ✢ To Mrs Crewe afterwards Lady (I)

Augt 8th 1773

Dear Madam.

As nothing has been a more constant source of mortification to me than the fear[2] of being forgotten by you in the very long Interval which has elapsed since I had the Honour of seeing you, so no circumstance within my recollection ever afforded me a more sincere Pleasure than the Receipt of your Letter,[3] which has *renovated* as Dr Johnson w^d have said the remembrance of the many happy Hours I enjoyed in Days of ease & carelessness under the same Roof with yourself! [4]My early attachments have taken such deep hold in my

[11] Hutton had begun his letter of 2 July with the self-introduction: 'Mr Hutton of Lindsey House Chelsea (whom Dr Hawkesworth takes friendly notice of) begs Dr Burney to excuse the trouble of this'. John Hawkesworth (1720–73), LLD (1756), man of letters, had just published (9 June) his three-volume *An Account of the Voyages undertaken by order of his present Majesty for making Discoveries in the Southern Hemisphere* (1773). CB, whose friendship with Hawkesworth dated from about 1748 when CB belonged to Fulke Greville's household at Wilbury, had been instrumental in securing for Hawkesworth the authorship of the *Voyages*. See Lonsdale, pp. 21, 111–12; J. L. Abbott, *John Hawkesworth: Eighteenth-Century Man of Letters* (Madison, 1982), *passim*; *EJL* i. 173–4, 325–7 and *passim*.

Hutton eventually became a great favourite of the Burneys whom he delighted with his endearing eccentricities (*ED* i. 303–12; *EJL* ii).

[1] Frances Anne Crewe, née Greville (1748–1818), the beautiful daughter of CB's patron, Fulke Greville, had married (1766) John Crewe (1742–1829), of Crewe Hall, Cheshire, MP (1765–1802), created Baron (1806). She was a lifelong friend of the Burney family, and in CB's later years one of his most faithful correspondents (Namier and Brooke, ii. 276–7; Lonsdale, pp. 20, 133; *JL* i. 2).

[2] MS fear] *alternative* reflexion

[3] Mrs Crewe's letter is not preserved.

[4–4] MS My . . . oak.] *originally* early attachments have ever been with me, that tho' accidents may break them, like oak, it is with the utmost difficulty that the Root can be torn up *altered by*

affections that though untoward accidents may break them yet they are as difficult to tear up by the Root as an old oak.[4]

I no sooner heard from M[r] Price[5] that [6]you sometimes condescended to mention my name[6] with your usual Goodness & partiality but I flew to your Door; yet alas I was not only unfortunate in this first attempt, but in a 2[d] w[ch] I made the Day after you had set out for France; & in still another upon hearing you were returned two Days after you had quitted London.

This is a long History to write & still a longer for you to read, but this renewal of our acquaintance suggests so many things to say, & we seem to have so long an acc[t] to settle that I scarce know where to begin or End.

You have probably heard of the hardy work I have undertaken in the way of a *History of Music*: I am now got into a Country Village at a Friend's house[7] in order to work at it in Peace & Quiet after all my summer rambles & the hurry & Fatigue of a long winter in London—

I never durst ask if you had read my *first* publication, the musical Journal of my Italian Tour—I rather supposed you had not, and imagined you were afraid to meet with the Jargon of hard words & the unintelligible Giberish of affected Science wth w[ch] Books on the subject of music are usually crammed; but tho' I'll answer for Nothing else I will venture to tell you that there is nothing more difficult to understand in the Books w[ch] I have hitherto published, than in the adventures of Giles Gingerbread, or the history of Good two shoes.[8] & indeed Many of the readers of these last delectable Works have flattered me so far as to say that the stories of singing men & singing women in my Book afforded them some amusement even *after* the perusal of the other great works,[9] tho' of an inferiour kind: but what fed my Vanity most was that none of them have ever complained of not understanding me.—[10]Of this Trifle ab[t] Flutes & Fiddles I have not one copy left,

---

deletion and interlineation to early attachments are so deeply rooted with me, that tho' untoward accidents may break them, like an oak, it is almost as impossible to tear them up by the Roots *further altered to* early attachments have taken such fast hold of me, that . . . Roots *finally fair copy written out* My early . . . old oak.

[5] Doubtless Uvedale Price (1747–1829), created Baronet (1828), writer on 'the picturesque' (*DNB*), who occasionally attended the Sunday evening concerts in the Burney home at this period. Fanny describes him as 'a young man of Fashion . . . very intelligent, sensible & clever. . . He is kinsman to M[r] Greville' (*EJL* i. 148, 218).

[6–6] MS you . . . name] *altered from* you mentioned my name to him

[7] William Bewley's at Great Massingham, Norfolk.

[8] Two of the most popular children's books: *The Renowned History of Giles Gingerbread* (1764), and *The History of Little Goody Two-Shoes* (1765), both published and possibly written by John Newbery (1713–67). See S. Roscoe, *John Newbery and His Successors, 1740–1814, a Bibliography* (Wormley, 1973), pp. 135–7, 200–1; *DNB*.

[9] MS great works] *interlined above deleted* Books

[10–10] MS Of . . . printing] *altered from* a new Edition of the Tour is printing

however a new Edition is now printing,[10] & if you sh^d not have hitherto had the courage to attempt reading it, I shall be extreamly happy in being allowed the honour of laying a Copy of it at your Feet, next winter.[11] As to my German Tour, I have ordered a Copy of it to be packed up & sent to Grosvenor Square, in order to [ensure] its being forwarded to you in Cheshire by the first conveyance, and am extreamly flattered by your Wish to see it, & the kind opportunity you afford me of furnishing you with it: I have no other wish now to make on the occasion but that it were less unworthy of your Time & attention.

You laugh at your poor old acquaintance, & he laughs at himself (he was always a *gigler* you know) when you tell him of his being in the list of *Great Men*[12]—well, this Life, as far as I know of it, is a strange mixture of sense & nonsense—Joy & sorrow—affliction & Farce—a meer Tragi-Comedy, at which one is inclined to cry & to laugh, all in a Breath.—You will perceive, my dear Madam, in the perusal of my Nonsense, how far I was forced to go *out* of my way, in order to get *into* a little Notice.—I remember the Time of your bearing a very good share[13] in a *Philosophising* Party; and yet, it is so long since that I fear you have forgot it; I don't mean *how* to philosophise, for Time [14]makes it necessary to us all by the frequent occasion it gives[14] us of doing it; but alas my fear is that you have forgot when I used to have the honour of performing a small part in such discussions.

Your humility of only wishing to be my Critic in the style of Moliere's *Old Woman*[15] has a Contrary Effect on me, by making me very Proud, & almost young enough to cut my Joaks ab^t it in the old way; but when I recollect that your little Acquaintance Hetty has dignified me with the Venerable name of *Grandfather*,[16] I assume a proper Gravity on the occasion, which reminds me that it is high Time to conclude this long & rodamontad[17] Letter by seriously assuring you that I have the honour to be,

---

[11] 'The Second Edition, Corrected' of the *Italian Tour* was to come out on 18 Dec. 1773. See CB to Arthur Young, 11 Oct. 1773, n. 2.

[12] Perhaps an allusion to CB's candidacy to the Royal Society, for which see CB to Twining, 30 Aug. 1773, n. 54.

[13] MS share] *interlined above deleted* part *and* performance

[14-14] MS makes ... gives] *altered from* makes us all Philosophise, at least gives us occasion for it;

[15] Tradition has it that Molière, as a test of their comic effectiveness, would read his plays after composition to his devoted servant, La Forèt. See J. Palmer, *Molière* (1930), p. 403.

[16] Hetty's first child, CB's first grandchild, Hannah Maria ('Marianne') was baptized on 16 July 1772 at St Paul's Church, Covent Garden (*The Registers of St. Paul's Church, Covent Garden, London, Vol. II.—Christenings, 1752–1837*, ed. W. H. Hunt, Harleian Society's Publications (1906), p. 65; *JL* i, p. lxix).

[17] MS & rodamontad] *interlined below deleted* & foolish

with the truest respect
& most sincere regard
dear Mad^m
y^r most Obliged & most devoted Servt
& obed^{t18}

I hope the last acc^{ts} of Mrs Greville were favourable & that all the Wilbury Family, as well as your own enjoy Perfect Health.

I am sorry & ashamed to detain you a Moment Longer, but I must add that, I was astonished that your Letter found me out, having been directed to my old House in Poland[19] Street, wch I have quitted more than 3 years, for one in

Queen Square, Bloomsbury—

my head Quarters, however will be at Lynn Regis Norfolk, till ab^t Mich^s.

To Thomas Twining[1]

Great Massingham, 30 August 1773

ALS (BL Add. MS 39929, fos. 59–64).
Docketed by Richard Twining: 1773–Aug^{st} 30. 1773; *by* Richard Twining, Jr.: (to Rev. T. Twining). | (30 Aug. 1773) | (30 Aug 1773)   *Also* AL incomplete draft (Berg).   *Docketed by* FBA: × Mr Twining.   *Also* AL copy extracts (Berg).
Endorsed by CB: Extracts from a Lett^r to the Revd Mr Twining Augt 1773; *And by* FBA: ×   *Publ.:* Scholes, *Hawkins*, pp. 239–40 (in part).

Dear Sir.
My Friends often upbraid me for not more frequently partaking of the Diversions of the Times, and the Pleasures of Society by an interchange of Visits. Upon this occasion I have but one short & true answer to make, which is, that 'I have no Time to be happy.'[2]
It amazes me when I reflect on the great number of different, &

---

[18] CB added beside this elaborate complimentary close a marginal memorandum: 'Jokes'.
[19] MS Poland] *interlined above deleted* Queen

[1] Following his first letter to Twining of 28 Apr. (see *ante*), CB received three letters from his new friend, dated 8 May, 28 May, and 22 July 1773. These three letters are partially preserved in copies made by Twining's half-brother, Richard Twining (1749–1824), the tea-merchant, whose unfortunate transcription practice it was to omit passages he considered uninteresting or indiscreet. Thomas Twining's letter of 8 May is preserved intact (BL Add. MS 39933, fo. 72^v); only extracts are preserved of his next two letters, 28 May (fos. 73–8^v), and 22 July (fos. 79–82^v).
[2] The source of this quotation has not been traced.

most of them disagreeable, avocations which necessity has imposed on me since the Rec^t of your admirable Letter of May 28th, without allowing me Leisure to acknowledge it; though I was so highly delighted with its contents, that if I were either K. of England, or his Prime Minister, I would give you the first vacant Bishoprick,[3] with an Exemption from Preaching anywhere, except in my Chapel, upon Condition that you w^d write me one as long every week.

I have been pretty much *repandu*, as a Correspondent, since I first communicated to the Public my design of attempting a Hist^y of Music. My two Journeys on the Continent have procured me many foreign Letters, and my small previous publications have been the occasion of many of my Countrymen honouring me with their voluntary Notice;[4] yet, I can say with the utmost sincerity that, among all these Letters, several of which I was very much pleased with, no one afforded me so perfect and heart-felt a satisfaction as I rec^d from the Perusal of yours. You seem to me to get to the Root of my *Besogne*, while others are playing at See-saw on the Branches. I have often seen with disgust the *grossierté* of Strong Compliments; ⌜[5]and think it as indecent to praise a⌝[5] man to his Face, ⌜as to talk B——y[6] to a modest woman, or blasphemy to a Clergyman; &⌝ yet I long to tell you what I discovered in your Lett^r but dare not. However, I will say that I wish you had been obliged to write a Hist^y of Music yourself. It is abominable of People, possessed of every Quality for writing well, to spend their whole lives in reading the nonsense of others, in search of perfection & Information wch they are sure not to find.

After this, shall I dare to say that our sentiments are congenial? and that, though I am unable to execute such difficulties as you, yet, I c^d relish them in your Performance?[7] All I have for it in attempt[ing] such difficulties as I have to encounter, will be to aim at that inoffensiv[e] pruden⟨ce⟩ which avoids doing mischief.

Swift has thrown a Ridicule upon our approbation of Persons who think like ourselves;[8] but there is no other Criterion of our approbation

---

[3] Twining had introduced the droll notion of his elevation to the episcopacy in his letter of 8 May 1773: 'I would have got a frank if possible, but I could as soon get a Bishoprick.' This 'Bishoprick' was to develop into a constant source of merriment in Twining's correspondence with CB.

[4] For the reception of the Italian and German *Tours*, see Lonsdale, pp. 101, 104–5, 120–30.

[5]–[5] MS and . . . a] *obliterated by Richard Twining who interlined* and shrink from praising a

[6] CB's copy (Berg) of extracts from this letter makes clear that 'Bawdy' is the word intended.

[7] In his reply of 16 Oct. 1773 (copy, BL Add. MS 39933, fos. 83^v–92^v), Twining modestly observed: 'I can't help saying, . . . as to your notion of my being qualified for such a work as you are engaged in, that there is a monstrous stride between seeing what *should* be done, & doing it.'

[8] '*That was excellently observed*, say I, when I read a Passage in an Author, where his Opinion agrees with mine. When we differ, I pronounce him to be *mistaken*' (*Thoughts on Various Subjects*, in *The Prose Works of Jonathan Swift*, ed. H. Davis (Oxford, 1939–68), iv. 248).

than correspondent sentiments & Ideas. Whether an author says what we have said, or thought, or *should* have said or thought in similar Circumstances, or upon similar occasions, it is much the same, if it satisfy our Minds. To admire a writer's reasoning, or Wit, or Humour, or penetration, which we could never attain, is from the same mental Satisfaction arising from his having improved our own Thoughts.

ᴵ I ought here to give you a sketch of my Life and Conversation since I rec^d your Letter, in order to account for the late arrival of my answer; But Time is not to be lost on either side, by writing or reading such stuff. I will only say that after quitting the Tourbillon of London, I went into another at Oxford,[9] which though of a less magnitude was equally rapid in its Motion. From thence I journeyed to Worcester— Then back to London for a few Days; After wch I went to Lynn in Norfolk, from whence in a fortnight or 3 weeks I made my escape to the House of a Friend in a small Village, ten or twelve Miles from a Market Town, where I rec^d your last kind communication, & where I am at work upon the *opus Magnum*, in Peace and Quiet, for I can do nothing at it in London on acc^t of eternal Interuptions, nor at Lynn for eating & drinking.

Concerning your Letter of May, I c^d write a Volume with more ease than a Single Page of Nonsense that is to be printed; for you kindly give me leave to write not only *when* I will, but *what* I will. Do, pray keep on your Gown,[10] not the Clerical one, & let the case be reciprocal. Let us slap down our Thoughts as they come, without the Trouble of seeking or arranging them. I lament the distance between us, & the want of your Conversation & Counsel. I question whether we should recognize each other if we were to meet; and yet I feel so entirely off my guard with you that like some of our Common People and Servants, who, when they like Folks, give them, in the first Hour's Acquaintance, a History of all their Misfortunes, ill-usages, bad places, & bodily complaints.—So I seem *inside-out* with you, & inclined to tell you every secret of my *Life*.—But to Business—And first, let me thank you for the Honour of your Name, and for that of Mr Wegg;[11] and tell

[9] A tiny fragment from CB's MS 'Memoirs' preserved in the Berg Collection shows that CB had journeyed to Oxford in early July to attend Encaenia and see 'Ld North Installed at Oxf. —73'. Lord North had been elected Chancellor of Oxford University on 3 Oct. 1772, and his installation at Encaenia (7–9 July 1773) was 'said to have been the grandest that ever was celebrated in that University' (*GM* xliii. 350; A. Valentine, *Lord North* (Norman, 1967), i. 263, 302). Anxious at this period to seize every opportunity to solicit subscriptions to his *History*, CB was careful to insert advertisements for his subscription list in the *Oxford Journal*, 3 and 10 July (*EJL* i. 299, n. 7).

[10] MS Gown] *originally* Night-Gown. In his letter of 28 May, Twining had said, 'your obliging letter has . . . put me at once *en robe de chambre* & at my ease.'

[11] Twining had written (28 May): 'pray put my name into your list:—my mother, or my

you that I find my Fr^{ds} better disposed to forward my Subscription than the Public at large. Between 2 & 300, chiefly among my ac- quaintance, have already given in their Names; but I believe I could have ensured full that number, If I had chosen to employ personal Interest that way, for a set of Lessons or Concertos, which w^d have cost me but little money to print, & less labour to compose. People lye by, and wait to be asked—& if I were to spend my Time in soliciting subscriptions, how, or when w^d my work be executed? But many even of those who, I have reason to think intend to read & to purchase the Book if 'tis published, are slack in sending in their Names: Is it that they are sore from former ill-usage in Subscriptions? or are they fearful that I should become too fat and Lazy to write, if the *great profits* of my work poured in upon me too fast, *d'avance*? However this may be, I must confess that the Zeal of a few *private* Friends, though a grateful Circumstance to my Heart, is not an Incence of so sweet smelling a Savour to my Vanity, as an Author, as the voluntary Offerings of the public would be. Indeed, next to such a Dread as yours of being thought a *Pushing Fellow*,[12] there is nothing that would Mortify me more than to find myself *à Charge* to my Friends. The last thing, & the least I thought of was what I should *get* by my undertaking. To say the Truth, I have been long too certain of *Loss*, to have the least hope on the side of Filthy Lucre. After fourteen or fifteen hundred pounds kicked down in my rambles & Bibliomania, with a certainty of sinking Eight or 900 more, if I print two 4to Volumes, besides the Loss of Time, Ease, Sleep, &, perhaps, Reputation, I could hardly, when I contented myself with requiring only 500 Subscribers,[13] expect to

---

brother, will convey the subscription to you. I have the honour to be the *prôneur* of your work wherever I have opportunity. One friend of mine told me he should certainly subscribe.'

George Wegg (d. 1777), of Colchester; his second son was Samuel Wegg (1723–1802), lawyer, Fellow (1753) and for 34 years Treasurer of the Royal Society (*GM* xlvii (1777), 459; Venn, under 'Wegg, Samuel'). Both father and son are included in the list of subscribers to the *History of Music*.

[12] Recalling in his letter of 28 May his first introduction to CB, Twining explained why he had not kept up the acquaintance: 'every man has his dreads, & his antipathies about him; some are afraid of spiders, some of cats &c—of all things in the world there is nothing that throws me into such a panic as the idea of being thought what is called a *pushing* man.'

[13] CB had stated in his 'Proposals' (see CB to Twining, 28 Apr. 1773, n. 4): 'It is the author's intention to publish the first volume in the course of next year, 1774. But, as the printing of it will be attended with too great an expence for him to risk it against the public opinion, though the work is in great forwardness, he cannot venture to send it to the press before *five hundred copies*, are subscribed for. ... And in order to render security reciprocal, between the public and the writer, if the number of copies specified be not ascertained by next Christmas, he will abandon the enterprize, and return the money to the subscribers.'

Twining had commented (28 May): 'The very mention, in your proposals, of abandoning the enterprise, hurt me; but I hope there is not the least doubt of your securing, without difficulty, the number you have fixt upon. You have deserved everything of the musical public, by the uncommon pains & expence you have been at, in order to procure them authentic information. It is a respect that is *seldom* paid to the public, & they ought to be grateful for it.'

grow rich by the Trade of an Author. However, I am now too far waded in Ink to retreat;[14] & therefore pursue the undertaking with all the Vigour of a Man in sight of the two Temples of Fame & Fortune, with the Goddess at the Door of each, beckoning him to come in.⌐

Your approbation of as much of my Plan as I think practicable & defensible myself, gave me great pleasure, and rubs off a considerable Part of the *public Debt* wch I have been talking of. ⌐If I could know when the Knight's *last sheet* was in the press, I would perhaps retouch & publish my Plan.⌐[15]—I like you for disliking my medling with the *Old Stuff*.[16] However, I wish you could see what I *have* done, before it is too late to change my Manner, & with what Humility I begin & end every thing I hazard on the Subject. One Comfort I have in this part of my work is, that the *Confession of Ignorance*[17] in speaking of Greek Music will be at least as *new* to the public as the conjectures of my predecessors, which, as you observe, are given with all the solemn and decisive assurance of Certainty & Demonstration.[18]

My present Idea is [19]to take your advice and to throw into[19] a Dissertation, or preliminary Discourse, what guess-work, & ancient Authorities, have furnished me concerning the Doctrine of Modes, Systems, & Genera, and to confine my narrative to Circumstances meerly historical. And these I shall treat with more familiarity,[20]

---

[14] Cf. 'I am in blood ┃ Stepp'd in so far that, should I wade no more, ┃ Returning were as tedious as go o'er' (*Macbeth*, III. iv. 136–8).

[15] Twining had written in his letter of 28 May: 'Your plan gave me much pleasure; it is unlucky that prudence prevents your publishing it as you intended; because it is such as certainly promises more entertainment, & a better *sort* of information than people, left to their own ideas, expect from such a Work.'

[16] 'Your idea[s] of a history of music, in general, I am much pleased to find coincide so nearly with my own. All the articles that relate to your principal object, the history of *modern* music (I mean as distinguish'd from the Greek &c) I think excellent' (ibid.).

[17] Samuel Johnson had written to CB on the subject of the notes to his edition of Shakespeare: 'where I am quite at a loss, I confess my ignorance, which is seldom done by commentators' (8 Mar. 1758, Berg; Johnson *Letters*, i. 106). This sentiment CB echoed: '. . . it appeared likewise necessary, before I attempted a history of ancient Greek music, to endeavour to investigate its properties, or at least to tell the little I knew of it, and ingenuously to confess my ignorance and doubts about the rest' (*Hist. Mus.* i, p. x; Mercer, i. 16).

[18] 'What disgusts & provokes one', Twining had observed, 'is the *gravity* of the writers of ancient music who *will* talk about the scale, the genera, the modes &c, as if they really knew what they meant, & were present at Greek concerts every evening of their lives. All sides, I think, both the defenders & the opposers of *harmony* in the ancient music, are too positive' (28 May 1773).

[19–19] MS to take . . . into] *interlined above deleted* to, give in

[20] Twining's advice to CB to 'throw' the obscurities and uncertainties of ancient music into a preliminary 'Dissertation' was omitted by Richard Twining when he made the copy of his brother's letter of 28 May. Richard Twining did, however, copy Thomas Twining's concurrence with CB as to the best manner of treating the subject: 'Obscurity & nonsense itself, will cease to offend, or even become amusing, when they are in the hands of a writer who sees them with unprejudiced eyes, gives them for what they are, & helps the reader to laugh at them. You cannot have much hope of instructing your readers in this part; but you will have many fair opportunities of diverting them by *just* ridicule.'

perhaps, than will be approved of by those who venerate the *Puerilities* of the Ancients more than the most manly Efforts of *grown-Gentlemen* among the Moderns.

If I am sure of anything ab[t] the Ancient Music, it is what you suggest concerning the Scale.[21] And I think the very passage in Euclid[22] upon which those who think otherwise have founded their opinions, is in our Favour. He says that the Diatonic Tetrachord moves from the acute to the grave by the Intervals of Tone, Tone, & Semitone: κατα τόνον, καὶ τονον, καὶ ἡμιτόνιον. Now the writers who take it for granted one after the other that **B** was the first & lowest Tone of the ancient Tetrachord are sure in that Case that **E** w[d] be the highest. So that **E D C B** give the Tone, Tone & Semitone required. But I rather think the Scale was quite the reverse, and instead of the Semitone being at the bottom was at *our* Top. **C D E F**, is a Series composed of Tone, Tone & Semitone. Add to this another disjunct Tetrachord of the same kind **G**[T]**A**[T]**B**[S]**C** and we have our complete Diatonic Octave, in an order of sounds much more likely to occur to the Musicians of Nature in remote ages of antiquity than the insipid Scale w[ch] the moderns have invented for them: I have not Time to give you all my reasons. Rousseau, I find, supposes the Gr. Scale retrograde to ours; and yet talks of their Tetrachords as if they moved in the order w[ch] I have just placed them in.[23]

When I read the passage in your Letter which says that 'it always makes you Sick to hear People talking about the *Invention* of Music.'[24] I recollected that I had not only had the like sickness formerly, but that I had written down something ab[t] it in my Memorandums.—I c[d] not

[21] Richard Twining did not transcribe what Thomas Twining suggested concerning the scale in ancient music in his letter of 28 May. In his reply dated 16 Oct., however, Twining counselled caution in dealing with the Greek scale: 'What hopes can we have of inverting this obstinate scale, While it is thus pinned down by this confounded long peg of a Proslambanomenos? ... When a man finds that a thing *will* be, in spite of his teeth, otherwise than he wishes it to be, it is the best philosophy to seek for reasons why it should be so.' CB accordingly found 'an infallible rule ... in the works of the great Euclid'. See *Hist. Mus.* i. 14–18; Mercer, i. 33–6.

[22] CB refers to the *Introductio harmonica*, for a long time attributed to Euclid by, among others, CB's source, Marcus Meibom in his *Antiquae musicae auctores septem* (Amsterdam, 1652). The author of the *Introductio* was in fact Cleonides (*fl. c.*100). See O. Strunk, *Source Readings in Music History* (1952), pp. 34–46; also *Hist. Mus.* i. 446–8; Mercer, i. 353–4.

[23] See Rousseau, *Dictionnaire de musique*, under 'Gamme', 'Genre', and 'Tétracorde'.

[24] In his letter of 28 May Twining had written: 'The *invention* of music, too, which was surely never invented at all, always makes me sick', and elaborated on this statement in his reply of 16 Oct.: 'People talk about *music* in *general*, as if Amphion, or Apollo &c, had sat themselves down, & *contrived* it, as they might have done a pocket boot jack, or a cucumber cutter. If there was any *inventor* of *music*, it was the first man who found that he could sustain his voice in one tone; but one may as well talk of a first inventor of eating.'

find it then, but a few Days since found among my loose Thoughts the following, which is perhaps too wild for use, in its present form; but it will serve as a part of my *Profession de Foi*, to you, who will, if I am erroneous, lead me in the right way.—[25]'Music seems a part of Nature as much as Light or Heat; and to number either among human Inventions is equally absurd. The Invention of all Science must be referred to the Author of Nature; for what is *Geometry* but the study and imitation of those proportions by which the world is governed? *Astronomy* but reflecting upon and calculating the Motion, Magnitude and Distance of those visible, but wonderful parts of Nature which are placed before our Eyes? *Theology*, but contemplating the works of the Creator, and adoring him in his attributes? *Medicine*, but the discovery & use of what inferior beings instinctively find in every Wood and Field through which they range, when the animal Oeconomy is disturbed by accident or Intemperance? The ancients by experiments on a single-string found out the relations and Proportions of one sound to another; but the moderns have gone further, & discovered that nature in every sounding Body has herself arranged and settled all these proportions, in such a manner, that each single sound is composed of the most Perfect Harmonies; and where two concordant sounds are produced in just proportion, nature gives a *Third sound*, which is their true & fundamental Base.'[25]—If you mean that the *Art* of music was never invented, I am likewise of your opinion for that must have had its Infancy, childhood, & youth, before it arrived at Maturity.—

> 'By slow degrees the arts are won,
> By slow degrees e'en Hercules grew strong.'[26]

I thank you for Mottos—they are admirably well chosen for the Purposes you mention.[27] When I quit the Greeks and Romans, I shall most assuredly adopt the verse in Homer[28]—and the passage in Dante[29] when I *board* Counterpoint. The English of my German Motto[30] is this—'Be proud Germany of the Musicians to which thou

---

[25-25] This passage found its way, virtually unchanged, into *Hist. Mus.* i. 187–8; Mercer, i. 164.

[26] Not identified.

[27] Much of what Twining had to say about mottos appears to have been omitted in Richard Twining's transcription. A few disjointed sentences are preserved. Twining wrote (28 May): 'As to Mottoes I own I rather like them, when they are very pat & not blown upon.'

[28] Twining had suggested (ibid.): 'I have often thought that the best motto for a history of Greek music would be this line in Homer, "Ημεις δε κλεος οιον αχουομεν, ουδε τι ιδμεν"': 'we hear but a rumour and know not anything' (*Iliad*, ii. 486). CB did not use this motto in the *History of Music*.

[29] Twining, in his letter of 28 May, had commended CB's quotation from Dante's *Purgatorio*, ii. 113–14, on the title-page of his *Italian Tour*: 'I thought you happy in the motto of your first journal.' See *Tours*, i, p. [v].

[30] On the title-page of the *German Tour*. See *Tours*, ii, p. [v].

hast given birth; in France & Italy there are none greater.'

Your *scale* of admiration at Blainville's Hist^y, though I cannot *compose* my Muscles in it, has *worked* 'em *soundly*. He seems just the reverse of the Knight—the one tells you *nothing*, & the other *everything*.[31]

I now come to your last Letter,[32] wch has been so long on the road, waiting in London for a parcel, or some such nonsense to be full freighted, ere it was shipped that I have but just rec^d it.—I am happy again in finding our Musical opinions congenial. Corelli & Geminiani, I believe, hold the same rank in my List of favourite Composers as in yours. We owe almost all Grace & Simplicity in modern Music to the one, and a great deal of the art & contrivance to the other. Indeed the advancem^t of the Violin, & its Family, towards perfection in this Country, for the 1st 40 or 50 years of this Century, in short, till the arrival of Giardini, was in a great Measure the Work of Geminiani.[33] But as a player, he was always deficient in *Time*; as a composer, *laboured*; & as a Critic, *jamais de bonne Foi*, changing his opinions according to his Interest, as often as Caprice.[34] One Day he w^d set up French Music against all other—the next, English—Scots—Irish, anything but the best Compositions of Handel & Italy. You know, I dare say, how much he preferred the Character of a Picture-dealer, without the least knowledge or Taste in Painting, to that of a Musician, by which he had acquired his reputation & importance. I am afraid there is such a *penchant* in the generality of Italian artists towards Chicane, that they w^d rather trick a Man out of a Guinea than get it fairly, in a John-Trot[35] way. & when Geminiani's Musical decisions ceased to be irrevocable, he tried his Hand at painting.[36]

[31] Twining's comments on Blainville have been omitted in the copy made by Richard Twining. For CB's comments on Blainville, see CB to Ebeling, Nov. 1771, n. 9. Later he called Blainville's writings on music 'compilations without taste, which teach nothing new to those who know any thing about music already; and not enough to those who know nothing' (Rees).

[32] Of 22 July 1773 (see n. 1). Richard Twining copied out only some of the passages in the letter dealing with Geminiani's opinions, which Twining had gleaned in conversation (see CB to Twining, 28 Apr. 1773, n. 13). CB himself, however, published other sections from Twining's letter under his discussion of Corelli in the *History of Music* (iii. 552–4, 557–8; Mercer, ii. 439–40, 442–3).

[33] Francesco Xaverio Geminiani (1687–1762), a pupil of Corelli, arrived in London in 1714, and established himself as a violin virtuoso, composer, teacher, musical theorist, and art dealer (*New Grove*). In 1751 Geminiani published in English his violin method, *The Art of Playing on the Violin*, 'which was a very useful work in its day; the shifts and examples of different difficulties, and uses of the bow, being infinitely superior to those in any other book of the kind, or indeed oral instruction, which the nation could boast, till the arrival of Giardini' (*Hist. Mus.* iv. 643; Mercer, ii. 992).

[34] In his letter of 22 July, Twining wrote, 'As to Geminiani's *opinions* of music & musicians, I fear they were often governed too much by caprice or prejudice.'

[35] CB's use of 'John Trot', with the connotation of an honest English yeoman, differs from the definition in *OED*, 'John', 4: 'a man of slow or uncultured intellect, a bumpkin, a clown.'

[36] CB repeats almost verbatim this characterization of Geminiani in *Hist. Mus.* iv. 645; Mercer, ii. 993–4; Rees.

⌐The acc[t] of Corelli's Inferiority in Execution to the Neapolitans of his Time, is truely Characteristic.[37] The Roman School of Music *now*, tho' superior in Grace, taste & refinement, has neither the Fire, Invention, nor Art of the Neapolitan. The Genius of Corelli was perhaps limited by Nature to a small range; but his chast[e] & timid selection of passages narrowed it still more.—With respect to his plagiarism, I believe nothing of it.[38]—Every age has it's phraseology—Corelli's is that of his Time. Geminiani multiplied Notes, rather than improved Melody, of w[ch] he had very little. Old Roseingrave[39] used to talk of an old Church double Fugue by Negri or Carissime,[40] I forget w[ch], exactly upon the same Subjects as that in the best of Geminiani's Concertos—the 6th in the 2[d] Set. in **E** natural.

His favourite Minuet

is very like one in the same Key, among old Scarlatti's Concertos, in Melody & Conduct.[42]—But he was a great Master of Harmony & very useful in his Day.—

When He told you of poor Corelli's *Disgrazia* at Naples, I suppose he *sunk* his own, at the same place.[43] Barbella[44] assured me that his

[37] Although omitted in Richard Twining's MS transcript, Twining's communication of Geminiani's anecdote about Corelli's inferiority to the Neapolitans of his time is published in *Hist. Mus.* iii. 552–4; Mercer, ii. 439–40.

[38] In his letter of 22 July, Twining had written, 'Geminiani asserted that Corelli availed himself much of the compositions of other masters, particularly of the Masses in which he played at Rome; that he got much from *Lulli* (particularly the method of modulating in *legatura*) & from Bononcini's famous Camilla'. CB published this passage in *Hist. Mus.* iii. 557; Mercer, ii. 442 with footnotes that indicate he modified his scepticism regarding Corelli's 'plagiarism'. See also Rees.

[39] Thomas Roseingrave (1688–1766), English composer and organist. As a young man, CB had frequently visited Roseingrave, whose 'conversation was very entertaining and instructive, particularly on musical subjects.' See *Hist. Mus.* iv. 262–6; Mercer, ii. 703–6; Rees; Lonsdale, p. 11.

[40] Marc'Antonio Negri (*fl.* 1608–21), vice *maestro di cappella* at St Mark's, Venice (1612–20); Giacomo Carissimi (1605–74), of whom CB declared, 'no composer of the last century was more the delight of his contemporaries or more respected by posterity' (*Hist. Mus.* iv. 141; Mercer, ii. 607).

[41] CB quotes the second movement, *Allegro assai*, from Geminiani's *Concerto grosso*, Op. 3, no. 6 (1733). This concerto, CB asserted, was 'the most pleasing and perfect composition of the kind, within my knowledge' (*Hist. Mus.* iv. 645 n.; Mercer, ii. 994 n.).

[42] According to CB, Geminiani studied counterpoint under Alessandro Scarlatti (*Hist. Mus.* iv. 641; Mercer, ii. 991). The finale, marked *Allegro cantabile*, of Geminiani's *Concerto grosso*, Op. 2, no. 1 (1732), was popularly known as 'Geminiani's Minuet' (see CB to Case, 23 July 1759, n. 8). Geminiani's *Concerti grossi*, Opp. 2 and 3 were well known to English audiences, being widely used as interval music in the theatres (see R. Fiske, *English Theatre Music in the Eighteenth Century* (1973), p. 107).

[43] For the anecdotes relating how Corelli and Geminiani disgraced themselves at Naples, see *Hist. Mus.* iii. 552–3, iv. 641; Mercer, ii. 439–40, 991.

[44] Emanuele Barbella (1718–77), Neapolitan violinist and composer, whom CB had met at

Father told him he remembered Geminian[i] coming to Naples (before his arrival in England) to seek employment; but he was so inferior to the performers of that place that he was never allowed a better part there than that of the Tenor.[45] They allowed him indeed to have a strong Hand; but thought him too wild & unsteady to be trusted as a leader, or even 2ᵈ Fiddle.

I shall *Boar* you to death abᵗ him.—He *bothered* poor Worgan[46] so much formerly, that, after he had studied the *Modulation* of Palestrina; the *organ playing* of Handel, & the *Scores* of Geminiani, & shᵈ have begun to *think for himself*; he tells him that the Spaniards were the only Composers in the world: That if he had a mind to know anything of the matter, he shᵈ first learn to read the Spanish Language; & then Study a Book called *El porque della Musica*[47]—wᶜʰ he wᵈ part with to him, as his particular Frᵈ, for the small price of 20 Guineas.—What Effect had this, but to spoil the Vaux-hall Ballads?[48]—Having now dispached Corelli & Geminiani, I must bestow a few words on the Knight, who, par Parenthese, has borrowed of Worgan the Book of Books, *El porque della Musica*; but declared to me that he found nothing extraordinary in it; he shᵈ have added, *except the difficulty of readᵍ it.*— What pity it is that his Majesty, wᵗʰ his Title cᵈ not bestow on him the Gift of Tongues.[49] For my own part I find more are wanting in pursuing my work than were necessary to stop the Bricklayers at Babel.ꞌ—Among your Acquiremᵗˢ have you any Hebrew to spare?— if you have, for Charity, give me an explanation of the words used in the Titles of the *Bible psalms*, to save me the trouble of applying to any

Naples in Oct. 1770, and who furnished CB with 'much biographical knowledge concerning old Neapolitan musicians' (*Tours*, i. 264–5, 282, 284). 'He corresponded with me in London, ... communicating to me, by letter, several other particulars of the Neapolitan school' (*Hist. Mus.* iii. 569–70; Mercer, ii. 451–2). His father, Francesco Barbella (1692–1733), was also a violinist at Naples.

⁴⁵ The viola.

⁴⁶ John Worgan (1724–90), Mus.B. (1748), Mus.D. (1775), English organist and composer, 'was first taught by his brother, and afterwards by Roseingrave, till getting acquainted with Geminiani, he swore by no other divinity ... [He] composed innumerable songs and concertos for Vauxhall' (*Hist. Mus.* iv. 665–6; Mercer, ii. 1009).

⁴⁷ *El porqué de la música, en que se contiene los quatro artes de ella, canto llano, canto de órgano, contrapunto, y composición* (Alcalá de Henares, 1672), by the Spanish organist and theorist, Andrés Lorente (1624–1703). CB's copy is listed in 'Cat. Fac. Mus.', item 84.

⁴⁸ From 1751 to 1774, Worgan served as organist and composer to Vauxhall Gardens (*New Grove*). In his article on Worgan in Rees, CB was to write: 'The knowledge of Spanish and study of Lorente seem to have had no other effect on Worgan's compositions, than to spoil his Vauxhall songs; which though sung into popularity by dint of repetition, had no attractive grace, or pleasing cast of melody.'

⁴⁹ Sir John Hawkins wrote of *El porqué de la musica*: 'This book, of which the late Mr. Geminiani was used to say it had not its fellow in any of the modern languages, is questionless a very learned work; it is in truth a musical institute, and may be said to contain all that is necessary for a practical composer to know' (Hawkins, iv. 265).

one else. Is *Gittith*, Neginoth, Nehiloth, or Sheminith the name of an Instrument or a Place? and what do you say *Selah*, so often used in the psalms, means? Calmet & all the Commentators are gravelled.—The Polyglott, as well as other Translations confound the Names of Instruments—Lute, Harp & Psaltery, are all alike[50]—ᶠI like yʳ Accᵗ of the Knight's Erudition much—& his own Specimens of English, as well as the importance of his Conjectures & discoveries, in the notes upon Walton do not repress my Scribling ardor perhaps so much as they ought.[51]

The First Time I saw him, I was such a Fool, in the course of our Conversation, as to *bolt out* that *Fontanini*, wᵗʰ Apostolo Zeno's notes,[52] was a useful Book for Lovers of Italian Literature.—& likewise that the Italians & French had quarrelled abᵗ music so long since as in the Time of Charlemagne.—The next Time I saw him he told me, as *News*, that Apostolo Zeno's notes on Fontanini (neither of whose Names he seemed to have heard of when I first saw him) had supplied him wᵗʰ much knowledge of Ital. Musical authors. & that he had found an accᵗ of the Quarrel between the Roman & Gallic Singers. I suppose in Ro[u]sseau. You will find that he'll make a huge pother abᵗ a MS. which the late Mʳ West[53] lent him, at the request of Mʳ Daines Barrington,[54] after he had put it in my Hands, just before I set out for

[50] For CB's amusing survey of Biblical commentary on the Psalm titles, 'Selah', and ancient Hebrew instruments, see *Hist. Mus.* i. 236–43; Mercer, i. 199–204; for Antoine Calmet, see CB to Crisp, [31] May [1771], n. 14. It may be added that with regard to 'Selah', modern biblical scholarship is equally 'gravelled'.

[51] Twining's account of Sir John Hawkins was, unfortunately, not transcribed by Richard Twining. For Hawkins's edition (1760) of Walton's *Complete Angler*, see CB to Twining, 28 Apr. 1773, nn. 8, 9; Lonsdale, pp. 189–91.

[52] *Biblioteca dell'eloquenza italiana . . . con le annotazioni del Signor Apostolo Zeno*, 2 vols. (Venice, 1753). These volumes are based on *Della eloquenza italiana*, first published in Rome in 1706 by Giusto Fontanini (1666–1736), titular Archbishop of Ancyra, scholar and critic. The Venetian poet and literary historian, Apostolo Zeno (1668–1750), revised the work of Fontanini, and provided copious notes (see *Biografia degli italiani illustri*, ed. E. de Tipaldo (Venice, 1834–45), vii. 25–40, 438–50). CB's copy of the *Biblioteca* fetched 16s. at the dispersal of his library (*Cat. Misc. Lib.*, lot 663).

[53] James West (1703–72), lawyer, politician, antiquary, and bibliophile, MP for St Albans (1741–68), Boroughbridge (1768–72), FSA (1727), Fellow (1726), Treasurer (1736–68), and President (1768–72) of the Royal Society (*DNB*; Namier and Brooke, iii. 624–6).

The manuscript volume referred to, the Waltham Holy Cross Abbey MS, is now in the British Library: Lansdowne MS 763. Hawkins describes its provenance and contents at great length in his *History*, i. 353–5; ii. 142–3, 175, 201–47; and CB relatively briefly in *Hist. Mus.* ii. 412–27; Mercer, i. 685–95. See also CB to Martini, 20 Oct. 1779, n. 7.

[54] The Hon. Daines Barrington (1727–1800), judge, naturalist, and antiquary, had written on 24 June 1773 to his antiquarian friend, Samuel Pegge (1704–96): 'I believe that both Sʳ John Hawkins's & Dʳ Burneys History of Music will have their distinct merit' (Bodleian, MS Eng. lett. d. 44, p. 371). Fanny Burney records that it was Barrington who had introduced CB and Hawkins to one another (*EJL* i. 147).

On 20 May 1773, Barrington had proposed CB as a candidate for the Royal Society. The

Italy. He told me at my return that this MS, not a word of which he c^d read, had been 'of singular service to him respecting English Music'— I c^d not give much Time to the Book while it was in my Hands; but I took a list of its Contents—among other things there was a Tract which he took for the Micrologus of Guido, & which was only by somebody else upon his principles. Another by John de Muris, because somebody helped him to make out his name in it.—The MS. was written, I mean transcribed, but a little while before the Invention of printing, in the 15th Cent^y—I have seen in Italy much older Copies of Guido's Micrologus in Padre Martini's Collection & in the Lorenzinian Library at Florence[55] than S^r Jn° can have met wth. And of John de Muris besides the Copy in the King's Library at Paris, I saw a very good one the other Day in the Bodleian at Oxford.[56] All these matters must perhaps be mentioned; but to dwell upon them in my Hist^y, as an antiquarian, w^d be but adding one volume more to the long list of *unread* Books, already written on the subject of Music.

The Knight's reasoning ab^t Musical Expression is curious. For my part I think good Music well executed wants *no words* to explain its meaning to me—it says everything that the Musician pleases.—And Addison & others who make such a Fuss ab^t not understanding words, when People sing, say, perhaps, only that they Love Poetry better than Music.[57] Handel's air, 'Return o God of Hosts',[58] is a fine supplication, & whether it was first made to a Mistress or to the Divinity proves nothing against Music being capable of expressing the passions.

By this Time I suppose you have had partly enough—I am as much ashamed of the Length of this Letter as of the Time you have waited for it. I did not think I either w^d or c^d write so long a one to any body, over head & Ears, as I am, in Debt with Correspondents; but what we do *con amore* is usually done at a Jerk & with all our Might.—

certificate, in Barrington's hand, reads: 'Charles Burney Mus. D: of Queen Square Bloomsbury well known to the litterary world by the travels through France Italy & Germany which he hath lately publish'd, as well as by his knowledge in various branches of science being desirous of becoming a Fellow of the Royal Society we the under written on our personal knowledge recommend him as highly deserving of that honour' (Royal Society of London, MS Certificates, III. 172). Supported by the signatures of nine other Fellows, CB was elected on 16 Dec. 1773. On 23 Dec., he 'Paid 5 Guineas signed Bond & [was] Admitted' as a Fellow of the Royal Society.

[55] For Guido's *Micrologus* in Padre Martini's collection, and the Laurentian Library, see *Tours*, i. 147, 185.

[56] Writing in his *History of Music* about the theoretical treatises attributed to Johannes de Muris, CB gave 'a complete list of his works that are still preserved in the several libraries of Europe' (ii. 198–201; Mercer, i. 545–7).

[57] See *The Spectator*, ed. D. F. Bond (Oxford, 1965), Nos. 18, 29, 251, 405 by Joseph Addison (1672–1719); and Nos. 258, 278 by Sir Richard Steele (1672–1729). For CB's spirited rejoinder to the *Spectator* censure of Italian opera, see *Hist. Mus.* iv. 225–9; Mercer, ii. 675–8.

[58] An air sung by Micah in the oratorio *Samson*, composed in 1741–2.

Do, let me entreat you before I sign & seal, never to think of paying postage, or waiting for Franks. Does not one pay a shilling portrage for a ⌜Cursed stinking⌝[59] Hare not worth Sixpence, when sweet; and shall I *begrudge* portrage for a Feast of Soul?—pray write, whenever you can, without wishing the Letter to *miscarry*; & when you come to Town for Heaven's sake call in Queen Square, without the wicked wish that I may be out.[60]—We c^d do more Business in an Hour's Conversation by interchanging & comparing sentiments, than in a week of such Work as this. I am,⌝

Dear Sir, wth great regard,
y^r obliged & most humble Servt
Ch. Burney.

Great Massingham, Norfolk. | 30th Aug^t—my head Quarters | will be, at Lynn R^s, till towards | the End of September, when I | intend returning to London.

To Arthur Young[1] Queen Square, 11 October 1773

ALS (BL Add. MS 35126, fos. 157–8^v).
Addressed: Arthur Young Esqr | at Bradmore Farm | North Mimms | Herts   *Pmk:*
12 OC   *Docketed by* ?: Copied Jany 20th 1834   *Publ.:* Mercer, ii. 1029–30.

Queen Square
Oct. 11 —73

Dear Sir.
You understand the Arcana of the Bibliopolean Tribe so much better than myself, that I want your Counsel. I shall state my present situation, as an Author, & then beg of you to tell me how, under Similar Circumstances, you w^d act.

My Italian Tour is reprinted & ready to deliver,[2] not one copy of

---

[59] MS Cursed stinking] *deleted by Richard Twining who interlined* wretched
[60] Expatiating on his horror at being considered a '*pushing* man', Twining had confessed in his letter of 28 May: 'When I knock'd at your door, I half wish'd you might not be at home; & when I put my letter in the post, that it might miscarry.' This instance of Twining's shyness became a standing joke among the Burneys. See Fanny Burney to CB, [6 July 1778], (Berg).

[1] Arthur Young (1741–1820), a leading figure in the English Agricultural Revolution, traveller, whose constant stream of publications had begun in 1758, was CB's brother-in-law. In 1765 he had married Martha Allen (1741–1815), younger sister of CB's second wife. See J. G. Gazley, *The Life of Arthur Young, 1741–1820* (Philadelphia, 1973).
[2] The second edition of the *Italian Tour*, printed for T. Becket, J. Robson, and G. Robinson,

the first Edit. being left. I have corrected & somewhat enlarged it, to the amount of 10 or 12 Pages.[3]—The German Tour has gone off so well, that of 1000 Copies, Robertson[4] says he imagines not one will be left by Jan[y] next.

Now Becket[5] has called once or twice when I was out, as Hami[l]ton[6] tells me, to sound me as to disposing of the Copy-right, or 2[d] Impression of both Tours.

What w[d] you do? w[d] you dispose of the new Edit: of the Italian, & stand the rest? or w[d] you dispose of *all*, or *Stand all*? I sh[d] be Sorry to throw away two B[ks] that have made their way, without Bookselling, or other Craft. & yet I want all my Time & Thoughts so much for my History, that I sh[d] be glad If I c[d] cleverly wash my Hands of all Trouble ab[t] former Publications.—The advertising, & sale, however of these Tours will awaken attention in some to the Subject of my great undertaking, & keep it alive in others.[7] & it will become the Bookseller's interest to push, if they Purchase, the former works, which will be serving me in spite of & wth themselves.—If you advise *selling* Copy-right or Edition-right, what sh[d] I ask in either Case?—Suppose the Trade w[d] take off my Hands not only this new impression of the Italian Tour, but that now on sale of the Germ. Tour, concerning which I have settled with nobody, nor nobody wth me?—suppose I say, Gentlemen, what will you give me.

and priced 6*s*. bound, was published on 18 Dec. 1773 (*Public Advertiser*; *Morning Chronicle*). For the clearly strategic purpose of this publication date, see n. 7 below.

[3] A short notice in the Jan. 1774 issue of the *Critical Review* (xxxvii. 77) informed the reading public, 'In this new edition of Dr. Burney's Italian Tour, though the title-page promises only corrections, we find several additions in different parts of the work, which has extended it twelve or fourteen pages more than the first edition'. The additions are then listed, and the notice concludes with a genial comment by 'The Reviewers' (see Lonsdale, p. 130, n. 3).

[4] A slip for George Robinson (1737–1801), who had set up in 1764 a publishing and wholesale bookselling business at Addison's Head, 25 Paternoster Row. CB's slip was no doubt due to the fact that Robinson was in partnership with John Roberts (d. *c.*1776), trading as 'Robinson and Roberts'. See *DNB*; Plomer, p. 215; Maxted, pp. 191–2.

[5] Thomas Becket (*c.*1721–1813), bookseller and publisher at Tully's Head (corner of Adelphi) in the Strand, imported many books from overseas, and published CB's *Tours*, and the first volume of the *History* in conjunction with Robinson, and James Robson (1733–1806), whose shop was situated at 27, the Feathers, New Bond Street (Plomer, pp. 20–1, 216; Maxted, pp. 17, 192–3; *GM* lxxxiii (1813)[2], 630; J. Taylor, *Records of My Life* (1832), i. 383–5).

[6] Archibald Hamilton (*c.*1720–93), editor and publisher of the *Critical Review* (see CB to Crisp, [31] May [1771], nn. 7, 13).

[7] As CB's deadline of Christmas 1773 for the accumulation of 500 subscribers to the *History of Music* approached (see CB to Twining, 28 Apr. 1773, n. 4; 30 Aug. 1773, n. 13), the newspapers in mid-December carried heavy advertising for the second edition of the *Italian Tour*, published on 18 Dec. (see *Public Advertiser*, 16 Dec. et seqq.; *Morning Chronicle*, 17 Dec. et seqq.; *St. James's Chronicle*, 14–16 Dec. et seqq.). These newspapers also advertised CB's 'Proposals', giving the full text of the expanded version as it is found facing the title-page of the second edition of the *Italian Tour*. Although still dated 'London, April 20th, 1773', the expanded 'Proposals' added a fourth 'Condition': that the names of the subscribers would be published in the *History of Music*, and that non-subscribers would have to pay more for the projected two volumes.

For the 2ᵈ Edition of Ital. Tour,⎫
paying all the Expences of it? ──⎭
What for the Copy right of Dᵒ? ─
or Conditionally, allowing something for⎫
every new Impression, provided I ────⎬
prepare it for the press ? ────────⎭
For the 1ˢᵗ Edit. of Germ. Tour?
For 2ᵈ Dᵒ?
or for Copy-right, in perpetuity?
But in every Case shᵈ not something be
allowed for preparing a new impression?

Now, opposite to these Questions, if you wᵈ be kind enough to specify a fair & practicable sum,[8] by wᶜʰ I mean one that will neither fright the Trade, nor Injure myself, you would very much oblige

Dear Sir
Your affectionate Servᵗ
Ch. Burney.

I beg you to present my best Compᵗˢ to Mʳˢ Young—you have not mumbled tough Beef-steaks, nor eat Cold Meat, nor taken Pot-Luck in Qu. Sq. a great while

To [Brigg Fountaine?][1] [Queen Square], 3–[4] November 1773

ALS (Berg).
Docketed by ?: Original letter from Dʳ Burney ┃ (Author of this histʸ of Music) ┃ to his friend Mʳ Bewley, Surgeon ┃ at Massingham—Norfolk—   *And by* ??: Dʳ Burney to B.F

---

[8] Young did not fill in the blank spaces left for his estimates. For the outcome of CB's negotiations with the booksellers, see CB to Robinson, 9 Dec. 1773.

[1] The probable recipient of this letter, Brigg Price Fountaine (*c*.1745–1825), educated at Clare College, Cambridge, had assumed in 1765 by Act of Parliament the surname and arms of Fountaine. His mother was a niece of Sir Andrew Fountaine (1676–1753), of Narford Hall, one of CB's early Norfolk patrons. A cultivated and learned man, Brigg Fountaine later published a translation of the sequel to *Don Quixote* by the pseudonymous author, Alonso Fernandez de Avellaneda, entitled *The Life and Exploits of the Ingenious Gentleman Don Quixote . . . Translated from the Spanish* (Swaffham and London, 1805). See *GM* xcv (1825)¹, 477; Lonsdale, p. 41.
  The conflicting evidence in the dockets identifying the recipient of this letter (see headnote) may stem from Bewley's friendship with Fountaine. Bewley was fond of playing duets with Fountaine during visits to Narford Hall (Bewley to CB, [Nov. 1778], Osborn). CB's later letter to Brigg Fountaine of 5 Apr. 1776, which discusses a German publication, supports the testimony of the 'Dʳ Burney to B. F' attribution. It seems likely that CB, possibly with Bewley's assistance, had enlisted Fountaine's help with German during his summer stay in Norfolk.

Dear Sir.

When I sent you the German Books, I hardly knew what a dry & tiresome Piece of work I had Cut out for you. I now pity you, & blush for myself. Old Printz[2] is hitherto as dry as the 10th Chapt. of Nehemiah, or the 1st of St Mathew. He gives little else but a List of Names, of anc^t Poets & Musicians wch every school-boy has read of with the entertaining addition of their marvellows abchievements. Brossard, in his Musical Dict^y said that Printz & Bontempi were *two Jewels*, that he prized more than all the rest of the Authors (to the amount of 1500) in his Collection.[3] This, & Marpurg's flourish, made me Curious to see Printz's Hist^y wch is very scarce[4]—(Bontempi I found in Italy.)—It was absolutely necessary for me to know how he treated the Subject, & I thank you heartily for wading thro' so much of him. Indeed there seems to be more Merit in his Plan than Execution,—tho' perhaps he becomes more entertaining as he advances towards Modern Times.— I sh^d like to know his notions of Greek Modes & Counterpoint, as I am drawing to a Focus whatever has been said by writers of Eminence *on* those Subjects, & not till I have examined the Evidence, on both sides shall I dare to pass Judgment.—

The articles I marked were chosen merely from the Titles, for I had no Time to puzzle out the rest—when you find, as you often will, among these Germans, that the Tracts I have fixed on are long-winded, dry, unentertaining, & useless to my work; don't meddle with them, but merely tell me how d——d bad they are—or favour me with the *precis* only—When there is anything Singular, or interesting from the manner in which it is treated, I sh^d wish it entire—not else, for your Eyes', & patience sake—I thank you for Comparing

Bewley himself does not appear to be a likely recipient: in none of his letters to CB does Bewley show a knowledge of German; CB and Bewley had long since replaced the salutation 'Dear Sir' with 'Dear Bewley' and 'Dear Burney'; and the tone of the letter as a whole, while friendly, is not intimate as was the CB–Bewley correspondence.

[2] Wolfgang Caspar Printz (1641–1717), *Historische Beschreibung der edelen Sing- und Kling-Kunst* (Dresden, 1690), the first major German history of music. See n. 4 below.

[3] Sébastien de Brossard (1655–1730), French ecclesiastic, composer, and writer on music, compiled the first dictionary of musical terms under the title *Dictionaire de musique, contenant une explication des termes . . . et un catalogue de plus de 900. Auteurs, qui ont écrit sur la musique* (1703). Many subsequent editions appeared (*DBF*; *New Grove*). CB rather exaggerates Brossard's high opinion of Printz's *Historische Beschreibung* and Bontempi's *Historia musica*. Brossard wrote: 'Ce sont deux excellents Livres, que j'estime & conserve très-cherement' (*Dictionaire* (3rd edn., Amsterdam, [1707?]), p. 369). CB owned a copy of this Amsterdam edition of Brossard's *Dictionaire* ('Cat. Fac. Mus.', item 22).

[4] As CB was to explain in *Hist. Mus.* iii. 576; Mercer, ii. 459–60, he never managed to see a copy of Printz's *Historische Beschreibung*, and had to rely on the two-part summary with extracts given of it in Marpurg's *Historisch-kritische Beyträge zur Aufnahme der Musik*, i (1754–5), 172–9, 479–500. CB had received a set of Marpurg's essays from Ebeling (CB to Ebeling, Nov. 1771, n. 20), and was now having Marpurg's summary of Printz translated, as well as other articles in Marpurg's periodical.

dates with Blair[5]—I have not his B^k, 'tis cursed dear—I believe 5 G^s—Usher, S^r Is. Newton & Priestly will be my principal Guides in Chronolog.[6]—but, will you look into Blair, & tell me what he says of *Sesostris?*[7]—

Don't be nice at all ab^t your future Translations—you may imagine that such long winded Gentry as these Germans must be sparingly used in my Work, wch I shall wish to have *read*.—Therefore the Chief use I shall make, unless of very tid-bits, will be to consult them & squeese their opinions into a Nut-shell.—

I now Come to your 2^d kind Communication, wch is so much the more welcome for coming so soon— *bis dat* &c[8]—I think this Lute Historian[9] makes but a dull Business of it—by giving so many Proofs, he proves nothing. What a pack of Stumping Stories does he give!—none ab^t *Cocks* indeed, but *Bulls* in abundance.[10]—Well, the greater the *seccatura*, the more I am obliged to your Perseverence.—The Hist^y of the Lute was a promising Title.——But his manner of writing it is truely German—tedious, dull, & Circumstantial—always supposing his reader ignorant of the most common incidents relative to his subject, he gives you *all* that he can possibly scrape together—& 'tis ever so wth German Writers—I wonder they do not begin every Book they write, by the *Alphabet*, & a few easy rules of orthography.—As to the Tract on Anc^t Harmony,[11] if 'tis only *Harmonics*, don't bestow a

[5] The Revd John Blair (d. 1782), LLD, author of *The Chronology and History of the World, from the Creation to the Year of Christ, 1753, Illustrated in LVI Tables* (1754), which went through several later editions.

[6] Dr James Ussher (1581–1656), Archbishop of Armagh. The *Annales*, his great work of chronology adopted in the margins of the English Bible, translated from the Latin into English appeared as *The Annals of the World. Deduced from the Origin of Time, and continued to the beginning of the Emperour Vespasians Reign* (1658). The book is lot 2060 in *Cat. Misc. Lib.*, and was sold for 18*s*.

CB owned two copies of *The Chronology of Ancient Kingdoms Amended* (1728) by Sir Isaac Newton (1642–1727), as well as a copy of the 1728 abridgement (*Cat. Misc. Lib.*, lots 1345–7).

The Revd Joseph Priestley (1733–1804), dissenting divine and scientist now best remembered for the discovery of oxygen, was a friend and correspondent of William Bewley. CB refers to Priestley's two publications on chronology: *A Description of a Chart of Biography* (Warrington, 1764), and *A Description of a New Chart of History* (1770). These popular pamphlets accompanied and explained engraved sheets bearing diagrammatic tables of chronology.

[7] In his attempt to date the invention and use of musical instruments in ancient Egypt, CB needed to know when the legendary King Sesostris lived. In the *History of Music*, CB draws upon Blair, saying this 'excellent chronologer fixes the reign of Sesostris 1485 years B.C.' (i. 204 n.; Mercer, i. 176 n.). See Blair, *Chronology*, plate 2.

[8] 'Bis dat qui cito dat' ('He gives twice who gives soon'), a proverbial saying attributed to Publilius Syrus (*fl.* 1st cent. BC).

[9] Ernst Gottlieb Baron (1696–1760), *Historisch-theoretisch und practische Untersuchung des Instruments der Lauten* (Nuremberg, 1727), to which Baron later added a supplement under the title 'Beytrag zur historisch-theoretisch- und practischen Untersuchung der Laute', published as an article in Marpurg's *Historisch-kritische Beyträge*, ii (1756), 65–83. CB refers to this supplement, which bears the running-title 'Hrn. Barons Beytrag zur Historie der Laute'.

[10] See *OED*, under 'bull' *sb.* 4, in the sense of a 'ludicrous jest' or unconscious 'inconsistency'; and under 'cock-and-bull'.

[11] F. W. Marpurg, 'Ob und was für Harmonie die Alten gehabt, und zu welcher Zeit dieselbe zur Vollkommenheit gebracht worden', *Historisch-kritische Beyträge*, ii (1756), 273–322.

moment upon it—I am at this Inst^t overwhelmed with *Sections of the Canon-divisions of the Monochord*, & *Harmonical* & *Arithmetical proportions*.[12] —Who the d—l will read anything ab^t 'em?—none of my subscribers, I am sure—not even Mathematicians, who will never imagine *I* can tell them anything new ab^t Such matters. Never mind explaining Greek Terms—I have been drumming over them so much lately that I know them now as well as ever I shall—

I have been in Possession of the Life of Ptolomy Auletes[13] some Time, but thank you for your Information concerning it—there is a great deal Ab^t Anc^t Music in it—

I need not tell you that I write in great Haste, tho' it is necessary to beg of you to excuse it. If I were to wait till I had more Leisure, God knows when I sh^d thank you for all the Trouble you have taken; therefore I must entreat you to accept of my best acknowledgm^{ts} in this rough way, & that you will believe

me to be your much obliged & Obed^t Servt

Chas Burney.

can you in the Vol^s under examination fish out Marpurg's *own* opinion, as to the ancients having known *Counterpoint?*

Thursday Morn^g I open my Letter to add a word or two to tell you that the acc^t of Castration[14] having been practiced, *for the use of the Voice*, so early as the Time of Severus,[15] awakened my Curiosity very much, for I have been long in search of Proofs upon that subject, & those wch the German author alledges had hitherto escaped me. I therefore went eagerly to Work in verifying them; but to my Mortification, cannot, in a Latin Edit. (I have not the Greek) find a word ab^t this matter in Herodian.[16]—& in Dion Cassius[17] the Passage seems to me only to say that 'Plautian invited to his House a hundred Citizens of good Families, & had them all *castrated*. Upon this occasion he not only used Boys in this manner But Married Men, that the Number of Euneuchs in the service of his Daughter Plautella might be encreased'— 'I have seen some of these Men who were at once Euneuchs, Hus-

---

[12] i.e. chapter V of his history of Greek music (*Hist. Mus.* i. 430–53; Mercer, i. 342–58).

[13] Charles-César Baudelot de Dairval (1648–1722), *Histoire de Ptolemée Auletes. Dissertation sur une pierre gravée antique du cabinet de Madame* (1698).

[14] In the *Historisch-kritische Beyträge*, i (1754–5), 353, where Marpurg gives Herodian and Cassius Dio as his authorities for asserting that boys were castrated in order to preserve their voices early in the third century AD in Rome.

[15] Lucius Septimius Severus (AD 146–211), Emperor of Rome from AD 193 until his death.

[16] There is, indeed, no account of castration in Herodian's history of the Roman empire. This scholarly red herring was probably spawned by a confusion on Marpurg's part (see n. 14) between Herodian and Herodotus. An account of castration appears in Herodotus (VI. 32), which CB later cites in *Hist. Mus.* iv. 42 n.; Mercer, ii. 529 n.

[17] See Cassius Dio's *History*, 76. 14. 4.

bands, & Fathers, who had Beards.'—This is given as a proof of the
Power & cruelty of Plautius, not of Luxury & refinem* as to *Singing*.
Nor do I find a Word concerning the Effect wch this operation had on
the voice, in Dion Cassius. Now it is well known that Castration will
not *give* a Voice; it will only *preserve* that of a Boy, & keep it from
breaking, as it is called, at the Time of Puberty. & the Italians never
Perform this operation upon adults.—The Roman Emperors imitated
the Custom of Eastern princes in having Euneuchs for Chamberlains
ab^t their Women, as Guards upon their Chastity, a practice of the
highest antiquity. & I beleive no instance of Singers can be found in
a[n]cient History that were Castrated, except the Enthusiastic Priests
of Cybele, the *Galli*, who performed the operation upon themselves, at
their Initiation in a fit of Frenzy, without the least Idea of improving
the Voice.[18] Indeed I suppose these were initiated young, as they are
called *Squalling* Euneuchs; & you perceive from Dion that the operation
had no Effect but *impuissance* upon *grown Gentlemen*, who still continued
to have *Beards*, & I suppose a rough & Manly Voice.—I wish you w^d
examine again what this German says on the subject, wch is an important one in the Hist^y of *vocal Music*. Does he jump from the 3^d Cent^y
to modern Times?—no *Evirati* were used in the Pope's Chapel till the
year 1600[19]—nor on the Stage till after that Time.—The point I want
to prove is, *when Castration was first performed, meerly on acc^t of the Voice*.—
I find every Day the necessity of examining what writers assert *roundly*,
as to doubtful Facts. If I were to content myself with *hear-says* & *Pre-
sumptions*, my Book w^d be a tissue of Lies & blunders, & not of the least
use, unless printed on *Soft Paper*.

To George Robinson[1] [Queen Square],
9 December 1773

ALS (Hyde).

London Decr 9th 1773.

Rec^d of Mr George Robinson the Sum of One hundred & fifty
Pounds, being in full; for one Half of the Sole Copy-Right of my Tour

[18] See *Hist. Mus.* iv. 41; Mercer, ii. 528–9.
[19] See *Hist. Mus.* iv. 40–1; Mercer, ii. 528. Recent studies place the emergence of musical 'evirati' about half a century earlier. See 'Castrato' in *New Grove*; F. Rogers, 'The Male Soprano', *Musical Quarterly*, v (1919), 413–25; A. Heriot, *The Castrati in Opera* (1956), chs. 1–3.
[1] George Robinson (see CB to Young, 11 Oct. 1773, n. 4), an enterprising businessman, paid his authors well, and in the vigorous purchase of copyrights, rapidly established himself as one of

Through France & Italy in one Volume, Octavo; and also for my Tour through Germany & the Netherlands in 2 Vol^s Octavo, with any Corrections that may be necessary in any future Editions. & I likewise promise any further Assignment for the said Copy Right on Demand.

Chas Burney

To [Daines Barrington]^1 Queen Square,
28 December 1773

ALS (Dr Johnson's House, 17 Gough Square, London).

Queen Square, 28–Dec.
1773

Dear Sir.

Day after Day I have been in hopes of thanking you personally at your Chambers for the Letter & Information with which you have kindly favoured me;^{2} but so many accidents & unexpected hindrances incessantly occur that I find it impossible to get at you so soon as I wish—No other method is left therefore but to make the Penny Post my Proxy, in Mitre Court^3—if I were a Parson I sh^d not *Court the Mitre* with more Zeal than I w^d now your Company & Friend^p. If I had Time to be happy. But, *ma chienne d'Histoire*, et toutes mes Chiennes d'Affaires, so plague & harrass me at present, that I have scarce Time to eat or sleep^4—but what business has an author to be hungry? whoever takes up that Trade sh^d get rid of such a hopeless Concupiscence—& then as to Sleep: to fit himself for the Company of Apollo & the Muses, he sh^d try to divest himself of such infirmities of Nature as celestial Beings never feel—he sh^d Spiritualize—he sh^d—by the L^d I know not what he sh^d do; but he certainly sh^d *not boar* his Fr^{ds} with

---

London's leading booksellers (see J. Nichols, *Literary Anecdotes of the Eighteenth Century* (1812–15), iii. 445–9).

^{1} The recipient of this letter was most probably Daines Barrington (see n. 3). Proposed by Barrington, CB had just been admitted FRS (CB to Twining, 30 Aug. 1773, n. 54).

^{2} Preserved in the Osborn Collection is a MS memorandum prepared for Barrington, which he passed on to CB, entitled 'The Antiquity of the *Violin*'. CB may be referring to this document.

^{3} Barrington occupied chambers in the King's Bench Walks, Inner Temple, access to which was gained from Fleet Street through the wicket doorway of Mitre Court (J. Nichols, *Literary Anecdotes of the Eighteenth Century* (1812–15), iii. 8–9; R. A. Roberts, ed., *A Calendar of the Inner Temple Records*, iv (1933), p. ii; v (1936), index under 'Barrington' and 'Mitre Court').

^{4} For confirmation of CB's amazing industry, late hours, and how 'he Uses his thin Carcass most abominably', see *EJL* i. 311, 318, 321; Lonsdale, p. 140.

long Lett^rs & so if you are now disposed to Cook, I wish you a Good Stomach.—

and am most sincerely y^rs

C. Burney.

To Thomas Pennant[1]

Queen Square,
4 January 1774

ALS (BL Add. MS 52540 J).
Addressed: To ⎮ Thomas Pennant ⎮ Esqr   *Docketed by* CB: Pîb gorn   *And by*
Pennant: Doctor Burney ⎮ on Bagpipes.   *Also* LS copy (Osborn: 'Letterbook,
Musical Correspondence').   *Addressed*: To Thomas Pennant Esqr   *Docketed
by* FBA: ×   This copy, which omits the first sentence of the letter, dates merely
'Jan. 1774'.

Sir.

Few Consequences of my undertaking have flattered me more than
the Interest which you have been pleased to take in it. If your kind
offer of favouring me with a sight of the two Welch Instrum^ts can be
accepted without occasioning much trouble to you, I shall be much
pleased with a sight of them.[2] I have already seen the Crwth wch M^r
Daines Barrington has presented to the Society of Antiquarians, &
I was favoured by that Gent^n with his printed description of the
Instrum^t before publication[3] as well as with his acc^t of it vivâ voce;
but I know very little of the *Pipe-Corn*, & indeed have not had sufficient
Leisure, nor occasion as yet to consider the Crwth: upon the antiquity
of which the more early use of the *Bow* upon this Island than on the
Continent seems to depend. Your truely Philosophical Spirit of Enquiry, & the perspicacious Manner in which you have been long
accustomed to regard objects of art & nature make me very ambitious
of your Counsel & Communications in Many parts of the work I
have undertaken; a work of wch the Difficulties are so multiplied &

---

[1] Thomas Pennant (1726–98), Welsh traveller and naturalist (*DNB*), had written to CB
([late Dec. 1773], Osborn), asking to be included in the list of subscribers to the *History of Music*.

[2] Pennant had written in his letter of [late Dec. 1773] that he had 'in his possession two welch
instruments now almost obsolete, the Crwth & Pipe-corn: which if the Doctor wishes to see M^r
Pennant will bring up from the Country.'
The crwth is a stringed instrument, and the pibgorn a single-reed wind instrument (*New
Grove*; H. Panum, *The Stringed Instruments of the Middle Ages*, trans. J. Pulver, [1941], pp. 124–7,
239–45; A. C. Baines, *Woodwind Instruments and Their History* (3rd edn., 1967), p. 223).

[3] 'Some Account of two Musical Instruments used in Wales', *Archaeologia*, iii (1775), 30–4.
Barrington had presented this paper at the Society of Antiquaries of London in Chancery Lane
on 3 May 1770.

magnified by examination & Reflexion that I despair of having either Leisure or Abilities to accomplish it in the manner such readers as your self may expect, or indeed in such a way as will at all satisfy my own Idea of what is wanted.

As to the Bagpipe[4] I have several proofs of its having been in use among the Ancients, besides those in Monfaucon.[5] Among others, Blanchini, de tribus generibus Instrumentorum Musicæ Veterum Organicæ;[6] Ficorone, delle Maschere;[7]—& Bonanni, Gabinetto Armonico;[8] have given drawings from antique representations of this Instrum[t]—it is mentioned by Suetonius, *in Nerone*, where it is called *Utricularius*.[9]—Mr Morrison[10] shewed me at Rome a fragment of a most beautiful Basso rilievo, in White Marble, in which there is a Bagpiper playing upon his Instrument, *tale quale* like a highlander—& that excellent Antiquarian assured me that this was Greek Sculpture of the highest Antiquity.—With respect to its' Modern use on the Continent, they have it in the south of France under the denomination of *La Musette*, & it is used in several parts of Italy, particularly in the Kingdom of Naples, where it is called the *Piva*, or Cornamusa—in France it is very frequently called *la Cornemuse*[11]—

I do not recollect the Meeting with it in Germany, nor can I speak to its use in Denmark, where I have never been; but a learned Friend

---

[4] Pennant had asked CB in his letter of [late Dec. 1773] if he had 'any other evidence of the Antiquity of the Bagpipe than what is in Monfaucon'; whether it was currently in use in Italy; whether any other nation used it apart from the Scots and the Irish, 'if so he begs the local name'; and if CB had travelled in Scandinavia, 'for Mr P. thinks that he was misinformed when he was told it was a danish instrument.'

[5] Bernard de Montfaucon (1655–1741), *Supplément au livre de l'antiquité expliqée et représentée en figures* (1724), iii. 188, and plate 73, figs. 1, 2.

[6] Francesco Bianchini, the elder (1662–1729), *De tribus generibus instrumentorum musicae veterum organicae dissertatio* (Rome, 1742), p. 11, and plate 2, fig. 12. CB's copy of this volume is listed in 'Cat. Fac. Mus.', item 160.

[7] Francesco de Ficoroni (1664–1747), *Le maschere sceniche e le figure comiche d'antichi Romani descritte brevemente* (Rome, 1736), pp. 214–17, and plate 83. CB owned the Rome, 1748 edition (*Cat. Misc. Lib.*, lot 660).

[8] Filippo Buonanni (1638–1725), *Gabinetto armonico. Pieno d'instromenti sonori* ... (Rome, 1722), pp. 73–5, and plates 30, 31. CB's copy is listed in 'Cat. Fac. Mus.', item 17.

[9] Suetonius, *The Lives of the Caesars*, vi. 54.

[10] An antiquary whom CB had met in Rome in 1770 (*Tours*, i. 203, 212, 226–8). Not otherwise identified.

[11] Pennant incorporated this information from CB in the second edition of his *A Tour in Scotland, and Voyage to the Hebrides* (1776), i. 348–9. In his reply (11 Jan. 1774, Osborn), Pennant wrote from Downing, Flintshire: 'You satisfy me that we have no claim to the melodious instrument the Bagpipe. Greece probably gave it to Rome. Rome to us. We to Norway & Sweden, for it is (as D[r] Solander tells me) common there. It was doubtlessly brought there by the crowd of arctic adventurers that invaded Scotland & the Hebrides from the 8th to the 13th century.

I shall bring up the Pip-corn with me: & next summer strive to get for you some old welsh musick lurking in an old house amidst our Hills.'

of mine, who is in a public Character at one of the Northern Courts[12] has promised me some particulars relative to the National Music of Sweden & Denmark—& of the Instruments in use there.—I have already been furnished with some Russian Instrum^ts & an Acc^t of the State of Music in that Country from an Englishman who has long resided there.[13]

I beg you will excuse the haste with which I am obliged to mention these particulars; but I w^d rather appear guilty of inaccuracy than Insensible of the Honour you have been pleased to confer upon, Sir,

your obliged
& most Humble Servant.
Chas Burney.

Queen Square | Bloomsbury | 4th Jany 1774

To Samuel Crisp

Queen Square,
21 January 1774

ALS (Berg).
Addressed: To | Saml Crisp, Esqr | at Mrs Hamilton's, Chesington, | near Epsom, | Surry   *Pmk:* 21 IA   *Docketed by* Crisp: 21. Jan. 1774   *And by* FBA: # singularities | & excentricities | of Fulke Greville— | & extraordinary | anonymous | Patronage | of the | History | of Music. | N° 4

Qu. Square. 21
Jany 1774

My dear Friend.

I have long seen a Storm of Business brewing for this winter—the Cloud grows blacker & blacker, & I sh^d not wonder if the D——l were to carry me away in a high wind.—It is now high Time to put you out of your fright concerning Greville[1]—for a sore fright you seemed to be

---

[12] Louis Devisme had been given diplomatic instructions as British Envoy Extraordinary to the Swedish Court in Dec. 1773. He arrived in Stockholm on 15 Mar. 1774, and died there on 4 Sept. 1776 (Horn, p. 144).

[13] Doubtless the Revd John Glen King (1732–87), DD, FRS, FSA (1771), a native of South-acre, Norfolk, and friend of the Burney and Allen families. Since 1764, King had been chaplain to the English factory at St Petersburg. See *CB Mem.*113; *EJL* i. 150, n. 25 and *passim*.

[1] Fulke Greville, at whose country house at Wilbury CB had been introduced to Crisp, had paid Thomas Arne £300 for the transfer of CB's indentures at Michaelmas 1748. Although CB had then completed only 4 of his 7 apprentice years, Greville waived all further obligations 9 months later when he permitted CB to marry Esther Sleepe in June 1749. Over 20 years later, however, Greville, in financial straits, asked CB to repay the £300. This CB refused to do (Lonsdale, pp. 20–3, 232).

in—however if a Trial were to come on at Westminster Hall where w^d be the harm of your declaring what you thought of the Transaction between him & me & Arne, at the Time it happened? You did or did not think the money G. paid to Arne for the residue of my Time ⌜as an apprentice for⌝ *a Loan* from G to me.—But to cut Matters short—such revolutions happened soon after my last Letter to you, that before I had your answer he was in Town & we had an Interview together 1st at his House in Brook Street & 2 Nights after he supped wth me & Family in Queen Square!!!—I see you arch your Eye-Brows—stare—& cry—prodigious!—

Well—it will only cost you two pence or 3 pence extraordinary[.] I'll e'en send you his Letters.[2]—Read'em as numbered.—I had not answered the fury he had sent me, & wch you saw, when N° 1 arrived.—Astonished, & indeed pleased as I was with this Letter, I readily accepted of his proffered Friendship; but in the Course of my answer stated the whole transaction ab^t Arne; & his demand just as I had done to you—told him what I then & always thought of it—of the full use he had of my Time as an equivalent for his Money—of the sacrifices I made of all kind of Business in order to ⌜attend⌝[3] him in Town & Country, without ⌜wages⌝[4] or even Cloaths, except now & then one of his old Coats—of[4] my present Circumstances, ⌜far from affluent⌝[5]—with 8 Children[6] for whom eternal Drudgery was ever in all likelihood to be my Lot—&c &c—Now read his 2^d Letter—he had not rec^d mine when he came from Wilbury—& I knew not how it w^d operate upon so warm a Temper—however, now was the Time to get rid of his preposterous demand forever—I obeyed his summons &

Although it is now impossible to establish the exact chronology of the ensuing dispute, the surviving evidence suggests that Greville may have made his demand initially as early as 1771 (*EJL* i. 32, 262–4, 322–3). Matters seem to have come to a head in early 1773. Fanny d'Arblay, confusingly telescoping events, gives an account of the quarrel and reconciliation in a passage intended for her *Memoirs*, but which she finally omitted (BL Egerton MS 3696, fos. 127ʳ–130). There she relates how Greville had demanded repayment on a visit to CB in Queen Square, and followed the visit with 'a Letter that seemed dictated by frantic fury . . . treating the cancel of the Articles as a Loan, & denouncing a public trial for repayment in Westminster Hall.' In 'extreme perturbation', CB consulted Crisp, who 'strongly counselled Dr. Burney to avoid all discussion, all representation, & to leave to the simple & unenforced operation of Time such a recollection of the business as might restore Mr. Greville to more sane ideas'. This stratagem worked.

[2] Not preserved. In 1812 CB destroyed the bulk of his correspondence with Greville. See *ED* i. 220 n. 2; *JL* xi. 186.

[3] MS attend] *obliterated by FBA who interlined* be with

[4–4] MS wages . . . of] *obliterated by FBA who interlined* any emolument whatever—of

[5] According to Fanny d'Arblay, Greville had acted on the assumption that CB was now 'a man of easy fortune' (BL Egerton MS 3696, fo. 128).

[6] In addition to the six children who survived his first wife, CB's second wife had now presented him with two more: Richard Thomas (1768–1808), and Sarah Harriet (1772–1844).

spent a very agreeable Evening with him till 2 o'Clock in the Morn^g without a word of our Quarrel or his secret—this was Sunday Night— on Tuesday he supped with us—on Thursday he got my Lett^r from Wilbury—& on Friday I rec^d the facetious Note (N° 3) in the style of Flash to Fribble, wch parts at Wilbury we used to be fond [of] acting— & Mrs G. was Miss Biddy Belair[7]—We met after this at his Lodgings & at the opera, & all smooth & well—but no Secret—however, in ab^t 10 Days he went out of Town; but before his Departure he came to my House with a large Bundle of Papers, sealed up, which, I being out he left wth Mrs B. to deliver carefully into my own Hands[8]—The Contents I must not tell—but I had much rather not have had them—however it was a strong Mark of his Confidence—we corresponded freely in the Country—he wants too much of my now, more than ever, precious Time—that's the worst of it—or else, while he's thus his *old self*, I can't help giving him my old Esteem. —— He came to Town to the Birth Day[9]—& I have had 2 or 3 Lett^{rs} from him, but am unable to read much less answer all that so prolific a pen of Leisure produces.— He's not ab^t to publish anything he now writes, I must tell you—& so Basta—'all's Well that Ends Well'—[10]

Well, but a word or two ab^t 'Scrip:[11]—⌐& that too goes on well—my N° is now ab^t 490 honestly, & Moderately speaking.⌐—Last summer, ⌐I wanted to tell you that⌐ 2 great Merch^{ts} in the City wrote me the following Letter.

Sir.

We are directed by a friend of ours to give you th⟨is⟩ Notice, that if you will be pleased to keep open your subscript⟨ion⟩ until X^{mas} next for y^r History of Music, we will & do, hereby engage to you to make good to you any deficiency that may arise from the want of 500 subscribers, in the whole, agreeable to your Proposals, & to the

[7] These are characters in David Garrick's farce, *Miss in Her Teens*. See CB to Mrs Greville, [?July 1756].

[8] Since Mrs Burney left London to spend the summer at Lynn in mid-May 1773 (*EJL* i. 265), all these events must have taken place before that date.

[9] The Queen's official birthday was celebrated each year on 18 Jan. (Olwen Hedley, *Queen Charlotte* (1975), p. 67).

[10] CB may have composed on this occasion his verses 'To Fulk Greville Esqr upon the termination of a long contested difference', preserved in a 'Poetical Notebook' in the Osborn Collection (shelves c 33, pp. 143–4). Two lines indicate that CB's estrangement from Greville extended over a considerable period of time:

How many years, alas! I strove in vain
Once more our past coincidence to gain!

[11] i.e. subscriptions to the *History of Music*.

performance of which you may have any further satisfaction you may desire at our Hands.

We are very respectfully, S^r y^r Most Obed^t hum^{ble} ser^{ts}
Chandler & Davidson

Fenchurch Buildings
30th July 1773.
Dr. Burney.

What think you of an offer from one unknown to me[12] wch might involve him in an Expence of 4 or £500?—I want to tell you the whole transaction but have not room nor Time—I am yet ignorant to whom I am so much obliged—I have seen Mr Davidson 2^{ce}—he's quite a Gentleman in appearance & behaviour—says his Fr^d wishes still through Delicacy to lie concealed, but interests himself so much ab^t my Publication that he cares not what it costs him, provided I carry the work into execution—told me that he was a young Man of Family & large independant Fortune—and upon my telling at X^{mas} the real state of the subscription wch then barely amounted to 400, & saying that I had promised the Public to advance or retreat at that Time, & might be called on—'well, S^r you have an answer ready—we are impowered to beg you to go on'—'but S^r, I sh^d be sorry to be a weight upon any Fr^d, whose partiality may over-rate my abilities[']—'S^r replied M^r D: he does not care if it was the whole—Pray advertise[13]— I shall wait on you very soon'—he our conversation Ended, & here we Parted—thus Ends my story—

⌐If this Incognito does anything it will surely be to subscribe for 100 sets, to make up the deficiency, as the scrip stood at X^{mas}⌐ Fashion begins, I think now, to operate—I have had the most flattering Letters imaginable from all Quarters ⌐& from⌐ people of rank, & high in Literature.—Johnson puffs my Books—Mrs Montagu[14] has desired my acquaintance—Mr Pennant has wrote a flomery Letter, ⌐with his subscription⌐[15]—& hundreds more—Greville has subscribed for 5 sets—Ld Sandwich sent me 18 ⌐great⌐ Names from Hinchinbroke[16]

---

[12] CB's unknown benefactor remains anonymous to this day. See Lonsdale, pp. 139–42. His agents, the City merchants Chandler and Davidson had offices at 14 Fenchurch Buildings (*Kent's Directory* (1780), pp. 37, 50; *Universal British Directory* (1790), p. 121). Duncan Davidson (d. 1799), of Tulloch, Scotland, and Bedford Square, London (*GM* lxix (1799)^2, 726; lxxxi (1811)^2, 394), is listed among CB's subscribers. Chandler is not identified.

[13] CB's advertisement informing the public he would proceed with the *History* appeared in the newspapers in early Jan. See, for example, *Public Advertiser*, 6 Jan. 1774; *St. James's Chronicle*, 11–13 Jan. 1774. For the text of CB's notice, see Lonsdale, p. 141.

[14] Elizabeth Montagu, née Robinson (1720–1800), authoress and acknowledged 'Queen' of the bluestockings (*DNB*).

[15] See CB to Pennant, 4 Jan. 1774, n. 1.

[16] CB had visited Lord Sandwich at his seat, Hinchingbrooke in Huntingdon in the autumn

—& has since subscribed for 5 sets for himself, ⌈& given me two more Names⌉—Boone[17] takes 12—Cox[18] 2 doz &c &c

y^{rs} most affectionately
C.B.

To Thomas Twining [Queen Square], 21 January 1774

L copy extract (Osborn: 'Twining Letterbook No. 2', pp. 3–5).

21. Jany 1774.

... [Ba]ckers[1] makes the best Piano Fortes, but they come to 60 or 70 £, with 3 unisons—& of the Harpsichord size — Put *them* out of the question, & I think Pohlman[2] the best maker of the small sort, by far. Z[u]mpe[3] was the best, but he has given up the business.—Pohlman

of 1771, and there had met Captain James Cook (1728–79), recently returned from his first voyage of discovery (*Frag. Mem.*, Osborn; Lonsdale, pp. 111–12).

[17] Charles Boone (*c.*1729–1819), educated at Eton and Trinity College, Cambridge; on Lord Orford's interest, MP for Castle Rising (1757–68 and 1784–96) and for Ashburton (1768–84). Boone, his wife, and his daughter are listed as subscribers to the *History of Music* (see Namier and Brooke, ii. 101; Walpole *Corresp.* x. 7–8). According to Fanny d'Arblay (*Mem.* i. 59), CB as a young man had met Boone at Wilbury; with Boone, John Hawkesworth, and Richard Cox he formed 'connections of lasting and honourable intimacy'.

[18] Richard Cox (*c.*1718–1803) of Quarley, Hampshire, army agent and founder (1758) of the bank which to this day functions as agent to H. M. Forces. CB had met Cox at Wilbury, and the two men had become firm friends. According to Mrs Thrale, Cox was 'Musick-mad' (*Thraliana*, i. 455). In the 1790s CB was to spend part of his summer holidays every year with Cox at Quarley (Lonsdale, pp. 21, 362, 418; F. G. Hilton Price, *A Handbook of London Bankers* (1890–1), p. 48; see also K. R. Jones, 'Letters of Dr. Burney to Richard Cox, Army Agent', *Notes and Queries*, ccx (1965), 221–5). Cox is listed as having subscribed for three copies of the *History of Music*. Boone and Cox seem to have collected lists of subscribers for CB.

[1] MS copy gives 'Ruckers' in error. Americus Backers (*fl.* 1759–81), Dutch harpsichord and pianoforte maker who settled in London in Jermyn Street, invented the 'English' grand piano action. CB (*Tours*, ii. 179) mentions Backers's instruments with approval, but changed his mind later (see Rees, under 'Harpsichord'). See *GM* lxxxii (1812)[1], 11; Rosamond E. M. Harding, *The Piano-Forte: Its History Traced to the Great Exhibition of 1851* (Cambridge, 1933), pp. 54, 57–8; D. H. Boalch, *Makers of the Harpsichord and Clavichord, 1440–1840* (2nd edn., Oxford, 1974), p. 7; *New Grove*, under 'Pianoforte: England and France to 1800'.

[2] Johannes Pohlmann (*fl.* 1760–1807), who conducted his business in Compton Street, Soho and 113 Great Russell Street. Pohlmann's square pianos were almost as popular as Zumpe's (Harding, *Piano-Forte*, pp. 54–6, 402), though CB later thought them 'very inferior in tone' (Rees, under 'Harpsichord'). Twining bought an 18-guinea Pohlmann piano (see Twining to CB, 31 Jan.; 7 Mar. 1774, copies, BL Add. MS 39933, fos. 93^v–95^v, 96^v–97^v), which arrived in Colchester in late Mar. or early Apr. (Twining to CB, 4 Apr. 1774, in *Country Clergyman*, pp. 25–6).

[3] MS copy gives '*Zempe*' in error. Johann Christoph Zumpe (*c.*1735–*c.*1800) came to England about 1760. His own business was conducted in Prince's Street, Hanover Square. Zumpe

then for 16 or 18 Guineas makes charming little Instruments, sweet & even in Tone, & capable of great variety of piano & forte, between the two extremes of pianissimo & fort^{mo}. Those for 16 Gn^s only go down to double G, without a double G♯; but for the 2 gn^s more he has made me two or three with an octave to double F & F♯ with a double G♯ —

You talk so much what I think about Geminiani & Corelli that if we had had sufficient intercourse together I should have said your words had suggested my thoughts, or è contra.[4] I have long found out that, as Geminiani was a bad Timist in playing, he but ill attended to Rhythm in writing: his movements are not *phrased*, as Rousseau well expresses it,[5] and that merit of measured periods, of accenting melody, & rendering it more poetical than formerly (if I may so say) is, to my apprehension, the chief characteristic of modern music, & what it most excels the old music in. How much more easy it is for a man with a tolerable ear to *get in*,—if in playing a part in a full piece he happens to be out,—now, than formerly!—What you say about a degree of simplicity necessary to longevity in musical compositions, has often struck me.[6] Corelli is so plain & simple that he can always be made modern,—whereas Purcel is so elaborate in his melodies, by having written down all the fashionable Graces & embellishments of his time, that he soon grew obsolete; for it is not so easy, nor perhaps warrantable, to simplify Music, as to embroider & adorn it. Jackson's[7] poor

pioneered the manufacture of 'small-piano-fortes of the shape and size of the virginal, of which the tone was very sweet, and the touch, with a little use, equal to any degree of rapidity' (Rees, under 'Harpsichord'). Zumpe's pianos were in great demand. William Mason owned one (Gray *Corresp*. iii. 957–8). See *New Grove*; Harding, *Piano-Forte*, pp. 36–7, 53–6, 76, 409.

[4] In his letter of 16 Oct. 1773 (copy, BL Add. MS 39933, fos. 83^v–92^v), Twining had written of Geminiani, 'As to his melody, I wonder whether you will agree with me in my distinction—I think that he cannot so much be said absolutely to *want melody*, as to want a *continuance* of melody; he has *bars* of fine melody frequently, but few *melodious movements*'.

[5] 'It is in the invention of musical phrases, in their proportion and texture, that the true beauties of music consist. A composer who accents and phrases his passages well, is, according to Rousseau, a man of wit. Upon this principle, Haydn's music is full of *bon mots*' ('Phrase' in Rees: largely a translation from Rousseau's *Dictionnaire de musique*).

[6] Twining had written (16 Oct. 1773): 'As to Corelli, he deserves, I think, a far higher place, & did every thing that could be expected from a composer in *his* day: & I never hear his concertos without being astonished how *little* they grow old to *my* ear. I fancy there is a certain dose of *simplicity* necessary to the longevity of music; the modern compositions are of a more refined & perishable construction, &, I doubt, will never attain to the "viridis senectus" of Corelli'.

[7] William Jackson (1730–1803), of Exeter, organist and composer. His set of twelve *Songs*, first published in 1755, established his popularity throughout Britain (*New Grove*). Among others, he composed music to poems by Pope and Joseph Warton. Twining (16 Oct. 1773) had elaborated on simplicity in music with unfavourable reference to Jackson: 'And yet, how impossible, if one tries ever so, to get the least idea of a modern overture become *fogrum*? . . . en tout genre, those who set out with the *design* to be *simple*, are insipid & abominable. ⌜Mr J. has this affectation⌝'.

stuff made it's way by the excellence of the words to which he has applied it, which had never been well set before. But I tell his admirers to play his airs *without* words, & tell me what they think of them. Now there are Italian & German airs, which, detached from the divine Poetry of Metastasio, will be still full of Passion, pathos, or hilarity. Abel is, (though sometimes tame) beautifully simple, polished, & refined.[8]—But for instrumental music, are you much acquainted with that of the Hamburgh Bach—of Haydn—Vanhall—Ditters—Hoffmann[9] &c?—their compositions never consist of *Notes*, et RIEN que *des Notes*.—Scrip goes on rather swimmingly, now folks are come to Town. Have you seen my declaration for going to the Press as soon as I can?[10]

Yrs in all haste & affection
C. Burney.

To Charles Davy

[Queen Square,
March 1774?][1]

AL draft fragment (Osborn).
Endorsed by CB: Mem. for beginning of a Letter to | Revd Mr Davy.   *And by* FBA: ✳ Fragm^t

... I have not Leisure to discuss here the Use for wch providence allowed us to discover & practice music. But I will confess that I see no perversion of the Designs of providence in applying it to the purpose of an innocent amusement.[2] I always regarded Vocal Music as superior to Instrumental, & Church Music when well composed & executed as the noblest & most affecting kind of all musics. Thus far

---

[8] Twining had written (ibid.): 'Abel is, in a degree, simple by nature in his compositions, & *this* simplicity being joined, as I think, with great beauty, sets him high in my scale of modern composers'.

[9] C. P. E. Bach; Franz Joseph Haydn; Jan Křtitel Vaňhal (1739–1813); Karl Ditters (1739–99), ennobled (1773) as 'Ditters von Dittersdorf'; Leopold Hofmann (1738–93). See *MGG*; *New Grove*. For a study of the development of CB's progressive views on instrumental music, see Grant, pp. 203–19.

[10] See CB to Crisp, 21 Jan. 1774, n. 13.

[1] The date is conjectural. In CB to Davy, 3 Nov. 1774, CB alludes to a letter from Davy received 'last March', and also refers to 'a slight difference of opinion' concerning music. CB perhaps refers to the disagreement evident in the present undated fragmentary draft over the relative merits of vocal and instrumental music, a subject on which Davy and his friend Christopher Smear wrote an 'Essay' (see CB to Davy, 3 July 1772, n. 2).

[2] '*What is* MUSIC? An innocent luxury, unnecessary, indeed, to our existence, but a great improvement and gratification of the sense of hearing' (*Hist. Mus.* i (1776), xiii).

perhaps we agree. But as nature has denied a good Voice to 99 persons at least out of a 100, of the Inhabitants of the Globe & the knowledge of its use, in our Country, to almost all those to whom a Voice has been granted, it seems to me no abuse of our musical faculties to supply the defects of Voice by Instruments—& in meer Instrumental music it seems a certainty that the mind cannot be corrupted. If vocal Music has more Power over the Soul, that power is sometimes abused by making it the vehicle of licentious Poetry ...

To Regina Mingotti[1]   [Queen Square], 3 May 1774

ALS draft (Osborn).
Endorsed by CB: To Madame Mingotti | at Munich   *And by* FBA: *1* ○

London May 3ᵈ
1774.

Dear Madam.

It is now more than 12 Months since I confided to the Care of a Friend in the Secretary of State's Office[2] a Parcel for M. de Visme at Munich, but by a chain of Accidents this parcel was prevented from ever arriving at the first place of its destination & is now performing a Voyage in search of M. de Visme at Stockholm.[3] It's contents were 2 Printed Volˢ of my remarks on the present State of Music in Germany, & The Netherlands [and] a Letter to M. de Visme, in wᶜʰ I had entreated him in a particular manner to make my best acknowledgments to you for your kindness & hospitality during my short residence at Munich. I had likewise charged our late Minister there with my respects & thanks to several persons in that city from whom I had recᵈ

---

[1] Regina Mingotti, née Valentini (1722–1808), soprano, had first appeared in London in 1754. As a singer of international repute, her profession took her all over Europe. In Dresden in 1747, she performed in the première of Gluck's *Le nozze d'Ercole e d'Ebe* in which Gluck included a part written for her voice. See A. Einstein, *Gluck*, trans. E. Blom (1964), pp. 28–32. In 1772, she had settled in Munich, where CB met her (*Tours*, ii. 45–6). Mingotti gave CB an account of her life (ibid., pp. 54–8), and, among other courtesies and assistance, arranged two concerts for his benefit (ibid., pp. 60–1). See also, *Hist. Mus.* iv. 463–8, 483–4, 671–2; Mercer, ii. 852–5, 867, 1014; and Rees.
[2] Probably Anthony Chamier (1725–80), described by Fanny Burney in 1775 as 'an intimate friend of my father's' (*ED* ii. 106). Chamier was Deputy Secretary at War (1772–5) and Under-Secretary of State for the Southern Department (1775–80); MP for Tamworth (1778–80). See *DNB*; Namier and Brooke, ii. 207–8; Hill–Powell, i. 478 n. 1.
[3] See CB to Pennant, 4 Jan. 1774, n. 12.

Civilities. Besides the Books & this Letter to M. de V., there was a Letter to yourself wch Lady Edgcumbe[4] had desired me to enclose in my packet to M. de Visme. Nothing gave me more concern than the miscarriage of this Letter, as you w^d have perceived by its Contents the regard wch her Ladyship still retains for you. I had the Honour of dining wth her in Company with Mrs Brudenal[5] and several of your Friends soon after my return to England from Germany, & the satisfaction of perceiving that my Acc^t of you, & your remembrance of them, afforded them the highest pleasure; & it was then that L^y Edgcumbe promised to write to you on my acquainting her Lad^p that I sh^d soon be able to forward her Letter to you in a Parcel wch I had an opportunity of sending to M. de V. at Munich.

It is by means of Mr Elliot,[6] the son of Sr Gilbert Elliot, Bar^t a Gentleman much esteemed by all who know him, and who is now setting off for your Court in order to supply the place of M. de Visme, that I have the Honour of writing to you & of sending you my two Vol^s concerning the pres^t state of Music in Germany, of wch I beg your acceptance. You will oblige me by presenting my best respects to the Intelligent Father Kenedy,[7] & giving him a Permission to peruse my hasty remarks. I know that I can tell you nothing new concerning Germany or the subject of Music; but I write to my Countrymen, ignorant of both, to whom everything is new. Et pour le reste cet ouvrage est destiné comme avant *Coureur*, to my greater under-taking—& it is only *pour sonner le Tocsin*, that it is published.

[4] Emma Edgcumbe, née Gilbert (1729–1807), daughter of John Gilbert (1693–1761), Archbishop of York, married (1761) George Edgcumbe (1721–95), 3rd Baron Edgcumbe of Mount Edgcumbe (1761), created Viscount (1781), Earl of Mount Edgcumbe (1789), admiral (*DNB*). According to CB, Lady Edgcumbe was an accomplished harpsichordist, and performed at the private concerts organised in the 1750s by Mrs Harriet Fox-Lane (1705–71), later (1762) Lady Bingley. The main attractions at these 'academias' were Giardini and Mingotti (*Hist. Mus.* iv. 671–2; Mercer, ii. 1013–14). For CB's account of Lady Edgcumbe, who 'was one of the great patronesses of Giardini and Mengotti', see *Mem.* iii. 375–6.

[5] Anne Brudenell, née Legge (d. 1786), married (1760) the Hon. James Brudenell (1725–1811), created Baron Brudenell of Deene (1780), 5th Earl of Cardigan (1790). 'She was a scholar of La Signora Mingotti, and, my father told her, reminded him of the *good old school* of singing. She has a fine voice, and has great merit, for a *lady singer*; but . . . was not by any means steadily in tune, and sung with her mouth shut, which has never a good effect' (*ED* ii. 109). See Joan Wake, *The Brudenells of Deene* (2nd rev. edn., 1954), pp. 287–9, 315–16.

[6] Hugh Elliot (1752–1830), diplomatist, second son of Sir Gilbert Elliot (1722–77), 3rd Baronet of Minto (1766), statesman, philosopher, and poet (*DNB*). Hugh Elliot had been appointed to succeed Louis Devisme as British Minister to the Imperial Diet, and Minister Plenipotentiary to Bavaria. He arrived in Munich in mid-June 1774 (*DNB*; Horn, pp. 42, 46).

[7] Ildephons Kennedy (1722–1804), a Scottish Catholic, had emigrated from his native Perthshire to Bavaria at the age of 13, and had joined the Scottish Benedictines at Ratisbon. A renowned scientist and natural historian, he was elected a member of many European learned societies. He was a founder member and Secretary of the Munich Academy of Science, established in 1761. Kennedy took up residence in Munich, where Regina Mingotti had introduced him to CB (*Tours*, ii. 52, 57; *ADB*; Michaud).

M. de Visme when he did me the Honour to send me some Music from his serene hig[h]ness the Elector of Bavaria,[8] told me that orders were or w^d be given to M. le Compte Haslang[9] to subscribe for my Hist^y of Music; but as yet I have heard nothing from him. The subscription has filled in a very Flattering manner; I have 7 or 800 Names already of the first persons of this Country for Rank & Talents in my List, & our Queen has not only subscribed but given me permission in a Most Gracious Manner, to dedicate my Work to her Majesty.[10] I shall be proud of your permission to insert y^r Name in my List, without involving you in any expensive Consequences, as a Person for whom I have a very great regard, & to whom the Subject of my Work has such great obligations.[11] I hope you will pardon what I have taken the Liberty of saying with respect to yourself in my German Tour: I knew it w^d be well rec^d in my Country, & I meant to contribute my mite towards recording your Merit & Talents as a Person at the Head of a Profession, wch I wish to make respectable.

If you w^d honour me with a Letter & communicate to me any particulars, worth recording relative to my Subject either of Past or present Times, I should be extreamly obliged to you, & shall readily acknowledge or conceal the source from whence I obtain[e]d such Information in the exact manner that you shall direct.

I am dear Madam wth great Consideration, your obed^t & much obliged serv^t

Chas Burney

To Thomas Twining

Queen Square,
13 July 1774

L copy extract (Osborn: 'Twining Letterbook No. 2', pp. 6–8).

[8] Maximilian III Joseph of Bavaria had sent a *Litany* and a *Stabat Mater* of his own composition to CB (*Tours*, ii. 51; see also CB to Hutton, 17 July 1773, n. 10). Devisme had long ago told CB that Maximilian meant to subscribe to the *History of Music* (Devisme to CB, 20 Sept. 1772, Osborn). He did.

[9] Josef Franz Xaver, Graf von Haszlang (*c.*1700–83), Bavarian Envoy Extraordinary and Minister Plenipotentiary to the Court of St James's from 1741 to his death (*Repertorium der diplomatischen Vertreter aller Länder, III. Band, 1764–1815*, ed. O. F. Winter (Graz–Cologne, 1965), pp. 22, 304; Walpole *Corresp.* ix. 185; xxxiii. 178; *GM* liii (1783), 454, 540).

[10] Samuel Johnson composed for CB the Dedication of the *History of Music* to the Queen. See Hill–Powell, iv. 546–7; *Thraliana*, i. 204; Lonsdale, pp. 168–9.

[11] Regina Mingotti's name is included in the list of CB's subscribers.

Qu. Sq. 13th July 1774.

Shall I scribble a few words to you, en attendant a longer letter?—
you say, yes.—Well you are a jewel of a man, to drudge for me in
these pitch-dark & coal-black mines.—Your letter[1] I have been not
only reading a 2nd time, to day, but have interleaved it, & scribbled
assents & dissents; a very few of these last,—all which I hope to live to
discuss with you. But, why are you so perverse & singular as to fear a
journey in summer more than winter?[2] Now, though I am still sore
from the kicks of German waggons,[3] I long to be a vagabond in
summer 10,000 times more than winter.—But your Dissertation on
Enharmonic[4] is charming! & your whole letter.—But you would be
ashamed to hear all the good I think of it.—Is it not odd that *you*
should write down your *Creed* about ancient music, & that *I* had done
the same 3 or 4 years ago. Your creed consists of more articles & is
better founded than mine,[5]—but some time or other we'll compare
'em.—Do you know that I really believe I should have loaded a chaise
with books & bestrode old Wallis,[6] upon finding you inexorable to my
entreaties about rummaging in Qu. Square—but—(I wish there was
no such word in any language)—a business kicked up, which I least
expected, at the very instant I was going to threaten you with my

---

[1] Twining's letter to CB is only partially preserved in a copy made by Richard Twining (BL
Add. MS 39933, fos. 106^v–11^v), who transcribed the date: 'Fordham July 3–4.5.6 &c 1774'.
Also preserved are Thomas Twining's own notes for the letter (BL Add. MS 39936, fos. 51^v–53),
which he dated 'July 8. 1774'. The letter CB refers to can thus be dated 3–8 July 1774.

[2] Twining explained in a letter of [14] July 1774 from his country vicarage at Fordham: 'It is
not a journey that I fear in summer, but a journey to London, and being there in summer. Here
we shall be quite snug; I have seldom visitors, and no neighbours' (*Country Clergyman*, p. 31,
which gives 10 July as the date of this letter. Twining's notes show 14 July as the correct date.
See BL Add. MS 39936, fos. 53–4).

[3] 'So hard are the seats of German post-wagons, that a man is rather kicked than carried from
one place to another' (*Tours*, ii. 136).

[4] Twining had sent in his letter of 3–8 July 1774, his observations on the Enharmonic Genus,
calling his treatise 'my best *hit* about the Greek music: & the only thing *like* a discovery that I
have made in it'. Twining's notes for his letter (BL Add. MS 39936, fos. 51^v–53) correspond
closely to the discussion of the Greek Genera included in *Hist. Mus.* i. 27–35; Mercer, i. 43–9. In
order to include Twining's 'discovery', CB was obliged to cancel three leaves (Sigs. E4, F1 and
G2) in *Hist. Mus.* i (1776), 31–34, 43–44. See Lonsdale, pp. 148–9, 161–3, 491–2.

[5] Twining had professed in his letter of 3–8 July a long and preposterous 'creed in Greek
music', ending with the observation: 'Sir—there is nothing too hard for my belief.—'Here have
I been sweating to form new articles of faith for you, &' I am to be called a sceptic 'for it!—And
you wish me a Bishop too!'

[6] Twining had advised CB (ibid.): 'Wallis seems to me, the safest guide, & most to be
depended on, as to the etymology of the Greek names of notes'.

John Wallis (1616–1703), DD (1654), FRS (1663), Savilian Professor of Geometry at Oxford
(1649–1703), mathematician, and scholar. His edition of Ptolemy's *Harmonica* (Oxford, 1682),
was included in his collected *Opera*, published at Oxford (1693–9) in three huge folio volumes
which CB may well have envisaged himself 'bestriding'. CB's copy of these volumes was sold for
19s. (*Cat. Misc. Lib.*, lot 2066).

company for a few days. This business is nothing less than the establishing a Conservatorio in London, after the manner of the Music Schools of Italy.[7] Ever since my return from that country the Idea has haunted me. I drew up the sketch of a plan immediately, & communicated it to Giardini, who saw as well as myself the want & feasibility of it.—We had an idea of the K. or Q. by the interest of the D. of G & C————d patronizing it,—but the Family Quarrel destroyed our hopes from that quarter.[8] We next thought of getting the Governors of the Fund for decayed Musicians to join us, but difficulties occurred there, & the mode of a public subscription was next thought of: but that having likewise its difficulties, the plan slept till within this week. Our present hopes are from the Foundling Hospital.[9] A House, a Chapel, a number of Children to choose out of, a want of Musical Exhibitions & employment for Orphans, from the time they quit the nurse, till they are 21—all this makes that Hospital the properest place for our establishment. We are now in treaty. Last night I read the plan, in confidence, to a Select Committee,[10] which was well received, & next wed^y the fate of this important business to the Musical Art in Great Britain is to be determined by a General Court of the Guardians & Governors of the Hospital.[11] Pray sit X legged for it. If it had not been for this enterprise I should have tried

[7] See CB to Giardini, 21 June 1772.

[8] William Henry (1743–1805), younger brother of George III, created Duke of Gloucester (1764), had secretly married (1766) Maria Walpole (1736–1807), 2nd illegitimate daughter of Sir Edward Walpole (1706–84), and therefore Horace Walpole's niece. She was the Dowager Countess Waldegrave, having first married (1759) James Waldegrave (1715–63), 2nd Earl Waldegrave (1741). Gloucester informed the king of his marriage in September 1772.

Henry Frederick (1745–90), another younger brother of George III, created Duke of Cumberland (1766), also secretly married (1771) a widow, Anne Horton, née Luttrell (1743–1808), who had first married (1765) Christopher Horton (1741–68) of Catton, Derbyshire.

Rumours of Gloucester's clandestine marriage and scandalous news of Cumberland's provoked the King to push through Parliament the Royal Marriages Act of March 1772 (12 Geo. III, c. 11), whereby no member of the royal family under the age of 25 could contract a valid marriage without the consent of King and Parliament (*DNB*, under 'Henry Frederick' and 'William Henry'; J. S. Watson, *The Reign of George III, 1760–1815* (Oxford, 1960), p. 155).

[9] Established by Royal Charter dated 17 Oct. 1739, and supported by an Act of Parliament of 1740 (13 Geo. II, c. 29), the Hospital for the Maintenance and Education of Exposed and Deserted Young Children, known as the Foundling Hospital, was situated in a 56-acre site at the northern end of Lamb's Conduit Street. See R. H. Nichols and F. A. Wray, *The History of the Foundling Hospital* (1935), *passim*.

[10] On 6 July 1774, a meeting of the Court of Governors of the Foundling Hospital had authorized 'Sir Charles Whitworth, Mr. Scott and Mr. Harrison ... to receive ... [CB's and Giardini's] Proposal in order to report the same to the General Committee in case it should appear to them proper to be adopted by this Corporation' (Foundling Hospital Library, 40 Brunswick Square, London: MS 'Minutes of General Court', vol. iii, pp. 172–3).

[11] The General Court duly met on Wednesday 20 July 1774, and accepted CB's plan. The Court also resolved to open a subscription roll to raise money for the initial expenses of the Music School, set up a Special Committee to direct its establishment, and proposed that CB should be elected a Governor of the Hospital, an honour already conferred on Giardini in Mar. 1770. All these schemes collapsed when the following General Court held on 3 Aug. 'Resolved

ere now to find Fordham.—Well I shall hold my hand about old Greek stuff till you answer this letter.

Nothing I say in the Dissert: can be taken as positive or dogmatical assertion after my bit of Spanish[12]—nor in the Hist of Gr. Music after the Motto with which you have furnished me from Homer.[13] ...

To William Hunter[1]   Queen Square, 29 July [1774][2]

L 3rd person (Osborn).
Addressed: Dr. Hunter, | Windmill Street | Haymarket.

Dr. Burney presents his Comp^ts to Dr. Hunter, & will be very glad of the pleasure of seeing him to morrow, with the Young Person[3] he mentioned, to Drink Tea, if convenient to the Doctor.
Queen Square | Friday Evening. July 29th

To Thomas Twining   [Queen Square, late August 1774][1]

L copy extract (Osborn: 'Twining Letterbook No. 2', p. 9).

that the Minute of the last meeting ... relative to the said proposal of Dr. Burney & Mr. Giardini be vacated; [and] that the said Plan be returned to Messrs. Burney & Giardini' (MS 'Minutes', iii. 177–8). See *Mem.* i. 233–44; Nichols and Wray, *History*, pp. 247–8; Scholes, i. 261–3; Lonsdale, pp. 149–53; Jamie C. Kassler, 'Burney's *Sketch of a Plan for a Public Music-School*', *Musical Quarterly*, lviii (1972), 210–34; Ruth K. McClure, *Coram's Children: The London Foundling Hospital in the Eighteenth Century* (1981), pp. 230–1.

12 'De las cosas mas seguras | Le [*sic*] mas segura es dudar', quoted in the Introduction to the 'Dissertation on the Music of the Ancients' in *Hist. Mus.* i (1776), 4, and there translated: 'The most certain of certain things, is doubtful'. In the 'Errata' to this volume, CB revises the translation to: 'The most secure of all secure things, is, to doubt', but neglects to correct the misprint 'Le' to 'La' in the Spanish. The correct 'La' and the improved translation appear in the second (1789) edition of the first volume of the *History* (p. x; Mercer, i. 17). See also CB to Twining, 3 Feb. 1776, n. 6.

13 See CB to Twining, 30 Aug. 1773, n. 28.

1 William Hunter (1718–83), MD (1750), FRS (1767), anatomist, obstetrician, and antiquary. Since 1770, his anatomy school occupied a building in Great Windmill Street. See Sir Charles F. W. Illingworth, *The Story of William Hunter* (Edinburgh, 1967).

2 During the years of CB's residence in Queen Square, 29 July fell on a Friday only in 1774.

3 Not identified.

1 Although Daniel Twining (see Lonsdale, p. 134 n. 1) does not date his transcription of this paragraph, and copies the text as following on from CB's letter of 13 July, it is clear from internal

... After playing a piece of Music by heart a long while, if by chance I look at the notes, *memory* is unhinged.—After reading the thoughts and opinions of others, I have none of my own.[2]—After conversing with a man of whose knowledge one has a high opinion one is afraid of thinking,—*Why* all this?—I have been poring over the Modes, & what authors have said of them, these 3 or 4 days, till I have not a single idea left about 'em,—though, while I was with you, I thought myself so clear, that I would not trouble you with much discussion upon that subject, but hastened from it to something else.[3] Did you ever feel anything like this?[4]—I believe the best way would be to burn all my books, & think for myself.[5] The *authorities* one is obliged to give in these matters for every *nothing* one says is ruination to all original thought, or connexion of matter: The whole will be shreds & patches.[6] ...

To James Lind[1]

[Chessington],
19 September 1774

Source: Monthly Magazine, l (1820–1), 531–2.
Addressed: Dr. James Lind, Edinburgh.　　*Also* LS draft, in FB's hand (Osborn), with FBA editorial alterations.　　*Endorsed by* CB: Copy of ⌐ Letter to ⌐ Dʳ Lind *And by* FBA: To *Dr. Lind* ✳ 1774 or 5　　*Editor's note:* The text is taken from the printed source, with insertion of the musical example, complimentary close, and paragraphing from the MS draft. Significant variant readings from the draft are footnoted. See Textual Introduction.

and external evidence that the present fragment comes from a separate letter written in late Aug. 1774, after CB's week-long first visit to Fordham early in the month.

[2] Twining replied on 30 Aug. (BL Add. MS 39933, fo. 113): 'What a strange thing this brain of ours is? I know well What it is to keep cramming ones head till ones ideas stick together.'

[3] Twining begins his answer of 30 Aug. with: 'And so now we begin again with this miserable poking, creeping, tortoise work of manual *correscondence*. Ah!—this is nothing like talking together in my parlour, with the table cover'd with books & papers—I never go into the room, but I see you in your linen Dressing gown.'

[4] Twining answered (ibid.): 'Full many a time have I begun reading with no ideas,—read on till I had got all I *could* get—kept pushing on to get more, till the line of *clear* information, was left behind me, & read myself back, at last, into an ignorance ... the ignorance of a full brain, is worse than that of an empty one.—However—this is only temporary: let your skull alone a little, & things set themselves to rights.'

[5] 'It is the being pressé to write your thoughts down *immediately* in this state of indigestion, that as you say is the ——.' (ibid.).

[6] See *Hamlet*, III. iv. 102.

[1] James Lind (1736–1812), MD (1768), Fellow of the Edinburgh College of Physicians (1770), FRS (1777), had visited China in 1766 while serving as a surgeon in an East Indiaman. In addition to medical treatises, Lind published the results of his astronomical observations (*DNB*).

[Chessington],[2] Sept. 19th, 1774.

Sir.

In the summer of 1772, I had the honour of dining with you at the Admiralty,[3] and in the course of a very agreeable evening afterwards, we had some conversation concerning Chinese music, in which you dropt several particulars relative to it, that excited my curiosity the more, as you soon convinced me that you were a thorough master of the subject. But I was obliged to steal away from the company in order to prepare for a tour into Germany, upon which I set out next morning; since which time I have not been able to discover that you have been in London, or I should have applied to you for some further information relative to the national melody and musical instruments of China.[4] I have sent some queries to intelligent persons in that country by two or three ships, but whether an answer can be returned previous to the publication of my work, is uncertain.

I think you told me that the Chinese had a kind of musical drama,[5] and that their melodies very much resembled the old Scots tunes. Have I permission for quoting your authority for this circumstance?[6] I think you likewise said they had no music in parts, either moving in different melodies, or in counterparts?[7] But the fact which I am most eager to ascertain, and of which I am most immediately in want, is, whether their scale moves in pure *diatonic without semitones*,[8] as has been

[2] [Chessington]] *publ. source gives* London *in error.*
From early Sept. to about 8 Oct. 1774, CB was at Chessington suffering from a severe attack of rheumatism (*EJL* ii). The MS draft of this letter shows that CB dictated it to Fanny Burney who helped to nurse her father during his illness.
[3] This dinner party probably occurred on 2 July 1772, the day before CB's departure for Germany. At that time, Lind was in London preparing to accompany Joseph Banks (1744–1820) on an expedition which sailed soon afterwards for Iceland (H. C. Cameron, *Sir Joseph Banks, K.B., P.R.S., the Autocrat of the Philosophers* (1952), pp. 47, 56, 295, 302–3).
[4] From about 1777, Lind settled at Windsor and became Physician to the Royal Household. Fanny Burney was to record a visit to Dr Lind to view his Eastern 'curiosities': 'I was extremely well entertained there. His collection is chiefly Chinese' (*DL* ii. 339 *et passim*; v. 440).
[5] In his reply, dated from Edinburgh, 11 Nov. 1774 (Osborn), Lind wrote: 'All the Plays which are exhibeted at Canton are Musical Dramas, such as our Begger's Opera &c generaly Tragedy or much filled with Tragical incidents; . . . The Chinese who speak English call a Play a Sing Song which name applies very well to a Musical Drama'.
[6] 'With respect to the music of China, Dr. Lind . . . assured me that all the melodies he had heard there bore a strong resemblance to the *old Scots tunes*' (*Hist. Mus.* i. 32; Mercer, i. 46). Dr Lind actually wrote (11 Nov.): 'Some of their Music, but I cannot say wither all, resembles very much that of the Highlands of Scotland.'
[7] counterparts] counterpoint *MS draft.*
Lind replied (ibid.): 'Their Music has no parts, an Octave is sometimes indeed introduced, and some of their Instruments, the Chinese Organ is capable of playing at one time several unisons.'
[8] 'As to Your most material question wither their Scale is purely Diatonic without Semitones? is a question in which I cannot solve you' (ibid.). Lind goes on to give CB the scales of two Chinese organs in his possession. The Chinese and the Scots both employed the pentatonic

asserted by many writers, and which a Chinese instrument that I saw at Paris, in the possession of the Abbé Arnaud, in a manner confirmed.[9]

This instrument was a kind of *Sticcardo*, consisting of bars of hard, sonorous wood of different lengths laid over a hollow vessel like the hull[10] of a ship, and its compass was about two octaves, [11]& the scale moved in this manner

or

Now it is impossible to produce any melody from these scales which will not resemble that of the ancient Scots. I should be glad to know if you have any such instrument in your collection, and whether this is the general scale of all their instruments.[12] May I take the liberty of troubling you with a few more questions? Is music much cultivated among them,[13] and have you had any opportunity of proving whether the European melody and harmony are more grateful to their ears than their own?[14] Have they any notation for this music? Or is it traditional, learnt merely by the ear, and retained by memory?[15] You have doubtless reduced to European characters some of their melodies. If you could furnish me with 2 or 3 genuine examples, you would be a real benefactor to my work.[16]

I am the less ceremonious in my manner of putting these questions to you, as such a lover and successful cultivator of arts and sciences as yourself, will the more readily pardon in another that curiosity

scale, which has five pitches to the octave, thus giving a similarity to their melodies. See 'pentatonic' in *New Grove*.

[9] See CB to Suard, 24 May 1771, n. 6.

[10] hull] hulk *MS draft*.

[11-11] & the scale ... [*musical example*]] *MS draft. Omitted in publ. source. FBA later edited the MS draft to read* ... & the scale moved in a manner to make it impossible to produce any melody from it .˙.

[12] Lind enclosed in his letter of 11 Nov. 1774, a diagram of 'Seven different Gamuts for the Chinese Flute'.

[13] Lind informed CB that there were 'frequent opportunities' to see Chinese Opera, and that 'Music is not only used in their Plays, but tunes are also play'd, at Marriages, Funerals, and in all Proc[e]ssions. ... Many Chinese who are not Musicians by profession Sing, and generaly some other one plays the tune on the Flute along with them, ... I beg to observe to you that the Chinese always Sing with a FEIGNED VOICE' (ibid.).

[14] 'The Chinese are much pleased with a simple Scotch tune, and with them only; other music being much above their comprehension' (ibid.).

[15] 'Music is a Profession in China, and is taught partly by certain Characters, and partly by the Ear. The notes being taught by the Characters, but the time or quantity of each note by the Ear alone' (ibid.).

[16] Lind also enclosed in his letter some 'Examples of the Chinese notation of Music', with explanatory observations: 'The Characters used for that purpose, and which signify such a note, or such a hole in a wind Instrument &c are variously used by different Authors ... The Characters are Common Chinese Characters—signifying things which have no connection with Music or musical Instruments. The ordinary meaning of such of them as I am acquainted with I have subjoined at the end of each example.' See Illustration 2.

2. An example of Chinese musical notation sent to Burney by James Lind, 11 November 1774. Burney: 'Have they any notation for this music?' Lind: 'The Characters used for that purpose . . . are Common Chinese Characters. . . . The ordinary meaning of such of them as I am acquainted with I have subjoined at the end of each example.'

and eager desire of information by which alone knowledge can be acquired.

[17]If at your first Leisure you w^d Honour me wth an answer to these particulars, you w^d extreamly serve & oblige

S^r, y^r Obed^t
& most Humble serv^t[17]
Chas. Burney.

To [Charles Davy]

St Martin's Street,
3 November 1774

ALS (Osborn).
Endorsed by Davy: Burney Novr 3^d | 1774

St Martin's Street, Leicester Field⟨s⟩
3^d Novr 1774

Dear Sir.

I hasten to thank you for the Pleasure you have afforded me of shewing my readiness to be a Subscriber to the Work you mention. Indeed, had I known of your Sons intention sooner I sh^d, unsolicited, have begged to have been honoured with a place in their List.[1]

I have a great many Apologies to make for not answering a very kind Lett^r I rec^d from you ever since last March,[2] in wch you were so obliging as to inclose some Designs of ornaments fit for a Musical Work; but that unremitting hurry in wch the Multitude of my affairs throws me prevented me for some Time; after wch your Letter was mislaid, & though ten Times more of my little summer Leisure was spent in seeking it than w^d have sufficed to have written a dozen Answers, I was unable to find it till very lately in moving House,[3] it

---

[17–17] If ... serv^t] *MS draft. Omitted in publ. source which gives* Your obliged and obedient servant.

CB, crippled in the shoulder by rheumatism, signed the MS draft with a tremulous 'C.B.'.

[1] Charles Davy's two sons, Charles (*c.*1757–1836) and Frederick (b. 1759), were translating into English the *Description des glacières, glaciers & amas de glace du duché de Savoye* (Geneva, 1773), by Marc-Théodore Bourrit (1739–1819), Swiss artist and pioneer in Alpine exploration (*DHBS*; Michaud). The Davy brothers' translation appeared as *A Relation of a Journey to the Glaciers, in the Dutchy of Savoy* (Norwich, 1775).

[2] Not preserved.

[3] CB moved into his new residence in St Martin's Street on 8 Oct. 1774. For a description of this famous dwelling, built by Sir Isaac Newton, see *ED* i. 313–14, 328; Constance Hill, *The House in St. Martin's Street* (1907), pp. 1–5; *HFB*, pp. 51–2; *EJL* ii.

was discovered among other lost Things by one of my Daughters; that Daughter to whom you were so polite, & so unjust as to apologize for an imaginary offence with wch your delicacy had charged yourself; but I can venture to say that your Peace is entirely made both wth her & me, if ever it c^d be broken, by a slight difference of opinion concerning *Flutes* & *Fiddles*.[4]—My Work has been very much impeded by a Long & severe indisposition, wch for more than two months disabled me, Body & Mind. A Fever with a most acute Rheumatism fixt in my right Shoulder were my Complaints, wth the Dregs of which I am still confined to my Room.[5] I fear this will prevent my keeping my Word, wth my Subscribers, by publishing the 1st Vol. of my Hist^y so Soon as X^{mas}; however, I have been in the Press some Time, & hope I shall not be obliged to Trespass much upon their Indulgence. I sh^d have been extreamly glad in the course of the summer to have seen your Translation of Euclid,[6] & indeed sh^d yet, if a safe & favourable conveyance sh^d offer; for though the greatest part of what I have to say ab^t the Theory of Anc^t Music is already Printed, there are certain things which I wish to see over & over again not only with my own Eyes, but with the Eyes of all my learned Friends.

You were so obliging as to remind me of a promise in one of your Letters, to transmit to you my last Proposals.[7] I now take the Liberty of enclosing two or three & beg your Pardon for not doing it sooner. I have purchased at so great an expense 6 ornamental Plates for my two Vol^s engraved by Bartolozzi from designs of Cipriani,[8] that I fear I must hold my Hand as to further ornaments. The rest must be confined to useful, such as representations of Anc^t Instrum^{ts} from

---

[4] Davy's 'slight difference of opinion' with, presumably, Fanny, is otherwise unexplained; that with CB is possibly explained by CB to Davy, [Mar. 1774?].

[5] For an account of this breakdown of CB's health, see Lonsdale, pp. 155–8.

[6] Charles Davy's translation reached print only thirteen years later: *Letters, addressed chiefly to a Young Gentleman, upon Subjects of Literature: including a Translation of Euclid's Section of the Canon; and his Treatise on Harmonic; with an Explanation of the Greek Musical Modes, according to the Doctrine of Ptolemy* (Bury St Edmund's, 1787). CB's copy of this work is listed in *Cat. Misc. Lib.*, lot 492. It fetched 4s. For CB's review of Davy's *Letters*, see *Monthly Review*, 2nd ser., i (1790), 78–84; 144–50.

[7] After the deadline for collecting 500 subscribers for the *History of Music* at Christmas 1773 had passed, CB issued a revised set of 'Proposals' dated 'London, Jan. 10th, 1774.' This version stated that 'The first volume is in the press, and will be published with all possible expedition', and that non-subscribers would have to pay 3 guineas for the two volumes instead of the 2 guineas for subscribers. The text of this revised 'Proposals' was also printed facing p. 1 of the second volume of the second edition of the *German Tour* (1775).

[8] Giovanni Battista Cipriani (1727–85), RA (1768), painter and engraver, had come to England in 1755. He is best known for his drawings, most of which were engraved by his Florentine contemporary, and lifelong friend, Francesco Bartolozzi (1727–1815), RA (1768), who had settled in England in 1764 as 'engraver to the King'. For accounts of the six ornamental plates CB bought, see *Hist. Mus.* i (1776), 517; Lonsdale, p. 493.

drawings made abroad under my own Eye, for the 1ˢᵗ Vol. & Examples of Music for the 2ᵈ.

> I am, dear Sir,
> With great respect, yʳ obliged
> & Most Obedᵗ Servᵗ
> Chaˢ Burney.

To James Lind

St Martin's Street,
26 November 1774

ALS (Osborn).
Docketed by Lind: answered 8ᵗʰ Decʳ 1774
532–3.

Publ.: Monthly Magazine, l (1820–1),

> London. Sᵗ Martin's
> Street Leicester Fiēlds.
> 26ᵗʰ Novʳ 1774.

Sir.

The post that brought your kind & obliging Communications[1] should not have returned empty Handed if I cᵈ have procured a Frank in which to have inclosed my sincere thanks for the Pains you have taken in order to gratify my curiosity with respect to Chinese Music; but so few of my Parliamentary Friends were then in Town that I was obliged to Postpone my Acknowledgemᵗˢ till now.

The accounts with wᶜʰ you have favoured me are very curious & satisfactory, & will enrich my 2ᵈ Volume, in which I shall have occasion to speak of modern national Music.[2] And they are the more to my purpose as they corroborate accᵗˢ I have already recᵈ from intelligent Persons in these Matters with whom I have both conversed & Corresponded, some of whom like. yourself have been in China. With respect to the Scale abᵗ which you speak with some diffidence,[3] I have no doubt as far as I am able to Judge by the Instrumᵗ I saw at

---

[1] Lind's long letter of 11 Nov. 1774 (Osborn) included as enclosures examples of Chinese musical notation, drawings of Chinese instruments, a Chinese music book, the words of the songs in a Chinese play, and 'the favouret Moorish Tune which is Sung over all Indostan'. See Illustration 2.

[2] CB never succeeded in his plan to include chapters on National Music in his *History*. Thirty years later, when he wrote the articles on the music of various nations for Rees's *Cyclopaedia*, CB penned one on 'Chinese Music'. By that time he had accumulated much more material on the subject, and Dr Lind's observations are not mentioned.

[3] See CB to Lind, 19 Sept. 1774, n. 8.

Paris, & the Tunes given by Duhalde,[4] & 12 more wch I have just rec^d & concerning the authenticity of wch there is not the least room to doubt, confirm not only my opinions ab^t the Scale but convince me of the strong resemblance between the Chinese Melodies & those of Scotland.

The Moorish Tune wch has been in such favour all over Indostan,[5] I take to have been formed upon a different scale from all the Chinese Tunes I have ever seen.

I have been long confined at Home by a most severe fit of the Rheumatism, & have not as yet been able to consult the Gentlemen whom you mention in order to furnish me with more particulars on the subject.[6] But I shall avail myself of all your hints as soon as ever I am able to go out. A Nobleman of my acquaintance[7] has a large room hung with some of the most beautiful India Paper I ever saw, upon wch are represented several Concerts performed upon various Instruments by Figures as big as the Life, & the Instruments proportionably Large: I suppose one may depend upon these being exact representations from Nature? if they are, a very good Idea of the Instrum^ts of the Country, & the Manner of Playing upon them may be acquired from these representations. I have procured the Chinese Novel, wch becomes very curious & Instructive ab^t Chinese Matters from your recommendation.[8] Otherwise I sh^d have had no Idea of it's being Genuine, or of more authority than a *Conte, fait au plaisir*.

The only part of my work wch is, as yet, printed, is a Dissertation upon the Music of the Ancients, in wch having had occasion to Compare one of the Greek Scales wth one sent me from China, I have taken the Liberty of quoting your authority for a Confirmation of the strong resemblance between the Melodies of Scotland & those of China. This I durst not do till I had the honour of y^r Letter, tho' I remembered

---

[4] See Jean-Baptiste Du Halde, SJ (1674–1743), *Description géographique, historique, chronologique, politique, et physique de l'empire de la Chine et de la Tartarie chinoise* (1735), iii. 265–7. CB's set of the 1736 edition of Du Halde, published at The Hague, sold for £1. 11s. 6d. (*Cat. Misc. Lib.*, lot 645).

[5] See n. 1.

[6] Lind had written in his letter of 11 Nov.: 'For further information I recommend to you Mr Grill, a Swadish Gentleman, he was a Swadish Supercargo and lived a good time in China, he is an excellen[t] Musician and studied Chinese Music. He lives in Swaden, but his brother to whom Dr Solander will introduce you, lives in London at Mr Lindigrien's Deventer Court Mincing Lane[.] There are likewise in London, Mr Fitzheugh a very inteligent man, who was our Chief Super-Cargo at China when I was there; and M^r McKienzie an other Super-Cargo, which last I believe can furnish you with some of their tunes, those I had being lost.'

[7] Not identified.

[8] Lind had recommended for CB's perusal ('if you wish to know Chinese manners, and love to be entertained at the same time') the first work of Chinese fiction translated into English: *Hau Kiou Choaan or The Pleasing History*, trans. James Wilkinson, ed. with notes by Thomas Percy (4 vols., 1761). CB's copy fetched 17s. (*Cat. Misc. Lib.*, lot 767). See also L. F. Powell, 'Hau Kiou Choaan', *RES* ii (1926), 446–55.

your saying something to that Purpose at the Admiralty.[9] I sh[d] be very happy in an opportunity of talking over these matters wth you in S[t] Martin's Street, if, luckily, you sh[d] have a call to London. I can throw out no temptation so great to an astronomer perhaps as telling you that I now inhabit the House where S[r] Is. Newton long lived, & where he remained till within a few Days of his Death. His Observatory on the Top of the House is a conspicuous Object in Leicester fields.—

If, *en attendant* a London Journey, anything concerning the *Materia Musica* sh[d] occur to you I shall be very much obliged to you for a further Communication, but at any rate shall be happy in hearing from you when you have a Quarter of an hour to bestow, on Sir,

Your obed[t] &

Most obliged humble Serv[t]

Cha[s] Burney

To Samuel Crisp[1]

[St Martin's Street,

late March 1775][2]

AL and ALS (BL Egerton MS 3694, fos. 25–30[v]).

Docketed by FBA: ✳ N[o] I of Mr. Bruce. 2ce with Mr. Twining, M[rs] Strange, &c | & M[r] Bruce, Nesbit, &c | *March* 1775 | 1775 / By Dr. Burney   *And by* Crisp: N[o] 17 ⌐I believe about March or April⌐   *Publ.: ED* ii. 34–6 (in part); Constance Hill, *The House in St. Martin's Street* (1907), p. 32 (in part).

Here Fan desires me to write the Prologue to I know not what she's going to give you—& with my Paw too!—not one strait Finger have I on my right Hand!—however, I want just to give you some Signs of Life after so long an absence, & silence.—I have a Million of things to say to you ab[t] myself & others, but such a hurried, shattered, worn-out posthorse as I am at present crawls not on the Earth.—Yet even Leisure to attend to bodily hea[l]th cannot exempt poor mortals from pain! for you, poor soul, I hear are laid up—I w[d] it were Summer & I'd come and Con ailments with you—I know not what Effect it w[d]

[9] See CB to Lind, 19 Sept. 1774, n. 6.

[1] This letter extends to 12 pages in the MS, of which CB wrote the first half-page, and a concluding page. Fanny fills the intervening 10½ pages with her account of the first three occasions on which she met James Bruce. See *EJL* ii.

[2] Constance Hill erroneously dates this letter 12 Mar. (*House in St. Martin's Street*, p. 32). Fanny, in her section of the MS, anticipates 'Next Sunday' as the day fixed for Bruce's 'second appearance in St. Martin's Street', which occurred on Sunday 26 Mar. (*ED* ii. 31–2). Crisp's reply is dated 'Ches[sington] Mar. 27' (ibid., p. 37). CB's and Fanny's joint letter to Crisp can therefore be dated sometime in the preceding week: 19–25 Mar. 1775.

have on your Gout, but it w^d certainly comfort my Bowels to chat & philosophize with you—It seems a long life since I saw you—& I have to tell you of my poor Book—at a dead stop now—page 352[3]— but what think you of the King of Abyssinia[4] who has at length indulged me with 2 Charming drawings of Instrum^ts! an Abyssinian *Lyre*[5] now in Common use, & the Theban Harp,[6] most beautiful indeed, though drawn from a painting in Diospolis, at least 3000 y^rs old—a Letter of description too! wch I have leave to print[7]—God bless you.

[*The letter is continued for 10½ MS pages by Fanny Burney, after which CB concludes:*]

Thanks for Theocritus—I must now throw it in the Cauldron till an opportunity offers of using the passage[8]—my dissertation has been long closed, otherwise it w^d have done nicely in the Section upon anc^t Harmony. But a Time will come perhaps when I may resume the subject of dispute concerning the question whether the Greeks & Romans knew *Counterpoint*, or *music in parts.*—I am got now to the Olympic & Pythian Games,[9] whose Musical Contests wd perhaps furnish some Biographical amusement, at least, to my readers, whom

[3] i.e. at sig. Yy, towards the end of the third chapter, 'Concerning the Music of Heroes and Heroic Times', in 'The History of Greek Music' (Mercer, i. 283). CB's printer was clearly waiting to receive the fourth chapter, there being insufficient copy left in the third to print sig. Zz. CB was now working on the musical contests associated with the Olympic and Pythian Games, which constitute part of the fourth chapter. See n. 9; and *Hist. Mus.* i (1776), 353–60.

[4] James Bruce (1730–94), of Kinnaird, African traveller and author, called 'His *Abyssinian Majesty*' by his kinswoman, Isabella Strange, née Lumisden (1719–1806), wife of the engraver, Robert Strange (*ED* ii. 13; *JL* i. 142 n.). Bruce had returned to England in June 1774, after some 10 years spent in North Africa, Egypt, and Abyssinia, and had been lionized by London society eager to hear the account of his exploits. Mrs Strange introduced CB to Bruce (*Mem.* i. 297), who, as Fanny records, soon became 'very intimate with my father' (*ED* ii. 7), and a frequent visitor at the Burney house in St Martin's Street. See Lonsdale, pp. 160–1; A. A. Moorefield, 'James Bruce: Ethnomusicologist or Abyssinian Lyre?', *Journal of the American Musicological Society*, xxviii (1975), 493–514.

[5] See *Hist. Mus.* i (1776), plate V, item 6; Mercer, i. 396.

[6] *Hist. Mus.* i (1776), plate VIII; Mercer, i. 391. Bruce includes descriptions and illustrations of the harps he discovered at Thebes in his *Travels to Discover the Source of the Nile* (Edinburgh, 1790), i. 127–33.

[7] Bruce to CB, 20 Oct. 1774 (Osborn). The inclusion of an expanded form of this letter in the *History* under the chapter 'Of Egyptian Music', obliged CB to cancel the original sig. Ee, and add two more gatherings: *Ee and *Ff, bearing pagination *217–*232. See Lonsdale, pp. 492–3.

[8] Theocritus, *Poems*, xviii. 7. CB placed this description of 'the bride-maids of Helen in the act of dancing and singing altogether, *one and the same melody or tune*' in the Additional Notes, *Hist. Mus.* i (1776), 500. In the second edition of the first volume, the reference is incorporated in the discussion of whether the ancient Greeks had harmony in their music (*Hist. Mus.* i. 131; Mercer, i. 121).

[9] i.e. to the fourth chapter, 'Of the State of Music in Greece, from the Time of Homer, till it was subdued by the Romans, including the Musical Contests at the Public Games', in 'The History of Greek Music' (Mercer, i. 294–316). See n. 3.

I must endeavour to *divert* wh⸍n I have not the least chance of *Instructing* them. My 1ˢᵗ vol. will necessarily consist more of the History of Poets & Musicians than of Music; for till frequent specimens can be given how is it possible to reason upon the kind of Music that was in use & admired at any distant period of Time: 'what can we reason but from what we know?'[10]—'answer me that, & un-yoke'.[11]—My Paw akes already. So, once More God bless you—best remembrance to Madᵐ Ham:[12] & the Cap:[13]—

⸢P.S. I have not wrote so much *History* this month. My plates are in great forwardness. I have already got a double one from Grignion[14] of Instruments, & the Busts of the figures playᵍ upon them—from antiques.[15] & Strange has been so kind as to take 2 more over to Paris for me, which he has got engraved there, & will bring back 2 or 3 soon.[16] the Theban Harp is Engravᵍ[17] [xxx *two words*]. I'll send you a proof of it, one of these Days.⸥

[*Fanny Burney's 4-line conclusion is omitted.*]

To Thomas Twining

[St Martin's Street, mid-June 1775][1]

L copy extracts (Osborn: 'Twining Letterbook No. 2', pp. 13–14). *Docketed:* Memᵈᵘᵐˢ for Twi[2]

[10] Pope, *An Essay on Man*, i. 18.

[11] 'Ay, tell me that, and unyoke' (*Hamlet*, v. i. 52).

[12] Sarah Hamilton (*c.*1705–97) had inherited Chessington Hall from her brother, and kept the old mansion as a country boarding-house. Samuel Crisp rented a suite of rooms from her (see *ED* i. 125 and n. 2; *HFB*, p. 17; *JL* i. 144 n. 4; *EJL* i. 8 n. 24, 158 n. 43; *CB Mem.* 105).

[13] Probably John Frodsham (*c.*1737–91), of the Royal Navy, commissioned (1758), Commander (1779), Post-Captain (1782), related to Crisp by marriage (*Burford Papers*, pp. 15, 42–3, and *passim*). After Frodsham's death in 1791, CB transcribed into one of his MS 'Poetical Notebooks' an 'Inscription & Epitaph on Captain John Frodsham' (Osborn: shelves c 33, pp. 226–8).

[14] Charles Grignion the elder (1717–1810), line-engraver whose studio was situated in James Street, Covent Garden (*DNB*).

[15] See plate IV in *Hist. Mus.* i (1776); Mercer, i. 394–5.

[16] Robert Strange, partly because of his Jacobite sympathies, spent long periods on the Continent. Plates V and VI in the first volume of *Hist. Mus.* (Mercer, i. 396–8), were engraved by his French pupil, Pierre Maleuvre (1740–1803). See E. Bénézit, *Dictionnaire critique et documentaire des peintres, sculpteurs, dessinateurs et graveurs* (1966), v. 733.

[17] By Grignion. See nn. 6, 14.

[1] Written in reply to Twining's letter of 9 June 1775 (copy extracts, BL Add. MS 39933, fos. 136ᵛ–137ᵛ, and Osborn), and before Twining's next letter of 22 June (copy, BL, ibid., fos. 138ᵛ–139ᵛ), this letter can be dated between *c.*10 and *c.*20 June 1775.

[2] This letter probably accompanied proof sheets of the 'Dissertation on the Music of the

. . . Our harmony of ideas will appear from the very few alterations I have made, either in the thoughts or words of your MS. I have likewise adopted almost every correction offered for the cancelled ½ sheet[3] except the rejection of Note (y) which contains an Idea that I am loth to part with.[4]

*   *   *

I shall send you a charming Symphony of Vanhal—make it into a Lesson for the P. Forte;—it will go sweetly upon it, & so will that you already have,—by taking in parts you may produce.

Would you have not only thought of a Translation of Plutarch, but executed it long ago![5] What a help it would have been to me, poking in the dark about Greek!—I have wanted you to write something *de votre propre façon*, ever since I have known you. Translation is unworthy of you—but let's have it, rather than nothing, I entreat you. Your notes will give you an opportunity for a display of all your musical & other eruditions, as well as taste: so go to work. . . .

To Thomas Twining

[St Martin's Street],
28 June 1775

L copy extract (Osborn: 'Twining Letterbook No. 2', p. 14).

June 28. 1775

. . . You work & mortify me by saying that my being in possession of your Enharm: System partly prevents your translating Plut[s] Dial.[1]

Ancients' in which CB included almost verbatim Twining's 'Enharmonic Hypothesis'. See Lonsdale, pp. 161–2.

[3] CB refers to the cancellation of his original sigs. L3 and L4, and their replacement by a new sheet, comprising L3, L4, and two unsigned leaves, together with an extra leaf signed *L. The cancellation, which obliged CB to introduce double pagination numbered *81–*86, was made necessary by Twining's observations on classical metre. See A. T. Hazen, *Samuel Johnson's Prefaces & Dedications* (New Haven, 1937), p. 27; Lonsdale, pp. 491–2; Mercer, i. 74–82.

[4] *Hist. Mus.* i (1776), 78 n.; Mercer, i. 76 n. CB was unwilling to part with his observation that in the English language 'an *accented* and a *long syllable* are by no means to be confounded, at least in setting words to music.'

[5] In his letter of 9 June (copy extract, Osborn), Twining had written: 'Q. would Plut[arch]'s dial[ogue] on Music translated into readable English, yet as fairly as possible—without dark patches & *dissembled difficulties* left to plague a reader—egayé with notes musical, critical, explanatory,—avoiding bothers, & owning unintelligibilities wherever they are, which editors and translators never do— . . . would it make a readable book? would it do? would anybody buy it? be entertained with it?—Such a fancy has sometimes floated in my brain. Tell me.—'

[1] In copying Twining's letter of 22 June (copy, BL Add. MS 39933, fos. 138ᵛ–139ᵛ), Richard Twining omitted the passage to which CB refers. See Lonsdale, p. 163. Twining had evidently

— — If I acknowledge it in the Preface,[2] which I will, & every thing
else most readily & gladly, if I have your leave, it will be yours *again* to
do what you please with do, do, do,—don't lay such a weight on my
conscience.[3] Nay, I'll certainly tell all with 10,000 Comp[ts] of erudition,
perspicacity Taste &c &c &c if you don't go to work upon that, or
something else, *immediately*. . . .

To [Charles Davy]   Chessington, 2 August 1775

ALS (Cambridge University Library, MS Add. 4251, fo. 181).
Docketed by Davy: D[r] Burney Aug[st] 2 1775

Chesington, near Epsom, Surry
Aug[t] 2[d] 1775.

Dear Sir.

It has given me great Concern that I have been unable to return
your MSS.[1] sooner; but your Letter[2] did not find me for a Considerable
Time after it was written, & when I rec[d] it, I was in the Country &
you[r] books being carefully locked up in London, I c[d] give no orders
about them.

I had great Pleasure in the perusal of them, & am sorry the Pains
you & your learned fellow-Labourer[3] took in illuminating such dark
subjects sh[d] be so long witheld from the Public. Unluckily for me &
my work, all I had to say on these matters was printed before I was in

mentioned that in handing over to CB his 'discovery' regarding the Enharmonic Genus of the
Greeks, his intended edition of Plutarch's *Dialogue on Music* became superfluous.

[2] Twining replied: 'Go to—you & your preface;—I desire none of your palaver. You had
better have an engraving of my *joulter*, had not you? along with your own, in an oval frame, with
Lyres & hautbois & trumpets & flying Music-books all round it;— the motto—"caput inter
nubila condit," [*Aeneid*, iv. 177]—to denote the sublimity, darkness, & out-of-sightedness of my
researches.—Peste!—' (24 July 1775, copy extract, Osborn).

[3] Twining wrote in reply (ibid.): 'My jokes taken seriously again. It was always about as
probable that I should translate Plutarch, as that I should fly. When I give a man a thing, &
wish it back again, it must be something of more value than my Enharmonic hypothesis.'

[1] In his letter to Davy of 3 Nov. 1774, CB had expressed a desire to see Davy's translation of
Euclid's writings on music. These translations are doubtless the MSS to which CB refers.

[2] Not preserved.

[3] Christopher Smear, with whom Davy collaborated in writing 'An Essay upon the Principles
and Powers of Vocal and Instrumental Music' (see CB to Davy, 3 July 1772, n. 2). When writing
about ancient Greek music, Davy consistently defers to his 'ingenious friend Mr. C.S.', a circumstance which confirms Smear as Davy's 'learned fellow-Labourer' to whom CB refers. See
C. Davy, *Letters, addressed chiefly to a Young Gentleman* (Bury St Edmund's, 1787), i. 295, 305, 333,
338, 355; ii. 204, 410.

Possession of your MSS, so that I was unable to avail myself of your ingenious Labours.

My Health has never been established since the severe attack I had last Autumn, and I am seldom well enough [to] give that close application to my Book or to pursue my enquiries with the vigour I wish. I have been ordered to Buxton,[4] to wch Place I hope to be able to go next Week. Though my 1st Vol. is in great forwardness yet I fear this Journey will prevent its being published till after Mich^s.

I am much obliged to you for inserting my Name in the list of Subscribers to the excellent translation of an enterta[in]ing work by your Sons,[5] wch I doubt not will be thankfully rec^d by the Public, and do them as much honour as they have done the Author Justice. I see no London Bookseller's name in the Title,[6] & am ignorant to whom my Subscription is to be paid; I beg you to take the trouble of letting me know, at your Liesure to whom I shall discharge my debt. Y^r 3 Vol^s will be sent by to Morrow's Coach.

I am, dear Sir,
with great regard
your Obedt &
Most faithful Servt
Chas Burney.

When you next honour me | with a Lett^r if | St Martin's Street | Leicester Fields be | put upon it, I shall | have it sent after me.

To [James] Lind[1] — St Martin's Street, 12 August 1775

ALS (Dixson Library, State Library of New South Wales, Sydney, Australia: DL MS Q160).

Addressed: To | Dr John Lind | at | Edinburgh — *Endorsed by* CB: single sheet

Pmk: 12 AV — *Publ.: Monthly Magazine*, li (1821), 343–4 (in part).

[4] CB was to spend nearly 3 weeks at Buxton, the spa in the Peak District of Derbyshire, seeking further alleviation sea-bathing at Cley next the Sea in North Norfolk (*ED* ii. 85).

[5] *A Relation of a Journey to the Glaciers, in the Dutchy of Savoy* (Norwich, 1775). See CB to [Davy], 3 Nov. 1774, n. 1.

[6] The first edition (1775) of the Davy brothers' *Relation* was printed by Richard Beatniffe (1740–1818), who, since 1773, had conducted his printing, bookselling, and publishing business at 1 Cockey Lane, Norwich (Plomer, p. 20). CB's own publisher, George Robinson, brought out the second revised edition (London, 1776), which includes CB's and Fanny's names in its list of subscribers.

[1] CB, in error, addresses his letter to Dr 'John Lind'. This letter clearly belongs to CB's correspondence with James Lind (1736–1812), the physician and astronomer whom he had met at the Admiralty in 1772.

London. St Martin's Street
Leicester Fields.

Dear Sir,

It has frequently given me great Concern that your last Letter[2] was not immediately answered; but for some Time past the want of health & of Leisure have made me guilty of many omissions of that kind wch are painful to reflexion. After so long a Silence I sh^d have been ashamed to address you without some excuse, which seems as necessary now for my Letter appearing at all as for its not appearing sooner.

When you last favoured me with a Letter I remember, & have constantly remembered that you wished to be apprised whether any new Expedition was in meditation for the South Seas.[3] I c^d get no intelligence worth communicating sooner as nothing was resolved on during the Absence of Capt. Cook;[4] but now he is come home & has made considerable discoveries another Expedition is not only talked of, but *determined* to take place between this Time & next X^{mas}—I yesterday Dined at the Admiralty & had (I speak it *inter nos*) the Information from Ld Sandwich himself. Two Ships are to be sent out, in one of wch I believe my Son, who has already been a circumnavigator wth Capt. Fourneaux,[5] will go out Lieutenant.

He sailed last Tuesday in the Cerberus for Boston[6] but is expected

---

[2] Of 8 Dec. 1774. Although Lind's letter is missing, he had endorsed CB's previous letter of 26 Nov. 1774, 'answered 8th Decr 1774'.

[3] Lind's interest in plans for South Sea expeditions was more than purely academic. In 1772 Lind had been recruited by Joseph Banks (1744–1820) as naturalist in his team of experts who were to have sailed in HMS *Resolution* with James Cook (1728–79) on his second voyage of discovery. Parliament had also made a special grant of £4000 to defray Lind's expenses. Difficulties over accommodation aboard the *Resolution*, however, had caused Banks and his team to withdraw from the expedition. Lind, who had disbursed considerable sums of his own money on preparations and equipment, was left in financial straits. See H. C. Cameron, 'The Failure of the Philosophers to Sail with Cook in the *Resolution*', *The Geographical Journal*, cxvi (1950), 49–54; H. C. Cameron, *Sir Joseph Banks, K.B., P.R.S., the Autocrat of the Philosophers* (1952), pp. 47–56, 294–6, 302–3; J. C. Beaglehole, *The Life of Captain James Cook* (1974), pp. 292–3, 303.

[4] In consort with HMS *Adventure*, Cook in the *Resolution* had sailed from Plymouth on 13 July 1772 with instructions to discover, if possible, the unknown great southern continent, *Terra Australis Incognita*. In the course of the voyage, the two ships parted company. The *Adventure* returned to England on 14 July 1774, more than a year earlier than Cook, who, in the *Resolution*, anchored at Spithead on 30 July 1775 (Beaglehole, *Cook*, chs. 13–17; *GM* xliv (1774), 330).

[5] Tobias Furneaux (1735–81), circumnavigator, had commanded the *Adventure* into which Cook had promoted James Burney as second lieutenant when the expedition was at anchor in Table Bay on 18 Nov. 1772. James had sailed in Cook's own sloop, the *Resolution*, at the beginning of Cook's second voyage of discovery. See Manwaring, pp. 13–47; R. Furneaux, *Tobias Furneaux, Circumnavigator* (1960).

The private journal of James Burney as second lieutenant in the *Adventure* has been published as *With Captain James Cook in the Antarctic and Pacific*, ed. B. Hooper (Canberra, 1975).

[6] HMS *Cerberus*, 28-gun frigate, in which James Burney was second lieutenant, sailed on 8 Aug. 1775 from Portsmouth with stores, medical supplies, and money for the British forces in North America. On arrival in Boston Harbour on 26 Sept., James Burney was promoted first lieutenant. In this capacity he served on the American station until early Dec., when he availed

back in Nov^r, wch will be Time enough Ld S. says for the new Southern Expedition.[7] Capt. Cook has been made a Post Capt. since his arrival, & so has Capt. Fourneaux.[8]

If this Intelligence will be of the least use or satisfaction to you, it will afford me a very sensible Pleasure, being, Dear Sir with sincere regard

your much obliged
& most obed^t Servt
Chas Burney

12th Aug^t | 1775.

The same want of Health wch has made me a bad Correspondent, will prevent me from publishing the 1st vol. of my Hist^y of Music, I fear, before Nov^r; as I am now ordered to Buxton for 3 Weeks or a Month, wch will Stop the Press till my return. The B^k, however, is in great forwardness, the Plates being all nearly ready & more than 400 pages of Letter press printed.

To Thomas Twining

[St Martin's Street, *c.*12] October 1775[1]

L copy extract (Osborn: 'Twining Letterbook No. 2', p. 17).
Docketed by Daniel Twining: D^r B to T. T.

Oct. 1775

It grieves me sorely, my dear Friend, to be under the necessity of breaking in upon you with a request that may seem unreasonable & importunate, but the Press standing still just at the time when I can best attend to it, makes me wish now that you would be so kind to

himself of Lord Sandwich's permission to return to England to join Captain Cook's last expedition (Manwaring, pp. 52–61). See also G. R. Barnes and J. H. Owen, eds., *The Private Papers of John, Earl of Sandwich, First Lord of the Admiralty, 1771–1782*, Navy Records Society (1932–8), i. 80–1.

[7] James Burney was to sail as first lieutenant in the *Discovery* under the command of Charles Clerke (1743–79). The *Resolution* under Cook, and the *Discovery* finally departed England on 12 July and 1 Aug. 1776 respectively. See Beaglehole, *Cook*, pp. 498, 506–10; *ED* ii. 38.

[8] Cook was promoted post-captain on 9 Aug., and Furneaux on 10 Aug. 1775 (*The Commissioned Sea Officers of the Royal Navy, 1660–1815* ([Greenwich], 1954), i. 193, 341).

[1] The approximate date of this letter may be inferred from the following circumstances: Fanny reports towards the end of Oct. 1775 that CB had 'been returned home about a fortnight' (*ED* ii. 85) after his summer visits to Buxton and Norfolk; Twining's reply, dated 16 Oct. 1775 (BL Add. MS 39933, fos. 148^v–151^v; Osborn) provides the *terminus ante quem*; and it is unlikely that Twining delayed this reply, in view of CB's urgent call for the return of his MS.

make two parcels of my MS copy,[2] & send me that which you said in your last was done with.[3]—I have not been visible to a creature in London since I came out of Norfolk, for when once I open the door to interruption, or cross the threshold in the way of out-work, there's an end of any kind of regular study, or of sleep & refreshment.—If I don't get this vol. out before X^{mas} I shall break my heart—& there is so much to do to it, & printers, if all was done on my part, are so little to be depended on, that I expect to be harrassed to death by 'em, if I do not first wear myself out.[4]

To Thomas Twining   [St Martin's Street],
                                                            18 October 1775

L copy extracts (Osborn: 'Twining Letterbook No. 2', pp. 18–20).
Docketed by Daniel Twining: D[r] B to TT

Oct. 18 1775

I am quite ashamed to see how much there was to *do* at my MS, & still more to see how much you *have done*.[1]—I would not plague you with this so soon but to let you know all came safe,—and *sound*, no doubt, after such Cathartics as you have administered.—You have treated me with all the sincerity of a true friend. In matters of blunder & ignorance I submit implicitly—in matters of opinion I am now & then a patriot, & for Wilks & Liberty.[2]—The want of room is the

[2] Twining's notes for his correspondence with CB show that he had received CB's MS of the last three chapters on 'The History of Greek Music' by late Aug. 1775: 'About marking his MS.—Of printing the Gr[eek] text of translations &c.' (BL Add. MS 39936, fo. 58).
[3] Neither the extracts copied by Richard Twining from his brother's letter of Sept. 1775 (BL Add. MS 39933, fos. 144[v]–147[v]), nor Thomas Twining's own notes for the letter (BL Add. MS 39936, fo. 58[v]) reveal precisely which portion of CB's MS had been 'done with'.
[4] Responding immediately to CB's plea, Twining observed, 'You will think me the most poking, dawdling, tiresome animal!—You & I draw together like a racer, & a cart horse; but then remember what it is we are drawing:—none of your light postchaises, or flimsy phaetons, but a great heavy-loaded broad-wheeled waggon, swagging & creaking thro' terrible deep roads! Agree that my *pace* is better suited to the work' (16 Oct. 1775, copy extracts, BL Add. MS 39933, fo. 148[v]; and Osborn, 'Twining Letterbook No. 2', p. 18).
[1] Twining had written to CB enclosing part of the MS of the last three chapters of 'The History of Greek Music' on 16 Oct. 1775 (copy extract, BL Add. MS 39933, fos. 148[v]–151[v]): 'Knowing the haste in which you are forced to work, I kept a watchful eye upon mistakes of all sorts; & I think verily, there are none but what I have detected, unless your chronological dates are any of them wrong: *this* is the only part which I did not, indeed *could* not,—minutely examine.'
[2] For the origin of this political slogan, coined in May 1763, see G. Rudé, *Wilkes and Liberty, a Social Study of 1763 to 1774* (Oxford, 1962), pp. 26–7.

greatest of all my distresses, for upon a new reading I see several places I could mend & enliven, if I durst say a word more. . . .

With respect to Bruce's flummery[3]—I think the only way to make it pass unnoticed is, to print at the beginning *Letters from the learned* on the Continent—*Testimonials* from foreign & domestic Journals, Joel[4] included, & *Verses* in Greek, Latin, French, Italian, German, & English.

TO THE AUTHOUR

Pray get a good handsome copy ready, if you have a mind to be taken in tow to immortality. I am sorry Gray is dead[5]—otherwise, perhaps, you'd have been so kind to have got a few lines from him in behalf of me & my work. Mason I am sure of—& Johnson—if he won't write, I have such fine things under his hand, already written![6]— O, Sir! I could fill a 3[d] Vol[7] with the most honourable Testimonials—

[3] Writing about the Theban harp he had discovered, Bruce had said in his letter to CB of 20 Oct. 1774 (Osborn): 'I shall say nothing of the capabilities of this Instrument, nor what may be provd from it relative to the State of Musick, at a time when they were able to make such an Instrument, I shall with Impatience Expect This detail from you, Better Qualified than any I know now In Europe, for this disquisition, tis a curious one, & merits Your utmost Reflection, & Attention'.

In quoting Bruce's letter, CB printed verbatim this flattering testimonial (*Hist. Mus.* i (1776), *224; Mercer, i. 183), much to Twining's discomfort. In his letter of 16 Oct. Twining declared his concern that CB had not 'stuck in some little bit of a *blushing* note about the compliment . . . One should not *seem* to consent to a man's saying that in ones own book. Not that I should know at all what to say about such a thing. You might have just said that M[r] B[ruce] was of such an immense size that you could not possibly venture to desire him to leave it out.' See also Lonsdale, p. 168; and below n. 10.

[4] 'Joel Collier', pseudonym for John Bicknell (*c.*1746–87), *Musical Travels through England*. This ribald parody of CB's continental *Tours*, had first appeared on 20 Aug. 1774. For the identification of 'Joel Collier', and CB's reaction to the parody, which also mocked CB's scheme to establish a music conservatory at the Foundling Hospital, see Lonsdale, pp. 153–7; R. Lonsdale, 'Dr. Burney, "Joel Collier", and Sabrina', in *Evidence in Literary Scholarship: Essays in Memory of James Marshall Osborn*, ed. R. Wellek and A. Ribeiro (Oxford, 1979), pp. 281–308.

CB may have had in mind Twining's soothing observation on the appearance of Collier's *Musical Travels* that parody is itself an oblique form of compliment: 'No mans merit is completely confirmed, till he has received two sorts of praise: The *direct* praise of the generality, & the *inverted* praise, if I may call it so, of one or two particular detractors . . . ·Is not Virgil burlesqued very laughable, & Virgil very admirable?' (Twining to CB, 17 Sept. 1774, copy, BL Add. MS 39933, fos. 114[v]–151[v]).

[5] Thomas Gray died on 30 July 1771 (Gray *Corresp*. iii. 1269–82). Twining's acquaintance with Gray dated from his undergraduate years at Cambridge, where Gray played an influential part in the formation of Twining's musical taste.

[6] CB included a set of musical definitions 'with which I was some years since favoured by Mr. Mason, in consequence of a conversation on the subject of ancient music' in *Hist. Mus.* i. 124–5; Mercer, i. 117.

Johnson's authorship of the Dedication to the Queen is discussed in Lonsdale, pp. 168–9. See also *Hist. Mus.* i (1776), pp. iii–v; Mercer, i. 9–10.

[7] Although mentioned here in jest, CB has clearly taken note of Twining's warning: '2[d] Vol. to begin with Guido, or else there will be 3 Vol' (notes for Twining to CB, 21 Aug. 1775, BL Add. MS 39936, fo. 58). Twining's alarm over the increasing bulk of the first volume and the prospect that the *History* would require a third volume now became a major concern in his letters to CB.

from your Padre Martinis—your Prince Abbots[8]—your Rousseaus—Diderots—&c. &c. These with a *beautiful* print of the Author, engraved, from an original painting of Battoni,[9] by Bartolozzi, & published at the *request of the Subscribers*, will make Bruce, great man as he is, shrink into a grain of mustard seed.[10]—If you behave handsomely I'll join your Effigies to my own in that very Archiepiscopal wig of which you are so *fond*.[11]

To Thomas Twining [St Martin's Street], 15–[16?] November 1775

L copy extract (Osborn: 'Twining Letterbook No. 2', pp. 21–4).

15 Nov. 1775.

... I was carried out of a sick-bed to the Opera on Saturday.[1] The public was in general disappointed. They expected a Giant in Gabrielli, & behold! a pigmy. I was more pleased than surprised or disappointed. A little, dapper, short-armed, elegant, appetissante figure, was not likely to have the voice of a Stentor. She had a cold, & was put out of

---

[8] Martin Gerbert von Hornau (1720–93), Prince-Abbot (1764) of the Benedictine monastery of St Blasien in the Black Forest, historian of church music (*New Grove*). Although CB had not met Gerbert on his German journey (*Tours*, ii. 236), 'an intercourse has been opened between this learned prelate and myself, by means of a German gentleman ... resident in London; to whom the prince-abbot has applied for books and information, relative to the history of church music in England'. Preserved in the Osborn Collection ('Letterbook, Musical Correspondence') are copies of two letters from Gerbert to Rodolph Valtravers (*fl.* 1747–76), Bavarian Agent and Consul in London, dated 9 Apr. and 25 May 1774, in which CB figures prominently. Gerbert also wrote to Padre Martini, 20 May 1774 (Bologna: H. 86. 133), saying that he did not know precisely what topics CB's *History* would cover (see Anne Schnoebelen, *Padre Martini's Collection of Letters in the Civico Museo Bibliografico Musicale in Bologna: an Annotated Index* (New York, 1979), item 2276).

[9] CB refers ironically to Pompeo Girolamo Batoni (1708–87), Italian painter, celebrated in his time for his portraits of the wealthy and the aristocratic (*DBI*). A portrait of CB had in fact recently been requested by Padre Martini in a letter dated 19 Aug. 1775 (Osborn). See Brofsky, p. 327.

[10] James Bruce was a huge man, 6 feet 4 inches tall, and Twining's humorous comment on his size (n. 3) was based on personal recollection. Twining had met Bruce at the Burneys on 5 Mar. 1775 and had whispered to Fanny: 'This is the most awful man I ever saw! ... I never felt myself so little before' (*ED* ii. 21–2).

[11] Twining himself had started this exchange of drollery. See CB to Twining, 28 June 1775, n. 2.

---

[1] On Saturday 11 Nov. 1775, the famous soprano Caterina Gabrielli (1730–96) made her London Opera début singing Dido in Sacchini's setting of Metastasio's *Didone abbandonata* (*The London Stage*, IV. iii. 1927–9). For a full account of the performance, see *ED* ii. 91–3; *EJL* ii. See also *Hist. Mus.* iv. 502–4; Mercer, ii. 881–2; Rees; *New Grove*.

humour by the brutality of John in the Gallery hissing her Sister.[2] But through all clouds & storms I discovered a voice more like Mrs Sheridan's[3] in the clear places, than any one I know of: an execution rapid & neat to a very superior degree. After a very long swell in her cadence which I thought had wholly exhausted her air-pump, she set off with such a *Volata* as arracher'd des louanges from her greatest enemies. Her Cantabile melted me: and I was ready to pronounce her to be *two distinct singers*: and in the Duet, her & Rauzzini[4] to be only *one*,—so delightfully did they breath the first part, which was exquisite, together,—& so admirably *contend* in the 2nd for preeminence in rapidity & neatness. But all this while power of voice was wanting to stun the Galleries. And then her accustomed *nonchalance* offended John. [5]G—D—me! was[5] there ever such insolence!—to shew such little respect & fear. In the last scene the *witch* escaped *burning*, & every one went home dissatisfied thereat.—& so ends my present account;—the news will be that she's hissed off the Stage, or so insulted that she'll never sing a note more to such *maladette bestie*! for John often quarrels with his bread & butter, and would much rather fast than not have it entirely to his palate.[6]

We had all the great Volk here on Sunday[7] to nothing but Harp^{d} Lessons & duets,[8]—and a song or two by Mrs Brudenel. But all were so charmés that I shall be forced to sacrifice another blessed day to let some other great volk hear our rumbles. L^{y} Edgcumbe almost downed

---

[2] Francesca Gabrielli (*fl.* 1755–82), mezzo soprano, sister to Caterina, who frequently employed her as the *seconda donna* (*New Grove*). In *Didone*, Francesca sang the part of Selene (*The London Stage*, IV. iii. 1927).

[3] Elizabeth Ann Sheridan, née Linley (1754–92), soprano, had married in 1773 Richard Brinsley Sheridan (1751–1816), after which she retired from public performances. See Rees, under 'Linley, John', and 'Sheridan'; *New Grove*, under 'Linley (2)'; *The Letters of Richard Brinsley Sheridan*, ed. C. Price (Oxford, 1966), i. 20, 79–81; iii. 301; Margot Bor and L. Clelland, *Still the Lark, a Biography of Elizabeth Linley* (1962).

[4] Venanzio Rauzzini (1746–1810), Italian castrato and composer whom CB had met in Munich (*Tours*, ii. 46–8, 50, 54), first appeared in London in Nov. 1774 (*New Grove*; *BD*). Rauzzini sang the male lead, Aneas, in *Didone*. See also *Hist. Mus.* iv. 501; Mercer, ii. 880; Rees; A. Heriot, *The Castrati in Opera* (1956), pp. 175–7.

[5]–[5] MS G— ... was] *oath deleted and* was *altered to* Was

[6] Twining had grumbled to CB about John Bull's temperament in a letter dated 31 Oct. 1775: 'We are the most sour headed, bull-dogly, ill-tempered people upon earth' (BL Add. MS 39933, fo. 164^{v}).

[7] This concert on 12 Nov. 'was occasioned by the desire of Dr. King to have Prince Orloff of Russia hear Mr Burney & my sister in a Duet before he left England' (*EJL* ii). For the guest-of-honour, Count Alekseĭ Grigor'evich Orlov (1737–1808), whose visit to England lasted from 29 Sept. to 12 Dec. 1775, see *EJL* ii; and for an account of the whole evening, see *ED* ii. 93–9, 102–13, 117–21; *Mem.* ii. 43–60.

[8] The '*great Feast*' or 'great gun' at the Burney evening concerts during 1775 was Johann Gottfried Müthel (1728–88), *Duetto, für 2 Claviere, 2 Flügel, oder 2 Fortepiano* (Riga, 1771), performed on two harpsichords by Charles Rousseau Burney and his wife, CB's eldest daughter, Hetty (*ED* ii. 60; *Mem.* ii. 17, 61; see also *Tours*, ii. 240–1).

on her scraggy knees to me this morning to let M de Guignes, Mad Diaden, & Count Bruhl hear 'em.[9] If I wanted anything of them how they'd hang an ere they'd let me enter *their* doors, much more ere enter mine. Yet we must submit to the world's humours, when they produce nothing but Vanity,—if one can keep off the *Vexation*,—of Spirit. . . .

Nov [16?] 1775.[10]

. . . O!—the awkward scrawls you wish to have fingered,—where are they?—aye—here they are—what queer toads!—yet they are Bach's[11]—would one not think they were written by a man who had never laid his hand on a keyed instrument?[12]—I stept in to the Comic opera for ½ an hour to night,[13] & was very much pleased & entertained—It was during the first act, which I had not heard rehearsed. Trebbi[14] is really a good singer of the kind, & an excellent actor. She[15] silver & *tuneable* as usual—The voice of Cabbage, Savoi,[16] divine—& the Quartetto truly amusing—addio—

[9] Lady Edgcumbe got her way, and another concert took place on Sunday 26 Nov. 1775. For an account of the soirée at which Monsieur de Guines and Madame von Diede were present, see CB to Twining, [30] Nov. 1775. Hans Moritz, Graf von Brühl (1736–1809), Saxon Envoy Extraordinary to England from 1764 till his death (*DNB*), does not appear to have attended the concert.

[10] Daniel Twining transcribed the following paragraph (Osborn: 'Twining Letterbook No. 2', p. 24) as part of a separate letter, giving it a conjectural date, 'Nov 19? 1775.' This date is clearly in error, for no public performances were given at the Opera on 19 Nov., which was a Sunday. A more convincing editorial conjecture places the paragraph as a postscript written on Thursday 16 Nov. 1775, on which date the pasticcio comic opera *La Sposa Fedele* was performed at the King's Theatre (*The London Stage*, IV. iii. 1930).

[11] C. P. E. Bach, of whom Twining had written (13 Oct. 1774, copy, BL Add. MS 39933, fo. 117ᵛ), 'I find the Carlophilipemanuelbachomania grow upon me so, that almost every thing else is insipid to me'. In his letter of 31 Oct. 1775 (ibid., fo. 156ᵛ), Twining reported he had 'been playing *Emanuel* on my Piano forte', and his letter of 3 Dec. 1775 (ibid., fo. 170ᵛ) makes clear that CB had been fingering some of C. P. E. Bach's keyboard concertos for him: 'the parcel arrived safe last night.—How good of you to send me those Concertos!—these are your true "*dona mellita*" to *me*. I have an eager, craving appetite about me for *that* man's music, that I never felt for any other'.

[12] The first chapter of C. P. E. Bach's *Versuch über die wahre Art des Clavier zu spielen* (Berlin, 1753, 1762), gives Bach's own method of correct keyboard fingering. See Bach, *Essay on the True Art of Playing Keyboard Instruments*, trans. W. J. Mitchell (2nd edn., 1951), pp. 41–78.

[13] *La Sposa Fedele* had its first performance at the King's Theatre on 31 Oct. 1775 (*The London Stage*, IV. iii. 1925).

[14] Giuseppe Trebbi (*fl.* 1775–82), the first *buffo* at the comic opera. This was his first London season. He appeared again in 1776–7, and 1779–81, without great success (*Hist. Mus.* iv. 502, 516; Mercer, ii. 881, 891–2; *The London Stage*, IV. iii. 1910; v. i. 16, 282, 370).

[15] Doubtless the first *buffa*, Giovanna Sestini (*fl.* 1775–91), who had first appeared on the London comic opera stage on 7 Mar. 1775 (*Hist. Mus.* iv. 502; Mercer, ii. 881; *The London Stage*, IV. iii. 1874). Twining had probably seen her perform then, when he, 'grinning like a dog, & running about the city' (Twining to CB, 26 Mar. 1775, copy, BL Add. MS 39933, fo. 132ᵛ), had paid one of his rare visits to London from Jan. to early Mar. 1775. This circumstance would explain CB's off-hand allusion to Signora Sestini.

[16] Gasparo Savoi (*fl.* 1765–77), the serious man in the comic opera, had first appeared in London in 1765 (*Hist. Mus.* iv. 488–90; Mercer, ii. 870–2; *The London Stage*, IV. ii. 1127, 1149).

To Thomas Twining [St Martin's Street, 30] November 1775

L copy extract (Osborn: 'Twining Letterbook No. 2', pp. 25–6).

end of Novr 1775

... The Gab. comes on, I think, in favour.[1] She has changed a bad Rondeau, however, for one not much better by Giardini

&c the 3rd bar, in spite of

And^te motion is *hornpipish*, to my ears—the 2nd part has some pretty divisions in it, however, which she executes very neatly.—Well but we had Grand Volk again on Sunday[2] to hear little volk play Harp^d duos—Son Excellence M de Guignes[3]—M^r le Baron & Mad^e la Baronne Dieden[4]—L^ds Sandwich—Ashburnham[5]—Barrington[6]—& Edgecumbe with his Lady—& Mrs Brudenel[7]———————— with Rauzzini all were molti contenti—as I believe.[8]—M^r B[urney] has made a new Duo,[9] less recherché than that of Müthel, consequently, easier to comprehend,—but Basta.

I have now a request to make to you with respect to Preface which I do hope devoutly you will not refuse me. It will comfort my bowels,— ease my heart of a load, & flatter my vanity exceedingly if you will but just let me mention your name with only 3 words of acknowledgment

[1] Caterina Gabrielli had sung in *Didone* at the Opera each Saturday since her début (*The London Stage*, iv. iii. 1929 ff.).

[2] For an account of this concert on 26 Nov. given in honour of the French Ambassador, see *ED* ii. 114–16, 121–6; *Mem.* ii. 61–7; *EJL* ii.

[3] Adrien-Louis de Bonnières (1735–1806), comte (later, 1776, duc) de Guines, French Ambassador to England from 1770 to 1776 (Michaud). See also *JL* v. 271.

[4] Wilhelm Christopher, Baron von Diede (1732–1807), Danish Envoy Extraordinary to England from 1767 to 1776, had married (1772) Ursula Margrethe Constantia Louise von Callenberg af Huset Muskau (1752–1803), an accomplished amateur harpsichordist (*Dansk biografisk leksikon*, ed. C. F. Bricka and S. Dahl (Copenhagen, 1933–44), vi. 9–12). This was the second evening concert they attended at the Burneys (*ED* ii. 56–60, 123–4).

[5] John Ashburnham (1724–1812), 2nd Earl of Ashburnham (1737), courtier, had recently (1775) been appointed First Lord of the Bedchamber and Groom of the Stole (*ED* ii. 121).

[6] William Wildman Barrington (1717–93), 2nd Viscount Barrington (1734), statesman, Secretary at War since 1765 (*DNB*; Namier and Brooke, ii. 55–9). He was the eldest brother of CB's good friend, Daines Barrington.

[7] See CB to Mingotti, 3 May 1774, nn. 4, 5.

[8] Venanzio Rauzzini was also present at the concert, but suffering from a bad cold, declined repeated invitations to sing: '... he told us that nothing made him so miserable as *refusing*; ... He said that he must retire, and immediately go to bed; ... And so he went, leaving every body monstrously disappointed, and nobody displeased' (*ED* ii. 126).

[9] Not identified.

for your intelligent & friendly zeal, & kind communications. Why not a book has been lent me by anyone else that I have not acknowledged, & would you have me groan under the weary load of ingratitude to You,—a legion of friends?—Do not deprive me of the Pride & Happiness of numbering you among my friends & the well-wishers of my enterprize. Your delicacy shall be menagée; but my friendship & gratitude must not be quite starved.[10] ...

To Thomas Twining [St Martin's Street], 3 December 1775

L copy extract (Osborn: 'Twining Letterbook No. 2', p. 27).

3 Decr 1775

... The Gab sang divinely last Sat[y][1] the delightful Duo between her & Rauzzini, encored universally. Tis delicious. In the close to her

Cantabile air she began wth which she swelled out for

½ an hour. Grumblers begin to come about & allow that it is just possible she may once have been a fine Singer.[2]—

To Thomas Twining [St Martin's Street, mid?]-December 1775[1]

L copy extracts (Osborn: 'Twining Letterbook No. 2', pp. 30–1).

[10] Twining, in his reply of 3 Dec. 1775, relented: 'If ... it is necessary for your comfort & *soulagement* to mention my name, I cannot *reasonably object*. I know you can do nothing grossly: do *just* what is necessary to satisfy your own mind: ... my inclination was to say *no*: but a little change of place made me see clearly that to do so, would be *injustice* to you, & giving myself airs.—Be *decent*,—is all I beg. One may *thank*, without *praising*' (BL Add. MS 39933, fo. 171ᵛ). For CB's acknowledgement of his obligations to Twining's 'zeal, intelligence, taste, and erudition', see *Hist. Mus.* i (1776),'xviii–xix; Mercer, i. 19. See also CB to Twining, 28 June 1775, n. 2.

[1] 2 Dec. 1775 (*The London Stage*, IV. iii. 1935).

[2] 'Tell me truly, is or has the Gabrielli been a great singer? She has at least not honoured us but with a most slender low voice. Her action is just, but colder than a vestal's. However, as you know, she carries the resemblance no farther, ... We import superannuated sirens, and spoil them more than the Italians can afford to do, who at least enjoy them young' (Horace Walpole to Sir Horace Mann, 8 Dec. 1775, *Walpole Corresp.* xxiv. 148–9).

[1] The conjectural date is determined by the publication of Steele's *Essay* on 5 Dec. (n. 3), and Twining's allusion to it in his letter of 8 Jan. 1776 (see CB to Twining, 3 Feb. 1776, n. 12).

Dec. 1775.

... I remember 30 years ago in some ridiculous variations I made to Shilan O Guira,[2] using the same mark for a rapid & regular flight, up or down, as Squire Steele[3] does for his quarter tones

The sliding up and down the finger-board to imitate speech,[4] is an old trick, that, in my boyish days I have often practised myself to the great delight of private audiences

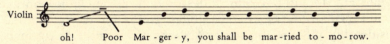

But if this had ever any other than a buffoon & ridiculous effect, I shall wonder!—Indeed tragic declamation is so drawled out that it may be easier imitated than common speech or reading—Dr Johnson says 'If any man were to speak in conversation like players on the Stage he would be sent to Bedlam[.']⁵

And what a notion he (Steele) has of melody!⁶—A man who has been in the way of good Music & good Musicians all his life, & who has worn holes through the finger-board of his Baseviol & worked one hole of his Germ. flute into another by hard practise!! ⌐Bravo! my Lord!⁷—what precise & clear Ideas he has of Music!—& yet he must talk about it.¬

---

² Not identified.

³ Joshua Steele (1700–91), writer on prosody, whose *An Essay towards establishing the Melody and Measure of Speech to be expressed and perpetuated by peculiar Symbols*, published on 5 Dec. 1775, roused considerable interest (*DNB*; *Public Advertiser*, 5 Dec. 1775). CB's copy is listed in 'Cat. Fac. Mus.', item 140. Steele proposed a system of notation for recording the sounds of speech. See Kassler, ii. 974–8.

⁴ Steele, *Essay*, pp. 15–16.

⁵ The printed source of this quotation is unidentified. CB may well have heard it in conversation with Johnson, who 'at all periods of his life . . . used to talk contemptuously of players' (Hill–Powell, i. 167).

⁶ 'The *melody of speech moves* rapidly up or down by *slides*' (Steele, *Essay*, p. 4). It is instructive to contrast Steele's definition with CB's: '*What is Melody?* A series of sounds more fixed, and generally more lengthened, than those of common speech; arranged with grace, and of proportional lengths, such as the mind can easily measure, and the voice express' (*Hist. Mus.* i (1776), xiii; Mercer, i. 21). See also Hill–Powell, ii. 327 n. 2.

⁷ James Burnett (1714–99), Lord Monboddo (1767), had published in 1773 and 1774 the first two volumes of his *Of the Origin and Progress of Language* (Edinburgh, 1773–92). Steele's *Essay* takes the form of remarks on Monboddo's volumes, followed by an exchange of open letters and observations between the two authors on the melody and rhythm of speech. See Kassler, i. 125–8.

To Thomas Twining [St Martin's Street], 24 December 1775

L copy (Osborn: 'Twining Letterbook No. 2', pp. 28–9).
Also AL verse copy (Osborn: 'Poetical Notebook', pp. 1–2).

24 Dec 1775

If my book & self should live till a 2nd Edit.[1] is wanted, not a tittle of your Criticisms & corrections shall be neglected; but at present more I could not do without ruin & destruction of the whole impression. 20 cancelled pages. 11 of addit. notes. 26 double & 2 of errata, will considerably inflame the reckoning with the printer & stationer, & make my book, as I feared some time ago *600* instead of 500 pages.[2]

Noel

>May each hare & each pheasant
>Arrive sweet & pleasant;
>May turkies from Norfolk
>In plenty come for folk;
>And may the minc'd pies
>On your stomach neer rise;
>May mirth & fat ale
>Your neighbours regale,
>May gambols abound
>And puns fly around
>But when dulness retards
>Then call in the Cards
>Not to make your purse bleed
>Or your Av'rice to feed
>But to keep the house quiet
>From noise & from riot.
>May the friends whom you see
>To love Music agree
>And ceasing to laugh
>May they call for a Bach
>And to heighten the treat
>May Pohlman[3] be sweet,

---

[1] The second edition of the first volume of CB's *History of Music* appeared in 1789. For a discussion of CB's plan to publish a corrected second edition soon after the first, a scheme abandoned in favour of a second impression of the first edition, see Lonsdale, pp. 184–7.

[2] For a full discussion of the bibliographical complexities of *Hist. Mus.* i (1776), see Lonsdale, pp. 491–4. [3] Twining's pianoforte.

As the pine-apples Juice,
And quite ready for use;
May the Temper & Tone,
Accord with your own;
Then let fingers take flight
And fill with delight
Each vibrating ear
Till the exquisite tear
Impetuous shall rush
With a rapturous gush:
   No languor 'twill leave
   Like the apple of Eve
   But benignant & pure
Why who can endure —— such stuff as this!
A thousand thanks for all your *sayings* & *doings*.
                    John! Stop the post-man.

To Thomas Twining   [St Martin's Street], 3 January 1776

AL copy incomplete (Osborn).
Docketed by CB: To the Revd T. Twining, Jany 3^d 1776.

My dear Friend ——— How fares it wth your cold?[1] are you
   Still moaping, sulky, motionless & dumb,
Broiling each eye, & each revolving thumb?
Solemn as Puss, who fourteen years has told,
On hearth reclines, when pinch'd with winters cold?
    But now in *Allegro*
    I'll call you a Negro
    And tell you in Quavers
    I like not your 'hav'ors. 🎵
Flowing may the numbers glide
As the graceful Heinel's[2] stride:
Though the movement be *Andante*

[1] In reply to CB's Christmas verses (24 Dec. 1775), Twining had sent some of his own ([late Dec. 1775], Osborn), complaining at the same time, 'I have got a horrid cold, & am as stupid as a post, & sit twirling my thumbs, with my mouth wide open, & my eyes fixed upon the fire'.
[2] Anne-Frédérique Heinel (1753–1808), dancer, whose first appearance at the King's Opera House in the 1771–2 season had caused a sensation (*The London Stage*, IV. iii. 1569, 1644; *BD*; *Hist. Mus.* iv. 498; Mercer, ii. 878; Walpole *Corresp.* xxxii. 66).

May your conscience prick & haunt ye;
Till you write a letter ample,
As the last I sent for sample;
Not of humour, wit, or sense
Such as gods to you dispense
In such overflowing tide
As to others is denied.—
Be your letters long or short
Still they're full of pun & sport, ...

To William Bewley [St Martin's Street], 30 January 1776

AL copy extract (Osborn).
Docketed by CB: Extract of a Letter to Mr Bewley sent Jany 30th 1776.

My dear Bewley

I cannot find in my Heart to let this *Child* of my brain[1] approach you without a word of recommendation. Pray receive him as the offspring of your old Friend. If his language should be incorrect, or abound w^th *naughty words*; If he sh^d sometimes be *dull* & *stupid*; & at others *pert* & *trivial*; If he should discover a want of *knowledge* & *Reading*; or sh^d incline to *severity* & *calumny*; If you sh^d discover in him a propensity to *lying*, or hazardé assertions; a want of *diligence* in search of Information, or that he deals in old stories, & turns out a mere *Boar*; pray exscuse his *errors* & *defects*, in consideration of the little Health & leisure I have had to render him more polished & fit for the world.[2] I think *I* can answer for his *Fidelity, good Intentions, & Candour*; & I think *you* will readily allow that I have spared no pains or expense in furnishing him wth specimens of the polite arts, both ancient & modern; Such as *drawing, Engraving, Music* & *Poetry*. It has always been my ambition to make him a welcome guest where ever he goes, & that neither Friends nor foes sh^d complain of his being useless or burthensome to them—Yet with all my anxiety & care his reception in the

---

[1] CB habitually used the metaphor of childbirth when referring to the publication of his literary productions. The first volume of the *History* was officially published on 31 Jan. 1776 (*Public Advertiser*; Lonsdale, p. 173), under the full title, *A General History of Music, from the Earliest Ages to the Present Period. To which is prefixed, a Dissertation on the Music of the Ancients*. The title-page shows that it was 'Printed for the Author: And sold by T. Becket, Strand; J. Robson, New Bond-Street; and G. Robinson, Paternoster-Row.'

[2] Cf. '... should the materials be found ill-digested, or the diction incorrect; it is humbly hoped that part of these, and other defects, will be attributed to want of leisure and health, as well as want of abilities, to render it less unworthy the public patronage' (*Hist. Mus.* i (1776), xi).

world may perhaps be Such as will cover me with dishonour, &, instead of being a credit & comfort to me, corrode my heart wth chagrin, & bring my grey hairs wth sorrow to the Grave!³ In such a case you will, perhaps, heave a Sigh for the fate of an Industrious & well intentioned Parent, whose Child was not *Spoiled* for want of such wholesome correction as his affection & leisure w^d allow! But *You*, who will now *view*, & perhaps *review*⁴ him without parental blindness or solicitude, will be more able than me to judge of his vices, & Virtues, if he has any; & to recommend him to y^r Friends & to the world in general, if you sh^d find him worth y^r notice; &, Friendship to me apart, sh^d be able, without putting violence on y^r taste, Judgement, & sincerity, to say any good of him.

God bless you my Dr Friend—I wish my lubberly Boy may be honoured wth y^r attention in an auspicious time, when y^r Fire burns well; When y^r Dinner has been well cooked & eaten; When a Glass or two of good old Lynn Port has put you in humour wth Yourself & the world; When Mrs Bewley's⁵ room is quite tidy; & all y^r Litters & nonsense out of the way; When she, Good soul! is at leisure to take a little notice of my Brat's collection of prints, & to hear a little about him. For, entre-nous, my d^r Friend the learned & outlandish lingos out of the question, She's full as able to judge of his sense & parts as any individual in the critical *Quorum.*⁶ &c &c &c

To Thomas Twining [St Martin's Street], 3 February 1776

L copy (Osborn: 'Twining Letterbook No. 3', pp. 1–4).
Docketed by Daniel Twining: Dr Burney to the Rev^d T: T.

³ CB quotes *Genesis* 44:31: '. . . thy servants shall bring down the gray hairs of thy servant our father with sorrow to the grave'.
⁴ Bewley did review the *History of Music* in the Mar. and June issues of the *Monthly Review*, liv (1776), 203–14, 438–46. See also Lonsdale, pp. 177–8.
⁵ Barbara Bewley, née Green (d. 1797), had married William Bewley in 1749, according to a letter from Bewley to CB, 26 Oct. 1771 (Osborn), where he mentions his 'two & twenty years' of matrimony. Bewley's obituary in *GM* liii (1783)², 805, written by CB, points out the remarkable circumstance that his death on 5 Sept. 1783 'happened upon his birth and wedding days'. Mrs Bewley's will (PRO, Prerogative Court of Canterbury, Walpole 236) reveals her maiden name, as does an Assignment preserved in the Norfolk Record Office (Bradfer-Lawrence Collection, Shelf X (11)).
⁶ Bewley wrote to CB (30–1 Jan. 1776, Osborn): 'I long with no small impatience to see your book . . . You have a warm friend in the Wife of your future judge.' Bewley in a subsequent letter dated 3 Mar. 1776 (Osborn), provides further evidence of CB's real anxiety over the critical reception of the *History*. Having read the volume, Bewley comments: 'You astonish me with your *repeated* croakings . . . about *disgrace.*—From what quarter must it come? & on what account?'

3 Feby 1776

That I should ever live to see the day when my ebullitions of Crambo nonsense should be so highly honoured!—why there now!—it never rains but it pours! If I am not in the *Poet's Corner* of that *judicious, candid,* & *decorous* paper the Morning Post[1] to day I'm a rogue!—*You* pretend to taste, & judgment, & all that!—Why this sensible gentleman the Editor has selected the very *thing* which you rejected![2] Pray read Mimnermus again, & again, & confess you were mistaken.[3]— But to be *serus*. The house is a Fair, from morning to night; torn to pieces, Sir! The impatience of the public!! Would you believe it? People (so turned are the tables) with whose names I should, a month ago, have thought myself highly honoured, as well as gratified, are now begging as for our alms, during the frost, to be admitted as subscribers. The fame of the work, & the additional half guinea in its price, work prodigiously.[4] All goes on smoothly yet—but I dread what may come for all that.—I want to tell you the reception of our book most minutely, but it would fill a volume as big as itself to do it. 'Tis now the Town's talk, & none of the abuse reaches my Ears. I have had a great deal of flummery of people of high rank—but here's a promise from Kenrick of a Critique upon it in his London Review next month.[5] How I shall fare is in the Stars.—I almost wish I could provoke you to give the Reviews a dose of your Salt of Wormwood, for Hamilton, the publisher, as good as told me the other day, that *they* wished to mention it in next month's R.,[6] but at the same time said that none of the *Confrairies* understood the subject.

[1] The *Morning Post* had printed CB's translation, 'Aristotle's Hymn to Hermias' (*Hist. Mus.* i (1776), 470; Mercer, i. 363), to the inclusion of which Twining had objected as irrelevant. See Lonsdale, pp. 173, 175.

[2] In his reply of 19 Feb. 1776 (BL Add. MS 39929, fo. 73ᵛ), Twining echoed CB's biblical allusion: 'Thank you for your *head stone* of the *corner*—Well, why those people you know, have always a very pretty taste. ... I wonder'd at the condescension of Mr Morning post.' See *Psalm* 118:22; *Acts* 4:11.

[3] Mimnermus of Colophon (*fl.* 632–29 BC), Greek elegiac poet and musician. CB's meaning here is explained by a passage in Twining's letter of 31 Oct. 1775 (copy, BL Add. MS 39933, fos. 156ᵛ–165ᵛ): 'I have just taken up the Greek of Mimnermus, & must make a reflection *là dessus*. Things fade in ones memory. The Greek is really pleasing, & speaks *feelingly*, & there is some elegance in the *expression*. It did not appear in the same light when I read your translation, & contented myself with only a vague recollection of the original. Yet, by what I remember, your translation does not want spirit, & I find no fault with it'. CB's verse translation of a fragment of Mimnermus appears in *Hist. Mus.* i (1776), 392 n.; Mercer, i. 309 n. For Twining's general disapproval of CB's verse translations, see Lonsdale, pp. 165–7, 170–1.

[4] To non-subscribers, the first volume of the *History* cost 1½ guineas.

[5] William Kenrick (*c.*1725–79), LLD (1761), miscellaneous writer, founded and edited the *London Review* (*DNB*). CB's *History* heads the 'List of Books and Pamphlets, recently published, of which a more particular account is deferred', published at the end of the Jan. issue of the *London Review*, iii (1776), 80. A two-part critique duly appeared in the Feb. and Mar. issues (pp. 102–10, 194–203). See Lonsdale, p. 179.

[6] From Feb. to June 1776, a five-part review appeared in Archibald Hamilton's *Critical Review*,

The Gab sang divinely on Saturday in Ventos feeble opera.[7] The man has neither learning nor invention, but he cannot for the Italian blood of him be vulgar! He's just the contrary of a german composer, who never lets the ear have what it expects; for on sçait par cœur all Ventos Music. He never disappoints you, nor gives the lie to memory.[8]

I have just got from Rome Eximeno's book,[9] the size of my own. He has the sourness of a German & the arrogance of a Frenchman. He says cutting & decisive things. What think you of the Qualifications of a supreme musical Dictator who sets off by telling you that a Combination of Circumstances too tedious to tell the reader 'mi fecero quattro anni sono volgere uno sguardo alla Musica'?[10] Do *you* think it possible for even a Newton to be critically master of every branch of Theoretical & Practical Music & to have read all the best books on the subject with care & attention in four years?—He treats Rules & harmonical laws with too much contempt. Licence is allowable only to great Genius arrived at a certain height.[11]—You may have heard me say I believe, that a good composition might be made of such things as old Theorists have prohibited both in harmony and melody. Music has its Grammar & Syntax as well as other languages;—but where am I running?

xli (1776), 81–90, 185–93, 271–80, 337–44, 433–42. See Lonsdale, pp. 178–80. Lonsdale's suspicion that 'some friend of Burney' wrote this review is confirmed further by the writer's inclusion in his first article (p. 86) of the passage in *Hist. Mus.* containing CB's 'bit of Spanish' (see CB to Twining, 13 July 1774, n. 12). Not only does the reviewer go to the trouble of substituting in his quotation CB's revised translation from the 'Errata', he also unobtrusively corrects the misprint 'Le' to 'La' in the Spanish, an alteration not even prompted by the published 'Errata' list.

[7] *La Vestale*, the new serious opera by Mattia Vento (1735–76), Neapolitan composer and opera director who had settled in London in 1763 (*New Grove*), had its first public performance on Tuesday 6 Feb. 1776 (*The London Stage*, iv. iii. 1950) at the King's Theatre, after a series of postponements (*Public Advertiser*, 25, 27, 30 Jan.; 3, 5, 6 Feb. 1776). CB must have heard Caterina Gabrielli rehearsing in *La Vestale* on Saturday 27 Jan., the date on which she also performed publicly in Sacchini's *Didone* (*The London Stage*, iv. iii. 1948).

[8] See *Hist. Mus.* iv. 506–7; Mercer, ii. 882. In his article on Vento in Rees, CB wrote: 'he set "La Vestale," in his usual easy style; and when we told him that his airs were somewhat too familiar for great singers, he said, "God forbid I should ever compose difficult music!"'

[9] *Dell'origine e delle regole della musica colla storia del suo progresso, decadenza, e rinnovazione* (Rome, 1774), by Antonio Eximeno y Pujades (1729–1808), Spanish Jesuit mathematician and musical theorist (*New Grove*). In proposing to abolish the strict laws of counterpoint and harmony and to apply instead the rules of prosody to musical composition, Eximeno's publication provoked considerable controversy. See *Hist. Mus.* iv. 575–6; Mercer, ii. 939; Rees. CB's copy of Eximeno is 'Cat. Fac. Mus.', item 43.

[10] Eximeno, 'Prefazione', *Dell'origine*, p. 1. CB never forgave Eximeno for this claim: '. . . too confident of his own powers, he imagined himself capable, with four years study only, intuitively to frame a better system of counterpoint than that upon which so many great musicians had been formed' (*Hist. Mus.* iv. 575–6; Mercer, ii. 939).

[11] Twining wrote in his reply of 19 Feb.: 'O! Your Abbate Eximeno is a jewel of a man, I see. No writers so entertaining & picquants as these railing, decisive, tear-away fellows . . . Why, to be sure his *4 years*, looks a little coxcombical; if he means that he had within that time made himself Master of the subject, & got *all* his knowledge of it.'

I read Squire Steele[12] with two days attention, & liked very much several things in the latter part of him, which put me more in humour with his work than I thought I should be. For knowing his arrogant & dogmatic turn in Conversation, I was surprised to find some modesty & fair reasoning. But my Lord Monboddo,[13] what business had he ever to talk about Music?—without knowing its principles or feeling its power? I would not be bound to read his nonsense, & I much wonder at Steele's patience with him. Indeed his last letter[14] lets one know that he has stirred not an inch, tho' he has often turned on his pivot.[15]

Adieu.

To Mrs Ord[1]

[St Martin's Street,
early February 1776][2]

AL draft (Osborn).
Docketed by FBA: ✳

Dr B. presents his Respects to Mrs Ord & has the Honour to send her two Copies of his Book: one for Mrs Bigge,[3] & one for Mrs Ord's

---

[12] For Joshua Steele's *Essay towards establishing the Melody and Measure of Speech* (1775), see CB to Twining, [mid?]-Dec. 1775, n. 3. In his letter to CB of 8 Jan. 1776 (BL Add. MS 39929, fos. 65–8^v), Twining had included Steele in some doggerel verses:

> '*Thesis* is heavy, *arsis* light,
> Says Joshua Steele; & very right;
> But not in *Preaching* as in *Music*;—
> When *up* we mount to make each pew sick.'

[13] See CB to Twining, [mid?]-Dec. 1775, n. 7.

[14] i.e. Monboddo's last letter and enclosed 'Observations' printed in Steele's *Essay*, pp. 174–80.

[15] Twining replied (19 Feb.): 'Ld *Monboddo* seems to be a simple, fogrum kind of antient-led good man. Your *pivot* is an excellent thought: 'tis the blind horse in the mill, that thinks he is going forward all the time; the top that turns & sleeps: &c. I don't think Steele's *book* is dogmatical at all: but sure there are *some* very absurd things in it: & Ld M. is right in thinking that he goes too far in his application of music to speech.'

[1] Anna Ord, née Dillingham (*c.*1726–1808), bluestocking, was the widow of William Ord (d. 1768), whom she had married in 1746. She 'was turned of forty before' CB met her, but she soon became a close friend, and an intimate of the Burney family. See *ED, DL, JL, passim*, and CB's 'Memoir' of Mrs Ord in *GM* lxxviii (1808)[2], 581–3.

[2] CB's letter is a reply to a letter from Mrs Ord, dated merely 'Sunday' (Osborn). In her letter, Mrs Ord informs CB she has read the *History*, and thanks him for 'affording her so early a perusal' of it. CB had probably sent Mrs Ord her copy of the *History* before the publication date, and her letter, written soon after her perusal, can be dated conjecturally [early Feb. 1776]. CB's reply, drafted on the verso of Mrs Ord's letter, can also be so dated.

[3] Jemima Bigge, née Ord (1749–1806), Mrs Ord's eldest daughter, had married (1772) Thomas Charles Bigge (1739–94), of Benton, Northumberland, High Sheriff of the county in

Clerical Fr^d in the Country.⁴ Dr B. will not attempt to say how grateful the Nectar & ambrosia of Praise from such a Candid & intelligent Judge of his Work as herself, is to his Vanity.⁵ His first wish in undertaking it was to merit such Praise; but that was soon changed into the more humble hope of avoiding Disgrace.⁶ As *after-pains* are incident to other *Labours*, he must not expect to be exempted from them; however, a few cordials like that which Mrs O. has kindly administered, will, he hopes, enable him to bear the Evils that may be still in store for him.

To [Lord Mornington]¹   St Martin's Street, [20] February 1776²

ALS draft incomplete (Osborn), dated 18 Feb. 1776.

... and condescend to Interest yourself in my Enquiries, I shall think myself extreamly honoured by such a Correspondent, and Benefactor to my Work.

The Question wch I had the honour to propose to your Lord^p concern^g The Time when the Harp was first Quartered in the arms of Ireland, & upon what occasion, is still among the problems of Musical History. Your Lord^p's Conjecture is ingenious,³ & has a very probable

---

1771 (*GM* lxxvi (1806)², 1173; G. F. R. Barker and A. H. Stenning, *The Record of Old Westminsters* (1928), i. 87). Mrs Bigge's name is listed among CB's subscribers.

⁴ Not identified. Mrs Ord had requested in her letter, 'If Dr Burney has one Copy left undispos'd of, Mrs Ord will be greatly obliged if he will favor her with it, & thereby enable her to make a present of it to a worthy Friend of the Muses (a Clergyman in the Country) whose taste in the polite Arts Prudence forbids him to indulge, at the expence of his Pocket; on which a numerous family hath a prior claim'.

⁵ Mrs Ord wrote (ibid.) that she had derived 'pleasure, as well as Improvement' from CB's 'most Learned, Elegant, & Entertaining History of Music; which the ignorant in that Science may read with Delight; & the most informed genius with Profit'.

⁶ For CB's fear of 'disgrace', see CB to Bewley, 30 Jan. 1776, n. 6.

¹ Garrett Wellesley, or Wesley (1735–81), 2nd Baron Mornington (1758), created Viscount Wellesley and Earl of Mornington (1760), keen musician and amateur composer (*DNB*; *New Grove*; D. Barrington, *Miscellanies* (1781), pp. 317–20). Through the good offices of Richard Rigby (see n. 14), CB had sent Lord Mornington in Ireland in 1773 a list of queries about Irish music. Mornington had replied on 30 Dec. 1773 (Osborn).

² Although the draft is dated 18 Feb. 1776, the date of the letter (not preserved) actually sent was evidently 20 Feb., as is made clear by Mornington's reply, 30 Mar. 1776 (Gerald Coke Collection): 'I receiv'd your Letter of the 20th of last month with very great Pleasure'.

³ MS ingenious] *interlined above deleted* far from improbable

Mornington had written in his letter of 30 Dec. 1773 (Osborn): 'a King of North Wales call'd Griffin apConan [Gruffydd ab Cynan (*c*.1055–1137)] being by his Mother & Grand mother an Irishman carried over from Ireland several expert Musicians who deviz'd all the instrumental Musick in Wales ... Geraldus Cambrensis likewise says that The Irish were incomparably well skill'd on The Harp—now it occurs to me that after that Welsh King had carried musicians

foundation; but I have made it my rule hitherto never to recur to Conjecture & ingenuity where Facts or Proofs can be attained. The Question has been sported at the Antiquarian Society; & Mr Daines Barrington has sent it over to some of his Fr^{ds} in Ireland, but I hear, as yet, of no satisfactory solution of the Difficulty: and I own, the Circumstance seems to me in itself so honourable to Music & of such importance to its History, that I cannot help wishing very much to trace it to its source. With respect to the difference between the Welsh & Irish Harps your Lord^p has already been so kind as to give some Criteria[4]—The Welsh Harp is *doubly strung* wth strings made of the Intestines of animals, commonly called *Bowel-strings*, & more commonly, though erroneously, Cat-Gut strings, & the Irish Harp *singly*, wth those of metal. I sh^d be very glad to know when the Compass of the Instrument was extended to 4 octaves in Ireland, whether there are any anc^t representations of it in painting, or sculpture with so great a Number. In none of the illuminations of Anc^t Manuscripts that I have seen in England does the Compass of the Harp appear so extensive, nor c^d it be necessary for a single part or melody unaccompanied with a Base.[5] The Tunes of Carrolan,[6] so much celebrated in Ireland, I have been informed were printed at [7]Dublin; but[7] I have never yet been able to obtain a sight of them. Copies of the

from hence to Wales which was a great proof of the Superiority of the Irish over the Welsh in point of musick I say perhaps they at that time when their musical Glory was so high took for their Ensign the Instrument upon which they were so remarkably famous—'.

[4] Mornington had written (ibid.): 'the Improvements made upon the Harp by the Welsh make it a very Different Instrument from the Irish Harp which I believe has chang'd little of its ancient form or Powers'.

[5] Mornington had informed CB in his letter of 30 Dec. 1773: 'An Irish Harp is something about the size of a small German Harp—its Compass properly about 4 octaves strung with Brass in the Bass & Tenor & Steel in the Treble—of a melancholy jingling tone tune'd in C$^\sharp$ 3^d only one Row of Strings and no Semitones the performer In general plays an extempore thrumming Bass to the Tune he means to perform'. In his reply dated 30 Mar. 1776 (Gerald Coke Collection), Mornington admitted he had never come across an Irish Harp with a four-octave compass. See also CB's article in Rees, under 'Harp'.

[6] Mornington had written (30 Dec. 1773): 'as to Irish national musick I can and will procure for you some of our best native Airs but what I have been searching up & Down this Island for is a Collection of tunes compos'd by one Carrolan who was a Blind itinnerant Harper whose compositions are exceeding extraordinary'.

For Turlough Carolan (1670–1738), the most famous of the Irish harper-composers, see *New Grove*; and D. O'Sullivan, *Carolan: the Life, Times, and Music of an Irish Harper* (1958).

[7-7] MS Dublin; but] *altered by deletion from* Dublin ab^t the latter End of the last Century but

Prior to the publication of *A Favourite Collection of . . . the original and genuine compositions of Carolan* (Dublin, [1780]), printed books containing Carolan's tunes were extremely rare. CB doubtless refers to the book of Carolan's music known to have been published in Dublin in 1748 by Carolan's son, a unique imperfect copy of which has recently been identified in the National Library of Ireland ('Carolan' in *New Grove*). Mornington, in his reply to CB of 30 Mar. 1776, refers to this publication: 'As to the Collection of Tunes of Carolan, I well remember to have seen, nay to have had in my own Possession about 18 or 19 years ago, some Copies of a Sett of his Tunes publish'd in Dublin, for the Benefit of a Son or nephew of his, but not being then as

most anc[t] Irish Tunes & such as are most esteemed by the Natives & allowed by intelligent Lovers of Music among them to be genuine, are what I very much wish to obtain, that I might select a few to engrave for my 2[d] Vol. as Specimens of the national Melody of Ireland.[8]

I am very much Mortified that your Lord[P's] Name did not arrive[9] Time enough to be inserted in the List of Subscribers, w[ch] has been printed near two months. I had the Honour to present the B[k] to her Maj[ty], to whom it is dedicated, the 25th of Jan[y] & it was published the 31st.[10]

The Subscription was closed the 1st Week in Jan[y] & the vol. sells now for £1.11.6. but few Books of the Impression besides what are appropriated to the Subscribers remain for sale, & those are now in the Hands of the publishers. No Copies were printed on large Paper, & there was no difference of Price to Subscribers: all I am able to do now for your Lord[P] in order to shew my respect & the sense I have of y[r] kind & generous Intention of subscribing for the work on Large Paper, is to select two sets of the best Impressions of the Plates for your Lord[P's] use among those that were first taken off. & to admit your Lord[P] as a Subscriber to the 2[d] Vol. at 1 Guinea for each Copy. I shall forward two copies of the 1st Vol. by the Assistance of M[r] Robinson Bookseller in Paternoster Row, who will adress them to M[r] Wilson[11] Bookseller in Dublin, & it will afford me a very singular Satisfaction when you shall have had Leisure to peruse it, to [12]be honoured w[th][12] the remarks of so intelligent a Judge of the Subject as your Lord[P]—My good Friend M[r] Chamier, under-secretary of State in L[d] Weymouth['s] office,[13] & a particular Fr[d] of M[r] Rigby,[14] has

curious as I am at present about Musick and the Tunes being most wretchedly sett, I neglected to take care of the Books, and so they were lost: this now obliges me to hunt up and down in old musick shops, amongst their Rubbish, to see if I can find a Copy, and if I meet with one, will send it to you in its original Dress.'

[8] CB had informed the readers of the first volume of his *History* that he intended to include 'examples of national music in the second volume' (i (1776), 38). CB's chapters on national music never materialized in his *History*.

[9] This communication from Mornington, presumably of late Jan. or early Feb. 1776, has not been located.

[10] In old age, CB, in his 'Memoranda from Pocket book' for 1776, jotted down the proud entry: 'Jan[y] 25 present 1st Vol. of Hist[y] of Music to her Maj[ty] at S[t] James's in full drawing room' (*Frag. Mem.*, Berg). See also *Mem.* ii. 71–2; Lonsdale, p. 173.

[11] Peter Wilson (*c*.1719–1801), conducted his bookselling and music publishing business in Dame Street, Dublin. He took into partnership William Wilson (*fl.* 1769–1801), presumably a kinsman, whose name alone appears in the imprint from 1772 onwards (Plomer, pp. 407–8; *GM* lxxi (1801)[2], 1213).

[12-12] MS be honoured w[th]] *interlined above deleted* receive

[13] Thomas Thynne (1734–96), 3rd Viscount Weymouth (1751), created Marquess of Bath (1789), statesman, held the post of Secretary of State for the Southern Department from 1775 to 1779 (*DNB*).

[14] Anthony Chamier (1725–80) had been recommended to Lord Weymouth in 1775 for the

kindly offered to forward my Letters to your Lord^P & has given me permission to request y^r L^P to Honour me wth your Commands & Communications under Cover addressed to him—(Anthony Chamier Esqr at Ld Weymouths Office, Cleveland Row)

I have the Honour to be

with the greatest Respe[c]t & Consideration

My Lord, y^r Lordship's most Obliged

& most Obed^t Servant.

Ch. Burney

St Martins Street, | 18th Feby 1776.

To Brigg Fountaine   St Martin's Street, 5 April 1776

ALS (Osborn). Mounted.
Docketed: To Brigg Fountaine Esq | Dr Burney.

St Martin's Street
Apr. 5th 1776

Dear Sir.

I witheld my Thanks for the kind trouble you have taken, in translating my little German 9 shill^g Pamphlet,[1] till I supposed you arrived at Bath—it must have cost you much more trouble than it's worth—I find in it no new Ideas—The grand principle that vocal melody sh^d imitate the natural Tones of Passion, wch has been so long & so often recommended to Composers, is much superior to his leading precept of imitating oratory & declamation. For these are as often affected, unnatural, & vicious as vocal melody. Stage declamation in England, for Example, if introduced by any one into Society w^d endanger his being sent to Bedlam[2]—and in France, Italy, & Germany orators seem still more unnatural—& to have a Cant & a *tune* that is to the last degree offensive to me.

appointment as Under-Secretary by Richard Rigby (1722–88), MP, of Mistley Hall, Essex, politician, and Paymaster-General of the Forces from 1768 to 1782 (BL Add. MS 35509, fo. 248; *DNB*; Namier and Brooke, ii. 207–8; iii. 354–60; see also n. 1). Chamier and Rigby belonged to a highly convivial circle of friends who called themselves 'the Gang' (*Memoirs and Correspondence . . . of Sir Robert Murray Keith, K.B.*, ed. Mrs Gillespie Smyth (1849), ii. 32–46, 70–7).

[1] *Von der musicalischen Declamation* (Göttingen, 1775), published anonymously by Jacob Schuback (1726–84), lawyer, Syndic of Hamburg, diplomatist, and amateur musician (*MGG*; *New Grove*). Schuback had sent CB his treatise with a covering letter (not preserved) dated 16 Feb. 1776 (see CB to [Schuback], 12 Feb. 1779).

[2] Samuel Johnson had made this observation. See CB to Twining, [mid?]-Dec. 1775, n. 5.

If you take a Master for the Violin, during your Residence at Bath, I w^d recommend to you Mr Linley Junior,³ who is a Charming Performer, and of a Good School, having been under Nardini, Tartini's best Scholar,⁴ in Italy, a considerable Time. I therefore Enclose a Letter to him⁵ upon a supposition that he is by this Time returned to Bath, after leading at the oratorio in Drury Lane & at 2 or three Hospitals⁶—I am dear Sir

in great haste but with great Truth
your obliged & affectionate Servt
Chas Burney

To Mrs Raper¹   St Martin's Street, 12 April 1776

ALS (Berg).
Addressed: To | Mrs Raper | China Row | Chelsea   *Pmks:* 7 O'CLOCK W ⟨?⟩HOLSON PENY POST PAY⟨D⟩

Dear Madam,

It gave me great Concern that I had not the happiness of meeting you in Stratton Street on Tuesday,² & still more at the Cause of my disappoin[t]m^t. You have already done the little Lady³ much good in

³ Thomas Linley (1756–78), violinist and composer, second son of Thomas Linley (1733–95), composer and singing-master at Bath. In Sept. 1770, CB had met the 14-year-old Linley at Florence, where he was studying under Nardini (*Tours*, i. 184–9). Earlier that year, Linley and his contemporary, Mozart, had met and become firm friends (*The Letters of Mozart and His Family*, ed. Emily Anderson (2nd edn., 1966), i. 129–30, 160–1). Linley returned to England in 1771 to resume his career as a concert violinist and orchestral leader (*DNB*; *New Grove*; G. Beechey, 'Thomas Linley, Junior. 1756–1778', *Musical Quarterly*, liv (1968), 74–82). See also Clementina Black, *The Linleys of Bath* (rev. edn., 1971).
⁴ See CB to Garrick, 17-[18] Oct. 1770, nn. 21, 39.
⁵ Not preserved.
⁶ At the London theatres the oratorio season ran on Wednesdays and Fridays during Lent, which ended in 1776 on Easter Sunday, 7 Apr. Since 1774, in collaboration with John Stanley (1712–86), Thomas Linley senior had managed the Drury Lane oratorios, in which his son led the orchestra and frequently performed a violin concerto 'between the acts' (see Garrick *Letters*, iii. 1064 n.; *The London Stage*, IV. iii. 1954–65). During the 1776 oratorio season, Linley junior also led the orchestra in *The Messiah* on 2 Apr. at the Foundling Hospital (*Public Advertiser*, 2 Apr. 1776).

¹ Katherine Raper, née Shepherd (1735–1823), had married (1763) Henry Raper (1717–89), of Chelsea. Their son, Charles Chamier Raper (c.1777–1845) was to marry (1807) CB's granddaughter, Frances Phillips (1782–1860). See *GM* xxxiii (1763), 465; xciii (1823)², 477; *Cat. Corr.*, index; *JL* v. 157 n.
² Possibly at the London residence, 10 Stratton Street, Piccadilly, of Richard Bull (1721–1805), MP (1756–80), for whom see CB to FB, 6 Nov. 1782, n. 19.
³ Not identified.

the steps that have been taken towards her Musical Studies; but it seems to me as if you might advance still further with great safety, by superintending her practice of my Evolutions of Fingering till such Time as she can execute them with precision & Rapidity, always recommending to her the keeping her Hands *round*, wch can only be done by the Thumbs' constantly hanging over the Keys.[4] It w^d also be of great service to her, If you w^d likewise teach her the Common Chords, radically; that is by counting the semitones of each Interval at first, & afterwards practicing them till she can play them with speed & facility all over the Instrument; then applying them to the Hexachords in all the 24 Keys,[5] all wch you are as able to teach her as any professed master in Europe. When she has accomplished these matters, I will give her another Meeting & further prescriptions. In the mean Time I would recommend to her slow practice both with her Fingers & Voice, a true & open shake[6]—& when she can play such Hexachords as are in her Compass, she will be able to accompany herself in singing them to the well-known Syllables Do, re, mi, fa, sol, La—The best fingers for playing the Chords, in order to keep the

Hand round & snug are, for the 1st face,[7] 1 — 2^d $\overset{4}{\underset{+}{2}}$ — 3^d $\overset{4}{\underset{+}{2}}$ — & if

---

[4] CB as a young man 'had invented a mode of adding neatness to brilliancy, by curving the fingers, and rounding the hand, in a manner that gave them a grace upon the keys quite new at that time, and entirely of his own devising' (*Mem.* i. 29). For CB's keyboard technique and teaching method, aspects of which he derived from François Couperin (1668–1733), *L'Art de toucher le clavecin* (2nd edn., 1717), see the articles 'Doig[h]ter' and 'Fingering' in Rees; *CB Mem.* 41 n. 3; 84 n. 9.

[5] CB wrote in Rees: 'Hexachord, from the Greek, is a term, in *Music*, implying . . . a scale of six sounds. In the general system, the scale of Guido had originally only the Roman literal notation; and it was some time after its invention that it was divided into these relative hexachords, which were interwoven into each other, and called by these several names: as the *durum* hexachord, from gammut, or G to E; the *natural* hexachord, from C to A; and the *molle* hexachord, from F to D, in which B is flat . . . The syllables . . . *Ut re mi fa sol la* . . . being applied to each of these hexachords, was to give articulation to sounds in singing, and assist the student in hitting distances.' See also 'hexachord' in *New Grove*.

[6] i.e. a trill. See *OED*, under 'shake', 5. An 'open' shake is a trill of a tone or semitone, as distinct from a 'closed' shake, or vibrato involving a smaller interval. See Rees, under 'shake': 'There are two kinds of shakes, the continued, and the transient. The continued shake, upon a long note, must be practised at first by incipients, slow, and accelerated by degrees . . . The two tones or semitones that constitute the shake major or minor, should be equally loud and distinct; but above all, perfectly in tune with the notes of the general scale and particular key in which the performer is singing . . . If the singer is not possessed of a true and good shake, he or she had best refrain from ever attempting it; . . . Shakes upon keyed instruments are best practised at first with the second and third fingers; holding down at the same time the fifth below with the thumb, to keep the hand and the wrist quiet. And we recommend, contrary to the usual practice and precepts, beginning the shake with the lowest note; otherwise, in rapid transient shakes on semiquavers, there is not time for returning to the upper note; so that the shake is reduced to a mere appogiatura.'

[7] French technical term in music 'used to distinguish the different forms of the triad, or ways

she were to practice frequently with both Hands such passages as the following, she w^d acquire strength, & an equal touch & spring in All her Fingers.

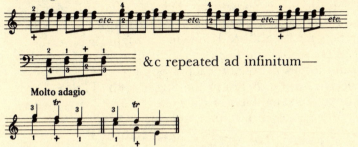

&c repeated ad infinitum—

Molto adagio

I taught Mr Burney in this manner many years ago, at the Distance of 200 Miles[8]—surely, wth your assistance, & frequent Interviews, our little Friend may be forwarded greatly in her Musical Studies. It will afford me great Pleasure to shew my Zeal for her service, & how sincerely I am on all occasions, Dear Mad^m

Your Obed^t & affectionate Servt

Chas Burney.

I beg my best Comp^ts to Mr Raper.

St Martin's Street. 12th Apr. 1776

To Susan Burney[1]

[St Martin's Street],
23 May 1776

AL verse (Berg).
Addressed: Miss S. Burney.   *Endorsed by* CB: To Sue on her recovery.   May 23^d 1776.   *Docketed by* FBA: ⚹ ✖ From the Jaundice.   *Also* AL verse copy

of taking the common chord; as 1re face $\frac{8}{5}$, 2de face $\frac{3}{8}$, and 3me face $\frac{5}{3}$; or, as we should say, first stage or station of a chord, &c. A chord has as many faces or forms as it has notes' ('face' in Rees).

[8] At about the age of 6, CB's nephew, Charles Rousseau Burney (1747–1819), 'began to show symptoms of . . . an extraordinary ear for music, . . . for which he had talents very uncommon at his age' ('Worcester Memoranda'). Soon after, in 1754–5, CB's brother, Richard (1723–92), moved his family from London to Worcester. CB himself then lived in King's Lynn, Norfolk; the '200 Miles' to which he refers represents the distance between Lynn and Worcester.

[1] 'Somewhere about May or June Mrs. C. R. Burney [Hetty] & her sister Miss Susan Burney took a small house very near Barborne Lodge, where they resided for the summer months, change of air being recommended for themselves & the children' ('Worcester Memoranda'). CB's daughters returned to London in Sept. For Susan's jaundice while she was at Worcester, see *ED* ii. 193; *EJL* ii: 'Pray, Miss Fanny . . . how does the *Yellow lady* do?' '*Yellow lady?*—' 'Yes,—didn't you know your sister turned yellow while she was in Worcester?'

(Osborn: 'Poetical Notebook', shelves c 33, p. 95).   *Entitled by* CB: To my
daughter Susan, [|] on her recovery from the Jaundice.   *Docketed by* FBA: ✳·

When the Crocus & Snow-drop their *white* have display'd
Come the Primrose & Cowslip, in *Yellow* array'd;
Then the bowing Jonquil, & Kingcup so bright
With *golden* enamel gleam forth to the Sight.
With Nature to vie, & to gain each a Spark,
Thus bedeck'd are the Belles in the Street & the Park
All ambitious the same kind of Liv'ry to wear
& all, like my Susan, in JAUNDICE appear:
Till more vertical suns give a glow to all Nature,
& bestow vivid Tints on each Flow'r & each Feature:
Then blushes the Rose in its own healthy Red;
Then the Pink & Carnation their gay Colours spread;
The Tulip with these helps to paint the parterre
& the Poppy's *vermilion* the Corn-fields all share.
　　To give to my Susan her vigour & force
May her blood & her Juices resume their right Course!
& to make her Cheek blooming, & pleasing her smile,
Be her Face like her heart free from Gall & from bile!
May the Roses & Lillies which now just appear
In her Countenance revel & laugh all the year!

London, May 23^d 1776.

To Jean-Baptiste-Antoine Suard[1]   St Martin's Street, 25 May 1776

L (Département de la Musique, Bibliothèque Nationale, Paris), in the hand of
Fanny Burney.
　　Addressed: A Monsieur [|] Monsieur Suard, [|] Suffolk Street.　　*Docketed:* Mad.
D'arblay (Miss Burney)　　*Also* ALS draft (Osborn), *written on an old address sheet,
addressed:* To [|] d^r Burney [|] St Martins Street [|] Leic^r fields [|] London　　*Pmk:* 24 MA
LYNN　　*And docketed* Single　　*Docketed by* FBA: I　　*Publ.:* Leigh, pp.
193–4.

[1] Suard, who is not listed among the subscribers to CB's *History*, had written to David Garrick
on 28 Feb. 1776, asking for assistance in obtaining a copy of the volume. Suard intended to have
the *History* translated, 'avec des notes de mon ami l'Abbé Arnaud, un des hommes de l'Europe
qui entend le mieux et l'art et l'histoire de la musique' (Boaden, ii. 614). Garrick complied with
his friend's request (Garrick *Letters*, iii. 1078), but Suard's intended translation never appeared.
Suard paid a visit to England from mid-Apr. to early June 1776 in order to attend Garrick's
farewell performances at Drury Lane (F. A. Hedgcock, *A Cosmopolitan Actor: David Garrick and
His French Friends* [1912], p. 338; Leigh, p. 192; *The London Stage*, IV. iii. 1907 ff.).

St Martin's Street
Leicester Fields.
Sat^y Night, May 25th—76

Dear Sir,

As you can read English with infinitely more facility than I can write French, I shall make no apology for addressing you in my own Dialect: & if I might hope that you would sometimes Honour me with a Letter from Paris, I should wish that it might be written in French, a Language which, though I fear to write, yet I read with pleasure.

I have the honour to send you a Volume of my History of Music, for our worthy Friend, M. Diderot,[2] & a set of Scots Songs[3] for yourself. Some of the airs are very ancient, but are corrupted by Modern Embellishments, which, as the 4th & 7th of the key are introduced in them, destroy the character of the Melody. I have Marked with a Cross such Tunes as are most genuine; &, if I had had Time, I would have restored the original *Chant* as it is Sung by the Highlanders, & written in ancient MSS. But the Words are as rustic & curious as the Music, being in a *Patois*, as different from Modern English, as the Peasants' Language of Gascony, is from good French.

The perusal of your excellent Academic *Discours*[4] has afforded me a pleasure which I never before received from any writing of the same kind. It breathes a truly philosophic spirit throughout, & the sentiments are as free & enlarged as the Religion & Government of your Country could possibly allow. The Character of Voltaire [5]& of Rousseau,[5] & the defence of Philosophers, are admirable.[6] I shall communicate it to my Literary Friends whose judgment & Taste stand highest in my opinion, as a Patern of French Eloquence, liberality of Thought, & delicacy of Expression.[7] I wished to have given you my Thanks for it in Person, but as I have an Engagement to go into the Country to-morrow Morning with Lord Sandwich, for a few Days,[8] &

---

[2] On his return to Paris, *c*.2 June 1776, Suard faithfully delivered the *History* to Diderot, who acknowledged the gift before reading it in a letter to CB which can be dated [early June 1776] (Osborn). See Diderot *Corresp.* xiv. 195–7.

[3] Not identified. No volume of Scottish songs is listed in the *Catalogue des livres de la bibliothèque de feu m. J.B.A. Suard* (1817).

[4] *Discours prononcez dans l'Académie françoise le jeudi 4 août 1774, à la réception de M. Suard* (1774). See also Garrick *Letters*, iii. 969–70; D.-J. Garat, *Mémoires historiques sur la vie de M. Suard, sur ses écrits, et sur le XVIIIe siècle* (1820), i. 322–42.

[5–5] MS & . . . Rousseau,] *interlined in CB's hand.*

[6] Suard's *Discours*, a defence of philosophy against accusations that it enfeebled the arts, attacked religion and morals, and fomented revolutions, attracted considerable attention. Voltaire penned a congratulatory letter to Suard, 16 Aug. 1774 (*Voltaire's Correspondence*, ed. Th. Besterman (Geneva, 1953–65), lxxxviii. 163–4; see also, A. C. Hunter, *J.-B.-A. Suard, un introducteur de la littérature anglaise en France* (1925), p. 130).

[7] Suard sent CB another copy of the *Discours* together with his reply 27 [May 1776] (Osborn).

[8] CB's MS 'Memoranda from Pocket book' for 1776 (*Frag. Mem.*, Berg), records the destination

am in fear of your being gone before my return, I beg you to forgive me for taking this method of conveying to you my real Sentiments, as well as my best wishes for your good Journey, Health & Felicity, & assurances of my being,

with great Regard,

Dear sir,

your obliged & affectionate Servt

Chas Burney

In the course of your extensive Reading & Researches, if you should meet with any thing curious & *piquant* relating to my Historical Enquiries concerning music, you will greatly oblige me by communicating it to me by Letter. & if you could make me *bon à quelque chose*, by pointing out to me any English wants you may have, which it shall be in my power to supply, you will always make me very happy.

To Lord Mornington [St Martin's Street, *c.*late May 1776]¹

L and ALS incomplete draft (Osborn).

Docketed by FBA: Ld Mornington credo. *I* | ✳ 1775 or   *Editor's Note:* The surviving fragment of the draft begins on the fourth page of a double folio sheet in FB's hand. The hurried nature of the writing suggests that FB wrote while CB dictated. FB's hand is discernible from 'dignity …' to '… advance further in the Work'. Alterations were made by CB, who also indicated an insertion after '… Singer I have ever known'. This insertion, comprising the two paragraphs on Crosdill and modern oratorios, is in CB's hand, written on the second page of the sheet. The conclusion of the letter from 'The approbation …' is also in CB's hand.

… dignity, though her stature is short, & she is, alas! near 40.² However, il y a de beaux restes, & her profile is beautifully Grecian. I have given my opinion of Rauzini in my German Tour, article Munich,³ to wh^{ch} I shall only add, as I have nothing to take away, that he is so good a musician, & is posessed of so modern & exquisite a Taste, that whatever state his voice may be in, he never offends, & almost always gives very great pleasure, in every thing except his

of this jaunt: 'wth Ld Sandwich to … Hampton'. From 1775, Sandwich had 'inhabited a retired mansion … on the edge of Hampton Green' (J. Cradock, *Literary and Miscellaneous Memoirs* (1826), i. 153). See further, CB to Mrs Thrale, 1 Nov. 1777, n. 10.

¹ CB wrote this letter in reply to two letters he had received from Mornington: 30 Mar. (Coke) and 16 May 1776 (Osborn). Mornington's letters are addressed from Dangan Castle, Co. Meath, Ireland.

² Caterina Gabrielli, who was actually 45 years old.

³ See *Tours*, ii. 46 ff.

shake, wh^{ch} I doubted of before, but am now convinced is too close, &, properly speaking, rather a flutter than a true shake.[4] Yet his Execution of rapid passages is wonderful & only inferior to that of Gabrielli, wh^{ch} is more articulate. Rauzini has more Merit as a Composer than any *professed* Singer I have ever known.

Crosdill,[5] whom your Lord^P may have heard on the Violoncello in Ireland, is very much improved: The great Performers whom he has constantly heard & with whom he has been associated[6] at Bach & Abel's Winter Concerts[7] have polished his Taste & The amazing force & precision of Duport's[8] Tone & Execution upon the same Instrument have excited in him an Emulation wch has had a great Effect in stimu-lating him to hard practice in wch he has been so successful as to approximate Duport in Tone & execution—in his Taste he is far superior, being of a better School.[9]

With respect to Modern Oratorios,[10] I, who endeavour as much [as] I'm able to divest myself of prejudices of all kinds, cannot say much in their Favour. The Dignity & learning of Handel's Chorusses will certainly not be reached by his *imitators* of this Country, if they ever are by more original Composers in any other. With respect to Fugues, so fitted for Church Music, & now with Propriety wholly devoted to its Service, all other writers seem Children, learning the 1st rudiments of Composition when they attempt them. His subjects are so bold & varied that those of others wch are not stolen from him, seem

---

[4] 'I think his shake is not quite open enough' (ibid., p. 54). CB wrote in his article 'shake' in Rees: 'The Italians call a bad shake, or no shake at all, but a quivering upon the same note, *tosse da capra*, a goat's cough'.

[5] John Crosdill (1751?–1825), English violoncellist, had been principal 'cellist at the Three Choirs Festival since 1769 (*New Grove; DNB; BD*).

[6] Some notion of the calibre of Crosdill's musical associates may be gained from the list of instrumentalists who participated in Crosdill's benefit concert on 19 Apr. 1776 in the Assembly Rooms, Hanover Square (*Public Advertiser*, 19 Apr. 1776). In addition to J. C. Bach, pianoforte, and K. F. Abel, viola da gamba, the performance included the eminent violinists Wilhelm Cramer (1746–99) and Felice de'Giardini, and the oboist Johann Christian Fischer (1733–1800).

[7] J. C. Bach and K. F. Abel conducted their season of subscription concerts each Wednesday evening at the Assembly Rooms, Hanover Square. In 1776 they gave fifteen concerts between 17 Jan. and 8 May (see *Public Advertiser, passim*). See also R. Elkin, *The Old Concert Rooms of London* (1955), pp. 92–104.

[8] Jean-Pierre Duport (1741–1818), French violoncellist who first appeared in London in 1769 (*New Grove; BD*). Duport's younger brother, Jean-Louis Duport (1749–1819), was also a cele-brated violoncellist, friendly with Crosdill, but since he did not visit London before 1782, it seems likely that CB's reference is to 'Duport l'aîné' rather than 'Duport le cadet'. See also, *DBF*.

[9] Although Crosdill had studied the cello under Jean-Pierre Duport, he received his early musical education in the Westminster Abbey choir under John Robinson (1682–1762) and Benjamin Cooke (1734–93). See *BD*, under 'Crosdill'.

[10] Mornington had written in his letter of 30 Mar.: 'pray what Idea am I to form of the new oratorios that are springing up every Day [?]—The King of Harmony died when Handel died, we shall never have such Choruss Musick again'.

always feeble & Common. With respect to most of Handels airs, they by frequent imitation and performance are become common; & indeed Time has rendered many of them ungraceful & even uncooth: however, those which have been lately made tho' of a more modern Cast are in a frivolous, light, & improper Style for the words to which they are set, as well as for the general Subject of a Sacred Drama. Your Lordship will often find me a Defender of the *Moderns* against the Prejudices of outrageous admirers of antiquity—here I must give them up. The modern oratorios of Italy are in general too light & are too much in the style of Theatrical Music.—A Line sh^d certainly be drawn between the Church & Stage; but, as the French say of the universal finery & Foppery of all ranks of People: 'il n'y a Point d'Etat.'—Jomelli & Bach have Composed some admirable Oratorios,[11] in the true Church Style, with Good Chorusses, & slow airs that are truely pathetic, [12]with others that are[12] full of Passion, or chearful, *Cum dignitate*.

Y^r L^dship's queries[13] have brought this long Lett^r upon yr. self, therefore I shall make no apology, but for its late arrival; wh^ch was occasioned by Indisposition & extreme hurry. I am greatly flattered by y^r L^dship's favourable opinion of my literary labours, & have only to hope for its continuance as you advance further in the Work.[14] The approbation of Your Lord^p is so much the more grateful to me from your Taste & Knowledge in the subject upon wch I write,[15] as well as from the great ambition I have to merit in some small Degree the notice with wch you have honoured me. Permit me to assure your Lord^p that the frankness, & unrestrained manner in wch you condescend to write, & permit me to reply, renders our Correspondence extreamly pleasing as well as honourable to him who is with the highest respect & regard, My L^d, y^r Lord^p's

> most obliged & affectionately
> Devoted Servant.
> Chas Burney.

[11] CB refers to Jommelli's *La Betulia liberata* (Venice, 1743); *La Passione* (Rome, 1749); and *Isacco figura del Redentore* (Rome, 1750). See *Hist. Mus.* iv. 562–3; Mercer, ii. 928–9.

The Bach allusion is to J. C. Bach's oratorio, *Gioas, Rè di Giuda*, first performed on 22 Mar. 1770 during the oratorio season at the King's Theatre in the Haymarket (*The London Stage*, iv. iii. 1463). See also *Hist. Mus.* iv. 497; Mercer, ii. 877.

[12–12] MS with ... are] *interlined above deleted* & the quick

[13] In his letter of 30 Mar., Mornington had requested 'that when you have an Idle Hour you will be so good as to give me your opinion of the vocal & Instrumental Performers who^s names I see in the papers for ye opera and the oratorios'.

[14] Acknowledging receipt of the first volume of CB's *History*, Mornington wrote on 16 May: 'I never read any thing with more pleasure than your Elegant and judicious Dissertation, ... there is a vein of spirit that runs through it which is admirable. Your dedication to the Queen is the only Dedication I ever saw that was good and Complimentary without Flattery. When I have proceeded a little further in the History I shall do myself the pleasure of writing to you again'.

[15] Trinity College, Dublin, conferred the degree of Mus. Doc. on Mornington in 1764, and made him Professor of Music (1764–74). See *New Grove*.

To Thomas Twining

[St Martin's Street,
June 1776][1]

AL verse copy (Osborn: 'Poetical Notebook', shelves c 33, pp. 106–7).
Docketed by FBA: *I* ○

To the Same.
On Sir Thomas Robinson making reparation for
a breach of Promise.[2]

My furrow'd brow, & shrivell'd hide
Are now made smooth & sleek with pride

---

[1] CB included these verses in a letter not now preserved to Twining, who went on holiday to Yorkshire in late June or early July 1776. Twining's reply from Yorkshire, dated 28 July 1776 (BL Add. MS 39929, fos. 101–2), makes clear that CB's letter and verses had reached him before his departure from Fordham. Twining commented, 'Your jeu d'esprit upon his [Robinson's] embonpoint diverted us much'.

[2] Sir Thomas Robinson (?1702–77), MP, of Rokeby, Yorkshire, called, on account of his height, 'long Sir Thomas', created Baronet (1731), Governor of Barbados (1742–7), amateur architect. Sir Thomas, a major shareholder in Ranelagh Gardens, directed its entertainments (*DNB*).

Although CB's letters to Twining from late Feb. 1776 to Nov. 1778 have not been preserved, it is possible to reconstruct from the evidence of Twining's replies (20 Mar.; 28 Mar.; 9 Apr.; 27 Apr.; 18–20 May; 28 July; 22 Aug.; 17 Sept.; 7 Oct.; 21 Oct.; 29 Nov. 1776; 24 Jan.; 17 Dec. 1777: BL Add. MS 39929, fos. 80–157 *passim*) the story of CB's efforts to advance the career of James Fisin (see n. 3), a young and impoverished Colchester musician befriended by Twining.

It emerges from Twining's letters to CB that Sir Thomas Robinson had asked CB to recommend a musician for his 'domestic wants', a request that CB passed on to Twining who wrote in Mar. 1776 that Fisin, then organist at Colchester, 'is a very decent, well-behaved, modest young man' who sought 'opportunity of improvement'. CB judged the position of 'Sr T.'s domestic poodle poo' as a 'good opening' for the young man, especially in view of Sir Thomas's assurance that he 'wou'd get him [Fisin] into the Ranelagh band . . . at *parting*.'

Seeing that 'the thing has a face that promises', Twining encouraged Fisin to go up to London at the end of March, introduce himself to CB, and open negotiations with 'Sr T. Rob. surnamed *the Long*', who seemed 'disposed to be friendly & kind to a young [man] who shou'd please him'. But Sir Thomas reneged on his offer and Twining wrote to CB on 9 Apr.: 'Poor Fisin!—well, you have been, & are, very kind about him; who cou'd help, or foresee all this? . . . Well, it helps to confirm me in my prejudice against very tall persons . . . & in my hypothesis, that the seat of conscience is in the extremity of a man's longest toe.' The baronet's rebuff still rankled when Twining wrote again (18–20 May) that 'Sr Thomas Longshanks was a shabby fellow . . . As for poor Fisin, if you can do anything to help him, I know you will . . . His situation is none of the most comfortable; for *two* scholars, I believe, are, at present, his whole musical employment; & he has no means of getting forward, but private practice.'

About early June, however, the unpredictable Sir Thomas, possibly pressured by CB, engaged Fisin. This turn of events occasioned this poetical 'jeu d'esprit' from CB to Twining, who replied (28 July): 'I had the satisfaction of hearing, from a Colchester man who had seen Fisin in London, that he was much pleased with his situation, & prospects, & with the *plump* Knight's behaviour to him.'

CB's and Twining's satisfaction was short-lived. On 17 Sept. 1776 Twining wrote again to CB: 'You have perhaps heard Fisin's story by this time, from himself. He wrote me word, that

To think what Joy my Twi's in
At finding that the recreant Knight
Has done, at length, the thing that's right
By honest, humble, *Fisin*.[3]

No more a *chetif miserable*,
L'*Amande* he makes, is *honorable*
  His conscience seems to prick him;
He's white-wash'd by regeneration,
And now I gulp my indignation
  Nor longer wish to kick him.

He's now not quite devoid of grace,
Less frightful than the head of base,
  Less lank than Calascione;[4]
He's now unlike a long-legg'd Harry,[5]
Nor w^d he make a maid miscarry
  Who saw his carcase bony.

I do believe no child in fits
W^d instant fall, or lose its wits,
  Who saw a thing so frightful;
No gentle dog w^d howl and bark
Who spied him stalking through the Park—
  No, no, he's grown delightful!

No more, dear Twi,
Cry on him fie!
  His legs seem somewhat shorter;
His stature dwindles,
And his spindles,
  W^d serve an Irish porter.

the K^t dismissed him suddenly, without giving any reason, good or bad.' Fisin, however, had by now attracted the attention of other wealthy patrons so that 'his dismission from Father Longlegs is no misfortune'.

  [3] James Fisin (*c.*1750–1847), of Colchester, violinist and keyboard player. He was a pupil of the English bass and organist Frederick Charles Reinhold (1737–1815). Fisin's early career in London is the first documented instance of CB's musical patronage, and a good indicator of CB's rising eminence and influence in London musical life. In 1823, Fisin gratefully remembered in an autobiographical account that in 1776 he had been 'placed under the auspices of the late Dr. Burney, from whom he experienced infinite advantages' (*BD*).

  [4] 'A species of guitar, with ... a very long neck ... sometimes six feet long' (Rees). See also 'Colascione' in *New Grove*.

  [5] The cranefly or daddy-long-legs (*OED*, under 'Harry', 8). Twining (29 Nov. 1776) was to refer to Sir Thomas Robinson as 'Sr T. Spider-legs'.

His figure lean
Creates no spleen
Robust he seems as Carman;[6]
Nay more, seems plump
On rib & rump, ——
Son embonpoint est charmant!

To Elizabeth Allen[1] [St Martin's Street, summer?] 1776

AL verse copy (Osborn: 'Poetical Notebook', shelves c 33, p. 96).
Docketed by FBA: ○ *and deleted.*

Playful Epistle, To Miss Eliz. Allen.
at a boarding-school in Paris, 1776. Ætat. suæ 14.

'Ma-de-moi-selle,
I love you well.'
John Bull.[2]

And believe me, dear Bess
I wish happiness
May attend you through life,
Whether spinster or wife.
If your hand you ne'er give,
But single sh^d live,
May no care or restraint
Your pleasures e'er taint;

---

[6] Garman (or Carman) was the name of a family of theatrical and fair-ground entertainers. CB may refer specifically to Peter (or Francis) Garman (*fl.* 1742–97), clown, tumbler, actor-dancer. See *BD*, under 'Garman'. See also 'carman' in *OED*: a carter, carrier.

[1] Elizabeth ('Bessie' or 'Bessy') Allen (1761-*c.*1826), younger daughter of CB's wife by her first marriage, was born on 13 Nov. 1761. A 'spoiled' child, 'conceited' and 'pert', Bessy Allen had been sent to Paris in 1775 to refine her 'unformed & backward' manners. See *HFB*, pp. 25, 61; *EJL* i. 22 n. 57.

In a letter from Paris, dated 9 July 1776 (Osborn), the Jacobite, Andrew Lumisden (1720–1801), wrote to CB: 'Miss Allen is perfectly well. She is much improved since she has been here. Blessed with an amiable mild disposition, she will gain the affections of all who know her.'

[2] To the strains of the National Anthem, John Bull, the generic 'plain dealing' Englishman, warns Bessy against excessive gallic influence.

But may whim & vagary
Your joys ever vary
While o'er bed & o'er board
You're both lady & lord.
   Yet if you sh^d chuse
To be tied in a noose,
May the cordage ne'er gall,
But of silk soft & small,
May your neck or your heel
The knot never feel.
Be your partner ne'er dull
But his head as brimful
Of wisdom & knowledge
As the *head* of a College.
Be with kindness his heart
As full as a tart.[3]

To Thomas Twining   [St Martin's Street, *c*.11] September 1776[1]

AL verse copy (Osborn: 'Poetical Notebook', shelves c 33, p. 105).
Docketed by FBA: Animated Friendship | For Poems | ✳   *Also* AL verse draft
(Osborn).   *Endorsed by* CB: Post Chaise. Septr 1776   *Docketed by* FBA: ✳

To the Revd Thos Twining.[2]

Friend of my heart! whose pen, like magic wand
Has ev'ry mental treasure[3] at command:

---

[3] Bessy Allen's subsequent marital escapades and troubles were to prove only too painful and embarrassing to her family. See *HFB*, pp. 70–2; *JL* iii. 4 n. 12; xi. 447 n. 5.

[1] Dated from Twining's reply of 17 Sept. 1776 (BL Add. MS 39929, fos. 105–7), acknowledging receipt on 14 Sept. of CB's 'sweetmeat of a letter', only the poetical part of which is now preserved in CB's draft and copy.
   CB and Mrs Burney had set out for Bristol on 27 July 1776 (*ED* ii. 141–2), where they parted company. CB proceeded on to Worcester and Gloucester, arriving at Buxton in mid-Aug. (*Frag. Mem.*, Berg). CB's 'Post Chaise' notation indicates that he drafted these verses on his way back to London in early Sept.

[2] Twining comments in his reply of 17 Sept.: 'And pray are not *you* satyrical, with your fine verses?—Well, I thank you for 'em: they were of great service. I had a little sickness at my stomach just when I read your letter.—I filled three large basons, & was charmingly after it. I own you make your emetics of well-tasted materials. I can see good lines, & ingenious thoughts, when I forget whom they are applied to. As for *truth*—I declare I shou'd have thought you just as near the mark, if your verses had been intitled an address to my worthy friend T.T. upon his discovery of the longitude, & quadrature of the circle.'

[3] MS treasure] *draft reads* talent *interlined above deleted* pleasure

Wit, humour, learning, sense, all wait its motion,
And dance, like Merlin's Sprites, at its devotion.
    ⁴What envy w^d thy partial love excite
Thy *Cheese* bestowing on a single *Mite*!
A gift, wch freely didst thou but concede,
W^d foster worlds, & hungry myriads feed.⁴
Did all mankind, like me, thy powers know,
And what delight thy talents can bestow
What wonder⁵ w^d thy partial love create
Among the learned, witty, wise, and great!
    Thy genius gleams a pure & lambent flame
Free from the gross concupiscence of fame:
Though sedulous the public eye to shun,
Peeping through narrow apertures, its Sun
Prismatic tints emits with niggard hand
Would lighten worlds, if suffer'd to expand.⁶
    Blest with thy friendship, let its vivid rays
⁷On me and mine continue still to blaze;⁷
For where they penetrate, no sullen gloom
Can long subsist, were Erebus⁸ the room.

To Thomas Twining   [St Martin's Street,
                                       c.1 January 1777]¹

AL verse copy (Osborn: 'Poetical Notebook', shelves c 33, pp. 109–16).

New-year's Ode for 1777.
To the Revd Thos Twining.

⁴⁻⁴ MS What ... feed.] *inserted in draft from bottom of the page.*
⁵ MS wonder] *draft reads* envy
⁶ On his self-effacing shyness, Twining replied (17 Sept.): 'I know myself, my *goods*, & my *bads*, pretty well. No man wou'd like fame, & the eyes of ye world, better. But I am timid, & indolent,—& moreover, have all possible reason to doubt very much whether I *cou'd* acquire any fame, worth having, if I were to *try*. As for *vanity*—every man living, I hold, is vain; all ⟨the⟩ difference is, that some are vain with decency, & some without. If my vanity ⟨w⟩as as *indecent* as yo⟨ur⟩ Panegyric!—why then, it w^d not all have *come* up.'
⁷⁻⁷ MS On ... blaze;] *altered from* Continue in my mansion long to blaze; *so also draft.*
⁸ In Greek mythology, a place of darkness between Earth and Hades.

¹ Twining had received CB's New-year's Ode by 24 Jan. 1777 (BL Add. MS 39929, fos. 120–4). In this reply Twining thanks CB for his 'last delightful communication, prosaic, poetical, & musical'. Only the Ode is now preserved in CB's copy.
    On CB's poetical offering, Twining commented: 'you hit off better & more *piquant* lines, & thoughts with ease, & en *badinant*, than many a *famous* poet can shew, with all his effort, & *apprêt*. I wish they were to anybody but me; peste! I can't read them to any one, because of your confounded compliments.'

'I'll have one every year, mind![']
Twi.[2]

Prologue.

An Ode, in true form,
Sh^d ferment to a storm;
Sh^d growl & sh^d grumble,
Sh^d roare, rant, & rumble,
And the elements jumble,
As if nature w^d tumble
To pieces & crumble ——
But my muse is too humble,
Too placid & quiet,
To kick up a riot.
Each line & each *strophe*
Sh^d swell like a Sophy;[3]
Proudly big in each stanza,
As a Duke of Braganza.[4]
The *antistrophe* too
Sh^d have its full due;
And the breath of the god
Sh^d inspire the *Epode*,
In *trimetric, dimetric*
Iambics symmetric.
Then the verses alternate
No critic will spurn at.

Ode.[5]

Strophe.

Chief of Winter's comforts, Fire,
Claims each shiv'ring mortals praise;

---

[2] Thanking CB for his 'Noel' at Christmas 1775, Twining had written on 27 Jan. 1776 (BL Add. MS 39929, fos. 71–2): 'You are my laureate;—I'll have an New year's ode ⟨every⟩ Year, mind!'

[3] A Persian monarch (*OED*).

[4] *Braganza*, a tragedy by Robert Jephson (1736–1803), had its first performance at the Drury Lane Theatre on 17 Feb. 1775 (*The London Stage*, IV. iii. 1869–70). It met 'with prodigious success' (Walpole *Corresp.* xxviii. 176).

[5] MS *CB's footnote*: Imitations. Ἄριστον μεν ὕδωρ—Pind. Olym. I.

CB's ode is a loose imitation of Pindar's 'For Hieron of Syracuse', *Olympian Odes*, I.

Wood & Sea-coal can inspire
    Though depriv'd of Phœbus' rays.
Social chat and solace sweet
    During night's Cimmerian gloom[6]
Kindred souls incline to meet ——
    Festive mirth then fills the room.
Take the poker, stir the fire,
    Let the Broom its office fill;
Draw your chair a little nigher
    Wintry breezes makes one chill

Antistrophe.

Let some trusty, sober fellow
    In the nether regions chuse
Wine that's genuine, old & mellow
    Fit for Bacchus' self to use.
Let the spiral engine quick
    Free the liquor from its cork,
Gently, lest you make it thick—
    Lay each guest a knife and fork.
Range your friends around the board
    Plac'd contiguous to the fire;
Give whate'er the house afford,
    Cram them to their hearts desire.

Epode.

But lest some morsel in its way sh[d] stick
    With gen'rous wine to lubricate the parts
Let ev'ry glass be will-nigh fill'd, & quick,
    To help digestion, & to cheer their hearts.
All pleas'd, and ended the repast
    Let vocal harmony resound,
And many a Catch & Glee go round ——
Then 'bless our Landlord, Heav'n'! will be the last.[7]

---

[6] In Greek mythology the Cimmerii were a people who lived in perpetual darkness. See also Pope, *The Dunciad*, iv. 532.
[7] MS *CB's footnote*: Imitation. O bless my country, Heav'n! &c Pope.

Cf.   'And you! brave COBHAM, to the latest breath
       Shall feel your ruling passion strong in death:
       Such in those moments as in all the past,
       "Oh, save my Country, Heav'n!" shall be your last.'
          (Pope, *Epistle to Cobham*, ll. 262–5).

But I have no time
To make rhyme nod at rhyme,[8]
Nor genius to dash
Like the light'ning's fleet flash
Through earth, air, & Sea,
Yet make all agree,
And assign in the pother
To each strophe its brother.[8]

When out of breath, with awkward grace,
To ease my Nag, I change my pace.
Sometimes I *amble*, sometimes gallop,
Or croud my sail in little shallop.[9]
Sometimes I tamely take a *walk*
In verse as mean as common talk;
Thus *trot* through rough roads, full of ruts & rude stones
Which threat dislocation, & fracture of bones.
Losing leather,
Here my tether
Seems to make a final close;
Tamely creeping,
Soundly sleeping
Till recruited by repose.
When I think o'er all your kindness,
Friendly zeal, good-natur'd blindness,
All your virtues, winning ways,
All your claims to honest praise;
Then on Pegasus' back with fresh vigour I scramble
And fancy again round Parnassus I amble;
On tiptoe exalted, I stand in each stirrup
Supported by thoughts that are sweeter than syrrup
Which vanity flatter, & whisper to pride
That we oft times together the same Hobby ride.
You conundrums love, & joking,
I in Books am ever poking.

---

[8] Cf.

'No pleasing Intricacies intervene,
No artful wildness to perplex the scene;
Grove nods at grove, each Alley has a brother,
And half the platform just reflects the other.'
(Pope, *Epistle to Burlington*, ll. 115–18),

and

'A place there is, betwixt earth, air, and seas,
Where, from Ambrosia, Jove retires for ease.'
(Pope, *The Dunciad*, ii. 83–4).

[9] A sloop, or dinghy (*OED*).

You the Muses seek, & court,
Not in earnest, but in sport.
You, my friend, I'm proud to tell ye,
Possess with me the *idem velle*;
And still alike in ev'ry folly,
We seem to have the *idem nolle.*[10]
You music of all kinds detest
But what's refin'd, and well express'd.
The Masters of your youth respect,
Yet all their errors can detect.
Regard for those you've always nurs'd
Who of their age & place were first;
Yet think it no atrocious crime
To travel with the present time.
    If genius is immortal, why
Suppose he did with Handel die?
Does he not his gifts diffuse
In concert with the heav'nly Muse,
And all his glowing colours spread,
Wherever Science lifts her head? ——

Here the parallel must end.
Love and friendship both depend
On whim, caprice, & things amusing,
Which influence ev'ry heart in chusing:
Gifts & acquirements great & solid,
Art oft possess'd by Beings squalid;
Which none can love, though all pretend
Uncommon talents to befriend.
To genius, learning, wisdom, sense,
As great as yours, I've no pretence;
But yours, though great, w^d ne'er alone
Have made my heart & soul your own:
    Sans le penchant, sans la rage
    Pour l'aimable Badinage,
Which, in spite of all repulse,
Oft your inward man convulse.
Join to these your upright mind
Your certain *tact*, and taste refin'd—
    Nor sh^d your *squareness* be derided,[11]

[10] 'Nam idem velle atque idem nolle, ea demum firma amicitia est' (For agreement in likes and dislikes—this, and this only, is what constitutes true friendship). Sallust, *Catiline*, 20. 4.
[11] An allusion to the close of Twining's letter of 28 Mar. 1776 (BL Add. MS 39929, fos.

Though once, *en badinant*, I chided;
For though on *Method*-ism it border,
The principle, is love of order.

Deep in the commerce of the world,
To w^{ch}, by Fate, I've long been hurl'd;
True Friendship's source I find so various
And its duration so precarious,
That many a wight who entertains
For *half an hour*, oft wants the brains
To instruct or please a minute more,
Though with him years you live threescore.
Others can for *a day* endear,
And some *a week, a month, a year*;
But then, alas! their pow'r is spent,
Disgust ensues, & discontent. ——
    To you, dear friend, as to my wife,
I neck & heels am tied *for life*.
Did not your heart to Friendship's call
Beat like the Clock-work of St Paul
Constant & true, your parts[12] are sure
To make the union long endure;
For more than twice ten thousand ways
You bind with skrews, with cramps, & stays,
Of genius, learning, taste, & wit,
From wch no mortal can get quit:
Take these away, your fun & humour
To fix affection sure w^d do more
And make it bear all wind & weather,
Than all the lib'ral Arts together.

Epilogue.

Under our signet & sign manual
Kindly receive this Tribute annual;

82–3): 'You shall hear from me again when my *squareness* will permit. Sir, do you know that Simonides (in a pass. quoted by Aristotle & Plato) speaking of a thorough good man, calls him ἀνηρ τετραγωνος, i.e. a *square* man?' Twining signs the letter with a cartoon figure of a man with outstretched arms and a square torso which also resembles his usual 'T. T.' signature.

[12] Twining replied (24 Jan.): 'Really, Sir, some of your lines are perfectly *indecent*;—they amount to a kind of *bawdry*;—ay, & I see, just this moment, how I can prove it; for they talk of my *parts*, & if ever any man's parts were *private* parts, I *do* think mine are: & I believe always *will* be; my mind, I fear, will never shed it's breeches!'

And as you chose me for your Colley[13]
With Christian patience bear my folly;
The Sack[14] in wch he us'd to paddle
Made with its fumes his head quite addle,
And whate'er *from* him, came so sweet
And mawkish, all condemn'd the treat.[15]
  So fares it with each scribe Empiric,
Who deals out drugs of panegyric;
Who does to Dulness altars raise,
Or slavers Kings with pseudo praise.
As patron, *You* I may commend,
Who are not my King, or Lord, but Friend:
An *alter idem*, letter'd guide,
Whom more I've lov'd, the more I've tried!
For such your heart, that nice dissection
Augments your claims to my affection:
Receive it then, without controul,
Warm from the bottom of my Soul.[16]

To Charles Grant[1]

[St Martin's Street,
early? 1777][2]

AL and L draft (Osborn).
Docketed by FBA: ✳ To Mr Grant. | on the | loss of a | beloved child— | I believe |
excellent   *Editor's Note:* The MS shows that while CB was drafting this letter he

[13] CB, appointed Twining's 'laureate' (n. 2), refers to Colley Cibber (1671–1757), Poet Laureate (1730), the hero of Pope's *Dunciad*.
[14] The Poet Laureate's perquisites include a butt of sack. See *The Dunciad*, ed. J. Sutherland (3rd edn., 1963), p. 415.
[15] Cf.   'Flow Welsted, flow! like thine inspirer, Beer,
            Tho' stale, not ripe; tho' thin, yet never clear;
            So sweetly mawkish, and so smoothly dull;
            Heady, not strong; o'erflowing, tho' not full.'
                (Pope, *The Dunciad*, iii. 169–72).

[16] In a postscript to his letter of 24 Jan., Twining wrote: 'Last night, in a chosen circle ... I was so hard prest, that I was forced to lay aside all mod[e]sty, & read your Ode myself. It was *encored*, & I never saw people more pleased, or wondered less at it; for upon my life you are —— I won't be indecent.'

[1] Charles Grant (1746–1823), statesman and evangelical philanthropist (*DNB*). Later to rise to eminence and fortune, Grant served at this time as Secretary to the Board of Trade at Calcutta in the East India Company Civil Service. See H. Morris, *The Life of Charles Grant* (1904), pp. 38–40, *et passim*. The Grants were to assist the Burneys in the late 1780s by helping to 'recover' young Dick Burney who had to be packed off to India after committing some mysterious crime. See Lonsdale, p. 333; Morris, *Grant*, p. 156.
[2] The date is deduced from the accounts rendered (n. 18), and reference to the death of Grant's infant daughters (n. 5).

found he had no time to finish it. He deleted the detailed accounts and called on FB to take down from dictation a hurried concluding paragraph to the letter. FBA in later years deleted the entire second page from 'As soon as it was rec^d ...'.

Dear Sir.

³It is my fervent Wish³ that the Letter wch I have now the honour to write will find you & my dear & most amiable Fre^d Mrs Grant⁴ in a more tranquil & comfortable state of mind than you Enjoyed when the last Lett^r wth wch you favoured me was written. *Time*⁵ only can blunt the Arrows of misfortune; Reason helps us but little ⁶during great Calamities;⁶ & Philosophy, I fear operates ⁷still less⁷ in favour of feeling Minds under the ⁸pressure of affliction.⁸ Sorrow, as Sterne well observed, must be digested ere it can be soothed:⁹ that is, Time must have prepared & steeled the heart a little before the balm of counsel or Pity can have any Effect. Grief described with so much sensibility as yours must have taken deep root; & yet, such are the terms of our Existence! Calamities succeed each other so rapidly that however any *one* may stand against the Powers of Time, reason, & philosophy, it *must* give way to a 2^d as that will to a 3^d & so on to the end of our sublunary warfare!¹⁰ If each single misfortune were to continue to torture us wth equal force to the end of our Lives what must the accumulation be! & what the aggregate of Sufferings 'wch Flesh is Heir to!'¹¹ All we can hope is for ¹²an Interval¹² of ease to refit, & enable us to bear new shocks! May heaven allow you one as long as can be granted to our frail Existence!—And if this melancholy preface to my Letter sh^d find your Minds in a Calm & comfortable State, it w^d grieve me very much to ¹³turn your¹³ attention to Painful subjects—I shall therefore hasten to Business; one of the best Champions against

---

³⁻³ MS It ... Wish] *altered from* I sincerely hope

⁴ Jane Grant, née Fraser (*c.*1756–1827), whom Charles Grant had married on 23 Feb. 1773. With his bride, Grant took passage to return to India in May 1773 (Morris, *Grant*, pp. 29–32, 392). Grant and his wife are each listed as having subscribed for two copies of CB's *History*.

⁵ MS *Time*] *FBA added* & Religion

The letter from Grant is not preserved. It clearly bore sad news of the Grants' infant daughters, Elizabeth (1774–6) and Margaret (1775–6), who both died from smallpox within nine days of each other in Apr. 1776. This family calamity wrought a great change in Grant's life and conduct (see Morris, *Grant*, pp. 56–66).

⁶⁻⁶ MS during ... Calamities;] *initially* on great occasions *altered to* in Times of Calamity *finally altered to present reading.*

⁷⁻⁷ MS still less] *altered from* but little

⁸⁻⁸ MS pressure ... affliction] ... *altered from* tortures of Calamity Misfortune

⁹ 'Before an affliction is digested—consolation ever comes too soon;—and after it is digested—it comes too late' (*Tristram Shandy*, vol. iii, ch. 29).

¹⁰ MS warfare] *interlined above deleted* race

¹¹ *Hamlet*, III. i. 63.

¹²⁻¹² MS an Interval] *altered from* a little time *and* a small Interval

¹³⁻¹³ MS turn your] *interlined above deleted* awaken

226

Evils wch prey on the heart with double fury when they monopolise our whole Time & thoughts.

And first let me acknowledge & thank you for the remittance of £250 wth [w^{ch}] you favoured me, & wch was duly paid. As soon as it was rec^d I called on Mr Becher,[14] both at his Compting House in the City, & at his House in Portman Square in order to refund the surplus in your Favour, but never was so fortunate as to meet with him before I [15]was made acquainted wth[15] your wish to present my good & Excellent Scholar[16] with an Organ. I then grew more indifferent ab^t adjusting this difference between us, as I imagined, as you had done before me, that the ballance in your Favour w^d nearly serve for defraying that Expense. When I called on Mr Becher I had [17]an exact[17] State of our Money Concerns to lay before him.[18]

I have not now Time allowed me to transcribe it for your inspection, as my Letter is called for much sooner than I expected. I can only add that since the calculation you made of there being a surplus of £78 in y^r favour I have pd. 2 Bills for Music &c, sent to Calcutta.
one, of   £10: 2: 0   Feb. 1776
                          which leaves me in possession
& another of £31: 7: 6. Nov. 1776
of ab^t £37 of y^r property, wh^{ch} I will keep towards the organ, or at any Time pay to Mr. Becher, or any one else whom you shall authorise to receive it.

---

[14] Richard Becher (d. 1782), trader, and civil servant in the East India Company, befriended the young Charles Grant and advanced his career in Bengal. When Grant first arrived in India in 1768, Becher served as a Member of Council at Calcutta, then became Political Resident at the Court of the Nawab of Bengal at Murshidabad (1769–70). Blamed for the Bengal famine of 1770, Becher was dismissed from the Company on his return with Grant to England in 1771. Reinstated, Becher was appointed a Director of the Company in 1775, returned later to Bengal, and died there in Nov. 1782, 'leaving a wife and seven children destitute of worldly provision' (Morris, *Grant*, pp. 10, 14–22, 27–9, 79; CCR (1776), p. 211; HMC, *Palk* (1922), pp. 130–1, 389; *GM* liii (1783)^1, 540).

[15-15] MS was . . . wth] *interlined above deleted* received

[16] Doubtless Mrs Grant, who was highly accomplished (see Morris, *Grant*, pp. 30, 56–7).

[17-17] MS an exact] *interlined by FB above deleted* the following

[18] Deleted from the MS draft is the following detailed account:

Rec^d of Mr Grant	£250. 0. 0
For myself on acc^t of Subscriptions	170. 0. 0
Paid a Bill for Music sent to India, Feby 1776	10. 2. 0
D^o Novr in the same year	31. 7. 6
	211. 9. 6

It is unlikely that the huge sum of £170 was paid to CB for subscriptions to the *History of Music* alone. CB may have been involved in some of Grant's financial speculations in India.

To———Baker[1]   [St Martin's Street],
                                 17 March [1777?][2]

L, in the hand of an amanuensis (Osborn).

D[r] Burney presents his Comp[ts] to M[r] Baker, & is extremely Sorry
that so imperfect a Book happened to be delivered to him; he has the
honour to send him another, which has been examined, & found free
from Book Binder's blunders.—
Monday March 17th

To Gabriel Piozzi[1]   [St Martin's Street],
                                 5 August 1777

ALS draft (University of California at Berkeley, Bancroft Library: 76/31 Z).
Docketed by FBA: To Piozzi. 77

[1] The recipient is not identified. Two 'Bakers' are listed as subscribers to the *History of Music*:
William Baker and John Baker; but it is unlikely (see the conjectural dating in n. 2) that the
present note was addressed to either, for subscribers received their copies early in 1776. CB presumably sends the recipient a copy of the second impression of the first edition of *Hist. Mus.* i.
For this second impression, advertised in mid-Nov. 1776, see Lonsdale, pp. 187, 198–9.

[2] Of the years in which 17 Mar. fell on a Monday, 1777 appears the least unlikely to fit the
circumstances of CB's note.

[1] Gabriele Mario Piozzi (1740–1809), Italian tenor, harpsichordist, and composer who married
(1784) Mrs Thrale. The fortunate preservation of some consecutive pages from CB's MS *Frag.
Mem.* (Berg) provides details of CB's first meeting with Piozzi, the progress of their early
friendship, and the background to this letter (see also, Lonsdale, pp. 280–1).
    CB first heard Piozzi sing on 18 Nov. 1776 'to a large & splendid company' at the house of
William Douglas (1725–1810), 3rd Earl of March, later (1778) 4th Duke of Queensberry, who
'desired me to mention him to my friends'. CB 'liked [Piozzi's] manner of singing extreamly; his
taste and expression were new and extremely elegant.' And so, during the 1776–7 season, CB
'made several Concerts at my own house . . . for him to be heard by leading people of high rank'.
    'In quitting London late in the summer of 1777', Peregrine Bertie (1714–78), 3rd Duke of
Ancaster and Kesteven, 'applied to me to recommend a good Musician to go with the family into
Lincolnshire . . . to play & sing to himself & the Duchess at Night' and also to assist the musical
studies of his daughter, Lady Priscilla Barbara Elizabeth (1761–1828), who was one of CB's
own pupils during the London season.
    As Piozzi 'had not long been come over . . . [and] had few patrons & no scholars,' CB relates,
'⟨I⟩ spoke of him to the Duke of Ancaster as a singer wth whose performance his Grace w[d] be
much pleased, ⟨a⟩nd if he sh[d] like to go into the country for ⟨2⟩ or 3 months, as he was
likewise a good ⟨p⟩layer on the har[p][d] he might be very useful to Lady Priscilla on that
Instrum[t]'. Piozzi accepted the Duke's offer, and left London on 5 July with Ancaster's party for
Grimsthorpe Castle, the family seat in Lincolnshire (*Public Advertiser*, 5 July 1777).
    'He had not been t⟨here⟩ a week before he wrote me a letter full of complain⟨ts⟩ of the
uncomfortable manner in w[ch] he was trea⟨ted.⟩ He was sent to the 2[d] table and kept at a great

Amico Mio Carissimo.

Ho ricevuto le sue stimatis⟨sim⟩e Lettere tutte due[2] quasi al me-
desimo Tempo perche avendo fatto una visita di villeggiature per
qualche Giorni non son tornato che Ieri mattina.[3] Mi dispiace molto
che la sua residenza *Ducale*[4] si trova un si tal seccatura—ma ci vuol
pazienza in questo Mondo. Non c'è niente di perfetto, da per tutto.—
Se la sua dimora in Campagna fornisce che pochi Piaceri, bisogna
sperar vantaggi in Conseguenza di questa Penitenza, che pagaranno
bene il Fastidio. Una vita simmetrice, o sia una troppa granda *Mono-
tonia* nelle cose Casareccie, non è, in generale, il vizio della Nobiltà
Inglese—al Contrario, una disordine universale regna nelle sue Case,
anche come negli loro Costume.[5] Si dice che al Duca di *Devonshire*[6] non
si vede nè il padrone nè la padrona della Casa, tutto il Giorno ni alla
Collazione, ni al Pranzo od alla Cena—tutta la Compagnia è in *piena
Libertà* o di Mangiar o di Morire di Fame. Giardini e partito di godere
di Questa Libertà. Credo io, che Grimsthorp[7] sarà una bella Scuola
di Pazienza e di Filosofia—E, che bella Cosa sarebbe di devenire
veramente *Filosofo di Campagna!*[8] Spero almeno che la Mancanza di
Conversazione, e di Parole d'esprimere li suoi bisogni, sarà un stimulo
d'incitarvi al Studio di nostra Lingua Gottica, della quale avrete gran
bisogno tornando in Londra. La Gabrielle sta in abbandono del suo
Amico,[9] chi come si dice va maritarsi fra poco alla sorella di Milord
Monson.[10]—L'*Incantatrice* Catarina a presa una Casa in Suffolk Street,
dove piena di Maledizioni resta, adesso con tutta la santa Famiglia.

distance from the Duke & Duchess. He was expected to devote his whole morning to L^y
Prisci⟨lla⟩ and at Night was never sent for by the Duke till 9 or 10 O'Clock, before wch time he
used to lock and barricade his chamber door with trunks, boxe⟨s⟩ and all the lumber he c^d find
that he may not be forced to quit his gite like ⌈a dog or⌉ an anima⟨l⟩ to shew his tricks.'

[2] Not preserved, but see n. 1.

[3] Evidence to establish exactly where CB's visit had taken him is lacking. He may have gone
to Chessington to start writing the second volume of the *History* (See Lonsdale, pp. 238–40).

[4] MS *Ducale*] *interlined above deleted* presente

[5] Piozzi had already complained to CB about what he considered the loutish behaviour of the
English upper classes at home: 'he had brought over letters of recommendation from English
travellers wch he had met with at Milan, Brussels, Spa, & Paris in his route to this country; but
he had no opportunity of delivering them—*que*[*st*]*i Sig^ri Inglesi* (he said) had a custom *molto
particolare*—they were "*sempre* not at home"' (*Frag. Mem.*, Berg). The Burneys gleefully adopted
Piozzi's macaronic phrase as a standing family joke.

[6] William Cavendish (1748–1811), 5th Duke of Devonshire, married (1774)Lady Georgiana
Spencer (1757–1806).

[7] When Piozzi 'came away he protested that he hated the place so much, that "if he had left
an eye behind him, he w^d not go back to fetch it"' (*Frag. Mem.*, Berg).

[8] Baldassare Galuppi's comic opera of this name achieved great popularity when it was first
performed in London in Jan. 1761 (*Hist. Mus.* iv. 474–5; Mercer, ii. 860; *The London Stage*, iv. ii.
836).

[9] Caterina Gabrielli 'is kept by a Mr. Piers, a very rich gentleman of Yorkshire' (Walpole
Corresp. xxiv. 148). CB's use of 'abbandono' is an allusion to Sacchini's opera *Didone abbandonata*
in which Gabrielli had made her London début in Nov. 1775.

[10] Henry Peirse (*c.*1754–1824), Caterina Gabrielli's 'Amico', of Bedale, Yorkshire, MP for

Non son arrivati fin qui gli novelli soggetti dell'opera. Hò sentito cantar 2 o 3 arie la Giorgi[11] la settimana passata e mi pare che a molta profitata delle Lezzione del Maestro Sacchini.[12]—Venga la Todi[13] per far La parte della 1ma Donna nell'opera Buffa. Per il 1mo Buffo, non mi ricordo il suo nome Tedesco.[14]

Ma che bel sogno! a fatto, lei!—ho fatto ieri sera un Viaggio aposta nella Citta per cercar il Numero 31[15]—ma si ridono a tutti l'Offizi di Loteri⟨a⟩ dov'io lo domandato.—E un pezzo che qualche Migliaia di biglett⟨i⟩[16] son sparsi per tutt'il Mondo.[17] Ma senza un avertimento nelle Gazette che costerà quattrini non e creduta possibile di trovar⟨e⟩

Northallerton, Yorks (1774–1824), married on 16 Aug. 1777 the Hon. Charlotte Grace Monson (d. 1793), sister to John Monson (1753–1806), 3rd Baron Monson of Burton (Namier and Brooke, iii. 256; J. Foster, *Pedigrees of the County Families of Yorkshire* (1874), vol. iii).

[11] Brigida Banti, née Giorgi (*c.*1756–1806), soprano singer and actress, began life as 'a piazza performer' in Venice. After her discovery and triumphant début at the Paris Opéra on 1 Nov. 1776, the Proprietors of the Pantheon in London engaged her 'merely on speculation ... for three seasons, at 800l. a year, upon condition that 100l. should be deducted each season out of her salary, for the payment of an able master to cultivate her voice' (Rees). See *New Grove*; *BD*. CB presumably played a major part in these negotiations, for from 1773 to 1776 he drew an annual salary of £100 for conducting foreign correspondence for the Pantheon proprietors (Lonsdale, pp. 227–8).

[12] CB wrote of Brigida Giorgi-Banti's succession of singing masters: 'Sacchini was the first appointed to this office; but soon found her so idle and obstinate, that he quitted her as an incurable patient. She was next assigned to Signor Piozzi, whose patience was likewise exhausted before she became a perfect singer'. She also received instruction from Karl Friedrich Abel (*Hist. Mus.* iv. 507–8; Mercer, ii. 885; Rees).

Although Miss Giorgi was now still under Sacchini's tutelage, Piozzi clearly had a professional interest in her progress. When the Pantheon season of Subscription Concerts opened on 24 Nov. 1777, the vocal soloists included 'Signora GIORGI, (being the 1st Time of her performing in this Kingdom) ... and Signor PIOZZI' (*Public Advertiser*, 24 Nov. 1777). CB's nephew and son-in-law, Charles Rousseau Burney, also appears in this advertisement as playing a concerto on the harpsichord.

[13] Luísa Rosa Todi, née d'Aguiar (1753–1833), Portuguese mezzo-soprano singer, 'failed to please' her London audiences in 1777 (see *Hist. Mus.* iv. 509; Mercer, ii. 886), though she won warm admiration elsewhere (*New Grove*; T. Borba and F. L. Graça, eds., *Dicionário de música* (Lisbon, 1956–8), ii. 629–31).

[14] Mme Todi's partner as first *buffo* in 1777–8 was an Italian tenor named Guglielmo Jermoli (*fl.*1777–9), of whom nothing is known apart from CB's crushing comment: 'The manner of singing of the tenor Jermoli, more resembled that of a German, than an Italian; but neither in voice, taste, nor action, did his performance ever surpass mediocrity' (*Hist. Mus.* iv. 509; Mercer, ii. 886; *BD*).

[15] Fifty thousand tickets at £10 each for the State Lottery of 1777 'began to be delivered out at the Bank' to subscribers on 4 Aug. (*Lloyd's Evening Post*, 4–6 Aug. 1777; see also C. L'E. Ewen, *Lotteries and Sweepstakes* (1932), p. 203). Piozzi had evidently dreamt that ticket No. 31 would be 'lucky' in the drawing which commenced on 17 Nov. (see also *The Spectator*, No. 191, ed. D. F. Bond (Oxford, 1965), ii. 248–52).

[16] MS biglett⟨i⟩] *alternative* bulletti

[17] 'When the Parliament have resolv'd on a Lottery for raising Part of the Supplies for the Year, A Subscription is set on Foot,' payable in instalments, the first deposit usually made in Apr. 'At the Payment of the first Subscription at the Bank, the Subscribers receive Receipts for the Sums and Numbers of Tickets subscribed for ... As soon as the Subscribers have got these Receipts, some of them, after adding what they think a reasonable Profit to the Subscription Price, put them into the Hands of the Brokers for Sale, so that Tickets are nominally selling

un qualsisia numero particulare. Però ho pregato un *Sensale* (Broker) di cercarlo al Banco di Londra dove gli Mercanti son forniti di bulletti all'ingrosso. Ed il mio servo va adesso per domandar risposta del successo degli ricercamenti—ed eccolo tornato—e dice che il Bulletto N° 31 si trova nelle Mane del Sig[r] Wenham & Co. at the Lottery Office in the Poultry[18]—ma non e possibile di comprarlo, essendo venduto a qualche persone in *piccole porzioni*.[19]—Adesso bisogna far un altro sogno ed in Caso che quel Oracolo dà Coraggio di solecitare la Fortuna, non a altra Cosa a fare che di dirmi la sua Voluntà. Ma non scorda che andrò in Campagna la settimana Ventura.[20]

La mia Moglie e tutta la famiglia *Bernesca*, strettamente mi chiedono di farle i suoi Complimenti più distinti.—Amatemi, comandatemi, e crediate che niuna cosa può essermi piu gioconda quando lo impiegarmi in vostro servizio. Viva felicie. Pieno di stima ed amicizia mi raffermo

Di Vos[ria]

Londra 5 Aug[to] 1777

umil[mo] devot[mo] Serv[re]

Carlo Burney

To Matthew Raper[1]   [St Martin's Street, ?September–October 1777][2]

ALS draft (Osborn).
Docketed by FBA: *I* To— Mathew Raper—

sometimes for Months before they have any real Existence' (*The Lottery display'd, or the Adventurer's Guide* (1771), pp. 8–9).

[18] John Wenham (*c.*1730–96), conducted his lottery-ticket and stock-brokerage business at 11 The Poultry. He was one of the leading London lottery-office keepers of his time (*GM* lvii (1787)[2], 836; lxvi (1796)[2], 709; Ewen, *Lotteries*, p. 271).

[19] Since lottery tickets were expensive, and beyond the purses of the majority of people, the brokers 'instituted the system of dividing a ticket into aliquot parts, charging adequately for the accommodation, and reaping an enhanced profit' (Ewen, *Lotteries*, p. 246). Tickets were in this manner divided into 'shares' which were sometimes as small as a sixty-fourth part of a whole ticket.

[20] In late August, CB spent a week with the Thrales at Streatham (*ED* ii. 284; Clifford, pp. 154–5; Lonsdale, p. 240).

[1] Matthew Raper (*c.*1741–1826), FRS (1783), FSA (1785), antiquary, miscellaneous writer, and merchant, had joined the Council of the East India Company supercargoes at Canton in 1767. From 1777 he served as Chief of the Council until his return to Britain in 1781. Raper, mentioned in CB's will (Scholes, ii. 271), obtained for CB most of the information on China contained in the second edition of the first volume of *Hist. Mus.* (pp. 31–5; Mercer, i. 45–9), and in the article on 'Chinese Music' in Rees. See *GM* xcvii (1827)[1], 378; H. B. Morse, *The Chronicles of the East India Company trading to China, 1635–1834* (Oxford, 1926–9), vols. ii and v *passim*; G. Lipscomb, *The History and Antiquities of the County of Buckingham* (1847), ii. 482.

[2] In his article 'Chinese Music' in Rees, CB mentions two communications from Raper 'dated

Sir.

Such active Zeal as you have kindly manifested for the service of a Man whom you never saw, & of whose undertaking you c^d have been animated only by a slight sketch, is as difficult to acknowledge as to Parallel. Indeed the little Claim I have to your Friendly offices at the same Time that it greatly exalts *your* disinterestedness, a little humiliates & mortifies *me*, particularly when I consider how impossible it is for me ever to get out of Debt.

The answers to my Queries[3] made in Italian at Pekin, wch you were so kind to send me in Dec. 1775[4] are Curious & in a great Measure satisfactory. My chief difficulty in reading them is in reconciling the answer to my 2^d Query—whether the Chinese have any Semitones? wch is positively answered in the Negative: *Gli Cinesi nella loro Musica non hanno Semituoni*. And yet in the scale & appogiature to the Air wch accompanies it, I find Semitones. Perhaps in the *anc^t* National Music of China, like that of Scotland, these Intervals were avoided; but either by Corruption, Refinem^t, or imitation, of other Music, the Moderns not only use the Semitones in their *New Melodies*, but apply them, in varying & gracing the ancient. [5]Indeed your French Correspondent[6] seems to Confirm this Conjecture when he observes 'que l'ancienne Musique Chinoise a soufferte surement beaucoup de chang[e]ments, et qu'il est bien difficile de la bien verifier.'[5] As the

Canton, 1775 and 1777'. The trading season closed at Canton on 5 Mar. 1777 (Morse, *Chronicles*, ii. 23), when the last East Indiaman sailed for Britain. Six months have to be allowed for the passage. CB also received a letter from Twining, 31 Oct. 1777 (BL Add. MS 39929, fos. 147–8), complimenting him on the '*bonbons*' he had received from China. CB's letter of thanks to Raper can therefore be dated, conjecturally, Sept. or Oct. 1777.

[3] When CB finally made full use of Raper's information in Rees, 'Chinese Music', he explained: 'The author of the present article, when collecting materials for his "General History of Music in every civilized part of the Globe," did not forget China ... He sent queries to an English gentleman, a good judge of music, who had resided many years at Canton, and who transmitted them to different distant provinces, whence he obtained answers in French and Italian, from missionaries long resident there'.

[4] Not preserved, but the contents of Raper's consignment to CB are known: 'our correspondent at Canton not only transmitted to us [the missionaries'] answers, but sent with them a complete set of Chinese instruments; among which there was every species of flutes, several stringed instruments of the lute and guitar kind, the *pao*, formerly called *yu*, *tcheo*, *he*, and *ching* ... [which] is a beautiful instrument, which has a gourd, or bamboo for its basis, and represents in the arrangement of its reeds or bamboo pipes, the column of an organ: with these we received the largest gong which had ever been brought to England. These instruments were accompanied by Chinese airs in Chinese characters of notation, and in those of Europe ...' (ibid.).

[5-5] In the MS draft, CB signals the insertion of this comment from the foot of p. 2 of the MS with an asterisk.

[6] Probably Jean-Joseph de Grammont (1736–*c*.1808), French Jesuit missionary to China, with whom Raper was in correspondence. Fr de Grammont was a competent musician. See J. Legge, *The Texts of Tâoism* (Oxford, 1891), i. 12; E. H. Pritchard, *The Crucial Years of Early Anglo-Chinese Relations, 1750–1800*, Research Studies of the State College of Washington, vol. iv, nos. 3–4 (Pullman, Washington, 1936), p. 208; L. Pfister, *Notices biographiques et bibliographiques sur les Jésuites de l'ancienne mission de Chine. 1552–1773* (Shanghai, 1932–4), ii. 958–62.

Person who answers these Queries is an Italian[7] who seems to understand my Subject, & is himself a *Practical Musician*, his answers have
greater weight wth me (Entre nous) than those made by a Native
of France, who declares his want of Skill. The Italian mentions a
circumstance relative [to] some young Euneuchs of the Emperors
Court having been taught to play upon our Instrum[ts] in the European
Manner, ab[t] 30 years ago. Now, I wish I c[d] know whether this was the
first Time they were so employed, & whether it became a Custom & is
still continued for them to practise Music?—Whether their Voices are
cultivated like those designed for the operas & the Churches of Italy?
& whether Evirati are ever made in China merely for the Preservation
of the Voice, as well as to render them *Safe-Guards* to the Chastity of
their women?[8]

The *Memoire sur la Musique des anciens*—par l'abbé Roussier,[9] mentioned by the Italian Missionary, I have not only read, but have long
been personally acquainted with the Author. So much for your first
kind Communication: I come now to the 2[d], wch is not only extreamly
ample, but Curious.[10]

But here again I am perplexed ab[t] the semitones, as I find in the
Gamut Equivalents to so ut, & mi fa, of the Fr. Scale & BC–EF of
ours; & yet y[r] correspondent says 'the Chinese are astonished & unable
to give a satisfactory answer when interrogated ab[t] Semitones.[']—
& allows that their Scale is not in tune with ours &c—A Chinese
Instrum[t] I saw at Paris of the *Sticcado* kind[11] has absolutely no more
than 6 Sounds in the octave, & the Intervals were the same as those
between the 5 flats & sharps, or short Keys of our Keyed Instruments.
If I knew the Scale of the little organ, the Flutes or other Instrum[ts] w[th]
w[ch] you have been so kind as to furnish me this Doubt w[d] be fully
cleared up[12]—as it is, if I am unable to make a scale from the Flutes I
must have recourse to Conjecture, on Probability—Rameau & the

---

[7] Not identified.

[8] '"It was asked, whether eunuchs were employed as singers on the stage, or in the palace;
and the answer was, that some from Europe had been introduced in the palace early in the reign
of the late emperor, as musicians, to sing, play on instruments, and teach others; but that was
not of long continuance; and now, as formerly, no other use is made of them than as guardians of
the wives and concubines of the emperor and of great personages." This communication bears
date, Peking, 1780' (Rees, under 'Chinese Music').

[9] The Abbé Pierre-Joseph Roussier (1716–*c*.1790), *Mémoire sur la musique des anciens, où l'on
expose ... de divers systêmes de musique chez les Grecs, les Chinois & les Egyptiens* (1770). CB's copy is
listed in 'Cat. Fac. Mus.', item 126. CB had met Roussier at Paris in June 1770 (*Tours*, i. 25,
30–2), and Roussier's name appears in the list of subscribers to CB's *History*.

[10] Not preserved, but see nn. 2, 4.

[11] See CB to Suard, 24 May 1771, n. 6, and *Tours*, i. 317.

[12] CB never 'cleared up' this problem with regard to the *ching (shêng)*, the free-reed mouth-
organ: 'The scale to this sweet little instrument, remains the grand desideratum in Chinese
music' (Rees, under 'Chinese Music').

Abbé Roussier both affirm that the Chinese Scale & Music is without semitones.[13]

It seems, from the Specimens of Chinese Music with wch I am favoured from y^r Fr. Correspondent, that to reduce it to European Intervals & Measure is a very difficult Task; for by its wildness in these particulars, I am convinced that it is very different—& I suppose both can only be expressed in our Characters, *à peu prés*.

In short, except the Difficulty of Semitones, y^r two Communications have amply furnished me wth materials sufficient for as long an Article concerning the National Music of China, as I shall be able to find room for in the Sequel of my Work,[14] & I hold myself extreamly obliged to you & your Fr^{ds} for enabling me to gratify the public Curiosity on a subject so new to my Countrymen & to the Inhabitants of the rest of Europe. The Royal Poem wth wch you have been so good to furnish me wth a translation[15] is extreamly original & Curious, & if I can possibly allow it Room in my work I shall insert the whole.

I have nothing more to solicit, except it were possible whenever you write again to Europe to oblige me with a scale of some of the Instrum^{ts} [with] wch you have so liberally enriched my Collection, particularly the little organ—& the Manner of blowing it—are there not Concords, or a kind of Music in Parts produced by it?[16]—I have seen some of the same kind of Instrum^{ts} before: our Queen has one, but no one here can judge of its Effects for want of skill in playing upon it.—I was sorry to hear that my 1st Vol. had been sent to you,[17] as I hoped to have been the first to beg of you to allow it a place in your Library—I shall, however, have the honour, if I live to Complete my Plan [to] send you the whole either in 2 or 3 Vol^s as well bound as it can be here, & wth the best Impression of the Plates, not as an Equivalent for all your kindness & assistance, but as a Mark of my Gratitude & a Testimony of the Esteem & respect of, S^r,

Your most obliged
& Obed^t Servant
Chas Burney.

[13] Jean-Philippe Rameau (1683–1764), *Code de musique pratique, . . . avec de nouvelles réflexions sur le principe sonore* (1760), pp. 191–3, 226; and Roussier, *Mémoire*, pp. 14–16. Rameau's *Code* is listed in 'Cat. Fac. Mus.', item 120.

[14] The section on National Music which CB intended to include in a later volume of his *History* never materialized. About 30 years later, CB incorporated Raper's findings in his article 'Chinese Music' in Rees, there calling him 'our zealous friend (Mr. R.)'.

[15] *Éloge de la ville de Moukden, et de ses environs* (1770), a poem by Ch'ien Lung (1711–98), Emperor of China (1736–96), translated into French by Jean-Joseph-Marie Amiot (1718–93), French Jesuit missionary at the Chinese Court (*DBF*). CB mentions the *Éloge* in Rees, under 'Chinese Music'.

[16] For CB's description of the *ching* (*shêng*), 'the only instrument that we have received from China which would please European ears', see Rees, under 'Chinese Music'.

[17] Matthew Raper appears in the list of subscribers to the *History*.

The Instrum^ts rec^d some damage from the length of the voyage & Dampness of the place where they were stowed on Ship-Board; but I hope to get them repaired & to find out the Scales of some of them. Few things Sir w^d make me more happy than to have an opportunity afforded me of being of some use to you here, or, at least, of showing my Zeal, & the sense I have of the uncommon assiduity with wch you have executed a troublesome Commission.

To Mrs Thrale[1]   St Martin's Street,
                                          1 November 1777

ALS (Rylands, English MS 545, no. 1).

                                          St Martin's Street.

Dear Madam.

If my long Silence has *traust* into your head any suggestions of my Friendship being like that of many others, only local & temporary, believe them not; for something tells me Daily that however business, disagreeable Situations, or a relaxed & flaccid Mind may prevent me from writing, you will never be forgotten. When I was at Bright^n,[2] I was too happy to write; Time flew as smooth & swift as the *Glid*[3] we saw in our last ride. One Peg lower w^d perhaps have made me wish

---

[1] In CB's doggerel autobiography for 1776 (*Mem.* ii. 100), he wrote: 'This year I acquaintance began with the Thrales, | Where I met with great talents 'mongst females and males: . . .'. CB's meeting with Henry Thrale (*c.*1728–81), wealthy brewer and MP for Southwark, took place at a dinner party given by Sir Joshua Reynolds on 8 Jan. 1776 (MS 'Memoranda from Pocket book', *Frag. Mem.*, Berg). Later in the year, CB was introduced to the Thrale home at Streatham, where he met Hester Lynch (Salusbury) Thrale (1741–1821), Henry Thrale's accomplished and literary wife whom he had married in 1763 (*Thraliana*, i. 136). On 12 Dec. 1776, CB journeyed to Streatham to give his first music lesson to the Thrales' eldest daughter, Hester Maria (1764–1857), called by Johnson 'Queeney'. Mrs Thrale recorded in her 'Children's Book' that Queeney had 'begun studying Musick under Dr Burney, who is justly supposed at present the first Man in Europe, & whose Instructions I have long been endeavoring to obtain for her' (Hyde, *Thrales*, p. 172).
[2] CB had travelled on 30 Sept. with the Thrales to Brighton (Clifford, p. 155), and stayed with them for a fortnight, returning to London on 12 Oct. (Johnson *Letters*, ii. 221). At Brighton, Mrs Thrale had presented a gold pen to CB, who duly wrote an appreciative poem dated 7 Oct.: 'To Mrs Thrale on her presenting the Author with a Gold Pen' (*Thraliana*, i. 216; MS holograph draft in *Frag. Mem.*, Berg; MS holograph copy in 'Poetical Notebook', Osborn shelves c 33, pp. 117–18; 3 MS copies by Mrs Thrale, Rylands (Eng. MS 545, nos. 16, 16a), Yale).
On 11 Oct., while still at Brighton, on the occasion of the Thrales' fourteenth wedding anniversary, CB also presented them with some 'Stanzas on the Anniversary of M^r & Mrs Thrale's Wedding day' (Osborn: 'Poetical Notebook', shelves c 33, p. 122).
[3] The common kite, in the Shropshire dialect of CB's youth (see *The English Dialect Dictionary*, ed. J. Wright (1898–1905), under 'gled(e)').

for Pen Ink & Paper; but two or three lower have made me shudder at the thoughts of them.[4] So it is—our Reason, Resolution, & the Proofs, even of our Affection, are the Slaves of Circumstance! That we are *Journaliers* in the performance of mental as well as bodily Feats, every retailer of Saws will allow; but that there are certain *Diavolini degl'Impedimenti*, or mischievous Sylphs & Gnomes that successfully forge Fetters for Resolution, even wise Folks will deny; & yet, I seem surrounded with an Army of them, that prevent me from doing every thing I wish & intend.

> 'This erring Mortals levity may call,
> 'O blind to Truth! the Sylphs contrive it all.'[5]

You were very good ('but, tis a way you have')[6] to try to comfort poor Madam after her unfortunate Campaign on the Continent.[7] She changed her Resolution, & came to London the [day] after her Landing,[8] & the Day following we went together into Surry, for a Week. She is now in Town, but invisible: 'Tis humiliating to tell melancholy Stories ab^t one's self, & more so to hear People pretend to pity one, when we know they have no more Feeling than *Punch*.[9] I hate to think of the Trick that has been played her, & still more to talk

---

[4] For one source of CB's despondency, see n. 7. It is unlikely that by this date he had received news that his son, Charles, had been sent down from Cambridge for stealing books from the University Library. Although documentary evidence is lacking, it seems probable that CB heard of this family catastrophe in mid-November (see Lonsdale, p. 241; R. S. Walker, 'Charles Burney's Theft of Books at Cambridge', *Transactions of the Cambridge Bibliographical Society*, iii (1962), 313–26).

[5] Pope, *The Rape of the Lock*, i. 103–4.

[6] Possibly an allusion to Marlow's 'It's a way I have got' in Goldsmith's *She Stoops to Conquer*, II. i.

[7] Mrs Burney had journeyed to France in Aug. to bring back her daughter, Bessy Allen, who had been sent to school in Paris. Bessy, however, had eloped to Ypres, where on 12 Oct. she married one Samuel Meeke (d. *c.*1796). Distraught, Mrs Burney returned '*all alone*' to England, arriving at Brighton on 17 Oct. in the belief that her husband was still there with the Thrales. Mrs Thrale wrote of Mrs Burney to Johnson: 'greater, & more real Distress have I seldom seen' (Johnson *Letters*, ii. 225; see also *ED* ii. 284; *HFB*, pp. 70–2; Lonsdale, pp. 240–1; *JL* iii. 4 n.).

[8] Mrs Thrale's letter of 18 Oct. from Brighton to Johnson explains Mrs Burney's 'Resolution': 'She *did* come yesterday, expecting to find the D^r with us, but he was gone; ... but She resolved not to go home however, but to a Friend's House where She would stay She said till her Husband came to fetch her, for She could not bear to go tell *her Story* among his Girls—& receive their Consolations' (Johnson *Letters*, ii. 225).

On their reunion, CB composed for his wife an affectionate poem, 'On My Wife's Birth Day. Octr 20th 1777', the holograph draft of which is preserved in the Osborn Collection. One stanza reads:

> May black ingratitude no more torment
> Or Reminiscence petrify thy heart!
> May fruitless Sorrow ne'er deplore the Event
> Which late bereav'd thee of so dear a part.

[9] Dr Johnson commented on Mrs Burney's 'calamity' in similar vein in a letter to Mrs Thrale dated 22 Oct. (Johnson *Letters*, ii. 226).

about it. When things go wrong, I find relief from nothing so much as Silence and Sulkiness.

While I was out of Town this last Time, I made a Visit to Lord Sandwich at Hampton, of 3 Days, & was ill of a Fever the whole Time. His Lord^{p's} is a good house for the Robust & the Jolly, but a very bad Hospital.[10] If I had not crawled to Mrs Garrick[11] to beg a paper of James's Powders,[12] I might have been there now, or in my Grave.

I very much want some Bright^n news, however; for one can read, you know, & still be silent & sulky—& yet a Letter from you w^d let me be neither.[13]—'Confidence begets Confidence'—Chearfulness, chearfulness, &c &c[14]—I wish you were at Streatham:[15] I w^d then fly thither, & if the foul Fiend followed me, you w^d instantly send him a packing.—You w^d ferment Pleasanter Ideas, & set me a prating as usual—& we'd have our Pastoral, & our Rondeau again; *that's* what we w^d. And let those be wise that will. My Master,[16] though he pummels one sometimes has a good bottom, & though he does not come into all one's *Schto-fe* at once, he lets one defend one's self, without remembering it the next Day, or indeed the Next Hour. I know not how it is but I feel less sore after a beating from him than any one else who can hit hard.

But the Comic opera you talk of?[17] If I had been admitted of the

[10] From 1775 to 1780, Lord Sandwich occupied 'a retired mansion . . . on the edge of Hampton Green' (J. Cradock, *Literary and Miscellaneous Memoirs* (1826), i. 153), to which he and his mistress, Martha Ray (*c.*1745–79), frequently withdrew (H. Ripley, *The History and Topography of Hampton-on-Thames* (1884), pp. 11, 90; G. D. Heath, *Hampton Court House*, Borough of Twickenham Local History Society, Paper no. 20 (1971), pp. 6–7). For an account of Sandwich's heartiness, see G. Martelli, *Jemmy Twitcher: A Life of the Fourth Earl of Sandwich, 1718–1792* (1962), pp. 84–7.

[11] For the villa at Hampton purchased by the Garricks in 1754, see Ripley, *Hampton*, pp. 12–18; and Garrick *Letters*, i. 205, n. 4. From about 1765, CB had been a frequent guest of the Garricks: '. . . of a Sat^y evening when he did not act or Sunday morning, he used to carry me with him to Hampton, and brought me back to town on Monday' (*CB Mem.* 108).

[12] The famous febrifuge patented (1746) by Robert James (1705–76), MD (1728), physician (*DNB*), contained antimony oxide powder diluted with calcium phosphate. The powder had a diaphoretic, cathartic, and, in large doses, an emetic effect. A paper of the powder contained about twenty grains, and a normal adult dose for fever was a third to a half of a paper every 6 hours (R. James, *A Dissertation on Fevers* (8th edn., 1778), pp. 135–6).

[13] Mrs Thrale's reply, containing news from Brighton, is dated 6 Nov. (Osborn; extracts in C. Hill, *The House in St. Martin's Street* (1907), pp. 189–91).

[14] Not identified.

[15] CB recounts his rapid assimilation into the intimate circle of Thrale friends at Streatham: 'After teaching Miss Thrale some time by the lesson or journey ⟨to⟩ Streatham, Mr Thrale proposed [a] . . . stipend of £100 per. Ann. for going ⟨th⟩ither once a week dining there, and returning to Town the next day as early as I pleased. This continued to the end of Mr Thrale's life' (*Frag. Mem.*, Berg).

[16] Henry Thrale. Johnson's appelation gained wide currency in the Streatham circle (Clifford, p. 65).

[17] In a letter not now preserved, Mrs Thrale had evidently complained to CB, as she had to Johnson, about a 'Dinner of Rakes' hosted by the notorious John Wilkes. Henry Thrale, despite

Junto, in my present humour, I must have begged the under-plot or serious part of the Farce: & you who well know how Mawkish that usually is, *nelle Drame Buffe*, w^d not have denied me that department. Is Mr Murphey[18] still with you?

And so you w^d neither stare at Johnny Wilkes for fear of your Eyes? nor converse with him for fear of your Mind?[19] Well, I believe I sh^d have been of your party, for even City patriots are now ashamed to be seen in his Company.[20]

I am glad you bear your Sickness[21] so heroically; if either Master *J: Acky*[22] or *Lickle Sooky*[23] sh^d come in your way at such Times, who c^d help the Consequences? They will excuse you, I dare say, if you tell them it is a present from the Young Lord of old Bachygraig.[24]

You kindly desire me to make every body I love, love You; as if you wanted help for that! I never knew you make so useless a request; & can only say that all under my Roof are already in your Chains.— Indeed if I knew any Beings who did not love you, that were at all acquainted with you, I sh^d hate them. When I put Comp^{ts} to my

---

his wife's valiant efforts to 'keep him out of such Company', had attended. See Johnson *Letters*, ii. 225; Clifford, p. 156; Hyde, *Thrales*, p. 194.

[18] Arthur Murphy (1727–1805), Irish lawyer, author, dramatist, and actor (*DNB*), was an old friend of Henry Thrale's from his bachelor days. Murphy had introduced Dr Johnson to the Thrales (Clifford, pp. 53–5). When Murphy joined the party at Brighton, Mrs Thrale reported to Johnson (11 Oct.) that he and CB 'like one another much' (Johnson *Letters*, ii. 221). In her reply of 6 Nov. to CB, Mrs Thrale wrote: 'Mr Murphy leaves ... tomorrow'.

[19] John Wilkes was notoriously ugly. Mrs Thrale related to Johnson her meeting with Wilkes at Brighton in her letter of 16 Oct.: 'I have seen the famous J. Wilkes, he came hither to wait on Murphy: I like him not: he professed himself a Lyar and an Infidel, and I see no Merit in being either' (Johnson *Letters*, ii. 224).

[20] Wilkes's popularity with the voters of the City of London suffered a decline between 1776 and 1779. Staggering under debts incurred during his Lord Mayoralty of London (1774–5), Wilkes had scandalized his followers by offering himself in 1776 for the lucrative Chamberlain-ship of London. He was twice defeated in 1776, and again in summer 1777, polling only 1,228 votes against 2,132. In these repeated bids against the incumbent Chamberlain, Wilkes further dismayed his supporters, for the office was traditionally held for life. On his fifth attempt, Wilkes finally became Chamberlain in 1779 (see H. Bleackley, *Life of John Wilkes* (1917), pp. 306–13).

In late 1776, CB had himself dined with Wilkes. Samuel Crisp mocked CB for it in a letter dated 17 Dec. 1776 (Osborn and Berg): 'Well Done Burney!—Crack'd two Bottles with Catiline! what a Strange power of Fascination he must possess! to transform a Milksop, that I have seen almost kick at the proposal of a second Glass, into a bottle Companion! I must no longer wonder at his leading fat-headed, Turtle-eating Aldermen by the Nose—'.

[21] Mrs Thrale was in early pregnancy (see Hyde, *Thrales*, pp. 189–90, 196, 198).

[22] Probably CB's own son, Richard Thomas, now aged nearly 9, a very beautiful child, and a great favourite of Mrs Thrale, who proposed to CB at about this time that she 'would have his little Son *Dick* to spend some holy days ... with my Children' (*Thraliana*, i. 219).

[23] Mrs Thrale's second surviving daughter, Susanna Arabella (1770–1858), Dr Johnson's favourite (Johnson *Letters*, ii. 219–20), now aged 7, pined after young Dick Burney (*Thraliana*, i. 423, 443, 481–2).

[24] Throughout her pregnancy, Mrs Thrale 'prayed hard for a Son' (Hyde, *Thrales*, p. 190), who would inherit her own Salusbury family estate of Bach-y-Graig in Flintshire, North Wales, with its valuable forest of 15,000 oak trees (*Thraliana*, i. 275–6, 315–18, 320; Clifford, pp. 128–9).

Master into your hands, who know how dearly he loves them, I need not fear his being over-dosed. Pray administer to him just as many as you can get him to swallow without Nausea.[25] To Miss Thrale,[26] Miss Owen,[27] & Mr Cotton[28] you may perhaps be a little more liberal.—But, Mercy on us! you have peradventure been all carried away in the high wind, & are now, like Micromégas, travelling from Planet to Planet, pour achever de se former l'*Esprit et le Cœur*.[29] If that shd be the Case, when you have done frisking about, if you find your way back to Brightn you will probably find this Letter there, & perhaps, in answering it favour me with some Acct of your adventures, & future designs.[30] I want to know when you intend turning your Faces towards Streatham, & les Hôtes de vos bois? Whether you have heard from Miss Stretfield?[31] Whether Mr Seward has found his way to Brightn?[32]

---

[25] Mrs Thrale wrote in reply (6 Nov.): 'Mr Thrale accepts your *good* Words, and says I may send you some in return; the *rough* Ones have been liberally bestowed on Mr Murphy—but my Master has a real Regard for both of you, only somewhat an *odd* way of shewing it.—'

[26] Hester Maria ('Queeney') Thrale (see n. 1).

[27] Margaret Owen (1743–1816), from Penrhos, distant cousin and childhood playmate of Mrs Thrale, known in the Streatham circle as Peggy Owen. Fanny Burney observed, '[she] is good-humoured and *sensible enough*; she is a sort of butt, and, as such, a general favourite' (*ED* ii. 152). Johnson thought her 'empty-headed' (Hill–Powell, iii. 48, 478). A 'woman of family and fortune' (*Mem.* ii. 88), she was constantly in the company of Mrs Thrale, who considered Peggy a possible second wife for her husband should Mrs Thrale die in childbirth (Clifford, pp. 140, 148–51; Hyde, *Thrales*, pp. 157, 175). For Peggy Owen's mistaken notion (and Queeney Thrale's ghastly pun thereon) that the Burneys were of Irish origin, see *Thraliana*, i. 49–50 and Hyde, *Thrales*, p. 172.

[28] Thomas Cotton (d. 1820), civil servant, held a clerkship in the Office of the Treasury (*CCR*, 1777, p. 94). He was later promoted a Chief Clerk (*GM* xc (1820)², 477). Cotton, a first cousin to Mrs Thrale on her maternal side, maintained at the time of the present letter cordial relations with the Thrales (see Hyde, *Thrales*, pp. 147, 178, 204, 217; *Thraliana*, i. 103–4, 193, 348, 356).

[29] The hero of Voltaire's satirical tale, *Micromégas* (1752), banished from the court of his native planet, Sirius, 'se mit à voyager de Planète en Planète pour achever de se former l'*esprit et le cœur*, comme l'on dit' (see I. O. Wade, *Voltaire's Micromégas, a Study in the Fusion of Science, Myth, and Art* (Princeton, 1950), pp. 22–3, 121). The phrase ridiculed by Voltaire and quoted by CB is drawn from the title of Charles Rollin (1661–1741), *De la manière d'enseigner et d'étudier les belles-lettres, par rapport à l'esprit et au cœur* (1726–8), a celebrated pedagogical treatise generally called the *Traité des études*. CB's copy of *Micromégas* is listed as lot 1918 in *Cat. Misc. Lib.*

[30] Mrs Thrale answered (6 Nov.) in part: 'The Balls are over, and the Rooms expire tonight; but Mr Thrale does not mean to stir till next Monday or Tuesday sevennight—we have a *Lame* Lord left, a *deaf* Gentleman, and Mr Palmer who *squints*; my Master therefore *compels* them to come in & we play at Cards in the best Parlour.'

[31] 'Miss Streatfield would suffer our Acquaintance to drop, but I who have long been a Nurse by Profession have written a short letter just to support the young Creature from falling, & I hope it will have its Effect' (ibid.). Sophia Streatfeild (1754–1835), a beauty and a scholar, had been tutored by Mrs Thrale's own mentor, Dr Arthur Collier (1707–77). The two ladies had recently met by chance at Brighton, and the acquaintance progressed rapidly into friendship (*Thraliana*, i. 323, *et passim*; Clifford, p. 168; Hyde, *Thrales*, pp. 193–4).

[32] William Seward (1747–99), author, amateur physicist, and hypochondriac (*DNB*), had introduced CB to the Thrale household (*Thraliana*, i. 136) where Seward was 'a great favourite'

&, above all whether our great & good Doctor has yet taken possession of the Comfortable bed wch I had the honour of Airing for him.[33] I fear mine is a bad Soil, for neither at Streatham, nor Bright^n, did I feel, as I ought, the Effects of those Emanations wch must escape him where so ever he resides; & which, like the beams of the Sun, sh^d fertilize, invigourate, & meliorate every Spot on which they fall. But not a Chip, a Shaving, or Diamond-filing did I pick up in either of his work-shops!—

Adieu, dear Madam, pray do me the honour to number me among your Most zealous &

faithful Servants
Chas Burney.

1st Novr 1777.

To Mrs Thrale

[St Martin's Street,
*c.*8 November 1777]

AL verse copy (Osborn: 'Poetical Notebook', shelves c 33, p. 123).
Docketed by FBA: ✳

Extract of a letter[1] to Mrs Thrale, who had complained of the fading honours of Brighthelmstone; where the whole company was reduced, one by one, to a *lame Lord*.[2]

So have I seen, but not at Streatham,
When fruits are bad, that folks have eat'em:
On Goosb'ries amber, green, & red
The humble guests have eager fed.
At first, they seek with curious pry

(Hill–Powell, iii. 123). During the summer of 1777, he toured the Highlands of Scotland, 'enkindled by our travels', as Johnson wrote to Boswell (28 June, Johnson *Letters*, ii. 181), and also journeyed in Wales where he had inspected Mrs Thrale's property, Bach-y-Graig (Hyde, *Thrales*, pp. 184–5).
[33] Johnson visited the Thrales at Brighton from 14 to 18 Nov., and returned with them on the latter date to Streatham (Johnson *Letters*, ii. 232–4).

[1] Mrs Thrale had concluded her letter to CB from Brighton of 6 Nov. (Osborn): 'Let me have one Letter more before I listen once again to the Pastoral & Rondo, and before I make you listen to the Nonsense of Your most Faithful | humble Servant | Hester: L: Thrale.' CB's compliance with this request is preserved only in these verses which he transcribed into his MS 'Poetical Notebook'.
[2] See CB to Mrs Thrale, 1 Nov. 1777, n. 30.

What's bright & blooming to the eye:
Selecting with a greedy gripe
The sweet, the clean, the plump, the ripe—
L'*Esprit de comparaison* still
Excites desire, and guides the will;
Till wither'd, flaccid, stale & crude
Alike, by turns, are suck'd & chew'd.
And, ere the poor desert is done,
'Tis *Hobson's choice*—the *maim'd* or none.

To Mrs Thrale

St Martin's Street,
11 January 1778

ALS (Yale University, BRBL: MS Vault File). Mounted.
Publ.: A. M. Broadley, *Dr. Johnson and Mrs. Thrale* (1910), pp. 127–9.

St Martin's Street.
Jany 11th 1778.

Dear Madam.

What a *way you have*[1] to make obligations of the greatest weight sit lightly on the Stomach of those who receive them at your Hands!— And then our good, great, & dear Doctor, so readily to second your Kindness, & my wish to be obliged to you both![2]—You are delightful Folks, & have so rivetted the affection of all under this Roof, who were before your willing Captives, that your names are never mentioned without such Gleams of Pleasure appearing in every Countenance; such smirking & smiling, that a by-stander, unacquainted with the Cause, w^d think us all bewitched: as, indeed, I believe we are.

My Conscience w^d not let me rest till Thursday without thanking you for all you *have* done, & Dr J. for all he so kindly *intends* to do, for our little Boy.[3] You love Children too well not to know how nearly

---

[1] See CB to Mrs Thrale, 1 Nov. 1777, n. 6.

[2] CB refers to Mrs Thrale's assistance in plans to send young Dick Burney to Winchester, where Dr Johnson's friend, Dr Joseph Warton, was Headmaster. See *ED* ii. 284–6; *Mem.* ii. 81–4; Hill–Powell, iii. 367; Clifford, p. 158; Lonsdale, p. 242. See also CB to Mrs Thrale, 25 [Sept. 1778].

[3] Johnson needed much prodding to bestir himself 'to write a recommendatory letter' for Dick, as Mrs Thrale was to relate in her *Anecdotes of the late Samuel Johnson, LL.D.* (1786): '. . . after he had faithfully promised to do this prodigious feat before we met again—Do not forget dear Dick, Sir, said I, as he went out of the coach: he turned back, stood still two minutes on the carriage-step—"When I have written my letter for Dick, I may hang myself, mayn't I?"—and turned away in a very ill humour indeed' (*Johnsonian Miscellanies*, ed. G. B. Hill, (Oxford, 1897), i. 280).

Benefits conferred on them come to a Parent's Heart. Heaven grant that the Ricciardetto[4] may become worthy of such Patronage!

I am wholly in Leading-Strings as to the disposal of this Dicky-Bird. He shall certainly go no more to Hendon,[5] if he can be received at Winchester after the Holydays. As I am entirely ignorant of the Institution, I know not at what Age, upon what Notice, or what Conditions Children are admitted. Something makes me fear there may not be an immediate vacancy, & in that Case, what is to be done? I think Dr J. said he w^d be rec^d as a Boarder, by Dr Warton[6]—But, why do I talk of things beyond my Ken? The business is in such excellent Hands that it cannot go amiss, and I comfort myself, & quiet all Doubts with that Consideration.

But now, to transfer my Thoughts in a more particular Manner to Streatham: Do you know, my good Mad^m, that I returned from that dear Habitation more dissatisfied with myself than usual, at the thoughts of the little Service I had been able to do Miss T. during my last Visit? It is neither pleasant to a Pupil to hear, nor a Preceptor to tell Faults, in *Public*—Pray, if you can, let us fight our A, B, C-Battles in private, next Time. Miss B——ns[7] are very goodnatured Girls, & as little in the way as Possible; but yet it is not easy for Miss T. or myself

Johnson evidently got round to writing the letter about 25 Jan., for Warton's reply (MS Winchester College) is dated 27 Jan. See also Lonsdale, p. 242.

[4] Niccolò Forteguerri (1674–1735) wrote a poem entitled *Ricciardetto* ([Venice], 1738), in the burlesque genre devised by Francesco Berni (*c.*1497–1535). For Mrs Thrale's punning jest to which CB here makes reference, see *Thraliana*, i. 219.

[5] At this period there were two elementary schools in Hendon, Middlesex: an old charity school in existence since 1685, and a second school founded in 1766 by one John Bennett (d. 1777) who built his schoolhouse on a plot of waste ground donated by David Garrick, owner of Hendon Manor and its estates. In view of the keen interest Garrick took in CB and his family, it seems most likely that Dick was a pupil in Bennett's school. See G. C. Tyack, 'Hendon' in *The Victoria History of the Counties of England. A History of Middlesex*, vol. v. (1976), pp. 43–4, 47; F. Hitchin-Kemp, 'David Garrick and Hendon', *Notes and Queries*, clxiii (1932), 310–11; D. Lysons, *The Environs of London*, vol. iii (1795), p. 20.

[6] The Headmaster of Winchester, Dr Joseph Warton, explained the process of admission to scholarships at the school in his letter to Dr Johnson of 27 Jan. (MS Winchester College): 'There are six Electors—the Warden of New Coll. the Warden of Winchester Coll. myself, our Sub-warden, & two fellows annually elected at New College called Posers. Each of these six electors has an equal power of Nomination. There are 70 fellows of New College, & 70 Scholars of this college from whence, when Vacancies happen, the Oxford college is supplied. But you easily see that there do not happen Vacancies enough at New College to provide for all *our* 70 Scholars.... I shall be very glad to receive Dr Burney's Son into my House till a Vacancy happens.'

Dick Burney clearly failed to obtain a scholarship on the Foundation of Winchester College, and his association with Warton's house was of short duration. See CB to Mrs Thrale, 25 [Sept. 1778].

[7] One of these 'goodnatured Girls' may be tentatively identified as Fanny Browne (*fl.* 1777–1811), of Wimbledon, an intimate of the Streatham household (*Thraliana*, i. 222; Hyde, *Thrales*, pp. 214, 217). She had a 'wild, careless, giddy manner, ... loud hearty laugh, and general negligence of appearance' (*DL* i. 234), eloped in 1779, and disappears from the Johnsonian circle (see *Thraliana*, i. 407; and *DL* i, *passim*).

to forget that they are in the Room. When *real Business* is over, I shall rejoice to talk, laugh, sing, or play with them, till the Instant I am obliged to depart—But let our downright *Drumming* be first finished.

You must by this Time have seen, my dear Madam, that the Language of Music, like every other that has been cultivated, has its Letters, Syllables, Words, Phrases, & Periods; with Grammatical Difficulties equivalent to those of Declensions, Conjugations, Syntax, &c. The *Theory* of these is an Employment for the *Head*, only; but The *Practice* upon Instruments, Embarrasses the *Hand* as much as the Pronunciation of a new Speech does the Tongue. If my Utility in smoothing the road for my Fair Pupil to Musical knowledge & Abilities did but correspond wth my Zeal, she would then be exempted from that Progressive Drudgery to wch even Orpheus & Amphion must have been obliged to submit—But I forget that I am writing, & my Pen prattles away your Time about *Tweedledum* & *Tweedledee*[8] with as much sober sadness as if you were a Musical Rapturist, an Enthusiastic *Dilettante*—Perdona! amica mia Colendissima! & remember that as yours was the first Letter of mere business wth wch you have honoured me,[9] so this is the first from me to you without attempts at *Badinage*; but if any Terrestrial Concerns merit seriousness, & awaken sensibility, it must be such as relate to our Children; such Kindness as yours & our revered Friend Dr Johnson's; & such Gratitude as that of, dear Madam,

> your obliged and
> most obedient servant.
> Chas Burney.

To Mrs Thrale

[St Martin's Street],
22 February [1778][1]

AL (Rylands, English MS 545, no. 2).

To cut short all *Hes* & *Shes*, & equivocal Relatives, let me address you, Dear Mad^m, in the 1st person, & tell you that tho' I gave the

---

[8] See John Byrom (1692–1763), 'Epigram on the Feuds between Handel and Bononcini', in *Miscellaneous Poems* (Manchester, 1773), i. 343–4: 'Strange all this Difference should be, | 'Twixt Tweedle-dum and Tweedle-dee!' See also *OED*, under 'Tweedle–'.

[9] Mrs Thrale's letter does not appear to have survived.

[1] The year is determined by 22 Feb. falling on a Sunday only in 1778 during the years of CB's intimacy with Mrs Thrale. For seven weeks, from late Jan. to the first week in Mar. 1778, the Thrales stayed in London (Clifford, p. 157; Hyde, *Thrales*, pp. 198–200). CB's reference to Mrs Thrale's rash also confirms the date of the present letter. Mrs Thrale makes reference to 'this tingling Rash' in a letter of 20 Feb. 1778 to Johnson (see Johnson *Letters*, ii. 244).

Thing up last Night, & stayed at Home to Coddle my cold instead of
going to the Opera,[2] and that I have been snivelling & sulking at
Home all the Morning, I neither can nor will relinquish the design of
waiting on you to Night; & if you sh^d not have a Creature with you,
why so much the better—for I never remember our being in want of
Subjects or Words for Conversation—& now we are both *invalidisk*,
we may *con Ailments* you know. I hope y^r Rash is literally walked off, &
not retired into yourself.—I shall neither detain you nor your Mercury
longer than to say à l'Honneur de vous voir.—O yes, but I must say a
Word for Mad^m & the Girls, or they'll tear my Eyes out.—They beg
you to accept of their best Respects & the L^d knows what besides—
but I must say Addio—

Sunday 22^d Feb.

To Mrs Thrale

[St Martin's Street,
4 March 1778][1]

ALS (Rylands, English MS 545, no. 10).
Addressed: To ¦ Mrs Thrale.   *Endorsed:* Dr Char^s Burney.

What a too good Creature you are to enquire after your seemingly
Naughty Friend![2] Well, but 'tis now near one & I am still in my Robe
de Chambre—But you know *that* gives one an opportunity of saying
foolish things—indeed I fully intended doing *wise* ones this Morning—
Mr Wyatt[3] came to me wth his *Lancelot*[4] in his Hand, for I engaged him
last Night by your orders to come & use his friendly Dagger—but,
behold! on feeling my Pulse he told me I was too low already, & that
he w^d not advise bleeding at present—I took something Cooling last

---

[2] Sacchini's *Erifile* was performed at the Opera on Sat. 21 Feb. (*The London Stage*, v. i. 149).

[1] External and internal evidence points to 4 Mar. 1778 as the date of this letter. CB's comments
on Mrs Thrale's verses (see n. 7), and the paragraph in the *Morning Post* about Johnson's illness
(see n. 10), reply to a letter from Mrs Thrale, Friday 27 Feb. [1778], (Platnauer). The presence
of Mrs Thrale's 'Messenger' on CB's doorstep indicates that the Thrales were still in town. They
returned to Streatham on or before Saturday 7 Mar. (Hyde, *Thrales*, p. 198). The Wednesday
during the intervening week was 4 Mar.

[2] Mrs Thrale's messenger had evidently brought to CB an enquiry from her about his health.
She had written in her letter of Friday 27 Feb.: 'do not plague yourself to answer all this Folly, &
say *see*? here's another *Letter* for me to write—no Peace &c.' CB clearly took Mrs Thrale at her
word, and had still made no reply by Wednesday.

[3] Probably John Wyatt (*fl.* 1777–90), FRS (1778), listed as a surgeon at the Middlesex
Hospital in *CCR*, 1779, p. 230. He appears to have resided in Essex Street, the Strand (P. Barfoot
and J. Wilkes, *The Universal British Directory of Trade and Commerce*, vol. i (1790), p. 447). Another
John Wyatt, of Mansell Street, Goodman's Fields, also practised surgery in London at this time
(ibid., p. 451; see also Garrick *Letters*, i. 367–8).

[4] *OED*, under 'lancelet', recognizes CB's spelling as an alternative.

Night, & hope to do well yet—& *so much Care*[5] ought to be rewarded; for here I have been Idle a whole blessed Morning.—If anything w^d make one fond of Life, it must be such Fr^{ds} as You, who interest themselves ab^t one, & render Existence desirable by telling one they wish its Continuance.[6]—The plagues, the pains, the vexatious & difficult roads one meets wth in this sublunary Journey, will not break my Spirit, as I am now an *old Traveller*, if that Comfort remains.

Thank you many many Times for your pretty Verses.[7] They are delightful—clean, neat, & happy—you must never again talk to me of Care[8]—where confidence is placed, you[r] bureau is more likely to betray you than me—that may be broke open—but who can pick a heart-lock?—very few can mine—much fewer than are likely to attempt your bureau—

Our dear Fr^d at Bolt's Court was dosing in his Chair upstairs when I called last Night: so I did not see him—but I chatted ½ an hour with Mrs Williams,[9] forbidding every one to disturb him by any Information of my Visit—He had been at a full dose of Opium, again—wch says he suffered previously—But thank God not a word more of the Paragraph in the Morn^g Post[10] is true than we have long known, to our great Sorrow.—He is *not well*—nor perhaps ever will be much better than he has been for some time past—& *that* is melancholy & heart-breaking to us who so truely Love & honour him. — —

Addio—Mad^m is gone to Bethnal Green,[11] but charged me wth millions of Respects & Comp^{ts}—& Susan if she was not ashamed to be so troublesome to both, w^d do the same—poor Fan has a worse cold than mine.—I am ashamed to keep y^r Messenger longer or w^d

[5] See n. 6.

[6] Mrs Thrale had written in her letter of 27 Feb.: '... take care of your health, pray do, for the sake of your truly amiable Family, for your Friends sakes, & if you loved Flattery half as well as I should love to flatter you, I could add for the sake of the *World* in general; but I hope you would rather I should say for the Sake of your Friends at *Stretham*'.

[7] Enclosed in her letter of 27 Feb., Mrs Thrale had sent CB her verse translation of an epigram attributed to the French classical scholar Claudius Salmasius (1588–1653). The translation is included in *Thraliana*, i. 234.

[8] In sending her verses, Mrs Thrale had cautioned: 'I *think* you have too much regard for me to let any Nonsense of mine go among People less partial to me than yourself, so I will say no more of the *Schtoffe*.'

[9] Anna Williams (1706–83), blind poetess who lived in Johnson's house at 8 Bolt Court (*DNB*).

[10] 'It is with infinite concern we hear that the public is likely to suffer an irreparable loss, by the death of that great Luminary of the English language, Dr. Johnson, the Author of the celebrated dictionary, he being now attended by Dr. Jebb, without the smallest hopes of ever restoring him to a tolerable state of health' (*Morning Post*, 27 Feb. 1778). Mrs Thrale had commented in her letter of 27 Feb.: 'See how the people are killing poor dear Johnson in the Morning Post! it shocked *me* tho' I knew it could not hurt *him*.' The *Morning Post* news item was picked up by the *Public Advertiser* the next day, but refuted in the *London Chronicle*, 26–8 Feb. 1778. See also Hill–Powell, iii. 221–2, 515; Helen L. McGuffie, *Samuel Johnson in the British Press, 1749–1784, a Chronological Checklist* (New York, 1976), p. 218.

[11] Mrs Burney's trip to Bethnal Green is not otherwise explained.

carry on the Chat much further—but—I must, & ought to run away as I did yesterday—so once more addio—& portez vous bien—

C.B.

Wed^y Noon

To Mrs Thrale

Turnham Green,
8 March 1778

ALS (Rylands, English MS 545, no. 4).

Turnham Green.[1] Sunday
8th Mar. 1778—

Why, what a Lady Bountiful you are! most People content themselves & others by giving *Boxes* & *Turkies* at X^{mas}; but you are an endless Giver[2]—never waiting for Times, Seasons, or occasions, but making them at your pleasure. It was doubly kind of you to tell us that you were arrived at dear Str[e]atham both *safe* & *well*[3]—I hope to God I shall find you so on friday next.—What weather have the poor Girls & I had for our wild expedition—to be shut up in a house worse than one's own, without usual Conveniences & Comforts—& without appetite to be always in duty bound to be talking of eating & drinking for the Good of others, is queer & unpleasant.[4] I had almost given up all thoughts of pursuing the Idea of coming hither, till on my arrival at home your Note was a Stimulus wch cured me of the *Poltronnerie* of retreat.—I brought Books with me without curiosity to look in them—I brought writing Work, but was too *lache* to meddle with it. The few paltry Sprigs of Laurel I sometimes fancied I saw trembling before me in some degree of Verdure, have seemed shrivelled & withered so much of late, that I came hither to *Turn'em Green*—but alas! in vain, as I shall shew you over the Leaf. However, you will see at the same time how I amused myself here, & what was the chief Subject of Contemplation to dear Mad^m your obliged & affectionate Servt

Chas Burney.

[1] CB's friend, the editor of the *Monthly Review*, Ralph Griffiths (1720–1803), resided at Turnham Green, in a mansion called Linden House (T. Faulkner, *The History and Antiquities of Brentford, Ealing, & Chiswick* (1845), pp. 466–7; *DNB*).

[2] Mrs Thrale's gift may have been a gold-headed cane, in gratitude for which CB penned a poem, 'On receiving from her a Gold-headed Cane, immediately after a severe fit of Sickness' (MS 'Poetical Notebook', Osborn shelves c 33, p. 119).

[3] Mrs Thrale's letter is not preserved. The Thrales returned to Streatham at the end of the first week in Mar., probably on the 7th (see *Thraliana*, i. 234; Hyde, *Thrales*, pp. 198, 200).

[4] 'Dr Griffiths was a steady advocate of literature; a firm friend, a cordial lover of the enjoyments of domestic happiness, and a zealous and successful promoter of the charms of social intercourse' (J. Nichols, *Literary Anecdotes of the Eighteenth Century* (1812–15), iii. 507).

To Mrs Thrale.[5]

Not more the hungry pilf'ring wretch
His brain can rack, or fancy stretch
How best his neighbour's Goods to seize
Than You, your Friends to serve & please.
Forever on the watch to find
New ways & means their hearts to bind
You eager seek with Argus' pry
Each wish to know, & want supply.
   When Wealth is lodged in hands like yours
With patience Envy's self endures
The Serpents which her heart devour
At sight of such superior pow'r.
Humiliation ne'er corrodes
The Mind of those your bounty loads
But grateful Souls your Boons receive
With Joy as pure as you can give
Proud of the Notice you bestow
Which Kindness only taught to flow.
While some, to whom Fate grants the purse
Contrive to make each gift a curse;
And Conflicts raise in ev'ry breast
Whether to love or to detest
The Cold, ungraceful, clumsy hand
Which Pride & Insolence expand.
   Insolvent, yet I ne'er repine
At Favours heap'd on me & mine,
And though both numerous & great
They no remorse or shame create
For, by the Manner you bestow
The Hearts acquire so warm a glow
Of all who benefits rece[i]ve
As makes them feel like those who give.
   La Rochefoucault has sourly said
That 'Man, by selfishness misled,
Sees those he has serv'd with more delight
Than such as to his thanks have right.'[6]
However false the Maxim be,
As far as *I* can feel or see,
I most devoutly wish that *You*
May ever find the Doctrine true,

---

[5] This poem, entitled 'On her Munificence', is also included in CB's MS 'Poetical Notebook', pp. 120–1 (Osborn: shelves c 33).

And that to Friendship what you give
May prove a strong provocative
And make you eager wish to spy
The Joy that sparkles in the Eye
Tho' vulgar praises to elude
You silence prating Gratitude.

To Padre Martini   [St Martin's Street],
                                        22 June 1778

ALS (Bologna: I.1.28).
Publ.: in English translation: C. S. Terry, *John Christian Bach* (2nd edn., 1967), pp. 159–60); Brofsky, pp. 328–30.

Reverendissimo Padre e Pad^ne mio Colendissimo.

Siccome niente mi sia più prezioso della cara rimembranza di V. Paternità la sua de' 13 Gennaro[1] non fin adesso sarebbe restata senza Risposta, se io non fossi stato impedito dell'imbarazzo di tanti affari varij e inevitabili. Ma ora trovandomi un poco meno impiegato, e stimolato dall'occasione, che si presenta di servirmi della cortesia dell'amabile Signore Roncaglia,[2] chi fa conto di partirsi senz'indugio per Bologna; in verita resterei senza scusa s'io omessi piu d'assicurarla del mio rispetto, é venerazione e di renderle le grazie debite del caro dono del suo stimatissimo *Saggio di Contrāpunto*;[3] un'opera per la quale io sento la più grande impazienza—l'esemplare destinato a me, e commesso alla cura del Signore Vergani,[4] non m'e ancora capitato

---

[6] François (1613–80), duc de La Rochefoucauld, author and moralist, first published his celebrated *Réflexions ou sentences et maximes morales* in Paris in 1665. CB paraphrases Maxim No. 558 in the standard numbering: 'Nous aimons mieux voir ceux à qui nous faisons du bien que ceux qui nous en font', which first appeared in the posthumous 1693 edition of the *Maximes* (*Œuvres complètes*, éd. Pléiade (1964), p. 482). CB owned a copy of the English translation of La Rochefoucauld published in London (1706), under the title *Moral Reflections and Maxims, ... Newly made English from the Paris Edition*. The volume fetched sixpence at the dispersal of his library (*Cat. Misc. Lib.*, lot 1518).

[1] Padre Martini's letter, thanking CB for the first volume of the *History of Music*, dated Bologna 13 Jan. 1778, is preserved in the Osborn Collection.

[2] Francesco Roncaglia (*c.*1750–*c.*1800), castrato, 'of the Bologna school' (*Hist. Mus.* iv. 508; Mercer, ii. 886), had just completed his first season at the London Opera (*The London Stage*, v. i. 112). See Fétis; A. Heriot, *The Castrati in Opera* (1956), pp. 177–8.

[3] Padre Martini had written in his letter of 13 Jan.: 'Procurarò per mezzo del Sig. Vergani spedirle i due Tomi della mia Opera: Saggio di Contrappunto.' Martini's two-volume collection of contrapuntal models, *Esemplare o sia saggio fondamentale pratico di contrappunto sopra il canto fermo* (Bologna, 1774–5), is listed in 'Cat. Fac. Mus.', item 96.

[4] Possibly Angelo Vergani (d. *c.*1813), Italian grammarian (Michaud).

alle mani; Ma spero che fra poco la terrò poi che ne hò bisogno grandissimo, ni posso per mezzo di Libraro alcuno in questo paese procurarlo per molti mesi.

Il Tomo terzo di sua dotta e inestimabile Historia[5] mi sarebbe della piu grande utilita nella Fabbrica della mia se fosse ancora dato alla luce. Spero che l'impatienza del Pùbblico, come quella di me stesso saranno subito sodisfatte dall'apparenza di quella opera pregiatissima.

Se fossi stato avertito più a tempo del proposito del Signore Roncaglia d'andare a Bologna subitamente mi sarei tenuto molto onorato della sua richiesta lusinghiera del mio ritratto.[6] Spero pero fra poco di poter trovar l'occasione di mandarnele qualche disegno rassomigliante. Hò fatta l'ambasciata sua al Signor Bach,[7] il quale secondo il suo promesso s'é fatto depingere.

S'assicuri, Signore mio Rev[issimo] delle mie supplicazioni a Dio, congiunte con quelle di ogni fautore di musica, Erudizione è Virtù, che la sua Providenza le conceda, Vita, Salute, e perseveranza, per compire al suo bel agio, la sua impresa stupenda, & rendere così cari alla posterità il suo nome e Carattere come sono a quest'ora Rev[mo] & Degnissimo mio Padre al di V. P[a]

Londra li 22. Giugno 1778
Um° dev° & obligat° Servidore
Carlo Burney.

To Padre Martini

[St Martin's Street],
29 June 1778

ALS (Bologna: I.1.29).
Addressed: Al Reverendissimo, Colendissimo, e molto | Rinomato Padre Martini. | Minor Conventuale | A Bologna. | *Italy.*   *Docketed by* ?: pp[sh] Wishart   *Also* AL draft (Osborn), of the second paragraph of the letter only.   *Docketed by* CB:

[5] The third volume of Martini's *Storia della musica* appeared in 1781.
[6] Padre Martini, requesting that a likeness of CB should be sent him, had explained in his letter of 13 Jan. that he was collecting portraits of eminent ancient and modern musicians. Almost 6 years were to pass before he received in late 1783 one of the copies of Reynolds's portrait of CB executed by Edward Francesco Burney. See CB to Charles Burney, 25 Feb. 1781, n. 28.
[7] i.e. J. C. (the 'London') Bach. Martini had written, 'Se ha ocasione di vedere il Sig. Bach, li dica si ricordi sollecitare a spedirmi il suo Ritratto, come lo pregai tempo fà.' J. C. Bach had been a pupil of Padre Martini in the 1750s (see CB's MS 'Materials Towards the History of German Music & Musicians' (Osborn: shelves c 100, pp. 23–4, 56); Terry, *Bach*, pp. 14–50). A copy of Thomas Gainsborough's (1727–88) portrait of Bach was duly dispatched under Roncaglia's care to Padre Martini (J. C. Bach to Martini, 28 July 1778 (Bologna, MS 1. 24.86), English translation in Terry, *Bach*, p. 160). The painting now hangs in the Civico Museo Bibliografico Musicale, Bologna.

Biglietto al ˡ Padre Martini ˡ Giugno 1778   *Publ.:* Brofsky, p. 330, in English
translation, omitting the postscript.

Reverendissimo Padre e Pad^ne mio Colendissimo.

Avendo scritto una Lettera pochi giorni fà alla Sua Paternità per
favore del Sig^r Roncaglia, ringraziandola pel sua bontà nel mandarmi
graziosamente il suo eccellentiss^mo Saggio di Contrãponta, il quale
non è ancora ricevuto, hò gran pauro che questo Biglietto sara di
sproposito. Ma avendo scordato di fare a V.R. una richiesta di pre-
mura, io preso la confidenza di pregarla perdonarmi questa Seconda
Lettera.

Se il Reverendo e molto Venerato Padre vorrebbe farmi la grazia
d'instrurmi, per la posta, della differenza fra il *Canto Ambrosiano* ed il
Gregoriano,[1] mi sarebbe di grandiss^mo servitio nel componimento della
mia Storia della Musica. Gli Autori Musicali non parlano chiaramente
nè del Canto Ambrosiano antico, nè di quello che si pratica nel Duomo di
Milano adesso; òve si dice che la maniera di cantar il Sant'Uffizio
all'ambrosiana è conservata nella sua pristina purità.[2] Ma io non sò se
i tuoni o siano i modi Ecclesiastici Ambrosiani sono otto, come quelli
del Canto Gregoriano, nè se la differenza consiste negli Chiavi, Cantilena, ò Finali dei stessi tuoni. Un brevissimo Esempio scritto nelle
note, di questa differenza è una grazia che non ho corraggio di sperar
della di lei bontà, ma se non sarebbe darla troppo fastidio, prenderebbe
la licenza di pregarla di solvere questi dubbij al suo bell'agio in quella
maniera che a lei sarà più commodo. Con pieno Rispetto mi dichiaro
di V^a P^a

Londra 29 Giugno. ˡ 1778.
l'umilissimo e devotissimo
Servidore
Carlo Burney

Questo Biglietto era mandata alla picola posta di Londra in dirizato,
innavedutamente ad una signora Inglese[3] in luogo d'un altro che
n'era commesso alla cura del Sig^r Roncaglia chi era partito primo di
scoprire la sbaglia.

[1] CB had recently discussed this problem with Thomas Twining, who duly 'poked my marrow-
spoon into Boethius, & Franchinus, but nothing very savoury or smack-chappy has come out'
(Twining to CB, 15 Apr. 1778, BL Add. MS 39929, fos. 163–5). See *Hist. Mus.* ii. 11–14 and list
of Corrections and Additions; Mercer, i. 416–18, where CB acknowledges 'a long letter on the
subject' from Padre Martini. This letter is not preserved. See also R. Allorto, 'Il Canto Ambrosiano
nelle lettere di G. B. Martini e di Charles Burney', *Festschrift für Erich Schenk, Studien zur Musik-
wissenschaft, Beihefte der Denkmäler der Tonkunst in Österreich*, xxv (1962), 1–4; CB to Martini, 20
Oct. 1779, n. 13.
[2] One of CB's main objectives during his Italian tour was to discover how the Ambrosian
Chant was preserved and performed in Milan (*Tours*, i. 65, 76–7, 83).
[3] Mrs Thrale. See CB to Mrs Thrale, 29 June 1778, n. 1.

To Mrs Thrale[1]

[St Martin's Street],
29 June 1778

ALS (Bologna).
Addressed: Biglietto—o sia aggiunta alla ˡ Lettera del Dottor Carlo Burney ˡ Al molto reverendo Padre Martini. ˡ A Bologna.

Dear Madam

Since the departure of my Letter[2] this Morning, several awkward businesses have kicked up, w^(ch) oblige me, much against my Inclination, to postpone our Visit till Friday; when I hope we shall find you still more robust than we sh^d have done on Wed^y, & obtain your Pardon for this disagreeable procrastination, w^(ch) of itself is sufficient punishment to dear Madam,

Yours in all truth & Zeal.
Ch. Burney.

Monday Even^g ˡ 29^(th) June, 1778.

If one were to send Comp^(ts) to Mr Thrale, he w^d only pooh! pooh! at such diddle me daddle me stuff; But pray make speeches for me to Miss Thrale for not making a tender of my services at the Piano Forte on Wed^y, as I had promised to do. Oh! but the grand new Instrum^(t)[3] is ready to be sent home upon very short Notice. If my Master w^d give his royal leave it might be at Streatham before my arrival—or shall Merlin[4] keep it till you are able to quit y^r Bower,[5] & descend into the nether Regions?

[1] As CB explains in the postscript of his letter to Padre Martini of the same date, this letter to Mrs Thrale was given by mistake to Roncaglia, who then dutifully delivered it to Padre Martini. This circumstance explains the oddity of a letter from CB to Mrs Thrale (which she presumably never received) preserved in Bologna.

[2] Not preserved.

[3] Mrs Thrale had ordered a 'fine Harpsichord' for Streatham for CB's use in teaching Queeney (see Johnson *Letters*, ii. 248; Clifford, p. 166). Although Mrs Thrale calls the instrument a 'Harpsichord', it is more than likely that the 'grand new Instrum^(t)' to which CB refers was a combined pianoforte-harpsichord patented in 1774 by John Joseph Merlin (n. 4). On 4 Jan. 1781, Mrs Thrale wrote to Fanny Burney from Streatham: 'Merlin has been here to tune the Fortepianos' (Berg; *DL* i. 458). See also Rees, under 'Harpsichord'.

[4] John Joseph Merlin (1735–1803), Flemish instrument maker and inventor, had arrived in London in 1760, and stayed till his death, conducting his business from 1773 in Queen Ann Street East, and from 1783 in Prince's Street, Hanover Square. By 1775 he had become a 'great favourite' of the Burney family. Merlin was the maker of CB's harpsichord and six-octave pianoforte which graced the library at St Martin's Street. See *ED* ii, *passim*; Scholes, ii. 202–9. For a full account of Merlin's life, inventions, and relations with the Burneys, see the exhibition catalogue by Anne French, *John Joseph Merlin, the Ingenious Mechanick* (1985).

In 1777, 'when Dr. Burney first composed and published duets "à quartre mains," or for two performers on one instrument [*Four Sonatas or Duets for two Performers upon one Piano Forte or Harpsichord* (1777)], the ladies, at that time wearing hoops, which kept them at too great a

1778

To Fanny Burney[1]   [St Martin's Street, *c*.17 July 1778][2]

L extracts (Berg).

Publ.: in part, *Mem.* ii. 148; *DL* i. 45.   *Editor's note:* Extracts from CB's letter with paraphrase of other parts of it are included in a paragraph of Fanny Burney's Journal for 20 July 1778. The whole paragraph is given here, with Fanny's commentary printed in italics.

At the same Time [*19 July*],[3] *I had also a Letter from my beloved Father,—the kindest, sweetest Letter in the World!—in which he says* 'Thy *schtoff (for the* German *pronunciation of* stuff,*)* reads better the 2ᵈ Time than the first,[4] & thou hast made thy old Father Laugh & Cry at thy pleasure.' *All tenderness & goodness is his dear Heart. He tells me, too, that he found Mrs. Thrale*[5] 'full of *Ma foi's* jokes, the Captain's brutality, 'Squire Smith's gentility, Sir Clement's outdaciousness, the Branghton's vulgarity, & mother Selwyn's sharp knife, &c, &c.' *He then says that he wishes to tell Lady Hales,*[6] *though she cannot be made more fond of the Book by a personal*

distance from each other, had a harpsichord made by Merlin, expressly for duets, with six octaves; extending from the octave below double C in the base, to the octave above C in alt. in the treble' (Rees, under 'Ravalement'). This famous instrument is mentioned in CB's will as his 'large Piano Forte with additional keys at the top and bottom, originally made by Merlin, with a Compass of six Octaves, the first that was ever constructed, expressly at my desire, for duets à Quatre Mains, in 1777' (Scholes, ii. 268). CB had taken delivery of the instrument by Sept. 1777, for on 6 Oct. Twining wrote to him: 'It was unlucky that I could not have a peep at you in town; but indeed I very little expected it. I had the satisfaction however of darkening your doors, ... & I went up stairs, & tried Merlin's new inst[rument] that goes up to the clouds at one end, &·down to the center of the earth at the other' (BL Add. MS 39929, fo. 146).

⁵ Mrs Thrale had given birth on 21 June to her twelfth child, Henrietta Sophia (1778–83). See Hyde, *Thrales,* pp. 203–5. CB celebrated Henrietta Sophia's birth in a 62-line poem entitled 'June' (MS holograph, Rylands, Eng. MS 545, no. 15; MS holograph copy, 'Poetical Notebook', Osborn shelves c 33, pp. 124–6). CB probably presented the verses to Mrs Thrale at the christening of the infant at Streatham on 12 July, when Mrs Burney stood proxy for Mrs Montagu as godmother (Mrs Burney to Fanny Burney, 13 July [1778], Hyde).

¹ Fanny Burney's first novel, *Evelina,* had appeared anonymously on 29 Jan. 1778 (*EJL* iii). For the account of its success and the discovery of the identity of its author, see *HFB,* chs. 4, 5; Lonsdale, pp. 243–4. In early May Fanny had gone to Chessington to recover from illness. There she received from her sister Susan in London long accounts of the progress of *Evelina's* reception (Berg; *ED* ii. 220–54).

² See nn. 3, 5, and 6 for the circumstances that lead to the conjectural date of CB's letter.

³ Fanny had received on this date a letter from Mrs Burney written at Streatham on 13 July, but postmarked '18 IY' (Hyde).

⁴ CB had first read *Evelina* in early June, and again in early July (*ED* ii. 222, 235–46).

⁵ CB and his wife had spent a few days at Streatham from Saturday 11 to Tuesday 14 July. On the way to Streatham, CB had revealed Fanny's authorship to Mrs Burney, and on Monday 13 July to Mrs Thrale (*ED* ii. 246), who had exclaimed, 'Lᵈ! Dʳ Burney! we must be acquainted—do pray bring her with you the next time you come to Streatham' (*Frag. Mem.,* Berg).

⁶ Mary (Coussmaker) Hales, née Heyward (*c.*1741–1803), widow of Sir Thomas Pym Hales (*c.*1726–73), MP, 4th Baronet (Namier and Brooke, ii. 566). CB had first read *Evelina* in

partiality for the author. He concludes with—'I never heard of a novel writer's statue,—yet who knows?—but above all things take care of your Head; if that should be at all turned out of it's place by all this intoxicating success, what a figure would you cut upon a Pedestal! prenez y bien garde! — —'

To Mrs Thrale

[St Martin's Street], 25 [September 1778][1]

ALS (Rylands, English MS 545, no. 6).
Addressed: To | Mrs Thrale

Friday—25

You are a good Creature for thinking of us before the Dun arrived: for there is no appearance, either by Word or date,[2] that Madam's[3] Letter & a parcel to Evelina sent into the Borough[4] on wed^y had made their appearance at Streatham. You will learn from that Letter, that before my return to St Martin's Street,[5] or determination ab^t Westminster was known, Dick had been placed under the Care of a Clergyman (of the *Church of Eng^d*) whom I had ferreted out before my departure, as a proper person to keep him out of Idleness till he went into Yorkshire. And now, as he has been learning a different Grammar from that used at Westminster, I think it will be for his advantage to work at the Books used in that School, with the assistance of Mr Pitt,[6] the Gentⁿ mentioned above, who is Curate of St George's Church Han^r Square, & has 5 or 6 Children ab^t the Age of Dick, at £100 p^r

company with Lady Hales and her daughter by her first marriage, Catherine Elizabeth Coussmaker (*fl.* 1764–1803). See *ED* ii. 223–32; *JL* i. 164 n. 54.
On his return home from Streatham on 14 July, CB had said to Susan Burney, '"I suppose Fanny'll give me leave to tell her secret to L^y Hales"—I tried to dissuade him—but don't know whether I succeeded' (Susan to Fanny Burney, 16–19 July [1778], Berg; *ED* ii. 247).

[1] CB's use of 'Evelina', referring to Fanny and her stay at Streatham, gives the year; and 'Friday—25' gives the month of this letter.
[2] Mrs Thrale was notorious for not dating her letters. CB replies here to an undated letter from Mrs Thrale, published in A. M. Broadley, *Doctor Johnson and Mrs. Thrale* (1910), pp. 129–30, which may now be dated [23 Sept. 1778]. For 'Dun', meaning a horse, see *OED*.
[3] CB's wife. In her letter of [23 Sept.], Mrs Thrale had asked, 'What does Mrs. Burney say to the new scheme for Dick?'
[4] Southwark, Henry Thrale's constituency in which was located his brewery and town house.
[5] On Monday 21 Sept., from Streatham.
[6] The Revd Richard Pitt (*fl.* 1776–91), clergyman, appears for the first time in the Marriage Registers of St George's Church, Hanover Square, as performing a wedding on 16 Apr. 1776, and for the last time on 5 Mar. 1791. He signs himself simply as 'Rd. Pitt, Curate', appending no degree, as was the custom of his fellow curates.

ann.—as by this means he will perhaps obtain a better place at school, on his arrival, than if he was utterly ignorant of all that is taught in it; &, moreover, it will be a trial of his diligence and punctuality, as he is only to be a Day scholar with Mr Pitt. Between this Time & X^{mas} I shall try to make an acquaintance wth the Master at Westminster under Whose Care he is at first to be placed, & information concerning several circumstances relative to that school of wch I am utterly ignorant. Dr J. says he knows Dr Vincent,[7] the under Master a little; if by chance he sh^d meet wth him I know it w^d be a Stimulus to his future kindness & attention if he w^d do Dick the honour to say he knew him, & wished him Well. He seems now to set off with Spirit, & to get his tasks tolerably well—If, at last, egregiâ et præclarâ indole,[8] Dick *sh^d* astonish the world by his Erudition, I shall with equal humility & gratitude sing non Nobis &c[9]—

I have my Eye on Streatham for Tuesday or Wed^y next,[10] & shall beg house-room there till the end of the Week. I shall take the Liberty of bringing work with me, but with no great expectation of consequences—for who can Patiently dig among the dead for Information or amusem^t when living sources are running to waste in one's reach? I have not set pen to paper for the press since I came home; but have idled my Time away in hunting old B^{ks} for intelligence, wch I have but seldom found, & still more seldom secured. The Eel of Science to me becomes more slippery every Day — — my hooks are broken & decayed; and, from want of success, my former eagerness after this kind of fishing is greatly diminished.

I am glad my Master keeps off the foul Fiend[11]—& that you are all going to amuse yourselves;[12] & my Joy in this is purely selfish, as your happiness will ever contribute to that of Dear Mad^m

Yours in all Truth & affection.
C.B.

[7] William Vincent (1739–1815), DD (1776), classical scholar, second master (1771), head-master (1788) of Westminster (*DNB*).

[8] Cf. Cicero, *De Oratore*, i. xxix. 131. CB's use of the phrase may be rendered: 'by outstanding and brilliant natural ability'.

[9] Psalm 115 (113). 'Non nobis, Domine . . .': 'Not unto us, O Lord, not unto us, but unto thy Name give the praise'.

[10] Tuesday 29 or Wednesday 30 Sept. In her letter of [23 Sept.], Mrs Thrale had asked, 'When will you come and take up your abode with us?'

[11] Mrs Thrale wrote in her letter of [23 Sept.]: 'I doubt not but you see his [Thrale's] spirits much mended already'. For Henry Thrale's financial worries during 1778, see Clifford, pp. 164–73; Hyde, *Thrales*, pp. 201–9.

[12] In her letter of [23 Sept.], Mrs Thrale had mentioned plans to visit her cousin, Sir Robert Salusbury Cotton (*c.*1739–1809), 5th Baronet (1775), now a colonel in the Guards (Namier and Brooke, ii. 260–1) on their way to Tunbridge Wells and Brighton for a holiday: '. . . we are to set out a colonelling on Monday 5, of Oct., as my master tells me: he will do himself good by change of Place I think'. See also Hyde, *Thrales*, pp. 209–10.

To Francesco Roncaglia [St Martin's Street],
6 October 1778

ALS draft (Osborn).
Docketed by CB: (Al Roncaglia) *And by* FBA: 78

Cariss^mo Amico.

La ricordanza sua mi sta molto a Cuore, e le novelle del suo fortunato
viaggio a Bologna mi son gratissime recavano grandissimo Piacere.[1]
E un Pezzo che il suo amichevole foglio mi è venuto in mano, e non
avrebbe perduto un momento a rispondere toccante Il Sig^r Benedetti[2]
se un altro soggetto anche a Bologna non avessi avuto proposto, dal
quale io aspettavo una risposta in pochi Giorni dopo l'arrivata della
sua stimatissima Lettera. Questo soggetto è la Marchet⟨ti⟩[3] la quale
mi Scrive che non a esita un Momento ad Abbraciare il progetto
di Cantar al Panteon l'Inverno venturo, e che alla fine del mese di
Settembre interprenderà il viaggio, senza aspettar altra Lettera della
parte mia. Mi dispiace di non essere in Libertà per adesso di profittare
della sua amicizia riguardando il Sig^r Benedetti; ma spero, un altra
volta, di far sapere la mia obbedienza in di lei Servizio e di mostrar
che niuna cosa lusinga tanto Piacevolmente l'animo mio quanto il
darmi occasioni di credere che io possa essere altrui di qualche utilità.

I soggetti Cantanti del Panteon per la Stagione ventura saranno La
Marchetti, Miss Harper,[4] Inglesina,[5] e Piozzi. L'Inglesina a una voce

---

[1] Roncaglia had written to CB from Bologna, 29 Aug. 1778 (Osborn).

[2] Michele Benedetti (*fl.* 1778), a castrato who sang in Rome at this time (*Enciclopedia dello spettacolo* (Rome, 1954–62), ii. 235), is not otherwise identified. In his capacity as a Proprietor of the Pantheon, CB had clearly asked Roncaglia to make enquiries in Italy about suitable singers for its subscription concerts. In his letter of 29 Aug., Roncaglia suggested 'un bravo cantante chiamato Benedetti, . . . Questo canta il Soprano e suona bene il cembalo, in somma io lo trovo capace per il Panteon'.

[3] Apart from what CB published about Marchetti (*fl.* 1773–81) in *Hist. Mus.* iv. 500; Mercer, ii. 880; Rees; and information gleaned from letters in CB's correspondence, little is known of this singer: 'She had a powerful, brilliant, and sweet-toned voice, with which she might have become a singer of the first class, if want of health had not prevented her from that persevering practice, which is so necessary to the vanquishing of vocal difficulties' (Rees). She appeared first at the Pantheon in 1774, returned from Italy in 1778, married one Luigi Mattei Marchetti, and, for reasons of ill health, returned to her native Bologna in 1780. See CB to Martini, 20 Oct. 1779; 1 June 1780 (Bologna); Martini to CB, 7 Nov. 1779 (Osborn); and Luigi Mattei Marchetti to CB, 22 May 1781 (Osborn).

[4] Elizabeth Harper (1757–1849), actress-singer, who married (1783) the comedian John Bannister (1760–1836). In the summer of 1778 she had been engaged by the proprietors of the Pantheon for two years at the salary of £1000 (*BD*, under 'Bannister').

[5] Cecilia Davies (*c.*1753–1836), soprano, 'known in Italy by the name of L'Inglesina . . . Miss Davies has the honour of being not only the first Englishwoman who has performed the principal female parts in several great theatres of Italy, but who has ever been thought worthy of

graziosa e dolce, senza i difetti ordinarij della Natione nostra, ed e scolare de Sacchini. L'Orchestra sarà ancora sull'Imperio del Caro Giardini,[6] e mi son nella speranza che col questa dispositione delle Cose il publico sarà contento.[7] La Harper è impiegata per dui Anni.

La Bernasconi[8] prima Donna dell'opera di Londra è arrivata ma non ancora il Pacchierotti.[9]

Quando vedrà La Gabrielli[10] la prego de presentarla i miei Complimenti piu distinti, e di far la sapere ch'io fo somma stima del suo gran Merito. Tutta la Famiglia mia anno per lei una stima particulare e mi pregano di ringraziarlo la sua ricordanza. Ed io, che ella a fatto suissimo, la supplico di non scordarmi, ma di amarmi, commandarmi, e credermi quale Sono e Sarò sempre di Cuore e colla piú verace amicizia, sua

Londra 6 Ottobre 1778
Dev͞mo ed aff͞mo Serv^e
Carlo Burney.

To Mrs Thrale [St Martin's Street], 16 October 177[8][1]

ALS (Osborn).
Docketed by unknown hand *in pencil*: Dr Chas Burney

singing there at all ... Her voice, though not of a great volume, or perhaps sufficiently powerful for a great theatre, yet was clear and perfectly in tune' (*Hist. Mus.* iv. 499–500; Mercer, ii. 879). See also *BD*; *New Grove*; *EJL* ii.

[6] In his letter of 29 Aug., Roncaglia had asked CB to present his compliments 'al Caro Giardini'.

[7] The performers listed here by CB did appear at the Pantheon when its season of winter subscription concerts opened on 25 Jan. 1779 (*Public Advertiser*).

[8] Antonia Bernasconi (1741–1803), a German soprano who adopted the name of her stepfather, had just arrived in England for a two-season engagement at the Opera (*New Grove*; *BD*). CB found 'she had a neat and elegant manner of singing, though with a voice that was feeble and in decay' (*Hist. Mus.* iv. 509; Mercer, ii. 886; Rees).

[9] Gasparo Pacchierotti, or Pacchiarotti (1740–1821), Italian castrato, who CB stated categorically to have been 'one of the most scientific, expressive, and finished singers, which Italy ever produced' (Rees). London audiences were keenly awaiting Pacchierotti's arrival, for his praises had been proclaimed by Patrick Brydone in his *A Tour through Sicily and Malta* (1773), ii. 254–6. Gabriel Piozzi had also been pleasing London audiences by singing 'several airs after his [Pacchierotti's] manner, in a style that excited great ideas of his pathetic powers' (*Hist. Mus.* iv. 509–13; Mercer, ii. 886–9). Lord Mount-Edgcumbe said of Pacchierotti that he was 'the most perfect singer it ever fell to my lot to hear' (*Musical Reminiscences* (2nd edn., 1827), pp. 23–7). See also, *New Grove*; A. Heriot, *The Castrati in Opera* (1956), pp. 163–71.

[10] In his letter of 29 Aug., Roncaglia informed CB of his plan to travel in Sept. to the region of Venice and to meet Caterina Gabrielli, who, it was said, was to perform at the opera at Mestre.

[1] Although CB dates his letter clearly '1779', it belongs to 1778.

Lord bless me! & so you waited for a Letter!² & there was I wondring, & wondring what was become of you, & feeling uncomfortable at the Idea of being forgotten. The Period of Absence³ already seems long, & full of Events. After coddling myself, & getting tolerably well, what does my I, but accept of an invitation from an old Friend at Thistleworth⁴ to eat Venison; to take Mad^m with me, & have a little Fun—well, but you know the rest, for I find that my adventures have already been recorded by an illustrious historian⁵—for this Even^g as I suppose Fan will tell you,⁶ we drank Tea with our dear Doctor, who says that he has written you the longest Letter he has been guilty of this great while⁷—& that in it he had set forth as how I had been robbed, &c—So there's an end of that; but in spite of my Information to Justice Fielding,⁸ & desire that he w^d let proper officers try to prevent others from being treated in the same manner, M. Le Texier⁹ was divested of his purse exactly on the same Spot, & by the same Persons I am sure, tho' he has dignified the acc^t by calling them *Highwaymen*—but to Foreigners a *highway robbery* does not imply that it was committed by Gent^n of the Equestrian Order.

On Sunday I went out again to have a little More Fun—at Chelsea,

² Mrs Thrale had written to CB on 14 [Oct. 1778], (Comyn), from Tunbridge Wells: 'When every body goes to look for their Letters here at the Booksellers Shop ... poor I have no Letters to fetch ... no Truths to please myself with concerning the health & Welfare of my Friends'.
³ The Thrales had set out from Streatham probably on 5 Oct. (see CB to Mrs Thrale, 25 [Sept. 1778], n. 12) to visit Sir Robert Salusbury Cotton at his military camp (see Johnson *Letters*, ii. 257, 260–1). They then proceeded to Tunbridge Wells where they enjoyed 'the sweet Society' for a fortnight before going on to Brighton (Clifford, p. 172; Johnson *Letters*, ii. 261; and CB to Mrs Thrale, 6 Nov. 1778, n. 10).
⁴ Thistleworth, near Isleworth in Middlesex. CB's old friend is not identified.
⁵ Johnson had written to Mrs Thrale on 15 Oct., 'When I called the other day at Burneys, I found only the young ones at home, at last came the Doctor and Madam from a dinner in the country, to tell how they had been robbed as the⟨y⟩ returned. The Doctor saved his purse but gave them three guineas and some silver, of which they returned him three and sixpence unasked to pay the turnpike' (Johnson *Letters*, ii. 257).
⁶ No letter from Fanny Burney to Mrs Thrale at this time appears to have been preserved (see *Cat. Corr.*, p. 70).
⁷ Johnson concluded his letter of 15 Oct. to Mrs Thrale with the observation: 'I never said with Dr. Dodd that *I love to prattle upon paper*, but I have prattled now till the paper will not hold much more ...' (Johnson *Letters*, ii. 258).
⁸ Sir John Fielding (1721–80), Kt. (1761), magistrate, half-brother of the novelist Henry Fielding (1707–54). See *DNB*; R. Leslie-Melville, *The Life and Work of Sir John Fielding* (1934).
⁹ Antoine-A. Le Texier (*c.*1737–1814), French actor celebrated for his solo performances of all the characters in various plays, had come to England in Sept. 1775. He served as acting Manager of the Opera at the King's Theatre in the Haymarket for the 1778–9, part of the 1779–80, and the 1795–6 seasons (*The London Stage*, v. i. 201, 282; iii. 1791), a position for which CB initially thought him totally unfit (see *Thraliana*, i. 268). For Le Texier, see F. A. Hedgcock, *A Cosmopolitan Actor: David Garrick and His French Friends* (1912), pp. 267–74; A. D. Wallace, 'Le Texier's Early Years in England, 1775–1779', in *Studies in Honor of John Wilcox*, ed. A. D. Wallace and W. O. Ross (Detroit, 1958), pp. 71–89; *BD*.

where I dined with my Fr^{ds} the Rapers,[10] & met Chamier;[11] but was so silly as to come home in a high Fever which was worse than being robbed; so I went to bed at 9 o'Clock, & was not able to quit that & my room till Wed^y — — However, I am better now, & intend to continue mending till I am quite *Charmingly* — — & so do you know that I have let Miss Reynolds[12] behold my Charms twice, for 2 Hours together, by Shrewsbury Clock?—& have not killed her yet![13]—Oh— but the tol der rol March?—why ay—now you'll have another very good excuse for writing ab^t *that*[14]—does the all Charm^g S.S.[15] wish to have any more of it than the Abridgment in Miss Thrale's Book? or *joost Thautt*? The original you may remember was considerably longer—it was shortened for every-Day use, & the convenience of my Fr^d Sr Jno Wodehouse's[16] Band, *en attendant* a better—so now do y zay wch it shall be.[17]—How can you be so ungrateful to complain of the Emptiness of the Place you are in,[18] when surrounded with Wisdom, Learning, & Beauty; to wch you can, ad Libitum, contribute the *Seasoning* of Wit. — — I feel very comfortable that you and the dear & sweet Mrs Crewe club Chata*tion* together.[19] Pray put her in mind of me again & again. And don't let my Master think to diddle

---

[10] Henry Raper (1717–89), his wife Katherine (1735–1823), and their family.

[11] Anthony Chamier (1725–80), Under-Secretary of State for the Southern Department (*DNB*), had recently (10 June 1778) entered Parliament as MP for Tamworth (Namier and Brooke, ii. 207–8). His friendship with the Rapers is reflected in the naming of their son Charles Chamier Raper (*c.*1777–1845), who married CB's granddaughter Frances Phillips (1782–1860) in 1807 (*JL* v. 157 n.).

[12] Frances Reynolds (1729–1807), amateur painter and author, for whom Mrs Thrale had 'a great regard' (Johnson *Letters*, ii. 143), youngest sister of Sir Joshua Reynolds, for whom she had kept house for many years (see *Thraliana*, i. 79–80).

[13] See *1 Henry IV*, v. iv. 146: '. . . and fought a long hour by Shrewsbury clock'. CB was sitting to Miss Reynolds for his portrait, and the sessions may indeed have seemed interminable: Miss Reynolds was notoriously indecisive and tiresomely fidgety (see *Mem.* i. 331–4; *JL* iv. 256; and CB to Fanny Burney, [26? July 1782], n. 3). None of the portraits of CB known to be preserved is by Frances Reynolds.

[14] Mrs Thrale had written (14 [Oct.]): '. . . I have at last however light on an Excuse to write to *you*; Miss Streatfield falls in love with your Norfolk Militia March & begs me to make Interest that she may have it.' Nothing is known of CB's Norfolk Militia March, other than is contained in this correspondence.

[15] For Sophia Streatfeild (1754–1835), see CB to Mrs Thrale, 1 Nov. 1777, n. 31. Sophy's charms ensnared the affections of most men, including CB's (see *Thraliana*, i. 523).

[16] Sir John Wodehouse (1741–1834), of Kimberley, Norfolk, 6th Baronet (1777), MP (1784–97), created Baron Wodehouse of Kimberley (1797), scion of the leading Tory family in Norfolk (Namier and Brooke, iii. 653).

[17] It is not known which version CB transcribed for Sophy Streatfeild. In her reply, dated 28 Oct. (Osborn) from Brighton, Mrs Thrale wrote: 'Your sweet Letter followed me hither & gave me a Pretence to write to my lovely Friend enclosing the March.'

[18] Mrs Thrale had written in her letter of 14 [Oct.] from Tunbridge Wells: 'As for News I have none; Mrs Crewe is the handsomest Woman here & Mrs Montagu the wisest—but the Place is so empty that it is no Praise to be either.'

[19] Mrs Thrale wrote (ibid.): 'Mrs Crewe is delighted that your Daughter is the Author [of *Evelina*], . . . She & I talk of you & yours all Day long.'

me daddle me out of all my breeding—Cook up I entreat you, selon son goût, mille Jolies Choses de ma Part—here comes the postman, or I sh^d have been my own Cook—But Miss Thrale—& Miss Streatfield must not forget the old Grand Father—well God bless you my dear Madam—believe me & mine to be yours in all affection—

Ch. Burney—

Dick & Mr Pitt are on the best Terms imaginable—how happy you made the little scoundrel with your Present![20]—but 'tis your way—
16 Octr 1779[21]

To Mrs Thrale   Oxford, 6 November 1778

ALS (Rylands, English MS 545, no. 5).
Addressed: To | Mrs Thrale

Oxford 6th Novr 1778

Dear Madam.

Having commissioned Secretary Fanny to answer your last Charming Letter,[1] or at least to thank you for it in her best Eveline Manner,[2] I came hither on Tuesday Even^g to run my Nose into Cobwebs, & consult the Learned. Our dear & Good Doctor gave me Letters[3] to Drs Wheeler & Edwards whom I like extreamly. The former[4] is a polite & agreeable Man of the World, as well as a good Scholar & Christian; the latter[5] almost an old School-Fellow, having left Shrewsbury School

---

[20] When Dick Burney had been placed under Dr Joseph Warton at Winchester in early 1778, Mrs Thrale had 'not only made him a present of a piece of fine holland to set him up in shirts with but ... likewise furnished him with an intire set of school books' (*ED* ii. 286). Mrs Thrale had probably now made a similar gift to Dick as he started to prepare for Westminster.

[21] In error: see n. 1.

[1] Of 28 Oct. [1778], (Osborn). Mrs Thrale wrote from Brighton, shortly after her arrival there from Tunbridge Wells. See also n. 10.

[2] Mrs Thrale had written (ibid.), 'how is my sweet Evelina?' and had instructed CB, 'when you have been kept up late either by Business or Prattle make her write to me, & do not wear your Eyes out to delight mine.' If 'Secretary Fanny' did write to Mrs Thrale on CB's behalf between 28 Oct. and 6 Nov. 1778, the letter has not been preserved (see *Cat. Corr.*, p. 70).

[3] For these letters dated 2 Nov. 1778, see Johnson *Letters*, ii. 264–6; Hill–Powell, iii. 366–7.

[4] Benjamin Wheeler (*c.*1733–83), DD (1770), Professor of Poetry (1766–76), Regius Professor of Divinity and Canon of Christ Church (1776–83). Through Wheeler's connection with Christ Church, CB gained access to the musical library formed by Dr Henry Aldrich (1648–1710), and bequeathed to the college. For Wheeler, see Foster; Johnson *Letters*, iii. 429; for Aldrich, see *DNB*; *New Grove*. See also CB to Charles Burney, 25 Feb. 1781, n. 12.

[5] Edward Edwards (1726–83), DD (1760), of Jesus College, where he was Vice-Principal (1762–83), classical scholar. Johnson introduced CB to Edwards, who came from Talgarth, Merioneth, North Wales, and could therefore help with a Welsh MS in the Bodleian. Edwards's

just when I entered it[6]—he is moreover I find a remarkable good Græcian, & I trust a Special Tory.—M[r] Monkhouse[7] of Queen's Coll. whose Guest I usually am, is a hospitable, worthy Man, who hates Presb————ns, & is thoroughly *honest*.—With these, & with other Good Folks, how Charming a place w[d] Oxford be, if they had but the sense & Politeness of Italy, & gave Degrees to learned Ladies!—Then there w[d] be some chance of meeting with a Dottoressa here equally deserving of the honour with the Laura Bassi[8]—the Corilla[9]—or any modern Minerva of them all. Lord! it w[d] have been so nice if you & my Master & the sweet Queeny, & all, were here now instead of being blown to Pieces in that Capital of the 4 Winds Bri[gh]ton[10]—!

But Mum! it is only in Stormy Weather, & at this distance that I dare speak irreverently of B————n. And it is very ungrateful to do it at all for I was very happy there last year, & sh[d] be so now in the same Company. But I owe every place a grudge that takes you out of reach—I tried to persuade Seward to come hither & refresh his memory concerning wigs, Tobaco, and other parts of recondite Learning,[11] of w[ch] y[r] fine Gent[n] who live in the great world have no Notion.—But though I dined with him on Sat[y] & coaxed him all I c[d] he was inexorable, & thought, I suppose, that the Doctors here, who are reputed Gourmands, w[d] have eat *him* up.—On Sat[y] Even[g][12] determining to make a kind of Streatham Day of it, I took Fan in my hand

edition of Xenophon's *Memorabilia* was published posthumously in 1785. See Foster; Hill–Powell, iii. 367, 529.

[6] A difficulty arises here with respect to the dates of CB's attendance at Shrewsbury School. In the incomplete register of Salopians at this period, Edward Edwards is listed as entering the school during the academic year Nov. 1738–Nov. 1739 (J. E. Auden, ed., *Shrewsbury School Register. 1734–1908* (Oswestry, 1909), p. 4). CB's name is nowhere to be found in the extant school lists. It is known, however, that CB entered Chester Free School on 25 Dec. 1739 (Lonsdale, p. 4). If CB's chronology is accurate in stating here that he entered Shrewsbury just after Edwards's departure, we have to conclude that both Edwards and CB spent only a brief period at the school during 1739.

[7] Thomas Monkhouse (*c*.1726–93), DD (1780), of The Queen's College, where he had been a Fellow since 1760 (Foster; *GM* lxiii (1793)[1], 479, 496). He edited the third volume of *State Papers collected by Edward, Earl of Clarendon . . . from which his History of the Great Rebellion was composed* (Oxford, 1786). CB later wrote of Monkhouse in *Frag. Mem.* (Berg): 'D[r] Monkhouse & I became acquainted at the Installation of L[d] North. He was a very good judge of Music and a great collector of curious compositions of w[ch] he liberally let me take copies. In my Ital. Tour, as I had picked up many very scarce and curious b[ks] & Musical Comp⟨o⟩sitions not in *his* collection, there was an unr⟨e⟩served commutation between us.'

[8] See CB to Garrick, 17–[18] Oct. 1770, n. 31.

[9] See ibid., n. 37.

[10] In her letter of 28 Oct. [1778], (Osborn), Mrs Thrale had written: 'Our Tunbridge Set broke up in the last Storm, & the Wind drove us hither [Brighton]; where though there is a great deal of Company I do not expect such Society as I had the luck to enjoy for this last fortnight—'. The Thrales returned to Streatham on 26 Nov. (Hyde, *Thrales*, p. 213).

[11] William Seward matriculated from Oriel College on 4 June 1764, aged 17 (Foster). He took no degree.

[12] 31 Oct. 1778. See also Johnson *Letters*, ii. 263.

& went to Bolt Court—where the good Soul rec^d us with open Arms, & was so pleasant & Comical!¹³—but you know him when he is off the great Horse, & condescends to tittup on a little Welsh Kephel¹⁴ — — But avast! as my son¹⁵ w^d say—I must go to Christchurch—& more-over cease talking Nonsense or I shall have my Tongue and Pen hacked off, & my Gown stripped over my Ears—and so adieu Dear Madam!—Say kind Things for me—get well & rosy—& let us live in hopes of a laugh ere long at dear Streatham — —

C.B.

To Mrs Thrale

[St Martin's Street,
19 November 1778]¹

ALS (Osborn).
Addressed: To⏐Mrs Thrale   *Docketed by* unknown hand: Dr Burney⏐born. 1726 died 1814.

Ah, my dear Madam! it is lucky for you that I am not an idle man, for you w^d then be *so* pestered with Letters in order to provoke you to quick & ample returns as w^d make you rue the Day you ever learned to write or read. As it is, my Cacoethes scribendi² is kept in pretty good bounds; for perpetually jumbled from pillar to post, by certain, as well as accidental Diavolini degl'impedimenti, I am not likely to overwhelm my Friends with Letters; however I may wish to be always scribling to certain People.

Luckily for you, I did not receive the Letter addressed to me at Oxford³ till Sat^y Night—I arrived in Town on tuesday last week,⁴ & by *Catholicking*⁵ the thing over, It seems near a demonstration that

---

¹³ It was doubtless on this occasion that CB asked Johnson to write his letters of introduction to Oxford friends (see n. 3). Johnson also wrote to CB on Monday 2 Nov., assuring him of a warm welcome at Oxford through the good offices of Thomas Warton (1728–90), of Trinity College, the historian of English poetry (Johnson *Letters*, ii. 266).
¹⁴ The modern spelling for 'horse' in Welsh is 'ceffyl'. During the summer of 1774, Johnson had toured North Wales in company with the Thrales (see A. M. Broadley, *Doctor Johnson and Mrs. Thrale* (1910), pp. 155–219; Hill–Powell, v. 427–61).
¹⁵ James, the naval officer.

¹ The year, month, and week in which this letter was written is established from Dr Johnson's correspondence with Mrs Thrale (Johnson *Letters*, ii. 269–71); the day is given by CB's 'Thursday Night'.
² 'The itch of writing'. See Juvenal, *Satires*, vii. 52.
³ Not preserved.
⁴ i.e. 10 Nov. On Saturday 14 Nov., Johnson reported to Mrs Thrale CB's experience of trying to work in the Bodleian: 'Dr Burney had the luck to go to Oxford, the only week in the year when the library is shut up' (Johnson *Letters*, ii. 269).
⁵ The verbal form 'to catholic' is not listed in *OED*. CB's meaning, however, is clear: he examined the postmarks stamped all over Mrs Thrale's re-directed letter.

your kind Memento reached Oxford ab^t the same time. I have been all hurry & bother ever since I came home. The Evenings wch I had allotted for Letter writing have been swallowed up I hardly know how—2 of 'em however I recollect with pleasure—our Fr^d Seward drank Tea with us on Sunday, & had a good natured plan for lessening Becket's Debt[6] by taking B^{ks} of him, & paying me for them—I had but little stomach to set ab^t it—however he called on Monday, consulted Catalogues, & made out a List, wth wch he insisted on my going to B. directly—I wanted both Whip & Spur in this Business—But he spared neither, finding me a *craving* Nag—he *stuck* close to me, & laid me on wth *double* Thong—& to my great astonishm^t I found myself in B——'s shop & in Conversation wth him ere I had time to shake my Ears—& in a few minutes more, to my still greater astonishm^t I found myself in a Hackney Coach loaded with Books of all sizes to the amount of more than 20 Vol^s! These were all I c^d find in his shop of those that were specified in my *order*.—However he promises to get others to the amount of more than double his debt to me, for many of wch he will touch the ready.[7]—In the Even^g in Comes Seward again to enquire how I had behaved in the Execution of his orders, & we had scarcely done laughing at the good Effects of my Prowess, when Johnson & Baretti adjourned here from Sr Joshua's[8]—well, this *was* a nice Even^g, & full of Chat & good humour—& the Triumvirate stayed till near 12.—Baretti asked me if I sh^d be at home Tuesday Night,[9] as he had something to shew me—I c^d not say him nay—& after working all the Morn^g at the Museum, I was entrusted in the Evening with his whole plan for obliging the learned & musical world with the Carmen Seculare & other poems of y^r Fr^d Horace—set by Philidor[10]—as you have already heard—Baretti shewed our Dr Doctor 4 additional complimentary verses to the English, wch were intended for the *Coro finale*— & these he has not only very much altered for the better, but translated

---

[6] The financial troubles of CB's publisher, Thomas Becket (*c.*1721–1813), led to his being declared a bankrupt in Mar. 1779 (*London Gazette*, 6–9 Mar. 1779). Preserved in the Bodleian is a MS letter from Becket's former business partner, Peter Abraham Dehondt, to Ralph Griffiths, which gives some indication of the rapidly worsening state of Becket's affairs during 1778: 'a little more than a Year before Mr Becket was declared Bankrupt . . . his Debts . . . amounted to £14176 and the value of his Stock to £12576' (Bodl., MS Add. C. 89, fos. 32–3); yet only five shillings in the pound were allowed creditors after the liquidation of Becket's assets. Becket's imprint, from now on, disappears from the title-pages of CB's publications.

[7] i.e. 'ready money' or 'ready cash' (*OED*).

[8] Informed about London events by this letter, Mrs Thrale wrote to Johnson from Brighton on 21 Nov.: 'And so I heard of you at Reynolds's with Burney Baretti &c. I was glad on't' (Johnson *Letters*, ii. 271).

[9] i.e. 17 Nov.

[10] For a full account of the Baretti–Philidor adaptation of the *Carmen Saeculare*, see C. M. Carroll, 'A Classical Setting for a Classical Poem: Philidor's *Carmen Saeculare*', in R. C. Rosbottom, ed., *Studies in Eighteenth-Century Culture*, vi (Madison, Wisconsin, 1977), 97–111.

in such a manner as you know he is able to do in his most Poetical & lucky Moods.—4 lines are I think the best in our Language[11]—but you'll both see & hear by & by.—I hope, with the patronage of the learned, his Fr[ds], that this plan will be acceptable to the Public,[12] who are to be *told*, you know, what they are to admire—what they are to say, & how they are to *seem* to feel.[13]—If it puts money into Baretti's purse,[14] what does it signify whether affectation or Judgm[t] pays the Piper?

Thursday Night 10 O'Clock—I am just come from our Fr[d] in Bolt Court, who has agreed to go with me to dear Streatham this Day 7 Night[15]—so tell my Master that I shall obey his orders with much greater Pleasure than Seward's—O, but à propos to Seward—I was pleasantly surprised to see him at the R. S. to Night, & still more to find him a Candidate for the honour of becoming a *Confrere*—he's gibetted already—& I w[d] not quit the room till I had under-written him[16]—But the rogue will soon have a surfeit of queer Wigs, thread-bare Coats, Fluxions, Logarithms & Cockle-shells.—These will not Stir his blood half so much as a good sonorous Chorus of Handel a dui Cori, con Trombetti, Timpani, e Corni da Ca⟨c⟩cia—

We must brush up our *feeble* Music, though, at Streatham—tell Miss Thrale I have a Power of Musical news for her—I have heard the Bernasconi—Pacchiarotti[17]—& the new Comic Opera[18] rehearsed

---

[11] See 'Epilogue to Horace's "Carmen Seculare"', in D. Nichol Smith and E. L. McAdam, eds., *The Poems of Samuel Johnson* (2nd edn., Oxford, 1974), pp. 218–19.

[12] Johnson wrote to Mrs Thrale on 21 Nov.: 'Baretti has told his musical scheme to Burney, and Burney *will neither grant the question nor deny*. He is of opinion, that, if it does not fail, it will succeed, but, if it does not succeed he conceives it must fail' (Johnson *Letters*, ii. 270–1).

In her reply to CB of 21 Nov. [1778] (Comyn), Mrs Thrale wrote, 'I wish Baretti Success, and if it lies in my way will do more than wish it.'

[13] The advertisements for the three performances on 26 Feb., 5 and 12 Mar. 1779 in the *Public Advertiser* included the announcement, 'The Learned and the Elegant are invited to this Exhibition as to a new Mode of Pleasure, arising from the Union of ancient Poetry with modern Music.' Baretti also published *The Introduction to the Carmen Seculare* [1779], setting forth his ideas. This *Introduction*, in the form of an essay entitled 'Joseph Baretti to the English Reader', was issued separately in an octavo format (14 pp.) and appeared also as the prefatory material in the quarto libretto distributed (price 1s.) at the performances in Freemasons' Hall.

[14] An allusion to *Othello*, 1. iii. 333ff. Baretti 'seriously hoped to make his fortune' by this scheme (L. Collison-Morley, *Giuseppe Baretti and His Friends* (1909), pp. 321–3), an ambition that was thwarted (see Hill–Powell, iii. 373 n. 3; *GM* lix (1789)[1], 569; HMC, *Charlemont*, i (1891), 375; Johnson *Letters*, ii. 281).

[15] i.e. Thursday 26 Nov. Johnson had written to Mrs Thrale on 14 Nov., 'And on the 26. Burney is to bring me. Pray why so. Is it not as fit that I should bring Burney?' (Johnson *Letters*, ii. 269). Mollified by CB, Johnson wrote again on 21 Nov., 'Burney and I have settled it, and I will not take a postchaise merely to show my independence' (ibid., p. 270).

[16] Seward was duly elected FRS on 11 Feb. 1779 (*DNB*).

[17] Antonia Bernasconi and Gaspare Pacchierotti had been engaged for the serious opera as principal vocalists for the 1778–9 season (*Public Advertiser*, 24 Oct. 1778).

[18] The comic opera that opened the season at the King's Theatre in the Haymarket on 24 Nov. was Sacchini's *L'Avaro Deluso* (*The London Stage*, v. i. 217).

to Day — — — Well, but are you to look *Hecklich*, now?—*Interesting* you are sure of—But I love the roses better than the Lillies, remember that, & don't part with 'em all, I beseech you.—I fear the *Poets* do not live so *fast* now as formerly — — Whether Johnson can tell you that the Hist^y of Music is in a *thriving* state or no, I very much doubt.— But we'll discuss these Points & a 1000 more anon—& so without a flourish I end *tout plat*, with only a hearty wish that now your frolick is nearly at an end, you may be eager to enjoy your own domestic comforts, & even long for a homely Chat with your constant & every-Day Friends, including the Cats, Dogs, chickens, & your affectionate & faithful Servt

C.B.

To Lord Sandwich

[St Martin's Street],
22 November 1778

AL 3rd person (Osborn).
Endorsed by unknown hand: Dr Burney | to | Ld Sandwich

Doctor Burney presents his humble respects to Lord Sandwich, & has the honour to acquaint his Lordship that he has been canvassing for Mr Banks ever since he knew the Chair at the R.S. was likely to become vacant.[1] Dr B. from a Personal regard for Mr B. & a conviction of his Abilities to succeed Sr Jno Pringle,[2] spoke to all his acquaintance in his Favour, without waiting for Solicitation. And though he is extreamly happy to find that his opinion coincides wth that of Lord Sandwich, he is sorry his Lord^p has put his Gratitude & obedience to so small a trial, as the request wch he has done him the honour to make to him now, is only confirming & flattering the wish of his heart.

22^d Novr 1778

---

[1] Joseph Banks (1743–1820), FRS (1766), created Baronet (1781), KB (1795), naturalist and explorer. On 30 Nov. he was elected President of the Royal Society, a dignity he retained till his death (*DNB*). Banks was a particular friend of Lord Sandwich, who had permitted him to accompany James Cook on his first voyage of exploration (1768–71). For an account of the canvassing and political manoeuvres preceding Banks's election, see H. C. Cameron, *Sir Joseph Banks, K.B., P.R.S., the Autocrat of the Philosophers* (1952), pp. 112–22.
[2] Sir John Pringle (1707–82), MD (1730), FRS (1745), created Baronet (1766), physician to the King (1774), had been President of the Royal Society since 1772. Failing health forced Pringle to resign his Presidency (*DNB*; *DSB*).

To Thomas Twining [St Martin's Street],
1 December 1778

L copy extract (Osborn: 'Twining Letterbook No. 3', pp. 7–8).
Also L copy extract, of the postscript only (Osborn: 'Twining Letterbook re. *Evelina & Cecilia*', p. 1).

1. Dec. 1778.

... Now for a little opera music. Come along as fast as you can. Lock up your doors: take the clapper out of your Church Bells: give your flock a hearty benediction & come along!—Why such a Singer as Pacchierotti has never been heard by such young fellows as you or me.—The old codgers who can remember your Niccollinis Senesinos & Farinellis[1] may pretend perhaps that they have heard a better, but I who have a distinct idea of the powers of every first Singer from Monticelli[2] to the present time do say that for taste, refinement, originality of expression & invention of passages and above all for feeling, & the power of getting at one's *Entrailles* I have never known his equal. In short Piozzi whom we so much & so justly admire is but a faint Copy in his best slow songs of Pacchierotti.[3] I used to think Mrs Sheridan's[4] voice as sweet as sugar — — but his has the elegant sweetness of a pine-apple.[5]—If he were to sing the same air 100 times he would disdain repeating it in the same way. His variety is incredibble without being heard. Then,—I say,—come away!—The first woman la Bernasconi has no great voice, but she has a very elegant style of singing, & many embellishments & refinements that are wholly new

[1] Three Italian castrati at the height of their powers in the early eighteenth century:
Nicolò Grimaldi, called Nicolino or Nicolini (1673–1732), 'the first truly great singer who had ever sung in our theatre' (*Hist. Mus.* iv. 207–9; Mercer, ii. 661–2), first came to London in 1708. His last appearance in England occurred in 1717 (*New Grove*; A. Heriot, *The Castrati in Opera* (1956), pp. 123–9).
Francesco Bernardi, called Senesino (*c.*1680–*c.*1750), performed in London from 1720 to 1737 (*New Grove*; Heriot, *Castrati*, pp. 91–5).
Carlo Broschi, called Farinelli (1705–82), appeared in London 1734–7 (*New Grove*; Heriot, *Castrati*, pp. 95–110).
[2] Angelo Maria Monticelli (*c.*1715–64), arrived in London in 1741 and remained until 1746 (*New Grove*; Heriot, *Castrati*, pp. 162–3). Monticelli was thus the reigning castrato on the London stage when CB, aged 18, arrived in the city in 1744.
[3] Piozzi had 'excited great ideas of [Pacchierotti's] pathetic powers' in London audiences, for, having heard Pacchierotti in Milan, Piozzi had 'sung several airs after his manner' (*Hist. Mus.* iv. 510; Mercer, ii. 887).
[4] Elizabeth Ann Sheridan, née Linley (1754–92).
[5] CB relished this gustatory image when writing about Pacchierotti's voice, 'that is as superior to the generality of vocal sweetness, as that of the pine apple is, not only to other fruits, but to sugar or treacle' (*Hist. Mus.* iv. 511; Mercer, ii. 887; Rees).

here,[6]—& yet such a giant as Pacchierotti makes her a pigmy. With Roncaglia she would have captivated every hearer, but the comparison is now against her.—The music,[7] chiefly of Bertoni,[8] who is come over with Pacchierotti, is really good. Misero Pargoletto is by Monza,[9] & an exquisite composition: the duet very pleasing of Anfossi,[10] and a prodigious fine tune for the Tenor[11] by Paesiello[12] &c &c so come along I entreat you,—Mrs Twi[13] & all.[14]

C.B.

If ever you are so idle & so silly as to read novels, let me beg you to run over Evelina. I have much to say to you about it, if already it has not been said.[15] Addio.

To Dorothy Young [St Martin's Street, late 1778][1]

ALS fragment (BL Egerton MS 3700A, fo. 17). Torn.

[6] But see CB to Roncaglia, 6 Oct. 1778, n. 8.

[7] The opera which opened the serious opera season at the King's Theatre in the Haymarket on 28 Nov. 1778 was *Demofoonte*, a pasticcio, with Pacchierotti and Bernasconi in the leading parts (*The London Stage*, v. i. 218).

[8] Ferdinando Gasparo Bertoni (1725–1813), Italian composer and organist, had been engaged as the house composer at the King's Theatre, in which capacity he served 1778–80 and 1781–3 (*New Grove*; *BD*). 'Almost every great singer unites himself in interest and friendship with some particular composer, who writes to his peculiar compass of voice, talents, and style of singing. Thus ... Pacchierotti and Bertoni, were closely connected' (*Hist. Mus.* iv. 513–14; Mercer, ii. 889–90).

[9] Carlo Monza (*c.*1735–1801), Milanese organist and composer (*MGG*). CB had listened to a Mass composed and conducted by Monza during his Italian tour (*Tours*, i. 72–3).

[10] Pasquale Anfossi (1727–97), prolific opera composer was later (1783) to come to England as composer to the Opera (*New Grove*; *BD*).

[11] The title-role in *Demofoonte* was sung by Valentin Adamberger (1743–1804), German tenor (*New Grove*; *BD*), 'who with a better voice would have been a good singer' (*Hist. Mus.* iv. 514; Mercer, ii 890).

[12] Giovanni Paisiello (1740–1816), composer of about a hundred operas and as many other works of different kinds (*New Grove*).

[13] Elizabeth Twining, née Smythies (1739–96), whom Twining had married in 1764 (*JL* iii. 161–2 nn. 4, 7).

[14] Twining wrote on 19 Dec. 1778 in reply: 'Your Opera news was a great feast to me;—I had not heard so much as the *name* of Pacchierotti. His being the best singer *you* ever heard ... is a character that, of course, gives me the highest possible idea of him ... Bertoni, I am totally unacquainted with ... Paesiello is one of the names that I respect most; he pleases me more than Nanny Fossi' (BL Add. MS 39929, fos. 185–8).

[15] Twining replied (ibid.): 'I hope I never shall attain to that degree of *wisdom*, as to despise a good Novel; nobody can do me a greater kindness than to tell me of a work of genius, in that *genre*; which, with all it's abuses, & the inundation of miserable trash that the *apparent* facility of ye thing has occasioned, is, still, an admirable *genre*; ... I have made our Bookseller send for Evelina. Tell me about it; I have heard nothing. Will it make me cry?—Has it filled your parlour with blubber?—I loves wastly to be moved!'

[1] Two indications point to this fragment as part of a letter sent to the old Lynn friend of the

Addressed: ⟨Miss⟩ D. Young ∣ ⟨?⟩ Street, Lynn Regis ∣ Norfolk   *Endorsed by*
Dorothy Young: Answered Jany 24 17⟨79⟩

... a *conversation suivie* of 7 or 8 people, no one says what any one of the rest w^d have said in the same situation. Every speech is appropriate. Then her invention in varying situations and events, wch though all natural & likely, seeming to rise out of each other, but few w^d have thought of Her Hero, Ld Orevill,[2] is the perfection of a well educated man of honour and parts. And Evelina herself with all her mistakes from innocence & inexperience, is every thing that such a man c^d wish.—But I seem reviewing the book, in wch though I am now so partial, I was once afraid of looking.—What c^d such an ignorant chit as my daughter tell the world, wch somebody had not better told before?[3]

I have written lately to Mr Maxey Allen[4] to thank him for a present of the same kind as yours;[5] but pray my love to Mr Stephen Allen & his family.[6] If any one else is alive at Lynn that knew and remembers me I sh^d wish you to give them the Comp^ts & thanks

Of your ever obliged, faithful, & affectionate friend

Chas Burney.

To Thomas Lowndes[1]

St Martin's Street,
27 January [1779]

L, in the hand of an amanuensis (Comyn).
Addressed: Mr Lowndes ∣ Bookseller ∣ Fleet Street   *Publ.: DL* i. 193 n.

Burneys, Dorothy Young (*fl.* 1750–1806), late in 1778. Miss Young's endorsement gives the time of year. A letter to CB from William Bewley, [Nov. 1778], in the Osborn Collection reveals that the authorship of *Evelina* was common knowledge amongst the Burneys' Norfolk acquaintance by late 1778.

[2] Lord Orville, the hero of *Evelina*.

[3] CB recounts in his MS *Frag. Mem.* (Berg) his first impressions of *Evelina*: 'I opened the first Vol. with fear & trembling, not supposing she w^d disgrace her parentage, but not having the least idea, that without the use of the press, or knowledge of the world, she c^d write a book worth reading. The dedication to myself, however, brought tears in my eyes, and before I had read half the first Vol. instead of being frightened I was delighted'.

[4] Maxey Allen (*c.*1730–1804), Lynn merchant and distiller, Mayor of King's Lynn in 1771, 1779, and 1792, was the younger brother of CB's second wife (Bradfer-Lawrence, table between pp. 188–9). CB's letter to Maxey Allen is not preserved.

[5] Doubtless a Norfolk turkey for Christmas.

[6] CB's stepson, the Revd Stephen Allen (1755–1847), son of CB's second wife by her first marriage, educated at Harrow and Christ's College, Cambridge (Venn), had married (1772) Susanna Sharpin (*c.*1755–1816) at the age of 17 at Gretna Green. Stephen Allen received deacon's orders on 2 Aug. 1778 and the curacy of Edgefield, Norfolk. Of his twelve children, the first two had been born by the time of this letter: Stephen (*c.*1775–1855), and Edward (1777–1815). See *JL* i, p. lxxiv, and genealogical table facing p. lxix.

[1] Thomas Lowndes (1719–84), bookseller and publisher at 77 Fleet Street from 1756 until his

Doctor Burney sends his Comp^{ts} to Mr Lowndes and acquaints him that by the Manner in which Evelina has for some time been advertised in Company with the Sylph, it has generally been imagined that both these Novels have been written by one, & the same Author.[2] Now, as Mr Lowndes must be *certain* that they are the Works of two different Writers; and as accident has now made the Author of Evelina pretty generally known, who by no means wishes to rob the writer of the Sylph of whatever praise may be his due, Dr B..begs Mr L. will not only cease to advertise these books in an eq[u]ivocal way, but inform the Public in some *clear and decisive manner*, that they are the works of two different Writers.[3]

St Martins Street: Jany 27th

To William Hunter[1]

St Martin's Street,
9 February 1779

ALS (The Royal Society, 'Letters and Papers', decade VII, no. 91, fo. 1).
Addressed: To Doctor William Hunter, F.R.S.   *Docketed*: Read Feby 18. 1779.
Also ALS copy (The Royal Society, 'Letters and Papers', decade VII, no. 103).
Publ.: Philosophical Transactions, lxix (1779), 183.

death (Plomer, p. 159). For Fanny Burney's secret negotiations with Lowndes over the publication of *Evelina*, see *HFB*, pp. 62–7, 76–7, 87–9, 492.

[2] *The Sylph: a Novel* in two volumes, sometimes attributed to Georgiana Cavendish, née Spencer (1757–1806), Duchess of Devonshire (*DNB*). Although the title-page bears the date 1779, *The Sylph* had been first announced as 'This Day is published' in the *Public Advertiser*, 4 Dec. 1778: 'Printed for T. Lowndes, No. 77, in Fleet-street. Where may be had, just published, in 3 Vols. Evelina, a Novel'. Lowndes retained this wording of the advertisement in subsequent issues of the *Public Advertiser* until 28 Dec., when the notice was revised to read, 'THE SYLPH, a Novel; and in three Volumes, Price 7s. 6d. sewed, EVELINA, a Novel.' See also *DL* i. 192–3.

[3] In his reply, dated 27 Jan. 1779, Lowndes wrote to CB, 'The Sylph is wrote by an Es⟨?⟩ Lady I beg Miss will accept of one it may amuse—you shall approve of my future advertisement before Printed' (BL Egerton MS 3695, fo. 12). No mention is made of *The Sylph* when the advertisement for the third edition of *Evelina* duly appeared in the *Public Advertiser*, 26 Feb. 1779.

Lowndes's ambiguous advertising did mislead the public into thinking Fanny Burney had written *The Sylph*: 'Just this instant . . . a Novel was put into my hands called the *Sylph*, AVERRED to me to be the production of the same *Artist*. . . . Tell the Damsel that I will be her Knight Errant, & will protect her spotless fame against the *Silphites*, who profane her name' (Bewley to CB, 29 May 1779, Osborn).

[1] This letter was sent as a covering note to CB's paper on the musical powers of the child prodigy William Crotch (1775–1847). The paper was read to the Royal Society on 18 Feb. 1779, and officially published under the title 'Account of an Infant Musician', *Philosophical Transactions of the Royal Society of London*, vol. lxix, pt. I (1779), 183–206. CB also had the *Account* printed separately for his own use by John Nichols (1745–1826), in a quarto format. See also Lonsdale, pp. 249–50. The *Account* was reprinted in Dodsley's *Annual Register . . . for the year 1779* (1796), pp. 75–86; and extracts were included in *GM* xlix (1779), 588–91. For Crotch, see *DNB; New Grove*; M. Raeburn, 'Dr. Burney, Mozart and Crotch', *Musical Times*, xcvii (1956), 519–20; J. Rennert, *William Crotch (1775–1847) Composer, Artist, Teacher* (Lavenham, 1975).

Sir.

As your curiosity seemed much excited by the extraordinary Accounts of the Norwich Musical Child,[2] & as you expressed some
desire to know in what particulars his performance was wonderful, &
disposition to Music superior to that of other Children of the same
age; after making all the enquiries my leisure & opportunities would
allow, & repeatedly hearing & studying him, I have drawn up the
following account, which, if it does not appear too trivial, I should be
glad if you would do me the honour of presenting to the Royal Society,
as a mark of my respect & veneration for that learned Body, who, as
their enquiries extend to all parts of Nature, will perhaps not disdain
to receive a narrative of the uncommon exertions of the human faculties
at a more early period of Life than they usually develope.

I have the honour to be, with great regard,
Sir, your obedient & most humble servant.
Cha[s] Burney.

S[t] Martin's Street. | Feb[y] 9th 1779.

To [Jacob Schuback][1]   [St Martin's Street],
                                    12 February 1779

AL draft (Osborn).
Docketed by FBA: *I*

12me Fev[r] 1779—A Londres.

Monsieur.

Je[2] ne veux pas perdre une occasion nouvelle de vous remercier de
la Lettre[3] dont vous m'avez honoré, et qui me fut rendû Mardi[4] au
Soir a mon retour au logis, quand il etait trop tard pour profiter alors

---

[2] Hunter's interest in infant prodigies was not confined to William Crotch: he had already
consulted CB about some other child. See CB to Hunter, 29 July [1774].

A fragment of CB's MS memoirs provides further information. CB recorded that on Sunday 7
Feb. 1779 he had 'Examined little Crotch the Musical Child of 3½ old. Th⟨is⟩ was previous to
writing, at the request of D[r] W: Hunter, an account of this infant Musician for the Royal
Society.' CB went on to note that on 14 Feb. 'The Hon[ble] Daines Barrington & D[r] W: Hunter
came to my house to hear the paper read, which was afterwards printed in the Philosophical
Transactions' (*Frag. Mem.*, Folger: MS Y. c. 377(1)).

[1] Jacob Schuback (1726–84), to whom C. D. Ebeling and J. J. C. Bode had dedicated their
German translation (2 vols., Hamburg, 1773) of CB's *German Tour*, was a lawyer, Syndic of
Hamburg, a diplomatist, and amateur musician (*MGG*; *New Grove*).

[2] MS Je] Malgre la Mortification avec laquelle Je *deleted*.

[3] Schuback's letter is not preserved, but CB published an extract from it in *Handel Commem.*,
p. 56 n.

[4] MS Mardi] *interlined above deleted* Vendredi

To ~~ Hist   London, Feb? 21ᵗʰ 1779.

Sir   St Martins Street,
                                     Lincoln Fields.
(a beautiful letter)

If you imagine my Silence has been Voluntary, since the Letter & Sonatas wᶜʰ you did me the honour to submit to my Inspection came to hand, you neither think justly of yourself nor of me.

3. Burney to Benjamin Archer, 21–28 February 1779. The manuscript bears Madame d'Arblay's docket, 'a beautiful letter' and shows her characteristic editorial obliteration of her father's text.

de la poste etrangere; Je suis pourtant bien mortifié des reproches que vous me faites, et le suis encore plus de ce qu'il ne me sera pas possible de me justifier entierement a vos yeux. Il est vrai, Monsieur, et Je l'avoue [5]avec confusion,[5] que Je reçus la Lettre dont vous voulâtes bien m'honorer du 16 Fev. 1776:[6]—Votre *Traité sur la declamation*[7] m'est aussi parvenû, et m'a fait le plus grand plaisir; Mais la Multiplicités de mes affaires M'embarrasserent alors tellement qu'ils m'ont empéché de vous marquer combien j'etais sensible a l'honneur que vous me faisiez, et ayant été forcé de defferer ainsi de Jour en Jour ma reponse Je devins enfin si honteux de l'apparence qu'il y avait de Negligence dans mon procedé que Je n'eus plus le courage de vous addresser. A l'egard de votre Traité admirable, il est ecrit sur un Sujet que Je n'ai pas encore eu occasion de traiter dans Mon Histoire de la Musique, dont [8]Je n'ai encore pû offrir que le 1r Tome au Public.[8] Je suis actuellement[9] occupé à preparer le 2d[10]—et quand le tems sera arrivé pour [11]ecrire sur la Declamation[11] Je serai charmé de profiter de vos lumieres, et des idées dont vous avez favorisé le public sur ce Sujet.

En Attendant, Je vous prie Monsr de croire que Je serai toujours sensiblement flatté d'avoir de vos nouvelles, et que vous me trouverez toujours aussi prompt et aussi exact qu'il me le sera possible a executer aucune commission dont vous voudrez bien me chargez en Angleterre.

J'ai l'honneur d'etre Monsieur
&c—[12]

To Benjamin Archer[1]   St Martin's Street, 21–28 February 1779

ALS (Osborn)
Docketed by FBA: ✗ To ~ ~ Hist | (a beautiful letter)   *Also* LS copy (Osborn: 'Musical Letterbook').   *Addressed*: To Benjamin Archer Esqr—March the 1st

[5–5] MS avec confusion,] *interlined above deleted* a ma honte
[6] Not preserved.
[7] Schuback's anonymous treatise *Von der musicalischen Declamation* (Göttingen, 1775), had been translated for CB by Brigg Price Fountaine (see CB to Fountaine, 5 Apr. 1776, n. 1).
[8–8] MS Je . . . Public.] *interlined above deleted* le 1r Vol apparût il y a 2 ou 3 ans—
[9] MS actuellement] *interlined above deleted* maintenant
[10] Thomas Twining's letter to CB dated 1 Feb. 1779 (BL Add. MS 39929, fos. 191–2; and notes, Add. MS 39936, fo. 65v) shows the precise stage at which CB had arrived in the composition of the second volume of the *History of Music*: on that date, Twining returned to CB the printed proofs of the first chapter, and the completed MS of the second.
[11–11] MS ecrire . . . Declamation] *interlined above deleted* traiter sur cette matiere,
[12] CB's draft omits the full complimentary close and signature.

[1] Benjamin Archer (d. 1814), of St Kitts, Leeward Islands, West Indies, merchant and amateur musician, had had a set of *Six Sonatas for two Violins and a Violoncello with a Thorough Bass*

1778.   *Docketed by* FBA: × NB. parts to be taken for fragm[ts] musical.   *Editor's note:* The original letter is heavily obliterated by FBA. With the assistance, however, of the copy in the 'Musical Letterbook', the text of the original may be restored.

London, Feb[y] 21th 1779.[2]
S[t] Martin's Street,
Leicester Fields.

Sir.

If you imagine my Silence has been Voluntary, since the Letter & Sonatas[3] w[ch] you did me the honour to submit to my Inspection came to hand, you neither think justly of yourself nor of me. ⌐It was late in the summer ere the Parcel arrived at my house, at w[ch] time I was in Hampshire, & did not see it till autumn. It was my real wish & intention to answer your Letter immediately on the perusal of your Compositions, in the gratification of w[ch] wish I sh[d] have had the more pleasure, as they discover knowledge⌐ in ⌐Counterpoint, an acquaintance with the works of good Masters, & a considerable share of Genius. But, unluckily, after a long absence from home I was then oppressed wth business & engagements of various kinds, w[ch], without making me forget your request, mortified me incessantly at not being able to comply with it. And still to make me suffer more in your Opinion, when I *did* get a few minutes w[ch] I intended to employ in giving my honest Sentiments on your productions, I was unable to find either them or your Letter: both having been mislaid, & mingled with heaps of other Papers, w[ch] form such a Chaos in my house as renders the meeting wth any particular thing subservient to mere Chance.[4]

for the Harpsichord published at London with a dedication page dated 'S[t] Christophers July 26th 1770.' A single copy of this publication is preserved in the Rowe Music Library, King's College, Cambridge (*BUCEM*). On 27 June 1812, 'being about to depart from' St Kitts, Archer made his will (PRO, Prerogative Court of Canterbury, 170 Pakenham), bequeathing to his natural son the proceeds from the sale of several lots of land in Basseterre, St Kitts, and securities. He died 'at an advanced age' in London on 13 Dec. 1814 (*GM* lxxxiv (1814)[2], 677). Included in the sale of CB's musical library (*Cat. Mus. Lib.*, lot 656) is a 'Sonata by a Gentleman at St. Kitt's, *in score*, MS.', doubtless one of Archer's compositions.

[2] CB's MS presents a problem in the second digit of his date. He appears to have written originally 'Feb[y] 20th', then to have altered the 'o' to '1' with several strokes of the pen that produced what can only be described as a messy blot. In changing the date from 20 to 21 Feb., CB furthermore failed to alter the superscripted '[th]' to the grammatical '[st]'. Matters are not helped by the MS 'Musical Letterbook' copy: this letter is there firmly dated 'March the 1st 1778', clearly in error.

[3] Archer's letter is not preserved. In his comments on Archer's compositions, it is illuminating to compare what CB said with regard to Handel: 'it is impossible for any composer to invent a GENUS of composition that is *wholly and rigorously new*, any more than for a poet to form a *language, idiom, and phraseology*, for himself. All that the greatest and boldest musical inventor *can* do, is to avail himself of the best effusions, combinations, and effects, of his predecessors; to arrange and apply them in a new manner; and to add, from his own source, whatever he can draw, that is grand, graceful, gay, pathetic, or, in any other way, pleasing' (*Handel Commem.*, p. 39).

[4] Twining affords us a neat characterization of the chaos in CB's study (or, as he liked to call

And now having fortuitously laid my hands on them, I shall not let them escape from me till I have given them a 2ᵈ perusal.

Feb. 28.⌉ You will now, Sir, have a few reflexions, dictated by that Probity wᶜʰ the modesty & diffidence wᵗʰ wᶜʰ you have appealed to my opinion, require. I can perceive in your Harmony, & disposition of the parts, an ingenious design, & a use & facility in the exercise of your Pen. ⌐& with respect to the *Mechanical* part of each Sonata, there are but few things to censure, and not many to mend. If I were within the reach of conversation I shᵈ take the liberty perhaps of specifying the very few places I have in my Eye, while I say this; but unfortunately that not being the Case, my Leisure will not allow me to set abᵗ a regular Criticism in writing.⌉ As to *Invention* in Music, after all that has been produced by the happy Effusions & Enthusiasm of the great Masters of the Art in Europe, it is extreamly difficult to extend its Limits, without violating the rules of Composition, & preferring the Grotesque to the Graceful, the crude to the natural, & adopting, for the sake of Novelty, what has often presented itself to others, but wᶜʰ sound Judgment, & good taste have rejected. No ambition of this kind appears in your Pieces; the Subjects of wᶜʰ are natural & often grace-ful, though, perhaps, not always new. However ⌐no marks of direct *Plagiarism* appear—though persons well-read in the favourite authors of the present times may perhaps in some places imagine particular Passages & Effects to have proceeded from *Imitation*, & may think that Schobert, & Eichner[5] stand high in your favour.⌉ However, we often remember what we have read, without recollecting that we *have* read it. And it is perhaps right for a young Composer, as well as Poet, to have some Model of imitation in his Eye, as Pope had Dryden; yet there is a Time for Originallity to break the Trammels of Authority & for Genius to go alone. It has always appeared to me necessary for a

it, 'spidery'), as well as a rare glimpse of CB at work on his *History*: '. . . keep writing on, & don't let yourself cool. But I feel for the *rinforza* of chaos that all these accessions will produce in your poor crammed study—you will find nothing—and, la pauvre bibliothecario be expected to find everything! "Fanny, what *have* you done with that MS of Thingumtide there.—God bless my soul, now this is very extraordinary.—I had it but this minute—you *must* have poked it into some hole or other"' (Twining to CB, 19 Dec. 1778).

⁵ Johann Schobert (*c.*1735–67), harpsichordist (*MGG; New Grove*) whose compositions show the characteristics of the Mannheim school, 'is well entitled to a niche in an English history of Music, his pieces for the harpsichord having been for many years the delight of all those who could play or hear them. . . . In 1766, I was the first who brought his works to England from Paris. His style never pleased in Germany so much as in England and France' (*Hist. Mus.* iv. 597; Mercer, ii. 956).

Ernst Eichner (1740–77), bassoon player, and composer of the younger Mannheim school (*MGG; New Grove*), 'introduced a style between that of Schobert and the present; with less fire than Schobert, and more taste and expression' (*Hist. Mus.* iv. 598; Mercer, ii. 957).

CB himself employed Schobert's and Eichner's sonatas as pedagogical tools, as is shown in a signed MS Receipt dated 30 Sept. 1779 (Osborn) of payment for harpsichord lessons and music given to one Miss Hoare. See also CB to Twining, 14 Dec. 1781, n. 30.

young Musician to study the works of all the great & favourite Masters of his Art; but not to adhere to the style of any one long enough to become a servile Copy. Rather let him endeavour to incorporate all their beauties & perfections in his own Store-house of Invention; & then give way to his native temper & powers, & try to form a manner of writing peculiar to himself.

If it were possible to wait till fermentation came on, & the mind laboured with some new & striking Subject, Composers of the first Class w^d not so frequently repeat themselves & others as they do, when like Piccini, Paesiello, & Sacchini they engage to furnish more operas & other Compositions, in one year, than a Single Copyist c^d fairly transcribe.[6]

When a young composer first begins to arrange his Ideas & pour them on Paper it is necessary to examine the Works of others, to know what *may be done*; but when he is sure of his Harmony & Modulation, he sh^d perhaps only look in them to see what to *avoid*: not because unwarrantable on the side of rule, but because it has been already done. By this reflexion I w^d by no means be understood to insinuate that you are never to write a passage that has already appeared on Paper, as y^r Music w^d be detestable if that were the Case; for there are certain Traits in Melody & Combinations in Harmony wch are as much in Common wth all Composers, as the single words & phrases of a Language are to all Writers, whether in Verse or Prose. At the time of Conception a Composer perhaps feels passages, subjects, & particular movements stronger than he can hope a cool hearer will do, or than he himself will do in a different disposition at another Time. Till a reputation is established it appears necessary for a new Candidate for musical fame to present the public with only such specimens of his abilities as will make them hunger after more; & as have evident

[6] Niccolò Piccinni (1728–1800), 'may be ranked among the most fertile, spirited, and original composers that the Neapolitan school has produced. ... Sacchini assured me, in 1776, that Piccini had composed at least three hundred operas, thirteen of which were produced in seven months' (*Hist. Mus.* iv. 619–20; Mercer, ii. 974). Piccinni wrote 139 operas. See CB to Garrick, 17–[18] Oct. 1770, n. 56. Since 1776, Piccinni had been employed in Paris as opera composer, a circumstance which precipitated the 'querelle célèbre' between his admirers and those of Gluck (*New Grove*).

Giovanni Paisiello (1740–1816), who at Naples had found in Piccinni a formidable rival, had journeyed in 1776 to St Petersburg at the invitation of the Empress Catherine II (1729–96). See *New Grove*. His numerous compositions included about 100 operas. CB considered Paisiello 'gifted with as much fertility of invention for dramatic compositions as nature ever bestowed on an Italian opera composer' (Rees).

Antonio Sacchini (1730–86), had come to London in 1772 as Italian opera composer. He 'had a taste so exquisite, and so totally free from pedantry, that he was frequently new without effort. ... In the year 1770, when I saw Sacchini at Venice, he told me that he had composed near forty serious and ten comic operas; and in 1778, upon enquiring of him to what number his dramatic works then amounted, he said to seventy-eight, of which he had forgot even the names of two' (*Hist. Mus.* iv. 520; Mercer, ii. 894). See *New Grove*; and CB to Garrick, 17–[18] Oct. 1770, n. 28.

marks of Originality on the side of Melody, Harmony, Contrivance or Modulation. & as the fundamental rules of Composition seem familiar to you; & your mind & memory are stored with such examples of writing as are allowed to be excellent; there appears to me no reason for your not continuing to record your Feelings, when they are really the offspring of Passion, & are excited without Effort. ⸢Many of your 1ˢᵗ Movements I think if weeded of a few passages that are perhaps a little too familiar, & many parts of your other movements, if published, wᵈ certainly do you credit. Examine them yourself, coolly, & deliberately; & reject what you can recollect to have seen elsewhere, for wᶜʰ your own resources will easily supply you with substitutes. You have in general steered clear of vulgarity, & are often graceful & elegant. There is no pedantry, or affectation in your style, & if you are a severe Critic on yourself, you will have nothing to fear from others. These are my real sentiments, & given with that freedom & sincerity wᶜʰ I wᵈ use to a son or a scholar whom I wished to become a favourite of the public, & an ornament to his Profession.⸣

I am, Sir, your Obedᵗ & most

Humble Servant.

Chaˢ Burney.

To Paul Panton[1]

St Martin's Street,
21 June 1779

AL (City of Liverpool Public Libraries, The Hornby Library: HL 18–4).
Addressed: To ┃ — Panton Esqʳ ┃ Nº 12 Serle Street ┃ Lincoln's Inn ┄┄ *Endorsed by* Panton?: From Dʳ Burney ┃ (June 21ˢᵗ 1779)

Doctor Burney presents his best Compᵗˢ to Mʳ Panton & returns him Mʳ Morris's[2] Welsh MS with many thanks for permitting him to be so long in possession of it.[3] Unfortunately Dʳ B. has been in such a

---

[1] Paul Panton (1727–97), of Plas Gwyn, Pentraeth in Anglesey, Welsh barrister, antiquary, and collector (*DWB*; *DNB*; HMC, *Welsh*, vol. ii, part 3 (1905), pp. 801–70). Sometime in late Apr. or early May 1779, CB had spent a Sunday morning with Panton, probably trying to make sense of the Welsh MS (see nn. 3, 4) which is the subject of the present letter. Twining wrote to CB on 12 May: 'And your Sunday morning—the Sabbath of your studies—lost upon Mʳ Panton!' (BL Add. MS 39929, fo. 200). Panton was a friend of the Morris brothers and of Thomas Pennant.

[2] Richard Morris, or Morys (1703–79), Welsh scholar, founder of the Cymmrodorion Society, had held the post of chief clerk of foreign accounts in the Navy Office since 1757, and dwelt in a house within the precincts of the Tower (*DWB*; *DNB*; J. H. Davies, ed., *The Letters of Lewis, Richard, William and John Morris, of Anglesey, 1728–1765* (Aberystwyth, 1906–9), i, pp. xii, xviii–xxi). On the death of his scholarly brothers, Lewis (1701–65) and William (1705–63), Richard Morris had secured their collections of MSS, which added to his own form the Morrisian collection now in the British Library (Add. MSS 14866–961; see H. Owen, ed., *Additional Letters*

Constant hurry since he was first favoured wth this curious MS. as not to have been able to study it wth the attention he wished in order to decypher the Musical Characters. He has however acquired some Idea of their import, & reduced to Modern Notation a few Fragments.[4] As his Leisure time is now coming on, when he intends resuming his Historical Enquiries & making a considerable progress in his 2^d Vol. if he c^d again be indulged with the MS. he w^d try to make himself Master of its musical contents. He will certainly ere long do himself the honour of waiting upon Mr Morris at the Tower[5] in order to solicit this Favour.

If the sending the MS. to the Tower will be attended with any inconvenience to Mr Panton, D^r B———'s Servant will carry it on if he has instructions given him by M^r P.

St Martin's Street | Monday 21. June 1779

To Mrs Thrale
[Chessington],
29 [August 1779]

ALS (Rylands, English MS 545, no. 3).

of the Morrises of Anglesey (1735–1786) (1947–9), i, pp. vii–xi). For the lives and activities of the Morris brothers, see *DWB*.

[3] This small folio MS volume bears the title 'Musica neu Beroriaeth' and is now BL Add. MS 14905. For a description of this 'Robert ap Huw's MS' and its significance, see *New Grove*, xx. 161–2, and under 'Ap Huw'. Although CB's letters to Twining relating his discovery of the MS, and his struggles with having it translated and interpreted are not preserved, Twining's replies (19 Dec. 1778, 8 Jan., 12 Mar., 12 May 1779: BL Add. MS 39929, fos. 185–8, 189–90, 193–6, 199–202) furnish a good deal of information. In his letter of 19 Dec. 1778, Twining wrote 'O but this Welch MS is *una gioia*, & worth a little hunting after. . . . You must get that Mr Jones to translate for you.' On 12 Mar. 1779, Twining complained, 'As to Mr Jones's 2 letters, they give me not the least satisfaction. . . . He neither *proves* anything, nor *explains* anything. . . . Can you find nobody that understands *Welch*, but a *Welchman*? The MS is surely a great curiosity & deserves a little groping.' CB was still troubled in May: Twining wrote on 12 May, 'I can't help being diverted to see you sticking your quill into the brains of every *Welch Man* you come near, & sucking them 'till your cheeks meet, squeezing their poor heads with your two thumbs as a school-boy serves an orange, to make more come out than is in—& all to no purpose!' See also Lonsdale, p. 249.

[4] CB's circumspect treatment of Morris's MS, with 'specimens' of Welsh notation 'explained in modern musical characters' is included in *Hist. Mus.* ii. 110–14; Mercer, i. 484–7. CB later on in the volume (ii. 352; Mercer, i. 647) admitted 'that though the gravity or acuteness of the several notes can be ascertained, yet their lengths, or duration, cannot be established with any degree of certainty.' In a letter to Panton dated 31 Jan. 1786 (Hyde), CB still had not solved the problem: 'I am pretty certain of the notes, c^d I but discover a method of knowing their duration.' He never did (see Rees, under 'Wales—Language, &c.').

[5] Richard Morris's residence in the Tower of London had caused Twining to comment in his letter of 8 Jan. to CB: 'I shall be glad to hear you are committed to the *Tower*—but take care of your *head*! old MSS have brought many a one to a *block*.'

Sunday 29th as I
really believe—

I thought, as how, we were to *throw notes* at each other. I have so
long been a dealer in Notes, & am now so beset wth them,[1] that if you
liked their fashion, I w^d send you some to *un*bother, as I have had
partly enough of them. But, unluckily, a million of my notes w^d not be
worth one of yours—*such* a one as I carried off with me, unread, on
Tuesday, dated 18 Aug^{t2}—& I found your sweet, dear, innocent,
sportive little *Soul*, wrapt up in it![3]—Well, 'tis a good little Soul, as
eefer vaas—& I likes it.—Who, but a Swan, c^d sing so sweetly, when
dying?—indeed who but the truely innocent & tranquil can sing at
all, in such a situation?[4]—Pray content yourself, as you will delight
me, with singing *worse*, & being *better*.

Here's no news yet! & so we'll have no Politics[5]—they sour the
blood, & are not half so exhilerating as Quibbles & nonsense—à
propos—here has been our Fr^d Jemmy Mathias[6] to day, singing like
a bird—of wisdom, as he is—& has taken up all the precious time I
intended to bestow on you, with his old songs & saws—'Honour &
Aaa Aa Aaa AaArms'[7]—&c—Well, you may not like his *Vox taurina*,
but you *must* allow that his *Manner* is good, & that he sings in a *very
pretty Taste*.[8]

---

[1] On 31 July 1779 CB had retired to Chessington by way of Streatham (*ED* ii. 255–60), and
was now actively engaged in writing the third chapter of the second volume of the *History of
Music*: 'Of the formation of the Time-table, and state of Music from that discovery till about the
middle of the fourteenth century'. See Lonsdale, pp. 250–1.

[2] Now in the Osborn Collection. Mrs Thrale entered an almost verbatim transcription of her
letter into *Thraliana*, i. 402. CB had spent a week in town in mid-Aug., returning to Chessington
with Mrs Burney on Tuesday, 24 Aug. (Susan to Fanny Burney, 25–26 Aug. [1779], BL
Egerton MS 3691, fo. 11).

[3] Mrs Thrale included in her 18 Aug. letter her 6-line translation of the celebrated epigram
'Animula vagula blandula', attributed to the dying Emperor Hadrian (76–138) by Aelius
Spartianus in his *De Vita Hadriani*, xxv. 9 (*The Scriptores Historiae Augustae*, ed. D. Magie (1922–32),
i. 78).

[4] On 10 Aug. at Streatham, Mrs Thrale had 'miscarried in the utmost Agony ... after
fainting five times ... a Boy quite formed & perfect' (*Thraliana*, i. 400–1).

[5] See n. 15; and CB to Fanny Burney, [29 Aug.] 1779, n. 12.

[6] James Mathias (*c.*1710–82), wealthy Hamburg merchant, of Freeman's Yard, Cornhill,
and formerly business agent to Mrs Thrale's uncle, Sir Thomas Salusbury (1708–73). Mathias
was a friend of the Burneys (*ED* ii. 306), given to singing: 'The same tongue which so often
uttered melodious sounds, and advanced the empire of harmony, prevented discord and the
calamities of vexatious suits', according to an obituary notice in *GM* lii (1782), 311, by Jonas
Hanway (1712–86). See also Clifford, pp. 32, 107; *Thraliana*, i. 26; Johnson *Letters*, i. 237; ii. 337,
420; A. L. Reade, *The Reades of Blackwood Hill and Dr. Johnson's Ancestry* (1906), pp. 240–1.

[7] Not identified.

[8] 'This James Mathias was eminently skilled in Musick I asked Dr Burney about that—Yes
says he the Man has Knowledge enough, but no more Taste than a Bull' (*Thraliana*, i. 148).
  In her reply dated 30 Aug. [1779] (Osborn), Mrs Thrale wrote, '... but if you cou'd bear
Mathias indeed who'll pity you?

Well, but I forgot to tell you that your 'Good Night'![9] is got about—
that is, the *good report* of it—& I was entreated to make use of my
interest with you in favour of a very good Fr^d & man of taste[10] to
obtain a Copy of it for him—do you know, my dear Mad^m, that I
have not one myself—I lost mine with the silly tune I set to it[11]—pray
let me have another, & I'll promise never to sing away the sense
again. When you have leasure, do favour me with another Copy, à
Coté de l'original—& tell me if I may communicate [it] to the Elect—
none other shall ever be thought dign⟨e.⟩[12]

Ab^t to morrow 7 night, if matters & things go well—what think you
of taking a peep at the old Castle & Philosopher of Chesington?[13]—*do*
y, if you can—& I'll stick as close to you as a Harvest Bug—till you
get to Streatham & as long as I can afterwards. — — I am *in* for
another Sunday at Epsom[14]—this Day fortnight—I hope you got our
D^r again safe & sound, after a frightful fall he got at Chamier's[15]—'all
so long as he vaas—'[16] pray remember me in all kindness to my

> For not more loud and deep the Lay
> Which Bulls can roar and Asses bray.

I was talking of him last Night to Miss Burney; odd enough! for to be sure I do not think of the
Man twice a Year, & who would have dream'd that he was ever admitted at Chessington!'

[9] Mrs Thrale's translation of a French poem by Chrétien-François de Lamoignon (1644–1709),
jurist, friend of Racine and Boileau, and President (1705) of the Académie des inscriptions
(Michaud), was entered into *Thraliana* (i. 348–9) in Dec. 1778. The refrain in the French
original, 'Bon soir la Compagnie', is rendered by Mrs Thrale, '. . . bid the Company Good
Night'.

[10] Possibly Samuel Crisp.

[11] Of her translation, Mrs Thrale wrote, 'Burney has set these Lines to Musick & says they
make an admirable Song' (*Thraliana*, i. 349). CB's setting does not appear to have survived.

[12] In her reply of 30 Aug. (Osborn), Mrs Thrale complied with CB's request, with the
comment, 'And so I will to be sure, & so here is the *Schtofe* just as you wish'd & desired—Be the
Song whose it will, the Confidence is yours, & in you I always willingly confide.' She copied out
Lamoignon's poem as well as her own translation.

[13] The present letter, and one from Mrs Thrale dated 27 Aug. (Osborn) crossed in the mails.
In Mrs Thrale's letter, she too declared 'Well! if nothing important happens before, I do intend
treating Miss Burney with a Sight of her Friend Mr Crisp, & myself with a Drive to Chessington
next Monday Morning.'

In her reply of 30 Aug. (Osborn), Mrs Thrale confirmed the arrangements for her first visit to
Chessington, proposed for Monday 6 Sept.: '. . . on Monday next you shall present a Friend who
loves you well, to a Friend who has loved you long'.

The Thrale visit appears to have taken place as planned. CB himself 'from multiplicity of
avocations, was forced, when the day arrived, to relinquish his share in the little invasion' (*Mem.*
ii. 183). See *HFB*, p. 116.

[14] Anthony Chamier had a house at Epsom (Samuel Johnson, *Diaries, Prayers, and Annals*, ed.
E. L. McAdam, Jr., *et al.*, in *The Yale Edition of the Works of Samuel Johnson*, vol. i (New Haven and
London, 1958), pp. 298–9).

[15] Dr Johnson's fall probably occurred on Sunday 22 Aug. Susan Burney records that CB on
that date 'was at Mr. Chamier's' (*ED* ii. 263). As Under Secretary of State, Anthony Chamier
was in a position to inform Johnson and his circle of the latest developments and activities of the
Franco-Spanish fleet which in mid-Aug. 1779 threatened England's southern shores (Johnson
Letters, ii. 302; A. T. Patterson, *The Other Armada: the Franco–Spanish Attempt to Invade Britain in
1779* (Manchester, 1960), ch. 10).

[16] This quotation is not identified.

Master—Miss T. & the *Ting forte* are both, I hope, in perfect tune—& that you may have recovered all you[r] Lillies & Roses[17] & be delightfully *made up*[18] ere this, is the fervent Prayer of dear Mad^m yours

in all Friendship
& affection,
Ch. Burney.

To Fanny Burney[1]   [Chessington, 29 August] 1779[2]

ALS (BL Egerton MS 3690, fos. 4–5).
Addressed: To | Miss Burney   *Docketed by* FBA: on | a project | of writing — | by the | instigation | of | Mr. | Sheridan— | a | comedy. ✖ ✠ VIII—79

Sunday Night—

My dear Fan—
  I love originals of good Things & good Folk so much better than Copies, that I cared not a farthing for Mrs Thrale's Letter,[3] or yours,[4]

---

[17] Cf. Robert Herrick (1591–1674), 'To the Virgins, to make much of Time', in *Hesperides* (1648):

> Gather ye Rose-buds while ye may,
>   Old Time is still a flying:
> And this same flower that smiles to day,
>   To morrow will be dying.

[18] Mrs Thrale described her own appearance in May 1778: 'The Neck rather longish, and remarkably white—so much so as to create Suspicions of its being painted ... The Complexion however is perfectly clear—the Red very bright, & the White eminently good & clean' (*Thraliana*, i. 321).

[1] Following the success of *Evelina* and her entry into the Streatham circle, Fanny had been encouraged to write a comedy by Dr Johnson, Mrs Thrale, Richard Brinsley Sheridan, Sir Joshua Reynolds, and Arthur Murphy. Early in 1779, she started writing 'The Witlings', a satiric comedy about a set of bluestockings. CB took the completed play with him to Chessington and there on 2 Aug. read it to 'Daddy' Crisp and the assembled company (Susan to Fanny Burney, 3–6 Aug. [1779], BL Egerton MS 3691, fos. 9–10). After an initial favourable reception, however, CB, in consultation with Crisp, vetoed Fanny's hopes to have the comedy staged the next season. Mrs Thrale noted the objections succinctly: 'Mr Crisp advised her against bringing it on, for fear of displeasing the female Wits—a formidable Body, & called by those who ridicule them, the *Blue Stocking Club*' (*Thraliana*, i. 381, n. 3). The MS of the abandoned play is now in the Berg Collection. See *HFB*, pp. 129–38. See also CB to Fanny Burney, [27 Nov. 1779], for Mme d'Arblay's misplaced endorsement, which should belong to this letter.
[2] CB's 'Sunday Night' can only refer to Sunday 29 Aug. The 'Combined Fleets', to which he makes reference in this letter, 'frighted the whole Nation' by appearing off Plymouth on 16 Aug. (n. 12); the following Sunday, 22 Aug., CB was engaged at Anthony Chamier's (CB to Mrs Thrale, 29 [Aug. 1779], n. 15).
[3] Of 18 Aug., which CB 'carried off with me, unread' (see CB to Mrs Thrale, 29 [Aug. 1779], n. 2). MS Letter] *altered by FBA to* Letters
[4] Not preserved. Fanny, who had spent the first half of Aug. in town nursing her sister Hetty,

while I was near you.[5] My Stomach came down afterwards to the level of *both* your Letters—⌈I have been very hot & *flabby*,[6] or I sh^d have answered both sooner — — Yours is rather serious, & requires Care in preaching an answer — — I am glad the objections all fall on [7]the Stocking[7]-Club-Party—as my chief & almost only quarrel was with its Members. As it is, not only the Whole Piece, but the *plot* had best be kept secret, from every body—As to finishing another upon a *new Story*, in a *hurry*, for next winter, I think it *may* be done, & w^d be not only feasible but desirable at any other Time than the present—But public affairs are in such terrible Confusion, & there is so little likelihood of People having more money or more spirits soon,[8] that I own myself not eager for you to come out with any kind of Play, *next Winter*. Many Scenes & Characters might otherwise be preserved, & perhaps save you time—though I am not sure of it — — for the adjusting, fine-drawing, & patching neatly is teadious work—

Crisp has been out of spirits & sorts the whole week,[9] & in such a humour I did not chuse to teaze him ab^t writing—nor to send a Letter to Streatham without writing myself—so take this in part of an answer[10]—the House has been brim-full all Day—& I c^d not speak even to Crisp—& it is with difficulty I get this ready for the *Parson*⌉[11]— I had not read, ⌈or even opened⌉ your Letter, when we last Conversed

returned to Streatham on Tuesday 17 Aug. (Fanny Burney to Crisp, [*c*.13 Aug. 1779], Berg; *DL* i. 260). On 18 Aug., Mrs Thrale noted with satisfaction in her journal: 'Fanny Burney has pleased me today—She resolves to give up a Play likely to succeed; for fear it may bear hard upon some Respectable Characters' (*Thraliana*, i. 401). Mrs Thrale then apparently suggested to Fanny an 'idea—of new modelling the play' (*DL* i. 262), which with 'hard fagging' Fanny might accomplish in time for the following theatrical season. Fanny evidently set all this down in a letter addressed to CB who was in town from about 17 until 24 Aug.

[5] CB and Mrs Burney evidently had called in at Streatham on their way to Chessington on Tuesday 24 Aug.

[6] 'Here is the hottest Weather that England ever knew', wrote Mrs Thrale on 1 Sept. 1779 (*Thraliana*, i. 403).

[7-7] MS the Stocking] *altered by FBA to* the Blue Stocking

[8] CB was himself feeling the hardness of the times. Mrs Thrale noted in July 1779 with reference to him: 'Poor dear Man! he is sadly pressed for Pelf . . . the Times go *so* hard with him' (*Thraliana*, i. 395).

[9] For an account of Crisp who at this time 'spends his life in perpetual apprehension of terrible national calamities', see *ED* ii. 261–3.

[10] Fanny's missing letter to CB (n. 4) was also intended for Crisp's perusal. The original condemnation of 'The Witlings' had been conveyed in a joint letter (not preserved) described by Fanny as 'that hissing, groaning, catcalling epistle' which 'my two daddies put their heads together to concert' (*DL* i. 260).

Crisp eventually wrote to Fanny. His letter is printed, undated, in *DL* i. 261–4. 'Your other Daddy (who hardly loves You better than I do) I understand, has wrote You his sentiments on the Subject of your last letter—I cannot but be of the same opinion' (Berg: Diary MSS I, p. 1007).

[11] Not identified, other than that he acted as the postman for Liberty Hall, Chessington, which was notoriously remote and inaccessible. Susan Burney observes of this local vicar: 'Surely Fielding never drew a more poor creature than this man among his country parsons!' (*ED* ii. 260).

on the subject—& I believe you wondered at my taking no Notice of your new Project—indeed it was what at first struck me as the most feasible & desirable—But the Combined Fleets had not then frighted the whole Nation[12]—But all this is no reason why you sh^d not write— tho' it is one against doing anything of such Consequence to your Fame &c—in a *hurry*—don't fear that the Author of Evelina will be soon forgotten! —— Come out When you will—something Good, & pleasing, will be expected—You have resources sufficient for Writing a great deal—only, for the stage, I w^d have you very Careful, & very Perfect—that is, as far so as your own Efforts, & the best advice you can get, can make you. In the Novel Way, there is no danger—& in that, *no Times* can affect ye.[13] Adieu—my dear Fan—

Believe me most affect^{ly} yrs.
C.B.

To [William Colman?][1]   [St Martin's Street, mid-October 1779][2]

AL draft (Osborn).
Docketed by FBA: ✳ on Crotch ┃ NB. ┃ To some ┃ Learned Cambridge ┃ Professor on ┃ the musical ┃ tracts ┃ in the ┃ Cam. Libraries.

Dear Sir.

As you seemed to interest yourself ab^t little Crotch the Infant-Musician, concerning whom, at the desire of some ³respectable persons³

---

[12] On 16 June 1779 Spain had declared war, thus formally joining the Franco-American alliance against Britain (*Public Advertiser*, 17 June 1779; Walpole *Corresp.* xxiv. 482–5). British fears of an invasion reached a climax when in mid-Aug. the combined fleets of France and Spain, comprising an armada of 66 ships of the line with attendant lesser vessels, slipped past the British fleet, entered the English Channel, and appeared off Plymouth on 16 Aug. (A. T. Patterson, *The Other Armada: The Franco–Spanish Attempt to Invade Britain in 1779* (Manchester, 1960), *passim*).

[13] MS ye] *altered by* FBA *to* you

[1] The unnamed recipient of this letter may have been William Colman (1728–94), DD (1778), who had been elected Master of Corpus Christi College, Cambridge, on 25 June 1778 (J. Lamb, ed., *Masters' History of the College of Corpus Christi and the Blessed Virgin Mary in the University of Cambridge* (Cambridge, 1831), pp. 253–7; Venn).

[2] The date of this letter is conjecturally determined by the following circumstances: CB recorded in his doggerel autobiography for 1779, 'In September, to *Cambridge* I fly for a week ┃ Fresh materials for Volume the second to seek' (*Frag. Mem.*, Berg). He then visited Oxford, returning to London before the end of the month (MS Receipt for Miss Hoare's account, 30 Sept. 1779, Osborn). James ('Hermes') Harris wrote to CB on 14 Oct. (Osborn), to thank him for a copy of the *Account of an Infant Musician*, to enclose which CB had delayed sending the present letter to Cambridge.

³⁻³ MS respectable persons] *interlined above deleted* Friends in the R.S.

281

I drew up an acc^t, for the R. S. wch will soon appear in the Trans-actions; yet as I am allowed a few Copies[4] for the use of my Fr^{ds} I cannot resist the ambition of including you among them. Indeed the many civilities & Kind offices wth wch you honoured me during my late[5] visit to Cambridge w^d sooner have vanquished all scruples ab^t the propriety of making my best acknowledgem^{ts} to you in this manner if I had not waited for the little Paper to be printed wch accompanies this Letter.

And now I have broken in upon your retirement, [6]it seems in gratitude but right to say a few words ab^t the Musical MSS[6] wch I consulted in your Curious Lib^{y7} wch I cannot help wishing were more particularly described in your Lib^y Catal. & assigned to the true Authors.[8] & if Mr Nasmith sh^d ever give another Edit. of the excellent Cat. he lately published,[9] as I have not the honour to know [him] I sh^d through your means perhaps acquaint him with the discoveries I made in perusing N° 210. Musica Hogeri.[10]

The title of this MS has long puzzled the learned, for I find it the subject of a Cor[r]espondence between Baptista Doni[11] of Florence &

---

[4] See CB to Hunter, 9 Feb. 1779, n. 1.

[5] MS late] *interlined above deleted* short

[6-6] MS it ... MSS] *interlined below and above deleted* I cannot help taking the Liberty of acquainting you that

[7] The library of Corpus Christi College, Cambridge, to which Matthew Parker (1504–75), Archbishop of Canterbury (1559–75), had bequeathed his magnificent collection of manuscript and printed books (Lamb, *Masters' History*, pp. 103–5). CB evidently related his experiences in this library to Twining, who in reply laughed at 'Your *getting leave* to *be locked* up in C.C. lib^y from 9 in ye morn^g till 5 in the afternoon' (3–4 Nov. 1779, BL Add. MS 39929, fos. 214–17). By the terms of Archbishop Parker's bequest, strict conditions for the safe keeping of the collection had to be observed. The Master of the College was entrusted with the key of one of the three locks under which the Collection was kept (Lamb, *Masters' History*, p. 104). To gain access to the Parker MSS, CB must therefore have had dealings with Dr Colman.
The account of the Corpus MSS that follows is included almost verbatim in *Hist. Mus.* ii. 121–2; Mercer, i. 492–3.

[8] CB recounts the pleasure he took in his scholarly triumphs: 'I had in my researches dis-covered curious and rare MS. tracts on Music of the Middle Ages before the invention of the press not mentioned in any of the printed or manuscript Catalogues & wch the most learned Librarians did not know were in existance: owing to several different Tracts & Treatises in Latin, French, & obsolete English being bound up in one Vol. & only the first of them mentioned in the lettering or title of the Volume' (*Frag. Mem.*, Osborn).

[9] James Nasmith (1740–1808), DD (1797), Fellow of Corpus Christi College, Cambridge (1765), antiquary (*DNB*; Lamb, *Masters' History*, pp. 406–7), published at College expense *Catalogus librorum manuscriptorum quos collegio Corporis Christi et B. Mariae Virginis in Academia Cantabrigiensi legavit reverendissimus in Christo Pater Matthaeus Parker, archiepiscopus Cantuariensis* (Cambridge, 1777).

[10] Actually, no. 260, described in Nasmith's *Catalogus* (p. 308) as 'Musica Hogeri, *sive* excerp-tiones Hogeri abbatis ex autoribus musicæ artis.' For a full description of this MS volume, see M. R. James, *A Descriptive Catalogue of the Manuscripts in the Library of Corpus Christi College Cambridge* (Cambridge, 1909–12), ii. 10.

[11] Giovanni Battista Doni (1595–1647), Florentine patrician and scholar, whose passionate interest in and championship of ancient music led him to construct a double lyre, and publish in

Dr Thos Rigel[12] of London in 1639.[13] Doni who had Emissaries all over Europe at this Time in search of Musical curiosities upon being told of this MS by Dr Rigel, says: De Hogerii Abbatis Excerptis (siquidem exstarent) brevia quædam Specimina dumtaxat cuperem: quum enim autor sit mihi plane ignotus, affirmare non ausim, an talia sint ejus scripta, ut totus exscribi mereatur.—The D[r] in his reply to Doni the same year tells him that after making all possible enquiry in the Library at *Cambridge*—nullum Hogerii scriptum in ea Bibliotheca inveniri.[14]—Whether this was true, or only a short way of getting rid of the trouble incident to such enquiries, I know not, but I find the B[k] entered in the Catal. that goes under the Name of Dr Gale[15] thus: Excerptiones *Rogeri Baconis* ex auctoribus Musicæ Artis.[16] & it is possible that this Book may have been transcribed by, or for, this wonderful man; it is the more possible as he admitted Musica among

his lifetime the *Compendio del trattato de' generi, e de' modi della musica* (Rome, 1635); the *Annotazioni sopra il compendio* (Rome, 1640); and *De praestantia musicae veteris* (Florence, 1647), among other works (*New Grove*). For CB's severe comments on Doni, see *Hist. Mus.* i. 111–13, iv. 20; Mercer, i. 107–8, ii. 511.

[12] Thomas Ridgley, or Rugeley (*c.*1575?–1656), physician, musician, and scholar, educated at St John's College, Cambridge, MD (1608), FRCP (1622), of whom his contemporary Dr Baldwin Hamey (1600–76) wrote: 'Medicus bonus musicusque, linguæque Latinæ facultate vir præstans' (W. Munk, *The Roll of the Royal College of Physicians of London* (2nd rev. edn., 1878), i. 180; Venn).

[13] MS 1639.] *CB has a footnote mark* (a) *but no note.*

[14] This exchange between Doni and Ridgley was printed in *Io. Baptistae Donii patricii florentini Commercium Litterarium*, ed. A. F. Gori (Florence, 1754), cols. 127, 133. Five years later, in 1644, Ridgley wrote again to Doni with the news that he had managed to get some extracts from the MS in question, 'ex Bibliotheca Collegii Cantabrigiensis, quod Corporis Christi titulum praefert' (ibid., cols. 167–8). CB owned a copy of the *Commercium Litterarium*, which is listed in 'Cat. Fac. Mus.', item 38.

[15] MS Gale] *is followed by a deleted footnote mark* (b) *but CB omitted to delete the footnote itself which reads* Catalogi Libror̄ MSS[torum] Angliæ—1697.

The learned antiquary and collector, Thomas Gale (*c.*1635–1702), DD (1675), Dean of York (*DNB*), had nothing to do with the catalogue entry quoted. It is possible, however, to retrace CB's steps and explain this curious error. When this passage appeared in *Hist. Mus.* ii. 122 (Mercer, i. 493), CB footnoted his reference, as he does here, to the *Catalogi Librorum Manuscriptorum Angliae et Hiberniae in unum collecti*, ed. E. Bernard, *et al.* (Oxford, 1697). In this collection of catalogues of manuscripts, the spurious entry (see n. 16) 'Excerptiones Rogeri Baconi ...' appears under the numbers 1466. 189 (vol. i, pt. 3, p. 138), i.e. item 1466 in a continuous numbering of Cambridge MSS, and manuscript 189 in Corpus Christi College, Cambridge. Having taken this reference, CB subsequently mistook the numeral '189' as a *page* reference, and in turning again to the *Catalogi Librorum Manuscriptorum*, opened the book inadvertently to vol. ii, pt. 1, p. 189, saw there the running-title 'Codices Manuscripti Thomæ Gale', and concluded, without checking, that his reference appeared in the list of Gale's MS collection.

[16] This entry in the *Catalogi Librorum Manuscriptorum*, vol. i, pt. 3, p. 138, is a bibliographical ghost. It is a misreading of item 189 in the list of the MSS in Corpus Christi College, Cambridge, compiled by Thomas James (*c.*1573–1629), Bodley's Librarian (*DNB*). In James's list, item 189 is entered as 'Excerptiones *Hogeri* Abbatis, ex auctoribus musicæ artis' (*Ecloga Oxonio–Cantabrigiensis, tributa in Libros duos* (1600), bk. i, p. 83). Roger Bacon (*c.*1214–94), eminent English Franciscan philosopher (*DNB*). For his interest in music, and the attribution to him of *De valore musices*, see, for example, S. Jebb, ed., *Fratris Rogeri Bacon ... Opus majus* (1733), sig. d2[v], and pp. 111, 149.

[his] studies, & is said by his Biographers to have written *De Valore musices*, pr. secundum Boëtium et cæteros Auctores. However this may have been I can venture to pronounce that upon collating the MS in Benet Coll.[17] Library wch is called *Musica Hogeri* with a transcript of part of it wch I had obtained from the K. of France's Lib^y at Paris,[18] & with the Quotations of Padre Martini[19] & the Abbot Gerbert[20] in their musical Histories I find that it contains *two distinct Treatises* of great antiquity & value: the first, *De Harmonia Institutione*, or the Enchiridion of Hubald,[21] monk of St Amand in Flanders, who died in 930 at near 90 years of age. & the 2^d by St Odo,[22] Abbot of Cluni in Burgundy, who died at the age of 64, in 942. The first is entirely perfect, & the 2^d wants but a few lines at the end, to be complete.

I have likewise a Word or two to say concerning N° 410. 25N.[23] wch not only contains a very ample & scarce Treatise on Music by Walter Odington, Monk of Evesham, who flourished early in the 13th Cent^y[24] but two other Tracts, wch want but little of being perfect. The first of these, wch begins *Quilibet in Arte*, is said in the Margin, & in the

[17] Corpus Christi College, Cambridge, was popularly called 'Benet College' by virtue of its foundation: the Cambridge Guild of Corpus Christi, centred in the parish Church of St Benedict, with the Guild of the Blessed Virgin Mary, successfully interceded in 1352 for a licence to establish a College from King Edward III. See Lamb, *Masters' History*, pp. 7–22.

[18] CB refers to the MS volume now preserved in the Bibliothèque Nationale, Paris, MS lat. 7202.

[19] *Storia della musica*, vol. i (Bologna, 1757), pp. 180, 183, 235.

[20] *De cantu et musica sacra a prima ecclesiae aetate usque ad praesens tempus* (St Blaise, 1774), ii. 56, 58–9, 112–16. CB's copy is listed in 'Cat. Fac. Mus.', item 56.

[21] Hucbald (*c*.840–930), Benedictine monk of St Amand in Flanders, musician and theorist (*MGG*; *New Grove*). CB here confuses (as he does in *Hist. Mus.* ii. 122; Mercer, i. 493) two distinct works: *De Harmonica Institutione* is the only work certainly attributable to Hucbald; the *Musica Enchiriadis*, a different treatise of great importance for its introduction of explanations of part-singing, is not the work of Hucbald. See R. Weakland, OSB, 'Hucbald as Musician and Theorist', *Musical Quarterly*, xlii (1956), 66–84; C. V. Palisca, ed., *Hucbald, Guido, and John on Music* (New Haven, 1978).

[22] CB describes this musical treatise attributed to Odo at length in *Hist. Mus.* ii. 126–8; Mercer, i. 495–7. St Odo of Cluny (879–942), Abbot (927) of the Benedictine monastery of Cluny in Burgundy, monastic reformer (Michaud; *Butler's Lives of the Saints*, ed. H. Thurston, SJ and D. Attwater (1956), iv. 384–6), was a poet, musician, and composer. Tradition has it that Odo was also a musical theorist, and wrote notably the *Enchiridion musices*, also called the *Dialogus de musica*. Conclusive evidence of Odo's authorship of this and other tracts attributed to him is wanting. See *MGG*; *New Grove*; O. Strunk, *Source Readings in Music History* (1952), pp. 103–16; M. Huglo, 'L'auteur du "Dialogue sur la Musique" attribué à Odon', *Revue de musicologie*, lv (1969), 119–71.

[23] For a description of this MS volume, see M. R. James, *Descriptive Catalogue*, ii. 295–6. CB refers to the manuscript under its Nasmith numbering 410, as well as 'N.25', which was the numbering given to it in the *Catalogus* (p. 45) by William Stanley (1647–1731), published in 1722 (*DNB*).

[24] Walter Odington (*fl.* 1298–1316), Benedictine monk of Evesham Abbey (*New Grove*), whose musical treatise, *Summa de speculatione musicae*, is preserved in this unique copy. CB describes this important MS in detail in *Hist. Mus.* ii. 155–61, 192–4; Mercer, i. 515–19, 542–3. See F. F. Hammond, ed., *Walteri Odington Summa de speculatione musicae (Corpus scriptorum de musica*, vol. xiv), American Institute of Musicology, 1970.

body of the Work to have been written by John de Muris, a writer upon music of very great Eminence in the 14th Century.[25] I saw this M.S. in the Vatican Lib^y where it is ascribed to the same Author. N° 5321. Joannis de Muris Practica Cantus Mensurabilis. pr. *Quilibet in Arte.* The last is a Fragment only, of a Treatise upon Discant in very old & uncouth English, for wch alone it is curious.[26]

I am sorry to have detained you so long ab^t Matters concern^g wch you can be but little interested; however I hope to be excused in behalf of my zeal for the honour of your invaluable Library.

It w^d afford me great pleasure to have some *Shropshire* talk[27] with you in St Martin's Street, & to be allowed an opportunity at any time or place of manifesting with what truth I have the honour to be ...

To Padre Martini

[St Martin's Street],
20 October 1779

ALS (Bologna: L. 117.34).
Publ.: Brofsky, pp. 331–2, in English translation.

Molto reverendo e dotto Padre.

L'inestimabile Lettera, ed anche l'eccellentissimo Saggio di Contrappunto[1] di VS. onorat^{mo}, mi furono consegnati dal Sig^r Mattei[2] lungo tempo fa; ed io, pieno di sensibilità e di riconoscenza della di lei bontà, sarebbe stato piu pronto di ringraziarla se non fosse per mancanza d'un Occasione di mandare una Lettera della parte mia. Adesso è per favore d'un degnissimo mio amico, uomo di garbo, e molto intelligente nell'antichità di tutte le belle arte, ch'io ho l'onore di scrivere. Questo Signore tornando di Londra a Roma dove è stato Citadino 14'anni, e che si chiama *Giacomo Byers*,[3] va passare subito per Bologna, ed è molto ambitioso di riverire una persona tanto rinomato che VS.

[25] For Johannes de Muris (*c.*1300–*c.*1350), see CB to Crisp, [31] May [1771], n. 16. CB gives an account of this find in *Hist. Mus.* ii. 202–3; Mercer, i. 548.

[26] The tract in English commences: 'Here begynnes a schorte tretys of the reule of discant. It is to wit þat þere are acordance w^t outen nowmber' (M. R. James, *Descriptive Catalogue*, ii. 296).

[27] This allusion is unexplained. No Fellow of Corpus Christi, Cambridge, at this time came from Shropshire.

[1] Padre Martini's letter is not preserved (but see n. 13). For his *Saggio di contrappunto*, see CB to Martini, 22 June 1778 n. 3.

[2] Luigi Mattei Marchetti (*fl.* 1779–81), husband of the singer who had appeared at the Pantheon in 1774. See CB to Roncaglia, 6 Oct. 1778, n. 3.

[3] For James Byers (1734–1817), Scottish architect and archaeologist, see CB to Crisp, 19–24 Dec. 1770, n. 14.

Siccome sua reverenza sta sempre molto curioso di Sapere tutte le circostanzie straordinarie toccando la Musica ho l'onore di mandarla per Questo Signore un piccolo Saggio[4] fatto all'istanza della nostra Società reale, sopra un Fenomeno musicale, del quale il Publico d'Inghilterra e stato molto occupato. Mi dispiace che non ho tempo di farne una traduzione in favella Italiana, ma spero che non sarà difficile di trovare qualche Amico suo, intendente nella nostra Lingua, chi lo spiegararò.

É un pezzo che il 1mo Tomo della mia Storia generale della Musica è uscito dal Torchio, e ch'io ho principiato a far stampare il 2do; ma scrivendo di secoli mezzani, i materiali interessanti son difficili a trovare, e quando son trovati, ancora piu difficili a mettere in ordine. Ma dopo i miei Viaggij in Francia, Italia, Allemagna, &c mi sono stato determinato a cercare Codici Musicali nel Paese mio, e per questo ho visitato le nostre Università d'Oxford e Cambrigge, ed anche il Museo Britannico, &c. dove si trova Copia de Manuscritti rari, e curiosissimi spettando l'opera mia: per esempio, quelli d'Ubaldo, di S. Odo, Guido, Franco, Giov. di Muris;[5] oltreche degl'altri, scritti da Compatriotti miei, cio e dal Gio. Cotton, Gualtiero Odington[6] monaco d'Evesham nel 13° secolo—del Tomaso di Teuksbury, Simon di Tunsted, Lionel Power, Gio. Torkesey, Tomaso Walsingham,[7] e molti altri de secoli 14° e 15° degli quali io darrò Conto nel mio 2do

---

[4] CB's *Account of an Infant Musician*. See CB to Hunter, 9 Feb. 1779, n. 1.

[5] For Hucbald, see CB to [Colman?], [mid-Oct. 1779], n. 21.

For St Odo of Cluny, see ibid., n. 22.

For Guido d'Arezzo, see CB to Mason, 27 May 1770, n. 16. CB here had in mind 'a small volume of MSS. in the British Museum [Harleian MS 3199], which contains fifteen of the twenty chapters of Guido's *Micrologus* . . .' and 'a tract of great antiquity in the library of Baliol College, Oxford [MS 173A, fos. 100–6], which . . . I once imagined to have been written by Odo; but am now convinced that it is the work of Guido himself' (*Hist. Mus.* ii. 79–80, 120; Mercer, i. 463, 491–2).

Franco of Cologne, known as Magister Franco (*fl.* mid-13th cent.), credited with the authorship of the *Ars cantus mensurabilis*. CB refers to the MS in the Bodleian (MS Bodl. 842) which he describes in *Hist. Mus.* ii. 179–92; Mercer, i. 532–41. See *MGG*; *New Grove*.

CB's list of the MSS of works attributed to Johannes de Muris preserved in English collections is given in *Hist. Mus.* ii. 198–204; Mercer, i. 546–9; Rees, under 'De Muris, John'.

[6] John Cotton (*fl. c.*1065–*c.*1121), English Benedictine monk, student of St Anselm at Bec in Normandy. The musical tract, *De Musica*, is treated at length by CB in *Hist. Mus.* ii. 142–6; Mercer, i. 506–9. For problems of attribution, see E. F. Flindell, 'Joh[ann]is Cottonis', *Musica Disciplina*, xx (1966), 11–30; *MGG* under 'Johannes von Affligem (Affligemensis)'; *New Grove*; and C. V. Palisca, ed., *Hucbald, Guido, and John on Music* (New Haven, 1978).

For Walter Odington, see CB to [Colman?], [mid-Oct. 1779], n. 24.

[7] 'Tho: de Tewkesbury', written in a bold seventeenth-century hand on the fly-leaf of MS Digby 90 in the Bodleian Library has misled scholars into attributing to him the musical treatise therein contained, *Quatuor principalia musice*. The name arose probably from a confused misreading of a memorandum in MS Digby 90, fo. 6^v: a mistake corrected by CB (*Hist. Mus.* ii. 393–6; Mercer, i. 673–5), who ascribes the work instead to Simon Tunstede (d. 1369), Franciscan friar, scholar, and musical theorist (*DNB*; *New Grove*), on the corroborative evidence of MS Bodl. 515. In CB's article in Rees (under 'Tunstede'), he declared he made the discovery in 1780. It is

Tomo. Ma spero ardentemente d'essere illuminato dal 3ᶻᵒ Tomo della *sua Storia*[8] prima di terminare le miei fatiche.

Ho trovato il Signor Mattei, sposo della Marchetti,[9] uomo veramente degno de Lodi che VS. venerandissima l'a onorato. Adesso egli stà in Scozia, insieme colla molta Stimata Moglie.

Fino a quest'ora i Signori professori di Violino[10] li quali VS. mi raccommanda non son arrivati in Londra, altramente null'Occasione che dipenda di me sarebbe perduta d'essere di qualche giovamento a quei Signori.

Infelicemente in tempo di Guerra i Teatri ed altri luoghi di recreazione vanno male,[11] e già son più professori di Musica in Inghilterra che possono trovar Pane.

Intorno il ritratto mio, il quale VS. mi fa l'onore di bramare, sono stato ultimamente si occupato di varie fatiche ch'io non ho avuto tempo di farmi pignere; ma spero subito di secondare la richiesta lusinghievole di VS. riverendᵐᵃ—frattanto ò l'onore di consignare al cura del Sigʳ Byers una stampa del nostro Dottor Boyce, defunto fra poco, ma gia Maestro di Capella reale, uomo degno, buon Contrappuntisto, e molto intendente della Musica di Chiesa.[12]

Non posso dar fine a questa Foglia senza dire quanto mi son preziosi la di lei informazione toccando il Canto Ambrosiano[13] ed anche il

therefore understandable that in 1779 he should now be writing to Martini about the non-existent 'Thomas of Tewkesbury' as a musical theorist.

The names of Leonel Power, John Torkesey, and Thomas de Walsingham are associated with various tracts included in the Waltham Holy Cross Abbey MS (now BL Lansdowne MS 763), of which CB gives an account in *Hist. Mus.* ii. 412–27; Mercer, i. 685–95 (see CB to Twining, 30 Aug. 1773, n. 53). Leonel Power (d. 1445), was a composer and author of the treatise included in the Waltham MS in English *Upon the Gamme* (*DNB*; *New Grove*; S. B. Meech, 'Three Musical Treatises in English from a Fifteenth-Century Manuscript', *Speculum*, x (1935), 235–69). Nothing appears to be known of John Torkesey apart from his appearance in the Waltham MS. Thomas Walsingham has been identified (*New Grove*) with the historian and Benedictine monk (d. 1422?), precentor and superintendent of the scriptorium of St Albans Abbey (*DNB*).

[8] The third volume of Martini's *Storia della musica* appeared in 1781.

[9] See n. 2.

[10] Not identified.

[11] For a similar observation, see CB to Fanny Burney, [29 Aug.] 1779.

[12] Since 1755 Boyce had held a royal appointment as Master of the King's Band, to which post CB had aspired on Boyce's death on 7 Feb. 1779 (see Lonsdale, pp. 294–5; *GM* xlix (1779), 103). Personally and professionally, CB held Boyce in very high esteem (Rees; CB to Callcott, 29 Jan. 1802, Osborn).

CB probably sent Padre Martini the engraving of Boyce's portrait by John Keyse Sherwin (*c.*1751–90). The earliest date listed for the Sherwin engraving is 1775 (F. O'Donoghue, *Catalogue of Engraved British Portraits preserved in the Department of Prints and Drawings in the British Museum* (1908–25), i. 223).

[13] See CB to Martini, 29 June 1778, n. 1. CB discusses the difference between the Ambrosian and Gregorian chants in the first chapter of the second volume of the *History* (pp. 11–14; Mercer, i. 416–18). Since the chapter was already in print when he received Martini's communication, CB was obliged to include it in a page of 'Corrections and Additions' appended to the volume. There he states that 'the learned Padre Martini . . . honoured me with a long letter on the

Saggio di Contrappunto, Lib° utiliss° e pieno di dottrina. Receve, molto venennato Padre, con l'accostomata sua benignità la mia ricono-scenza, e degna, delle volte, onorarmi della sua gratiss^{ma} ricordanza, e la supplico di somministrarmi Occasioni di corrispondere a tanti obblighi ch'io le professo con tenere esercitata la Mia obbedienza nella esecuzione dei suoi commandi, e insieme di considerarmi quale con tutto il rispetto ed ossequio mi do l'onore di protestarmi

Di VS. reverend^{mo}

Londra il 20° Ottobre 1779

umill^{mo} Dev° ed obligat^{mo} Serv^{re}

Carlo Burney, dottor

della Musica.

To Mrs Thrale [St Martin's Street, 28 October 1779][1]

AL (Rylands, English MS 545, nos. 8 & 9).[2]

Thursday Night.

I did not like the *Tone* of your Letter[3] at all, it was out of tune—&, without a figure, made my heart ache—you are out of health, & out of spirits,[4] & all who know you must participate of your sufferings, as you constantly under happier circumstances have a way of making them partakers of all the Good things in your possession. But Courage! our Master gets better,[5] & thats worth a victory by sea or by Land.—

subject; in which, after acknowledging that the *Cantilena Ambrosiana* is, in general, the same as the *Canto Romano*, except in the *Finals*, he has favoured me with copious extracts from a scarce book, entitled *Regole del canto fermo Ambrosiano dal Camillo Perego*, *In Milano*, 1622, *in 4to*' (Mercer, i. 416 n.).

[1] Susan Burney's journal letter to Fanny (n. 12) and CB's 'Thursday Night' give the date of this letter.

[2] Although catalogued as fragments of separate letters (see *Cat. Corr.*, p. 17), the line of CB's thought and progressive looseness of his handwriting show clearly that Rylands Eng. MS 545, no. 9 is a continuation of no. 8. See also n. 10.

[3] This letter is not preserved. On 5 Oct., the Thrales, together with Fanny Burney, had left Streatham. They visited Knole and stayed at Tunbridge Wells for 3 nights, arriving on 8 Oct. at Brighton whence Fanny wrote to CB on 10 Oct. (Berg), and Mrs Thrale on 13 [Oct.] (Osborn). See *Thraliana*, i. 409; Clifford, p. 180; *DL* i. 268 ff. Mrs Thrale had clearly written again, but her letter has not survived.

[4] Fanny Burney had reported in her letter of 10 Oct.: 'Here we are, all safe & all well,—*Mrs*. Thrale excepted, who is grievously tormented with the Tooth ache.'

[5] On 8 June 1779, Henry Thrale suffered his first stroke, which left him more sullen and taciturn than usual. His depression of spirits, alleviated only by convivial company and constant travel, induced his family to seek diversion for him in and around Brighton (Clifford, pp. 175–80).

Let us still hope that public Concerns being as bad as they *can* be, *must* mend,[6] as nothing in the solar system stands still. Planets & stars are sometimes s^d to be *stationary*, but from a *deceptio visus*—for all is in motion—& all the inhabitants of these orbs, I'll warrant you, like those on our own D—ghill, are either mounting to Maturity, or tottering towards decrepitude!

And so I am just come from our dear Doctor—I visit him as oft as ever I can, but no *return*—a naughty Man! After all his swaggering, & saying he sh^d hang on the Burneys in your Absence—so far from a hanger on, he has never once filled my great Chair or darkened my door[7]—I send the young Mercury Dick to invite him in form this Morning, & after consenting to come, Mr Frank[8] ran after him to say that the D^r had just recollected he had taken Physic[9] & c^d not come out—so what does my *I*, as the next best thing but d'on my great Coat & approach the Mountain—

[10]Hey day! here's a trick indeed! I began my Letter on the 1st paper I c^d find, & the other ½ sheet happen'd to have a Page of Hist^y on it—& I am in too great a hurry to be able to take a fresh sheet—I c^d not get out till near 9—I had a Congress of out-landish folks at Tea— a Sig^r Fontana, a very intelligent Florentine[11]—a Germans *Meister das Sprache*—an Irish Gent^n—wth a Portugal, & a Dutch Jew, his Companion.[12]—

Both Fanny Burney and Mrs Thrale in their letters (see n. 3) to CB from Brighton had reported on the immediate salutary effect of the place on Henry Thrale's mood.

[6] Fears of invasion were revived in late Oct. when the *Daily Advertiser* (26 Oct. 1779) reported renewed French plans to invade England (Walpole *Corresp.* xxiv. 525; xxxiii. 131). See CB to Fanny Burney, [29 Aug.] 1779, n. 12. CB can certainly be counted among the alarmists in the invasion scare of summer 1779. His friends, recognizing his great fears for England's safety, did not fail to mock him gently for them (e.g. Anthony Chamier to CB, 15 Sept. 1779, Osborn; Twining to CB, 29 Sept. 1779, BL Add. MS 39929, fos. 208–11: 'Bravissimo!—You really croak in a masterly manner,—considering the little time you have practised').

[7] Johnson was to confess to Mrs Thrale on 2 Nov., 'I know not well how it has happened, but I have never yet been at the B⟨urney⟩s. ⟨The Doctor⟩ has called twice on me ...' (Johnson *Letters*, ii. 318).

[8] Francis Barber (*c.*1742–1801), Johnson's negro servant.

[9] Apart from an attack of gout, Johnson declared on 19 Oct., 'I am very free from some of the most troublesome of my old complaints, but I have gained this relief by very steady use of mercury and purgatives, with some opium, and some abstinence' (Johnson *Letters*, ii. 309).

[10] At this point, CB turned over his page only to discover the conjugate leaf had writing on it. He filled the second page, cut away the conjugate half-sheet, and proceeded to complete his letter on another single leaf. This bibliographical tangle has led to the separate cataloguing of the two single leaves which taken together carry the complete text of the present letter (see n. 2).

[11] Felice Fontana (1730–1805), physiologist and biologist, was a Tyrolean by birth. Since 1766 he had settled in Florence to organize and develop the physics laboratory and museum of natural history at the Florentine court. Fontana had been travelling in France and England since 1775, and was to return to Florence early in 1780 (*DSB*).

[12] Susan Burney's journal letter to Fanny of 3–[27] Nov. [1779] (BL Egerton MS 3691, fos. 22–50) gives a full account of this 'Congress': 'Tuesday Se'nnight [26 Oct.] in the Eve^g M^r

I dined wth Sr Jos. on Sunday[13] & a small party the best of wch was our Doctor—& that w^d have been the Case, had the house been full—Sr Jos. has seen 2 or 3 of my Nephews[14] academy drawings & has lent him Birk's portrait[15] to Copy—I asked him to send him a picture, & he very kindly desired him to come & chuse—upon seeing the timid Young Man's drawings—he asked if he had been under Cipriani[16]—said they were in a grand style—& told him he w^d lend him a more pleasing Subject next Time[17]—&c—this I know will

Fontana called with a German Gent^n to speak concerning a Piano Forte, which my Father promised to procure for the former, to take with him abroad . . . My Father was not visible—however as Foreigners you know are never at a loss, they sate down & stay'd Tea . . . Wednesday Eve^g just before tea these two Gent^n call'd again to enquire after *Dr Borne*, & tho' he was again *notàtom* as Piozzi writes it, they enter'd, drank tea with us, & stay'd pretty late . . . Thursday Eve^g I really could scarce forbear laughing when Mr Fontana & his German Friend were again announced—3 Days following! . . . however *this* Eve^g Mr Kirwan [Richard Kirwan (1733–1812), FRS (1780), chemist and philosopher, CB's tall neighbour] accomp^d them—Soon after their arrival came a Mr Franco, a Jew, not quite so tall as Mr Wafer, but with a better face, & fortunately not depressed by the consciousness of the particularity of his figure, & another Gentleman, with a face *very* like an Owl, & a gravity & steadiness of Countenance worthy that venerable Bird.—These came by appointment, so that my Father appeared at Tea, & we had a very *singular* party—Italian, French, Irish, English—Jews, Protestants, Catholics, *Deists*—What Not! . . . the conversation was entirely in French.'

[13] On Monday 25 Oct. Johnson wrote to Mrs Thrale, 'Yesterday I dined with Sir Joshua' (Johnson *Letters*, ii. 312).

[14] Edward Francesco Burney (1760–1848), artist. The 'Worcester Memoranda' records under 1776: 'In May Mr. Richd Burney sent his 4th son Edward Francisco to London, to study Drawing at the Royal Academy, for which art he had given proofs of a very superior talent.' Richard Burney does not appear to have been happy with his son's sojourn in London, for Charlotte Burney wrote in her 'Diary' (Berg) on 7 Nov. 1779: 'Our Cousin Edward has been introduced by my Father to Sir Joshua Reynolds—has shewn him some Drawings of his, concerning wch Sir J: told my father that they were "*finely done*, ['']—that there was *great feeling in them*, & that he did not believe there was any one in the Royal Academy that c^d Draw better!—on wch acc^t my father has been so kind as to write a most charming letter to my uncle to entreat him to let Edward continue in Town at his Studies—the answer to wch is not yet arrived, but wch we all wait for most impatiently:—Surely if old Worcester, (as Daddy Crisp calls him) can withstand such a letter his "*heart* must be composed of flint," & his *head* of no softer materials!' See also *ED* ii. 289–93; Patricia Crown, 'Edward F. Burney: An Historical Study in English Romantic Art' (Univ. of California, Los Angeles Ph.D. thesis 1977), and her 'An Album of Sketches from the Royal Academy Exhibitions of 1780–1784', *Huntington Library Quarterly*, xliv (1980–1), 61–6.

[15] The portrait of Edmund Burke (1729–97) which Reynolds executed in 1773–4 for the Thrale library at Streatham is now in the Scottish National Portrait Gallery (see Burke *Corresp*. iii. 8 and frontispiece). Susan Burney wrote to Fanny (1–[2] Nov. [1779], BL Egerton MS 3691, fos. 19–21) that on 23 Oct. 'my Father called at Sir Joshua Reynolds' to borrow one of his Pictures for Edward to Copy—Sir Joshua desired he might come & choose for himself—He did so, & by my Father's desire carried with him some drawings—Sir J: behaved with the utmost good-humour—s^d his drawings were *in a Grand Style* & ask'd him *if he had not taken Lessons from Cipriani*—& gave him a Portrait of Mr Burke to copy.'

[16] Giovanni Battista Cipriani (1727–85), historical painter and engraver, three of whose designs, engraved by Bartolozzi, had graced the pages of the first volume of CB's *History*. See Lonsdale, p. 493; CB to [Davy], 3 Nov. 1774, n. 8.

[17] In her journal letter to Fanny (n. 12), Susan Burney records a visit on 30 Oct. to her aunts in York Street, Covent Garden 'where I found Edward hard at work copying Sir Joshua's Portrait . . . he is to shew his Copy when it is finished to Sir Joshua, who has very goodnaturedly

please you & our Fan, to whom I beg you to tell it, as I have not Time—'tis a modest lad of real merit—I dare not say Genius—but I will say his disposition towards the brush is strong[18]—

I hope you'll be soon well enough to get into the sea[19]—'twill drive away Rheumatism better than any thing you can do.—

I did not like your party—but hope it is mended ere now by augmentation or diminution[20]—

Do you know that I went to Murpheys Yesterday to enquire when he went to Brigh'ton, not being sure if the Chaise had been at the Door, but that I sh^d have stepped in, & told my Family of my Journey when it was performed—but behold he's still at Sr Paddy Blake's, & not expected in Town this Week[21]—& then I shall be hemmed in

promised him *a more pleasing Subject next time.*' On 24 Nov. Susan wrote, 'Edward by appointment breakfasted with my Father, & carr^d the original & Copy of Mr Burke's portrait to Sir J: Reynolds—by whom he was very kindly received, & who, of his *own accord*, gave him Dr *Johnson* to copy—'twas just what my Father wished—& we shall soon have a Copy of this most admirable Portrait.' CB eventually bequeathed Edward's copy of Reynolds's *Johnson* (now Yale: BRBL) to Fanny (Scholes, ii. 271). See also, K. K. Yung, *Samuel Johnson 1709–84: A Bicentenary Exhibition* (1984), pp. 117–18 and frontispiece.

[18] In her letter to Fanny (see n. 15), Susan wrote: 'My Father called again on Sir Joshua a few days ago ... mentioned Edwards strong preference & *propensity* to painting before every other—"The propensity is *so* strong, s^d Sir Joshua, that, *in the present case, I believe we must call it GENIUS.*" In consequence of all this our Dear Father is become so interested in Poor Edward's continuing sometime longer in town that he has written a very long & charming Letter on the subject to my Uncle.' CB's letter to his brother is not preserved.

[19] Johnson wrote to Mrs Thrale on 7 Nov., 'I hear ... that you have at last begun to bathe. I am sorry that your toothach kept you out of the Water so long, because I know you love to be in it' (Johnson *Letters*, ii. 322).

[20] Fanny Burney had written in her letter of 10 Oct. from Brighton, 'Since we came hither, I have seen nobody that I know, & Mr. & Mrs. T. very few'. Mrs. Thrale must also have complained to Johnson, who wrote back on 21 Oct.: 'The want of company is an inconvenience, ... make the most of what you have' (Johnson *Letters*, ii. 311). Finally, on 9 Nov., Mrs. Thrale was able to write to CB, 'Our Society rather mends now, & the Cecchina gets more Fun I hope, for I was sadly afraid she would find it a very dull party for some Time' (Hyde).

[21] A barrister by profession, Arthur Murphy had been retained in 1764 as lawyer and steward of the estates of his wealthy kinsman, Sir Patrick Blake (*c*.1742–84), of Langham, Suffolk, MP for Sudbury (1768–84), created Baronet (1772). See Namier and Brooke, ii. 98; J. Foot, *The Life of Arthur Murphy, Esq.* (1811), pp. 371–84; J. P. Emery, *Arthur Murphy* (Philadelphia, 1946), pp. 85, 140, 148.

As Murphy himself explained in a letter to Mrs Thrale, from his chambers in Lincoln's Inn, 5 Nov.: 'I have not been able to follow my inclinations and fly to you and Doctor Burney's Tenth Muse at Brighthelmstone ... I am heartily tired of the long and painfull attendance in the Affair of the Arbitration between Sir P. Blake and Adml. Keppel. How preposterous! They are disputing about the Boundaries of their Manors, at a time when the Grand Question is What are the Boundaries of the British Empire, or indeed, whether such an Empire is to exist' (A. M. Broadley, *Dr. Johnson and Mrs. Thrale* (1910), pp. 130–2).

In her reply to CB of 9 Nov. (Hyde), Mrs Thrale wrote, 'Now my Dear Sir, Mr Murphy will soon I hope have his Chaise at the Door, and you will jump into it who knows—& come & see us.' The 'chaise at the door' alluded to by both CB and Mrs Thrale appears to have been an in-joke of the Streatham coterie. Murphy was fond of characterizing the ingratitude of 'those Blakes' by telling a long story of how he and a Blake might be shipwrecked together and finally struggle ashore, only to be abandoned there by his kinsman in favour of a mere acquaintance whose 'chaise is at the door' (Foot, *Murphy*, p. 384).

by a Family coming to town to work hard with me every Day while they can stay—indeed I have now got my Litters ab^t me, & what is more the D——l in humour—of whom I have lately had 3 sheets²²—amounting in the Course of the whole summer to 5!—Wonderful!—

& so that *Frelon* C————d²³ does not like Evelina—nor her parent—hang him—tis an innocent, tho' a Common Enemy to all who drive the Quill, good bad & Indiff—'here break we off'—but you shall soon say 'Lo! here he comes again.'²⁴—

To Fanny Burney   [St Martin's Street, 27 November 1779]¹

AL (BL Egerton MS 3690, fo. 3).

Addressed: Miss Burney   *Docketed by* FBA: ✗ ✳ VII 1779 On the subject of a *Comedy,* ⌐which F.B. had been pressed to⌐write by most of the celebrated⌐Authours to whom she had the ⌐ honour to be known, *between* ⌐ the Compositions of Evelina & Cecilia—Namely *Dr. Johnson, Mrs Thrale. Mr Sheridan,* ⌐ *Mr Murphy.* Sr Joshua Reynolds.²

Sat^y Night

⌐Dear Fan—I have had a sad drabbled tailed Fag—& am now, without much Stomach, dressing to go to *shop*—that is, the opera

---

²² In Johnson's letters to Mrs Thrale of 21 Oct. and 2 Nov. he mentions that CB 'has sent me another sheet', and 'I have seen some more sheets' of the second volume of the *History of Music* (Johnson *Letters*, ii. 311, 318). Twining also makes mention of these proof sheets in his letter to CB of 17 Nov. (BL Add. MS 39929, fos. 218–19).

²³ Richard Cumberland (1732–1811), playwright and miscellaneous writer (*DNB*). Fanny Burney gives a long account of Cumberland and his family's rudeness to her at Brighton (*DL* i. 282–98). Cumberland appears to have been envious of Fanny's success, and suspicious of her as a rival dramatist (ibid., pp. 286–7).

CB's '*Frelon*' is a clear allusion to the famous caricature of Cumberland as Sir Fretful Plagiary in Sheridan's *The Critic* (1779). See also Lonsdale, p. 435; CB to Fanny Burney, [27 Nov. 1779], nn. 6, 9; 'Richard Cumberland as Sir Fretful Plagiary', in *The Plays & Poems of Richard Brinsley Sheridan,* ed. R. Crompton Rhodes (Oxford, 1928), ii. 252–9.

²⁴ *Hamlet,* i. i. 40, 126.

¹ This letter is a reply to a letter from Fanny dated merely 'Streatham. Sat. Morn^g 2 o'clock'. There Fanny writes, 'We have this moment finished the Critic. . . . If you mean to let Mrs. Crewe know of this indulgence, I am sure you will tell her how much I am obliged to her for allowing it'. Mrs Crewe had lent CB her copy of Sheridan's *The Critic* (first performed at Drury Lane on 30 Oct. 1779), on 18 Nov. (Susan Burney to Fanny, 3–[27] Nov. [1779], BL Egerton 3691, fo. 35^v). The Thrales with Fanny had returned to Streatham from Brighton on Tuesday 23 Nov. (*Thraliana*, i. 409–10), and on Thursday 25 Nov. Johnson and CB visited Streatham, where CB had clearly left his borrowed copy of *The Critic* for Fanny and Mrs Thrale to read. Fanny's letter and CB's hasty reply written the same day can therefore be dated by editorial conjecture the following Saturday, 27 Nov.

² This docket and a footnote appended to this letter (n. 8) show that Mme d'Arblay in later years completely misread this letter.

³ The 1779–80 opera season opened on Saturday 27 Nov. with a performance of the pasticcio *Alessandro nelle Indie* (*The London Stage,* v. i. 299), with Pacchierotti among the principal singers.

House[3]—however, I must thank you for your Lett[r] & Comf. ab[t] our good Master[4]—& pray, wth my Affectionate Comp[ts] to our dear Mistress, tell her not to fret & worrit herself[5]—for, *je pretend moi*, to have discovered by more than 50 Years study, Labour, & expence of mental & Corporal Strength, this great Secret: That there's never nothing to be got by FRETTING.[¶6]

& so Johnson's *first rate*[7] is to take your little skiff in tow?[8] Oh rare you! to be convoyed to Posterity by a Vessel of such force! well, bon voyage!—I dare say you'll give S[r] Fretful[9] the go-by—or be strong enough to *run him down* if he sh[d] come in the way. Addio—And may you long—

> 'attendant sail,
> Pursue the Triumph, & partake the gale![']¹⁰

To Daines Barrington   [St Martin's Street, January 1780?][1]

Source: Daines Barrington, *Miscellanies* (1781), p. 288. A similar account appears also in CB's MS 'Materials towards the History of German Music & Musicians' (Osborn shelves c 100, p. 11).

[4] Fanny had written in her letter of [27 Nov.]: 'Our dear Master came Home to Day quite as well as you saw him yesterday. He is in good spirits & good humour,but I think he looks sadly.'

[5] Henry Thrale had returned from Brighton in a very alarming state of health, and Fanny reported in her letter (ibid.) that Mrs Thrale 'agitates herself into an almost perpetual Fever.'

[6] CB also adroitly alludes to Richard Cumberland, caricatured as Sir Fretful Plagiary in *The Critic*. Mrs Thrale commented in a letter to CB, which can now be dated [c.28 Nov. 1779] (Osborn): 'How tender & kind is your good Advice! and how *new* your Argument against fretting: well! but really fretting does do no good, & I will be wise & think on my Friends & worry as little as I can.'

[7] i.e. the largest and most heavily armed line-of-battle ship (*OED*).

[8] At this point in the MS, Mme d'Arblay appended a note: 'Dr. Johnson had been so kind as to consent to Mrs. Thrale's desire of looking over the Comedy FB was urged to write. But the design was relinquished. Those who in Chief recommended a Dramatic Attempt were *Sheridan*: Sir *Joshua Reynolds. Murphy. Johnson* himself.' Mme d'Arblay, re-reading the letter many years later, thought by mistake that CB referred to her suppressed play 'The Witlings'. CB in fact refers to *Evelina* which had been placed by Bodley's Librarian 'in his noble Library'. Fanny had written in her letter of [27 Nov.]: 'Dr. Johnson ... says the Bodleian Librarian has *but done his Duty*,—& that when he goes to Oxford, he will write *my* name in the Books, & my age when I writ them; & sign the whole with his *own*;—"& then," he says; "the World may know that we

> So mix'd our studies, & so join'd our Fame—
> for we shall go down Hand in Hand to posterity!!!"'

(Fanny slightly misquotes Pope, 'Epistle to Mr. Jervas', l. 10.) If Johnson carried out his intention, no evidence of it is to be found in any of the Bodleian copies of *Evelina*. See also Hill–Powell, iv. 223, n. 4.

[9] MS Fretful] *FBA footnotes* Mr. Cumberland.

[10] Pope, *An Essay on Man*, Epistle IV, ll. 385–6.

[1] When Daines Barrington reprinted his 'Account' of Mozart from the *Philosophical Transactions*

... Mozart being at Paris, in 1778, composed for Tenducci[2] a scene in 14 parts, chiefly obligati; viz. two violins, two tenors, one chromatic horn, one oboe, two clarinets, a Piano forte, a Soprano voice part, with two horns, and a base di rinforza.[3]

It is a very elaborate and masterly composition, discovering a great practice and facility of writing in many parts. The modulation is likewise learned and recherchée; however, though it is a composition which none but a great master of harmony, and possessed of a consummate knowledge of the genius of different instruments, could produce; yet neither the melody of the voice part, nor of any one of the instruments, discovers much invention, though the effects of the whole, if well executed, would, doubtless, be masterly and pleasing.

To Thomas Twining   [St Martin's Street, 3–10 March 1780][1]

L copy extracts (Osborn: 'Twining Letterbook No. 2', pp. 10–12). The first extract is dated '28 Feb. 1775', clearly in error.

of the Royal Society of London, lx (1770), 54–64, in his collection of essays, *Miscellanies* (1781), pp. 279–88, he appended a note (p. 288) dated '*Jan.* 21, 1780', which includes CB's communication. Barrington explains in his note: 'On this republication of what appeared in the LXth volume of the Philosophical Transactions ... I have ... been favoured by D. Burney with the following account of one of [Mozart's] latest compositions.' The date of Barrington's note suggests the approximate date of CB's letter.

[2] Giusto Ferdinando Tenducci (*c.*1735–90), Italian castrato and composer, 'whose voice was a high soprano of a clear silvery tone, which by great pains he had rendered very flexible' (Rees), had come to London in 1758 as 'second man' for the serious opera, and remained in the British Isles for most of his subsequent career. He had befriended the Mozarts in London in 1764 (*New Grove*; A. Heriot, *The Castrati in Opera* (1956), pp. 185–9). For Mozart's meeting with Tenducci and J. C. Bach in Paris in Aug. 1778, see A. Einstein, *Mozart: His Character, His Work* (2nd edn., 1956), pp. 47–9; *The Letters of Mozart and His Family*, ed. Emily Anderson (2nd edn., 1966), ii. 606–7.

[3] CB elsewhere provides more details of this *scena*. He describes it as 'a *Scene*, for a Soprano Voice accompanied by 2 Violins, 2 Tenors, one Hautbois, 1 Chromatic Horn, 1 Bassoon, a piano forte, & Base, all obbligati in the Recitative—& 2 Violini, 2 Viole, Oboe, Corno, Piano forte—2 Clarinetti—obbligati—with 2 Corni i Basso di Rinforza in the Air. Tenducci lent me the original score in the Author's own Hand writing. Signed or rather superscribed "Di Wolfgango Amadeo Mozart. St Germian 1778['']' (MS 'Materials towards the History of German Music & Musicians', Osborn shelves c 100, p. 11). For a discussion of the possible survival of this *scena*, see C. B. Oldman, 'Mozart's Scena for Tenducci', *Music and Letters*, xlii (1961), 44–52; but see Grant, pp. 277–80.

[1] Daniel Twining's transcription of extracts from this letter is highly misleading. He unaccountably dates the first extract '28 Feb. 1775', and treats the second extract as a separate letter dated 'Friday—Mar. 10th'. The suggestion provided by CB's text ('Here's another week gone ...') that his letter was written in at least two sittings each a week apart, is borne out by the dates of the events described (nn. 4, 11), and Twining's reply of 22 Mar. 1780 (BL Add. MS 39929, fos. 224–6) which makes clear he was responding to a single '*parcellina*' from CB com-

It is only in the broken-stick way[2] that I can now say a word to you:—out every day before 9, & hardly ever at home before 11. What a Tourbillon is London to me at this time of the year![3]—

But I must hasten to tell you a piece of intelligence I heard last night at Piozzi's Benefit[4] which vexes me very much. In a conversation with Giardini[5] concerning some comical mistakes that were made in the night's bill of fare, he said he would send it to Dr Arnold[6] to be explained in his Dictionary. 'Dict^y? what dict^y!?' quoth I.—'Why he is going to publish an explanation of Musical Terms, & has been with me, to consult me about several.'—*is* not this vexatious? It seems as if somebody or other were to spit in every mess of porridge I intended to taste.[7]—And now the injury to you and the Public, of which I was guilty, in making *you* give up the design you had formed of compiling a Musical Dictionary stares me in the face, & smites my very heart.[8] Why, if I had hallooed you on, your work might have been out by this time, or at least in such forwardness as to make it a vain attempt for any one to think of getting the start of you.—Surely Arnold can go little further than the little Glossaries prefixed to shilling books of Instructions for the Flute, Violin, &c, or at most than to take what he may want more from the Translations of Brossard & Rousseau.[9]—It

prising this letter (written 'in the broken-stick way') and a few pages of the *History of Music* in manuscript.

[2] From the French expression 'à bâtons rompus' or 'à bâton rompu': intermittently, in fits and starts. The phrase was a favourite jest between CB and Twining who, apologizing for the tardiness of his reply of 22 Mar., wrote, '. . . you will think me long: but I have had many interruptions, & the *stick* has *been* often *broken*: (about my back, you hope!)'.

[3] Johnson gives a vivid description of CB's industry at this period. On 15 Apr. he wrote to Mrs Thrale at Bath, 'There has just been with me Dr Burney, who has given. What has he given? Nothing, I believe, gratis. He has given fifty seven lessons this week. Surely this is business' (*Johnson Letters*, ii. 341).

[4] Piozzi's benefit concert was held at the Hanover Square Rooms on Thursday 2 Mar. 1780 (*Morning Chronicle*), an event which dates this letter.

[5] Giardini was one of the instrumental performers at Piozzi's benefit.

[6] Samuel Arnold (1740–1802), D.Mus. (1773), English composer, conductor, organist, and music scholar (*DNB*; *New Grove*; *BD*). In collaboration with Thomas Busby (1755–1838), Arnold brought out in parts an incomplete musical dictionary (*c*.1783–6), which ran to 197 numbers (*DNB*; *New Grove*, under 'Busby'; K. G. F. Spence, 'The Learned Doctor Busby', *Music and Letters*, xxxvii (1956), 143; Kassler, i. 22, 141–3).

[7] See John Dryden, 'Prologue to *Albumazar*', ll. 37–40:

> They make the benefits of others studying,
> Much like the meales of Politick, *Jack Pudding:*
> Whose Dish to challenge, no man has the courage,
> Tis all his own, when once h' has spit i' th' Porredge.

[8] For an account of Twining's ambition to compile a musical dictionary, and CB's opposition to the plan in 1777, see Lonsdale, pp. 238–9, 253, 407.

[9] Sébastien de Brossard (1655–1730), *Dictionaire de musique* . . . (1703), translated by James Grassineau (*c*.1715–67) and published in London in 1740. The second edition (1769) of Grassineau's *A Musical Dictionary* adds an appendix, containing articles from Rousseau's dictionary (*New Grove*, under 'Grassineau'; Kassler, i. 409–10). For Brossard, see CB to [Fountaine?],

always appeared to me an undertaking more fit for such an universal knowledge of Music & Languages as you are possessed of, than for any one else.—I suppose the work will still remain to be done, after Arnold's is out, though no one for many years to come may be bold enough to set about it.[10] ...

Friday—Mar. 10th

Here's another week gone, & it is in vain I find now to wait any longer for leisure to write more. Every day increases my hurry, & narrows my meals & repose by new & unexpected engagements. Last night I had 3 patients to visit ere I could get to Pachierotti's Benefit,[11] in spite of all my arrangements & diligence.—However between 8 & 9 I had the great satisfaction to find the house well filled, & to hear him more applauded in Sacchini's Se cerca, se dice[12]—set formerly for Millico[13]—& Paessiello's divine Rondo, *Ti seguiro fidele*[14] than ever he, or almost any performer I ever heard, was before. Such an encore to this last! had any one disputed it, or dared to hiss I do believe he would have shared Marsyas's fate.[15]

3–[4] Nov. 1773, n. 3. CB's copy of the 1740 edition of Grassineau is listed in 'Cat. Fac. Mus.', item 60.

Jean-Jacques Rousseau's *Dictionnaire de musique* (1768), was translated into English by William Waring, c.1775. A 'second edition' appeared in 1779. See Kassler, ii. 911–12, 1236–7.

[10] Twining consoled CB in his reply of 22 Mar.: 'D[r] Arnold!—I can't think he will do anything terrible;—tho', I know nothing of him, his abilities, or attainments.—You need not care about him, in all probability;—besides, you will not be ready for the business, I suppose, 'till you have hawked & *grous'd* up all your *great* gob, which will stick in your throat for some time yet. And by the time you can set about it, D[r] A.['s] book will have had time to shew people that such a work is wanted.' See also, R. Lonsdale, 'Dr. Burney's "Dictionary of Music" ', *Musicology*, v (Sydney, 1979), 159–71.

[11] Pachierotti's benefit, held at the King's Theatre, Haymarket, on Thursday 9 Mar. 1780, was a performance of the serious opera *L'Olimpiade*, a pasticcio setting of Metastasio's libretto with music chiefly by Ferdinando Gasparo Bertoni, who directed the orchestra. See *The London Stage*, v. i. 323.

On a recent visit to London in Jan.–Feb. 1780, Twining had at last heard Pachierotti: 'I heard him six times, one of which was at Dr. Burney's, in a snug way' (*Country Clergyman*, p. 76). In his reply to CB dated 22 Mar., Twining wrote, 'I rejoiced to hear Pachierotti had so good a benefit, & so much applause. How much I am obliged to you for procuring me a meeting with him in so snug & comfortable a way!' Susan Burney in her MS Journal (BL Egerton 3691, fos. 70[v]–72[v], 75–76[v]) gives detailed accounts of the soirée at St Martin's Street on Sunday 13 Feb. 1780 at which Pachierotti and Twining had met, as well as of the Pachierotti benefit on 9 March.

[12] From Sacchini's setting of *L'Olimpiade* (1763), text by Metastasio (A. Loewenberg, *Annals of Opera, 1597–1940* (2nd edn., Geneva, 1955), vol. i, col. 271).

[13] Vito Giuseppe Millico (1737–1802), Italian castrato and composer, had made his first appearance in London in 1772 in the same season as Sacchini (*New Grove*; A. Heriot, *The Castrati in Opera* (1956), pp. 161–2; *Hist. Mus.* iv. 497–8; Mercer, ii. 877–8; Rees).

[14] '*Ti seguirò fedele*, in Olimpiade, by Paesiello' was, according to CB, one of the four 'airs in which Pachierotti's natural sweetness of voice, taste, expression, and general powers of pleasing seem to have made the deepest impression' (*Hist. Mus.* iv. 515 n.; Mercer, ii. 891 n.; Rees).

[15] Marsyas, for losing a musical contest to Apollo, was flayed alive by the deity (*The Oxford*

To Mrs Thrale

[St Martin's Street,
13 March 1780]¹

ALS (Rylands, English MS 545, no. 11).
Addressed: To | Mrs Thrale

Monday Morn^g

'Still harping on my Daughter'!²—Ah! my dear Madam, If his Majesty c^d as easily vanquish his Enemies as you can your silly Friends who attempt to resist the power you have over them, how soon w^d they be disarmed!—*Your Influence*³ w^d be truely dangerous if you chose to exert it to its utmost extent — — — & then lest it sh^d fail in its Effects, steps in my Master!⁴ — — no, no, that I cannot help calling *undue* Influence — — — I see there's no chance of counteracting either; & therefore have a design to apply to Burke to insert an additional Bill in his 'Plan, for the better Security of the Independence'⁵ of Friendship — — — 'though I shall advance to it with a tremor that will

Classical Dictionary, 2nd edn., ed. N. G. L. Hammond and H. H. Scullard (Oxford, 1970), p. 652). For CB's account of the legend, see *Hist. Mus.* i. 275–82; Mercer, i. 227–33, where he observes of Marsyas's fate, 'This punishment has frequently been inflicted in modern times upon inferiority, not only by rival musicians of great talents, but by fashion.'

   At their meeting at the Burney's on Sunday 13 Feb., Pacchierotti had asked Twining where he had sat in the Opera House. Twining replied, 'in the 3sh^g Gallery where he tho^t he heard better than any where else—"Indeed," s^d Pac. looking chagrin'd—"It is from there comes all the *Issing*!"—We had then much talk on this disagreable subject—I find he attributes it to some personal enemies, who take advantage of his being encored to vent their spite' (Susan Burney's Journal, BL Egerton MS 3691, fo. 71).

¹ The publication of Burke's *Speech* on Monday 6 Mar. 1780 (see n. 5); the departure of the Thrales with Fanny Burney for Bath on Tuesday 28 Mar. (*Thraliana*, i. 436), for which arrangements had been 'settled' by the evening of 13 Mar. (Susan Burney's Journal, BL Egerton MS 3691, fo. 79^v); and CB's 'Monday Morn^g', all point to Monday 13 Mar. 1780 as the probable date of this letter.

   It is now possible to date a hitherto undated letter from Mrs Thrale to CB (Osborn), [*c.*13 Mar. 1780], which Fanny took home to her father that morning. Mrs Thrale writes of her 'Request & desire you will *bid* her [Fanny] go to Bath with me, . . . I have sent her home to tell her own Story, for I can't go without her & there's an End.'

² *Hamlet*, II. ii. 187.

³ In her letter of [*c.*13 Mar.], Mrs Thrale concluded her request for Fanny's company at Bath with the observation, 'I *used* to have some Influence over you, & if true Affection for all belonging to you can purchase it I'll have it still.'

⁴ Mrs Thrale wrote (ibid.): 'My Master who does not understand soliciting and being refused talks of going thro' Windsor & Oxford & tempts her [Fanny] with twenty Things—'.

⁵ Edmund Burke, *Speech . . . on presenting to the House of Commons (on the 11th of February, 1780) a Plan for the better Security of the Independence of Parliament, and the Oeconomical Reformation of the Civil and other Establishments*, published in its authorized text on 6 Mar. 1780 (W. B. Todd, *A Bibliography of Edmund Burke* (1964), pp. 100–4; *Public Advertiser*, 6 Mar. 1780). Included in the sale of CB's Library was a collection of fifteen of Burke's 'Political Pamphlets and Speeches' (*Cat. Misc. Lib.*, lot 278).

shake me to the utmost Fibre of my Frame —— for I feel that I shall engage in a Business in itself the most ungracious —— & I really think, the most completely adverse that can be imagined, to the natural turn & temper of my Mind.'[6] But at present I feel no power of resistence, & therefore shall say to you & my good Master as the Anatomist does to Mons[r] Gerard —— 'You shall have my *daterre* —— you may depenne upon it M. Gerard, you shall ⟨have⟩ my daterre'[7]—. & much good may she do your Hearts!

C.B.

To Thomas Twining [St Martin's Street, April? 1780][1]

L copy extract (Osborn: 'Twining Letterbook No. 3', p. 25).
Docketed by Daniel Twining: D[r] B to T.T. no date

... every one I talk to on the subject frights me about the impossibility of getting all my necessary matter into one Vol. more. Johnson says it would be like a writer of the Hist. of Eng[d] giving one Vol. to the Heptarchy,[2] & *only* one to all the rest of our annals. What shall I do? I dread having another Vol. on my hands, as well as the clamour of subscribers, who expected the work would be completed in 2 Vols. *Well, j'irai mon train*[3]—I shall neither squeeze violently,

[6] Burke, *Speech*, p. 2. Mrs Thrale was familiar with Burke's *Speech*, calling it 'his famous Speech of this Year upon the Reform Bill' (*Thraliana*, i. 434).

[7] CB quotes from memory from the popular one-act farce, *The Anatomist: or, The Sham Doctor*, published in 1771, an adaptation of the three-act farce (1696) of the same name by Edward Ravenscroft (*fl.* 1671–97). Ravenscroft's Doctor in the original play is turned in the adaptation into a French 'Monsieur Le Medicin', whose 'Daughtère' is sought in marriage by Old Gerald, consistently called by the French doctor 'Monsieur *Girarde*': '. . . depen upon it, you sall ave my Daughtère' is the French doctor's reiterated assurance (*The Anatomist* [1771], p. 8).

[1] The approximate date of this fragment is determined from its contents and letters from two of CB's correspondents. On 10 July 1780, Andrew Lumisden wrote to CB from Paris: 'I return you a thousand thanks for your obliging letter of April 25th . . . I am happy to find that your great work is so far advanced. You surely judge properly not to crowd the whole history of modern music into one volume. I am persuaded that the public will much approve of your plan, and willingly pay for a 3[d] volume . . . this additional volume will be indispensable' (Osborn). William Bewley wrote on 24 May 1780: 'if you give us two [more volumes], as you now propose' (Osborn). It seems evident that CB decided in Apr. 1780 to discard his original plan of completing his *History* in two volumes. See also Lonsdale, pp. 255–6.

[2] i.e. Anglo-Saxon England. It was formerly thought there were then seven kingdoms in England. CB later included Johnson's observation in his apology to subscribers for not completing the *History* in two volumes as originally envisaged. See *Hist. Mus.* ii. 585–6; Mercer, i. 808.

[3] This idiomatic French expression appears to have been a favourite between CB and Twining. Twining uses it also in his letter to CB of 21 Nov. 1780 (BL Add. MS 39929, fos. 244–5).

nor amplify more than seems necessary for explaining, confirming, & illustrating in such a manner as to make my book intelligible & amusing—if I can.

To [Sir Joshua Reynolds?][1]   [St Martin's Street,
                                                          c.24 April 1780][2]

AL draft (Osborn).
Docketed by FBA: × on Dr. Franklin's | idea for a Cantata | at Somerset House

Dear Sir.

I am sorry to say that a week will not be sufficient for a *Cantata* to be composed, transcribed, practiced by the Singers, & rehearsed with a *Band*, wch that Species of Composition seems to require. Even a *Catch* of one movement, though it might have been composed in a short time, c^d hardly have been fit for so public a performance in a week. But the Cantata wch Dr Franklin[3] meditates being intended as a Species of Dialogue, will require several different Airs, & perhaps a·Duet or Trio; wch I sh^d not be able even to *transcribe* in the little leisure I shall have between next Sat^y & the Day of Performance, if they were already composed. Indeed at the opening of your new Exhibition-room,[4] so splendidly furnished, the *Eye* will be so busy that it w^d be difficult to interest the *Ear*. & tho' Dr Franklin's Idea, of making the Arts dispute the Palm seems happy; yet in a Contention between the objects of these senses at such a time, I fear those of the Ear w^d be utterly

---

[1] The most likely recipient of the present letter is Sir Joshua Reynolds (1723–92), first President of the Royal Academy, with whom CB had been on terms of close friendship since the publication of the *German Tour* in 1773 (see Lonsdale, pp. 128–9). A possible alternative recipient would be Francis Milner Newton (1720–94), portrait-painter and Secretary of the Royal Academy (1768–88). See *DNB*; J. E. Hodgson and F. A. Eaton, *The Royal Academy and Its Members 1768–1830* (1905), pp. 49–51.

[2] Internal evidence suggests a date about a week before the public opening of the new rooms of the Royal Academy in new Somerset House on Monday 1 May 1780 (see n. 4).

[3] Thomas Francklin (1721–84), DD (1770), miscellaneous writer, Regius Professor of Greek at Cambridge (1750–9), an intimate friend of Sir Joshua Reynolds. On the death of Oliver Goldsmith in 1774, Francklin had succeeded to the honorary office of Professor of Ancient History to the Royal Academy (*DNB*; Hodgson and Eaton, *Royal Academy*, p. 369; *Letters of Sir Joshua Reynolds*, ed. F. W. Hilles (Cambridge, 1929), pp. 181–2; Hill–Powell, iii. 483; *ED* ii. 296, 302).

[4] 'The Twelfth Exhibition of the Royal Academicians was opened yesterday, and for the first time the Publick were invited to see it at the superb and stately mansion erected for the use of the Academy, on the seite of ground formerly occupied by Somerset House' (*Morning Chronicle*, 2 May 1780). For a description of the new rooms, see W. Sandby, *The History of the Royal Academy of Arts* (1862), i. 154–60; Walpole *Corresp.* xxix. 33.

neglected. If the Cantata however had been ready sooner I sh^d certainly have done my best to shew the zeal & regard I have for the R. Academy; and I shall still be ready to do on any future occasion on w^ch ...

To Padre Martini

[St Martin's Street],
1 June 1780

ALS (Bologna).
Publ.: Brofsky, pp. 333–4, in English translation.

Dottoss^mo e molto venerando Padre.

Son passati più di otto Mese ch'io avesse l'onore di Scrivere una Lettera[1] assai lunga alla Sua Reverenza, consegnata alla cura del Sig^r Byres, degniss^mo Scozese, ed Amico mio, che tornando a Roma per via di Bologna m'a fatto promessa di presentar quella Lettera più volontiere dal gran desiderio ch'avesse di vedere una Persona tanto rinomata come V.R. Sarebbe molto afflitto e vergognoso se questa mia Foglia, contenanda gli miei ringraziamenti più umili per la sua preziossiss^ma Lettera sopra il Canto Fermo Ambrosiano, ed anche per il dottiss^mo Saggio di Contrapunto non fosse ricevuta.

Adesso che la Marchetti va tornare à Bologna col' suo Sposo[2] Io mi fo un dovere di salutar V:R: e di dire che questi degniss⟨mi⟩ Soggetti correspondono in tutte cose alla bontà della quale a parlato a proposito loro. La povera Marchetti pure non a fatta gran fortuna in questo Paese; non per mancanza di talento Ma salute, perche quasi tutto quest'Inverno e stata amalata. Son Gente veramente di buon Cuori, e Stimatissime di me anche della mia Famiglia; e mi farebbe sempre gran piacere di loro mostrar la mia amicizia.

Si dice che V:R: a terminata felicissimamente la sua grand'Opera, la *Storia della Musica.*[3] Questa Intelligenza mi da il più gran Piacere, e mi fa molto impaziente di vedere i suoi nuovi Volumi avanti di publicar il Secondo Tomo della mia Storia, il quale e più che mezza uscito dal Torchio. Ò dato commissione al mio Libraro di procurarmi l'ultimo

---

[1] CB to Martini, 20 Oct. 1779.
[2] For Marchetti and her husband, Luigi Mattei Marchetti, see CB to Roncaglia, 6 Oct. 1778, n. 3.
[3] CB's information was not necessarily incorrect. Padre Martini may have completed in MS the third volume of his *Storia della musica*, which appeared in the following year, 1781. Martini informed CB on 6 Oct. 1781 (Osborn), that he hoped to send the third volume of the *Storia* in a few days.

Volumi dell'inestimabile Opera Sua quanto prima. Ma il comercio de' Libri forestieri e molto difficile e tedioso in tempo di Guerra. Se dunque un'occasione si presentera di passarle da Bologna, la prego coll'istanza di farmi questo favore.

Sarebbe grandissimo il contento ch'io proverebbe nella Lettura delle ricercate sue, R:P: sopra la Musica, s'io non fosse occupato nell'istesso stessissimo Spezie di Lavoro; Ma nella prosecuzione del mio Piano io mi confido tanto sopra la dottrina, la probità di citazione, ed i materiale varij, curiosi, e preziosi che si trovano negli scritti suoi, ch'io gli trovo affatto indispensabili.

La supplico di sominstrarmi occasioni di mostrar la mia riconoscenza per tanti Oblighi ch'io devo alla bontà sua, e di considerarmi quale con tutta la venerazione ed ossequio mi do l'onore di protestarmi

Di V: Reveren^{mo}

Londra 1 Giugno 1780
Umiliss^{mo} Obligatiss^{mo}
e devotiss^{mo} Serv^{re}
Carlo Burney.

To Thomas Twining

[St Martin's Street],
11 [June] 1780

LS copy (Osborn: 'Twining Letterbook No. 3', pp. 9–20).
Publ.: Country Clergyman, pp. 80–4 (in part).   *Editor's Note:* The text is transcribed from the MS copy. Significant variants in the *Country Clergyman* (*CC*) text are noted.

May 11. 1780[1]

Ah my ever dear & worthy friend, into what a situation are we brought by the pusillanimity of one party & the malignity of another! The newspapers must have told you of the outrages committed by Ld G. Gordon's mob on public buildings & persons of high rank,[2] as well

---

[1] The incorrect 'May' in the date, which appears in Daniel Twining's MS copy as well as in *Country Clergyman*, p. 80, clearly stems from CB's original letter, now lost.

[2] In June 1778, the Roman Catholic Relief Bill, which proposed the removal of certain disabilities imposed on Roman Catholics, received the royal assent (18 Geo. III, c. 60) after an easy passage through both Houses of Parliament. In opposition to this new toleration law, a Protestant Association was formed in London in Feb. 1779, and in the following Nov. elected as its President Lord George Gordon (1751–93), MP (1774–80) for Ludgershall (*DNB*; Namier and Brooke, ii. 513–15; P. Colson, *The Strange History of Lord George Gordon*, 1937).
On Friday 2 June 1780, Lord George Gordon presented to Parliament the petition of the Protestant Association for the repeal of the toleration act. He was accompanied to Westminster

as of the *general confusion* that has reigned here ever since Friday 7 night, when he was suffered to head[3] the fanatics in S[t] George's Fields; but you can have no conception of the particular consternation, distress, & danger into which the inhabitants of Newton-House[4] have been involved by the fury of the miscreants who on Monday night assailed[5] the house of Sir Geo. Saville[6] in Leicester Fields, & on Tuesday that of Justice Hyde[7] in our very Street: making bon-fires of their furniture, & in this last not leaving a floor, shutter, door, window-frame, or any thing which could feed 6 or 7 fires in the street at first, & afterwards one great fire at the top of it, in Leicester fields from 6 in the evening till 2 o'clock the next morning, at the same time obliging all the inhabitants to illuminate for this victory over all Law & Government,[8] while Newgate was broken open, 2 or 3 hun[d] prisoners set at liberty, & the building set on fire.[9] Wed[y] night will be remembered by all the present inhabitants of London & Westminster to their latest hour for the horrors & calamities with which it abounded.[10] The furniture, books & MSS of L[d] Mansfield had been destroyed in the morning, together with his house in Town,[11] where[12] himself & L[y]

by a crowd of 60,000, which had assembled earlier in the day in St George's Fields. The demonstration got out of hand, and the Gordon Riots began. See De Castro; C. Hibbert, *King Mob: the Story of Lord George Gordon and the Riots of 1780* (1958).

[3] MS head] muster and head *CC*.

[4] CB's house in St Martin's Street had belonged to Sir Isaac Newton, from whose observatory atop the building CB and his family watched the progress of the rioting. CB's account in this letter is well supplemented by Susan Burney's long journal-letter to Fanny Burney, 8–12 June [1780] (BL Egerton MS 3691, fos. 132–47).

[5] MS assailed] assaulted *CC*.

[6] Sir George Savile (1726–84), 8th Baronet (1743); MP (1759–83) for Yorkshire (*DNB*; Namier and Brooke, iii. 405–9), had introduced the Roman Catholic Relief Bill in the Commons on 14 May 1778. He was therefore a primary object of the rioters' fury (see De Castro, pp. 8–9, 63–4).

[7] William Hyde (d. 1805), magistrate, had been one of the few Justices of the Peace to perform his duty in the face of the rioters. On Tuesday 6 June he had read the Riot Act and then ordered the Horse Guards to disperse the mob. Not only was his house in St Martin's Street destroyed, his country residence in Islington was similarly wrecked the following night (De Castro, pp. 82–4, 122; Hibbert, *King Mob*, pp. 66–7, 70–2; *GM* lxxv (1805)[2], 880).

[8] Susan Burney witnessed the disturbance in St Martin's Street with Charles Rousseau Burney and Hetty: 'While M[r] B: My Sister & I stood at the Window, ... I saw about 10 Men & Women in a Groupe looking up at Our Windows—"*No Popery*," cried they—& repeated this 2 or 3 times ... we had no idea that we were ourselves addressed at this time, till one of the Men s[d] to the rest pointing to us, "*They are all 3 Papists*."—"for God sake, cried poor Etty, M[r] Burney call out *no Popery* or anything"—M[r] B—— accordingly got his Hat & Huzza'd from the Window ... "*God bless your Honour*," they then cried, & went away very well satisfied' (BL Egerton MS 3691, fos. 134[v]–35).

[9] For the attack on Newgate prison, see De Castro, pp. 88–92; Hibbert, *King Mob*, pp. 74–7.

[10] Horace Walpole named this night '*Black Wednesday*, the most horrible night I ever beheld, and which for six hours together I expected to end in half the town being reduced to ashes' (Walpole *Corresp.* ii. 224).

[11] William Murray (1705–93), created (1756) Baron Mansfield, Earl (1776) of Mansfield, Lord Chief Justice of the King's Bench (1756), known for his approval of the Roman Catholic

4. The fore parlour from the Newton–Burney house in St Martin's Street, Leicester Fields. Re-erected at Babson College, Wellesley, Massachusetts. The room measures approximately 24 feet long, 14 feet wide and 10 feet high. Above the fireplace hangs a copy of the portrait of Sir Isaac Newton at the age of eighty-three, attributed to John Vanderbank.

narrowly escaped with their lives.[13] Caen-wood[14] had likewise been devoted & beset, but was preserved by a regiment of Militia.— However, at night, there were no less than 5 or 6 dreadful fires raging at the same instant. The King's-bench, Marshalsea, & Fleet Prisons;[15] —the dwelling-house, shop, & distillery of a Roman Catholic in Holborn,[16]—the house of another in great Queen Street,[17] & of a third in the Poultry![18] all these, & more, furnished a sight from my observatory, particularly that of the distillery, which surpassed the appearance of Mount Vesuvius in all its fury. There was not I believe during this day & night a thinking or sober inhabitant in any part of the Town, who was a house-keeper, or in possession of anything valuable, that thought himself safe. Every one moved his papers & most valuable effects to the dwelling of some friend, whose situation was equally dangerous: for what street or quarter of the Town could

Relief Bill, and obnoxious to the mob for his partiality in favour of a Catholic priest recently tried before him for saying Mass (*DNB*; De Castro, pp. 36, 95–102).
'About eleven o'clock [on Tuesday night], a very large body attacked Earl Mansfield's house in Bloomsbury-square, the furniture of which took them a long time destroying. ... After this, the mob set the house on fire, when there being two engines arrived, ... the mob would not suffer them to play till it was reduced to ashes' (*Morning Chronicle*, 8 June 1780). 'Lord Mansfield's loss is estimated at 30,000l. as every book of his valuable library, which cost him 10,000l. was burnt, among which were a collection of the choicest manuscrips ever known in the possession of an individual; his fine collection of pictures shared the same fate. ... The note books, to the number of 200, of Lord Mansfield, in his Lordship's hand writing, were consumed in Bloomsbury-square, which is an irreparable loss to the Gentlemen of the Bar' (ibid., 9 June 1780).
[12] MS where] when *CC*.
[13] 'Lord and Lady Mansfield escaped but a few minutes before the rioters broke open and entered the house' (*Morning Chronicle*, loc. cit.). William Murray had married (1738) Lady Elizabeth Finch (1704–84).
[14] Lord Mansfield's country seat between Highgate and Hampstead (also spelt 'Kenwood'). See Walpole *Corresp.* xxxiii. 184 n. 5; De Castro, pp. 103, 112–13.
[15] For the attacks on and firing of the prisons, see De Castro, pp. 110, 135–9. 'The burning of the Fleet prison, the King's Bench prison in St. George's fields, the prison called the Borough Clinck, in Tooley-street, the New Bridewell, in St. George's fields, on Wednesday evening, (all being on fire at the same time) together with the other conflagrations, afforded from every point of view one of the most dismal and painful spectacles ever exhibited in or near this metropolis' (*Morning Chronicle*, 9 June 1780).
[16] This was Thomas Langdale (*c.*1714–90), 'an eminent distiller' (*GM* lx (1790)², 1151). 'The same evening [Wednesday], ... some persons among the mob, either wilfully or accidentally set fire to Mr. Langdale's house and warehouse at Holborn-bridge, which presently communicating to his vast stock of spirituous liquors, set the whole of the premises in one dreadful flame' (*Morning Chronicle*, 9 June 1780). See also De Castro, pp. 87–8, 131–5; Walpole *Corresp.* xxxiii. 187.
[17] 'The house of Mr. Cox, in Great Queen-street, Lincoln's inn-fields, was yesterday [Wednesday] morning gutted of all its furniture, and a bonfire made of it opposite the house' (*Morning Chronicle*, 8 June 1780). According to De Castro (p. 111), Cox was a brewer, a Catholic, and a Justice of the Peace. He may be identified as Robert Quay Cox, brewer, listed in *The Universal British Directory* (1790), p. 115. It is possible that Robert Quay Cox is a variant spelling of Robert Kilbye Cox (*c.*1746–1829), who is listed in *Publications of the Catholic Record Society*, vol. xii, *Obituaries* (1913), p. 185.
[18] Not identified.

be found without a Justice of Peace, a Judge, a Minister of State, an Ambassador, a Bishop, or a Roman Catholic? The houses & furniture of all these were devoted to the flames —— & unluckily for me in particular one of the tenants of 2 tenements adjoining to my house, & part of the same estate, is a Roman Catholic,[19] & among the proscribed! So that whatever is the fate of his habitation, will be that of mine! The first things I removed to the house of a friend, were the valuable books & MSS which had been lent to me—the next some writings to another[20]—& 3[dly] a coach-ful of the MSS I had collected for my History in France, Italy, Germany & elsewhere during my travels & the greatest part of my life, I sent to M[r] Burney,[21] supposing him in a quiet part of the town, & intending to send more, but the 2nd load was brought back, as likely to be more safe in my own house, there being a riot in his street, and a banditti levying money at pleasure upon the inhabitants.[22]

[Thursday][23] things remained pretty quiet after the military ventured to fire at these free-born Englishmen on their attempting the Bank.[24] The Blue cockades however, those signals of sedition, rapine, & plunder, abounded in the streets,[25] to my great annoyance & astonishment, till evening, when near a hundred of the perpetrators of these[26] mischiefs being found drunk about Fleet-ditch & secured;[27] &

[19] Susan Burney's journal-letter to Fanny furnishes the name of this tenant: 'M[r] Porter, the poor Man whose Wife keeps a China Shop in one of the Houses belonging to my Father, just at the back of ours' (BL Egerton MS 3691, fo. 138).

[20] According to Susan Burney (ibid., fo. 140), these friends were: John Bogle (*c.*1746–1803), miniature painter, who married (1767) May or Mennie Wilson (d. 1823). The Bogles lived close by at 1 Panton Square (see *JL* i. 89). The other friendly household was that of Richard Kirwan (1733–1812), FRS (1780), LLD (1794), chemist and natural philosopher. The Kirwans lived in Newman Street.

[21] Susan Burney wrote: 'I assisted my Father to pack up his MS: Papers in large Bags, w[ch] we sent by W[m] in our Coach to my Sister's—where they were taken in' (BL Egerton MS 3691, fo. 140). Charles Rousseau and Hetty Burney lived at this time in Tavistock Street, Covent Garden.

[22] Susan Burney relates: 'We now sent a 2[d] Coachfull, wth my Father's Cloaths, my Mother's & some other portable things ... William soon came back, wth all the things he had taken in this 2[d] Journey, & told us Tavistock Street was so full of Rioters, who were knocking at several doors wth great fury, that he tho[t] it was not safe to carry them into M[r] Burney's House'. When CB visited Hetty the next day, she told him 'that the Rioters in her street the preceding Night came for *Money*—which they demanded wth Authority, & said it was *for the poor prisoners* they had rescued from Newgate!' (BL Egerton MS 3691, fos. 140–2).

[23] Daniel Twining mistranscribed 'Tuesday'.

[24] For the attacks on the Bank of England on Wednesday night and early Thursday morning, see De Castro, pp. 141–3, 154.

[25] Susan Burney wrote: 'Thursday the 8th of June, a Memorable Day, My dear Father rose & went out early—he return'd home to Breakfast ... My Father had been on foot into the City, & visited every spot where the Rioters had been most busy' (BL Egerton MS 3691, fo. 141). The blue cockade, originally adopted by the Protestant Association 'to know their friends from their enemies', had by now become odious as an 'ensign of rebellion' (De Castro, pp. 25, 117).

[26] MS of these] of all these *CC.*

[27] MS & secured] were secured *CC.*

a Proclamation[28] published that the Soldiers were ordered to fire on all rioters, without waiting for a civil Magistrate to read the riot-act, with a rumour that Martial Law would be enforced,[29] not a vestige of the £2500's worth of blue ribbon[30] purchased by Ld G.G. & his friends was to be seen in the streets. Friday & yesterday all was quiet in London & Westminster, except the seizing delinquents & entering the house of one More,[31] a rascally Printer, who dispersed hand-bills to encourage the friends of L^d [Gordon] & Protestantism to liberate him from the Tower.[32] In the Borough[33] however there were disturbances both these days; & even yesterday 3 or 4 fires were made in one of the streets with the furniture & effects of an unfortunate Roman Catholic. However at night all seemed perfectly quiet, & I was one of the few who ventured to go to the Opera,[34] where all the Performers, being guilty of a religion & country different from the mad bull, John, sang & danced with the utmost fear & trembling. Yet Pacchierotti is as superior in courage to the rest as in talents.[35] He says that he should be much more frightened in Italy, or any where else than England during such disturbances, as the English are not *sanguinary* upon these occasions.[36] No soldiers could be spared for the usual opera-guard & all was melancholy & forlorn. I began however to tranquilize, &

[28] The Royal Proclamation, given at St James's on Wednesday 7 June, threatened 'to employ the Military Force . . . by an immediate Exertion of their utmost Force'. See the *London Gazette*, 6–10 June 1780; De Castro, pp. 114, 126–7.

[29] Martial law was not enforced (De Castro, pp. 172–5, 202–8).

[30] 'The cockades were made by Washington & Wharton, milliners, of 100 Salisbury Court, Fleet Street, at a cost of £2500' (De Castro, p. 29, n. 2).

[31] 'Last Saturday night [10 June] Mr. Moore, (author of a scurrilous paper called the *Scourge*) was apprehended by virtue of a warrant issued by John Wilkes, Esq; for causing inflammatory hand bills to be distributed about the metropolis, recommending the assemblage of a mob to relieve Lord George Gordon from his present confinement in the Tower.' Wilkes spent most of Sunday at the Globe Tavern, Fleet Street, examining this publisher, William Moore (*fl.* 1768–80), who was committed for trial on Monday (*Morning Chronicle*, 12 and 14 June 1780; De Castro, pp. 191–3, 230; Plomer, p. 175).

[32] 'Yesterday [Friday 9 June 1780] Lord George Gordon was apprehended by order of Government, and after an examination of some hours before the Privy Council, was sent to the Tower' (*Morning Chronicle*, 10 June 1780). See also De Castro, pp. 180–2, 190–1.

[33] i.e. Southwark. For the Friday disturbances there, see De Castro, pp. 171–2.

[34] CB attended a performance of Sacchini's *Rinaldo*, first performed on the London stage on 22 Apr. 1780. Under the title *Armida*, this opera had been performed at Milan in 1772 (*The London Stage*, v. i. 335–6, 349).

[35] Pacchierotti sang the title-role in *Rinaldo*, 'where he sung with as much energy, taste, and expression, as ever it was possible for him to manifest on any occasion' (*Hist. Mus.* iv. 513; Mercer, ii. 889).

[36] On Wednesday 7 June, as Susan Burney relates it, Pacchierotti arrived on foot at the Burneys. Horrified, the family remonstrated with him, pointing out the danger to him, a foreigner and a Catholic. '"To say the truth," s^d he, "I am not alarmed, because The English Nation it seem to me composed of Good hearted, Mild people—In my Country such a tumult as there is here now, would cost the lives of 10 or 12000 People—but it seem to me that the English are not a *Sanguinary* People"' (BL Egerton MS 3691, fo. 137).

imagine all was over; but, alas! the mischief[37] is gone into the Country! for an express arrived last night from Bath in 8 hours,[38] with the news of the colliers having entered that City, beaten the Queen's Rangers, who were quartered there, and imitating all the outrages against the poor defenceless Catholics, which have been practised in London![39] Where will all this end? and what is it for? The Protestants feel no more inconvenience from the tolerating Bill in favour of Papists,[40] than from the Talmud or Alcoran, and the cry of *No Popery* can only be construed into *No Loyalty* and No KING! The Oliverian & Republican spirit is gone forth, and Religion is a mere pretence for subverting the Government & destroying the Constitution. [41]This should be more generally known than it is by the friends of the Church.[41] Men seem, in this country, not to enjoy the happiness that lies fairly within their reach, or else why should a D. of R———d,[42] a L^d R————m[43] Sh———n,[44] R———r,[45] Ab———n,[46] a L———er[47] or a S——lle,[48] who have so much to lose ⟨ally⟩ themselves with Scoundrels & Traitors, nay, with devils, by devising, encouraging, & abetting these evils.[49] And

[37] MS the mischief] like a new cap, the mischief *CC*.
[38] The fact that Fanny was in Bath with the Thrales made this information all the more alarming to CB. He heard the news from Richard Brinsley Sheridan at the Opera, and on his return home, as Susan Burney records, 'told us that Mr Sheridan had informed him an express was arrived from Bath, in wch place the *Colliers* had risen, & beaten out the King's troops that were station'd there' (BL Egerton MS 3691, fo. 146^v).
[39] A long 'Extract of a letter from Bath, June 10' appears in the *Morning Chronicle*, 13 June 1780, in which the disturbances at Bath and the destruction of the new Catholic chapel in St James's Parade are described. Fanny Burney's eyewitness accounts are contained in her letters to CB, 9–10 June, and 11 June 1780 (Berg), published in part in *DL* i. 422–8.
[40] i.e. the Roman Catholic Relief Act of 1778 (see n. 2).
[41-41] *Country Clergyman*, p. 84, gives a variant reading: 'This should be more generally known and counteracted than it is by the friends of Church and State'. It then leaves out the rest of the letter, but concludes with a short paragraph not transcribed by Daniel Twining. I insert this paragraph editorially in the appropriate place (see n. 51–51).
[42] Charles Lennox (1735–1806), 3rd Duke of Richmond and Lennox (*DNB*).
[43] Charles Watson-Wentworth (1730–82), 2nd Marquess of Rockingham (*DNB*). Lord Rockingham had introduced the Roman Catholic Relief Bill in the House of Lords (De Castro, p. 9).
[44] William Petty (1737–1805), 2nd Earl of Shelburne (1761), created (1784) Marquess of Lansdowne (*DNB*; Namier and Brooke, iii. 271–2).
[45] Jacob Pleydell-Bouverie (1750–1828), 2nd Earl of Radnor (Namier and Brooke, iii. 302–3).
[46] Willoughby Bertie (1740–99), 4th Earl of Abingdon (1760), a political associate of Lord Rockingham (*DNB*), and an enthusiastic music-lover.
[47] Sir James Lowther (1736–1802), 5th Baronet, later (1784) created Earl of Lonsdale (*DNB*; Namier and Brooke, iii. 56–60). Sir James supported Lord George Gordon (De Castro, pp. 47–8, 187).
[48] For Sir George Savile, see n. 6.
[49] CB's list of prominent leaders of the Opposition stems from rumours and suspicions that they had 'countenanced' the rioters for political gain (De Castro, pp. 229–33). The political effect of the Gordon Riots was in fact quite the opposite: Lord North's administration received a surge of popular support (see I. R. Christie, 'The Marquis of Rockingham and Lord North's Offer of a Coalition, June–July 1780', *English Historical Review*, lxix (1954), 388–407).

are these infernal mobs *The People* to whom the Good Ld Melborne[50] & others threaten to appeal? or if as they say more than 100,000 worthy dissenters & republicans have signed the petition & joined the associations for repealing the late act, will they not lick up in their progress all the dirt & filth that's in their way? And supposing the nation to consist of 7 or 8 millions of true protestants & friends of the established Church, are *they* to lose their share in the Government, & suffer their Church to be stript of all its honours & venerable remains to please Puritans, Knaves, & Fanatics? If we are to be allowed any Religion at all, let it be supported with a Dignity worthy of the Being whom we worship, & not degrade its Temples into Barns & Granaries, & its Priests into Tradesmen & Mechanics.

[51]Your kindest of all letters arrived before all this violence and fury began to rage openly, and comforted, pleased, and amused me beyond measure.[51]

The great Concert[52] at which Pacchierotti & Miss Harrop[53] met was at the Opera House for the joint & Common Benefit of Cramer, Crosdill, Cervetto & Fischer.[54]

---

[50] Peniston Lamb (1745–1828), MP (1768–93), 2nd Baronet (1768), created Baron (1770), Viscount (1781) Melbourne in the Irish peerage, and Baron (1815) in the peerage of Great Britain (Namier and Brooke, iii. 17–18).

[51-51] This sentence, omitted in the MS transcript by Daniel Twining (Osborn), is given as a concluding paragraph in the shortened printed version of CB's letter in *Country Clergyman*, p. 84. It is here inserted editorially at what appears to be the appropriate point in the letter. See n. 41–41.

Twining's letter, to which the next four paragraphs of CB's letter are a reply, is dated from Fordham, 18 May 1780 (BL Add. MS 39929, fos. 229–32).

[52] Twining had written (ibid.), 'a hamper of thanks for your account of Pacchierotti &c &cᵃ,' referring to a letter now lost. 'But I am a poor ignorant creature, behind-hand in all the affairs that occupy your London world—pray, what was the "*Great concert*" at which Pacch. & Miss Harrop met? I see no *London* papers here.'

The 'Grand Concert of Vocal and Instrumental Music' at the King's Theatre, Haymarket, was held on Friday 14 Apr. 1780 (*Morning Chronicle*; *Public Advertiser*).

[53] Sarah Harrop (*c.*1755–1811), English soprano, who married (1780) her music-master the conductor Joah Bates (1741–99), was also a pupil of Sacchini (*New Grove*; *BD*). According to CB, she had a 'seraphic voice', was 'one of the most enchanting singers which this or perhaps any country ever produced', and was famed 'particularly in the pathetic songs of Handel' (Rees, under 'Bates'). Susan Burney, however, thought 'every now and then things escaped her that were really *vulgar*' (*ED* i. 210 n.).

[54] These leading London musicians were associated with Bach and Abel's weekly subscription concerts in Hanover Square.

Wilhelm Cramer (1746–99), violinist and composer, of the influential Mannheim 'school', had come to London in 1772, and from 1779 to 1796 was first violinist and leader of the band at the Opera, among other appointments and engagements (*DNB*; *New Grove*; *BD*).

The violoncellists, John Crosdill (1751–1825) and James Cervetto (1749–1837) were linked by CB: 'The rivalry between the admirable Crosdil and the younger Cervetto, in their youth, did them as much good in their struggles for excellence, as in riper years their friendship has done honour to their hearts' (Rees, under 'Cervetto'). See also *DNB*; *New Grove*; *BD*.

CB considered Johann Christian Fischer (1733–1800), who came to England from Germany in 1768, 'the most pleasing and perfect performer on the hautbois, and the most ingenious

Le Texier,[55] a Frenchman famous for reading plays written in his own language in such a manner, as if heard by persons blind-fold, would be imagined to be declaimed by a complete Troupe of Actors & Actresses. He has by this talent, & the difficulty he makes of exercising it, gained great favour among the nobility & gentry, who have lent him money to purchase the patent of the Opera-house when M[rs] Yeats & Brook[56] parted with it, had not Sheridan out-bid & out-jockeyed him.[57] However, he made him some amends. He was appointed director & super-intendant of the Opera at a Salary of 300, or 600, I forget which, a year. Not content with this, finding himself little minded by the performers, with whom he had quarelled, & who all hated him cordially, he prevailed on Sheridan to allow him a share in the profits, & the rank of joint-manager & patentee. But soon after this a quarrel arose, & he was dismissed; but still was allowed to advertise a splendid *Fete* at the Opera-house for his benefit,[58] in which every part of the entertainment was manquée, & he hissed, & nearly tossed in a blanket;[59] and this is the *disgrazia* I alluded to supposing

composer for that instrument that has ever delighted our country during full sixty years', even though his conversation left much to be desired: 'he had not a grain of sense but what he breathed through his reed' (Rees). See also *DNB*; *New Grove*; *BD*.

[55] For A.-A. Le Texier (*c*.1737–1814), see CB to Mrs Thrale, 16 Oct. 177[8], n. 9. Twining had asked in his letter of 18 May, 'And who is M. Le T., who was so ill treated, or well treated at ye play-house?—I had heard not a syllable about, & you have excited my curiosity.'

[56] Mary Ann Yates, née Graham (1728–87), actress, and Frances Brooke, née Moore (1724–89), author and actress (*DNB*), had jointly managed the Opera in the King's Theatre, Haymarket, since 1773 (*Hist. Mus.* iv. 499; Mercer, ii. 879).

[57] Le Texier had consulted, among others, Horace Walpole (see Walpole *Corresp.* xxviii. 364–5). On 4 Feb. 1778, R. B. Sheridan and Thomas Harris (d. 1820), the proprietor and manager of Covent Garden Theatre (*DNB*), had purchased for £22,000 the King's Theatre in the Haymarket. The transaction was finalized the following June (*The London Stage*, v. i. 192–3; Garrick *Letters*, iii. 1231; *The Letters of Richard Brinsley Sheridan*, ed. C. Price (Oxford, 1966), i. 116 n. 3; W. Sichel, *Sheridan* (1909), i. 46–7, 529; ii. 391). For an account of Le Texier's attempt to purchase the Opera franchise, and the ensuing quarrel which ran in the pages of the *Morning Post* in Feb. and Mar. 1778, see A. D. Wallace, 'Le Texier's Early Years in England, 1775–1779', in *Studies in Honor of John Wilcox*, ed. A. D. Wallace and W. O. Ross (Detroit, 1958), pp. 82–8.

[58] In, for example, the *Public Advertiser*. The fête took place on Monday 10 Apr. 1780.

[59] In the *Morning Chronicle*, 12 Apr. 1780, appeared a critical 'account' of the fête: 'About nine o'clock the Fete opened with an overture exceedingly long and tedious.—Then four figure dancers, in shabby dresses, came down a few steps out of a kind of gate set in the middle of the stage, and exhibited an awkward fighting match among themselves, which was succeeded by an assault between two fencing-masters. And this, Monsieur Le Texier had dignified with the appellation of Olympic Games ... These ridiculous representations began to put the audience out of humour, but the hunting songs in the second act, and the Italian cantata exhausted the patience of every auditor, and an universal discontent prevailing in the house, Monsieur le Texier was called for several times. He at length stepped forth and addressed the Assembly ...'. Le Texier's speech is reported, ending with '*On a fait tant de cabales contre moi.* ... This apology did not mend the matter at all, the Company, which was of the first kind, and extremely numerous, treated the apology with the utmost contempt, and hissed the apologist out of their presence; indeed they were so exceedingly disgusted ... that had they not been superior to vulgar means of gratifying their resentment, they certainly would have done violence to the

you had known his story, which is not of the most honourable kind.—
He is said to have been in trade at Lyons, but always passionately
fond of the Stage. In order to gratify this propensity he has strolled
about with provincial companies of players. Some story or other is
told about his having broken open the strong box of a Merchant or
Company at Lyons, by whom he was trusted,[60]—for which he was
forced to quit France, whither 'tis said he dares not return. However I
make no doubt but that he is now good Frenchman enough to act as a
Spy in favour of his Country; & being admitted much into the first
Company of this Kingdom, he must pick up plenty of intelligence
which must be useful for his countrymen to know. A propos to the
Strong-box story. On the 1st of April he had a box sent to him her-
metically sealed, after being filled with filth; & on opening it, over the
Contents he found this Inscription '*Reste de la caisse de Lions.*'—On his
being appointed manager of the opera, he stopt Cramer in every
movement to say this was too fast, that too slow, & something else did
not go well &c. Cramer only cut him short with saying that it was *his*
affair, not M. le Texier's, how the band went.[61]—But Giardini on
hearing of this impertinence, told me that he could not have let him
off so easily;—for he should have said, when he pretended to say
anything about Music, 'Monsieur, laissez-moi faire: le violon est a
moi—mais, pour la Caisse, a la bonne heure.'

I will condescend to allow that Pacc's Cadences are not *always*
equally happy:[62] that, sometimes, when well intended they are *manquées*

theatre. An end being thus put to the Fete, the company repaired to the *Temple of Plenty* in the
painted rooms, where they found a scarcity of every thing, and especially of wines.'

[60] Le Texier had been receiver-general of the taxes of Lyon. Madame du Deffand wrote to
Horace Walpole, [11] Dec. 1776: 'Il a volé la caisse de la recette et de plus M. Boutin, qui s'était
rendu sa caution; en un mot c'est un fripon' (Walpole *Corresp.* vi. 378).

[61] Susan Burney reports a conversation on 28 Apr. 1780 between CB and Cramer: 'my Father
mentioned Tessier's *Fete*—& Cramer exclaim'd against it—"I told him, sd he, 3 or 4 Days
beforehand that he had better give it up—indeed it was such nonsence I was *sure* it wd not
succeed however I had promis'd to play for him, & I did my best to serve him—& after that he
told every body it was my fault that it did not succeed—Indeed, he treated me very scandalously,
& I told him so—& then to make me *mad* he sent me money the next day to *pay* me—But I sent
it him back again—I wd not take a farthing from such a Rascal—However I made him pay the
Band double price, wch indeed they very well deserv'd there were so many Rehearsals—I made
him *promise* to do it before the time & made him *perform* too!"' (Susan Burney to Fanny, 24 Apr.–
9 May 1780, BL Egerton MS 3691, fo. 112).

[62] Twining had written about Pacchierotti in his letter of 18 May: 'I wish I cou'd hear you
allow me *one* thing— ... that his cadences are not quite upon a level with the rest of his
singing;—are not what one wou'd expect from his *shorter* passages of embellishment. At least I
own I did not hear one cadence from him that thoroughly pleased me; they were not of the *kind*
that I like, & that I shou'd suppose *he* wou'd like.—((—Miss B!—does your father double his
fist?—))'.

CB had very decided views on what a 'close' was and should be: 'Close, in *Music*, simply
means an end or termination to a movement, vocal or instrumental. ... But since the establishment of the opera, ... by a close or cadenza is understood such an extemporaneous effusion of

from defect or infirmity of voice; but I'll knock down any one that shall scruple to allow that *I* have sometimes heard him make closes, which, to my judgment & feelings, were the most learned, the most pathetic, the most original & fanciful, or the most brilliant I ever heard in my life from any Singer:—now, take care how you dispute this matter with me, je vous en avertis.[63] I know that Mad[e] Le Brun's are very good Hautbois-Closes[64]—& that Miss Harrops would be tolerably good on the Harpsichord, whence they are derived;[65] but for truly vocal closes, such as are human, & discover the performer to have kept good company, to be of a good school, & to be possessed of a creative genius & unbounded invention, Pacchierotti against the field.

Rinaldo is a charming Opera,[66] full of fine things in a variety of styles. As a whole it is admirable; but the Recitative accomp[d] in the last act is higher wrought, & more interesting & learned than I ever heard in any Opera.[67] The author was literally & figuratively full of

taste and fancy, terminated by a shake, as could be executed in one breath. ... A few select notes, with a great deal of meaning and expression given to them, is the only expedient that can render a cadence desirable, as it should consist of something superior to what has been heard in the [air], or it becomes impertinent. ... But, to length is now added another complaint, ... which is, the taking breath, sometimes even more than once, before the concluding shake is made, after which the performer expects to be "welcomed home"' (Rees).

[63] Twining wrote in reply on 14 July (BL Add. MS 39929, fos. 235–7): 'You terrified me with your held-up fist, about Pacchierotti's cadences;—but *I* am safe, & *you* are very reasonable; for, certes, the man who denies that *you* have heard &c[a], *deserves* to be knocked down. I was out of luck, I suppose.'

[64] Franziska Lebrun, née Danzi (1756–91), German soprano and composer, had married (1778) Ludwig August Lebrun (1752–90), oboe virtuoso of the Mannheim orchestra. CB had heard the soprano on his German tour at Schwetzingen on 9 Aug. 1772 and thought her then 'a very engaging and agreeable performer, and promises still greater things in future' (*Tours*, ii. 34). She appeared at the London Opera during the 1777–8 season, and had returned for the 1779–80 season, singing opposite Pacchierotti (*New Grove*). CB, however, thought that Mme Lebrun was 'so cold and instrumental in her manner of singing, that they did not well accord together.' He judged 'the natural tone of her voice ... not interesting ... constantly imitating the tone and difficulties of instruments ... forgetting that she is not a bird in a bush or a cage'. She 'copied the tone of [her husband's] instrument so exactly, that when he accompanied her in divisions of thirds and sixths, it was impossible to discover who was uppermost' (*Hist. Mus.* iv. 513, 508, 509 n.; Mercer, ii. 889, 886 and n.).

[65] Sarah (Harrop) Bates's technique was trained by her husband, Joah Bates, conductor and keyboard player (see n. 53). CB clearly had expressed some reservations about Miss Harrop in private to Twining, who wrote in his letter of 18 May: 'I am sorry Miss H., in your opinion, loses ground: I was not sensible of the defects you mention'. Twining had heard Miss Harrop in early 1780 on one of his rare visits to London (see *Country Clergyman*, pp. 74–5).

[66] Twining had enquired in his letter of 18 May: 'How turned out Rinaldo?—a great deal of *gout* in it? Not performed to *roomatic* houses, I hope?' Sacchini's *Rinaldo*, in which Pacchierotti and Mme Lebrun starred, enjoyed a run of ten performances between 22 Apr. and 24 June 1780 (*The London Stage*, v. i. 281, 335–51). The first night received a favourable review in the *Morning Chronicle*, 24 Apr. 1780.

[67] CB refers to 'Questa e dunque la selva?' (*The Favourite Songs in the Opera Rinaldo Composed by Sig[r] Sacchini* [1780], pp. 42–65).

gout when he composed it.[68]

I ventured in my great hurry to send a proof of nearly the beginning of the present Chapter[69] to Johnson, begging him to correct it for me, & point out anything he disliked. However, he altered not a tittle, & wrote at the bottom—'this is an Excellent sheet indeed'. This I have put up in lavender, & shall bequeath it to the Museum or Bodleian library. I never would consult him about anything where Music is concerned, as he is wholly deaf & insensible to it. But this Chap on the origin of modern languages is certainly within his ken, & he has convinced me that he has an *excellent Taste*, which I hope you will not dispute in the sentence he has so *justly* passed on my sh[eet.][70]

God bless you. Send me word how things go on in your part of the world as to commotions, Associations, &c[71] A letter I received from Yarmouth[72] yesterday says 'there is terrible work at Norwich.['] There must have been great pains taken to render this fury so general concerning a mere phantom, which though all fancy they see, yet is so incorporeal that not a human creature can feel it. Addio

C.B.

To Fanny Burney [St Martin's Street, 12 June 1780][1]

AL (Berg, Diary Mss I. 1281–4).
Addressed: To¦Miss Burney   *Endorsed by* FBA: From¦Dr. Burney¦and Charlotte Burney¦on Lord¦George¦Gordon's¦horrible¦Mobs ✗ ✳ IX 1780   *Docketed by* CFBt: Dr Burney to Miss F. Burney.   *Publ.: DL* i. 428–9.

---

[68] Twining replied (14 July): 'Your account of Rinaldo makes my mouth—no—makes my *ears wax*. I am fond of *propriety*!'

[69] The fourth chapter in the second volume of the *History of Music*: 'Of the Origin of Modern Languages, to which written Melody and Harmony were first applied; and general State of Music till the Invention of Printing, about the year 1450'. See also Lonsdale, pp. 254–5.

[70] Twining wrote in reply (14 July): 'I am glad your sheet was *proof* against Dr Johnson's criticism: I believe his eulogium to be strictly true, & I hope you felt yourself fillip'd on by it.'

[71] Twining, writing from Fordham in Essex, reassured CB in his reply of 14 July, 'We have been all peace, in this part of the world. The *association* for redress of grievances, with y^r friend Sr Rob. Smyth in the chair—has been silent & inactive of late. I hope that *associating* spirit will be quenched by the terrible effect of the Protestant association. It *must* open ye eyes of many well-meaning people who had before joined in them.'

[72] Not preserved.

---

[1] The date of this letter is established by CB's 'Monday Afternoon', and Charlotte Burney's continuation, which is a direct reply to Fanny Burney's letter of 9–10 June to her father (see n. 2).

St Martin's Street. Monday
Afternoon—y^r Lett^r just rec^{d2}

My dear Fan.

We are all safe & well, after our heartachs, & terrors. London is now the most secure residence in the Kingdom. I wrote a long Lett^r to our dear Mrs T. on Friday night, with a kind of detail of the Week's transactions.[3] I am now obliged to go out, & shall leave the Girls to fill up the rest of the Sheet[4]—all is safe & quiet in the Borough.[5] We sent W^m thither on Sat^y — — God bless you — — all affection & good Wishes attend our dear Friends. — — I s^d that riot w^d go into the Country like a new Cap, till it was discountenanc[e]d & out of Fashion in the Metropolis. I bless every Soldier I see. We have no dependence on any defense from outrage, but the Military.[6]

[*Charlotte Burney completes the letter.*]

To Thomas Twining[1]   [St Martin's Street], 23 October 1780

L copy extract (Osborn: 'Twining Letterbook No. 3', p. 26).

23 Oct. 1780

. . . In the mean time comes home my eldest son after a 2nd circumnavigation. Apprehensions for his safety had long kept me comfortless, & for some time hopeless—however, he is now safe in old England, & arrived in the Thames, Master & commander of the Ship '*The Discovery*', of which he went out first Lieu^t.[2] He is an honest worthy young man,

---

[2] Fanny Burney to CB, 9–10 June 1780 (Berg). This letter, sent from Bath, bears Henry Thrale's frank, and postmarks FREE, BATH, and 12 IV. The last mark shows that the letter arrived in London on 12 June. Fanny's letter is published almost complete in *DL* i. 422–6.

[3] Not preserved.

[4] Charlotte's continuation of this letter is printed in *DL* i. 429–31, which omits the concluding reassurance to be found in the MS: '. . . you see there is no occasion to be *Molloncholly* about *us*!'

[5] The Thrale brewery in Southwark had barely escaped destruction on 6 June (see *Thraliana*, i. 437; Clifford, pp. 185–6; *DL* i. 421).

[6] London, lacking a regular police force, looked to the military for protection in time of crisis. In the aftermath of the Gordon Riots, the metropolis appeared to contemporary observers to be like a garrison. See De Castro, ch. 6.

---

[1] Twining's reply to this letter, dated 4 Nov. 1780 (BL Add. MS 39929, fos. 242–3), reveals that CB's letter accompanied a 'parcellina' containing a further portion in MS of the fourth chapter of the second volume of the *History of Music*. CB evidently also included news of his son, Charles, and of Anthony Chamier's death on 12 Oct. 1780.

[2] For James Burney's departure on Cook's third voyage, see CB to Lind, 12 Aug. 1775, n. 7. The day after Charles Clerke's death on 22 Aug. 1779, James Burney had been transferred to the

& if I may be allowed the expression, as good a Seaman & Subject as I could wish him to be. I really believe him to know his business thoroughly. His Journals & Charts[3] are such as you, who in spite of learning & refinement can love an honest Tar, & a plain unvarnished Tale,[4] free from flourish & palaver, would like: indeed, I think his account manly, candid, plain, & above all things—TRUE—.[5] ...

To Thomas Twining [St Martin's Street], 7 November 1780

L copy extract (Osborn: 'Twining Letterbook No. 3', pp. 27–9).

7. Nov. 1780

... The passage from Euripides[1] was first pointed out to me by D[r] Johnson; and it struck me as so beautiful that I beg[ged] him to give me a Translation of it.[2] There is a word in it that I want to change '*o'erful*[3] the saturated soul',—I like not—the rest I think charming—

Resolution as first lieutenant. On re-entering home waters in Aug. 1780, contrary winds drove the two vessels to seek shelter in the Orkneys, whence James King (1750–84), now in command of the *Discovery*, 'was sent away in a small vessel to aberdeen with the charts, Journals, &c to carry up to the Admiralty; and M[r] Burney 1st Lieu[t] of the Resolution took the command of the discovery in His absence' (*The Journals of Captain James Cook on His Voyages of Discovery*, ed. J. C. Beaglehole (Cambridge, 1955–69), iii. 716–17, 1462, 1471). Burney's commission as commander was dated 2 Oct. 1780 (*The Commissioned Sea Officers of the Royal Navy, 1660–1815* ([Greenwich], 1954), i. 129). The *Discovery*, under his command, 'Lash'd along side the sheer hulk at woolwich' on 7 Oct. 1780 (Beaglehole, *Journals*, iii. 717). See also Manwaring, chs. 4 and 5.
  Samuel Crisp wrote to his sister Sophia (Crisp) Gast (*c*.1706–91) on 24 Sept. 1780: 'Jem Burney is come home from rounding the world, ... the Dr. had a letter from him (the first these 4 years), dated from the Orkneys, about a week ago' (*Burford Papers*, p. 47).
  [3] James Burney's MS journals and charts of this voyage are preserved in: PRO, Adm. 51/4528/45; BL Add. MS 8955; Mitchell Library, State Library of New South Wales, Sydney, MS M.L. Safe 1/64, 79. For a description of these MSS, see Beaglehole, *Journals*, iii, pp. clxxxii–clxxxiii.
  [4] Cf. 'I will a round unvarnish'd tale deliver': *Othello*, i. iii. 90.
  [5] Twining wrote in reply on 4 Nov.: 'Lord, how I cou'd devour that journal, & *circumnavigate* the author with 10,000 silly questions, that he w[d] be glad to take refuge among mountains of ice from the persecution of my hungry curiosity!—I give you joy, of your comfort on this occasion.'

  [1] The *Medea*, ll. 193–203, quoted with Johnson's translation in *Hist. Mus.* ii. 340; Mercer, i. 638–9. Twining had written in his letter of 4 Nov. 1780 (BL Add. MS 39929, fos. 242–3): 'The passage from the Medea of Euripides, I have written in the blank space, ... to compare with the translation, which, whoever did it, is well done: an *imitation* it is rather, with much *rencherissement* (not *wrong*-cherissement) upon y[e] Greek. And, I am persuaded, every *verse* transl., to be readeable or worth a farthing, *must* be so. Pray, now, tell me, (if there is no mystery) *cujum pecus?*'
  [2] See Lonsdale, pp. 250–1, 257–8, 269 for an account of Johnson's translation of Euripides for CB. See also *ED* ii. 256–7; *Thraliana*, i. 397–8.
  [3] Twining wrote in a letter dated 4 Dec. 1780 (BL Add. MS 39929, fos. 246–7): 'The passage in Euripides is charming, & Dr Johnson has translated it very agreeably. The expression you

there's the true Smack of la belle antiquité in it, according to my feelings—but you are so hackneyed in Greek beauties, that like a player at draughts of my acquaintance, who was such a master of the game, that after the first 2 or 3 moves he knew how the game must go, and left off playing entirely as it ceased to afford him any kind of amusement—so I suppose you'll serve not only your Homer, but your Fiddle & Harpsichord by & by.[4]—How in one part of our lives, we complain of labour & difficulties, which at another are wanted to stimulate attention & pursuit!

I am glad to find it your opinion that no Poetry will admit of literal translation.[5] It must be paraphrase to be pleasant reading in any but its mother tongue. What makes Pope's Homer & Dryden's Virgil fasten on every reader but the licentiousness of their Translations? With respect to my numerous Translations of old Stuff[6] though its darkness to most readers was an excuse, yet in the Song on Roland[7] 'Je me rends—& Cry you mercy['][8]—I liked the Song as a Military war-whoop, for which I give it, & it diverted me to try, one hot day, when I was able to undergo no harder labour, whether, totidem verbis, I could not make it English. Once more, perdona, in the original 'tis a good song.[9]—

Would that you and Mrs T. could come and see my circumnavigators

---

dislike, I disliked too. But I read it—*ò'er-fill?*—'tis queer; & the *expression* is saturated, & *plethoric.*' 'O'erfill' is the reading in *Hist. Mus.*

[4] To this accusation, Twining replied in his letter of 4 Dec.: 'No, No—indeed I am far from callous to *la belle antiquité*. I am very fond of Euripides, in particular; but at the same time I cannot join in the language of those prejudiced admirers of the Antients who represent them as almost faultless *models*. Great beauties, & great defects, side by side, is the *general* & fair character of the Antients, by no means excepting Homer.'

[5] See n. 1.

[6] In his letter of 4 Nov., Twining had written, 'Upon the whole, it rather struck me that too large a part of the pages You sent me was occupied by *language*, & *Poets*; & to[o] small a portion by *Music*.' CB misinterpreted this observation as a criticism of his poetical translations, and Twining was obliged to clarify his position in his reply of 21 Nov. 1780 (BL Add. MS 39929, fos. 244–5), 'I never objected, nor meant to *hint* objection, to y^r translations; I think as you do about the necessity, or at least, the amusement of them.'

[7] See *Hist. Mus.* ii. 275–80; Mercer, i. 597–600. Twining makes no specific mention of this long poem and its translation in his letter of 4 Nov. He may, however, have objected to their inclusion in a marginal note in CB's MS which he returned 'by the usual Colch^r Coach on *Monday* [6 Nov.], & with it my annotations, good or bad.' Twining's notes to his correspondence with CB show that his letter of 4 Nov. was sent 'With MS of 4th Chap.' (BL Add. MS 39936, fo. 69); the letter itself bears a London postmark of 6 Nov.
Mrs Thrale noted in *Thraliana* (i. 458) in Sept. 1780: 'Doctor Burney has translated the famous old French Chanson Militaire—*all about Roland*: how happy, how skilful, how elegant is that dear Creature's Pen!'

[8] Proverbial: a humorous non-apology. See *The Oxford Dictionary of English Proverbs*, rev. F. P. Wilson (Oxford, 1970), p. 159; *King Lear*, III. vi. 51—'Cry you mercy, I took you for a joint-stool'.

[9] Twining replied on 21 Nov., 'As for ye Song of *Roland*, it is delightful;—I wou'd never converse with you more, if you were to cut it out.'

Museum ere 'tis broken up![10] He has given many things to the Museum, many to Sir Ashton Lever,[11] & to private friends;[12] yet still, I think, he could make you stare if not laugh.—Well but here's a good discovery made in the voyage[13] for the *Old Book*:—a narrow passage through Behring's Straits only 14 leagues wide between *Asia* and *America*, with 2 or 3 Islands by way of stepping-stones,[14] which will get over the difficulty concerning the manner in which America was peopled;—a stumbling-block which had been removed by supposing two Creations.[15] Johnson, a good believer, says this discovery alone pays the voyage & makes it of great consequence.[16] ...

C.B.

To Charles Burney   [St Martin's Street], 25 February 1781

ALS (Comyn), first sheet; (Department of Western Art, Ashmolean Museum, Oxford), first leaf of second sheet.

[10] Twining wrote on 4 Dec.: 'I am sorry to say, that you will hardly see me by your comfortable fire-side *this* winter. I sh^d rejoice to see the *outlandish* curosities, & a *Burney* that I don't yet know. But—"it *mun'-not* be."'

[11] Sir Ashton Lever (1729–88), Kt (1778), collector, whose museum, which he called the Holophusikon, was situated in Leicester House, Leicester Square. See *DNB*; *DL* ii. 167–8; Hill-Powell, iv. 335.

[12] One friend who reaped some benefit from James Burney's souvenirs was Mrs Thrale, who appeared at Court on 18 Jan. 1781 in a gown of 'striped sattin Otaheite pattern'. See Clifford, p. 194; *ED* ii. 265–6; *DL* i. 460; *Thraliana*, i. 480–1.

[13] The principal purpose of Cook's third voyage was to try to discover the North-west Passage, from its Pacific end. See J. C. Beaglehole, *The Life of Captain James Cook* (1974), ch. 19. Thirty-nine years later, James Burney published his *A Chronological History of North-Eastern Voyages of Discovery; and of the Early Eastern Navigations of the Russians* (1819), which includes an account of the voyage (pp. 202–70).

[14] James Burney's own chart of Kamchatka, the Bering Strait, and the coasts of America and Asia, showing the tracks of the *Resolution* and *Discovery* from 3 July to 4 Aug. 1779 is included in his MS journal preserved in the Mitchell Library, State Library of New South Wales, Sydney, MS M.L. Safe 1/64, 79. The chart is reproduced in *The Journals of Captain James Cook on His Voyages of Discovery: Charts & Views*, ed. R. A. Skelton (Cambridge, 1969), chart LVI.

[15] The creation theory which posited two Adams is attributed to Theophrastus Philippus Aureolus Bombastus von Hohenheim, called Paracelsus (*c.*1493–1541), the famous Swiss physician, medical reformer, and alchemist (*DSB*), by Georg Horn, called Hornius (1620–70), in his *De originibus americanis libri quatuor* (The Hague, 1652), p. 8: 'Omnium stultitiam Theophrastus Paracelsus exhausit, qui duplicem Adamum, alium in Asia, in America alium creatum asserit.' The origin of the American Indians was the subject of much controversy and speculation. See Edward Stillingfleet, *Origines sacrae, or a Rational Account of the Grounds of Christian Faith* (1662), pp. 575–6, for references to 'the bandyings of this Controversie in the many Writers about it.'

[16] Dr Johnson had written to Mrs Thrale on 16 Oct. 1780: 'I have seen Captain Burney and his cargo' (Johnson *Letters*, ii. 406). For a discussion of Johnson's otherwise dim view of Cook's voyages, see T. M. Curley, *Samuel Johnson and the Age of Travel* (Athens, Georgia, 1976), pp. 35–6, 221–6.

Editor's Note: The first four pages of the MS, up to '. . . by Ld Bruce,' are preserved in the Comyn Collection; the last two, from 'now Earl of Aylesbury . . .' in the Ashmolean fragment.

Dear Charles.

Your present situation is doubtless very critical, & requires the assistance of the most cool reflexion & deliberate reasoning & Calculation.[1] I wish I were able to set ab^t it for you, & like the great Præcursor, St John, prepare the way, & make the Path strait[2] to prosperous happiness, founded on honour & Virtue. But if I had the leisure for such meditations, I have not the Means of discovering the Longitude by wch you ought to sail. I am utterly unacquainted wth the Character of L^d F————ter[3] wth whose patronage, you have hitherto had such reason to be flattered. You speak like a credulous young Man, with a warm heart, when you say in such positive terms—that 'you *perfectly* know wth whom you shall have to act'—'that you trust his Friendship, from the incorruptible integrity of his heart, will *never* be diminished'—&c &c—all this *may* be true—but wiser People than you or me, have been, ere now, deceived by appearances on so short an acquaintance.—Indeed for, my own Part, I know not 'why the *Poor* sh^d be flattered'—None are treated in such a Manner as you have been, by several great Personages in Scotland, but for something wch they are pleased to admit as an equivalent—Pure Friendship is imagined to be the most disinterested of all affections; but I fear when accurately examined it will turn out to be as selfish as many other Passions of a grosser Name—& be only proportioned to the pleasure we receive in doing acts of kindness to Beings that have a latent power of attaching us. As there are many Bipeds who are insensible to the Charms of Wealth, Honour, Ambition, & even Love, so there are others that know not the fascinating Power of certain Figures, & dispositions over our souls, when the Congenial Spirit, the Idem velle

[1] CB's second surviving son, Charles, had entered Caius College, Cambridge, in 1777 at the age of 19. Only a few months later, the Burneys' hopes that Charles would pursue a successful ecclesiastical career were shattered when he was sent down in Oct. for stealing books from the University Library. Charles subsequently gained admission to King's College, Aberdeen, where he was admitted MA on 31 Mar. 1781. He was now, therefore, exploring the possibility of taking orders, an ambition that was not to be fulfilled until 1807. For a full account, see R. S. Walker, 'Charles Burney's Theft of Books at Cambridge', *Transactions of the Cambridge Bibliographical Society*, iii (1962), 313–26. See also, Scholes, i. 344–8; *HFB*, pp. 72–7, 144–6, 330–1, 406, 492–3; Lonsdale, pp. 241–2; *Thraliana*, i. 360–1.

[2] Matthew 3:3.

[3] James Ogilvy (1750–1811), 7th Earl (1770) of Findlater, who had befriended Charles in Scotland. Preserved in the Osborn Collection is a letter from Charles to Lord Findlater, Aug. 1781, requesting a loan. According to his obituary in *GM* lxxxi (1811)[2], 657, Lord Findlater 'resided chiefly on the Continent . . . [and] was esteemed a good classical scholar.' His estates in Scotland were worth £30,000 a year.

et idem Nolle,[4] operate in favour of those we call our Friends—the thing, however subsists, & its effects have been so often proved, & recorded that there can be no doubt of its having always existed. It has been said that *equality of Condition*, as well as similarity of disposition is necessary to firm & lasting Friendship—but call the Partiality of the Great by the name of Patronage, or what you will, it must still be a desirable thing in your Present Circumstances. I know L^d F—e's[5] character & disposition pretty well, & never expected from him any very solid Benefits—but even his Notice & Countenance, were flattering & desirable favours in y^r situation. Many such in the course of my Life have made me a Castle-builder. But I still remain a drudge amid the smiles of Wealth & Power. As to Ld Fin——ter's affection for you it seems like that of David for Jonathan, so 'wonderful as to surpass the Love of Woman'.[6] If it is but founded on such a basis of rectitude, reason, & reflexion, as will make it durable, it may be the means of y^r pas[s]ing through the world with honour, Comfort & happiness; but if by some false calculation, Caprice, fault or offence, on either side, it sh^d be suddenly withdrawn it will certainly leave you more miserable, & less fit to buffet with the World, than it found you. It is not from a natural distrust, or bad opinion of Mankind that I remind you of that being Possible, & preparing you for such a Mortifying & perhaps ruinous reverse, but from long experience, & an intimate acquaintance with the vicisitudes of human affairs.

My opinion however is, that if your business at Aberdeen can be wholly completed in time, your Degree obtained, & you can quit the place with credit & propriety, that you w^d do well to avail yourself of L^d F——ter's proffered kindness & Condescension of introducing you to the Archb^p of York,[7] & bringing you on to the Capital, or such Part of England as his Lord^p shall be bound. To obtain Orders from the Archb^p during your abode with him, is a Consumation devoutly to be wished;[8] as difficulties & disagreeable impedim^ts may happen as you come nearer home of wch there is no possibility of thinking without

---

[4] Sallust, *Catiline*, 20. 4: 'idem velle atque idem nolle, ea demum firma amicitia est'.

[5] James Duff (1729–1809), 2nd Earl Fife (1763) in the peerage of Ireland, created Baron Duff of Fife (1790) in the British peerage, MP (1754–90), agricultural improver. Charles had spent the summer of 1780 at several of Lord Fife's mansions in Banffshire and Aberdeenshire (Walker, 'Theft', p. 316). Lord Fife was known for his great wealth and generosity (*DNB*; Namier and Brooke, ii. 346–9).

[6] 2 Samuel 1:26.

[7] William Markham (1719–1807), DCL (1752), Headmaster of Westminster School (1753–64), Dean of Rochester (1765–7), Dean of Christ Church, Oxford (1767–76), Bishop of Chester (1771–6), Archbishop of York (1776–1807). See *DNB*. Dr Markham was Dean when James Ogilvy, later Lord Findlater, matriculated at Christ Church on 8 Apr. 1769 (Foster). See Sir Clements Markham, *A Memoir of Archbishop Markham 1719–1807* (Oxford, 1906); and *Markham Memorials* (1913).

[8] *Hamlet*, III. i. 63–4.

dread. That important business done, whatever change may happen in the affection & Conduct of y^r present noble Patron, a Curacy, or a school, at least, will, it is to be hoped, not be difficult to obtain, for present Assistance. Wherever you are, & with whomever connected, pursue your Studies with diligence, & try every thing in your power to render yourself a useful Member of Society; &, with Innocence, & Propriety of Conduct, you have no reason to fear the neglect or unkindness of the World.

You have never yet Mentioned L^y F——ter—is my L^d a Married Man? has he Children? or of what does his Family & Household consist?[9] All I have yet heard of his L^p is good—I am told that he has lived abroad a good deal—My Friend Seward knew him in Italy—& spoke well of him—as being a person of a grave & studious cast— When you next write, I sh^d be glad if you w^d tell me his favourite pursuits, & general manner of passing his time. Is he a sportsman, or fond of Classical knowledge, antiquities, or the Beaux-Arts? Travelling through Italy often gives & ferments a pas[s]ion for anc^t Lore as well as modern Arts and refinements. Does his Lord^p or any of his Family play on any Musical Instrument, or seem in a particular manner captivated by Music of any kind?—God bless you, my dear Charles; continue your endeavours to deserve, & you shall never want, the affection, & support of y^r

Fr^d & Father

Ch. Burney.

Write either to me or your sisters immediately, & often, & let us know your plans adventures & progress towards the Capital.

Sunday 25th Feby 1781.

I must tell you that I am known to the Archb^p of York, who is always very civil to me, whenever we meet. Before I knew his person, while he was Dean of X^t Church Oxford, he did me the honour to send a Message by Ld Bruce, now Earl of Aylesbury, & Chamberlain to the Queen,[10] 'that there was a great Collection of Anc^t Music at X^t Church, wch had been bequeathed to it by Dr Aldrich,[11] & wch if I wished to examine, he w^d give orders for my admission'—It was many years ere I c^d avail myself of this liberal & voluntary offer—

---

[9] Lord Findlater had married (1779) in Brussels, Christina Theresa Josepha Murray (*c*.1755–1813), 'with whom he lived but a short time' (*GM* lxxxi (1811)^2, 657). There were no children of the marriage.

[10] Thomas Brudenell-Bruce (1729–1814), 2nd Baron Bruce of Tottenham (1747), created (1776) Earl of Ailesbury, Governor to the Prince of Wales (1776), Chamberlain to the Queen (1780), Lord Chamberlain (1781–92), Treasurer (1792–1814), had frequented the Sunday musical soirées at the Burneys in the mid-1770s. See *ED* ii. 98, 108, 118; *JL* iv. 90.

[11] Henry Aldrich (1648–1710), DD (1682), Dean of Christ Church, Oxford (1689–1710), divine, scholar, collector, architect, and musician (*DNB*; *New Grove*).

indeed the Archb^p had quitted Oxford before I presented myself to one of the Canons of X^t Church, Dr Wheeler, with a Letter, from Dr Johnson,[12] to beg his assistance in Facilitating my Enquiries, wch so Perfectly answered the purpose, that a Vote or order [was] passed by the present Dean,[13] that I sh^d not only have leave to examine Dr Aldrich's Collection of Music, but be permitted to take home any part of it to transcribe or consult at my leisure—& I have now a considerable number of these curious vol^s in my Possession—last Summer, & the two summers before, I made a Catalogue of the excellent collection of old Music at X^t Church, of wch I shall present the College with a Copy[14]—I tell you all this to furnish you with a little conversation ab^t me & Oxford, when you shall see the Archb^p—& then you must not forget to tell his Grace how much flattered I was with his liberal offer, & wth his thinking my undertaking Worth his Notice. You must likewise say how much I have been always served in my Enquiries at X^t Church by the Revd Mr Jackson,[15] who was at first Librarian to the College, but the summer before last I found him a Canon—you may say with truth that he is a great favourite wth me as I know he is wth his Grace—you know, I dare say, that this Mr Jackson was Sub-preceptor to the P. of Wales & B^p of Osnaburg,[16] when Dr Markham was Preceptor.[17]—You may likewise say that Counsellor Batt[18] of X^t Church, is my Particular Friend.—& that I have been working in the Bodleian & other Libraries at Oxford the last 3 Summers successively. That I am very fond of Oxford, where I had my Degree, & where I have many Friends, &c &c—

[12] See CB to Mrs Thrale, 6 Nov. 1778, nn. 3, 4. Johnson's letter of 2 Nov. 1778 to Dr Wheeler specifically mentions that 'Dr. Burney, who . . . is engaged in a History of Musick; and having been told by Dr. Markham of some MSS. relating to his subject, which are in the library of your College, is desirous to examine them' (Johnson *Letters*, ii. 264–5).

[13] Lewis Bagot (1741–1802), DCL (1772), succeeded Dr Markham as Dean of Christ Church (1777–83), Bishop of Bristol (1782), of Norwich (1783), of St Asaph (1790). See *DNB*.

[14] CB's catalogue is still in Christ Church Library and has the shelfmark Library Records 12.

[15] Cyril Jackson (1746–1819), DD (1781), Canon (1779), then Dean of Christ Church, Oxford (1783–1809). A protégé of Dr Markham, Jackson had served under Markham as sub-preceptor (1771–6) to the two eldest sons of George III (*DNB*).

[16] George (1762–1830), Prince of Wales, afterwards George IV; and Frederick Augustus (1763–1827), elected Bishop of Osnaburg (1764), by which title he was generally styled until created (1784) Duke of York and Albany. Prince Frederick relinquished the bishopric of Osnaburg in 1803. See *DNB*.

[17] On the recommendation of his friend Lord Mansfield, Dr Markham had been appointed on 12 Apr. 1771 preceptor to the Prince of Wales and Prince Frederick. Markham retained the post until 28 May 1776 (Markham, *Memorials*, ii. 25–7).

[18] John Thomas Batt (1746–1831), educated at Westminster School under Markham, and Christ Church, Oxford (BA 1766; MA 1769), admitted to Lincoln's Inn (1763), called to the bar (1770). Together with his Westminster schoolmate, Dr. Cyril Jackson (n. 15), Batt served as one of Markham's executors (Markham, *Memorials*, ii. 46–7). A friend of the family, Batt advised the Burneys on legal matters (*DL* iii. 128; iv. 426). For Batt's career and wide acquaintance, see *GM* ci (1831)^1, 274; G. F. R. Barker and A. H. Stenning, *The Record of Old Westminsters* (1928), i. 62 and *Supplement* [1938], p. 12; Foster; Walpole *Corresp.* xi. 17.

I have lately sate for my Picture to Sr Jos. Reynolds,[19] for my Friend Mr Thrale (for wch he has 50 G^s)[20] who has a Library furnished wth 12 or 14 portraits of Persons with whom it is a great honour to be placed[21]—Such as Drs Johnson—& Goldsmith—Garrick, Murphey, Baretti, Sr Robt Chambers,[22] Sr Jos. Reynolds, Burke, Sr Richd Jebb,[23] Ld Westcote[24] & Ld Sonds[25]—y^r Coz. Ned is now making *two Copies* of my picture,[26] (wch every body says is very like,[27] & the Judges are of

[19] The Reynolds portrait of CB, now in the National Portrait Gallery, London (no. 3884), reproduced as the frontispiece in Lonsdale, was painted in Jan. 1781 at Streatham. Mrs Thrale wrote to Fanny on 4 Jan. 1781, 'my master ... has *ordered* your father to sit to-morrow, in his peremptory way; and I shall have the dear Doctor every morning at breakfast. I took ridiculous pains to tutor him to-day, and to insist, in *my* peremptory way, on his forbearing to write or read late this evening, that my picture might not have blood-shot eyes' (*DL* i. 458; MS now Berg). See also, C. R. Leslie and T. Taylor, *Life and Times of Sir Joshua Reynolds: with Notices of Some of His Cotemporaries* (1865), ii. 313. The portrait was exhibited at the Royal Academy, 1781, and judged 'Excellent' by Horace Walpole (A. Graves and W. V. Cronin, *A History of the Works of Sir Joshua Reynolds P.R.A.* (1899–1901), i. 134–5). Bartolozzi made an engraving (1784), included as frontispiece to the last volumes of *Hist. Mus.* (see CB to Mrs Phillips, [25]–26 Apr. 1784, n. 3). A miniature is in the Comyn Collection. See Frontispiece.
[20] Examination of Sir Joshua Reynolds's accounts reveals a discrepancy. Sir Joshua records a payment of 35 guineas from 'Mrs Thrale of Dr Burney' on 10 Feb. 1781 ('Ledgers, 1760–1792', vol. ii, fo. 72, Fitzwilliam Museum, Cambridge, Founder's Library MS 25 D).
[21] For the Streatham library portraits, see *Thraliana*, i. 470–6; Clifford, p. 157; Mary Hyde, 'The Library Portraits at Streatham Park', *The New Rambler*, ser. C, xx (1979), 10–24; Nadia Tscherny, 'Reynolds's Streatham Portraits and the Art of Intimate Biography', *Burlington Magazine*, cxxviii (1986), 4–11; *Mem.* ii. 80–1. There were thirteen pictures in the collection.
[22] Sir Robert Chambers (1737–1803), Kt (1777), BCL (1765), Vinerian Professor of Common Law, Oxford (1766), judge of the Supreme Court in Bengal (1774–99), a close friend of Johnson, who helped Chambers with his law lectures (*DNB*; *Thraliana*, i. 204, 473). See Sir Robert Chambers, *A Course of Lectures on the English Law Delivered at the University of Oxford 1767–1773*, ed. T. M. Curley (Oxford and Madison, 1986).
[23] Sir Richard Jebb (1729–87), MD (1751), FRCP (1771), created Baronet (1778), physician to the Prince of Wales (1780), to George III (1786). Sir Richard was the Thrale family physician, and currently much in favour with Mrs Thrale for his efforts to preserve her husband's health. A characteristic comment may be found in Mrs Thrale to CB, [17? Jan. 1781], (Osborn): 'What a fine Fellow is that sweet Sir Richard Jebb?' CB is mistaken in his list: the Streatham library pictures did not include a portrait of Sir Richard. See *DNB*; W. Munk, *The Roll of the Royal College of Physicians of London* (2nd rev. edn., 1878), ii. 291–3.
[24] William Henry Lyttelton (1724–1808), colonial governor, diplomatist, and MP (1748–55; 1774–90), created Baron Westcote of Ballymore (1776), Baron Lyttelton of Frankley (1794), was now a Lord of the Treasury (1777–82). Lord Westcote had made the Grand Tour in company with Henry Thrale (*DNB*; Namier and Brooke, iii. 76–7; *Thraliana*, i. 200, 471; Clifford, p. 35).
[25] Edwin Sandys (1726–97), 2nd Baron Sandys of Ombersley (1770), MP (1747–70), 'an admirable Scholar' whose 'Friendship with Mr Thrale is of long standing' (*Thraliana*, i. 471), was 'immensely rich'. See *GM* lxvii (1797)^1, 255; Namier and Brooke, iii. 403–4.
[26] Edward Francesco Burney eventually executed three copies of his uncle's portrait by Reynolds. In addition to the two copies noted below (nn. 28, 29), a third copy remained in the family until 1930. It subsequently passed into the hands of the New Haven, Connecticut, booksellers, C. A. Stonehill, Inc., from whom the portrait was purchased in 1952 by the late J. M. Osborn, who reproduced it in a Christmas greeting card.
[27] Except Dr Johnson, as CB was later to recall: 'Johnson grumbled at it much—"we want to see *Burney* & he never comes to us in that dress"' (CB to Charles Burney, [12 Oct. 1801], Osborn).

opinion that it is higher finished than any one of Sr Jos.'s Works) one for Padre Martini at Bologna, who has many years been desiring to have my Picture,[28] & another for the Music School at Oxford,[29] at the request of Dr Hayes[30] the present Music Professor, who has lately had the Music-School repaired & furnished.

To Mrs Thrale   [Chessington,
19? August 1781][1]

ALS (Rylands, English MS 545, no. 7).
Addressed: To | Mrs Thrale

                                                            Sunday

I was, for once in my life, sorry to see your hand writing:[2] supposing you had not rec^d my Letter,[3] & must think me an ingratitude man—

---

[28] The Martini copy of CB's portrait is preserved in the Civico Museo Bibliografico Musicale, Bologna. It is reproduced in Vernon Lee (pseud. Violet Paget), *Studies of the Eighteenth Century in Italy* (2nd edn., illustrated, 1907), facing p. 107; and as the frontispiece of Scholes. Padre Martini had first requested a portrait of CB in Aug. 1775, but had to wait, despite his repeated pleas, until late 1783, when Ferdinando Gasparo Bertoni delivered Edward Francesco's copy together with the second volume of CB's *History*. See CB to Martini, 22 June 1778, n. 6; 20 Oct. 1779. For Martini's letters to CB on the subject of the portrait (all preserved in the Osborn Collection), see Brofsky, pp. 313–45.

[29] The copy CB presented to the collection of musical portraits in the Music School at Oxford was transferred together with the collection in 1884–5 to the Examination Schools. In 1909 it was moved to the Ashmolean Museum, where it is now preserved in the Department of Western Art. See Mrs R. L. Poole, *Catalogue of Portraits in the Possession of the University, Colleges, City, and County of Oxford*, Oxford Historical Society, vol. lvii (Oxford, 1912), pp. xii, 137, 193–4; and 'The Oxford Music School, and the Collection of Portraits Formerly Preserved There', *Musical Antiquary*, iv (1912–13), 143–59. The Oxford copy is reproduced in the *Illustrated Catalogue of a Loan Collection of Portraits of English Historical Personages ... Exhibited in the Examination Schools, Oxford ...*, introd. L. Cust (Oxford, 1906), pl. XIX.

[30] Philip Hayes (1738–97), D.Mus. (1777), succeeded his father, Dr William Hayes (1708–77) in 1777 as organist of Magdalen College, and Heather Professor of Music, Oxford (*DNB*; *New Grove*). For Philip Hayes's renovation in 1780 of the Music School in the Schools Quadrangle, and his additions to the collection of portraits and busts, see *The History and Antiquities of the University of Oxford ... by Anthony à Wood, M.A.*, ed. J. Gutch, vol. ii, pt. 2 (Oxford, 1796), pp. 888–94. CB had contributed five guineas towards the purchase of a set of forms for the School (ibid., p. 889), and gives an unflattering account of Philip Hayes in Rees.

[1] Fanny's week-long attendance on Esther and her newborn son (n. 10) gives mid-Aug. 1781, and CB's 'Sunday' gives the 19th as the probable date of this letter. CB's letter is evidently written at Chessington. See *DL* ii. 32–3, 52; *HFB*, p. 144; Lonsdale, p. 264.

[2] CB writes in reply to a letter from Mrs Thrale dated 'Sunday' (Osborn). Mme d'Arblay subsequently added the erroneous date '[17]82'. Mrs Thrale's letter can now also be dated [19? Aug. 1781].

[3] Not preserved. The absence of CB's missing letter renders his following comments on Thomas Pennant unclear.

but all is right, & I love & thank you for so soon enabling me to think of Pennant without unchristian Malice.[4] & so in the fortuitous concourse of letters, & jumble of things, the appellation of *blue-stocking* has been heretofore in Y^r Family?[5]—well, 'tis very *Nod*—I think this *must* set you at the head of the Order, joined to your other indisputable Claims. 'And so master Pennant I shake you by the hand—& will try some time or other to read your Book,[6] in spite of your enmity to *Pronouns*—indeed I began to think you too *personal*, but, in future am ready to allow that you are a good honest sort of a shop-keeper, a man of real business, who hates to waste Peoples Precious time in palaver, & useless words'—Quid multa? Pauca Verba[7]—shall be his Motto.

And so what a power of business you have contrived to do on this blessed Day![8]—I need not ax vaat is all dat Schtof?—'tis very ostensible — — here's stuff for the Mouth, & Stuff for the Pocket — — special *hard wear*—safer & more likely to mend, than mar, my Garments, like your nectareous fruit.—But I must be serious, these Money Matters, & Executor folks[9] must not be trifled wth—& there are no transactions I hate so much, with those I love, as these.—I shall write

[4] In 1781 Thomas Pennant published the first part of the second volume of his *A Tour in Wales* under the separate title *The Journey to Snowdon*. Pennant included (pp. 22–3) a description of Bach-y-Graig, the family estate of his cousin, Mrs Thrale, which CB and Crisp presumably thought unflattering. Pennant, for example, called the rooms of Bach-y-Graig 'small, and inconvenient'; he also noted: 'The country people say, that it was built by the devil, in one night, and that the architect still preserves an apartment in it'.

Mrs Thrale, referring to CB's missing letter, had written in her reply of [19? Aug. 1781], 'your friendly Wrath against Pennant flattered me into a Notion that you *do* care for me ... Poor Pennant! he has done much Good in exciting your kindness & Mr Crisp's partiality, & no harm in the World has he done'.

[5] CB and Crisp must also have objected to Pennant's account of the Salusbury family (*Tour in Wales*, ii. 25 ff.), which included a description of a portrait of Sir Henry Salusbury (d. 1632) of Llewenny, the 1st Baronet, showing 'his stockings purple'. Mrs Thrale had written in reply: 'the Book is filled with Anecdotes of the Salusbury Family, ... & the Jest is that one of our Ancestors God knows how long ago was *really* surnamed Salusbury *Blue-Stocking* which he mentions in the Course of his Enquiries, without either Malice or Merriment.'

[6] Mrs Thrale had urged CB in her letter of [19? Aug. 1781], 'do read the Book'. CB and Crisp must have heard of the contents of Pennant's *Tour* by repute, or read an extract in an untraced newspaper.

[7] The source of this Latin tag is not identified.

[8] Henry Thrale had died on 4 Apr. 1781, having appointed Mrs Thrale and Dr Johnson among the five executors of his estate (Clifford, pp. 198–205; Hyde, *Thrales*, pp. 226–33). The brewery in Southwark was sold on 31 May, but the business of winding up her husband's affairs continued to occupy Mrs Thrale throughout the summer. In her letter of [19? Aug.], Mrs Thrale settled her outstanding account with CB (the crucial 4 lines were obliterated later by Mme d'Arblay): 'Now I begin in my serious Character ⌜& have enclosed your Account with a Draft for £(?) for which I must have returned me a proper Receipt. ...⌝ In future dear Sir let our Money Matters be always settled half Yearly'.

[9] Of John Cator (1728–1806), MP (1772–80, 1784, 1790–3), timber merchant, one of Thrale's executors, Mrs Thrale had written in her letter of [19? Aug.], '⌜Mr Cator is excessively exact & all these Transactions pass through his Hands.⌝' See also *Thraliana*, i. 418, 491; Namier and Brooke, ii. 198–200.

a rec^t—I hope a *proper one*, on the bill—I w^d you had given me the form, if 'tis not a common one.

I know but little ab^t Family *consarns* in Town, except that poor Hetty is likely to lose a fine boy;[10] & tho' the house is brimful already,[11] & she has nothing to give 'em but her blessing, yet she's such a *Natural* as to fret as much as if he were sole Heir to a large Estate.—I believe you w^d do justement comm⟨e⟩ ça—& so will the more readily excuse Fanny's staying to coddle & comfort the poor soul, under a Weak body, & strong apprehensions.[12]

Well, God bless you, dearest Madam, we have nothing but airy thanks to send for all your solid benefits. But you shall have no lack of them—O yes, you shall have ten thousand *Lacs*,[13] though not so valuable as Roupees—What a nonsense Letter is this to send to a learned Lady! Well, vive la bagatelle! & now you have enabled us to live 'as Country Gentlefolks *sh^d* do',[14] we'll not only drink your health as usual, but Prosperity to the blues, & the Whole blue-stocking Family!

I hope soon to hear of our truely good & great Doctor's perfect health—& that we shall see you all here as soon as the Tyo[15] can get *home* to you. You see it is not for *self* that she's torn from you—I know if all was well in Denmark[16] she'd go barefoot to Streatham immediately, rather than wait for Shoes.

And so believe, dear Madam, not

only her, but me, to be ever yours

in all Affection

Chas Burney

---

[10] After fears of a miscarriage (*Burford Papers*, pp. 59, 64), Esther gave birth prematurely to Henry, baptized on 19 Aug., and buried on 25 Aug. 1781. See *HFB*, p. 144; *The Registers of St. Paul's Church, Covent Garden, London*, ed. W. H. Hunt, Harleian Society Publications (1906–9), ii. 98; v. 125.

[11] Charles Rousseau and Esther Burney had already presented CB with five grandchildren: Hannah Maria (1772–1856); Richard Allen (1773–1836); Charles Crisp (1774–91); Frances (1776–1828); and Sophia Elizabeth (1777–1856). See *JL* i, p. lxix.

[12] After Thrale's death, Mrs Thrale came to rely increasingly on Fanny's company at Streatham, and strongly resented any separation. Samuel Crisp wrote to his sister, Mrs Sophia Gast (*c.*1706–91), on 4 June: 'Fanny is now there, and I believe is likely to become at Last a sort of Fixture to the house. Mrs. Thrale and Dr. Johnson can't breathe without her' (*Burford Papers*, p. 63). Mrs Thrale stormed at about this time, 'What a Blockhead Dr Burney is, to be always sending for his Daughter home so! what a Monkey! is not She better and happier with me than She can be any where else? Johnson is enraged at the silliness of their Family Conduct . . .' (*Thraliana*, i. 502).

[13] A lac or 'lakh' was reckoned £10,000 or 100,000 rupees (*OED*).

[14] Not identified.

[15] Mrs Thrale writes about Fanny Burney in *Thraliana*, i. 487: '. . . dearly, very dearly, do I love my little *Tayo*, so the People at Otaheite call a *Bosom Friend*.' The word, brought from the Pacific by James Burney, is not listed in *OED*. See also *DL* i. 491; ii. 22.

[16] An allusion not only to *Hamlet*, i. iv. 90, but also to Denmark Court in the vicinity of Esther's house in Covent Garden.

I return my Bill, with a rec^d under the Articles; & that for the Books, as well as Merlin's,[17] that you may *collate* at a future time.

To Thomas Twining [St Martin's Street, mid/late October 1781][1]

L copy (Osborn: 'Twining Letterbook No. 3', pp. 5–6).

... When I read your account of yourself I felt very uncomfortable at your having written so *long* a letter in spite of prudence & injunctions.[2] But you still have courage to ask after opus Mag: & friendship to encourage the author to the old practice of employing you.[3] I believe I ought not to abuse your kindness so far as to accept it,—& yet every sheet would terrify me that had not gone thro' your hands previous to printing.

What you say of Johnson's severity to Gray[4] I join in, and have

[17] John Joseph Merlin had made the pianoforte that Mrs Thrale ordered for Streatham. Merlin's bill may have been for his tuning the instrument on various visits to Streatham. See *DL* i. 458, 503–5; ii. 13–14.

[1] This letter was written in reply to Twining's letter of 10 Oct. 1781 (BL Add. MS 39929, fos. 274–8). Daniel Twining's extract copy shows an obliterated date, which possibly reads 'O^ct 31'.

[2] Twining had been seriously ill for most of 1781. A 'violent cold towards the end of February, attended with a cough that shook me to pieces, & *ne finissoit jamais*, but I thought it wou'd have finished *me*' had left him unable 'to bear any sort of *fagging*, mental or bodily,' and 'obliged to indulge myself in writing lazily, & a little at a time'. In July he had visited friends in Yorkshire in an effort to restore his health (Twining to CB, 4 May, 8 June 1781, BL Add. MS 39929, fos. 254–7, 260–5). Twining's ten-page letter to CB of 10 Oct. contains a long account of his illness during his Yorkshire jaunt, 'exceedingly dejected, languid, tremulous, breathless with the least motion, starting from sleep, flutters, *defaillances* &c^a', and his slow convalescence, his doctor's advice to '*burn my books*', and his finding that '*Writing* long together ... hurts me much more than reading'.

[3] Twining had enquired after the progress of 'the *Opus magnum*' in his letter of 10 Oct.: 'I shall be exceeding glad to hear how you go on; I hope you are now in sight of publication. If you have anything that you wou'd give a farthing to have me read, make not the least scruple of sending it, at any time. For I both read & write, in a moderate way, though I cannot *fag* at anything. You may do anything with me, but hurry me; & you might hurry me, if anybody might ... let me hear what you have been groping & poking at.'

[4] Twining had written in his letter of 10 Oct.: 'I am sorry to say I am, & must be, very angry with Dr J. for his unjust & narrow critique upon Mr Gray. I highly respect him, on many accounts; but a *Poet* he never was, only a good *Versifier*; & every man *relishes*, in proportion as he can *do*. Dr J. criticizes Gray, as a common Organist wou'd criticize Em. Bach.' For Twining's friendship with Gray, see CB to Twining, 18 Oct. 1775, n. 5; and 14 Dec. 1781, n. 5.

Johnson's critical biography of Gray appeared in the tenth volume of his *Prefaces, Biographical and Critical, to the Works of the English Poets*, of which the first four volumes had appeared in Mar. 1779, and the remaining six in May 1781. The animadversions on Gray raised a storm of protest. See Hill–Powell, i. 404; iv. 64; W. P. Courtney and D. Nichol Smith, *A Bibliography of Samuel Johnson* (Oxford, 1925), pp. 129–41; *Lives of the English Poets by Samuel Johnson, LL.D.*, ed. G. B.

likewise the same complaints to make of his treatment of Prior—the delight of my youth,[5] as Gray was of my riper years. I hope you'll keep your word in the notes to your Aristotle.[6] For tho' I revere Johnson on many accounts, I think his severity here mischievous. The Nation is relaxed & fastidious enough already; & he is only teaching the taste-less & unfeeling to be more dainty & difficult to please. I have often had battles with him about Prior & Gray, & during the time he was writing the Character of the latter often begged he would spare him, & made Mrs Thrale join with me; but his opinion was rockey.[7]— G. was a Cambridge man—a friend of Mason—& had been, as he thought—I suppose—too violently praised.—La *pauvre humanité*!— Johnson, with more wisdom and penetration than his share, is not perfect in either.—Yet he is surely a great, a *very* great man, with all his prejudices, & imperfections. His lives of Dryden, Milton, Cowley, Waller, & Pope, surely are delightful.[8] I want his prejudices to be always attacked, & yet I wish his Genius & Virtues to be spared. He has many that the world knows nothing of, nor perhaps ever will believe. He is in private often pleasant, candid, charitable, to a degree of weakness, & as good-natured as a family mastiff, whom you may

---

Hill (Oxford, 1905), iii. 421–45; R. Lonsdale, 'Gray and Johnson: The Biographical Problem', in *Fearful Joy*, ed. J. Downey and B. Jones (Montreal, 1974), pp. 66–84.

[5] CB's youthful enthusiasm for the poetry of Matthew Prior (1664–1721) is recorded in a preserved portion of his *Frag. Mem.*, which appears to refer to events in 1742, when he was 16: '... verses I liked were Prior's, wch I borrowed; & not being rich enough to purchase even a 2^d hand set I transc[r]ibed the whole two Vol^s entirely' (*CB Mem.* 14). See also Lonsdale, p. 7.

[6] Twining had been working since 1778 on a translation and commentary on Aristotle's *Poetics* (Lonsdale, p. 248). By the time he wrote his letter of 10 Oct. 1781, Twining had almost completed the translation and was looking forward to writing his commentary, of which, referring to Johnson's strictures on Gray, he declared, 'If ever I write my notes upon A., I shall have something to say upon the subject of this sort of *prose Criticism*.' Twining's *Aristotle's Treatise on Poetry, Translated: with Notes on the Translation, and on the Original; and Two Dissertations, on Poetical, and Musical, Imitation*, appeared in 1789. In his commentary, Twining mentions and quotes Johnson several times with approval, with the single exception of pp. 385–6, where Twining defends Gray against an unnamed critic who sneered at Gray's *Agrippina*, and 'pronounced, also, that the Bard of Gray, only "*endeavours* at sublimity;" who saw in the juvenile Poems of Milton "*no* promise of Paradise Lost;" and who has admitted, with seeming complacence, into the catalogue of English Poets, such names as *Blackmore, Yalden*, and *Pomfret*'. The critic thus castigated in the body of Twining's text is carefully identified in the index to the volume, under 'Johnson, Dr.—his censure of Mr. Gray's Agrippina'.

[7] As Mme d'Arblay recalled in *Mem.* ii. 177–8, Dr Johnson would permit proof-sheets of his *Lives of the Poets* to be read aloud at Streatham 'to embellish the breakfast table', a custom that led to 'discussions ... in the highest degree entertaining'. Mrs Thrale noted in Oct. 1780, 'Mr Johnson's Criticism of Gray displeases many people; Sir Joshua Reynolds in particular' (*Thraliana*, i. 459). See also Clifford, pp. 196–7.

Twining would come under Boswell's category of 'some Cambridge men' who 'arraigned' Johnson 'of depreciating Gray' (Hill–Powell, iv. 64).

[8] Twining replied in his letter of 8–10 Dec. 1781 (BL Add. MS 39929, fos. 287–90): 'To shew you that I have no quarrel with Dr J., I have just bought his *Lives*, & am delighted with his account of the Metaphysical Poets in his *Cowley*; which is all I have yet read.'

safely pat & stroke at the fire-side, without the least fear of his biting you. The utmost he will do if you are a little rough with him is to growl. . . .

To Thomas Twining [St Martin's Street], 14 December 1781

L copy (Osborn: 'Twining Letterbook No. 3', pp. 30–6).

14. Dec. 1781

—You think of the old Stuff just as I wished, that is, just as I did myself.[1] I have scored them all, & transcribed them[2] for you without trial of effect, except in my *minds ear*; but, as you very comically say, by long habit & experience one's *Ear* gets up into one's *Eye*.[3]—My P. F. is always so loaded with books, & so out of tune, that I have neither industry nor inclination to unload & put it in order for a momentary use. In the summer, however, I did try the effects of Old Okenheem's Conundrum after I had decyphered it, & found it quite as nasty as you have done: and yet so few fragments of this composer are to be found, I believe I shall print it.[4] Indeed it seems as if the Pedantry

[1] CB replies to Twining's letter of 8–10 Dec. (BL Add. MS 39929, fos. 287–90; *Country Clergyman*, pp. 104–10), which followed the return of CB's manuscript of part of the fifth chapter of the second volume of the *History*, 'Of the State of Music, from the Invention of Printing till the Middle of the XVIth Century'. For an account of CB's and Twining's growing admiration for sixteenth-century music, see Lonsdale, pp. 264–6; Grant, pp. 125–32. Twining had written, 'I found your MS prodigiously entertaining, & I have nothing but approbation & praise to give you. . . . Your *musical* criticisms upon the specimens, indications of unusual discords, & the gradual & progressive *advances* of the art, are among the most valuable parts of your work. . . . I was much diverted to see how similarly we were both served by this old Ecclesiastical Music. In y^r last letter, you tell me how it *stole* upon you as you studied it, after a long inte[r]mission perhaps, &, from some prejudices against it, brought you to relish its *real beauties*, & be its apologist.—I was served just so.'

[2] Eleven MS volumes now preserved in the British Library (Add. MSS 11581–91) contain CB's copies and scores of the polyphonic and later compositions that he used as examples in the last three volumes of the *History of Music*. This set is listed in *Cat. Mus. Lib.*, lot 624; the individual compositions are identified in A. Hughes-Hughes, *Catalogue of Manuscript Music in the British Museum* (1906–9).

[3] Twining, apologizing for keeping CB's MS for a long time, explained in his letter of 8–10 Dec.: '. . . y^r MS w^d have been returned much sooner, but for the *musical* Specimens, which neither y^r request, nor my own curiosity, w^d suffer me to return unexamined. You, from long habit, have your *ear in your eye*; & can, perhaps, *hear* all the effect of complicated Harmony, by *reading* it. So can I, *tolerably*, in *mod*. Music, & *mod*. notation: but in this old church music . . . I can do nothing but at a keyed instrument; & even so, I cannot with much *readiness*, get through the harmony.'

[4] Referring to a list of notes and comments (not now preserved) on CB's MS and musical

& false Taste of each century should be recorded as well as the excellencies in Music.

The history of your Musical Studies and attachments is fair & curious.[5] Mine, if I had time to recollect & write it, would shew the same flexibility & openness to conviction.[6] Handel, Geminiani & Corelli were the sole Divinities of my Youth; but I was drawn off from their exclusive worship before I was 20, by keeping company with travelled & heterodox gentlemen, who were partial to the Music of more modern composers whom they had heard in Italy.[7] And for songs those of Hasse[,] Vinci, Pergolesi, Rinaldo di Capua, Leo, Feo, Selli[t]i, Buranello, with a few of Domenico Scarlatti, won my heart,[8]

examples, Twining wrote in his letter of 8–10 Dec., 'You will see plainly that I was in a *pet* with *Ockengheim*'.

Johannes Ockeghem (*c.*1410–97), Franco–Flemish composer and teacher, from about 1451 composer and 'premier chapelain' to three successive Kings of France; in 1459 made treasurer of the Abbey of St Martin-de-Tours. He was the leader of the second generation of the Franco–Flemish school of the fifteenth century, and is notable for his achievements in the art of imitative counterpoint (*New Grove*). CB's incorrect solution to Ockeghem's celebrated three-voice canon (incipit 'Prenez sur moi') is given in *Hist. Mus.* ii. 475–7; Mercer, i. 729–30. See Fétis, under 'Okeghem' for the correct solution; *MGG*.

[5] Twining had related in his letter of 8–10 Dec. his progress from a youthful interest in polyphonic music to a fondness for 'the *Cantata* style of [Alessandro] Scarlatti, Gasparini, Lotti &c&ᵃ', and that 'It was Mr Gray, principally, who made me first turn my back upon all this, by his enthusiastic love of *expressive* & *passionate* Music, which it was hardly possible for me to *hear* & *see* him *feel*, without catching something even of his *prejudices*. For Pergolesi was his darling: he had collected a great deal of him, & Leo, in Italy, & he lent me his books to copy what I pleased. This was the *bridge* over which (throwing bundles of old prejudices in favour of Corelli, Geminiani & Handel, into the river) I passed from *Antient* to *Modern* Music.' See also CB to Twining, 18 Oct. 1775, n. 5; [mid/late Oct. 1781], n. 4; Lonsdale, p. 265.

[6] Since his arrival at the conviction that 'the Pergolesis & the Leos had carried vocal music to its utmost perfection, & that nothing was to be done after them', Twining admitted in his letter of 8–10 Dec., '*Now*, I *venture* to *think* myself free from all musical *prejudice*; & though a man must have neither ear nor soul who is insensible to the wonderful improvements in Melody, grace, expression, rhythm & *even harmony itself* in *some* respects,—which have been going on gradually to the present time,—yet I can still see beauties of *another* kind in the antᵗ *harmonious* style, which make me listen to it with great pleasure.'

[7] These gentlemen were CB's early patron, Fulke Greville, and his friend, Samuel Crisp (see Lonsdale, pp. 15, 18–19). CB in later years wrote of visits to Wilbury where 'besides lessons, I had to play & to hum a great deal of vocal music, wᶜʰ Mr Greville had brought from Italy, and both Mr Crisp & Mr Greville who had heard it sung in Italy by great singers, with their voice & advice, gave me a good notion how to express it on the harpᵈ' (*CB Mem.* 43).

[8] With the exception of Baldassare Galuppi, called 'Il Buranello' (1706–85), who was chiefly associated with Venice, CB's list comprises musicians belonging to the 'Neapolitan school'. They composed in 'the natural, simple, and elegant manner of writing for the voice' (*Hist. Mus.* ii. 470 n.; Mercer, i. 726 n.). For CB's comments on the individual composers, see his chapter 'Progress of the Musical Drama at Naples, and Account of the eminent Composers and School of Counterpoint of that City' in *Hist. Mus.* iv. 544–72; Mercer, ii. 914–36. See also Rees, under 'Naples'; M. F. Robinson, *Naples and Neapolitan Opera* (Oxford, 1972).

Johann Adolf Hasse (1699–1783); Leonardo Vinci (*c.*1690–1730); Giovanni Battista Pergolesi (1710–36); Rinaldo di Capua (*c.*1705–*c.*1780); Leonardo Ortensio Salvatore di Leo (1694–1744); Francesco Feo (1691–1761); Giuseppe Sellitto (1700–77); Buranello (see above); Giuseppe Domenico Scarlatti (1685–1757). See *New Grove*.

& weaned me from the ancient worship. However, at all times in my life I honoured an elaborate & learned composition for the Church whatever its age & country,[9] & at all spare hours I was scoring pieces of Bird, Morley, Luca Marenzio, Stradella;[10] and studying Palestrina,[11] Steffani's admirable Duets,[12] with Cantatas by old Scarlatti, Gasparini, the Baron D'Astorga, & Marcello.[13] Before I was 18 I scored Geminiani's 2 sets of Concertos,[14] for improvement in Counterpoint,

[9] Twining had written in his letter of 8–10 Dec. with reference to polyphonic church music, 'As *religious* music, I really think we have had nothing comparable to it since: and *more* than that may be said in its praise'.

[10] William Byrd (1543–1623), celebrated English composer, appointed (1570) Gentleman of the Chapel Royal. CB owned 'My Ladye Nevells Booke', a MS collection of Byrd's keyboard music (see *Hist. Mus.* iii. 91; Mercer, ii. 79–80; E. H. Fellowes, *William Byrd* (2nd edn., 1948), p. 197).

Thomas Morley (1557–1602), B.Mus. (1588), English composer and theorist, pupil of Byrd, and Gentleman of the Chapel Royal (1592), wrote the treatise *A Plaine and Easie Introduction to Practicall Musicke* (1597).

Luca Marenzio (c.1553–99), Italian composer, who brought the art of madrigal composition 'to its highest degree of perfection' (*Hist. Mus.* iii. 201; Mercer, ii. 165).

Alessandro Stradella (1644–82), Italian composer, violinist, and singer. 'His compositions, which are all vocal, and of which I am in possession of many, and have examined a great number more in other collections, seem superior to any that were produced in the last century, except by Carissimi' (*Hist. Mus.* iv. 100; Mercer, ii. 574).

[11] Giovanni Pierluigi da Palestrina (c.1525–94), maestro of the Cappella Giulia, St Peter's, Rome (1551–4, 1571–94). 'It would be endless to transcribe all the eulogiums that have been bestowed upon Palestrina, ... [who] merits all the reverence and attention which it is in a musical historian's power to bestow.' See *Hist. Mus.* iii. 185–98; Mercer, ii. 153–63; Rees.

[12] Agostino Steffani (1654–1728), Italian composer and diplomat, priest (1680), bishop (1706). 'Near the latter end of the last century a species of learned and elaborate *Chamber Duets* for voices began to be in favour. ... those of the admirable Abate Steffani were dispersed in manuscript throughout Europe. ... There are perhaps no compositions more correct, or fugues in which the subjects are more pleasing, or answers and imitations more artful, than are to be found in the duets of Steffani, which, in a collection made for Queen Caroline, and now in the possession of his Majesty, amount to near one hundred' (*Hist. Mus.* iii. 534–5; Mercer, ii. 424–5). See W. B. Squire, *British Museum Catalogue of the King's Music Library. Part II. The Miscellaneous Manuscripts* (1929), pp. 196–200, 205–6.

[13] See 'Of Cantatas, or narrative Chamber-Music', the fourth chapter in vol. iv of *Hist. Mus.* (Mercer, ii. 601–38), in which CB declared, 'We are now arrived at the golden age of cantatas in Italy, a species of Music that was brought to the greatest degree of perfection, without accompaniments, about the end of the last century and beginning of the present, by the genius and abilities of Ales. Scarlatti, Francesco Gasparini, ... the Baron d'Astorga, and Benedetto Marcello'. CB then proceeded to discuss the relative merits and shortcomings of the cantatas of Alessandro Scarlatti (1660–1725), 'the most voluminous and most original composer of cantatas that has ever existed'; Francesco Gasparini (1668–1727), whose cantatas 'are graceful, elegant, natural, and often pathetic; less learned and uncommon than those of Ales. Scarlatti; but, for that reason, more generally pleasing'; Emanuele Gioacchino Cesare Rincón, barone d'Astorga (1680–c.1757), whose cantatas 'are much celebrated; yet several that I have lately examined did not fulfill the expectations excited by ... his elegant and refined *Stabat Mater*'; and 'the illustrious' Benedetto Marcello (1686–1739), who 'composed a great number of cantatas, of which the vigour of conception and ingenuity of design please me more than his celebrated psalms.'

[14] Francesco Geminiani (1687–1762), *Concerti grossi*, Opus 2 and Opus 3. 'It was not till the year 1732 that Geminiani published his first six concertos, which he called his *Opera seconda*, and dedicated to the Duchess of Marlborough. Soon after this, his *Opera terza*, or second set of concertos, appeared, which established his character, and placed him at the head of all the

& I remember when he was about to print them in score, with new *readings*, he borrowed my MS which he never returned.[15]

As to Harpsichord music[16] besides the study of Handel's *Lessons*,[17] which in that elaborate style are admirable, I was early a great admirer of the original Fancy, boldness, delicacy, & Fire of Domenico Scarlatti,[18] so different from all lessons before & since!—Then the Taste, refinement, & elegant *Chant* of Alberti,[19] struck me as new in instrumental music; & tho' the easy monotony of his division Bases is so easy to imitate,[20] yet none of those who have used the like expedient for supplying the short-lived tone of the Harpsichord by this kind of bustle, have equalled him in the taste & elegance of his treble

masters then living, in this species of composition' (*Hist. Mus.* iv. 642; Mercer, ii. 991). See also W. C. Smith and C. Humphries, *A Bibliography of the Musical Works Published by the Firm of John Walsh during the Years 1721–1766* (1968), nos. 690, 695. Preserved in the British Library (Add. MS 39957) are transcriptions of twelve Geminiani sonatas, among other music, made by the 18-year-old CB at Chester in 1744 (Grant, p. 190; *CB Mem.* 19 n. 5).

[15] CB wrote in *Hist. Mus.* iv. 644; Mercer, ii. 993, of Geminiani, '. . . he went to Paris, where he continued till 1755, when he returned to England, and published a new edition of his two first sets of concertos.' In a footnote, CB recorded, 'This edition was prepared from a score which I had made for my own improvement, and of which, upon Geminiani complaining, in 1750, that he had lost his *original*, I was much flattered by his acceptance.' These two sets of concertos were printed by John Johnson in Cheapside in [1755?] with the respective title-pages: *Six Concertos, . . . Opera seconda. The second edition, Corrected and Englarged, with some new Movements, by the Author; And now first Published in Score*; and *Six Concertos, . . . opera terza. The second edition, Revised, Corrected, and Enlarged, by the Author; And now first Published in Score.* The musical plates were engraved in France, by Marie-Charlotte Vendôme (*fl.* 1744–86), Parisian music engraver (C. Hopkinson, *A Dictionary of Parisian Music Publishers 1700–1950* (1954), pp. 116–17).

[16] 'Handel's compositions for the organ and harpsichord, with those of Scarlatti and Alberti, were our chief practice and delight, for more than fifty years' (*Hist. Mus.* iii. 510; Mercer, ii. 405).

[17] Handel's *Suites de Pièces pour le Clavecin* appeared in three collections; the first book, printed by John Cluer (1720); the second book, printed by John Walsh (1727; 2nd edn., 1733); and the third book by Witvogel (Amsterdam, 1733). See A. C. Bell, *Handel Chronological Thematic Catalogue* (Darley, 1972), pp. 116–25; T. Best, 'Handel's Keyboard Music', *Musical Times*, cxii (1971), 845–8.

[18] Giuseppe Domenico Scarlatti (1685–1757), 'the most illustrious, original, fanciful, and powerful performer on the harpsichord in Europe, during the early part cf the last century. . . . The Lessons of M. Scarlatti were in a style so new and brilliant, that no great or promising player acquired notice of the public so effectually by the performance of any other music' (Rees). CB's youthful enthusiasm for Scarlatti was fostered by conversations with Thomas Roseingrave (1688–1766), a great admirer, and editor of Scarlatti's *XLII Suites de Pieces Pour le Clavecin* [1739]. See *Hist. Mus.* iv. 262–7; Mercer, ii. 703–6; R. Kirkpatrick, *Domenico Scarlatti* (Princeton, 1953), pp. 101–4, 401–3; *CB Mem.* 36, 41, 46.

[19] Domenico Alberti (*c.*1710–40), Venetian composer, whose name is associated with a style of keyboard accompaniment consisting of broken chords for the left hand (see *New Grove*; *DBI*). For CB's comments on Alberti, see *Hist. Mus.* iv. 540: Mercer, ii. 910. Many years later, he wrote a fresh article on Alberti in Rees: 'At a time when there was little melody in harpsichord lessons, he brought about a revolution in the style of playing that instrument, by giving a singing treble to a rapid base, . . . none ever composed such elegant treble parts for keyed instruments; the melody of which still stands its ground, through all the vicissitudes of 60 years.'

[20] CB, complaining that he had 'neither met with a *great* player on the harpsichord, nor an *original* composer for it throughout Italy' in 1770, remarked in a footnote, 'It seems as if Alberti was always to be pillaged or imitated in every modern harpsichord lesson' (*Tours*, i. 236 and n. 1).

part. From the time his pieces were first printed[21] Composers of all kinds seem only to pour water on the *leaves* of others till the German Symphonies appeared by Stamitz, Filtz, Haultzbaur, Canabich, &c.[22] The two Martinis indeed had original merit, the one on the old plan, & the other on the new;[23] but the Sonatas of Zanetti & Campioni[24] seemed models of grace & elegance till those of Schwindl & Abel appeared.[25] After these, however, came Haydn, Vanhal & Boccherini for bowed-instruments,[26] & for vocal music after Pere[z], Jomelli,

[21] For the introduction of Alberti's keyboard music to English audiences in 1745, see *Hist. Mus.* iii. 569; iv. 664; Mercer, ii. 451, 1008. Alberti's *VIII Sonate Per Cembalo Opera Prima* was published by John Walsh in Nov. 1748 (Smith and Humphries, *Walsh*, no. 15).

[22] 'At the court of Manheim, about the year 1759, the band of the Elector Palatine was regarded as the most complete and best disciplined in Europe; and the symphonies that were produced by the maestro di capella, Holtzbaur, the elder Stamitz, Filtz, Cannabich, ... became the favourite full-pieces of every concert, and supplanted concertos and opera overtures, being more spirited than the one, and more solid than the other' (*Hist. Mus.* iv. 582; Mercer, ii. 945). See also, for CB's visit to Mannheim, and his comments on its celebrated orchestra, *Tours*, ii. 30–6, 134.

Johann Wenzel Anton Stamitz (1717–57), founder of the 'Mannheim school', violinist and composer; Anton Filtz (1733–60), a pupil of Stamitz, cellist in the Mannheim orchestra (1754); Ignaz Jakob Holzbauer (1711–83), Austrian composer, joined the Mannheim orchestra as its conductor in 1753; Johann Christian Cannabich (1731–98), a pupil of Stamitz, succeeded (1757) his master as first violinist in the Mannheim orchestra, conductor (1774). See *New Grove*.

[23] The Sammartini (or San Martini) brothers were: Giuseppe Sammartini (1695–1750), oboist and composer, who came to London in 1728. 'As a composer Martini was possessed of all the learning of the old school, with infinitely more invention, taste, and grace than any other Italian of his time.'

Giovanni Battista Sammartini (*c.*1701–75), of Milan, whom CB had met on his Italian tour (see CB to Garrick, 17–[18] Oct. 1770, n. 13), whose 'violin music, ... particularly his symphonies, concertos, and notturni, composed about the middle of the last century, was full of fire, invention, and beautiful melodies.' See CB's articles on both Sammartinis in Rees, under 'Martini'.

[24] Francesco Zannetti (1737–88), Italian composer, violinist, and singer, whom CB had met in 1770 (*Tours*, i. 319) in Perugia, where Zannetti had been *maestro di cappella* at the Duomo since 1760 (UTET; *New Grove*). In an article on Zannetti in Rees, CB wrote, 'He has composed much natural and pleasing music for instruments', and noted that 'some elegant and easy sonatas of his composition were published by Bremner'. For Zannetti's chamber music published in London in the 1760s and 1770s, see *BUCEM*.

Carlo Antonio Campioni (1720–88), French-born Italian composer, whom CB had met in Florence (see CB to Garrick, 17–[18] Oct. 1770, n. 40). CB wrote, 'his printed trios were in the modern Italian style, and in great favour in England, for more than 10 years, during the middle of the last century. They were in an easy and graceful taste, and pleased universally till the superior force and genius of the elder Stamitz and Boccherini, created new wants and expectations' (Rees; see also *BUCEM*).

[25] Friedrich Schwindl (1737–86), Dutch composer, violinist, flautist, and harpsichordist, whose compositions enjoyed a vogue in England in the third quarter of the eighteenth century, championed by Giardini (see *Hist. Mus.* iv. 599;Mercer, ii. 957–8; Rees). For Karl Friedrich Abel (1723–87), the German viola da gamba player and composer who had settled in England in 1759, see CB to Crisp, [31] May [1771], n. 10; *Hist. Mus.* iv. 678–80; Mercer, ii. 1018–20. See *BUCEM* for the many London editions of Schwindl's and Abel's trio sonatas to which CB appears to make specific reference.

[26] Franz Joseph Haydn (1732–1809), some of whose symphonies and quartets CB had heard in Vienna on his German tour in 1772 (*Tours*, ii. 75, 100, 124), was now *kapellmeister* to Prince

Piccini, Sacchini, Monza &c[27] out skips me Paesiello,[28] more original, bold, yet natural & pleasing, than any one of them. As to Harpsichord music you know my opinion of our friend Em. Bach.[29] Schobert, Eichner, & now & then Echard, are *stock* composers for the P. F. with me,[30] and since then I can recollect nothing like a new *genre* struck out. Here's my Profession de Foi musicale, & if it deserves the Inquisition, I think you would equally deserve the danger of fire & faggot.

I have found a Motet of Josquin[31] superior to all I sent you; but it vas too long to print or even transcribe,[32] but I hope to shew it, & chew it with you some time or other. Oh! I like of all things to compare

Nicolaus I Esterházy (1714–90). For an indication of CB's present familiarity with Haydn's works, see CB to Twining, 6 Sept. 1783.

Johann Baptist Vanhal (1739–1813), Bohemian composer whom CB had sought out in Vienna (*Tours*, ii. 120–1). Vanhal's symphonies were popular at the Pantheon concerts in London (Rees), and CB commented, 'The quartets and other productions for violins by this excellent composer certainly deserve a place among the first productions, in which unity of melody, pleasing harmony, and a free and manly style are constantly preserved' (*Hist. Mus.* iv. 599; Mercer, ii. 958).

Luigi Boccherini (1743–1805), Italian composer and violoncellist, 'has perhaps supplied the performers on bowed-instruments and lovers of Music with more excellent compositions than any master of the present age, except Haydn. His style is at once bold, masterly, and elegant' (*Hist. Mus.* iii. 573; Mercer, ii. 455).

[27] i.e. the generation of 'Neapolitan school' opera composers succeeding those listed in n. 8: David Perez (1711–78); Nicolò Jommelli (1714–74); Niccolò Vito Piccinni (1728–1800); Antonio Maria Gasparo Gioacchino Sacchini (1730–86); Carlo Monza (*c*.1735–1801). See *New Grove*.

[28] Giovanni Paisiello (1740–1816), 'a Neapolitan, and gifted with as much fertility of invention for dramatic compositions as nature ever bestowed on an Italian opera composer ... he has justly been regarded at the head of vocal composition of the present time [1804], as Haydn of instrumental' (Rees).

[29] Carl Philipp Emanuel Bach (1714–88), whom CB had met in Hamburg (*Tours*, ii. 211–20), 'the greatest composer and performer on keyed-instruments in Europe' (*Hist. Mus.* iv. 594–5; Mercer, ii. 954).

[30] See CB to Archer, 21–28 Feb. 1779, n. 5. Johann Schobert (*c*.1735–67), whose works were brought from Paris to England in 1766 by CB, who claimed that Schobert's style 'never pleased in Germany so much as in England and France'. Ernst Eichner (1740–77), had 'less fire than Schobert, and more taste and expression'. Johann Gottfried Eckard (1735–1809), Schobert's rival in Paris, whose compositions 'manifest great skill, refinement, and knowledge of his instrument'. See *Hist. Mus.* iv. 597–8; Mercer, ii. 956–7; Rees.

[31] Josquin des Prez (*c*.1440–1521), composer of the Franco–Flemish school, 'who may justly be called the father of modern harmony' (*Hist. Mus.* ii. 485; Mercer, i. 735). CB's admiring comments on, and musical examples of Josquin had elicited from Twining an equally enthusiastic response in his letter of 8–10 Dec.: 'As for Master Josquin, I go all lengths with you: he was an admirable fellow, & I had no conception that such Harmony existed near a century before Palestrina.' CB plays an important part in the revival of interest in Josquin (see D. Harrán, 'Burney and Ambros as Editors of Josquin's Music', in *Jòsquin des Prez*, ed. E. E. Lowinsky (1976), pp. 148–77).

[32] Josquin's setting of the penitential fiftieth (or fifty-first) Psalm, 'Miserere mei, Deus', for five voices. In *Hist. Mus.* ii. 507 (Mercer, i. 749–50), CB devotes a paragraph to this motet, calling the setting 'truly admirable', but adding with regret, 'as it consists of three movements, is too long to be inserted in a work of this kind, but appears to me a model of choral composition, without instruments ...'. CB's transcription of Josquin's 'Miserere' is preserved in the British Library (Add. MS 11582, fos. 69–72ᵛ), with an appended comment (fo. 72ᵛ): 'This Miserere is a Model of Ecclesiastical Music, without Air, or secular levity & refinements. The Style is truely

notes, & sentiments about these matters, & am extremely pleased with your comments, & remarks.[33] They proceed from great knowledge of Harmony, & experience in musical effects in full compositions. When I work at your remarks on my MS I'll have a letter on the stocks, & tell you all my feelings whether similar, or different from yours.

But who writes perfectly well for an instrument of which he is not an entire master?[34] When Sacchini, Vanhal, Jomelli, Piccini, or any first rate Composer for voices or other instruments writes for the Harpsichord, what flimsy, awkward stuff it is.

If Pacchierotti goes on singing clearer & clearer, & louder & louder every night, you'll hear him by & by, at Colchester without an Acousticon.[35]

But I must give you some account of the Comic opera, *I Viaggiatori felici*, by Anfossi,[36] which was performed the first time, here, last Tuesday.[37] The Music is polished, graceful, & pleasing, as are all his

grave, & reverential; the Harmony pure; the imitations are ingenious, & all constructed upon a fragment of Canto fermo, to wch the 2^d Tenor is wholly confined ...'.

[33] From Twining's letter of 8–10 Dec., it is clear that CB had sent for special comment the three major musical examples of Josquin's compositions, which were included in the *History of Music*.

The motet 'La Déploration d'Ockeghem' (*Hist. Mus.* ii. 480–4; Mercer, i. 732–4), with which Twining was 'half angry & half pleased'; the *Osanna* and *Benedictus* from the 'Missa Faisant regretz' (*Hist. Mus.* ii. 499–500; Mercer, i. 743–5), with which Twining was '*much* pleased'; and the motet 'Misericordias Domini' (*Hist. Mus.* ii. 503–6; Mercer, i. 747–9), with which Twining was '*delighted*'.

Twining's general comments are illuminating, and serve to explain CB's eventual inclusion of several more musical examples from Josquin: 'Surely, there is nothing of [Palestrina's] *superior*, in richness, sweetness[,] clearness of harmony, & ingenuity of contrivance, to Josquin's "*Misericordias Domini*"?—is there? ... Publish *that* Motett, & *I* will give you a receipt in full for Josquin: Tho' I care not how *many* specimens of him you can afford to give us. But as you say you must be as oeconomical here as you can, I sh^d think that *2* specimens—the *Motett* of his *best* style, & the *unfettered* powers of his genius—& the *Hosanna*, of his *technical* style, & his tyrannical mastery over difficulties,—wou'd be enough to give an adequate idea of his merit & rank.'

[34] Referring to an unidentified set of duets, Twining had written in his letter of 8–10 Dec.: 'I thank you much for sending me those Duetts; I am sorry I can not in conscience make a good report of them. ... They have all the *appearance* of being composed by a man either knowing little of the instrument, or composing without his fiddle in his *hand*, or in his *mind*.'

[35] In his letter from Colchester, Essex, of 8–10 Dec., Twining had written, 'Tell Pacch. to sing so loud that I may hear him here.' Pacchierotti, after an absence of one season, returned to the London stage on 17 Nov. 1781 in the title-role in *Ezio*, a pasticcio with music composed mainly by F. G. Bertoni (*The London Stage*, v. i. 476–7). Soon after his return to London, Pacchierotti called on the Burneys in St Martin's Street, a visit recorded by Fanny Burney in a letter to Mrs Thrale, 4 Nov. [1781], (Berg), printed (in error under 1780) in *DL* i. 451–3.

[36] Pasquale Anfossi (1727–97), Italian composer, who in 1783 came to London as composer to the Opera (*BD*): 'at an unfavourable time ... his reputation was rather diminished than increased in this kingdom' (*Hist. Mus.* iv. 523–4; Mercer, ii. 897).

[37] *I Viaggiatori felici*, a comic opera in two acts, was one of Anfossi's most successful. First presented in Venice in Oct. 1780, it was brought over to London and produced on Tuesday 11 Dec. 1781. During the 1781–2 London season it was sung no less than twenty-eight times (*The London Stage*, v. i. 451; A. Loewenberg, *Annals of Opera, 1597–1940* (2nd edn., Geneva, 1955), vol. i, col. 382).

compositions, without much originality. But the first woman *Allegranti*[38] is truly charming, in figure, gesture, & vocal performance. Her voice is not powerful, but so flexible, that she seems to do with it just what she pleases—She occasionally goes up to G in altissimo, but with this difference from Mad. le Brun,[39]—that her performance & manner are so interesting, animated, & agreeable, do what she will, elle *a toujours raison.* The applause she received amounted almost to acclamation: for the audience not content with encoring several songs, particularly one introduced by a long scene, with accompanied Recitative, in the mock-heroic Style, where she counterfeits madness, when she returned upon the Stage after a considerable absence, while other scenes were performed, renewed their violent applause before she had said a word, or sung a note.—If I had a mind to criticise with rigour, I should say that she had but few real notes in her voice—that the bottom is weak & meagre, the top all falsetto, & that her execution was but a pretty *flutter,*—yet, with all this, the ensemble is delightful, & in her style, she is an exquisite performer,—in age considerably under 30, I should think.—It is from the thinness, or, as Sir Fr. Bacon would say, *exility*[40] of her voice, that she is enabled to get into such crannies & by-places in her divisions & riffioramenti.[41] Indeed she seems to me original— her graces and embellishments do not appear to have been copied from any other singer, or to have been mechanically taught by a master. What a Country is Italy, for talents in the fine arts! After so much *croaking* of old people, that la vera scuola della musica e ⟨rovinata⟩, to have two such composers as Boccherini & Paesiello, & singers in totally different Styles, as Pacchierotti & l'Allegranti!

[38] Teresa Maddalena Allegranti (1754–*c*.1802), Italian soprano, whom CB had heard on his 1772 German tour (*Tours*, ii. 34), and described her then as singing 'in a pretty unaffected manner; and though her voice will not allow her to aspire at the first part in an opera, she seems likely to fill the second in a very engaging manner.' Her London appearance made CB change his mind: he found her 'a very captivating *prima buffa*' (*Hist. Mus.* iv. 516; Mercer, ii. 892). For Allegranti, see *New Grove*; *BD*; and n. 41.

[39] For Franziska Lebrun, née Danzi (1756–91), see CB to Twining, 11 [June] 1780, n. 64. CB makes the comparison between Mlle Allegranti and Mme Lebrun for two reasons: Lebrun had been the leading lady on the London Italian opera stage during the previous seasons; and both Allegranti and Lebrun had been associated with the Elector Palatine's troupe at Mannheim and Schwetzingen in 1772, when CB first heard them together in the same opera (*Tours*, ii. 33–4).

[40] 'For exility of the voice or other sounds; it is certain that the voice doth pass through solid and hard bodies, . . . and through water, . . . But then the voice, or other sound, is reduced by such passage to a great weakness or exility' (*Sylva Sylvarum*, para. 154, in *The Works of Francis Bacon*, ed. J. Spedding, R. L. Ellis, and D. D. Heath (1857–9), ii. 401).

[41] 'Her voice was very sweet and flexible, though not very powerful. Her taste, closes, and variety of passages in the *Viaggiatori Felici*, . . . were universally admired. However, after she had been heard in the *Contadina in Corte*, of Sacchini, and in Anfossi's *Vecchi Burlati*, it was found by some that her *riffioramenti* were not inexhaustible, and by others, that she did not always sing perfectly in tune' (*Hist. Mus.* iv. 517; Mercer, ii. 892). In CB's usage (see n. 42), 'riffioramenti' means extempore embellishments of the vocal line by the singer.

The first Buffo, Viganoni,[42] is a young man, a pretty figure, good actor, & with a much better voice & manner of singing than any one we have had since Lovatini's[43] best days. Old Morigi[44] keeps the spectators in a broad grin as usual. The dancing pleases just as much as it should do, not exclusively, as last year;[45] though Noverre[46] has very good resources, as a Ballet-Master, and the Theodore[47] is a Butterfly, in agility.

To Thomas Twining [St Martin's Street], January 1782[1]

L copy extract (Osborn: 'Twining Letterbook No. 3', p. 37).

[42] Giuseppe Viganoni (before 1762–1823), Italian tenor, whose début on the London stage occurred in this performance described by CB. Viganoni also sang in the following London season, 1782–3, and returned again to London in 1796 (see *The London Stage*, v. i. 460, 552; v. iii. *passim*). The Irish tenor and composer Michael Kelly (1762–1826) became a friend of Viganoni (see Kelly's *Reminiscences*, ed. R. Fiske (1975), *passim*). CB had no high opinion of Viganoni (*Hist. Mus.* iv. 516; Mercer, ii. 892). In Rees, CB wrote of Viganoni, 'his style of singing was what painters would call *manière*: for with all his *riffioramenti*, or embellishments, of which he was so lavish, his performance seemed monotonous.'

[43] Giovanni Lovattini (1730–after 1782), Italian tenor, had first appeared in London in 1766, and performed regularly there until 1775 (*The London Stage*, IV. ii. 1182; IV. iii. *passim*). 'Lovattini's voice, which was a sweet and well-toned tenor, with his taste, humour, and expression, insured him great and constant applause' (*Hist. Mus.* iv. 490; Mercer, ii. 872). When Michael Kelly met Lovattini in his native Bologna in 1782, he 'had retired from public life with very ample means' (Kelly, *Reminiscences*, p. 60). See also *Hist. Mus.* iv. 516; Mercer, ii. 891–2; Rees; Walpole *Corresp.* xxii. 474.

[44] After a 9-year absence, this performance marked the return to the London stage of Andrea Morigi (*fl.* 1766–93), Italian bass, who had first appeared in London in 1766 with Lovattini. CB classified him as a '*buffo caricato*', and admired his performance. Morigi performed in England for the last time in 1793 after many seasons in Italian comic opera (see *Hist. Mus.* iv. 490, 514–15; Mercer, ii. 872, 900; Rees; *BD*).

[45] For CB's complaint at the popular ascendancy of the ballet over the singing in the attention of London opera audiences, see *Hist. Mus.* iv. 517–18; Mercer, ii. 892–3; and CB to Twining, 24 Feb. 1782; to Mrs Phillips, [7 Dec. 1783].

[46] Jean-Georges Noverre (1727–1810), celebrated Swiss–French dancer, choreographer, and reformer of ballet had last worked in London in 1757. In the 1781–2 season he re-staged seven of his most famous compositions and introduced three new ones (*The London Stage*, v. i. 451). See Michaud; *New Grove*; D. Lynham, *The Chevalier Noverre, Father of Modern Ballet* (1950); M. H. Winter, *The Pre-Romantic Ballet* (1974).

On 11 Dec. 1781, a *Divertissement* composed by Noverre was danced after the end of Act I of *I Viaggiatori felici*, and at the end of the opera was presented Noverre's *Les Petits Riens*, originally created for the Paris Opéra in 1778, and now revived to music by François-Hippolyte Barthélemon (1741–1808). See *The London Stage*, v. i. 482; Lynham, *Noverre*, p. 170.

[47] Madeleine-Louise Crespé, called Théodore (1760–99), French ballerina, had made her début in 1777 at the Paris Opéra. She had come to England with Noverre, and married (1783) the male dancer and choreographer Jean Bercher, called Dauberval (1742–1806). See *DBF*, under 'Dauberval'; *BD*; Lynham, *Noverre*, pp. 101–4, 187–8.

[1] Jan. 1782 must be accepted as the date of this extract of a letter copied by Daniel Twining, who deleted '15. Oct. 1781', a date which does not necessarily belong to this extract.

Jan. 1782

... With respect to the application of *shouting* to the English,[2] I have lately found that we were so stigmatised proverbially,[3] & the Italians still worse, with imitating in their singing the noise of *goats*;—from which Pietro Aaron seriously defends them.[4] The following national Characters must certainly have been given first by a *Frenchman*. 'Galli cantant, Angli jubilant, Hispani plangant, Germani ululant, Itali Caprizant'—As it is certainly to these provincial characters that Tinctor alludes,[5] we must gulp, & not take the *Cant* from the French.[6] ...

To Thomas Twining [St Martin's Street], 24 February 1782

L copy extract (Osborn: 'Twining Letterbook No. 3', pp. 37–9).

Feb. 24. 82.

... But there is a fade[1] & pumpkin-kind of sweetness in ⟨?⟩ which my lugs dislike hugely.—Tis but reversing the passage, which in falso

[2] 'This alludes to national characters which I have seen in several books that were written during the fifteenth and sixteenth centuries, and which were at first probably circulated by one of the natives of France, as no others are allowed to *sing*' (*Hist. Mus.* ii. 450 n.; Mercer, i. 712 n.).

[3] The source of the saying is not identified, though CB's quotation in this letter closely resembles the version given in Andreas Ornithoparchus (b. *c.*1490), *Musice active micrologus* (Leipzig, 1517), bk. IV, ch. 8 (sig. M2). Ornithoparchus's popular treatise was translated into English by the great lutenist and composer John Dowland (1563–1626) as *Andreas Ornithoparcus His Micrologus, or Introduction: Containing the Art of Singing* (1609), in which the passage in question is rendered (p. 88): '... divers Nations have divers fashions, ... Hence is it, that the English doe carroll; the French sing; the Spaniards weepe; the Italians, which dwell about the Coasts of *Ianua* caper with their Voyces; the other barke: but the Germanes (which I am ashamed to utter) doe howle like Wolves.' CB's copy of Dowland's translation is listed in 'Cat. Fac. Mus.', item 105.

[4] Pietro Aaron (*c.*1480–*c.*1550), Italian musical theorist (*DBI*; *New Grove*; *Hist. Mus.* iii. 154–7; Mercer, ii. 131–3). CB refers to Aaron's *Lucidario in musica di alcune oppenioni antiche, et moderne* (Venice, 1545), bk. IV, ch. 1 (fo. 31). CB owned a copy of the *Lucidario*, listed in 'Cat. Fac. Mus.', item 5.

[5] Johannes Tinctoris (*c.*1435–1511), Franco–Flemish theorist and composer (*New Grove*). CB quotes Tinctoris's allusion to these alleged national singing characteristics in *Hist. Mus.* ii. 450; Mercer, i. 712. See also, Johannes Tinctoris, *Proportionale musices*, in *Johannes Tinctoris: Opera Theoretica*, ed. A. Seay (1978), vol. iia, p. 10 (*Corpus Scriptorum de Musica*, 22); O. Strunk, *Source Readings in Music History* (1952), p. 195.

Twining had discussed this passage, and CB's translation, in a letter dated 8 June 1781 (BL Add. MS 39929, fos. 260–5).

[6] For a similar play on words, see *Thraliana*, i. 268, where Mrs Thrale wrote in 1778: 'Mr Tessier was talked of for Manager to the Opera—Lord says Dr Burney now we shall have our Ears grated with French Musick, & what will the poor Italians do then?—why *cry* quoth Mr Seward: for Ut. Gallus cantat,—flet Petrus! You know.'

[1] For the adjectival 'fade', meaning 'feeble', 'insipid', 'commonplace', or 'uninteresting', see *OED*.

bordone is good, & common: ⟨?⟩[2] But the *common* was what he wished to avoid, I suppose, at any rate. Mimo Scarlatti[3] in his *rapid* lessons has worse things of this kind: yet even *he* would not in *slow* movements, I fancy hazard a similar passage to that of Worgan.[4] I have not seen the Lessons whence you give it; but did you ever discover *real Genius* in W———'s compositions? I mean real enthusiastic ebullitions of Spirit, Grace, Dignity, Pathos? I own I never did: now all imitation of Geminiani; now of Scarlatti, & now of Handel, or somebody else. All his endeavours at novelty are clumsy & awkward, like Mr Vellum's pleasantry—'you'll excuse my being jocular, Mrs Abigail.'[5]

I am going to Lord Archer's,[6] where the Concert des dames is held to night. Pacchierotti sings, & the band is the best that can be selected as well as the Company, who being all of the Meilleur *Ton*, must, you know, greatly meliorate the concert. The opera does not go on to my wish. The Town is all Cabal. Alegrante[7] by small judges is malevolently pitted against our friend,[8] & she is no more to be compared

[2] In the MS copy, Daniel Twining left blank spaces where CB had written out musical examples which would have explained his point about Worgan. For 'falso bordone', a fifteenth-century term for harmonizations of liturgical chants, see 'Faburden' in Rees; 'Fauxbourdon' in *New Grove*.

[3] CB occasionally uses this diminutive for Domenico Scarlatti in his published works. See, for example, *Tours*, ii. 191 n. 2.

[4] John Worgan (1724–90), Mus.B. (1748), Mus.D. (1775), English organist and composer (see CB to Twining, 30 Aug. 1773, n. 46). A pupil of Thomas Roseingrave, Worgan 'was impressed with a reverence for Domenico Scarlatti ... and afterwards he became a great collector of his pieces ... [and] editor of twelve at one time and six at another' (*Hist. Mus.* iv. 666; Mercer, ii. 1009). See R. Kirkpatrick, *Domenico Scarlatti* (Princeton, 1953), pp. 122, 124–5, 408–9.

CB wrote of Worgan: 'his style of composition was not pleasing; his melody was often uncouth, never graceful; and his harmony & modulation, like that of his master Roseingrave, too studied & unnatural to please the public, or even connoisseurs of good taste' (*CB Mem.* 36). See also Rees, under 'Worgan', where CB writes of Worgan's originality as 'original awkwardness, and attempts at novelty without nature for his guide.'

[5] Joseph Addison, *The Drummer; or, The Haunted-House* (1716). Vellum, the ponderous steward in this five-act comedy, relishes his characteristic line: 'Ha, ha, ha! You will pardon me for being jocular.' See *The Miscellaneous Works of Joseph Addison*, ed. A. C. Guthkelch (1914), i. 448, 450, 455, 462, 470, 480.

[6] i.e. the late Lord Archer's residence. Andrew Archer (1736–78), 2nd Lord Archer, Baron of Umberslade (1768), had married (1761) Sarah West (1741–1801). The widowed Lady Archer was notorious in fashionable London society for her excessive use of rouge. See *DL* ii. 178–80; Walpole *Corresp.* xxxiii. 500; and CB to Fanny Burney, [13 Nov. 1782], n. 4. In 1782, Lady Archer's town residence was in Portland Place. See M. Dorothy George, *Catalogue of Political and Personal Satires Preserved in the Department of Prints and Drawings in the British Museum*, vol. v (1935), No. 6114. CB, in an undated paragraph of his *Frag. Mem.* (Berg), gives a long account of how he would give Lady Archer's three daughters music lessons 'in the evening, from 6 to 9; wch luckily was more convenient to L^y A.'s late hours & deep play and more agreeable to the young Ladies, who doated on Music ... I never had more pleasure in giving instruction than to these diligent & amiable Ladies.'

[7] For Teresa Maddalena Allegranti, see CB to Twining, 14 Dec. 1781, nn. 38, 41.

[8] Pacchierotti.

with him, than Mrs Clive was to Mrs Cibber.[9] He is an excellent
Comic singer, with good taste, & many pretty & new passages, but
she sings chiefly in falset, has no shake, & has neither the resources
nor divine enthusiasm of our friend. I want to be pleased with both in
their several *genres*; but I am not allowed, for by asking too much for
Alegrante, I am perhaps inclined to give too little, and by speaking
irreverently & unfairly of the Pacch. I am perhaps too red hot in his
praises. The opera, however, is dwindling again into a mere Dancing
Entertainment.[10] The Ballets historique fill the house more than the
singing. Mad^e Theodore[11] is truly charming in the Demi-Caractere. It
is exhilerating to see her legereté of motion. She heres & theres it like a
butterfly, & yet dancing at an Opera is at best but a secondary thing,
& should ever strike the flag to Music. ...

To William Mason   [St Martin's Street, mid-April 1782][1]

ALS draft (Osborn).
Docketed by FBA: ※ To the Revd Mr Mason

Dear Sir.

It w^d subject me to great self-reproach if I did not seize the first
moment of leisure wch the multiplicity of my present occupations &
engagem^ts will allow, to thank you for the valuable present wch you
have kindly bestowed upon me.[2] I have long flattered myself with

[9] Mrs Catherine Clive, née Raftor (1711–85), universally known as Kitty, the vivacious and
celebrated female comic singer and actress (*DNB*; *BD*); and her contemporary, Mrs Susannah
Maria Cibber, née Arne (1714–66), singer, playwright, and actress who built up her repertory
to include almost all the great tragic roles for women on the English stage (*DNB*; *BD*; Mary
Nash, *The Provoked Wife: The Life and Times of Susannah Cibber*, 1977).

Mrs Clive's singing 'was intolerable when she meant it to be fine, in ballad farces and songs of
humour was, like her comic acting, every thing it should be' (*Hist. Mus.* iv. 654; Mercer, ii.
1000). Mrs Cibber, on the other hand, had a voice 'which was a mezzo soprano, almost, indeed,
a contralto, of only six or seven notes' but was 'touching' in her 'simple, but pathetic, style of
singing' (Rees; see also *Hist. Mus.* iv. 526, 657–8; Mercer, ii. 899, 1003). For the youthful CB's
acquaintance with Mrs Clive, and friendship with Mrs Cibber, see Lonsdale, pp. 11, 17–18, 57,
71 n. 2, 489; CB to Fanny Burney, [mid-June 1763], n. 1.

[10] See CB to Twining, 14 Dec. 1781, n. 45; to Mrs Phillips, [7 Dec. 1783].

[11] For Madeleine-Louise Crespé (1760–99), who took the stage-name Théodore, see CB to
Twining, 14 Dec. 1781, n. 47.

[1] The publication dates of Mason's *Essay on Cathedral Music* and the second volume of CB's
History of Music determine the approximate date of this letter (see nn. 2, 4, 14).

[2] William Mason's *A Copious Collection of those Portions of the Psalms of David, Bible, and Liturgy,
which have been set to Music, and sung as Anthems ... and published for the Use of the Church of York, under*

imagining that there was some similarity in our Ideas of Music in general; but as to the particular part of it wch you have so well discussed in your Essay, you will find disseminated through the 2^d Vol. of my Hist^y & still more in the 3^d so many reproaches against the old Composers for the Want of *accent* & *propriety* in the setting of words, that it will almost seem to have arisen from a conference or previous communication of sentiments.[3] The last sheet of my 2^d Vol. was in the press[4] when I had the honour of receiving your B^k otherwise I sh^d have spoken of it as I thought on perusal & backed my opinions by your authority. However this will be done with more force & propriety in my 3^d Vol. as the work in the II^d is brought down no lower than the time of the Reformation.[5] You know, I believe, my very worthy Fr^d the Revd Mr Twining,[6] wth whom I have long been in the habit of corresponding & communicating my Musical Ideas; & he has now in his hands, [7]a paper of mine written[7] at least 6 months ago containing my undisguised opinions upon the defect of simplicity in full Church

---

the Direction of William Mason, M. A. Precentor of that Cathedral. By whom is prefixed, a Critical and Historical Essay on Cathedral Music, was published at York, c.10 Apr. 1782 (see Walpole Corresp. xxix. 226; P. Gaskell, The First Editions of William Mason (Cambridge, 1951), pp. 27–8). CB's copy, presumably this presentation copy, 'with MS. Remarks', was sold for 4s. 6d. (Cat. Mus. Lib., lot 904).

Mason included a revised version of this essay in his Essays, Historical and Critical, on English Church Music (York, 1795), a volume reviewed severely by CB in Monthly Review, n.s. xx (1796), 398–408. See also The Works of William Mason, M. A. (1811), iii. 327–59; CB's article on Mason in Rees; and J. W. Draper, William Mason. A Study in Eighteenth-Century Culture (New York, 1924), ch. 13.

[3] Mason objected to polyphonic church music, 'which combines a variety of parts in various intricate manners, and gives to the different voices that perform those parts different words to express at the same time, which occasions ... a confusion which constantly perplexes the common ear, and which the most practised in harmony cannot always easily develope' (Essay on Cathedral Music (1782), p. xxii). CB expresses a similar sentiment, to take only one example, in Hist. Mus. ii. 173; Mercer, i. 528: '... it seems as if the perfection of *figurative Counterpoint*, and the invention of Fugues, had utterly diverted the attention of the composer, performer, and public, from poetry, propriety, and syllabic laws; to this may be added the use of the Organ in accompanying the service of the church, which ... rendered the words that were sung difficult to be understood.'

[4] On 14 Feb. 1782, Twining had written to CB (BL Add. MS 39929, fos. 293–4): 'Well, but I wish you joy of your arrival at the *end* of Vol. II.—I hope now the Devils will work hard, & deliver you handsomely of this bouncing brat e'er long.' A month later, on 18 Mar., Dr Johnson returned with his emendations the MS of the last pages of the second volume of the History, which carry CB's apology to his subscribers for the necessity of a third volume. See Johnson Letters, ii. 468; Hist. Mus. ii. 585–6; Mercer, i. 808; CB to Twining, [Apr.? 1780].

[5] Mason's Essay opens: 'At the time of the Reformation Cathedral Music was extremely intricate' (p. xv), and then proceeds to censure the persistence in the Church of England of polyphonic church music. CB mentions Mason's views, with guarded approval, in Hist. Mus. iii. 146, 480 n., 600, 609; iv. 11–12, 191 n.; Mercer, ii. 125, 383 n., 478, 485, 504–5, 648 n.

[6] Twining had been at Sidney Sussex College, Cambridge, from 1755 to 1764, during which years he became acquainted with Mason. See Country Clergyman, pp. 156–7; Draper, Mason, p. 123.

[7-7] MS a ... written] altered from in a Letter written to him,

Music and its remedies, [8][and on the] absurdity[8] of Fugue, Canon, & other Gothic Contrivances, in rendering the words of vocal music unintelligible. I have no copy of this Paper now in my Possession; but as my Friend seems to approve ⟨o⟩f it, I shall find a place for it in the 3^d vol. where during the reigns of Eliz. ⟨& James⟩ the 1st the abuse of Fugue & multiplied parts seem most loudly to call for it.[9] I own that the great ingenuity of Josquin, Palestrina, Tallis & Bird, sometimes get the better of my objections & soften my censures: who, as a musician, nursed in Fugue, cannot perhaps help having some lurking prejudices in favour of the art, craft, & Mystery of multiplied melodies in this kind of writing. Indeed I sometimes wish the art of Fugue to be cultivated *only* for the use of the Church, where being banished the Theatres & other public places it might under proper restrictions preclude the levity of Secular Melodies.[10] If the words are well set & well articulated in leading off the subject, their meaning w^d be as well conveyed to the Congregation as if read by a Minister or Clerk. And as most anthems are taken from the Psalms contained in the Common prayer book wch few go to Church without, [11]it will perhaps be s^d that no greater[11] reproach falls to the share of a Composer & singer when it is used during an Anthem or service in a Cathedral than to the reader in the Desk of a Parish Church, during divine service.[12] I shall however continue to recommend more Simplicity, and attention to accent than has hitherto been observed in our own Church Music, or that of the Catholics Lutherans or Calvinists. I hope ere long to have an opportunity of discussing these points wth you vivâ voce, & of shewing you the thoughts I had committed to Paper as mentioned above; of wch my Fr^d T. is pleased to say:[13] ⟨?⟩

I hope my II^d Vol. will be ready for publication before the expiration

---

[8–8] MS [and ... absurdity] I have long seen the absurdity *deleted. CB's draft leaves the sense of his sentence incomplete. The words within square brackets are editorially supplied.*

[9] See *Hist. Mus.* iii. 144–9, 395–6; Mercer, ii. 123–7, 311–12, where CB softens his intended censure of 'Gothic Contrivances'.

[10] 'The fugues and canons of the sixteenth century, like the Gothic buildings in which they were sung, have a gravity and grandeur peculiarly suited to the purpose of their construction; and when either of them shall, by time or accident, be destroyed, it is very unlikely that they should ever be replaced by others in a style equally reverential and stupendous. They should therefore be preserved as venerable relics of the musical labours and erudition of our forefathers, before the lighter strains of Secular Music had tinctured melody with its capricious and motley flights' (*Hist. Mus.* iii. 145; Mercer, ii. 124).

[11–11] MS it ... greater] *altered from* it is no more a subject of

[12] Mason argued that the very publication of an anthem book showed in Anglican church music 'the defect of intelligibility ... which, if it did not really subsist, would give ... no occasion to supply the congregation with an Anthem-Book, as the ear would not then require the assistance of the eye, in order to be convinced (as a good Protestant ought) that what was sung was not sung in an unknown tongue' (*Essay on Cathedral Music* (1782), p. xxiv).

[13] CB leaves a gap in the MS draft, with no indication of which Twining letter he meant to quote.

of next month:[14] I now only wait for the Plates of Music wch amount to near 60, & wch are almost all engraved & ready for the rolling Press.[15] It has always appeared to me that no descriptive praise or censure of Music c^d be so satisfactory to a Musical reader as the Compositions themselves, & of these I have given examples in score from the most anc^t scarc[e] & curious I c^d find.[16]

I have the honour to be wth great regard
dear Sir, y^r obliged & most
Obed^t Servt
C.B.

To Thomas Twining

[St Martin's Street],
21 April 1782

L copy extract (Osborn: 'Twining Letterbook No. 3', pp. 39–40).

Ap. 21. 1782

... Mr Mason's work[1] is well digested, & contains many useful criticisms & ingenious thoughts, but he seems too *Calvinistical* a reformer of Church Music,[2] as he wishes to exterminate Fugue & contrivances, where alone I wish them to remain. A Fugue, now it is banished profane places, seems venerable & fit only for the Church like the old Scripture language.[3] Elementary sounds, one to each syllable, will render Music *seche* rough, inelegant, & angular, as long notes & divisions are likewise to be excommunicated.[4]—I agree with

---

[14] It was published on 29 May 1782 (Lonsdale, p. 268; *Morning Chronicle*, 29 May 1782).

[15] For a description of the rolling press and copperplate printing, see P. Gaskell, *A New Introduction to Bibliography* (Oxford, 1972), pp. 156–8.

[16] For CB's published declaration of this principle, see *Hist. Mus.* ii. 439–40; Mercer, i. 705.

[1] See CB to Mason, [mid-Apr. 1782], n. 2.

[2] CB wrote in Rees (under 'Mason'): '... his ideas of reforming cathedral music would reduce it to Calvinistical psalmody. He wished for nothing but plain counterpoint in the services and full anthems, and dull and dry harmony in the voluntaries, without melody, accent, or measure.'

[3] See CB to Mason, [mid-Apr. 1782], n. 10. See also, *Hist. Mus.* ii. 508–9; Mercer, i. 751.

[4] Mason also objected to vocal display in anthems for soloists: 'Where a voice (considered a an instrument) is to be shewn, the frittering of one syllable into perhaps almost a century o semiquavers, is perhaps the best and only expedient for shewing its executive powers ... and the quicker the succession of notes in these divisions, the more perfect are deemed the performers powers in this point. This being the case, ... a too great indulgence, or indeed any at all, to the performer in these instrumental tricks, must not only greatly diminish the gravity and solemnity of Church Music, but also render it, as a vehicle for words, much less intelligible' (*Essay on Cathedral Music* (1782), pp. xxxix–xl). For CB's later comments on this proscription, see *Monthly Review*, n.s. xx (1796), 404.

him in my censures as I remember, of want of attention to the accent and expression of the words, by our old Masters, & in the unintelligible confusion occasioned by the singing different words at the same time, in Canons & fugues, as well as other improprieties,[5] but I now forget all about it. At the close of his Essay, he says very civilly.

'When D[r] B, in the course of his Musical History, treats this part of his subject, I have good reason to hope that whatever I may have here advanced consonant to true taste, will be supported by more scientific argument.'[6] . . .

To Fanny Burney and Mr & Mrs Phillips[1] [St Martin's Street, *c*.22 July 1782][2]

AL (Hyde).
Docketed by FBA: Delightful Kindness from Dr. Burney to his happy Daughter, when with her dear bridal | Sister, Susanna E. Phillips, at Ipswich, immediately after the publication of Cecilia, which she | took to Ipswich for a first reading with her beloved Sister. | in July, 1782 ✳ ✖ (2) XI

---

[5] See *Hist. Mus.* ii. 170–4, 552 ff.; Mercer, i. 526–9, 784 ff. CB wrote of Mason: '. . . we never could subscribe to his reform of cathedral music, farther than in the accentuation of the words, and distinction of long and short syllables, in which our old cathedral composers, as well as psalmodists, are egregiously defective' (Rees).

[6] *Essay on Cathedral Music* (1782), p. lii. In the revised version of this treatise, published as the second essay in his *Essays, Historical and Critical, on English Church Music* (York, 1795), Mason politely but firmly maintained his point of view: '. . . though I cannot withdraw the strictures I made on many of our Composers, in point of Vocal Intelligibility; I entirely submit to his [CB's] superior judgment in every thing, that respects scientific Harmony' (p. 159; see *The Works of William Mason, M. A.* (1811), iii. 359).

---

[1] In the MS CB's salutation 'Dear Folks' is glossed by Mme d'Arblay: 'Capt. & Mrs. Phillips & F.B.'

CB's third and favourite daughter, Susanna Elizabeth, had married on 10 Jan. 1782 Molesworth Phillips (1755–1832), of the Royal Marines, who now held the rank of Captain (see *JL* i, pp. lxx-lxxi). Phillips was a friend and shipmate of James Burney, having served as Lieutenant in command of the marines on Cook's last voyage. After a month-long honeymoon at Chessington, the couple had moved in early Feb. to Ipswich, where Capt. Phillips had been posted with a recruiting party (*HFB*, pp. 142, 145–7; *Burford Papers*, pp. 72, 74–6).

Fanny Burney's second novel, *Cecilia, or Memoirs of an Heiress*, in five volumes, published by Thomas Payne (1719–99) and Thomas Cadell (1742–1802), appeared on Friday 12 July 1782 (*Public Advertiser*; A. Ribeiro, 'The Publication Date of Fanny Burney's *Cecilia*', *Notes and Queries*, ccxxv (1980), 415–16). A week after the publication of her novel, Fanny travelled to Ipswich on Friday 19 July to visit Susan, by now pregnant, and to share with her the first perusal of *Cecilia* (Fanny Burney to CB, [17 July 1782], Berg).

[2] The date is deduced from Fanny's journey to Ipswich, and a letter from Fanny and Susan to CB, 21 July [1782] (BL Egerton MS 3690, fos. 11–12[v]), directed to Chessington, re-directed to St Martin's Street, and bearing a London postmark of 22 July. As CB's letter clearly crossed Fanny's and Susan's in the mail, Monday 22 July 1782 is its probable date.

Dear Folks,

I came from Ches.[3] this morning where I left your Mother *rather* better than she has been for some time: that is, rather more alive than dead. I thought it impossible, & so did all here, that she c^d survive the 2^d attack—recovery of appetite, sleep, & strength will inevitably be slow—Life, & ease, are the present blessings to be sought—ꟾwe have not s^d a word of your departure from London—but laid your continuance in it on Cadell's absence, & backwardness in settling with you.ꟾ My Susey & her Cappy are well I hope—& laughing, & crying, by turns at your pleasure—ꟾMiss [xxx *2 words*]ꟾ Mrs Rishton, writes word to D.Y.[4] that she has read Cicely 3 Times over, herself, & her sposo, like Sr Jos. wth Evelina is unable to eat & drink for it[5]—he brings the b^k constantly to table at dinner & supper—But this is nothing to what I have heard from y^r Friend (*you*, Fan, I now speak to) Sr Josh—I had not been ½ an hour come home ꟾin the houseꟾ ere he shot me flying, by a Message desiring me to dine wth him, & meet Dr Warton,[6] just come to Town.—Miss Palmer's brother,[7] just come also from Ireland & the D^r were all the Company—Sr Josh—had the 5th vol. in his Painting-room—in wch he is now ab^t ½ way.[8] He intends sending you in a Bill—for damages—the B^k has already Cost him at least £100. Well, he is so full of it—& absorbed by the Characters that he can think of nothing Else—he & Miss P. now, more than ever, cry out for y^r writing a Comedy.[9] Sr J. says he never yet read a book in wch the Characters are so supported, & discriminated. He s^d something good of them all, separately—but particularly Albany[10]—

[3] CB, Mrs Burney, and Dorothy Young had journeyed to Chessington in early July, intending to stay for only a few days. CB's wife, however, fell dangerously ill there, and could not be moved. See *Burford Papers*, pp. 83–4; *HFB*, pp. 153–5.

[4] CB's step-daughter, Maria Allen (1751–1820), had married (1772) Martin Folkes Rishton (*c.*1747–1820). See *JL* i, p. lxxiv. Mrs Rishton's letter to Dorothy Young is not preserved.

[5] For Sir Joshua Reynolds's distraction over *Evelina*, see *DL* i. 60–1, 106.

[6] The Headmaster of Winchester, Dr Joseph Warton (1722–1800), for whom see CB to Warton, 12 Aug. 1771; to Mrs Thrale, 11 Jan. 1778.

[7] Sir Joshua Reynolds's niece, companion, and heiress, Mary Palmer (*c.*1751–1820), had lived with Sir Joshua almost continuously since 1773. In 1792 she married Murrough O'Brien (1726–1808), 5th Earl of Inchiquin (1777), created (1800) Marquess of Thomond. Mary Palmer's elder brother was the Revd Joseph Palmer (1749–1829), author, educated at Exeter College, Oxford, MA (1772). He was Rector of Killinick, co. Wexford, and among other church preferments was Chancellor of Ferns (1779–1801), and Dean of Cashel (1787). See *DNB*, under 'Palmer, Mrs. Mary'; *Letters of Sir Joshua Reynolds*, ed. F. W. Hilles (Cambridge, 1929), pp. 40–2, 55, 110–11, 157, 162; Burke *Corresp.* iii. 275–6; v. 252; Garrick *Letters*, iii. 954–5; Foster; F. T. Colby, *Pedigree of the Palmer Family, formerly of Southmolton and Great Torrington, Devon* (Exeter, 1892).

[8] Fanny Burney had reported to CB in her letter of [17 July 1782] that Sir Joshua was 'still only in the first vol:'.

[9] For the calls on Fanny to write a comedy after the success of *Evelina*, see CB to Fanny Burney, [29 Aug.] 1779, and [27 Nov. 1779].

[10] 'My father's present favourite is the old crazy moralist, Albany' (*DL* ii. 86). In Fanny's

343

who has a Methodistical cast, without disgusting or putting one out of humour with religion—& nothing but religion, says the K^t, c^d so totally vanquish the fear of the World, & give courage to oppose its habits. Hobson he says is an admirable ale-house Philosopher—& young Belfield[11] an excellent expansion of a Truth: that, take a man of Genius from his natural bent, & he never pursues anything else with success—Miss la Rolles & Lady Onoria, he finds so like, & so different!—Monkton not an uncommon *worldly* Man of the World—&c &c &c—this is not a quarter of what was said by him & his niece all dinner & Tea-time—Mrs Burke[12] delighted—*He*[13] wont let any one speak of it yet, till he has time to read it—Gibbons[14] read all the 5 vol^s in one Day !!!!!![15]—I suppose a day in the new Planet—of wch the year is fourscore times as long as ours, & Perhaps the days of the same proportion[16]—all like *Cicy* better than Evelina—& say, though *younger* she is much more matured—Gibbons says it is admirably *written*—& that, he is so nice in language, he perhaps more particularly attends to—Warton is eager from the acc^t he heard, to begin—he goes to Winchester to Morrow, & takes it with him—God bless you all—& send you as happy as I wish you—When Susan can spare you—we must produce you at Ches. Hetty & Nancy[17] came away with me—

reply from Ipswich, 25 July [1782] (BL Egerton MS 3690, fos. 13–14^v), she commented: 'I am mightily pleased, also, to have such a supporter for Albany, who is too excentric a Character for popularity, & who I expect will be as generally criticised by one set of people, as Briggs will by another. *Those* are the two personages for whom I have always had the most apprehension, though for each I have had *myself* a sneaking liking that has made me willing to risk them.'

[11] According to Fanny, CB's favourite character after Albany was Belfield: 'The tradesman *manqué*, he says, is new, and may be not uninstructive, and he is much pleased with his various struggles, and the *agrémens* of his talents, and the spirit, yet failure, of his various flights and experiments' (*DL* ii. 86–7).

[12] Jane Mary Burke, née Nugent (1734–1812), had married Edmund Burke (1729–97) in 1757 (*DNB*; Burke *Corresp.* i. 115).

[13] Edmund Burke, Paymaster General in the second Rockingham Administration, had recently resigned after Lord Rockingham's death on 1 July (Burke *Corresp.* iii. 423; v. 3–25). Fanny had met Burke for the first time in June 1782, when she accompanied CB to a dinner party at Sir Joshua Reynolds's country house in Richmond. Fanny on that occasion fell 'quite desperately & outrageously in love' with Burke (*DL* ii. 87–92; *HFB*, p. 151).

[14] The celebrated historian, Edward Gibbon (1737–94), had also been present at Sir Joshua's dinner party (*DL* ii. 90, 92). At this date, Gibbon was writing the fourth volume of *The History of the Decline and Fall of the Roman Empire*, 6 vols., 1776–88 (*DNB*; J. E. Norton, *A Bibliography of the Works of Edward Gibbon* (Oxford, 1940), p. 57).

[15] See also *DL* ii. 141: ' ". . . Gibbon says he read the whole five volumes in a day." "'Tis impossible," cried Mr. Burke, "it cost me three days; and you know I never parted with it from the time I first opened it." '

[16] Uranus, which orbits the Sun in 84.01 years but rotates rapidly on its axis in about 10.75 hours, had been discovered on 13 Mar. 1781 by William Herschel (1738–1822), musician and astronomer. See *DNB*; *DSB*; J. L. E. Dreyer, ed., *The Scientific Papers of Sir William Herschel* (1912), *passim*. For CB's lifelong interest in astronomy, and his friendship with Herschel, see Lonsdale, pp. 80–3, 331, 348, 381–406.

[17] CB's elder sister, Ann Burney (1722–94), the sensible 'Aunt Nanny' described by Fanny

Jemm took an ½ hour's peep at us on Sat[y]—& is in high spirits—& in seeming good humour wth the world & Consequently himself[18]—he saw L[d] Keppel[19] 2[ce] & told him he was ready, if wanted to put to sea wth L[d] Howe[20] in an hour's time—he was sent for to consult ab[t] convoying 10 India men to Madrass—& had 2 Conferences wth M[r] Stephens[21] & the Chair-man of the India Comp[y22] w[ch] gave him a Dinner in the City—they have furnished him with Charts—& it seems to me as if the ⌜⟨admiral?⟩⌝[23] was a GREAT MAN made—say nothing of all this to a 4th Person—Jemm did not enjoin *secrecy*—but he *ought* to have done it; & therefore let us suppose ourselves sworn to it—

To Fanny Burney

[St Martin's Street,
26? July 1782][1]

AL (Osborn). Mutilated fragment.
Addressed: Miss Burney | at M[rs] Philips's | Ipswich   *Frank:* Free P: J: Clerke
Pmk.: ⟨26?⟩ IY FREE   *Docketed by* FBA: VI Dr. | Johnson— | *Hobson* | Cecilia,
| Mrs. Reynolds ⧺ ✳ 1782.

---

as 'my good Aunt Nanny, who is the best Nurse in England, tender, careful & affectionate & but too well experienced in illness' (*EJL* i. 52, 156).

[18] James Burney had been appointed in May to the command of HMS *Bristol*, 50 guns; was posted Captain on 18 June 1782; and had been busily engaged at Plymouth and later at Spithead in fitting out his new command for sea. The *Bristol* was to convoy a flotilla of East Indiamen to Madras. See Manwaring, p. 166 ff.; *Burford Papers*, p. 81; *The Commissioned Sea Officers of the Royal Navy, 1660–1815* ([Greenwich], 1954), i. 129.

[19] Augustus Keppel (1725–86), Admiral of the White (1782), had been appointed First Lord of the Admiralty on the formation of Rockingham's second Administration in Mar. 1782. In Apr. he was created Viscount Keppel of Elveden, and remained in office after Rockingham's death until Jan. 1783 (*DNB*; Burke *Corresp.* v. 24 n. 2).

[20] Richard Howe (1726–99), Admiral of the Blue, created Viscount (1782), Earl (1788) Howe of Langar in the Peerage of Great Britain, at this time Commander-in-Chief of the Channel Fleet (*DNB*). When the British fleet sailed on 11 Sept. 1782 for the relief of Gibraltar, James Burney's convoy accompanied Lord Howe until 1 Oct., when the *Bristol* and the fourteen ships under her protection proceeded on their voyage to the East Indies (Manwaring, pp. 169–70).

[21] Philip Stephens (1723–1809), Secretary to the Admiralty (1763–95), MP (1759–1806), FRS (1771). On his retirement from the Admiralty in 1795, he was created a Baronet and appointed one of the Lords of the Admiralty (*DNB*; Namier and Brooke, iii. 475).

[22] Sir Henry Fletcher (c.1727–1807), of Clea Hall, Cumberland, MP (1768–1806), created Baronet (1782), Director of the East India Company (1769, 1771–5, 1777–80), Deputy Chairman (Apr.–July 1782), Chairman (July 1782–Nov. 1783). His early career had been spent as an officer in the Company's naval service (*DNB*; Namier and Brooke, ii. 439–40; *CCR*, 1783, p. 211).

[23] Mme d'Arblay altered the MS, converting CB's 'the' to 'He' and heavily overscoring what appears to be CB's joking reference to Jemm as an 'admiral'.

---

[1] Internal evidence and the postmark provide the year and the month. The date on the postmark is very faint, and is tentatively read as '26'. See also n. 10.

Dear Folks.

I have been trapsing & sweltering all over London to day & am truly dog-tired; Yet I hate to let a frank[2] budge without a shake by the Hand. I have been sitting likewise (I hope to the Lord for the last time) to Mrs Reney who now thinks she has made me d——d handsome indeed —— & that she has given me a *sweet look*.[3] Not a word said ab^t Cicely, to be sure, except what c^d be uttered from my first entrance into the house, to my quitting it. She is all for you (Fan) ⟨pu⟩tting the whole into a play, immediately, without altering the Names, & with as little al⟨ter⟩ation in the Dialogue, as possib[l]e. She is sure all the world will be more delighted in seeing these Characters realised, than any others that c^d be represented—pensez-y —— Dr Johnson is still all for Hobson[4]—but I am much pleased that he likes, quite as well as *I* do the 1st meeting of Cecilia & Henrietta.[5] Another scene (I now forget w^ch) he said was *very fine*.[6] At parting this morning (though he was far from well yesterday, & had not had a good night) his last words were 'remember me to Fanny! a rogue!!' The sweet Mrs Crewe, in a note ab^t other Matters,[7] says, 'a Thousand thanks for Cecilia, w^ch *I* can only praise like a Miss Larolles: "it is

---

[2] As the address panel shows, CB had obtained a frank from Sir Philip Jennings-Clerke (1722–88), MP (1768–88), created Baronet (1774), politician and friend of the Thrales (Namier and Brooke, ii. 680–1; Hill–Powell, iv. 80–1, 487; *Thraliana, passim; DL* i. 199–201).

[3] For Sir Joshua's sister, Frances Reynolds (1729–1807), and her portrait of CB, see CB to Mrs Thrale, 16 Oct. 177[8], nn. 12, 13. CB's exasperation with Miss Reynolds is reflected in a passage of his MS *Frag. Mem.* for 1792 (Berg), written after the death of Sir Joshua: 'His Sister Miss Reynolds had genius and a masculine understanding. But her character was very singular, for indecision. "My Sister (Sir Joshua used to say) who is always in a wonderment." ... She did Dr Johnson, Mr Burk, Mr Hoole and even myself, the honour to ask us to sit to her for our portraits, calling us her *worthies*. Yet in spite of this flattering title, she thought me a much greater coxcomb than I proved to be: for after sitting to her one day, longer than usual, she said: "I'll only give the *wig* a little touch, and let you off["]—and upon seeing me smile, she said: "why is not it a Wig?" I said I believed not, the hair-dresser never took it off my head to dress it—"What! I must not call it a wig, then?" She said nothing more; and I thought she was convinced of her mistake. But a few days after, standing talking with her at the window of her brother's dining room, while it was full of Company, she suddenly caught hold of my queue, and gave it so violent a tug, that I thought she w^d have pulled off my head. However she doubtless intended to expose me as an artificial beau to the company, all in full dress and ready to laugh at a bald head. I never had worn a Wig since I was at school, ... But whether she thought my Wig was on a block with a peculiar fastening to it, or that she had not pulled hard enough, I know not; but she never made the least apology for her mistake or uttered a single word to convince me that she thought my coifage was natural. ... she was not very successful in these *worthy* portraits.'

[4] Fanny had reported in her letter to CB of [17 July 1782] (Berg): 'Dr. Johnson supports Hobson at the Head of the tribe, & says it is a very *perfect* character'. See also *HFB*, pp. 151, 161–3.

[5] See *Cecilia*, bk. iii, ch. 3.

[6] Probably the scene in Vauxhall Gardens (*Cecilia*, bk. v, ch. 6) already referred to by Fanny in her letter of [17 July 1782]: Dr Johnson 'said "I have again read Harrel's Death, it is finely done,—it is *very* finely done!" with a very emphatic voice & manner.'

[7] Not preserved.

so *monstrously* charming, you've no Notion."'—I saw her yesterday morning, & consul⟨ted⟩[8] . . .

[*The rest of the page has been cut away. On the verso the first half of the top line of text has similarly been removed.*]

. . . ⟨Ches.⟩ to morrow—a Letter from ⌐Hemming[9] written yesterday is not pleasant—your mother's lowness, & *epuisement*, though the Fever is off, continues in a terrible degree. Stephen Allen is with her now[10]— & you shall hear from me, or somebody, how she is, after my arrival. When the fortnight you (Fannykin) talked of is expired, if your taking a peep at Chesington sh^d be wanted⌐ . . . [*cut*] . . . Mr Cadel of ⌐whom you have⌐ . . . [*cut*]

[P.S.] ⌐No news, (my dear *Cappy*) from the Fleet, yet;[11] & I fear Gibralter[12] is out of the reach of ⌐ . . . [*cut*]

To Mrs Phillips

Chessington,
22 September [1782]

AL (Berg). Mutilated and obliterated.
Docketed by FBA: Dr. Burney to⌐Mrs Phillips.⌐Dr. Johnson & Mr. Burke⌐on Cecilia. ✳ 1782.   *Editor's Note:* This fragment is pasted into a Scrapbook preserved in the Berg Collection. The curators do not permit the removal of the fragment for inspection of the verso, which carries 17 lines of obliterated text.

Ches. Sunday 22 7^ber

My ever dear Sue.

You must not think yourself forgotten, or less beloved by me than usual, on acc^t of my long silence. I have not till this morning written a Letter to a single creature for more than a month. I liked, very much, your Critique on Cicely[1]—our Feelings I found have been very similar

---

[8] CB may have enlisted Mrs Crewe's help in his attempt to obtain the organist's post in the Queen's Band and also of St Martin's-in-the-Fields. See Scholes, ii. 324–5; Lonsdale, p. 295.

[9] Thomas Hemming (*c.*1728–1810), surgeon and apothecary at Kingston, Surrey, attended Mrs Burney during her illness (*Burford Papers*, pp. 83–4; *GM* lxxx (1810)[2], 596; W. Munk, *The Roll of the Royal College of Physicians of London* (2nd rev. edn., 1878), ii. 418).

[10] Samuel Crisp wrote of Mrs Burney on 29 July 1782 (*Burford Papers*, p. 83): 'Her son was sent for up out of Norfolk and is gone again this morning.' This reference to Stephen Allen helps to date CB's letter.

[11] i.e. news of Molesworth Phillips's friend, James Burney, who was to sail in Lord Howe's fleet. See CB to Fanny Burney and Mr & Mrs Phillips, [*c.*22 July 1782], n. 20.

[12] Gibraltar had been besieged by the Spanish since July 1779. See J. Drinkwater-Bethune, *A History of the late Siege of Gibraltar* (1785).

[1] Susan's critique of *Cecilia* is not preserved, but Fanny reported to CB in her letter of 25 July [1782] (BL Egerton MS 3690, fos. 13–14^v): 'Susan is yet but in the 4th Volume, . . . Capt.

—'tis an admirable work—no B^k of ⌜such high⌝ amusement ever had, I believe more merit. Nay, it is not confined to *amusem^t*—tis an excellent moral production—*Burke* thanked Fanny for her *Instruction*,[2] & when I told *Johnson* this—he s^d, ''tis very true, Sir; no Man can read it, without having Ideas awakend in his mind that will mend the heart. When Fanny reasons, & writes from her own feelings, she is *exquisite.'*—*There's* approbation for you!—well, the Reviews, I believe, are afraid of treating her like a novellist—. & condemning or approving in a summary way—for I hear she'll neither be in the *Monthly* nor *Critical*, next Month[3] ⟨—⟩ But my sweet Sue!—when you told me that Ca⟨ppy⟩ ... [*cut*]

To Fanny Burney [St Martin's Street], 6 November 1782

AL fragment (BL Egerton MS 3690, fo. 18). Second leaf missing.
Docketed by FBA: on ⌐ Cecilia's ⌐ early favour XIII ✳ ✗ a ⌐ Kind ⌐ Kind ⌐ Letter ⌐ on ⌐ Cecilia, ⌐ in its ⌐ first ⌐ year. ⌐ 8. Nov. 1782.

6 Novr 1782—

My dear Fan—It makes me feel uncomfortable to let your Letter[1] lie unanswered, or your thoughts unemployed in my favour. But though I have but one solitary scholar in Town, after so long an absence, I plunged into London Concerns & interruptions the instant I arrived.—⌜I have long thought & think still that Payne & his Partner[2]

Phillips is all for Morrice,—Susan for Lady Honoria & *Simkins*,—but Delvile is the God of her Idolatry. The marriage ceremony in the 4th volume has half destroyed her. Till that Event, Harrel's Death, in the 3^d volume, haunted her as if she had herself heard the report of the Pistol.'
  [2] Edmund Burke had written to Fanny on 29 July 1782 (PML), thanking her 'for the very great instruction and entertainment I have received' from reading *Cecilia* (Burke *Corresp.* v. 25–7; *DL* ii. 92–4). Fanny had been staying at Ipswich with the Phillipses when she received Burke's letter, and wrote to CB on 4 Aug. (BL Egerton MS 3690, fos. 15–16^v) of her delight in it: 'O, dearest Sir, for elegance of praise no such a one was ever written before. ... Did I not say well when I said Mr. Burke was like *You*? ... he is, indeed, a delightful creature, & as sweet in his disposition as he is rare in his abilities. I could not, for some time, believe my own Eyes when I looked at his signature.' See also *DL* ii. 138–41; *HFB*, pp. 153, 157–8; *JL* iii. 222.
  [3] Both periodicals carried notices of *Cecilia* in Dec. See *Monthly Review*, lxvii (1782), 453–8; *Critical Review*, liv (1782), 414–20; *HFB*, p. 163 n. 1. The author of the review in the *Monthly Review* was the theological and literary critic Samuel Badcock (1747–88). See *DNB*; B. C. Nangle, *The Monthly Review, First Series, 1749–1789: Indexes of Contributors and Articles* (Oxford, 1934).

  [1] Of 3 Nov. 1782 (Berg), from Brighton, where Fanny Burney had joined Mrs Thrale and Dr Johnson on 26 Oct. (*DL* ii. 102).
  [2] The publishers of *Cecilia*, Thomas Payne (1719–99), and his son Thomas Payne, the younger (1752–1831), 'at the Mews-Gate', and Thomas Cadell (1742–1802), 'in the Strand'. See *DNB*; Plomer, pp. 41–2, 195.

are mean *Creetters* after such a thumping Edition[3] going off so soon, to take your Copy & new arrangements without paying you the poor £50 ab^t wch they have all along been so shabby, puts me quite out of Charity with them.[4] If they keep you 6 months out of it after publication, according to Mr Cadel's liberal Notion, their saving of Interest will not amount to above 12 or 13 shillings. & can they be so miserably poor in purse or spirit as to think *that* an object worth disgusting a successful author for? you were too mealy mouthed by far[5]—but, perhaps, as the difference in profit to you, of receiving the 50 now, or 6 months hence, is but reciprocal to their gain, it was hardly worth the disagreeable taste of Discussion.⁋ I hope our dear Mrs Thrale & Co. are all well. We had Mrs Williams[6] to dine here yesterday wth M^r & Mrs Maxey Allen,[7] & Mrs Foster[8] of Windsor—(a daughter of Alderman Exton[9] of Lynn) & as our good humoured & pleasant Capt. Phil. was in Town, the Day passed off very tolerably. I hope Dr J. has had no relapse or illness of any kind since you wrote last[10]—Mrs W. c^d tell me nothing new ab^t him. I love him more than ever for speaking so

---

[3] 'Of Cecilia the first Edition was reckoned *enormous* at 2000. . . . It was printed . . . in July, & sold in October,—to every one's wonder' (*JL* iii. 206). See also *ED* ii. 307; *HFB*, pp. 148, 151–2.

[4] Samuel Crisp had written on 23 May 1782: 'Mr. Payne told me . . . that he and his Partner . . . did not intend to limit their generosity to the bare price stipulated (£250) if the work answer'd . . . but that they intended (privately) to present her with a handsome pair of Gloves over and above—this he whisper'd to me in Confidence as a secret—this I guess will be t'other £50—a pretty Spill (£300) for a young girl in a few months to get by sitting still in her Chamber by a good Fire!' (*Burford Papers*, p. 81). It was probably the payment of this £50 bonus that was now irritating Fanny and CB. In later years Fanny wrote of the '*enormous*' first edition of *Cecilia*: 'as a part of payment was reserved for it, I remember our dear Daddy Crisp thought it very *unfair*' (*JL* iii. 206). A receipt dated 19 Dec. 1782 (Berg) shows that Fanny sold the copyright of *Cecilia* to Payne and Cadell for £250. This sum, invested in 'a well-secured annuity' (*DL* ii. 99), yielded an income of £20 per annum (*JL* ii. 82).

[5] Fanny had written to CB on [17 July 1782] (Berg), 'Miss Palmer tells me it is reported about Town I have had £1000 for the Copy! Mrs. Cholmondeley told me she understood I had behaved like a *poor simple thing* again, & had a Father *no wiser than myself*!—I wonder what *would* content the people!'

[6] Anna Williams (1706–83), the blind poetess who had lived in Johnson's house since 1752. See *DNB*; Hill–Powell, i. 232–3.

[7] For Maxey and Sarah (Bagge) Allen (1728–1806), Mrs Burney's brother and sister-in-law, see CB to Dorothy Young, [late 1778], n. 4; *EJL* i. 6 n. 15.

[8] Not otherwise identified.

[9] John Exton (d. 1759), surgeon and apothecary of King's Lynn, Mayor (1735 and 1750). His will was proved in 1759 (Norfolk Record Office: Consistory Court of Norwich, 46 Gooch). See Norfolk and Norwich Archaeological Society, *A Calendar of the Freemen of Lynn, 1292–1836* (Norwich, 1913), pp. 225, 235, 238, 244; T. F. Barton, *et al.*, *Index of Wills Proved in the Consistory Court of Norwich 1751–1818* (1969), p. 70.

[10] Fanny had reported in her letter of 3 Nov.: 'Dr. Johnson has his Health wonderfully well.' For Johnson's state of health during this visit to Brighton, see Samuel Johnson, *Diaries, Prayers, and Annals*, ed. E. L. McAdam, Jr., *et al.*, in *The Yale Edition of the Works of Samuel Johnson*, vol. i (New Haven and London, 1958), pp. 338–51.

In her reply, 8 Nov. 1782 (Berg), Fanny wrote: 'Our Dear Doctor Johnson keeps his Health amazingly, &, with *me*, his good humour; But, to own the truth, with scarce any body else. I am quite sorry to see how unmercifully he attacks & riots the people. He has raised such a general

plainly & favourably of our Ciceley[11]—why sh^d Mrs T. be tired of hearing it commended?—I hardly think if it was her own, she would.[12]

Well Fan—but though your praises were not *sung* at the opera on Sat^y Night,[13] I heard nothing else *talked* of—& I protest I was so far from being tired at the end, that I sh^d not have been sorry if all had been encored! First, the Eldest Miss Bull,[14] who has a delightful Box on the ground floor just over the Orchestre, prince's side[15]—in Co. wth L^y M. Duncan,[16] ⌈Miss B.⌉ said 'she was sure you c^d never have acquired so much knowledge of the world & of Characters in the short life you had lived in your present form & figure—it must have been during a preexistent state'—there! put that in your pocket. L^y Mary —to whom it was, I believe the 1st B^k she ever read since the Bible—I found well acquainted with several of y^r Characters,—particularly your Meadowses & Harrels—

alarm, that he is now omitted in all cards of invitation sent to the rest of us. What pity that he will never curb himself! nor restrain his tongue upon every occasion from such bitter or cruel Speeches as eternally come from him!' See also *DL* ii. 107–9, 112–15, 122.

[11] See *DL* ii. 116. In Fanny's reply from Brighton, 8 Nov. 1782 (Berg), she wrote, 'Dr. Johnson does me the highest honour upon every occasion: &, like You, dearest Sir, never wearies of either hearing or saying or spreading kind things upon this Subject.'

[12] Fanny replied (8 Nov.): '. . . there is a certain levity mixt with her noble qualities in Mrs Thrale that would, I do really believe, make *her* tired if it were her own; for her excess of fondness & regard for me can only by your's & my sister's be equalled.'

[13] i.e. Saturday 2 Nov., when the 1782–3 opera season opened with a performance of Bertoni's comic opera *Il Convito* (*The London Stage*, v. i. 566). The *Public Advertiser*, 4 Nov. 1782, reported a relatively low attendance at this opening night: 'The Pit had not above 150 Persons in it; those however who were there, were a Corps of *pick'd Men*—' among whom 'Dr. Burney' is mentioned by name. See also, *Morning Chronicle*, 5 Nov. 1782.

[14] Elizabeth Bull (*c.*1750–1809), elder daughter of Richard Bull (see n. 19). She and her sister, Catharine Susanna (see n. 17), were devoted admirers of Pacchierotti, and early in 1783 overcame 'the awkwardness of our acquaintance and no acquaintance' to become friendly with Fanny of whom they had initially been 'dreadfully afraid' (*DL* ii. 147–8, 151, 174, 223–4; *GM* lxxix (1809)^1, 386).

[15] i.e. Box number 28, on the right-hand side of the house, facing the stage. See the floor plan in *The London Stage*, v. i, between pp. 102 and 103.

[16] Lady Mary Duncan, née Tufton (1723–1806), daughter of the 7th Earl of Thanet, widow of Sir William Duncan (1707–74), MD (1751), created Baronet (1764), whom she had married in 1763 (*JL* i. 136; Hill–Powell, ii. 354; W. Munk, *The Roll of the Royal College of Physicians of London* (2nd rev. edn., 1878), ii. 211–12). Lady Mary was an eccentric but devoted friend and admirer of CB (*Mem.* iii. 32–7; Lonsdale, pp. 274, 315, 459). They had met in Mar. 1779: 'Our acquaintance was brought about in the following manner. Happening to sit by her Ladyship in the Pit at the Opera, unknown to each other, we agreed so entirely in our approbation of Pacchierotti, that we mutually enquired of persons near us, who our neighbour was? And the next day, I was honoured with an invitation from her Ladyship to Music at her house the middle of the ensuing week. I thought it right to wait upon her previous to this Concert, as a usual mark of civility & respect, & I believe for the rest of her life, she never had a great singer, great Assembly, or Conversazione, without including me in her invitations—Whether Pacchierotti, Marchese, Rubinelli, or the Banti were in favour' (*Frag. Mem.*, Berg). For Lady Mary's admiration of Pacchierotti, which was the talk of the town, see Walpole *Corresp.* xxix. 174; see also Illustration 5.

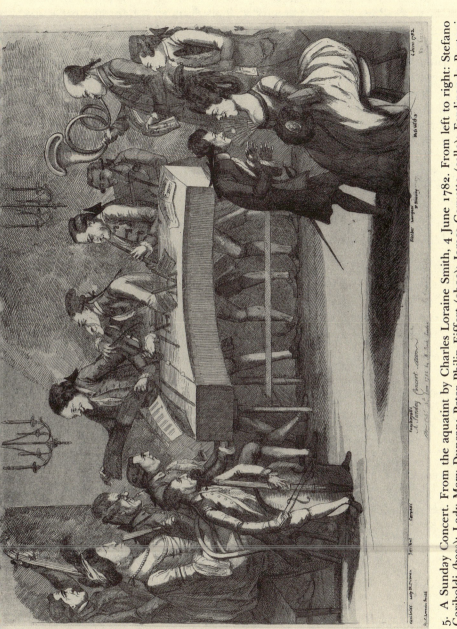

5. A Sunday Concert. From the aquatint by Charles Loraine Smith, 4 June 1782. From left to right: Stefano Gariboldi (bass); Lady Mary Duncan; Peter Philip Eiffert (oboe); James Cervetto (cello); Ferdinando Bertoni (keyboard); Gasparo Pacchierotti (singing); Giovanni Salpietro (violin); Johann Christian Fischer (oboe); Vincenzo Lanzoni (violin); Dr Burney; Mary Wilkes; Pierre-Joseph Pieltain (horn); an unidentified spectator.

After this I made a Visit to the other Miss Bull,[17] who was in Lady Clarges's Box, wth M[r] Skreen[18] & her Father[19]—here again Cecilia was instantly of the Party—I was very glad to find M[r] Bull extreamly well acquainted with her—& M[r] Skreen said he c[d] not get a word from his Daughter, L[y] C. for a week after the Book came out—Here I met with Pach.[20] for the first Interview—the ⸢rogue⸣ looks well, though he does not allow himself to be so—Well, but the Opera house[21] is so improved that I thought myself in Italy[22]—There is so much symmetry & Elegance in the Whole building, that it seems to me, though *in little*, compared with the Italian Theatres, to be equal in beauty to any one I ever saw on the Continent.—⸢This will not I fear⸣ ...

[*The second leaf is cut away*]

To Mrs Phillips[1] [St Martin's Street, 11 November 1782][2]

ALS fragment (Comyn). First leaf missing.
Docketed by FBA: Dr. Burney to his Daughter Susanna on Sir Joshua Reynolds. | Sir

[17] Catharine Susanna Bull (d. 1795), younger of the 'two very accomplished Daughters' (*JL* v. 430) of Richard Bull (see n. 19). It was Catharine Bull who lent Fanny her opera ticket (*DL* ii. 147–8, 151), thereby gaining her friendship. Catharine Bull died on 13 Oct. 1795 'of a consumption' at North Court House, Shorwell, Isle of Wight, a Jacobean mansion which her father had bought for her health. See *GM* lxv (1795)[2], 971; *JL* v. 430 n. 9.

[18] Lady Louisa Clarges, née Skrine (1760–1809), had married (1777) Sir Thomas Clarges (1751–82), 3rd Baronet (1759), MP (1780–2). Her father was William Skrine (*c.*1721–83), MP (1771–80). See Namier and Brooke, ii. 216; iii. 443. Lady Clarges's box was numbered 33 and situated in the second range on the Prince's side (*The London Stage*, v. i, between pp. 102–3).

[19] Richard Bull (1721–1805), of Ongar, Essex, and North Court, Shorwell, Isle of Wight, MP (1756–80), was one of England's foremost collectors of prints and engraved portraits. See W. P. Courtney, 'Richard Bull', *Notes and Queries*, 11th ser., vii (1913), 170–1; *GM* lxxvi (1806)[1], 289; Namier and Brooke, ii. 130–1; Walpole *Corresp.* xli. 414 *et passim*; J. M. Pinkerton, 'Richard Bull of Ongar, Essex', *The Book Collector*, xxvii (1978), 41–59.

[20] Lady Clarges was a particular friend of CB's daughter, Mrs Phillips, and an admirer of Pacchierotti (*JL* v. 387).

[21] For an account of the 1782 reconstruction of the King's Theatre interior, and the ruinous expense of the renovation for the proprietor, see *The London Stage*, v. i. 542–3; W. Taylor, *A Concise Statement of Transactions and Circumstances respecting the King's Theatre, in the Haymarket* (1791). For other contemporary comment on this 'sumptuous and magnificent' edifice, see *Public Advertiser*, 2, 4, 6, 9, 11, 13 Nov. 1782. See also D. Nalbach, *The King's Theatre, 1704–1867: London's First Italian Opera House* (1972).

[22] 'A certain Nobleman, ... made it his Business upon every Occasion to depreciate our Theatres, and in the same Breath extol to the very Skies the Superiority of Foreign Edifices. He was, however, prevailed upon to visit the King's Theatre on the first Night of its being open. He was hardly entered when he exclaimed, in a Kind of enthusiastic Rapture, "I am still in Italy"' (*Public Advertiser*, 9 Nov. 1782).

[1] Susan had written to CB, [10 Nov. 1782], (BL Egerton MS 3700A, fos. 54–5[v]), from Chessington, where she was convalescing after the birth of her first child, Frances (1782–1860), born on 5 Oct. 1782. See *HFB*, p. 156; *JL* i, p. lxxi.

[2] The date is established by Sir Joshua's stroke, CB's 'to day when I called myself', and his

Joshua died in Feby 1792 | Sir Joshua Reynolds. ✳ ✕   *And by* ?: peculiar | Lett^rs
Dr B. | p. 25

... ⌜why Dr Hunter[3] will be quite *ondone* without him⌝—I am
heartily grieved to tell you that poor Sr Jos. has had a paralitic stroke,
wch drew his mouth very much out of its place, & distorted his whole
Countenance![4] He is better, & I dined with him, & a very small party,
on Saturday,[5] only his Physician, Sir Geo. Baker,[6] Will. Burke,[7] & his
relation E[d]mund's Son[8]—It was then resolved that he was to go out
of Town to Morrow at farthest—He was to stop a Week at Burke's[9] to
give Miss Palmer time to meet him at Bath[10]—he was far from being
in spirits as you may imagine—& told me, if it went no farther, he sh^d
think himself very well off.—Yesterday on Enquiry, he was said to be
better—& to day when I called myself, he said he was so much better
that he believed he sh^d not go to Bath—however he promised me, if S^r
Geo. Baker made a very serious point of his going, he w^d not rebel—
Though I am extreamly pleased to find him so much better, yet after
such an attack the sword hangs over his head by such a feeble Hair,
that he's never safe—He says he had a slight stroke of the same kind

letter to Fanny of Wednesday [13 Nov. 1782], where CB refers to his visit 'on Monday Morn^g',
which could only have been Monday 11 Nov. 1782.

[3] William Hunter (1718–83), MD, FRS, who had attended CB's first wife in her last illness.

[4] Edmond Malone (1741–1812), the great Shakespearian scholar and critic, and Reynolds's
literary executor, wrote in the biography of his friend: 'He was ... in the year 1782 distressed for
a short time by a slight paralytick affection; which, however, made so little impression on him,
that in a few weeks he was perfectly restored, and never afterwards suffered any inconvenience
from that malady' (*The Works of Sir Joshua Reynolds, Knight* (4th corr. edn., 1809), i, p. cvii). See
also C. R. Leslie and T. Taylor, *Life and Times of Sir Joshua Reynolds: with Notices of Some of His
Cotemporaries* (1865), ii. 379–80; Johnson *Letters*, ii. 515.

[5] i.e. Saturday 9 Nov. 1782.

[6] Sir George Baker (1722–1809), MD (1756), created Baronet (1776), FRS (1762), Fellow
(1757) and nine times President (1785–90, 1792–3, 1795) of the Royal College of Physicians,
also treated the King and Queen (*DNB*; W. Munk, *The Roll of the Royal College of Physicians of
London* (2nd rev. edn., 1878), ii. 213–18).

[7] Not certainly identified. He was not William Burke (1728–98), who was at this time in
India. He may have been the otherwise unidentified Irish cousin of Edmund Burke, one 'Will
Burke' who appears fleetingly in 1759 in Burke *Corresp*. i. 125–6. Perhaps CB mistook Richard
Burke (1733–94), barrister, younger brother of Edmund Burke—but then CB would have said
'& his nephew' in referring to the younger Richard (n. 8), Edmund's son. See also CB to Fanny
Burney, [13 Nov. 1782], n. 8; D. Wecter, *Edmund Burke and His Kinsmen. A Study of the Statesman's
Financial Integrity and Private Relationships* (Boulder, Colorado, 1939).

[8] Richard Burke (1758–94), only son of the statesman, educated at Westminster and Christ
Church, Oxford (BA, 1778), of which he was a Student (1772–81), admitted to the Middle
Temple (1775), called to the Bar (1780), had served as Deputy Paymaster to his father (Mar.–
July 1782). In May 1782 he had sat for his portrait to Sir Joshua (Leslie and Taylor, *Reynolds*, ii.
374–5, 387). See Burke *Corresp.*, *passim* and Index; *GM* lxiv (1794)², 770.

[9] Edmund Burke's country house at Beaconsfield, purchased in 1768, was 'not the worst
Hospital for convalescents' (Burke *Corresp*. i. 351–2; v. 239, 433).

[10] Mary Palmer had set out on a visit to Devonshire on 14 Aug. (Leslie and Taylor, *Reynolds*,
ii. 379).

in his face 30 years ago[11]—& I now can fancy that on[e] side was fuller than the other before this last accident—He goes to Burke's to Morrow, but fights off the Bath Journey.

God bless you my dear Susey—Love to all from C.B.

To Fanny Burney [St Martin's Street, 13 November 1782][1]

ALS (BL Egerton MS 3690, fo. 17). First leaf missing.
Addressed: To∣ Miss Burney∣ at Mrs Thrale's∣ Brighthelmstone∣ Sussex   *Pmks.:* 13 NO IM   *Docketed by* FBA: On an Epilogue for a private play acted at the Honble ∣ Mrs. Hubbard's—written by Miles Andrews. 1782 XII

Dear Fan—I wished you to see what Charlotte to save post, has transcribed from yesterday's *Morn^g Herald*,[2] as it is such an hon^ble Testimony of Cecilia's *Notoriety* & *publicity* among *les Gens comme il faut*, as I never remember of any book so soon after publication—For It must be supposed that all the Characters mentioned, in this Epilogue[3]

[11] Sir Joshua appears to have suffered a slight stroke in the summer of 1764 (Leslie and Taylor, *Reynolds*, i. 229–30; Johnson *Letters*, i. 169; D. Hudson, *Sir Joshua Reynolds, a Personal Study* (1958), pp. 86–7).

[1] This letter is dated by its postmark, the reference to the poem in 'yesterday's' *Morning Herald* (nn. 2, 3), and the advertisement 'to Day' of the second edition of *Cecilia* (n. 6).

[2] CB's letter begins on the second of what were two conjugate leaves, with the direction panel on the verso.

The missing first leaf doubtless bore Charlotte's transcription of an 'Epilogue' by Miles Peter Andrews (d. 1814), dramatist (*DNB*; *GM* lxxxiv (1814)², 190–1), printed in the *Morning Herald*, 12 Nov. 1782. The 'Epilogue' had been spoken by Albinia Hobart, née Bertie (c.1739–1816), wife of the Hon. George Hobart (1731–1804), later (1793) 3rd Earl of Buckinghamshire (*DNB*), at a private performance of Arthur Murphy's *All in the Wrong* (1761) before a fashionable audience at their 'house at Ham-Common'.

Fanny replied on 14 Nov. [1782] (Yale: BRBL), that she had accidentally seen the verses when a copy of the *Morning Herald* had arrived in Brighton: '. . . you may believe I was not a little astonished . . . It was an awkward thing enough at the time, though very pleasant afterwards'.

[3] The allusions to *Cecilia*, 26 lines in all, in Andrews's 'Epilogue' begin with:

'At the Opera assembled, some smart Maccaroni,
Begins with some Belle, the gay *conversazioni*;
"Fore Gad, that *Cecilia's* a charming young woman!
Were you, Miss *Larolles*, at the play at Ham-Common?
Oh, yes to be sure! you can't think how delightful,
The men were so bad, and the women so frightful,
Such a croud, so much heat, and so little to drink,
The time pass'd so pleasantly on, you can't think—'

and proceed in similar vein with references to Meadows, Lady Honoria Pemberton, the elder Delvile, and Morrice. The lines are footnoted: 'Alluding to the Novel of Cecilia from whence the characters are taken' (*Morning Herald*). The 'Epilogue' was also published in the *Public Advertiser*, 13 Nov. 1782.

were well known to the Company, wch L^y Archer[4] at the opera on Sat^{y5} told me was very numerous, or else there w^d have been no fun in the Allusions.

And so here's a 2^d Edit. advertised to Day to be published with *all possible expedition*[6]—by wch I conjecture that it is now out of Print[7]— Poor Sr Jos. has been very ill—but is better now—I dined with him, his Physician, Sr Geo. Baker, young Burke, & Will. Burke,[8] only, on Sat^y—& he is now gone out of Town, by advice—he was ordered to Bath—but ⟨told⟩ me on Monday Morn^g that he found himself so much better⟨r that⟩ he thought he sh^d Rebel[9]—Not a word ab^t Ciceley, to be sure!—except that nothing else was talked of!—What makes the Reviews alone silent I cannot imagine[10]—never heed,—the public cannot be said to have taken its opinion from them.—Miss Benson & Mrs Hatsel,[11] only behaved, as two Ladies at Colchester (accord^g to Twi.) you know had done before.[12]—I am glad to hear D^r

[4] For Lady Sarah Archer (1741–1801), see CB to Twining, 24 Feb. 1782, n. 6. She occupied Box number 76, in the third range on the Prince's side (*The London Stage*, v. i, between pp. 102–3).

[5] At the third performance of *Il Convito* (see CB to Fanny Burney, 6 Nov. 1782, n. 13).

[6] 'In the Press, and with all possible Expedition will be published, in five vols. 12 mo. price 12s. 6d. sewed, The Second Edition of CECILIA ...' (*Morning Chronicle*, 13 Nov. 1782).

[7] *Cecilia* was 'printed ... in July, & sold in October' (*JL* iii. 206).

[8] Fanny wrote in her reply of 14 Nov.: 'But surely it must have been *Richard* not *Will*. Burke you met at Sir Joshua's for *Will*. I thought was in the East Indies, whither Jem had dispatches for him from his Brother.' For this unresolved problem of identification, see CB to Mrs Phillips, [11 Nov. 1782], n. 7.

[9] Fanny wrote in her reply of 14 Nov.: 'I am very sorry for poor Sir Joshua,—Lord Ashburton has written to Dr. Johnson that the illness was a stroke of the Palsey:—I hope it was nothing so serious. It will bring Miss Palmer, I suppose, in all haste from Devonshire.' After Fanny's return to London on 20 Nov., she relates that on Wednesday 4 Dec., 'I called in the morning upon Miss Palmer ... Her uncle has been very dangerously ill, but is now quite recovered.' Four days later, she reported Sir Joshua as looking 'vastly well, and as if he had never been ill' (*DL* ii. 131, 137).

[10] The Oct. issue of *GM* lii (1782), 485, gave a half-column of 'warmest commendations' to *Cecilia*, which it declared, 'holds up a mirror to the gay and dissipated of both sexes, in which they may see themselves and their deformities at full length, and exhibits more knowledge of the world, or the *ton*, than could be expected from the years of the fair authoress.' For other reviews, when they finally appeared, see *HFB*, p. 163 n. 1.

[11] Fanny had written in her letter of 8 Nov. (Berg), 'Miss Benson arrived on Monday, she told me, at the last volume; & cried & roared so vehemently that she could not make her appearance, & was forced to give up going to the last Ball: & Mrs. Hatsel, to whom she was reading aloud, ... gave up the Ball also, to stay with her & finish it.'

'Miss Benson', an acquaintance of the Thrales (see *DL* i. 445, 465; ii. 104, 106, 116, 122–3, 148; *Thraliana*, i. 455), may have been Ann Benson (*c*.1740–1814), of Green Park Place, Bath.

'Mrs Hatsell', née Ekins (*c*.1731–1804) had married (1778) John Hatsell (1733?–1820), Chief Clerk (1768–97) of the House of Commons (*GM* xlviii (1778), 45; lxxiv (1804)^2, 1176; *DNB*; Burke *Corresp.* vi. 209; A. R. Ingpen, *The Middle Temple Bench Book* (1912), p. 272).

[12] Twining had written to CB, 18 Sept. 1782 (BL Add. MS 39929, fos. 299–303^v): 'I know two amiable sisters in Col^r, sensible & accomplished women, who were found *blubbering* at such a rate one morning!—the tale had drawn them on 'till near the hour of an engagem^t at dinner, which they were actually obliged to put off, because there was not time to recover their red eyes & swelled noses.' For Fanny's evocation of the 'tender pathetic' in *Cecilia*, see *HFB*, pp. 158–9.

Johnson is so well; but grieved that he is such a raw-head & bloody bones, to his acquaintance.[13] But—you Fan—you say not a Word of your return? When? hah!—tell us in your next, if it begins to be in Contemplation[14]—I had a Lett^r from the dear Sue by the same post as your pale faced Scrib[15]—worse than Master Briggs's Ink[16]—do, put a little Lamp-black in it—or it will never hide the clean, light-coloured dirt of Brighton[17]—adieu

y^{rs} very affectionately—

Charles Burney

[*Charlotte Burney completes the letter with news of Pacchierotti who 'was here yesterday'.*]

To Henry Blencowe[1]   [St Martin's Street], 23 February 1783

ALS draft (Osborn).
Endorsed by CB: To | Henry Blencowe Esqr | Feb. 23. 1783.   *And by* FBA: ✳
Blencowe | Memoirs ⌗

It is a little cruel to throw the sins of a Man's youth into his Face, at a time when he ought to be most inclined to blush at their remembrance So much is the Style of every species of Musical Composition changed ⁓ ⁓ce the Juvenile productions wch you have *deterré*, [2]first saw the light⁚ ⁚hat they now seem a fitter present for the Antiquarian

---

[13] See CB to Fanny Burney, 6 Nov. 1782, n. 10. In her reply of 14 Nov., Fanny wrote: 'How your *raw Head & bloody bones* made me Laugh!—He is still, however, as kind & as soft as ever to your F.B.' The phrase denotes a nursery bugbear or bogy-man (*OED*, under 'raw-head').

[14] Fanny replied (14 Nov.): 'We shall be in Town next Wednesday, Novr 20th'.

[15] i.e. Mrs Phillips to CB, [10 Nov. 1782], (BL Egerton MS 3700A, fos. 54–5^v); and Fanny Burney to CB, 8 Nov. 1782 (Berg). Both letters show the London postmark '11 NO'. Fanny's faint writing obliged her in later years to ink over her letter again.

[16] The miserly Mr Briggs, one of Cecilia's guardians, who used shoe blacking for ink. See *Cecilia*, bk. ii, ch. 9.

[17] Fanny begins her reply (14 Nov.): 'I have this moment been in search of a little fresh *blacking*, Dearest Sir, that my thanks for your kind Letter may not sink without making any impression.'

---

[1] Henry Prescott Blencowe (1752–87), of Blencowe Hall, Cumberland, and Thoby Priory, Essex, was matriculated at Queens' College, Cambridge (1772), and admitted to the Inner Temple in 1774 (Venn; S. Jefferson, *The History and Antiquities of Leath Ward, in the County of Cumberland: with Biographical Notices and Memoirs* (Carlisle, 1840), pp. 382–6). In the absence of Blencowe's letter and of any further correspondence between him and CB, it is not possible now to identify the 'Hebdomadary' musical society on whose behalf Blencowe had written. For CB's early compositions, see Scholes, ii. 340 ff.

[2-2] MS first ... light] *altered from* were first produced

Society than a regale for the author. It is so long since ³my literary pursuits have allowed me leisure to be³ guilty of composing for Violins, except as accomp^ts to the Harp^d,⁴ that I can recollect nothing in my Possession worthy the notice of your Musical Society, wch is not at least 20 years old. At this Time of the year I am whirled ab^t in the Tourbillon of the Capital with such rapidity that I can seldom get a tranquil Moment for the revival of old Friendships or the cultivation of new, or it w^d afford me very great Pleasure to wait on you & talk over old times as well as to make myself better acquainted with your Hebdomadary Institution; of wch at present I am so ignorant that whether the Mite you wished me to throw in w^d be most acceptable if produced on a *Cheshire* or a *Parmasan* Cheese, I know not—nor whether your wants are Vocal or Instrumental; &, if the latter, whether for *bowed*, *keyed*, or *Wind* Instruments? of all these particulars I would instantly enquire *vivâ voce*, had I leisure to gratify your wish or my own heart; but between this time & the 27th Instant my Engagements of various kinds are so numerous as scarcely to afford me leisure to eat drink or sleep sufficiently to support Nature. When the winter hurly burly is done,⁵ & the storm in wch I now live, is a little abated, it will afford me a very sensible pleasure to renew our acquaintance, & personally to assure you how flattering the honour of your remembrance is to dear Sir, your obliged &

most humble Servt
C.B.

To Jacques-Pierre Brissot de Warville¹

[St Martin's Street, *c.*17 March 1783]²

LS draft, in the hand of FB (Osborn).
Endorsed: Reply.

³⁻³ MS my ... be] *altered from* I have been
⁴ CB refers to his *Two Sonatas for the Harpsichord or Forte Piano with Accompanyments for a Violin and Violoncello* (*c.*1770?) and his *A Second Number of Two Sonatas for the Harpsichord and Forte Piano, with Accompanyments for a Violin and Violoncello* (1772). See Scholes, ii. 347–8.
⁵ *Macbeth*, 1. i. 3.

¹ Jacques-Pierre Brissot, called Brissot de Warville (1754–93), French *philosophe*, author, and later leader of the Girondins (*DBF*). Brissot was currently in London, and had written to CB, 16 Mar. 1783 (Osborn), asking for a portrait of Fanny which he intended to reproduce in an unnamed forthcoming periodical, probably his *Journal du Licée de Londres, ou Tableau de l'état présent des sciences et des arts en Angleterre* (Paris, 1784). See also *Mem.* ii. 334–7.
² CB's reply is drafted by Fanny on the second leaf of Brissot's letter of 16 Mar. There is no reason to suspect any delay in the reply to Brissot's formal request.

Monsieur,

Le ressouvenir du plaisir que Je ressentis chez M. Linguet,[3] quand heureusement je vous y ai rencontré, m'a rendu d'autant plus sensible à l'honneur de votre Lettre; et j'espere qu'il ne vous sera pas difficile de croire que ma fille est flattée autant que je puis l'être moi-même de l'intention qui en est le sujet: mais quel que soit sa sensibilité de l'honneur que vous la faîtes, elle n'a ni l'ambition ni la vanité de desirer une marque d'approbation si signale et si public que celle que vous l'offrez. Son Libraire, M. Cadell, il y a quelque tems, lui [a] demandé son portrait, afin de la faire graver pour la quatrieme edition de Cecilia;[4] mais y ayant une repugnance invincible, elle lui a donné un refus absolu. Elle n'a même jamais voulu consentir à avoir son Nom mis à la tête de ses œuvres,[5] et ne desir rien si ardemment que d'eviter toute sorte de distinction public. Nous ne pouvons, donc, Monsieur, que Vous offrir nos remercimens sincères pour l'honneur que vous avez desiré de la faire, et de vous assurer qu'elle est vraiment mortifiée de vous refuser une demande qui lui est neanmoins très flatteur.[6]

J'ai l'honneur d'être, Monsieur, &c

Chas Burney.

To Samuel Crisp [St Martin's Street], 12 April 1783

ALS (Berg). First leaf: Fanny Burney's letter. Second leaf: CB's letter.
Addressed: Samuel Crisp Esqr | at Mrs. Hamilton's, | Chesington, | Kingston, | Surry
Docketed by CFBt: Dr Burney to Mr Crisp | (written on the same sheet with the foregoing)
Publ.: DL ii. 210–11.

[3] Simon-Nicolas-Henri Linguet (1736–94), French lawyer, pamphleteer, and controversialist, whose notorious writings forced him to seek refuge in England (Michaud). Brissot, in his letter of 16 Mar., had reminded CB that they had met 'chès M. Linguet il y a un mois ou 6 semaines,' and that the topic of conversation had been 'L' interessant roman de Cecilia'.

[4] Published in 1784.

[5] *Evelina* was published anonymously, and *Cecilia* 'by the Author of Evelina'.

[6] The Burneys remained for a while on cordial terms with Brissot, who wrote again to CB, 29 July 1783 (Osborn), enclosing 'un mercure d'allemagne où Je trouve L'eloge de Cecilia'. In a long note appended to the letter, Mme d'Arblay wrote of a subsequent 'Evening Rendez-Vous' at which 'Brissot de Warville was rather agreeable, from fullness of literary information.—Poor Man! . . . how happy at that moment with his adored young Wife, & his Studies, & his *Hermitage* at Brompton! . . . Ten years after this peaceful Meeting, & these literary & philosophic enjoyments, sweetened by conjugal endearments, he was Guiliotined, with 20 other members of The Convention!—' Mme d'Arblay eventually recalled this evening with distaste (*Mem.* ii. 336–7).

Sat^y Night—12 Apr.
1783

My dear Friend.

Though the incessant hurry I have for some time been in has exceeded that of former Years, wch I then thought impossible to be exceeded, yet I have hardly ever had your sufferings and situation[1] a moment out of my mind—& the first Question I have constantly asked at my coming jaded home of a Night, has been: 'What news from Chesington?' I do hope most fervently that you will still weather this terrible attack, and that in a very few months I shall see you w⟨ell⟩ and happy in my favourite retreat, wch has been always rendered so superior to all others by your Presence—

Susey was desired to ask you if I had any kind of book that was likely to afford you any amusement, & it is with extreme Pleasure that her answer is in favour of Mem: de Petrarque[2]—I will not only send that with the greatest pleasure, but a Cart-load of the choicest & best books in my Collection, if you will but furnish a list—

Adieu my ever dear & honoured Friend! may your recovery be not only sure but speedy! is the most hearty wish of him to whom your loss would be the most painful & severe *amputation* wch misfortune could perform upon my affections[3]—

C.B.

My Wife as well as all around me have been greatly allarmed for you, & entreat me to send their warmest and most affectionate wishes for your speedy recovery.

C.B.

---

[1] In Fanny's preceding portion of this letter, she commences: 'I am more grieved at the long & most disappointing continuation of your illness than I know how to tell you'. See also *DL* ii. 208–10; *Mem.* ii. 315–24.

[2] Susan Phillips had written to Fanny from Chessington, 11 Apr. [1783] (Berg): 'He sends his love to my Father too, & begs if he has Petrarca's life at home that he will be kind enough to send the 1st Vol: or all of them, by Cooke's Kingston Stage on Monday, wch sets out from the One Bell Inn, near the new church in the Strand. I rejoice that he expresses any desire of this kind, & so I am sure will you'.

The Abbé Jacques-François-Paul-Aldonce de Sade (1705–78), *Mémoires pour la vie de François Pétrarque* . . ., 3 vols. (Amsterdam, 1764–7). CB's set fetched £3 18s. (*Cat. Misc. Lib.*, lot 1540). CB cites this work in *Hist. Mus.* ii. 333; Mercer, i. 634.

[3] Susan Phillips wrote in reply [14 Apr. 1783] (Berg): 'Our poor sufferer does not seem to get much worse, but Nature is I fear wholly exhausted, & that to recover him is quite beyond the power of Man!—He heard y^r letter this morning, tho' my voice failing me towards the end of it, I was obliged to sink some part of it, lest it sh^d excite an emotion in him wch might do him harm.—When I had done reading it, "Well," s^d he, "I have some that love me yet!—that's a great comfort!—" —& a little after—"True friendship is I find to be purchased in this world!"'

To Fanny Burney

[St Martin's Street,
24? April 1783][1]

ALS (Berg).
Docketed by FBA: ⌜On the last illness—& approaching Death, of my truly loved ┆ & ardently admired & faithfully honoured Mr Crisp.— ┆ Received at Chesington— ┆ where I was devoting myself, in deep affliction, to his last Days.⌝ I XIV ✕ 1783. *And by* CFBt: From Doctor Burney ┆ to Miss F. Burney—   *Publ.: DL* ii. 211–12.

Ah! my dear Fan, your last Letter has broke all our hearts—Your former acc^ts kept off despair—but this brings it back in all its horrors![2]— I wish, if it were possible, that you w^d let him know how much I loved him, & how heavily I shall feel his loss, when all this hurry subsides & lets me have time to brood over my sorrows—I have always thought, that in many particulars his equal was not to be found—his wit, learning, taste, penetration;[3] &, when well, his conviviality, pleasantry, —& kindness of heart to me & mine, will ever be thought of, with the most profound & desponding regret!—

I know not what to say that will not add to your own affliction, & all around you—what in the way of comfort *can* be said, at present?— or at least be believed, & rec^d?—

I can only wish you all possessed of fortitude sufficient to bear, what now appears inevitable, & almost immediate!—'tis terrible, when no good can be done, to be in the way of such Scenes—& yet,—we reason ourselves into the belief of its being right.—

Poor Mrs Thrale returned to Bath yesterday[4]—[she] called between

[1] Samuel Crisp's death on 24 Apr., and Mrs Thrale's return to Bath on 23 Apr. (n. 4), give the probable date of this letter.
[2] Fanny had 'hastened to Chessington' (*DL* ii. 211) on 14 Apr., in company with Captain Phillips and Dr George Fordyce (1736–1802). On her arrival, she appended a hasty report in Susan's letter to CB of [14 Apr. 1783] (Berg): 'We are just arrived—& this dear Dr. Fordyce gives us some hope!—he says all is very *bad*, but not *desperate*.—We are here in extacy—& have some thoughts of Burning Mr. Hemmings in Effigy at least, for he has given him over, & advised *against* having a Physician all the Time.' On Easter Sunday, 20 Apr., Fanny wrote to CB (Berg), 'I intended returning to Town on Saturday with Dr. Fordyce, as I think my Daddy in as fair a way as we have any right to expect; but he has himself quite entreated me to stay a little while longer ... that he *will* recover I do indeed believe'. The postmark shows that CB received this letter on Monday, 21 Apr. A subsequent letter, not now preserved, must have informed CB that Crisp was sinking.
[3] See CB's obituary notice of Crisp in *GM* liii (1783)[1], 452, where he writes of Crisp's conversation, 'which was rendered captivating by all that wit, learning, a professed knowledge of mankind, and a most exquisite taste for the fine arts, could furnish.' See also, *Mem.* ii. 323–4.
[4] Mrs Thrale had taken up residence at Bath with her three eldest daughters in early Apr., but had had to hurry back to Streatham School on 19–20 Apr., where her youngest daughter, Henrietta Sophia (1778–83), had died from whooping-cough, and another, Cecilia Margaretta

9 & 10—I was gone out & no one else up—she was much disappointed at y^r not being at home—Charlotte has, I suppose s^d the rest—of her sending a Coach from Streatham &c[5]

Love to dear Susey & Capt. Phillips—I pity you all, as well as myself—God bless, & give you powers to support your situation! is all I have time to say—C.B.

⌐I am waited for below—¬ Miss Rose has been here to Day—who is much liked[6]—

To Fanny Burney [St Martin's Street, May 1783][1]

ALS draft (Berg).
Docketed by FBA: XIV 2 ⌗ ✗ 1783 | on my Grief after the death of my first dearest Friend | Mr. Crisp—& on the subject of a long. From my truly | admirable Father *Publ.: DL* ii. 212–13; *Mem.* ii. 319–20.

I am much more afflicted than surprised at the violence & duration of y^r sorrow[2] for the terrible Scenes & Events of Ches. & not only pity you, but participate in all y^r feelings. Not an hour in the Day has passed *as you will some time or other find*—since the fatal Catastrophe in wch I have not felt a pang for the irreparable Loss I have sustained.[3] However as something is due to the *living*, there is perhaps a boundary at wch it is right to *endeavour* to stop, in lamenting the dead. It is very hard, as I have found it all my Life, to exceed these bounds in our duty or attention without its being at the expence of others. I have [4]experienced the loss of one[4] so dear to me as to throw me into the

(1777–1857), had been dangerously ill. Mrs Thrale returned to Bath 'on the Wednesday 23^d' (*Thraliana*, i. 560–5; Clifford, pp. 219–20; Hyde, *Thrales*, pp. 237–8).
    [5] Charlotte's letter is not preserved.
    [6] Sarah Rose (1759–1821), called 'Rosette', daughter of Dr William Rose (1719–86), schoolmaster and translator, was to marry CB's son, Charles, on 24 June 1783 (*JL* i, p. lxxi; *DNB*, under 'Rose, Samuel'; Hill–Powell, iv. 509). Charles was now employed as an assistant master in Dr Rose's school at Chiswick.
    [1] The present letter was probably written a few weeks after Crisp's death. See n. 2.
    [2] According to Mme d'Arblay, after Crisp's death, Fanny, 'in the depth of her grief, had shut herself up in mournful seclusion', from which prostration CB's 'mild and admirable exhortation effected fully its benevolent purpose.' (*Mem.* ii. 318–20).
    [3] For CB's 'Elegy' and the inscription he composed for Crisp's monument, see *Mem.* ii. 321–3; *Burford Papers*, p. 85. Two holograph copies of CB's 'Elegy' are preserved in the Osborn Collection.
    [4]–[4] MS experienced ... one] *CFBt stets CB's deleted* lost in my time persons
    CB refers to his grief over his first wife, Esther.

utmost affliction & despondency which can be suffered without in-
sanity—but I had Claims on my life, my reason, & activity, wch drew
me from the Pit of despair & forced me, though with great difficulty,
to rouse & exert every nerve & faculty in answering them. It has been
very well said of mental wounds that they must digest like those of the
body before they can be healed⁵—⌐The Pultice of⌐ *necessity* can alone
perhaps in some cases bring on this digestion. But we sh^d not prevent
it by caustics or corrosives—let the wound be open a due time, but
not treated wth violence—to quit all metaphor we must, alas! try to
diminish our sorrow for one Calamity, to enable us to support another—
as a national Peace⁶ is but time to *refit*—a mental is no more!—So far
however am I for blaming your indulgence of sorrow on the present
occasion that I both love & honour you for it—& therefore shall add
no more on that melancholy subject.

C.B.

⌐With respect to the other, to you no less melancholy subject,⁷ I will
write a few words when I can get time.⌐

To Sir James Lake¹

St Martin's Street,
25 May 1783

ALS draft (Osborn).
Endorsed by CB: Copy of a Letter | To Sir James Lake, relative to | little Crotch—
May 1783.　*Docketed by* FBA: 23—May 1783. | To Sr J^s Lake

Dear Sir.
The perusal of your friend's² humane & excellent Letter concerning
the unfortunate little Crotch³ has afflicted me extremely. I have always

---

⁵ *Tristram Shandy*, vol. iii, ch. 29. See CB to Grant, [early? 1777], n. 9.
⁶ The preliminary articles of peace, ending the War of American Independence, had been
signed at Versailles on 20 Jan. 1783, and ratified in Feb. (*Annual Register . . . for the Year 1783*,
pp. 148 ff.; Walpole *Corresp.* xxv. 356–7, 365; xxxiii. 381).
⁷ Possibly an allusion to the undeclared intentions of George Owen Cambridge (1756–1841)
towards Fanny, an account of which is given in *HFB*, pp. 187–93.

¹ Sir James Winter Lake (*c.*1742–1807), 3rd Baronet (1760), of Edmonton, Middlesex,
Governor of the Hudson's Bay Company, FSA (1782), antiquary and collector. See Venn; *GM*
lxxvii (1807)¹, 390; *A Catalogue of the Genuine and Extraordinary Collection of British Portraits and
Historic Prints . . . Collected . . . by the Late Sir James Winter Lake, Baronet* (1808); *Bibliotheca Lakeana.
A Catalogue of the . . . Library of . . . Sir James Winter Lake* [1808]. Listed as a subscriber to the *Hist.
Mus.*, Sir James and Lady Lake are also mentioned among CB's engagements for [Apr.] 1776 in
his MS 'Memoranda from Pocket book' (*Frag. Mem.*, Berg).
² Not identified. He was plainly the 'benevolent & feeling Mr F.' (n. 11).
³ William Crotch was now nearly 8 years old, and accompanied by his mother, Isabella

lamented his situation, without seeing the least Possibility of amending it: as this is not an age for the *solid* Patronage of uncultivated [4]Genius, any further[4] than by transient admiration, & the immediate gratification of curiosity. The Persons who have had the managem^t & Guidance of this wonderful Child must inevitably have checked & impeded the progress of his reasoning as well as Musical faculties. But, who, in a free Country, has a right to take a Child from his Parents without consent or ample indemnification? When Gravina[5] the Civilian heard the young Metastasio sing in the streets of Rome, & by a closer examination in his own house, had discovered his great natural Genius & tendency to Poetry, he enquired of his parents, who were supported by his Talents, how much a year they imagined his performance produced; wch when they had specified, he told them, that he w^d allow them an equivalent sum, & take upon himself the Care of the Boy's Education; wch it is well known was such as rendered him & his writings the delight & ornament of all Europe. Mrs Crotch[6] w^d doubtless have been glad to have transferred to such a Patron the superintendence of her son's Education; but having been long maintained, though often miserably, by his premature Talents, it is natural to suppose that she w^d be unwilling to part with him, merely for his *own sake*, without thinking of *herself*, & the loss of profit & importance she sh^d sustain by placing him in other hands. If therefore any great nobleman were disposed to patronise the boy, by taking him into his house or being at the expense of his board & Education elsewhere; (a species of patronage at present very difficult, I fear, to be found;) if he did not likewise support the whole family, my opinion is that he w^d not be allowed to adopt or appropriate the Boy. Our sovereigns of the Tudor Race exercised a power of impressing singing boys, for the service of the Chapel Royal,[7] & I believe this Tyranny extended to the Dean & Chapter of Cathedrals till the beginning of the last Century; & hard as such a prerogative might fall upon worthy & fond

Crotch (d. 1830), and his elder half-brother, John Beale Crotch (b. 1764), travelled ceaselessly, performing as a self-taught musical prodigy. See J. Rennert, *William Crotch (1775–1847) Composer, Artist, Teacher* (Lavenham, 1975), pp. 19–20.

[4–4] MS Genius ... further] *interlined above deleted* Talents

[5] Giovanni Vincenzo Gravina (1664–1718), Italian scholar, man of letters, and jurist, was a founding member of the Academy of the Arcadians in 1695 (*Biografia degli italiani illustri*, ed. E. de Tipaldo (Venice, 1834–45), viii. 367–75). For CB's account of Gravina's discovery and adoption of Metastasio, see his *Memoirs of Metastasio*, i. 1–15, where he declares (p. 12): 'Gravina rendered his name more celebrated by educating and forming the taste of Metastasio, than by all the productions of his own pen.'

[6] See n. 3. Mrs Crotch, according to Rennert, *Crotch*, p. 70, died in 1830 'having survived well into her nineties'.

[7] See *Hist. Mus.* ii. 432–3; iii. 24–5; Mercer, i. 698–9; ii. 30–1; Rees, under 'Chapel, Royal Establishment'.

parents, it might have been happy for little Crotch if he had been taken from his vulgar & foolish family many years ago.

When I formerly s^d that a master was unnecessary,[8] my opinion was not only founded on his extreme youth, but on the utter neglect there had been in his education of inculcating obedience, or attention to the precepts of those that were older & wiser than himself. Indeed the boy discovered very early that his understanding was superior to those ab^t him, & therefore he not only despised their orders but acquired a habit of frowardness & disobedience to all kinds of admonition. Whether his own reason as yet has corrected this early defect I know not; but it is much to be feared that the admiration & applause wch his great natural but artless attempts publickly acquired for what nothing but infancy w^d make wonderful, have rendered him as much satisfied wth his own imperfections in performance, as contemptuous of all such instructions as his weak & vulgar mother or her connections c^d supply.

With respect to his health; the first thing to be thought of, & the terrible accident wch was brought ab^t by his awkward, or brutish brother,[9] I am extremely shocked, & w^d do anything in my small power to alleviate his sufferings & secure a life wch by its premature indications promised so much honour to himself & human nature. But as for 'sending for the boy up to London, or its neighbourhood,' while his Mother & family can be supported by exhibiting him to the public elsewhere, it is only in the blind zeal of humanity & tenderness that one can see it possible. If a subscription were opened for bringing him & his relations up to Town for the sake of quiet & medical assistance I w^d contribute my mite wth great alacrity; or, if his Mother *ex mero motu*, were to bring him hither, I w^d procure him the best advice possible, either by my purse or influence.[10] More seems not in my Power. If the benevolent & feeling Mr F.[11] were to signify this to the Mother & Child, if still in his Neighbourhood, it may, perhaps accelerate their motions towards the Capital, before it is too late. At

[8] CB had written of the 3½-year-old Crotch: '... at present, he plays nothing correctly, and his voluntaries are little less wild than the native notes of a lark or a black-bird. Nor does he, as yet, seem a subject for instruction: for till his reason is sufficiently matured to comprehend and retain the precepts of a master, and something like a wish for information appears, by a ready and willing obedience to his injunctions, the trammels of rule would but disgust, and, if forced upon him, destroy the miraculous parts of his self-taught performance' ('Account of an Infant Musician', *Philosophical Transactions of the Royal Society of London*, lxix (1779), 201).

[9] CB perhaps refers to a thigh wound which Crotch sustained in Feb. 1783 at Derby, when the bayonet fixed to a toy gun fell from the top of his bed as he sat on it to undress. What part his half-brother John Beale Crotch (n. 3) played in the incident is unknown (see Rennert, *Crotch*, p. 21).

[10] According to Rennert (*Crotch*, p. 27), CB's wife agreed to give Crotch some French lessons.

[11] See n. 2.

present, I know not the place of their residence; & indeed have not time, consequence, or abilities, to take the whole upon myself, however my fervent affection for the boy & admiration of his great natural powers, & intellectual Capacity may incline me to wish it. When his health is well established If I can chalk out such a line for his future conduct & the further pursuit of his Musical Studies as, under the unfavourable circumstances of his situation may be practicable, it will afford me very great satisfaction.

I beg you will do me & my family the honour to present our best respects to Lady Lake,[12] & believe me to be, with great regard, dear sir,

Your obliged &
most obed^t humble Servt
C.B.

St Martin's Street | May 25th 1783.

To Sarah (Rose) Burney [St Martin's Street, 31 July 1783?][1]

ALS (Berg).
Addressed: To | M^{rs} Ch. Burney | at Mrs Hamilton's, Chesington | near Kingston, | Surry   *Pmk.:* 31 IY

Thursday Night.

Having, perhaps, nothing better to do, it was very kind of you, my dear daughter, to bestow your charity[2] on a correspondent, who, I fear, will turn out not worth powder & shot. In the perpetual bustle in which I am involved, & the employment I have for my Pen, whenever I can snatch it up, I have very little time to bestow on my friends in answering Letters, whenever they are so kind as to write to me. Indeed your near Neighbour, the dear Mrs Phillips, has heavy claims upon me of that sort, concerning wch my heart frequently smites me; but she knows, and all my acquaintance know, that I am unable to be punctual and honest in paying such debts, & therefore frequently let

---

[12] Lady Joyce Lake, née Crowther (*c.*1747–1834), had married Sir James in 1764. See *GM* xxxiv (1764), 302; n.s. ii. (1834), 447.

[1] CB's 'Thursday Night' and the postmark '31 IY' coincide with the calendar for 1783. The tone of the letter to Rosette also suggests a date shortly after her marriage to Charles on 24 June 1783 (see CB to Fanny Burney, [24? Apr. 1783], n. 6). For Charles's courtship of Rosette, and her uneasy relations with his sisters, see R. S. Walker, 'Charles Burney's Theft of Books at Cambridge', *Transactions of the Cambridge Bibliographical Society*, iii (1962), 318–19.

[2] Rosette's letter is not preserved.

me off by an *Act of Grace*. Why now, I shall not be able to pay *you* at the rate of 7 shillings in the pound; which is bad encouragement for continuing the Commerce wch you have generously opened between us. Well, all I can say is that I w^d do better by you if I c^d—at present all I can add is to thank you for you[r] intentions, for your enquiries after health, & for not only letting me know that your own is better, but that you are all happy, & that time does not hang heavily on your hands.

I soon got rid of my *Feverette*, & am now tolerably well after being roasted & boiled by the late intense heat. Pray give my love to all around you. I am sorry to say that there is not the least chance of my getting out of Town for some time; having business to do at the Museum, w^ch, if omitted, now, I shall never be able to accomplish. Unexpected engagements break in upon all my plans every day, while I am here, & I do nothing according to my intentions & wishes. May your time never be too little for your wants, or too much to be filled up happily, is the hearty wish of

Yours very affectionately
Chas Burney.

To Charlotte Burney   Chessington, 31 August 1783

LS verse copy (Harvard University, Houghton Library: MS Eng 926, pp. 111–14).

Elegiac Epistle to my daughter Charlotte
on the Loss of my *Bowman*. Aug^st 31st 1783.

Dear Charlotte how awkward life seems without thee,
Who about me art ever as busy as Bee!
No Minister e'er was so missed by a King
Or Infant so helpless without a back string
As I, far from thee both in country & Town,
When I hardly know how to go upstairs or down.
My Study like Chaos, I warrant now looks
And, freed from thy Rummage the worms eat my books;
In Town, not a thing without thee can be found,
And here though less littered, I'm often aground:
For Fanny is walking when weather is mild,
And Sue must attend on her husband & child[1]

---

[1] Frances ('Fanny') Phillips (1782–1860), born on 6 Oct. 1782.

To an *Authress*, a *Wife*, & a *Mother*, you know
Some kind of respect one at all times must shew;
Nor must with their time too much liberty take,
Tho' I know they ne'er wish their old Dad to forsake.
And there's Phillips to trouble & danger all blindness
Whenever he thinks he can do one a kindness.—
Yet my *Habits* are such, from beginning to ending,
When thou art away, they seem all to want *mending*.
　　To what good natured Critic, whatever is spoke
Shall I henceforth appeal, howe'er doubtful the Joke;
And boldly, like Chalkstone,[2] with energy say,
Quite sure of success, the words—'Heh! Charlotte, heh!'
Alas! now thou'rt absent my d[r] little *Bowman*,
My quibbles are flat, and my Puns liked by no Man!
So in silence I'll bottle them up for the winter,
Nor give the unworthy a chip or a splinter,
Of *Black*, or *Forecastle*, or honest *Joe Miller*:[3]
For Fanny's so squeamish, such rubbish w[d] kill her;
And while Madam Susan is using her thimble
And *Cappy* performing the part of Will Wimble,[4]
Honest Kate[5] is not always quite quick at a Joke,
And into the ears of poor *Ham*,[6] who can Poke?—
[xxx *2 lines*]
Where your mother good soul, tho' she huff & she ding,
Will give us I warrant, as 'good as we bring.'
As for Hetty, we're certain, *she'll* be of the Party,
And approve by a chuckle & laugh the most hearty
While Dick like a Stentor will Roar & will hollow,
And what is most filthy[7] most greedy will swallow.
As to Charles, if from Chiswick he happen to pop in,
While he waits for the devil, or wife goes a shopping,
Unless we can give him some joke from the Greek
Away to his Printer he'll quietly sneak:
So the Town is our own, Girl, in spite of the Fates
Let us hoist up the drawbridge & lock up the Gates.

---

[2] Lord Chalkstone and Bowman, his sycophantic friend, are characters in the 1756 revision of David Garrick's farce *Lethe*.

[3] For *Joe Miller's Jests*, see CB to Mrs Phillips, [26? Dec. 1784], n. 26.

[4] Introduced in *The Spectator*, No. 108, good-natured Will Wimble is a character who obliges everyone by trifling services. See *The Spectator*, ed. D. F. Bond (Oxford, 1965), i. 446–9.

[5] Papilian Catherine Cooke (1730–97), who assisted in the management of Chessington Hall (see *EJL* i. 8 n. 24).

[6] Sarah Hamilton (*c.*1705–97), resident manager of Chessington Hall (see *JL* i. 144).

[7] MS filthy] *obliterated and* stupid *interlined*.

Of the kindhearted Hoole[8] & his Reverend Son[9]
A word must be added, & then I have done.
I heard from your Mother, with heart felt delight,
That the elder in London arrived T'other night,
Much better in health than I feared he would be;
And as to the younger, Pray tell him from me,
'Tis my wish step by step he may mount to y[e] Top,
Of the Protestant Church, e'er the Curtain shall drop.
And now having acted the part of *Tom Fool*,
'Tis time to be serious, & greet Madam Hoole.[10]
Pray present her my love & a shake by the hand,
And a wish that with pleasure her heart may expand
As long as she likes to remain here below,
And then that she strait may to Paradise go;
Where I hope we shall meet, & talk of old Times,
And read Ariosto—and laugh at these *Rhymes*.
Chesington.   Charles Burney. Mus D

To Lord Orford

[St Martin's Street,
5 September 1783][1]

AL draft (Osborn).
Endorsed by CB: Copy of Lett[r] | to L[d] Orford concerning | the death of my poor
Friend | Bewley.   *And by* FBA: on | the Death | of Mr. Bewley L[d] Orford #

[8] John Hoole (1727–1803), translator of Italian classics (*DNB*), whose complete verse-translation of Ariosto's *Orlando Furioso* was first published in 1783. Charlotte Burney was particularly friendly with the Hooles.

[9] The Revd Samuel Hoole (*c.*1758–1839) had matriculated from Magdalen Hall, Oxford, on 14 July 1780, aged 22 (Foster). He became Curate (*c.*1786) of Abinger-Wotton, Surrey, and Rector (1803) of Poplar, Middlesex. See Hill–Powell, iv. 442; Johnson *Letters*, iii. 98; *JL* i. 242 n. 31. A minor poet, Samuel Hoole anonymously published *Aurelia; or, The Contest: An Heroi-Comic Poem; in Four Cantos* (1783) in which (pp. 62–3) the Genius speaks the following lines about Fanny Burney's *Cecilia*:

'I stood, a favouring muse, at BURNEY's side,
To lash unfeeling Wealth and stubborn Pride,
Soft Affectation, insolently vain,
And wild Extravagance with all her sweeping train;
Let her that modern Hydra to engage,
And point a HARRELL to a mad'ning age:
Then bade the moralist, admir'd and prais'd,
Fly from the loud applause her talent rais'd.'

[10] Susannah Smith (*c.*1726–1808), a Quaker of Bishop's Stortford, had married John Hoole in 1757.

[1] Bewley's death on 5 Sept. 1783 (see *GM* liii (1783)[2], 805), gives the date of this letter. Obituary notices of Bewley also appeared in the *Public Advertiser*, 8 Sept. 1783; and the *Morning Chronicle*, 9 Sept. 1783. See also CB to Parr, 7 Sept. 1783; to Charles Burney, 12 Sept. [1783].

My Lord.

After so long an absence, & privation of the honour of all kinds of intercourse, it grieves me to address your Lord^P on a subject wch from the well-known steadiness & sincerity of your attachment to those whom you have once honoured with your regard, I am certain will very sensibly affect you.

My very old, worthy & truely scientific Friend Mr Bewley after having it so long in meditation, as your L^P already knows, came to London, first visiting his Friend Dr Priestley[2] at Birmingham. I was extremely happy to embrace him after so many years absence, but saw with Pain that he was very much ematiated, & was extreamly allarmed to hear him say that he had a long time laboured under a complaint wch he thought out of the reach of medicine.[3] However, he was not quite without hope of Chirugical help, & was at last he believed unrooted from Massingham by the melancholy necessity of consulting Pott[4] or Hunter.[5] This, however, he postponed in spite of admonition, got into Spirits, seeming to forget his complaints, & I spent three or four Days with him in the same chearful & cordial manner as 30 years ago, when we used, now & then, to have a musical & literary debauch, at Lynn. Sunday was 7 night,[6] & monday were almost wholly spent in hearing & playing his favourite authors. Tuesday Morning at the Museum—the Evening at Dr Johnsons[7]—wed^y morning he saw

[2] The Revd Joseph Priestley (1733–1804), LLD (1764), FRS (1766), author, divine, and scientist with whom Bewley had been in correspondence on scientific matters for 15 years. Priestley later wrote of Bewley: 'All that he published of his own were articles in the *Appendixes* to my volumes on air, all of which are ingenious and valuable. Always publishing in this manner, he used to call himself my *satellite*. There was a vein of pleasant wit and humour in all his correspondence, which added greatly to the value of it' (*Memoirs of Dr. Joseph Priestley, to the Year 1795, Written by Himself: with a Continuation, to the Time of His Decease, by His Son, Joseph Priestley* (1806–7), i. 66). See also *DNB*; *DSB*; Lonsdale, p. 277; R. E. Schofield, *A Scientific Autobiography of Joseph Priestley (1733–1804)* (Cambridge, Mass., 1966), pp. 130–1; CB to Twining, 6 Sept. 1783, n. 9.

[3] Lord Orford wrote in reply to CB on 9 Sept. 1783 (Osborn) about Bewley: 'The weak state of his Health made it Easy to forsee that his Final Dissolution coud not be at any Great Distance, & He was Himself so much Persuaded of his Approaching End, that He told us the very manner in which He apprehended it wou'd happen.'

[4] Percivall Pott (1714–88), FRS (1764), of St Bartholomew's Hospital, one of the most eminent surgeons of his day (*DNB*).

[5] John Hunter (1728–93), FRS (1767), anatomist and surgeon, a pupil of Percivall Pott, had been appointed (1776) surgeon extraordinary to the King (*DNB*; Jessie Dobson, *John Hunter*, Edinburgh, 1969). John Hunter's elder brother, Dr William Hunter, CB's friend and correspondent, had died on 30 Mar. 1783.

[6] CB's chronology is defective. In CB's letter to Twining of 6 Sept. 1783, he states that Bewley arrived about '3 weeks ago', which signifies Sunday 17 Aug. 1783. Instead of '7 night', CB should have written 'a fortnight'.

[7] Bewley had long been an admirer of Johnson, and had for some years suffered agonies of indecision over how best to thank Johnson for a presentation set of the *Lives of the Poets*. See R. Lonsdale, 'Johnson and Dr. Burney', in *Johnson, Boswell and Their Circle*, ed. Mary Lascelles, *et al.* (Oxford, 1965), pp. 21–40; Hill–Powell, iv. 134; Johnson *Letters*, ii. 431; *ED* i. 176; Lonsdale, pp. 277–8.

Barry's paintings,[8] & had an interview with the Duc de Chaulnes[9]—in the Evening saw the principal Squares, Merlin's curiosities,[10] & the Pantheon.[11] All wch he seemed to enjoy as much as a young man of five & twenty. On Thursday, as he had other f[r]iends to see, I went into the Country.[12] And in a Day or two he went on a visit to his Friend Mr Griffiths's[13] the Editor of the Monthly Rev. at Turnham Green. He was, however, very far from well, I found, during this visit—in wch he had long promised himself great pleasure—He & the good Mrs B.[14] return'd to my house in London on Thursday was 7 night[15]—much worse than he left it. He then began seriously, with much teasing, to think of a Consultation wch however was not brought ab^t for some Days. He was not absolutely confined to the House till Sunday. On Monday Pott examined him, & declared that his complaint whatever it might be was wholly out of his reach. He now grew so bad that on Tuesday Mrs Burney sent for me by express. I arrived in Town a little before 2 o Clock, at wch hour a meeting had been arranged between Dr Warren,[16] Dr John Jebb,[17] & Mr Pott. Dr Jebb I

---

[8] James Barry (1741–1806), RA (1773), painter (*DNB*), had just completed his series of six canvasses on the subject of 'Human Culture' (1777–83) to decorate the walls of the Great Room of the Society for the Encouragement of Arts, Manufactures, and Commerce. CB, who had been a member of the Society since 1764, is incongruously portrayed in the fourth picture, 'Commerce, or the Triumph of the Thames', as the representative figure of English music. See J. Barry, *An Account of a Series of Pictures, in the Great Room of the Society of Arts, Manufactures, and Commerce, at the Adelphi* (1783), pp. 62–5; Sir Henry Trueman Wood, *A History of the Royal Society of Arts* (1913), pp. 36, 70–82; D. Hudson and K. W. Luckhurst, *The Royal Society of Arts 1754–1954* (1954), pp. 22–8; *Mem.* ii. 340–2; Scholes, ii. 14–17; Lonsdale, pp. 274–5.

[9] Louis-Marie-Joseph-Romain d'Albert d'Ailly (1741–92), duc de Pecquigny, succeeded (1769) as duc de Chaulnes, had previously visited England in 1763–4 (Walpole *Corresp.* xxxviii. 215, 295–6, 306–7, 313, 322); FRS (1764). Like Bewley and Priestley, M. de Chaulnes was an enthusiastic experimental scientist (*DBF*; Michaud). For an account of his introduction to CB in 1783, see *Mem.* ii. 337–40; Scholes, ii. 11–12. See also CB to Twining, 10–12 Nov. 1783.

[10] For an account of Merlin's shop in Princes Street, Hanover Square, see Sophie von la Roche, *Sophie in London, 1786*, trans. Clare Williams (1933), pp. 139–41.

[11] Situated on the south side of Oxford Street, the Pantheon, designed by James Wyatt (1746–1813), RA (1785), had opened in Jan. 1772 as a theatre and fashionable public assembly rooms. It became noted especially for the masquerades held there. Wyatt's splendid building was destroyed by fire on 14 Jan. 1792 (P. Cunningham and H. B. Wheatley, *London Past and Present* (1891), iii. 24–5; A. T. Bolton, 'The Pantheon in the Oxford Road. James Wyatt, R. A., Architect, 1770–2', *London Topographical Record*, xiii (1923), 55–67). In 1776 CB had bought a share and became a Proprietor of the Pantheon (Lonsdale, pp. 227–8; Crisp to CB, 17 Dec. 1776, Osborn and Berg).

[12] To Chessington where CB stayed between 21 Aug. and 2 Sept.

[13] Bewley had been a regular contributor to the *Monthly Review* since Dec. 1766.

[14] Barbara Bewley, née Green (d. 1797), who had been married to Bewley for 34 years.

[15] i.e. Thursday 28 Aug. 1783.

[16] Richard Warren (1731–97), MD (1762), FRCP (1763), FRS (1764), physician in ordinary to the King since 1762, was much sought after as an outstanding medical practitioner (*DNB*; W. Munk, *The Roll of the Royal College of Physicians of London* (2nd rev. edn., 1878), ii. 242–7).

[17] The Revd John Jebb (1736–86), MD (1777), FRS (1779), theological and political writer

found already arrived & the others came soon after. They examined the Patient very minutely, & with uncommon deliberation; & afterwards consulted together, in all near an hour & half. When the Consultation was over they informed me that my friend's Case was very difficult & dangerous; that he had a Fever sufficient to allarm; but that besides the Fever there was some latent Disease wch they c^d neither get at, nor, with great certainty, give it a Name—however they feared it was a Cancer on the Colon or principal intestine, wch perhaps might be paliated, but *never* c^d be cured. After this he hourly grew worse. His pain at times excruciating, fever more strong, & himself of course more debilitated. He was attended by all the three Eminent Gentlemen above mentioned very assiduously, and with as much care & tenderness as if like me they had known him in his better day.

I am extremely afflicted to come to the Catastrophe; but last night he suddenly grew easy, his Fever seemed to subside, & he lay perfectly quiet: but alas! these seeming favourable circumstances were only the consequences of a Mortification; in the morning his pulse, wch last night Dr Jebb found intermit once or twice while he was feeling it, sunk very much & on sending for the same Physician at 8 o'clock, as he was the nearest,[18] he passed the dreadful sentence of an approaching dissolution! which melancholy prediction was fulfilled ab^t 11 o'Clock.

My Letter is insensibly run into length & minuteness, for wch I hope to be pardoned. But my heart is at present so full, & my remembrance of his uncommon virtues & science so recent that though it was painful to begin this Letter it would have been much more to have said less on the melancholy subject, knowing how long & truely your Lord^{P's} regard for him had subsisted.

Poor Mrs Bewley who in the midst of her affliction begs me to present her humble respects to your Lord^P remains at my house till the last scene of the Tragedy is over, & will receive every consolation & comfort in our Power to bestow[19]

I have the honour to be with
the greatest respect &c

My poor Fr^d will be opened by Pott to morrow in order to discover the cause & ravages of so uncommon a complaint.

---

and physician, had turned to medicine as a profession in 1775 after resigning his ecclesiastical preferments on conscientious grounds (*DNB*; Munk, *Roll*, ii. 309–11).

[18] Jebb's practice was situated in Craven Street, the Strand.

[19] Mrs Bewley eventually returned to Norfolk and settled in Swaffham, where, when CB met her in 1789, she seemed to be 'comfortably situated and as happy as one can expect after such a loss' (CB to Fanny Burney, 2 Oct. 1789, Yale: BRBL).

To Charles Burney[1]   St Martin's Street,
6 September 1783

ALS (Osborn).
Addressed: To | Mr Burney | at Doctor Rose's Academy | Chiswick—

St Martin's Street.
Sat^y Morn^g Septr 6th
1783.

Dear Charles.

I was sent for hither on Tuesday, in a great hurry, on a very melancholy occasion. My poor Fr^d Bewley's Illness became so allarming that there was little expectation I sh^d find him alive, on my arrival. Dr Warren, D^r Jn° Jebb, & Mr Pott, had a consultation immediately on my coming to Town, ⟨but⟩ encouraged no hope of his recovery. They have all attended him ⟨with⟩ as much Care & anxiety as if they, like me, had known ⟨him⟩ in his better Day. After suffering most excruciating Pain till Thursday Night, a Mortification came on, wch gave him that dreadful ease for wch he often wished during his illness; & yesterday at ab^t 11, he breathed his last! I am quite worn out with grief & *Hypochond[r]ia*, and unable to perform the last act of friendship—that of attending his funeral on Sunday. I wish, my Dear Charles, you would take this Cup from me[2]—&, for the love he bore all my family, & wch every part of it who knew him, w^d willingly repay, come hither to go in the Coach with another of his friends to St Martin's Church. If you are in want of anything *black* for the occasion, you can be furnished here. My love to your wife, & Comp^ts elsewhere, and assure yourself of my being very affectionately yours.

C.B.

Dick is too young for this Office,[3] or Poor Mrs Bewley & her brother, Mr Green,[4] w^d accept of him.

---

[1] CB's second son, Charles, now settled as an assistant master in the school at Chiswick run by his father-in-law, Dr William Rose, would certainly have known of Bewley's visit to Ralph Griffiths in the neighbouring village of Turnham Green. Rose and Griffiths were close friends, brothers-in-law, neighbours, and associates in the establishment of the *Monthly Review* (T. Faulkner, *The History and Antiquities of Brentford, Ealing, and Chiswick* (1845), pp. 349–68; B. C. Nangle, *The Monthly Review, First Series, 1749–1789: Indexes of Contributors and Articles* (Oxford, 1934), pp. 37–8).

[2] See Matthew 26:39.

[3] CB's youngest son, Richard Thomas (1768–1808), was still in his 15th year. He had returned in June from Geneva where he had been sent in early 1781 to 'finish his Studies' (*Thraliana*, i. 481 and n. 2; Johnson *Letters*, iii. 42; *Burford Papers*, p. 60).

[4] Joseph Green (*fl.* 1783–1801), of East Street, Red Lion Square, and later of Turnham Green, Middlesex, who appears in Mrs Bewley's will as one of her executors, as well as in an

To Thomas Twining

St Martin's Street,
6 September 1783[1]

L copy (Osborn: 'Twining Letterbook No. 4', pp. 1–5) and AL (BL Add. MS 39932, fos. 165–6), numbered *by CB*: 2.

Editor's Note: Daniel Twining, the copyist of the 'Twining Letterbook' in the Osborn Collection, did not transcribe the second sheet of this letter, which has survived and is preserved in the British Library. He also left blank spaces in his transcript where CB's letter had probably been mutilated. Conjectural readings are supplied within angle brackets.

St Martin's Street—6th Sepr 1783

I had some thoughts of going ⟨into Norfolk⟩ this summer & carrying work with me; for Chesington had ⟨lost its⟩ ornament & temptation.[2] But my friend Bewley & fr⟨iends whom⟩ I wanted to see were on the wing themselves & very uncle⟨ar as to plans⟩ so I remained *roasting* in London, during the furious ⟨heat of the⟩ summer. However about the middle of last month my daughter ⟨& her⟩ Captain[3] begged so hard that I would go to Chesington that I determined to ⟨bow to their⟩ wishes however painful it would be to go thither so soon after the loss of my ⟨dear friend Crisp.⟩

Just before the time I had fixed for leaving London, I heard that my Friend Bewley was on the road thither from Birmingham, where he had been visiting Dr Priestley. About 3 weeks ago he & Mrs Bewley arrived. I found him much ematiated, & ill; however, we embraced most cordially, got into our old habits of Music,—Books,—& nonsensical talk—& we spent 4 days together with great felicity.

As he had not been in London for 30 years,[4] & never seen much of it, I went about with him to see places & persons, which he seemed to enjoy as much as a young man of 25, having an insatiable curiosity,

Assignment dated 8 Aug. 1801 preserved in the Norfolk Record Office (Bradfer-Lawrence Collection, Shelf X(11)).

[1] Although it may seem odd that CB should describe Bewley's death so movingly in the portion of the present letter transcribed by Daniel Twining (Osborn), and then proceed to discuss so brightly detailed musical matters in the undated portion preserved in the British Library, the conclusion that both fragments belong to the same letter is inescapable. In both sections CB replies to Twining's letter of 5–[6] July (BL Add. MS 39929, fos. 316–19), and is in turn answered by Twining's letter of 22 Oct. (ibid., fos. 320–3). The BL fragment is moreover dated by CB's 'flight' to Chessington 'to Morrow' (n. 46): his letter to Parr is dated from Chessington, on 7 Sept. 1783.

[2] Twining had referred to a letter, not now preserved, from CB, in his letter of 5–[6] July: 'Your character of your poor friend, Mr Crisp, is most amiable. . . . I felt for you, & for all of you, my dear friend, when I read your letter. As to myself, I don't know whether I was most glad that I *did* not know Mr C., or sorry that I *cou'd* not.'

[3] Susan and Molesworth Phillips.

[4] Fanny Burney records one brief visit to London by Bewley on 26 June 1774 (*ED* i. 316–17).

not only in scientific researches, but vulgar things with which he was unacquainted. At the end of 4 days, he having other friends to see in London & its Environs, I left him in order to go to Chesington; but by the time I had been there a week, He & Mrs Bewley returned to my house, where I had left Mrs Burney & Charlotte. He was now worse in health than when he came to Town, & on Sunday 7 night began to be wholly confined to the house. By Tuesday he was so ill that Mrs Burney sent for me by express; & on my arrival in Town he was too ill to see me, & there was a Consultation between Dr Warren, & Dr Jno Jebb; & Mr Pott the Surgeon, who gave me little hope that he would ever recover. He had a fever that was very alarming; but besides that, there was some latent disease, to which they could not give a name with any certainty.[5] [...] I will not lengthen the tragic tale⟨. On Thursda⟩y night after excruciating torture, there was all at once a cessation ⟨of pain⟩ & I feared a mortification was come on. He lingered ⟨until about⟩ 11 o clock yesterday morning, & then expired! I am ⟨sure you will⟩ pity us all. He now lies dead in the house! & ⟨also his⟩ disconsolate widow stupified with grief. I did not in⟨tend to prac⟩tice on your sensibility with so circumstantial a story, but my heart is so full of it that it boils over.—I had not had sufficient time to refit between the loss of Crisp & this *ami de trente trois ans*. I have told you my sentiments of him before privation had increased tenderness, & magnified his virtues.[6] He was born the same year as myself;— loved every thing that you & I love—Music—Books—fun—& had an *extent* & *depth* of Science that I have never met with. [7]In Electricity he has made as many discoveries as Franklyn,[8] & in fixt Air as Priestley:[9]

[5] MS certainty.] *Daniel Twining then deleted* but feared it *which gives evidence of a silent omission of a portion of CB's letter.*

[6] CB had contrived to keep Bewley and Twining, his closest advisers in the writing of the *History of Music*, in almost total ignorance of each other's assistance. For an account of CB's motives, see Lonsdale, pp. 218–19, 252. See also CB to Twining, 31 July 1784, n. 30.

Twining replied in his letter of 22 Oct.: 'Alas! your poor friend, Bewley! Your story was sad, indeed.—I did not know him—but from your account of him, as well as what I had heard from other people, I loved the *idea* of the man. I read your letter when I was weak & low, & consequently more open than usual to impressions of the melancholy kind. I did not read it with dry eyes. It affected me very much.—I say no more—for alas what is to be said?—The best thing we can do, on such occasions, is to thank God that we *have* had such friends, and to cherish the *recollection* of them as long as we live:—to say to ourselves,—I have *lost* my friend,—but I thank God I can't *forget* him.'

[7-7] This passage closely resembles in organization and phrase CB's 'Acc^t of the death of my poor friend Bewley Sent to the papers', a MS copy of which is preserved in the Osborn Collection. CB's obituary notice served as copy for the announcements which appeared in the *Morning Chronicle*, 9 Sept. 1783, and *GM* liii (1783)[2], 805. See also CB to Parr, 7 Sept. 1783; to Charles Burney, 12 Sept. [1783], n. 7.

[8] Benjamin Franklin (1706–90), the celebrated American scientist and statesman (*DAB*; *DSB*), whose discoveries in electricity were first published in London under the title *Experiments and Observations on Electricity* in 1751, and reached a fifth edition in 1774. Bewley had reviewed the

an excellent anatomist, of course, but for experimental philosophy, there was no end or limit to it, and with all this a humanity, & goodness of heart; & a simplicity of character, enlivened by natural & original wit & humour, which delighted every body who conversed with him.[7] I am now, you'll think, running into panegyric. I beg pardon. There is no likelihood of my speaking to you soon of two such friends as Crisp & Bewley. I know you'd have liked them, & they you, had you ever met. Indeed memory furnishes me with no two, of all my acquaintance, so likely to have won your heart. You speak warmly of old friends:[10] I know you will forgive me. But they knew us, & we knew them before a lock was put upon the heart by experience & distrust; and they had ever since the *entrée*, as *amis de la maison*.

How delightfully have you described Dr Loftus's[11] performance on the violincello! The Baron Back,[12] Dr Grey[13] of the Museum told me t'other day used to have great concerts in London at which he would

fourth (1769) edition in the *Monthly Review*, xlii (1770), 199–210, 298–308. See I. B. Cohen, ed., *Benjamin Franklin's Experiments* (Cambridge, Mass., 1941); B. C. Nangle, *The Monthly Review, First Series, 1749–1789: Indexes of Contributors and Articles* (Oxford, 1934), pp. 110–11, but see also R. Lonsdale, 'William Bewley and *The Monthly Review*: a Problem of Attribution', *Papers of the Bibliographical Society of America*, lv (1961), 309–18.

[9] 'Fixed Air' is the obsolete term for carbonic acid gas (CO_2). For Bewley's relations with Priestley and reviews of his work, see CB to Orford, [5 Sept. 1783], n. 2; Nangle, *Monthly Review*, pp. 179–80. Bewley's chemical researches were published in the Appendixes of Joseph Priestley's *Experiments and Observations on Different Kinds of Air* (1775–7), i. 317–21; ii. 337–60, 382–99; iii. 386–411.

[10] Twining had written in his letter of 5–[6] July 1783: 'M[rs] T. & I are going on Monday to pay a visit of a week or two to D[r] Hey at Passenham near Stony Stratford, Bucks; & M[r] Elmsall comes out of Yorkshire to meet us there. These are old & most intimate friends, whom I meet with great joy; but much more seldom than I cou'd wish. What a dirty trick it is of that blind jade, Fortune, to take up two friends, one in one of her great fists, ... & t'other in t'other, & throw them with all her might to opposite corners of the kingdom!'

[11] MS Loftus's] *Daniel Twining footnotes this allusion by quoting Twining's letter to CB of 5–[6] July:* 'Do you know a certain D[r] *Loftus Wood?*—M[rs] Ch. Burney does, I believe.—He is settled at Colchester, & plays the violoncello — — bon Dieu!—dat is such ting vat I never vas hear in my *loife!*—I reckon myself thoroughly *broke* to *out-of-tuneity* in playing. But the D[r]!—I never heard anything like it!—he knows very well that to make D he must put his finger down a little nearer to the bridge than when he makes C; but for the rest he leaves the precise *place* entirely to providence,—but I *must* say providence is a little ungrateful to him.'

Loftus Wood (*c.*1738–1804), MD, of Colchester, Essex, physician and medical author (*GM* lxxiv (1804)[2], 888). His most recent publication was *The Valetudinarian's Companion; or, Observations on Air, Exercise, and Regimen* ... (1782).

[12] Charles Ernest, Baron de Bagge (1722–91), wealthy amateur violinist, composer, and patron of musicians. Born in Kurland in Scandinavia, Bagge settled in Paris (*c.*1750) where he established a celebrated musical *salon*. He visited England in the summer of 1778. Michael Kelly wrote of Bagge, '... his performance was as bad as any blind fiddler's at a wake in a country town in Ireland; but he was a man of immense fortune, and kept open house. ... In my life, I never knew any man who snuffed up the air of praise like this discordant idiot' (*Reminiscences*, ed. R. Fiske (1975), p. 117). See *New Grove*.

[13] Edward Whitaker Gray (1748–1806), MD, botanist, Fellow (1779) and Secretary (1797) of the Royal Society, was Keeper of the Department of Natural History and Antiquities in the British Museum (*DNB*).

always play the first fiddle though Giardini, Cramer, & la Motte,[14] were in the band.

—I love Boccherini, as I have told you before[15] very—very much, but I think I shall live to make you eat your words about his pathetic being superior to Haydn's, whose fort you say is not pathos.[16] I will undertake to prove, however, when we meet, that you have not seen his merit in adagio & Cantabile movements, for want of reading more of his music.[17] ...

[*Daniel Twining's transcription ends here with an interpolated signature* C. B. *The second sheet, in CB's hand, preserved in the British Library, follows:*]

... by Longman, to the 3 sets of his Lessons, wch from my fondness for them I was at the trouble of making[18]—If I dont mend a passage, I hope you'll allow that I have been tender of the author, & done no mischief noise & impertinence.

There have been 6 or 7 of Haydn's symphonies tolerably cooked for the

[14] Franz Lamotte (*c*.1751–81), Flemish violinist and composer, had appeared in London in 1776, and again in 1778–9 (*New Grove*; *MGG*). CB had first heard Lamotte perform in 1772 on his German tour: 'La Motte, a Flamand, the best solo player and sightsman, upon the violin, at Vienna' (*Tours*, ii. 125). Under [Apr.] 1776 'La Motte leads at Pantheon' is an entry CB made in his MS 'Memoranda from Pocket book' (*Frag. Mem.*, Berg). See also Rees.

[15] See CB to Twining, 14 Dec. 1781, n. 26.

[16] Twining had written in his letter of 5–[6] July: 'Haydn & Boccherini, spoil me for all other fiddle music. Haydn, I think, is much *oftener* charming than Boccherini. Yet when Boccherini *is at his best*, there is a force of *serious* expression, a pathos, that is not so much Haydn's fort, I think. I never see a *smile* upon Boccherini's face; he is all earnestness, & Tragedy. Haydn leans to Comedy: even in his adagio he is wanton, playful, & never forgets his *tricks*.—It is, now & then, *serious* comedy, but seldom, I think, amounts to Tragedy, or even to the Comedie *larmoyante*.— Not that I mean to find fault; he is, to me, delicious, & I wish for nothing better while I am playing him. For variety, & endless *resources*, I know no composer like him.'

[17] Twining stoutly defended himself in his reply of 22 Oct.: 'Sir?—*eat my words?*—"make me eat my words," I think you said?—I fancy, Sir, you will not find that so easy. ... "When we meet" you say?—But alas! when shall we meet? ... as to my *words*, I scarce know what they were;—but I think I am yet upon firm ground; for I *do* not say, nor, I verily think *did* say,—that Haydn was *never* pathetic, or that he was *always* leaning to the comic—but only that, in his *general cast & manner*, Boccherini is a more serious, *earnest* composer.'

CB doubtless proceeded to give musical examples of Haydn's slow movements which Daniel Twining omitted in his transcription, for the next sentence in Twining's reply of 22 Oct. reads: 'All the movements of Haydn you mention, I know very well; I allow them to be very fine,— serious, & pathetic:—but I spake of *general* style & character only; & it still appears to me that Boccherini's genius is Tragic, & that in Haydn the graceful, the fanciful, the enjoué, the playful &c.—prevails upon the whole.—Such is my idea still—not from obstinacy, Dieu scait—but from the impression which these two charming composers make upon my ear & mind.' See further CB to Twining, 10–12 Nov. 1783, n. 71.

[18] CB refers to his violin accompaniments to three sets of Haydn's keyboard sonatas, published by Longman and Broderip as Opp. 13, 14 and 17 (Hoboken XVI: 21–26; 27–32; 35–39, 20), each set bearing the title *Six Sonatas for the Forte Piano or Harpsichord with an Accompaniment for a Violin Composed by Giuseppe Haydn* ..., and advertised in the *Public Advertiser*, 5 Jan. 1784 as 'Haydn's Lessons for the Harpsichord, Op. 13, 14, and 17, with a Violin Accompaniment, by Dr. Burney, each 10s. 6d. or the Accompaniments separate, each 3s.' See Hoboken, vol. i, pp. 733, 753, 757, 762–3; and CB to Twining, 10–12 Nov. 1783, n. 75.

Harp[d] or P. forte—But whole movements being omitted, in 3 of them, for the sake of my scholars, I have adapted & given him them to print & will let you know when they are ready.[19] The 1st symph. you know.[20]

It begins thus, in D &c[21]

but the 1st Movem[t] is omitted, of w[ch] the Base begins thus:

[22] Giordani[23] & Carter[24] have both

adapted this symph. entirely, but *secondo di me*, very ill—both having taken unwarrantable liberties wth the Author. 2 of the 3 Charming symp[s] w[ch] you purchased in Parts[25] have been likewise printed for the P. forte, but without adagio to either. These you will soon have, entire—

There is a delicious symph In E♭ adapted by Giordani

[19] CB's keyboard arrangements of Haydn symphonies raise perplexing problems. Longman and Broderip published *The Celebrated Overture, Composed by Sig[r] Haydn, and Performed at Mess[rs] Bach & Abel's Concerts; Adapted for the Piano Forte or Harpsichord*, which comprised Symphonies 53, 68, 66, and Hob. I:B2, discussed by CB in this letter. The Longman and Broderip publication was advertised, however, in the *Morning Herald* for 30 Dec. 1782: too early a date for this letter. See Hoboken, vol. i, p. 69.

[20] Haydn's Symphony No. 53 ('L'Impériale') in D, was first performed in London at the Bach–Abel concerts in 1781. It was an immediate success, and greatly enhanced Haydn's reputation amongst English music-lovers. For an account of this symphony, and the complexities of its different versions, see Hoboken, vol. i, pp. 66–73, 282–5; H. C. Robbins Landon, *The Symphonies of Joseph Haydn* (1955), pp. 364–8; *idem, Haydn at Eszterháza, 1766–1790* (1978), pp. 560–3, 595.

[21] CB quotes the opening bars of Haydn's Overture (Hoboken Ia:7), which serves as the Finale to Versions B′ and B″ of Symphony No. 53. The same Overture, however, displaces the first movement of the symphony in Versions E′ and E″. CB presumably refers to some arrangement of the symphony in one of the E versions.

[22] i.e. the 'Vivace' opening of the first movement in Version B″, in which the introductory 'Largo maestoso' is omitted.

[23] None of the anonymous keyboard arrangements of this symphony listed in Hoboken, vol. i, p. 69 is attributed to Tommaso Giordani (*c*.1733–1806), Neapolitan harpsichordist and composer closely associated with the opera in the King's Theatre in the Haymarket (*New Grove*; *BD*). The *Morning Chronicle*, 15 July 1783, advertises however, 'Three favourite Overtures, composed by the celebrated Guiseppe Haydn, of Vienna, adapted for the Harp or Piano Forte, by Signior Giordani'. The compositions thus adapted were Haydn's Symphonies Nos. 63, 75, and 69 (see Hoboken, vol. i, p. 89).

[24] *Haydn's Celebrated Overture, adapted for the Harpsichord or Piano Forte; in an easy style by Tho[s] Carter*, published by John Preston (*fl.* 1774–98), was advertised in the *Morning Herald*, 5 May 1783. See Hoboken, vol. i, p. 69.

Charles Thomas Carter (*c*.1740–1804), Irish composer and keyboard virtuoso, had settled in London in the early 1770s as a composer of comic operas, and songs for Vauxhall (*DNB*; *New Grove*; *BD*).

[25] Possibly the set published by Longman and Broderip in 1781 under the title *Three Simphonys in Eight Parts, for Violins, Hoboys, Horns, Tenor and Bass . . . Op. XV*, which included Symphonies Nos. 67, 66, and 68. See Hoboken, vol. i, p. 97.

1783

&c get it.[26]

Another of the 3 in parts set by D[r] Hayes—'tis in F

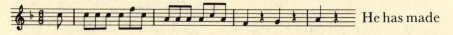

He has made

it very hard and awkward; but you can simplify—'tis delightful.[27]

There are two printed by Bland[28] for the Harp[d] one in G[♮]—w[ch] is begun by the Fr. Horn. I forget how. But something like this

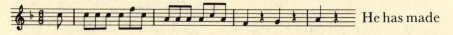

&c[29] The slow movem[t] on an old

org. Point is admirable for that Instrum[t][30] 'Seek, & ye shall find.'[31] In this last only mind in the last Allegro en Rondeau, how he returns to the Subject. There is another in B[♭] wch begins with a short Ada[o] of only 2 or 3 Bars that I do not like so well[32]—however among old & common things there is much good & new.

I know nothing of any modern Ricci[33]—there were Concertos à

[26] CB quotes the opening bars of the first movement of Haydn's Symphony No. 74. Giordani's arrangement is not traced.

[27] Haydn's Symphony No. 67, arranged by Philip Hayes. *Jackson's Oxford Journal*, 20 Jan. 1781, advertised Hayes's arrangement, which appeared under the title *A Favourite Symphony of Giusseppe Haydn, adapted to the Harpsichord or Piano-Forte*, 'Printed for W. Mathews in the High Street, Oxford'. See also Hoboken, vol. i, p. 97; Rosemary S. M. Hughes, 'Haydn at Oxford: 1773–1791', *Music and Letters*, xx (1939), 242–9.

[28] John Bland (c.1750–c.1840), engraver, printer, music seller and publisher, the recipient of Haydn's 'Razor' Quartet (Hoboken III:61), in whose house at 45 High Holborn, Haydn stayed on his arrival in England on 1 Jan. 1791 (*New Grove*; P. A. Scholes, 'Burney and Haydn', *Monthly Musical Record*, lxxi (1941), 155–6; H. C. Robbins Landon, *Haydn in England, 1791–1795* (1976), pp. 27, 31–5).

[29] CB quotes, accurately, the opening of Haydn's Symphony No. 47, adapted for the keyboard by William Tindal (c.1756–1804), and published by Bland under the title *Sig[r] Haydns Grand Orchestre Sinfonie as performed at the Nobility's Concerts; adapted for the Organ, Harpsichord, or Piano Forte*. Bland also issued keyboard arrangements of Haydn's Symphonies Nos. 69, 73, and 85 (see Hoboken, vol. i, p. 58; vol. iii, p. 269). For the Revd William Tindal, MA, FSA, see Foster; *GM* lxxiv (1804)[2], 889–90.

[30] Marked 'Un poco adagio', this slow movement remained one of CB's favourites. See Landon, *Haydn at Eszterháza*, pp. 304–5. For 'org[an] Point', see Rees, under 'Point d'Orgue', where CB defines it as 'a pause ∩ upon a note in the base ... when the treble part ... is allowed to wander about ... after the manner of a cadenza or close'.

[31] Matthew 7:7.

[32] Haydn's Symphony No. 71.

[33] Twining had enquired in his letter of 5–[6] July: 'What is your idea of Ricci? I have some Quartetts of his that are, to me, very pleasing; like no other music that I know of; & tho' simple & of very easy execution, by no means trite or insipid.' Twining referred to a set of six string quartets (Op. 8), published at The Hague (c.1773) and later by Welcker in London, composed by Francesco Pasquale Ricci (1732–1817), Italian Franciscan, and composer, who in 1759 had become *maestro di cappella* of the Duomo in Como (*New Grove*; *MGG*).

Capella, I think by one Ricci published ab^t 30 years ago[34] in w^ch *Non Nobis domine*, ascribed to Palestrina, was the subject of a Fugue.[35]

I fear your Fr^d Jones[36] will turn out a mere *Grumbling Fogrum*. And I am sorry: as, when men of Letters, with a spice of Philosophical Enquiry, takes *Miss*, that is Instrumental, or Mad^m music when wedded to Poetry by the Hand, one w^d hope that he w^d do her some good; enlarge her Ideas; & extend her dominions; but alas! instead of that, he gives her while single the *Cramp* in her fingers—a *numbness* in all her joints, & when married a *locked-Jaw*.—Master Hopkins[37]—no, I begs pardon Simpkins, says very truely, that 'this is what one may call a very disagreeable thing.'[38]

You speak of Barry's book so exactly as I think that I can add nothing on the subject.[39]—Sir Jos. Reynolds *jealous* of him! and his

---

[34] In Twining's reply of 22 Oct., he wrote correcting CB: 'There *is* a modern Ricci: I have his Quartetts.—I believe you mistake about the Concertos à Capella; I think you mean the Concertos published under the name of *RicciOTTI*, but composed, (as I have always understood,) by Count *Bentinck* to whom they are dedicated. ... But perhaps you are acquainted with these Concertos—if so—& if I am wrong in my judgment—send me back this part of my letter, & I will *eat* it.' CB was indeed thinking of the six *Concerti armonici*, formerly attributed to Pergolesi, as well as to the obscure Italian violinist, Carlo Ricciotti (*c*.1681–1756), called 'Bacciccia', who had the set published at The Hague in 1740. The *Concerti* are now firmly attributed to Count Unico Wilhelm van Wassenaer (1692–1766). See A. Dunning, *Count Unico Wilhelm van Wassenaer (1692–1766). A Master Unmasked, or: The Pergolesi/Ricciotti-Puzzle Solved* (Buren, 1980). See also CB to Twining, 10–12 Nov. 1783, n. 70.

[35] The fugue in the first movement of the Concerto No. 3 in A major is marked 'Da Capella Canone di Palestrina'. The subject is the celebrated canon 'Non nobis Domine'. CB's copy of 'Ricciotti's' *Concerti armonici* is listed in *Cat. Mus. Lib.*, lot 800.

[36] The Revd William Jones (1726–1800), BA (1749), FRS (1775), Perpetual Curate of Nayland, Suffolk (1777), prominent divine and musician (*DNB*; *New Grove*). In Jan. 1784 he was to publish at Colchester *A Treatise on the Art of Music; in which the Elements of Harmony and Air are practically considered* ..., the manuscript of which he had shown Twining, who wrote to CB (5–[6] July 1783): 'My friend Jones is publishing his *Analysis* of Air & Harmony, ... You *must absolutely review* this book, when it comes out. I have reviewed it in private; *my* mouth is shut. I must not be treacherous. Yet, you see I have no objection to setting *you* upon my friend's back! ... The truth is, Mr J.'s absurd prejudices, & obstinate immobility of opinion, are provoking. I know if his brain cou'd be laid open & inspected, the first thing one shou'd see wou'd be a number of great iron opinions, in religion, necessity for a man's cock—but here, for a to go for to drive a , such as one sees upon houses, cramping down all his Politics, Music &c &c. To be sure there is no ideas to be always whirling about like a weatherman as soon as ever he gets an opinion into his head, great bolt into it, & make it as fast as the mainmast of a Ship—why, if so be I may be so bold to say so, it's quite what you may call a *disagreeable* thing.' See further, CB to Twining, 31 July 1784, n. 32; Kassler, i. 601–7.

[37] Actually, Mr Hobson, the retired 'man of business' in *Cecilia*, bk. v, ch. 6.

[38] A characteristic remark of Hobson, echoed by his cringing sycophantic friend Simkins. CB replies in kind to Twining's verdict on William Jones (see n. 36).

[39] For James Barry's *Account of a Series of Pictures* (1783), see CB to Orford [5 Sept. 1783], n. 8. Twining had written in his letter of 5–[6] July: 'I read Mr Barry's wild book, & was entertained by it in spite of its failings. Surely he is a very Rousseau-ish being? Is there,—*can* there be, any foundation for his complaints of envy, persecution &c^a?—of Sr J. R. in particular? ... Though he seems romantic, & visionary in his views & expectations, there is an appearance of integrity, & of a moral & generous way of thinking in him, that, I own, interest me more than his faults

persecutor![40]—downright madness & self-over-rating Pride.—But besides this the *Potatoe* often appears elsewhere—& yet as you say there is spirit & a seeming integrity & indignation in his book that dazzle one. As to Swift I think him so right that I clapt him on the back for what he says, of the late fashion in lowering his merit & downing with him.[41]—I *do* and ever *did* like & love Swift—and am not sure that I ever rec^d equal pleasure from any other writer—in wit & humour I am most certain I never did, and so here's entire unisonous Coincidence between us.

I believe the very thoughts of profit, have terrified Fanny's muse or Genius,[42] to such a degree that she's flown out of sight, like the new French Kite filled with Gas, or inflamable Air[43]—for I cannot discover the least tendency towards scribbling in *any shape of Life*.[44]

I hope your Jaunt[45] turned out to you & M^r[s] T. pleasant & Comfortable.

offend me.—For his indignant defence of Swift, that capital man, who has lately been so unfairly attacked, by Harris, Beattie, &c^a—I honour him ... I deny that Swift's writings have any one bad tendency; I deny that he was a Misanthrope; ... What connection is there between indignation at the vices of mankind, & hatred of mankind? ... pray, now—do y now—agree with me about all this ... You *do* love Swift now, don't you?—ay, ay, I knew it.—And yet,—can *you* possibly love an *ill-natured* man? No. *Ergo*, he was *not* an ill-natured man.'

[40] Although Barry does not accuse Sir Joshua Reynolds by name in his *Account* of the set of paintings executed for the Society of Arts, he hints darkly at 'underhand malevolent attentions from a certain quarter' (p. 25); writes of himself as being 'powerfully and artfully opposed' (p. 28); and in a clear allusion to Reynolds states: 'we every where meet with those who are all virtue, candor, and amiability, out of their profession, where there is no rivalship, though they scruple not to practise every baseness and treachery within, when it can be done with sufficient concealment; and that the complaints of the injured may be made to appear nothing more than the barkings of envy, and mere professional clamour' (p. 76).

[41] Barry included Swift's portrait in the sixth picture of the series, 'Elizium, or the State of final Retribution', in which, as Barry explains in his *Account*, he sought to 'bring together in Elyzium, those great and good men of all ages and nations, who were cultivators and benefactors of mankind' (p. 116). Barry's lengthy and spirited argument in favour of Swift is found in his *Account* (pp. 122–6), and concludes: '... my indignation has been greatly roused at some late scurrilities; and I could not withold myself from flinging out these few hints, as a justification of my intention of adding Dr. Swift' (p. 126).

[42] Twining wrote in his letter of 5–[6] July: 'As for Miss B. if there is any body that wou'd be better pleased than I sh^d be to see both her pockets bunching out with money, like a pair of panniers—I'll be hanged. And yet I cannot find in my heart to be angry with her for objections & delicacies qui lui siedent si bien.'

[43] The first public launching of an experimental balloon filled with 'inflammable air' (hydrogen), took place on 27 Aug. 1783 at the Champ de Mars in Paris (see L. T. C. Rolt, *The Aeronauts: a History of Ballooning, 1783–1903* (1966), pp. 31–7). Reports of the historic flight reached London in early Sept. and were published in the newspapers. See, for example, *Public Advertiser*, 6 Sept. 1783: '... Two Cannons were fired as a Signal for the Globe to be let off, when the Inventor cutting a Cord that held it, it immediately mounted into the Air, and turning occasionally round its own Axis, it was in about a Minute carried completely out of Sight.'

[44] Twining replied in kind in his letter of 22 Oct.: 'Oh—never fear, never fear: when Miss B.'s *Kite* has taken it's *train* in the air, it will come down again, & be found, un beau jour, when we are not looking for it. She has powers of mind that cannot, I hope, let her rest long.'

[45] The Twinings had gone on a 'summer jaunt' to Passenham, Buckinghamshire, in mid-July (see n. 10). In his reply of 22 Oct., Twining assured CB that the visit had been 'very pleasant'.

380

I shall fly 'from these dread scenes', to Morrow[46]—& try to be quiet at Ches. a little while longer—will you let me *expectorate* by & by, if *Gobbs* should arise? I had made a beginning in the memorandum way of the Chap. on the rise of the Musical Drama, by the Invention of *Recitative*—but not a Page written, or digested yet[47]—however this will, I foresee be more pleasant work to me, than rummaging old Engl. *Madrigals* by your Weelks's—Kirbies—Wilbies—& Bennets.[48] What a mob of them have I been forced to score, in order to be able to say that they are all so *alike* that they might pass for the productions of an Individual![49]—

It was my Intention to go to Farnham with Fanny on a Visit to the B^p of Winchester[50] ab^t the middle of this Month—but accident having layed violent hands on the time I intended to bestow on my *sequel*—I hardly think I shall find [it] in my heart to go.

What disputes & Squabbles ab^t opera Management![51] If Gallini's

[46] The source of the quotation is not identified. The 'dread scenes' refers to Bewley lying 'dead in the house! & ⟨also his⟩ disconsolate widow stupified with grief'. CB's intended 'flight' to Chessington 'to Morrow' (i.e. Sunday, 7 Sept.) also explains his plea to Charles Burney to represent the family at Bewley's funeral 'on Sunday' (see CB to Charles Burney, 6 Sept. 1783). See also CB to Parr, 7 Sept. 1783.

[47] Twining, in his reply of 22 Oct., wrote encouragingly: 'Well—but I am glad to hear you talk of pursuing clues, & such things, & that you have a *gob* in your throat ... *Slam* it at me whenever you please ... I long for the advancement of your 3^d Volume; the work will grow more & more interesting at every step, not to me only, but to all your readers ... your Dramatic chapter must be highly interesting. Above all let us have as many specimens as you can afford us.'

CB's chapter 'Of the Invention of Recitative, and Establishment of the musical Drama, or Opera, in Italy' eventually appeared as the first chapter in the fourth volume of the *History of Music*.

[48] Thomas Weelkes (*c*.1576–1623); George Kirbye (*c*.1565–1634); John Wilbye (1574–1638); John Bennet (*fl.* 1599–1614), English Elizabethan madrigal composers, for whom see *DNB*; *New Grove*. 'Of these four composers, the best madrigalists of our country, many productions have lately been revived at the Concert of Ancient Music, and Catch-Club; where, by the perfection of performance, effects have been produced, of which it is probable the authors themselves, even in the warm and enthusiastic moments of conception, had but little idea ... it may perhaps with truth be said, that they are not only renovated, but rendered much better compositions than the authors intended them to be' (*Hist. Mus.* iii. 123; Mercer, ii. 106).

[49] CB wrote of the Elizabethan madrigalists: '... they all resemble each other so much in modulation and style, that they might very well pass for the productions of one and the same composer. There is no one that towers above the rest sufficiently to give a modern ear the least idea of invention or originality' (*Hist. Mus.* iii. 131; Mercer, ii. 112).

[50] Brownlow North (1741–1820), DCL (1770), Dean of Canterbury (1770), Bishop of Coventry and Lichfield (1771), of Worcester (1774), of Winchester (1781). See *DNB*. The growing friendship between Dr North's family and the Burneys is shown by a pressing invitation from the Bishop of Winchester to CB, 27 Dec. 1782 (Osborn), to join a house party at Farnham Castle, the episcopal palace of the Bishops of Winchester.

[51] The expenses incurred in the renovation of the King's Theatre in 1782 (see CB to Fanny Burney, 6 Nov. 1782, n. 21) had bankrupted the proprietor, William Taylor (*c*.1754–1825), who, while imprisoned for debt, saw his share in the theatre purchased by Giovanni Andrea Battista Gallini (1728–1805), dancing master and impresario. Taylor, however, functioning from prison through a board of trustees, denied the legality of Gallini's purchase, and reclaimed the right to manage the Opera. Complicated litigation and a furious pamphlet war ensued

Claims to the Theatre are valid, we shall have the dear Pacchierotti another year, by a Contrivance of mine & another of his Friends[52]— but mum—more in my next on this & other matters.—I have stimulated a wish to get Haydn over as opera Composer[53]—but mum mum—yet—a correspondence is opened, & there is a great likelihood of it, if these Cabals, & litigations ruin not the opera entirely. M[rs] B. joins me in best Comp[ts] to M[rs] T. The Girls are luckily all out of Town—but wherever they are you are sure of their love—& so take my benediction, though you can *give* a better yourself.

vive felice.

To Samuel Parr[1]   Chessington, 7 September 1783

Source: The Works of Samuel Parr, LL.D., ed. J. Johnstone (1828), vii. 383–4; with enclosure, p. 385.

At Mrs. Hamilton's, Chessington, near Kingston,
Surrey, Sunday night, Sept. 7, 1783.

Dear Sir,

   I am sorry to rush in upon you with a tragical tale, but hope you will forgive me in favour of a most valuable friend who is its hero. You have doubtless, ere now, heard of the death of poor Bewley, who had

between the Taylor and Gallini factions. CB refers to the hottest exchange of claims and insults publicly conducted in the advertisement columns of the *Public Advertiser*, 2, 3, 4, 5, 6 Sept. 1783. For the details of the controversy, see D. Nalbach, *The King's Theatre, 1704–1867: London's First Italian Opera House* (1972), pp. 50–3; *The London Stage*, v. i. 542–3, ii. 634; *BD*, under 'Gallini'; *Morning Chronicle*, 9 Sept. 1783. See also CB to Twining, 10–12 Nov. 1783, nn. 57, 76.

   [52] Not identified, possibly Lady Mary Duncan.

   [53] Although CB's attempt to engage Haydn for the London opera in the 1780s has hitherto passed unnoticed, the efforts of other music lovers are described in C. Roscoe, 'Haydn and London in the 1780's', *Music and Letters*, xlix (1968), 203–12; C. B. Oldman, 'Haydn's Quarrel with the "Professionals" in 1788', in *Musik und Verlag*, ed. R. Baum and W. Rehm (Kassel, 1968), pp. 459–65; and Landon, *Haydn at Eszterháza*, pp. 595–602. See also CB to Twining, 10–12 Nov. 1783, n. 76; Grant, p. 280.

   CB's account of earlier negotiations with Haydn is contained in his MS 'Materials Towards the History of German Music & Musicians' (Osborn shelves c 100, p. 7): 'He was engaged to Compose for Ld Abingdon's Concert and was expected in England ab[t] the end of the year 1782; but did not come, as the security for his money: (£300, & travelling expenses from Vienna; & at the end of the season £100 more for Copy-right, of the 12 Pieces he was to compose for the concert, of whatever kind he pleased, if he c[d] not dispose of them more to his advantage.)'

   [1] The Revd Samuel Parr (1747–1825), LLD (1781), Headmaster of Colchester Grammar School (1777–9), and of Norwich Grammar School (1779–85), scholar (*DNB*; W. Derry, *Dr. Parr, a Portrait of the Whig Dr. Johnson*, Oxford, 1966). Twining, who knew Parr at Colchester, had introduced the Burneys to him (Twining to CB, 28 Dec. 1781; 14 Feb., 5 May, 18 Sept., 28 Nov. 1782; 27 Jan., 19 Feb. 1783: BL Add. MS 39929, fos. 291–313, *passim*).

been at Birmingham on a visit to Dr. Priestley; whence he came to London in a very alarming state of health, just as I was on the point of quitting it for some time. It was with great joy that I postponed my journey in order to enjoy his company, after so long an absence, a few days, all he had to spare; and, though feeble, he seemed very much amused with old conversation, new music, and the sight of remarkable persons and things. From Monday was seven-night[2] to Thursday we continued together; but then, having other friends to see and visits to make in the environs of London, he and Mrs. Bewley left us, and I set off for the country, after they had promised to follow me, or at least return to my house in town if they should have any more time to bestow on us.

A week after they did return, but he was much worse in health than before; and the Wednesday[3] following he was so ill that Mrs. Burney sent for me home by express. I just arrived time enough to meet my friend Dr. Warren, Dr. John Jebb, and Mr. Pott; who, in examining the patient and in consultation, remained near two hours in my house. They gave me but little hope of his recovery; however, they attended him to the last with as much punctuality and solicitude as if, like me, they had known him in his better days. The poor soul suffered excruciating torture till Thursday night; when he became suddenly so easy that I dreaded a mortification, which, however, on being opened, was found not to have taken place, though he died the next morning, Sept. 5th, at the age of fifty-seven.

The seat of his disorder was in the colon, or principal intestine; where a cancer had for some time been formed, and whence a violent inflammation had spread itself almost through his whole frame. I staid in St. Martin's-street to help to console and comfort poor Mrs. Bewley, till within an hour of the funeral; which leaving my two sons[4] to attend, and Mrs. Burney having prevailed on Mrs. Bewley to quit the house during this last act of the tragedy, I flew away from such scenes of horror, and am come hither to brood over my loss, and meditate on the wretchedness and calamities to which the best of mortals are subject!

In youth men of parts and enterprise court the world; in age, if they have useful talents, the World courts them. Bewley, in spite of diffidence and obscurity, and wholly careless of fame or fortune, was just arrived at this last period; and if he had survived ten or twelve years

---

[2] For CB's defective dating, see CB to Orford, [5 Sept. 1783], n. 6.
[3] Actually, Tuesday, for which see CB to Orford, [5 Sept.]; to Charles Burney, 6 Sept.; to Twining, 6 Sept. 1783.
[4] i.e. Charles and Richard.

more, as in the common course of things he had a title to expect, they would have been glorious to himself and useful to mankind.

Those men, however, who having deserved well of society have neglected themselves, should not be suffered instantly to drop into oblivion, but should have their dividend of well-earned fame honestly paid to their memory, if the world, during life, has withheld it from them, or they themselves have omitted to ask for it. I must therefore, my dear Sir, intreat you to obtain a place in the Norwich paper for the following hasty attempt at a character of my excellent friend,[5] if a better has not already been furnished by his Norfolk acquaintance.

Mrs. Burney and the rest of my family, particularly Charles, whom you have honoured with your notice,[6] beg your acceptance of their best compliments, and, on my own behalf, I entreat you to believe me to be with great regard, dear Sir, your obliged and most obedient servant,

CHA. BURNEY.

[*Enclosure:*][7]

London, 1783.

'On Friday last, Sept. 7th,[8] died at the house of his friend Dr. Burney, in St. Martin's-street, where he was upon a visit, Mr. William Bewley, of Massingham, in Norfolk, whose death will be very much lamented by all men of science to whom his great abilities, particularly in anatomy, electricity, and chemistry, had penetrated through the obscurity of his abode, and natural modesty and diffidence of his disposition. Indeed, the depth and extent of his knowledge in every useful branch of science and literature, could only be equalled by the goodness of his heart, simplicity of character, and innocence of life, seasoned with a natural unsought wit and humour of a cast most original, pleasant, and inoffensive.

---

[5] CB's enclosed obituary is that printed in *GM* liii (1783)[2], 805. See also CB to Orford, [5 Sept. 1783], n. 1; to Twining, 6 Sept. 1783, n. 7–7.

The *Norwich Mercury*, 13 Sept. 1783, printed an obituary which reads: 'Yesterday se'nnight died, on a visit to his friend Dr. Burney, in St. Martin's-street, Leicester-square, London, Mr. William Bewley, of Massingham, in this county; who was justly eminent for his great skill in Natural Philosophy and Chemistry, as well as for his exquisite taste in almost every branch of literature. This, however, was his least praise; he was not only one of the most accomplished, but one of the best of men. By his death, society, and especially those who had the happiness of conversing and corresponding with him, must sustain a loss, which, it is to be feared, will not soon be repaired.'

[6] See CB to Twining, 10–12 Nov. 1783, nn. 61, 62.

[7] Minor variants excepted, the text of this enclosure, including CB's explanatory footnote (n. 10), corresponds with the holograph 'Acc^t' of the death of my poor friend Bewley Sent to the papers' preserved in the Osborn Collection.

[8] CB confuses the date of Bewley's death and that of this letter to Parr.

Hobbs,[9] in the last century, whose chief writings were levelled against the religion of his country, was called, from the place of his residence, the Philosopher of Malmsbury; but with how much more truth and propriety has Mr. Bewley, whose life was spent in the laborious search of the most hidden and useful discoveries in art and nature, in exposing sophistry, and displaying talents, been distinguished in Norfolk by the respectable title of the Philosopher of Massingham.'[10]

To Charles Burney

[Chessington],
12 September [1783]

ALS (Berg).
Addressed: Mr. Burney, | Chiswick, | Middlesex   *Pmks:* ⟨12⟩ SE EPSOM

Dear Charles.

I thank you for your two Letters.[1] The copy you have sent of what you intend to insert in y^r next publication[2] seems very fit for the purpose—and the only alterations I shall propose are, 1st—in mentioning his age to change 58 to 57.[3]—I think 'at the *zenith* of vigour'— had better be 'in *full* vigour'.[4]—Is it very modest for you to talk of *delivering* anything to *posterity?*[5]—I only ax—

Period 2^d Pray let his *Anatomical* abilities stand first in the list,

---

[9] Thomas Hobbes (1588–1679), philosopher (*DNB*).

[10] An asterisk indicates a footnote appended by CB: 'Mr. Bewley, for more than twenty years, supplied the Editor of the Monthly Review with an examination of innumerable works in science, and articles of foreign literature, written with a force, spirit, candour, and, when the subject offered occasion, humour not frequently found in critical strictures.' For a study of Bewley's contributions to the *Monthly Review*, see R. Lonsdale, 'William Bewley and *The Monthly Review*: a Problem of Attribution', *Papers of the Bibliographical Society of America*, lv (1961), 309–18, which corrects the survey and index given in B. C. Nangle, *The Monthly Review, First Series, 1749–1789: Indexes of Contributors and Articles* (Oxford, 1934), pp. 4–5.

[1] Not preserved.

[2] *The London Magazine, Enlarged and Improved*, edited by CB's son, Charles, carries in its third (Sept. 1783) issue a glowing obituary of Bewley under the title 'Character of the Philosopher of Massingham' (pp. 258–9). As this letter shows, Charles had written the 'Character' and had submitted the draft to his father for CB's comments and corrections. See Lonsdale, p. 279; and CB to Twining, 10–12 Nov. 1783, n. 62.

[3] 'He died on the 5th of September, 1783, while he was paying a visit at the house of his friend Dr. Burney, in St. Martin's-street, London, at the age of fifty-seven years' (*London Magazine*, loc. cit.).

[4] 'His fancy retained its wonted liveliness: his ardour for acquiring knowledge continued unabated; and his faculties were in full vigour, until a few hours before his dissolution' (ibid.).

[5] This phrase was either deleted or heavily revised in Charles Burney's 'Character' of Bewley.

as anatomy was his immediate profession.[6] And as this has been in several News-papers[7] it sh[d] be marked as quotation, with inverted Commas.?[8]

3[d] period—instead of saying 'he cultivated *this* Art'—w[ch] applies to the *Violin*—you had better say—'He cultivated the art & science of Music &c'[9]

Period 6—I wish you w[d] say after 'His love of every liberal art & science',—(and insatiable curiosity concerning every thing that was connected with them, were his ruling Passions—) 'so strongly indeed did *they* &c'[10]

In the last period—Is it necessary to say M[r] Hobbs?—because my poor Fr[d] is called M[r] Bewley?—it seems queer to me—After Massingham sh[d] not there be a note of interrogation? or admiration! The Question is asked 'w[th] *How much more Truth* &c?['] This is only a Query.[11]

D[r] Jebb has left in S[t] Martin's Street a description of the state in w[ch] my poor friend's body was found, on dissection—but I fear M[rs] Bewley has carried it with her into Norfolk—

I have not time to add a word more but best Comp[ts] to Chiswickers & Turnham-greeners[12]—love to the Rosette & to yourself from

Y[rs] affectionately C.B.

Friday Even[g] | 12th Sept[r]

[6] 'Mr. William Bewley, of Massingham in Norfolk, will be long lamented by all men of science, to whose notice his great abilities, particularly in anatomy, electricity, and chemistry, had penetrated through the obscurity of his abode, and through the natural modesty and diffidence of his disposition' (ibid.). See n. 7.

[7] The *Morning Chronicle*, 9 Sept. 1783, for example, which listed, however, Bewley's 'great abilities, particularly in electricity, chemistry, and anatomy'. See CB to Orford, [5 Sept. 1783], n. 1; to Twining, 6 Sept. 1783, n. 7–7. CB's MS 'Acc[t] of . . . Bewley' (Osborn) has the passage in the corrected sequence: 'anatomy, electricity, & chemistry'.

[8] Inverted commas do not appear around this paragraph of Charles Burney's 'Character' of Bewley.

[9] 'Mr. Bewley had naturally a fine ear, and was particularly fond of music. He was not only an excellent judge of compositions, but also a good performer on the violin. He cultivated the art and science of music, as a relief from severer pursuits; and applied to it, in his hours of relaxation, with that ardour which characterised all his undertakings' (*London Mag.* iii. 258–9).

[10] 'A love for every liberal science, and an insatiable curiosity after whatever was connected with them, were his ruling passions. So strongly indeed did they operate, that he desired some books might be brought to him, on the evening before he died, when the excruciating pains of his disorder had a little abated. He was, however, unable to read himself, yet, still drank in knowledge at his ears, with his wonted eagerness' (ibid.).

[11] 'In the last century, Hobbes, whose chief writings were levelled against the religion of his country, was called, from the place of his residence, *The philosopher of Malmesbury*. The life of Mr. BEWLEY was devoted to laborious researches. . . . With how much more truth and propriety has such a writer, and such a man, been distinguished in Norfolk by the respectable title of THE PHILOSOPHER OF MASSINGHAM!' (ibid.).

[12] i.e. to Charles Burney's in-laws, the family of Dr William Rose at Chiswick, and that of Ralph Griffiths at Turnham Green. See CB to Charles Burney, 6 Sept. 1783, n. 1.

To Thomas Twining

[St Martin's Street],
10–12 November 1783

AL (BL Add. MS 39929, fos. 324–6). Second leaf of second sheet missing.
Docketed by ?: (Dr Charles Burney to Rev. Thomas Twining)   *Also* L copy
extract (Osborn: 'Twining Letterbook No. 4', pp. 7–10).

Novr 10th 1783.

At length, dearest friend, I take my large sheet, & begin my excuses
for letting so kind, so afflicting, so comforting, & so admirable a
Letter,[1] remain near 3 weeks unanswered, at this time of the year,
when the Misses are far off, & it must seem as if I had nothing else to
do than gratify my heart in the way I liked best.—It is so seldom that
I am not ashamed of running you so soon in debt, that perhaps I
ought to make a merit of my forbearance; but you shall have my short
hist^y, for the ease of my Conscience. You were so kind to give me leave
to send you a Gobb or two;[2] and though several have been ready, as I
thought, for some time, yet It seemed expedient to overhaul them
first—& upon a revisal of what my daughter Susan had transcribed
from my very foul Copy, when I was not within reach to explain
darknesses & difficulties, I found so much to fill up, and so much old
ground to go over again in sea[r]ch of what I had been long trying to
forget, that I have not been able to accomplish my task till this very
night. The Copy I now send, amounting to near a 100 Pages finishes
Italy wch the last Parcellina had left imperfect, by breaking off in
the middle of the Neapolitan School, art. Venosa. You are now to be
bothered wth the Lombard, Bolognese & Florentine Schools, up to the
year 1600—wth Germany, France, & Spain, to the same Period.[3]

Even *you* can hardly imagine the versatility necessary to fly from
one Kingdom, Language, Style & Century to another. What little I
have done lately has been to poke out & pore over English Fogrums of
the last Century, wch has driven every Idea out of my head ab^t the
times & Countries included in the papers I now send, as if my brains
had been taken out & washed. You will see what Susan had left me to
do by the Crimes of *deeper die*. To furnish dates & authorities required
such different Books & papers from those I have lately been dirtying
my fingers that I dreaded the task I had to perform, wch turned out

---

[1] Twining's letter of 22 Oct. 1783 (BL Add. MS 39929, fos. 320–3).
[2] See CB to Twining, 6 Sept. 1783, n. 47.
[3] i.e. the completion of the second chapter, together with the third, fourth, and fifth chapters
of the third volume of *Hist. Mus.* (iii. 217–99; Mercer, ii. 177–241).

quite as tiresome and tedious as I expected.—So much for Gobbs—now to other Matters—

The melancholy acc^t you gave of your own health in the 1st page of your letter afflicted me most sincerely[4]—I have never recovered my spirits since the fatal Scene I was in here last Sept^r—& everything seems to lead to it, when I have a moments time for reflexion. I used to laugh at low Spirits & thought it impossible I sh^d ever indulge them; but alas! if I did not keep off foul fiends by forcing myself & by being forced into employm^t I sh^d sink under them. To see how easily the thread of life is snapped! to feel infirmities dayly encreasing—the time of Life—Constitution—& a thousand gloomy Ideas crowd incessantly into my mind and devour me![5]—I felt as you have kindly said you felt—that though not absolutely a Lett^r in debt, yet I dayly accused myself of not writing to enquire what, where, & how?[6]—But I had not power or spirits to do the very thing I most wished & thought most necessary.

Wed^y [12 November]

I hope to God you continue recovering your health, strength and Spirits. Your poor shin too![7] how much more that accident makes me hate Figs than ever! I have *always* hated them, & hardly ever c^d be brought to taste them till I was at Florence, where there is a small kind of Green Fig that is much more sightly & tastely than our *soft Soap*, to wch you admirably compare their appearance.

When I was at Chesington, I worked as much as affliction w^d let me at the origin of the musical Drama in Italy, & had got to ab^t the middle of the last Cent^y—when I returned to London I made a thorough muster of all my material for Engl. Mus. during the last Cent^y, w^{ch}, except a few compositions for the Church by Pelham Humphrey,

---

[4] Twining had written (22 Oct.) of repeated 'fits' of fever that had 'attacked' him since early Sept., which 'had such an effect upon me, that I never was so thoroughly pull'd down, weaken'd, unnerved, *abattu*, by any illness that I remember.'

[5] CB's gloom was not alleviated by Samuel Johnson, who, mourning the death of Anna Williams, wrote in sombre tones to CB on 20 Sept.: 'You and I have lost our Friends ...' (Comyn; Johnson *Letters*, iii. 70).

[6] Twining had written (22 Oct.): 'It is true, I was not in your debt—but *your* silence being longer than usual, I began to be restless—to wonder what was the matter—&, at last, to fear that you were ill;—with these apprehensions I *felt* in your *debt*—I felt that I *ought* to say—Well —what?—how?—where are you?—what is it?'

[7] Twining (22 Oct.) ended the account of his fever fits and slow recovery: 'There's my historiette—except a terrible broken shin which I *procured* by being fool enough to stand upon a tottering stool to gather a fig for my lady Mother.—(I hope you hate figs as I do—else—don't tell me—for it may *make* a *coolness* between us, in spite of our sympathy in other matters.—I can *make* as good a fig as ever was eat, with a little soft soap, red wine, & sugar, & a bit of cabbage-leaf to tie it up in.)'

Wise, & Blow,[8] are from Orlando Gibbons to Purcell,[9] unmeaning, dull, & despicable. Do you know much ab^t 'em?—The Knight has been very pompous & minute in his Hist^y of men who have done nothing[10]—now I sh^d like to speak of them & their Works published by Playford 1653[11] in the following Summary way:

> The Base of *Laniere*[12]
> Is too frequently queer,
> And the Treble he gives
> Too like Recitatives.
> Of the dull Doctor *Wilson*[13]
> Our ears get their fill soon;
> His Passages old
> Stuff'em up like a cold.
>   The renown'd Harry *Lawes*[14]
> You will find has his flaws,
> For his Treble's Psalmodic
> & Base immethodic.
> While *William*'s too rude
> To be patiently chew'd;

[8] Pelham Humfrey (1647–74), Michael Wise (*c.*1647–87), and John Blow (1649–1708), were contemporaries, and at the Restoration became choristers in the Chapel Royal under Henry Cooke (*c.*1615–72), who 'had the merit, or at least good fortune, to be the master of three boys among the children of the chapel, who gave very early testimonies of their genius and progress in composition. These were Pelham Humphrey, John Blow, and Michael Wise, who, even while they were choristers in the chapel, produced verse-anthems far superior in melody and design to any that our church could boast anterior to Purcell.' See *Hist. Mus.* iii. 444–57; Mercer, ii. 349–59; *DNB*; *New Grove*.

[9] Orlando Gibbons (1583–1625) and Henry Purcell (1659–95): that is, between 'the best English composer for the Church, during the reign of James I' and Purcell, 'who is as much the pride of an Englishman in Music, as Shakspeare in productions for the stage, Milton in epic poetry, Lock in metaphysics, or Sir Isaac Newton in philosophy and mathematics' (*Hist. Mus.* iii. 328, 485; Mercer, ii. 264, 380).

[10] See Sir John Hawkins, *A General History of the Science and Practice of Music* (1776), vols. iii and iv *passim*.

[11] CB himself footnoted this allusion: '*Musical Ayres and Dialogues*', referring to *Select Musicall Ayres and Dialogues, in Three Bookes*, published in 1653 by John Playford (1623–86). CB's copy of this collection is listed in *Cat. Mus. Lib.*, lot 27. Of this publication CB wrote scathingly: 'the whole collection does not contain one ayre which now seems worth engraving, either as a specimen of individual genius, or national taste' (*Hist. Mus.* iii. 417; Mercer, ii. 329).

[12] Nicholas Lanier (1588–1666), English composer, lutenist, and painter, Master of the King's Musick to Charles I and II (*DNB*; *New Grove*). See *Hist. Mus.* iii. 346–7; Mercer, ii. 277–8.

[13] John Wilson (1595–1674), D.Mus. (1645) and 'Musick Professor' at Oxford (1656–61), lutenist, singer, and composer (*DNB*; *New Grove*). See also *Hist. Mus.* iii. 3[9]9–401; Mercer, ii. 314–16.

[14] Henry Lawes (1596–1662), English composer who wrote the music for Milton's *Comus* (*DNB*; *New Grove*). 'All the melodies of Henry Lawes remind us of *recitative* or *psalmody*, . . . As to his knowledge and resources in counterpoint, I am certain that they were neither great nor profound' (see *Hist. Mus.* iii. 393–[9]8; Mercer, ii. 310–14).

But since knock'd on the head
There's no more to be said.[15]
  Billy *Webb*[16] is a Bumkin
Insipid as Pumkin.
I own I am loth
To call *Colman*[17] a Goth;
But you'll see by his paces
He knew not the Graces.
And yet master *Ned*
In his heels has more lead.[18]
  With Jeremy *Savill*[19]
E'er far I w^d travel,
I'd freely submit
To have my Nose slit.
  Then for *Child*, & for *Rogers*[20]
Two fumble-fist Codgers,
They're only prolific
In Strains soporific,
Which, Sleep to procure,
Are than opiates more sure.
  As to *Jenkins*,[21] he seems
But a dreamer of dreams;
And the Scrapers sh^d fly all
From Kit *Simpson*'s[22] Viol,

[15] CB here appended a footnote: 'Wm Lawes was killed at the Siege of Chester 1645.' William Lawes (1602–45), younger brother of Henry, composer, served in the Royalist army in the Civil War (*DNB*; *New Grove*). See also *Hist. Mus.* iii 391–3; Mercer, ii. 309–10.

[16] William Webb (*c.*1600-after 1656), English singer and lutenist, a Gentleman of the Chapel Royal, and (in 1637) a wait of the City of London (*MGG*; *New Grove*).

[17] Charles Coleman (*c.*1605–64), Mus.D. (1651), violist and composer, was a chamber musician to Charles I, and after the Restoration, composer to Charles II (*New Grove*; *DNB*).

[18] CB footnotes here: 'Edward Colman, the Son of Dr Chas Colman.' Edward Coleman (*c.*1633–1669), singer, lutenist, violist, and composer, appointed one of the Gentlemen of the Chapel Royal at the Restoration (*MGG*; *New Grove*; *DNB*).

[19] Jeremy Savile (*fl.* 1651–65), English composer of songs, of whom little is now known (*New Grove*).

[20] CB here drops a footnote: 'Both *brother Doctors*'. William Child (1606–97), D.Mus. (1663), organist and composer chiefly of church music; and Benjamin Rogers (1614–98), D.Mus. (1669), organist and composer (*DNB*; *New Grove*). 'Rogers and Child were too near each other to differ much in the style of their Church Music; and, indeed, they trod on the heels of our own times too much, for their modulation to have that solemn, and seemingly new, effect, on our ears, which the productions of the sixteenth century now afford' (see *Hist. Mus.* iii. 363–4, 461–3; Mercer, ii. 289–90, 362–4).

[21] John Jenkins (1592–1678), performer on the lute and viol, and 'voluminous composer of *Fancies* for viols, which were in great esteem during this rude state of instrumental Music' (*Hist. Mus.* iii. 408–14; Mercer, ii. 321–6; *DNB*; *New Grove*).

[22] Christopher Simpson, or Sympson (*c.*1605–69), English composer, theorist, and viol player (*DNB*; *New Grove*; *Hist. Mus.* iii. 421–2; Mercer, ii. 332–3). CB punningly alludes to

And ev'ry *Division*
Regard with derision.
   Coperario's a fop
Whose Ears I c^d crop,
For forging a name
And bringing to shame
Two Countries at once,
Yet *still* be a Dunce.[23]
   The bold blade *Captain Cook*,
Who his King near forsook,
And when all was despair
Kept his dread *Nom de Guerre*,[24]
Only fit seems through Life
For a Drum or a Fife:
The *Canons* he fir'd
'Twas Mars that inspir'd;
A God who Apollo
Could always beat hollow.—
Yet, when Charles was restor'd,
.Cook as Sovereign Lord
Was anointed the King
Of the Pipe and the String. — —

— — And there's 'a Complete list of all the running horses, & colours of the riders' on our Musical course; where the *course Music* w^d make any one *start*, go off *at scores*, and *run* at such a *rate* as to *distance* Pegasus himself[25] — — But, such rubbish apart—do tell me, dear Friend—are you much acquainted wth Purcell?[26] If you are not, for heaven's

Simpson's *The Division-Violist: or an Introduction to the Playing upon a Ground: Divided into Two Parts* (1659), of which CB's copy is listed in *Cat. Mus. Lib.*, lot 916.

[23] CB appends a footnote here for Twining's benefit: 'His name was *Cooper*, but having been in Italy, changed it to *Coperario*.' John Cooper, called 'Coprario' (*c.*1575–1626), English viol player, lutenist, teacher, and composer, had adopted the pseudonym 'Coprario' by 1603. Although details of his Italian sojourn are wanting, he became on his return the principal promoter of fantasias for viols which enjoyed a vogue in England during the seventeenth century (*DNB*; *New Grove*).

[24] Henry Cooke (*c.*1615–72), English bass singer, choir trainer, and composer, fought for the Royalists in the Civil War, rising to the rank of Captain. CB's footnote in the MS reads: 'Cook was originally a Musicia[n]; but having nothing to do in that Capacity, during the rebellion, he obtained a Captain's Commission in the Kings Army; and never parted with the Military title.' See *DNB*; *New Grove*; *Hist. Mus.* iii. 443–4; Mercer, ii. 349.

[25] CB's manifest familiarity with horse-racing is not remarkable in view of his early friendship with Fulke Greville, and later acquaintance in the 1750s with Lord Orford in Norfolk.

[26] Twining replied, 3 Feb. 1784 (BL Add. MS 39929, fos. 327–31ᵛ): 'Yes,—I am well acquainted with him [Henry Purcell], if one can be *well* acquainted with him without an *extensive* knowledge of his works.'

sake! get every note you possibly can of his, *curled* or *uncurled*[27]—why 'tis another Haydn. In the midst of barbarians, in savage times, before an opera, an opera singer, or the works of Corelli had been heard on the Island, to have such resources of force and expression, is more wonderful than that Haydn, who with his own property has incorporated the best of all others during the present century, sh^d be so perfect, so bewitching & Charming!!!—I shall speak of Purcell from an *actual survey*, or *review* of all his works, consisting, 1st of his *Church Music*, or Anthems & Services, printed by Boyce,[28] 10 or 12—as many more in the MS. Collection made by Dr Tudway for Ld Harley, Brit. Mus.[29]—others printed by Walsh in different Collections[30]—& still more preserved in MS. at Ch. Ch. Oxford,[31] wch I have now, on *loan*, here—& 2 or 3 in my own Collection,[32] wch I have seen no where Else—these, with his Printed *Te Deum*,[33] form a large body of Church Music, of a more expressive & varied kind than I have ever seen of

[27] By '*curled*', CB means Purcell's adherence in some compositions to 'the elaborate and learned style of . . . Tallis, Bird, and Gibbons, in which . . . the several parts are constantly moving in fugue, imitation, or plain counterpoint'; and by '*uncurled*', CB means Purcell's 'giving way to feeling and imagination' by adopting in other compositions 'the new and more expressive style of which he was himself one of the principal inventors' (*Hist. Mus.* iii. 479; Mercer, ii. 383).

[28] William Boyce, ed., *Cathedral Music: being a Collection in Score of the Most Valuable and Useful Compositions for that Service, by the Several English Masters of the last Two Hundred Years* (3 vols., 1760–73). For a list of Purcell's works included in this collection, see F. B. Zimmerman, *Henry Purcell, 1659–1695: an Analytical Catalogue of His Music* (1963), pp. 516–17. CB subscribed to Boyce's *Cathedral Music*, and his set fetched 7 guineas in 1814 (*Cat. Mus. Lib.*, lot 181).

[29] 'A Collection of the most celebrated Services and Anthems used in the Church of England from the Reformation to the Restauration of K. Charles II . . .', compiled in 6 vols. (1715–20) by Thomas Tudway (*c.*1650–1726), Mus.D. (1705), Professor of Music at Cambridge (1705), for Edward Harley (1689–1741), 2nd Earl of Oxford (1724), collector, and friend of Pope and Swift (*DNB*; *New Grove*). The volumes are now BL Harley MSS 7337–42. For the Anthems and Services of Purcell transcribed by Tudway, see A. Hughes-Hughes, *Catalogue of Manuscript Music in the British Museum* (1906–9), i. 53–62, 405–8; Zimmerman, *Purcell Catalogue*, pp. 454–5. CB compiled a thematic catalogue of the Tudway volumes with critical notes (BL Add. MSS 11587, fos. 37^v ff.; 11589, fos. 2–19). This work he probably accomplished when he was granted permission to borrow the Tudway collection from the British Museum ('Minutes of the Standing Committee', 23 Dec. 1785, p. 1919).

[30] John Walsh the elder (*c.*1665–1736), began his celebrated music publishing business in 1695 at about the age of 30 (*MGG*; *New Grove*). He published Purcell's *Te Deum* (see n. 33), and other Purcell sacred music in *Musica Sacra* (1724), and *Harmonia Sacra or Select Anthems in Score* (*c.*1730). CB's copy of this last-named collection is listed in *Cat. Mus. Lib.*, lot 214. See Zimmerman, *Purcell Catalogue*, pp. 508, 510; W. C. Smith and C. Humphries, *A Bibliography of the Musical Works Published by the Firm of John Walsh during the Years 1721–1766* (1968), pp. 116, 279.

[31] CB wrote, '. . . in a manuscript bequeathed to Christ-church College, Oxon. by Dr. Aldrich, there are two motets and a *Gloria Patri* for four and five voices, in Latin, with seven psalms and hymns for three and four voices, by our fertile and diligent composer' (*Hist. Mus.* iii. 483 (duplicate pagination); Mercer, ii. 386). CB refers to Christ Church Library, Music MS 628.

[32] CB refers to a collection of Anthems, '*in score*, MS.', sold as *Cat. Mus. Lib.*, lot 223. The Anthems are not individually identified.

[33] *Te Deum & Jubilate, for Voices and Instruments, made for St Caecilia's Day, 1694*, first 'printed by J. Heptinstall, for the Author's Widow, . . . 1697'. Purcell's *Te Deum* in D major (Z. 232) was subsequently reissued and republished frequently under the Walsh imprint (W. C. Smith, *A Biblio-*

any Composer, of any Country. Palestrina was Grave, Sweet, & sublime in his way; but it was all in *one* way. Carissimi & Stradella,[34]
more constantly elegant & polished than Purcell; but with less feeling
& variety. Handel more grand, masterly, full, & flowing; but by no
means so original, so impassioned, so superior to Art & study, yet at
times discovering effects of the deepest labour & Meditation. Purc[e]ll's
Expression of English words must I think frequently make Englishmen
feel what Handel with all his Harmonical resources c^d never arrive at.
At least he frequently *shivers* me: makes my hair creep, & gives me
sensations beyond those of the utmost elegance & refinement.—Now
for his *Dramatic Music*[35]—Orpheus Britannicus 2 vol^s Folio.[36]—12
Overtures, Entries or *symphonies*, with sets of Tunes in 4P^ts called *Musicks*[37]
made expressly for new & revived Plays during the time that he &
Dryden worked for the Theatre—Including his Engl. operas, of King
Arthur, Dioclesian, Bonduca[38] &c. These, considering he had never
heard or seen an Italian or French opera, are wonderful Productions,
if compared with what *had* been done by others in our own Country:[39]
the Effects of various kinds, without much *Instrumental* Assistance, w^ch
he knew not how to draw, are of such a kind as must have enchanted

graphy of ... *John Walsh* ... *1695–1720* (1948), nos. 108, 248, 276, 595; W. C. Smith and C.
Humphries, *A Bibliography of ... John Walsh ... 1721–1766* (1968), pp. 280–1). CB's copy of one
of the Walsh editions is *Cat. Mus. Lib.*, lot 213. He gives a full account in *Hist. Mus.* iii. 483–7
(duplicate pagination); Mercer, ii. 386–8.
[34] Giacomo Carissimi (1605–74), Italian composer, *maestro di cappella* at Sant' Apollinare,
Rome, noted for his contributions to the development of the chamber cantata and oratorio (*New
Grove*).
Alessandro Stradella (1644–82), Italian singer, violinist, and composer (*New Grove*). 'His
compositions ... seem superior to any that were produced in the last century, except by Carissimi'
... 'Purcell manifestly formed his style on the productions of Carissimi and Stradella, particularly in his recitative and secular songs' (see *Hist. Mus.* iv. 100–10, 141–51; Mercer, ii. 574–81,
607–15).
[35] For a study of Purcell's music for the stage, see R. E. Moore, *Henry Purcell and the Restoration
Theatre* (1961).
[36] *Orpheus Britannicus. A Collection of All the Choicest Songs for One, Two, and Three Voices*, first
published in 2 books, 1698 and 1702. CB's set is listed in *Cat. Mus. Lib.*, lot 36. For his account of
these volumes which 'treasured up the songs from which the natives of this island received their
first great delight and impression from the vocal Music of a *single voice*', see *Hist. Mus.* iii.
489–500; Mercer, ii. 390–7.
[37] *A Collection of Ayres, compos'd for the Theatre, and upon other Occasions* ... (1697), comprising
'the chief part of his instrumental Music for the playhouse' (see *Hist. Mus.* iii. 487–8; Mercer, ii.
388–9). CB's set of the four parts is *Cat. Mus. Lib.*, lot 795. CB miscounts slightly: there are in
fact thirteen 'Musicks' in the collection.
[38] *King Arthur; or, The British Worthy*, text by John Dryden (1631–1700), first performed in
1691; *The Prophetess; or, The History of Dioclesian*, staged in 1690 to a text adapted by Thomas
Betterton (1635–1710) from the play by John Fletcher (1579–1625) and Philip Massinger
(1583–1640); *Bonduca; or, The British Heroine*, brought out in 1695, based on the play by Francis
Beaumont (1584–1616) and John Fletcher, the adaptation published by George Powell (*c.*1658–
1714). See *The London Stage*, i. i. 395, 382, 452–3; E. W. White, 'Early Theatrical Performances of
Purcell's Operas', *Theatre Notebook*, xiii (1958–9), 43–65; Moore, *Purcell*, chs. 3, 5.
[39] For a survey of early opera in Britain, see E. J. Dent, *Foundations of English Opera* (Cambridge, 1928).

lovers of Music, his Cotemporaries, & rendered him the National Idol—As to his *Chamber Music*,[40] Odes on St Cecilias Day, wth many of other kinds; single songs, Duets, CATCHES, and Sonatas, altogether, very numerous, considering his short Life, as he died at 37, were sufficient in that single Species of Composition to entitle him to the first Place among the Musicians of this Country.—And here, for the present, ends my Rhapsody on PURCELL.[41]

I pack up in the Parcellina, a new set of Em: Bach's Pieces[42]—chiefly Rondeaus—with many new *kicks*, & *detours*—But he seems reduced to *recherche* & caprice in order to be new—& to say the truth, his Eleve Haydn[43] seems to have given him the *go by*, on his own ground. However, the great Man frequently appears, & there are charm^g things par-ci par-là in this collection.

While I think of it, let me ask you whether I did or did not a good while ago send you a course translation of Salvator Rosa's course verses on Cathedral singing?[44]—If I did, & the Letter wch contained them is in being, I sh^d be obliged to you for them in the next *paquet*; for I am unable to find 'em, & have no stomach for a 2^d translation.

But what say you, my Friend, to the *Ballons*? Heres Penneck[45] of the Museum just come from Paris, who on the faith of a Clergyman protests that he last week saw one mount 500 feet in the Champs de Mars, with two Gentlemen, one a Chevalier de St Louis, in the Pockets; thus: and these Gentlemen, who were succeeded by others, had the means of renovating the buoyant power of the *Gaz*, from time to time, by the Smoke of Straw,[46] wch they were furnished with, and burned at the bottom of the Ballon. ----------

---

[40] For CB's discussion of Purcell's chamber music, see *Hist. Mus.* iii. 489–503; Mercer, ii. 390–400.

[41] Twining wrote (3 Feb. 1784): 'Your "Rhapsody on Purcell," is no Rhapsody; for woe to the man who can praise him coolly. Every word you have said is delightful to me; & I prophecy that no part of your work will afford a more precious morsel—or be a more relishing *gob*—than that which will contain your account of this interesting man, & YOUR observations upon his works.'

[42] Doubtless C. P. E. Bach's fourth collection of keyboard pieces, published at Leipzig in 1783 under the title *Clavier-Sonaten und Freye Fantasien nebst einigen Rondos fürs Fortepiano für Kenner und Liebhaber, . . . Vierte Sammlung* (Wq. 58). See A. Wotquenne, *Thematisches Verzeichnis der Werke von Carl Philipp Emanuel Bach (1714–1788)* (Leipzig, 1905), pp. 14–15.

[43] 'If Haydn ever looked up to any great master as a model, it seems to have been C.P.Em. Bach' (see *Hist. Mus.* iv. 596, 600; Mercer, ii. 955, 958).

[44] Salvator Rosa (1615–73), Italian painter, poet, and musician (*New Grove*), whose satire on church music is translated by CB and included in *Hist. Mus.* iii. 148; Mercer, ii. 126. CB was mistaken in thinking Rosa a composer (see F. Walker, 'Salvator Rosa and Music', *Monthly Musical Record*, lxxix (1949), 199–205; lxxx (1950), 13–16, 32–6).

[45] The Revd Richard Penneck (*c.*1728–1803), of Trinity College, Cambridge, MA (1753), FRS (1768), Chaplain in the Navy (1756) and of Trinity College (1757–1802), was Keeper of the Reading Room at the British Museum (Venn; *GM* lxxiii (1803)^1, 94, 189–90).

[46] CB's recollection of Penneck's story appears here as a slightly garbled account of the events

394

An acc[t] of the principal experiments that have been made at Paris by M. Mongolfier[47] & others, was read on Thursday last at the Royal Society, in a Letter from the old Philosopher & Politician D[r] Franklin— It was some times so comical & jocose as to make the whole learned body laugh more perhaps than Philosophers ought to laugh.[48] The chief Facts, however which you have seen related in the news Papers,[49] are seriously confirmed. There is a Philosophical French Duke here at present, The Duc de Chaulnes, who has been in Egypt to visit the Pyramids, & has printed a memoire,[50] presented to the Fr. Academy on a curious piece of antiquity found in a subterraneous building under one of them—a Memoire on Chinese Colours,[51] w[ch] his Grace being a great Chymist has discovered the art of making—He has been 2 or 3 times at my house to see the Hotel du grand Newton—I have returned his Visits; & the day before yesterday he shewed me a very curious book of Chinese Drawings,[52] chiefly of Imperial buildings & Palaces—Copied at Paris with his *own Colours*, from the originals in the Possession of M. Bertin[53] of Paris—who being minister of state

in Paris on Sunday 19 Oct. 1783. On that day, in the Réveillon gardens, rue de Montreuil, faubourg Saint-Antoine, the world's first aeronaut, Jean-François Pilatre de Rozier (1754–85), made four captive ascents in a hot-air balloon. After two solo ascents, he took one Giroud de Villette as a passenger, and on the fourth ascent, François-Laurent (1742–1809), marquis d'Arlandes de Salton, who was to accompany Pilatre de Rozier on 21 Nov. on the first manned balloon flight. See *Journal de Paris*, 22 Oct. 1783, pp. 1216–17; *Public Advertiser*, 8 Nov. 1783; B. Faujas de Saint-Fond, *Description des expériences de la machine aérostatique de MM. de Montgolfier* (1783–4), i. 268–80; T. Cavallo, *The History and Practice of Aerostation* (1785), pp. 77–81; L. T. C. Rolt, *The Aeronauts: a History of Ballooning, 1783–1903* (1966), pp. 44–5.

[47] The brothers Joseph-Michel (1740–1810) and Jacques-Étienne (1745–99) Montgolfier, ennobled in Dec. 1783 to 'de Montgolfier', paper-makers and inventors of the hot-air balloon (*montgolfière*) had successfully launched their first experimental balloon from their native town of Annonay on 5 June 1783 (Michaud; *DSB*; L. Rostaing, *La famille de Montgolfier, ses alliances, ses descendants*, Lyons, 1910).

[48] Benjamin Franklin to Sir Joseph Banks, dated Passy, 8 Oct. 1783 (Royal Society of London: Letters & Papers, VIII. 37). The comedy would have been provided by Franklin's description of the experiment at Versailles on 19 Sept., when in the presence of the King and Royal Family, a *montgolfière* took flight carrying a basket containing a live sheep, a duck, and a cock. All three animals survived the flight (Faujas de Saint-Fond, *Description*, i. 36–48; W. R. Dawson, ed., *The Banks Letters* (1958), p. 346).

[49] See, for example, *London Chronicle*, liv (1783), 246, 256, 298, 310, 316, 394, 418, 437.

[50] *Mémoire sur la véritable entrée du monument égyptien, qui se trouve à quatre lieues du Caire, auprès de Saccara, & qui a été consacré par la superstition à la sépulture des animaux adorés pendant leur vie* ... (1777); 2nd edn. (1783). M. de Chaulnes had travelled to Egypt in 1765 (*DBF*).

[51] M. de Chaulnes had sent his 'memoire sur les couleurs des chinois' for CB's perusal with a covering note dated 20 Oct. [1783] (Osborn). Although this paper is listed among 'les Mémoires que l'Académie a approuvés en 1781, & qu'elle a destinés à être imprimés dans le Recueil des Ouvrages qui lui sont présentés', no printed version has been found (see *Histoire de l'Académie royale des sciences. Année M.DCCLXXXI* (1784), p. 52).

[52] Not traced. The account which follows is riddled with error (see nn. 53, 54).

[53] Henri-Léonard-Jean-Baptiste Bertin (1720–92), French statesman, who held besides other posts that of Contrôleur Général des Finances (1759–63), was Ministre et Secrétaire d'État to Louis XV and Louis XVI from 1764 until his retirement in 1780. He was an agricultural

some years ago, had prevailed on 6 or 8 young men Natives of China
to come into France, to learn European Arts—They arrived just 3
Days after his dismission from his Office—however the Fr. King took
them under his Protection, & they remained in France 5 years—Two
of these[54] being excellent draftsmen, having regularly learned perspective, in gratitude to their Patron M. Bertin, have sent him 7 or
8000 original drawings, made with the advantage of truth & perspective wch no designs hitherto brought from that Country have
had—the Book of architectural drawings made here in the Colours of
M. de Chaulnes, is an exact Fac-simile of one sent into Europe by the
2 young men above mentioned—I wish you c^d see the Book, it is
extremely beautiful, & gave me more pleasure than anything of the
kind I ever saw. The Taste and ornaments of the Chinese buildings is,
I think, *here*, superiour to every other that I have seen, except Grecian
—& I dare say very suitable to the Climate. Well, but while I was
looking at these, a Letter was brought to the Duc from a celebrated
Physicien, with a printed proposal for a subscription of 400 Louis d'ors,
entered into by a 100 Gent^n a[t] 4 G^s each, for a larger Ballon than has
hitherto been exhibited[55]—the Cover contained besides the Printed

reformer, collector, and patron to French missionaries, whose work in the Far East fell within
the compass of his ministerial duties (Michaud; *DBF*; J. Silvestre de Sacy, *Henri Bertin dans le
sillage de la Chine (1720–1792)* (1970)). Passionately interested in things Chinese, Bertin instigated
and fostered the publication of the important series *Mémoires concernant l'histoire, les sciences, les arts,
les mœurs, les usages, &c. des Chinois: par les missionaires de Pekin*, 16 vols. (1776–1814). See also H.
Cordier, *Bibliotheca Sinica* (2nd edn., Paris, 1904–24), cols. 64–5, 1041–5; F.-M. Grimm, *Correspondance littéraire*, ed. M. Tourneux (1877–82), xiv. 286–8.
[54] Louis (Aloysius) Kao Jen (1732–after 1795) and Étienne Yang Tche-teh (1733–*c*.1798),
Chinese Jesuit priests. Together with one Louis Tcheng (who did not remain to take orders),
Kao and Yang were sent by the French Jesuit missionaries at Peking in 1751 to France to study
for the priesthood. After their ordination in 1763, Kao and Yang applied to Bertin for leave to
return to China in Jan. 1764. The Minister proposed that they should remain an extra year in
France to undergo an intensive course of study in order to equip the two Chinese priests in
various Western arts and crafts. In Feb. 1765, Kao and Yang finally sailed for China with gifts
for the Emperor, a royal pension of 1200 livres per annum, and formidable lists of questions
about China, which, Bertin hoped, they would be able to answer from personal observation. For
the success of this enterprise, which bore fruit in the *Mémoires concernant les Chinois*, largely
through the active cooperation of the entire French Jesuit mission in Peking, see H. Cordier, 'Les
Correspondants de Bertin', *T'oung Pao*, 2e sér., xiv (1913), 227–57, 465–72, 497–536; xv (1914),
307–38; xvi (1915), 27–60, 229–35; xviii (1917), 295–379; xxi (1922), 394–8; J. Dehergne, SJ,
'Voyageurs Chinois venus à Paris . . .', *Monumenta Serica*, xxiii (1964), 372–97; Silvestre de Sacy,
Bertin, ch. 14. For Kao and Yang, see H. Cordier, 'Les Chinois de Turgot', in *Florilegium . . .
Melchior de Vogüé* (1909), pp. 151–8; J. Dehergne, SJ, *Répertoire des Jésuites de Chine de 1552 à 1800*
(Rome and Paris, 1973), pp. 133–4, 301.
[55] The subscription was launched by the Robert brothers, Paris artisans, who helped construct the first manned hydrogen balloon, designed by the physicist and aeronaut, Jacques-
Alexandre-César Charles (1746–1823). Charles and the elder Robert were to ascend in their
balloon from the gardens of the Tuileries on 1 Dec. 1783 (*DSB*; Rolt, *Aeronauts*, pp. 49–54). For
the terms of the subscription, see *Journal de Paris*, 19 Nov. 1783: 'Les articles principaux por-
toient que le nombre de ces Souscripteurs seroit fixé à cent; que chacun d'eux payeroit quatre
louis . . .'.

396

Paper 3 sheets of writing *par rapport des Experiences Phy[s]iques*. But before half this was read a Gent[56] was announced of whom, if one may judge by the cordiality of the *Embrassades*, the Duc is very much attached—& who sh[d] this be but the Collegue of M. de Mongolfier in all his Areostatical discoveries & experiments?—He is a lively youngish man—& speaks English tolerably well—is come here to pass the winter, and in all probability will push on to unknown Regions, & make more Celestial discoveries than Cook has terrestrial.—Where will all this End?—set your imagination to work—let me know what are your chief hopes & expectations from this very great discovery & you shall be gratified in all that is reasonable. Barring accidents if no Necks are broken, or lives lost in early experiments a *Diligence* to the moon will ere long be established—I know well enough that your timid & sober Philosophers will tell you that such are the properties of Air that respiration cannot be performed, beyond a certain height in our atmosphere—but that's a difficulty w[ch] will be easily obviated—have we not Means of subsisting *under* Water in diving Bells, by supplying fresh air to those who are in them? Lord! Sir, we shall soon have a *Moon* Gazette instead of that published at Noon—How pretty it w[d] be to be carried up to heaven, body and Soul, without the pain of dying!—

But, en attendant, let me tell you that our dear Pacchierotti is come back, (entre nous, par une *Trame* de ma façon) Though such is the distracted state of Opera Governm[t], it is very doubtful whether any Theatrical use will be made during the whole winter of his Talents[57]—but he is *here*—& I shall now & then hear him—I have made him very fond of a Cantata by Haydn, lately come from Vienna. 'Ah, come

---

[56] Not certainly identified. He may have been the adventurer, the 'learned Chevalier de Moret, a genius for distinguished discoveries', who, from Jan. 1784, announced the construction of an aerostatic machine in the form of a 'Chinese Temple'. This impostor's attempt to fly the Chinese Temple met with disaster in Aug. 1784. See V. Lunardi, *An Account of the First Aërial Voyage in England* (1784), pp. 14–15; J. E. Hodgson, *The History of Aeronautics in Great Britain* (1924), pp. 111–13; M. Dorothy George, *Catalogue of Political and Personal Satires Preserved in the Department of Prints and Drawings in the British Museum*, vol. vi (1938), pp. 165–6.

[57] 'Pacchierotti and Allegranti are both to stay two more Years at the Opera. The Former of course spends his Summer with his usual Patroness, Lady Mary Duncan' (*Public Advertiser*, 18 July 1783). The appointment of performers for the Opera season of 1783–4 was caught up in the Taylor-Gallini feud. In the *Public Advertiser*, 29 Sept., Gallini announced a cast-list for the season, naming Pacchierotti as First Man for the serious opera. This announcement was immediately discounted by the Taylor faction in the issue of 1 Oct., where they announced that 'A complete List of the Performers will be laid in due Time before the Public'. Subsequent negotiations between the warring parties had broken down, according to a further advertisement by Gallini, dated 4 Nov., first published in the *Public Advertiser*, 5 Nov., and in subsequent issues. Gallini wrote that 'the Business remains at present totally unsettled, and that I will very soon submit . . . a Plan for conducting Operas for the ensuing Season.' See also CB to Twining, 6 Sept. 1783, n. 51.

il core mi palpita'[58]—It is so much in his best style of singing that it seems *fatta apposta per lui*—I made him the other Day, in my *Spidery*, admire some fragments of Purcell's Recitativo such as the opening of Mad Bess[59]—of 'Ye twice ten hundred Deities',[60] &c—He said it was the kind of *Recitativo Cantante* of the old Masters that he had studied & chiefly formed himself upon.—

My son Cha[s] seems in high favour with *Parr*—they are in correspondence[61]—& Johnson has lately taken to him very much—Speaks of him to every body with uncommon warmth & energy, for him— invites him to call frequently on him to talk *Philology*—He is at present a little bewitched with the Study of Greek—did I ever whisper to you that he is Editor of the London Magazine? for w[ch] he has £100 a year[62]—My Fears are that these 2 pursuits will interfere with his zeal & attention to the school, which D[r] Rose talks of quitting—But this all *entre nous*—

Poor M[r] Burney my eldest daughter's Husband has been in a bad state of Health all the summer, & allarmed us all very much—bad digestion and frequent *defaillances*,[63] are his chief complaints—D[r] Warren whom he has been obliged frequently to Consult, says however, he can cure him.

I have not the honour of knowing M[rs] Lort—w[ch], if she's half as agreeable as Mrs Smythies, is a great Loss[64]—I saw the D[r65] last

[58] *Cantata per un Soprano con Accompagnamento* ..., published by Artaria in Vienna, 1783 (see Hoboken, vol. ii, pp. 204–5, 400–3), based on Celia's *scena* from Act II of Haydn's opera *La Fedeltà premiata* (1780). See H. C. Robbins Landon, *Haydn at Eszterháza, 1766–1790* (1978), pp. 439–45.

[59] Purcell's solo song *Bess of Bedlam* (or *Mad Bess*), 'From silent shades and the Elysian groves' (Z. 370), included in *Orpheus Britannicus*, vol. i, pp. 126–9, is described by CB in *Hist. Mus.* iii. 493; Mercer, ii. 393 as 'a song so celebrated, that it needs no panegyric'. See also Moore, *Purcell*, pp. 9–10.

[60] '"You twice ten hundred deities," opens with what seems to me the best piece of recitative in our language. The words are admirably expressed throughout this song, by modulation as well as melody' (*Hist. Mus.* iii. 492; Mercer, ii. 392). Ismeron the Conjurer's bass aria in the third act of the operatic adaptation (1695) of *The Indian Queen* by Dryden and Sir Robert Howard (1626–98), is included in *Orpheus Britannicus*, vol. i, pp. 25–8. See also Moore, *Purcell*, pp. 164–6.

[61] Parr's handwriting is notoriously illegible. Twining, in his reply of 3 Feb. 1784 wrote of Parr: 'I am glad your son & He are so good friends. But how does M[r] B. manage to *read* his letters?—his Greek especially, is absolutely undecypherable. This circumstance is really a considerable *drawback* upon the value of his correspondence. I have had scrawls from him which I have been a week in reading, without being able to read *all*. A dog might be taught to write better. If Parr had written the *hand-writing upon the wall*, Daniel might have guessed long enough to no purpose.' For Charles Burney's correspondence with Parr, see *Cat. Corr.*, pp. 242–96; and *The Works of Samuel Parr, LL.D.*, ed. J. Johnstone (1828), i. 532–8; vii. 385–418; viii. 265.

[62] See CB to Charles Burney, 12 Sept. [1783], n. 2. Charles Burney had obtained the editorship of the *London Magazine, Enlarged and Improved* on Parr's recommendation (R. S. Walker, 'Charles Burney's Theft of Books at Cambridge', *Transactions of the Cambridge Bibliographical Society*, iii (1962), 319).

[63] See *OED*, under 'defail' and 'defailance', meaning loss of vigour, weakness.

[64] Twining had written (22 Oct.): 'O—have you seen M[rs] *Lort*?—& how do you like her?— and do you know that She is *own* Sister to the M[rs] Smythies whom you saw, & fell in love with, at

Thursday at the R.S. just returned from a Tour on the banks of the Rhine from Dusseldorf to Coblentz—wth wch he seems to have been much amused. We have long been de bons amis. He lends me queer & out-of-the-way books—and laughs *pianiss°* like a Hyena with Fanny at Mrs Thrale's—Is the Dr Price[66] you fiddled with a Son of the late Mr Price of Herefordshire[67]—the great Friend of Wyndham, Stillingfleet & Smith?[68]—If he is, my Brother at Worcester knows him well—he is nephew to Ld Barrington[69]—I meet with People every Day who play & sing tolerably, nay *greatly*, without *feeling*. The executive part of music is so *mechanical*, that a great deal is done without soul or sentiment—It was but last winter that I discovered wth what precision many of my Scholars played the Harp^d by the mere assistance of the *Eye*, without the least use of the *Ear*.

Fordham?' Susannah Norfolk (*c.*1742–92), had recently married (May 1783) Dr Michael Lort (n. 65). Her younger sister, Jane Strange Norfolk (1743–1824) had married (1771) Francis Smythies (1742–98), of Headgate House, Colchester, Town Clerk and Recorder (1787–98) of Colchester, and younger brother of Twining's wife, Elizabeth, née Smythies (1739–96). See *DNB*, under 'Lort'; *GM* lxxxi (1811)[1], 526; R. H. R. Smythies, *Records of the Smythies Family* (1912), pp. 14, 18, 46, 48–9.

[65] The Revd Michael Lort (1725–90), DD (1780), FRS (1766), Regius Professor of Greek at Cambridge (1759–71), antiquary, bibliophile, and collector (*DNB*). Charlotte Burney thought him 'a droll quiz' (*ED* ii. 297), and Fanny found him 'comical and diverting' (*DL* i. 476). 'One has many Chances for Improvement and almost a Certainty of being amused by a Conversation with Mr Lort' (*Thraliana*, i. 381).

[66] Twining had written (22 Oct.): 'Our summer jaunt to Passenham was very pleasant. I met with the best Dilettante player on the Violoncello in Northamptonshire, that I ever heard: a Dr Price—a man as little like a Doctor of any kind as can be imagined: a young, lively clergyman, in his own hair & buck-skin breeches. He has learned of both Cervetto & Crosdill. I played Quartetts very comfortably with him: & yet—what is very extraordinary—the man does not appear to *feel* Music.—But I talk foolishly—why is it *extraordinary*?—nothing seems less extraordinary than a Musician with every requisite *but* feeling. Crosdill, to me, has absolutely *none*: nor Cramer. Their ears, as the Abbé Du Bos says, are at a great distance from their hearts.'

[67] Robert Price (d. 1761), of Foxley in the parish of Yazor, Herefordshire, was a keen amateur musician and artist. He married (1746) Sarah (d. 1759), eldest daughter of John Shute Barrington (1678–1734), 1st Viscount Barrington (1720). Sir Uvedale Price (1747–1829), CB's friend, and writer on 'the picturesque' was Robert Price's eldest son. Another son, Robert (*c.*1748–1823), was doubtless Twining's 'cellist. The younger Robert Price matriculated at Christ Church, Oxford, in 1765, took the DCL in 1782, was Chaplain-in-ordinary to the King, Canon of Salisbury (1785), and Prebendary of Durham (1795). See *DNB*, under 'Price, Sir Uvedale'; Foster; *GM* xxix (1759), 146; xxxi (1761), 538.

[68] William Windham (1717–61), of Felbrigg, Norfolk, Colonel, father of the statesman. Windham's tutor and lifelong friend was Benjamin Stillingfleet (1702–71), naturalist and dilettante, some of whose texts were set to music as oratorios by John Christopher Smith (1712–95), English organist and composer. For the close friendships that existed in this circle, formed in 1740 and called The Common Room at Geneva, see *DNB*; W. Coxe, *Literary Life and Select Works of Benjamin Stillingfleet* (1811); and *Anecdotes of George Frederick Handel, and John Christopher Smith* (1799).

[69] William Wildman Barrington (1717–93), 2nd Viscount Barrington (1734), statesman (*DNB*), whose sister, Sarah, had married Robert Price the elder (n. 67). Lord Barrington frequented the musical evenings at the Burneys. Fanny wrote of him: 'To *look* at this nobleman, you would swear he was a tradesman, and by no means superior to stand behind a counter' (*ED* ii. 124).

Ricciotti's Concertos[70] came into my head, when you mention[ed] those of Ricci—of wch I know nothing. Ricciotti's were the *last polish* of elaborate Music in Fugue & full Harmony.

I'll allow that Boccherini is more constantly serious than Haydn[71]— nay that he is always serious & Charming—but in Haydn's works, more serious Compositions in the true gran Gusto, may be selected, than Boccherini has ever produced—& then you have all his fun, fancy, extravagant if you will & Capricious, for Gigantic players, *di plus*—God bless 'em both, I say; but if I were forced to part with one of them—I sh^d not hesitate a moment in locking Haydn fast in my Arms, & only sending a sigh after the other.[72]

I am extremely glad that Merlin has doctored you[r] Violin satisfactorily[73]—The dog has just finished a small Piano forte, so loud, sweet, & beautiful, that I c^d sit & divert myself upon it without food for 24 hours—Ma—ma—the price is — — — £40!

What you say of high Notes is as true as it is punnish & Comical[74]—

My Accomp^{ts} to Haydn are not yet out, though engraved[75]—but

[70] In clearing up CB's confusion in identifying Francesco Pasquale Ricci with Carlo Ricciotti, Twining had written (22 Oct.) a brief appreciation of the *Concerti armonici*, to which CB here makes reply. Twining wrote: 'The Ripienos are often obligati—at least, have their *own* melody— so that the composition is in 6 parts. The effect, in *some* movements, is very fine: there is a fullness & glow of harmony, without confusion, & with very beautiful melody in the principal parts.' See also CB to Twining, 6 Sept. 1783, nn. 33, 34.

[71] Twining had written on the relative merits of Haydn and Boccherini in his letter of 22 Oct.: 'I am so far from meaning to disparage Haydn, that were I obliged to give up him, or Boccherini, I do believe I shou'd turn to Haydn in preference. His wonderful variety, & *intarissable* fancy w^d turn the scale.' See also CB to Twining, 6 Sept. 1783, nn. 16, 17.

[72] For studies of the relations between CB and Haydn, see Rosemary S. M. Hughes, 'Dr. Burney's Championship of Haydn', *Musical Quarterly*, xxvii (1941), 90–6; P. A. Scholes, 'Burney and Haydn', *Monthly Musical Record*, lxxi (1941), 155–7, 172–8; Grant, pp. 213–15. CB, always interested in the personal characteristics of musicians, carefully recorded two reports of Haydn in the mid-1780s: 'Clementi, who saw him in Hungary at Prince Esterhausi's says he is a little, brown complexioned Man, turned of 50—wears a wig—and when he hears any of his own Pieces performed that are capricious he laughs like a fool. ... The Mara says when any one praises him to his face, he runs away & hides himself. He is so modest & humble as to fear to quit the Prince of Esterhausi, lest he sh^d starve' (MS 'Materials Towards the History of German Music & Musicians', Osborn shelves c 100, p. 7).

[73] Twining had informed CB (22 Oct.), 'I am *quite* satisfied with Merlin's operations upon my Stainer. The tone is not quite so loud & piercing as before, but, en revanche, has gained a great deal of sweetness, & *some* breadth;—the *shape* of the tone is altered for the better,—and it is smoother, more oily, &, what is a great matter, far pleasanter to the player, than it was. I easily conceive tho', that the new neck wou'd have hurt a fiddle that had not tone to spare.'

[74] In his letter of 22 Oct., Twining had written of Haydn: 'His Quartetts spoil me for almost all other music of the kind. There are, in *them* too, some very fine, *serious* Cantabiles;—yet now & then in the midst of them, he takes a freak up to the top of the finger-board—& then, (to *my* ear, at least) the charm is dissolved—trick, caprice, & the difficulté vaincue, take place of expression & pathos.—It seems to me as if no Composer, or player cou'd be in earnest, in *altissimo*:—it is

not the $\left\{ \dfrac{\text{climb-at}}{\text{climate}} \right\}$ for it.'

[75] See CB to Twining, 6 Sept. 1783, n. 18.

though I wrote them in a very short time, without a Score, except the two p^{ts} of the Lessons to look at—I have left out bars, & blundered so much that some of the plates must be broken & newly engraved.

Did I tell you that Gallini's agents shewed me a Letter from Haydn, in wch he was in treaty to come over for the opera[76]—all is in such Confusion now that there remains no hope, for this Winter—but— who knows, when I have mounted my *Ballon*, but he may yet come?

Not a word have I said all this while in reply to your very kind and tempting invitation to Fordham.[77] Ah my Fr^d I had not Spirits for Enterprise—I was to have visited my Friend Mr Cox in Wiltshire—& Fanny & I were to have gone to the Bishop of Winchester's at Farnham but I was forced to excuse myself to both[78]—and then my poor wife has been in a drooping languishing way, that has confined her to her Room 5 or 6 Weeks—No—Thanks—thanks, 10,000—but it c^d not be with any Comfort.

To Mrs Phillips [St Martin's Street, 7 December 1783][1]

AL (Osborn).
Addressed: To | Mrs Phillips   *Docketed by* SBP: Decr 17th 1783.   *And by* FBA: Gay & enlivening Letter on Baloons—Duc de Chaulnes | Dr. Johnson—Pac-chierotti—Vestris, Dancers &c | 17. Decr 1783. | Dr. B. | to Mrs. Phillips ✲

[76] CB reports: 'In 1783, Gallini wrote to him [Haydn] to come over as Composer to the opera: I saw his answer; he asked £600. Gallini was then in Italy. Since that according to Fischer he had asked him £1000 for coming over expressly for the opera' (MS 'Materials Towards the History of German Music & Musicians', Osborn shelves c 100, p. 7). See CB to Twining, 6 Sept. 1783, nn. 51, 53. The earliest letter from Haydn to Gallini hitherto recorded is dated 19 July 1787 (H. C. Robbins Landon, ed., *The Collected Correspondence and London Notebooks of Joseph Haydn* (1959), pp. 66–7).
[77] Twining in his letter of 22 Oct. had actually invited the Burneys to Colchester: 'But *is it— is it absolutely* impracticable for you to throw yourself, one of these days, into one of the con-venient & comfortable vehicles that travel to Colchester, & take a peep at us in our town cabin?—& Mrs B. with you?—I fear I am *impurent* & *d——d insurance*—but it wou'd be so pleasant & pretty—& no running away after Misses &c —— but days of solid, unbroken *jaw*— (except our jaws break in the eagerness of chattering—)—Is it impossible?—pensez-y: & desire Mrs B. to persuade you, —& herself.' As an added enticement, Twining assured CB he would meet Mrs Smythies (n. 64) again at Colchester.
[78] For Richard Cox (*c.*1718–1803), the Army agent, and the Rt Revd Brownlow North (1741–1820), Bishop of Winchester, see respectively CB to Crisp, 21 Jan. 1774, n. 18; to Twining, 6 Sept. 1783, n. 50.
[1] CB's 'Sunday night'; dinner party with the duc de Chaulnes; and account of Pacchierotti at the opera 'last night', provide a definite date for this letter. Susan Phillips's docket, followed by Mme d'Arblay, almost certainly indicates a slip of the pen. See n. 18.

How much pleasanter an employm^t would it be, if I had time for it, my ever dear & darling Susey, to scrible nonsense to Thee, than either to write Hist^y or read lectures on its alphabet, from door to door, as I now begin to do! Engagem^{ts} come on too, much faster than either my health or spirits can fulfill, without effort, & inconvenience. Every day is broke into—the heavy coach Jobb begins on Tuesday, at 4 Guineas a week, & 7^s the driver! my back aches at the Idea of the number of hours I must fag for this—indeed for the 1st month all my profits will hardly suffice—but I am unable to trapes through dirt & wet—& I am more likely to get cold in damp hacks, (wch cannot always be got at the moment I want 'em) than in the streets[2]—oh that I had no visits to make but to little Fan,[3] her Nurse, Flaxen & Piggy Wiggy! of wch sweet society your acc^{t4} pleases & diverts me hugely—The dear little bratty being so fond of *you* makes me willing to forgive all her *eloignement* & *cruelty* to me.

I inclose Cappy a paper on *Meteors*, sent me by Dr Maskelyne,[5] as He is the likeliest, man I know, to turn it to acc^t—

I am just going to dine wth the Duc de Chaulnes, where probably I shall pick up some *Balon* news. The Duke's note of invitation is so curious that I shall transcribe it *literally*

'The Dukes of Chaulnes best Compliments to Doctor burney. he desires the favour of his company to dinner, with Dr Johnson, on sunday next, between about three, and four o clok, which is the hour convenient to the excellent old Doctor, the best piece of man, indeed, that the Duke ever saw -/-'[6]

Tell Cap. that I have no doubt but that his little Fan will live to see a regular Balon stage established to all parts of the universe that have ever been heard of. And that if she ever goes to the places where these stages *Inn*, she will hear the Book-keeper ask to what part of the Solar-system those who apply for places chuse to go? where your Military men will cry out, to *Mars* Lechers to *Venus*—Men of Pleasure, in pain from mysterious diseases, to *Mercury*. Your sour & melancholic folks will pay earnest for a place to *Saturn*—& the *Jovial* to *Jupiter*. Others will be enquiring whether a stage or Dilly is yet established to the

---

[2] For an assessment of CB's present financial standing in relation to the necessity to maintain his 'situation in the world', see Lonsdale, pp. 292–4.

[3] Frances ('Fanny') Phillips (1782–1860), Susan's first child, now aged 14 months.

[4] Not preserved.

[5] The Revd Nevil Maskelyne (1732–1811), DD (1777), FRS (1758), Astronomer Royal since 1765 (*DNB*; *DSB*). Maskelyne's paper on meteors, dated 6 Nov. 1783, appeared under the title *A Plan for observing the Meteors called Fire-Balls*. It gives a set of instructions for 'proper observations' of meteors in order to make progress 'towards accounting for their phænomena'.

[6] The note, dated 'thursday evening' [4 Dec. 1783], is now preserved in the Osborn Collection. See also *Mem.* ii. 337–9.

Georgium sidus[7]—& Lunatics, will secure a passage in one to the *Moon*—while others will be yet curious in their enquiries after a Balon being sent out on discoveries and in pursuit of Comets, Meteors, & double-stars.—Tout cela viendrâ, soyez sure—and Fanny, or at least, her Children, will live to see many things in these Aerial voyages wch elder sons & daughters of mother *Earth* have hitherto thought beyond the reach of human ken.

Sunday night

The dinner did not go off so lightly as the last Balon; the *inflammable Air* of Johnson, that was to lift us all up, was damped by sickness. He spoke but little, & that not in his best manner. The Duke however shewed me all his Correspondence *à la Balonade* with Mongolfier,[8] M. Charl,[9] & others of the principal Physiciens de Paris—there was one to be sent up the end of last month 70 feet high, & 40 in diameter—that was to lift 2500 weight[10]—of the success of this, no acc^t has yet been rec^d—I was in great hopes that the last wch was let off here, from the artillary ground & was carried southward[11] w^d have found its way to Chesington—M. de Rosiers, at Paris has pledged himself to mount in the next, and trust himself to the mercy of the atmosphere, without cords or any check whatever, except what is in his own power—& Mongolfier can depress or raise his balon at pleasure.[12] But the giving

---

[7] The planet Uranus was given this name by its discoverer, William Herschel, in honour of George III. See Herschel's letter naming the planet in *Philosophical Transactions of the Royal Society of London*, lxxiii (1783), 1–3; *London Magazine, Enlarged and Improved*, i (1783), 17–21, 506–7; and CB to Fanny Burney and Mr & Mrs Phillips, [c.22 July 1782], n. 16. 'Uranus', the name that finally triumphed, was proposed by Johann Elert Bode (1747–1826), German astronomer, of the observatory of the Berlin Academy (*ADB*; *DSB*).

[8] CB does not specify which of the Montgolfier brothers (see CB to Twining, 10–12 Nov. 1783, n. 47).

[9] Jacques-Alexandre-César Charles (1746–1823), inventor of the '*charlière*', or hydrogen-filled balloon.

[10] Reports of the dimensions and weight-bearing capacities of the early balloons are notoriously inaccurate and contradictory. CB's description seems to accord with the hot-air balloon in which Pilatre de Rozier performed his captive ascents in mid-Oct. (see CB to Twining, 10–12 Nov. 1783, n. 46), and in which he made the first flight on 21 Nov. from the gardens of the Château de la Muette, a royal palace near Paris (B. Faujas de Saint-Fond, *Description des expériences de la machine aérostatique de MM. de Montgolfier* (1783–4), ii. 11–30).

[11] CB refers to the first public launching in England of an experimental hydrogen-filled balloon from the Artillery Ground in Moorfields on 25 Nov. 1783. Designed by Count Francesco Zambeccari (1752–1812), an Italian currently resident in London, the balloon descended 48 miles away at Graffham, near Petworth, Sussex (J. E. Hodgson, *The History of Aeronautics in Great Britain* (1924), p. 102; L. T. C. Rolt, *The Aeronauts: a History of Ballooning, 1783–1903* (1966), pp. 61–2; *London Chronicle*, 27–9 Nov. 1783; *Public Advertiser*, 26 Nov. 1783; *Morning Chronicle*, 26 Nov. 1783).

[12] Although a full report of the first manned balloon flight by Pilatre de Rozier and the marquis d'Arlandes on 21 Nov. had appeared in the *London Chronicle*, 29 Nov.–2 Dec. 1783, CB's own newspaper, the *Morning Chronicle* did not report the event.

it a Horizontal motion seems still to find[13]—However, it was a long while after the invention of a boat before sails were invented.—But, by this time you have perhaps had partly enough on this *light* subject.— If I had wit enough, or energy of mind sufficient to be *mad* ab^t anything now, it w^d be ab^t *Balons*[14]—I think them the most wild, Romantic, pretty playthings for grown Gentlemen, that have ever been invented. & that the subject, as well as the thing, lifts one to the Clouds, whenever one talks of it.

I have not wondered so much at having no Letter from Jemm since I saw the acc^t[15] of his having been sent with the Isis to Mangalore with Troops & stores[16]—as that expedition may have taken place a considerable time before the ship sailed wch brought the news to Europe; & in that Case he may be out of the reach of means to send a letter if he had been disposed to write one—which is not at all certain.

I was much pleased last night[17] with Pacchierotti at the opera—I had so bad a cold as not to be able to go the 2 first nights[18]—His voice was in good order, & he sang divinely—his 1st song a Grasiosa—or rather mezza bravura Air of Bertoni, which I had never heard before; but so elegant & fanciful that I sh^d have been less surprised had I been told that the Catilena was Pacchierotti's—his 2^d Air a Cantabile in the gran gusto by Anfossi—and the 3^d air, Rasserena il mesto ciglio, of Gluck,[19] wch we got encored. He sang in a truely grand style

[13] Dr Johnson, CB's dinner companion, made a similar comment: 'In amusement, mere amusement I am afraid it must end, for I do not find that its course can be directed' (Johnson *Letters*, iii. 227; see also J. E. Hodgson, *Doctor Johnson on Ballooning and Flight* (1925)).

[14] Horace Walpole wrote on 2 Dec.: 'Do not wonder that we do not entirely attend to the things of earth: fashion has ascended to a higher element. All our views are directed to the air. *Balloons* occupy senators, philosophers, ladies, everybody' (Walpole *Corresp.* xxv. 449).

[15] A dispatch from India dated 19 July 1783 was printed in the London newspapers of 26 Nov. It reported that 'A detachment of 300 Europeans, together with a supply of powder and provisions, are sent from Madras to Mangulore in his Majesty's ships Bristol and Isis' (*Morning Chronicle*; *Public Advertiser*). James Burney had last written home from on board the *Bristol*, 'at Sea', on 7 May 1783 (PML).

[16] In overall command of the *Bristol* and the *Isis*, also of 50 guns, James Burney had sailed on 10 July 1783 from Madras with a detachment of Hanoverians and supplies of gunpowder and provisions for Mangalore, then under siege. The expedition arrived at its destination on 18 Aug. (Manwaring, pp. 175–7).

[17] CB heard *Silla*, a pasticcio opera, libretto by Giovanni de Gamerra (1743–1803), with music chiefly by Pasquale Anfossi (1727–97), who in this production made his London début as composer and musical director to the King's Theatre (*The London Stage*, v. ii. 661–2, 664; *BD*, under 'Anfossi').

[18] *Silla* had been performed on Saturday 29 Nov., and Tuesday 2 Dec. The third performance, which CB attended, took place on Saturday 6 Dec. This circumstance dates CB's letter.

[19] This aria from Gluck's *Artamene* (1746) was a great favourite. Although CB is severe in his criticism of it: 'The motivo of this air is grateful to every ear; but it is too often repeated . . . The second part is good for nothing' (*Hist. Mus.* iv. 454; Mercer, ii. 845), he had prevailed on Gluck to sing it when they met in Vienna in 1772 (*Tours*, ii. 91). The aria had appeared in *The Favourite Songs in the Opera call'd Artamene by Sig^r Gluck*, published by Walsh in 1746, and also appeared now as *Rasserena il mesto ciglio. The Favourite Song sung by Sig^r Pacchierotti in the Opera of Silla*, published

the whole night—with too little applause & attention—though there was some of both—The first woman Lisini,[20] has a brilliant toned voice—a little shrill—but in tune and of a *bel metallo*, but rough, course, & unfinished in all her Passages—she is often near right, but never quite right in anything. The 2[d] woman[21] is not sure of singing one note in tune—The 1st Tenor[22] the worst in voice, figure, & manner of singing I ever heard at the opera. I think he has less voice than Piozzi—& far less taste—it seem[s] a worse & Courser Voice in decay—there was a most Charming Quartet by Sarti[23] at the End of the 2[d] act, full of new passages & Effects, which was wholly ruined by the Tenor, who sang the lowest part or base. He wanted strength to support the harmony of the other parts, & when he was heard it was only to make one execrate his intonation—the other 3 parts in the harmony were charming, that is the 2 1st men & 1st woman.[24] But the Dancing![25] what extacy, exclamation & acclamation at the sight of young Vestris![26] I sickened with disdain when I recollected how little had been bestowed on our friend.—But think how these 2 Dances were filled; besides the 2[d] rate & Figuranti,[27] there was Le Piq, Vestris Junior & Slingsby; with Mad. Simonet, Theodore, & Rossi[28]—If it

[1783] by Wright and Wilkinson. See *BUCEM*; A. Wotquenne, *Thematisches Verzeichnis der Werke von Chr. W. v. Gluck (1714–1787)* (Leipzig, 1904), pp. 29, 191–2.

[20] Caterina Lusini (*fl.* 1781–4), Italian soprano (*BD*), was one of the 'female singers, [who] were tried with Pacchierotti before his departure, but unsuccessfully' (*Hist. Mus.* iv. 515; Mercer, ii. 891). She stayed only for the 1783–4 season.

[21] Maria Catenacci (*fl.* 1783–6), sang for three seasons at the King's Theatre, from 1783 to 1786 (*BD*).

[22] Vincenzo Uttini (*fl.* 1783–4), Italian tenor, who sang the title role of Silla, appeared at the King's Theatre for this one season. 'Signor Uttini is very indifferent' (*London Chronicle*, 29 Nov.–2 Dec. 1783).

[23] Giuseppe Sarti (1729–1802), Italian composer, now at the height of his powers, and *maestro di cappella* of the Duomo in Milan. He composed about seventy-five operas besides church and chamber music (*New Grove*). CB commends Sarti, who 'set, in the manner of cantatas, several of Metastasio's charming little poems, which he calls *canzonette*. These exquisite compositions were produced by Sarti expressly for the voices of Pacchierotti, Marchesi, and Rubinelli, and are, in all respects, the most perfect and complete models of *chamber Music* that have ever come to my knowledge' (*Hist. Mus.* iv. 179; Mercer, ii. 637). CB wrote later of Sarti: '. . . a sweet, tender, and graceful composer . . . His harmony was sweet and simple, and his melody truly vocal' (Rees).

[24] i.e. Pacchierotti; his fellow castrato, Vincenzio Bartolini (*fl.* 1782–92), who sang the role of Cinna (*DB*); and Caterina Lusini.

[25] Two ballets devised by Jean Bercher, called D'Auberval (1742–1806), were performed for the first time at the King's Theatre on 6 Dec.: *The Pastimes of Terpsycore* was danced after Act II of *Silla*, and after the end of the opera, *Friendship leads to Love* (*The London Stage*, v. ii. 664; *BD*, under 'D'Auberval'). The reviews in the newspapers of 8 Dec. (*Morning Chronicle*; *Public Advertiser*) were glowing: e.g. 'never was there such a groupe of dancers.'

[26] '*Vestris* was received with acclamations that were prodigious! and indeed, his performances were prodigious also! . . . In feathered agility, and in the firmness of vigour, he not only exceeds all other dancers, but even what we, a year or two past, used to see in himself' (*Morning Chronicle*, 8 Dec. 1783). See n. 28.

[27] See *OED*, 'figurant', 2: 'a supernumerary character'.

[28] Charles LePicq (1744–1806), French dancer and choreographer, Noverre's favourite pupil,

were not for Pacchierotti this affected & silly stuff w^d triumph over Music indeed—God bless you dear Susey—remember me heartily to the Cap, and give Bratty 2 or 3 Kisses de plus foll me—

Poor Mrs Ham[29] has I hope ere this recovered her bruises. Hoops have often bruised the poor *Min*, but I never heard of their attacking the Ladies, whom they were intended to guard—O yes, now I think of it Jobson threatens Nell—that he'll 'ten times a day *hoop* her barrel['][30]—Love to honest Kate,[31] & so addio—addio.

To Lord Sandwich[1]

[St Martin's Street], 11 February 1784

ALS (Montagu: 36/95).

Wed^y Night. 11th Feby 1784.

My Lord.

I have the honour, in obedience to your Lord$^{p's}$ Commands, to inclose an extract from my daughters Letter concern^g Capt. Phillips's

starred in *Friendship leads to Love*, partnered by Geltruda Rossi, later to become the second Mme Charles LePicq (M. H. Winter, *The Pre-Romantic Ballet* (1974), p. 123).

Marie-Jean-Augustin (called Auguste) Vestris (1760–1842), French dancer and teacher, for whom D'Auberval composed *The Pastimes of Terpsycore*, was the leading male dancer of his time. He partnered Mlle Théodore (for whom see CB to Twining, 14 Dec. 1781, n. 47).

Simon Slingsby (*fl.* 1758–93), was probably the first British dancer to have a successful career in France as well as in London (C. W. Beaumont, 'Simon Slingsby', *Ballet*, iv (Nov. 1947), 13–19). He was partnered on 6 Dec. by one of the Simonet sisters: Léonore or Rosine.

For LePicq, Vestris, Théodore, and Slingsby, see *Enciclopedia dello spettacolo* (Rome, 1954–62); G. B. L. Wilson, *A Dictionary of Ballet* (3rd edn., 1974); H. Koegler, *The Concise Oxford Dictionary of Ballet* (1977).

[29] Sarah Hamilton (*c.*1705–97), who kept Chessington Hall as a country boarding-place (see *JL* i. 144).

[30] Thus does Zekel Jobson, 'a Psalm-singing Cobler', terrorize in song his wife Nell, 'an innocent Country Girl', in the immensely popular ballad-opera *The Devil to Pay; or, The Wives Metamorphos'd* (1731) by Charles Coffey (d. 1745), John Mottley (1692–1750), and Theophilus Cibber (1703–58), based on *The Devil of a Wife, or A Comical Transformation* (1686), by Thomas Jevon (1652–88).

[31] Papilian Catherine Cooke (1730–97), assisted her aunt, Sarah Hamilton, in the management of Chessington Hall (see *EJL* i. 8 n. 24).

[1] Although Lord Sandwich had lost Office as First Lord of the Admiralty on the fall of Lord North's Administration in Mar. 1782, he continued to supervise the preparation of the official account of Captain Cook's last expedition for the press (J. C. Beaglehole, *The Life of Captain James Cook* (1974), pp. 691–2). This publication was to appear under the title *A Voyage to the Pacific Ocean* ..., in June 1784, in three volumes, the first two based on Cook's journals, and the third on those of Captain James King (1750–84), who had assumed command of the *Discovery* in Aug. 1779 (*DNB*). Sandwich and King had sought CB's advice on the subject of music among the South Sea Islanders (King to Sandwich, 30 Jan., 6 Feb. 1784, Montagu: 36/93, 94).

opinion of the Music of the South sea Islanders.[2] Some of the circumstances seem, indeed, worth mentioning. Each performer having only one note consigned to him, which is regulated by the sound of his Bamboo, is something like the limited power of our ringers in a Belfry, where no one has more than a single Sound to his share. During the infancy of Music, in Greece, the Syrinx had a Pipe for every sound, before a single pipe, by being perforated, produced the whole scale. Capt. Phillips's Bamboo Story implies infancy in the South sea Music.

I have written to him in the Country to ask whether this method of singing in parts, as it is called, was peculiar to any one place or Island in the South seas, or whether he recollects the having heard it elsewhere. As soon as I receive his answer[3] I shall communicate it to your Lordship; and have the honour to be with great respect, My Lord,

your Lordship's obliged & most devoted Servant

Cha[s] Burney.

To Lord Sandwich

St Martin's Street,
17 February 1784

ALS (Montagu: 36/98).
Addressed: To | The R[t] Hon[ble] | The Earl of Sandwich

My Lord.

I have the honour to inclose the Fragment of a Letter w[ch] I last night rec[d] from my daughter, M[rs] Phillips, containing some further particulars & *eclaircissemens* concerning the Music of the South sea Islanders, w[ch], if they sh[d] be of any use in the approaching publication, will afford me great pleasure.[1]

---

[2] Since CB's son, James, was in India at this time (see CB to Mrs Phillips, [7 Dec. 1783], nn. 15, 16), CB had had to consult instead his son-in-law, Molesworth Phillips, on the question of the music of the Islanders. The two-page enclosure which CB sent Sandwich is preserved in the Montagu Collection together with the present letter. It reads in part: 'In The Islanders regular Concerts Captain Phillips says each man had a Bamboo, which were of different lengths & gave different tones—these they beat against the ground, & each Performer assisted by the note given by this instrument, repeated the same note, accompanying it with words, . . . in this manner they sung in Chorus, & not only produced octaves to each other, . . . but fell on concords such as were not disagreable to the Ear.'

[3] See CB to Sandwich, 17 Feb. 1784.

[1] Susan's clarification that Molesworth Phillips's comments applied only to the music of the Friendly Islands is preserved together with this letter in the Montagu Collection. Her letter can be dated [16? Feb. 1784]. Phillips's information was not included in the *Voyage to the Pacific Ocean.* King wrote to Lord Sandwich, 14 Feb. 1784: 'I have omitted the paragraph from Capt. Philips because it appears to be only a repetition of what is said before' (Montagu: 36/97).

I have the honour to be with great Respect, my Lord, your Lordship's
obliged & most devoted Servant
Chas Burney.

St Martin's Street [|] Feby 17th 1784.

To Mrs Crewe[1] [St Martin's Street], 19 February [1784][2]

ALS (Osborn).

Dear Madam.

There is no picking up anything in the way of news, worth transmitting to you; as all my acquaintance seem as ignorant of what has
happened, or is likely to happen, as myself. Doubt, mystery, & indecision travel from the Cabinet to other places, & we are sure of
nothing but that the kingdom is in strange disorder, & that 'Chaos is
come again.'[3]

Last Night it was imagined (as Sr Jos. R———ds had picked up
among the Politicians of his acquaintance) that this Day the L^{ds} w^d
address the K— to dissolve the P————t, in consequence of the
Commons refusing to grant the Supplies moved for yesterday.[4] This

---

[1] Daughter of Fulke Greville, CB's early patron, Frances Anne (Greville) Crewe (1748–1818)
had married in 1766 John Crewe (1742–1829), of Crewe Hall, Cheshire, MP for Stafford
(1765–68), for Cheshire (1768–1802). Crewe was on intimate terms with Charles James Fox
(1749–1806), supporting him financially and politically. Fox rewarded his friend with a Barony
in 1806 (*DNB*; Namier and Brooke, ii. 276–7; *JL* i. 2–3). Mrs Crewe was active in political
circles as a great Whig hostess, and a staunch supporter of Fox.

[2] 19 Feb. falling on a Thursday, and the political events discussed in the letter, admit no
doubt that 1784 is the correct date.

On the King's dismissal of the Fox and North Coalition and the appointment of the 24-year-
old William Pitt (1759–1806) as First Lord of the Treasury and Chancellor of the Exchequer to
head a minority Government in Dec. 1783, the country had been thrown into a constitutional
crisis. A period of intense political strife followed, leading to the general election of 1784 which
produced a landslide victory for Pitt. For the issues, personalities, and political manoeuvres at
this period, see J. S. Watson, *The Reign of George III, 1760–1815* (Oxford, 1960), pp. 266–72;
Namier and Brooke, i. 87–96; *Annual Register ... for the Years 1784 and 1785* (2nd edn., 1795),
pp. 58–99.

Mrs Crewe had said to William Wilberforce (1759–1833) on 22 Dec. 1783: 'So your friend Mr.
Pitt means to come in, ... well, he may do what he likes during the holidays, but it will only be a
mince-pie administration, depend on it' (R. I. and S. Wilberforce, *The Life of William Wilberforce*
(1838), i. 48).

[3] *Othello*, III. iii. 93.

[4] On 18 Feb. 1784, the House of Commons had voted by 208 to 196 to postpone the passage of
the annual Supply to the Crown (*Journals of the House of Commons* (1803), xxxix. 934). This drastic
measure, which blocked the payment of public money, as well as the threat that the House might

Morn^g I saw M^r B——ke,[5] & he seemed to think that some such measure w^d be pursued in the House of L^{ds} to day—This Even^g I drank Tea wth D^r W————n[6]—who thinks otherwise—& that such a procedure was so new, for one part of the Legislature to interfere wth another, that he c^d not think it probable—Ld Bathurst,[7] however is to make a Motion in the House of L^{ds} to day, the subject of wch is kept a profound secret; but many I find imagine it like to be for addressing the K. to dissolve the P————t.—Dr W. saw in the K——'s own Hand writing the instructions he gave Ld Sidney[8] for proposing a meeting between the D. of P————d[9] & Mr Pitt—& the Duke's answer;[10] both of wch you will find discussed and misrepresented in the Papers[11]— But it appears to me as if there was never any serious wish or design for union[12] on the part of the Cr——n.—and that the D—— has done

indeed refuse to appropriate funds, were greeted by Pitt's supporters with horror: '. . . in the present state of our government, to deny the ordinary annual supply, would be, in fact, to dissolve the whole fabric of government' (*Annual Register, 1784–5*, p. 91). See also *The Parliamentary History of England*, vol. xxiv (1815), cols. 595–617, for the report of the Commons debate of 18 Feb.

[5] Burke's last act as Paymaster General in the Fox–North Coalition Ministry had been to secure for CB the appointment of Organist at Chelsea College with a salary of £50 per annum. See Burke to CB, [19] Dec. 1783, in *Mem.* ii. 374, and Burke *Corresp.* v. 120; Lonsdale, pp. 295–6.

[6] Richard Warren (1731–97), MD (1762), was the King's physician (*DNB*).

[7] Henry Bathurst (1714–94), 2nd Earl Bathurst (1775), Lord Chancellor (1771–8), Lord President of the Council (1779–82), was politically a supporter of Lord North (*DNB*). For a report of Lord Bathurst's proposed motion, the intention of which he refused to reveal to the House of Lords on 19 Feb., see *Morning Chronicle*, 20 Feb. 1784. Bathurst's secrecy caused concern and suspicion in the upper chamber: 'Lord Temple . . . expressed a hope, that the noble Earl had no intention to bring forward any motion likely to promote disunion between the two Houses of Parliament'. He did not.

[8] Thomas Townshend (1733–1800), created Baron (1783), Viscount (1789) Sydney, Secretary of State for the Home Department (1783–89) in Pitt's Administration (*DNB*). In an attempt to solve the constitutional crisis by the formation of a coalition ministry, a move vigorously urged by a group of independent Members of Parliament (*Annual Register, 1784–5*, pp. 87–91, 265–72), the King on 15 Feb. had sent the Duke of Portland (n. 9) a message delivered by Lord Sydney. George III asked Portland to confer with Pitt to work out a plan for 'the formation of a new Administration on a wide basis and on a fair and equal footing' (*The Later Correspondence of George III*, ed. A. Aspinall (Cambridge, 1962–70), i. 35).

[9] William Henry Cavendish Bentinck (1738–1809), 3rd Duke of Portland (1762), as First Lord of the Treasury (Apr.–Dec. 1783), had been the nominal head of the Fox–North Coalition, and was now the titular leader of the Opposition forces (*DNB*). Portland was passionately fond of music, and on CB's meeting him at Bulstrode in 1793, the two became firm friends. See Lonsdale, p. 366.

[10] Portland's answer to Lord Sydney, 15 Feb. 1784, pointed out 'the impossibility of my conferring with Mr Pitt on any plan of ministerial settlement untill he shall have signified . . . his inclination to comply' with the wishes of the Opposition majority in the Commons. In effect, it was a call for Pitt's resignation. Portland pointedly omitted the word 'equal' in the assurance of his willingness to submit to His Majesty 'such advice . . . as most likely to promote the formation of a firm, efficient, extended and united Administration'. See *Later Corresp. of George III*, i. 35–6; *Morning Chronicle*, 3 Mar. 1784.

[11] See *General Evening Post*, 14–17 Feb.; 17–19 Feb. 1784; *Morning Chronicle*, 18 Feb. 1784. Among other slight inaccuracies, the *General Evening Post*, for example, reported the King as 'most solicitous of establishing' a Portland–Pitt Coalition Administration.

[12] i.e. the formation of a Coalition Administration.

wisely & honorably to avoid the Snare—There seems at present an artificial hue & Cry against the H. of C——ns—they have so long had on their hands the odious employm^t of Taxing the People, though for the Support of Governm^t & Ministers, that the public at large perhaps think the chief part of their grievances proceed from that House, the sole barrier between them & despotism—How all this will terminate,^{13} I know not; but I cannot help thinking, what I heartily hope, that the Eyes of this same public will ere long be opened, & that all will once more be right; ere it is wrong forever—adieu—dear Mad^m—excuse these hasty Scrawls, but I have time for no more—never being able to get home of a Night till 'tis time to send a Letter away—I Thank you for your last,^{14} & am y^r most affectionate

& Devoted Servt

C.B

Thursday Night. | Feby 19th

To Edmond Malone^1

[St Martin's Street, 17 March 1784 *or post*]^2

ALS (PML: RV Autographs Misc. Musicians).
Addressed: To | Edmond Malone Esqr | Queen Anne Street East   *Also* L copy (Berg).

My dear Sir.

I am sorry that I cannot be as obedient to you, as Bentley's friend^3 was to him, when he cried out—'Walker, our hat.[']^4

---

^{13} Pitt's tenacity, the influence of the Crown and moneyed men, and the erosion of support for Fox both within and without the House led to the dissolution of Parliament on 25 Mar., followed by the general election of 1784. Pitt triumphed. See Watson, *Reign of George III*, pp. 270–2.

^{14} Not known to be preserved. The Crewe papers are not open to inspection.

^{1} Edmond Malone (1741–1812), scholar-collector, critic, and author, had settled permanently in London in 1777 as a man of letters, elected to The Club in 1782 (*DNB*; Sir James Prior, *Life of Edmond Malone* (1860)).

^{2} CB's 'Wed^y Morn^g', the name of the recipient, and The Club Minutes give the earliest possible date of the present letter. The Club met on Tuesdays during the Parliamentary session. Proposed by George Colman the elder and seconded by Sir Joseph Banks, CB was elected on 17 Feb., and attended his first meeting on 2 Mar. 1784. Malone and CB met at The Club for the first time on 16 Mar., after which meeting (or at any number of subsequent meetings when both were present) members' hats got mixed up. CB and Malone were two of the most regular members at The Club. See Lonsdale, p. 283; J. M. Osborn, *The Club: The Founders' Era* (forthcoming).

^{3} The Revd Richard Bentley (1662–1742), DD (1696), classical scholar and critic, Master of Trinity College, Cambridge (1700–42), was staunchly supported in his quarrels with the Fellows of Trinity by the Revd Richard Walker (1679–1764), DD (1728), Vice-Master of Trinity (1734–64). See *DNB*.

^{4} This anecdote of Bentley calling for his hat and walking out on a tiresome visitor is enshrined

My 'first best Beavor' is too shabby at present to be owned by you
or any of our brethren—my name too is written on the lining—I wish
you better luck in your future enquiries, & am in great haste

> Y^{rs} with true regard
> Ch^{as} Burney

Wed^y Morn^g

To Mrs Phillips

[St Martin's Street,
25]–26 April 1784^1

AL (Osborn).
Addressed: To | Mrs Phillips, | at Mrs Hamilton's, Chesington, | near Kingston, in |
Surry.   *Pmk:* 26 AP   *Docketed by* SBP: April 27th 1784.   *And by* FBA:
Sweet Baby Fanny description ⌜For Fanny Raper⌝ ✗ ✳

> Sunday Night. 26 Apr.
> 1784

What Pity it is, my ever dear Susey! that such Scenes as you have
sent me cannot be as well acted as written. I never was more pleased
or interested by any domestic situation of the same kind as that w^{ch}
you have so nicely described between yourself & your clever little
Girl. I never lost sight of her for a moment during the perusal of your
Letter.^{2} Her first shiness, its diminution, recognition, & returning
affection, are all painted in such a manner as none but a witnessing &
feeling mother, just while the transaction was recent c^d delineate. I
thank you for it heartily. And will soon shew my gratitude by giving
you, in return, an excellent engraving, according to Sr Jos. of your
aged parent, of w^{ch}, at length (tell Cappy) I have just got a Proof from
Bartolozzi.^{3} It was very kind & good of you to let us know how [you]

in Pope's *Dunciad,* iv. 273–4:

> 'Walker! our hat'—nor more he deign'd to say,
> But, stern as Ajax' spectre, strode away.

---

^{1} CB's 'Sunday Night', and his '⟨M⟩onday Even^g' dating show that this letter was written
over a period of time from 25 to 26 Apr. 1784.
^{2} Not preserved.
^{3} For Sir Joshua Reynolds's portrait of CB (1781), now engraved by Francesco Bartolozzi, see
CB to Charles Burney, 25 Feb. 1781, n. 19. The plate is dated 1 Apr. 1784. Twining, to whom
CB gave a copy later this year, wrote of the engraving: '. . . everybody that has seen it, & seen
you, are agreed with me in *two* things—1. that the print is, *all-together,* a strong, & striking
likeness, that is recognised au premier coup d'œil; & 2. that, notwithstanding that, upon examination, the likeness is not complete—their is *some* unlikeness mixed with it; & it is, I think,
principally about the nose.—What says Mrs B. & all those who are most intimately acquainted
with that *bel volto* of yours?' (Twining to CB, 12 Nov. 1784, BL Add. MS 39929, fos. 342–3).

fared on the road, & what was the state of your health after your bad journey. There have been a few warm & good days lately, wch I hope you enjoyed, & benefitted by—The agues you talk of seem to be epidemical among Children—Mr Lock[4] told me yesterday at the R. Academy dinner,[5] that agues were never known before, in Surry. Tell Cap. that he made apologies for not having waited upon him. But said that he did not know of his staying so much longer in town than he talked of, till it was too late.

Election not yet over![6] Both sides, however, have ceased to Canvas me—But it is, & will be so hard a run thing, that I fear for my little preferm^{ts}—as it is s^d an order will be sent to all the *Household*[7] to vote for Sr C. Wray—If so, I shall certainly be congedié, as I have made up my mind, & determined to quarrel with any body rather than myself, & my own feelings in performing an act of ingratitude to the few benefactors I have had.[8]

Tell my dear Capt. that I hope he will remind his Fr^d Mr Webber[9]

---

[4] William Lock, or Locke (1732–1810), of Norbury Park, Surrey, art amateur (*DNB*), whose wife, Frederica Augusta, née Schaub (1750–1832), was soon to become Fanny Burney's closest friend, supplying the place of Mrs Thrale in her affections (*DL* ii. 253–4; *HFB*, pp. 183–4). A man of great inherited wealth, William Lock had married in 1767, and purchased the Norbury estate where he built in the 1770s an elegant house for his family. See The Duchess of Sermoneta [Vittoria Caetani], *The Locks of Norbury* (1940).

[5] At the opening of the 1784 Royal Academy Exhibition on Saturday 24 Apr., the Academicians 'gave a great entertainment'. The names of CB and William Lock are listed in the newspaper accounts of the occasion. See, for example, *General Evening Post*, 24–6 Apr. 1784.

[6] Voting in the 1784 general election for the two Westminster seats in Parliament had begun on 1 Apr. Pitt's ministerial candidates were: Rear-Admiral Lord Samuel Hood (1724–1816), created Baronet (1778), Baron Hood in the Irish Peerage (1782), and later (1796) Viscount, who had family connections with Pitt; and Sir Cecil Wray (1734–1805), 13th Baronet (1752), who, since 1782 had represented Westminster (*DNB*; Namier and Brooke, ii. 636–7; iii. 663–5). Charles James Fox stood in opposition. It soon became clear that the naval hero Lord Hood would head the poll, leaving Wray and Fox to battle it out for the remaining seat. A struggle of epic proportions ensued: the voting lasted the full 40 polling days permitted by law, with vigorous canvassing, notably on Fox's behalf by Georgiana, Duchess of Devonshire. See *Annual Register, 1784–5*, pp. 174–80*, 279–80; Namier and Brooke, i. 335–7; Earl Stanhope, *Life of the Right Honourable William Pitt* (1879), i. 163–6, 177–8; L. Reid, *Charles James Fox: a Man for the People* (1969), pp. 198–213.

[7] CB was technically a member of the Royal Household: since 1774 he had been a 'Musician in Ordinary in the King's Band', a sinecure worth £40 a year. See Scholes, ii. 321–3; Lonsdale, pp. 168–9, 294–5.

[8] CB's determination to vote for Fox was based on his gratitude to Burke and the Fox–North Coalition for the organist's post at Chelsea College (see CB to Mrs Crewe, 19 Feb. [1784], n. 5), and on grounds of friendship for Mrs Crewe, a staunch campaigner for Fox and daughter of CB's early patron, Fulke Greville. Fox, in addition, was a fellow member of The Club to which CB was proud to belong. As Samuel Johnson put it: 'I am for the King against Fox; but I am for Fox against Pitt ... the King is my master; but I do not know Pitt; and Fox is my friend' (Hill–Powell, iv. 292). Moreover, Wray had spoken out against the maintenance of Chelsea Hospital (College). See Reid, *Fox*, p. 200; *DNB*. CB's political affiliation is also revealed by an entry in his pocket-book: 'May 18th [1784] Mrs Crewe's Buff & blue ball, on acc^t of C. Fox having gained his Election' (*Frag. Mem.*, Osborn).

[9] John Webber (*c*.1750–93), RA (1791), artist, had accompanied Captain Cook on his third and last voyage as draughtsman. On his return in 1780, Webber was engaged by the Admiralty

of the set of 1ˢᵗ impressions he spoke to him abᵗ for Mʳ Smith,[10] as I perceive the Voyage is to be published next Month.[11]

This is a terrible hurrying time of the year, in Conversationi Concerts & calls, as well as Scholaring. You may judge a little by a Sketch of last weeks accidental engagemᵗˢ—*Monday* dined at Dʳ Warrens—*Tuesday* at Mʳ Cox's—after wᶜʰ at a grand Conversatione at Mʳˢ Wilmots,[12] where Mʳˢ Montague, Vesey, Carter, H. Moore, Mʳˢ Walsingham, Garrick, Ord;[13] Sʳ Jos.[,] Horace Walpole, Bᵖ of Sᵗ Asaph,[14] Soame Jennings,[15] & all the conversation People and Wits one had ever seen

to make finished drawings from his sketches to illustrate the official account of the expedition which appeared in 1784 under the title *A Voyage to the Pacific Ocean . . . for making Discoveries in the Northern Hemisphere*. Webber's drawings of views, portraits of natives and their habitations, customs, rituals, and implements, and Pacific flora and fauna were engraved, the plates forming a magnificent supplementary volume to the three-volume *Voyage*. See *DNB*. Molesworth Phillips, as Lieutenant in command of the marines aboard the *Resolution*, had been Webber's shipmate.

[10] Not certainly identified. Perhaps he was Anker Smith (1759–1819), engraver (*DNB*).

[11] The *Morning Chronicle*, 23 Apr. 1784, first advertised *A Voyage to the Pacific Ocean* as 'In the course of next month will be published'. CB's copy of the three volumes, with the plates in a separate folio volume, fetched £6 10s. (*Cat. Misc. Lib.*, lot 434).

[12] Sarah Wilmot, née Morris (*c.*1724–93), descended from a family of wealthy plantation-owners in the West Indies, had married Henry Wilmot (1710–94), of Farnborough Place, Hampshire, and Bloomsbury Square, solicitor. The Wilmots were great friends of the Garricks. See V. L. Oliver, *The History of the Island of Antigua* (1894–9), ii. 273, 275, 279; Gertrude Lyster, ed., *A Family Chronicle Derived from Notes and Letters Selected by Barbarina, The Hon. Lady Grey* (1908), pp. 3–6; Garrick *Letters*, ii. 534, 698; *GM* lxiii (1793)¹, 378; lxiv (1794)², 770.

Of his social life in 1784, CB later noted: 'My dinners & Conversations increased this year so much, that to 21 houses of old acquaintance 16 new were added, where I dined & spent evenings for the 1ˢᵗ time' (*Frag. Mem.*, Osborn).

[13] This formidable array of Blue Stockings may be identified as:

Elizabeth Montagu, née Robinson (1720–1800), the acknowledged 'Queen of the Blues' (*DNB*; R. Blunt, ed., *Mrs. Montagu* [1923]).

Elizabeth Vesey, formerly Handcock, née Vesey (*c.*1715–91), whose husband, Agmondesham Vesey (d. 1785), a friend of Burke's, had been present at CB's first attendance at The Club (*DNB*).

Elizabeth Carter (1717–1806), poet and miscellaneous writer, noted Greek scholar (*DNB*; M. Pennington, *Memoirs of the Life of Mrs. Elizabeth Carter* (2nd edn., 1808)). Together with Hannah More and Mrs Garrick, CB in later years regarded Elizabeth Carter as one of his 'old sweet hearts' (*JL* iv. 133–4).

Hannah More (1745–1833), poet, dramatist, and religious writer, a favourite of Samuel Johnson (*DNB*; W. Roberts, *Memoirs of the Life and Correspondence of Mrs. Hannah More* (3rd rev. edn., 1835)). She had written 'Bas Bleu', her poem on the Blue Stockings at Bristol in July 1783. The poem, after circulating widely in MS, was published in 1786 under the title, 'The Bas Bleu: or, Conversation. Addressed to Mrs. Vesey.'

Charlotte Boyle-Walsingham, née Hanbury-Williams (1738–90), widow of the Hon. Robert Boyle-Walsingham (1736–80), MP (1758–80), Captain (1757) in the Royal Navy who was lost at sea in Oct. 1780 (Namier and Brooke, iii. 603–5). Mrs Walsingham was a friend of Horace Walpole (see Walpole *Corresp.* xxxi. 251).

Eva Maria Garrick, née Veigel (1724–1822), ballet dancer and David Garrick's widow.

Anna Ord, née Dillingham (*c.*1726–1808), widow of William Ord (d. 1768). Mrs Ord was a particular friend of the Burneys.

[14] Jonathan Shipley (1714–88), DD (1748), Bishop of St Asaph (1769–88), member of The Club and intimate friend of Burke and Reynolds (*DNB*).

[15] Soame Jenyns (1704–87), MP (1741–80), miscellaneous writer (*DNB*; Namier and Brooke, ii. 681–2).

were assembled. *Wed^y* at L^y M. Duncan's—*Thursday* Pantheon[16]—
Friday dined at Mr Hanbury's[17] wth the D. of Dorset, just arrived from
Paris[18]—his Mother, Lady Sackville,[19] my friend & Countryman S^r
Charlton Leig[h]ton[20] &c—after w^ch & music, went to Mrs Veseys &
met all the *blues*[21]—H. Walpole & I after all the rest were gone sate
the Candles out in talking over old times & old operas—Sat^y dined
at the R. Acad^y where the Prince of Wales was expected, but after
keeping the best Comp^y I ever saw there till past 6 o'Clock till they
were ready to eat each other, he sent word that he had forgot it, & c^d
not come[22]—Notwithstanding Gainsborough's ⌜insolence in sending
orders for placing & ill-humour⌝ in withdrawing his Pictures,[23] the
exhibition is very splendid—Sr Jos. is truely great[24]—West[25] better

---

[16] i.e. on Thursday 22 Apr. when a 'Grand Concert' was given (*Morning Chronicle*, 22 Apr. 1784) at which the star attraction was Gertrud Elisabeth Mara, for whom see n. 32.

[17] William Hanbury (*c.*1748–1807), of Kelmarsh, Northamptonshire, amateur dramatist, and from 1790 to 1799 British agent and consul to the Circle of Lower Saxony (Foster; *GM* lx (1790)², 962; lxxvii (1807)², 1176; Garrick *Letters*, iii. 951–3, 955–7; Walpole *Corresp.* xxxii. 168–9).

[18] John Frederick Sackville (1745–99), 3rd Duke of Dorset (1769), whom CB had met at Rome (see CB to Garrick, 17–[18] Oct. 1770, n. 45; *Tours*, i. 201 ff.), at present British Ambassador Extraordinary and Plenipotentiary to France (1783–90), had taken leave of absence from the French Court on 20 Apr. (Horn, p. 26).

[19] Lady Frances Sackville, née Leveson Gower (d. 1788), a daughter of John Leveson Gower (1694–1754), created Earl Gower (1746), had married in 1744 Lord John Philip Sackville (1713–65), MP (1734–47), second son of Lionel Cranfield Sackville (1688–1765), created Duke of Dorset (1720). See G. F. R. Barker and A. H. Stenning, *The Record of Old Westminsters* (1928), ii. 812; Sedgwick, ii. 400; *GM* lviii (1788)², 660.

[20] Sir Charlton Leighton (*c.*1747–84), 4th Baronet (1780), of Wattlesborough, Shropshire, MP (1774–5, 1780–4) for Shrewsbury, CB's native town (Namier and Brooke, iii. 33).

[21] Mrs Vesey's parties at her house in Clarges Street were noted for their informality. Horace Walpole, CB's interlocutor for the evening, referred to them as 'Mrs. Vesey's Babels' or 'the Vesey-Chaos' (Walpole *Corresp.* xxix. 104; xxxv. 495).

[22] 'The Prince of Wales had promised to be there; but when we had waited an hour and half, sent us word that he could not come' (Johnson *Letters*, iii. 159). Contemporary gossip had it that the Prince of Wales had nominally accepted the Academy's invitation in order to win Sir Joshua Reynolds's vote and influence on behalf of Fox in the Westminster election (W. T. Whitley, *Artists and Their Friends in England 1700–1799* (1928), ii. 13–15).

[23] Thomas Gainsborough (1727–88), RA (1768), had quarrelled with the Royal Academy over the hanging of his full-length portrait group, *The Three Eldest Princesses: Charlotte, Princess Royal, Augusta and Elizabeth*, painted for the Prince of Wales and intended for the State Room at Carlton House. Gainsborough had maintained that his picture was executed 'in so tender a light' that it could not be 'placed higher than five feet & a half'. The Hanging Committee for the Academy Exhibition of 1784, however, refused to make an exception to the rule at Somerset House that full-length portraits should be hung above the level of the tops of the doorways so that their bases were 8 or 9 feet above floor-level. In high dudgeon, Gainsborough withdrew the eighteen pictures he had intended to exhibit. See W. T. Whitley, *Thomas Gainsborough* (1915), pp. 212–25; *The Letters of Thomas Gainsborough*, ed. Mary Woodall (rev. edn., 1963), pp. 28–31; O. Millar, *The Later Georgian Pictures in the Collection of Her Majesty the Queen* (1969), i. 40.

[24] Sir Joshua's most important exhibit this year was the celebrated *Mrs. Siddons as the Tragic Muse* (C. R. Leslie and T. Taylor, *Life and Times of Sir Joshua Reynolds: with Notices of Some of His Cotemporaries* (1865), ii. 420–6, 435–6).

[25] Benjamin West (1738–1820), RA (1768), historical painter born in Pennsylvania, had

than usual—Loutherberg[26] charming—&c &c—The dear good Johnson was able to be there,[27] & I sate by him, & facing Mr Lock, all dinner time—you will probably see a list of the Comp^y, so as time is very short I shall say no more ab^t it.—From the Acad^y I drove to the opera just to shew myself to L^y M. Duncan, as it was Demofonte[28]—I c^d not stay till Pacch. came off the stage, to speak to him, as Fan was waiting for me to accompany her to a blue Party at Mr Burrows's,[29] where we were invited to meet Mr Montague[30]—& where we likewise found Mrs Garrick—H. Moore, the Pepys's[31] &c—was not this a good days work after the usual dayly Labour was over?—& indeed was not the whole week a busy one?—Well—I am not likely to be much more at leisure next week—to Morrow am to meet the Mara[32] at Mr Hanbury's who as well as the D. of Dorset who is to be there, was acquainted with her at Berlin. Tuesday I am to carry Johnson to the Literary Club.[33] Wed^y to dine with Sr Geo. & L^y Beaumont[34]—

arrived in England in 1763. He became a founder member of the Royal Academy of which he was elected President in 1792 after the death of Sir Joshua Reynolds (*DNB*).

[26] Philippe Jacques de Loutherbourg (1740–1812), RA (1781), painter born in Germany of Polish descent, had come to England in 1771. Garrick employed him as chief scenery designer for the Drury Lane Theatre. De Loutherbourg exhibited extensively at the Royal Academy (*DNB*).

[27] 'The Academicians had the pleasure of seeing again amongst them their Professor of ancient Literature Dr. Johnson, compleatly recovered from his late indisposition, though he appears to be much emaciated' (*General Evening Post*, 24–6 Apr. 1784). See also, Johnson *Letters*, iii. 158–9.

[28] *Demofoonte*, a pasticcio, was performed on 24 Apr. (*The London Stage*, v. ii. 698).

[29] The Revd John Burrows (1733–86), BCL (1762), Rector of St Clement Danes (1773–86), friend of Mrs Montagu and tutor to her nephew Matthew (n. 30). See *JL* iv. 141; Blunt, *Mrs. Montagu*, i. 274; ii. 189; M. Burrows, *History of the Family of Burrows* (Oxford, 1877), pp. 33–152.

[30] Matthew Montagu, formerly Robinson (1762–1831), nephew, adopted son and heir of Mrs Elizabeth Montagu, who directed him to change his name in 1776. He was MP (1786–96, 1806–12), and 4th Baron Rokeby (1829). See *DL* ii. 180–1; Namier and Brooke, iii. 157; Blunt, *Mrs. Montagu*, i. 301 *et passim*.

[31] William Weller Pepys (1741–1825), a Master in Chancery (1775–1807), created Baronet (1801), had married (1777), Elizabeth Dowdeswell (*c*.1748–1830). Although Pepys was a member of the Blue-Stocking circle, and a friend of Mrs Thrale, neither Johnson nor CB was fond of him. See Walpole *Corresp.* xi. 30; Hill–Powell, iv. 487–8; *JL* i. 93; *Thraliana*, i. 379; Alice C. C. Gaussen, ed., *A Later Pepys* (1904).

[32] The German soprano, Gertrud Elisabeth Mara, née Schmeling (1749–1833), had been engaged to sing 6 nights at the Pantheon for her first season in London. The performances were, however, poorly attended owing to the current political upheaval. See *Hist. Mus.* iv. 519; Mercer, ii. 893; *New Grove*; *MGG*. While negotiating to come to England, Mme Mara had written to CB from Ostend a letter full of complaints against Gallini, Abel, and Pacchierotti dated 12 Nov. 1783 (Osborn).

[33] Johnson had not been at The Club since 2 July 1783: his physician had forbidden his attendance, 'not caring to venture the chillness of the evening' (Johnson *Letters*, iii. 158). The Club Minutes show that Johnson and CB were present on 27 Apr. 1784. See J. M. Osborn, *The Club: The Founders' Era* (forthcoming).

[34] Sir George Howland Beaumont (1753–1827), 7th Baronet (1762), connoisseur, patron of art, and landscape painter, had married Margaret Willes (*c*.1756–1829). The Beaumonts had set out on the Grand Tour in 1782 (*DNB*; *GM* xcix (1829)², 92).

she was the 2^d Miss Willes, a beauty & a Paintress—& he one of the best dilettante Painters in Europe—they have been for some time in Italy, & are just returned. Thursday another *Pantheen*,^{35} as W^m the black-guard used to call it^{36}—Friday is as yet open, but Sat^y is big with blue; at Mrs Montagues—

Adieu—*my* Susey! Love me, & teach your Husband & Bratty to love me as well as I love ye all, & shall be Molto Contento—Love to the good Mrs H. & honest Kate^{37}—

⟨M⟩onday Even^g Mr Fox polled 39 more than Sr C. Wray, to day; ⟨co⟩nsequently the majority of the latter is reduced to 27.^{38}

To [Sir Joseph Banks]^1 [St Martin's Street], 26 May 1784

ALS (Hyde). Mounted.

Wed^y Morn^g 6 O'Clock

Dear Sir

I was not five minutes at home the whole day, yesterday, and all this day I shall not be within a mile of my own house. I sh^d have been very happy in the honour of meeting you at the Club yesterday, but had long been engaged to dine at Mr *Bowles*'s,^{2} & to day, if we sh^d meet at Westminster Abbey,^{3} we sh^d not be able to talk ab^t business. Entrons nous donc en Matiere—

^{35} For another 'Grand Concert', at which Mme Mara was to perform (*Morning Chronicle*, 29 Apr. 1784).
^{36} William, CB's servant, had performed heroic deeds for his master during the Gordon Riots (see CB to Twining, 11 [June] 1780, nn. 21, 22).
^{37} For Sarah Hamilton and her niece Papilian Catherine Cooke, see CB to Mrs Phillips, [7 Dec. 1783], nn. 29, 31.
^{38} CB was justifiably excited. After trailing behind Sir Cecil Wray for 3 weeks, Fox was now catching up. On Monday 26 Apr., the 22nd day of the poll, Wray collected 40 and Fox 79 votes, giving them respective totals of 5777 against 5750. Fox was to overtake Wray on Tuesday and maintain his lead to the close of the poll on 17 May. See *Morning Chronicle*, 26, 27, 28 Apr.

^{1} The recipient of this letter is identified by CB's references to fellow-membership of The Club and to Lady Banks in the postscript.
^{2} William Bowles (1755–1826), of Heale House, Wiltshire, Sheriff of Wiltshire (1782), friend and admirer of Johnson, who had visited Bowles at Heale in Aug.–Sept. 1783. In Feb. 1784, Bowles had been elected to Johnson's Essex Head Club, of which CB was also a member. See Hill–Powell, iv. 234–9, 522–4; Johnson *Letters*, iii, *passim*; *DL* ii. 204; Lonsdale, pp. 282–3.
^{3} i.e. at the first of the performances in commemoration of Handel. Subsequent performances took place on 27 May at the Pantheon, and on 29 May, 3 and 5 June at Westminster Abbey. The celebrated Handel Commemoration of 1784 was one of the most notable musical events of the century in England, involving over 500 musicians at each performance, and audiences of about

Your Correspondent[4] seems very unwilling to be satisfied wth anything less than good Music, a good Price, & a power of Praise for his pious compilations; & I fear his cravings in these respects are not very likely to be gratified: Stanley[5] has said, as plainly as a civil man can speak, in one of his Letters to me[6] wch I communicated to you, that he did not chuse to set these Oratorios: 1st because he had not time; 2dly because the public was unwilling to like any other compositions of that kind than those of Handel, though they have heard them so long, that they are heartily tired of them. If this letter is not destroyed, I wish you w^d send it to your Friend. Indeed nothing but royal Patronage or uncommon excellence in the Performance can ensure a full house to any of Handel's best Oratorios. And I own that my expectations of a more satisfactory answer from Stanley are very small. If there is any other adventurer in Compositions of this sort: such as Dr Arnold, young Arne, or Linley,[7] to whom he wishes they sh^d be shewn, I w^d willingly communicate to them the MSS.

I have the honour to be, with great regard, dear Sir,

> Your obliged
> and most zealous servant
> Chas Burney

I am extremely sorry for the Cause of L^y Banks's[8] affliction—H⟨er⟩ Ladyship's Lessons this Winter, I believe, only amount to 17. And as to either them or the B^{ks}, she is so exact and faithful a steward that I wish very much to have the whole matter arranged from her own memorandums & recollection.

May 26th 1784.

3000. The fullest account is given by CB himself in the *Handel Commem.*, as the following letters show. See also Lonsdale, pp. 296 ff.

[4] Not identified.

[5] John Stanley (1712–86), blind English organist and composer, was, since 1779, Master of the King's Band of Musicians (*DNB; New Grove*), a post to which CB himself aspired (Lonsdale, pp. 294–5, 319–20). Since 1760 Stanley had organized the annual oratorio season in Lent, in collaboration with J. C. Smith, and then with Thomas Linley the elder (see n. 7).

[6] Of the two oratorios in question, Stanley had written to CB on 21 Apr. 1784 (Coke) in the third person that '. . . his time will not Admit of any new business, . . . And indeed M^r S thinks there is little reason to suppose that any other than Mr Handels Musick would succeed, as people in general are so partial to that, that no other Oratorios are ever Well Attended.'

[7] For Samuel Arnold (1740–1802), D.Mus. (1773), see CB to Twining, [3–10 Mar. 1780], n. 6.

Michael Arne (*c.*1740–86), natural son of CB's master, Thomas Augustine Arne, was a harpsichordist and composer 'always in debt, and often in prison' (Rees; *DNB; New Grove; BD*).

Thomas Linley the elder (1733–95), singing-master, composer, and since 1774, joint manager with Stanley of the Lenten Oratorios which Linley continued after Stanley's death in 1786 with the assistance of Dr Arnold (*DNB; New Grove*).

[8] Dorothea Weston-Hugessen (1758–1828), had married Joseph Banks in Mar. 1779. She was a collector of antique china (*JL* iv. 493; H. C. Cameron, *Sir Joseph Banks, K.B., P.R.S., the Autocrat of the Philosophers* (1952), pp. 254–7; *GM* xcviii (1828)^1, 647).

To Lord Sandwich   St Martin's Street,
                                  20 July 1784

ALS (Montagu: 52/15).

St Martin's street, July 20th
                                      1784.

My Lord.

I have the honour to acquaint your Lordship that on Sunday last, at a very numerous general meeting of the members of the Society of Musicians,[1] after a vote of thanks had unanimously passed to your Lordship & the rest of the Directors of the musical performances in commemoration of Handel, by which their Fund has been so greatly augmented, the Earl of Exeter[2] was unanimously elected honorary President of the Society for the year ensuing, & your Lordship, with the Earl of Uxbridge,[3] Sir Watkin Williams Wynn,[4] & Sir Richard Jebb,[5] Bar^{ts} vice Presidents: an office wch they presume to hope, from your Lordship's great zeal & kindness for their Institution, you will not disdain to accept.

> I have the honour to be, with
> the most profound respect, my Lord,
> your Lordship's obliged &
> most devoted Servant,
> Chas Burney.

[1] The General Meeting of the Society for the Support of Decayed Musicians and their Families, held on 18 July 1784, at the Feathers Tavern in the Strand, with seventy-three members present, had unanimously voted CB to the Chairmanship. CB enclosed in this letter a signed copy of the resolutions passed at the meeting which thanked the Directors of the Handel commemoration and Joah Bates, the Conductor, and elected the Honorary President and Vice-Presidents as set forth in the present letter. The resolutions also appeared in the newspapers. See, for example, *Morning Chronicle*, 27 July 1784. See also CB to Twining, 31 July 1784, n. 24.

[2] Brownlow Cecil (1725–93), 9th Earl of Exeter (1754), who together with his fellow directors of the Concert of Ancient Music, had undertaken the arrangement and management of the Commemoration performances. See *New Grove*, under 'London, §VI, 4(i); §VI, 6(i)'; *Handel Commem.*, pp. 4, 16; R. Elkin, *The Old Concert Rooms of London* (1955), pp. 82–91.

[3] Henry Paget, formerly Bayly (1744–1812), 10th Baron Paget (1769), had been created Earl of Uxbridge of the second creation on 19 May 1784.

[4] Sir Watkin Williams Wynn (1748–89), 4th Baronet (1749), MP, for whom see CB to Twining, 31 July 1784, n. 35. Sir Watkin was an art collector and interested in drama and music (Namier and Brooke, iii. 671–2).

[5] Sir Richard Jebb (1729–87), MD (1751), created Baronet in 1778. See also CB to Charles Burney, 25 Feb. 1781, n. 23. Sir Richard, according to his entry in *DNB*, was 'fond of conviviality and music'.

To Fanny Burney and Mrs Phillips

Queen Anne Street West,
24 July 1784

ALS (Berg).
Docketed by FBA: Dr. B | Most | Kind Parental | Letter to S.E.P. | and F.B. at Chesington—XV ※

Queen Ann Street West. Sat^y
24th July 1784.

All my fine Castle, built as I thought with such excellent Materials, so well planned & constructed with all the Architectural skill I was able to muster, is tumbled down! crumbled into dust, & annihilated! Il caro Amico[1] va partire subito, subito, & there is not the least hope of getting a day for the party I had planned—It has been so uncertain where you w^d be,[2] that I hung back, & said Nothing to him ab^t our expedition, till I was sure where I might find you—he now talks of going on monday or Tuesday, & so there's an end of that dream!—& now, being wide awake, let one tell you that in ab^t a week or ten days, I hope to get my MS.[3] so forward, that I can leave it with the Printer, if it gets out of royal Hands, & can receive the Proofs & correct them at Ches.—I have greatly enlarged my plan in the Sketch of Handel's Life—& the book, will now, wth the 7 prints,[4] be at least ^s15.—God bless you! I write this to my 2 dear good Girls—& am happy in the Bill of health you sent last—L^y Mary[5] has to night none but the *very* elect. L^y Cadogan,[6] & the 2 Miss Bulls.[7] — — addio — I have 2

[1] Pacchierotti, who had given his last performance for the season on 19 June at the King's Theatre (*The London Stage*, v. ii. 716). CB had hoped to accompany Pacchierotti on a visit to Norbury.

[2] Although Mme d'Arblay's subsequent docket indicates that she and the Phillipses were at Chessington, the available evidence points to Norbury Park. Fanny and Susan wrote to CB from Norbury Park, [26 July 1784] (BL Egerton MS 3690, fo. 19): 'These *insinuating* Lockes grow dearer to us all Daily', and CB himself in his postscript appears to refer to the Locks and Norbury Park rather than to Chessington. In the spring of 1784, Phillips had settled his family in a cottage in Mickleham, adjoining the Locks' estate. See *HFB*, pp. 183–4.

[3] Of *An Account of the Musical Performances in Westminster-Abbey, and the Pantheon, May 26th, 27th, 29th; and June the 3d, and 5th, 1784. In Commemoration of Handel* (1785). CB himself dates the text of the *Handel Commem.*, p. 139, 'St. Martin's-street, July 1784.'

[4] For the description of the seven plates included in the book, see *Handel Commem.*, p. [viii].

[5] Lady Mary Duncan, from whose house in Queen Anne Street West CB pens this letter.

[6] Mary Cadogan, née Churchill (1750–after 1803), Horace Walpole's niece, had married (1777) Charles Sloane Cadogan (1728–1807), 3rd Baron (1776), created Earl Cadogan (1800), MP, from whom she was divorced in 1796 for adultery (Namier and Brooke, ii. 169–70; Walpole *Corresp.* xxxii. 368).

[7] For Elizabeth and Catharine Susanna Bull, see CB to Fanny Burney, 6 Nov. 1782, nn. 14, 17.

Copyists at work, as I believe, I said last Night—at present I outrun them—& hope they will not overtake me till I am arrived at my goal.

Susey–Fanny—& Fanny–Susey—love y^r old Dad, & believe him most affect^{ly} y^{rs} C.B.

The Hettina is with the Fitz,[8] & writes funnically to the Ottenburg — — she talks of taking a Peep at Ches. I hope it will be when I am there that I may embrace the 3 witches, the 3 sluts — — I mean the 3 Graces—together—remember me very heartily to Cap. Susey's Night-Cap—& Day Cap. to us all—I hope ere long to *see* those sweet & Charming folks[9] who inhabit so enchanting & Enchanted a Castle.

To Fanny Burney

[St Martin's Street], 27 July [1784]

ALS (BL Egerton MS 3693, fos. 16–17^v).
Addressed: To | Miss Burney | at William Lock's Esqr | Norbury Park, near Leather-head | Surry   *Pmk.:* 27 IY   *Editor's Note:* The first two pages (fos. 16–16^v) carry Charlotte's portion of this joint letter to Fanny. Esther's brief note occupies the top half of p. 3, and CB continues and concludes the letter on the bottom half of p. 3 and top strip of p. 4 (fos. 17–17^v).

Hetty says there never was such nonsense as ⟨the⟩ above[1]—now I'll hold 5 to 4 that the below will beat it hollow, in that shape—for she is just comed home, merry funnical, & we have mustered 2 or 3 hold-fashioned laughs—Well—but the dear Pac. came here this morning for the melancholy business of taking leave! — — he goes the 1st fine day—& there is not the least chance of my seeing [him] again!!—I am grieved that our party[2] c^d not take place on all acc^{ts}— When I shall get out of the hands I am now in, God knows—Day, after day passes on & I seem but more distant from my Goal—Ches.

---

[8] As Hetty herself explains in the joint letter to Fanny, 27 July [1784] (see *post*), she was visiting Mrs Fitzgerald at Cookham, Berkshire. This was probably Mrs Mary Fitzgerald (*fl.* 1779–84), daughter of Keane Fitzgerald (d. 1782), FRS (1756). Mary had married (1779) John Fitzgerald (1760–1818), a close friend of Captain Phillips. The Fitzgeralds of Poland Street and Cookham were long-standing family friends of the Burneys: the two families were next-door neighbours in the 1760s. See *ED* i. 178; ii. 144–6, 305–6; *DL* ii. 128, 148, 172–3, 180; *JL* i. 72, 186; iii. 260–1.
[9] The Locks of Norbury Park.

---

[1] Hetty had penned a few lines in the style of Miss Larolles in *Cecilia*: 'I am this minute come from Mrs. Fitzgerald's ... *Write* says my Father,—I am so bother'd I can't think of any thing ... & then my Father is to write *under* neath, Consequently will read my Letter.'
[2] Charlotte had written in her section of the present letter: 'How sorry I am that you were disappointed of the great pleasure you promised yourselves in seeing him [Pacchierotti] at Norbury!'

Love to Sue—I am so glad to hear of all your healths, that I care not so much for the rest as I sh^d otherwise be—God bless!—I find by the direction of M^rs T's Letter³ that she is gone back to Bath;⁴ but if she were still in London, I don't think I sh^d break in upon her, bon gré mal gré—I never had the least hint from herself that she was here—& *he*⁵ has been in Town, & seen by thousands, without ever calling—so that I suppose he's out of humour, and does not wish to renew the acquaintance—'tis perhaps lucky—for I sh^d not dissemble well.

Let us know of your arrival at Ches. as soon as you can, if you don't write before—I want very much to let those angellic People you are with know what a reverence I have for their Virtues & Character, but I know not how, without more acquaintance—mais cela viendrâ—I hope some time or other—& so once more God bless you—hearty love to Sue—and Cap.—is all the needful from y^r most affectionate old dad.

C.B.

To Mrs Piozzi
[St Martin's Street],
30 July 1784

ALS (Rylands, English MS 545, no. 12).
Addressed: To | Mrs Piozzi, | at Bath *Pmk.:* 31 IY *Publ.: The Piozzi Letters*, ed. E. A. and L. D. Bloom, vol. i (Newark, Del., 1989), p. 105.

Friday Night
July 30. 1784

Dear Madam.

If my wishes for your felicity sh^d seem to arrive late, I hope you will not imagine that I was slow in forming them; but ascribe my silence to the true cause: my not being certain that the Event had taken place.

---

³ Mrs Piozzi to Fanny Burney, 25 July 1784 (Berg).
⁴ Mrs Thrale had arrived in London from Bath on 11 July, in company with Piozzi. On 23 July they were married by a Roman Catholic priest, and returned immediately to Bath, where the marriage service according to the Church of England's rite was performed on 25 July. See *Thraliana*, ii. 611; Clifford, pp. 228–9.
⁵ Piozzi. On a previous visit to London in May 1784, Mrs Thrale had revealed to CB her passion for Piozzi and her intention to marry him. CB had 'behaved with the utmost Propriety' (*Thraliana*, i. 594). Fanny reported, 'My Father was too much prepared by the universal voice of rumour to be *much* surprised;—yet surprised he still was,—& never speaks to me of the matter but with a sigh for the frailty of human nature!' (*The Queeney Letters*, ed. The Marquis of Lansdowne (1934), p. 99). Mrs Piozzi wrote to Queeney Thrale on 25 July 1784, immediately after the Bath ceremony: 'I always *thought* I could manage with Charles well enough, but dear Fanny Burney wonders he softened so soon' (ibid., p. 171).

For, till this evening that I saw it announced, seemingly with authority, in my own Paper, the Morning Chronicle,[1] I had nothing but slight & uncertain rumour to depend on. Fanny is still at M[r] Lock's, & I have been shut up in the *Spidery* scribling in the utmost hurry an Acc[t] of the late Commemoration of Handel, for immediate publication, so that I gain but little information from mixing wth the world, & still less from news-papers, into w[ch] I have hardly time to look once in a Week. This it seems necessary to say in apology to you, dear Mad[m], & my friend, M[r] Piozzi, to whom I most heartily wish every species of happiness w[ch] this world can allow.

I fear M[r] P. is displeased with me for not writing to him at Milan in answer to the Letter wth w[ch] he favoured me from that City early last Winter;[2] but you can explain to him my situation, & the eternal hurry of my Life; w[ch] so far from affording me sufficient time for my friends & for Social happiness, scarcely allows me leisure to support existence by the necessary aliments of sleep & food. I was mortified to hear of his arrival in England from any one but himself. Make my Peace with him, dear Mad[m], I entreat you. And prevail with him to partake of the assurances of my esteem & regard jointly with yourself.

I had not time to thank you for your last Letter,[3] or the agreeable Visit it procured me from M[r] Lysons,[4] who is a charming young man. I had the honour of sending to you, by him, a *proof Print* from Bartolozzi's engraving of me from your picture by S[r] Joshua.[5] It will not be published or presented to any one else till my last Vol.[6] comes out; an event not yet within my ken. Bartolozzi has the Picture still; but is to return it to Sir Jos. & your orders for its future disposal will be instantly & implicitly obeyed.

---

[1] Of Friday, 30 July 1784: 'On Sunday last, and not before, was married, at St. James's-church, Bath, Gabriel Piozzi, Esq; of that parish. to Mrs. Thrale, widow of Henry Thrale, Esq; of St. Saviour, Southwark.'

[2] Piozzi's letter is not preserved.

[3] Of 7 June [1784], from Bath (Osborn).

[4] Mrs Thrale had written (7 June): 'My dear Doctor Burney who never forgets a Friend, will remember all I said to him of Mr Lysons; ... talk with him of painting, of Language, of Medals or of Fossils—*præsto est*: no one can talk so well on so many Subjects as yourself, and none can judge better of another's Merit. Esteem him for his own sake then, and love him for mine.'

Samuel Lysons (1763–1819), antiquary, lawyer, and painter, FSA (1786), FRS (1797). See *DNB*. Lysons had met Mrs Thrale in Bath in Jan. 1784, and rapidly became a close and faithful friend for whom Mrs Thrale wrote letters of introduction when he left Bath to pursue a legal career at the Inner Temple. It was Samuel Lysons who was to oversee the publication of Mrs Piozzi's *Anecdotes of the late Samuel Johnson, LL.D.* (1786). See *Thraliana*, i. 586, 598; ii. 630, 681; L. Fleming, *Memoir and Select Letters of Samuel Lysons, V.P.R.S., V.P.S.A., 1763–1819* (Oxford, 1934); Johnson *Letters*, iii. 171–2.

[5] See CB to Charles Burney, 25 Feb. 1781, n. 19; to Mrs Phillips, [25]-26 Apr. 1784, n. 3.

[6] Of the *History of Music*, published 30 Apr. 1789 (Lonsdale, p. 341), in which Bartolozzi's engraving is in some copies used as frontispiece. See also CB to Twining, 25 Dec. 1784, n. 30.

422

I beg you will present my best Comp^{ts} of congratulation to Mr Piozzi, & ever regard me as your most obliged & affectionate Servant.[7]

Chas Burney.

To Thomas Twining   [St Martin's Street], 31 July 1784

ALS (Berg).

Sat^y July 31. 1784.

Ah my good & ever dear Friend, what a while it seems since I rec^d your last kind and comfortable Letter,[1] without being able to thank you for it, or tell you what I was about! You don't know how much I wish always to answer your letters in the margin, on the 1st perusal, as the King of Prussia does all that are addressed to him; but I know you to be too honest a man to like to be *run in debt* so soon, without Rhyme or Reason; & therefore, when it happens that I c^d find time to write to you by return of Post, I have not impudence sufficient to make use of it.

You ask my opinion of the *Commemoration* Performance[2]—have a little patience, my dear friend, & you shall have it *in print*. W^d you believe it, that after expecting little more than noise & confusion, as I believe I told you in my last letter, things went so much better, & afforded me so much more pleasure & satisfaction than I expected, that in a kind of Rodemontade gratitude I told Lord Sandwich I had some notion of writing an acc^t of the Commemoration Performances for immediate publication, & shewed him the sketch of some such promise wch I intended putting into the Papers, to prevent others from spitting i'th' Porridge?[3] He jumpt at the Idea—said it was just what

---

[7] Mrs Piozzi wrote to her eldest daughter on 4 Aug.: 'Dr Burney has written a most affectionate Letter indeed, *he* as well as everybody else took kindly to young Lysons, they think him as I do a very promising Creature' (*The Queeney Letters*, ed. The Marquis of Lansdowne (1934), p. 176).

In Mr and Mrs Piozzi's joint letter of thanks to CB, 2 Aug. [1784] (Osborn), Mrs Piozzi added, ominously, 'I long however for the good Wishes of your amiable Daughter more than I can express'. Fanny Burney and Mrs Piozzi were never fully reconciled.

[1] Of 26 June 1784 (BL Add. MS 39929, fos. 334–7), in reply to an earlier CB letter (probably of 9 May 1784), not now preserved.

[2] Twining had written (26 June): 'O—but the Westminster-Abbey *Charivari*—how was it?— I long to hear your account of it. ... I own I had never any great idea of the scheme. I considered mere *loudness* as it's object. And, moreover, I doubted much whether such a monstrous Orchestra cou'd be kept in tolerable order. ... I'll be hanged if I did not *wish* that your prophecy—"I foresee that it will be *manqué*"—might be fulfilled, merely for their abominable neglect of your opinions, & hints.'

[3] Dryden's 'Prologue to *Albumazar*', ll. 37–40, for which see CB to Twining, [3–10 Mar. 1780], n. 7.

he & the rest of the Directors[4] wished—& desired that he might put my slip of Paper[5] in his Pocket, to shew his Collegues. But not contented with this he carried it up into their Majesty's Box in the Abbey, where it was 1ˢᵗ mentioned, & upon the King saying that all went so well that they shᵈ get an historian to write an accᵗ of it, Lᵈ S. told his Majesty that it was what he had been just talking of, & shewed him & the Q. the slip of paper—The K. was pleased to say he was glad it wᵈ be in such hands; & wished to see it, when written, in MS.—Here you see I was bound 'with Styx nine times round me'[6]—& there was no getting loose if I had wished it. Now my first Idea was to make out a 2 or 3ˢ pamphlet—Lᵈ S. & the rest of the managers sᵈ I shᵈ have the 3 Ticket Plates wᶜʰ were elegant & well engraved, wᵗʰ wᶜʰ to ornament my accᵗ—Then I thought, *as how* a Sketch of *Handel's* Life wᵈ be necessary to accompʸ this narrative—& what does my *I*, but I leaves everything at sixes & sevens, & ran away for the sake of quiet, to Chesington, for a week leaving between 20 & 30 scholars in Town, thinking that I shᵈ finish the whole in that time—but, alas! new things, at least different things from what I at 1ˢᵗ saw, were dayly licked up as I explored & meditated on the subject, & now my pamphlet will be a ˢ15 4ᵗᵒ (the size of my Histʸ) will be ornamented wᵗʰ 7 elegant Copperplates—a Life of Handel—a longish Preface, and Introduction—an accᵗ of all the 5 Days performances, with remarks on every Piece that was well performed—&c &c—and is with permission already given, to be dedicated to his Majesty[7]—who has already seen the Preface, wᶜʰ he took with him to Windsor to read at his leisure—He has now there the Life of Handel & the 1ˢᵗ Day's performance—I employ two transcribers & cannot get them to keep pace with me—Yesterday I had a single Page composed by the Printer, in order to have it to say in advertising, that it is in the press & will be speedily published.[8] But hard & incessantly as I work, I see wᵗʰ grief that it trenches on my poor dear Histʸ & will employ all my time &

---

[4] For the Directors of the Commemoration, see CB to Sandwich, 20 July 1784.

[5] CB's draft proposal for an account of the Handel commemoration may well lie behind the wording of a news article which appeared in the *Morning Chronicle*, 7 June 1784. The article commented, among other observations: 'The Commemoration of Handel is a circumstance by no means below the dignity of the Historic Muse, and it is with anxious pleasure we look forward to Dr. Burney's intended history of a transaction so extraordinary in the harmonic world.'

[6] See Pope, 'Ode for Musick on St. Cecilia's Day', ll. 90–1:

'Tho' Fate had fast bound her
With *Styx* nine times round her'.

[7] For this Dedication, CB enlisted the help of Johnson. See Lonsdale, pp. 285, 307–8; Johnson *Letters*, iii. 191, 206, 209–10, 215–16; Hill–Powell, iv. 544–7; R. Lonsdale, 'Dr. Burney and the Integrity of Boswell's Quotations', *Papers of the Bibliographical Society of America*, liii (1959), 327–31.

[8] An advertisement to this effect appeared in the *Morning Chronicle*, 9 Aug. 1784.

thoughts for a long time to come. How I wish for you at my Elbow!—
& how I lament the want of time to plague you with every page as fast
as it is scribled!—Indeed the chief part [h]as been written on scraps of
Paper wth a Pencil, *chemin faisant*, in going from scholar to scholar
— — the instant a sheet is written it is given to be transcribed on gilt
Paper for the Royal Eye — — Bates[9] was to have read it to the King;
but his Maj^y finds that [he] has no time for such things in Town, &
therefore carries off every *gob* of MS. to Windsor as fast as he gets
it—A Mr Nicolay,[10] one of the Pages, a German Musician originally
ab^t the late Prince of Wales[11] is the go between—*Entre nous*, I wish
there was any other mediator than B[ates]—whom I perceive no
praise either of himself or Handel can satisfy—& the K. is full as
intoleratingly fond of the old Saxon as B.—so that, if I was to act
politically & *wisely*, I sh^d openly abuse all other Music, Musicians, &
lovers of Music in all parts of the world, but Handel & his insatiable
& exclusive admirers. And in that Case sh^d not you think me a very fit
person to write a *general Hist^y* of Music—to do justice to Genius &
Talents in every Time & Country where I c^d find them? I see that I
am in great danger of doing myself more harm than good by this
Business,—however circumspectly I may Act. But I will not write like
an Apostate—I will not deny my liberal principles—I will not abuse
the lovers of the best Music of Italy & Germany, & say that they are
only admired *through fashion*, & want of good taste & judgment.—I
will ransack the language for terms of praise, in speaking of his best
works—& the Manner in wch they have been lately performed; but
cannot, will not say that there is no other Music fit to be heard, or as
well performed.[12]

[9] Joah Bates (1741–99), English musician, admitted to King's College, Cambridge (1760),
where he met Twining (Rees, under 'Bates'), BA (1764), MA (1767), private secretary to Lord
Sandwich, who procured for him various posts in the civil service. Bates was the conductor of
the five performances which comprised the Handel Commemoration (*DNB*; *New Grove*).

[10] Frederick Nicolay (*c.*1729–1809), of the Royal Household, Page of the Back-stairs, and
member of the Queen's Band of Musick (1762), later violinist in the Queen's Chamber Band. A
man of cultivated tastes, Nicolay was an adviser to their Majesties on collecting, and served as
unofficial royal music librarian (A. Hyatt King, 'Portrait of a Bibliophile V, Frederick Nicolay,
1728/9–1809', *The Book Collector*, ix (1960), 401–13; reprinted in *Some British Collectors of Music,
c.1600–1960* (Cambridge, 1963), pp. 115–29). It was Nicolay who transmitted to CB two
'critical notes' in the hand of George III, commenting on passages of the *Handel Commem.* while it
was being composed. See *Mem.* ii. 384–6; *Handel Commem.*, pp. 80, 105.

[11] i.e. Frederick Louis (1707–51), Prince of Wales, eldest son of George II, and father of
George III (*DNB*). Nicolay had been brought to England in 1736 by his parents, when they
accompanied Princess Augusta of Saxe-Gotha (1719–72) to the Court of St James's for her
marriage to the Prince of Wales (King, *British Collectors*, p. 120).

[12] For CB's diplomatically worded dissociation of himself from 'bigotry' in favour of Handel,
see *Handel Commem.*, p. xv. For his further comments on Handel, see *Hist. Mus.* iv. 222 ff.;
Mercer, ii. 672 ff.; and especially Rees, for his final assessment of Handel.

Franks will no longer than next week, I fear, be of any use but to Members of Parl^t themselves,[13] or I w^d send you scraps of MS. or proof sheets as fast as they c^d be spared—I long for your *vardy* ab^t millions of things; and having so long leant on you as my Crutch, I limp & stumble at every step I take without you.

But you have been at work for *nown self*, like a very good Boy.[14] And you have been tolerably well too, like a still better boy[15] — — & you still think of me & my dirty *Gobs*, like the best of all Boys![16]—I have not been able to bestow the most distant thought on my MS. concerning old times—& in trying this Morn^g to find the *Gob* I wished to send you ages ago have not been able to find it — — — where it lies buried—under what heap of rubbish, God knows — — If I can find it, this Letter shall be in the Parcellina—If not I have a Frank—for I will not longer postpone telling you of my present doings.—I hope to God you have had no return of your cursed *viscous* Fever[17]—& that Aristotle & you have continued Hand & Glove ever since the paroxysm began[18]—In looking over you[r] last Letter I find some allusion to what I had said I suppose in my last Letter ab^t Tassoni & Scots Music;[19] but if I can recollect what, I'll be hanged. This one new business has put all other businesses out of my head—& if my brain were microscopically exam[in]ed, *Handel* and *Commemoration* w^d be

---

[13] CB's fears were slightly premature. The Franking Act of 1784 (24 Geo. III, c. 37) received the Royal Assent on 20 Aug. 1784 (*London Gazette*, 17–21 Aug. 1784). Designed to check the abuse of Members' Franks, the Act required each Member of Parliament to write out in his own handwriting the entire superscription of each letter, adding the place and date of posting 'in Words at Length', and to sign the address panel. The Act attempted to make franking 'as troublesome as possible'. See *Journals of the House of Commons* (1803), xl. 407; K. Ellis, *The Post Office in the Eighteenth Century, a Study in Administrative History* (1958), p. 42; H. Joyce, *The History of the Post Office* (1893), pp. 216–17.

[14] Twining wrote in his letter of 26 June: 'Since I left Colchester, a fit of industry has seized me, & I have been getting on a little, *testudines* gradu, with my Notes.'

[15] 'As to health, I have, thank God, been quite comfortable for a long time,—'till Sunday last, when I had a return of my ague, but not a violent one' (ibid.).

[16] 'I ought, ages ago, to have desired you to send the *gob* you talked of . . . Pray send your papers whenever it suits you . . . To look over your MS will be *pure* amusement & gratification to me; & it will be kindness to furnish me with so pleasant a relief from my own faggings, & book-huntings, & groperies & pokeries & sweepings & cobweb-catchings' (ibid.).

[17] Twining had grumbled in his letter of 26 June about his recurring fits of ague: 'I wish I cou'd, by any means, overcome the *viscosity* of this plaguy disorder which persecutes me Winter, & Summer.'

[18] About his work on Aristotle's *Poetics*, Twining had written (ibid.): 'I was willing to make the most of an indust[r]ious paroxysm that seldom lasts me long.'

[19] 'By the bye—as to the passage of Tassoni, which you mention—you say, in your *last* letter that all the Scotch writers since, have boasted of the *royal* descent of their national Music. As to the *fact*, whether *James* did, or did not, invent the Scots Melodies I leave that to you to settle;—I dare say you are right. The passage of Tassoni undoubtedly does prove that *Tassoni understood* James to have been the inventor of them; this however is no proof that it *was* so' (ibid.). See *Hist. Mus.* iii. 218–20; Mercer, ii. 178–9, where CB discusses this problem arising from the Italian poet and critic, Alessandro Tassoni (1565–1635), in his *Dieci libri di pensieri diversi*, bk. X, ch. xxiii (4th rev. edn., Venice, 1627, p. 664).

seen clinging to every fibre. One thing I have discovered (and a most melancholy one it is, fait comme je le suis) that neither his M———y nor M[r] B. has the least notion of a *Joke*—not the most innocent or insipid smile must be put on a single period—*one Key* of Panegyric is all they want.—fine!—very fine!—charming! exquisite! grand!! Sublime!!!—These are all the notes (a Hexachord) I must use—Some time or other I'll shew you a passage or two that I have been obliged to expunge, or render utterly insipid, because they smiled a little[20]— Now B. can smile & smile & still be dissatisfied[21]—But then the K—— — — does not like it.—Into what a Scrape am I got?—I may do myself irreparable mischief—& *can* I fear derive no good—considering the hands I am in. I set out with the design of praising honestly & heartily what I felt deserving—& to be silent as to the rest.—After I had read my Preface, & fragments of the rest to L[d] Sandwich, S[r] W. W. Wynn, Bates &c—L[d] S. said—'you intend giving the profits of this Acc[t] to the Fund, D[r] B.—don't you?'—'No, my L[d]—I had no such intension—It will be a drop in the Ocean, after the Thousands it has gained by the Commemoration—& yet though little for them to receive, it will be a great deal for me to give—There is not a Bookseller in London who w[d] not readily give me a £100 for a Pamphlet on the subject. By paying a Guinea for my admission at each Performance, & the loss of 4 entire days business my Sacrifice to the Commemoration & Fund has already been considerable, & the giving up my Copyright to the Pamphlet will make my contribution much higher than my share, or that of any one else.'—'His Majesty expects it'—says my L[d]—'you w[d] not I dare say be the only one who benefitted by the Commemoration.' — — This staggered me—& made me feel very uncomfortable—though it did not convince me that I ought to comply. I fretted afterwards, & grumbled in the gizzard—till tired of both—I made up my mind ab[t] it—& perhaps more heroically than wisely determined to sacrifice my youngest babe to please his M———y & their Lord[ps] & Baronetships. And an errant Slave has it made me.[22]

[20] Twining wrote in reply, 27 Aug. 1784 (BL Add. MS 39929, fos. 338–9): 'Well—I long to *see* y[r] book.—Some day or other we'll have an Edition *non chatrée*, with *all* the *original jokes* in it.'
[21] Cf. *Hamlet*, I. v. 107–8: '. . . meet it is I set it down That one may smile, and smile, and be a villain'.
[22] CB probably meant 'arrant', with an echo of *Hamlet*, II. ii. 543: 'O, what a rogue and peasant slave am I!' Twining's reply of 27 Aug. expressed suitable indignation: 'But who can expect feeling, or delicacy in these *great* people? . . . I do maintain, that what you urged to L[d] S. was unanswerable. . . . What arrant nonsense to talk of your being "*the only one benefitted by the Commemoration*"! . . . If you got £100 for y[r] copy, wou'd the Charity have had £100 the less? . . . And then, your *Critics*!!—to clap one padlock upon your pocket, & two more *tumpers* at each corner of your poor dear mouth—or rather two great *cramps* to prevent the least simper of the muscles—'tis *too* much. When I read your *moving* complaint about this *defense* of joking, *de par le Roi* . . . I laughed with one eye, & cried with the other.'

All my other concerns neglected—Hist^y forgotten—a pile of letters 12 or 14 Inches high, unanswered on my table—kept in Town at a time I want, & used to enjoy, tranquility & whol[e]some Air—running a risk of offending the ———— & quarelling wth B.—a slave to other peoples opinions & prejudices!—in short all that is uncomfortable attends this business—thus far—What the future may produce, I know not. My heart & pen are locked up.—I wrote the Preface, Life of Handel—Introduction & 3 1st Days wth my heart *au bout de la langue.*—But now, I am terrified at every word I write—my playful & folatre way of expressing myself taken from me, reduces me to the state of a hireling ministerial Scribler, without the Pay—Every man not merely 'a fellow without mark or likelihood'[23] has a way of expressing himself as of looking—I can no more help aiming at bad jokes in writing than you the making good ones. Ma—ci vuol Pazienza. —Because I had not writing enough—being summoned to a Genl meeting of the Musical Fund, after the Commemoration, & suspecting that I sh^d be called to the Chair, I prepared a kind of discourse, as I am not accustomed to public Speaking—& this after much debate, folly, & illiberality, was called for by one of the Members to whom I had slightly mentioned my design.—Part of it will appear in the next London Magazine,[24] in wch I must whisper to you, my son Chas has some concern,[25] & pressed me to let him make use of it, rather than leave it to the mercy of News Papers—There is nothing in it but a wish to make the Members of a Society now suddenly enriched[26] a little more liberal & Charitable than when they were Poor; which I find very hard to do.[27] Besides this, as Chairman, I had the Minutes

[23] Cf. *I Henry IV*, III. ii. 45.

[24] See CB to Sandwich, 20 July 1784, n. 1, for the meeting on 18 July 1784. CB's prepared speech as well as an account of the proceedings appeared in the July issue of the *London Magazine, Enlarged and Improved*, iii (1784), 73–4. CB's ally to whom he had 'slightly mentioned' his idea was the bassoonist, John Ashley, for whom see CB to Sandwich, 2 Aug. 1784, n. 8. The evidence for this identification is contained in a letter from Ashley to Sandwich, 25 Dec. 1784 (Montagu: 52/34). See also n. 27.

[25] See CB to Twining, 10–12 Nov. 1783, n. 62.

[26] 'The decayed Musicians fund bids fair to be one of the most thriving institutions of an eleemosinary kind. It was in a good way before the late Commemoration, which added to it so very largely as a nett annual produce of 300l. and it is now understood to be the determination of their Majesties, to patronize the yearly concert of the fund, and the performances on that occasion are to be selections from Handel; the band to be as full a one as can be got together' (*Morning Chronicle*, 31 July 1784). See also CB to Twining, 1 Sept. 1784, n. 14; 25 Dec. 1784, n. 26.

[27] CB had urged that in view of the £6000 that had come to the Society from the Handel Commemoration, 'the public will be much more pleased and served by the sums we shall *spend*, without diminishing our capital, than by those we shall *save*'. He advocated increases in the sums paid to present pensioners, the diminution of the '*difficulties* which new candidates for admission into the Society have heretofore met with', and the readmission of '*seceders back* to our Society, and to *rescind* all harsh and hasty *acts of expulsion*' (*London Magazine*, iii. 73–4). CB's rage at the

& 6 Letters of Thanks to write to the Directors & Conductor[28]—my hand, head, & heart are alike crippled.

You mention the Cheek-by-jowlliad between me & the Knight[29]—. Did I tell you of a real one lately between us twain?—I met him at Dr Johnson's & did not know him, he's grown so thin & old since I came from Italy. He came up to me—shook me by the paw—& more politely than I thought he c^d truckle to, told me he [was] glad to see me &c—I believe it was poor Bewley who wrote the monthly Review of S^r Jno[30]—& himself the Critical[31]—

I had wholly forgotten y^r Fr^d Jones & his book,[32] till you put me in

Society's illiberality is illuminated by John Ashley's letter to Lord Sandwich, 25 Dec. 1784 (Montagu: 52/34). Ashley wrote: 'After they had received the Donation from the Jubilee which almost doubled their Capital, Doctor Burney and myself thought it a good time to propose an Act of Grace, and remission of Sins; which was my Lord, to reinstate those poor Members who from indigent circumstances had been unable to pay their Arrears therefore expelled the Society. The Doctor drew up the Motion in Writing and at the General Meeting (Appointed to receive the Account of the Commemoration) it was received with the greatest bursts of Applause, and Humanity, and Charity, Echo'd from every part of the Room; but in less than a Week after the first Governors Meeting, a party was raised against it and the Doctor affraid of Worse consequences was Obliged to withdraw his Motion'.

[28] See CB to Sandwich, 20 July 1784. CB's five other letters were doubtless addressed to the Earls of Exeter and Uxbridge, to Sir Watkin Williams Wynn, Sir Richard Jebb, and to Joah Bates.

[29] Twining had informed CB, 7 Apr. 1784 (BL Add. MS 39929, fos. 332–3): '. . . now Sr John's *price* is so reduced, I have condescended to purchase him; . . . So, henceforth, you may say, *See* Sr J. H. p. &c.'; and in his letter of 26 June: 'Well—but I congratulate you, & the Knight, upon your being such good friends. There you are, upon my shelf together, like Pylades & Orestes. You have not turned your *backs* upon each other once. Think of *my* taking off Payne's hands, to his great joy, the *last* lingering copy of Sr John's book.'

[30] Twining had written (26 June): 'My brother had a curious conversation with Payne about the Knight, at the play, not long since. Do you know that Payne thought, & had been told so, that I wrote the criticism upon Sr J.'s book in the M.R.?—I wish it were true, for it was an excellent thing. I *have* been told that your poor friend Bewly wrote it; but I forget by whom. I think I never read *you* say.' For a full account of Bewley's devastating review of Hawkins's *History* in the *Monthly Review* for 1777 (lvi. 137–44, 270–8; lvii. 149–64), see Lonsdale, pp. 208–19. See also CB to Twining, 6 Sept. 1783, n. 6.

[31] The laudatory notices of Hawkins's *History* appeared in the *Critical Review*, xlii (1776), 401–14; xliii (1777), 34–44, 98–109, 267–74, 442–5, much to CB's annoyance. See Lonsdale, pp. 208–9.

[32] For the Revd William Jones (1726–1800) of Nayland, and his *Treatise on the Art of Music* (1784), see CB to Twining, 6 Sept. 1783, n. 36. Despite his protestations in the present letter, CB did in fact maul Jones's *Treatise* in the *Monthly Review*, lxxv (1786), 105–12, 174–81. CB's copy of the *Treatise* is listed in 'Cat. Fac. Mus.', item 71.

Twining had written in his letter of 26 June a long condemnation of Jones's *Treatise*, in reply to CB's comments in his missing letter (see n. 1). Twining wrote: 'Nothing can be so applicable to J—— as y^r quotation—"authors before they write shou'd read."—This he never does.' Jones, in the Introduction to his *Treatise* had uttered such heresies as: 'We are now divided into parties for the old and the new Music . . . I confess very freely, that my feelings give their testimony to the Style which is now called ancient; . . . I think the Golden Age of Music is past . . . we are fallen into the Silver age . . . Doctor *Burney* has also done great justice to the old Ecclesiastical Composers, in his learned commentaries on the works of *Josquin de Prez*; and if he carries his work down to later times, I hope he will do the same Justice to the Fathers of Instrumental Harmony

mind of it—Why it died still-born—I never heard it cry—or be cried-up—What is become of it—sh^d it be allowed X^tian burial, with so much unchristian spirit in it against modern Music — — Peace to its ashes, if they burned sufficiently to produce any—but I rather think it fizzed a little whil[e], & moldered away, without leaving a $\left.\begin{array}{c}\text{wreck}\\\text{reck}\end{array}\right\}$ behind. It did *smoke* however for you saw the *Vapour*—he might be smoked in his turn—but ere I'll meddle with it I'll be smoke dried—no, no—I have other Game to pursue—& therefore shall not make game of him.—Was the reviewing his book one of the many things you wanted me to write—when my Hist^y was [*here CB missed a page. He noted on it:* This page was missed *par megard*—avancez toujours—sans y penser.] finished?—or did you foresee that the Directors & Conductor of the Commemoration of Handel w^d want an Historiographer?—I want you to mention some undertaking or other to keep me from that root of all Evil—Idleness.

In my late conversations with Bates, I find you meant *him*, not Jones in your last letter[33]—'d'ye think I did not know him?' Yes, yes, he has made up his mind, *avec une vengeance*—my God!—what contraction, & childish prejudices—how deaf, as well as how blind are both to real Genius!— These people in fastening on Handel & Clinging so closely to him, are sure of being right sometimes—& if they were to let go their hold, what w^d become of 'em?—They will be too insolent now. Les grands Hommes! qu'ils sont![34] — — That Sr W. Sea-calf, as Pac. calls the *true* Prince of Wales—Sr Watty—do you know him—or did you ever see a sea-Calf—?[35] I was invited to meet them as I told you before, to 5 or 6

in the last age, whose excellencies he is well able to distinguish and recommend for imitation' (pp. iii–v).

[33] Twining had written of Jones in his letter of 26 June: 'He is one of those men who, when once they have *made up their minds*, as they call it, upon any subject, never *unmake* it upon any account.'

[34] Twining replied (27 Aug.): 'My friend Jones is not a bit more prejudiced than Bates, & has a good deal of sense, & pleasantry about him, *de plus*. I knew B. well at Camb., & was glad to meet him as a *Musician*, but the *man* I never *took to*; & he is now *more* offensive to me by a sort of unmeaning *courtly palăver* that he has picked up of late years. Of humour he never had a glimpse; & in point of sense & abilities is quite a *common man*. But there is nothing in human conduct, that answers so well as the being overbearing. Since the beginning of the world, all mankind have agreed to give way to a pushing, over-bearing, man.' See also CB to Twining, 30 Aug. 1773, n. 12.

[35] Twining wrote in reply (27 Aug.): 'Sr Watty, I never saw. I have seen the great fat-ar—d Hippopotamus at Sr Ashton Lever's.' Sir Watkin Williams Wynn (1748–89), of Wynnstay, Denbighshire, MP (1772–89), Lord Lieutenant of Merioneth (1775–89), was a scion of one of the wealthiest and most influential Welsh families (Namier and Brooke, iii. 671–2). His father, Sir Watkin Williams Wynn (1692–1749), 3rd Baronet (1740), an active Jacobite, was called the 'Prince of Wales' by virtue of his vast estates in North Wales (Walpole *Corresp*. xxx. 292; xxxiv. 4, 95; *DNB*). See also B. Ford, 'Sir Watkin Williams-Wynn, a Welsh Maecenas', *Apollo*, xcix (1974), 435–9.

Dinners;[36] but so far from doing any good, I cd not edge in a Word—all I had to do was to stuff—drink—& be a witness to their importance & blunders—

I have been dining with Sir Jos. Reynolds & an agreeable set of his Frds & have staid so late that I shall not have time to look out—to deterré my MS. or to add a word more having several other Letters to write—so God bless you—I'll send my Parcel per favour of yr Brother if Possible—Mrs Burney is gone to Hastings, to try Sea Air.

I intended filling my 3 sheets, but have not a moment[.] Have you the Baron d'Astorga's Stabat Mater? 'tis of the most exquisite & recherché kind, when recherche was most in fashion—yes, yes, his Cantatas of wch I have many are very fine—I collected at Rome 8 or 10 by him[37]—as many by Gasparini—Marcello[38]—& *Hen*del, some of wch none of the Collectors of Handel here ever saw—These were certainly made while he was at Rome—1709.[39]

Fanny & Mrs Phillips have been at Mr Lock's on a Visit 4 or 5 weeks— There is a *viscosity* in their friendship—Do you know anything of Mr Lock? He fills my Idea of an accomplished Man more than any gentleman I was ever acquainted with—The Artists all bow down to his Judgment in Sculpture, Painting, Architecture, & Antiquities—In Music his Taste is nice, refined, & certain—& in Literature all you'd love—Addio—must run from you—best respects to Mrs T.

& beleive me ever yrs with
the most hearty & Cordial affection.
C. Burney.

You will instantly perceive that all I have written abt his M——y & Bates is rigorously Sub sigillo—

Won't you let a body hear from you soon?

[36] Earlier in the year, CB had noted in his pocket-book for Mar.–Apr.: 'Dine with directors of the Com. of Handel during its arrangement' (*Frag. Mem.*, Osborn).

[37] For Emanuele Gioacchino Cesare Rincón, barone d'Astorga (1680–c.1757), see CB to Twining, 14 Dec. 1781, n. 13. Twining had written (26 June): 'I hope the Baron D'Astorga stands well in yr good-liking. He is one of my favourites. I have many Cantatas of his, some of which are, (allowing always for the improvements of air since his time—) to me, charming; especially his recitatives.' In reply to CB's enquiry, Twining wrote (27 Aug.): 'I *have* D'Astorga's *Stabat*, copied by my own painful paw. *Besides* learning & recherc[h]e, there is, I think, considerable expression, & elegance of melody.'

[38] For Francesco Gasparini (1668–1727), and his pupil, Benedetto Marcello (1686–1739), see CB to Twining, 14 Dec. 1781, n. 13.

[39] 'In 1770, I purchased at Rome, among other manuscript compositions by old masters, six cantatas, *a voce Sola*, del Georgio Federigo HENDEL, *detto il Sassone*, which were, probably, produced in this city during his residence there, about the year 1709: by the yellow colour of the ink, they seem to have been long transcribed. Some of them I have never seen in any other collection' (*Handel Commem.*, p. [*8] n.). This MS volume of cantatas is listed in *Cat. Mus. Lib.*, lot 610, and fetched 6*s*.

To Lord Sandwich   [St Martin's Street],
                                        2 August 1784

ALS (Montagu: 52/20).

My Lord.

Besides returning your Lordship my humble acknowledgments for
the letter wth wch I was honoured from Burleigh by Saturday's post,[1]
there appears a necessity for troubling your Lord^P with a letter on
another account: wch is to beg your Lord^P to acquaint our worthy
President Lord Exeter, that in my Conversations with Mr Nicolay
concerning his Majesty's gracious inclination to become the Patron of
our Society, he told me that his Majesty in speaking on the Subject
had said that the regular channel through wch our petition sh^d be conveyed to him w^d be through the mediation of the Lord Chamberlain.[2]
This I thought right to communicate to your Lordships as soon as
possible, after reading in the letter wth wch I was honoured from
Burleigh that it was the intention of Ld Exeter to lay our request
before his Maj^{ty} *without delay*, through the *Duke of Montagu*.[3] Your
Lord^P I am sure will see my reason for hastening to forward this
information to Burleigh, lest irregularity in application might impede
in[s]tead of forwarding our important business. I saw Mr Nicolay &
conversed with him on the subject, late on Sat^y Night. He thinks all
will go on smoothly & expeditiously through the channel indicated by
his Majesty himself.

I have worked double tides[4] at my acc^t of the Commemoration
Performances since I had the honour of seeing your Lordship. His
Majesty has read & returned the Preface, of wch I have since had a

---

[1] Lord Sandwich's letter, written at Burghley House, Northants, seat of the Earl of Exeter
(Walpole *Corresp.* x. 344–7), in reply to CB's letter of 20 July is not preserved.

[2] The Lord Chamberlain of the Household at this time was James Cecil (1748–1823), 7th
Earl of Salisbury (1780), created Marquess (1789). Lord Salisbury, appointed in 1783, held the
post till 1804.

[3] George Brudenell, afterwards Montagu (1712–90), 4th Earl of Cardigan (1732), created
Duke of Montagu (1766), Governor to the Royal Princes (1776), Master of the Horse (1780–90),
Governor of Windsor Castle (1752–90). See *DNB*, under 'Montagu (formerly Brudenell)'.
Warned by this letter, Lord Sandwich, who had just left Burghley House, evidently wrote to
Lord Exeter, who said in a reply dated 5 Aug. 1784 (Montagu: 52/21): 'Whenever business of
any kind is to be done I always endeavour to use expedition which was the reason I wrote to the
Duke of Montagu the same morning that I inform'd Dr Burney of my readiness to accept the
favour confer'd on me by the Society for the Musical Fund therefore cannot apply to the L^d
Chamberlain till I receive an answer from His Grace having mention'd this circumstance to D^r
Burney I hope He will communicate it to Mr Nicolai'.

[4] See *OED*, under 'tide', *sb*. 14.

single page *printed*, in order to advertise *with truth*, that the pamphlet is in *the Press*, & will be speedily published.[5] I have drawn up an advertisement ready for Mr Simpson[6] to have inserted in all the Papers. His Maj^ty has now in reading the Sketch of the Life of Handel, & the acc^t of the 1st Day's performance, wch when returned will be printed with all possible expedition. I keep two transcribers hard at work—the 2^d Day is already copied fair for his Maj^ty; & the 3^d & 4th Days are now transcribing. The 5th & last Day, wth a translation of Count Benencasa's Letter,[7] and a summary acc^t of the Musical Fund—the rec^ts, expences, surplus, it's disposition &c will be more bulky than any of the other 4, though but little was left to be said of the performance, as it had been minutely described in speaking of the 3^d day. This will be ready for transcription by the time either of the Copyists returns with the 3^d or 4th day.

When my work of writing & revisal is over, I shall closely attend to the press, & the Engravers, rolling-press printers, &c.

Much will depend on the expedition wth wch his Majesty peruses & returns the MS. But with all the hast[e] possible of every one concerned, I perceive with sorrow that the whole summer will melt away before I shall be able to quit London, or resume the thread of my long neglected History.

I have the honour to be with the greatest respect, My Lord,

your Lordship's obliged
& devoted Servant.
Chas Burney.

London, | Monday 2^d Aug^t | 1784.

I sh^d be very remiss if I did not entreat your Lord^P to accept of my most grateful thanks, for thinking me worthy the honour of a *Gold Medal*, wch was delivered to me by Mr Ashley,[8] & wth wch I am very much flattered.

[5] See CB to Twining, 31 July 1784, n. 8.

[6] Redmond Simpson (d. 1787), oboist and member of the Queen's Chamber Band, was, according to his obituary in the *Scots Magazine*, xlix (1787), 51, 'the first performer on the hautboy in this kingdom; ... he was one of the musicians who attended her Majesty from the continent'. As sub-treasurer, Simpson had assisted Sir Watkin Williams Wynn in keeping the accounts of the Commemoration (*Handel Commem.*, p. 125), and served as treasurer to the Musical Fund. See Rees, where CB wrote of Simpson as 'an active and important personage at the meetings of the musical fund'. See also CB to Sandwich, 25 Dec. 1784, for CB's blunt comments on Simpson.

[7] Of 7 June 1784, most of which CB included, together with a translation from the original French, in *Handel Commem.*, pp. 115–23. Count Bartolomeo Benincasa (1746–1816), Italian man of letters (*DBI*), had written a complimentary letter to CB, comparing the Handel Commemoration favourably with other musical celebrations on the Continent. The letter is now preserved in the collection of Gerald Coke.

[8] John Ashley (1734–1805), bassoon-player, assistant conductor of the Handel Commemoration performances (*DNB*; *New Grove*). Letters from Ashley to Lord Sandwich preserved in the

To Sarah (Rose) Burney [St Martin's Street], 1 September 1784

ALS (Burney-Cumming).
Addressed: To | Mrs Burney

My dear Rosette.

The letter to wch you allude, luckily, never came to hand; wch spared me great uneasiness, & now exempts you from all apology for its contents.[1] I have been extremely concerned to hear of your indisposition, & sh^d have been still more afflicted had I thought you ever fancied me cold, indifferent, or unkind towards you. For God's sake my dear daughter, drive away all such groundless suppositions, & assure yourself of my affection & friend^p as long as you think them worth having. As the wife of my beloved son Charles, the daughter of my honoured friend Dr Rose, & the adopted Child of my bosom, you are sure of a warm place in my heart: therefore banish all suspicions of coldness or neglect, for wch you have not, to my knowledge, the least real cause. Professions of kindness are easily made; but why sh^d I make them, if not Sincere? or why sh^d you torment yourself with imaginations of unkindness that was never meant, and for wch I am utterly ignorant of having given cause even for suspicions. Complaints of want of kindness in a lover or a friend, if well founded, I believe never brought back the heart of one or the other. Affection must be gained & kept by constant & reciprocal confidence & agreeable qualities, or it is held by a rope of sand. Even reason, wch may teach disguise & dissimulation, can never govern the heart. The undefinable something, wch is stiled *affection*, depends on many latent causes; but on none that are obvious, I believe so much as openness, and a constant wish to please.

To fancy ourselves slighted & ill-treated without perfect demonstration & conviction, is not only tormenting to ourselves but so displeasing oftimes to others, as to lay a foundation for the very thing of wch we are most in dread.

---

collection of Victor Montagu show that Ashley was responsible for liaison between the Directors of the Handel Commemoration and the various engravers and minters who executed the illustrated tickets and commemorative medal. The medal, which is illustrated in the Frontispiece to *Handel Commem.*, has not been traced among the Burney family mementoes. See also CB to Sandwich, 27 Nov. 1784, n. 2.

[1] Neither Rosette's letter to which the present one is a reply, nor her former letter, appear to have survived. Rosette Burney, CB's daughter-in-law, at times highly excitable, was also prone to bouts of deep depression (see *JL* i. 81; CB to Fanny Burney, [24? Apr. 1783], n. 6).

This is the language I w^d use to my own Child, & such as I w^d not address to you, my dear Girl, if I was not interested in your happiness as much as if you really stood in that relation. Endeavour by all possible means to tranquilize your mind; and, by becoming calm & happy yourself, you will render others happy: the most satisfactory felicity we can enjoy in this world.

Adieu my dear daughter, & that returning health of body may be accompanied with every mental comfort & gratification wch rational & innocent beings are allowed to enjoy, is the hearty prayer of yours most affectionately.

Chas Burney.

Septr 1st 1784.

To Thomas Twining [St Martin's Street], 1 September 1784

L copy extract (Osborn: 'Twining Letterbook No. 4', pp. 11–15).

Sep. 1. 1784

About the 13th you say.[1] Why I am obliged to be in Town to attend the press every 3 or 4 days, and I'll contrive to be there the *very* day of your arrival, or any other day that you think more likely for you to take a peep at me in my spidery. I have so many things to say & to shew to you, that I do hope you will do your part towards a meeting *there*. Otherwise I have been thinking that through Isleworth is one of the roads to Chesington, & about half way thither. Why now how nice it would be, if you would let me call & carry you off to my hiding place for a day or two!—it would be all in the change of air-way. Perhaps Fanny & the Philipses may be there, & we should so chat, & lounge, & laugh, & be idle & foolish that all the boys & girls in the Parish would cry shame on us.

After this if you go to Malvern, you will stand no chance of escaping Burneys. My brother[2] lives at Worcester and has a large family of very

---

[1] Twining had written to CB on 27 Aug.: '... if I am otherwise stout, shall run away from this land of agues for a few weeks; ... I shall probably go to my brother's at Isleworth, ... So that I comfort myself with the thoughts of having a peep at you, at Newton House, or somewhere.' His doctor 'recommends *Malvern*, as the purest, & most *anti-agueish* air in the kingdom.... Are not there *Burneys* at Worcester? Lord, how impertinently & cavalierly I wou'd exercise my prerogative of knowing all sorts & sizes of Burneys,—if I went into that part of the world! ... I hope e'er long to see you. I shall *probably* be in town, (if at all) by y^e *13*^th Sept^r.'

[2] Richard Burney (1723–92), of Barborne Lodge, Worcester. For the 'Worcester' Burneys, see 'Worcester Memoranda', and *JL* i, pp. lxxiv–lxxv. Richard Burney was a music and dancing master by profession.

worthy & ingenious young men & women. Mr Burney,[3] whom you know, is the eldest son. The rest of the boys are dispersed, one at Glo[u]cester,[4] another at Shrewsbury,[5] a third[6] a student in the R. Acad. of Painting & a lad of very great Genius, who has made 3 drawings for my Commemoration account, that the King & Queen have seen, & I was told, were *highly delighted* with:—but what is still more & better, Sir Jos. Reynolds[,] Mr Strange,[7] Bartolozzi, Wyatt,[8] & other very eminent artists have said very kind & flattering things of them, but the difficulty is in meeting with good engravers that will undertake to do them justice at such short notice as this. I am almost afraid they must be sent to France.—Let me see,—I left off at my Brother's 4th Son. He has a 5th who lives with him at Worcester,[9] a lad of great Genius, likewise, for drawing, & if you should make an excursion to Worcester, my brother will shew you such a collection of prints & drawings as would take 2 or 3 days at least to examine. He has 3 daughters,[10] all amiable & sweet girls that you would like to chat with: the 2nd I believe is with my brother in that city, and the third keeps her brothers house at Shrewsbury; but they are always scampering about & will certainly ride over you some day or other while you are at Malvern. M^r B & my daughter are just returned from Worcester,[11] where they went on a family visit, & where all the Patriarchal family met.—Thank you for your pity & the charming Stanza of Ariosto.[12] Indeed this Commemoration business lies very

[3] Charles Rousseau Burney (1747–1819), harpsichordist and music teacher, who had married CB's daughter Hetty.

[4] Richard Gustavus Burney (1751–90), music and dancing master, had close connections with musical societies in Gloucester as well as in Worcester where he resided with his father ('Worcester Memoranda').

[5] James Adolphus Burney (1753–98) had settled at Shrewsbury in 1778 as a music and dancing master. His sister Rebecca (n. 10) joined him there the following year as his housekeeper ('Worcester Memoranda').

[6] Edward Francesco Burney (1760–1848), the artist, for whom see CB to Mrs Thrale, [28 Oct. 1779], n. 14. E. F. Burney eventually executed four of the illustrations for *Handel Commem.* (see CB to Sandwich, 27 Nov. 1784).

[7] Robert Strange (1721–92), Kt. (1787), engraver, one of CB's oldest friends (*DNB*).

[8] James Wyatt (1746–1813), RA (1785), architect (*DNB*).

[9] Thomas Frederick Burney (1765–85), who, 'at the age of about 15, display'd an uncommon genius for pen & ink drawings' ('Worcester Memoranda'). In the autumn of this year he started to learn the art of engraving, but died of consumption in Oct. 1785.

[10] Ann, or 'Nancy', Burney (1749–1819), who had married (1781) the Revd John Hawkins (d. 1804), of Nash Court, Kent; Elizabeth Warren Burney (1755–1832), called 'Blue'; Rebecca Burney (1758–1835), who was to marry (1788) William Sandford (1759–1823), surgeon.

[11] This visit is also recorded in the 'Worcester Memoranda' for the summer of 1784: 'Mr. & Mrs. Charles Rousseau and Edward Francisco, (who then resided with them) paid a visit at Barborne. Rebecca gave them the meeting'.

[12] In reply to CB's long lamentations of 31 July 1784, Twining had written (27 Aug.): '... your description of your situation, perplexities, & uncomfortable *gêne*, went to my very heart; but indignation came to my relief. I felt like Ariosto's Bear defending her wounded young ones—half

heavy on my shoulders, for now tis all written, & Royally read & approved, yet my whole time, thoughts, and summers retreat are gobbled up by it, in attending the press. Then there are Tweedle-dum & Tweedle-dee quarrels in the Musical Society[13] which plague, mortify,—& employ my time & thoughts.[14] Wrong-headed people there are every where, but in such abundance as in this Society, I believe no where.

—I have reserved to myself, for the sequel of my History, the critical examination of Handel's works in general,[15] and then shall 'extenuate nothing, nor set down aught in malice'.[16]

I must do his Maj. the justice to say that he is much better acquainted with Handels works & merit than any of the noble or gentle Directors. Right or wrong, he gives reasons for his admiration; & the great crime of *exclusive liking*, (particularly in a King) excepted, I can heartily subscribe to most of his notions. He hears no other Music if he can help it, & therefore knows every movement of Handel's popular works.

I have been lately on a visit at M*r* Lock's of Norbury in Surry, whom you must at least have heard of, as a man of such taste & real judgment in the fine arts, that the first artists in Europe bow down to his decisions; which are so liberal, reasonable, & convincing that I never felt the least inclination to dispute them. He is in taste, elegance, good-breeding, & gentlemanly accomplishments at the head

pity, & half rage—Lord, now I must find the lines, because they are so charming; & I remember nothing *en detail*.' He then quoted the *Orlando Furioso*, 19. 7.

[13] CB's analogy in this instance is particularly felicitous:

'Some say, compar'd to Bononcini,
That Mynheer Handel's but a Ninny;
Others aver, that he to Handel
Is scarcely fit to hold a Candle:
Strange all this Difference should be,
'Twixt Tweedle-dum and Tweedle-dee!'

See John Byrom (1692–1763), 'Epigram on the Feuds between Handel and Bononcini', in *Miscellaneous Poems* (Manchester, 1773), i. 343–4; *OED*, under 'tweedle-'.

[14] Preserved in the Osborn Collection is a speech CB delivered to the Society from the Chair on 12 Sept. 1784, which shows the problem at hand (MS 'Speech at the Royal Society of Musicians, 1784'). The Society was wrangling over its expression of thanks to '*all* the great personages to whom we are obliged' on the occasion of the King and Queen becoming Patrons of the Society. It was finally agreed to request the Earl of Exeter, Honorary President of the Society, to transmit its 'most humble and grateful acknowledgements'. See also CB to Twining, 31 July 1784, n. 26; to Sandwich, 2 Aug. 1784; and to Twining, 25 Dec. 1784, n. 26.

[15] CB wrote in the 'Preface' to his *Handel Commem.*, p. xvi: 'And though I reserve the critical examination of the entire works of HANDEL for the last volume of my History, yet, as indiscriminate praise is little better than censure, I shall specify such beauties of composition and effect as I felt most forcibly in attending the performance of each day, and for which, by a careful perusal of the score, I have been since enabled to assign reasons.'

[16] *Othello*, v. ii. 345–6.

of humanity, in my eyes. His place a paradise. His family angelic. His collections of all kinds of fine things prodigious. He & his stout wife have taken to Fanny & the Philipses, & lock 'em up in their celestial abode: addio: best respects to M^{rs} T.

C.B.

To Sarah (Rose) Burney [St Martin's Street, 4 September 1784][1]

ALS (Burney-Cumming).
Addressed: To | Mrs Burney | at Mr Wallace's, Lisson Street, Edgware road, near | Tyburn Turnpike

My dear Daughter.

Your letter,[2] wch I have just rec^{d}, has given me very great pleasure; & I hasten, not only to thank you for it, but to assure you that there is nothing I more wish than that you should coalesce and incorporate so intirely wth my family, that no want of consanguinity sh^{d} appear to ourselves or others.

Let me entreat you to lay no kind of stress on Mrs Meeke's[3] nonsensical & Groundless insinuations, whatever they were: If I know anything at all of my family, it is that my children are not addicted to Dissimulation or duplicity; and that as they all very sincerely love one another, they must wish to love & be beloved by one so nearly allied to them as yourself. I think I know, likewise, that they are neither so irrational nor unjust as to dislike, without a cause, any fellow creature, though a mere stranger: why then an aversion to the beloved wife of a brother for whom they have a great affection, & for whose happiness they are always anxious? The mere Idea does not deserve a serious thought, & therefore I shall never think more of it, unless it is forced on my mind.

To give you an early instance of the sincerity with wch I wish ever to regard you as my *own daughter*, I shall go on, as you give me encouragement, in saying every thing wch I w^{d} say to a child who has called me father from her birth, that seems likely to contribute to her happiness.

And I'll tell you what strikes me as very likely to contribute to yours, at present. It seems to me as if you were likely to spend many

---

[1] CB's 'Sat^{y}' and his plan to go 'again' to Norbury on 'Tuesday' (see also CB to Fanny Burney, 4 Sept. 1784) revealed in the postscript, give the date of the present letter.
[2] Probably in reply to CB's letter of 1 Sept. Rosette's letter is not preserved.
[3] CB's step-daughter, Elizabeth Meeke, née Allen (1761–*c*.1826). See *JL* i, p. lxxiv.

hours alone, on acc^t of your husband's being so constantly engaged, either in School, or at his books & other studies & employments, wch necessarily deprive you of his company or conversation. Now, in order not to be wholly *dependent on others for amusement*, at such times, I w^d advise you to undertake a course of *reading, study, ingenious* work, or amusing employment of some kind or other; wch will totally preclude, or, at least, diminish all kind of sorrow or complaint at the absence of *your* family or *mine*, as well as of your friends, & soon enable you so to divert yourself, as hardly to wish for their assistance.

What this self-diversion is to be, your own inclination must determine. A course of reading I have mentioned, as well as some kind of ingenious work, with or without the needle. And I will just add, that the study of French or Italian w^d be an ornament, & not only furnish rational amusement, but extend the limits of Reflexion, by enabling you to know the Manners & sentiments of a whole polished & neighbouring Nation.

I'll say no more on the subject at present, except reminding you, my dear Rosette, as an apology for your not seeing my daughters in the way of visit, more frequently, that they are constantly occupied in some way or other, wch takes from them the power of bestowing much time on any person or thing, out of their own Family. Hetty, you know, & Susey, have their Husbands & Children; Fanny her own books, & Charlotte mine to think of: so that, having little leisure for external amusement, they seek it at home, where it is always most likely to be found, when wanted. Some of them find it in Music; but *all* have a taste for reading, wch is a never-failing resource against the horrors of loneliness & Solitude.

God bless you, my dear Rosette—here's a hasty Specimen of *Parental Affection*—take it, I entreat you, as it is meant, in kindness of heart, & as an instance of the most sincere solicitude for your comfort and happiness, from your ever affectionate Relation

Chas Burney.

Sat^y near 3 o'Clock.

If Possible, I'll take a Peep at you on Monday—as I go again to Mr Locke's, for a few days, on Tuesday—Love to Charles—

To Fanny Burney   [St Martin's Street], 4 September 1784

AL (Osborn). Second leaf missing.
Docketed by FBA: on | Sir Joshua | Reynolds | Norbury Park, & | Edward Burney's | Drawings. ⧧ XVI (I)

Sat^y Night—4th Sept^r
1784.

Dear Fan.

I shall take your advice, & venture to take another peep at Paradise, that I may clearly know what is meant by *Paradise regained*. The weather is now delicious, and though I hate being in London, yet I feel but little appetite for Ches. when neither yourself nor the Phills are there— don't tell Kate—& therefore I have made a bargain wth Sir Jos. at a venison dinner he gave yesterday, to club horses, & go in his Chariot, like *Cavalieri*, to Norbury. He has long promised, he says, & long wished, to go thither; & it is now determined that we get there by dinner, on tuesday, & stay till thursday. I wish him to see the sweet place & sweeter people during this delicious weather, w^{ch}, as so much is due, I *do* hope will continue. I promised the dear Sir Jos. to acquaint Mr L. with the plan, wch commission I now transfer to you & Susey. I hope our visit will occasion no inconvenience to those angellic folks that I *do* affection most cordially—The sweet *Willie-ho*[1] will not, I hope, be gone—I long to see his Witch—his Sylphes, & the rest of his Witchcraft in the Portfolio. They are all *household* Gods at least—& you & I & the rest the *mortals* who inhabit under their sacred roof & protection.

Sir Jos. too has a bit of divinity in his heart as well as *hand*—for he very kindly & good-naturedly, after praising Ned's drawings in a tone of wonder, desired me to bring him to dine with him—& we had a very pleasant party & dinner—There are so many delays & difficulties in getting his drawings well engraved in any moderate time, that Sr Jos. has, I think, persuaded him to *etch* them, himself—& says, very wisely, that though ignorant people love a neat finical engraving, that artists & Judges will be much better pleased with an *etching* by the draughtsman or inventor of the design. '& then, says the dear Sir Jos. it will be *all his own*.' This was Strange's original Idea—or, at least, that he sh^d make an *out-line* for whoever engraved them—wch in fact w^d have been nearly as much trouble—Etching is but making an out-line, I believe, with a needle instead of a pen or pencil. One difficulty there is: that his plate will not bear 2000 Copies to be worked off without retouching or renewal—But this he may do, even at Worcester —if a plate will stand 500 Copies, that N^o will serve the 1st demand, & give time for preparing another Plate, wch indeed may be previously prepared.

[1] William Lock, the younger (1767–1847), eldest son of CB's host, now aged nearly 17, together with his two younger brothers, Charles (1770–1804), and George (1771–1864), was at school near Cheam. William was noted for artistic precocity (Duchess of Sermoneta, *The Locks of Norbury* (1940), pp. 25–7; *DL* ii. 266).

As to work, if Sir Jos. is at Norbury, joined to the bewitching tricks of the Family, I do not build on a great deal being done.—Well—I must pay it off at Ches. when I get there for good—but God knows when that may be—Twi—is coming hitherward the 13th—& I shall try to get him to Ches. for 2 or 3 Days, if, in my way thither I can steal him from his Brother,[2] . . .

To Charles Burney

[St Martin's Street],
24 September 1784

ALS (Osborn).
   Addressed: To | Mr Burney | at Dr Rose's | Chiswick   *Pmks.:* PENNY POST PAID
V8M 2 O'CLOCK M

Dear Charles.

I have never been in great intimacy with Dr Warton since Dick was with him,[1] though we are *enchanted* when we meet each other. I have therefore procured a Letter of recommendation for you to his acquaintance from Mr Hool,[2] who *providentially* called on me this Evening—without exaggeration I rec^d 10 letters during the short time I was at Ches[3]—found 12 on my Chimney yesterday on my arrival in Town, & 4 to day—all wch oppress, bother, & distract me—they are all answerable on my Peril, & yet there is not one in wch my heart, or my immediate interest, has the least concern. Considering it is the most vacant time of the year for the real Scholaring business, 'tis hard to be so pestered—proofs & revises likewise have a plentiful share of my time—Alas! poor Hist^y! if it reach posterity, there will be more books wanting than of Livy.[4]

I never was on the Isle of Wight, tho' I have been on the opposite shore frequently—I sh^d like such a retirement as you describe hugely,

---

[2] Richard Twining's home was at Isleworth (see CB to Twining, 1 Sept. 1784, n. 1).

[1] In 1778. See CB to Mrs Thrale, 11 Jan. 1778, nn. 3, 6; Lonsdale, p. 242.

[2] John Hoole (1727–1803), accountant and auditor at the East India Office, translator of Tasso, Ariosto, and Metastasio, friend of Johnson (*DNB*). In 1757 Hoole had married Susannah Smith (*c.*1726–1808), of Bishop's Stortford, a Quaker. Charlotte Burney was particularly friendly with the Hooles, at whose house she met 'Dr. Warton of Winchester School, a very pleasing man' (*ED* ii. 301).

[3] CB had been at Chessington since at least 20 Sept. Twining's letter of 18 Sept. 1784 (BL Add. MS 39929, fos. 340–1), informing CB that illness had delayed his visit to London, bearing a London postmark of 20 Sept., was re-directed to CB at Chessington.

[4] Of the original 142 books of the *History of Rome* by Livy, only 35 books and fragments of others survive.

provided there was no Post to it from England to pester me with Letters & businesses concerning wch it is my wish ever to be ignorant & out of reach.

It gives me great pleasure to find that the Rosette performed her Journey so well—the benefit from Bathing does not always manifest itself immediately. I hope hers is not far off—pray my love to her & best Comp^{ts} to Miss Harriot.[5]

Fan & the Phills come to Town next Thursday—The latter set off for France in ab^t a week after[6]—Y^r Mother & Sal talk of returning to London[7] ab^t the 2^d or 3^d of next Month. Twining is in Town backwards & forwards. Isleworth is his head Quarters. Poor Johnson is very low spirited, but not worse in health or symptoms.

Printing goes on so slow though it constantly wants my attendance, that I fear it will be near X^{mas} ere the book & *plates* are ready.

Rare Balloon fun, however. Lunardi's day was admirable.[8] I went with Sr Jos. Mr Burke sen^r & Junr Mrs Burke, Ld Inchiquin,[9] & Mr Wyndham.[10] After we quitted the Artillery Ground, & had seen the Horses taken off Chas Fox's Hackney Coach by the Mob who found him out, or rather in it, & carried him I know not whither—We went in Corpo to see the Lions at the Tower, and thence to Sr Joshua's to dinner, where Dr Fordyce[11] gave us the Meeting, & an excellent party, Dinner, and *Balonade* we had. The 1st intelligence of Lunardi's safe arrival on Earth came from Charlotte, who at ab^t 4 o'Clock walking with M^r & Mrs Hoole in their Garden 'never thinking of nothing at all'[12] saw the Baloon just over their heads at a great height—& after-

---

[5] Not identified.

[6] The Phillipses were to set off in early Oct. 1784 for Boulogne, where they stayed for about a year for the benefit of Susan's health (*DL* ii. 262–5; *HFB*, p. 187 n.).

[7] From Hastings, where Mrs Burney had gone with her youngest daughter, Sarah Harriet Burney (1772–1844).

[8] On 15 Sept. 1784, the first successful manned balloon flight in England was performed by Vincenzo Lunardi (1759–1806), Secretary to the Neapolitan Envoy Extraordinary. Lunardi rose in a hydrogen-filled balloon from the Artillery Ground at Moorfields, watched by an immense crowd. He remained airborne for over 2 hours, travelled about 24 miles, and descended in a field near Ware in Hertfordshire. See *DNB*; V. Lunardi, *An Account of the First Aërial Voyage in England* (1784); J. E. Hodgson, *The History of Aeronautics in Great Britain* (1924), pp. 117–24.

[9] Murrough O'Brien (1726–1808), 5th Earl of Inchiquin (1777) in the Irish Peerage, created (1800) Marquess of Thomond. In 1792 he married his second wife, Mary Palmer, Sir Joshua's niece and heiress (Namier and Brooke, iii. 222).

[10] William Windham (1750–1810), of Felbrigg Hall, Norfolk, MP (1784–1810), statesman (*DNB*; Namier and Brooke, iii. 648–50), had journeyed to London on this occasion specifically to witness Lunardi's balloon ascent (*The Diary of the Right Hon. William Windham, 1784 to 1810*, ed. Mrs Henry Baring (1866), p. 22).

[11] George Fordyce (1736–1802), MD (1758), FRS (1776), physician and chemist (*DNB*), a member of The Club (Hill–Powell, v. 109 n.), had designed the apparatus for and directed the inflation of Lunardi's hydrogen balloon (Hodgson, *History*, pp. 98, 121).

[12] The source of this quotation, a favourite with the Burneys, has not been identified.

wards saw it descend ab^t 4 or 5 Miles off. Geo. Cambridge[13] foll^d it on horseback—& at Ware conversed with the Aerial Traveller. Charlotte saw him, & was more delighted than if the Man in the Moon had quitted his satellite to visit the neighbourhood of Amwell.[14]

God bless you—tis very late, & I must scratch Paper for others—so health & pleasure attend you & yours.

C.B.

Friday Night $^|$ 24th Sept^r $^|$ 1784

Mr Hoole had not time to write to yourself, but desires his best Comp^{ts} to you & sposa—

To Lord Sandwich [St Martin's Street], 14 October 1784

AL draft (Gerald Coke).
Docketed by FBA: To Ld Sandwich. ✕

Thursday Octr 14th 1784.

My Lord

The Letter with wch your Lord^p honoured me[1] w^d have been sooner answered had I been in Town when it arrived in St Martin's street; but being in the Country for a few days only, it was not sent after me, & I now find it at my return. I am very sorry that your L^p & your friends have had your patience put to so severe a trial by the slow Progress of the Press in printing the Acc^t of the Musical Performances in commemoration of Handel; no time however has been lost. The acc^t was written, perused by his Majesty, & returned, more than two Months ago; but the number of copies of wch the impression consists,[2] & the engraving of the Plates render the whole a slow & operose business. The letter-press is however now in great forwardness: more

[13] The Revd George Owen Cambridge (1756–1841), MA (1781), later Rector of Elme, Prebendary of Ely, and Archdeacon of Middlesex (Foster), with whom at this time Fanny was in love (*HFB*, pp. 187–93).

[14] Situated only 1½ miles distant from Ware in Hertfordshire, the village of Amwell had been celebrated in a descriptive poem (1776) of the same name by the Quaker poet, John Scott (1730–83), whose posthumous *Critical Essays on Some of the Poems, of Several English Poets* (1785) carries a biographical preface of the poet by his intimate friend, John Hoole. See *DNB*. The Hooles, with Charlotte in tow, were probably visiting Scott's widow and daughter, who continued to live at Amwell House after the poet's death (L. D. Stewart, *John Scott of Amwell* (Berkeley and Los Angeles, 1956), p. 201).

[1] Not preserved.
[2] Two thousand (see CB to Fanny Burney, 4 Sept. 1784; to [Keith], 9 Nov. 1784).

than 160 4to pages are printed, including the Preface, Life of Handel, introduction & acc^t of all the 3 first days performances. The 4th day is now in hand, and I fancy that in ab^t a fortnight or 3 weeks the printer's work will be done. The plates I fear will not be ready so soon; it was extremely difficult to find any Artists of eminence who w^d undertake to engrave one of them in less than 4 or 5 Months. After preparing the acc^t for the press, the correction of the proofs & attention to engravers have wholly occupied my time & thoughts ever since I had last the honour of seeing your Lord^p; nor have I been able to be absent from London a whole week at a time since the Commemoration. So that I shall gain easy belief when I say that I am very anxious to have the work ready to present to his Maj^{ty} to your L^p & the rest of the Directors, as well as to the Public; as I find the pursuit of my gen^l Hist^y of Music impossible, while this recent & particular Event constantly[3] draws off my attention from remote periods of time.

[To Johann Joachim Eschenburg][1]   [31 October 1784]

Editor's Note: Original MS not traced. Eschenburg gives a German translation of extracts of CB's letter to him in a MS preserved in the Gesellschaft der Musikfreunde in Vienna (MS 1325/43 cat.).

... Seit der musikalischen Aufführung zum Andenken Ihres berühmten Landesmannes Händel bin ich mit meiner Allgemeine Geschichte der Musick nicht viel weitergekommen, weil ich vornemlich mit der Ausarbeitung einer nächstens herauszugebenden Nachricht von dieser Feier beschäftigt gewesen bin, die ich eine nun verfertigte Lebensbeschreibung dieses Lieblingskomponisten unsers Landes beifügen werde. Solten Sie Zeit and Lust haben, diese Schrift ins Deutsche zu übersezen; so werde ich

---

[3] MS constantly] *alternative* dayly

[1] Johann Joachim Eschenburg (1743–1820), German critic, literary historian, and poet, Professor at the Collegium Carolinum in Brunswick, noted for his German translations of English writers. He had recently published the first complete German prose translation of Shakespeare entitled *William Shakespear's Schauspiele* (Zürich, 1775–82). When the first volume of CB's *History* appeared, Eschenburg translated the opening 'Dissertation on the Music of the Ancients' as *Dr. Karl Burney's Abhandlung über die Musik der Alten* (Leipzig, 1781). And now, at CB's invitation, he was to publish his translation of the *Handel Commem.*, under the title *Dr. Karl Burney's Nachricht von Georg Friedrich Händel's Lebensumständen und der ihm zu London im Mai und Jun. 1784 angestellten Gedächtnissfeyer* (Berlin and Stettin, 1785). See Lonsdale, pp. 499–501; *ADB*; *NDB*.

Ihnen mit vielem Vergnügen eins der ersten Exemplare über-senden.—Mit Händels Leben und der Nachricht von den fünf Konzerten werde ich eine summarische Anzeige von der gegen-wärtigen Verfassung der musickalischen Sozietät verbinden, die bei uns zur Versorgung abgelebten Tonkünstler und ihren Familien bestimt ist, und die gegenwärtig weitbeträchtlicher, als vorher, werden wird, nicht nur durch die geschirmte Ver-mehrung ihres Fonds durch die geschenkten 6000 Pfund, sondern auch durch die dem Institut neulich wiederfahrne grosse Ehre, da beide königliche Majestäten gnädigst geruht haben, die Protektion desselben zu übernehmen ... Mein Buch, dem der König die Ehre erwiesen hat, es in der Handschrift Bogen für Bogen, wie sie fertig wurden, durchzulesen, wird Sr. Maj. gewidmet, und mit sieben Kupfer-tafeln geziert werden, die von den besten englischen Meistern gezei-chnet und gestochen sind. Um zu unsrer milden Stiftung auch mein Scherflein beizutragen, habe ich den Gewinn, der etwa durch den Verkauf dieser Schrift zu erhalten steht, für den musikalischen Fond bestimt. ...

To [Sir Robert Murray Keith][1] St Martin's Street, 9 November 1784

ALS (BL Add. MS 35532, fos. 364–5).
Endorsed by Keith?: Dr Burney Nov. 9 | St Martins Street | Leicester Square. 1784.

London, Novr 9th 1784.
St Martin's Street, Leicester Square.

Sir.

You formerly honoured me with such testimonies of zeal for the success of my musical enquiries, & gave me so much encouragement to apply to you for succour in future wants, that being utterly unable here to clear up a point of musical history, wch concerns Vienna, I cannot resist the temptation of throwing myself on your clemency in my present distress.

You have doubtless, Sir, heard of our musical performances, last summer, in Commemoration of Handel, and of their Success; w^{ch}

---

[1] Sir Robert Murray Keith (1730–95), KB (1772), soldier and diplomatist, had been, since 1772, British Envoy Extraordinary and Plenipotentiary to the Imperial Court at Vienna (*DNB*; Horn, p. 39). CB was to acknowledge Keith's assistance in gathering particulars about Haydn for him in 1778 (*Hist. Mus.* iv. 599 ff.; Mercer, ii. 958 ff.).

indeed so far surpassed expectation, that the most sanguine abettors of the enterprise were nearly as much astonished as incredulous Theorists, who thinking the undertaking too gigantic & unwieldy had predicted its failure.

You must long have observed, Sir, that there are partisans for every kind of music as well as Sectaries of every religion, and that the followers of Handel are very numerous in England: indeed the belief in his infalibility & *supremacy* forms a part of our national musical creed. But even those who being accustomed to more modern, and, as they contend, more graceful, elegant and fanciful music; & who call his style of composition Gothic, inelegant & clumsy, readily allowed that the effects in performance by a band of voices & instruments in Westminster-Abbey, amounting to 525, were such as they had never experienced, & excited sensations of delight for which they were wholly unable to account.

I own that previous to performance, regarding most of the singers that were to be employed as birds of ill-omen, & reflecting on the number and distance of the performers, I had not allowed imagination to run riot, or anticipate many great & good effects, unless from the aggregate of sound in the Choruses. The Solo parts, I thought would be lost in the expanse through wch they had to travel to a great Part of the company, unless very coursely performed; and with the *ensemble* I expected to be stunned. But incredulity is silenced, and experience & speculation overturned. The loud was *not* course, nor the soft *inaudible*. The general Mass of Harmony attracted & impelled, with a kind of centripetal power, all the parts of this immense band to keep together; &, from the happy construction of the building, the most gentle vocal breathing and inflexion of sound was augmented without reverberation, & conveyed to the most distant hearers more sweet & full than it was delivered.

Indeed the success of this enterprise has been so complete as to induce me to prepare a detailed account for immediate publication, wch his Majesty, to whom permission is granted to dedicate it, has honoured so far as to peruse in MS. sheet by sheet, as fast as it was written. And it seems as if an event so honourable to the Art, to our country & to national gratitude, would form an Æra in the annals of Music.

In my preface I have enumerated the chief musical Musters on record, as well as such others as I c^{d} get well authenticated;[2] but last week, after the greatest part of my Work was printed, I accidentally met with an account in a book of Letters, written in German: *Briefe*

---

[2] See *Handel Commem.*, pp. viii–xi.

446

eines reisenden Franzosen über Deutchland an seiner Bruder zu Paris, in wch it is said that there is an annual Musical Performance at Vienna, for the benefit of the Widows of deceased Musicians, by a band of 400 performers.[3] An anonymous book is no authority; if there *is* such a performance every year, I should be extremely glad to mention it in my commemoration account, & you w^d confer a very great favour upon me, Sir, if you w^d honour me with an answer to the following queries, from *your own knowledge*, as much as possible, as *patriotism* almost always inclines the natives of every country to exaggerate whatever will redound to its honour—and be reflected back on themselves.

1. How long has this extraordinary congress of Musicians been established?

2. What is the exact number of performers imployed, vocal and Instrumental?

3. Where, & what music, do they generally perform?

4. About what sum, *communibus annis*, is raised by this meeting? and how disposed of?

5. To what number does the *most probable* calculation of the Inhabitants of Vienna & its suburbs amount?

My book, though the writing was finished in July, as the impression is to consist of 2000 Copies, & it is to be ornamented with 7 Copper plates by the best artists, approaches publication but slowly; and though it has been promised in the News-papers *in the course of the present month*,[4] I have reason to fear that the Engravings will not be ready. If therefore your Excellence w^d be so indulgent to my wishes as to honour me wth an *immediate* answer to my queries, and it arrives before publication, I w^d add a leaf to my acc^t in order to mention this Vienna musical assembly, wch I shall do with the more pleasure, as the School of Instrumental Music in that City stands very high in my esteem; indeed it not only seems to me the first in Europe of the present time, but of all times, since the invention of Counterpoint.

I have not only endeavoured within these few days to obtain information from German Musicians here, but have applied to Lord

---

[3] See *Handel Commem.*, p. 48, where CB adds in a footnote '2 vols. 8vo. 1783', referring to *Briefe eines Reisenden Franzosen über Deutschland an seinen Bruder zu Paris* (2 vols., [Zürich], 1783), by Johann Kaspar Riesbeck (1754–86), German man of letters and traveller (*ADB*; Michaud). Riesbeck's volumes were translated into English by the Revd Paul Henry Maty (1745–87), *Travels through Germany, in a Series of Letters* (1787). The passage to which CB refers occurs in Letter xxvii, translated by Maty (i. 309): 'There are about four hundred musicians here . . . On a particular day of the year they have a general concert for the benefit of musicians widows; . . . the four hundred play together as distinctly, as cleanly, and as justly, as when there are only from twenty to thirty. This is certainly the only concert of the kind in the world.'

[4] CB had advertised the appearance of the *Handel Commem.* in the *Morning Chronicle*, 26 Oct. 1784, under the heading: 'In the Course of next Month will be published'.

Stormont,[5] as well as the Corps Diplomatique,[6] without having acquired, as yet, such satisfactory answers to all my questions as I wished.

It w^d afford me a very great gratification if your Excellency w^d honour me so far as to present my most humble respects to my musical patroness & St Cecilia of Vienna, the Countess Thun,[7] by whose remembrance I sh^d be extremely flattered.

I had last year hopes that the admirable Haydn the chief ornament of the Vienna School & of the Age, w^d have made us a visit; If the universal admiration & performance of his works w^d be a temptation to visit us, I can as[s]ure him of that claim to his favour; but as to the opera, at present, its regency is in such confusion that it is hardly certain whether its existence will be ascertained during the ensuing Winter.[8]

I have the honour to be, with the most profound
respect & regard, Your Excellency's obliged
& most devoted Servant
Chas Burney.

To Lord Sandwich   **[St Martin's Street],
27 November 1784**

ALS draft (Gerald Coke).
Docketed by FBA: ✕ To Ld Sandwich. | 27 Nov.—1784

[5] For David Murray (1727–96), 7th Viscount Stormont (1748), who was Keith's predecessor at Vienna, see CB to Firmian, 22 June 1772, n. 3. Lord Stormont was now active in the House of Lords in opposition to Pitt (*DNB*).

[6] *Handel Commem.*, pp. 48–9 shows that CB eventually obtained the answers he sought through the good offices of Friedrich, Graf von Kageneck (1741–1800), Austrian Envoy Extraordinary and Minister Plenipotentiary to England from 1782 to 1786 (*Repertorium der diplomatischen Vertreter aller Länder, III. Band, 1764–1815*, ed. O. F. Winter (Graz–Cologne, 1965), p. 76).

[7] Maria Wilhelmine, Gräfin Thun-Hohenstein, née Ulfeld (1744–1800), pupil of Haydn, patroness of Mozart, and friend of Beethoven. Lord Stormont had introduced CB to her in 1772 at Vienna, and 'she did everything in her power to procure me entertainment and services', including an introduction to Gluck, 'a very dragon, of whom all are in fear' (*Tours*, ii. 76, 89–90, 100–1). See A. Orel, 'Gräfin Wilhelmine Thun', in *Mozart-Jahrbuch 1954* (Salzburg, 1955), pp. 89–101; C. von Wurzbach, *Biographisches Lexikon des Kaiserthums Oesterreich* (Vienna, 1856–91), xlv. 22–3.

[8] For the troubles over the management of the Opera House, see CB to Fanny Burney, 6 Nov. 1782, n. 21; to Twining, 6 Sept. 1783, n. 51. Gallini, in Nov. 1784, was still involved in litigation over the King's Theatre (*The London Stage*, v. ii. 728). As CB later wrote, it was in the summer of 1785 that 'the whole opera machine came to pieces, and all its springs, disordered by law suits, warfare, and factions, were not collected and regulated, till the next year,' when Gallini was finally 'invested with the power of ruining himself and others' (*Hist. Mus.* iv. 524; Mercer, ii. 897).

My Lord.

The time being nearly elapsed, when my Commemoration acc^t was promised to the public,[1] it seems necessary to acquaint your L^p wth the reasons of a further inevitable delay.

I have this day sent my last corrections to the Printer, & if the Plates had been ready, sh^d just have been able to keep my word; but, at present, 3 of the 7 plates are still in the hands of the engravers, who are, how[ev]er hard at work upon them. It was the wish of Sr W. W. Wynn that Bartolozzi sh^d engrave the medal & reverse to serve as one of the ornamental plates;[2] but Bartolozzi, whose hands are always full, had not made a beginning 10 Days ago, & threw the blame on Mr Wyatt[3]—who, beat it back on Bartolozzi. And this last, when my nephew had an opportunity of talking with him on the subject at Fulham, the place of his abode, very justly, I think, observed, that the Medal only, with a naked head of Handel, neither very remarkable for likeness nor workmanship, on one side, & a mere inscription on the other, w^d cut but a small, & no very interesting, figure, on a whole 4to Page. He therefore desired my Nephew to draw a design for ornamenting the plate, & in a very short time he carried 3 for Bartolozzi's choice: who has chosen one of these, w^{ch}, by so good an engraver, will make a beautiful Plate, & serve as a Frontispiece to the Work. He w^d not, however, undertake to do it in less time than 3 Weeks—one of wch expires next Monday. The other two plates (the Orchestra, and Monument of Handel, in Westm^r Abbey,)[4] will certainly be finished in that time.

This, my Lord, is the present state of things, of wch his Majesty has from time to time known the progress. Mr Nicolay has been with me

[1] See CB to [Keith], 9 Nov. 1784, n. 4.

[2] See the Frontispiece to *Handel Commem.*, and its description (p. [viii]): 'The MEDAL struck on occasion of the Commemoration of HANDEL, and worn by their Majesties and the Directors, on the Days of Performance.' See also n. 4.

[3] Although James Wyatt is not credited with any of the ornamental plates in CB's publication, he had been deeply involved in the Commemoration as architect for the stage, boxes, and galleries constructed for the occasion in Westminster Abbey and the Pantheon (see *Handel Commem.*, pp. 8–11, 46–7, 125). See also CB to Orford, [5 Sept. 1783], n. 11.

[4] i.e. Plates VII and II respectively in *Handel Commem.* The Frontispiece (n. 2), however, was much delayed. John Ashley wrote to Lord Sandwich, 25 Dec. 1784 (Montagu: 52/34): 'May it please Your Lordship, To give me leave to explain the Situation of Doctor Burneys Book at this time. His part of it is intir[e]ly finished and printed off. But I perceive We shall stay a great while for the plates except your Lordship will take the trouble to write to Bartolozzi to finish the Medal Plate directly. For there is no relying on his promises—He had the Ticket Plate to retouch, and after keeping it seven Weeks, sent it back again without any amendment, He has since done justice to it, and it is now near equal to the first impression, and has left it with Borghi with an Order not to let it go without twenty Guineas, (which I have not got for Him) there is impressions sufficient of this Plate to bring out the Book, if We could but get Him to finish the Medal Plate'.

this morning, & had full information concerning all circumstances of procrastination.

And ever since July that the work has been in the press, I have attended to nothing else. Indeed I have hopes that the *Life of Handel* will be greatly improved by the delay.[5] For not having been able to find some German b^{ks} wch I wanted to consult while I was writing it, but w^{ch}, since it was printed have come to hand, I have cancelled the 1st sheet, new written it, & added 18 or 20 pages of new matter to other parts, *deterrée* from Mattheson[6] & different German Musical Writers, concerning Handels youth, of w^{ch}, being spent on the Continent, little or nothing is known in England.[7]

I c^d furnish your L^P & the rest of the Directors, next week, perhaps, with a complete Copy of my Book in sheets, without the plates, if that c^d be done with propriety, before his Majesty, to whom the book is dedicated, shall be presented with a Copy, splendedly bound, and ornamented wth first impressions of the plates. You my L^d are so perfect a judge of what I ought to do in this respect that I shall wholly regulate my proceedings by your L^{P's} counsel, If you will condescend to honour me with it. No one of the directors, as yet, has asked for the book in sheets, as fast as printed, except Sr W.W. to whom a few have been sent; but I really think that an exclusive distinction of this kind, if due to one, is due to *all* the directors; & feel as if there was something against strict propriety in sending the complete book, or even particular sheets, to any one before the King has rec^d his Copy.

To Mr Bates, who is so deeply engaged in the honour of the enterprise, I have wished to keep open a communication, when he was in Town, & the distance of our abodes w^d allow it; but to none else, except to Mr Nicolay in order to obtain his Majesty's opinion of additions or alterations since my MS. was read & returned, have I been very communicative of my printed sheets or proceedings.

I have the honour, &c
C.B.

To the Earl of Sandwich ∣ Novr 27. 1784.

---

[5] Samuel Johnson had written to CB on 1 Nov. 1784: 'That your book has been delayed I am glad, since you have gained an opportunity of being more exact' (Comyn; Johnson *Letters*, iii. 243).

[6] For Johann Mattheson (1681–1764) and his work on Handel's biography, see CB to Ebeling, Nov. 1771, n. 28; B. C. Cannon, *Johann Mattheson, Spectator in Music* (New Haven, 1947).

[7] CB added a footnote to this effect in his 'Sketch of the Life of Handel' (*Handel Commem.*, p. 7 n.). See also Lonsdale, pp. 306–7.

To Lord Sandwich   [St Martin's Street],
                                    19 December 1784

ALS (Montagu: 52/32).

                                        Sunday 19 Dec^r
                                        1784.

My Lord.

In obedience to your Lordship's commands,[1] & with great zeal for the service of the arrangements in meditation, I immediately acquainted Mr Bates that I sh^d be happy in surveying Bloomsbury Church in his company this morning; but he being engaged, I went thither myself, during service time, & from thence directly to St George's Hanover Square, to form a comparative view, & think Bloomsbury church very little bigger than St George's. And as there is *no Organ* in it, & the west Gall^y where it is usually placed being small, & fitted up with Pews, w^d occasion great expense & confusion to make a place there for the reception of an Organ & a large band. There is likewise but one entrance into Bloomsbury Church, wch w^d render the admission of company a very slow process. The Organ Gallery at St George's Church seems much too small for such a band as will be necessary to keep up the reputation acquired by the Commemoration performances, & to render the next a model for *annual* exhibitions of the same kind.

From this last church I went immediately to Westminster abbey, the sight of wch renewed my affliction that there sh^d be so many impediments to the use of a building so happily constructed for the Purpose of Charitable musical performances on a great scale, worthy

---

[1] Following the great success of the 1784 Handel Commemoration performances, plans were set in motion to make a large-scale musical performance in aid of the Society of Musicians an annual event. The problem, which caused much controversy, was to find a suitable venue. Lord Sandwich wrote to CB on 14 Dec. 1784 (Comyn) from Hinchingbrooke: 'Before I left London I got hold of Mr Wyatt, and went with him to St Martins Church, and allso to St Georges Hanover Square: I own I think that the wretched access that there is to the former will spoil the whole festival and discourage people from attending again. Only consider that there is no way for coaches to get to the door of the former but thro' the narrow part of St Martins Lane where two carriages can barely pass one another; consider allso that most of the trade of the city of London from the west passes up the narrow part of the Strand, and will obstruct our company, or be obstructed by them which will be equally matter of inconvenience and complaint. St Georges Hanover Square is built exactly on the same plan as St Martins but is not quite so spacious; tho' I am of opinion it will hold more company than will give guineas for admission, and the avenues to it are excellent from all quarters. I am unacquainted with Bloomsbury church but perhaps that might do, as the access to it is as good as to the other. I wish you would turn this matter in your thoughts, and talk to some of your Musical friends about it; I have written to Mr Bates on the same subject'.

of their Majesties presence, & the Nation's Patronage! But with the utmost oeconomy, if there were no other objection to get over than the expense of building Galleries & an orchestra, wth the occasional erection of an Organ, I question much whether the produce of one or two performances only, w^d be sufficient to pay the Carpenters, & contribute any very great sum to charitable uses.

But my chief reason for going into the Abbey to day was to see whether the Tablet was replaced,[2] & I find it put up, but so high that from my being very near-sighted, I was unable to read it, even with my concave Glass. The inscription however, at the bottom of the monument, I was sorry to find had not been corrected, as I understood it was ordered to be in consequence of the discovery I had made very early in the summer, of Handel having died on *Good-friday* the *13th*, & not on Sat^y the *14th* of April 1759, as erroneously engraved on the Tablet at the bottom of his Monument.[3]

From the Abbey I went to St Margaret's Church, in wch I had never entered before; & I am clearly of opinion, that, next to the Abbey it is the fittest place for the intended performances. The architecture, though not strictly Gothic, is venerable, & the Size unexceptionable; being at least one 3^d larger than any of the Parish Churches in Question. The side Galleries are deep, & capable of containing great numbers of auditors, &, what is best of all, the Organ Gallery is uncommonly roomy, & fit to be formed into a great orchestra. I know that the great objection to this Church is the high pitch of the organ, & its imperfections in other particulars; but even if the repairs & additions necessary to make it fit for the next & for all future annual great performances sh^d amount to the considerable sum of £300, it w^d be worth while to sacrifice that sum, if the use of the Instrument & the Church c^d be secured for all such future occasions. Perhaps the parish w^d contribute towards this expense in consideration of the advantage it might be to the Benefit for the Westminster infirmary.[4] But even if they did not, such is the public hope & expectation of hearing something like the commemoration Performances of last summer, that I do believe the first of that kind next year, be it what & where it will, as it is sure

---

[2] The mural tablet recording the Commemoration was placed above Handel's monument in Westminster Abbey, and illustrated in *Handel Commem.*, facing the first page of the 'Sketch of the Life of Handel' (plate II).

[3] CB gives an account of this 'discovery' in *Handel Commem.*, p. 31. Handel in fact died at eight in the morning on Saturday 14 Apr. 1759 (O. E. Deutsch, *Handel, a Documentary Biography* (1955), p. 816), which is the date carved in the inscription beneath his monument in the south transept of Westminster Abbey. CB, however, clearly prevailed on his nephew, E. F. Burney, who designed the plate illustrating the monument, to alter the 'XIV' to 'XIII' in the engraving.

[4] £1000 of the profits from the 1784 Commemoration had been donated to the Westminster Hospital (*Handel Commem.*, pp. 4, 125).

of the Patronage & presence of their Majesties, will infallibly draw together a great deal of Company, even at a Guinea a Ticket; but if the inferiority in the performance sh^d be very considerable, there will be an end of all hope for succeeding years.

Your Lordship's objections to St Martin's Church are certainly insuperable, unless the plan wch has so long been wished & in meditation sh^d take place in time for the Performance; wch is the opening St Martin's Lane, opposite the Portico of the Church, into the Mews. At present this fine building, his Majesty's Parish Church, is suffocated by miserable tenements, with the Stocks & watch-house only in sight. In all respects but the approach, this Church is fitter for the purpose than either that of Hanover Square or Bloomsbury; but after examining them all this morning, St Margaret's appears to me not only preferable internally but externally, as it has every convenience of approach, that there is to Westminster Abbey.

My Commemoration book has been quite ready for the Plates more than a week, & when these will be all finished & worked off, I know not; as I have no reliance on the most solemn promises of Engravers. I now almost wish, if a Copy of the Acc^t is not ready for presentation[5] before the expiration of the present year, that the ceremony may be delayed till your Lordship's arrival in Town; as it w^d make me very happy to be honoured with your Lordship's countenance on that occasion.

I have the honour to be with very great respect, My Lord, your Lordship's obliged

and devoted Servant
Chas Burney.

Mr Ashley has been with me since the above was written[6] & I desired him to communicate to Mr Bates[7] my opinion of St Margaret's Church. Ashley thinks the Organ might be made concert-pitch by

[5] i.e. to the King. See CB to Twining, 25 Dec. 1784, n. 4.

[6] Ashley, who emerges as CB's closest ally, gives some indication as to the conversation at this meeting. He wrote to Lord Sandwich, 25 Dec. 1784 (Montagu: 52/34): 'Mr Simpson wishes Me to begin to solicit such Performers as are not Members of Our Society directly for the next Benefit, but if it meets your Lordships Approbation, I will defer it, till I have Doctor Burneys Book ready to deliver them, for at present my Lord I dont meet a Musician but He asks me when the Book is to make its appearance.—Dr Burney joins me in Opinion my Lord, that there can not be any thing done about the Benefit till your Lordship and the other Directors come to Town, and think the Committee should not be too precipitate in fixing on a Church till it meets with the inter Approbation of the Directors— . . . I know Dr Cooke thinks the Orchestre at St Martins can not contain so many Performers as St Margarets, and as to the expence of the Organ (in my Opinion) would be very little, as the Organ is half a tone too sharp, yet by transplanting the Pipes and adding only one New Pipe to each Stop, it would Answer the purpose, at least it appears so to me, but I imagin[e] Mr Green would rather have One of his Own'.

[7] Ashley had been assistant conductor to Bates at the 1784 Handel Commemoration.

transplanting the pipes; placing, for instance, those that belong to B flat into the Sockets of B Natural, & those of A$^\flat$ into the places of A natural. This being done (& it seems very possible) there w^d only be one set of Pipes wanting for the lowest note in the Instrum^t—I have begged him likewise to mention this circumstance to Mr Bates, who will perhaps prevail on Green[8] to undertake it.

To Lord Sandwich

[St Martin's Street],
25 December 1784

ALS (Montagu: 52/33).

X^{mas} Day, 1784

My Lord.

There is not a single Idea in your Lordship's letter which does not beam conviction on my mind.[1] But I fear that precipitate judgments have been formed, & that they will be precipitately followed. There have been 4 Meetings, I find, of the *Concert Committee*, at each of wch St Margaret's Church seems to have been wholly out of the Question. Mr Simpson told me on thursday morning that it was in vain to visit Churches by way of choice, as the King had fixed on St Martin's. Mr S. is zealous & active in any cause, as long as it is connected with importance; but he is impetuous & not the deepest & closest reasoner. Either he has taken upon trust the prejudices of others, or he is very much prejudiced himself: for, to my apprehension, he speaks very unfairly of St Margaret's Church, & is very much prejudiced in favour of St Martin's.[2] According to Mr Wyatt's calculation the building in

---

[8] Samuel Green (1740–96), celebrated organ builder, patronized by George III. Green was given to designing cases in the Gothic style. The organ he built in 1784 was 'opened' at the Handel Commemoration in Westminster Abbey before transportation to Canterbury Cathedral (*DNB*; *New Grove*; *Handel Commem.*, p. 8; C. Clutton and A. Niland, *The British Organ* (1976), pp. 83–4, 191, 233–4).

[1] In reply to CB's letter of 19 Dec., Lord Sandwich had written from Hinchingbrooke on 22 Dec. 1784 (Burney-Cumming): 'Your letter has much good matter in it, & treats the subject in question with fairness, judgement, & depth of reasoning, which is by no means the case of that I enclose to you, which ... is satisfied with the assertion of Mr Wyatt, that the objection to the avenues of St Martins is trifling & easily got over: I wish Mr Wyatt would shew how it is to be got over; as to its being trifling I am sure the fact is otherwise, & that the confusion among the carriages will utterly ruin the undertaking. ... I was allways of opinion that Saint Margarets Westminster was the best church next to the Abbey, and I think I can plainly see that the objections raised against it have their origin in some private predilection for St Martins'.

[2] Redmond Simpson had been rebuffed by the Parish of St Margaret's. John Ashley wrote to Lord Sandwich on 25 Dec. 1784 (Montagu: 52/34): 'from some Words which fell from Mr Simpson

this Church will amount to £1000. The organ, not being of the right Pitch will incur the same expense as that at St Margaret's. How many this Church will contain commodiously, I know not; but if expenses amount to 15 to £1600, I have no Idea that the residue will furnish a very splendid sum to the Fund.

I had this morning a long Conversation with Mr Bates on the subject—I think he under-rates the size of St Margaret's Church, & sees, by tradition, St Martin's in too favourable a light.[3] The difficulties of approach to this last Church are too much overlooked, I think, by every one I have talked with, except your Lordship. Mr Bates however agrees wth me, that, as the Performance is so distant,[4] nothing should be absolutely & *finally* determined ab^t the Church till your Lordship & the rest of the Directors come to Town at the opening of Parliament;[5] & then I am certain that many difficulties & prejudices will vanish, wch at present embarrass & distract the Committee. He agrees with me that it w^d be madness to think of having a Performance in a church till May or June; & that it is of the utmost importance to the establishing an *annual* performance of the same kind, that it sh^d be in a very grand style & to a numerous & splendid audience, for whom every possible convenience of access & station sh^d be contrived.

I called yesterday & to day on Mr Nicolay, but, unluckily missed him; however soon after Mr Bates quitted me he called at my house, & I had a long conversation wth him on the subject of the ensuing Performance. & I began by begging to know whether his Majesty had absolutely *fixed* on St Martin's Church, in preference to any other; as, in that case all discussion of the subject w^d naturally drop. And I find that his Majesty inclining to one Church more than another was merely in consequence of Mr Nicolay's representation of the superiority of St Martin's Church to that of Hanover Square or Bloomsbury, without anything being said, as far as I can find, of St Margaret's. &

the other day I imagin[e] He has been treated a little cavalierly by some of St Margarets Parish, but the Directors will easily surmount any difficulty that may have been thrown in his Way if they perfer that Church to St Martins'.

[3] Sandwich had written in his letter of 22 Dec.: 'I wish you would trouble yourself to see Mr Bates again, and if you can get the opinion to lean for St Margaretts, let the arguments on each side be fairly stated in writing, and then I dare say that Ld Uxbridge will undertake to get them laid before his Majesty for his finally deciding the matter. I will write to Mr Bates by this Post, and will enclose to him the letter from you which I now am answering, and I will tell him in the strongest terms in which I can express myself, that I am by no means satisfied with Mr Wyatts loose declaration that by management the objections to St Martins are easily to be removed; but on the contrary that I still remain firm in my idea that they are absolutely *insuperable*'.

[4] On Friday 3 June 1785, 'A grand musical concert, from Handel's Works, was performed in Westminster Abbey to a most brilliant audience of more than 2000 persons, many of them of the highest rank, and patronized by the royal family. The instrumental performers amounted to 600' (*GM* lv (1785)^1, 484).

[5] The new session of Parliament opened on Tuesday 25 Jan. 1785 (*GM* lv (1785)^1, 72–3).

Mr Nicolay seems to have retailed the opinion of Mr Simpson, & Mr Simpson that of Mr Wyatt. I cannot however help thinking that M^r S in applying for St Margaret's Church has met with some personal rebuff or disagreeable treatment, wch has warped his judgment;[6] & I am not sure that Mr W. has not come to the shortest conclusion, without sufficiently measuring or surveying the several premises. I know he's an artist of exquisite taste, but, from the constant hurry he is in, liable to go the shortest way to work in order to save time. His calculation both at the Abbey & Pantheon were last year inaccurate. The former was laid at 4000, & the latter at 2000—and your Lord^p knows how short of that number the amount was, when both seemed stuffed as full as possible. I sh^d be extremely glad to have St Margaret's Church & St Martin's carefully and accurately measured, by some indifferent surveyor before the Point is determined not by the Eye but actually by Line & rule. Mr Nicolay has been made to believe that St Martin's will contain more People than St Margaret's: a fact as repugnant to my belief as that it's approach is more convenient. I have entreated Mr Nicolay, who is of the Committee, to try to stop further, or at least final proceedings, ab^t the place of Performance [till] the Directors[7] are all in Town; & then, I still hope that more accuracy, & fairness of investigation will take place in deliberations on the subject, & that all will at last be determined for the general good of the Fund & the honour of its great Patrons & Protectors.

My book still waits for plates, & the plates already done for money; as no proper measures have been taken by the Society for paying any of the bills consequent to getting the work ready for publication, though it was expected to be finished 3 Months ago. However, when the plates are quite finished I have determined to redeem them myself, rather than the Publication shall be delayed a single day longer than is absolutely necessary for the engravers to finish their work.[8] The story of the last performance will become little more interesting

[6] See n. 2.

[7] Lord Sandwich had canvassed his fellow Directors for support. Lord Uxbridge wrote to him on 26 Dec. 1784 (Montagu: 52/35): 'St Margarets Ch: West^r against the field'. And Lord Exeter wrote the same day (Montagu: 52/36): 'their cannot be a moments dispute in giving the preference to St Margaret'.

[8] CB's friend and ally in his irritating relations with the Society of Musicians, John Ashley, wrote to Lord Sandwich, 25 Dec. 1784 (Montagu: 52/34): 'Doctor Burney has been used very illiberally in my Opinion by the Society. When he found Mr Simpson had not been provident enough to leave Money in his Hands to defray the expence of the Engraving Printing &c. a Message was sent to the Governors of the Fund to desire them to lodge a Sum of Money with Mr Barrow or Mr Simpson, that the Bills might be paid when due, this is more then two Months ago, yet when Delattres Plate came Home this Week, the Doctor had no Cash to pay Him, this has hurt Him exceedinly and I plainly see He wishes He had not promised to give his Work to the Fund'. See also CB to Twining, 25 Dec. 1784, n. 4.

than an old almanac, when the next becomes the general Topic of conversation.

> I have the honour to be with the highest respect,
> My Lord, your Lordship's obliged
> and devoted Servant
> Chas Burney.

To Thomas Twining [St Martin's Street], 25 December 1784

Source: Country Clergyman, pp. 125–31.
Also L copy extract (Osborn: 'Twining Letterbook No. 4', pp. 15–17). *Editor's Note:* Although Daniel Twining's MS copy of this letter only gives an extract from 'Poor Johnson . . .', he seems to have followed CB's emphatic punctuation, ignored in *Country Clergyman*, which also omits the postscript. Significant variants are noted.

Christmas Day, 1784.

Ah! my ever dear friend, that I should be fated to let the sweetest and most gratifying letter[1] I ever received from you remain, *invita Minerva*,[2] so long unanswered! We have nothing to do with free will, I'll maintain it; all our actions have been predestined, from eternity; else would not I instantly have told you that I had thought you a 'leetle' naughty, and the time betwixt your departure and my receipt of your letter a great while;[3] but that your hand instantly wiped away all naughtiness from the score between us, and so far from its seeming a great while since I saw you, this same letter brought you so full to my view that I was ready to swear you were present during the perusal of it, and to knock any one down who should dare to prove an *alibi*. Day after day, week after week, month after month have I expected to be able to present my Commemoration Account to you and to his Majesty, and though my Epistle Dedicatory to you is not yet written, that to his Majesty has been printed more than a month, and all the letterpress of my book ready for binding; but engravers and other

[1] Twining had written from Colchester, 12 Nov. 1784 (BL Add. MS 39929, fos. 342–3). CB endorsed Twining's letter 'answered Decr 26. 1784', indicating probably the date of posting of the present letter.
[2] For this Latin tag, meaning 'contrary to one's natural inclination' or 'against the grain', see Cicero, *De Officiis*, 1. 31. 110; Horace, *Ars Poetica*, l. 385.
[3] Twining had evidently managed to visit London in the autumn. He wrote in his letter of 12 Nov., 'I'm afraid I am a naughty boy—I promised you, & I promised myself, to write *soon*.— I'm afraid it is not *soon*, is it? . . . forgive me; & remember how prettily I behaved in town, & how I plagued & interrupted you at all hours.'

diavolacci degl'impedimenti swore bloodily it should not appear till next year. What bitter histories I could give you of unforeseen plagues in this business, besides those which from the beginning stared me full in the face! I shall only say, in few, that besides the disappointments of engravers, the grateful Musical Society for whom I have been royally commanded to write have as yet taken no proper measures for defraying the expenses of printing, paper, and plates; so that unless I redeem the sheets and plates, when finished, with my own credit and purse, the book will remain some time unpublished for want of money to pay the artists that have been employed.[4]

The next subject of my scribble shall be your *protégé*, the painter.[5] If any possible means of serving such a man as you describe had occurred to me on or since the perusal of your letter you would certainly have heard from me sooner; but, alas! I have long seen and predicted that the polite arts have been fostered, cherished, and are arrived almost at maturity in this ruined country merely to be starved to death! The swarm of young artists who have been students in the Royal Academy has over-stocked the capital and country so much that I am told many of them are at present in the utmost indigence. Zoffani[6] and Humphreys[7] are gone to the East Indies, and Pine,[8] with several others, to the West. It is the same with music; many masters, once in great business, are now wholly scholarless, without any other cause assigned but the general declension of the kingdom. Schools are indeed multiplied; but their existence is of short duration. The governesses, beginning on credit and a little money borrowed at very exorbitant interest, never subsist above three or four years, running in debt with every one that will trust them, and then suddenly disappearing. The

---

[4] CB finally presented the *Handel Commem.* to their Majesties on 17 Jan. 1785 (Lonsdale, pp. 310–11). The presentation was reported in the *Morning Chronicle*, 22 Jan. 1785, and the book first advertised as 'This Day is published' on Monday 24 Jan. 1785. See also CB to Sandwich, 25 Dec. 1784, n. 8.

[5] In his letter of 12 Nov., Twining had asked for CB's 'opinion & advice' about the career prospects in London for 'a young man' of Colchester, 'a painter; a sensible, modest, quiet man', who 'wishes much to be *etabli* in London, if he cou'd get employment there as a drawing Master. . . . If he cou'd get a *School*, to begin with, I believe he wou'd be glad to try his fortune. . . . He has true *Musical* feelings, . . . loves humour, & has that modest quietness, & *unpushingness* (a pretty vocable!) about him, that never did anything but harm to it's possessors since the world stood.'

[6] Johann Zoffany (1733–1810), painter of Bohemian descent, had migrated to England in 1758, RA (1769), travelled to Italy in 1772, returning to England in 1779. He left for India in 1783 (*DNB*). The *Morning Chronicle*, 17 Jan. 1785, reported, 'The unexpected great gains which Zoffani's pencil has acquired during his short stay in the East Indies, have tempted other painters to the same venture—Humphry, the miniature painter, Smart, and Engleheart, all are going in the present fleet to the East Indies.'

[7] Ozias Humphry (1742–1810), portrait painter, notably of miniatures, RA (1791), was about to depart for India, encouraged by Robert Strange (*DNB*).

[8] Robert Edge Pine (1730–88), painter, had emigrated to Philadelphia in 1783 (*DNB*).

poor masters are certain sufferers on these occasions. I have felt their bankruptcies a little; but Mr. Burney very heavily. To such unestablished schools as these I should be sorry to recommend your friend; and to others of long standing the masters are generally of the highest rank in their profession. A man who has a name to make, whatever his intrinsic worth and abilities, will never get into a great school but as an assistant. After this gloomy description of the general state of the arts and their votaries in London, you may be assured, my dear friend, that any person recommended by you can never be out of my thoughts, and if anything should offer within my ken and power of influence it shall be instantly communicated to you. Poor Fisin,[9] who has always done your patronage credit, seems to find it more and more difficult to subsist in London, and is languishing for a quiet organist's place in the country. I tried to get Newcastle for him some years ago, but was foiled. He was not, however, rejected for want of splendid abilities, as might naturally be expected; but for want of friends powerful enough to overset the natural interest of a man in the neighbourhood, not much his superior in talents, and greatly his inferior in good qualities.

Poor Johnson is gone![10] I truly reverenced his genius, learning, and piety, without being blind to his prejudices. I think I know and could name them all. We often differed in matters of taste, and in our judgments of individuals. My respect for what I thought excellent in him never operated on my reason sufficiently to incline me to subscribe to his decisions when I thought them erroneous. The knight, Sir John, and I met two or three times during his sickness, and at his funeral.[11] He steps forth as one of poor Johnson's six or eight biographers,[12] with as little taste or powers of writing worthy of such an occupation as for musical history. The Dean and Chapter of Westminster Abbey lay all

[9] James Fisin (*c.* 1750–1847), for whom see CB to Twining [June 1776], nn. 2, 3. In the autumn of 1776, CB had tried, unsuccessfully, to have Fisin appointed to Newcastle, but was successful many years later in obtaining a teaching post for him at Chester in 1801.

[10] Samuel Johnson had died about seven in the evening on Monday 13 Dec. 1784 (Hill–Powell, iv. 417). For the account of CB's last visits to Johnson, see Lonsdale, pp. 285–90.

[11] On Monday 20 Dec. 1784 (Hill–Powell, iv. 419). CB's name is included in the list of 'gentlemen who attended as mourners' in the account of the funeral which appeared in the *General Evening Post*, 18–21 Dec. 1784. Both CB and Charles Burney are listed in the official account of the 'Ceremonial of Dr. Johnson's Funeral' which Sir John Hawkins published in *GM* liv (1784)[2], 947. CB's son, Charles, included this 'Ceremonial' in the June 1785 issue of his *London Magazine, Enlarged and Improved*, iv (1785), 401–2, with the significant addition of a paragraph regretting 'that the cathedral service was withheld from its invariable friend; and the omission was truly offensive to the audience at large.'

[12] See CB to Mrs Phillips, [26? Dec. 1784]. For a listing of the announcements by those who intended to write Johnson's biography, see Helen L. McGuffie, *Samuel Johnson in the British Press, 1749–1784, a Chronological Checklist* (New York, 1976), pp. 330 ff.

the blame on him for suffering Johnson to be so unworthily interred.[13] The knight's first inquiry at the Abbey, in giving orders, as the most acting executor, was—'What would be the difference in the expense between a public and private funeral?' and was told only a few pounds to the prebendaries, and about ninety pairs of gloves to the choir and attendants; and he then determined that, 'as Dr. Johnson had no music in him, he should choose the cheapest manner of interment.' And for this reason there was no organ heard, or burial service sung; for which he suffers the Dean and Chapter to be abused in all the newspapers,[14] and joins in their abuse when the subject is mentioned in conversation. Dr. Bell[15] has stated the case, in a letter to my friend Dr. Warren, just as I tell it you. Again, I was told by a lady 'that she found Dr. Johnson had not been always so pious and good a Christian as in the latter part of his life.' 'How do you know, madam?' 'Why, Sir John Cullum[16] was told so by Sir John Hawkins, who says that when Dr. Johnson came up to London first he lived a very profligate life with Savage[17] and others, and was an infidel, and that he[18] (Hawkins) first

[13] CB's son, Charles, wrote to Dr Parr on 21 Dec. 1784, the day after Johnson's funeral: 'Ten mourning coaches were ordered by the executors for those invited. Besides these, eight of his friends or admirers clubbed for two more carriages, in one of which I had a seat. But the executor, Sir John Hawkins, did not manage things well, for there was no anthem, or choir service performed—no lesson—but merely what is read over every old woman that is buried by the parish. Surely, surely, my dear Sir, this was wrong, very wrong. Dr. Taylor read the service— but so-so' (*The Works of Samuel Parr, LL.D.*, ed. J. Johnstone (1828), i. 535). The meanness of Johnson's funeral rankled for years afterwards. Parr was to write to Charles Burney in 1792: 'Did you go to Sir Joshua's burial? I hope he had a complete service, not mutilated and dimidiated, as it was for poor Johnson at the Abbey, which is a great reproach to the lazy cattle who loll in the stalls there' (ibid., vii. 412).

[14] In, for example, the *Public Advertiser* and the *Morning Chronicle* (see McGuffie, *Checklist*, pp. 337 ff.), which appear to have led the attack. 'And his burial, *if a burial it could be called*,—in a cathedral, without an anthem, with the common service mutilated. . . . Each false emphasis and want of feeling, in the performance of the service . . . were such as the officiating Minister perhaps could not help. . . . The Chapter of Westminster . . . failed of attending on the funeral of such a man as Samuel Johnson—it is an imputation that never can be got over!' (*Morning Chronicle*, 22 Dec.). The cost of the funeral also provoked angry comment: charges were made for the organ, bellows blower, and wax lights—'There being *no Anthem*, there was *no* Organ, *no* Bellows Blower . . . The *fragment* of the burial service was done in the broad day-light of noon, when not a single taper was touched, nor a match lighted !!!' (ibid., 25 Dec.). See also J. C. Rowland, 'The Controversy over Johnson's Burial', *New Rambler*, ser. C, viii (Jan. 1970), 5–10.

[15] The Revd William Bell (1731–1816), DD (1767), divine, Prebendary of Westminster since 1765 (*DNB*; Venn). Bell's letter to Dr Richard Warren has not been traced. It doubtless contained an explanation such as appeared in the *Morning Chronicle*, 24 Dec.: '. . . the choir would have been summoned to assist, if Dr. Johnson's executors, who settled the business of the funeral, had chosen that it should: . . . the Dean's not officiating was owing to illness, . . . every prebendary who could, which were six in number, voluntarily attended'.

[16] The Revd Sir John Cullum (1733–85), 6th Baronet (1774), of Hawsted and Hardwick, Suffolk, FSA (1774), FRS (1775), antiquary and divine (*DNB*).

[17] Richard Savage (?1697–1743), poet (*DNB*). See also Johnson's *Life of Savage* (1744), in *Lives of the English Poets by Samuel Johnson, LL.D.*, ed. G. B. Hill (Oxford, 1905), ii. 321–440; C. Tracy, *The Artificial Bastard, A Biography of Richard Savage* (Toronto, 1953), pp. 11–27, 133–5.

[18] he] *he* (MS copy).

converted him to Christianity!'[19] This astonished me so much that I
could not help mentioning the story, and my authority, to Johnson's
oldest and most intimate friends, with whom I dined after attending
the funeral to Westminster Abbey,[20] and asked them if ever they heard
of Johnson having been a profligate and an infidel in his younger days,
and they one and all cried out, with astonishment and indignation,
'No!'[21] Dr. Scott,[22] one of the three executors, said that he had found
among his papers a great number of prayers, penned with great force,
elegance, and devotion, some of them as high up as the year 1738,
which would be a sufficient answer to such a charge; and I hear to-day
that Dr. Scott, without mentioning names, has said to the knight that
such a report had got about. 'Oh!' says Sir John, 'I[23] can best confute
such a rumour, who have so long known him, and ever found him a
man of the most exemplary life, and a most steady believer of the
doctrines of the Christian religion.' This strange story, for the honour
of Johnson and true piety, as well as the clearing up the point which
now lies between the reverend and irreverend[24] knight, I hope and
trust will be sifted to the bottom.[25] I shall write again in my book
parcel as soon as his Majesty is 'sarved,' and then tell you the upshot.
What an excellent writer and speaker is your (my) brother-chairman[26]

[19] Christianity!] Xanity!!! (MS copy).
[20] William Windham recorded the guests present at this dinner: 'We dined at Sir Joshua
Reynolds', viz. Burke and R. Burke, Metcalf, Colman, Hoole, Scott, Burney, and Brocklesby'
(*The Diary of the Right Hon. William Windham, 1784 to 1810*, ed. Mrs Henry Baring (1866), p. 35).
[21] No!] NO! (MS copy).
[22] William Scott (1745–1836), Kt (1788), created Baron Stowell (1821), DCL (1779), FSA
(1792), FRS (1793), maritime, international, and ecclesiastical lawyer, at this time Camden
Reader of Ancient History at Oxford (1773–85). He was a member of The Club and the Essex
Head Club, and rose to great eminence as a judge (*DNB*).
[23] I] *I* (MS copy).
[24] irreverend] *ir*reverend (MS copy).
[25] For the vexed question of what Boswell called Johnson's youthful 'indulgencies' (Hill–
Powell, i. 164) in company with Savage, see Sir John Hawkins, *The Life of Samuel Johnson, LL.D.*
(1787), pp. 54, 320–1; Hill–Powell, iv. 395–8, 551–2; *Johnsonian Miscellanies*, ed. G. B. Hill
(Oxford, 1897), ii. 212–13; J. L. Clifford, *Young Samuel Johnson* (1955), p. 203 (New York edn.,
p. 211); F. A. Pottle, 'The Dark Hints of Sir John Hawkins and Boswell', in *New Light on Dr.
Johnson, Essays on the Occasion of His 250th Birthday*, ed. F. W. Hilles (New Haven, 1959), pp. 153–62;
W. J. Bate, *Samuel Johnson* (1978), pp. 180–1.
[26] Twining's half-brother, Richard (1749–1824), head of the family tea business in the
Strand, was Chairman of the tea-dealers' Committee, at this time deeply involved in the
preparation and consequences of the Commutation Act of 1784 (24 Geo. III, c. 38) which had
received the Royal Assent on 20 Aug. (*London Gazette*, 17–21 Aug. 1784). The Act drastically
reduced the tea duty, thereby lowering its retail price in order to eradicate smuggling. The loss
in Government revenue was to be made up by a corresponding increase in window taxes. At the
East India Company's quarterly tea sale in Sept., however, certain unscrupulous merchants
combined to force up the price of tea. Richard Twining's efforts as Chairman of the tea dealers to
counteract this move were widely reported in the press (*Morning Chronicle*, 18 Sept. 1784, *et
passim*). At the Dec. sale, the dealers found certain lots offered for auction by the East India
Company to be spoiled. Richard Twining, in taking a firm stand against the Company, figured
conspicuously again in the newspapers (ibid., 17, 20, 21, 24 Dec.). He had also recently published

become in a short time! 'Oh! most righteous judge! a second Daniel!'[27] I wish I had leisure to follow him to the India House; but, alas! there would soon be a 'sale' at mine if I did!

A pit of destruction for the man who robbed us, in one year, of so many comforts! and, among the rest, of the power of tiring our friends to death with frequent and long letters, *à bon marché!*[28] Why, now I am but just got into my rate, and am obliged to pull up! I have lately had very pleasant accounts from (the) Philippi,[29] where I should like to meet you next summer. I have not been able to bestow a thought on my poor History, or the idea of a design for a frontispiece (which you do me the honour to remember better than myself),[30] since I saw you. Indeed, I once tried to find the sketch I read to you, in order to show it to Sir Joshua Reynolds, but could not. Shroeter's[31] second book of concertos has more nerves than the first, and the parts of both are well written and adjusted; but, I know not how it is, I tire of both very soon. I have not yet been at the opera. There is nothing new in the comic line; and Cherubini,[32] the second composer, with Crescentini,

two pamphlets in rapid succession: *Observations on the Tea and Window Act, and on the Tea Trade*, on 11 Dec.; and *Remarks on the Report of the East India Directors, respecting the Sale and Prices of Tea*, on 23 Dec. (*General Evening Post*, 11–14 Dec.; 21–3 Dec.). See also S. H. Twining, *The House of Twining, 1706–1956* (1956), pp. 45–9. CB also alludes to his own Chairmanship of the Musical Fund (see CB to Twining, 31 July 1784, nn. 24, 26; 1 Sept. 1784, n. 14), which, 'in consequence of royal patronage,' was soon to be named the Royal Society of Musicians. See the *London Magazine, Enlarged and Improved*, iv (1785), 229.

[27] See *The Merchant of Venice*, iv. i. 218–19, 296, 328, 335. CB conflates.

[28] CB refers to William Pitt's Franking Act of 1784, for which see CB to Twining, 31 July 1784, n. 13.

[29] i.e. from CB's favourite daughter, Susanna Phillips, at present in Boulogne. Susan's married name, as might be expected of the Burneys, gave rise to many a merry pun and allusion to *Julius Caesar*, iv. iii. Twining had written in his letter of 12 Nov.: 'I want sadly to hear of the good Phillipics:—you had not had any tidings of them when I left you, & seemed uneasy about it.'

[30] Twining had written (12 Nov.), '. . . tell me if your plan for a frontispiece to y[r] 3[d] Vol. is likely to be executed. . . . I liked the idea hugely.' These comments show that it was not CB's original intention to use as a frontispiece his portrait by Reynolds, now already engraved by Bartolozzi (CB to Mrs Phillips, [25]–26 Apr. 1784, n. 3; to Mrs Piozzi, 30 July 1784, n. 6).

[31] Shroeter's] Shroeter's *in CC in error*.

In his letter of 12 Nov., Twining had written: 'I brought home a 2[d] Set of Schroter's Concertos, at the instigation of M[r] & M[rs] B[urney] that please me much by a certain easy elegance, that avoids triteness, tho' it does not run *wide* of the common path, like Haydn &c[a]. One comfort is, where there is less originality, there is less difficulty: a thing very convenient to the limited power of my paw.'

Johann Samuel Schroeter (*c*.1752–88), German pianist and composer, had first performed in London in 1772. He succeeded J. C. Bach in 1782 as Music-master to the Queen (*New Grove*; *Hist. Mus.* iv. 682; Mercer, ii. 1022; Rees). CB and Twining discuss his *Six Concertos for the Harpsichord, or Piano Forte; with an Accompanyment for Two Violins, and a Bass . . . Opera III* [*c*.1774]; and *Six Concertos for the Harpsichord or Piano Forte, with Accompanyments for Two Violins, a Tenor and Bass . . . Opera V* [*c*.1777]. CB declared in Rees that Schroeter's style of composition 'was graceful and in good taste; but so chaste as sometimes to seem deficient in fire and invention.' See also K. Wolff, 'Johann Samuel Schroeter', *Musical Quarterly*, xliv (1958), 338–59.

[32] Luigi Carlo Zanobi Salvadore Maria Cherubini (1760–1842), Italian composer, was now in London for the first time, but did not achieve success (*New Grove*; *MGG*). As CB put it, he was

the first serious man, and the Ferrarese, the first woman,[33] being all principiants, I have no more desire to dress and go into the cold theatre to hear them than to go to a puppet-show, or to see the giants at Guildhall. Lolli,[34] the great violinist, is just arrived. Addio.

C.B.

[35]I love you the better for liking Berquin's touching simplicity.[36] Sir. Jos. Reynolds reads & cries like you.[35]

To Mrs Phillips

[St Martin's Street,
26? December 1784][1]

AL (Comyn). First leaf missing. FBA pasted a blank strip of paper to the top of the surviving second leaf. On top of this strip she pasted another strip from the bottom of the first leaf, beginning 'We have at length . . .'.

Docketed by FBA: *Death of Dr Johnson* | Dr. Burney to Mrs. Phillips—Boulogne Sur Mer, France | Part of a Letter of Dec[r] 1784. St. Martin's St ⌗ ⌗

. . . We have at length lost poor Johnson! he died as he lived, *en odeur de saintité*—I saw & rec[d] his Benediction on saturday,[2] and he expired

'a young man of genius, who had no opportunity while he was here of displaying his abilities' (*Hist. Mus.* iv. 527; Mercer, ii. 899).

[33] 'The Opera-house was opened in autumn, 1784, in no very auspicious manner: Pacchierotti being succeeded by Crescentini, with a feeble and uncertain voice, and the Lusini not much surpassed, by the Ferrarese del Bene' (*Hist. Mus.* iv. 523; Mercer, ii. 896–7).

Girolamo Crescentini (1762–1846), Italian male mezzo-soprano, made his début at the King's Theatre on 8 Jan. 1785, without success (*New Grove*; *BD*; *The London Stage*, v. ii. 763).

Adriana del Bene, née Gabrielli, called 'Ferraresi' (*c.*1755–after 1799), Italian soprano, who made her début in London with Crescentini, and stayed for two seasons (*New Grove*; *BD*).

[34] Antonio Lolli (*c.*1725–1802), Italian violinist and composer (*New Grove*), of whom CB wrote, '. . . so eccentric was his style of composition and execution, that he was regarded as a madman by most of his hearers. Yet I am convinced that in his lucid intervals he was, in a serious style, a very great, expressive, and admirable performer' (*Hist. Mus.* iv. 680–1; Mercer, ii. 1020–1).

[35–35] I . . . you.] *text from MS copy. Omitted in CC.*

[36] Arnaud Berquin (1747–91), French author, whose moral tales and romances for children became immensely popular (*DBF*). From Jan. 1782 to Dec. 1783, he published at Paris in 24 monthly instalments his *L'Ami des enfans*, which was also published in London in 1783, with each part bearing the original Paris publication dates. The London edition lists both CB and Fanny among Berquin's subscribers. The author had visited London in summer 1783 and called on the Burneys frequently (*DL* ii. 216; *Mem.* ii. 330–2). Twining was particularly moved by Berquin's tale of how an unloved little girl wins the affection of her mother and brother. He wrote in his letter of 12 Nov.: 'I don't read Aristotle & such old Bores; I read M. Berquin, & cry!—The little tale of *Phillipine* & *Maximin* (vol. [4])! how it choked me!'

[1] The probable date of this letter is inferred from Kearsley's announcement in the *Morning Chronicle*, Sat. 25 Dec. 1784, that 'Memoirs of the Doctor's Life . . . will be published on Monday next': i.e. 27 Dec. CB in the present letter refers to this publication date 'to Morrow'. See n. 21.

[2] i.e. Saturday 11 Dec. 1784. For Fanny's account of CB's visit to Johnson, see *DL* ii. 279–80. See also Lonsdale, pp. 285–90.

on Monday! He had been so bad for some days, as to be able to see none but medical People, & his constant attendants, the Hooles[3] & Langton;[4] however on my desiring Mr Hoole to let him know, if there was an opportunity, as he was said to be dozing, that I was in the next room, he soon returned & said he wished to see me—when he, sitting propt up in a great Chair, took hold of my hands & asked after the whole Family, particularly Fanny, who, I told him had been to enquire after him 2 days ago,[5] when he said 'I heard of it but hope she will excuse my not seeing her; for I was unable to talk with her'—& then said 'God bless you![']—after wch still holding my hands he made one of the most fervent & Eloquent Prayers that was ever uttered in the last moments of a Saint. I w^d give the world to remember it Verbatim, but it is impossible for memory to do it justice.[6] No one, I think was by, but his old friend Dr Taylor,[7] with whom he was in the summer at Ashburn in Derbyshire—whose intellects at present are not very powerful,—however he may have acquired the favour of Poor Johnson in his younger years. When I came away; he said '*come again*!'—though for several days he had taken a final leave of all with whom he was able to talk —& said 'tell Fanny I think I c^d throw the Ball to her yet'[8]—wch encouraged poor Fan to go to Bolt court next day, sunday;[9] but after staying more than 2 Hours in hopes of seeing him, Langton came out of his room to tell her it was impossible, as he was too bad to be able to speak to any one—this you may be sure over-set our poor Fan terribly. He went off on Monday in a sleep, without the knowledge of young Des Moulins, who only was in the room,[10] and imagined him still asleep some time after he expired. Though very uneasy for many years at the thoughts

---

[3] For John and Susannah Hoole, see CB to Charles Burney, 24 Sept. 1784, n. 2. Hoole wrote: 'Saturday, Dec. 11.—Went to Bolt Court about twelve; met there Dr. Burney, Dr. Taylor, Sir John Hawkins, Mr. Sastres, Mr. Paradise, Count Zenobia, and Mr. Langton. Mrs. Hoole called for me there' (*Johnsonian Miscellanies*, ed. G. B. Hill (Oxford, 1897), ii. 158).

[4] Bennet Langton (1737–1801), Greek scholar and member of The Club, one of Johnson's most intimate friends (*DNB*; Hill–Powell, *passim*).

[5] i.e. on Thursday 9 Dec. 1784, if CB's recollection is accurate. *DL* ii. 278 dates Fanny's unsuccessful visit 'Wednesday, Dec. 10', an impossibility in 1784.

[6] Johnson, as CB recalled many years later, 'uttered an exhortation, to philanthropy, & X^tian & social virtues ... & finished by this impressive precept—"Do all the good you can"' (CB to Lord Lonsdale, [?Mar. 1807], Hyde).

[7] The Revd John Taylor (1711–88), LLD (1752), of Ashbourne, Derbyshire, Johnson's Lichfield schoolmate and lifelong friend (*DNB*; Johnson *Letters*, *passim*). Since 1746 Taylor had occupied a prebendal stall at Westminster, and in that capacity read the service at Johnson's funeral. See also CB to Twining, 25 Dec. 1784, nn. 13, 14.

[8] MS yet] *FBA* interlined & his last words were 'Remember me to Fanny—',

[9] See *DL* ii. 280–2.

[10] John Desmoulins (*fl.* 1778–84), son of Elizabeth Desmoulins, née Swinfen (b. 1716), and grandson of Dr Samuel Swinfen (1679–1736), the Lichfield physician who was Johnson's godfather (*DNB*, under 'Swynfen'). Mrs Desmoulins, who had lived in Johnson's house until May 1783, had returned to Lichfield (Johnson *Letters*, iii. 239). Her son, John, who in Oct. 1778 had

of death, he at last faced it with great courage, & talked of that, his affairs and Funeral, with perfect composure. I shall say no more on this Melancholy subject till I know whether you see English Newspapers at Boulogne; if you do it will employ your time & mine very ill in tell⁸ you what you have already read, abᵗ his circumstances, Funeral, Biographers &cᴵᴵ—I will only tell you the Names of these last who are already writing his Life: Sir John *Hawkins*,¹² one of his Executors, wᵗʰ Dʳ Scott (who married Miss Bagnell)¹³ & Sir Jos. Reynolds—Dʳ Kippis;¹⁴ *Croft* whose life of the poet Dʳ Young is inserted in Johnson's Lives;¹⁵ Boswell;¹⁶ Tommy Tyers;¹⁷ The Editor of the Johnsoniana, a

been 'taken in *an undersomething* of Drury Lane' at 'five and twenty shillings a week' (ibid., ii. 260, 270; *BD*); witnessed Johnson's will on 8 Dec. 1784. Johnson, in the codicil to his will, left Desmoulins £200 consolidated 3% annuities. See Hill–Powell, iv. 402 n. 2, 442, 522.

CB's information that it was John Desmoulins, and not his mother, who attended Johnson in his last hours is corroborated by William Windham (*Diary*, ed. Mrs Henry Baring (1866), pp. 31–2) and, obliquely, by Sir John Hawkins (*Life*, 2nd rev. edn., 1787, p. 591), who refers to 'a young man that sat up with him'. Boswell (Hill–Powell, iv. 418) appears to have been misinformed by his brother, Thomas David (1748–1826), that Mrs Desmoulins was in attendance.

¹¹ For a detailed listing, see Helen L. McGuffie, *Samuel Johnson in the British Press, 1749–1784, a Chronological Checklist* (New York, 1976), pp. 329 ff. See also R. E. Kelley and O M Brack, Jr., *Samuel Johnson's Early Biographers* (Iowa City, 1971).

¹² MS *Hawkins* ... *Kippis* ... *Croft* ... *Boswell* ... *Tyers* ... *Cook*] *CB places numerals 1 to 6 over the names of these biographers.*

The *St. James's Chronicle*, 14–16 Dec. 1784, followed by other papers, reported: 'Biographers are very busy in preparing Materials for the Life of Dr. Samuel Johnson. Many, we are told, are the Candidates, but the principal which are mentioned are Sir John Hawkins, and James Boswell, Esq.' Hawkins's *The Life of Samuel Johnson, LL.D.*, was to appear in Mar. 1787, also issued as the first volume of his edition of Johnson's *Works*. A second revised edition of the biography was published three months later in June 1787. See B. H. Davis, *Johnson before Boswell, a Study of Sir John Hawkins' Life of Samuel Johnson* (New Haven, 1960); and *A Proof of Eminence: the Life of Sir John Hawkins* (Bloomington, 1973), chs. 20, 21.

¹³ Anna Maria Bagnall (*c.*1755–1809), of Erleigh Court, Berkshire, had married William Scott in 1781 (*DNB*). The Bagnalls had been acquainted with the Burneys since 1772 (see *EJL* i. 218–19).

¹⁴ The *Morning Chronicle*, 18 Dec. 1784, had reported: '... some authors of acknowledged ability have it in contemplation to favour the world with a Life of Dr. Johnson drawn from authentick sources ... Dr. Andrew Kippis is talked of in the literary circle, as the gentleman who has already determined to use his pen upon the subject.' The Revd Andrew Kippis (1725–95), DD (1767), FSA (1778), FRS (1779), nonconformist divine and biographer, editor of the second edition of the *Biographia Britannica*, of which only five volumes were completed (1778–93). See *DNB*; Hill–Powell, iv. 376. Nothing came of Kippis's projected Johnsonian biography, despite his public declaration of intent in the *Morning Chronicle*, 22 Dec. 1784. See also ibid., 25 Dec.

¹⁵ Herbert Croft (1751–1816), later (1797) 5th Baronet, author, barrister, and clergyman, had been a pupil of William Scott at University College, Oxford (1771). Johnson included Croft's life of Edward Young (1683–1765), the poet, in his *Lives of the English Poets*, ed. G. B. Hill (Oxford, 1905), iii. 361–99. See *DNB*. Croft did not write a biography of Johnson.

¹⁶ James Boswell (1740–95) published his *Journal of a Tour to the Hebrides with Samuel Johnson, LL.D.* on 1 Oct. 1785; and *The Life of Samuel Johnson, LL.D.* on 16 May 1791. See *The Correspondence and Other Papers of James Boswell Relating to the Making of the Life of Johnson*, ed. M. Waingrow (1969).

¹⁷ Thomas Tyers (1726–87), author, barrister of the Inner Temple (1757), and joint manager (1767–85) of Vauxhall Gardens (*DNB*). Tyers wrote 'A Biographical Sketch of Dr. Samuel

Mr Cook,[18] who does not set his name to it, but who suffered Kearsley[19] to advertise it as ready for publication the day after the good soul's death,[20] & it is to be published to Morrow.[21] Besides these a life of him is publishing every day in one of the News-papers. Not one of these Biographers has to my thinking a single Qualification necessary for the work he so flippantly undertakes; not one who sufficiently reverenced his learning, Genius, & Piety; or who is possessed of a style & abilities capable of doing them justice.[22] Hawkins & Kippis are both equally dry & dull—Croft, a fop who imitates Johnson's style without being possessed of one of his Ideas: ''twas very impudent, says Burke the other day at the Club, to take a man off in his own book'—meaning in his life of Young[23]—it was like Garrick taking off Gifford[24] the player before his face on his own stage when he was

Johnson', *GM* liv (1784)^2, 899–911, 982; lv (1785)^1, 85–7; partly reprinted in Charles Burney's *London Magazine, Enlarged and Improved*, iv (1785), 331–48. Tyers's *Biographical Sketch* was issued with revisions as a pamphlet in 1785, preserved only in a few copies. See the reprint, ed. G. D. Meyer, Augustan Reprint Society No. 34 (Los Angeles, 1952).

[18] William Cooke, or Cook (d. 1824), later known as 'Conversation' Cooke, from his didactic poem (1796) of that name, barrister of the Middle Temple, miscellaneous author (*DNB*). CB's assertion here that Cooke had edited *The Beauties of Johnson: consisting of Maxims and Observations, moral, critical, and miscellaneous* (1781), confirms A. T. Hazen's identification on circumstantial evidence in 'The *Beauties of Johnson*', *Modern Philology*, xxxv (1938), 289–95. In the fifth edition of the *Beauties* (1782), 'Memoirs' of Johnson had appeared (pp. vii–xv), about two-thirds of which was now incorporated in Cooke's anonymous *The Life of Samuel Johnson, LL.D. with occasional Remarks on his Writings* (1785; but published 29 Dec. 1784). See also Hill-Powell, iv. 437. CB's attributions to Cooke furnish weighty evidence: both belonged to Johnson's Essex Head Club (see Lonsdale, pp. 282–3; Hill–Powell, iv. 254).

[19] George Kearsley, or Kearsly (d. 1790), London bookseller and publisher, who currently conducted his business at 46 Fleet Street (Plomer, pp. 143–4; *GM* lx (1790)^2, 1150). He published the *Beauties of Johnson* (see also Johnson *Letters*, ii. 483), and Cooke's *Life*. CB had little reason to be enamoured of Kearsley, who had published the notorious parody of CB, the *Musical Travels* of 'Joel Collier' (see CB to Twining, 18 Oct. 1775, n. 4).

[20] Kearsley's advertisement in the *Morning Chronicle*, 15 Dec. 1784, announcing Cooke's *Life* for 'Next Week', is illuminating: 'To avoid the imputation of a catchpenny performance, which the speedy publication of this life might suggest, the publick are informed, that the whole has been drawn up, (the particulars of his death excepted) for some time, by a gentleman who has long lived in the habits of friendship with the Doctor, and who was only restrained by delicacy from publishing it during his life.'

[21] Kearsley advertised Cooke's *Life* on Sat. 25 Dec. as 'will be published on Monday next', a circumstance which helps to date this letter (n. 1). In the event, he had to postpone publication day to Wed. 29 Dec., as the 'Holidays have prevented a sufficient number of the LIFE of Dr. JOHNSON, being ready for delivery as intended This Morning' (*Morning Chronicle*, 27 Dec.). Cooke's *Life* was published 'This Morning' (ibid., 29 Dec.). CB's 'to Morrow' most probably refers to Kearsley's earlier advertised publication date.

[22] For a discussion of CB's intention to write a biography of Johnson himself, see Lonsdale, pp. 288–90.

[23] For other crushing comments by Burke on Croft's attempt to imitate Johnson's style, see Hill-Powell, iv. 59: '. . . it has all the nodosities of the oak without its strength . . . all the contortions of the Sybil, without the inspiration.'

[24] Henry Giffard (1694–1772), actor and theatre manager, in whose troupe at the Goodman's Fields Theatre Garrick made his sensational London début in 1741 (*BD*).

Master of Goodman's-fields Theatre—wch however produced a Duel, though Gifford had given Garrick leave to make the most of him, provided he would take off Ryan, Delany, Hales, Quin & others, in the Rehearsal.[25] Well, but to go on with these Biographers—Tommy Tyers is such a quaint, feeble, fumble-fisted writer, as is only fit for Mother Goose's tales—& Boswell with all his anecdotes, will only make a story book, a kind of a Joe Miller[26] the 2^d without address or dignity of introduction or application in relating his bons mots—and Cook, if we may judge of his talents by the Johnsoniana, will contrive to spoil the best stories he has picked up, by want of powers to relate them.

[25] Garrick first acted Bayes in Buckingham's *The Rehearsal* on 3 Feb. 1742 at Goodman's Fields (*The London Stage*, iii. ii. 965). There is much evidence that in this role he satirized the styles of fellow-actors such as Lacy Ryan (*c.*1694–1760), Dennis Delane (d. 1750), Sacheverel Hale (d. 1746), and James Quin (1693–1766). See *BD*; *DNB*; A. Murphy, *The Life of David Garrick, Esq.* (1801), i. 32–3, 50–6; G. W. Stone, Jr. and G. M. Kahrl, *David Garrick: A Critical Biography* (Carbondale and Edwardsville, 1979), pp. 476–80. The story of Garrick's duel with Giffard is probably apocryphal. See [J. Genest], *Some Account of the English Stage, from the Restoration in 1660 to 1830* (Bath, 1832), iv. 20–3; Carola Oman, *David Garrick* (1958), pp. 44–5, 388.
[26] i.e. a jest-book composed of stale jokes (*OED*, under 'Joe Miller'), from John Mottley (1692–1750), *Joe Miller's Jests: or, the Wits Vade-mecum*, which appeared first in 1739, and subsequently in many editions with additional feeble jokes and anecdotes of doubtful authenticity.

INDEX

Page references to Burney's letters are given under his correspondents' entries in bold type. Works are listed under the name of the artist, author, choreographer, composer, editor, or translator. Titles of works are abbreviated as far as possible. Performers are entered under their stage names where these are commonly used. Women are cited under their married names unless they first appear in this volume under their maiden names. British peerages are cross-referenced to family names and are abbreviated as follows: Abp = Archbishop; B. = Baron; Bns = Baroness; Bp = Bishop; Bt = Baronet; Cts = Countess; D. = Duke; Ds = Duchess; E. = Earl; M. = Marquess; Mns = Marchioness; Vt = Viscount; Vts = Viscountess.

'TORREY CANYON' POLLUTION
AND
MARINE LIFE

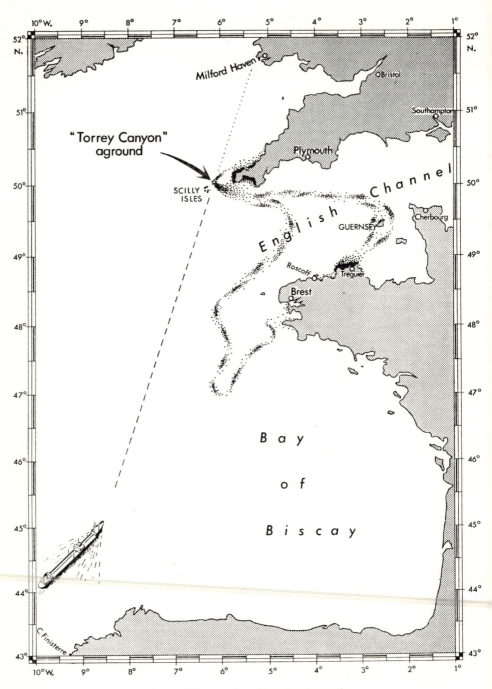

Fig. 1. The wreck and its oily aftermath.

'TORREY CANYON' POLLUTION AND MARINE LIFE

A Report by the Plymouth Laboratory of
the Marine Biological Association
of the United Kingdom

Under the general editorship of
J . E . SMITH, Sc.D., F.R.S.

Published for the
MARINE BIOLOGICAL ASSOCIATION
OF THE UNITED KINGDOM

CAMBRIDGE
AT THE UNIVERSITY PRESS

1970

Published by the Syndics of the Cambridge University Press
Bentley House, 200 Euston Road, London N.W. 1
American Branch: 32 East 57th Street, New York, N.Y. 10022

© Marine Biological Association of the United Kingdom 1968

Library of Congress Catalogue Number: 68–21400

ISBN: 0 521 07144 5

First published 1968
Reprinted 1970

Printed in Great Britain
at the University Printing House, Cambridge
(Brooke Crutchley, University Printer)

CONTENTS

LIST OF PLATES

PREFACE

This report is based on an intensive ten-week survey and analysis by the scientific staff of the Plymouth Laboratory of some biological consequences resulting from the release of 117000 tons of crude oil from the tanker 'Torrey Canyon' which, on 18 March 1967, was wrecked on the Seven Stones reef 15 miles from the Land's End of Cornwall.

The measures adopted by British authorities in dispersing oil at sea, and in the cleansing of the rocks and beaches along the 140 miles or so of the Cornish coastline invaded by oil during the week-end of 26–28 March, relied almost entirely on the liberal application of oil solvent/oil emulsifier mixtures (detergents). Detergents are toxic to marine organisms, and some $2\frac{1}{2}$ million gallons (more than 10000 tons) of detergents were used during the 'Torrey Canyon' operations. The greater part of this report is therefore concerned with the effect of detergents on marine plants and animals as revealed by field observations and laboratory experiments.

It was not the intention initially to include non-biological aspects of the 'Torrey Canyon' spillage within the Plymouth programmes. But the need to know the day-to-day distribution of the masses of oil released from the tanker, and the speed and direction of their movements, led to the development of methods of plotting and predicting oil movements which were encouragingly accurate and which have a clear relevance in the report to pollution of the Brittany beaches.

A brief comment may be offered in explanation of the way in which the report is presented. It was rarely possible during the period of the 'Torrey Canyon' investigations to make an observation or do an experiment under the terms that the investigator would have chosen, and in many instances observations had to be made well knowing that the means of fully understanding them were not available, either for lack of some necessary information or the absence at that time of suitable techniques of analysis and measurement.

In writing the report it was therefore thought best to describe the investigations as nearly as possible in the order in which they were done. This may help to explain some of the more obvious imperfections in the work reported, and will enable the step-by-step development of the programme to be the more clearly recognized.

The production of this report has been a truly corporate effort, not only in the field and laboratory work, but also in the preparation of the manuscript and in the editing.

STAFF PARTICIPATION

Almost all the members of the Plymouth Laboratory staff, and some of the long-term visiting scientists, participated in one way or another in the 'Torrey Canyon' investigations. The work was organized under the following headings:

> *Scientific Programmes*
> > (*a*) Sea surveys and plankton investigations
> > (*b*) Shore and near-shore (sublittoral) surveys
> > (*c*) Detergent toxicity testing
> > (*d*) Oil movements at sea
> > (*e*) Brittany surveys
>
> *Survey Samples and Records*
>
> *External Liaison*
>
> *General Organization*
>
> *Report Preparation*

The following took part: Pamela Ashton, Ann Baker, G. A. W. Battin, G. T. Boalch, Q. Bone, G. W. Bryan, E. I. Butler, L. H. N. Cooper, P. G. Corbin, E. D. S. Corner, A. G. Davies, E. J. Denton, G. R. Forster, J. Gage, P. E. Gibbs, J. B. Gilpin-Brown, J. E. Green, D. Harbour, Joan Hearn, Pamela Hobbs, N. A. Holme, J. V. Howarth, L. G. Hummerstone, Rosemary Jowett, Janet Kibble, R. G. Maddock, C. Manwell, A. D. Mattacola, B. J. Morgan, A. E. Nutty, Elizabeth Nybø, B. W. Osborne, Mary Parke, J. B. Pilkington, G. W. Potts, R.V. 'Sarsia' (Lt.-Cdr. C. H. White, R.N. (Retd.) in command), J. E. Smith, A. J. Southward, Eve Southward, G. M. Spooner, Molly Spooner, R. C. Swinfen, Susan Tibbits, A. Varley, F. J. Warren, D. P. Wilson, M. Alison Wilson.

COLLABORATIVE ORGANIZATIONS AND INDIVIDUAL CONTRIBUTORS

This record of indebtedness to the organizations and individuals who assisted the Plymouth Laboratory investigations by providing materials and information or by actively participating in surveys is by no means complete. The names attached to the organizations are often representative of a much wider indebtedness.

Collaborative Organizations

Ministry of Agriculture, Food and Fisheries (Mr A. C. Simpson)
Nature Conservancy (Mr W. O. Copland, Dr D. Ranwell, Mr F. R. Gomm)
BP Trading Company Limited (Mr G. C. Silsby)
Operations staff of Commander-in-Chief, Plymouth (Comdr. M. J. Garnett, R.N., O.B.E. and staff)
H.Q. 19 Group Coastal Command, R.A.F. Mount Batten, Plymouth (Sqdn.-Ldr. P. Halfacree, R.A.F.)
Meteorological Station, R.A.F. Mount Batten, Plymouth (all the staff)
Detergent Distribution Centre, Truro, Cornwall (Brigadier G. Lerwill, O.B.E., M.C.)
Admiralty Materials Laboratory (Superintendent)
Cornwall Naturalists' Trust (Mr J. K. Williams)

Toxicity Testing

Dr A. D. Boney (University College, Aberystwyth), Dr J. H. S. Blaxter (University of Aberdeen), Mr Norman Hendey (Admiralty Materials Laboratory), Dr Sheina Marshall (Millport Laboratory, Isle of Cumbrae), Mr B. W. Sparrow (International Paints Laboratory, Newton Ferrers), Mr P. R. Walne (Fisheries Experimental Station, Conway)

Bacteriology

Dr W. Gunkel (Biologische Anstalt, Helgoland)

Shore and Offshore Surveys

Dr J. N. Lythgoe (Institute of Ophthalmology, London), Mr G. Harwood (Kodak Limited, Harrow), Dr A. Nelson-Smith (University College, Swansea), Dr Gillian Matthews (Fowey), Dr Susan Vaidya (Marazion), Cornwall Sea Fisheries Committee with patrol boat 'Cornubia'

Brittany Survey

Prof. P. Courtot (Faculté des Sciences, Brest), M. Cabioch (Roscoff), Cdr. C. H. Brusson (Brest), M. Daniel (Morlaix)

Secretarial Assistance

Mrs S. E. Potts, Miss J. Penfold

Photographs illustrating this report have been kindly supplied by the following:

G. T. Boalch, Plate 7 A
Q. Bone, Plate 21 B
G. W. Bryan, Plates 2, 22 A, 23 A, 23 B
G. R. Forster, Plate 27 A
J. Gage, Plates 20 B, 24 A, 24 B
P. E. Gibbs, Plates 4 B, 5 B, 14 C, 18 C, 21 A
G. E. Harwood, Plates 6 C, 26 A, 26 B
N. A. Holme, Plates 1 C, 4 A, 6 A, 6 B, 7 B, 18 A, 22 B, 27 B, 27 C, 28 A, 28 B, 28 C, 29 A, 29 B
G. W. Potts, Plates 5 A, 17 B, 18 B, 25 A, 25 B, 26 C
A. J. Southward, Plates 9 C, 19 A, 19 B
F. G. M. Spooner, Plates 1 B, 3 A, 13 A, 14 A, 20 A, 26 D
G. M. Spooner, Plates 1 A, 3 B, 8 A, 9 A, 9 B, 13 B, 14 B
R. Swinfen, Plates 7 C, 8 B
D. P. Wilson, Plates 10 A, 10 B, 11 A, 11 B, 12 A, 12 B, 15 A, 16 A, 17 A
M. Alison Wilson, Plates 15 B, 15 C, 16 B

The copyright of the photographs belongs to those who took them.

CHAPTER I

INTRODUCTION

A BRIEF CHRONOLOGY
OF 'TORREY CANYON' EVENTS

Close to 09.00 hours on the morning of Saturday 18 March 1967 the
970 foot long tanker 'Torrey Canyon', bound for Milford Haven from the
Persian Gulf and carrying within her eighteen storage tanks some 117000
tons of Kuwait crude oil, ran aground on the Pollard Rock of the Seven
Stones 15 miles west of Land's End and 7 miles north-east of the Isles of
Scilly (see Frontispiece map). The tanker was travelling at about 17 knots
when she struck the reef. Six of her tanks were reported as having been
torn open by the impact and others were thought to be less severely
damaged. Engines hard astern failed to move the ship and she was to remain on the reef in progressive stages of disintegration until six weeks later,
a submerged and broken wreck, she was declared to contain no more oil.

Phase 1: 18–20 March

Oil began to escape from the ruptured tanks immediately after the
stranding, and by nightfall a narrow slick some 8 miles long had thrust
southwards from the Seven Stones to the east of the Isles of Scilly under
the influence of the fresh northerly wind. By the Sunday evening (19 March)
an estimated 20000 tons of oil had escaped from the tanker and 24 hours
later it was thought that almost 30000 tons had been discharged on to the
surface of the sea. The main oil mass was now 18–20 miles long and moving
to the south. But, with the wind freshening and backing to the west, the
escaping oil began to be blown eastward, more directly threatening the
southern shores of Cornwall, and causing serious concern for an extensive
contamination of more distant coastlines of the Channel.

It had thus become apparent within the first three days of the stranding
of the 'Torrey Canyon' (i) that an oil release was developing on an unprecedented scale, (ii) that it was occurring in a geographical situation
where, with the return of the prevailing south-westerly winds, there would
be an inevitable and heavy contamination of long stretches of the coastlines
of the English Channel and Bristol Channel, and (iii) that, in order to
minimize the effects of the invasion, urgent and energetic measures would
be needed to remove the oil at source or to disperse it from the surface
of the sea.

The first efforts to disperse the oil at sea had been made within 12 hours

I   TCR

of the grounding of the tanker. For some time past the Navy had been using mixtures of solvent and emulsifying chemicals (detergents) for cleaning up relatively small oil spills in harbours and coastal waters. It was therefore natural that they should use the detergent method of oil dispersal in dealing with the 'Torrey Canyon' efflux. Two naval vessels which began spraying on the evening of 18 March were joined by a progressively increasing number of large and small ships, and within three days some 15 000 gallons of detergent had been discharged on to the oil.

Meanwhile, there had been set up at Maritime Headquarters, Mount Wise, Devonport, a control centre where the measures needed to cope with the more immediate problems were being organized and co-ordinated. The Minister of Defence, Mr Denis Healey, placed the operations under the overall control of the Under Secretary of State (Royal Navy), Mr Maurice Foley. Mr Foley's first discussions with officers of the three Services, scientific advisers and representatives of local authorities were held at regional headquarters on 19 and 20 March. Press reports of the meetings gave especial prominence to plans for increasing the production of detergents, and for mobilizing stocks for use in the cleansing of beaches should oil be cast ashore in quantity.

Phase 2: 21–23 March

On the Tuesday and Wednesday (21 and 22 March) following the grounding of the 'Torrey Canyon' the fresh 15-knot westerly breeze of the previous day persisted. More oil was driven up Channel but it remained sufficiently distant from the shore not to threaten immediate danger. Moreover, with the wind veering to the north-west on the following day there came renewed hope that the fouling of the coastline might be further postponed. It was of course realized that so long as the 'Torrey Canyon' remained on the reef and charged with oil the invasion must surely come. But, if compressed air could be injected into the damaged tanker to give her added buoyancy in time for the onset of the spring tides, there seemed to be a reasonable hope that the ship would lift sufficiently to be hauled off the reef. Nevertheless, since there was no guarantee that the vessel would be freed, an official Committee of Scientists was convened on 22 March under the chairmanship of the Chief Scientific Adviser to the Government, Sir Solly Zuckerman, to advise on the actions to be taken if the measures already being considered were to fail. By Thursday 23 March (the last day of this second phase of the operations) the tensions had so far eased that *The Times* front page reporting of the 'Torrey Canyon' news was limited to a paragraph of a few lines. Some weeks were to pass before the 'Torrey Canyon' again achieved a comparable level of obscurity.

Phase 3: 24–26 March

During Friday 24 March (Good Friday) the wind backed from north-west to south-west and freshened to 25 knots. Oil newly released from the tanker, and the oil of previous days' release thrusting out to the east of the Seven Stones, began to be pushed inexorably towards the Cornish coast-line. By midnight on the Friday two large masses were standing off the Land's End peninsula, and the first thick oil came ashore near St Just on the morning tide of Saturday 25 March. The oil continued to come ashore in massive quantities throughout the day. Along the south coast heavy fouling affected the greater part of the coastline from Land's End to the base of the Lizard at the east end of Mount's Bay, the least affected being a stretch 12 miles westward of Penzance. To the north of Land's End oil was driven in a north-easterly direction parallel to the coast, and at some distance from the shoreline, as far east as Newquay.

During the following day, 26 March (Easter Sunday) the wind veered from south-west to west and increased to gale force. On the south coast the movement of oil into the eastern side of Mount's Bay and along the west coast of the Lizard was completed, while along the north coast of Cornwall the long-shore movement of the oil was continued almost to the entrance of the Camel estuary. This girdle of oil was driven ashore in quantity from St Ives to Trevone Bay two to three days later with the turning of the wind to the north-west. While few of the north- and east-facing bays were affected, shores open to the north-west and west received a heavy pollution.

By the late afternoon of Easter Sunday it was estimated that some 48 000 tons of oil had issued from the 'Torrey Canyon'. Most of the early release (about 30 000 tons) had, as we have seen, moved southwards, and was too distant from the mainland to be returned by the later-developing but short-lived south-westerly wind. Much of this oil was later (11 April onwards) to inflict upon parts of the coastline of Brittany a heavy and damaging pollution, the oil smearing in its passage across the Channel a part of the Guernsey coastline (7 April).

The south-westerly wind which blew throughout the Saturday and Sunday of the Easter week-end captured most of the remaining 18 000 tons of oil that had, up to that time, been released from the tanker and drove it rapidly towards Land's End. This 15 per cent or so of the oil carried by the 'Torrey Canyon' (now reduced a little by the evaporation of its lighter fractions) comprised, save possibly for some relatively small amounts that came ashore later, virtually the whole of the oil deposited on the British shoreline.

Almost all came ashore within the short space of four to five days, thereafter to be withdrawn and redeposited for a while with the rise and fall of the tides.

Phase 4: 27–30 March

Around 19.00 hours on the evening of Sunday 26 March, the 'Torrey Canyon', pounded by the heavy seas, broke her back, releasing an estimated 40000–50000 tons of oil into the sea. This immense mass of oil, at first driven in a south-easterly direction, was then, for two days, blown by a south-westerly wind towards the English coastline. Then, almost at the last moment, it was deflected seawards by the backing of the wind to the north. Thereafter, from 3 April, a north or north-easterly air stream persisted most uncharacteristically for a full 30 days, and the British coastline was relieved from further serious threat. For some weeks, at least, the greater part of this later outspill remained at sea. When in the Biscayan area it was treated extensively with powdered chalk by ships of the French navy and a substantial part of it was reported as having been sunk. A very small proportion of this oil eventually landed on the west coast of Brittany (Chapter 9).

The 'Torrey Canyon', her back broken and now almost beyond hope of salvage, was bombed on 28, 29 and 30 March. Oil in the ship and on the surrounding water was set alight, but in spite of the feeding on to it of aviation fuel the fires were not for long maintained. Thereafter, some oil continued to escape from the three separated sections of the wrecked tanker, which only gradually became submerged. The ship disappeared from view towards the end of April, by which time she was probably empty of oil.

THE PLYMOUTH LABORATORY
AND THE 'TORREY CANYON' INVESTIGATIONS

The Plymouth Laboratory is the research laboratory of the Marine Biological Association of the United Kingdom. The Association, founded in 1884, is supported by the subscriptions and donations of private members, universities, scientific societies, the Fishmongers' Company and other public bodies.

Nowadays the Laboratory, with an annual budget of about £250000, is financed almost entirely from government funds which since 1965 have been administered through the Natural Environment Research Council of the Department of Education and Science. As a grant-aided, independent institution the Plymouth Laboratory is thus in close liaison with the Research Council and its advisory committees, as well as with the Council of the

Marine Biological Association, and both bodies advise on the scientific programmes to be undertaken by the Laboratory.

The permanent staff at Plymouth includes some twenty-five scientists and an approximately equal number of supporting technical staff. Many visiting scientists from British and oversea universities and research laboratories work at Plymouth for longer or shorter periods, the visitors at times outnumbering the resident scientists. Two research vessels, 'Sarsia' and 'Sula', and a motor launch, 'Gammarus', are used to collect material for purposes of research and teaching, and to carry out, under the direction of the Laboratory's scientists, hydrographical and biological surveys and investigations of the sea and sea floor, mainly in the English Channel and the Atlantic approaches.

In broad terms the biological work of the Plymouth Laboratory includes ecological surveys of sea shores and of the sea floor; investigations of the floating populations of the (mainly minute) plants and animals of the phytoplankton and zooplankton; studies of the natural history, behaviour, development, physiology and biochemistry of many individual species, including important modern work on fishes, squids and cuttle fishes; and investigation of a variety of living processes and activities such as nerve conduction, muscle contraction and locomotion. On the physical side much work has and is being done on the cycling of nutrient salts in the sea; studies on the availability to and utilization by plants and animals of dissolved and suspended inorganic and organic substances; the identification and characterization of water masses of differing origins and properties; as well as many other types of study requiring the special expertise of chemists and physicists.

At the time of the stranding of the 'Torrey Canyon' none of the work of the Plymouth Laboratory was directly concerned with the effects on marine organisms of noxious substances discharged into the sea. The Laboratory nevertheless possessed in its facilities for scientific work on shore and at sea, and in its staff of scientists expert in a wide range of scientific disciplines and techniques, an organization which could usefully and without much difficulty turn its attention to the problems posed by the threat of the 'Torrey Canyon' oil.

The first steps in the involvement of the Laboratory in the 'Torrey Canyon' programme were taken on Thursday 23 March, five days after the stranding of the tanker, with a visit to regional headquarters at Mount Wise, Devonport. We were introduced to key personnel, learned of the essential arrangements for the control and co-ordination of operations, and declared our willingness to assist in any investigations that might be made of the biological consequences of the oil spill.

These opening inquiries were made towards the end of the second phase

(21–23 March) of the 'Torrey Canyon' events when the fear of an imminent flow of oil on to the Cornish beaches had in some measure abated, but when the continued use of detergents as a means of dispersing oil at sea had begun to raise publicly expressed fears about the damage they might cause to marine organisms and, in particular, to coastal fisheries. On Saturday 25 March it was reported that Scillonian fishermen were worried about the possible effects of detergents on their crab and lobster fisheries; and on the same day, in an article in the *Guardian*, Anthony Tucker severely criticized the view that had been expressed by Mr James Hoy, Parliamentary Secretary to the Ministry of Agriculture, Food and Fisheries, in a written answer to a parliamentary question, that detergents sprayed on to the surface of the sea would become so diluted that they would not be seriously harmful to marine life.

It was known from recent experience of three oil spillages in Milford Haven in which detergents had been used to clear the oil that crabs, barnacles, winkles, shore-living fishes and other animals, as well as some algae, were killed in considerable numbers. In the most recent of the spillages upwards of 250 tons of oil had issued from the damaged tanker 'Chrissi P. Goulandris', and 8000 gallons of detergent had been used to help clear it. The plants and animals which were affected by the detergent had, in this instance, previously been surveyed in detail by Dr Anthony Nelson-Smith of the University College of Swansea and, at the time of the 'Torrey Canyon' stranding, he was resurveying the shores for 'before and after' comparisons. The preliminary findings were kindly made known to us, and the full results are now being published (Nelson-Smith, 1968).

Very few quantitative data were available in March 1967 about the toxic effects of detergents. The main information came from some unpublished tests made by Mr A. C. Simpson, Director of the M.A.F.F. Laboratory, Burnham-on-Crouch, Essex. These showed that, over periods of 1–24 hours continuous exposure, solvent/emulsifying mixtures could be lethal to various commercially important shellfish in concentrations ranging from 3 to 250 parts per million (ppm). The tests had not, however, included the detergents mainly to be used on the Cornish beaches, nor were the commoner shore-living plants and animals among the organisms which had been tested. And among the many important questions which remained unanswered were the possible effects on animals of sublethal doses of detergent applied over a long period of time.

When a meeting of the staff scientists of the Plymouth Laboratory was held on Easter Monday, 27 March, to decide how far the Laboratory should be committed to the investigation of the biological consequences of the wrecking of the 'Torrey Canyon' and what its programmes should be, there were several matters which could be seen to be in urgent need of attention.

It was decided to divert the entire resources of the Laboratory to the 'Torrey Canyon' programmes for a period of six weeks, after which the position would be reviewed. Thoughts were turned to two aspects of planning. First, it would be necessary to decide on the scientific programmes of the Laboratory. Secondly, since the Laboratory would undoubtedly become, because of its situation, the regional centre for biological activities and information exchange, some sort of organization would be needed to cope with these requirements.

Scientific programmes

The Laboratory programmes were to be limited to the examination of oil/detergent pollution on the marine plants and animals living between tide-marks and in the offshore waters both in the open sea and on and within the sea floor. None of the investigations would be primarily concerned with commercially important species solely because of their commercial importance—this being the area of inquiry within the special competence of the Ministry of Agriculture, Fisheries and Food. Nor would the surveys overlap the special interests of the Nature Conservancy, the Cornwall Naturalists' Trust and the Cornwall Bird-Watching and Preservation Society in the effects of pollution on life in the border regions between sea and land and on sea birds.

Within our self-imposed terms of reference it seemed important to discover without delay whether the detergent-spraying of oil at sea had adversely affected the fish, crustaceans, molluscs and other animals living on the sea floor and the plants and animals living in the surface and intermediate waters in the neighbourhood of the oil cover. It was therefore decided that, on the following day, the laboratory's vessel 'Sarsia' should go to Mount's Bay and the Seven Stones to take plankton samples and trawl hauls both in areas uncontaminated with oil and in places where oil was present and detergent had been used. Samples of sea water were also to be taken for later laboratory testing of the concentration and toxic levels of the chemicals present at the various stations.

It was also decided to organize within the laboratory a programme of toxicity-testing of all the proprietary brands of detergent that were being used or would be used in dispersing oil at sea or on the beaches. The organisms to be tested were to include planktonic larvae of various kinds and as many as possible of the commoner plants and animals of the intertidal region and nearby offshore waters. During the course of these tests note would be taken of the varying sensitivities of the different organisms to known concentrations of detergents in order to select a few suitable examples to be used as indicators of the toxicity of sea-water samples

collected during cruises or shore surveys. Many extensions and developments of this kind of analysis were to be made during the course of these experiments. Although it would not be appropriate at this stage to mention them in detail, they included, for example, measurements of the toxicity of components of the various proprietary detergents and of the conditions of their persistence or decay in the sea and during laboratory experiments.

The third type of work in which it was important that the Plymouth Laboratory, situated as it was within working distance of the polluted beaches, should take the initiative was the survey of the effects of oil and detergent pollution on the plants and animals living between tide-marks.

The shore surveys had two main aims. First it was intended to put on record, in however brief a form, and for as many localities as could be visited, the extent of the initial oil pollution, the varying intensities and conditions of the subsequent detergent treatment, and the effect of the treatment on their resident populations of intertidal plants and animals. Secondly, it was thought important to survey in detail the effects of initial oil cover and of the subsequent detergent treatment in two or three localities chosen because they were well known beforehand and were therefore useful for making 'before and after' comparisons.

Other programmes which had not been thought out fully at the first staff meeting on Monday 27 March were developed later. These included underwater surveys with the main laboratory effort concentrated on the examination of the offshore movements and toxic effects of detergent used in beach cleansing at Porthleven, the plotting of the movements at sea of oil derived from successive phases of discharge from the 'Torrey Canyon', and the prediction of these movements in relation to the day-to-day variations in the speed and direction of the winds acting on the sea surface. Finally, there is included a report on the methods adopted in France for coping with oil at sea and with the oil deposited on the Britanny beaches.

Most of the work referred to in the foregoing paragraphs was completed for the purposes of this Report by the end of May, some ten weeks after the stranding of the 'Torrey Canyon', but observations of polluted shores are being continued. The chapter on the French experiences is based on a seven-day visit to Brittany by two members of the Plymouth staff in mid-June, during which they had many helpful consultations with scientists and representatives of the civil and service departments engaged in the anti-pollution operations. They were also able to visit a number of oil-polluted beaches and to inspect the methods of shore cleansing which were being used.

A list of members of the staff and long-term visitors who participated is given on page xii.

Some aspects of collaboration and liaison

The investigations planned in outline on 27 March involved from the beginning close liaison and collaboration with a number of scientific organizations, administrative authorities, consultative bodies and private individuals. Some indication of the indebtedness of the Laboratory for the help it received in carrying out its programmes from these external sources will be evident from the list given above (p. xiii).

The total participation of the Plymouth Laboratory in the 'Torrey Canyon' investigations had, at the outset, been assured of the active support of the Council of the Marine Biological Association through a message received from its chairman, Professor A. L. Hodgkin, F.R.S. On this being made known to the Natural Environment Research Council, its secretary, Mr R. J. H. Beverton, put at the disposal of the Laboratory the funds needed to get the programmes under way. Meanwhile, on Tuesday 28 March, the Director of the Plymouth Laboratory, Dr J. E. Smith, F.R.S., had been co-opted as a member of the official Committee of Scientists on the Scientific and Technological Aspects of the 'Torrey Canyon' Disaster which, under the chairmanship of Sir Solly Zuckerman, K.C.B., F.R.S., was required to review the consequences of the disaster; and to make recommendations for any future research needed and on necessary safeguards. The establishment of these initial conditions of programme recognition and support thereafter ensured a ready access to the bodies most directly concerned with the progress of the research and with its practical implications.

By comparison with the well-defined and largely predetermined channels of approach to these central advisory bodies the regional network of operational communications was more complicated and, for a time at least to the biologists requiring them, unfamiliar.

There may have been some aspects of the 'Torrey Canyon' operations which made little demand on outside sources for help and information, but this was certainly not true of the biological work. Each facet of the inquiry into the biological consequences of the sea and shore pollution relied in very large measure on assistance and information known or thought to be available and which had to be actively gathered in for the service of the work. There was a need to know how much oil was escaping from the ship; the latest reported positions of the oil masses; the kinds of detergents that were being used, in what quantity, and in what places; the composition of the detergents; the kinds of help that might be available for undertaking experiments which, either because of pressure of work or insufficient knowledge of specialized techniques, the Laboratory was unable to do.

And, in addition to these and many other outgoing lines of inquiry, there was, in reverse, a daily stream of incoming offers of help and requests for information. Could a place be found in the programme for a team of underwater divers? Would it be helpful if naturalists living in Cornwall were to survey the shores with which they were familiar, and what methods of survey should be used? Could the laboratory give information to fishing interests, to the press or to broadcasting agencies on particular questions or on the general situation? And could discussions be arranged with scientists from overseas—for example, from France, Germany and the United States?

It is not easy, in retrospect, to say exactly how or with what degree of efficiency these and many other aspects of co-ordination and information exchange were dealt with, but the nature and functions of the main channels of communication may be conveniently described by referring to the information on staff participation and collaborative organizations set out above (pp. xii and xiii).

During the early stages of the 'Torrey Canyon' operations the first three of the collaborative organizations listed, namely the Ministry of Agriculture, Fisheries and Food, the Nature Conservancy, and BP Trading Company Limited, had representatives resident in the Laboratory. This made for easy day-to-day liaison at a time when frequent consultations were particularly necessary.

The two-way communication with all other collaborative organizations and individual contributors was made in the first place by staff concerned with 'external liaison'. Much of this was effected by telephone and correspondence but some members of the staff spent a good deal of time going in search of information when it could only be obtained effectively by talking with people on their home ground (e.g. at Maritime H.Q., Mount Wise; H.Q. 19 Group Coastal Command; and in connection with the Brittany survey). Most of the information passing through 'external liaison' was subsequently recorded and distributed on the initiative of the people in charge. But when further advice was needed or matters of general policy were implicit in the inquiries the questions were passed to the members of the 'general organization' group for a decision.

All survey collections, samples of oil, detergents and reports relating to field studies were accepted and dealt with by the group 'Survey Materials and Records' for distribution within the Laboratory or for indexing for general use.

A collection of photographs relating to the various aspects of the 'Torrey Canyon' investigations has been assembled. It will be kept in the library of the Plymouth Laboratory where it will be available for reference.

CHAPTER 2

OIL AND DETERGENTS

On the Cornish beaches about 10000 tons of detergent fluids were used to treat about 14000 tons of crude oil. What were the properties of these two major pollutants?

It might have been supposed that a cut-and-dried answer could be given at least with regard to the physical and chemical properties of the oil, and that, although information might not be made public for trade reasons, it would be available also for the properties of the detergent components. This was, however, far from true. Moreover, little was known of the probable biological effects either of crude oil or of detergents.

The brief account in this chapter depends partly on the information kindly supplied by British Petroleum (Trading) Ltd (BP) and detergent manufacturers, and partly on the results of simple and often empirical tests in the Laboratory, prompted by field observations.

THE OIL

Kuwait crude oil is a dark-brown liquid smelling like diesel fuel and having the consistency of heavy engine oil. It is a complex mixture of hydro-carbons containing appreciable quantities of sulphur and traces of metals such as nickel and vanadium.

After it is discharged on the sea, crude oil undergoes a series of changes over a period of months. At least this can be said, but it is not yet possible to give a confident account of what exactly happens to an oil-spill that remains at sea. In the absence of artificial treatments its probable fate may be assessed by reference to its physical properties.

Table 1 shows the composition of Kuwait oil (specific gravity 0·869) in terms of boiling-point fractions. From this it may be inferred that the oil will lose about 25 per cent of its volume by evaporation within the first few days. Evaporation continues at a progressively diminishing rate for some weeks, during which the oil is further eroded by photo-oxidation and bacterial degradation. If the oil stays at sea for three months or more there should theoretically remain persistent asphaltic residue representing per-haps 15 per cent of the original amount. Similar residues collect on the sides and bottoms of the storage tanks of tankers, and in the fuel tanks of oil-burning ships. The black tarry lumps, now all too familiar on British shores, are normally derived from the latter source, but occasionally they may

Table 1. *Composition of crude oil in terms of boiling point of fractions*

Fraction	°C	Loss of wt (%)	Loss of vol. (%)	Specific gravity at 15·5 °C of residue
1	Up to 100	9·0	11·8	0·895
2	Up to 200	13·0	27·7	0·9255
3	Up to 300	38·1	43·6	0·955
4	Up to 400	53·1	58·5	0·983

represent the end-product of weathered crude oil. Indeed, N. K. Adam (1935), in a pioneer investigation of the oil-pollution problem on our coasts, and to whose account we still have to turn for a picture of the fate of oil at sea, believed that refined fuel oil, if remaining at sea, would ultimately end as a residue of small aggregated asphaltic lumps. Adam, having conclusively shown that the world's oceans had not acquired a continuous molecular film of oil, gave a coherent explanation in physical–chemical terms of how oil was steadily disappearing. It is curious that he gave no consideration to the possible role of bacteria in helping this degradation, though Orton (1924) had already appreciated that the weathering of floating oil involved bacterial decay. The importance of bacteria is now, of course, well recognized (see ZoBell, 1963); but many aspects of the changes crude oil may be expected to undergo after release on the sea surface are still obscure. Research on this problem is urgently needed.

In practice the actual time course of the degradation processes must be influenced by several environmental factors including temperature, wind, wave action, thickness of the oil and its degree of dispersion; but perhaps the most important factor is the tendency of the oil to form emulsions with sea water. Such emulsion may be oil-in-water (as is milk) or water-in-oil (as is butter), and the emulsification so modifies the physical properties of the oil as to render unreliable most predictions of the life of oil at sea. The oil from the 'Torrey Canyon' certainly formed water-in-oil emulsions of variable composition, and it is this which accounts for the thick consistency and variable colour, quite unlike the original, of the oil masses observed at sea and on the Cornish beaches (Plates 3A, 6C, 7A, B, C, 13A, 14A, B). Attempts in the laboratory to reproduce these water-in-oil emulsions by shaking with sea water, or by exposing oil and sea water in open containers out of doors for several days, all failed. Oil vigorously shaken with sea water immediately settled out, re-forming a layer of the same thickness as at the start. It remained the original very dark colour in all experiments. However, the chocolate-coloured type of stranded oil could be imitated by adding a little detergent (BP 1002) to the mixture.

The water-in-oil emulsion may contain up to 80 per cent water. It follows that whereas the mass of oil may be appreciably reduced by evaporation after a period at sea the bulk of the emulsified material may yet exceed that of the original oil. It is also noteworthy that as evaporation proceeds the mass of oil not only diminishes but its density increases (Table 1). This has practical consequences when attempts are made to sink the oil by application of dense powdered material. A sample of emulsion taken from the Bay of Biscay on 18 May (some 50 days after release) by R.V. 'Sarsia' contained 50 per cent sea water and the specific gravity of the oil fraction was 0·97. This corresponds to a loss of about 50 per cent of the original oil, the specific gravity of which is 0·869 at 15·5 °C (cf. Table 1). The French navy were successful in sinking oil emulsions of this kind by applying powdered chalk (Chapter 9), but to have sunk the same oil soon after release would have required six times as much chalk.

In the seas around Cornwall and on the Cornish beaches the principle of the cleansing operation was, in essence, to convert the viscous water-in-oil emulsion to a milk-like oil-in-water emulsion (Plates 4A, 5A, 10A, 22A, B, 23A, B, 28C) and so allow it to disperse in the great bulk of the sea.* This was achievable by treating the water-in-oil emulsion with detergent (Plate 5A) followed wherever possible by mechanical agitation. However, the emulsions were not readily formed under the conditions that obtained, and even when they were produced they were apt to be unstable (p. 21). Oil separated from unstable emulsions by floating upwards, just as the cream settles out on top of milk (Plate 1A, B). This oil, as seen in shallow shore pools, or in laboratory vessels, was black and fluid, much as it originally had been in the tanker. When separation occurred in the sea just offshore under different conditions a paler colour was typical (Plate 6A). Observations on the North Cornwall coast, in particular, showed that some of the oil very soon separated from detergent emulsions and that only a proportion could have been dispersed effectively. Aided by onshore winds the separated oil returned, either in a liquid condition or mixed with fine sand and fragments of seaweed, leading to secondary pollution (Plates 3B, 6A, B, 13B). Even as early as April oil masses weighted with sand were observed on the sea bed (Plate 6C).

Elsewhere in this report the water-in-oil emulsion which polluted the beaches is usually referred to as 'oil' and when reference is made to

---

* Dispersal in the sea, if effective, implies (1) that the small particles into which the oil is split are so scattered that they will not re-aggregate, and (2) that the oil is thus converted to the best possible state for attack by oil-consuming bacteria, which will eventually destroy any that has not evaporated. Thus the most ideal detergent cannot of itself destroy the oil.

emulsification it applies to the formation of a dispersible oil-in-water emulsion, unless otherwise stated.

Floating oil is not a serious hazard to marine life in the open sea save in the case of birds, thousands of which have died as a result of contact with oil from the 'Torrey Canyon'. Oil deposited on the coast is, however, severely damaging to coastal amenities and may affect shore animals by smothering them. Nevertheless, we were surprised how well such conditions could be tolerated and survived by many shore animals. Limpets, for example, were found to recover completely even after they had been left under an apparently continuous oil layer (Plate 9B). Indeed, limpets have been observed to be grazing on rocks coated with weathered oil, ingesting it without noticeable harm (Chapter 4; Plate 9C). No actual toxic effects of the oil have been noted either in shore or pelagic animals. Several intertidal algae survived after oil had settled on their fronds. In the splash-zone the lichen *Xanthoria* proved able to survive under a hardened oil layer (Plate 18C).

Stranded oil sticks all too readily to surfaces, offering considerable resistance to the force of waves and hoses. After settling, the oil layer becomes appreciably thinner, as it loses contained water and its own more volatile fractions. At the same time the oil becomes darker, whatever its original shade of brown, and eventually quite black. Typical examples of the blackened strand lines could be seen on granite boulders of the Land's End area, and around Hayle Estuary, where the oil had been left untreated. Plate 27 shows oil-blackened shores in Guernsey and Brittany.

DETERGENTS

Detergents are classified as ionic and non-ionic. Ionic detergents readily dissociate in solution and the effective portion may be positively (cationic) or negatively (anionic) charged. Non-ionic detergents, on the other hand, do not dissociate in solution to any significant degree.

The bulk of detergents used to deal with the 'Torrey Canyon' oil were non-ionic. When they were used no froth was produced, as so frequently with the more familiar household detergents. Household detergents release oil or grease from soiled articles by altering the surface tension of the oil so that it is no longer firmly held. Slight mechanical agitation will then dislodge the oil or grease, drops of which become dispersed in the form of an emulsion. It is not necessary for the emulsion to be stable, since it is normally quickly removed by rinsing.

However, for treatment of oil at sea, or on beaches, a stable emulsion is needed so that the oil may be more effectively dispersed. Some experiments

on the stability of detergent–oil emulsions are described later in this section. The detergents used for this purpose are mixtures of two or more compounds, a surfactant, an organic solvent and a stabilizer. The surfactant, often an ethylene oxide condensate, is the primary oil emulsifier; the solvent enables the surfactant to mix with the oil and form an emulsion. Substances such as coconut oil diethanolamide, when present, stabilize the emulsion formed.

All the solvents contain a proportion of aromatics. The higher the proportion of aromatics, the more effective is the solvent, but at the same time the more toxic.

The surfactants used, unlike those employed in household detergents, are 'hard'; that is, they are not readily destroyed by micro-organisms.

The following proprietary detergents were reported as having been used:

Gamlen Oil Spill Remover	Dasic Slickgone
Atlas	Petrofina Unisolva
Snowdrift	TC4 (Drew Chemicals)
Basol AD6	Esso F. 6155
Gramosol	Houghtosafe 112
BP 1002	Whittakers G.P. Degreasant

Some examples of the composition of these, indicated by code numbers not related to the above list, are:

Detergent no. 1: 66% solvent containing 24% aromatics, remainder cetyl phenyl ethylene oxide condensate

Detergent no. 2: 70% solvent containing 43% aromatics
15% tall oil
15% nonyl phenyl ethylene oxide condensate

Detergent no. 3: 75% solvent containing 76% aromatics
25% mixture of ethylene oxide condensate and calcium petroleum sulphonate

Detergent no. 4: 85% kerosene extract with a high proportion of aromatics
12% nonyl phenol ethylene oxide
3% coconut diethanolamide

Detergent no. 5: 75% solvent containing 83% aromatics
7·5% tall oil
2·5% triethanolamine
10% dodecyl benzyl sulphonate as the ammonium salt
5% non-ionic detergent

Some physical properties of BP 1002 and methods of estimation

The Laboratory experiments described in this section examine certain physical properties of the detergent BP 1002. This detergent was used on a much greater scale than any other, especially on the shore. Samples of the

detergent and its separate fractions were made available to us by BP Trading Limited, who also kindly undertook some of the analyses reported later.

Properties of solvent

(a) Density: 0·874 at 17 °C.

(b) Miscibility with sea water at 17 °C: 100–150 ppm (w/v) remain in the water phase some hours after shaking solvent with sea water.

(c) Boiling point: fractional distillation at atmospheric pressure yielded four fractions, of which the first two had a sulphurous smell.

Boiling point (°C)	% by volume of solvent	Toxicity compared with whole solvent as 100*
Below 120	1–2	45
Below 165	7	45
Below 185	18	80
Residue boiling above 185	74	78

* See page 143.

(d) The solvent has a characteristic smell, which can be detected at low concentrations. Sea-water solutions containing $\frac{1}{2}$ ppm BP 1002 are easily distinguished from detergent-free sea water by smell.

Rate of loss of solvent from sea water

Large volumes of a 10 ppm (parts per million) solution of BP 1002 in sea water were placed in open containers and exposed in the open air. Solvent concentrations at different depths in the solution were determined at intervals by the third method given below. Similar results were obtained in two experiments, using 70 and 30 l. of solution (Fig. 2). After 35 hours the concentration of solvent had fallen to 5 ppm; after 95 hours it had fallen to $\frac{1}{2}$ ppm. In the open sea evaporation would be more rapid. At concentrations around 10 ppm, the solvent tends to rise to the surface, as is seen by placing solutions in stoppered columns and determining solvent concentrations in upper and lower parts of the column after some hours. In one such experiment, where the initial concentration was 5 ppm, after

PLATE I

Treatment of oil with detergent may give varying results and mixtures of varying colours. **A**, Watergate Bay, 15 April: heavily oiled sand adjacent to rocks that had recently been hosed with detergent/freshwater mixture. The pool of white emulsion had patches of re-separated oil (resembling the original Kuwait crude oil) which had not formed an emulsion with the detergent as shown in Plate 2. **B**, Booby's Bay, 8 April: orange-brown partially emulsified oil floating on detergent solution in a high-water rock pool. **C**, Kynance Cove, 20 April: orange-brown oil emulsion after detergent treatment oozing down from boulders near high-water mark.

PLATE I

A

B

C

(*Facing p.* 16)

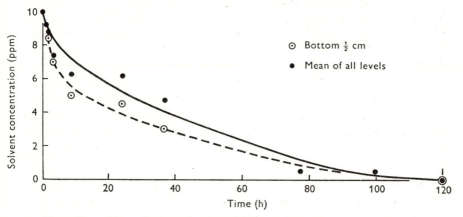

Fig. 2. Rate of loss of solvent fraction of BP 1002 from large volume of 10 ppm
solution in sea water in open container.

3 hours a sample from the upper part of the column contained 6 ppm, lower down the concentration was $2\frac{1}{2}$ ppm. Similar experiments with more concentrated solutions (e.g. 100 ppm) did not show layering.

Evaporation of detergent (BP 1002)

Some laboratory experiments were conducted on the undiluted detergent and its components to test their capacity to evaporate. The tests were carried out in a fume cupboard with air draught.

The whole mixture. Eighty ml (67·64 g by weight) was placed in an open Petri dish of 10 cm diameter. Half the weight was lost by evaporation in about 4 days, and 70 per cent in 11 days. The rate was continually becoming slower and in the next 11 days only an additional 5 per cent was lost. The graph was approaching exponentially a base-line representing 14 g (or 20·7 per cent by weight of the original sample).

The surfactant. This appeared not to evaporate at all.

The solvent ('Kex'). Eighty ml were placed in a Petri dish (experiment of 9 May). Sea water was used for comparison in a similar dish. It took $3\frac{1}{4}$ days for the sea water to evaporate to the point of leaving a deposit of moist salt crystals. In the same time the 'Kex' had lost barely half its volume; but it was steadily evaporating, and in 7 days had lost about three-quarters. From this point evaporation was hardly noticeable and at the end of the second week (23 May) the volume was measured at 17·5 ml (22 per cent of the original). This residue was found to be relatively persistent after transference to a small cylinder, which could be weighed easily. In this more confined vessel only 0·0176 g of the 'Kex' residue was lost between 31 May and 26 June, or 0·00068 g a day. It may be thought that 22 per cent was unduly high for the relatively persistent residue of a volatile solvent, and some allowance should perhaps be made for loss of the more volatile components from the can from which the sample was taken, since

it was not newly opened. Perhaps the figure should be halved, but, even if so, there is clearly a far-from-negligible fraction which might be liable to persist where the detergent was not exposed in thin films, and particularly if the detergent were buried. This fact helps to explain its persistence in sandy beaches (p. 79).

Surfactant distribution in sea water

Unlike the solvent, the surfactant component of the detergent is denser than sea water (D = 1·044 at 17 °C). Its capacity to sink both concentrated and diluted was simply demonstrated. It did not at all readily dissolve in, or mix with, sea water. Even at low concentrations therefore it may tend to settle in the sea; and there is some evidence from samples taken in Mount's Bay (p. 33) that this may have occurred under natural conditions.

In the laboratory successive turbid and clear layers may be produced by the addition of detergent to sea water in measuring cylinders under certain conditions, the differences between the layers presumably resulting from micelle formation.

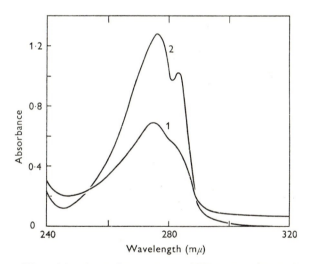

Fig. 3. Ultra-violet absorption spectrum of BP 1002 surfactant in sea water.
1, 50 ppm, 5 cm light path; 2, 500 ppm, 1 cm light path.

Micelle formation of surfactant

Determinations (by cryoscopic methods) of the molecular weight of the surfactant at concentrations above 1 per cent in sea water indicated an approximate molecular weight of above 10 000. Since the molecular weight of the surfactant is around 650 it is evident that molecular aggregates, or micelles, are formed. At lower concentrations the method used was un-

Table 2. *The relationship between the surfactant concentration and the ultra-violet absorbance at 275 mμ*

Concentration (C) (ppm)	Light path (L) (cm)	Absorbance at 275 mμ (A) corrected for turbidity	A/CL ($\times 10^{-3}$)
5	10	0·108	2·2
10	10	0·226	2·3
50	10	1·23	2·5
50	1	0·127	2·5
100	1	0·2	2·0
500	1	1·25	2·5

suitable, but further evidence of micelle formation was obtained by the use of ultra-violet spectroscopy. Fig. 3 shows the ultra-violet absorption spectrum of the major surfactant component of BP 1002 in sea water. Measurements in the range 5–500 ppm have been made. At 50 ppm a slight turbidity of the solution was apparent and at 100 ppm the turbidity was very marked. At 500 ppm the solution was clear and its spectrum indicated the formation of a new species of micelle in solution. At all concentrations examined except 100 ppm the absorbance at 275 mμ has been found to obey Beer's law (that is, was proportional to concentration) reasonably well after allowance has been made for the turbidity as estimated from the absorbance at 320 mμ (Table 2). The discontinuity found at 100 ppm is indicative of the formation of insoluble micelles at 100 ppm with subsequent regrouping to give a new dissolved species at higher concentrations. On the shore, concentrations of 100 ppm or greater were frequently observed.

By reducing the effective concentration of surfactant, micelle formation would be expected to reduce the toxicity of surfactant solutions in sea water, as well as affecting such physical properties of the detergent as its adsorption on to sand (p. 77).

Methods used in the determination of detergent concentrations in sea water

Three chemical methods were used, in addition to the bioassay methods described later (p. 141). The first two actually determine the amount of surfactant present and the third the amount of solvent.

Method 1

All the analyses by this method have been kindly made for us by BP Trading Limited at their Pumpherston laboratory. The method, devised by Conoco (Continental Oil Company), estimates surfactant in sea water and gives an accuracy and repeatability of ± 3 per cent relative at the 20 ppm level. The procedure is as follows.

Place 100 ml of sample solution into a separating funnel. Add 15 ml of ammonium cobaltothiocyanate reagent (prepared from 620 g reagent-grade NH_4SCN plus 280 g reagent grade $Co(NO_3)_2 . 6H_2O$ diluted to 1 l. and extracted twice with benzene) and 35–40 g of sodium chloride. Shake to dissolve the salt and allow to stand about 15 min. Accurately add 25·0 ml of benzene to the funnel. Shake for 1 min, then let stand to allow the layers to separate. Draw off and discard the lower aqueous layer. Transfer the benzene layer to a centrifuge tube, stopper, and spin at 500–700 rcf for 10 min. Read the peak absorbance at about 320 mμ against a reagent blank using a Beckman DB Ultraviolet Spectrophotometer with a deuterium lamp and 1 cm cells; 4 cm cells can be used to improve sensitivity. (The spectrophotometer connects to a 100 mV recorder through a Beckman Scale Expander accessory, to scan the region between 340 and 315 mμ.) Compare the absorbance with the reading obtained on a sample of known concentration.

Alternatively peak absorbance can be read at 625 mμ against a reagent blank using an infra-red tungsten light source and cell.

The instrument used at Pumpherston is a Cambridge SP 500. Present experience at Pumpherston indicates that in the range 0–10 ppm this procedure gives an accuracy within ± 20 per cent on samples obtained under practical working conditions.

This method determines only nonylphenol ethoxylate and is not effective at concentrations of 1 ppm or less.

Method 2

This simple method was developed in this laboratory at an early stage in the operation.

Add to 25 ml samples of the test solution in separating funnels 5 drops of an oil reagent ('3 in 1' oil saturated with Oil Red O and filtered through tissue). Shake vigorously for 15 sec. and stand for 3 min ± 10 sec. Separate and extract the aqueous layer with 4 ml chloroform. Read at 525 mμ in 1 cm cuvettes.

The calibration curves were linear over the range 0–5 ppm.

Method 3

This method was adapted from Gerade & Skiba (1960) and determines the amount of solvent present.

Using 50 ml test samples, extract into 3 ml of carbon tetrachloride. Shake the extract with 5 ml acid reagent (25 ml of 40 per cent formaldehyde in 500 ml concentrated sulphuric acid). Visual comparison with standards in the range 0–10 ppm gives values ± 5 per cent or better. The initial colour developed is pink, which after 30 min changes to orange brown.

The stability of detergent–oil emulsions

As already stated, the detergents act on the floating oil by producing a detergent–oil emulsion which is then supposed to be dispersed in the sea. The stability of such detergent–oil emulsions is important, for the more stable they are the better the dispersion. Some simple laboratory tests were made on this property.

Comparison between different detergents

A test was carried out on the stability of detergent/oil emulsions in sea water when there is no stirring; the results obtained give some indication of the relative efficiency of the different detergents tried.

Several detergents were used. In each case, 2 ml of detergent and 2 ml of Kuwait crude oil were mixed in a 100 ml measuring cylinder. Then 96 ml of sea water were added and the cylinder was sealed and shaken for 10 seconds. Oil started to settle out on the surface of the emulsion within a few minutes. As more oil settled out the emulsion column became lighter in colour and after about 2 hours there was considerable difference between the cylinders (Plate 2). In order of decreasing opacity of the emulsion the detergents were: Houghton, BP 1002, Gamlen, Gramosol, Whittaker, Slipclean, and Dasic.

These results suggest that Houghton detergent is best able to maintain an oil emulsion in sea water. It is also one of the most toxic detergents, as are BP 1002 and Gamlen. Dasic seems to be particularly poor in maintaining an oil emulsion in sea water and the water column cleared almost completely in a few hours. When the detergents only were added to sea water all except Dasic gave a milky emulsion. Dasic settled out on the surface of the water. It gave a perfectly good emulsion in fresh water and was extremely effective for washing off oil from all kinds of surfaces with warm tap water. The surfactant portion is largely anionic, and the preparation is presumably designed for use with fresh water.

Conductivity measurements made with 0·1 per cent solutions of detergent in distilled water verified that the surfactants of most of the detergents used are non-ionic; with the exception of Dasic and Teepol. These two detergents are least effective in sea water.

Deposited oil and BP 1002

The test reported above involved only 10 sec. shaking. Some other attempts were made to form a permanent emulsion with Kuwait crude oil and BP 1002, giving longer vigorous agitation and different amounts of sea water. With one mixture the emulsion, when left standing, showed no sign of separating until the next day, but the oil eventually layered out, and no better result was achieved than this.

With the oil collected on the shore, which, as has been explained, was already an emulsion of sea water in oil, the situation was appreciably worse. Though '*café-au-lait*' emulsions could be formed with different mixtures of oil, detergent, and sea water, these proved always to be very unstable and layering started at most within an hour or so. This was true

even when the oil was first soaked with the optimum amount of detergent for about half-an-hour before sea water was applied.

Further comments

The formation of persistent emulsions in sea water does not take place readily, and detergents were often applied by methods that were largely ineffective, uneconomic, and wasteful of effort. This was particularly true of the methods used in dealing with the oil stranded on the shore. Thorough agitation by hosing, or by the natural agencies of wind, waves, and tide is essential for effective dispersal of oil, and these conditions were not always ensured.

As to spraying at sea, we have no information about its eventual effectiveness. It was genarally agreed by those taking part in the sea operations that dispersal was often achieved in the immediate neighbourhood of spraying. However, despite the large quantities of detergents used, large areas of undispersed oil persisted for weeks as extensive and discrete patches.

CHAPTER 3

SEA SURVEYS

On 27 March when the 'Torrey Canyon' programmes of the Plymouth Laboratory were first discussed at a staff meeting there was one question that required an immediate answer. The question was this: to what extent is the crude oil which is escaping from the tanker and the detergents which are being used to disperse it affecting the planktonic plants and animals and the stocks of pelagic and bottom-living fish in the area of the polluted water? And so, in order to find out what was happening, it was decided to send the Laboratory's research vessel 'Sarsia', with a party of scientists on board, to the area of the Seven Stones to collect samples of water and of plankton for analysis and investigation. Trawl and dredge hauls would also be made for the examination of bottom-living fish and other animals.

CRUISE I

For some time past the Marine Biological Association had carried out five or six times a year a survey of the hydrographical conditions and plankton production of the western English Channel. A survey was in fact due on 28 March and to meet the needs of the occasion the route of the 28–30 March cruise was modified to work the stations shown in Fig. 4A. These included stations 1–5 of the regular survey, where the water was thought to be uncontaminated, together with stations A–M which lay within the area of visible or suspected contamination. At stations A, B, C, D, G, H, I and L a thin film of oil dotted with occasional patches of thicker oil covered the surface of the sea. Stations E and F, which were sampled on the morning of 29 March, were characterized by broken patches of rust-red oil (similar to that shown in Plate 7A), some $1\frac{1}{2}$–2 inches thick. Detergent was being sprayed at these stations and there was a strong smell of kerosene. Much more extensive areas of thick oil were found around stations J and K between 18.00 and 20.00 hours on 29 March. Because of the bombing of the 'Torrey Canyon' on this day the area north of a line from the Longships lighthouse to the Isles of Scilly had been closed to shipping. As the oil observed at stations J and K appeared from its direction of movement to have come from the closed area, it was thought at the time that this oil would have escaped treatment with detergent; but later calculations (as described in Chapter 8) show that the oil observed must have been released early on 27 March, and so would not necessarily have escaped spraying.

Distribution of detergent

At most of the stations water samples were taken in the normal way with hydrographic sampling bottles. At stations J and K, where samples were taken under the oil the open sampling bottle was lowered into the sea outside the oil area. The ship was then allowed to drift into the oil, and the bottle was closed. Finally the ship moved out of the oil and the bottle was raised.

Water samples taken on this cruise were sent to BP for chemical analysis of their detergent content. The analytical method used by BP measures the concentration of the *surface active (surfactant) component* of the detergent. It is important to bear this in mind in interpreting measurements given below since the two main components of the detergents, surfactant and solvent, may tend to separate at sea, the former sinking and the latter remaining near the surface and escaping by evaporation (Chapter 2). Samples were taken at seven depths between the surface and 70 m at station 2, at or near surface and at 50 m at stations A–D, at 1 m and 30 m at stations E–G and at the surface at stations H–M. With a single exception only, the results were completely negative, indicating that detergent was either absent or at most around 1 ppm. The only exception was station E at 1 m, where duplicated readings gave an equivalent of 1·2 and 6·0 ppm detergent (BP 1002).

This indicated that by 28–29 March the detergent might be accumulating locally to unwelcome concentrations, but it was not doing so at an alarming rate over a wide area.

Phytoplankton surveys

Tow-net samples of the small floating plants of the phytoplankton were taken at the surface, 5 m and 10 m at stations 2, 4 (uncontaminated water), A, B, C, D and M (under a thin oil film) and E (near to detergent-sprayed oil). They were examined on the ship under a microscope and were then stored at 5 °C for a more detailed examination in the laboratory on 30 March. Fig. 5 illustrates the appearance and size of some of the phytoplanktonic organisms referred to in this chapter.

PLATE 2

A comparison of detergent–oil emulsions in sea water 36 hours after the cylinders were shaken. Left to right: Houghton, BP 1002, Gamlen, Gramosol, Whittaker, Slipclean, Dasic, and control.

PLATE 3

A, Newly arrived splodges of oil deposited on sand at Marazion, 1 April. **B**, Marazion looking west after a gale, 5 May: strand lines of re-deposited treated oil mixed with fragments of torn weed.

PLATE 2

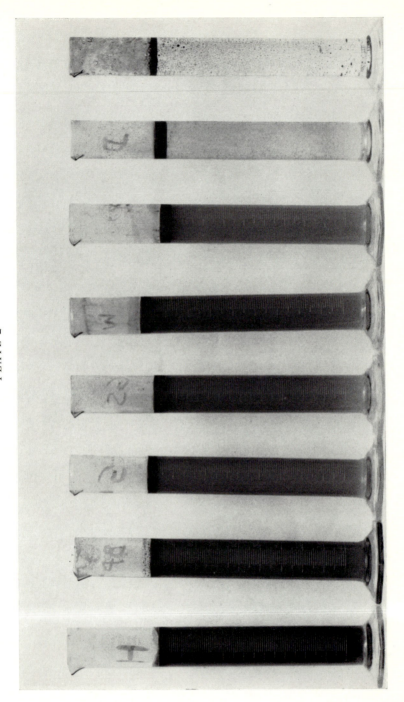

PLATE 3

A

B

PLATE 4

A

B

PLATE 5

A

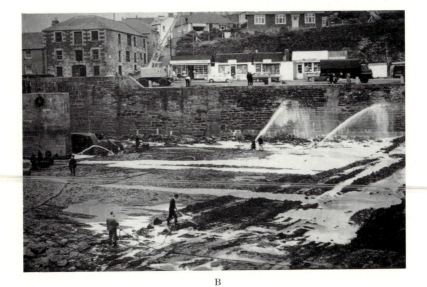

B

When the samples were examined on the ship and later on 30 March in the laboratory, all of them contained plant populations of the type normally found in the Channel in early spring and both diatoms (Bacillariophyceae) and dinoflagellates (Dinophyceae), appeared to be healthy at all stations. Cysts of the very small Prasinophyceae were examined with especial care for it was thought that their habit of floating on or near the surface might make them especially vulnerable to surface-sprayed detergent. They appeared, however, to be healthy at all stations except M, where some individuals of all the species in the group showed shrinking of the cell contents from the cell wall.

Thus, on first inspection, the phytoplankton was surprisingly normal. But, in order to test whether there might be delayed effects, specimens from the tow-net samples were cultured in the laboratory for a further week.

The first cultures contained cysts of the Prasinophyceae which had been picked out from the samples and placed in a stock culture medium. After seven days many had released viable motile cells. Only a few of the remaining cysts, however, were in a healthy condition and many of the younger cysts had died. This does not normally happen.

Four other series of cultures were also set up and the results are briefly reported. They were not aerated.

Series 1. Tow-net samples from stations A, B, C, D, E and M were cultured in equal volumes of the sample and culture medium. In three of the cultures most of the diatoms became abnormal or died within seven days; in the other three they remained healthy. The Prasinophyceae remained healthy in only one culture. Small colourless flagellates, on the other hand, prospered in all six cultures.

Series 2. Tow-net samples from stations A, B, C, D, E, M and 2 were cultured in one part volume of the sample to nine parts of the culture medium, a mixture favoured at Plymouth for the culture of diatoms and dinoflagellates. Except in two instances when a few diatoms appeared to be abnormal, all the organisms were healthy after seven days.

Series 3. Water samples from station J (under thick oil) and station D (where

---

PLATE 4

A, Detergent spraying in a remote cove near the Lizard, 22 April. Detergent drums are being ferried by helicopter to the cliff tops, from where it is piped down to the beach. Note the large patch of white emulsion in the sea.   **B**, Fishing Cove, Gunwalloe, 28 April, showing ridges bulldozed in the shingle for detergent treatment of this heavily-oiled beach.

PLATE 5

Cleansing operations at Porthleven Harbour, 28 April. **A**, Operator spraying detergent on harbour wall. The detergent is forming a white emulsion in the sea, with which are mingled streaks of re-separated oil and oil–water emulsion. **B**, Spraying detergent on the harbour walls at low tide. The floor of the harbour has been bulldozed.

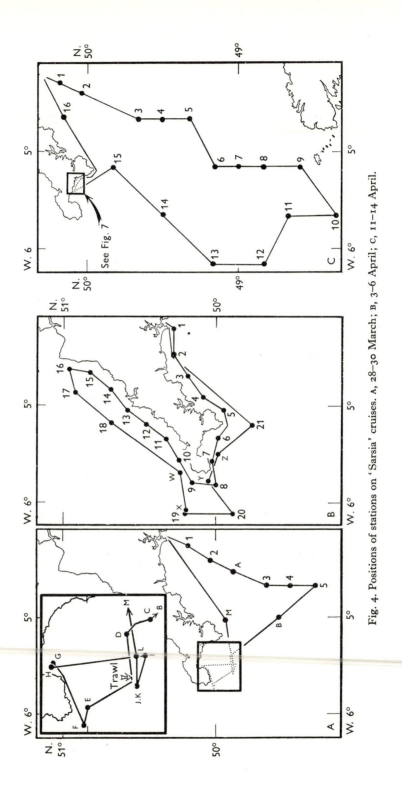

Fig. 4. Positions of stations on 'Sarsia' cruises. A, 28–30 March; B, 3–6 April; C, 11–14 April.

oil appeared to have been treated with detergent) were enriched with nutrients to encourage growth of the contained phytoplankton. All organisms were healthy after seven days.

Series 4. Water from stations J and D was filtered to remove the plankton and to the filtered water was added culture medium inoculated with planktonic algae grown in the Plymouth culture collection. Algae grown in an uncontaminated culture medium were used as controls.

The results of the series 4 tests span too many species to be set out in detail. A very brief summary of the results, however, is that, while the naked or scale-covered Prasinophyceae were killed in the stations J and D samples, the one species with a complete protective thecal covering that was tested grew better than in the controls. By and large all other forms prospered as well in the J and D water as in the controls.

The overall results and conclusions which follow from this phytoplankton survey may therefore be summarized as follows:

(1) There were deaths among the smallest flagellates (Prasinophyceae), often only after a period of some days in all the samples taken from areas of thin or thick oil cover, and there were no deaths at stations in the uncontaminated water. It is clear therefore that the Prasinophyceae can detect and respond to concentrations of toxic substances that are too low to be detectable by the method of chemical analysis that was available.

(2) Other phytoplanktonic algae (diatoms and dinoflagellates) were exposed at some stations to a lethal concentration of toxic substances; at others they were not. Those grown in the laboratory on a one-tenth concentration of the sea water in which they were taken survived. It may be concluded therefore that the concentrations of toxic materials in the water samples taken on cruise I were not much above the lethal level for the most delicate of the organisms examined.

(3) Most of the colourless flagellates were unaffected, and some of them grew rather better in the toxic sea water than in uncontaminated water.

Zooplankton surveys

Oblique tow-net hauls were taken at stations D and L (under thin oil) for the sampling of the plankton animals—mainly copepod crustaceans. The animals appeared to be of a normal abundance and all seemed healthy when examined immediately after capture.

Benthic organisms

Fish taken in the trawl at station D appeared to be healthy. No oil was found on the sea bed and there were no external signs of oil contamination

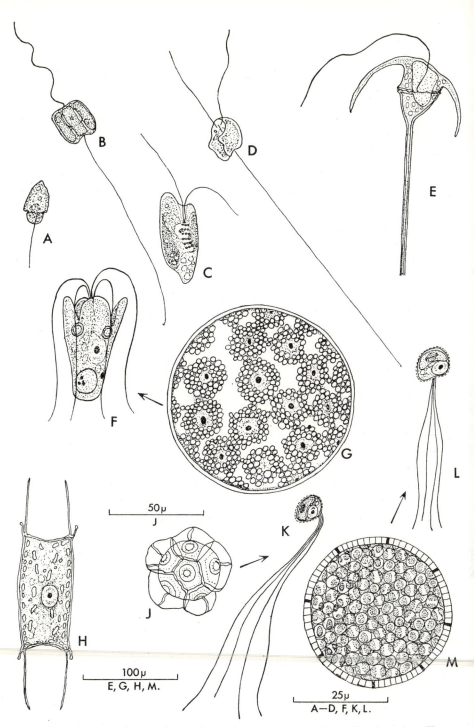

Fig. 5. Illustrations of some of the minute plants in the sea in the polluted areas. A, *Kato-dinium rotundatum* (Lohm.) Loeblich III (Dinophyceae). B, *Pseudopedinella* sp. (Chryso-phyceae). C, *Cryptomonas maculata* Butch. (Cryptophyceae). D, *Chrysochromulina ephippium* Parke et Manton (Haptophyceae). E, *Ceratium tripos* (O. F. Müll.) Nitzsch (Dinophyceae). F and G, *Halosphaera minor* Ostenf. (F = motile phase) (Prasinophyceae). H, *Biddulphia sinensis* Grev. (Bacillariophyceae). J and K, *Pterosperma marginatum* Gaarder (K = motile phase) (Prasinophyceae). L and M, *Pachysphaera marshalliae* Parke (L = motile phase) (Prasinophyceae).

on any of the fish or visible traces of oil within the gut. Several different types were boiled and eaten. They were much appreciated and there were no subsequent ill effects.

Investigations consequent to the cruise I survey

The laboratory studies of the toxicity of oil and detergents reported in Chapter 7, none of which, however, had been undertaken at the time of the first exploratory cruise of R.V. 'Sarsia', show that many kinds of zoo-planktonic organisms are in varying degrees susceptible to poisoning by detergents, the lethal doses depending on the detergent used, the concentration of the detergent, and the length of time the organisms are exposed to the toxic substances.

In addition, as is pointed out on page 145, laboratory experiments had shown that most of the very toxic organic solvent ingredient of the detergents tested is lost by evaporation within about two days. And so, although the first cruise of R.V. 'Sarsia' had demonstrated that the presence of oil on the sea and use of detergents had in the early stages produced little demonstrable adverse effect on any marine organisms, save for the smallest of the algae, it was not known how the continuation of spraying might alter the picture. It is possible also that seemingly healthy organisms might be harbouring deleterious effects which would only later become fully apparent. With these thoughts in mind it was decided to undertake further sea surveys and, at the same time, to carry out a series of laboratory experiments designed to examine the problem of possible long-term effects of detergents on planktonic organisms.

CRUISE II

On this cruise from 3 to 6 April twenty-one stations were worked with the Gulf III high-speed plankton sampler from Plymouth through the Seven Stones area round to Hartland Point on the north coast of Devon, and samples of water were collected. The stations at which samples were taken are shown in Fig. 4B.

Oil pollution was restricted to small patches, mainly of iridescent films containing a few small clots of thicker oil. They were present off the Lizard, near the Seven Stones, where surface and bottom 'drifters' were dropped, and off Trevose Head. Surface and bottom 'drifters' of plastic were dropped near the Seven Stones in the hope that they would drift with the oil and thus act as markers of the movements of the areas of contaminated water. These plastic 'drifters' are the modern version of the well-known drift bottles.

Table 3. *Detergent analyses*

Position	Station	Result
49° 56'N., 5° 02'W.	—	o
50° 10'N., 6° 04'W.	19 (W)	o
49° 56'N., 6° 01'W.	—	o
50° 03'N., 5° 47'W.	Y	+ve (3·3 ppm) and o*
49° 59'N., 5° 30'W.	Z	o

* These two samples may have been half a mile apart.

Samples of sea water collected from the polluted area were sent to BP for analysis. The results expressed as detergent concentrations (ppm) are shown in Table 3.

Four sets of phytoplankton tow-net samples (W, X, Y, Z) were brought back from the cruise and were examined in the laboratory on 6 April. The diatoms and dinoflagellates appeared to be healthy in all the samples, but cysts of members of the Prasinophyceae showed abnormalities. At stations W and Y there was an abnormally large number of empty outer walls of a size not consistent with their being from normal cysts. These were probably young *Halosphaera* cysts which had burst and exuded their contents. At station Y, in particular, there were many young cysts of *Pterosperma* spp. which were dead or in an unhealthy condition. One species of *Halosphaera* (a delicate one) also appeared to be adversely affected. The sample from station X, on the other hand, showed relatively fewer empty outer walls from abnormal releases of contents and all cysts appeared healthy. An abnormal contraction of cyst contents was more noticeable at station Z than at the other stations, but even so some individuals of both *Halosphaera* spp. and *Pterosperma* spp. released viable motile cells in the normal way after four days in the laboratory.

Thus, the observations made during the second cruise revealed abnormalities in one class of algae, the Prasinophyceae, especially at station Y where large quantities of detergents had been used. As mentioned already (p. 25), cysts of this class tend to float on or near the surface and this would make them particularly vulnerable to substances such as oil and detergents poured on to the surface.

Quantitative samples of the larger plankton animals were collected with a modified Gulf III high-speed plankton sampler (Southward, 1962) on 4 and 5 April, one or two days after the cessation of detergent spraying of oil patches at sea. These samples were examined for young fish, fish eggs and the larger zooplankton 'indicator' organisms (Fig. 6).

At two of the stations (7 and 8) nearly all the pilchard eggs (90 per

cent) were dead, compared with a figure of about 50 per cent mortality at
other stations where pilchard eggs were taken. Fish eggs tend to float near
the surface of the sea and would thus be expected to show any deleterious
effects of oil and detergent spraying. Young fish also tend to be found in
the surface layers in the first few days after hatching. The numbers of
young fish found in the samples taken on the second survey are shown in

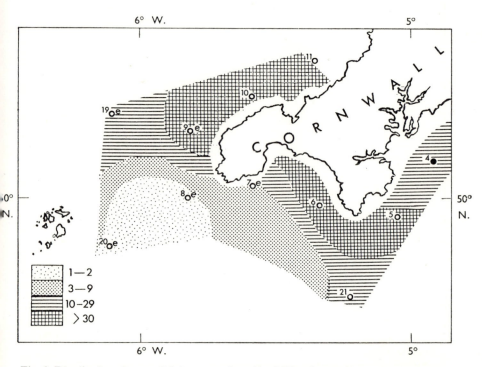

Fig. 6. Distribution of young fish (3–20 mm length) off West Cornwall, 4–5 April. Samples
taken with modified Gulf III high-speed sampler, fitted with 40 m.p.i. net. Results are
expressed as numbers per haul, corrected to a flowmeter reading corresponding to approximately 40 cubic metres of water filtered. All samples except one (solid black circle) were
taken in daylight. The letter 'e' shows the occurrence of north-western type of plankton,
a predominance of the arrow-worm *Sagitta elegans* and/or the presence of larvae of the
starfish *Luidia sarsi*.

Fig. 6. It is obvious that young fish were scarce or absent in the area to the
south and east of the Seven Stones, where detergent was used at sea. The
lack of young fish in this area bears no obvious relationship to the type
of plankton found and it seems an inescapable conclusion that the absence
of young fish south of the Seven Stones and the observed mortalities of
pilchard eggs at nearby stations was the effect of detergent spraying carried
out one or two days before the planktonic samples were taken.

CRUISE III

On Cruise III (11–14 April) series of stations across the Channel and in the Mount's Bay area (Figs. 4C, 7) were worked. One series of observations was made as close inshore as practicable (stations A–M), to coincide with

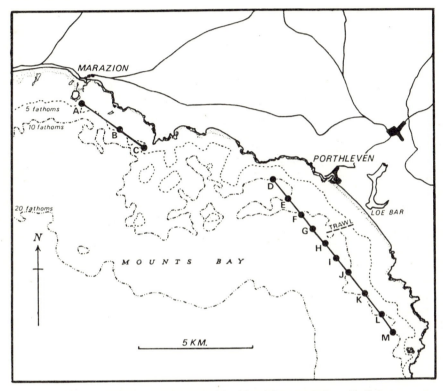

Fig. 7. Inshore stations worked by 'Sarsia' on 13 and 29 April.
The area shown here is indicated on Fig. 4C.

the activities of a party of aqualung divers working from the shore (see Chapter 6). At this time heavy detergent treatment was being applied in the Porthleven area.

Water samples from the Mount's Bay transect were again sent to BP for analysis, with the results, given in Table 4, expressed as detergent concentrations in parts per million.

In interpreting these figures it must be remembered that it was only the surfactant component that was being measured and that separation of surfactant from the solvent component may already have occurred. It is likely, therefore, that the detergent will have been underestimated at the surface

PLATE 6

A

B

C

(*Facing p.* 33)

Table 4. *Detergent estimations in Mount's Bay (ppm)*

Calculated from surfactant values

| | Mount's Bay stations | | | | | | | | | | | |
	A	B	C	D	E	F	G	H	I	J	K	L	M
Surface	7·8	6·7	5·1	5·1	2·4	2·4	0	0	0	0	0	0	0
Mid-water	6·7	2·4	0	0	0	0	0	0	0	0	0	0	0
Bottom	44·0	28·0	0	0	0	0	0	0	24	0	0	0	0

stations, and many times overestimated at some bottom stations where surfactant was detected. There is no doubt that the two most westerly stations at least (A and B) had been poisoned to a considerable degree. The high mortality of bottom-living animals recorded in Chapter 6 is readily understood. The toxic properties of the water in Mount's Bay clearly decreased eastwards, but zero readings should not necessarily be taken that no significant concentrations of the detergent (or some component of it) occurred.

Water samples from the same area were sent to Professor D. E. Hughes, of the Department of Microbiology, University College of South Wales and Monmouthshire, Cardiff, who reported that no oil-degrading bacteria were detectable. Such organisms are normally present in the sea in small numbers (ZoBell, 1963), and multiply as soon as any suitable substrate is provided. The present few results are too limited to be taken as indicating an effect of the detergent on oil-degrading bacteria in this area. The general subject of the effects of detergents on oil-degrading bacteria is being investigated by Gunkel (see p. 82).

On the cross-channel transect (Fig. 4C) no oil pollution was observed at stations 1 and 2. Stations 3-6 were worked during the hours of darkness, but no oil was observed during the stops on station. An oil film with occasional lumps—characteristic of oil treated at sea—was first observed at station 7 and this was found all the way along the route until just before station 12. Around station 8 there was an extensive area of thick oil (Plate 7A). This was of the same colour and general appearance as the oil observed on the first cruise, and once again it had a strong smell. Surface and bottom drifters were put down in this contaminated area.

PLATE 6

A, Trégastel-Plage (Côtes du Nord), 21 June. Oil–water emulsion which had re-separated after detergent spraying drifting on to the beach.   B, Salt marsh near Trégastel (Côtes du Nord), 21 June. A line of dark brown patches of re-separated oil deposited on the beach already blackened by the initial pollution.   C, Mullion Harbour, 6 April. Underwater photograph of an oil–water emulsion weighted with sand on the sea bed in the harbour mouth. Note the separated globule floating beside the main mass.

Phytoplankton tow-net samples were taken at stations 2, 4, 7 and 9–15, and examined immediately on return to the laboratory on 14/15 April. They contained organisms in varying quantities, but were all normal except that, as on previous cruises, there were some stations (2, 4 and 7) where the representatives of the Prasinophyceae were dead or abnormal.

SUBSEQUENT CRUISES

Later cruises by R.V. 'Sarsia' could not be diverted for long from normal oceanographic research work. However, some effort was devoted in three later cruises to a search for patches of oil that had disappeared to the south (see Chapters 8 and 9).

Water samples were taken on cruises on 28–30 April and in mid-May for oil content analysis of apparently clean water, at stations across the mouth of the English Channel. A closing water-bottle placed horizontally was used to sample the surface layer (top 10 cm at most). These samples contained crude oil at concentrations of 0·007–0·014 ppm at the end of April and 0·004–0·009 ppm in May. Subsurface samples contained negligible amounts of oil, no oil being detected in samples from 5 and 50 m depth (the lowest limit of detection being about 0·003 ppm).

We are indebted to the Superintendent, Admiralty Materials Laboratory for these analyses and also for the information that at a station 10 miles south of Portland Bill (*ca.* 280 kilometres up Channel from the Seven Stones) in surface samples taken weekly the concentration of crude oil was 0·003 ppm or less in March and April 1967, rising to 0·005 in June and returning to 0·003 in July, which is similar to the oil content of Channel waters sampled during recent years.

THE SEA SURVEY OBSERVATIONS IN RETROSPECT

The relatively little detected damage suffered by planktonic organisms in the western English Channel following the release of oil from the 'Torrey Canyon' and its treatment with detergent seemed, at the time of the surveys, to be rather surprising in view of the magnitude of the oil release and the large quantities of detergent used in an attempt to disperse the oil at sea. However, now that the circumstances of the pollution are better known it is possible to take a more informed view of its consequences.

Experiments reported in Chapter 7 show that many of the smaller planktonic organisms may be killed in a matter of a few hours in concentrations of detergent of 1–10 ppm. Zooplankton, however, are mostly active organisms which undergo marked vertical migrations and might well

escape toxic surface water by swimming downwards. But the more passive members of the plankton may really not have been so harmfully affected as might at first appear. Let us consider.

About 500000 gallons of detergent were used during the fourteen days or so of the sea-spraying operations. If all the detergent that had been used were spread evenly through the top 5 m of water (where the damage was mainly done) at a concentration of 1–10 ppm, an area of water 20–200 square miles would have been contaminated. Damage of this extent, bad, but far from catastrophic, was visualized at first.

But this is a wholly unreal picture, for detergents in sea water rapidly lose much of their toxicity (Chapter 7) and the patches of high concentration formed in the areas of spraying remain, for a time at least, coherent and do not readily disperse (Chapter 6). In Chapter 7 it is reported that the toxicity of detergents is mainly due to their aromatic components and in open dishes these are largely lost by evaporation within a period of from two to five days. Since in the sea the maximum solubility of aromatic hydrocarbons is of the order of 30–800 ppm the dissolved aromatics could, it is true, persist as a highly toxic system. But winds of a strength sufficient to achieve sufficient vertical convection to bring about a mixing to 5 m would also evaporate the toxic aromatics very rapidly from the sea surface to the air.

The effect of spraying oil patches, therefore, is to produce patches or tongues of oil and water charged with detergent which could be driven 30 miles or more downwind by a steady fresh breeze (Beaufort 6) lasting for two to three days. During this time much of the toxicity due to aromatics would be lost, though there would be a small proportion of aromatics remaining in true solution. In detail, much will depend on the stratification, cellular structure, and dynamic stability of the water, and these are dependent in turn on the relative sea and air temperatures by night and by day, and on the strength of tidal and residual currents. Thus, after a very few days, planktonic organisms are subject in the main to the much-diluted non-volatile and much less toxic surfactant constituents of the detergents.

The subsequent history and possible effects on organisms of these more persistent substances have not been studied during the present investigations.

CHAPTER 4

SHORE SURVEYS—ROCKY SHORES

On the Cornish coast there are two main types of substratum: (1) the rock of cliff bases, platforms, reefs or boulders, and (2) beach deposits usually of clean sand, or sometimes of pebbles. Rock is essentially stable whereas sands shift with the tides. On sandy shores there are seasonal changes, in that parts of the beach build up during the spring and summer under relatively calm conditions and are removed again during stormier periods of autumn and winter. Such different types of substratum obviously demand different cleansing procedures. The initial amount of exposure to, and damage to life by, detergent differs widely on rock and sand as does the degree to which the detergent persists. As, however, the two types occur in close proximity at any one locality this chapter is to some extent geographical in its approach. Attention is focused first on the more rocky shores; observations on sandy shores being given in the following chapter. Estuaries form yet a third type of habitat with quite different cleansing problems. The 'Torrey Canyon' pollution fortunately did not affect any of our major estuaries, but such effects as were seen are mentioned in Chapter 5.

ARRIVAL OF THE OIL

An account by a resident at Marazion stated that there was a smell of oil for a day before any actually arrived on the shore on 25/26 March. Dark blobs were seen silhouetted in crashing waves, and close inshore there was so much oil on the sea that the waves were smoothed, while elsewhere it was choppy with tan-coloured instead of white breakers (cf. Plate 13 B). The receding tide left a band about 5 metres wide of 'chocolate icing' (elsewhere described as 'chocolate mousse'). Some of this oil was washed off by the next tide, but some was left adhering to the seaweeds *Fucus* and *Porphyra*. Oil tended to be washed off barnacles but to be left in crevices on the rocks. Further landfalls of oil extended and thickened the coating, and then with gale-force winds behind a very high spring tide oil was flung right up the sea-walls and cliffs. But much of the oil brought into Marazion Bay did not settle, owing to a change of wind.

Along the coastline from the Lizard to Trevone pollution was general but far from continuous. A stretch of about ten miles of the coast on the west side of Mount's Bay, as well as many lesser areas, escaped. Winds concentrated the oil on to west-facing shores, or towards the eastern end of

bays facing north or south, pushing it into localized areas on a beach or into small coves. Later changes of wind direction caused more general pollution of northward-facing shores. This ghastly mess of oil, like thick blankets of 'chocolate mousse', presented a very different problem from the black tarry lumps of oil previously familiar along the drift line. Plates 3A, 8, 13 and 14 convey the appearance of the oil on the shore soon after arrival better than could any description.

Sennen was seen seven tides after the first oil-fall, and while more oil was still arriving and before any use of detergent. The boulders at high water were completely smothered in oil: the layer was estimated as about 1 cm thick, less on slopes, more in hollows (Plates 13A, 14A). On the sand there were large areas of oil about $\frac{1}{2}$–1 inch thick covering perhaps 50 per cent of the middle shore. At Gunwalloe Fishing Cove the oil was driven along the shore (Plate 4B), concentrated so that the breaking waves looked as if they were almost composed of oil, and their turbulence was markedly suppressed (Plate 8A). They swirled among the rocks, depositing a coating of oil on everything animate and inanimate. On the shingle they left a sticky blanket 1–2 inches thick which sank only slightly among the pebbles. But nowhere on the Cornish coast was oil nearly as thick as that which settled on parts of the Brittany coast (see Chapter 9, p. 160).

The 'chocolate mousse' was a mixture of oil, sea water and probably also detergent sprayed on at sea. Statements that this coating, usually referred to simply as oil, was up to 2–3 feet thick must have referred to very localized corners, or be erroneous. Oil floating on water in pools or, for example, in Porthleven harbour, could give a very misleading impression. Thicknesses and the area covered were very difficult to estimate and were subject to changes with each tide. Depths mentioned here were of oil seen after a few tides.

In most places the early deposits were mainly in the high-water zone and in the splash zone, but at Trevone where the oil was deposited on 29/30 March under calmer conditions the blanket of oil half an inch or more thick was spread over a wider tidal zone.

Treatment on the shore by detergents, usually hosed down with fresh water, produced milky streams running down the sands or retained in the rock pools (Plates 1B, 10A). It was this detergent mixture and neat detergent which proved so lethal to the fauna and flora.

As more oil arrived from the sea or was dispersed by detergents from one place to another pollution became more general. Even so there were stretches of shore and localized areas which escaped completely, providing a reservoir of organisms from which recolonization by the next generation of their larvae or spores can take place.

The zeal of the detergent users was such that even the most remote coves were often eventually tackled (Plate 4A), being incorrectly considered as the source from which 'new' oil was appearing. It is much more likely that the secondary deposit of oil on 'cleansed' beaches was in fact due to oil washed back by onshore winds or buried oil coming up from beneath the sands.

The map (Figs. 8–10) presents a synthesis of data from all reliable sources. It is based almost entirely on observations from Marine Biological Association workers, supplemented by records from the Nature Conservancy and from an Admiralty worker. The relative amounts of oil at different places are represented conventionally and were somewhat difficult to assess, but there seems little doubt that oil-falls were heaviest at Sennen Cove. The region of Cape Cornwall received a great deal and St Ives (Porthmeor Beach) had an exceptionally heavy plastering (Plate 8B), though the harbour and nearby beach escaped. Passing northwards along the coast there seemed to be rather less oil, but, owing to attempts to clean it during the long spell of northerly winds, relatively much more detergent was used, over a prolonged period. The degree of damage to life was much the same in all heavily treated areas. Two sharp spells of westerly wind caused heavy pollution along much of the eastern shore of Mount's Bay, but cleansing operations in this area were greatly helped by the long spell of northerly winds. The ten-mile stretch of coast from Penzance southwestwards escaped entirely and very little oil was deposited east of the Lizard. Only a few places, difficult of access, or lightly polluted, were left untreated by the end of the operation. Because detergent was distributed and used partly by the army and partly by local authorities (with frequent changes of personnel on the beaches) it has proved impossible to be exact about the amounts of detergent applied in the different areas and used on particular beaches. Figures are given (see page 42) for a few places where they seem to be reasonably reliable. For approximate totals of oil and detergent on Cornish beaches see Chapter 8. An essential contribution to the cleansing operations was made by the fire services using pressure hoses for delivering fresh water, or occasionally sea water, to wash the detergent and oil down the shore to meet the incoming tide. The methods of application varied widely as did the conditions and times relative to the tide. Local geography and weather were important. All these could make a great deal of difference to the effect on the flora and fauna as well as to the efficiency of oil removal.

AREAS STUDIED

Marine Biological Association workers between them visited sixty-five sites, many of them several times. Field work began on 28 March, and frequent journeys were made to West Cornwall until mid-May, since when studies have been continued by sporadic visits. The main sites studied are listed in Table 5.

The south coast is, in general, much the more sheltered from intensive wave action, has more localities with good weed cover, and is probably the richer in variety of species. The north coast is more open to powerful wave attack, tends to have on its rocky shores more barnacle and mussel coverage and less weed cover, and, while harbouring many plants and animals that are commoner there than on the south coast, is less rich in its variety of species.

On exposed shores the boulder zone near high water and also the inter-tidal sands have but a limited fauna. These were at first the hardest hit regions, but the spreading of the contamination, due largely to the use of detergent, meant that many rocky shores and sands became mildly con-taminated over nearly the whole of their tidal range.

Some of the places, particularly those on the north coast, and especially Trevone, have been visited regularly for a number of years by scientists from the Plymouth Laboratory, while for others there are detailed records of some of the commoner plants and animals which go back to the late 1940s and early 1950s (Crisp & Southward, 1958; Southward & Crisp, 1954, 1956; Southward, 1967) and in some cases to the 1930s (Fischer-Piette, 1936; Moore & Kitching, 1939). There was therefore a good back-ground of information available for detecting and assessing changes in the intertidal fauna and flora which could be attributed to the effects of oil pollution or of the cleansing operations.

From the field data currently available, a fourfold comparison has been attempted of shores or patches of them which (1) were completely un-touched and unspoilt, (2) had oil pollution alone, (3) had both oil pollution and detergent treatment, and (4) were affected by detergent but had never had any oil contamination.

Detailed surveys are given of two areas, Marazion and Trevone. Apart from visits paid by members of the Plymouth staff to Marazion, regular surveys were made by a local resident, Mrs S. Vaidya. Her studies of the algae and the commoner shore animals gave valuable continuity to the observations which covered a period of 20 weeks from the arrival of the first oil. This shore provided a range of habitats and showed a gradation of the effects of moderate pollution. In this it contrasted sharply with

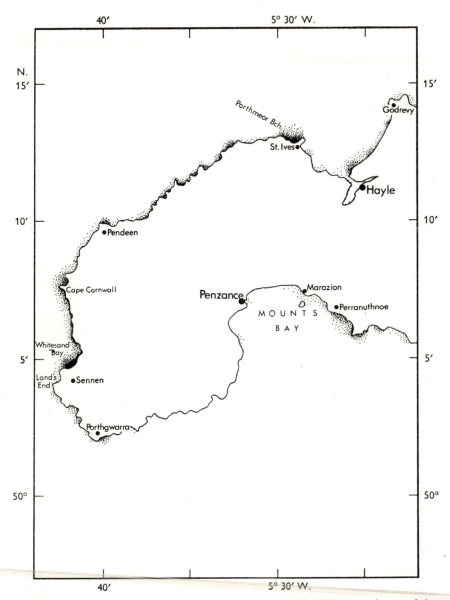

Fig. 8. The maps in Figs. 8–10 show the chief places studied by M.B.A. workers, and the amount of oil deposited on the beaches. The density of stipple indicates the relative degree of oil pollution. Scale, 2·5 kilometres to 1 cm. (approx. 4 miles to 1 inch).

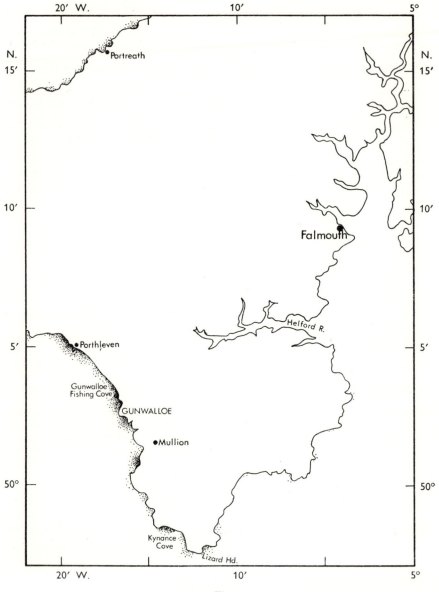

Fig. 9

Table 5. *List of main sites*

South coast eastward	
MARAZION (pp. 44–51)	Moderate pollution by oil and detergent. Hogus Reef slight oil-fall, no direct detergent treatment.
PERRANUTHNOE (p. 82)	Sandy shores and rocky reef, heavy pollution, at least 38 000 gallons detergent used.
PORTHLEVEN (pp. 57–61)	Reef beneath cliffs, harbour and beach, very bad pollution, 35 000 gallons detergent used on the reef alone, also vast amounts in harbour and on beach.
LOE BAR and GUNWAL-LOE FISHING COVE (pp. 79, 90)	Pebble beach, very badly polluted area. Detergent carried oil deep into beach, bulldozing alone more efficient.
KYNANCE (p. 63)	Bad pollution, much cleansing—continued late into May.
LIZARD POINT (p. 62)	Graded effects of damage away from site of detergent application.

Eastward of the Lizard there was only slight and isolated pollution, which did not reach as far as Helford Estuary.

North coast from Land's End	
SENNEN AND WHITESAND BAY (p. 81)	Boulders and sand and rocks; very exposed site. The worst polluted area, 164 000 gallons of detergent used up to 24 April. This was the only place where appreciable oil pollution was still visible in August.
CAPE CORNWALL (p. 65)	Heavy use of detergents and devastation of life.
PENDEEN WATCH (p. 62)	Small coves showing heavy oil not entirely cleaned.
ST IVES (PORTHMEOR SANDS) (p. 81)	Very heavily polluted and much detergent used, resulting in temporary quicksand formation. Re-polluted from buried oil.
HAYLE ESTUARY (p. 88)	High-level oil band deposited, no direct detergent treatment.
GODREVY POINT (p. 66)	On rocks, late cleaning.
ST AGNES (p. 64)	Contrast between two coves, Trevallis heavily treated, Trevaunance late careful treatment.
WATERGATE BAY (p. 81)	Sands and rocks, treatment over long period; repeated oil pollution.
MAWGAN PORTH (p. 78)	Sands and rocks, moderately heavy oil and treatment. A small corner escaped both, gave useful contrast.
BEDRUTHAN (p. 66)	Cove, difficult of access, some oil, no detergent used.
CONSTANTINE and BOOBY'S BAY (p. 65)	Patchily much oil and detergent, much of the shore escaped both.
TREVONE (pp. 51–57)	Much oil and detergent, mainly mid-shore damage.

No oil reached the Camel Estuary nor farther north.

Trevone, a heavily polluted rocky shore which is also described in detail as it was an area well known previously to the Plymouth staff making the survey.

Details are then given of the relative sensitivity of intertidal species found damaged by heavy pollution, especially from Porthleven (p. 57). Further examples of graded effects of damage are given, and then follow data collected from places where there was oil but no use of detergent. A summary of the conspicuous effects of heavy pollution is based on many observations on these and other sites (p. 67). Observations connected with

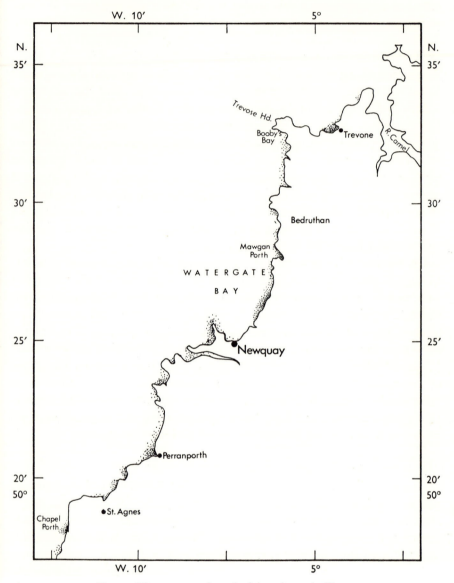

Fig. 10. The coast northward of that shown in Fig. 9.

the recovery and recolonization phase of rocky shores are summarized, followed by conclusions concerning the pollution and treatment of rocky shores.

MARAZION AREA

The area fronting the town between St Michael's Mount and the mainland has a wide intertidal zone with a varied topography, and has as diverse a flora and fauna as found anywhere on the oil-affected Cornish shores. Oil strandings over the rocks and sands tended to be rather patchy (Plate 3 A) and detergent treatment was restricted to particular areas. The heaviest mortality of marine organisms was largely localized in and adjacent to these areas; but a gradation could be detected towards more peripheral regions where plants and animals seemed to be little affected. The locality thus provided a wide range of conditions for study and the consequences of moderate pollution contrast sharply with areas of more general oil cover and heavy pollution by detergent.

On the sketch map (Fig. 11) letters mark areas of particular interest. Biological observations on the rocks in the upper part of the shore (A) were typical of a moderately polluted shore, and were in agreement with those in several other localities. A specially interesting low-water fauna (area B) showed the unfortunate indirect effects of spraying of detergents elsewhere. Hogus reef (C) formed something of a 'control', showing what happened when moderate oil deposits were left untouched by direct use of detergent. The sandy area (D) is in some ways different from most other sandy beaches. At Marazion, as elsewhere, early stages of recolonization were observed, and there were signs of biological degradation of oil by bacteria and also of the removal of oil by browsing animals.

Marazion—area A: upper part of main shore, rocky area

As elsewhere along the coast, damage to and destruction of life followed not so much the oil deposition as the application of detergent. Some algae were immediately bleached and some limpets killed, but many animals survived or escaped the first spraying. The worst effects in the Marazion area followed the intensive spraying in mid-April.

Among the algae the following effects were noted (for more detail see the account of algae at Porthleven, p. 58). Green filamentous algae were rapidly bleached as were encrusting coralline algae, particularly at the rims of pools where the detergent formed a toxic surface layer. Oil tended to cling to the thin fronds of laver (*Porphyra*), which after a few weeks became brittle and was washed away. The fucoids did not at once show the full extent of the damage; tips were soon discoloured (Plate 15 c), later they often lost

the blade of the frond, to be reduced to a midrib or stipe, and even this sometimes became readily detached from the rock; other plants survived and later put out new growth. There was considerable patchy loss of algae but not a complete devastation. There was also survival in the deeper parts of pools. By 23 April coralline algae in the pools were beginning to regain their normal pink colour. *Porphyra* and other red algae (for example *Chondrus* and *Dumontia*) were regenerating. Recolonization by sporelings of green filamentous algae (*Enteromorpha* and *Cladophora*) was beginning to show by the end of April but the rocks did not gain a heavy green cover (as they did at Trevone, for example), perhaps because some of the grazing population (chiefly the top-shells, *Monodonta*) were still present in appreciable numbers, although nearly all the limpets had been killed (Plate 9A).

Shore birds were observed pecking the upturned shell contents or the bodies of limpets occasionally left shell-less on the rocks (Plate 12A).* Many periwinkles and top-shells were also killed. Some mussels (*Mytilus*) were killed while others survived. The beadlet anemone (*Actinia equina*) gave sluggish reactions soon after use of detergent, but this resistant animal often survived when sited on the lower face of overhanging rocks. Barnacles were not all killed at Marazion, but crabs and shore fishes were much more often seen dead than alive. Some small crustaceans (gammarids etc.) which live in cracks in the rocks or under stones escaped the first application of detergent. Much later, in mid-July, what might be termed an indirect lethal effect of oil pollution was found. In the gullies between the rocks are flat stones under which oily drainage occurred. The deposit had become black and sulphurous and there was a complete dearth of animals due to the anaerobic conditions, that is oxygen lack. These were almost certainly brought about by bacterial degradation of the oil, some of which was still present, as indicated by vivid iridescence seen when stones were disturbed. By this date, the remains of paint-like oil patches on the rocks, except for those near and above high water, had mostly been worn off by wave action or other natural means.

Marazion—area B: low-water reef

The effects of detergent spread over the whole of the shore appreciably farther than the area where oil was deposited. This was apparent in the wide-spread effects mentioned above, and was also particularly well documented

---

* Dr Vera Fretter informs us that as a limpet dies the tonofibrillae—delicate structures which attach the columellar muscle to the shell—may be weakened whereas the mechanical suction and the secretion of the foot may still be effective in keeping the animal weakly attached. The loss of shells by limpets while still attached has been observed when they die in aquaria. It is not a specific effect of the detergent.

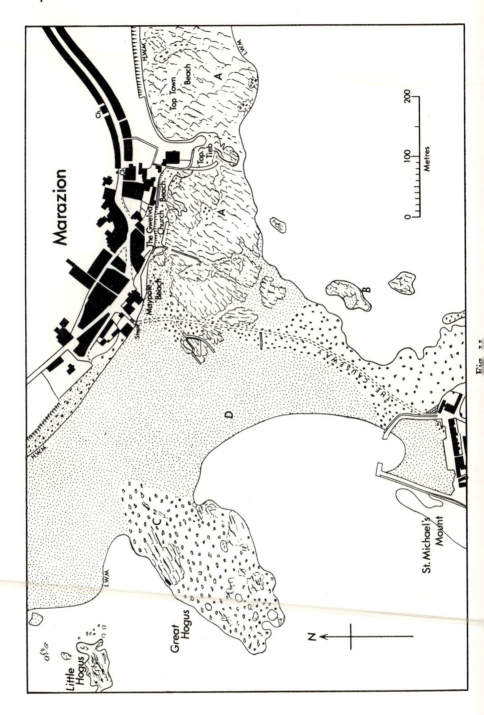

Marazion

Top Town Beach

Top Tieb

Church Beach

The Gwelva

Maypole Beach

Little Hogus

Great Hogus

St. Michael's Mount

A

B

C

D

N

0   100   200
Metres

Fig. xx

Table 6. *Summary of main events at Marazion*

(1) Oil deposited chiefly near high-water springs and in splash zone 25/26 March. Strong smell from volatile fraction of oil, which was ginger brown on arrival, gradually turning black on sea walls.

(2) First use of detergent 27 March chiefly at the town end of the Causeway, near the Top Tieb harbour, and between them, i.e. Maypole and Church beaches, also under the Mount.

(3) Lesser deposits of oil in splodges at high-water neaps during next few days (see Plate 6A, Maypole beach, 1 April). Subsequent tides (neaps) left thin layer of oil, which could be found over wider mid-tide zone.

(4) Widespread thin coating of oil on rock platform below the Gwelva and on Top Town Beach and in pools east of Causeway, 12 April. This oil was more viscous and mahogany-coloured. Probably some which had come out of emulsion after treatment elsewhere and was now redeposited.

(5) Moderate use of detergent on upper part of shore during mid-April; this moved most of the recent oil, some patches remained and there was still some buried in the sand (Maypole, Church and Top Town Beaches).

(6) Elements of oil–detergent mixtures were reappearing daily on the shore and on 26 April brown oil slicks with a detergent smell were close offshore.

(7) Secondary pollution after gale in early May (Plate 3B) on a long stretch of previously uncontaminated beach to west of area covered by map.

(8) Very heavy and extensive kelp (torn weed) deposited on sand (Maypole Beach to Great Hogus) by same gale, a normal seasonal occurrence.

(9) First faint signs of recovery, some return of pink colour to pools and of recolonization by very short green algae on rocks which lacked their normal browsing fauna, observed during last week of April.

(10) General greenness, especially on ungrazed rocks early July.

(11) Practically all oil removed by natural means from Hogus Rock by mid-July.

(12) Beach in full use by holiday makers, oblivious of such traces of oil as remain.

(13) Buried oil upshore being released by spring tides of larger amplitude, resulting in much stray oil and frothy oil seen in sea, 9 August.

(14) Abundant young fucoids replaced green weeds in early autumn in area *A*. Neither present in area *C*.

Caption for Fig. 11 opposite.

Fig. 11. Map of Marazion Beach showing places referred to in text. *A*, Upper and mid-tide rock platform with pools (see nos. 2, 4 and 5 of Table 6). *B*, Low-water reef, rich faunistically, no direct use of detergent, but showing serious indirect effects. *C*, Hogus Reef—patches of oil deposited 25/26 March, never any direct use of detergent, browsing fauna survived and helped in oil removal. *D*, Sand, some fauna affected temporarily at low level by detergent drifting with the tide. Buried oil at top of beach.

in the damage done to the low-water reef zone in the bay west of the Causeway, accessible only at very low tide. This area had been examined by
M.B.A. scientists on 28 February and a rich and abundant fauna recorded.
On 28 March it was free of oil. But by the time it was visited on 28 April,
after the main period of detergent application upshore, a considerable
change had occurred. Of the previously abundant snakelocks or opelet
anemones (*Anemonia sulcata*) there were now very few and those present
were only half expanded, with column and tentacle shrunken and not
showing typical turgidity. The habitat had been especially interesting and
rich in lucernarians, delicate little stalked jellyfish which live attached to
weeds. Four species, one of them present in thousands, had been seen in
February, but now they had all completely disappeared. Many of the algae,
including the oarweed, a *Laminaria*, were unhealthy, with large irregular
bleached patches of damaged tissue. The red weeds *Chondrus crispus* and
Calliblepharis jubata were unusually pale or showed bleaching or abnormal
red discoloration of the fronds. On this occasion a small colony of the very
local hermit crab *Clibanarius misanthropus* was found in a pool. Among
seven specimens there was a shell containing a dead individual. In natural
conditions shells containing dead hermit crabs are never found. This
example was probably a detergent victim.

Although there had been no oil deposited on this site and no direct application of detergent, polluted water could not have failed to have reached
it, and direct visual evidence of this was obtained when it was noted on
28 April that an oily film had accumulated against all windward facing rock
projections.

Marazion—area C: Hogus Reef

Great Hogus is a reef cut off from the shore at about half tide. The
original oil-fall, in discontinuous patches, had been moderate (up to
approximately ½ cm thick) and confined to the northern end of the reef
(area *C*). During the succeeding weeks the rock received only insignificant

---

PLATE 7

A, Oil emulsion on the sea surface about 20 miles north of Ushant, 12 April.   **B**, Isolated
patch of oil emulsion, about 1 metre across, floating a few miles south-west of Ushant
at 48° 22·6′ N., 05° 16′ W., 18 May.   **C**, Bay of Biscay, west of Pointe du Raz, 47° 22·6′ N.,
05° 20·5′ W., 12 May. Part of a dense patch of untreated oil emulsion, some 100 square
metres in area and perhaps 15 cm thick.

PLATE 8

A, Gunwalloe Fishing Cove, 30 March. Breaking wave heavily loaded with oil emulsion.
B, Porthmeor Beach, St Ives, 28 March. Beach polluted with untreated oil, deposited by
receding tide, prior to any cleansing operations. In the foreground the reflection of the
sky on the oil makes it appear blue.

PLATE 7

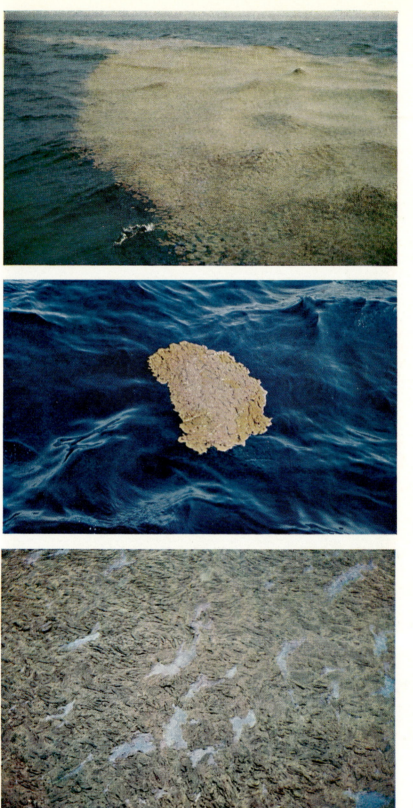

A

B

C

(*Facing p.* 48)

PLATE 8

A

B

additions of oil and detergents were never directly applied to it. It is probable, however, that the reef would on occasion have been washed by sea water containing detergent in low concentration when beach-cleaning operations were being carried out on the upper part of the tidal zone, some 300 metres distant.

Throughout the survey the absence of dead plants and animals in area *C* was in strong contrast to area *A*. On 28 March the flora and fauna seemed but little affected. Limpets which lay under a thin coating of oil were alive (Plate 9B) and reacted to touch, and some grazing tracks of top-shells through the oil were observed. Some of the limpets could be detached more easily than usual, and many of the top-shells (*Monodonta lineata*) had retracted within their shells and were remaining inactive at the bottom of pools.

Five days later the gastropod population of limpets, top-shells, periwinkles and dog-whelks, as well as small crustaceans, appeared to be entirely normal. Limpets gave their normal adhesion reaction, and *Monodonta* which had been taken to the laboratory on 28 March were now fully active. Oil patches were now somewhat thinner and darker. There was no evidence that any deaths of limpets or *Monodonta* had occurred as a result of the oil deposit. Indeed later in April limpets with their shells and the underlying rock still oil-coated had survived unscathed. Whatever indirect effects may have occurred temporarily during the height of the cleansing activities in mid-April, they had left no traces by 5 May, and limpets which had previously been photographed on a rock (Plate 9B) were all in their original seats. A hardened film of oil still covered shells and rocks seeming to offer inhospitable feeding conditions, for their usual food supply of algae and diatoms was smothered. If these could grow at all on the hardened surface of the oil, they were too scarce to be detected. That some of the limpets had in fact been grazing could be seen from the small partially cleaned areas around them (central limpet in Plate 9B; see also Plate 9C). A small boulder with four limpets attached was taken to the laboratory. These limpets had already cleaned a small area around themselves (cf. Plate 17B) and they continued to feed, browsing on the oily deposit and producing faeces containing oil. The presence of benzene-ring compounds in the faeces was demonstrated chemically. Similar observations were made on top-shells (*Monodonta*) and limpets (*Patella*) living on oily rocks at Perranuthnoe. They too produced oily faeces. The gut contents contained much brown-coloured matter, but the oily part could be distinguished by its solubility in benzene and by its taking up Oil Red O. The proportion of oil intake by these animals was estimated as about 20–30 per cent in *Patella* and 5–50 per cent in *Monodonta*.

4

When Hogus Reef was re-visited on 19 July the population of limpets and *Monodonta* was fully as abundant as before. It was very difficult to find an empty limpet seat (some always occur on normal shores). Practically the only traces of oil, now black, which could be found were on some of the *Monodonta* and limpet shells; the rocks and barnacles were clean. The oil may have been removed to some extent by wave action, but the distribution of the remaining traces is strongly suggestive that browsing played an important part in the cleaning, removing oil from the surfaces and binding it into small packages of faeces. As such, among other detritus, it would be readily accessible to bacterial oxidation. It is thus seen that the normal browsing fauna, left unkilled by detergent, can be effective cleaning agents, at least on rocks not too heavily oiled which are under water for some part (in this case about a third) of the tidal period. These observations confirm those made by George (1961) at Milford Haven.

Marazion—area D: sandy area

These sands differ in some ways from the usual Cornish sandy beaches which are of clean and often coarse sand (see Perranuthnoe fauna). A great deal of storm-torn seaweed is washed up here every year and much carted away by farmers; the 1967 kelp crop was normal and not considered by them to have been influenced by recent pollution. The sand here must receive much algal detritus and is greyish as a result; it also contains more silt than most beaches, thus making for stability. It is thus able to support an abundant polychaete worm population which was examined on 28 April. On this date there were only faint traces of detergent in the form of films on the surface of standing water near low-tide mark but no smell of detergent could be detected in the sand itself. The fauna within the medium-grade sand of which this beach is composed did not appear to have been affected. At about mid-tide level were bristle-worms, including lugworms (*Arenicola*), *Nerine* spp. and *Glycera convoluta*, all of which had survived such indirect effect of detergent as they may have encountered. *Arenicola* could have cut itself off from polluted water by ceasing to ventilate its burrow for a time. A single specimen of a sphaeromid crustacean and several of the bivalve mollusc *Venus striatula* were also found at this level. The *Venus*, though found on the surface, were apparently healthy.

At a low level on the same shore on 28 March, four specimens of the razor-shell *Ensis siliqua* had been found: three were protruding from their burrows and one was lying moribund on the sand (Plate 20A). This quite abnormal behaviour was attributed to effects of detergent spraying the previous day; two of the razor-shells recovered at least temporarily when put in clean sea water in the laboratory. As a result of the use of detergent

there was considerable destruction of *Ensis siliqua* in Marazion Bay during April (see diving record, p. 113). Large numbers of recently dead razor-shells were found thrown up in the drift line—gulls and a pair of crows were seen feeding on them. The sensitivity of this species to detergent was borne out elsewhere (Porthleven, Watergate, etc., and see toxicity tests, p. 137). As well as *Ensis*, the bivalve *Mactra stultorum* was also involved to some degree, the greatest number of empty valves being observed under the Mount on 16 April.

Another animal showing the effects of detergent, as elsewhere, was the heart-urchin, *Echinocardium cordatum*. The fragile dead tests do not normally remain long on the shore. Occasional ones were found during April, but towards the end of the month they were quite unusually numerous. This evidence of sensitivity is in agreement with the findings in the sublittoral zone at Porthleven (p. 140, and Plate 24). The last three animals mentioned are essentially shallow-water species, and as such they are probably much more sensitive to adverse factors (such as detergents) than are strictly intertidal species. The reported survival of many of the shore-living species may therefore give a false impression of the tolerance of marine organisms as a whole to potential poisons.

Razor-shells would be unable to close up completely as, for example, can mussels, which are therefore able to survive moderate doses of detergent (see p. 69).

TREVONE

The value of the Trevone survey derives mainly from the detailed knowledge which we had beforehand of the shores of this region and from the reliance that could therefore be placed in making surveys within this locality on 'before and after' comparisons. Trevone (Newtrain Bay to Porthmissen Beach) received a heavy oil pollution on 29 and 30 March (Fig. 12). The oil was said to be more than half an inch deep over all the rocks, with some patches of similar depth on the sands of Porthmissen Beach. Elsewhere there was a thin layer, and at first none at high water. When the first brief survey was made on 10 April, the shore had been subjected to detergent treatment for four days. There was a film of oil on the rocks at high-water neaps, and mixture of sand and oil up to a foot thick between high water of neaps and springs where spraying was in progress. A thinner film of oil was still present at the mid-tide level and on the seaward reefs near the sewer outlet. Water samples from pools on the lower part of the shore were not toxic, but a sample from a pool at high-water neaps, close to spraying operations, contained oil, about 60 per cent fresh water and (by bioassay) 700–800 ppm of detergent.

The only organisms in the vicinity that seemed unaffected at the time were the two common barnacles (*Chthamalus stellatus* and *Balanus balanoides*), mussels and fucoid algae. Some red algae were dying, 50 per cent or more of all three species of limpets had been killed, while most, if not all, top-shells, periwinkles and dog-whelks were already dead. No anemones

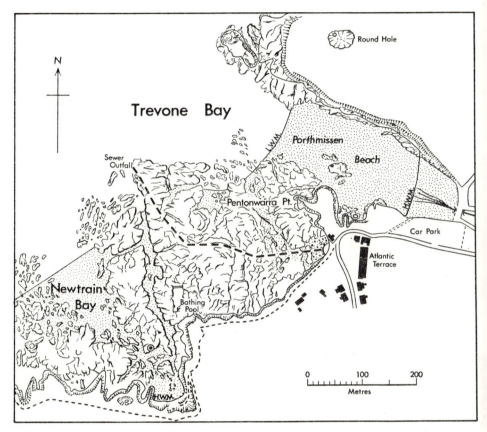

Fig. 12. Map of heavily oil-polluted and detergent-treated rocky and sandy shore at Trevone. – – –, Approximate line of sewer pipe. ⊙, Position of photographs reproduced in Plates 10B and 11 in Newtrain Bay.

were seen (alive or dead), nor intertidal fish, but among dead animals collected were the worm *Perinereis cultrifera*, the crabs *Carcinus maenas*, *Cancer pagurus*, *Porcellana platycheles* and the rare hermit crab *Clibanarius misanthropus*. Trevone was the only known locality for the latter on the north coast.

On 15 April firemen were still hosing detergent in fresh water over the rocks and sand of the rocky shore faced by Atlantic Terrace (Plate 10A),

and the sand here was full of oil. Porthmissen Beach, the main sandy beach adjacent to the car park, which had also been affected badly in places, was still being treated. Streams of fresh water mixed with detergent were flowing down it and a few workers were turning over the sand. But the main work had been done and the sand looked clean, though smelling strongly. The rocks to the west around the bathing pool and in Newtrain Bay had already been treated, but over some areas a thin film of oil remained.

Much biological damage had obviously been done to the mid-tidal region extending roughly from high- to low-water neaps, the region where the most intensive spraying had taken place. Rocks were denuded of molluscs and detergent-filled pools had only dead algae in them. Drifts of limpet shells, with and without soft parts inside, and separated soft parts, were washed with other molluscs into gullies, also one or two dead fish, dead crabs and a dead *Nephthys* worm. *Patella aspera* with flesh inside, and large tufts of *Fucus serratus* growing on these limpet shells, had here been washed up from lower levels or from pools. Around the bathing pool and near the Newtrain gully, where the oily film on some rocks perhaps indicated that spraying had been less intense, the damage seemed to be less severe. Even so, most limpets were easily detached by hand and the shells often lifted cleanly away from the soft parts on the rock (Plate 12A) (see p. 45). Among the dead algae found on 21 April were the green *Ulva* and red *Gracilaria* and *Ceramium*.

On 23 April, some days after the cessation of spraying, all the loose limpets had gone (Plate 12B) and only a few seated in sheltered crevices and on rocks still thinly covered with oil remained firmly attached. Everywhere many thousands of fresh clean limpet seats were clearly visible. Some examples of each of the top-shells *Monodonta lineata* and *Gibbula umbilicalis* survived, a mere remnant of their former abundance. Beadlet anemones, *Actinia equina*, although reduced in number, were fairly plentiful in pools and on oiled rocks in the Newtrain and bathing-pool regions. Here also the deeper pools contained *Bifurcaria bifurcata*, *Corallina officinalis* and other algae in apparently normal condition. Only one snakelocks anemone, *Anemonia sulcata*, usually common, was seen, unattached and looking sickly. Mussels on rocks near the sewer outfall, where a little oil was present, were as abundant as usual and alive, but scarcely any specimens of the dog-whelk *Nucella lapillus*, which in this area feeds mainly on mussels and is normally very common, could be found. Inactivated dog-whelks were lying loose and empty shells were seen (Plate 15B). Almost all the limpets had gone, leaving clean seats everywhere on the rocks. This visit coincided with low water of a good spring tide, and it was encouraging

to find all the plants and animals at the lowest levels more or less normal. Underneath-stones at the lower end of Newtrain gully were good growths of the ascidian *Botryllus* and, among other animals sheltering beneath stones were the crabs *Portunus puber, Carcinus maenas* and young *Cancer pagurus*, and some shore fishes including blennies and several *Lepadogaster lepadogaster*. The starfish *Asterina gibbosa* was present but no living sea-urchins (*Psammechinus miliaris*) were seen, though dead ones were found washed up in the gully. Similarly at the highest shore levels on the east side of Newtrain Bay, where it seemed that oil and detergent had not penetrated, there was a normal fauna with *Patella vulgata, Littorina saxatilis, L. neritoides* and *Chthamalus stellatus* all alive.

The visit on 29 April confirmed this general picture of a devastated middle shore flanked by relatively unaffected upper and lower regions. Individual *Actinia* and *Monodonta* which had been specially noted pre-viously were still in the same positions, and on the walls of the gully some patches of the sponges *Halichondria panicea* and *Hymeniacidon perlevis* survived. The floor of the Newtrain gully, however, contained moribund *Gibbula umbilicalis, Monodonta lineata* and *Patella vulgata* amid a drift of shells.

Certain shallow rock pools which had often been examined and photo-graphed had been known to contain *Actinia equina, Anemonia sulcata, Gibbula, Patella, Littorina littorea, Nucella, Corallina, Lithophyllum,* tufts of *Enteromorpha* and other seaweed. Small crabs, occasional prawns and small blennies were also among the usual inhabitants. After the deter-gent treatment, these pools for several weeks contained only beadlet anemones, *Actinia*, tufts of young *Bifurcaria, Corallina* and one or two other small algae. A microscopic slimy brown alga and diatoms began to coat over the apparently dead encrusting calcareous algae (*Lithophyllum*) and limpet scars. By July very young fishes and tiny crabs were hiding in the weed and one fair-sized gemmed anemone (*Bunodactis verrucosa*), one adult *Gibbula umbilicalis* and one *Littorina littorea* were seen.

In August 1966 a small patch of rock in Newtrain Bay, situated at roughly mid-tidal level, had been photographed to show the fauna (Plates 10B, 11A). This patch approximately 45 × 35 cm. set within a sloping rock face of about 100 square metres area was readily identifiable by the rock structure and photographed again on 23 April 1967 (Plate 11B). The rock still had traces of oil on it but had undoubtedly been heavily sprayed, though tufts of coralline algae, such as that shown in the photographs, were still soaked in oil and were dead. The single *Monodonta* shown in the photograph of 23 April was alive and in the same place on 29 April. The detergent treatment had almost completely cleared the rock of living organ-

Table 7. *Animals in areas photographed at Trevone* (Plates 11 A, B)

Species	Number present August 1966	Number present 23 April 1967
Actinia equina	1	0
Chthamalus stellatus	Many	Few (dead?)
Mytilus sp.	2 or 3 very small	1
Patella vulgata	24 medium and small	0
Monodonta lineata	11	1
Gibbula umbilicalis	1	0
Littorina saxatilis	4	0

isms and the two photographs are typical of the whole area before and after the spraying. Table 7 lists the animals shown in the two photographs (Plate 11 A, B).

On a further visit on 14 May 1967 a count was made of the surviving organisms on this particular rock face of approximately 100 square metres. There were 41 *Actinia*, 34 *Monodonta*, 2 *Patella*, a few *Gibbula*, a few small *Mytilus*, no *Littorina*, and it was almost cleared of acorn barnacles. The whole rock face looked strangely bare compared with its normal appearance.

The mussel-covered rocks near the sewer outfall, once drab-coloured, had a greenish look, due to young growths of *Enteromorpha* and *Ulva*, which mingled with brown growths of *Ectocarpus* and diatoms. These growths covered rocks and mussels and were particularly well developed in pools and all wet places.

The rocks at Pentonwarra Point which had been intensively treated with detergent, but had not been examined previously, had many areas with freely hanging byssal threads showing where mussels had been killed and had fallen off (Plate 15 A). Acorn barnacles had also been extensively destroyed, and the rocks were almost bare of life.

On 14 May sandy patches opposite Atlantic Terrace were still extremely oily with a strong smell, in Newtrain gully there was only a slight smell, less than before, and similarly on Porthmissen beach. Here the sand looked clean on the surface, but digging in the cove on the west side revealed a dark grey oily layer of sand having a strong smell of detergent. For the significance of this see page 81.

The rocky shore at Trevone was reinvestigated on 9 June. A few patches of hardened oil were seen around mid-tide level, and some small (2 cm in diameter) spots of new, soft oil were present at high water. The smell of detergent appeared to come mainly from the grassy cliff top where detergent drums had stood, but there were distinct traces of it in the coarse sand opposite Atlantic Terrace at the highest level of the tides.

Most of the fucoid algae had survived the cleansing treatment, and some re-growth of *Corallina* had begun in the pools. The overall effect, however, was of greenness, due to the unprecedented growth of *Enteromorpha* which had developed freely in the absence of limpets and other grazing molluscs. The growth was heaviest at low-water and mid-tide level, with some scattered patches above this level.

The few surviving limpets (less than one per 10 square metres) could easily be recognized from a distance, as they each occupied 'clearings' in the growth of green weed (Plate 17A). *Monodonta* was the commonest surviving mollusc, but a few *Gibbula umbilicalis* and *Nucella* were present. The beadlet, *Actinia*, was the only anemone observed. Settlement of young of the barnacle *B. balanoides* was quite heavy, and had continued after the cleansing operations as shown by their occurrence on limpet seats.

A month later on 9 July *Enteromorpha*, and in the lower places *Ulva*, were much further developed. An unusual carpet of vivid green covered almost the whole of the rocky shore from about half-tide level downwards (Plate 16B). Nothing like this has been seen here before (Plate 16A). Surviving mussels on rocks near the sewer outfall had almost disappeared beneath the green weeds growing on their shells. On the tops of the reefs near the sewer outfall the green algae were replaced by purplish-brown *Porphyra*, growing just as abundantly on rocks and mussels. Here and there a few solitary limpets or *Monodonta* still kept clear little areas of rock (Plate 17A).

Many of the oil film patches which had remained on high-level rocks after cessation of spraying had now gone, destroyed by natural agencies. Others were breaking down; they contained tiny grains of sand and could readily be rubbed off, often without staining the finger.

On this sunny July day Porthmissen Beach was crowded with holiday-

---

PLATE 9

A, Marazion, Church Beach, 5 May. Treated rocks, on which all limpets had been killed, but top-shells (*Monodonta lineata*) had largely survived. Old limpet seats show as oval pale areas.   **B**, Marazion, Church Beach, 5 May. Hogus Rock. Resident limpets surviving in oiled band, where the rock had not been treated with detergent. Note that the shells of the limpets are wholly or partly covered with oil. Oil has been grazed from the rock-face around the limpet in the centre of the picture. Others show it to a lesser extent.   **C**, Limpet tooth-marks in a film of oil on a vertical rock-face at Trevone, 9 June. This photograph shows how the natural grazing activities of limpets will help to cleanse a rocky shore, providing the animals are not killed or damaged by detergents.

PLATE 10

A, Spraying detergent on rocks and sandy patches opposite Atlantic Terrace, Trevone, 15 April. Note the white emulsion of detergent in the rock pools. At extreme top right men are spraying from Pentonwarra Point.   **B**, Sloping rock-face in Newtrain Bay, Trevone, on which a count of surviving organisms was made on 14 May (p. 55). The white rectangle marks the site of the photographs reproduced in Plate 11.

PLATE 9

A

B

C

PLATE 10

A

B

PLATE 11

A

B

PLATE 12

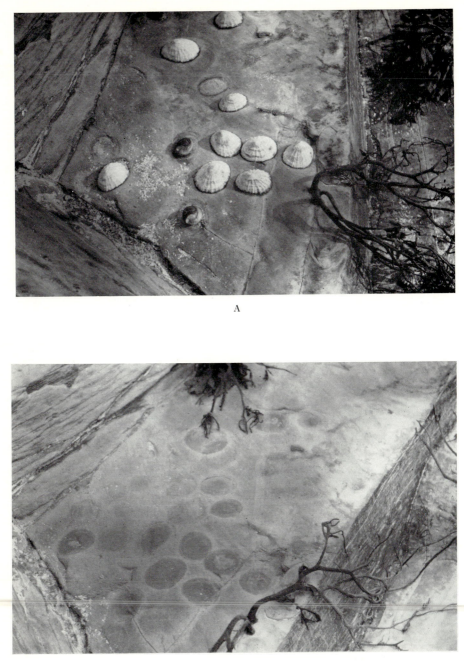

A

B

(*Facing p.* 57)

makers and children were happily playing even in the still stained and still slightly smelly sandy patches opposite Atlantic Terrace. For them the shore was back to normal.

RELATIVE SENSITIVITY OF
DIFFERENT SPECIES—PORTHLEVEN REEF

The field aspects of this problem were best studied at a place where the first visits could be paid while spraying was still in progress. The badly polluted area of Porthleven Reef (Fig. 17) was therefore chosen.

The first oil came in on 25/26 March on a high spring tide with a gale and was thus thrown about 20 feet up the cliffs to the thrift and turf. Lichens were largely smothered under this persistent blackening deposit. The bulk of the oil was near the base of the cliffs but on subsequent days much more oil was deposited—some of it probably being oil that had been washed out of the nearby harbour (see Plate 5 A, B)—so that nearly the whole reef had a slippery film of oil. Detergent was applied mainly in the higher regions of the shore, the most heavily treated area being between the monument on the cliffs and the harbour entrance (a distance of ½ km.) where it is estimated that a total of about 35 000 gallons of detergent were used·in the eight days between 4 and 12 April and on 25 and 27 April. Sea water and not fresh water was used to hose down these rocks after spraying, thus simplifying the understanding of the cause of mortality. The shore here consists of a rock platform gently sloping from above mid-tide level to below low water. It is crossed by deep gullies running seawards from the base of the cliffs. Some of the gullies consist largely of a series of pot-holes but others contain loose rocks and patches of gravel. Between the gullies there are some rock pools and individual pot-holes. The gullies were very efficient in transmitting concentrated detergent from the upper part of the shore to the low-tide region.

PLATE 11

A, A small area of mid-tidal rock at Newtrain Bay, Trevone, photographed in August 1966 to show the typical fauna of limpets, top-shells, etc. **B**, The same area of rock photographed on 23 April 1967 after treatment with detergent to remove oil. One top-shell and one small mussel (indicated by arrow) survive (see Table 7, p. 55).

PLATE 12

A, Mid-tide limpets at Newtrain Bay killed by detergent. Shells have been lifted off two of them leaving their soft parts *in situ* on the rock. Photographed 15 April, some days after cessation of spraying and typical of innumerable neighbouring limpets at that time. **B**, Scars of the same limpets eight days later. Photographed 23 April and typical of many rocks of the mid-tidal region after the washing away by the sea of limpets killed by detergent. Limpets on oil-coated rocks not detergent treated survived not far away.

The algae were most seriously damaged by the detergent at the higher levels on the shores. A high proportion of the *Porphyra umbilicalis* plants growing on the higher rocks were killed; so also were the *Enteromorpha* plants in the high-level pools. *Corallina*, with its associated epiphytes, and the encrusting calcareous algae on the bottom of these high-level pools were also killed (Plates 15 c, 18 a), but at mid-tide only their tips and some of their epiphytes were killed, while near low water the *Corallina* and its epiphytes appeared healthy. In the mid-tide pools the *Bifurcaria* and *Cystoseira* plants were either killed or had the young growing apices destroyed.

The fucoid vegetation on the rocks and its associated algal undergrowth was also more seriously damaged or destroyed at the higher levels. *Fucus spiralis* appeared to be more easily killed by the detergent than either *F. vesiculosus* or *F. serratus*. Even so, dead plants of all three species were recorded and a high proportion of the remaining fucoids higher on the shore had their young growing apices destroyed. In other areas *Pelvetia canaliculata* reacted to the detergent in a similar way to *Fucus spiralis*. *Ascophyllum nodosum*, rather local on these exposed shores, appeared to show fewer ill effects. At the lower levels on the shore the *Fucus vesiculosus* and *F. serratus* appeared healthy and the receptacular tissue was apparently undamaged.

Some of the algal species growing on the rocks beneath the fucoids appeared to have suffered little except some plants of a few of the species growing at the higher levels which had received the concentrated detergents.

The species of algae least affected by the detergent were: *Ahnfeltia plicata*, *Chondrus crispus*, *Cladostephus spongiosus*, *Dilsea carnosa*, *Furcellaria fastigiata*, *Gigartina stellata*, *Kallymenia reniformis*, *Laurencia pinnatifida*, *Polyides rotundus*, *Pterosiphonia complanata*, *P. thuyoides*, *Rhodymenia palmata*, *Schizymenia dubyi*, *Scytosiphon lomentarius*.

On the other hand many of the plants belonging to the following species had either been killed (bleached or tips bleached) or appeared very unhealthy: *Acrosiphonia arcta*, *Acrosorium uncinatum*, *Apoglossum ruscifolium*, *Callithamnion* spp., particularly *C. tetricum* on rock-faces, *Ceramium* spp., *Cladophora rupestris*, *Cryptopleura ramosa*, *Delessaria sanguinea*, *Dictyota dichotoma*, *Ectocarpus* spp., *Gastroclonium ovatum*, *Gracilaria verrucosa*, *Halurus equisetifolius*, *Hypoglossum woodwardii*, *Jania rubens*, *Laurencia hybrida*, *Lomentaria articulata*, *Membranoptera alata*, *Plocamium vulgare*, *Plumaria elegans*, *Polysiphonia* spp., *Ulva lactuca*. Lower on the shore, however, apparently healthy plants of most of the above species could still be found.

At low water in the *Laminaria digitata* zone the fronds of many of the

Laminaria plants were completely bleached, or green in colour, and the reproductive parts of their fronds had been killed, but a large number of plants still appeared healthy and bore living reproductive tissue. The young *Himanthalia* plants, *Cladostephus verticellatus*, *Furcellaria fastigiata*, *Phyllophora crispa* and *P. brodiaei*, all appeared to be in healthy condition.

It will be seen from this short description that the damage sustained by the algae has been extensive. For any one species (for example, *Corallina*) there is a gradation of effect, damage being most severe at the higher levels of the shore where the toxic concentration was greatest. It can also be seen that not all the species are equally sensitive: thus the very delicate filamentous membranaceous red algae seem to be particularly susceptible and in some cases have been completely destroyed.

A gradation of effect and variation in sensitivity to the detergent is also exhibited by the animals of the reef. Although there was much oil on the shore when this reef was seen on 30 March, the animals did not appear to have been affected. However, when the reef was again visited on 7 April, three days after detergent treatment started, most of the animals were dead or moribund. On subsequent visits on 11, 26 and 28 April far fewer dead animals were found because many had been washed along the gullies into deeper water or had been eaten by birds. This removal of dead animals to deeper water was confirmed by the divers (p. 109). This has meant that much of the evidence rapidly disappeared and may explain the absence of some species, such as small crustaceans. From material which was collected, the following list of the more common dead animals was made.

ANEMONES. The beadlet *Actinia equina* and the dahlia anemone *Tealia felina* are possibly the most resistant animals on the shore, being commonly found alive, and on 26 April they were found in pools between the tidemarks which appeared to be devoid of all other animals. Some *Anemonia sulcata*, *Sagartia elegans* and *Cereus pedunculatus* were found dead; few survived.

POLYCHAETE WORMS. *Lepidonotus clava*, *Eulalia viridis*, *Nereis pelagica*, *Perinereis marioni*, *Eunice harassii*, *Lysidice ninetta*, *Marphysa sanguinea*, *Arabella iricolor*, *Dodecaceria concharum*, *Potamilla reniformis* and *Dasychone bombyx* were found moribund or dead on 11 April and one or more specimens of practically all species were found alive later. To some extent these are examples of animals which live in micro-habitats, in crevices or among weeds deep in pools, where they would have been able to stay away from the worst of the poisonous water, but laboratory experiments showed that these worms were fairly resistant to poisoning by detergent.

CRUSTACEA. Dead *Ligia oceanica* and *Orchestia* sp. were littered among the rocks at high water. The larger mobile crustaceans, the lobster *Homarus*

vulgaris, and crabs *Porcellana platycheles*, *Cancer pagurus*, *Portunus puber*, *Xantho incisus*, *Pilumnus hirtellus* and *Carcinus maenas* were completely wiped out, only one living specimen of the last-mentioned and toughest crab being found. No shrimps or prawns were ever found nor were any gammarids seen. Barnacles appeared to have survived well on the main part of the reef, but near the old boat-house extensive patches of *Chthamalus stellatus* had been killed in this particularly bad area (Plate 19 A).

MOLLUSCA. The limpet population that had been killed comprised the three species of *Patella* in about the following proportions: *P. vulgata* 70 per cent, *P. intermedia* 20 per cent, and *P. aspera* 10 per cent. Of these three species together about 10 per cent were still alive on 11 April between the zones of mean low water and mean high water, whereas on 28 April there were none left alive in this main stretch of shore, there being only a few survivors at low-water springs and in the spray zone. An idea of the original abundance of the gastropods may be gained from counts which were made of dead bodies in two pot-holes on 7 April; these were only about 20 cm in diameter and 20–30 cm deep. Their combined contents included 269 *Patella* spp., 21 *Nucella lapillus*, 15 *Nassarius incrassatus*, 13 *Gibbula umbilicalis*, 10 *Gibbula cineraria*, 2 *Ocenebra erinacea*, and 1 *Monodonta lineata*. Other species of gastropods found dead were *Patina pellucida*, *Calliostoma zizyphinum*, *Tricolia pullus*, *Littorina littorea*, rissoid sp., *Trivia monacha* and *Aplysia punctata*. The sea hare, *Aplysia*, which would have been coming up the shore to spawn, was found alive on each visit, and was also surprisingly resistant in laboratory tests. Though there was high mortality among the gastropods between tide-marks some may have been only inactivated and recovered later (see p. 49). By 28 April only a few *Patella*, *Nucella* and *Monodonta* remained. Elsewhere *Monodonta* was a conspicuously resistant mollusc, perhaps because it has a very efficient operculum and is able to close itself off from the environment, in marked contrast to *Patella* (Plate 9 A). A limpet as soon as it ceases to hold its shell firmly against the rock would have all its delicate gills and the mantle edge—a large area—at once exposed to poisonous water, drawn in to its mantle cavity by ciliary activity. It is not therefore surprising that limpets are so vulnerable. The dog-whelk, *Nucella*,* has an operculum but does not seem to close it properly: despite this a few specimens were found alive on each visit, and at the end of April eggs were seen near low-water mark.

* Far more specimens of *Nucella* were found on the reef in October–November than in April–June. Apart from mature specimens their shells nearly all showed a marked groove (usually with inner teeth formation) after which new growth had clearly been added. This is unusual in normal habitats (Moore, 1936) and would seem beyond doubt to indicate that these *Nucella* had passed through a period of inactivity. They were probably washed into the depths of gullies at the time of spraying and took some weeks to recover. Similar grooved specimens were found on other detergent-treated shores.

The chiton, *Acanthochitona crinita*, was found dead and one found alive in its habitat under stones.

Among bivalve molluscs, no living specimens of the saddle oyster *Anomia ephippium* were recorded. Several living specimens of the very small species *Lasaea rubra* and *Turtonia minuta* were found among *Corallina* in the low-water region. A few of the crevice-dwelling *Hiatella striata* were also found alive, in addition to dead specimens. No mussels (*Mytilus*) were recorded from this shore. They were sporadic in their occurrence and are much more characteristic of the exposed northern coast, where they were found to be quite resistant to oil alone and to moderate doses of detergent, but not to repeated intense treatment. They can close up efficiently for hours at a time, but when open they draw large quantities of water through their mantle cavity, and thus might be sensitive to low concentrations of poison.

ECHINODERMATA. Many fragments of the starfish *Marthasterias glacialis* were found, but neither it nor the cushion-star *Asterina gibbosa*, nor the little urchin *Psammechinus miliaris*, were ever seen alive on the reef.

FISHES. The common blenny, *Blennius pholis*, the Cornish sucker-fish *Lepadogaster lepadogaster* and *Conger conger* were found dead; only one living fish was seen, on 26 April, and on 28 April what appeared to be healthy eggs of a shore fish were collected. It seemed as if the occasional active animal visited the shore.

On 8 May all mobile crustaceans were still missing (see page 71 for recolonization by them). There were a few *Actinia* and a few *Monodonta* and one or two specimens of *Patella* surviving in favoured places. Barnacles appeared to have survived well and there was some settlement of young *Balanus balanoides* taking place on clean surfaces. Such oil as was still present was in the form of a surface-hardened film.

We can see therefore that, as a result of the large amounts of detergent used on the Porthleven Reef, there had been widespread mortality of intertidal animals and plants.

As was pointed out on page 59, there is difficulty in finding evidence of dead animals, as their bodies are quickly washed away or eaten. In the case of active forms it is not easy to tell if their absence may not in fact be due to escape rather than death. The following records are therefore included here.

At Gunwalloe Fishing Cove on 2 April while there was much spraying the following dead fish were found: *Blennius gattorugine*, *B. pholis*, *Cottus* sp., *Gaidropsaurus* sp., *Zeugopterus punctatus*, *Ammodytes immaculatus*. One small lobster, starfishes and crabs were also collected.

In Porthleven harbour abundant dead sand eels, *Ammodytes*, had been seen and on Sennen beach twenty sand eels were washed up.

OTHER ROCKY AREAS

Of the shores so far studied in detail Trevone and Porthleven have shown the effects of heavy detergent treatment. Marazion had only moderate damage and graded effects were seen, and there was an area on Hogus where the oil was never treated. Some further examples will amplify the observations already recorded.

Graded effects of spraying

Graded effects could be seen in the proportion of dead and of living members of one species, and in the extent to which the more or the less resistant species had been able to persist.

The first area, Polpeor Cove, close to LIZARD POINT, is one previously well known to the investigators. By 8 May this cove had received much oil and probably a generous amount of detergent, the effect of which had seemingly spread beyond the original limits of the oil. The rocks to the immediate east of Polpeor Cove (at the Lizard itself), are partly sheltered from wave action by numerous outer reefs exposed at low tide, and before the 'Torrey Canyon' pollution the fauna and flora were very rich. The outer most accessible reefs at the point seemed relatively unaffected and the best-known reef seemed absolutely unchanged, though there was a slight film of oil in places towards high water. However, as the survey progressed round the point into Polpeor Cove the influence of the detergent became apparent. At first only the green algae and hermit crabs were missing; then all the limpets in pools and most of the top-shells disappeared, though in these tide pools the encrusting calcareous red algae and *Corallina* were alive. Closer into the cove, however, all these algae were dead and the pools were coloured white, and there were signs of mortality among the barnacles. In the cove itself, particularly on the rocks close to the old lifeboat slip, it was difficult to find a single living animal. Here even the barnacles were killed and the fucoids were dying; and the especially rich flora of the iridescent alga *Cystoseira* in the pools was very much reduced, only the bare stipes being visible, and these apparently dying.

In the vicinity of PENDEEN WATCH on the north coast there are several small coves which became badly polluted with oil. Cleaning was first carried out on the east side towards Portheras Cove, Morvah. The cleaning operations were later extended and, by the time of the final visit on 9 May, rather light spraying had been carried out over most of the area but there were still some oil-covered rocks on the east side. These rocks supported a good population of mussels and barnacles even though other animals as well as the green algae had vanished. Nearer the more heavily cleaned

areas, the barnacles began to show increasing mortality until close to the sandy coves even the hardiest of the barnacles, *Chthamalus stellatus*, were dead. In such places all the red algae had been killed and even *Fucus vesiculosus* (form *evesiculosus*) appeared to be dying.

In contrast to these barren shores to the east of Pendeen, Enys Cove to the west of the lighthouse showed hardly any deleterious effects, although there were traces suggesting that a small cleansing party had used a few drums of detergent where the small stream entered the cove. In spite of cleaning operations there was still a thick film of oil at high-water springs and a thinner layer extending down to mid-tide level. Most of the limpets and all of the barnacles seemed to be completely unharmed and patches of the green *Enteromorpha* were flourishing near high-water mark. Spat of *Balanus balanoides* were settling on oil-free patches of rock and periwinkles were present.

At FISTRAL BAY, NEWQUAY, the rocks of the Headland, as well as the sandy bay as a whole, had received much treatment and by 27 April most of the red and green algae were already dead, though some plants of the red alga *Gigartina* survived on vertical faces. On flat surfaces even the fucoid algae seemed to be dying. All the limpets had been killed. More than 50 per cent of the mussels had been removed from the rocks, leaving their byssus threads behind (cf. Plate 15A). On 22 April the empty shells had been conspicuous in the adjacent beach material. More than 50 per cent of the barnacles had died, including most of the *Balanus balanoides*, and all the purple-tinged *B. perforatus* of the more shaded and sheltered gullies. The settlement of young *B. balanoides* had begun on the seaward edges of reefs cleaned earlier. A few damaged anemones (*Actinia*) were still holding on.

On the south coast at POLDHU COVE there was still oil on the rocks on 7 April, though detergent had been used. The rocks on the north side of the bay showed a fairly good fauna, with limpets and anemones surviving in spite of a coating of oil, but the reefs on the south side were virtually denuded of animals. The oil fall and therefore the detergent treatment had probably been heavier on this side of the bay, while the direction of outflow of the tide and therefore of detergent drift may have affected this side more. The situation with regard to the organisms was relatively unchanged on 27 April. A similar state of affairs was seen at MULLION. It is thus seen that, although some areas were virtually stripped of living organisms, yet there are nearby regions which were relatively unaffected.

KYNANCE COVE suffered fairly heavy pollution during the first few days, and when examined on 20–22 April still showed much oil present on the rocks and in the sand (Plate 1C). Rocks at the centre and eastern end of

the cove had been heavily sprayed and further spraying was carried out well into May. On the large central reef all of the limpets and most of the mussels had been killed. Barnacles (mainly *Chthamalus stellatus*) showed nearly 100 per cent mortality and even many of the *Balanus perforatus* near low water were killed. The few snakelocks anemones (*Anemonia sulcata*) seen were in poor condition and none at all were seen on subsequent visits. Only a few beadlet anemones (*Actinia equina*) survived on this reef, some of them in the depths of pools. In some pools the encrusting calcareous algae were killed, in others they survived. The *Corallina* had turned white and later disintegrated, and other algae were also lost; thus the denuded pools offered no cover for small active forms such as young fish and prawns, which would usually hide in these pools as the tide recedes. Some of the *Pelvetia* and *Fucus vesiculosus* (form *evesiculosus*) were a rusty brown colour, with fronds disintegrating (cf. Plate 15 C). Some seem eventually to have died, others recovered. Not all these mortalities were observed until a later visit on 25 May.

In contrast to the heavily sprayed central and eastern reefs, on rocks to the north and west of the cove much of the flora and fauna remained untouched, though the rocks were still oily in places on the April visit. However, some 10 per cent of the mussels were gaping and probably dead.

Near St Agnes are two coves—Trevallis, which was heavily polluted and received intensive treatment, and Trevaunance, which had less oil, but where, owing to the private owner being averse to the use of detergent, the cove was at first not treated, and the common rocky fauna was reported to have survived well. Detergent was eventually used at Trevaunance, sparingly and with care, with little resulting damage to life. (For conditions later in the season see page 73)

Effects of oil without detergent

It had been amply demonstrated that treatment by detergent causes high mortality. It was therefore very interesting to try to observe what happened in the short term and in the long term if oil pollution were left untreated. In only a few sites was this possible because of the immense amount of detergent used even in remote places. However, in the first few days of pollution places were visited where oil was still untouched from the land.

The account by Richardson & O'Sullivan (1967) in which they compare the effects of pollution at Porthgwarra and Sennen before and after treatment was certainly borne out by our findings. The oil alone rarely seemed to have any ill effects during the first few days. At Cape Cornwall, however, moribund limpets under oil were observed; it is possible that they had been smothered very thickly with oil, or that the oil which

PLATE 13

A

B

PLATE 15

A

B

C

PLATE 16

A

B

PLATE 14

A

B

b

a

c

C

(*Facing p.* 65)

enveloped them contained detergent sprayed at sea and retained in more than usual quantity. The volatile and more poisonous fraction of detergent sprayed at sea would probably usually have evaporated away, and the observations already quoted are in keeping with the opinion that oil alone as it arrived on the shore was not harmful. This is not to say that crude oil, before it has lost its own volatile and acrid-smelling fractions, would not be toxic. A very thick layer would interfere with respiration and spoil normal food supplies for browsing animals. On sloping rock surfaces the oil deposit was usually not more than about 1 cm thick and soon became thinner. So far as limpets are concerned, they are unable to remain closed off from their environment for very long: the adductor muscles relax occasionally, thus lifting the shell very slightly. The viscous oil would not readily be drawn in under the edge of the shell by the ciliary currents in the mantle cavity, whereas detergent, alone or diluted in sea water, would creep in much more readily and be liable to kill the limpet. That this type of oil alone is not toxic to limpets is seen by the fact that they ingest it and pass it through their guts. This had already been noted with limpets from Hogus Reef, Marazion (p. 49), where the persistence of the full population into at least July is clear proof of the harmless nature of the oil to them. Evidence of limpets eating oil was seen also at Godrevy, Trevone (see Plate 9c) and elsewhere. That they could derive any food value from the oil seems unlikely.

The survival of mussels under heavy oil was seen at BOOBY'S BAY, in the first few days of pollution. On many occasions it was noted that oil remained among small mussel shells on rocks from which it had obviously been present more generally and had been washed off. In the absence of heavy detergent treatment these mussels had survived. At PORTREATH, in

---

PLATE 13

A, Whitesand Bay, Sennen, 28 March. Heavy oiling on boulders in the high-water region shortly after the initial deposition. Oily sand seen beyond.   **B**, Whitesand Bay, north of Sennen, 20 April. Oil-laden breakers in the foreground depositing oil on the shore to form characteristic wave marks. Note the contrast in the colour of the oily breaker with those behind. The mass of oil already treated at least once is being carried back on the shore by the rising tide.

PLATE 14

A, Sennen, 28 March. Viscous oil emulsion settled between boulders in the upper part of the shore.   **B**, Booby's Bay, Constantine, 29 March. Newly settled oil–emulsion dripping over rocks in the high-water region. Soldiers are seen in the background manhandling a detergent drum in readiness to start cleaning operations.   **C**, Oil-impregnated sand exposed along the upper shore at Sennen Cove on 23 August. A layer of sand impregnated with thick brown oil to a depth of about 15 cm is shown (*a*); this layer probably represents the beach level at the time of the oil deposition in late March. Subsequent to the deposition of oil, sand has accumulated on the upper shore covering the oiled sand and boulders (*b*). Water draining from this sand above the impermeable oil layer is removing oil and redepositing it below as a thin layer on the sand surface (*c*).

pools which had a film of oil, mussels were found alive and behaving normally, even though the mantle cavity contained globules of oil.

It was difficult to find areas on which oil had been left untreated. Up to 10 May no detergent appeared to have been used at GODREVY POINT itself. Most of the oil was in the form of a partly dried black surface layer about 2 mm thick coating the sides of gullies from extreme high water to mid-tide. Beneath the surface layer the oil was still brown and semi-liquid, and care had to be taken when walking on it. Below mid-tide the oil film was much thinner and light brown in colour. It appeared to be eroding away, the erosion being helped by feeding activities of the limpets, the tooth marks of which could be clearly seen in places (Plate 9 c).

As far as could be seen, the main deleterious effect of the oil on the fauna was physical rather than chemical. Where the layer was thick enough barnacles had been smothered, but more than 90 per cent of them had managed to clear an opening in the oil film. These were found to be in good condition when examined in the laboratory, and the gut did not appear to contain any oil. There were a few deaths among the *Balanus balanoides*, but *Chthamalus stellatus* seemed to be unaffected. Monterosso (1930) has shown that the latter is capable of surviving two months anaerobiosis under a film of petroleum jelly, and its survival in the present circumstances is not therefore surprising (Plate 19 B). Some mortality had occurred among the limpets on one vertical rock-face that had received heavy contamination by oil, but otherwise there were no obvious differences in the fauna and flora of oily rocks and adjacent uncontaminated surfaces.

It was known that at BEDRUTHAN, although much oil had entered the cove, relatively little had been stranded. Two patches had been photographed from the cliff top on 15 April. No detergent was used in the cove, which is difficult of access. It was interesting to see what had happened on these rocks after several months, and on 11 August they were examined from the shore. The patches of rocks which had been oiled were still recognizable, but the oil was much reduced, probably chiefly by sand abrasion, though the activities of limpets had undoubtedly played a part. On this very exposed shore they were practically the only browsers. A few *Littorina saxatilis* were also present. Rocks on which there was still a nearly complete cover of oil (with sand embedded in it) were seen to have no limpets (Plate 18 B). Rocks which were nearly clean had several limpets on them, there being markedly cleaner areas near the limpets and immediately round them (Plate 17 B). Most of the limpet shells had some traces of oil on them, but the contrast of still-oily limpets on clean rocks was not as marked here as it had been on Hogus, probably because of the greater importance of physical abrasion in this sandy exposed habitat.

These examples of cleansing of oil-polluted rocky shores without the use of detergent strongly support the observations by George (1961) in Milford Haven. It is a great pity that more areas were not left to be cleansed by natural agencies, not only because much time, trouble, money and shore life would have been saved, but also because such areas would have provided better 'control areas' to contrast with sites lethally sprayed and cleansed. Moderately polluted areas and remote and inaccessible stretches of shoreline could well have been left untreated, as in fact were the coves below precipitous cliffs on National Trust property between Navax Point (near Godrevy) and Portreath.

Between PORTHTOWAN and St Agnes Head lies another stretch of coast which received appreciable oil, but where detergent spraying was strictly localized and applied with care. This also lies on National Trust land. In Chapel Porth Cove the oil was reported as up to 2 inches thick on 29 March. There would have been rather less on adjacent rocks along the open stretches which were left unsprayed. In early September barnacles and limpets were surviving on the oil-blackened rocks near high water, but very little oil was left at lower levels. The fauna in the cove itself had suffered, as indicated by the absence of limpets, and the rocks were still a little oily. To the south of Chapel Porth the boundary between the unsprayed National Trust land and the detergent-treated shore adjacent to Porthtowan was clearly marked. In July and August the boundary was shown by a change from rocks having normal fauna and flora to unusually green rocks where *Enteromorpha* had developed prodigiously in the absence of browsers (see page 71).

The effects of very heavy oil-cover left untreated by detergent can perhaps better be studied on polluted parts of the Brittany coast (p. 168).

SUMMARY OF EFFECTS OF HEAVY DETERGENT TREATMENT

This summary is based on the numerous sites visited by several observers from Plymouth. Where spraying had taken place, the beaches or coves were usually identifiable at a distance by the numerous empty brightly coloured drums, or, if these had been removed, by patches of dead grass killed by spilt detergent, the smell of which persisted for months, quite apart from the smell persisting in the sands for at least three months. Evidence of deaths of animals in sandy shores is not readily obtained, the macrofauna always being very scarce in typical clean sands. On rocky shores the effect could be assessed over wide areas by simple inspection, so the following account applies chiefly to the latter.

Even if the shores had not been known previously, the ecologists visiting

them had a knowledge of what might reasonably be expected to be present. Where detergent had been used in any quantity the evidences of mortality could clearly be recognized and these signs were repeated all round the coast. The loss of limpets was at once obvious because of the many empty limpet seats, or 'scars', conspicuous in pools and detectable elsewhere (Plates 9A, 12B, 18A). Dead barnacle shells persisted for some time (Plate 19A), and, although it is usual to find a small number of dead and empty shells at times, a mortality of 50 per cent or more was clearly due to an unusual cause. Mussel shells gaped when dead. The rotting flesh did not take long to disappear, but, even when the shells had broken away, clumps of short straw-coloured byssus threads persisted for a few weeks, showing where mussels had died (Plate 15A). The absence of living winkles, top-shells and dog-whelks and the presence of many fresh shells of these and other species (Plate 15B) indicated the fate of such animals as have persistent hard parts. The absence of living crabs, shrimps, etc., and shore fishes might have been due in part to their quitting affected areas, but if killed their bodies would soon have been eaten by scavenging shore birds. Gulls were indeed seen feeding on dead limpets, even in water discoloured by detergent. In the early days of the disaster the presence of bleached weeds, particularly *Enteromorpha*, *Porphyra* and *Corallina*, and of discoloured wracks (fucoids), were sure signs of damage (Plates 15C, 18A). Later in the season an abnormal growth of the green weeds, developed in the absence of the normal browsing gastropods (Plate 16B), was seen on numerous polluted shores, but this evidence had to be examined carefully as it had in fact been an unusually good season in most localities for the growth of *Enteromorpha*. This greenness will probably not be a persistent feature, though the signs are that other algae will become unusually abundant before the browsing animals can recolonize the areas denuded of them (see Southward, 1964).

SUMMARY OF REASONS FOR SURVIVAL FROM DETERGENT POISONING

The occurrence of unharmed patches of shoreline with a full complement of species may be attributed to good fortune of geographical position. One side of a bay or even of a more localized rock formation often escaped both the oil and the subsequent effects of spraying. The drift of detergent from the upper part of a beach often affected one side of a cove and not the other because of the direction of tidal currents. The low-tide zone usually received no direct detergent treatment, and the mixtures which ran seawards while the tide was low were often channelled in gullies.

In moderately treated areas, differences of micro-habitat could be very important. The fauna on the undersurface of overhanging rocks quite often escaped, as did also some animals living in narrow crevices. In pools, the oil, detergent and fresh water all tended to stay on the surface, so that plants and animals in the depths of a pool stood a better chance of surviving. Animals, such as worms, burrowing in the depths of a fairly firm deposit (for example Marazion, area *D*) were probably below the level of influence of the poison.

The normal exigencies of shore life are such that only resistant species have been selected to live intertidally. Their adaptations often help, too, in their survival in poisonous water. The contrast between intertidal and sublittoral animals will later be apparent (Chapter 6). Animals which can close themselves off from their environment within resistant shells are at a great advantage, for example barnacles, mussels, and gastropods with well-fitting opercula. Limpets are at a disadvantage where poisonous water is involved, being dependent on maintaining a close adhesion to the rock during their period of exposure to the air. The beadlet anemone is normally able to survive long exposure to air, perhaps because of its mucoid cover: it was also a remarkably resistant animal to the unusual conditions of poisoned water. Some animals appear to be physiologically resistant; for example, the polychaete and oligochaete worms, despite their relatively unprotected bodies, were found to survive quite well. Such evidence as we possess suggests that nematodes also survived well, as would be expected from their known capacity to survive under difficult conditions.

This subject is discussed also on page 135 in relation to laboratory toxicity tests (Chapter 7) and with regard to sublittoral fauna (Chapter 6).

RECOVERY AND RECOLONIZATION

In most localities the existence of areas and pockets of surviving plants and animals gives hope of an eventual and perhaps an early recolonization and return to normal. How long this will be cannot be predicted, as natural balances have been upset even where there has not been complete destruction of life. These unharmed areas provide local sources for the spores of algae. Larvae of many shore animals often spend some weeks, if not months, in the plankton, in which case there is no question of immediate local recolonization. For mobile shore animals, such as fishes and crabs, and even for wandering gastropods, these local patches are important.

Where oil was left on rocks its fate was part of the recovery of the habitat. The very thin oily film which had often remained after cleansing was neither so persistent nor so continuous as to prevent some settlement of

alage and barnacles by the end of April. Brown oil films between tide-
marks on rocks and boulders were still occasionally present here and there
after several months. They had either been missed by detergent or secon-
darily redeposited. The oil underwent a gradual change, developing a
hardened skin, and the film decreased in thickness. Though dark on the
surface it remained, for a time, light-coloured and fluid below, and it often
had sand embedded in it. The decrease in quantity seemed to be due in
part to some erosion by wave action, assisted by sand abrasion, and perhaps
in part by evaporation, not to mention the action of browsing animals
where these had survived. In the splash zone there was also a decrease in the
blackened oil, so that by mid-summer it had become inconspicuous,
looking not unlike the black lichen *Verrucaria*. This oil, too, was weathering
away and the tiny winkles of this zone, *Littorina neritoides*, including (in
August) some recently settled (under 2 mm), were found living on and
among the black oil patches (see also page 72).

Flora

On the main part of the shore the algae will be considered first, because
in addition to their own intrinsic interest they form an essential part of
the habitat for the fauna, supplying cover and direct or indirect food
supply for many animals. Most of the fucoids were not completely killed,
commonly sprouting irregularly from distal parts. Thus in areas only
moderately affected no great overall change was apparent.

On a completely denuded reef at SENNEN, where there had been repeated
cleansings late into the summer, a very few fucoids were beginning to
sprout in lateral clusters of tiny blades from the stipe. *Ascophyllum* was in
a somewhat better condition, thus confirming a difference apparent elsewhere earlier in the season. Other reefs at Sennen, treated only lightly at
an early stage were in marked contrast to this barren reef; on them recovery
had brought the larger fucoid algae back to normal by mid-summer.

Where damage was more severe a distinction has to be made between
recovery, often from basal parts very closely applied to or actually in the
rock and recolonization by sporelings. An example taken from MAWGAN
PORTH is typical of rocks in the mid-tide zone at many other places. Rocks
which had lost their cover of *Porphyra* and *Enteromorpha* during April
by mid-May had occasional strap-shaped fronds of the former, up to 6 inches
long. These must have regenerated from basal parts of the *Porphyra* phase
or from the filamentous 'concocelis' phase on the rocks. By mid-August
these regenerated plants were common and well grown but darkly pig-
mented and reproductively immature. Besides the *Porphyra* there had
developed a very thick coating of *Enteromorpha*, from growth already started

by mid-May. This was one of the many places where there had been heavy loss of the browsing fauna with consequent rich development of the sporelings of green algae. A remarkable greenness was seen also, for example, at Porthleven, Cape Cornwall and Trevone. *Enteromorpha* and *Ulva* normally reproduce by frequent cyclical production of spores and they are prone to show very good growth in fine calm spells, so that reports of unusual greenness on the shores must be interpreted with care. Near Porthtowan a stretch of rocky coast which had been sprayed with detergent was markedly green in contrast to an adjacent unsprayed stretch with normal fauna and few green algae. As *Enteromorpha* dies soon after sporing and is soon reduced by storms the unusual greenness will not persist indefinitely. Sporeling fucoids (up to 3 cm) were becoming dominant in some affected areas (e.g. Trevone) by early September. The disturbance of balance, because of the lack of browsing fauna, may take a few years to redress. Elsewhere oil-spills have eliminated browsers and resulted in the abundant growth of the larger more persistent algae—for example, on the Californian coast (North, Neushul & Clendenning, 1965).

The recovery of algae in pools was very variable according to the degree of pollution. In mild cases there were early signs of recovery of calcareous encrusting algae, while it seems that *Corallina*, which grows relatively slowly, will take much longer to recover. Sporelings of *Ectocarpus* (a filamentous brown alga) were sometimes much in evidence, especially in the absence of browsers. The redevelopment of algae within tide-pools will be of importance to the life of the pools as a whole.

Fauna

There was evidence that some animals that suffered partial damage by detergent recovered in the field (gastropods on Hogus, p. 49, *Nucella*, p. 60). If there has been any cumulative poisoning to living animals it is not a phenomenon which could have been studied in the field in this present survey.

We have attempted to detect both the re-invasion of a denuded habitat by active adult animals and the recolonization by young stages—often, but not necessarily, of sedentary forms.

First there are the active swimmers, which may normally come and go with the tides. By 23 June some swimming crabs (*Portunus puber*) and shore fishes (*Blennius pholis*) had returned to Porthleven reef. Small fishes and active crustaceans need to have algal cover before they are likely to return. They were noticeably absent at Kynance from bare pools in July, while elsewhere (Trevone and Cape Cornwall) they were seen in August in pools previously barren and now surrounded by green algae. Animals

which by their own efforts could crawl a short distance might also be washed from undamaged areas on to previously denuded patches, where grazing forms would find a new growth of algae. The more resistant gastropods (*Nucella, Gibbula, Ocenebra, Monodonta* and *Littorina*) had become more frequent again as early as 23 June on the reef at Porthleven. Some juvenile winkles (*Littorina littorea*) were found in pools at Kynance on 23 July from which they were certainly absent on 20 May, but these species had by no means regained their former abundance. Both at Porthleven and Mawgan Porth, a few limpets had apparently wandered a short distance into unoccupied territory.

The recolonization by a new generation is dependent on the presence of a suitably oil-free and unoccupied area of substratum, and on the availability of the larvae. So far no newly settled limpets have been seen, but their main time for settlement is in the early months of the year and therefore no recolonization is expected before 1968. Other shore species often have larvae in the plankton in the spring and summer months, and of these species newly settled *Littorina saxatilis* and *L. neritoides* have been found. Many recently metamorphosed crabs were seen in 23 June at Porthleven, and larger ones at Sennen and Cape Cornwall in August.

Special attention has been given to the settlement of barnacle spat, since its abundance can be compared with what we know from previous years (Southward, 1967). It is clear that in general the larvae were not killed by the concentrations of detergent that they encountered at sea (see p. 93 and experiments on toxicity in Chapter 7). Moreover, it is probable that the planktonic larvae had either been liberated into the sea before pollution occurred, or else had come from adjacent unpolluted areas. Any differences from previous years could well be accounted for by difference in the direction of winds between the time of liberation of nauplii (first-stage larvae) and of settlement. In Cornwall, the settlement of *Balanus balanoides* occurs once a year in April and sometimes early in May. Along the south coast, in Mount's Bay in particular, including Porthleven, it settled more heavily than in previous years, occurring equally well in localities which had suffered pollution and those which had escaped. Along the north coast, settlement was not quite so heavy this year. The larvae require an oil-free surface on which to settle. Some were found on the seaward end of reefs which had been cleaned, for example, at Fistral Bay, Newquay, at Trevone, and at Enys Cove, near Pendeen. Where groups were seen occupying empty limpet seats it was a sure sign that they had settled in an area which had at some stage been affected by detergent. At Mawgan Porth they were found developing well on 14 May, being especially numerous on an uncontaminated area, whereas at Watergate none were

seen in suitable situations, but here cleaning had been delayed until nearly the end of April. For this species as a whole the pollution does not seem to have had any serious effect.

On 11 August a recent settlement of another species of barnacle, *Chthamalus stellatus*, was seen at Trevaunance in the mid-tide zone. Rocks at the same tidal level in the adjacent cove at Trevallis (where there had been heavy spraying) were smothered in green algae. In this part of the barnacles' tidal range its sites were therefore pre-occupied, but this may be only a very slight local effect as the species also settles abundantly higher on the shore later in the season.

SUMMARY AND CONCLUSIONS ON ROCKY SHORES

The lethal effects on the flora and fauna of heavy detergent treatment have been summarized above on page 67. Their seriousness for shore life is beyond dispute. Some of the reasons for escape or survival are set out on page 68. While in some places shore life escaped completely and serious damage was localized, yet the effects of detergent spread well beyond the extent of the original oil pollution. The second, man-applied pollutant was far more damaging than the accidental one. Recovery and recolonization is in progress but it may take some years before the normal balance of the population and the intricacies of the food chains are restored.

It has been seen that prolonged and repeated treatments do much harm even in a short space of time, and, while a region can recover gradually from one such onslaught, chronic oil pollution followed by repeated detergent treatment must do permanent damage. If large-scale and in-discriminate use of detergent were ever permitted as a standard method of treatment of oil-falls, shore life on one part of the coast after another could be disrupted and recovery would be far more prolonged and difficult. The risk of the loss of rare species and of species at the northern or southern limit of their geographical range would also be much greater.

We still do not know if there may be any long-term cumulative effects from the detergent persisting in the sands (see page 80).

Our survey shows that this type of *oil alone* has done little harm to shore life, and if the oil is left untouched there is clear evidence that browsing gastropods such as limpets and top-shells may remove and ingest oil without ill effects to themselves. The relative importance of the browsing fauna compared with physical agencies such as wave and sand abrasion, as well as evaporation, will depend on the locality and the tidal level. But left to themselves these physical and biological agencies have been able to effect the complete removal of moderate oil pollution in some places in three to

four months. Above the tide level aerial weathering is the chief agent on rocks. In other places the covering growth of salt-marsh plants (see page 89) has been remarkably effective in rendering the untreated oil innocuous and inconspicuous by the end of the summer.

The use of detergent should be considered only on shores of high recreational value, and then only after mechanical removal of as much oil as possible has been attempted (see page 90). It should be used in limited amounts and with care. The time of application relative to the tide and wind is of importance both for the efficacy of the detergent in making emulsions and for minimizing damage to shore life. The problem would of course be simplified if non-toxic detergents could be developed for general use. On other shores much greater advantage should be taken of natural cleansing.

SHORE SURVEYS—SANDY SHORES
AND ESTUARIES

SANDY SHORES

On sandy bays the oil arrived at first in drifts of generally half an inch up to a few inches thick in the high-water zone, often localized on one side of the beach. Some sank into the sand, making layers like sticky coffee grounds, and as such it was not difficult to scoop up (see page 170). This treatment was applied in a few places, the sand being dumped inland. For example, at MAWGAN PORTH some was put on marshy hinterland whence any eventual slow exudation would ultimately reach the sea, but where decomposition of the concentrated buried oil will be extremely slow. At TREVAUNANCE the owner of the mineral rights shovelled it up, putting it in an old mineshaft near the sea, where there is presumably no risk of contaminating springs and inland water supplies.

By far the more usual method was to push the oil back into the sea, by hosing or by using earth-moving equipment (Plate 4B). Deep furrows were made and the oil mixed with detergent was hosed down the shore. Alternatively, sand was shifted to near low water or into a stream where it was sprayed or otherwise mixed with detergent. This resulted in some oil being carried away to the sea as a dirty emulsion, especially if there was an off-shore wind, but it also spread unemulsified oil and detergent in various degrees of dilution and depth over the sands of the whole beach. In some places temporary quicksands were produced.

Wave action frequently buried untreated brown oily layers a few inches or even feet below the surface by depositing clean sand on top. There is a normal seasonal accumulation of sand at the top of beaches during the summer. This accumulation of clean sand helped greatly to give a 'cleansed' appearance to the shores. Offshore, water turbulence would occasionally mix oil and sand together so that the oil would be weighed down and has been seen resting on the bottom by divers (Plate 6C).

This movement of sand was clearly seen at SENNEN, where the whole of the boulder zone along the beach of Whitesand Bay had been exposed when the very heavy pollution of oil was deposited over the entire shore at the end of March (Plate 13A). By mid-summer sand had covered a great many of these boulders, but in July and August it was beginning to be eroded away and sticky oily layers were again appearing (Plate 14C).

This buried oil presented a considerable problem to the cleansers. Up to 24 April alone 164000 gallons of detergent had been used at Sennen and activities were continued at intervals during the early part of the summer as more oil drained out from among the boulders or otherwise reappeared.

The wisdom of the use of detergents on sandy beaches had been called in question, so, in addition to field observations, various laboratory experiments were set up to investigate the physical effects of oil and detergent in sands.

SOME PHYSICAL PROPERTIES OF SANDS CONTAINING OIL AND DETERGENT

Various experiments were devoted to the situation that might develop when oil, oil–detergent emulsions, and detergents themselves were in contact with sand.

The effect of oil alone on a sandy beach was examined by adding 5 ml Kuwait crude oil to the top of sand held in a glass column 3·75 cm in diameter. The sand was obtained from the shore at Duckpool (North Devon), an area free from the present oil pollution. The column was open at the top and the bottom, and was plugged with glass wool to prevent the sand flowing out. Tidal cycles were then simulated by mechanically raising and lowering the column in and out of sea water within a large measuring cylinder, the cycle time being 22 minutes. At the end of some 40 cycles, the oil had penetrated the top 3 cm of sand, but had not become further dispersed. Further cycling did not lead to more dispersion of the oil, and it seems likely that on the shore, in the absence of wave action, oil will not penetrate deep into sand and could therefore best be removed by mechanical means (see page 170; Plate 28 c). A similar experiment was set up, with the addition of 2 ml of BP 1002, and in this case the oil–detergent emulsion spread throughout the column in a short time. On beaches treated with detergent, oil has been found dispersed through a considerable depth of sand (see page 81).

The effect of detergent alone on a beach sand was also examined. Simple experiments were carried out in which weighed amounts of sand were shaken up with solutions of detergent in sea water, and then allowed to settle. A significant amount of the solvent was adsorbed on to sand, whereas less surfactant was adsorbed.

Other experiments, where detergent was added to watch-glasses with and without sand and the rate of evaporation followed by weighing at intervals (Fig. 13), showed that the rate of evaporation was less in the presence of sand, a result which again indicates adsorption by the sand grains.

It seemed probable from these results that retention of the solvent by adsorption on to the sand particles would prolong the period during which the sand would be toxic to organisms living in it. Moreover, the adsorbed solvent is not readily washed out from sand, as the following experiment shows: 100 g of sand were placed in a 500 ml flask and 1 ml of detergent added before the flask was filled with sea water and shaken; repeated washing of the sand by fresh sea water was carried out at intervals and, after

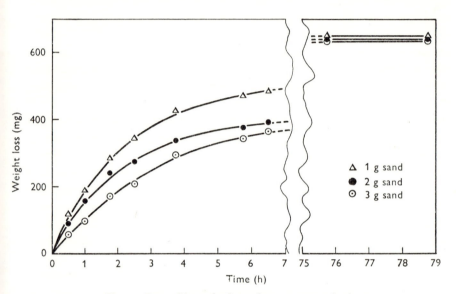

Fig. 13. Rate of loss of solvent from open watch-glasses
containing different weights of sand.

nine changes over seven days, 10 ppm of solvent was still present in the supernatant water while, after eleven changes, 4 ppm was present. Such experiments indicate that a number of tidal cycles and frequent flushing would be required to remove the solvent from beaches where the sand has been impregnated by detergent.

In another experiment sand 'castles' were made from uncontaminated sand soaked in detergent solutions of various strengths and all equally well drained. The experiment showed that the cohesiveness of the sand was markedly reduced by detergent even at 10 ppm concentration, presumably by alteration of the surface tension of the interstitial water. To this lack of cohesion may be added the flotation of oil-covered sand grains to which air is readily attached. Together they could give rise to enhanced mobility of sand under wave action. This is a fortunate feature in that more oil and detergent would be washed out of the sand than if the physical

properties had not been affected. Large movements of sand both up and down the shore have been noted, but whether or not these were abnormal is impossible to say without reliable long-term knowledge of the particular shores.

Some other field observations are especially relevant here. After the dispersal of detergent and oil through the sands quite unusual amounts of floating sand grains were noticed (similar to the little raft of sand grains seen in quiet corners soon after the turn of the tide) (see Plate 21 A). Scums of oil, air and sand were also very common. During the gales at the beginning of May the disturbance of sandy shores and also of the pebbles between Porthleven, Loe Bar and Gunwalloe was such as to cause a general strong smell of detergent all along that coast (see page 94 *et seq.*). These gales did much to cleanse the shores of both contaminants; they also redeposited oil on some previously unspoilt stretches of sand (Plate 3 B). Detergent was lost only slowly from the shore deposits: it was just detectable at about 30 cm depth near Loe Bar in the apparently clean pebbles near high water in mid-July; in a similar position in pebbly sand at Trevaunance (though only lightly treated) detergent could be smelt in August, and on more contaminated beaches it was easily traceable for more than three months after use. This smell of light aromatic oils almost certainly comes from the solvent fraction of the detergent; it is detectable somewhat below a half part per million and is readily distinguishable from any slight smell which the oil itself retained.

The production of temporary quicksands was seen on several beaches and was very pronounced at Porthmeor Beach, St Ives (see below). In Brittany quicksands were produced by oil alone.

The physical properties of sand deposits and some of their effects on the fauna have been studied by Chapman (1949). So far in our study only the purely physical effects of the use of detergent on sand have been considered, but there may be indirect biological effects in addition to the direct toxic effects on organisms living in the sand.

Oil content of sand

Rough estimates of the oil content of samples of oiled sand collected at various sites were made by weighing the sample, removing moisture by keeping at 37 °C until constant weight was attained, and removing oil by successive washing with solvents (petroleum ether and cyclohexanol). Very oily sand from Sennen contained 17 per cent by weight of water and 11 per cent by weight of oil; less heavily polluted sand from Porthmeor, St Ives, 8 per cent of water and 2–4 per cent of oil. Sand containing only 0·5 per cent oil was collected from an area where a quicksand had formed around

rocks at Porthmeor. In general, where there is more than 2 per cent of oil by weight of sand, the sand appears very heavily oiled, and oil can be squeezed out. The sand above high water at Sennen contained 0·6 per cent of oil (13 June). It felt oily and discoloured the hand, as did the sand collected earlier from Porthmeor. The lowest oil content was found in the surface layers at low water at Perranuthnoe (0·1 per cent). Oil present in similar small amounts in sands at low water was seen on digging pits in several beaches, where oil globules and an iridescent surface to the water-table were often observed. Similar traces of oil were present well into the autumn.

FURTHER OBSERVATIONS ON SANDY SHORES

An intensive study of a particular beach could have given useful information, but, because of shifting and mixing of sands under natural shore conditions, reliable quantitative work would have been difficult. It was not undertaken in the early stages of the survey partly because of lack of time and partly because of the distance of these shores from the Plymouth Laboratory. To make such a programme worth while some control over spraying activities would also have been desirable. As these factors were lacking, data collected from various beaches give an idea of the influence

Table 8. *Improvement in sand conditions at Mawgan Porth*

Date	Oil in sand (% oil/dry wt. sand)	Condition of water-table	Detergent
22 April	Brown layers and bands left after oily sand removed (on other shores 1–5 % oil in similar layers)	In area of quicksand and pools, oil floating on white detergent solution	Very strong smell in quicksand
14 May	Grey layers in above areas. Oily to touch. One sample 0·42 % oil	Iridescence in all parts, some blobs of oil on water collecting in pits. Quicksand area still 'soft'	General smell, chiefly subsurface
11 June	Vague greyness in above areas could be due to mixing or addition of sand. No widespread grey layer down to 30 cm	Iridescence general but less marked in pits. Quicksand area recovered	General, below surface, less marked than earlier
11 August	Grey layers at 20–40 cm over practically whole beach, surface in wide deep ripples, stability during calm spell. One sample 0·67 % oil	Ripple pools in firm sand with traces of oil on floating sand	Faint smell sub-surface, not confined to grey layer

Eurydice: several seen near low water 14 May; general over whole beach 11 August.

of treatment of sands over a period of time. MAWGAN PORTH is given as an example of the use of various methods and their effects on a moderately polluted sandy shore. For details see key to map (Fig. 14).

Observations at MAWGAN PORTH were confirmed by some at WATERGATE, which had received repeated oil-falls and prolonged treatment, spraying and bulldozing of sand to low water. There was relatively more oil and detergent in the water-table in May and June, and no grey sand was seen in subsurface layers in some thirty pits on 14 May. The impression was that recovery was taking place but not so rapidly as at Mawgan Porth. The temporary quicksands gradually recovered. At ST IVES, PORTHMEOR BEACH had been heavily coated with oil from top to bottom (Plate 8 B). From 28 March an enormous amount of detergent was used right through April into May, resulting in a temporary quicksand, and an immense amount of sand had been shifted mechanically. The beach was in full use by holiday-makers during the summer and only very slight traces of oil could be found by mid-August, but gales early in September disturbed much buried oil and the beach was again closed while oily sand was carted away. The very heavy pollution and prolonged cleaning at SENNEN and WHITESAND BAY has been mentioned above. In July and August there were widespread subsurface layers, often smelling distinctly of hydrogen sulphide, as well as brown oiliness in places, and oil was being redeposited on the surfaces of boulders, running out on to the sands (Plate 14C) or washing back as oily rims at wave edges. Despite this the beach was being used by holiday-makers.

At PERRANUTHNOE there is a long sandy stretch below low clay cliffs with flanking rocks. It was heavily polluted with oil: 34 700 gallons of detergent

---

PLATE 15

A, Trevone, 14 May. Byssal threads of mussels destroyed by direct spraying of detergent. Barnacles, *Chthamalus stellatus*, have also been killed. Some weeks later this rock was thickly covered with *Enteromorpha*, similar to the condition seen on Plate 16 B. **B**, Trevone, 23 April. A few days after spraying with detergent dead and dying dog-whelks (*Nucella lapillus*), top-shells (*Gibbula umbilicalis*) and limpets (*Patella*) found in a rock corner near the sewer outfall. **C**, Trevone, 23 April. Damaged algae after spraying with detergent. Species of *Fucus* have been reddened and subsequently little but the midribs of the fronds survived. The coralline weed *Corallina officinalis* and the encrusting coralline *Lithothamnion* sp. have been killed and bleached.

PLATE 16

A, Sewer rocks, Trevone, summer 1955. Normal appearance in the summer with brown fucoids, limpets and top-shells, etc. **B**, Sewer rocks, Trevone, 9 July 1967. Intensive growths of *Enteromorpha*, *Ulva* and some *Porphyra* (at highest levels) on the rocks and mussels, consequent upon destruction of most limpets and top-shells (see also Plate 15 B). A few limpets and top-shells survived and the occasional clean patches of rocks are mainly due to their grazing activities (see Plate 17 A). (N.B. These rocks were most probably not actually sprayed with detergent. They were affected by detergent washed over them from spraying nearby. This diluted detergent killed limpets and top-shells but the mussels survived.)

were used up to 18 April, and a further 2555 gallons before 10 May, but by 20 May spraying had stopped completely. On 28 April there was a widespread thin layer of oil on the sands and in the water-table. Between this visit and one on 10 May the strong south-west gales had carried away much sand from the top of the beach, exposing previously buried rocks. It is not known if this would have been a normal occurrence after such a gale at this time of year or if it might more probably be associated with abnormal mobility of the sands due to detergent treatment. Much torn weed was heaped up and also deeply mixed in the sand. Sand cores were taken and pits dug along a transect from high- to low-water marks to examine the fauna (see page 86 and Plate 21 B). The water-table contained floating oil at all levels down the beach; thin iridescent layers of oil often with thicker brown blobs collected in the pits. There were also discontinuous patches of thicker oil below clean sand. No grey sand layers were seen on 10 May a week after the gales, and there was no sulphide layer down to a depth of 60 cm. Near the base of the cliffs the sand was saturated with detergent. On later visits to Perranuthnoe grey oily layers were found, indicating that here as elsewhere decomposition of the oil was progressing. On 8 August the water-table still contained oil blobs on an iridescent layer, but the sulphide layer was now at around 40–50 cm below the surface. It seemed to be less oily, and less conspicuous except near low water.

BIOLOGICAL DEGRADATION

When the grey layers in the sandy shores were first found it was strongly suspected that biological degradation had been proceeding, both of the oil and of the detergent. Evidence for this important microbiological activity was sought and is given below.

Specialized bacteriological work was not carried out at Plymouth in the present survey as there was no member of the staff qualified to undertake such work. We are therefore grateful to experienced workers from other laboratories for their co-operation.

Dr W. Gunkel, of the Biologische Anstalt Helgoland, kindly permits us to give a brief account of his yet unpublished results. He collected twenty-three samples from different places on Cornish beaches towards the end of May and examined them at once for their bacterial content. In most sand samples there was obvious oil present and a smell of detergent (the exact amounts in the samples have not yet been determined). The numbers of aerobic oil-decomposing bacteria were determined using a dilution method without agar and with no carbon source other than the oil. Most oil-decomposing bacteria were found in samples which were heavily

6

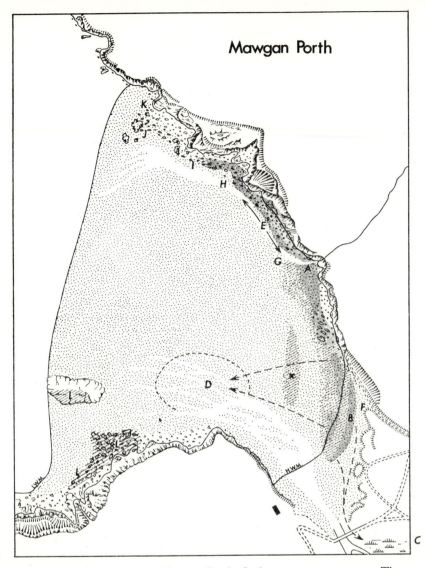

Fig. 14. Cleansing operations at Mawgan Porth. Scale 200 metres = 2·9 cm. The map shows low-tide conditions. High-water mark is above the boulder zone at the base of the cliffs except in the south-east part of the bay where there is sand rising into dunes. The main stream enters in the south-east corner and there is a side stream near *A*.

A Main area of contamination, $\frac{1}{2}$ inch of oil on rocks and boulders either side of *A*.
B, Patches of oil on sand $\frac{1}{2}$ inch thick, carted away and dumped on marshland in direction of *C*.
D, Sand pushed seawards, mixed with detergent and washed in stream.
E, Hosing with fresh water and detergent of main contaminated area. Boulders denuded of life, end of April.
F, Fires made of oil and drift-line weed (only a very small amount of oil destroyed).
G, Quicksand developed here, sand full of detergent and oil, April–May.
H, Milky stream at each low-tide period during hosing.
I to *J*, Boulders denuded by indirect detergent action. These, and those between *A* and *I* became very green with algae, June onwards.
K, Unspoilt 'control' area, not affected by detergent owing to direction of outflow.
L, Light spraying and some detergent damage.
x, Grey sand collected here, 14 May.

Sand over whole bay contained oil and detergent in May. Grey layer general in August after calm spell.

polluted or even consisted mainly of oil. The surprisingly high numbers found were much greater than ever experienced before elsewhere, the most numerous being over 400 million per 1 ml of wet sediment.

At Sennen: $1 \cdot 15 \times 10^8$, $6 \cdot 00 \times 10^6$, $2 \cdot 15 \times 10^6$, $4 \cdot 65 \times 10^6$;
Gunwalloe Fishing Cove: $3 \cdot 75 \times 10^7$, $4 \cdot 65 \times 10^6$, $9 \cdot 3 \times 10^6$;
Marazion Beach: $4 \cdot 65 \times 10^5$;
Pendeen: $8 \cdot 6 \times 10^6$;
Trenow Cove: $4 \cdot 2 \times 10^8$;
Prah Sands: $4 \cdot 65 \times 10^4$ (apparently no oil).

The so-called total number of other bacteria (heterotrophic-proteolitic types) was also determined. The average number of oil-decomposing bacteria ranged from about half to nearly three times as many as the other aerobes.

The only sample from which oil-decomposing bacteria were absent was of water from a rock pool which had much detergent in it. Subsequent experiments at Helgoland using bacteria from sea water (oil-free) showed that detergents, such as were commonly used against marine oil pollution, are capable of killing most oil-degrading bacteria even when used in fairly low concentration, e.g. 10 ppm. However, some bacteria survived even at 100 ppm and multiplied rapidly. At least some of them can use detergent as their only source of carbon. This must have happened on the shore except where detergent concentrations were very high as in the rock pool mentioned above. Because of the very high numbers of bacteria it is possible to assume that a fairly high rate of bio-degradation was taking place on the shores. In sand this process is not likely to be limited by the available nitrogen and phosphorus—as it may be in the sea (Gunkel, 1967). However, oxygen is likely to become a limiting factor. The presence of grey layers in the sand indicates an anaerobic condition subsequent to the activities of the main aerobic degraders. Aeration due to sand movement or water exchange would be important for the continuation of aerobic decomposition. Mechanical ploughing could help.

The development of grey layers was an abnormal and conspicuous feature of contaminated beaches from May and June onwards. The sands of a typical north Cornish beach are clean, i.e. with very low content of organic algal detritus, and, being generally devoid of silt, they are relatively mobile and well aerated. They do not normally develop grey sulphide layers because there is insufficient organic matter to provide sulphur for bacterial reduction. Such grey layers are characteristic of habitats rich in organic matter (Bruce, 1928).

In May sand-core samples and pits revealed only brown layers of buried

oil, no grey layers being present on several beaches (Watergate, Sennen, Perranuthnoe). Later digging revealed grey layers in places where there was known to have been oil. On microscopic examination of grey sand no algal fragments could be found, but there was a film of oil around the sand grains. The deposits were oily to the touch and smelt distinctly of the solvent fraction of the detergent. From some of the darker samples—for example, from Sennen—there was an unmistakable smell of hydrogen sulphide, and from near Sennen harbour the deposit was quite black. Table 9 shows percentages of oil in dry wt of sand (estimated on 14 August).

Table 9. *Oil in grey sands*

Sand from	Collected	Oil (%)	Appearance
Trevone	14 May	1·08	Dark grey when collected, surface became light, wet part became darker
Mawgan Porth	14 May	0·42	Grey when collected, became paler
Mawgan Porth	11 August	0·67	Grey when collected, became paler overnight
Watergate	14 May	13·91	Rich brown when collected, grey speckles developed on keeping

These samples were used in some simple bacteriological tests at Plymouth. Greying caused by bacteria (unidentified) working on oil anaerobically was confirmed under laboratory conditions. This seemed to show that destruction of oil may continue to some extent after oxygen is depleted. The intensity of greyness is of course not directly related to the oil content but rather to the lack of oxygen developed in relatively stable or deep sand. Under aerobic conditions black iron sulphide is decolorized by simple chemical oxidation. Grey sand samples from Sennen were found to contain only 20–50 ppm of sulphur in wet sand. This was kindly assessed at the Marine Sciences Laboratories, Menai Bridge, for us through Dr G. D. Floodgate to whom we are indebted for discussing the following matter. Kuwait oil contains about 2·5 per cent sulphur in various organic combinations, some of which are likely to be attacked by appropriate bacteria. This combined sulphur is mostly divalent so that its liberation as hydrogen sulphide is neither an oxidation nor a reduction. As a further source of hydrogen sulphide there could be anaerobic sulphate reduction by other bacteria which derive energy from oxidation of organic matter, in this instance paraffins and aromatic compounds in the oil or detergent. Any destruction of the oil in these two ways is, however, likely to be of less importance than the far more efficient aerobic processes whose existence on the shores was established by Dr Gunkel.

That the beaches are becoming cleaner is beyond doubt. How much of

this is due to bacterial degradation on the oil and how much to the washing out of oil from disturbed sands by wave action is unknown. The widespread presence of oiliness in the water-table and the smell of detergent suggests that a significant amount remained in the beaches below the normal level of disturbance in summer calm weather. During the autumn, until at least November, undegraded oil was still present on the very badly polluted beach at Sennen. Detergent treatment, by spreading oil thinly through a beach, may have aided bacterial oxidation of the oil.

The enrichment of the sand by oil and by all fractions of the detergent led to a great increase in the bacterial flora. This process may have been assisted by the poisoning of many or perhaps all of the smaller interstitial fauna which feed upon bacterial films on sand grains. As toxicity is lost and as oxygen becomes available again the way will be open for the re-entry of an interstitial fauna of microscopic predators.

FAUNA

In contrast with other shore environments mentioned in the previous chapter, it may be pointed out that these clean sandy beaches, being unstable and low in organic food content, do not support much animal life. The commonest detectable animal is a temporary inhabitant, the isopod crustacean *Eurydice pulchra* (about 3–6 mm long). When the tide is up it swims above the sand. As the water recedes it may be seen whizzing about in the ripple pools on sandy flats and leaving tracks before burying itself below the surface. Some specimens were seen on various visits to suitable sandy shores throughout the survey, but proper assessment of abundance would have been quite impracticable. It is, however, certain from the abundant tracks in pools at Mawgan Porth on 11 August that there was a numerous population over the whole of the lower part of the shore, in sand which still contained some oil and detergent, as indicated by discoloured floating sand grains and the faint smell. Toxicity tests on *Eurydice* (juveniles of *E. pulchra*) indicated that its survival after detergent treatment was above average for crustaceans (p. 134). All were killed at about 10 ppm after 24 hours exposure; at 5 ppm four out of five survived when transferred to clean sea water, while all survived at concentrations below this. In early days (23 April) a concentration of 4 ppm was found in sea water at either end of the bay on an incoming tide at least 24 hours after any spraying. Thus some individuals of the species would have been subjected to lethal conditions locally both in the sea water and in the sand, but some had survived (*Eurydice* were seen on 14 May near low water). The species had repopulated the whole beach by August. Although the sand still retained

some detergent during the summer the animals would have spent twice daily periods in almost uncontaminated water. Single large individuals of *Eurydice* spp. were also found at Sennen on 23 August despite markedly grey layers in the sand below them.

We have only scattered records of other members of the sparse macrofauna. Numerous sand eels were found dead at Sennen and Gunwalloe while detergent was being used. Empty carapaces of the small burrowing crab *Pirimela denticulata* were unusually common at Watergate soon after spraying as were also the empty tests of the heart-urchin, *Echinocardium cordatum*, and empty razor-shell (*Ensis siliqua*) and *Mactra* shells. All these animals are typical of clean sandy shores.

At Perranuthnoe, on 10 May, examination was made for fauna along a transect down a shore where there had been heavy treatment. Near high-water mark numerous small living oligochaetes and a few living nematodes were found where the water-table smelt strongly of detergent. At low-water mark similar fine sieving produced a live spionid worm. This suggests, as does evidence from Marazion and Porthleven and from toxicity tests, that worms can be fairly resistant to, as well as perhaps able to avoid, detergent damage. Animals under 1 mm in length, chiefly small crustaceans and nematodes, can be found by sieving many washings from normal sand through a fine net (see Delamare Deboutteville, 1960). At Perranuthnoe scarcely any fauna in this size-group was found, some dead foraminiferans and at one station live nematodes. At Sennen in August, similar washings produced a single nematode and three specimens of two species of *Eurydice* but no harpacticid copepods or cumaceans. It seems therefore that for the present at least there is a dearth of micro-fauna. At Sennen the production of hydrogen sulphide in subsurface layers might well be partly responsible.

THE INFLUENCE OF DETERGENT ON THE SETTLEMENT OF LARVAE AND THE RECOLONIZATION OF SANDS

Sabellaria is a polychaete worm whose behaviour at metamorphosis and settlement requirements had been previously investigated (D. P. Wilson, unpublished). It settles on rocky reefs protruding from sandy shores, building colonies of tubes of sand grains cemented together by an organic secretion. The crawling stage of the larva (about ½ mm long) settles readily in the presence of sand containing this cement. Here, therefore, was a clear-cut reaction on which the influence of detergent could be tested on a polychaete living associated with sand—the most suitable organism available at the time, though not a species typical of the sparse macro-fauna living in open sandy shores.

Ground-up and well-washed fragments of *Sabellaria* tubes were soaked in solutions of BP 1002 at 1000 ppm and 10 ppm for 90 minutes, and then thoroughly and repeatedly washed in clean sea water so that it could reasonably be expected that only adsorbed traces of detergent would remain. This sand was put into glass dishes of filtered sea water, and thirty crawling-stage larvae added to each as well as to a control dish with untreated sand made from *Sabellaria* tubes. When examined the next day the sand from the strongest solution was found to have had a marked detrimental effect, causing both delay in settlement and abnormalities of form and behaviour from which there was no recovery. Sand which had originally been treated with 10 ppm had caused but little difference in behaviour from that seen in the control dish (where there had been about 50 per cent settlement), healthy larvae continuing normal activity.

Five days later the sand which had originally been treated with 1000 ppm BP 1002 and had proved to be toxic was compared with newly prepared sand from *Sabellaria* tubes freshly treated, as before, with 1000 ppm and with 100 ppm followed by washing, and with an untreated control, using a fresh batch of larvae. The formerly toxic sand was found to have lost its poisonous effect, being similar to the new control, while the larvae in the other two dishes showed some abnormal effects, presumably from adsorbed detergent.

Hence it would seem that the major part of the toxicity of adsorbed detergent could be dissipated fairly rapidly (see page 145). However, in this case a very small amount of sand was lying in a shallow dish of sea water and conditions for loss of toxicity were therefore very different from those on the shore, where the bulk of the deposit retained traces of detergent for months. These experiments with *Sabellaria* have shown that even a trace of detergent present in or adsorbed on sand may well interfere with settlement and hinder recolonization perhaps for a year, because larvae of a species normally settle during a limited period of a month or two at a particular season of the year.

For microscopic animals whose habitat should be thought of in terms of individual sand grains, detergent both in the interstitial water and adsorbed on the grains is of much more significance than for larger animals which draw in water supplied from above or only burrow in the sand while the tide is out. The re-establishment of the full normal population involves all sizes of organisms: microscopic bacteria, protozoans (including ciliates and foraminiferans), and small crustaceans (including harpacticids and cumaceans), as well as those visible to the naked eye such as the isopod *Eurydice* and small worms, and finally the more obvious macro-fauna such as the occasional bivalve mollusc, burrowing crab and heart-urchin. Studies

on the recovery to normal physical and chemical conditions and on the recolonization of a sandy shore should include all these size-groups and work is in progress.

DRIFT LINE

The drift-line zone is evident on sandy shores where various small crustaceans and fly larvae play a useful part on the shore by acting as scavengers. Thick oil deposits at this level probably incapacitated and killed these small mobile creatures, but the sand hoppers (*Talitrus*) bury themselves in the sand, so some would probably be able to escape. Signs of damage from detergent were seen at Constantine where sand hoppers were found in a lethargic state at the base of the sand dunes soon after spraying. The same species was also found dead in quantity at Sennen.

It has already been reported that at Porthleven Reef *Ligia* and *Orchestia* were seen dead in quantities. They too are chiefly scavengers of the high-water zone.

In the Hayle Estuary the upper drift line was the only region badly affected by oil. It was left untouched by detergent and therefore formed an interesting 'control' area in which good recovery was observed in August (see below).

Very oily weed was sometimes thrown up. It is reported to have been collected and burnt at Mawgan Porth. This is a useful activity and practicable where quite small quantities of oil are concerned and dry weed is available, and providing burning is done well away from people as the fumes from partially burnt oil are considered noxious. It was not more widely attempted because of the trouble involved in the disposal of such a minute part of the oil stranded from the 'Torrey Canyon'.

ESTUARIES

The only estuaries to be polluted by oil were the small ones of the Gannel at Newquay and the Hayle Estuary. (Work on these is being carried out by the Nature Conservancy's Coastal Ecology Section.)

In the HAYLE ESTUARY oil was carried in on one of the very high spring tides, 28/29 March, and left as a blackening rim chiefly on walls and to some extent on saltings. Owing to a special request from the power station and to representations from biologically interested bodies no detergent was used within the estuary though there was lavish use on the sands at the mouth of the river. Traces of this were probably carried up some gullies where, on 30 March, some dead and moribund rag-worms (*Nereis diversicolor*) and some small crustaceans (*Corophium volutator*, and *Gam-*

marus spp.) were collected. When examined on 10 April the rich worm fauna in the sandy flats seemed unharmed. These worms form an important food supply for birds, one branch of this estuary being preserved as a bird reserve. Animals scavenging in the drift line would have encountered a blackened sticky mess of limited width and therefore perhaps not of much consequence to the area as a whole. When inspected in mid-August the black oily rim was still visible on the vertical walls around the estuary and harbour but aerial weathering had reduced it considerably. In places the orange lichen *Xanthoria* was growing through the oil (Plate 18c). The sticky deposit in the drift line had become innocuous and inconspicuous. Perennial salt-marsh plants, sea-plantain, beet, sea-aster and grasses had grown through it and annuals such as sea-milkwort and spurry—though delayed in developing—were spreading over the oil residue. The normal drift-line fauna of small jumping amphipods (*Orchestia*) and woodlice (*Oniscus*) were common under stones. These scavengers had perhaps not recovered by reproduction to a full normal abundance but they did not now seem incommoded by the texture of the oil residue. Where this had been washed by recent spring tides the crumbly oil and sand was being carried away. These are good examples of recovery by natural means in the absence of the use of any detergent.

At Hayle a boom was erected but no further oil approached the area after the first high-level pollution. The problem might have been much more serious had oil been driven in on a lower tide, or had detergent been used on these stable sandy flats in this enclosed area of water. It is here further stressed that it would be far worse than the effects seen on open sandy shores where, in contradistinction to estuarine conditions, instability of deposit and frequent complete changes of water have meant that oil and detergents are being washed or oxidized away (p. 84).

Oil pollution along the north coast did not extend quite as far as the Camel Estuary nor enter it. On the south coast the Helford Estuary (with oyster beds) was also beyond the limits of pollution. Great attention had been given to preparing a boom and suction-clearing apparatus should any oil arrive. Mopping up with straw was also considered. No detergent would have been used, not only because of its direct lethal effect on the oysters but because the spreading of a thin film of oil over the mud would have interfered with the surface micro-flora living there as well as affecting the infauna, thus seriously upsetting the food-chains for a long period, both for the oysters and for the life of the estuaries as a whole.

Local authorities should be aware of the disastrous results which the use of detergents in estuaries could produce since two Ministries have already stressed the dangers of applying detergents in estuaries and harbours (as

well as of applying neat detergent on rocks, etc.). Moreover, a general directive was issued that detergents should not be used in estuaries to combat 'Torrey Canyon' oil.

CONCLUSIONS ON THE USE OF DETERGENT AND OTHER METHODS OF TREATMENT OF SHORE AND ESTUARINE DEPOSITS

It may again be stressed that by good fortune the exposed conditions on the Cornish sandy shores were such as to lead to the ready flushing out of detergent and dispersed oil, providing the aeration necessary to aid bacterial decomposition without the production of much unpleasant smell of hydrogen sulphide. Had pollution occurred on more stable sheltered beaches and a similar enormous amount of detergent been used in dispersing the oil to depths (see experiment, page 76) the position would have been very different at the end of the summer. Likewise, if detergent had been used in estuaries and other enclosed waters, very long-term damage would have resulted.

We have seen evidence that oil left untouched as a black rim around Hayle Estuary at and above high tide has weathered and become innocuous in the absence of the use of detergent.

The removal of as much oil as possible *before* the use of detergent has proved worth while even on the few shores (Mawgan Porth and Trevaunance) where it was tried, and such procedure would have been an even more advisable method of dealing with oil on more stable sands or muds. On the shingle at Gunwalloe Fishing Cove it would have been possible to scrape up much oil from the surface if it had been attempted before detergent had been applied. The use of detergent caused the oil to sink very deeply into the beach so that very extensive mechanical shifting of shingle seawards was eventually necessary.

Some oil would be bound to remain, and, to aid its decomposition by bacteria, dispersal is desirable. This might well be accomplished much more cheaply by ploughing or otherwise mechanically mixing the oil and sand without the addition of detergents. There was no sandy beach on our Cornish coasts where detergents were not used which could be examined as a 'control'. Even if the cost of the procedure is ignored, the use of detergent is by no means the only and not necessarily the best way of treating oil on beaches. Other methods of treating sandy beaches were seen in Brittany (Chapter 9).

CHAPTER 6

OFFSHORE SPREAD AND TOXIC EFFECTS
OF DETERGENTS SPRAYED ON SHORES

The shore surveys reported in the previous chapter have shown that detergent cleansing of rocks and sands causes extensive damage to, and often total destruction of, the populations of intertidal plants and animals in and immediately adjacent to areas of intensive spraying. There was also evidence that, as a result of movements of toxic water, organisms living a quarter of a mile or more from the area of spraying may be damaged or killed.

It seemed important therefore to investigate in greater detail the patterns of flow of shore-originating polluted water under different conditions of wind and tide; the concentration and persistence of the component detergent fractions; and their possible effects on organisms living in the offshore waters. The investigations were undertaken during the month of April by teams working mainly in the Porthleven (South Cornwall) area. The teams, comprising shore-based parties and underwater divers, were aided by a ship survey (R.V. 'Sarsia' inshore stations A–M of 13 April, see Fig. 19) which included Agassiz-trawl sampling of the offshore benthic fauna. Laboratory measurements were made of the concentration of the component fractions of detergents present in the area of long-shore and offshore spread of the detergent-charged water.

Oil reached PORTHLEVEN on 25 March in considerable quantities during a period of spring tides and onshore winds so that in some places it was distributed well above the high-water mark. Very large amounts of detergent were subsequently used to combat the oil. According to the figure supplied by the local authority a total of 34 875 gallons were used between 25 March and 8 April at a rate of about 2500 gallons a day. Between 8 and 24 April another 10 800 gallons were used and the total issued for use in the area up to 9 May was given as 45 675 gallons. However, large amounts of detergents were used in the harbour on 26, 27 and 28 March, and these are not included in the daily totals provided by the local authority. In addition, the amounts of detergent used by the Army are not accurately known but usually seemed to equal or to exceed the local authority issue. A figure of 100 000 gallons would therefore be a reasonable estimate of the total amount of detergent used in the Porthleven area during the last week of March, April and the first week of May. It cannot, however, be considered

a final figure since detergent treatment was reported to be restarting on 10 May. The distribution of the detergent was probably as follows: 50000 gallons within the harbour itself, 35000 gallons on Porthleven Reef, to the west of the harbour, and 15000 gallons on the rocks and beach to the east.

In Porthleven Harbour spraying was carried out continuously from 25 March to 8 April and then again between 26 and 28 April. On the reef to the west and on the beach to the east of the harbour spraying began somewhat later, on 4 April. It was continued on the rocks of Porthleven Reef until 12 April and, after a break, was renewed for two days on 26 and 27 April. The maximum rate of application was 3000–4000 gallons a day, though these rates were not maintained throughout the period of cleansing. A similar intensity of treatment was for a time in operation at Halsfarren Cove, three miles south east of Porthleven, and some spraying was also reported at intermediate points (Figs. 15, 16, 17).

Shore surveys were made of the Porthleven Reef on 30 March before the cleansing operations on the reef had started and on subsequent occasions during the period of the detergent treatment (see page 57). Offshore dives, mainly off the Porthleven Reef and the harbour entrance, were undertaken during this period on 5, 7, 11, 13, 19 and 28 April, and water samples for chemical and biological assay were collected on 5, 7, 11, 13 and 19 April.

Observations relevant to the matters discussed in this chapter were also made on 23 April at the south end of Watergate Bay (North Cornwall).

The formation and behaviour of mixed oil and detergent patches

When oily shores are treated with detergent, clearly visible patches of detergent and oil emulsions develop in the sea. These patches are poisonous, for the solvents used in the detergents are toxic to marine organisms (Chapter 7). The development by the Laboratory, within a short time of the 'Torrey Canyon' stranding, of methods of biological assay for detergent toxicity thus enabled us to make quantitative determinations of the toxicity levels of the detergent/oil-polluted water. In this section, which deals with the formation, behaviour, and persistence of these areas of polluted water under different conditions of wind and tide, an important part of the observations was therefore to determine how far, both horizontally and vertically, the toxicity of the detergents would spread from treated shores.

In most of the cases to be described the detergent was sprayed after low water so that the oil could be emulsified as the tide rose and dispersed as the tide ebbed. Frequently fire hoses (Plates 5A, B, 10A), spraying either sea or fresh water, were used to help in emulsifying and dispersing the oil, particularly where it was near high-water mark. Milkiness due to

detergent usually started to develop in the sea shortly before high water and grew rapidly as the tide ebbed (Plate 23 A, B). Milky areas will be referred to as detergent patches. The oil in these patches, however, was often of three kinds: emulsified oil which stays in suspension (Plate 2), at least for some time; incompletely emulsified oil which soon floats to the surface; and oil which has been released from the shore by the cleansing operation but which is not emulsified (Plates 1 A, B, C, 5 A, B).

Methods

With the detergent patches concentrations of detergent (in ppm BP 1002) were measured by biological assay (p. 141), shrimps being used to cover the range 2–100 ppm and larvae of the barnacle *Elminius* to check concentrations over the range 2–10 ppm. A simple method for detecting kerosene (Gerade & Skiba, 1960) was also used successfully to check samples having low toxicities (p. 20). About 0·5 ppm of BP 1002 could be detected by this method, though interference was sometimes encountered from oil in the water. In many cases duplicate samples were analysed by British Petroleum Limited and by the Government Analyst, who used Method 1 (p. 19), which measured the concentration of the surfactant fraction rather than the more volatile toxic component.

Samples of water were collected in 200 ml glass clip-top bottles both from the shore and by the Laboratory's divers. At stations farther from the coast the samples were collected from R.V. 'Sarsia'.

By taking colour photographs of the detergent patches while surface samples were being collected it was possible to record the appearance of different concentrations of detergent. For instance, in calm water 25 ppm or greater usually gave the sea a milky appearance and 5 ppm was distinctly visible. The formation and development of detergent patches was therefore recorded on colour transparencies and these were sometimes used to estimate concentrations of detergent in inaccessible parts of patches.

Observations

The development and subsequent behaviour of these detergent patches is largely determined either directly, or indirectly, by the strength and direction of the wind. In presenting these results therefore the localities studied are grouped according to the wind direction relative to the shore.

The effect of cross-winds was observed at two places—Porthleven and Halsfarren Cove.

At PORTHLEVEN on 5 April (Fig. 15) an estimated 3600 gallons of detergent were used on a neap tide with a moderately fresh westerly wind blowing. There was brown oil on the rocks at either side of the harbour

entrance and on the sands for 1–200 metres east of the pier. The surface
of the outer harbour was also covered with brown oil and this surrounded
a large patch of black oil. All three regions were treated with detergent.

Even before high water a detergent patch which developed to the east of
the pier was extending eastwards along the shore, while later at about high
water separate patches from different treated areas were fusing together

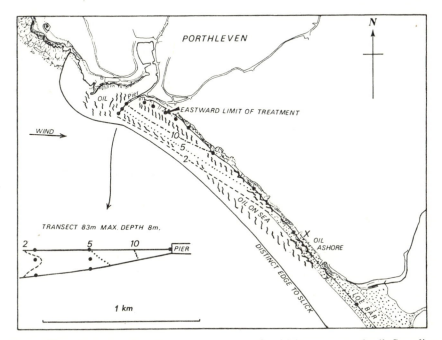

Fig. 15. The situation at Porthleven about 1 hour after high water on 5 April. Sampling
stations along the shore and in the transect are shown by closed circles. Numbers show the
concentrations of detergent in the water in ppm BP 1002. The scale refers to map, not
transect.

near the end of the pier. A transect through this region is given in Fig. 15
and shows that the toxicity of the patch extended through the water column
from top to bottom. The situation about 1 hour after high water is summarized in the same figure and also in Plate 22A. It will be seen that toxic
concentrations of the detergent were moving rapidly south-eastwards along
the shore and had already spread 1 kilometre from the nearest treated area.
In addition, a layer of thin oil, or some constituent of the detergent, extended along the surface of the sea close to the shore for about 4 kilometres
to the end of the bay. The movement of this detergent patch was mainly
due to the strong wind, although it was probably assisted by inshore
current. It was also noted that oil released from the rocks and harbour, but

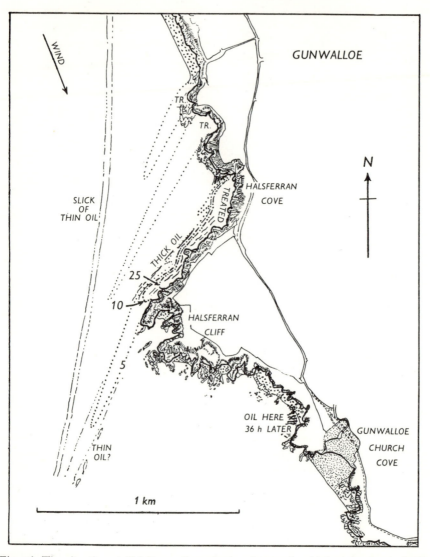

Fig. 16. The situation at Halsferran Cove about 2 hours after high water on 11 April. Numbers show the concentrations of detergent in the water in ppm BP 1002. Outlines of detergent patches from two other coves correspond roughly to concentrations of 5 ppm BP 1002. *TR.*, treated beaches.

not emulsified, was being blown rapidly along the surface of the sea and was already coming ashore on the sands to the east of the harbour (Fig. 15; Plate 22A).

At HALSFERRAN COVE on 11 April (Fig. 16) about 4000 gallons of detergent were used on a spring tide in the cove itself and more was used in the

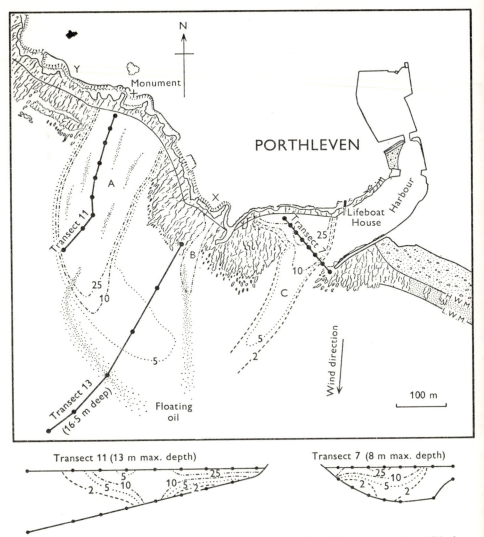

Fig. 17. Detergent patches at Porthleven about 2 hours after high water on 7 April. Black circles show the positions of sampling stations in a transect which was made on 7 April and also in transects made on 11 and 13 April. Results of transects made on 7 and 11 April are shown below the map. Numbers show the concentrations of detergent in the water in ppm BP 1002.

two coves to the north. The winds were light to moderate north-north-west. Brown oil up to 1 cm thick completely covered the intertidal and spray zones from Halsferran Cove to the base of Halsferran Cliff.

Under the influence of the wind, and probably also of the tidal current, the detergent patch which originated in Halsferran Cove moved along the

PLATE 17

A

B

PLATE 18

A

B

C

(*Facing p.* 97)

coast close to the base of the cliffs. It had a very distinct seaward edge. Beneath the cliffs 2 hours after high water (Fig. 16) the patch was mainly concentrated in the intertidal zone and, although there was very little wave action, it would almost certainly be toxic from top to bottom. The patch then continued out to sea and was more than 1 kilometre long, with large amounts of brown oil which had been released from Halsferran Cove floating in it and nearby. This patch, or possibly one developed subsequently on 12 April, may well have given rise to the fresh oil which appeared farther down the coast on 13 April (Fig. 16). This figure also shows how patches extending from other coves ran parallel to the patch from Halsferran Cove, and the position of a narrow band of thin oil (which was seen on a number of occasions) is also shown.

These two examples clearly demonstrate that, when winds are blowing along the shore, oil and toxic levels of detergent may be carried for some considerable distance parallel to the shore to pollute adjacent areas of coast.

The effect of offshore winds was studied at Porthleven on two occasions.

On 7 April oil was still present on the rocks and in the gullies to the west of the harbour and about 3000–4000 gallons of detergent were used, the largest detergent patch (A in Fig. 17) representing perhaps half of this. A similar amount of detergent was used when a detergent patch almost identical with patch A was produced on 11 April.

On 7 April three distinct creamy white detergent patches developed, from west to east (A, B and C). About 1½ hours before high water, patch B was well developed, and oil released from the shore and floating on the surface was being blown seawards (Plate 23 A). A photograph of patch A (Plate 23 B) also shows how, half an hour before high water, this released oil was being separated from the detergent patch by the wind. It also seems likely that,

---

PLATE 17

A, Detergent-affected rock near sewer outfall, Trevone, 9 July. A surviving limpet and a top-shell (*Monodonta lineata*) keep a small area of rock free from algal growth. The barnacles and the mussels are alive. B, Bedruthan Steps, 10 August. Two limpets on an oil-covered rock. The limpets have cleaned away oil from the region immediately around them. The oil is seen to be impregnated with sand from the surrounding beach.

PLATE 18

A, Kynance Cove, 20 April. Mid-tide pool on reef which had been heavily sprayed with detergent. The pool is lined with encrusting coralline algae, normally pink, which have become bleached, as have the tufted corallines, several small clumps of which may be seen. Both of these algae showed heavy mortalities on this reef. Oval patches where limpets had been living show up clearly. At this time these pools contained the bodies of limpets which had separated both from their shells and from the rocks, and one such body may be just seen below a tuft of coralline toward the lower right-hand side of the picture. B, Bedruthan Steps, 7 August. Oil impregnated with sand flaking off rocks at high-water mark as a result of natural weathering processes. C, Hayle Estuary, 23 August. Oily sea-wall, which had not been treated with detergent, showing distinct tide-line. The orange lichen *Xanthoria* is seen still living beneath a covering of oil.

in addition to the oil released from the beach, some oil was separating from the emulsion. Thus, close inshore, where there was a little wave action, there was no floating oil and the detergent patch was the colour of milk chocolate, yet at about 20 m offshore floating oil was present. Under the offshore wind the sea was calm and conditions were not ideal for creating or maintaining detergent–oil emulsions.

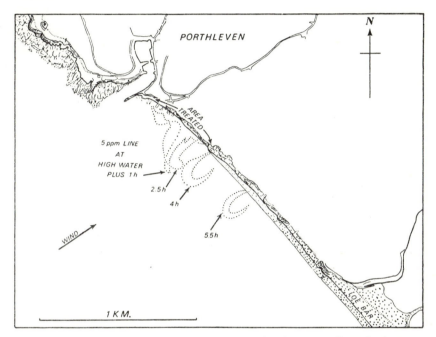

Fig. 18. Changes in the shape and position of a detergent–oil patch after high water at Porthleven on 19 April.

The situation at the surface of the sea 2 hours after high water on 7 April is summarized in Fig. 17. Each of the detergent patches had elongated, and all had very distinct edges, except at the seaward margin where some dilution and mixing seemed to occur. The largest patch (A) gradually turned eastwards and moved towards patch B, which was particularly well defined and was starting to constrict from the shore. Patches B and C did not turn eastwards because the wind blowing out through the harbour entrance was perhaps sufficient to counteract the eastward tendency of the tidal current.

A transect of patch C was made on 7 April, and on 11 April a transect was made of a patch which was almost identical with patch A as shown in Plate 23 B. Results from both transects are illustrated in Fig. 17. Both show

that most of the detergent–oil emulsion floats to the surface from the treated rocks. However, they also show that in the middle of each patch the toxic levels of detergent reached the bottom well seaward of the inter-tidal zone.

The effect of onshore winds was studied at two places—Porthleven Sands and Watergate Bay.

PORTHLEVEN SANDS were visited on 19 April on a neap tide with a light to moderate south-westerly wind blowing (Fig. 18). Detergent was being applied by pouring it on to the very coarse sand containing the oil and this was then covered by bulldozing on to it more oily sand. During this opera-tion only about 300 gallons of detergent were used. Separate small deter-gent patches formed along the beach and later fused into larger patches which then moved out as the tide started to ebb. About $2\frac{1}{2}$ hours after high water these had fused into a single patch having a very distinct eastward edge and a tendency to curve to the east. After 4 hours the patch had moved eastward and had almost separated from the shore. It had also developed a hooked shape—possibly because the end of the patch near the surface was being blown back on to the shore. The patch was still clearly visible about 5 hours after high water and had started to move down the coast more rapidly. This movement was probably caused by the tidal current, although the wind was in a direction which might have slightly assisted the movement. In its later stages the patch was only attached to the shore by a toxic strip about 10 metres wide and seemed to be shrinking in size. However, it still retained a distinct shape and the mixing was not as rapid as might have been expected with an onshore wind.

The southern end of WATERGATE BAY (near Newquay) was studied during a spring tide on 23 April. The winds were light north-westerly. Here oil was present on the rocks and in the sand at the bottom of the high cliffs. About 400 metres of shore were treated with what was reputed to be some 4000 gallons of detergent.

At high water, when the sea was breaking against the base of the cliffs, the detergent patch started to move seawards as a discrete finger which was much narrower than the treated area. About $1\frac{1}{2}$ hours after high water the shape of the patch was similar to that shown in Fig. 19, although the advancing tip had not yet reached Trevelgue Head. Both changes in the direction of movement of the patch probably resulted from the effect of the current sweeping through the bay. The detergent patch was coloured brown, and obviously contained a large amount of oil. As the sea is very shallow here the toxic effects would almost certainly penetrate to the bottom. About 3 hours after high water the patch was no longer visible at its seaward end, although this may have been due to its dark colour and

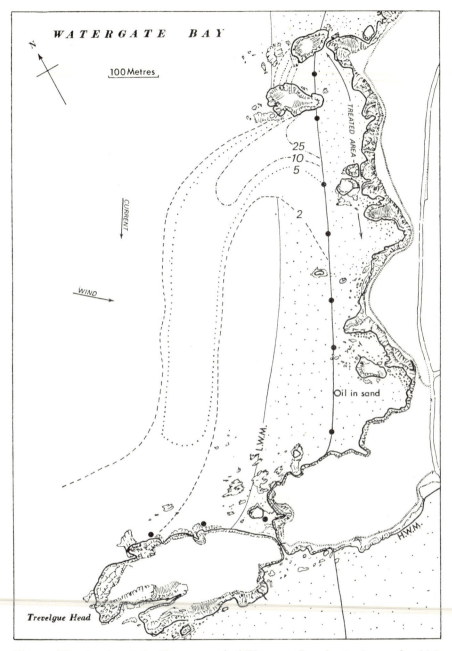

Fig. 19. The situation at the Newquay end of Watergate Bay about 3 hours after high water on 23 April. Black circles show the positions of sampling stations and numbers show the concentrations of detergent in the water in ppm BP 1002.

fading daylight. A series of samples was taken along the coastline as the tide ebbed. From the smell of detergent and the collecting of a toxic sample (greater than 2 ppm) near Trevelgue Head, it is almost certain that the patch was in the position illustrated in Fig. 19; but it was probably becoming progressively less easily defined as a result of mixing, evaporation and its movement out to sea. The figure clearly shows that the landward end of the patch did not spread farther along the shore but remained concentrated in the treated region. It seems almost certain that this part of the detergent patch would return on the following tide and that, in addition, detergent and oil were being left behind in the sand as the tide ebbed.

The persistence of detergent patches

Except where strong cross-winds were encountered (Fig. 15), the detergent patches have a fairly definite shape during their early history. It is difficult to discover just how long this shape lasts and what the ultimate fate of the patch is. Evidence from Figs. 17 and 18 shows that a constriction can eventually develop between a patch and the shore so that it could become detached and drift away. These patches are not visibly persistent, for no detergent patch was ever obvious on the day following its production. Presumably this is due to a combination of evaporation of the detergent and lateral and vertical mixing. However, mixing appears to be relatively slow, particularly in calm conditions, and individual patches may retain identity even when they are no longer visible.

There is some evidence to support this hypothesis. For instance, at low water on 7 April at Porthleven a transect was made by a team of divers with Dr Lythgoe with stations 120, 300 and 600 metres distant from the end of the pier. On the previous day the wind had been blowing off the shore and some detergent patches would have been expected to move through the region of this transect. Analyses by the Government Chemist of surfactant concentration gave equivalent total detergent concentrations at these stations of between 0·08 and 0·48 ppm. The results are summarized in Table 10 and show that the amount of detergent in the water decreases with depth. Concentrations of detergent of this order would probably not, however, be toxic to most species.

Further evidence for the persistence of an offshore detergent patch was obtained, again from Porthleven, on 13 April, on this occasion by a team of M.B.A. scientists. At low water a transect was taken from the reef to the west of the harbour along the line shown as transect 13 in Fig. 17. This extended 460 m from the tide line of low-water springs over a gently sloping rocky shelf to a sandy plane at approximately 16 metres depth. Toxicity equivalent to 2 ppm of BP 1002 detergent was detected along the

Table 10. *Concentrations of detergent (ppm) from a transect taken opposite Porthleven pier on 7 April*

(Concentrations were found by multiplying analyses for non-ionic surfactant by eight. At the most distant station the depth was about 20 m.)

Distance from pier (m) ...	120	300	600
Surface	0·4	0·48	0·4
1 m	0·24	0·40	0·32
½ depth	0·24	0·24	0·24
Bottom	0·16	0·16	0·08

shore, and at the surface stations 100, 300 and 400 metres, as well as at bottom stations at 300 and 460 metres distant from the shore. No detergent was used on 13 April. Detergent had, however, been used on 12 April, when it probably resulted in a detergent patch like A in Fig. 17, which passes through the region of this transect.

These two examples show that detergent patches may persist for at least 24 hours offshore. This may also be true for inshore patches. Thus, at high water at Mawgan Porth on 23 April the water at each end of the bay was toxic to the extent of about 4 ppm of detergent. This was at least 24 hours after the treatment of the sands with detergent. The detergent was probably still being leached from the treated sand and the onshore winds had probably prevented any seaward movement.

Evidence for a longer-term persistence of offshore patches is provided by R.V. 'Sarsia's' cruise III. On 13 April (p. 32) none of the samples collected off Marazion or Porthleven (Fig. 7) was toxic to shrimps. This suggests that there was very little detergent solvent in these regions and this was confirmed by using the test for it (p. 20). However, considerable amounts of the surfactant were found in some samples by the analysts of British Petroleum Limited. This was particularly evident in samples from the Marazion area (Table 4; Fig. 7). About 2 kilometres off Porthleven surfactant was only detectable at the surface, except in one instance where the equivalent of 24 ppm of detergent were found at the bottom. The only explanation which can be offered for this particular result is that it might be expected if the detergent moves in fairly discrete patches, as was suggested above.

Conclusions

From such a limited number of observations it would be dangerous to make any broad generalizations about the behaviour of detergent patches. As many different situations were examined as possible but in no cases,

except that of 5 April at Porthleven, were strong winds encountered. For example, it is not certain what the effect of a directly onshore gale-force wind would be.

What is certain is that toxic concentrations of detergent are not simply confined to the section of shore which is treated, or to the surface of the sea where the detergent patches are most obvious. Most of the evidence shows that detergent patches do not disperse very rapidly. Consequently, patches of water with some toxicity extending to the bottom can influence distant areas of the sea-bed or shore, under the influence of the wind and tidal currents. With cross-winds, toxic concentrations of detergent can be spread along the shore, probably for several kilometres. With offshore winds, distinct patches with some toxicity extending to the bottom move seawards and influence regions below the intertidal zone.

Residual toxicity can remain on shores, particularly in surface sand, for more than 24 hours. It has also been detected in offshore bottom samples 24 hours after treatment of the intertidal zone. Furthermore, when buried under fresh sand it can persist for many weeks.

Sometimes quite high concentrations of the non-volatile emulsifying agent (surfactant) from the detergent have been detected up to 2 kilometres offshore in the Porthleven and Mount's Bay areas. Emulsifying agents are not very toxic over short periods of time (p. 145) but we have no knowledge of their possible long-term effects.

It has been found that emulsification of oil is often incomplete and it further appears that, particularly in calm conditions, some oil separates from the emulsion—as it does in laboratory tests (p. 21). Whereas a detergent patch is influenced by tidal currents as well as the wind, the floating oil is moved solely under the influence of the wind (Chapter 8). As a result, floating oil can separate from the detergent patch and may then come ashore on another section of the coast (as seen in Plate 6A, B).

TOXICITY STUDIES ON OFFSHORE ORGANISMS

Our study of the initiation and subsequent fate of mixed oil and detergent patches has shown that relatively high concentrations of detergent can occur, not only at the point of application, but also some distance away. The question now arises: what will be the biological effects of the travelling patches of detergent? To examine this point further, toxicity experiments with representative offshore species were made in the laboratory (see Chapter 7, p. 137) in order to complement the offshore surveys made by various teams of divers which are reported later in this chapter.

BIOLOGICAL EFFECTS OF
OFFSHORE DETERGENT PATCHES

One of the most significant results from our studies of the transport of detergent patches was to show that these patches may persist as discrete bodies of toxic water for at least 24 hours and may, under appropriate conditions of wind and sea, extend well offshore. Moreover, as will be shown below and on page 137, their detergent concentrations are toxic to some at least of the sublittoral species of plants and animals.

It was important therefore to get direct evidence of mortalities in the sublittoral flora and fauna by means of underwater surveys. It was decided to examine one underwater region (Porthleven) in considerable detail, and to supplement this study with more generalized surveys elsewhere.

To some extent the areas chosen were determined by the weather, since diving in shallow sublittoral regions cannot be usefully carried on in rough seas when visibility is greatly reduced and turbulence prevents easy manipulation of equipment. In addition to the Porthleven surveys dives were carried out off Gunwalloe, Loe Bar, Marazion, Sennen Cove and Porthmeor Beach, St Ives (for maps see Figs. 8 and 9).

Offshore surveys at Porthleven

During April a long period of northerly (offshore) winds was favourable for diving in the Porthleven area. A diary of the Porthleven dives with notes on the condition of some of the plants and animals noted during the dives is given in Table 11. (For dates of spraying here see p. 57.)

The most detailed observations were made during the dives (nos. 5–10 in the Table) of 13 April along a transect extending from the seaward edge of the Porthleven reef to a station 460 metres from the shore and at a depth of 8·5 fathoms (16·5 metres). Fig. 21 (p. 109) shows a diagram of the distribution of the affected and unaffected animals and algae off

---

PLATE 19

A, Porthleven Reef, 8 May. Barnacles (*Chthamalus stellatus*) at high-water mark almost all killed by detergent-cleansing operations.   **B**, Godrevy Point, 10 May. Barnacles (*Chthamalus stellatus*) at high-water mark almost completely covered by oil, but untouched by cleansing operations, still alive after six weeks exposure to pollution.

PLATE 20

A, Marazion, 28 March. Razor-shell (*Ensis siliqua*) showing effect of detergent, which has caused it to come up out of the sand. Low water of spring tides on sand beach west of the Causeway.   **B**, Underwater photograph taken about 75 metres off Porthleven Sands at about 10 metres depth, 18 May. Dead shells of *Ensis siliqua*, *Mactra corallina* and one valve of *Lutraria* sp., together with fragments of tests of *Echinocardium cordatum*, which had accumulated in a gully between rocks.

PLATE 19

A

B

(*Facing p.* 104)

PLATE 20

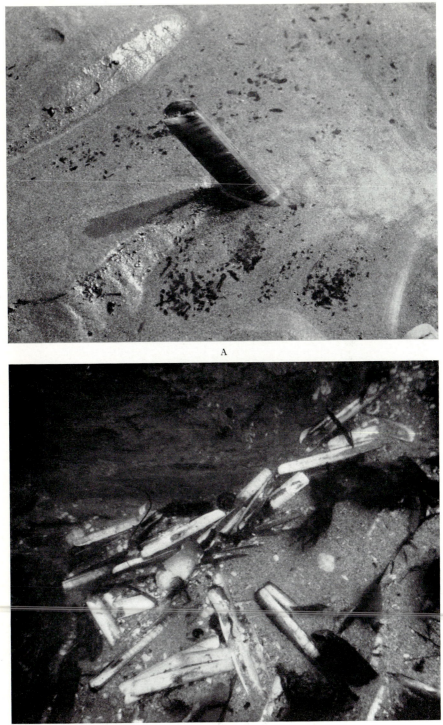

A

B

PLATE 21

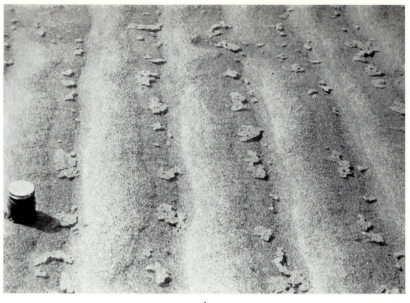

A

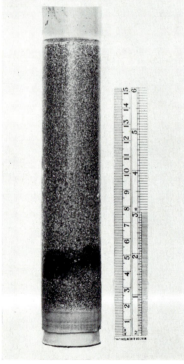

B

PLATE 22

A

B

Porthleven reef. The information is largely based on that gained from dives 5–10.

Dive no. 10 was made just below the low-water mark of spring tides at a station slightly to the north-west of the transect line.

Although the laminarians of wave-exposed shores, *Alaria esculenta* and *Laminaria hyperborea*, appeared healthy, the epiphytic red algae on the stipes of the latter, and also those on *Furcellaria* and *Cladostephus*, were either dead or had been seriously damaged. The only living species found as epiphytes were *Cryptopleura ramosa*, *Spermothamnium repens* and parts of some tufts of *Jania rubens*. Species which had been killed included the red algae *Apoglossum ruscifolium*, *Hypoglossum woodwardii*, *Polysiphonia* sp., *Ceramium rubrum*, *Plocamium vulgare*, *Delesseria sanguinea* and *Hetero-siphonia plumosa*, and the brown alga *Dictyota dichotoma*. Species brought up from the sublittoral fringe zone in healthy condition included *Laurencia pinnatifida*, *Gigartina pistillata* and *Phyllophora crispa*.

In slightly deeper water (dive no. 9, 2 fathoms) the plants were by contrast not visibly affected. As with the plants, animals in the first few feet below low-water mark suffered severely. During a dive on 11 April in the same area many dead decapods including crabs (*Portunus*, *Cancer*) and squat-lobsters (*Galathea*), a lobster (*Homarus*), and a few prawns (*Palaemon*) were found. Numerous dead specimens of the starfish *Marthasterias* were also collected; and others were seen in a moribund state. Several dead rocklings were also taken. It would seem that the strong ground-swell of 11 and 12 April may have swept to sea most of the casualties recorded on 11 April, presumably accounting for the lack of dead animals observed on 13 April (dive no. 9).

At the two succeeding stations along the transect (no. 8 in 5 fathoms, and no. 7 in 6·5 fathoms), which like the first had a dense canopy of *Laminaria*, there were again no toxic effects apparent on 13 April. Indeed, only one dead top-shell (*Calliostoma*) was seen. However, at the next station this type of habitat abruptly gave way to a level sandy bottom, unprotected by

---

PLATE 21

A, Sennen Cove, 23 August. Small rafts of floating sand grains on standing water in ripple 'troughs' at low tide.   **B**, Sand core from low-water mark at Perranuthnoe, showing layer of oil under clean sand, 12 May.

PLATE 22

A, View of detergent–oil patch taken from point X in Fig. 15 looking towards Porthleven. The patch, which originated in the region of the harbour mouth, is being blown along the coast past the camera. A, Harbour mouth; B, seaward edge of detergent–oil patch; C, oil in the waves; D, lines of oil deposited on shore.   **B**, Trégastel-Plage (Côtes du Nord), 21 June. Detergent emulsion spreading across the bay following spraying of oily rocks. This view is a little to the north of that shown in Plate 28c. The re-separated oil shown in Plate 6A was photographed an hour or two earlier beside the slipway seen in this view.

Table 11. *Summary of M.B.A. diving surveys—Porthleven*

Dive no.	Date: April	Position	Depth	Substratum	Results
2	7	(i) Off Porthleven reef	2 fm (4 m)	Rocks and gully	Collected dead crustaceans including one large lobster
3	7	(ii) Porthleven harbour entrance	2 fm (4 m)	Gravel	
4	11	Off Porthleven reef and harbour entrance	5 fm (9·5 m)	Rock shelf and gravel	Many dead decapods—*Portumus puber*, *Cancer pagurus*, *Galathea strigosa*, *Homarus vulgaris*, *Palaemon serratus*, *Xantho incisus*, also *Actinia equina*, *Marthasterias* sp. and *Onos* sp., *Delesseria sanguinea* affected, *Heterosiphonia plumosa* dead, *Hypoglossum woodwardii* bleached
5	13	Porthleven reef (i) 460 m from shore	8·5 fm (16·5 m)	Sand	Dead and dying *Echinocardium cordatum*, *Mactra corallina*, *Ensis siliqua* (19), *Marthasterias*. Apparently unaffected *Asterias rubens*, *Acrocnida brachiata*
6	13	(ii) 400 m	8 fm (16 m)	Sand	As above—fewer *Ensis siliqua*
7	13	(iii) 300 m	6·5 fm (13 m)	Rock	One dead *Calliostoma zizyphinum*. Two *Echinus esculentus*, one *Archidoris pseudoargus* apparently unaffected
8	13	(iv) 200 m	5 fm (10 m)	Rock	None apparently affected. *Calliostoma zizyphinum*, *Maia squinado* healthy
9	13	(v) 100 m	2 fm (4 m)	Rock	No obviously affected animals, casualties probably removed by ground-swell

10	13	Porthleven reef	0–2 fm (0–4 m)	Rock	Collected algae—mainly *Furcellaria fastigilda* and *Cladostephus verticillatus* which appeared normal. Epiphytes dead. *Delesseria sanguinea*—dead, *Gigartina pistillata* normal, *Laurencia pinnatifida* colour not normal, *Alaria* sp., good condition. Epiphytes: *Hypoglossum, Apoglossum, Polysiphonia, Ceramium, Plocamium,* and *Dictyota* all dead or dying
16	15	S. Porthleven (700 m offshore)	10·5 fm (21 m)	Fine sand	As for dive no. 15 (see Table 12) but with fewer *Ensis*
17	15	Porthleven sands	11·5 fm (22 m)	Fine sand	Dead and dying *Echinocardium cordatum* (23 in 5 samples of 1 m²), *Mactra corallina, Ensis siliqua. Acrocnida brachiata, Natica alderi, Corystes cassivelaunus* all appeared healthy
18	19	(i) Porthleven reef	7·5 fm (15 m)	Rock	*Echinus esculentus* on rocks—normal
19	19	(ii) Porthleven sands	7·5 fm (15 m)	Fine sand	Dead and dying *Echinocardium cordatum* (18 in 4 samples of 1 m²), *Ensis siliqua, Mactra corallina, Corystes cassivelaunus.* Healthy *Asterias rubens, Marthasterias glacialis, Acrocnida brachiata*—photographs taken (see Plates 24 A, B)
21	28	Porthleven reef (i) 375 m offshore	8·5 fm (17 m)	Sand	Accumulations of dead and dying *Echinocardium cordatum, Ensis siliqua, Mactra corallina.* Healthy *Acrocnida brachiata* and on a rock two *Cancer pagurus* present. *Gobius* sp. seen
22	28	(ii) 325 m offshore	7·5 fm (15 m)	Rock	*Laminaria hyperborea* forest with normal encrusting species. Eight *Echinus esculentus* healthy

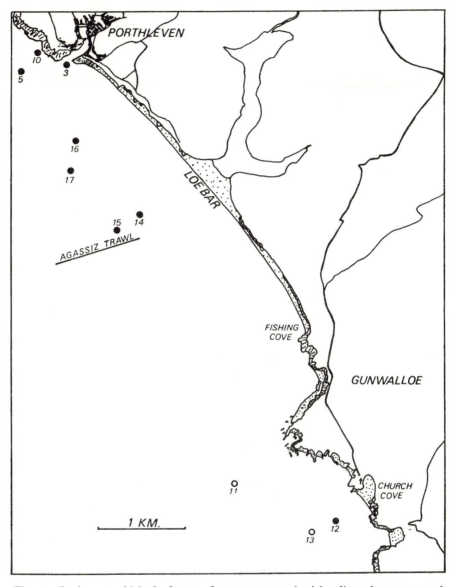

Fig. 20. Stations at which the bottom fauna were examined by divers between 7 and 15 April. Numbers correspond to those of the dives in the diving report (Tables 11, 12). Closed circles show that affected animals were found and open circles represent no effect or inconclusive evidence.

weed, and at the last two stations on the transect (6 in 8 fathoms and 5 in 8·5 fathoms) a totally different kind of fauna was found. Here there were found many dead and dying heart-urchins (*Echinocardium*), several bivalves

including *Mactra* and the razor-shell (*Ensis*), and two species of starfish (*Marthasterias glacialis* and *Asterias rubens*). At station 5 even more *Ensis* were found moribund and dead; and during a later visit to this station on 28 April large numbers of dead animals were taken here. Both the affected *Echinocardium* and *Ensis* (which live in considerable numbers within this fine sand) had taken up characteristic and unusual postures which are more fully described below (p. 113), and illustrated in Plates 20 B, 24 A, B and 26 C.

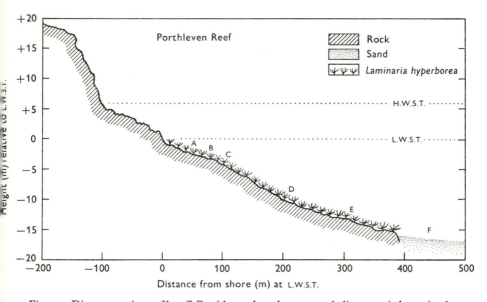

Fig. 21. Diagrammatic profile off Porthleven based on several dives carried out in the region. The nature of the bottom and distribution of organisms is shown. A, 0–2 metres depth: most crabs, starfish and other animals dead; many fine red seaweeds dead. B, 2–4 metres depth: some dead crabs, many others lacking limbs (?moribund); few dead rocklings; red seaweeds occasionally affected. C, 4–5 metres depth: some crabs lacking claws, others apparently unaffected; seaweeds also unaffected. D and E, 7–17 metres depth: no animals or seaweeds affected; edible sea-urchins present. F, 17–18 metres depth: many dead razor-shells and burrowing sea-urchins; brittle-stars and common starfish very little affected.

It will be seen that, in general, the immediate sublittoral fauna and flora of Porthleven Reef was markedly affected by the outflow of detergent— many animals being killed. However, the apparent diminution of effect close inshore (for example, at stations 7–9) is puzzling. The answer probably lies in the difference between the two habitats at the inshore and more distant stations—weed-covered rock inshore and open sand further to sea. In the first, many of the more obvious animals are free-ranging and when killed the carcases are probably washed to sea. In the second, much

Table 12. Summary of M.B.A. diving surveys—other localities
(For map, see Figs. 8–9.)

Dive no.	Date: April	Position	Depth	Substratum	Results
11	15	Gunwalloe (Church Reef)	6 fm (12 m)	Rocks and gullies	No sign of pollution, typical rocky bottom, fauna among *Laminaria hyperborea*. Fish present
12	15	Gunwalloe (600 m offshore)	5 fm (10 m)	Sand	Dead and dying *Mactra corallina*, *Echinocardium cordatum*, *Corystes cassivelaunus*. Healthy *Eupagurus* sp.
13	15	Gunwalloe (800 m offshore)	9 fm (18 m)	Packed sand	Worm burrows and one healthy *Cancer pagurus* seen
14	15	Loe Bar	6·5 fm (13 m)	Sand and rock	Dead and dying *Echinocardium cordatum*, *Mactra corallina*, many dead in gullies near rocks. Few *Acrocnida brachiata* which seemed healthy. Encrusting species on rock healthy
15	15	Loe Bar	9 fm (18 m)	Fine sand	*Echinocardium cordatum*, *Mactra corallina*, *Ensis siliqua* dead and dying on surface. Healthy *Asterias rubens* present
20	24	Sennen Cove	0–3 fm (0–6 m)	Sand and rocks (wreck)	Dead *Cancer pagurus*, *Portunus puber*, *Xantho* sp., *Patella vulgata*, *Echinus esculentus*, *Psammechinus miliaris*, *Actinia equina*. Healthy *Bunodactis verrucosa*, *Cancer pagurus*, *Labrus bergylta*, *Gadus pollachius*, *Marthasterias glacialis*, *Patella vulgata*, *Maia squinado* and worms. Red algae and *Corallina* sp. affected
23	28	St Michael's Mount (i) 250 m offshore	1 fm (2 m)	Coarse sand	Dead and dying *Ensis siliqua*, *Echinocardium cordatum*, *Mactra corallina*, *Venus striatula*, and *Portunus* sp. *Acrocnida brachiata* appeared normal

No.	Date	Locality	Depth	Substrate	Observations
24	28	(ii) 350 m offshore	2 fm (4 m)	Fine sand	Numerous dead and dying *Ensis siliqua* (90 % dead, 1–2/m²), *Echinocardium cordatum* (2–10/m²), *Mactra corallina*, *Portumnus* sp., *Donax vittatus*. Apparently healthy *Marthasterias glacialis*, *Asterias rubens*, *Natica alderi*, *Acrocnida brachiata*, *Crangon* sp., and *Zostera* sp.
25	29	Sennen (i) Lifeguard station	5·5 fm (11 m)	Rock reef and sand	Dead *Echinus esculentus*, *Marthasterias glacialis* abundant
26	29	(ii) Pedn-men-du	8 fm (16 m)	Rocks	Dead *Echinus esculentus*, *Homarus vulgaris* claw, *Alcyonium digitatum*. Healthy *Labrus bergylta* and two undersized *Cancer pagurus*
	1 May	Porthmeor 'Browther Rocks'	4–5 fm (8–9 m)	Rocks on sand	Two dead *Cancer pagurus*, one without legs, everything else normal
27	4	St Ives (i) 450 m off Porthminster Point	7 fm (13 m)	Fine sand	*Ensis siliqua*, *Echinocardium cordatum*—some dead, some on sand apparently unhealthy. *Dosinia lupinus* many dead shells, a few shells with dead tissues. One *Lutraria* sp. unhealthy. Hermit crabs healthy
28	4	(ii) About 350 m off Porthminster	7 fm (13 m)	Fine sand	Two *Echinocardium* within a 3 m radius, mollusc fauna as (i) but sparse. One young *Sepia* healthy
29	4	(iii) About 700 m south of Carrack Gladden	4·5 fm (8 m)	Clean sand	Fourteen *Echinocardium* covered with oil and sand. Two *Ensis* unhealthy. One *Corystes* healthy. One *Lutraria* possibly unhealthy, all in 3 m radius circle
30	4	(iv) About 500 m east of harbour light	9 fm (16·5 m)	Clean sand	One *Echinocardium cordatum* dead, one possibly unhealthy, two unhealthy *Ensis siliqua*, partly dead colony of *Hydractinia echinata*; whereas two hermit crabs, one *Corystes cassivelaunus*, two *Gari fervensis*, four *Dosinia lupinus* all apparently healthy. One shell with living goby eggs attached collected

of the fauna is less mobile and, moreover, contains mainly suspension and detritus feeders which sample considerable quantities of water.

The animals living in the fine sands off Porthleven demonstrated very clearly the toxic effects of the detergent patches at places far distant from the shore. Thus, affected animals (dead and dying *Echinocardium*, *Mactra* and *Ensis*) were found at all four of the diving stations off Loe Bar (Table 12, nos. 14–17; Fig. 20), two of which (15, 17) were more than a kilometre from the shore at about the 10-fathom line. Experiments (pp. 137, 140) have shown that these species are sensitive to only 0·5 ppm of detergent so that concentrations of this order presumably reached these offshore stations. Later dives on 28 April (Table 12, nos. 23, 24) showed that there had been a nearly complete mortality of *Ensis*. The numbers involved must be very great for there was often at least one dead animal to each square metre. It was also noted in the dives that fish were rare within a kilometre of the shore, yet when, on two occasions, the Agassiz trawl was used by R.V. 'Sarsia' 1–2 kilometres off Loe Bar (Fig. 20) living fish, such as plaice and dabs, were caught in normal numbers although one dead *Ensis* was seen. This would seem to indicate that for large animals the limit to which the toxic effects of the detergent had spread in this area was of the order of 1 kilometre from the shore.

It can be concluded then that the effects of the treatment at Porthleven were felt on the sea-bed at least as far as 2 kilometres south-east of the harbour and 1 kilometre from the shore. This is the direction in which the detergent would be expected to move because there is a net eastward flow of water in this region. At the end of the bay no effects were found at station 11 on 15 April. The detergents issuing from Porthleven had evidently not reached this area, and patches from Halsferran Cove (Fig. 16) may have passed between stations 11 and 13. Toxic effects found at station 12 were probably the result of treatment of Gunwalloe Church Cove.

In concluding this section of the report dealing with the offshore spread and toxic effects of shore-originating detergent patches, it may be of interest briefly to survey the consequences of the passage of the detergent patches, with some notes made at the time of the dives, on a few of the commoner animals of the sublittoral region.

PLATE 23

A, Shows detergent–oil patch B from Fig. 17 taken from point X on the cliffs about 1·5 hours before high water. Released oil is being blown rapidly seawards.   **B**, Detergent–oil patch A from Fig. 17 taken from point Y on cliffs about 0·5 hours before high water. Oil, which probably came out of emulsion, is being blown seawards as the detergent–oil patch swings to the east.

PLATE 23

A

B

(*Facing p.* 112)

Decapod Crustacea

Considerable mortality was noted in the squat-lobster, *Galathea strigosa*, and the swimming-crab, *Portunus puber*, as well as among young edible crabs (*Cancer pagurus*) during one dive from rocks 350 metres west of the harbour entrance at Porthleven on 11 April (dive 4, Table 11). Just below the lowest shore level down to about 1·5 fathoms (3 metres) virtually all crustaceans were dead, including one small lobster. At 1·5–2 fathoms (2·5–3·5 metres) some crabs were alive but incapacitated by loss of claws and legs, while at 2½ fathoms (4·5 metres) some *Portunus puber* and young *Cancer* were apparently unaffected. During a further search of nearby rocks on 13 April (dive 10) some more dead crabs were obtained but a ground-swell had swept away most of the casualties. A few dead *Cancer* and *Portunus puber* were found also at Sennen and two dead lobsters off Porth-leven. Dead specimens of the burrowing *Corystes cassivelaunus* were collected from Gunwalloe and Porthleven (Plate 25 A).

Bivalve molluscs

Observations at four different positions showed that *Ensis siliqua* and *Mactra corallina* had been seriously affected along much of Mount's Bay (dive 23), and also in St Ives Bay (dives 5, 27, 28, 29, 30), down to depths of 8 fathoms (14·5 metres). During the first few dives many specimens were still alive but in an apparently moribund state, the *Ensis* often pro-truding up to 5 cm above the sand and *Mactra* lying on the surface. Later dives on 28 April (dives 23 and 24) showed that there had been a nearly complete mortality among the *Ensis*. Many of the unhealthy *Mactra* were being attacked by small starfish (*Asterias rubens*) and it seemed probable that many, if not eaten by predators, might die from the effects of detergent poisoning. Off Marazion, in water containing up to 6 ppm of the surfactant fraction of the detergent, some dead *Ensis* were found. Tests had shown that *Ensis* were unaffected by exposure to 10 ppm surfactant for more than 24 hours. It seems likely therefore that the animals were killed by low levels of the solvent rather than by the surfactant component of the detergent. Follow-up dives in July and August established that at least a few *Ensis siliqua* and *Mactra* survived both off Porthleven and St Michael's Mount.

Echinoderms

Many dead specimens of the starfish *Marthasterias glacialis* were col-lected just below the low-water mark near Porthleven (dive 4), from 1–3 fathoms (2–7 metres) depth, and many more were observed in a moribund state. A few on the sandy ground at 6 fathoms (13·5 metres) were not healthy, whereas animals on rocks at 5–6 fathoms (12·5–13·5 metres) were

8   TCR

normal. At Sennen, however, moribund starfish were found in rocky areas from 3 to 6 fathoms (11–13·5 metres) depth (dive 25).

The burrowing heart-urchin, *Echinocardium cordatum*, was abundant (about six per square metre) on the fine-sand areas off Loe Bar, Porthleven, Long Rock and St Ives—most of the urchins were observed to have come out of the sand (Plate 24A), in which they would normally bury themselves to a depth of several centimetres; only a very few were collected in their burrows. Those on the surface were moribund; with a slow-moving animal such as the heart-urchin it is sometimes difficult to know its condition. There were, however, numerous recently dead tests, often aggregated by the ground-swell at the edge of rocks (Plate 26c). These and freshly dead animals washed ashore indicated widespread mortality. But dives later in the year showed many had survived.

Many recently dead tests of the large sea-urchin, *Echinus esculentus*, were seen off Sennen (dives 20, 25, 26) in depths of 3–8 fathoms (5·5–14·5 metres) together with live but moribund specimens (Plates 25B, 26B). Off Porthleven and near Gunwalloe, however, *Echinus* were common and apparently unaffected at 6–7 fathoms (13·5 metres) depth in the *Laminaria* zone. This would indicate a greater depth-penetration of the toxic concentration at Sennen than off Porthleven, perhaps because of the generally rougher sea on the west-facing coast during April, and also, no doubt, because of the extremely heavy spraying programme carried out at Sennen.

Algae

Apart from many of the delicate red algae at or near the shore margin the only species which seemed to be affected was *Delesseria sanguinea* in depths of less than 3 fathoms (6 metres) (Plate 26A).

In listing the offshore species which were adversely affected by detergents it should not be forgotten that many species were apparently quite resistant. Thus the spider-crab *Maia squinado* was found on several occasions in rocky areas apparently unaffected by the toxic chemicals which were killing *Cancer pagurus* and *Portunus puber* in the same region. Some spider-crabs were, however, found dead in heavily polluted regions. Among the echinoderms the common starfish *Asterias rubens* was very little affected, and healthy specimens were taken from sandy regions off Porthleven (dives 4 and 5) with dead spiny starfishes *Marthasterias glacialis* next to them. Mention should also be made of the brittle-star *Acrocnida brachiata*, which was found burrowing in an apparently healthy state in all the sandy areas examined. With the exception of *Delesseria sanguinea* and the smaller epiphytic algae almost all offshore seaweeds seemed to be unharmed.

CHAPTER 7

TOXICITY EXPERIMENTS

LABORATORY INVESTIGATIONS INTO THE TOXICITY OF OIL AND DETERGENTS

The spraying operations at sea and the detergent treatment of the beaches were mounted with one main objective in view, namely to preserve—or at least minimize the damage to—the amenity value of the coastal resorts. The amenity so seriously and blatantly threatened was the cleanliness of the beaches to which summer visitors flock for recreation. The removal of oil from the holiday beaches was an urgent objective, even at the risk of destroying or damaging other amenities, such as the incomparable wild life of the Cornish coast and shores. For even if the natural animal population around the treated beaches were largely destroyed, the effect on the tourist industry might be negligible compared with the prospect of an ever-oily beach. Few will have had serious doubts; to most only one course was right—to fight the oil with detergents regardless of the cost, in every sense.

But did these actions put at risk other and possibly greater interests? Was there a possible danger to public health? Was there a danger to off-shore and inshore fisheries? The answers to these and other vital and recurring questions had to wait upon the availability of accurate knowledge about the toxicity of the materials that were being applied, their persistence in the sea and the manner in which they spread.

We soon found that the scientific literature was deficient in relevant information and so a programme of toxicity tests was undertaken in the laboratory by several scientists whose previous experience enabled them to take up this work and develop it with the minimum delay. This work was carried out at the same time as the shore parties and the cruise personnel were making their observations on the beaches and at sea.

The urgency of the problem militated against the accurate refinement of the techniques employed, but in spite of this the experiments provided information of great value. In fact an answer to the all-important question of the persistence of the toxic qualities of the detergent emerged within the first few days.

From the toxicity experiments we were able to develop methods of bioassay which in turn made possible a more detailed investigation into the spread of the detergents.

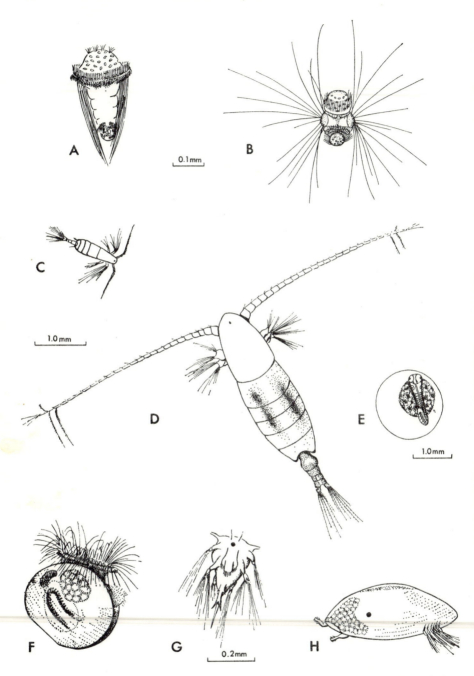

Fig. 22. Examples of zooplankton. A, *Sabellaria* larva, swimming. B, *Sabellaria* larva, irritated. C, The copepod *Acartia*. D, The copepod *Calanus*. E, Pilchard egg. F, Oyster larva. G, Nauplius larva of an acorn barnacle. H, Cypris stage of an acorn barnacle.

The results of the laboratory work are given in outline in the following pages; they represent much intensive effort. Where experiments are individually described they are examples of critical importance. It should perhaps be pointed out that when using living organisms as test material they are not necessarily continuously available; particularly is this true of larvae, which are of seasonal occurrence. Some zooplankton organisms tested are shown in Fig. 22 and phytoplankton in Fig. 5 (p. 28).

A survey of the contents of this chapter may help the reader to follow the somewhat complex subject-matter. The need for the analysis under section VI became obvious during early experiments in section I, and due care and allowance was made thereafter for the diversity of behaviour of the various ingredients of the detergents. At first several detergents were used and their toxicities compared. It became necessary to choose one detergent as a standard, and BP 1002 was chosen because it was one very widely used on the beaches, and with the willing co-operation of the BP Trading Co. Ltd its components could be separately investigated.

SUMMARY OF EXPERIMENTS

I. Toxicity studies on zooplankton
   Effects of detergents
      Elminius modestus larvae, barnacles
      Calanus finmarchicus and *Acartia clausi*, copepods
      Ostrea edulis and *Crassostrea gigas* larvae, oysters
      Lacuna vincta and *Nassarius reticulatus* larvae, shore gastropods
      Young fish
   Notes on toxicity of crude oil and of oil with detergent
   Conclusions from early experiments

II. Longer-term effects on zooplankton species during rearing
   Sabellaria larvae, polychaete worm, showing immediate transitory effects and longer-term effects (for transitory effects on settlement see page 86)
   Elminius larvae to metamorphosis
   Echinus esculentus larvae

III. Toxicity studies on phytoplankton

IV. Toxicity studies on intertidal and sublittoral organisms
   Intertidal algae
   Intertidal animals—toxic effects of BP 1002
      Various animals and in particular mussels, limpets, winkles and topshells, barnacles (both recently metamorphosed and adult)
   Sublittoral animals—toxic effects of BP 1002
      Various sublittoral organisms including *Echinocardium* (heart-urchin) and its commensals, and *Crangon* (shrimp)

V. Bioassay methods developed to enable water samples from the field to be assessed rapidly

VI. Toxicity and stability of components of BP 1002, etc.—solvent, surfactant
and stabilizer
   Elminius larvae
   Sabellaria larvae
   Crangon (shrimps)

I. TOXICITY STUDIES ON ZOOPLANKTON
Effects of detergents

Barnacle larvae

Stage II nauplius larvae of the barnacle *Elminius modestus* were used,
being obtained by hatching out fully developed embryos from the adult
barnacle. Preliminary tests showed that the detergents BP 1002, Gamlen
and Slipclean all rendered the larvae completely motionless in under 2 h,
at a concentration of 10 ppm. At high concentration (100 ppm) the animals
were rendered quiescent in a few minutes. By contrast, Teepol L, chosen as
an example of an ordinary domestic detergent, was found to be far less
harmful, concentrations between 27 and 270 ppm of active ingredients
being needed to stop swimming activity. Immobility was here taken to be
an indication of toxicity. Although a larva may regain mobility if removed
from dilute detergent solution and replaced in fresh sea water, it was
generally found that the loss of swimming activity was irreversible.

These hastily contrived experiments led us to more detailed studies. The
method followed that used by Corner & Sparrow (1956), but is here given
in outline.

In these later experiments a series of concentrations of each of several
detergents was prepared in sea water: about 100 nauplii were placed in
5 ml of sea water of each concentration contained in a corked tube. The
percentages rendered motionless were recorded for increasing times of
immersion. These data, when plotted as percentage motionless against
time, gave a sigmoid curve from which the time at which 50 per cent of the
test sample had lost all activity could be estimated. This time (i.e. TD 50)
was then plotted against concentration of detergent (as ppm) on a logarith-
mic scale. The results obtained are shown in Fig. 23. It is obvious from
this that Teepol L is far less toxic than any of the other detergents tested;
also that Teepol L may have a separate mode of toxic action, as the shape
of the dose/time curve is markedly different from those characterizing the
other four detergents, each of which has a sharp inflection above which the
concentration must be greatly increased in order to produce any sensible
change in TD 50. As these inflections occur at different points in each of
the four curves and as the slopes also vary, it is only possible to compare

Table 13. *Relative toxicities of detergents to* Elminius *nauplii*

TD 50 (min)	Number of times as toxic as active ingredients of Teepol L			
	BP 1002	Slipclean	Gamlen	Dasic
10	60	30	17	13
30	28	12	25	7

toxicities by referring to a particular TD 50 value. Thus, taking a TD 50 of 10 minutes, the relative concentrations needed (as ppm) are 7 (BP 1002), 14 (Slipclean), 24 (Gamlen), 32 (Dasic) and 1550 (Teepol L). By contrast, if a TD 50 of 30 minutes is used the concentrations are 3·5 (BP 1002), 3·9 (Gamlen), 7·8 (Slipclean), 15 (Dasic) and 370 (Teepol L). Relative toxicities based on these two TD 50 values are therefore different (Table 13).

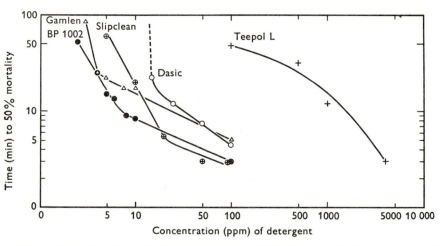

Fig. 23. Toxicities of various detergents to stage II *Elminius* nauplius larvae at 16–20 °C. Note: concentrations of Teepol L refer to the commercial preparation, which contains about 27 per cent active ingredients. The curve for pure Teepol L would be appropriately closer to those for the other detergents (as in Corner, Southward & Southward, 1968).

Copepods

These animals are important as food for pelagic fish and thus play a central role in the oceanic food-chain. Unlike *Elminius* their complete life-cycle is spent in the zooplankton: not just the young stages. The first experiments were 'rough and ready'. Samples of mixed zooplankton, mainly consisting of small copepods, were used in toxicity tests with BP 1002. Samples of the plankton were immersed in concentrations of 2·5 and 5·0 ppm of BP 1002 for 24 hours and then the fraction rendered inactive estimated by eye. The

indications were that both these concentrations had a deleterious effect on the animals.

(*a*) *Calanus finmarchicus* (Fig. 22 D). More detailed experiments were carried out at Millport by Dr S. M. Marshall, F.R.S., who has kindly allowed us to use her results. The test animal used was the copepod

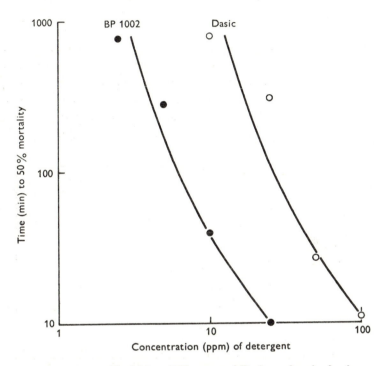

Fig. 24. Toxicities of BP 1002 and Dasic to *Acartia clausi*.

Calanus finmarchicus, and experiments with BP 1002, Gamlen, Dasic, Molyslip, and Houghton Solv. 112 showed that concentrations of 50 ppm were lethal in an hour; 5–10 ppm killed most specimens within two to three days, and 1 ppm, although not lethal, had some effect in that the

PLATE 24

PLATE 24

A

B

PLATE 25

A

B

(*Facing p.* 121)

treated copepods were not as active as those used as controls. These data indicate that *C. finmarchicus* is more resistant than *Elminius* nauplii to the various detergents used.

(*b*) *Acartia clausi*. Another species used as a food by fish, and one that spends its entire life-cycle as a member of the zooplankton, is the small copepod *Acartia clausi* (Fig. 22 c). Experiments with this animal were carried out by Mr B. W. P. Sparrow (International Paints Laboratory, Newton Ferrers), who has kindly allowed us to quote his results, summarized in Fig. 24. It will be seen here that the dose/time curves for BP 1002 and Dasic are almost parallel, so that their toxicity ratio can be stated for a wide range of values for TD 50. As in earlier studies with other species, BP 1002 is more toxic than Dasic, the ratio being approximately 5:1. Moreover, the resistance of the very small copepod *Acartia clausi* to detergents is far less than that of the much larger species *Calanus finmarchicus*: thus a concentration of 50 ppm BP 1002 was lethal to *Calanus* in 1 hour, whereas half this concentration (25 ppm) killed *Acartia clausi* in only a few minutes.

There is a general indication that among similar animals the resistance to detergent poisoning is related to size in such a way that the bigger the animal the more resistant it is.

Oyster larvae (Fig. 22 F)

Because of the possible effects of detergents on oysters, particularly when the animals might be spawning, experiments were carried out at the Fisheries Laboratory (Conway) by Dr P. R. Walne, who has kindly allowed us to quote his results. The animals used were embryos of the oyster *Crassostrea gigas*, a relatively warm-water Australian species. The developing eggs were placed in solutions of various detergents for 24 hours at 23 °C, and the proportion of swimming larvae that had developed to the so-called D-stage was then estimated. The results, shown in Table 14, demonstrate that all the detergents tested were toxic to oyster larvae at

---

PLATE 25

A, *Corystes cassivelaunus*, the masked crab. This specimen was alive when collected from Gunwalloe, 600 metres from the shore in 10 metres depth on 15 April (dive no. 12; see Table 12). It has an accumulation of black material on the setae of the ventral side which is not usual in healthy individuals. This material had collected along the region of the crab's respiratory currents.   **B**, A living edible sea-urchin (*Echinus esculentus*) collected from Sennen Cove on 24 April (dive no. 20; see Table 12). The animal is enfeebled and shows scars in which the surface epidermis and spines are gone and which are surrounded by an area of black tissue. The tube feet adjacent to these scars are responsive to tactile stimulation. Toxicity tests showed that the coelomic fluid of these urchins contained traces (2–5 ppm) of the kerosene fraction from the detergent. It is concluded that the scars are the direct or indirect result of pollution since these marks have not been previously recorded from normal populations.

Table 14. *Effects of detergents on development of oyster larvae*

Concn. (ppm)	Proportions of swimming larvae developed to D-stage						
	Control	Polyclens	Houghton Solv. 112	BP 1002	Slip-clean	Dasic	Gamlen
0	+++	.	.	.	.	.	.
0·5	.	o	o	+++	+++	+++	+++
1·0	.	o	o	+++	++	+	++
3·0	.	o	o	+	+	o	+

+++ = all, ++ = some, + = a few, o = none developed.

a concentration of 3 ppm and that some, particularly Polyclens and Houghton Solv. 112, appeared to have effects at 1·0 and 0·5 ppm.

In earlier experiments, made with *Ostrea edulis*, six types of detergent were tested for their effects on the growth of larvae of *O. edulis*. The results are shown in Fig. 25, from which it is apparent that concentrations of detergent in the range 2·5–7·5 ppm can halve the normal rate of development over two days.

Lacuna vincta (*the banded chink shell*) *and* Nassarius reticulatus (*the netted dog-whelk*)

These are larvae of shore-living gastropod molluscs, but like the nauplii of the barnacle *Elminius* they spend their life in the plankton until they settle on the shore and turn into adults. They were hatched from egg capsules and maintained in filtered sea water at 10 °C. When treated with detergent the larvae became opaque and were invaded by ciliates, which removed the soft tissues to leave an empty shell. The results are shown in Table 15.

Nassarius is obviously the more resistant species. Further experiments showed that at a concentration of 1·0 ppm of detergent the larvae of *Nassarius* recovered their customary activity after 36 hours and, ten days later, were still swimming and feeding normally.

Table 15. *Effect of BP 1002 on week-old larvae of* Lacuna *and* Nassarius

Species	Concn. (ppm)	% dead after:		
		2 days	4 days	10 days
Lacuna vincta (banded chink shell)	20	100	.	.
	2	100	.	.
Nassarius reticulatus (netted dog-whelk)	20	.	100	.
	10	.	.	70

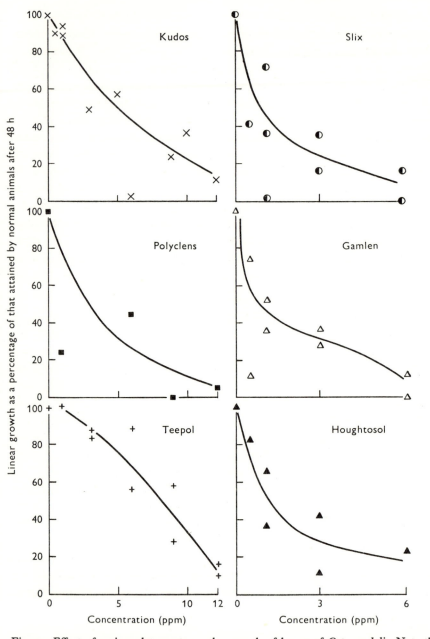

Fig. 25. Effect of various detergents on the growth of larvae of *Ostrea edulis*. Note the difference in the horizontal scale on the two sides of the figure, and the greater toxicity of the hard detergents on the right.

Young fish

It seemed essential to obtain information quickly on the effects of detergents on the early planktonic stages of fish, particularly of commercial species. Initial experiments on fish eggs at Plymouth indicated that fairly low concentrations of detergent (10, 1·0 and 0·1 ppm of Slipclean; 1·0 and 0·1 ppm of BP 1002) did not prevent the hatching of pilchard. Most of the hatched larvae survived up to resorption of the yolk sac, after which all died, including the controls. More detailed experiments, using larvae of sole and plaice, were made by Dr J. H. Blaxter (University of Aberdeen) and Dr J. Shelbourne (Fisheries Laboratory, Lowestoft), who have allowed us to quote their results. It was found that, with the exception of Polyclens, all detergents tested killed the larvae of both species within 24 hours at a concentration of 10 ppm. At higher concentrations (100 and 1000 ppm) death took place in a few minutes. At 'sublethal' concentrations (1–3 ppm) no effects were seen in experiments lasting for the short period of five days.

Note on the toxicity of crude oil

The toxicity studies so far described have dealt with detergents. Obviously it was important to know something about the toxicity of the oil itself, but the difficulty here was to prepare a satisfactory test solution. The method finally used was to add 1 g of the oil to 1 l. of sea water and shake the mixture vigorously for 30 minutes, by which time the oil had formed a pale-brown suspension. This was then used as the test medium. However, it should be noted that this suspension (1000 ppm) was only temporary: during long-term experiments the oil rose to the surface of the water where it remained as a dark-brown film, out of contact with the animals. Greater stability, however, was observed with lower concentrations (10 ppm), and in spite of experimental difficulties we were able to show that oil in higher concentrations (100 ppm) had no effect on the larvae of *Elminius modestus* after several hours, whereas detergents used at these concentrations killed the animals in a few minutes.

Further evidence of the comparatively low toxicity of the oil to marine animals is given in Chapter 4. Moreover, there is some evidence (cf. data for *Crangon*, p. 139) that under some conditions the addition of oil reduces the toxic effects of detergents.

Conclusions

The studies described in this section were of an exploratory nature, having been conducted over a period of ten weeks in response to a local disaster.

Nevertheless the results are unambiguous and the experiments left no doubt that the detergents used for emulsifying crude oil from the 'Torrey Canyon' were extremely toxic to marine planktonic animals. The experiments also showed that the very small members of the zooplankton are particularly susceptible to the toxic effects of detergents, and this could be serious in the sense that these animals—the microzooplankton—are now regarded as an extremely important part of the food-web in the sea (Johannes, 1961).

The overall biological effect of the detergents in the sea clearly depends on the persistence of the toxic principles. It was therefore desirable to know the relative toxicity of the several components of the detergents and their likely persistence. The experiments described in section V of this chapter are relevant to this question.

II. LONGER-TERM EFFECTS ON ZOOPLANKTON

In describing the experiments on the *Sabellaria* larvae (p. 145) the presence of a delayed effect was noted. To examine this further, and to see if it was evident in other species, some longer-term experiments were undertaken using sublethal concentrations of detergent. The species used for these experiments were *Sabellaria spinulosa*, *Elminius modestus* and *Echinus esculentus*. All are coastal animals having free-swimming planktonic larvae.

Sabellaria *larvae*

Larvae of *Sabellaria spinulosa* (Fig. 22 A) were placed in Monax dishes, about a third to a half full, loosely covered with watch-glasses. Concentrations of 1 ppm and 0·5 ppm BP 1002 were tested with thirty larvae per dish. There was an immediate reaction to 1 ppm detergent, the animals flexing their bodies ventrally and erecting their provisional bristles to point in all directions (Fig. 22 B). However, in the 0·5 ppm solution only about half the larvae reacted strongly: the remainder continued to swim but were irritable compared with the control animals. A little *Isochrysis* culture was added to all dishes after 2 hours, and overnight there was complete recovery of the larvae in 0·5 ppm, but not until two days had elapsed did those in 1 ppm appear to behave normally. At this time new larvae put into this dish showed no irritation, the irritant factor having disappeared. These two dishes and the control dish were kept supplied with *Isochrysis* for food, and all the larvae were apparently healthy and normal three weeks later. However, the experiment was continued, with the interesting result that after four weeks all the larvae in the solution which had originally contained 1 ppm of detergent were found to be lying motionless on the

bottom of the dish, in very poor condition. They were still surviving after six weeks, but were then in an even worse state and had hardly grown. Meanwhile, those which had originally been in a solution of 0·5 ppm detergent had become sluggish—but were still growing—after five weeks; however, during the sixth week they lay motionless, apart from an occasional twitch of the bristles. During all this time the animals used as a control sample were healthy, active and growing well.

The experiment therefore showed that the toxicity of BP 1002 still persisted, even after the organic solvent had evaporated, for after a prolonged period of apparent normality the larvae eventually succumbed.

Elminius *larvae*

Freshly liberated stage II larvae of *Elminius* (cf. Fig. 22 G) were reared in small vessels, with diatoms as food. The cultures were subsampled at intervals to estimate the percentage of mortality and the stage of development reached. All cultures were kept in loosely covered dishes and it is believed that the initial toxicity of those containing detergent was lost within the first few days. Thus, the experiments were equivalent to a short exposure to poison followed by a long period of recovery.

In the first series of experiments, using BP 1002, Gamlen and Slipclean at concentrations of 5·0, 1·0 and 0·5 ppm, and also 'Torrey Canyon' oil at 100 ppm, *Phaeodactylum tricornutum* was used as the main food. This diatom is known to be an indifferent food for *Elminius* (Moyse, 1963) and in addition the cultures were rather crowded. The final mortality was therefore high in all cultures, although initially much higher in those containing detergent at 5·0 and 1·0 ppm and oil at 100 ppm. The results are given in Table 16 and Fig. 26. At low concentrations of detergent (0·5 ppm) there was a slight delay in development compared with the controls, but after a week little difference was discernible. In the presence of oil and with medium concentrations of detergent (1 ppm) development was delayed by about two or three days throughout the experiment, the least effect being shown by Gamlen and Slipclean, and the most by BP 1002: all these cultures reached the cyprid stage, although those in BP 1002 failed to metamorphose and settle even when provided with suitably prepared surfaces—that is, cleaned shells of *Mytilus edulis* which had borne live *Elminius modestus* (see Knight-Jones, 1956). At the higher concentrations of detergent (5 ppm) more than 50 per cent of the larvae died the first day. Of the survivors, those in Gamlen failed to develop at all and died while at stage II. Most of the Slipclean survivors reached stage III four days behind the controls and then died, although a few individuals developed as far as stage VI. The survivors of BP 1002 recovered after seven days at stage II

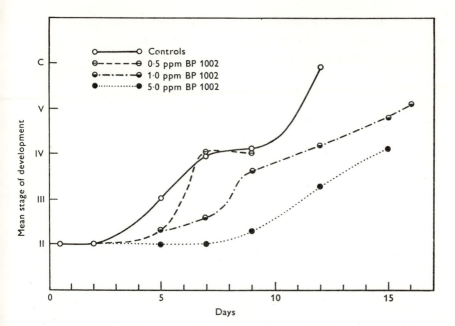

Fig. 26. Rate of development of larvae of *Elminius modestus* reared on *Phaeodactylum tricornutum* at 20 °C in the presence of different concentrations of BP 1002. Nauplius stages shown in Roman numerals; C, Cypris stage.

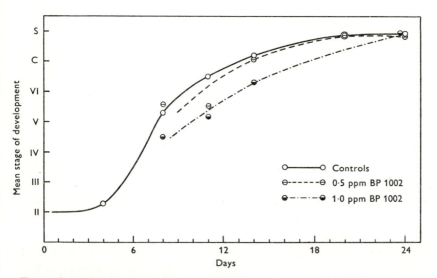

Fig. 27. Rate of development of larvae of *Elminius modestus* reared on *Skeletonema costatum* at 20 °C. Nauplius stages shown in Roman numerals. C, Cypris stage; S, settlement and metamorphosis.

Table 16. *Development of* Elminius *nauplii fed with* Phaeodactylum *at 20 °C*

(Time in days to the first appearance of each stage.)

Stage	Controls	Oil (100 ppm)	BP 1002			Gamlen			Slipclean		
			0·5	1·0	5·0	0·5	1·0	5·0	0·5	1·0	5·0
III	2	5	5	5	7	5	5	F	4	5	6
IV	4	6	6	6	11	6	6	.	5	6	7
V	5	7	6	7	12	6	7	.	7	7	7
VI	7	9	9	13	14	7	9	.	9	9	9
Cyprid	12	15	F	15	F	12	12	.	F	12	F

F = culture failed before reaching this stage.

and developed to stage VI still seven days behind the controls, but failed to reach the cyprid stage (Fig. 22 H).

In a second series of experiments using only BP 1002, a thick culture of *Skeletonema costatum* was available as food and the nauplii were less crowded. Consequently the final mortalities were much lower than in the first experiments and the growth faster. Nevertheless, the detergent caused delays in development, probably not significant at 0·5 ppm but of the order of three days at 1 ppm (see Fig. 27). At the latter concentration only a few cyprids were produced and very few of them metamorphosed and settled (0·6 per cent of the original larvae) compared with the controls (10 per cent of the original larvae).

Echinus esculentus *larvae*

Toxicity studies on *Echinus* were made on artificially fertilized eggs. A good fertilization was achieved using one female and one male. Approximately equal, small numbers of eggs were distributed among four 50 ml Monax dishes half-filled with sea water containing concentrations of 1·0, 0·5 and 0·1 ppm BP 1002 respectively. The eggs were scattered sparsely over the bottoms of the dishes, not longer than 35 minutes after fertilization and about an hour and a half before first cleavage.

The result of this experiment is summarized in Table 17. For the first five days, by which time the four-arm pluteus stage had been reached, no differences were observable between any of the dishes. The smell of organic solvent, present originally, disappeared quite early and water from dish 2 (1 ppm) tested after 48 hours did not irritate *Sabellaria spinulosa* larvae put into it. A little *Isochrysis* culture was now added as food at the pluteus stage, and larvae in all dishes fed on it. However, an hour or so before this food was added, and some hours after assessment of their condition recorded in Table 17, some of the plutei in dish 2 began to 'reduce' the lengths of their

PLATE 26

A

B

C

D

Table 17. *Development of* Echinus esculentus *in concentrations of BP 1002*

Date	Dish 1 (sea-water control)	Dish 2 (1 ppm)	Dish 3 (0·5 ppm)	Dish 4 (0·1 ppm)
5. iv. 67	Eggs distributed to all dishes half an hour after fertilization			
6. iv. 67	Normal blastulae	Normal blastulae	Normal blastulae	Normal blastulae
7. iv. 67	Normal gastrulae	Normal gastrulae	Normal gastrulae	Normal gastrulae
10. iv. 67	Normal plutei	Normal plutei	Normal plutei	Normal plutei
11. iv. 67	Majority normal, a few with reduced arms	All with much reduced arms	Majority with partially reduced arms	Majority normal, a few with reduced arms
12. iv. 67	Majority normal and growing	All poor, with stumpy arms	Majority with short arms, some normal	Majority normal and growing

arms; that is to say the flesh of the arms began to shrink down the skeletal rods, which, left protruding, broke off. This is always a sign of ill health. By next day all plutei in this dish had all their arms reduced to mere stumps, although their stomachs were well filled with food. In dish 3 (0·5 ppm) arm-reduction began later, not all plutei were affected and there was some recovery subsequently. But there was very little recovery in dish 2. Almost all the plutei in dish 1 (control) and dish 4 (0·1 ppm) continued to be in excellent growing condition, only a very few in both dishes having reduced arms (as almost invariably happens under even the best rearing conditions).

Too much should not be read into this single experiment. It is of interest only in that it confirms the earlier demonstration of a long-term toxic effect on other species of some component of BP 1002

III. TOXICITY STUDIES ON PHYTOPLANKTON

In order to grow phytoplankton organisms for experimental work it is necessary to keep the culture media well aerated by vigorous bubbling.

PLATE 26

A, 130–150 metres from the breakwater at Porthleven in 5 metres of water, 5 April. Fluorescent orange *Delesseria sanguinea* which has been affected by detergent and was found growing at the top of a gully on the sea-bed. The *Delesseria* is normally the same colour as the alga seen growing behind it. **B**, Sennen Cove, 7 April. Underwater photograph of a dead *Echinus esculentus* (edible sea-urchin) resting upside-down in a gully between rocks at a depth of 10–11 metres. Normally in healthy individuals the tube feet are conspicuously extended. **C**, Porthleven Reef, 28 April. Underwater photograph of the sea-bed at a depth of 17 metres (dive no. 21). Dead *Echinocardium cordatum* and *Mactra corallina* with healthy *Asterias rubens* and *Marthasterias glacialis* feeding on them. **D**, Constantine Bay, 8 April. Shells of recently killed molluscs in the drift line. Mussels, limpets, winkles and dog-whelks are all represented.

This greatly reduced the level of the organic solvent 'Kex' in BP 1002 (see page 145), and for this reason the following section deals in effect with only the surfactant components of the detergent.

The six following phytoplankton species were used: 64, *Phaeocystis pouchetii*; 81, *Dunaliella primolecta*; 85, *Chlorella stigmatophora*; 92, *Coccolithus huxleyi*; 205, *Halosphaera minor*; 207, *Gymnodinium* sp. The numbers are those used in the Plymouth culture collection.

The growth curves for each of these species were measured at 12 °C in sea water, initially filtered through an Oxoid membrane and autoclaved, and then enriched as follows: nitrate 10^{-4} g ions/l.; phosphate 10^{-5} g ions/l.; vitamin B_{12} 5·5 μg/l.; manganese 2 μg/l.; iron (as citrate) 50 μg/l. The cultures were subjected to alternating periods of 12 hours of darkness and 12 hours of light at about 600 foot-candles, and were vigorously aerated. One hour before inoculation, BP 1002 with known proportion of surfactant was added to the sea water at different concentrations. The aeration during the subsequent hour has been shown to cause the removal of most of the volatile kerosene solvent in the emulsifier. A fifth culture vessel containing no BP 1002 was used as a control.

Cell counts were made on each culture vessel 1 hour after inoculation and then daily for 12 days, using a Coulter Counter Model F; the inocula were obtained from Plymouth stock cultures.

From plots of the logarithm of cell numbers per ml against time, the length of the initial slow-growing phase (lag phase) and the mean generation time for each culture have been obtained. These are given in Tables 18 and 19.

Inhibition of growth is indicated by an increase in the length of the lag phase and the mean generation time in relation to the control. The two genera least affected by the surfactants were *Dunaliella* and *Chlorella*, both of which are characteristic of brackish-water plankton. At the highest concentration examined (1·2 ppm of surfactant) the lag phase for *Chlorella* was increased by a factor of three relative to the control, a result indicating some retardation in metabolism, but it grew at the same rate as in the other concentrations. At 1·2 ppm surfactant the other genera examined were destroyed in the hour between inoculation and the first cell count. The *Gymnodinium* proved to be the most vulnerable to the surfactant, with the growth rate almost halved at surfactant concentrations of $1·2 \times 10^{-2}$ and $1·2 \times 10^{-1}$ ppm, although, surprisingly, the length of the lag phase was about the same as in the control. An apparently paradoxical effect was noted at the lowest concentrations with certain species, notably *Coccolithus*. Here the mean generation time was shortened by about one-third, indicating a growth-promoting effect of the detergent. There are, however,

Table 18. *The length of the lag phase (in days) at various concentrations of the surfactant component of BP 1002*

Phytoplankton	Surfactant concentration (ppm)				
	0	$1\cdot2 \times 10^{-3}$	$1\cdot2 \times 10^{-2}$	$1\cdot2 \times 10^{-1}$	$1\cdot2$
64 *Phaeocystis pouchetii*	—	1·4	0·4	0·4	Cells killed
81 *Dunaliella primolecta*	2·2	1·2	2·0	2·0	2·5
85 *Chlorella stigmatophora*	0·8	0·9	0·9	0·9	2·5
92 *Coccolithus huxleyi*	0·25	0·35	0·35	0·35	Cells killed
205 *Halosphaera minor*	0·2	0·3	0·5	0·3	Cells killed
207 *Gymnodinium* sp.	1·2	2·6	1·7	0·9	Cells killed

Table 19. *The mean generation time (in days) at various concentrations of the surfactant component of BP 1002*

Phytoplankton	Surfactant concentration (ppm)				
	0	$1\cdot2 \times 10^{-3}$	$1\cdot2 \times 10^{-2}$	$1\cdot2 \times 10^{-1}$	$1\cdot2$
64 *Phaeocystis pouchetii*	—	1·0	1·0	1·0	Cells killed
81 *Dunaliella primolecta*	1·2	1·1	1·1	1·1	1·0
85 *Chlorella stigmatophora*	1·2	1·1	1·1	1·1	1·2
92 *Coccolithus huxleyi*	1·6	1·1	1·1	1·1	Cells killed
205 *Halosphaera minor*	1·6	1·5	1·2	1·6	Cells killed
207 *Gymnodinium* sp.	3·8	3·2	7·3	7·3	Cells killed

indications that cells grown under such artificial stimulatory conditions are abnormally fragile (Kidder, Dewey & Heinrich, 1954).

Non-ionic surfactants adsorb on to cell membranes by interaction of the hydrophobic portion of the surfactant with the lipoidal constituents of the membranes. This results in an increase in the permeability of the cell wall, facilitating the passage of dissolved substances both into and out of the cell. At sufficiently high surfactant concentrations the cell constituents are able to leak out from the cell, causing its death (Hotchkiss, 1946). The brackish-water *Dunaliella* and *Chlorella*, which proved the most resistant to the surfactant, are well adapted for ionic regulation (that is, controlling the passage of ions across their cell walls); they might therefore be expected to tolerate changes in the permeability of the cell wall more easily than the strictly marine species.

IV. TOXICITY STUDIES ON INTERTIDAL AND SUBLITTORAL ORGANISMS

Intertidal algae

The familiar seaweeds of the shore were often exposed to very high concentrations of detergent during the beach-cleaning operations. To

investigate the effect on the shore vegetation, detailed tests were made by Dr A. D. Boney of Aberystwyth on four chosen intertidal species. These were the green filamentous alga *Cladophora rupestris*, the brown knotted wrack *Ascophyllum nodosum*, the red algae *Polysiphonia lanosa* (a filamentous form often epiphytic on *Ascophyllum*) and the thalloid *Porphyra umbilicalis* (sometimes known as laver).

The technique employed was to immerse the weed in detergent solutions of a wide range of strengths for varying periods, usually 3 or 6 hours, in some ways simulating conditions which might have been encountered on the shore, except that no freshwater mixtures were used. After immersion the weeds were rinsed with clean sea water and any gross damage could be seen at once. They were kept in clean sea water for 24 hours before being examined microscopically for signs of cell damage, such as shrinking of the protoplasm, loss of pigment, etc. The results are here given only in outline. On the whole, seaweeds are very much more tolerant of detergent than are intertidal animals. Indeed *Porphyra umbilicalis* and *Polysiphonia lanosa* showed no damage detectable by the microscope even after 6 hours immersion in the undiluted detergent. These short-term experiments suggested an unexpectedly strong resistance to detergent treatment not in accord with the bleaching of *Porphyra* and discoloration of other red algae often seen on the shore, although this could generally have been due to the action of fresh water with which the detergent was diluted. Tests carried out on the sublittoral red alga *Delesseria* (see page 137) perhaps suggest a further reason for the apparent discrepancy, in that this alga may take several days to show the effects of damage in sea water. The cell walls of *Porphyra* and *Polysiphonia* must presumably be very impermeable to the constituents of the detergents when uninfluenced by fresh water.

With *Ascophyllum nodosum* (one of the brown shore weeds) the investigation was confined to the reproductive cells which were active at the time of the investigation and were chosen as being likely to be the most sensitive indicators of toxicity. Six hours immersion in a 25 per cent solution of detergent caused irreversible cell damage to the reproductive cells themselves and also to the cells of the receptacle in which the reproductive cells lie before release. In detergent at 12 per cent concentration cell damage was very slight or absent, depending on the type of detergent used. In fact six proprietary brands of detergents were used for all the tests, but the difference in the degree of damage caused by the different brands was not significant.

After they were released from the parent plant the reproductive cells, the spermatozoids and the oospheres, were extremely sensitive, a brief exposure to 0·01 per cent solutions (that is, 100 ppm) being sufficient to kill them.

The green seaweed *Cladophora rupestris* was the most sensitive of the species tested. Here the reproductive cells were not accessible to study and the examination was concentrated on the apical cells of the filaments, which, being the growing points, were judged to be the most sensitive. Here, severe damage was noted after 6 hours immersion in 6 per cent solutions of all detergents (except BP 1002, which was apparently harmless at this concentration). There was less severe, but irreversible damage down to about 1 per cent concentration.

Intertidal animals—toxic effects of BP 1002

During shore-spraying operations the intertidal animals and plants were exposed to very high concentrations of detergent for periods of up to several hours and the expected mortalities described in Chapter 4 were soon evident to the shore observers. Nevertheless, the intertidal species are, as a group, constitutionally very tough, and many of them, the bivalves for example, are able to seal themselves off from a hostile environment for long periods, later to emerge unharmed. It therefore seemed profitable to examine some of these animals for their resistance to detergent poisoning.

The first experiments were only crude, and involved placing animals in sealed containers filled with sea water to which various amounts of detergent were added. The concentrations ranged from 0·2 to 100 ppm. The animals were left in the sealed containers for 24 hours before being removed to fresh sea water and their recovery observed. The containers were large enough to avoid any danger of oxygen deprivation. The results of these preliminary tests are summarized in Table 20.

A few species were selected for more careful study.

Mussels. Specimens of the common mussel, *Mytilus edulis*, 40–50 mm long collected from low-water neap-tide level were used in two sets of experiments. All survived 24 hours exposure to 5 ppm detergent (BP 1002), but 10 ppm and over was lethal within 24 hours. A good guide to the condition of *Mytilus* is its ability to reattach itself to the substratum after disturbance by the extrusion of new byssal threads. In 1 ppm detergent all the mussels had attached in 24 hours and in 5 ppm 60 per cent of the animals had attached, but there was no sign of new byssal threads in 10 ppm and over. Exposed to crude oil in 1000 ppm suspension the mussels all survived the 24-hour period but there was no attachment.

Experiments with *Mytilus galloprovincialis* in the Black Sea (Aljakrinskaya, 1966) reveal that high levels of oil in sea water (up to 2 per cent) can be tolerated by mussels, which remove it from suspension by means of their cleansing mechanisms. It should not be overlooked, however, that

Table 20. *Toxicity of BP 1002 to some intertidal species at 12 °C*

Species	Popular name	Conc. (ppm) needed to kill majority in 24 h	Notes
Coelenterata			
Actinia equina	Beadlet anemone	25	Some young animals survived 25 ppm
Anemonia sulcata	Snakelocks anemone	50	Some looked dead but later recovered
Annelida			
Nereis diversicolor	Rag-worm	25	A few survived this concentration
Crustacea			
Eurydice pulchra	Isopod	10	Some killed at 5 ppm
Carcinus maenas	Shore-crab	25	—
Cancer pagurus	Edible crab	10	—
Palaemon serratus	Prawn	5	—
Crangon vulgaris	Shrimp	2	—
Mollusca			
Nucella lapillus	Dog-whelk	100 +	Became detached at 10 ppm
Monodonta lineata	Top-shell	100	—
Littorina littorea	Winkle	100	Some could recover from 100 ppm
Calliostoma zizyphinum	Painted top-shell	10	Became detached at 2 ppm
Aplysia punctata	Sea hare	50	Became detached at 10 ppm
Patella vulgata	Limpet	5	Dying limpets frequently but not always release their attachment to the substrate

even low levels of detergent may inhibit the natural cleansing mechanism and thus reduce the mussel's tolerance to oil.

Limpets. The common limpet *Patella vulgata* was found in abundance dead and dying on the detergent-treated shores.

Experiments were made with small animals (about 25 mm length) carefully collected from an unpolluted beach, while they were actively moving. This avoids damage to the foot, as occurs if the animals are prised from their seats. The limpets were allowed to attach to glass plates kept in clean sea water overnight, and the water was then replaced by the test solutions shown in Table 21, which summarizes the results of the experiments.

The sensitivity to low concentrations of detergent is in accord with the high mortality of limpets noted in the field observations.

Top-shells and winkles. An experiment on the top-shells *Monodonta lineata* and *Gibbula umbilicalis*, and the winkle *Littorina littorea*, showed that the normal climbing response, observed when the animals are kept in

Table 21. *Toxicity of BP 1002 to* Patella

		BP 1002		
	Control	100 ppm	10 ppm	1 ppm
Behaviour of pallial tentacles	All expanded	All withdrawn	All withdrawn	Withdrawn at first but 75% recovered after 3 h
% attachment of foot after 18 h	100% living	All dead	All dead or dying	80% recovered

Table 22. *Effect of oil and BP 1002 on cirral (limb) beat of very young* Elminius modestus

		BP 1002		Kuwait crude oil	
	Control	100 ppm	10 ppm	Film (1000 ppm)	Suspension (100 ppm)
Initial Activity	60–80% fast beat	50% stopped cirral beat	50% normal beat	50% normal beat	50% normal beat
1 h	60–80% fast beat	50% stopped cirral beat	Pumping beat only	50% normal beat	50% normal beat
24 h	.	Dead	Few active		
48 h	40% fast beat 40% normal beat		Dead	28% active	10% active

beakers of sea water, was inhibited by 10 ppm of BP 1002. The animals were partly withdrawn into the shell, and only the *Monodonta* survived three days immersion (by which time the toxicity was reduced by evaporation) and were able to climb out of the water. A detergent concentration of 1 ppm impaired activity in all three species but did not prove lethal.

The results of laboratory tests with the above species are again reflected in the observations on treated shores (Chapter 4) where there has been heavy mortality of winkles and top-shells. In places where the treatment has been light enough to give the animals a chance of survival *Monodonta* and *Nucella* have been the most tenacious.

Barnacles. Experiments made on *Elminius modestus* larvae (p. 118) were followed by others on the susceptibility of later stages to detergent poisoning. The effect on settlement and metamorphosis was first examined because this is a very critical stage in the life of a barnacle. Cleaned shells of *Mytilus* that had borne *Elminius* adults were placed in dilutions of BP 1002, and ten cyprids added to each. At 5 ppm and over the cyprids ceased swimming (see Fig. 30, page 141) and died in two days. At 3 ppm swimming stopped

after 24 h and the cyprids died in four days without settling. At 1 ppm swimming was unaffected and many of the cyprids settled and meta-morphosed. The newly settled adult form ('spat') is another critical stage on which experiments were also made. Shells bearing recently settled spat were exposed (1) to different concentrations of BP 1002, (2) to a film of Kuwait crude oil on the surface of sea water, and (3) to sea water that had been mechanically shaken for 5 minutes with the oil. The results are shown in Table 22, cirral activity (that is, limb movements) being assessed in the way described by Crisp & Southward (1961).

These data show that the young, recently metamorphosed barnacle is more resistant than the larval stages to poisoning by detergents. Neverthe-less, BP 1002 at a concentration of 10 ppm was ultimately lethal. Moreover Kuwait oil had an obvious depressing effect on cirral activity, and hence on feeding, and would thus inhibit growth.

Fully grown specimens of *Elminius* attached to mussel shells collected from low water of neap tides were also tested. They were treated with various concentrations of BP 1002, and with water that had been mechanically shaken for 30 minutes with 'Torrey Canyon' oil collected from a beach at St Ives during the first few days contamination. The vessels were not covered and so it is probable that the detergent lost toxicity in 24 hours. At a concentration of 100 ppm the barnacles became inactive and some died; the rest showed some cirral activity after 24 hours.

Detergent at concentrations of 5 and 10 ppm and oil at concentrations of 100 ppm slowed the rate of cirral beating by 25–35 per cent.

Sublittoral organisms—toxic effects of BP 1002

The observations reported in Chapter 6 show how detergents sprayed on the shore can lead to an expanding front of toxic water spreading to appreciable distances along the coast, over the surface and down to the sea-bed. Divers exploring offshore reaches of the sea-bed found a variety of dead and moribund animals whose habits and habitat precluded any sug-gestion that they had been killed on the shore and subsequently washed seawards. To complete this picture toxicity experiments were made with a selection of sublittoral species. The results of these are reported below and are sufficient to verify that the divers with their restricted range of vision and coverage saw a typical, but only a small, sample of the offshore consequences of the beach-cleaning operations.

Tolerance of various sublittoral species. The method used was the same as that already described on page 133. Table 23 gives some results for a number of species that live below the low-water mark. As might be expected, they are more sensitive than the intertidal animals. However, for a crustacean,

Table 23. *Toxicity of BP 1002 to some sublittoral species at 12 °C*

Species	Common name	Concn. (ppm) needed to kill majority in 24 h	Notes
Coelenterata			
Calliactis parasitica	Sea anemone	25	Stayed closed at 5 ppm
Crustacea			
Corystes cassivelaunus	Masked-crab	10	.
Portunus holsatus	Swimming-crab	5	.
Diogenes pugilator	Hermit-crab	25	.
Mollusca			
Nassarius reticulatus	Netted whelk	2·5	Some survived 2·5 ppm
Chlamys opercularis	Queen scallop	1	Affected at 0·5 ppm (tended to gape)
Laevicardium crassum	Smooth cockle	1	Affected at 0·5 ppm (tended to gape)
Spisula subtruncata	Trough-shell	2	Affected at 1 ppm (tended to gape)
Ensis siliqua	Razor-shell	0·5	.
Echinodermata			
Asterias rubens	Common starfish	25	Climbing stopped at 10 ppm
Ophiocomina nigra	Brittle-star	5	Affected at 2 ppm
Algae			
Delesseria sanguinea	Red seaweed	10	Took several days to change colour

Diogenes (a hermit crab) is remarkably resistant. Another fairly resistant species was the common starfish, *Asterias rubens*, which during the diving programme (p. 113) was seen feeding on other animals killed by the detergent.

Although it is one of the most sensitive seaweeds and becomes 'fluorescent' orange when killed (Plate 26A), the red weed *Delesseria* when treated with 0·001 per cent detergent took several days to change colour.

Bivalve molluscs were the most sensitive of the animals which were examined. Of these the razor-shell *Ensis siliqua* is the most susceptible to poisoning and was killed by 0·5 ppm of detergent. Results of the diving programme (p. 113) show that *Ensis*, together with the clam, *Mactra stultorum*, was killed at a distance of at least 1 kilometre off Porthleven. It therefore seems likely that detergent–oil patches having concentrations of about 0·5 ppm at the level of the sea-bed had moved through these areas.

Shrimps. Details of the use of the shrimp *Crangon vulgaris* in toxicity experiments are given under 'Bioassay'. The same method was used in order to test the relative toxicity of several detergents and the results are

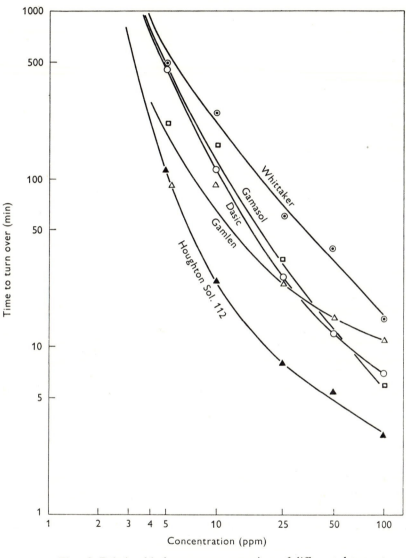

Fig. 28. Relationship between concentrations of different detergents
and the mean times taken by *Crangon vulgaris* to turn over.
(For 'Gamasol' read 'Gramosol'.)

shown in Fig. 28. As with similar experiments carried out on *Elminius*,
the curves were not parallel: thus, whereas Gamlen was less toxic than
Dasic and Gramosol at 100 ppm, it was more toxic at 5, 10 and 25 ppm.
Comparison of these data with those for BP 1002 in Fig. 29 shows that at
concentrations below 10 ppm BP 1002 was the most toxic detergent; this

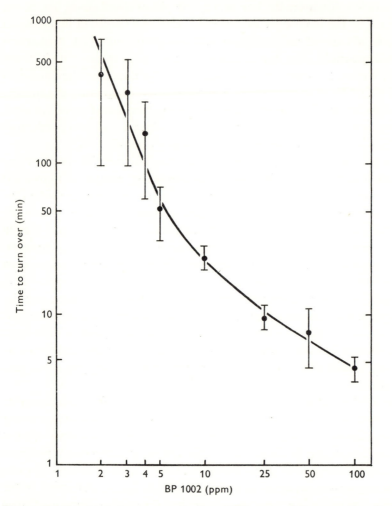

Fig. 29. Relationship between concentration of BP 1002 and the mean time for *Crangon vulgaris* to turn over. Vertical lines show the range of the standard deviation at each concentration.

again agrees in general with the *Elminius* results. In addition, it was found that a mixture of BP 1002 and Kuwait crude oil (equal volumes giving a concentration of 10 ppm detergent) was less toxic than the detergent used alone, the toxicity being reduced by some 30–40 per cent.

Sand-urchins and their 'commensals'. In view of the extensive mortalities of the heart-urchin, *Echinocardium cordatum*, off beaches cleaned with toxic chemicals, the effect of the detergent BP 1002 on it was tested in the laboratory.

The sand-urchin normally burrows to a depth of about 10–15 cm. It was maintained in the laboratory in covered bowls, each with an independent circulation of aerated sea water and containing sand in which the urchins burrowed naturally. The test animals, together with some of their native sand, were collected from an unpolluted area. Within a day, after sufficient detergent had been added to give a concentration of 10 ppm, the urchins died, either while still buried or after emerging to the surface of the sand. But at lower concentrations the urchins might emerge and then partly bury themselves again several times, although many eventually died.

It proved impracticable to seal the bowls effectively to prevent any evaporation of the volatile fraction of the detergent; and as each bowl was supplied with a stream of air bubbles this evaporation was considerable. In fact, the kerosene fraction in samples of both sand and water containing 5 ppm BP 1002 was estimated to have fallen to less than 10 per cent in five days; very little could have been present in those of lower concentration. Nevertheless the results indicate that BP 1002 has a toxic effect, even at a concentration of only 1 ppm.

To gain more information on the nature of the toxic effect, healthy urchins were put in breffits containing various concentrations (0·5–10 ppm) of BP 1002 in sea water. Each breffit held 2 l. of water, with a 2 cm layer of sand on the bottom. After 19 hours the urchins were transferred to a bowl with sand and circulating sea water to see if they recovered and would burrow.

Those urchins still living after exposure to 10 ppm for 19 hours were immobilized, with their spines and pincer-like pedicellariae barely moving and unresponsive to touch. There was a progressively less severe effect at lower concentrations. In clean water, although some partly recovered from the seemingly 'narcotized' state and re-burrowed, they all eventually came to the sand surface and died. The clearest initial effect of detergent on the activities of burrowed urchins was an arrested forward movement. A toxic effect was found above about 0·5 ppm. A small bivalve, *Montacuta ferruginosa*, and an amphipod crustacean, *Urothoë grimaldi*, both under 1 cm long, are common 'commensals' with the sand-urchin. Animals were tested in small, sealed bottles (150 ml capacity) holding various concentrations (0·1–50 ppm) of BP 1002, at least two specimens of each species being placed in each bottle for 12 hours. The *Urothoë* died when the detergent was above 5 ppm and appeared unaffected by lower concentrations. *Montacuta*, on the other hand, showed a graded effect: the bivalves died quickly in 50 ppm, but recovered in clean sea water from a 'narcotized' state with their valves gaping after exposure to lower concentrations. Concentrations below 1 ppm did not seem to have any effect.

V. BIOASSAY

The chemical methods of analysis described in Chapter 2 (p. 19) are potentially very accurate for estimating detergent concentration under well-controlled conditions, but they are attended by several defects which make them unsuitable for the testing of water samples, collected at sea or from the shore. The worst of these defects is that they estimate only

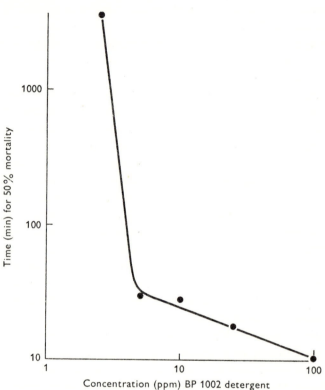

Fig. 30. Effect of different concentrations of BP 1002 on swimming activity of cyprids of *Elminius modestus* at 20 °C. See page 135.

one component of the detergent mixture; in two of the three methods this is the surfactant component which differs in density, persistence and toxicity from the main solvent component. Thus the concentration measured does not necessarily reflect the toxicity of the sea-water sample.

From the experience gained in the many toxicity tests earlier described we were able to devise simple methods of bioassay which, although they may fall short of the standards required in the analytical laboratory, are

easy to perform, are reliable, and directly measure the toxicity of the water sample. It was these methods which made possible the important series of observations on detergent drift reported in Chapter 6.

Several methods were tried. One which showed promise involved observing the effect of detergent solutions on the ciliary beat of isolated strips of the gill membranes of the mussel *Mytilus edulis*. However, the little time available in the early stages of the 'Torrey Canyon' operations prevented us from developing this method and, in the end, bioassay determinations were made by two methods using intact animals. These methods are described below.

Method 1 using Elminius *larvae*. Approximately 300 nauplii were used to test each sea-water sample. The animals were added to a 5 ml portion of the sample by pipette and the time taken for 50 per cent to be rendered motionless was noted. A calibration curve was prepared with known concentrations of BP 1002 (included in Fig. 31), and used to convert values of TD 50 into concentrations of detergent as ppm. An accuracy of about 10 per cent was achieved. This was poor by comparison with the standards usually required of chemical analyses, but sufficient for the purpose.

The main disadvantage of the method was the very narrow range of concentrations that could be tested. Thus, at values greater than 10 ppm, large differences in concentration had only a small effect on the TD 50 (see page 118): accordingly, test samples heavily contaminated with detergent had to be diluted with sea water until a concentration was attained representing approximately 10 ppm. At the other extreme, 2·5 ppm was the lowest concentration that could be estimated reliably: at values below this (for example 2·0 ppm) the animals showed spasmodic 'twitching' from which they later recovered.

Method 2 using Crangon vulgaris. Preliminary experiments on the toxicity of BP 1002 to a variety of common animals showed that the shrimp was one of the most sensitive (see Table 20). In toxic solutions the shrimp eventually becomes very agitated and, after a series of rapid flexions of the abdomen, turns over. Turning over is a fairly sharp end-point and the time taken for this to occur can be related to the concentration of detergent in the water. Occasionally, shrimps that have turned over in the presence of low concentrations of detergent subsequently recover if returned to fresh sea water. However, if at 25 ppm this recovery has not taken place after 5 minutes the toxic effect may be assumed to be irreversible.

Water samples for testing were collected in 200 ml clip-top glass bottles. The top 50 ml was removed for other tests and a shrimp weighing 1–2 g then placed in each bottle, which was subsequently sealed. Times for animals to turn over at 12 °C were recorded and converted into concen-

trations of BP 1002 as ppm using the calibration curve shown in Fig. 29. The method is not very accurate but seems to be reliable within its limits of accuracy. Thus, within 24 hours, 2 ppm of BP 1002 was always toxic but 1 ppm was not. Beyond this time, control shrimps died through lack of oxygen. The detergent does not seem to act on the respiratory system.

This second method has the same drawback as that using *Elminius* larvae, namely that the range of good sensitivity is restricted. In addition, as only one animal is used to test the sample the results are more variable; moreover, the volume of sea water needed to accommodate the test animal is much greater than the sample used in tests with *Elminius* (5 ml). However, a more serious criticism applying to both methods, when relating them to field observations, is that results are expressed as ppm BP 1002. In the field, toxic effects were often caused by some other detergent, or even by fresh water used in hosing down the beaches.

To sum up—in spite of their recognized limitations, two methods of bioassay were usefully applied in testing water polluted by detergents.

VI. TOXICITY AND STABILITY OF THE COMPONENTS OF DETERGENTS

Details have already been given in Chapter 2 of the chemical composition of various detergents, and it will have been noted that the largest constituent is the *organic solvent* (e.g. kerosene extract or 'Kex'). In addition there is a *surfactant* (or emulsifying agent); and a *stabilizer*.

None of the three components dissolves easily in sea water and stock suspensions were therefore prepared by mechanically shaking 1·0 ml with 1 l. of sea water for 30 minutes. These suspensions were then quickly diluted to provide test media representing an appropriate range of toxic concentrations. The organic solvent, 'Kex', was obviously unstable and evaporated continuously from the sea-water suspensions. Accordingly, all tests of the toxicity of the 'Kex' fraction were carried out in sealed vessels (the same precaution having been taken when tests were made with the whole detergent).

Studies with Elminius larvae

Toxicity. Stage II animals were used, as in the previous toxicity experiments. Data for the solvent 'Kex' are compared with those for BP 1002 in Fig. 31, from which it will be seen that 'Kex' used alone has a toxicity very close to that of BP 1002. By comparison, the stabilizer was notably less toxic than 'Kex' and the surfactant notably less toxic than the stabilizer (see Table 24). Figure 31 also includes data for Shellsol R, the organic solvent used to prepare the Dasic detergent. Compared with BP 1002,

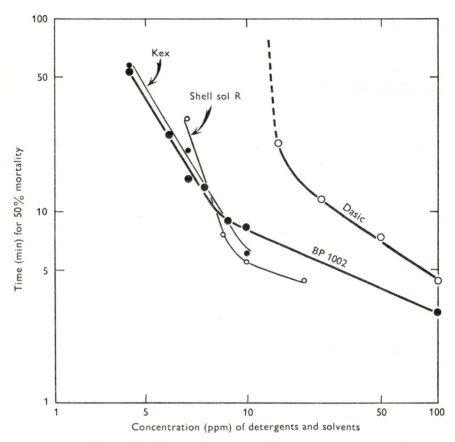

Fig. 31. Toxicities of detergents and their components to stage II
Elminius nauplius larvae at 16–20 °C.

Dasic is much less toxic, but somewhat surprisingly, its organic fraction Shellsol R has almost the same toxicity as 'Kex'. The proportion of Shell-sol R used in Dasic is slightly less than the proportion of 'Kex' in BP 1002. However, this difference is too small to account for Dasic being much less toxic than BP 1002. Possibly the other ingredients in Dasic may reduce the toxicity of Shellsol R.

Thus, in the case of BP 1002 and Dasic, and probably Gamlen and

---

PLATE 27

A, Oil residue on rocks west of Fort Le Crocq, Guernsey, 10 July. Shingle beach in distance mainly clear but with some residues above high-water springs. Rocky reefs were also oil covered at high-water neaps level.   **B**, Oiled rocks on Ile Renot (Côtes du Nord), 21 June. The oil darkened to this colour after two neap tides. Mean Ruz lighthouse in background. **C**, Oiled salt marsh and sand near Trégastel (Côtes du Nord), 21 June. Note that the rushes, although presumably oiled nearly two months earlier, appear healthy.

PLATE 27

A

B

C

Table 24. *Toxicity data for the components of BP 1002*

Concentration (ppm)	TD 50 (min)			
	Surfactant	Stabilizer	'Kex'	Total Mixture
500	50	—	—	—
50	120	18	2	4
25	200	38	4	5½
5	Non-toxic	212	21	17

Slipclean, the high toxicity of the 'detergent' is due mainly to the organic solvent on which it is based: in BP 1002, for example, the surfactant used is ten times less toxic (25 ppm) than the solvent (2·5 ppm). This finding appears to contrast with results obtained in fresh water, where some pure non-ionic surfactants, including the nonylphenyl-ethylene oxide condensate used in BP 1002, are toxic at concentrations below 10 ppm (see Marchetti, 1965). Possibly the cell membrane mechanisms are more sensitive in the fish that were used in Marchetti's freshwater experiments.

Stability. The stability of BP 1002, and of its three constituents, were also tested. Sea-water solutions were aerated for various periods of time in open vessels, and it was found that all the test solutions lost toxicity. The most marked effect was with 'Kex', a solution of 10 ppm (which originally killed 50 per cent of the test animals in 8 minutes) possessing no detectable toxicity after 2 hours aeration. The experiment was repeated using wide-mouthed dishes open to the atmosphere, but no aeration. The half-life of 'Kex' used at concentrations of 1–100 ppm was less than 24 hours in these conditions. The detergents Gamlen and Dasic also lost toxicity when similarly treated.

Solutions of the three components of BP 1002 were prepared with a heavy bacterial contamination by using sea water which had contained decaying barnacles. The stabilizer was found to have lost toxicity overnight, but the other components seemed unaffected.

Studies with Sabellaria *larvae*

Tests were made with *Sabellaria spinulosa* larvae that varied in the stage of their development from that figured by Wilson (1929, plate v, fig. 6) to the later stage drawn in fig. 7 on the same plate. The larvae had been reared in the laboratory from an artificial fertilization. The concentrations of BP 1002, and later of its constituents, were prepared in the same unfiltered sea water as used for the controls. All experiments were carried out under north-window illumination at a controlled temperature of about 15 °C.

To prevent loss of the toxic solvent during the course of the experiment, the sea water control and a solution of 1 ppm BP 1002 were each put into 100 ml glass-stoppered conical flasks, completely filled to leave no air-spaces under the stoppers. There were ten larvae in each flask, but no food was added. The larvae in the control were healthy and active three weeks later, although their flask was still well stoppered. But those in the detergent solution never recovered, remaining motionless on the bottom, bodies flexed ventrally and bristles erect. When the flask was unstoppered after 48 hours they were found to be dead. Moreover, water from the flask, shortly after unstoppering, was still extremely toxic to new larvae, quickly rendering them motionless with erect bristles. Air was now bubbled through the flask for several hours, the smell of the organic solvent disappeared and the water no longer had any toxic effect on fresh larvae immersed in it.

Tests were next made with sea-water solutions of the surfactant (10 and 1 ppm) and the stabilizer (10 ppm) prepared in open dishes. At 10 ppm both substances killed the larvae within a few hours, after first slowing their speed of swimming. There was no sudden raising of the bristles characteristic of treatment with the detergent. The larvae died with straight bodies, and with the bristle bundles only partly raised. In fact, in the solution of stabilizer, the bristles were barely lifted away from the sides of the body, the posture in death being almost as in life. In the 1 ppm concentration of surfactant, larvae showed no immediate reaction, but gradually their rate of swimming slowed and they became increasingly irritable. After 12 days, in spite of *Isochrysis* added for food, they were in poor condition and a few days later most were dead, the rest dying. All this time larvae used as a control were healthy, active and growing, and remained so five weeks after the experiment began.

A more extensive series of tests of the ingredients of BP 1002 was next made. These are listed in Table 25 and the results briefly summarized. 'Kex' at 2 ppm and 1 ppm had at first very little effect on the larvae: it merely made them slightly irritable. Overnight the slight smell of the solvent disappeared and from then on the larvae behaved normally for nearly four weeks; however, after this they lost activity until they lay motionless with only an occasional twitching of their bristles. The surfactant at 5 ppm and 2·5 ppm killed the animals, and the same concentrations of the stabilizer gradually slowed the swimming and killed within 20 hours. When treated with these components the larvae died as before with bodies straight and bristles scarcely raised. In another dish, containing 1 ppm of BP 1002, the immediate reaction was the usual ventral flexure of the body with well-raised bristles, the animals then remaining

Table 25. *Toxicity tests with BP 1002 and its components.*
(Ten larvae of *Sabellaria spinulosa* 29 days old were put into each dish.)

Date	Time	Dish 1: Control	Dish 2: 2 ppm 'Kex'	Dish 3: 1 ppm 'Kex'	Dish 4: 5 ppm surfactant	Dish 5: 2·5 ppm surfactant	Dish 6: 5 ppm stabilizer	Dish 7: 2·5 ppm stabilizer	Dish 8: 1 ppm BP 1002
14. iv. 67	3.00 p.m.	Put in	·	·	Put in	Put in	Put in	Put in	·
14. iv. 67	3.05 p.m.	Normal	·	·	Motionless	Normal	Normal	Normal	·
14. iv. 67	3.40 p.m.	Normal	·	·	Motionless	Slow	Slow	Slightly slow	·
14. iv. 67	3.45 p.m.	·	Put in	Put in	·	·	·	·	·
14. iv. 67	4.07 p.m.	·	Irritable	Irritable	·	·	·	·	Put in
14. iv. 67	4.25 p.m.	Normal	Almost normal	Normal	Dead	Poor	Dead	Dead	Motionless
15. iv. 67	10.08 a.m.	Normal	·	·	·	Dead	·	·	Slight recovery
17. iv. 67	2.30 p.m.	Normal	Normal	Normal	·	·	·	·	Poor
25. iv. 67	10.30 a.m.	Normal	Normal	Normal	·	·	·	·	Very poor
28. iv. 67	5.00 p.m.	Normal	Normal	Normal	—— Ten new larvae put into dishes 4–7 ——				Three dead
29. iv. 67	10.40 a.m.	Normal	Normal	Normal	Poor	Slow	Poor	Almost normal	Bad
1. v. 67	10.10 a.m.	Normal	Normal	Normal	Dead	Very slow	Dead	Slightly slow	Bad
2. v. 67	12.20 p.m.	Normal	Normal	Normal	·	Almost motionless	·	Slow	Bad
4. v. 67	10.50 a.m.	Normal	Normal	Normal	·	Five dead	·	Slow	Another dead
11. v. 67	12.15 p.m.	Normal	Less active	Less active	·	Eight dead	·	Slow	All dead
17. v. 67	11.45 a.m.	Normal	Motionless	Motionless	·	All dead	·	Almost normal	·

10-2

motionless for some considerable time. There followed a period of apparent partial recovery but progressive deterioration soon set in.

The animals were not fed for two weeks after the beginning of the experiment. Some *Isochrysis* culture was then added to all dishes. On the same day, healthy larvae were put into the dishes of surfactant and stabilizer (Table 25, dishes 4–7) where the original larvae lay dead and decayed. In both these components at 5 ppm the larvae soon died with straight bodies and bristles held almost normally. In dishes containing these components at a concentration of 2·5 ppm there was a more gradual slowing of the swimming speed and the larvae survived longer than did those originally put into these same dishes. In fact, although they eventually died in this surfactant concentration, the larvae in the 2·5 ppm stabilizer showed distinct signs of recovery by the end of the experiment. The stabilizer was evidently no longer present in toxic concentration.

These experiments, like those conducted with *Elminius*, demonstrate that the solvent fraction of BP 1002 is quickly lost from sea water exposed to air. But there is evidence of chronic poisoning resulting from fairly brief exposure. These open-dish experiments differ from those with *Elminius* larvae in that the effect of the whole detergent is considerably more severe than that of the 'Kex' alone.

Studies with Crangon

Methods described in an earlier section (see page 142) for estimating the toxicities of detergents to shrimps were used in further experiments concerned with testing the relative toxicities of the components of BP 1002 and the stabilities of these components in sea water. Experiments with shrimps showed that the organic solvent 'Kex' is the most toxic fraction; and that aeration of sea-water solutions of BP 1002 causes loss of toxicity.

CONCLUSIONS AND SIGNIFICANCE OF THE TOXICITY EXPERIMENTS

The account of the results of the range of toxicity experiments is already in a much summarized form. The results as a whole may be drawn together in a few comments.

They exhibit the expected variation of tolerance as between one species and another, and it would be impossible to define a generally 'safe level' of detergent concentration in sea water. All that can be said is that acute effects in some animals are detectable at less than 1 ppm of detergent and that as the concentration increases so the effects mount progressively and extend over a wider variety of species. At 10 ppm exposure for 1 hour is lethal to most planktonic and sublittoral animals and, whereas the inter-

tidal animals are more tolerant, they were exposed to much higher levels of detergent concentration in the type of beach-cleaning operation employed in the situation under study.

The experiments were conducted under conditions of great urgency, for the detergent spraying was begun in the absence of any detailed and reliable information on its likely biological effects.

There is, it is true, abundant information in the scientific literature on the toxicity of detergents. However, this is largely concerned with ionic detergents and with a freshwater environment. There are good physiological reasons for supposing that the action of non-ionic detergents in sea water could be very different.

The assumed toxicity was quickly verified in the first experiments and the effect of the operation hinged upon two interwoven questions. How far will the poison spread? And how long will it last?

The many experiments performed to establish toxic levels together with the observations reported in Chapter 6 throw light on the first question, and the experiments described under 'Toxicities and stabilities of the components of detergents' were undertaken to help answer the second.

The various reports in the literature describing toxicity experiments with detergents are almost wholly concerned with the surfactant fraction of the oil-spill detergents or their equivalent. It was therefore natural to suppose that the toxicity of the oil-spill detergents was largely in the surfactant fraction. The toxicity of this fraction to some species, at least, has been demonstrated, and the possibility of accumulation in food-chains, though perhaps slight in open waters, should not be forgotten. The surfactants used in the manufacture of oil-spill detergents are 'hard'; that is, only slowly degraded, so that it seemed that the toxicity was likely to persist in the coastal waters of the Channel, and the prognosis was indeed gloomy.

Hence it is of crucial significance that our experiments show that the toxicity of the oil-spill detergents in sea water is almost entirely in the organic solvent fraction and, moreover, that this fraction rapidly disappears by evaporation, at least when in low concentration. This result is of central importance for the whole of the spraying operation, for had it not been for this previously unknown and unsuspected fact the biological consequences in the English Channel would have been vastly worse than they were.

Nevertheless, it should be noted that besides this important demonstration of the severe but transient toxicity of the detergents used there is also a longer-term effect on the organisms tested.

THE PATTERN OF OIL DISCHARGE AND OIL MOVEMENTS FOLLOWING THE WRECK

The oil which escaped from the 'Torrey Canyon' was driven by the tidal movements of the water on which it lay and by the wind. Although, as is indicated later, tidal movements alone can give an appreciable to-and-fro movement of the oil with sometimes a residual movement remaining at the end of a tidal cycle, the movements of the oil over periods of several days will usually be determined mainly by the wind. In Fig. 32 are shown, from the excellent observations* made by R.A.F. Coastal Command based at St Mawgan, Cornwall, successive positions, for times between 20 March and 8 April 1967, of the very large patch of oil which was released from the 'Torrey Canyon' between the time when the tanker struck the Seven Stones Reef on 18 March and the evening of 20 March. By measuring the distances and directions between points marking the approximate centres of this patch on different occasions, the resultant oil movements between known times were determined. Over the same periods of time, vectors, giving wind distance (velocity of wind × time) and direction, were added geometrically to give resultant wind distances and directions with which the corresponding distances and directions of oil movement could be compared. For this purpose the wind velocities and directions were taken for 6-hourly intervals from the observations made at the land meteorological station nearest to the oil patch. The results of such comparisons are given in Table 26 (p. 161), which shows that the oil movement could have been very well predicted by assuming that the oil always moved in the same direction as the wind but with about 3·4 per cent of its velocity. This agrees well with the measurements made by Hughes (1956) on plastic envelopes floating close to the surface of the Atlantic Ocean. He found that the drift of such plastic envelopes was parallel to the surface winds, and that the velocity of drift was about 3·3 per cent of the velocity of these winds. The small difference between the factors 3·4 and 3·3 per cent indicates that the oil moves with almost, if not exactly, the velocity with which

---

* Different observers gave very consistent results for the positions of the heavier concentrations of oil. The observers themselves noted, however, that there was great difficulty in defining the areas of lighter pollution. Weather conditions, the state of the sea, and the criteria adopted by different observers all greatly affected the answers given.

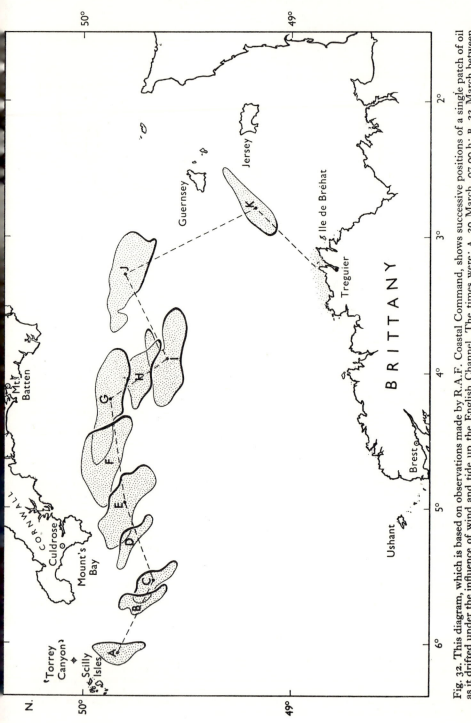

Fig. 32. This diagram, which is based on observations made by R.A.F. Coastal Command, shows successive positions of a single patch of oil as it drifted under the influence of wind and tide up the English Channel. The times were: A, 20 March, 07.00 h; B, 22 March between 06.00 and 08.00 h; C, 23 March, between 06.00 and 07.00 h; D, 25 March between 06.00 and 07.00 h; E, 26 March, 13.00 h; F, 27 March between 06.00 and 09.00 h; G, 28 March between 05.45 and 11.00 h; H, 30 March between 06.00 and 11.30 h; I, 1 April, 09.00 h; J, 4 April between 08.45 and 11.50 h; K, 8 April about midday.

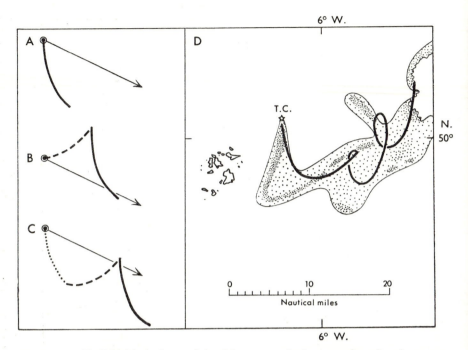

Fig. 33. A–C. If oil had leaked out of the ship at a steady *low* rate after 18.00 hours on 25 March and the wind had remained constant in direction and of strength 25 knots (in fact the wind was less strong and south-west over the first 6-hour period) the oil patch would be expected to have the shape shown: in A at about 00.00 h on 26 March, in B at about 06.00 h on 26 March, in C at about 12.00 h on 26 March. The patch of oil released in the first half tidal period is shown by the heavy black line; it is unchanged in successive periods of time but pushed by the tide first to the north and then to the south of a line in the direction of the wind and passing through the wreck.

Fig. 33D. Here we compare an actual R.A.F. plot of oil distribution close to the 'Torrey Canyon' made at 13.00 hours on 26 March with a line, calculated like those of A, B and C, but covering three full tidal periods before 13.00 hours on the 26th. We have taken account of the fact that over roughly the first two-thirds of this period the wind was south-westerly and of a force about 13 knots and later rose to 24 knots and became west-north-west. We have not allowed for the fact that the tidal streams closer to Land's End are stronger and have a set generally in a more westerly and easterly direction than those close to the wreck; if we had corrected for this, the calculated curve would certainly give a better fit to the actual observations. The oil was discharged in great quantities and has of course spread out after leaving the wreck.

surface water would move. There is therefore no reason to suppose that any change in the condition of oil as it becomes older would affect its velocity.*

Figures 33 A–C use these calculations to show the kind of effects which

* Following damage to the tanker 'Gerd Maersk' in 1955 8000 tons of crude oil were pumped into the North Sea. The German Hydrographic Institute of Hamburg followed the movement of the oil in the shallow coastal waters off Germany and Denmark and came to the conclusion that the oil moved with the wind at about 4·2 per cent of its velocity (Tomczak, 1964). It is hoped to discuss the differences between their results and those of this report in a later communication.

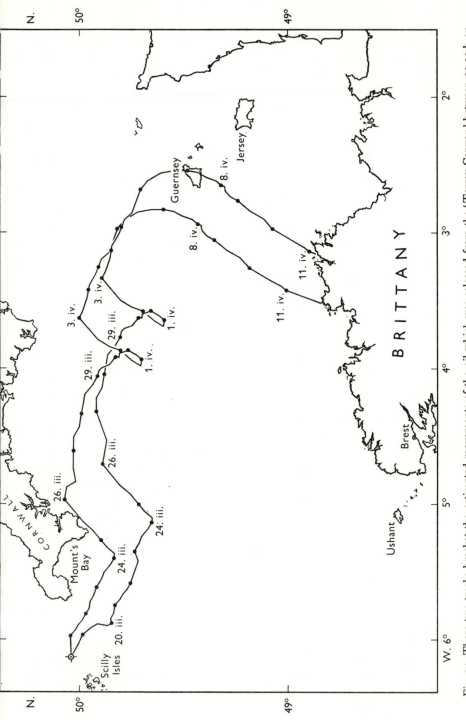

Fig. 34. These two tracks bracket the estimated movements of the oil which was released from the 'Torrey Canyon' between o9 oo h on 18 March and 12.oo h on 2o March. It has been assumed that the oil moved in the direction of the wind with 3·3 per cent of the wind's velocity. The dots on the lines mark oo.oo hours on successive days.

combined wind and tidal movements will have on oil movements, and Fig. 33 D shows a plot of oil distribution made by Coastal Command on the afternoon of 26 March together with an estimated pattern of oil movement. It will be seen that the agreement is good except that the oil patch widened considerably as it moved away from the ship. A great part of this widening must certainly be due to the spreading of oil under its own weight. The effect of tidal movements and spreading of oil meant that the patches were often several miles wide and this should be borne in mind in the discussion which follows.

Figure 34 shows how the oil released from the 'Torrey Canyon' between 18 and 20 March would have moved if it had been drifting under the influence of wind alone with a velocity equal to 3·3 per cent of the wind velocity. The plot shows that this oil, the first great volume released from the ship, would have failed to reach the English shoreline but that part would have fetched up on the Channel Islands and the rest around Treguier in Brittany on about 11 April, three weeks after release. (The oil did in fact land in Brittany around Treguier at this time, see Chapter 9).

Figure 35 plots, in a similar way, estimated oil movements for oil released between 21 and 25 March. This shows, for example, that oil released at the beginning of this period would have been blown on to the shores around Mount's Bay on 25 March while oil released later in this period would have been driven first along the north Cornish coast and then ashore on 26 March. There would, of course, be a great deal of oil driven on to the beaches around Land's End over this time. These estimates reflect very well the actual course of oil pollution over this period.

The two available official estimates of oil release agreed that the largest single loss followed the breaking of the 'Torrey Canyon' by storm on the evening of 26 March. This volume was given as 30000 tons in one estimate and 48000 tons in the other, and the later figure of about 48000 tons will be assumed below. Figure 36 shows how this oil would have moved under the winds which prevailed between 26 March and 12 April. For most of this time, since the oil was in the open sea, we have followed Hughes (1956) in taking our winds as two-thirds of the appropriate geostrophic winds calculated from the isobaric plots.* As the figure shows, this enormous volume of oil would have entered Mount's Bay, skirted the Lizard and then, during a long period of north-westerly, northerly and finally north-easterly winds, would have been pushed past Ushant well into the Bay of Biscay without touching land at all.

* The wind speeds calculated from isobaric plots agreed very well with the observations of neighbouring meteorological stations except for the sea area around Ushant, where the calculated speeds were consistently lower than those reported by the meteorological station at Ushant.

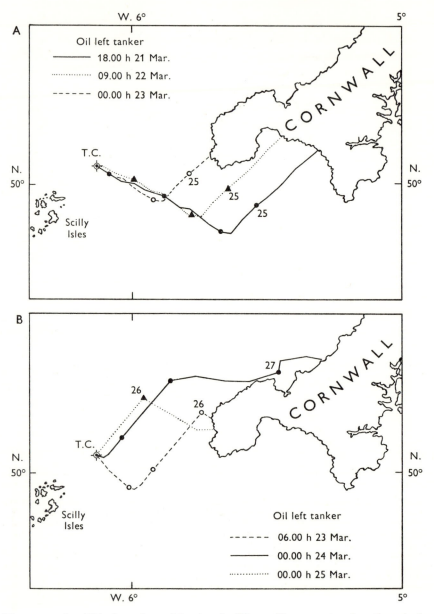

Fig. 35. A and B. This shows how oil leaving the 'Torrey Canyon', at various times in the period between 21 and 25 March, would have moved if it had travelled in the direction of the wind with 3·3 per cent of the wind's velocity. For an idea of how tides and the spreading of oil can affect such movements see Fig. 33 D. The symbols on the lines mark 00.00 hours on successive days.

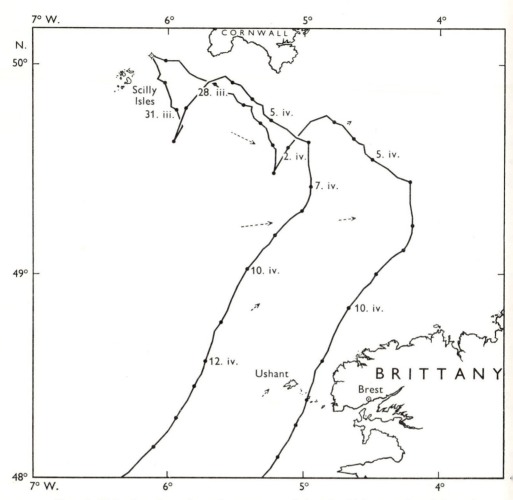

Fig. 36. This gives the estimated movements of the oil which was released from the 'Torrey Canyon' between 18.00 hours on 26 March and 00.00 hours on 29 March. This includes the oil released on the ship breaking up and most of the oil which was released (but not burnt) when the ship was bombed. It may be seen that this oil would not have reached any shore before passing Ushant. It has been assumed that the oil moved in the direction of the wind with 3·3 per cent of its velocity. The arrows give the directions of the tidal residuals at various places along the predicted path of the oil. The lengths of the arrows give the approximate distance by which the tides would have affected the oil movements. The dots on the lines mark 00.00 hours on successive days.

The air surveys showing oil distribution were mostly directed to finding the positions of patches of oil close to shore so that oil which had moved away from the shore is often not shown on the plots given by Coastal Command. It would have been almost impossible to interpret these surveys without some theory as to how the oil moved, and in no circumstance was

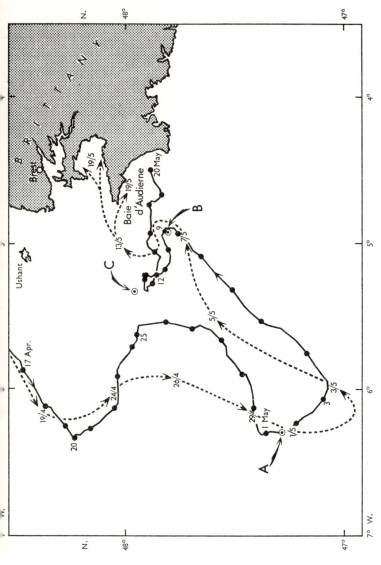

Fig. 37. This shows estimated movements of a large patch of oil which was observed in position A on 1 May by the French. It has been assumed that oil would move in the direction of the wind with 3·3 per cent of the wind's velocity. Estimates have been made working forwards to 20 May and backwards from 1 May to 17 April. B is the position of this oil on 9 May (given by French Navy). C is the position, on 12 May, of the largest 'patch' of oil seen from R.V. 'Sarsia' during a survey of oil in this region. The observed positions B and C are close to those predicted and the oil is shown as having come from the direction expected (see Fig. 36) of oil released from the 'Torrey Canyon' between 26 and 30 March. The dots on the lines mark 00.00 hours on successive days. The pecked line shows an actual track of oil movement as plotted by the French Navy and supplied to us after our own report had been completed.

this more true than in attempting to follow the oil released from the 'Torrey Canyon' during the period between 26 and 30 March. The air surveys do show, however, a very large patch of oil in Mount's Bay on 29 March and, at the same time, a large area covered with oil was seen in the same position (49° 35′ N., 05° 00′ W.) by the Plymouth Laboratory's vessel R.V. 'Sarsia'

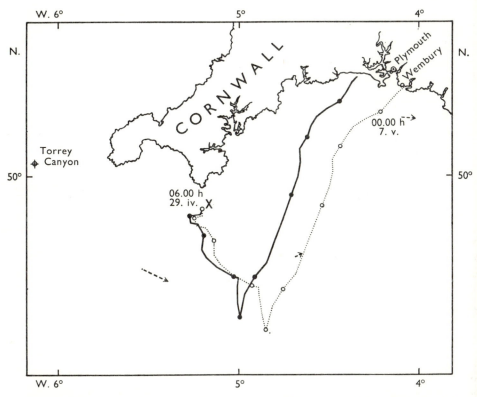

Fig. 38. This shows estimates of movements of the oil first observed from R.V. 'Sarsia' at position X on 29 April. The continuous line is that predicted by assuming that the oil moves in the direction of the wind with 3·3 per cent of its velocity. The dotted line is that given by correcting the continuous line for the effects of residual tidal movements. The dots on the line mark 00.00 hours on successive days.

(cruise I). This oil did not strike the Cornish coast, but later, on cruise III of R. V. 'Sarsia', oil was seen on 12 April extending from about 48° 50′ N. to the southern limit of the cruise at 48° 30′ N. The largest patch of oil seen was found at approximately 48° 50′ N., 05° 10′ W. This is most easily explained by its being 'Torrey Canyon' oil which had moved in the direction predicted by the plots shown on Fig. 36 but about 20 miles less far to the south. Beyond Ushant oil patches were followed by the French Navy and Air Force, and Dr P. Courtot of the Faculté des Sciences de

Brest has very kindly sent us some of their observations. On 1 May the French reported a main 'patch' of oil at 47° 17' N., 06° 17' W. (25 km by 1 km, with its long axis orientated at 260° and said later to consist of spots of oil 300 square metres in surface area and 3 cm thick) and secondary patches at 47° 35' N., 06° 05' W.; 47° 25' N., 06° 35' W.; and 47° 18' N., 06° 48' W. Starting from the position of the main patch of oil on 1 May, estimated positions of this oil, before and after this date, are shown on Fig. 37, where these estimates may be seen to agree well with observations of the oil patches.

On 29 April oil patches were observed off the Lizard and surface drifters were placed in the sea close to this oil. Figure 38 shows estimates of how this oil would have moved driven by wind alone (continuous line) and by wind and tide together (dotted line). These predicted that this oil would reach shores close to Plymouth on 7 May, and a little oil did in fact come ashore at Wembury three miles east of Plymouth Sound on 8 May. Several surface drifters were found close by in the days that followed but it is not known when these first came ashore.*

The observations and predictions shown on Figs. 32–38 and summarized in Table 27 are thus in good agreement with one another. If the main patch of oil reported by the French on 1 May (position A of Fig. 37) is identified as part of that found over a month earlier, on 29 March, in Mount's Bay, reliance on estimates based on the oil being driven by the wind alone at 3·3 per cent of its velocity would have indicated the direction in which the oil moved very well. It would, however, have overestimated the distance moved by about 20 per cent. Two likely explanations of this possible discrepancy are:

(1) A generally northerly current of the surface water opposing the southerly movement of the oil past Ushant. This current would have to have an average velocity of about $\frac{1}{20}$ knot to account for the whole discrepancy.

(2) A reduction in the ratio of oil velocity/wind velocity in conditions of sustained wind and high seas such as obtained in the seas around Ushant over the period following 6 April.

The Nature Conservancy report and our own observations show that, although the pollution was more extensive in Cornwall, the pollution was much heavier in Brittany. It was officially estimated that about 48 500 tons of oil were released between 18 and 26 March. Our estimates are that some 18 500 tons of this oil drifted towards the Cornish coast and that about 30 000 tons drifted up the Channel. Both of these masses oil were sprayed

* The first of them was found by a member of the general public at Wembury on 12 May, and the fact that a member of the Plymouth staff who looked for drifters a few days later found two more suggests that such drifters are not always quickly found by the general public.

at sea with large quantities of detergent. Even if we assume that detergent spraying at sea did not substantially reduce the oil mass, evaporation and detergent dispersal together would have reduced the weight of oil by some 30 per cent. Consequently, the maximum amount of oil which landed on the Cornish beaches can be estimated at some 13 000 tons, and the quantities reaching France and the Channel Islands at about 21 000 tons.

These estimates of the quantities of oil may be compared with the amounts of detergent used in Cornwall. Up to about 5 May about $2\frac{1}{2}$ million gallons of detergent were used—that is, about 10 000 tons—and a rough balance sheet would therefore read 13 000 tons of oil landing on our beaches with about 10 000 tons of detergent being used to disperse it. Now it seems that if the detergent is used to best advantage it can disperse about four times its volume of oil. We know, however, from our own and from other people's observations that ideal ratios of this kind would be impossible to achieve in practice and that detergent was often not used in the best conditions and was sometimes used in excess. The balance found between volumes of detergent and oil is therefore not a surprising one.

Thirteen thousand tons of oil may seem rather a small amount to cause so much damage but, when it reached the beaches, the oil was often in an emulsion whose composition was approximately 70 per cent sea water and 30 per cent oil, so that 13 000 tons of oil could give, for example, a continuous strip of oil-and-water emulsion 10 metres wide, 2 cm thick along a continuous length of over 200 kilometres of shore (cf. Figs. 8–10).

Although the pollution of our coasts was very serious we were greatly favoured by the fact that for most of the two months following the stranding of the ship the winds were northerly or north-easterly. If, for example, south-westerly winds had blown from 1 to 5 April the pollution along our shores would certainly have been three or four times heavier.

Conclusions

(1) Once a large patch of oil has been identified at sea its position subsequently can be predicted with fair accuracy by assuming that it moves in the direction of the wind at about 3·3 per cent of the wind's velocity. This means that very expensive blanket aerial surveys are not necessary since aircraft can be directed by predictions of the wind drift of oil. These predictions are simple to make and merely require wind speeds and directions which can be found either by calculation from the isobars on the meteorological charts or from the observations of wind by local weather stations. Allowance should, of course, be made for ocean currents and tidal streams where these are very strong.

(2) Patches of oil remain as patches for long periods. This is shown in

PLATE 28

A

B

C

Table 26. *Assessment of oil movement in terms of wind movement (see page 150)*

Change in position of oil patch (Fig. 32)	Vector distance in nautical miles		$\dfrac{\text{Oil velocity}}{\text{Wind velocity}} \times 100$	Direction of movement	
	Oil	Wind		Oil	Wind
A to B	23·3	834	2·79	116°	120°
B to E	23·8	911	2·61	69°	73°
E to G	29·9	633	4·72	81°	98°
G to I	20·3	556	3·65	145°	152°
I to J	27·1	849	3·19	63°	70°
J to K	41·7	1081	3·86	153°	123°
A to J	227	6687	3·39	91°	95°

the successive observations such as those described on Figs. 32 and 37. It is certainly not safe to assume, as many people have done, that oil patches become very rapidly dispersed at sea.

(3) Even with moderate winds the position of a patch of oil can change greatly in a relatively short time. Thus the patch shown in Fig. 32 moved about 90 nautical miles eastward between observations A and I in about 10 days and the patch whose movements are shown in Fig. 26 moved southwards from the Lizard to Ushant in about 14 days. This means that, if coastal authorities are to be given reasonable warning of threatened pollution, aerial observations should not be confined to waters close to shore but that the main patches of oil should be followed at intervals decided from estimates based on wind velocities and directions.

(4) Boom defences are very worthwhile for, if pollution can be held at bay even for a short time, a change of wind direction may remove the threat entirely.

(5) If pumping of oil on to the sea ('Gerd Maersk'), or the bombing of a wrecked tanker ('Torrey Canyon'), or any other process which would release oil at sea is contemplated, the time at which this is done should be chosen in the light of the forecasts of winds. If for example, the 'Torrey Canyon' had been broken by bombing on 24 March and the oil contained in the ship released, then several times more oil would have polluted the English coastline.

PLATE 28

A, Biscay, west of Pointe du Raz, 47° 55′ N., 05° 12′ W., 12 May. Dense swarm of the planktonic dinoflagellate *Noctiluca*, as seen from R.V. 'Sarsia's' bridge. The white powder is craie de Champagne. **B**, 47° 55·2′ N., 05° 19′ W., 12 May. Similar view of *Noctiluca* swarm, with small lumps of oil. **C**, Trégastel-Plage (Côtes du Nord), 21 June. Machine skimming off surface layers of oily sand. In the sea is a milk-white detergent/oil emulsion formed after recent spraying of rocks to left of photograph. This drifted across the beach on the rising tide.

Table 27. History of oil releases from the ship, and their subsequent fate

Date of oil release	How oil was released	Where oil was blown ashore	When first blown ashore	When wind set offshore	Where oil was on 8 May	Rough quantities of oil based on official estimates
18 March 19 March 20 March	Ship aground 09.00 h 18 March; some oil tanks breaking and then ship subject to wave action and losing oil	Channel Islands and N. coast of Brittany	7 April 11 April	3 May	Mostly ashore in Channel Islands or France	30000 tons (about 21000 tons after loss of more volatile fractions)
21 March 22 March 23 March 24 March 25 March		Land's End S. Cornish Coast N. Cornish coast	25 March 25 March 26 March	29 March 29 March 8 or 9 April	Some ashore on Cornish coast (largely mixed with detergent and washed into sand) or dispersed at sea and widely spread	18500 tons (about 13000 after loss of the more volatile fractions)
26 March 27 March 28 March	Ship broken by storm approx. 19.00 h 26 March	Not ashore on 8 May			In Bay of Biscay	48500 tons (loss by evaporation was probably over 50% before this oil was dealt with by the French)
29 March 30 March	Ship bombed at 16.00 h 28 March and again on 29 and 30 March	A little on S. Cornish coast	2 April	13 April		20000 tons said to be mostly burnt by bombing

CHAPTER 9

OIL POLLUTION IN FRANCE
AND GUERNSEY

From 18 to 25 June two members of the M.B.A. scientific staff visited
Brittany and met many of those concerned both scientifically and ad-
ministratively with oil pollution in France. They also visited polluted
beaches on the north and west coasts of Brittany.

OIL POLLUTION AT SEA

The French coast was threatened at different times by two separate bodies
of oil (Fig. 1). The first emerged after the original stranding of the 'Torrey
Canyon' and drifted up-Channel in the manner shown in Fig. 32, where it
was thought to be threatening the Channel Islands and Cotentin peninsula.
Its course was tracked by sea and air reconnaissance from England, and
it was also treated at sea with detergent. By 5 April when the oil mass lay
close to Guernsey the British ships treating it were withdrawn and it was
signalled to the French that they had emulsified all the oil they could, and
that in consequence spraying operations had ceased.

Aerial observations by the French showed much oil remaining and, with
the wind veering to the north-east, the coast of Brittany was threatened.
Emergency precautions were begun by the French on 8 April, but owing
to bad weather on 9 April, which prevented aerial reconnaissance, the first
oil reached the Côtes du Nord almost without warning, between Les Heaux
and the Bay of Lannion, on 10 April. Although hurried attempts were made
to treat the oil at sea with sawdust and with powdered chalk, there was
insufficient time to prevent the bulk of the oil (estimated at 15000 tons
by the French), from coming on the shore.

The second mass of oil to threaten the French coast almost certainly
issued from the 'Torrey Canyon' between 26 and 30 March. Its estimated
course is shown in Fig. 36. This oil does not seem to have been reported
to the French by the British, as the first warning received in France was
from a French fishing boat which reported dense patches of floating oil in
mid-Channel north of Ushant on 4 April.

First accounts were that it stretched over tens of miles and estimates of
its quantity varied between 'over 50000' and 80000 tons, several times as
much as was at that time drifting on to the Côtes du Nord. This oil would
comprise all that released from the 'Torrey Canyon' after she broke up.

11-2

The most recent British estimate of the oil released immediately after the ship broke apart on 26 March was 48500 tons (p. 162) and to this must be added any oil which was later released, but not burnt, when the ship was bombed on 28, 29 and 30 March.

The patches of oil were reported to be so dense and compact that vessels steaming into them were checked. The same oil was observed from R.V. 'Sarsia' on 12 April, about 20 miles north of Ushant (p. 33; Plate 7A).

From 11 April on the oil patches were reconnoitred and charted by the French Navy, with headquarters at Brest. The oil stayed at sea for a further five weeks (Fig. 37), during which it drifted to and fro off the west coast of Brittany. It was first treated by the French with sawdust, but from 18 April it was sprinkled with powdered craie de Champagne. This is natural chalk ($CaCO_3$) with about 1 per cent sodium stearate, which is normally added in the manufacture of blackboard chalk. In this instance the stearate seems to have made the chalk hydrophobic and oleophilic so that it was attracted to the surface of the oil, binding it into particles which sank after a few hours. The breaking up of the solid oil masses was facilitated by ships steaming through it, stirring up the mixture with their propellers. The French informed us that the 3000 tons used, if correctly applied, would sink 20000 tons of oil.

Because of the tendency of the dry chalk to choke the delicate machinery of the radar-operating gear and missile launchers of the larger warships it was found necessary to employ small but robust ships such as minesweepers and fishing trawlers to spread the powder on the oil.

In addition a 3000-ton coaster, the 'Petrobourg', was hastily adapted for pumping oil from the sea, and this came into service on 27 April. This ship had a hose with a special floating attachment for sucking oil from the sea surface. It was capable of collecting 1200–1500 tons daily, and operated by coming alongside an oil patch and allowing the wind to drift the oil against the side of the ship (causing the thickness of the oil to be increased to 60 cm), where it was held by a floating boom until sucked up. This method proved very effective when the layer of oil was sufficiently thick, but owing to the dispersion of the oil by the time the 'Petrobourg' was brought into use only 1200 tons in all were collected on the two days on which she was employed.

On 12 May R.V. 'Sarsia' steamed through the oil mass, which was centred at about 47° 58' N., 05° 22' W. The mass consisted of floating pieces of oil of varying sizes up to 'rafts' of some 100 square metres with a thickness of perhaps 10–15 cm and of the consistency of heavy grease (Plate 7c). It was estimated that at least 1000 tons of untreated oil was present in the area on that day.

The oil came ashore around the Pointe du Raz and the Crozon peninsula, south of Brest, on 19 and 20 May (Fig. 39), but the extent of beach contamination was small. One estimate was 300 tons in all, but the M.B.A. staff who visited certain of these beaches thought it might be much less.

It would therefore seem that the French were successful in preventing the bulk of this very large oil mass from coming ashore. This was possible because they had several weeks in which to apply the chalk and adapt a ship

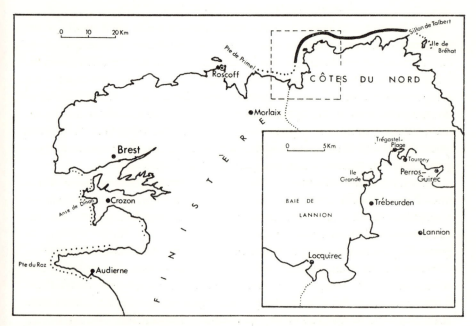

Fig. 39. Map showing oil pollution in Brittany, and some of the places visited by M.B.A. workers. The thick line shows the heavily polluted area on the Côtes du Nord. The dotted lines along the coast indicate slight or moderate pollution.

for pumping. Although the chalk would have sunk most of the oil it seems likely that in addition the remaining floating oil was broken up into small pieces which would soon become spread over a wide area and which, from the greater total surface area, would be more easily attacked by bacteria. An isolated patch of oil, still at sea on 18 May, is shown in Plate 7 B.

Observations from 'Sarsia' in mid-May indicated that there was a large area where the surface of the sea was very slightly oily, resulting in smooth slicks, but not opalescence. This area stretched westward from the Ushant–Penmarc'h area to the continental slope south of La Chapelle bank. It seems likely that a lot of the remaining oil had by this time become dispersed in this region.

Taking an estimate of 50000 tons of crude oil initially released and passing to the west of Ushant, the 'balance sheet' seems to have been:

Lost by volatilization (and perhaps by biodegradation) of lighter components	25 000 tons
Pumped by 'Petrobourg'	1 200 tons
Stranded on coast	300 tons
	26 500 tons

Leaving 23 500 tons to be accounted for.

The French estimated that the 3000 tons of chalk used could at the maximum have sunk 20000 tons of oil. Our analyses of a sample of the oil–water emulsion floating in the Bay of Biscay collected by R.V. 'Sarsia' on 18 May at 48° 05′ N., 05° 20′ W. suggest that by this time more than 50 per cent of the oil had evaporated and the density of the oil had so increased by loss of the lighter fractions (p. 13) that the chalk used could have sunk a maximum of 30000 tons. It seems therefore that the balance sheet for the oil which passed to the Bay of Biscay can be considered complete, and that there is no great quantity of oil still at sea.

Of the two methods used by the French, pumping seems useful where the oil forms a sufficiently thick layer. Sinking the oil with chalk is relatively cheap but might cause difficulties if much were sunk in an enclosed sea area, resulting in anaerobic conditions being set up. There is also the possibility that some might be washed up on the shore at a later date.

South of the main oil mass sighted on 12 May there was an area where slicks and small lumps of oil were present, and there was much chalk floating on the surface, indicating recent treatment of the oil. In the same area many dense patches of the planktonic dinoflagellate *Noctiluca* were seen, producing a 'red tide'. It is not known if the appearance of *Noctiluca* in the same area as the treated oil is anything more than a coincidence, but it is possible that conditions favourable to the rapid multiplication of *Noctiluca* were created by the presence of oil or by its treatment with chalk.

Details of the red tide were as follows. Red tide was first seen as R.V. 'Sarsia' was steaming towards the polluted area, at 15.15 hours G.M.T. on 12 May. The first patches seen were right at the surface, but from 17.57 hours on they were described as submerged just below the surface. Only one patch was seen after 18.57 hours, suggesting downward migration or dispersion in the evening.

Meteorological details at 15.00 hours were: wind S., force 1–2; bright; 6/10 cloud; smooth sea, very slight swell; barometer 1007; shade air temperature 17 °C.

At a hydrographic station at the edge of the polluted area sea temperatures were: at 5 m, 13 °C; at 50 m, 11 °C; depth 124 m.

The patches of *Noctiluca* occurred over an area estimated as eight miles from west to east and three miles from north to south, with centre at 57° 55′ N., 05° 16′ W. (about 22 miles off Pointe du Raz).

Individual patches of *Noctiluca* tended to be elongated, with long axis south-west to north-east. A typical fairly large patch was estimated as 3 × 30 metres, but some formed elongated streaks 100 metres or more long and a metre or two wide. Patches were orange-red in colour (Plate 28A, B) thinning to white at the edges, and were often associated with small pieces of floating oil or chalk. The *Noctiluca* was concentrated near the surface of the sea, except in the evening, when it submerged. The association between *Noctiluca* and floating oil or chalk is probably due to 'convection cells' as described for plankton patches by Bary (1953). These would tend to concentrate plankton and floating particles into bands or streaks at the surface during calm weather. This red tide was evidently non-toxic, as no dead marine animals were seen.

Information on the outbursts of dinoflagellates and other organisms causing red tides has been summarized by Rounsefell & Nelson (1966). Outbursts occur in calm weather, mainly in warm waters, and after diatom blooms have impoverished the water of nutrients. They often occur in coastal regions subject to run-off from the land. Surprisingly enough the level of phosphorus in sea water within the red tide area may be very high, as much as ten times the normal level, but whether this is a cause or an effect is not clear.

Without further information it is difficult to speculate about possible causes of the red tide observed around the treated oil. The chalk or the oil might be a source of substances favourable to *Noctiluca*; partially anaerobic conditions may have been produced through bacterial action on the oil masses (aided perhaps by the breaking up of the oil by the chalk, so increasing its surface area); or the *Noctiluca* may have been feeding on micro-organisms which were themselves attacking the oil.

One possibility seemed to be that the chalk was a source of phosphate, but an analysis showed a content of only 300 ppm.

Some laboratory experiments were carried out, oil and chalk being added to *Noctiluca* cultures. These failed to show that these substances appreciably affected the rate of multiplication of *Noctiluca* in culture.

BARRAGES AND BOOMS

The French had some success with booms, and the M.B.A. scientists had an account from M. Cabioch, sous-Directeur at Roscoff, of the booms set up to defend the harbour and laboratory foreshore at Roscoff. Some of the

oil from the Côtes du Nord, some 20 miles to the east, later drifted towards the Gulf of Morlaix and Roscoff, where it was under constant surveillance by local boats. The first boom was constructed in a great hurry, using straw covered with jute fibres buoyed up at intervals with tractor inner tyre tubes. The second boom had an expanded polyurethane core, surrounded by straw tied on, and a final covering of jute fibres. This boom was heavier, and according to M. Cabioch, less successful as a protection against oil. By means of these booms Roscoff was kept free of the oil, which for a time drifted in between the Ile de Batz and the mainland. The Biological Station at Roscoff is publishing an account of their experiences in a forthcoming number of the *Cahiers de Biologie Marine*.

CONDITION OF THE BEACHES

North coast

The beaches of the north coast of Brittany received about 15–18 000 tons of oil, which arrived on 10–12 April over about 60 miles of coast on the Côtes du Nord, between Trébeurden and the Sillon de Talbert (Fig. 39). Lesser amounts came ashore west of Trébeurden, and in Finistère as far west as Roscoff. There was a significant quantity on the shores of Finistère between Locquirec and the Pte de Primel, but very much less than in Côtes du Nord. Scientists from Roscoff were familiar with the beaches in Finistère both before and after the arrival of the oil, but had scarcely visited the polluted areas of Côtes du Nord, where the fauna was considered to be less rich.

From Trébeurden north and eastward to Perros-Guirec the M.B.A. scientists visited a number of beaches which were uniformly polluted, showing a dark brown-black band of oil about a metre wide on the rocks at high water for many miles. The oil had arrived in calm weather, so this band was quite level. The coast in this region is mainly rocky with large pink granite boulders, up to 15 metres or more across, and unlike Cornwall is readily accessible as there are no high cliffs. There are also stretches of sand or gravel between the rocks.

Little or no attempt had been made to clean most of the shoreline, so that its condition contrasted with that of Cornwall which had mostly been sprayed with detergent. In mid-June the oil on the rocks was almost black (Plate 27B). We were informed by M. Cabioch that it came ashore

---

PLATE 29

A, Steam-cleaning of oily rocks at Locquirec, Finistère, 20 June. B, North end of Trégastel-Plage (Côtes du Nord), 21 June. Troops wearing gasmasks spraying oily rocks with detergent.

PLATE 29

A

B

(*Facing p.* 168)

reddish brown in colour but after two days' exposure to the sun during neap tides it became blackened. The sandy regions had been to some extent treated with detergent and by mechanical means, but where they had not been so treated the surface of the sand was a dark blackish brown, sometimes with a thin hard crust of oil, with lighter brown oil in the top 10 cm of the sand (Plate 27 C).

At Ile Grande such an untouched beach of coarse sand showed some evidence of biodegradation of the oil in the sand (p. 81), as under some patches of oil a thin grey layer was present. Farther east near Trégastel, in a similar coarse sand beach, the layer of sticky brown oil showed no evidence of biodegradation at the time.

In general the impression was that pollution had been overall heavier than in Cornwall, although at some places, such as Sennen and Porthleven, worse conditions had been observed. It is likely that an earlier visit, when conditions would have been comparable to those first seen in Cornwall, would have suggested that pollution in Brittany was everywhere worse than in Cornwall, where a rather smaller quantity of oil was spread over a much longer coastline.

West coast

South of Brest, beaches polluted by oil which came ashore about 20 May were visited on 23 June. Beaches on the west coast of the Crozon peninsula were inspected, but not those around the Pte du Raz, where pollution on a similar scale has been reported. Estimates of 300 tons as the total for the western beaches suggested that pollution was light, and the oil which was found was more or less confined to the northern end of the beaches. Oiled rocks were black, and at one or two places were covered by up to 5 cm of thick viscous oil. At the north end of the Anse de Dinan, in addition to this type of pollution, there were small lumps of brownish oil on the strand line evidently drifted in at a later date than the main pollution. None of these beaches had been treated with detergent, but one beach had been treated mechanically by bulldozing, and at another some troops were collecting and burning small lumps of oil and driftwood.

The quantity of oil on each of these beaches appeared to be less than a ton, so that 100 tons may be a more realistic figure for the total drifted ashore from an original mass of over 48 000 tons.

METHODS OF TREATMENT

The following notes apply mainly to the north coast of Brittany.

Gorse and straw

Some sandy beaches had been cleansed of oil by laying a line of gorse or straw on the beach at low water. As the tide rose, these materials rolled up the beach and collected oily sand. They were then picked up and burned, and the process repeated. Repetition of this process over a month was said to be most effective, and the sandy part of the beach at Locquirec, for example, where this method had been used, was clean. Sawdust (of which there were traces on many beaches) was also tried in this way, but was not found to be effective.

Removal of upper layers of sand

When the oil arrived on sandy beaches it was reported to have sunk to about 15 cm below the surface. Cores taken at Ile Grande showed oil (in an untreated beach) in the top 10 cm. Since the beaches are mainly accessible to vehicles it had been feasible to bulldoze off the upper layers, repeating the process until all the oiled sand had been removed. In addition to bulldozers, two large machines flailing sand into a hopper were seen at Trégastel, the sand being carried away and dumped to aid land reclamation nearby (Plate 28 c).

Steam cleaning

On 20 June the M.B.A. scientists attended an experimental cleaning of oiled rocks at Locquirec (Finistère) under the direction of M. Daniel (head of Civil Defence for the department). Troops were using small trailer-mounted steam-cleaning equipment of the same kind as is used to clean the underside of vehicles (Plate 29 A). Steam at 140 °C and 8 kg/cm² was being delivered from small nozzles at the end of pipes held by the operators, who were equipped with oilskins and gasmasks (the latter not in use). A small quantity of Teepol (1 l. Teepol to 300 l. water) was added to the cold water used for rinsing the rocks after the steam treatment, and this produced a white foam around the treated areas. By this method 30 square meters of rock surface could be cleaned per hour per machine. An ample supply of fresh water, around 2000 l. per machine, was required.

The treated area was at high-water mark with few animals on it, and the steam treatment seemed to clean the rocks effectively. Below the treated reef, streams of water ran down through the sand, and in places the black sulphide layer in the fine sand had been washed up to the surface. It is

possible that this may have resulted from previous mechanical removal of sand, which had begun on 10 April, as soon as the beach had been polluted.

There was no evidence of plant or animal mortalities on this beach, although anything subjected directly to steam treatment would naturally be killed. The ultimate fate of the oil removed by steam treatment and washed down the beach is not known.

No detergents were being used for beach cleaning in the department of Finistère. Because of the important inshore oyster beds and shellfish industry of the area the civil defence authorities had been strongly advised against the use of detergents by scientists at the Roscoff Marine Biological station. A few miles to the east, however, in Côtes du Nord, detergents were being used for beach cleaning.

Detergents

Detergents were being used to clean rocky shores at various places on the coast of Côtes du Nord, the coast being much more heavily polluted than in Finistère. Detergent treatment began on 24 May and continued until the beginning of July. During this period some 2300 tons of detergent were reported to have been used. At the time of our visit detergents were being used more or less on an experimental basis under the direction of two experts from the Institut National de Recherche Chimique Appliquée, seconded to Roscoff from the Laboratory of the Ecole Polytechnique.

The chief detergents used were Oxane and Fina-sol, the latter being a dark red liquid, non-ionic, with a much less pronounced smell than BP 1002. The chemists from I.R.C.A. had been sent more than sixty types of detergent, of which Fina-sol had proved to be the least toxic. Toxicity tests carried out by M. Audouin of the Fisheries Laboratory at Roscoff confirmed the opinion earlier put forward in this report that the more efficacious the detergent the more toxic it is. Some experiments had been carried out upon emulsion stability, the conclusion being that few brands were capable of forming a stable emulsion of oil in sea water.

Drums of detergent were pumped into small trailers at the army camps, and these small trailer tankers were then moved by lorry to different sites, where spraying was carried out (Plate 29 B). A number of commercial tanker lorries were also employed. Operations were on a smaller scale than in Cornwall, spraying being from small nozzles by operators dressed in oilskins and wearing gasmasks. Only a limited area was treated at one time, the operators then moving elsewhere. On the badly polluted beach of Trégastel, spraying on the rocks produced sufficient detergent to form a white patch in the water which gradually filled the harbour (Plates 22 B, 28 C). The sand became impregnated with detergent from the water: it was

not sprayed directly. On this beach, dead limpets, other gastropods and crabs were found. Spraying had been carried on there for some time prior to the visit. At this site alone of those visited, oil layers were found buried below clean sand.

Despite the fact that the oil being treated by detergent was some two months old and had become black, the spraying seemed to be efficient at removing it. Fresh brown patches of oil (Plate 6A) some metres across were observed at Trégastel on the water in the harbour perhaps resulting from de-emulsified oil returning. Similar small patches were observed on the strand line near Ile Grande (Plate 6B). At other beaches, such as Perros-Guirec, detergent had been used, and a sulphide layer, 1 cm below the sand surface, smelt of detergent. An iridescent oil film was present on the water-table. In the harbours of Ploumenac'h and Tourony nearby the water was milky white and the sand smelt of detergent. Dead crabs were floating there, and a local resident reported that dead congers had been found. Although the lagoon of Tourony dries out at low tide, and although detergent-spraying had stopped there five days prior to our visit, the water was still milky with detergent at high tide. Spraying had been carried out here for the past month.

The general impression gained was that at Trégastel and certain other beaches much detergent had been used, and that similar effects to those observed in Cornwall were either observed or could be expected. It seemed probable that more detergent would be used.

No evidence was obtained of any effects of detergent upon the important lobster fisheries of the Côtes du Nord, but, if spraying were carried out elsewhere in the same manner as at Trégastel, it seemed likely that toxic effects would be observed.

OIL POLLUTION IN GUERNSEY

The following notes on oil pollution in Guernsey were made by a member of the M.B.A. scientific staff who visited the island on 10 and 11 July. He is indebted to Mr Guillaumette (States Supervisor), Mr Bichard (Department of Public Works) and Capt. Walker (Fishery Officer) for information and assistance.

Guernsey, the only one of the Channel Islands to suffer pollution, received a severe but localized shore fouling on 6 April. Shortly afterwards the very large mass of oil which later went ashore on the Côtes du Nord of Brittany (Fig. 34) passed very close to the Channel Islands and much of it was blown southwards through the channel between Guernsey and Sark.

The only badly affected area was a two-mile stretch of the west coast of

Guernsey from Saumarez Fort to the south end of Vazon Bay (Plate 27A). The intertidal reefs in this area are very extensive, up to half a mile wide in places, forming small north-facing bays and fortunately one of the least popular spots for holiday visitors. While the wind stayed onshore the most effective means of disposal was found to be the direct pumping of oil from the sea surface at high water and just after. Up to seventeen sewage tankers of 800–1000 gallon capacity were available and, fortunately, good access to the shore was possible from several slipways. A minimum thickness of oil of about 2 inches was necessary for successful pumping; so long as the wind stayed fresh the depth of oil built up at times to 4 inches. If the wind dropped or changed, pumping had to stop. Pumping was carried on until 24 April when the wind changed to south-east for less than a day, but the remaining floating oil was carried away to the south.

Some of the oil pumped from the sea was delivered through a large (4 inch) suction pump into a pit or tank from which the tankers filled up later, and small amounts of oil were pumped from pools with portable pumps. The total quantity of oil removed directly was 866000 gallons (*ca.* 3000 tons).

Steam-cleaning plant was tested on oil-covered walls but was found to be very slow compared to light detergent spraying coupled with pressure jets of water from a fire-hose.

The use of detergent was very strictly limited (it had to be paid for at 6*s.* per gallon) and was generally confined to slipways and sea-walls. Very extensive rock areas around the level of high-water neaps were still blackened on 10 July and will be left. The oil residues on the rock surfaces were dry to a light touch and slightly powdery. The oil took many days to adhere to the rock and did not affect lower parts of the shore.

Natural banks of broken kelp above high water absorbed the oil and cut weed was used deliberately to a small extent to absorb it.

Rock pools in the most heavily polluted reefs contained a normal fauna, including blennies, sea anemones, winkles, limpets, etc. Nearby several live ormers (*Haliotis*) were found during a short search just below low-water springs at Le Jaune Pont.

The total cost of the oil clearance work in Guernsey was estimated to be about £30000 (working out at roughly £10 a ton).

CHAPTER 10

SOME LESSONS LEARNT

SUMMARY OF MAIN RESULTS

The investigations reported in the previous chapters of this book have provided us with new information about the movement of oil at sea, about the properties of detergents and their dispersal in the sea, and about the effects that these two pollutants have had upon the animals and plants with which they have come into contact both at sea and on the shore. How can we profit from this information; what advice can we give for dealing with similar problems that arise in the future; and what can we suggest for further lines of research which ought to be put in hand?

Perhaps first it is convenient to refer to some of the more important points which have been discussed and emphasized in earlier chapters.

As regards the oil itself, the formation of emulsions of variable composition with sea water makes it difficult to predict the rate of loss of oil by evaporation. In connection with the drift of oil at sea a simple formula has been given which allows the movement of oil on the sea to be predicted. Pollution by the 'Torrey Canyon' oil was found to have little biological effect apart from the tragic destruction of sea birds.

The detergent used to treat the oil away from the coast was not noticeably injurious to marine life except in the extreme surface layers, where pilchard eggs and some phytoplankton were affected. The direct treatment of polluted shores, however, resulted in the death of a large number of shore organisms of many different kinds, and effects were also observed in the sublittoral zone. •

On shores left untreated, evidence has been obtained of removal of the oil by the fauna as well as by other natural agencies. In addition, on sandy beaches microbiological degradation has been occurring unhindered by detergent treatment.

Studies in the laboratory showed that, in addition to the immediate effects observed, longer-term consequences might be expected. It was found that the immediate toxicity of the detergent largely resides in the solvent fraction of the detergents, which is fortunately readily lost by evaporation from sea water, although it is adsorbed on to sand, and may have temporary physical effects upon sandy beaches. In general, treatment has been found to be most successful upon rocky shores; on sandy beaches the use of detergent has been less successful. On both types of shore, however, treatment has led to some degree of secondary pollution owing to

instability of oil–detergent emulsions which allow the oil to re-separate from the emulsion. Methods have been devised for the bioassay of detergents in sea water, and these have been used to follow the dispersion of detergents in the sea after use on the shore. These show that dispersion is largely dependent upon local weather conditions.

POLLUTION

These results have emerged from a study of some of the effects of a major instance of pollution. To be quite clear what we mean, pollution may be defined as 'an event or a continuing circumstance whereby there are introduced into the environments of air, land and water substances that may adversely affect the balance of nature and human well-being'. Pollution of the environment affects everybody. It may carry with it an actual or a potential danger to man's health and to his economy, and it may be damaging to or destructive of features of the natural environment that provide the means of recreation and aesthetic enjoyment. In a modern industrialized society the problems of pollution apply with especial force. They are, moreover, complicated by the fact that some forms of pollution are often permitted in the interest of one requirement but to the detriment of others.

The 'Torrey Canyon' disaster presented these aspects and problems of pollution in such an acute and severe form that it evoked two immediate and significant reactions.

In the first place the unexpected drama of the event, and the magnitude and variety of its possible consequences, showed that when the dangers of pollution are evident there is a widespread public concern for the formulation and development of a nationally conceived policy for dealing with pollution hazards. Secondly, the disaster necessitated the setting up at short notice of administrative arrangements, technological procedures and scientific programmes to asssess and, where possible, to counteract the consequences of the large-scale oil pollution. The 'Torrey Canyon' campaign has thus shown up the strength and weaknesses of a complicated collaborative exercise in ways which, if the lessons are properly learnt, will be of the greatest value in the framing of future procedures and policy for dealing with pollution problems generally.

THE BIOLOGICAL ASPECT

The Plymouth Laboratory was directly concerned with only a small sector of the 'Torrey Canyon' programmes. In association with scientists of the Ministry of Agriculture, Fisheries and Food and of the Nature Conser-

vancy, our primary purpose was to assess the damage done by oil and detergents to marine life and to make recommendations on the measures needed to reduce and alleviate such damage.

We soon found, however, that the need to obtain information on matters essential to our investigations—for example, the composition of detergents, the quantities used in different localities, the movements of oil at sea and its influx on to beaches—involved us intimately in all aspects of the remedial measures. And, in addition, we extended our investigations to the examination of some physical phenomena such as the movements of oil at sea and the stability of detergent-treated beaches which were not originally in our programmes. This has enabled us to view the problems of pollution in a broader perspective than at first we had thought possible. It is therefore thought appropriate to draw on these experiences, as well as on the results of our biological investigations, in commenting on the 'Torrey Canyon' procedures, to make suggestions which may be helpful in the planning of future programmes of work on marine pollution. We omit from our comments, however, reference to matters which are outside our scientific competence; for example, questions bearing on the salvage of the 'Torrey Canyon', the disposal of oil contained within the ship, and the efficacy of mechanical devices designed to prevent the spread of oil and to provide the means of collecting it. These matters are dealt with fully in the Report of the Committee of Scientists on the Scientific and Technological Aspects of the 'Torrey Canyon' Disaster (1967). Our comments are arranged under the following headings: 'Torrey Canyon' programmes and procedures in retrospect; organizational requirements for future emergencies; a final comment.

'Torrey Canyon' programmes and procedures in retrospect

The 'Torrey Canyon' marine pollution was caused by crude oil released on to the surface of the sea and by non-ionic detergents used in the dispersal of the oil. Oil, although it killed several thousand sea birds, was recognized from the outset of the 'Torrey Canyon' operations to be a pollutant mainly destructive of the amenities of shores and beaches; detergents, on the other hand, were known to be destructive of life.

There was therefore built into the operations, from the beginning, a division of effort and of purpose. Almost the entire complex machinery of policy-making, administration and technological procedures were focused on the problem of disposing of the oil, either by getting rid of it at source, by preventing it reaching shores, or if these methods failed by removing it from rocks and beaches. With the preservation of one kind of amenity the primary and most urgent objective of the operations, the biologists' role

was thus essentially to assess the effects of the oil pollution and of the use of detergents. A situation of this kind inevitably means, in a crisis, that the many bodies engaged in the preservation of 'amenity' have this purpose wholly in view and have little occasion to consult biologists for information which could assist them in their purpose. Biologists, on the other hand, must continually seek for information as to what is being done if they are to measure the effects of the pollutants and to recommend (as we were required to do) the measures needed to reduce and to alleviate the damage which they cause.

During the 'Torrey Canyon' operations we were fortunate in finding at Maritime H.Q. liaison personnel who were sympathetic and helpful in answering inquiries. Our work, however, would have been made easier, if from the beginning of the operations, there could have been established an interchange of personnel on a recognized basis between the Plymouth Laboratory, as the centre of biological operations, and Maritime H.Q. This would have needed one or two additional staff at H.Q. who could have spent some time each day at the Laboratory to see at first hand the nature and progress of the research going on and to discuss its implications with members of the staff. A direct contact of this kind would have been of particular value in assessing: the movements of oil at sea; the determination of its quantity in the travelling patches; in advising H.Q. on the routing of air reconnaissance flights; and in alerting authorities in France of the magnitude, rate of travel and direction of approach of oil patches threatening the French coastline.

Within the Laboratory itself our main need, once the programmes of investigation had been formulated, was to ensure (a) that we had expert advice available on all matters relevant to the study of pollution problems and (b) that the teams of workers in each field should be large enough to cover, in the limited time available, the work that had to be done. Pollution problems required the participation of organic and physical chemists, hydrographers, physiologists, pharmacologists and bacteriologists; and they involve the expertise of ecologists with a special knowledge of planktonic or of benthic organisms. So far as possible it is most important that all should work in a laboratory near the scene of operations. Only in this way can a problem which overlaps many scientific disciplines be fully probed, and the expert in each field be assured of the means of seeing the opportunities offered for study and for developing his investigations in his own way. During the 'Torrey Canyon' investigations we often felt the need for assistance in particular fields (e.g. bacteriology) and we should perhaps have been more active in recruiting it had we always known where to make the approaches.

We may now turn to some of the problems which had to be tackled in examining the biological consequences of the 'Torrey Canyon' pollution, and, in particular, to the effects of the use of detergents.

As has already been made clear in this report, the decision to use detergents for the dispersal of oil was taken on the view—with which there will be general agreement—that the preservation of coastal recreational amenities was of first priority, and in the hope that the effects of detergents on marine life would not be catastrophic. Let it be said straightway that the effects have not been catastrophic. But it would be wise not to take comfort from the outcome of an action taken largely in ignorance of its possible consequences. It is all the more necessary therefore in the light of our new-found knowledge of the nature and effects of detergents to examine (a) by comparison with other possible methods of oil clearance, the efficiency of the detergent method of dispersal, and (b) the possibility of the modification of detergents to reduce their toxicity.

Non-ionic detergents have been used for some years by the Navy and by harbour authorities for clearing small oil spills. Though detrimental to marine life if used repeatedly, they have been found to be convenient, efficient when properly applied, and relatively inexpensive to use when only small quantities of detergent (used in an approximate proportion of 1 part by volume of detergent to 2–4 parts of oil) were needed.

The decision to spray at sea the large oil masses which were escaping from the 'Torrey Canyon' was taken on the basis of these experiences. It has been argued that, if complete emulsification of the oil was, in fact, achieved, the 700000 gallons of detergent employed in the sea-spraying operations would have effectively dispersed up to 15000 tons of oil which might otherwise have been carried on to the neighbouring coastline (Committee of Scientists Report, 1967). However, the total cost of the sea operations was probably of the order of £400000 and the question arises as to whether the operation could have been done more cheaply and more effectively.

An alternative method of disposing of oil from the surface of the sea that was tried during the 'Torrey Canyon' operation was the French practice of sprinkling powdered natural chalk (with 1 per cent sodium stearate added) on to the oil. Our information was that 3000 tons of chalk were applied, and we estimate that up to 30000 tons of oil may have been sunk by this method (Chapter 9). Evidently, much more chalk would have been required to sink the same amount of freshly released oil, for the amount of chalk required depends directly upon the density of the oil to be treated; the longer that oil remains at sea the denser it becomes by evaporation of the lighter fractions. The cost of the materials has not been ascertained but it would undoubtedly have been but a small fraction of

the estimated £200000 spent on sea-sprayed detergents alone in the area of the Seven Stones. Possible disadvantages of the chalk-sinking procedure are that (1) the sunk oil may foul fishing grounds, and (2) the oil may subsequently be washed ashore. All that can be said at present is that there have been no reports that either has happened. There is at least a prima facie case for believing that oil patches moving into the open sea and away from the coast are best dealt with by sprinkling with chalk, or better still, a heavier material rendered unwettable by suitable pretreatment (for example, silicone-treated sand). Such methods might also be as effective as any other in dealing with oil patches driven towards the shore, though under these conditions the danger of sea-bed fouling, adverse to inshore fisheries, might render the chalk treatment undesirable. Nor might it be altogether suitable in shallow areas such as the Thames Estuary or off the Rhine delta. Much depends on how quickly the sunk oil is destroyed by bacteria.

In commenting on the use of detergents for the cleansing of rocky shores and sandy beaches, we fully agree with the point made in the Committee of Scientists Report that every attempt should be made to remove oil from shores and their approaches by mechanical devices and trapping materials, wherever they can be effectively used. It cannot be emphasized too strongly that detergents, at best, can only *disperse*—they do not *destroy* the oil. But where there is a need for the rapid cleansing of a shore the 'Torrey Canyon' operations have shown that detergent treatment can be very effective. There is, however, both for reasons of economy and the preservation of shore life, a need to employ detergents with discrimination.

We were told, at the beginning of the operations, that detergents are only effective in clearing oil from rock surfaces if applied quickly, and before the oil has undergone changes. This has been shown, in the course of 'Torrey Canyon' operations, not to be true. Oil can be cleared effectively from rocks weeks after deposition, provided always that the detergent is applied in a proper manner, and adequate agitation given to the oil–detergent mixture. As therefore a delay in spraying is permissible, the most favourable conditions of wind and tide can and should be selected. It would then not only be possible to consider the optimal conditions for dispersal of the oil, but also to give due regard to the effects of the spraying on the flora and fauna of the affected area. Some places, notably, inaccessible coves should be left undisturbed for, as shown in this report, natural processes including removal of oil by browsing intertidal animals and bacterial decomposition will in the course of a few months bring about a considerable recovery. The nature and time scale of these processes need further investigation. Where rocky shores are needed for holiday recreation there seems, however, to be a case for employing detergent

treatment to the point that they are again acceptable, although this may result in secondary pollution of adjacent sandy areas.

Oil on sandy beaches indeed presents an intractable problem. The difficulty here is that detergent-treated oil sinks into sand and may remain there for a considerable time to be uncovered at intervals by wave removal of the cleaner surface deposits. Moreover, oil mixed with sand may sink below low-tide mark and be subsequently washed back on the shore by gales.

The method of bulldozing oil-covered sand to the lower levels of the beach and there treating it with detergents met with some success, but owing to the instability of the oil–detergent emulsion the oil was apt to reappear and be redeposited elsewhere. An alternative method, if places for disposal are readily accessible, would be to remove the oily surface sand mechanically. Open coast beaches often have a sufficient cover to make this practicable without dangerously exposing the backing cliff to erosion, but the method would need to be used only when the conditions for sand removal are favourable.

We now consider the toxicity of detergents, with its attendant problems of (1) when, in their present form, their use would not be desirable, and (2) whether they could be modified to make them less toxic.

It may be supposed that the use of detergents for shore-cleansing becomes undesirable when the preservation of amenities is outweighed by other considerations of which the economic value of fisheries is probably the most important. The more cautious use of detergents by the French reflects the greater economic importance and the more open-shore siting of their shellfish industry. At the outset of the 'Torrey Canyon' operations it was very wisely decided, on the advice of Ministry of Agriculture, Fisheries and Food scientists that detergents should not be used in estuaries where there are commercially important shellfish beds. This should be a continuing directive to which greater point is given by the experiences gained from the 'Torrey Canyon' disaster. If they are protected by booms, estuaries are not likely to be polluted. Should oil enter, in small quantity, our evidence is that it would not kill shellfish, though it would probably make it undesirable for them to be eaten until the oil had been dissipated by natural processes of change and degradation.

The beaches and sea-beds affected by the 'Torrey Canyon' oil, and subjected to detergent treatment, were almost all of the clean, silt-free sand type characteristic of wave-exposed shores. The sand of these beaches is mobile and contains few animals other than minute interstitially living organisms. If, however, the pollution had occurred in a region of more heavily populated sandy muds and muds the high toxicity of the detergents

would have had a catastrophic effect. Oil deposited on the muddy sands and muds of quiet water regions might be very difficult to remove, but use of detergent is not likely to improve the situation.

Our investigations have shown that the toxicity of detergents resides mainly in their volatile aromatic components and we would advise that research is urgently needed to discover whether less toxic materials can be found as substitutes for the presently used solvent fractions. The surfactant components of detergents are much less toxic, but, since they are more persistent in sea water, further biological investigations are required in order to test their possible long-term effects on organisms and their concentration within the terminal organisms of food-chains.

We now comment on our organization of onshore and offshore surveys.

An essential requirement for a scientific analysis of an artificial change of environment on the populations of marine organisms is that the means shall be available for comparing the population changes with any alterations which would have occurred in the course of normal seasonal and other natural changes of the environment. In order to assess the effects of detergents on the populations of intertidal animals it is therefore necessary to have available for collateral study a nearby shore that has not been subject to detergent cleansing. It was a feature of the 'Torrey Canyon' shore-cleansing operations that they left hardly a single locality free from the suspicion of some measure of detergent treatment. If biologists are to report adequately on the effects of a pollution they must be left in possession of a control, and must be consulted before the operations have gone too far on the localities which are to be left untouched. From the few moderately oil-polluted sites that were in fact left untreated, the natural cleansing action of wave, sand, and fauna has become obvious.

A programme of regular surveys will be a continuing requirement if pollution effects are to be adequately assessed in the future. They will also be necessary in the immediate task of assessing the patterns of recolonization of shores following their treatment by detergent. There is therefore, in our opinion, an immediate need to provide by appropriate directives for the reservation of selected localities as 'protected' areas free from avoidable unnatural disturbance.

In carrying out our shore and offshore surveys we had two main purposes in mind: to report, in essentially qualitative terms, on the developing destruction in as many localities as could be visited by our few scientists in the limited time available to them; and to survey more continuously and in greater detail one or two localities which we had examined regularly for many years. The latter aim was only partly achieved because the oil did not reach our home grounds. The detailed survey of the progress of the

destruction of a rich and varied fauna and flora requires a concentrated and sustained attention, which can only be given by large teams working day by day on a shore and with well-prepared objectives, and where detergent-spraying or other treatment is carried out by authorities in collaboration with the scientists. This is a further example of the need for early discussion and collaboration of personnel at Operations H.Q. with the scientists involved in the biological surveys.

Our offshore surveys were limited in scope by the fact that only a single suitable research vessel was available; the cruise programme had therefore to be devised to cover as many different lines of investigation as possible, and this led to insufficient coverage of some important aspects.

Had our surveys been co-ordinated with other programmes including the aerial surveys, such important tasks as the collection of oil samples at sea to determine the progress of the ageing of the oil and its increase in density (relevant to decisions about the best method of treatment) could have been carried out more efficiently. We also think it important subsequently to follow not only movements of visible oil patches, but also the fate of very finely dispersed oil over the general sea surface.

Finally, some mention should be made of the observations and predictions made by scientists at the Plymouth Laboratory on the movements of oil at sea, the results of which are reported in Chapter 8.

As the laboratory nearest the scene of the wreck we began immediately to collect all the data relating to oil movements that we could lay hands on and we continued to collect records and to study them as a research project. By mid-April we had become seriously concerned that a very large amount of oil had disappeared from the scene, apparently without trace. The predictions shown in Figs. 32–38 were based on calculations from wind velocities and were intended as directives to further observation. Coastal Command of the Royal Air Force gave us most willingly all the assistance that it was in their power to give but their programmes did not allow them to fly the sorties which we needed. Our calculations remained therefore largely theoretical until at a later date oil stranded on the coast of Brittany and we established contact with the French Navy through Professor Courtot of the Faculté des Sciences, Brest.

We feel that the National Institute of Oceanography would have been admirably fitted not only to plot events but actively to advise the British and neighbouring governments on the air reconnaissance necessary for advising on the coasts which were at hazard.

It is, of course, easy to comment after all the facts have been collated and tested, but in any future incident of this kind we strongly urge the National Institute of Oceanography should at once be consulted as expert advisers

on the probable course of events. The Institute is well able to co-ordinate effort with its sister laboratories in neighbouring countries with which it has close contacts. Such international co-ordination was needed but was only slowly achieved.

Organizational requirements for future emergencies

Our commentaries on the lessons learnt from the 'Torrey Canyon' disaster and from the investigation of its biological consequences have included some suggestions and recommendations that may be of value in future emergencies of a similar kind. Oil pollution and the measures necessary to counteract it could, however, occur over any part of the British coastline, and it is appropriate to consider the means by which the investigation of the biological consequences might most effectively be organized on a regional basis.

We have given our reasons for believing that complex investigations of this kind, involving a wide range of scientific disciplines, need to be based on a laboratory with staff and facilities adequate to service these various requirements. It would seem desirable therefore in anticipation of future emergencies to prepare a list of regional centres upon which pollution investigations could be based. Such a centre would ideally be not more than 30–40 miles from the field operations, and would need to be of a size and scientific coverage such as is provided in Britain mainly by marine laboratories and universities. If the co-operation of suitably located universities could be sought in the provision of facilities for the conduct of emergency programmes a substantial part of the British coastline could be covered by a chain of regional centres. Within the framework of the present organization of civil science in the United Kingdom, the Natural Environment Research Council might well be thought to be the body best able to organize the regional arrangements and to provide such advice and assistance as would be needed in preparation for future emergencies.

A final comment

The 'Torrey Canyon' disaster highlighted with an exceptional clarity the unpleasantness (to put its consequences in the least emotive terms) that can arise when materials essential to man's industrialized society escape from the confines of their intended use to foul the environment.

The escape through human error or by unavoidable accident of dangerous or unpleasant pollutant materials are hazards which must be accepted and dealt with as the occasion arises and as best we can. Other forms of pollution are intentional and many are thought to be necessary. If we ask why they are thought to be necessary there can be but one answer: it is because

12-2

the easiest and cheapest way of disposing of unwanted materials is to throw them away. If materials so disposed of are harmless and unenduring no one minds very much. But, if they are injurious and persistent, acceptable means of disposing of them must be found even though it may be expensive to find the answer.

We are progressively making a slum of nature and may eventually find that we are enjoying the benefit of science and industry under conditions which no civilized society should tolerate.

BIBLIOGRAPHY

FURTHER READING

A general account of the shipwreck of the 'Torrey Canyon' and consequent fouling is described in:

GILL, C., BOOKER, F. & SOPER, T. (1967). *The Wreck of the Torrey Canyon.* Newton Abbott: David and Charles. 128 pp.

Recent reports on the subject of oil pollution also include:

BEYNON, L. R. (1967). *The Torrey Canyon Incident: A Review of Events.* British Petroleum Company. 20 pp.

BOURNE, W. R. P., PARRACK, J. D. & POTTS, G. R. (1967). Birds killed in the 'Torrey Canyon' disaster. *Nature, Lond.* **215**, 1123–5.

COMMITTEE OF SCIENTISTS (1967). Report on the Scientific and Technological Aspects of the 'Torrey Canyon' Disaster. H.M. Stationery Office, 48 pp.

DEVON TRUST FOR NATURE CONSERVATION (1967). Conservation and the 'Torrey Canyon'. *Suppl. Jl Devon Trust Nature Conserv.*, July 1967. 72 pp.

DREW, A., FORSTER, G. R., GAGE, J., HARWOOD, G. E., LARKUM, A. W. D., LYTHGOE, J. N., POTTS, G. W. & VINCE, M. (1967). 'Torrey Canyon' Report. *Underwater Association Report 1966–67*, edited by J. N. Lythgoe and J. D. Woods. P. G. W. Industrial and Research Promotions Ltd., pp. 53–60.

HOLME, N. A. (1968). Pollution par le mazout des côtes de Cornouailles anglaise à la suite du naufrage du 'Torrey Canyon'. *Penn Bed.* **6**, 88–94.

MELLANBY, K. (1967). *Pesticides and Pollution.* London: Collins. (New Naturalist Series.) 221 pp.

PILPEL, N. (1954). Oil pollution of the sea. *Research* **7**, 301–6.

The scientific names of the plants and animals mentioned in the text are those used in:

MARINE BIOLOGICAL ASSOCIATION U.K. (1957). *Plymouth Marine Fauna*, 3rd edition. Plymouth, xliii, 457 pp.

PARKE, M. & DIXON, P. S. (1964). A revised check-list of British marine Algae. *J. mar. biol. Ass. U.K.* **44**, 499–542.

Descriptions and illustrations of many of the organisms may be found in one or more of the following works:

BARRETT, J. G. & YONGE, C. M. (1958). *Collins Pocket Guide to the Sea Shore.* London: Collins. 272 pp. (For descriptions of the common plants and animals on British coasts. Illustrations of many species.)

DICKINSON, C. I. (1963). *British Seaweeds.* London: Eyre and Spottiswoode. (Kew Series.) 232 pp.

HAAS, W. DE & KNORR, F. (1966). *The Young Specialist Looks at Marine Life.* London: Burke. 356 pp. (Good illustrations of both shore and offshore organisms.)

HARDY, A. C. (1956). *The Open Sea: Its Natural History: Pt. I: The World of Plankton.* London: Collins. (New Naturalist Series.) 335 pp. (Contains illustrations of many planktonic organisms.)

WILSON, D. P. (1935). *Life of the Shore and Shallow Sea.* London: Ivor Nicholson and Watson. 150 pp. (Contains photographs of many shore species, many taken at Trevone (see Chapter 4).)

YONGE, C. M. (1949). *The Sea Shore*. London: Collins. (New Naturalist Series.) 311 pp. (General descriptions and illustrations of shore species.)

If further details are required the bibliographies in the above list of references should be consulted.

REFERENCES

Chapter 1

NELSON-SMITH, A. (1968). The effects of oil pollution and emulsifier cleansing upon shore life in south-west Britain. *J. appl. Ecol.* (in the Press).

Chapter 2

ADAM, N. K. (1936). *The Pollution of the Sea and Shore by Oil: A Report Submitted to the Council of the Royal Society*. London: Royal Society. 27 pp.

GERADE, H. W. & SKIBA, P. (1960). A colorimetric method for the determination of kerosene in blood. *Clin. Chem.* **6**, 327–31.

ORTON, J. H. (1925). Effects on marine organisms of oils discharged at sea. *Nature, Lond.* **115**, 910–11.

ZOBELL, C. E. (1964). The occurrence, effects, and fate of oil polluting the sea. *Proc. Int. Conf. Wat. Poll. Res.* 1962 (Pergamon Press, 1964), pp. 85–118. (*Contr. Scripps Instn Oceanogr.* **34** (1964), 1257–83.)

Chapter 3

SOUTHWARD, A. J. (1962). The distribution of some plankton animals in the English Channel and approaches. II. Surveys with the Gulf III high-speed sampler, 1958–60. *J. mar. biol. Ass. U.K.* **42**, 275–375.

Chapter 4

CRISP, D. J. & SOUTHWARD, A. J. (1958). The distribution of intertidal organisms along the coasts of the English Channel. *J. mar. biol. Ass. U.K.* **37**, 157–208.

FISCHER-PIETTE, E. (1936). Etudes sur la biogéographie intercotidale des deux rives de la Manche. *J. Linn. Soc. (Zool.)* **40**, 181–272.

GEORGE, H. (1961). Oil pollution of marine organisms. *Nature, Lond.* **192**, 1209.

MONTEROSSO, B. (1930). Studi cirripedologici. VI. Sul comportamento di *Chthamalus stellatus* in diverse condizioni sperimentali. *Atti Accad. naz. Lincei Rc.* **9**, 501–5.

MOORE, H. B. (1936). The biology of *Purpura lapillus*. I. Shell variation in relation to environment. *J. mar. biol. Ass. U.K.* **21**, 61–89.

MOORE, H. B. & KITCHING, J. A. (1939). The biology of *Chthamalus stellatus* (Poli). *J. mar. biol. Ass. U.K.* **23**, 521–41.

NORTH, W. J., NEUSHUL, H. & CLENDENNING, K. A. (1965). Successive biological changes observed in a marine cove exposed to a large spillage of mineral oil. *Symp. Commn int. Explor. scient. Mer Méditerr.*, Monaco, 1964, pp. 335–54.

O'SULLIVAN, A. J. & RICHARDSON, A. J. (1967). The 'Torrey Canyon' disaster and intertidal marine life. *Nature, Lond.* **214**, 448, 541.

SOUTHWARD, A. J. (1964). Limpet grazing and the control of vegetation on rocky shores. In *Grazing in Terrestrial and Marine Environments*. Brit. Ecol. Soc. Symp. no. 4 (edited by D. J. Crisp), pp. 265–73.

SOUTHWARD, A. J. (1967). Recent changes in abundance of intertidal barnacles in south-west England: a possible effect of climatic deterioration. *J. mar. biol. Ass. U.K.* **47**, 81–95.

SOUTHWARD, A. J. & CRISP, D. J. (1954). Recent changes in the distribution of the intertidal barnacles *Chthamalus stellatus* Poli and *Balanus balanoides* L. in the British Isles. *J. Anim. Ecol.* **23**, 163–77.

SOUTHWARD, A. J. & CRIPS, D. J. (1956). Fluctuations in the distribution and abundance of intertidal barnacles. *J. mar. biol. Ass. U.K.* **35**, 211–29.

Chapter 5

BRUCE, J. R. (1928). Physical factors on the sandy beach. II. Chemical changes— carbon dioxide concentration and sulphides. *J. mar. biol. Ass. U.K.* **15**, 553–65.

CHAPMAN, G. (1949). The thixotropy and dilatancy of a marine soil. *J. mar. biol. Ass. U.K.* **28**, 123–40

DELAMARE DEBOUTTEVILLE, C. (1960). Biologie des eaux souterraines littorales et continentales. *Actual. scient. ind.* no. 1280. Univ. Paris, Lab. Arago. Paris: Hermann. 740 pp.

GUNKEL, W. (1967). Experimentell-ökologische Untersuchungen über die limi- tierenden Faktoren der microbiellen Ölabbauses im Marinen Milieu. *Helgo- länder wiss. Meeresunters.* **15**, 1–4, 210–95.

Chapter 6

BELLAMY, D. J. and others (1967). Effects of pollution from the Torrey Canyon on littoral and sublittoral ecosystems. *Nature, Lond.* **216**, 1170–3.

Chapter 7

ALJARINSKAYA, I. O. (1966). On the behaviour and ability to filter of the Black Sea mussel *Mytilus galloprovincialis* in oil polluted water. *Zool. Zh.* **45**, 998–1003.

CORNER, E. D. S., SOUTHWARD, A. J. & SOUTHWARD, E. C. (1968). Toxicity of oil-spill removers ('detergents') to marine life. An assessment using the intertidal barnacle *Elminius modestus.* *J. mar. biol. Ass. U.K.* **48** (1).

CORNER, E. D. S. & SPARROW, B. W. P. (1956). The modes of action of toxic agents. I. Observations on the poisoning of certain crustaceans by copper and mercury. *J. mar. biol. Ass. U.K.* **35**, 531–48.

CRISP, D. J. & SOUTHWARD, A. J. (1961). Different types of cirral activity of barnacles. *Phil. Trans. R. Soc.* B **243**, 271–308.

HOTCHKISS, R. D. (1946). The nature of the bactericidal action of surface active agents. *Ann. N.Y. Acad. Sci.* **46**, 479.

JOHANNES, R. E. (1964). Phosphorus excretion and body size in marine animals: microzooplankton and nutrient regeneration. *Science, N.Y.* **146**, 923–4.

KIDDER, G. W., DEWEY, V. C. & HEINRICH, M. R. (1954). The effect of non-ionic detergents on the growth of *Tetrahymera.* *Expl Cell Res.* **7**, 256.

KNIGHT-JONES, E. W. (1955). The gregarious setting reaction of barnacles as a measure of systematic affinity. *Nature, Lond.* **175**, 266.

MANWELL, C. & BAKER, C. M. A. (1967). A study of detergent pollution by mole- cular methods: starch gel electrophoresis of a variety of enzymes and other proteins. *J. mar. biol. Ass. U.K.* **47**, 659–75.

MARCHETTI, R. (1965). Critical review of the effects of synthetic detergents on aquatic life. *Stud. Rev. gen. Fish. Coun. Mediterr.* **26**, 32 pp.

MOYSE, J. (1963). A comparison of the value of various flagellates and diatoms as food for barnacle larvae. *J. Cons. perm. int. Explor. Mer* **28**, 175–87.

WILSON, D. P. (1929). The larvae of the British sabellarians. *J. mar. biol. Ass. U.K.* **16**, 221–69.

Chapter 8

HUGHES, P. (1956). A determination of the relation between wind and sea-surface drift. *Q. Jl R. met. Soc.* **82**, 494–502.

TOMCZAK, G. (1964). Investigations with drift cards to determine the influence of the wind on surface currents. In *Studies on Oceanography*, dedicated to Professor Hidaka in commemoration of his sixtieth birthday, pp. 129–39. Tokyo: Hidaka Jubilee Committee, University of Tokyo.

Chapter 9

BERRY, B. H. (1953). Sea-water discoloration by living organisms. *N.Z. Jl Sci. Technol.* B **34**, 393–407.

ROUNSEFELL, G. A. & NELSON, W. R. (1966). Red-tide research summarized to 1964 including an annotated bibliography. *Spec. scient. Rep. U.S. Fish Wildl. Serv.* (Fisheries), no. 535. 85 pp.

INDEX

Acanthochitona crinita, 60
Acartia clausi, toxicity experiments on, 120, 121
Acrocnida brachiata, 106, 107, 110, 111, 114
Acrosiphonia arcta, 58
Acrosorium uncinatum, 58
Actinia equina, resistant, 45, 53, 54, 55, 56, 59, 61, 64, 69; damaged by detergent, 45, 63; killed, 106, 110; toxicity experiment on, 134
Adam, N. K., 12
Admiralty, the, 38; Materials Laboratory, oil in sea water, 35
Ahnfeltia plicata, 58
Alaria spp., 105, 107
Alcyonium digitatum, 111
algae, Plate 17; damaged or killed by detergents, 6, 44–5, 48, 52, 53, 62, 63, 68, Plate 15; survive with oil on fronds, 14; regeneration of, 56, 68, 73; resistant and sensitive spp. of, 58; underwater observations on, 105, 110, 114; intertidal, toxicity studies on, 131–3; *see also individual spp.*
Ammodytes, 61
anaerobic conditions, under flat stones, 45; in sand, 83, 85
Anemonia sulcata, 49, 53, 54, 59, 64; toxicity experiment on, 134
Anomia ephippium, 60
Aplysia punctata, 60; toxicity experiment on, 134
Apoglossum ruscifolium, 58, 105, 107
Arabella iricolor, 59
Archidoris pseudoargus, 106
Arenicola, 50
Army, application of detergent by, 38, 91
aromatics, in detergents, 15, 78; evaporation of, 34–5
Ascophyllum nodosum, 58, 70; toxicity experiments on reproductive cells of, 132
asphaltic residue of oil, 11
Asterias rubens, 109, 113; resistant, 106,

107, 110, 111, 114; toxicity experiment on, 137

bacteria, degradation of oil by, 11, 12, 13 n., 44, 82–5, 169; in sea water, 33; aerobic, influenced by detergent, 83; anaerobic, 84
Balanus spp., some survive detergent, 52; settlement of, 56, 61, 63, 72–3; killed by detergent, 63, 64; mostly survive under oil, 66
barnacles, killed by detergents, 6, 55, 60, 62, 68, Plate 19; oil washes off, 36; some survive detergent, 45, 52, 60, 61; survive under oil, 63, 66, 67, Plate 19; survival of larvae of, 72–3; *see also individual spp.*
Bedruthan, 42, 66, Plate 18
Beverton, R. J. H., secretary, Natural Environment Research Council, 9
Bichard, Mr, Dept of Public Works, Guernsey, 172
Bifurcaria bifurcata, 53, 54, 58
birds, floating oil as menace to, 14, 176; on shores, 45, 51, 68
Biscay, Bay of, oil in, 4, 156, Plate 7
bivalve molluscs, 60–1, 113, 133; *see also individual spp.*
Blaxter, J. H., toxicity experiments by, 124
blennies (*Blennius* spp.), 54, 61, 71, 173
Boney, A. D., toxicity experiments by, 132
Booby's Bay, 65, Plates 1, 14
boom defences, 89, 161, 180; in France, 167–8
Botryllus, 54
BP 1002 detergent, 15–20, 21; toxicity experiments with, 118–40
bristle worms, 50
British Petroleum Trading Co., Ltd, 10; information supplied by, 11, 16, 19, 117
Brittany, arrival of oil in, 3, 154; oil pollution on coasts of, 67, 78, 159, 163–9, Plates 27, 28, 29; oil on west coasts of, 4, 165; map, 165
Bunodactis verrucosa, 54, 110

Gigartina spp., 58, 63, 105, 107
Glycera convoluta, 50
Gobius, 107
Godrevy Point, 42, 66
Gracilaria, 52, 58
Gramosol, detergent, 15, 21, 24, 138
Guernsey, oil pollution in, 3, 172–3, Plate 27
Guillaumette, Mr, States Supervisor, Guernsey, 172
Gunkel, W., bacteriological investigations by, 81, 83
Gunwalloe Fishing Cove, 37, 42, 78, 86, 110, 114, Plates 4, 8; map, 108
Gymnodinium, toxicity experiments on, 130, 131

Halichondria panicea, 54
Haliotis, 173
Halosphaera, 30; toxicity experiments on, 130, 131
Halsferran Cove, map, 95; offshore observations at, 95–7
Halurus equisetifolius, 58
Hayle Estuary, 14, 42, 88–9, 90, Plate 18
Healey, D., Minister of Defence, 2
Helford estuary, 89
hermit crabs, 62; *see also individual spp.*
Heterosiphonia plumosa, 105, 106
Hiatella striata, 61
Himanthalia, 59
Hodgkin, A. L., President, Marine Biological Association, 9
Hogus Reef, Marazion, 46, 65; detergent not used on, 44, 47, 48–50, Plate 9
Homarus vulgaris, 59–60, 105, 106, 111
Houghton detergent, 15, 21; toxicity experiments with, 120, 122, 123
Hoy, J., Parliamentary Secretary of Ministry of Agriculture, 6
Hughes, D. E., Department of Microbiology, Cardiff, 33
Hydractinia echinata, 111
hydrogen sulphide, in sand, 83, 84, 86
Hymeniacidon perlevis, 54
Hypoglossum woodwardii, 58, 105, 106, 107

Île Grande, Côtes du Nord, 169, 170, 172
Île Renot, Côtes du Nord, Plate 27
Institut National de Recherche Chimique Appliquée, 171

Jania rubens, 58, 105

Kallymenia reniformis, 58
kelp, 47, 50
kerosene extract (Kex), organic solvent in BP 1002 detergent, 17, 129; toxicity and stability of, 143–8
Kudos detergent, 123
Kynance Cove, 42, 63–4, Plates 1, 18; recovery at, 71, 72

Labrus bergylta, 110, 111
Lacuna vincta, toxicity experiments on larvae of, 122
Laevicardium crassum, toxicity experiment on, 137
Laminaria spp., 58–9, 105, 107, 110
Land's End, 3, 14; map, 40
Lasaea rubra, 60
Laurencia spp., 58, 105, 107
Lepadogaster, 54, 61
Lepidonotus clava, 59
lichens, survive under oil, 14, 89
Ligia, 59, 88
limpets, 54, 55, 61; ingestion of oil by, 14, 49, 50, 65, 66, 73, Plate 17; killed by detergents, 45, 52, 53, 62, 64, 68, 110, Plate 12; survive oil coating, 49, 50, 56, 63, 66, 67, 173, Plate 9; susceptibility of, 60, 65, 69; reappearance of, 72; toxicity experiments on, 134, 135
Lithophyllum, 54
Littorina spp., 54, 66, 70; killed by detergent, 55, 60; reappearance of, 72; toxicity experiment on, 134
Lizard Point, 29, 42, 159, Plate 4; map, 41
lobsters, 59–60, 105, 106, 113, 172; fisheries for, 6
local authorities, application of detergent by, 38
Locquirac, Brittany, Plate 29
Loe Bar, 42, 78; underwater observations off, 110, 112; map, 108
Lomentaria articulata, 58
lucernarians, 48
Luidia sarsi, larvae of, 31
Lutraria, 111
Lysidice ninetta, 59

Mactra, 51, 86; underwater observations on, 106, 107, 109, 110, 111, 112, 113, 137, Plate 20